M000275859

OBSTETRIC ANESTHESIA

OBSTETRIC ANESTHESIA

Edited by

Mark C. Norris, M.D.

Associate Professor of Anesthesiology
Jefferson Medical College of Thomas Jefferson University
Co-Director of Obstetric Anesthesia
Thomas Jefferson University Hospital
Philadelphia, Pennsylvania

53 Contributors

J. B. LIPPINCOTT COMPANY
Philadelphia

Acquisitions Editor: Mary K. Smith
Assistant Editor: Anne Geyer
Project Editor: Barbara Ryalls
Indexer: Katherine Pitcoff
Designer: Doug Smock
Cover Designer: Leslie Foster Roesler
Production Manager: Helen Ewan
Production Coordinator: Nannette Winski
Compositor: Graphic Sciences Corporation
Printer/Binder: Arcata Graphics/Halliday

Copyright © 1993, by J. B. Lippincott Company. All rights reserved. No part of this book may be used or reproduced in any manner whatsoever without written permission except for brief quotations embodied in critical articles and reviews. Printed in the United States of America. For information write J. B. Lippincott Company, 227 East Washington Square, Philadelphia, Pennsylvania 19105-3780.

6 5 4 3 2

Library of Congress Cataloging in Publications Data

Obstetric anesthesia / edited by Mark C. Norris ; with 53
    contributors.
        p.   cm.
    Includes bibliographical references and index.
    ISBN 0-397-51115-9
    1. Anesthesia in obstetrics.   2. Pregnant women—Surgery.
3. Pregnancy—complications.   4. Labor (Obstetrics)—Complications.
I. Norris, Mark C.
    [DNLM: 1. Anesthesia, Obstetrical.   2. Pregnancy Complications-
-surgery.   3. Surgery, Operative—in pregnancy.   WO 450 N14232]
RG732.0263   1993
617.9′682—dc20
DNLM/DLC
for Library of Congress   92-49949
                                                                  CIP

The authors and publisher have exerted every effort to ensure that drug selection and dosage set forth in this text are in accord with current recommendations and practice at the time of publication. However, in view of ongoing research, changes in government regulations, and the constant flow of information relating to drug therapy and drug reactions, the reader is urged to check the package insert for each drug for any change in indications and dosage and for added warnings and precautions. This is particularly important when the recommended agent is a new or infrequently employed drug.

To my children:
Julia, Benjamin, and Daniel
Thank you for making it all worthwhile.

CONTRIBUTORS

George S. Allen III, M.D.
Instructor, Department of Obstetrics and Gynecology, University of Tennessee, Memphis, School of Medicine, Memphis, Tennessee

Valerie A. Arkoosh, M.D.
Assistant Professor, Department of Anesthesiology, Jefferson Medical College of Thomas Jefferson University, Philadelphia, Pennsylvania

Richard B. Becker, M.D.
Assistant Professor of Anesthesiology, George Washington University School of Medicine and Health Sciences; Co-Director, Obstetric Anesthesia, Co-Director, Intensive Care Unit, George Washington University Hospital, Washington, D.C.

Danny Bowen, M.S., C.R.N.A.
Staff Nurse Anesthetist, Section of Anesthesiology, Wright Patterson United States Air Force Medical Center, Wright Patterson Air Force Base, Ohio

R. Stuart B. Bramwell, M.D.
Assistant Professor of Anesthesia, Emory University, Director of Obstetric Anesthesia, Grady Memorial Hospital, Atlanta, Georgia

Walter U. Brown, M.D.
Associate Clinical Professor, Department of Anesthesiology, Vanderbilt University; Middle Tennessee Anesthesiology PC, Baptist Hospital, Nashville, Tennessee

Linda Chan, M.D.
Clinical Assistant Professor, Division of Maternal–Fetal Medicine, Department of Obstetrics and Gynecology, Jefferson Medical College of Thomas Jefferson University; Attending in Obstetrics/Gynecology, Thomas Jefferson University Hospital, Philadelphia, Pennsylvania

Theodore G. Cheek, M.D.
Associate Professor of Anesthesia and Obstetrics & Gynecology, Department of Anesthesia, University of Pennsylvania School of Medicine, Philadelphia, Pennsylvania

Doris Costello, M.D.
Staff Anesthesiologist, Women and Infants' Hospital of Rhode Island, Providence, Rhode Island

Richard Depp, M.D.
Professor and Chairman, Department of Obstetrics and Gynecology, Thomas Jefferson University Hospital, Philadelphia, Pennsylvania

M. Joanne Douglas, M.D.
Clinical Professor, Division of Obstetric Anaesthesia, University of British Columbia; Head, Department of Anaesthesia, Grace Hospital, Vancouver, British Columbia, Canada

John W. Downing, M.B., B.CH. Rand, F.F.A.(SA), F.F.A.R.C.S. (ENG), F.A.N.Z.C.A
Professor of Anesthesiology and Obstetrics, Vanderbilt University School of Medicine; Director of Obstetric Anesthesia Services, Vanderbilt University Medical Center, Nashville, Tennessee

Richard L. Elgart, M.D.
Instructor, Department of Anesthesiology, Jefferson Medical College of Thomas Jefferson University, Thomas Jefferson University Hospital, Philadelphia, Pennsylvania

Richard Flynn, M.D., F.F.A.R.C.S.I., D.C.H., D.R.C.O.G.
Consultant Anaesthetist, Bon Secours Hospital, Cork, Ireland

Marilyn J. Darby-Gage, M.D.
Assistant Professor, Department of Obstetrics and Gynecology, Jefferson Medical College of Thomas Jefferson University, Philadelphia, Pennsylvania

Raphael Y. Gershon, M.D.
Assistant Professor of Obstetrics and Gynecology, Emory University School of Medicine, Grady Memorial Hospital, Atlanta, Georgia

Beth Glosten, M.D.
Assistant Professor, Department of Anesthesiology, University of Washington School of Medicine, Seattle, Washington

Steven Goldberg, M.D.
Staff, Department of Obstetrics and Gynecology, Thomas Jefferson University Hospital, Philadelphia, Pennsylvania

William M. Grieco, M.D.
Resident, Department of Anesthesiology, Thomas Jefferson University Hospital, Philadelphia, Pennsylvania

Brett B. Gutsche, M.D.
Professor of Anesthesia, Professor of Obstetrics and Gynecology, University of Pennsylvania School of Medicine; Associate Director of Obstetric Anesthesia, Hospital of the University of Pennsylvania, Philadelphia, Pennsylvania

Barbara L. Hartwell, M.D.
Assistant Professor of Anaesthesia, Harvard Medical School; Staff Anesthesiologist, Brigham and Women's Hospital, Boston, Massachusetts

Joy L. Hawkins, M.D.
Associate Professor of Anesthesiology, University of Colorado Health Sciences Center, Denver, Colorado

Norman L. Herman, M.D., Ph.D.
Chief, Obstetric Anesthesia, Department of Anesthesiology, Wilford Hall United States Air Force Medical Center, Lackland Air Force Base, Texas; Clinical Assistant Professor, Department of Anesthesiology, University of Texas Health Science Center, San Antonio, Texas, and Uniformed Services University of the Health Sciences, Bethesda, Maryland

John E. Heusner, M.D.
Fellow in Obstetric Anesthesia, University of Utah Hospital, Salt Lake City, Utah

James E. Honet, M.D.
Instructor in Anesthesiology, Jefferson Medical College of Thomas Jefferson University; Staff Anesthesiologist, Thomas Jefferson University Hospital, Philadelphia, Pennsylvania

H. Jane Huffnagle, D.O.
Instructor in Anesthesiology, Jefferson Medical College of Thomas Jefferson University; Staff Anesthesiologist, Thomas Jefferson University Hospital, Philadelphia, Pennsylvania

Suzanne Lynne Huffnagle, D.O.
Staff, Jefferson Medical College of Thomas Jefferson University, Thomas Jefferson University Hospital, Philadelphia, Pennsylvania

Thomas H. Kramer, PharmD.
Research Assistant Professor, Departments of Pharmacology and Anesthesiology, University of Arizona College of Medicine, Arizona Health Sciences Center, Tucson, Arizona

Kathleen A. Leavitt, M.D.
Assistant Professor, Department of Anesthesiology, George Washington University School of Medicine and Health Sciences, George Washington University Hospital, Washington, D.C.

Barbara L. Leighton, M.D.
Associate Professor of Anesthesiology, Jefferson Medical College of Thomas Jefferson University; Co-Director, Obstetric Anesthesia, Thomas Jefferson University Hospital, Philadelphia, Pennsylvania

Ji-Bin Liu, M.D.
Research Assistant Professor of Radiology, Jefferson Medical College of Thomas Jefferson University, Thomas Jefferson University Hospital, Philadelphia, Pennsylvania

Andrew M. Malinow, M.D.
Assistant Professor of Anesthesiology, Obstetrics, and Gynecology, University of Maryland School of Medicine; Director, Obstetric Anesthesia, University of Maryland Medical Center, Baltimore, Maryland

Marianne P. Matthews, M.D.
Staff, George Washington University Medical Center, Washington, D.C.

Betty Lou Koffel Mokriski, M.D.
Assistant Professor of Anesthesiology, University of Maryland School of Medicine; Attending Anesthesiologist, University of Maryland Medical Center, Baltimore, Maryland

Holly A. Muir, M.D.
Staff Anesthetist, Victoria General Hospital and Grace Maternity Hospital, Halifax, Nova Scotia, Canada

J. Stephen Naulty, M.D.
Professor of Obstetrics and Anesthesia, George Washington University School of Medicine and Health Sciences; Director, Obstetric Anesthesia, George Washington University Medical Center, Washington, D.C.

Mark C. Norris, M.D.
Associate Professor of Anesthesiology, Jefferson Medical College of Thomas Jefferson University; Co-Director of Obstetric Anesthesia, Thomas Jefferson University Hospital, Philadelphia, Pennsylvania

Christopher Ernest Peter Orlikowski, M.B.B.Ch., F.R.C.Anaes.
Senior Registrar, Department of Anaesthetics, University of Natal Faculty of Medicine, Durban, South Africa

Pontus L. Östman, M.D.
Assistant Professor, University of Iowa College of Medicine, University of Iowa Hospitals and Clinics, Iowa City, Iowa

Craig M. Palmer, M.D.
Clinical Assistant Professor, Department of Anesthesiology, University of Arizona College of Medicine; Director of Obstetric Anesthesiology, University of Arizona Health Sciences Center, Tucson, Arizona

Jaya Ramanathan, M.D.
Associate Professor, Department of Anesthesiology; Director of Obstetrical Anesthesia, University of Tennessee, Memphis, College of Medicine, Memphis, Tennessee

Felicity Reynolds, M.B., B.S., M.D., F.F.A.R.C.S.
Reader in Pharmacology Applied to Anaesthesia, Honorary Consultant in charge of Obstetric Anaesthesia, St. Thomas Hospital, London, United Kingdom

D.A. Rocke, M.R.C.P. (UK), F.F.A. (SA)
Professor and Chairman, Department of Anaesthetics, University of Natal Faculty of Medicine, Durban, South Africa

Sheila L. Ronkin, M.D.
Assistant Professor, Department of Obstetrics and Gynecology, Hahnemann University; Acting Director, Maternal Fetal Medicine, Director, Fetal Well-Being Center, Hahnemann University Hospital, Philadelphia, Pennsylvania

C.C. Rout, F.F.A.R.C.S.
Lecturer, University of Natal Medical School Faculty of Medicine; Senior Specialist, King Edward VIII Hospital, Durban, South Africa

Jeannine C. Salvesen, M.D.
Assistant Professor of Anesthesiology, University of North Carolina and Hospitals, Chapel Hill, North Carolina

Divina Juson Santos, M.D.
Director of Obstetrical Anesthesia, Columbia Hospital for Women, Washington, D.C.

Timothy J. Schlairet, D.O.
Director of Obstetric Anesthesia, Section of Anesthesiology, Wright Patterson United States Air Force Medical Center, Wright Patterson Air Force Base, Ohio

Baha M. Sibai, M.D.
Professor and Chief, Division of Maternal Fetal Medicine, University of Tennessee, Memphis, College of Medicine, Memphis, Tennessee

Neil S. Silverman
Assistant Professor, Department of Obstetrics and Gynecology, Jefferson Medical College of Thomas Jefferson University; Division of Maternal–Fetal Medicine, Thomas Jefferson University Hospital, Philadelphia, Pennsylvania

Fred J. Spielman, M.D.
Associate Professor of Anesthesiology, Obstetrics, and Gynecology, University of North Carolina, Chapel Hill; University of North Carolina Hospitals, Chapel Hill, North Carolina

Christopher M. Viscomi, M.D.
Assistant Professor of Anesthesiology, University of Utah School of Medicine; Director of Obstetric Anesthesia, University of Utah Hospital, Salt Lake City, Utah

Jeffrey A. Weiss, D.O.
Staff Anesthesiologist, Palm Beach Heart Institute, Palm Beach Gardens Medical Center, Palm Beach Gardens, Florida

PREFACE

When I first told colleagues that I was going to edit an obstetric anesthesia textbook, they asked me two questions. The first was: "Does the world need another book about obstetric anesthesia?" If this book proves to offer something that the other available texts do not, then, yes, the world does need another obstetric anesthesia text. You the reader must decide.

The second question was: "How will your book be different from what is already available?" To that query, I have several responses. I have attempted to organize this book in the manner in which an anesthesiologist approaches a patient—preoperative evaluation, intraoperative management, and postoperative care.

The chapters in the first section of the book, **Preoperative Evaluation,** provide background information about both normal and high-risk pregnancies. In addition to a discussion of the physiologic changes that accompany normal gestation, there also are chapters examining how the woman with significant coexisting disease adapts to pregnancy and parturition. These chapters provide the information needed to evaluate and prepare a woman for obstetric anesthesia. Other chapters in this section focus on the fetus. Here the reader learns about routine fetal evaluation and surveillance and the in utero diagnosis and management of fetal anomalies and complications.

The next section of the text covers intraoperative management of the parturient throughout gestation and into the postpartum period. Although several of these chapters cover problems discussed in the first section of the book, the focus now shifts to anesthetic planning and management. Two chapters follow, covering postoperative analgesia and the complications that arise after an anesthetic has been completed. The final chapters discuss two important topics. Chapter 39 examines issues surrounding the provision of optimal obstetric anesthesia care in both community and university settings. The last chapter discusses pertinent legal and ethical issues that confront the obstetric anesthesiologist.

I hope this book is useful to both the anesthesia resident in training and the practitioner who frequently or occasionally cares for parturients. For the trainee, I hope this text fulfills several needs. First, it should explain how to prepare and anesthetize the healthy and complicated gravida. More importantly, however, it should explain why a given course of action is appropriate. For the practitioner, I hope this book will serve as both a review of obstetric anesthesia and a reference when she or he is faced with an unusual or difficult patient.

I would like to thank all of my contributors. I value each of their efforts. Without them, this book would never have happened. In addition, my deepest thanks to Suzanne Maiorano for her tireless help and support.

Mark C. Norris, M.D.

CONTENTS

SECTION TWO   Intraoperative Management

SECTION THREE   Postoperative Care

SECTION FOUR   Managing an Obstetric
Anesthesia Service

OBSTETRIC ANESTHESIA

SECTION

ONE

Preoperative Assessment

CHAPTER 1

Physiologic Adaptation to Pregnancy: The Healthy Parturient

Betty Lou K. Mokriski

The pregnant woman experiences physiologic changes in every organ system. Her body begins to transform in the early weeks after conception and continues changing into the postpartum period. Understanding the progressive nature of this metamorphosis helps the obstetric anesthesiologist approach not only the peripartum gravida but also the pregnant surgical patient with confidence. This chapter reviews the physiologic changes that occur in many organ systems, the hormonal, metabolic, or mechanical basis of these alterations, and their anesthetic implications.

CARDIOVASCULAR SYSTEM

Physical Examination

Heart sounds not routinely heard in healthy young women appear during gestation (Fig. 1-1). Even S_1 and S_2 change. Pregnancy amplifies the first heart sound as early as 12 weeks' estimated gestational age (EGA). Nearly all parturients have exaggerated splitting of the first heart sound. Respiratory variation of the second heart sound decreases. By 20 weeks of gestation, auscultation often (84%) reveals a third heart sound. The volume of S_3 peaks by 30 weeks. Ninety-six percent of pregnant women have a systolic murmur, most frequently of the ejection type. A diastolic "flow" murmur may be heard in 18% of patients.[1,2] The onset of these murmurs correlates most closely with rises in blood volume, not cardiac output.[1] Despite having normal electrocardiograms and systolic function, 9% of parturients will have a detectable pleural effusion (by echocardiography) in the third trimester.[3] The changes in heart sounds usually resolve within 4 weeks after delivery. A third heart sound, if present, usually disappears within 8 days of parturition.[1,2] Although an audible S_3, a diastolic murmur, or a pericardial effusion should not be overlooked during pregnancy, they may be "normal" and not signify cardiac pathology.

Hemodynamic Measurements (Table 1-1)

The cardiovascular system changes significantly within the first 8 weeks of gestation. Heart rate increases, and mean arterial pressure (MAP) decreases.[4] In fact, heart rate may rise as soon as 4 weeks after conception.[5]

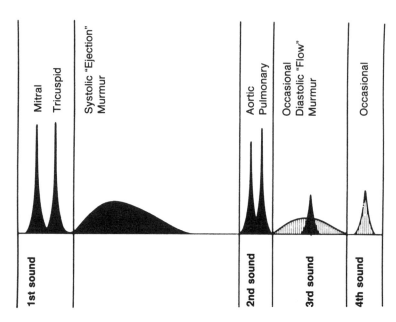

Figure 1-1. Auscultatory findings of the heart during pregnancy. (Hytten F, Chamberlain G, eds. Clinical physiology in obstetrics, 2nd ed. London: Blackwell Scientific Publications, 1991;4)

Longitudinal studies that evaluate the same women before and after they conceive provide particularly valuable information about the physiologic changes of pregnancy. (Many studies use postpartum measurement as a basis of comparison when evaluating the hemodynamic changes of pregnancy. Weight and activity changes influence "control" data obtained after delivery. The preconception state provides a more accurate comparison for the early weeks of gestation.)

Clapp *et al*[4] examined gravidae before conception and early in pregnancy. They found significant changes in heart rate (+17.5%) and MAP (−11%) by 7 weeks of EGA. The heart rate and MAP did not change further through the end of the first trimester.[4] Interestingly, pregnancies destined to fail did not exhibit these alterations at 8 weeks' EGA.

Early elevations in stroke volume[6,7] and cardiac output[7,8] (20%–40%) also have been noted. Walters *et al* studied women at monthly intervals beginning in the first trimester and found greater increases in stroke volume than in heart rate.[6] Capeless and colleagues confirmed the greater stroke volume using M-mode echocardiography.[7]

Cardiac Output

Cardiac output increases progressively throughout pregnancy.[6,9,10] Most reports show cardiac output peaking between 24 and 32 weeks' EGA.[6,11,12] However, early investigators often failed to consider the effects of maternal position on cardiac output. In the supine position, the enlarging uterus compresses the aorta and inferior vena cava. Decreased venous return then limits cardiac output. When measured in the supine position, cardiac output peaks in the late second trimester and then descends to nonpregnant levels by term. Today investigators and clinicians routinely attempt to limit aortocaval compression. Even so, cardiac output may crest before term.

In the lateral position, minute distance (a linear analogue of cardiac output measured by Doppler ultrasound) increases as early as 4 weeks' EGA, with maximum values occurring between 16 and 32 weeks.[10] Early elevation of stroke distance (a linear analogue of stroke volume) disappears after 32 weeks' EGA,[10] and then stroke distance shortens. By term, it decreases to values lower than in the nonpregnant state.

Left ventricular function (as measured by shortening characteristics) remains unchanged at term in spite of left ventricular enlargement.[13] Contractility decreases in the postpartum period, suggesting augmentation at term.[14] In spite of left ventricular volume overload (the increased plasma volume), pregnancy preserves or even augments myocardial function.[15]

Thermodilution cardiac output correlates well with pulsed Doppler[16] or suprasternal window continuous-wave ultrasound measurements.[17] However, during periods of hemorrhage, this consistency disappears,[18] making noninvasive measurements difficult during parturition.

Accurate cardiac output estimates with Doppler ultrasound require a constant aortic cross-sectional area. Variations in aortic area modify the estimated velocity

Table 1–1

Maternal Hemodynamic Changes with Pregnancy*

VARIABLE	PERCENT CHANGE COMPARED TO NONPREGNANT VALUE
Cardiac output	↑ 14%–50%
Heart rate	↑ 17%–26%
Stroke volume	No change – ↑ 32%
Mean arterial pressure	No change – ↓ 11%
Systemic vascular resistance	↓ 21%
Central venous pressure	No change
Pulmonary artery occlusion pressure	No change
Pulmonary vascular resistance	↓ 34%
Colliod oncotic pressure	↓ 14%

*Data from references 6, 8, 10, 12, 14, 22, and 28. Table excludes values obtained in the supine position.

of flow. Elevations in cardiac output detected by Doppler ultrasound could, then, be artifacts of an increasing aortic area; however, to mimic the changes in cardiac output reported during pregnancy, aortic cross-sectional area would have to expand by 30% to 45%.[10] Pregnancy does change aortic compliance and cross-sectional area. Compliance increases during pregnancy, and cross-sectional area decreases by 23% in the first 3 to 6 months postpartum. Aortic cross-sectional area seems to remain widened after pregnancy. Term values differ significantly between nulliparous and previously pregnant women.[19]

Pressures

Maternal systemic blood pressure reaches a nadir at 16 to 20 weeks' gestation and then increases toward term.[20,21] Diastolic pressure rises less than systolic pressure.[21] Central venous pressure[22] and pulmonary capillary wedge pressure[22,23] remain stable throughout pregnancy. Colloid oncotic pressure decreases by 14%.[22] Lower colloid oncotic pressure may predispose the gravida to pulmonary edema in the face of elevated pulmonary capillary wedge pressure.

Etiology

In pregnancy, the heart must supply both the gravida and her fetus. Augmented cardiac output improves peripheral and uteroplacental oxygen delivery. During most of pregnancy, however, oxygen delivery exceeds

fetal metabolic needs. During the first trimester, cardiac output increases 30% to 40%, whereas oxygen consumption grows only 10%.[8,24] The smaller a-v O_2 difference of early pregnancy also shows that oxygen delivery exceeds oxygen consumption.[9,25] Thus, the metabolic needs of the pregnancy do not provide an adequate explanation for the cardiovascular changes.

Expanded blood volume offers a mechanical explanation, but the early nature of the cardiovascular changes strongly suggests a hormonal etiology. Production of estrogen and other hormones rises rapidly early in pregnancy. Experimentally, these hormones modulate the cardiovascular system. In sheep, infusing conjugated estrogens for 4 hours elevates cardiac output (+32%) and heart rate (+50%) and lowers MAP (−10%) and systemic vascular resistance (−19%). Thus, even a brief exposure to estrogenic hormones can significantly modify the cardiovascular system and mimic term pregnancy.[26] In addition, estrogen enhances myocardial contractility.[27,28]

Effects of Positioning

In 1953, Howard *et al* described a tachycardic and hypotensive supine multigravida at term who complained of abdominal pain. She underwent emergency laparotomy and delivery for suspected ruptured uterus. A normal uterus and intrauterine pregnancy were found. Interestingly, a few days later he observed another patient with the same syndrome of "postural shock." Their investigation in dogs revealed that hypotension developed after inferior vena caval occlusion only during pregnancy. Howard *et al*[29] believed that caval occlusion deprived the pregnant dog of a greater proportion of her total blood volume compared to the nonpregnant dog. During the third trimester, the supine, lithotomy,[8,30,31] and even the right lateral[31] positions reduce maternal cardiac output, stroke volume, and systolic and diastolic blood pressure.[8,30,31] Peripheral vascular resistance increases significantly in these positions (Fig. 1-2).

Answers to the following questions about this phenomenon, which is now called the supine hypotensive syndrome or aortocaval compression, remain incomplete:

- Why do some patients exhibit the syndrome more often or more severely than others?
- What are the effects of labor on the syndrome?
- How can one prevent its occurrence?

Incidence and Etiology

Right atrial pressure declines in the supine position, limiting stroke volume and, subsequently, cardiac output (see Fig. 1-2). Hypotension follows unless compensatory tachycardia or peripheral vasoconstriction ensues. An increment in systemic vascular resistance offsets the decrement in cardiac output, and most patients maintain systolic blood pressure. In some patients, however, bradycardia or a decrease in systemic vascular resistance leads to significant hypotension.[32] Fifteen to twenty percent of third-trimester patients exhibit hypotension or tachycardia when supine.[32,33]

Interestingly, not all investigators have reported this syndrome.[10,34] McLennan and coworkers, for example, evaluated gravidae at 36 and 40 weeks' gestation. In this study, position did not affect minute distance (a linear correlate of cardiac output) in any of 45 patients.[10] These results show the inherent ability of many, but not all, parturients to compensate for aortocaval compression. Regional or general anesthesia compromises the gravida's ability to compensate for a fall in venous return. Labor, uteroplacental insufficiency, and fetal size also may affect the incidence and severity of supine hypotension.

Both occlusion of the inferior vena cava (IVC) and compression of the aorta play a role in the development of the aortocaval compression syndrome. At term, the gravid uterus obstructs the IVC when the parturient lies supine. The uterus commonly completely obstructs the IVC at its bifurcation. Blood returns to the heart through the azygous and vertebral veins. After delivery, angiography demonstrates a normal IVC. The previously large azygous and vertebral veins contain only minimal dye.[35]

Supine hypotension can occur without IVC obstruction.[29] In addition, IVC obstruction does not invariably lower blood pressure and cardiac output. In gravid ewes, when heart rate rose after IVC obstruction, the MAP remained stable. In contrast, when the ewe became bradycardic, MAP declined.[36] In chronically instrumented gravid ewes, cardiac output fell by **37%** and systemic blood pressure decreased by **24%** with suprarenal occlusion of the IVC. Infrarenal occlusion diminished cardiac output only.[29] In humans, im-

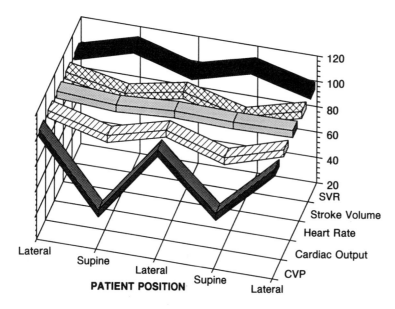

Figure 1–2. Changes in central venous pressure (CVP), cardiac output, heart rate, stroke volume, and systemic vascular resistance (SVR) with successive position changes. (Data from Lees MM, Scott DB, Kerr MG, Taylor SH. The circulatory effects of recumbent postural change in late pregnancy. Clin Sci 1967;32:453)

mediately after abdominal delivery, occlusion of the IVC lowered right atrial pressure but did not alter heart rate, blood pressure, or pulse pressure.[32] Thus, although IVC occlusion does decrease right atrial pressure, hypotension does not always follow.

Even in absence of hypotension, IVC compression may have adverse effects. Obstruction of the IVC decreases uterine artery perfusion pressure and uterine artery blood flow by raising venous pressure.[37] Inferior vena caval obstruction also may elevate uterine vascular resistance.[38] In gravid ewes, occlusion of the uterine veins without occlusion of the IVC did not alter stroke volume or cardiac output. Maternal arterial pressure actually rose.[37] Thus, it is unlikely that the effects of IVC obstruction are the result of decreased uterine venous blood flow.

Simultaneous or isolated compression of the aorta also may play a role in the supine hypotensive syndrome. Femoral artery hypotension occurs earlier and more often than brachial artery hypotension.[39] Usually, femoral artery systolic pressure decreases more than the diastolic pressure.[40] Angiograms show the uterus displacing the subrenal aorta laterally, cranially, and dorsally.[41,42]

Other work, however, suggests that aortic compression does not play a role in the genesis of supine hypotension. Recently, Kinsella *et al* studied 20 gravidas. They measured plethysmographic leg blood flow, continuous-wave Doppler ultrasound arterial flow, leg MAP, and heart rate. Heart rate increased in each position compared to the left lateral position. Leg blood flow was less in the supine, left pelvic tilt, and right pelvic tilt positions compared to the full left lateral position. However, position did not change leg MAP or arterial flow.[43] Acute aortic compression as an etiology of decreased leg blood flow is unlikely in the presence of normal leg MAP. Inferior vena caval compression explains the diminished blood flow and tachycardia.

Labor and Aortocaval Compression

Uterine contractions may be necessary to elicit the signs of aortic compression. In 70 angiograms, Bieniarz *et al*[41] showed that the relaxed uterus produced less aortic compression than the contracted uterus. During a contraction, this compression, mostly limited to L_{4-5}, can completely occlude the aorta.[41] Contractions seen during a non-stress test eliminated both foot pulse and oximeter tracings in 2 of 42 parturients.[33] In actively laboring women, dorsalis pedis artery ultrasound flow velocities decreased by 80% in both the supine and the lateral positions during contractions.[44] Painful uterine contractions may cause aortic compression through vasoconstriction by endogenous catecholamines. In 14 of 16 patients with continuous lumbar epidural analgesia, dorsalis pedis artery flow velocity remained high during contractions.[44] Although these observations strongly suggest that uterine contractions worsen aortic compression, others have reported an ameliorating effect of contractions.[29]

Labor also may alter IVC obstruction. In the supine position, uterine contractions augment cardiac output (25%) and stroke volume (33%) while lowering heart rate (15%). In contrast, in the lateral position, these values change very little with each contraction. These findings suggest that, in the supine position, uterine contractions relieve IVC occlusion.[45]

Perhaps IVC occlusion does not occur during contractions because the uterus is more easily supported by the vertebral column in the contracted state. In effect, the contraction lifts the body of the uterus off the inferior cava, but the firmly contracted uterus obstructs aortic flow more readily than does the relaxed uterus.

Prevention

Although nearly all obstetric anesthesiologists routinely advocate left uterine displacement (Fig. 1-3), the standard pelvic tilt position may not consistently relieve inferior vena caval compression.[34,46] Even the lateral position does not totally relieve compression of the IVC, at least as demonstrated by venogram.[35] The lateral position does completely prevent aortic compression as measured by angiography.[42]

Fetal position may explain some of the interindividual differences in response to the supine position. Maternal cardiac output and stroke volume are higher in the 45-degree left lateral position compared to the supine and 45-degree right lateral positions. The extent to which maternal cardiac output falls in the right lateral position depends on the location of the fetal body within the uterus. Cardiac output and stroke volume decline more if the fetal body lies to the right than the left in the uterus.[31] (The vena cava is on the right side of the vertebral column. A right-lying fetus will further compress the IVC when the mother is tilted to the right. If the fetus is on the left side of the uterus, right tilt still impairs venous return when compared to left tilt, but less so than if the fetal body was on the right.)

We can conclude that the supine position may harm some gravidae; perhaps up to 20% of these women will experience hypotension or decreased uterine blood flow. Inferior vena caval or aortic compression impairs venous return and, consequently, cardiac output. These changes ultimately decrease uterine blood flow and fetal oxygen delivery. Uterine contractions may alleviate IVC compression but exacerbate aortic com-

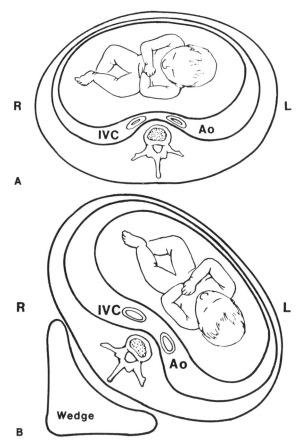

R

L

IVC   Ao

A

R

L

IVC

Ao

Wedge

B

Figure 1–3. **(A)** Diagram shows inferior vena cava (IVC) and aorta (Ao) compressed by the enlarged uterus when the gravida lies supine. **(B)** Diagram demonstrates lack of interior vena cava (IVC) and aorta (Ao) compression with a wedge under the gravida's hip. (Stoelting RK, Miller RD, eds. Basics of anesthesia, 2nd ed. New York: Churchill Livingstone, 1989;370)

pression. A 10-degree lateral tilt will eliminate aortocaval compression in most gravidae. Some will be asymptomatic only when they lie completely on their side. Depending in part on the position of the fetal body within the uterus, a given gravida may respond better in the left or right lateral position.

Anesthetic Implications

Normal cardiac output and uterine artery perfusion depend on adequate venous return. Regional anesthesia causes peripheral vasodilation and venous pooling secondary to the loss of sympathetic tone. Vasodilation increases the likelihood of supine hypotension. Acute intravenous hydration before induction increases blood volume and helps maintain normal maternal cardiac output.

Aortocaval compression may complicate maternal and fetal resuscitation. Partial IVC occlusion makes resuscitation of dogs given 20 mg/kg of intravenous bupivacaine more difficult and more prolonged.[47] Adequate maternal resuscitation may require delivery to eliminate completely the deleterious effects of aortocaval compression.[48]

Response to Vasoactive Agents

Pregnancy blunts systemic vasoconstriction and vasodilation in response to alpha- and beta-adrenergic stimulation.[49,50] Pregnancy also attenuates catecholamine secretion in response to physiologic stress.[51] The uterine artery dilates normally in response to sodium nitroprusside and hydralazine[52] and constricts normally with norepinephrine.[53]

Pregnancy markedly inhibits the chronotropic response to isoproterenol.[54] The degree of this effect greatly exceeds that expected due to the increased plasma volume. The chronotropic response to 15 µg of IV epinephrine also decreases at term.[55] A pregnancy-related inhibitory circulating factor may cause this effect. Cultured rat myocardial cells (a model of beta-adrenergic receptors) do not exhibit an isoproterenol-induced chronotropic effect when exposed to sera from term gravidae.[56]

The altered response to sympathetic stimulation has two significant anesthetic implications. Decreased responsiveness to alpha- and beta-adrenergic stimulation limits the precision of a chronotropic intravenous test dose. Beta-adrenergic agents are preferable for the treatment of maternal hypotension because alpha-adrenergic agents constrict the uterine arteries and impair uteroplacental blood flow.

Blood Flow

Uterine artery blood flow increases from 3.5% of cardiac output in early pregnancy to 12% at term. Uterine artery blood flow rises from 50 mL/min at 10 weeks' gestation to 200 mL/min at 28 weeks and 500 mL/min at term.[15,24] The resistance of the uterine artery to blood flow steadily declines during pregnancy.[57,58] Both direct arteriovenous anastomoses in the uterus and uterine artery vasodilation secondary to estrogens and angiotensin II account for this fall.[15]

Pregnancy does not change cerebral blood flow.[50,56,59] However, new noninvasive techniques detect decreases in Doppler-measured internal carotid artery flow velocity in the third trimester.[60] This technique uses mean velocity to estimate cerebral blood flow. If further investigations confirm this lowered flow, cardiovascular changes or the hypocapnia of pregnancy would provide an explanation.

Effects of Exercise

Pregnancy does not alter the physiologic responses to exercise, suggesting good myocardial reserve in the normal gravida.[25,61] The coupling of cardiac output to oxygen demand during exercise is unaffected by pregnancy.[61]

Effects of Labor

Labor further modifies the cardiovascular system (Table 1-2). Each contraction squeezes about 300 mL of blood from the uterus into the central circulation.[62] Uterine contractions also relieve IVC compression. Cardiac output (22%) and stroke volume (27%) rise during contractions in the first stage of labor. Maternal systolic and diastolic blood pressure increase 10 to 20 mm Hg during a contraction.[45] Cardiac output reaches

an apex 18 seconds before the uterus attains maximum amniotic fluid pressure.[62] Both the autotransfused blood and the augmented venous return that occur with each uterine contraction may explain these changes.

Both the process of labor and individual contractions affect cardiac output. Caudal analgesia prevents the progressive rise in cardiac output during labor but *not* the increases that coincide with each contraction.[63] Robson *et al*[64] measured stroke volume throughout labor using noninvasive techniques. All women labored in the left semilateral position with meperidine and nitrous oxide analgesia. Basal cardiac output increased 13% by 8 cm or greater of cervical dilation. Stroke volume, not heart rate, produced most of this change. Uterine contractions increased cardiac output in all patients throughout labor. The increment in cardiac output was greater at 8 cm or more and 4 to 7 cm of cervical dilation than at 3 cm or less (Fig. 1-4). Beyond 4 cm of dilation, the change in cardiac output with each contraction depended on significant increases in both heart rate and stroke volume (Figs. 1-5 and 1-6). At an earlier stage, stroke volume changes predominated.[64]

Maruta[65] confirmed increased cardiac output during contractions but found more significant increases in heart rate. In addition, *expulsive* efforts in the second stage of labor impaired cardiac output and

Table 1-2

Maternal Hemodynamic Changes with Labor*

	CARDIAC OUTPUT	STROKE VOLUME	HEART RATE
Early First Stage			
Basal[†]	No change	No change	No change
Contraction[§]	↓15% – ↑15%	No change – ↑8%	No change – ↑10%
Late First Stage			
Rest[†]	No change – ↑14%	No change – ↑12%	No change – ↑13%
Contraction[§]	↑20%	↑6%	↑13%
Second Stage			
Without expulsive efforts[†]	No change	↓13%	↑27%
With expulsive efforts[†]	↓23%	↓49%	↑48%

*Data from references 45, 63, 64, 65, and 66.
[†]Compared to resting values before labor.
[‡]Compared to between-contraction values in the same stage of labor.
[§]Compared to basal labor values.

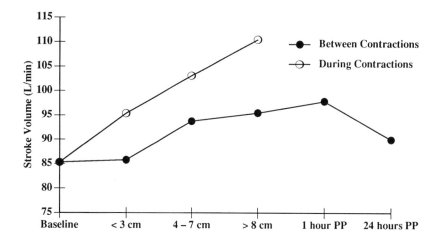

Figure 1–4. Cardiac output during labor. (pp = postpartum.) (Data from Robson SC, Dunlop W, Boys RJ, Hunter S. Cardiac output during labour. Br Med J 1987;295:1169)

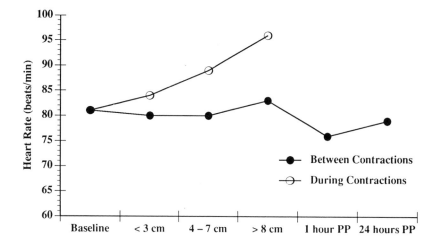

Figure 1–5. Stroke volume during labor. (pp = postpartum.) (Data from Robson SC, Dunlop W, Boys RJ, Hunter S. Cardiac output during labour. Br Med J 1987;295:1169)

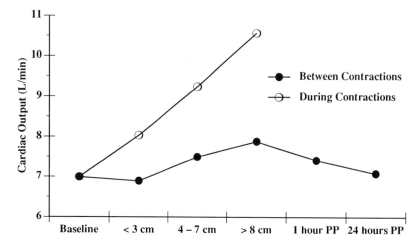

Figure 1–6. Heart rate during labor. (pp = postpartum.) (Data from Robson SC, Dunlop W, Bays RJ, Hunter S. Cardiac output during labour. Br Med J 1987; 295:1169)

Table 1–3

Maternal Hemodynamic Changes at Delivery Compared to Late in Pregnancy*

	CARDIAC OUTPUT	STROKE VOLUME	HEART RATE
Vaginal Delivery			
Immediate	↑23%–25%	↑12%	↑12%–18%
1 h	No change†	No change	No change
24 h	No change	No change	No change
Cesarean Delivery			
Immediate	↑9%–15%	No change	↑12%–16%
15–30 min	↑17%–37%		
1 h	No change		
24 h	No change		

*Data from references 64, 65, and 68.
†"No change" means values reported do not differ significantly from resting values obtained late in pregnancy.
Table does not include any parturients studied in the supine position.

stroke volume owing to hypovolemia from a decrease in venous return.

We can conclude that labor increases cardiac output with changes in both heart rate and stroke volume. Adequate analgesia may limit, but not prevent, these changes. Gravidae with limited cardiac reserve frequently benefit from early labor analgesia and limited expulsive efforts.

Effects of Delivery

Cardiac output, stroke volume, and heart rate all increase immediately after delivery (Tables 1-3 and 1-4).[65,66] By 24 hours, MAP and stroke volume also decline to their prelabor values.[64] Cardiac output rapidly increases owing to a central shift of blood from the now empty uterus and a marked decrease in IVC

Table 1–4

Maternal Hemodynamic Changes with Elective Cesarean Delivery*

TIME AFTER DELIVERY	CARDIAC OUTPUT	STROKE VOLUME	HEART RATE
Epidural Anesthesia			
15 min	↑37%	↑27%	No change
30 min	↑26%	No change	No change
60 min	No change†	No change	No change
24 h	No change	No change	No change
General Anesthesia			
15 min	↑28%	↑17%	↑11%
30 min	↑17%	↑14%	No change
60 min	No change	No change	No change
24 h	No change	No change	No change

*Data from reference 68.
†"No change" means values obtained did not differ from baseline values obtained before induction of anesthesia.

compression.[15] Reports that compared hemodynamics after delivery to values before delivery measured in the supine position found greater changes in cardiac output, heart rate, and stroke volume (+80%, +50%, and +80%, respectively).[63,67] The absolute value of postpartum cardiac output is the same regardless of maternal position before delivery.[63–68] Cardiac output returns to prelabor values within the first hour.[68]

During abdominal delivery, cardiac output, stroke volume, and heart rate change less than with vaginal delivery (see Table 1-3). The greater blood loss that occurs in cesarean section deliveries explains these differences.[65,68] The type of anesthesia does not influence the cardiac changes associated with cesarean delivery (see Table 1-4).[68]

Although postpartum hemodynamics return to term values within an hour, these are *not* nonpregnant values. Cardiac output remains increased for the first 24 hours postpartum and then progressively falls by the tenth postnatal day (25% decrease from term).[69] By 2 weeks after delivery, heart rate (−20%), stroke volume (−18%), cardiac output (−28%), and contractility all decrease.[14] Clark *et al*[22] measured pulmonary artery pressures and cardiac output at term and again 11 to 13 weeks' postpartum (in only the left lateral position). Cardiac output was 43% greater at term, heart rate was 17% higher, systemic vascular resistance was 21% lower, and pulmonary vascular resistance was 34% lower.[22] Maternal systolic and diastolic pressure may decrease for the first 2 postpartum days.[69] They significantly increase by the fourth to sixth postpartum day.[69,70] Central venous pressure rises in the first 24 hours postpartum if oxytocic drugs are given.[71] If excessive blood loss (>500 mL) occurs, heart rate increases and stroke volume falls for 48 hours.[69] Again, the type of anesthesia does not alter the effects of delivery on maternal hemodynamics (see Table 1-4).[68,72]

In summary, the immediate postpartum period brings the greatest cardiac output of pregnancy. Although well tolerated by most gravidae, this stress may necessitate close surveillance for at least 24 hours in the woman with preeclampsia or heart disease.

Plasma Volume

Plasma volume increases in the first 24 weeks of gestation.[73] Although some increment in plasma volume takes place by the end of the first trimester, most of this change occurs during the second trimester.[74,75] The third trimester brings only a slight further rise.[74,75] By 24 weeks the plasma volume is 1500 mL, or 50% larger

than before conception.[73,76,77] Plasma volume, when expressed in mL/kg, plateaus between 24 and 40 weeks' gestation at 70 mL/kg (Fig. 1-7, Table 1-5).[73]

The expanded plasma volume enhances circulation to the uterus, meets excretory needs of the kidneys, and helps to radiate body heat produced by the elevated metabolic rate.[77] The increased volume also serves to protect the fetus from the impaired venous return and decreased cardiac output of aortocaval compression. In addition, it provides a safeguard against blood loss at delivery.[15]

The phenomenon of aortocaval compression also flawed studies of plasma volume. The supine position delays mixing of tracer.[78] Indeed, *in the lateral position,* plasma volume does not decrease in late pregnancy.[76]

The rise of plasma volume with pregnancy has several possible etiologies. The fall in systemic vascular resistance and blood pressure produces a reflex rise in blood volume.[79] Estrogens also stimulate the renin–angiotensin system, resulting in sodium and water retention.[79,80] The influence of estrogens (whose precursors are formed in the fetal adrenal glands) has prompted Longo[79] to say that the fetus "through regulation of the hormonal milieu and in concert with the placenta, controls the maternal hematologic and cardiovascular adaptations to pregnancy." Progesterone does not influence blood volume unless combined with estrogens.[79]

Red Cells

During pregnancy, red cell mass increases by 18%.[75] Red cell mass and plasma volume exhibit no fixed rela-

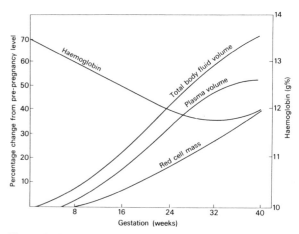

Figure 1–7. Progressive changes in hemoglobin, total body fluid, plasma volume, and red cell mass throughout pregnancy. (Crawford JS. Principles and practice of obstetric anesthesia. 5th ed. Oxford: Blackwell Scientific Publications, 1984;3)

Table 1-5

Plasma and Red Cell Volume Changes with Pregnancy*

	CHANGE AT TERM
Plasma volume	↑ 25%–80%
Red cell volume	↑ 20%

*Data from references 73, 74, 75, and 76.

tion to each other.[77] Red blood cell volume rises more slowly and to a lesser extent than plasma volume. This discrepancy causes the well-known decrease in hematocrit with pregnancy.[73,75,77,81] A normal or elevated hematocrit during pregnancy may signify intravascular volume depletion. However, when measured on a mL/kg basis, mean red cell volume remains constant at 27 mL/kg. Plasma volume changes from 50 mL/kg to 70 mL/kg.[73]

Erythropoietin, synthesized by the kidneys, stimulates red cell production.[82] Urinary excretion of erythropoietin peaks between 20 and 28 weeks of gestation. Human placental lactogen augments the action of erythropoietin.[82] Chorionic somatotropin, prolactin, and progesterone also stimulate erythropoiesis.[79]

White Cells

White blood cell counts also decline during pregnancy.[81,83] Neutrophils make up most of this elevated count. Monocytes may contribute, but lymphocytes, eosinophils, and basophils generally decline.[83]

Delivery

A gravida normally loses about 500 mL of blood with a vaginal delivery and close to 1000 mL with an abdominal delivery.[84] In response to the hemorrhage of delivery, blood volume rapidly decreases to normal and hematocrit changes very little.[75] This response to hemorrhage in the parturient differs from the nonpregnant patient in whom blood volume increases and hematocrit decreases.[84] Although total red blood cell volume falls rapidly,[84] red cell volume per kilogram of body weight remains stable.[73] Plasma volume declines over 3 to 5 days and reaches preconception levels by 8 weeks postpartum.[73]

Blood loss at delivery rarely necessitates transfusion due to the rapid decrement in plasma volume that helps maintain a normal hematocrit. Postpartum, a drop in hematocrit suggests that blood loss continues.

RESPIRATORY SYSTEM

Physical Examination

The increased volume of the intra-abdominal contents at term elevates the gravida's diaphragm and widens the transverse diameter of the chest 2 cm at term (Fig. 1-8). Gestation does not impair diaphragmatic motion. Roentgenogram reveals increased lung markings and a widened subcostal angle.[85] Hyperemia of the nasal turbinates and facial edema commonly complicate the airway.[86,87] A parturient may have severe laryngeal edema without stridor.[88]

Lung Volumes

Elevation of the diaphragm and changes in the chest diameter may alter dynamic lung volumes and gas flow in the airways, but, like the cardiovascular system, hormonal and metabolic factors play a major role. The progression of respiratory changes throughout gestation is not well understood. In one study, lung volumes did not change between the first and third trimester.[89] These results reflect the early onset of the respiratory changes of pregnancy.

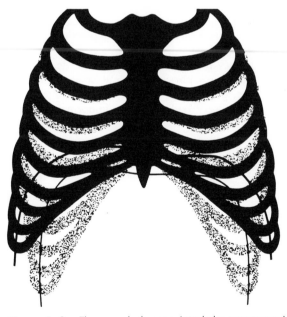

Figure 1-8. The normal rib cage (stippled = nonpregnant) showing raised diaphragm, increased diameter, and subcostal angle as seen with pregnancy (black). (Hytten F, Chamberlain G, eds. Clinical physiology in obstetrics, 2nd ed. London: Blackwell Scientific Publications, 1991;88)

Tidal volume begins to increase in the first trimester and rises to 28% above nonpregnant values at term.[90] Functional residual capacity (FRC) is progressively compressed throughout gestation.[90-93] Residual volume and expiratory reserve volume (ERV) also fall.[93-95] Total lung capacity and vital capacity change little with pregnancy.[85,93] Inspiratory capacity rises 10% at term, whereas expiratory capacity decreases 20% (Table 1-6, Fig. 1-9).[93]

Airway closure occurs during normal tidal breathing if closing volume exceeds ERV. This event adversely affects gas exchange. One study reported a rise in closing volume with pregnancy,[96] whereas another found no change.[92] Closing volume at term measures 8% of vital capacity, significantly higher than the 4.8% found 4 to 5 days postpartum.[96] Other investigators report that closing volume constitutes 10% to 11% of vital capacity when measured both in the third trimester and 2 days postpartum.[92] Perhaps the comparison to measurements made later in the postpartum period better reflects the nonpregnant (baseline) state.

The relationship between FRC and closing volume may explain the mild supine hypoxemia often seen in term parturients.[96] Airway closure can adversely affect gas exchange. Late in gestation, airway closure occurs above or closer to FRC than it does in the nonpregnant state.[97,98] This change may reflect not so much an alteration in closing volume as the smaller FRC.[97] In most patients, position does not alter closing volume but FRC falls further in the supine position. Hypoxemia often follows.

Pregnancy does not change anatomic dead space, but it decreases physiologic dead space (V_D/V_T). Therefore, pregnancy must considerably reduce alveolar dead space.[99] Wide variations in normal values of V_D/V_T make interpretation of these data difficult.[100] A smaller alveolar dead space improves the efficiency of ventilation and lowers the gradient between alveolar and end-tidal carbon dioxide.

Flow

Forced expiratory volume does not change (Table 1-7).[93-96,101,102] Pregnancy also does not alter flow measured at various lung volumes (flow–volume loops).[92] Lung compliance also remains unaffected by gestation. Total pulmonary resistance (made up of airway resistance and tissue resistance) falls significantly. Decreases in airway resistance predominate. Specific airway conductance rises during pregnancy, suggesting a greater cross-sectional area of the airway.[91]

Normally, bronchial muscle constricts in response to a decreased Pa_{CO_2}. Therefore, a bronchodilating mechanism must exist during pregnancy to explain bronchodilation in the face of hyperventilation.[103] Progesterone increases beta-adrenergic activity,[103] and smooth muscle relaxation occurs.[95] According to Rubin and colleagues,[95] "for a given 'alveolar' pressure, there is a significantly higher flow of air during pregnancy" due to smooth muscle relaxation.

Minute Ventilation

Minute ventilation rises 19% to 50% by term.[90,93,104] The increment in alveolar ventilation begins very soon after conception.[90,93,101,105] Respiratory rate increases 9% and tidal volume enlarges 28% (see Tables 1-6, 1-7).[93,106] Together they augment minute ventilation to above that required by oxygen consumption and carbon dioxide production.[104] Exercise further elevates minute ventilation[102,104,107] and oxygen consumption.[107] With greater workloads, however, a decrease in pulmonary reserve becomes apparent.[108]

The alveolar hyperventilation of pregnancy reflects hypersensitivity of the respiratory centers. Progesterone acts as a respiratory stimulant without changing the basal metabolic rate.[101] Carbon dioxide sensitivity curves shift to the left during pregnancy.[93] A parturient can hold her breath only until she attains a Pa_{CO_2} of 39.2 versus 48.2 mm Hg in nonpregnant subjects.[109] Progesterone administration to men and postmenopausal women duplicates these changes.[109] Sensitivity to carbon dioxide does not differ between the first and third trimester but dramatically falls after delivery.[89]

Nitrogen washout times also reflect alveolar hyperventilation. The time needed to reach an end-tidal ni-

Table 1-6

Changes in Lung Volumes and Capacities During Pregnancy*

	CHANGE AT TERM
Tidal volume	↑ 19%–28%
Expiratory reserve volume	↓ 17%
Residual volume	No change – ↓ 22%
Functional residual capacity	↓ 12%–25%
Vital capacity	No change – ↑ 6%
Inspiratory capacity	↑ 10%–19%
Expiratory capacity	↓ 20%
Total lung capacity	No change – ↓ 5%

*Data from references 85, 90 to 96, 99, 102, and 106.

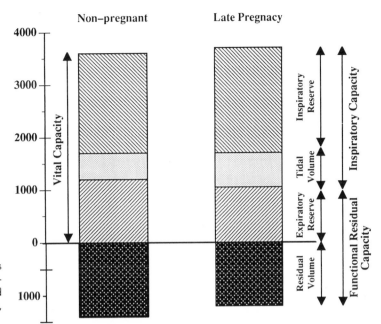

Figure 1–9. Lung volumes and capacities as altered by pregnancy. (After Hytten F, Chamberlain G, eds. Clinical physiology in obstetrics. 2nd ed. London: Blackwell Scientific Publications, 1991;84)

trogen of 2% when breathing 100% oxygen falls from 130 s before conception to 108 s at 13 to 26 weeks EGA to only 80 s at 26 to 42 weeks (Fig. 1-10).[110] Clinically, rapid nitrogen washout allows adequate maternal denitrogenation with four vital capacity breaths of 100% oxygen.[111] Four vital capacity breaths and 3 minutes of breathing 100% oxygen yield similar Pa_{O_2} values.[112]

Oxygen Consumption

At term the parturient consumes 20% to 30% more oxygen than at 12 to 14 weeks postpartum.[15,107] Most of this oxygen supplies the fetus. Demands by the placenta, uterus, and breasts account for most of the

Table 1–7

Ventilation Parameters at Term*

	CHANGE AT TERM
Respiratory rate	↑ 8.5%
Minute ventilation	↑ 19%–50%
Forced expiratory volume	No change

*Data from references 90, 92, 93, 104, and 106.

remainder of the augmented oxygen need (Fig. 1-11).[113]

Pulmonary Gas Exchange

Diffusion capacity does not change[114] or increases early in gestation.[98] Later decreases return the diffusion capacity at term to nonpregnant values.[98] The alveolar–arterial gradient (Pa_{O_2}–Pa_{O_2}) does not differ between the first trimester and term.[89] The Pa_{O_2}–Pa_{O_2} gradient increases in the supine position compared to the sitting position (20.0 mm Hg versus 14.3 mm Hg, respectively).[96] This effect most likely represents the relationship between a diminished FRC and a slightly elevated closing volume. At term, under general anesthesia for abdominal delivery, mean Pa_{O_2}–Pa_{O_2} gradient is 138 mm Hg at an inspired oxygen concentration of 67.5%.[100]

The hyperventilation of pregnancy lowers end-tidal carbon dioxide.[104] Gestation also affects the arterial to end-tidal carbon dioxide difference. In anesthetized, nonpregnant women, arterial carbon dioxide (Pa_{CO_2} is 3.5 to 5.3 mm Hg higher than the end-tidal carbon dioxide. After conception, this gradient narrows. Even early in gestation, Pa_{CO_2} is only 0.5 mm Hg higher than end-tidal carbon dioxide.[115] By the end of the first trimester, the end-tidal carbon dioxide approximates Pa_{CO_2}.[115] At term, under general anesthesia, the gradient can reverse and 50% of parturients have a higher

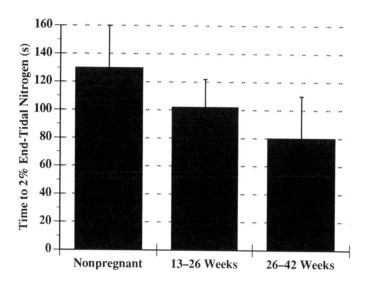

Figure 1–10. Time to 2% end-tidal nitrogen concentration in three groups of women. Pregnancy progressively shortens the time needed to attain adequate preoxygenation. (Data from Byrne F, Oduro-Dominah A, Kipling R. The effect of pregnancy on pulmonary nitrogen washout: A study of preoxygenation. Anesthesia 1987;42:148.)

end-tidal carbon dioxide than Pa_{CO_2}. The capnogram shows a steep phase III slope and end-tidal carbon dioxide can exceed mean alveolar (and arterial) P_{CO_2} (Fig. 1-12).[94,116,117] This trend reverses with delivery and mean Pa_{CO_2} rises from 0.03 mm Hg to 0.78 mm Hg above end-tidal carbon dioxide by 25 min postpartum.[116] Still, up to 31% of postpartum patients have higher end-tidal than arterial carbon dioxide.[117] During general anesthesia for postpartum tubal ligation, the mean Pa_{CO_2} gradient remains low, at 0.6 mm Hg.

Regression analysis suggests that the relationship between arterial and end-tidal carbon dioxide returns to normal by 8 days after delivery.[117]

Greater minute ventilation, cardiac output, and blood volume as well as the fall in alveolar dead space contribute to the smaller arterial to end-tidal carbon dioxide difference in pregnancy. End-tidal carbon dioxide values can accurately predict the degree of maternal hyperventilation and prevent uterine vasoconstriction induced hypocarbia.

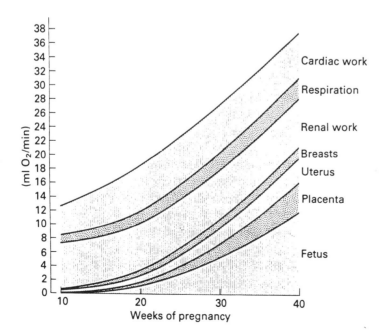

Figure 1–11. Partition of the increased oxygen consumption of pregnancy. (Hytten F, Chamberlain G, eds. Clinical physiology in obstetrics, 2nd ed. London: Blackwell Scientific Publications, 1991;91)

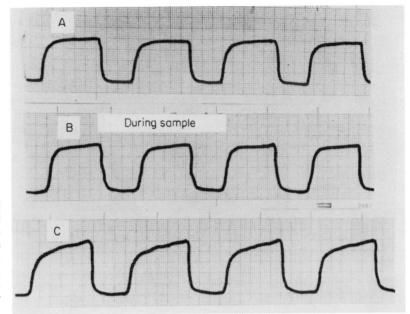

Figure 1–12. Capnograms during general anesthesia in a nonpregnant female **(A)** and gravidae **(B)** and **(C)**. Capnogram **(C)** demonstrates a steep phase III slope, resulting in a negative arterial to end-tidal difference. (Shankar KB, Moseley H, Kumar Y, Vemula V, Krishnan A. Arterial to end-tidal carbon dioxide tension difference during anaesthesia for tubal ligation. Anaesthesia 1987;42:482)

Maternal–Fetal Gas Exchange

The placenta consumes oxygen and produces carbon dioxide. Placental metabolism contributes to a considerable maternal–fetal carbon dioxide gradient. Fetal P_{CO_2}, but not P_{O_2}, correlates with maternal Pa_{CO_2}. Fetal P_{CO_2} averages 11.3 mm Hg higher than maternal Pa_{CO_2}.[118] The carbon dioxide gradient does not correlate with maternal Pa_{O_2}. Maternal–fetal oxygen gradient varies with maternal Pa_{O_2}. Umbilical vein P_{O_2} rises moderately in response to maternal hyperoxia.[118,119] Fetal oxygen uptake and uterine blood flow do not relate to maternal Pa_{O_2}.[119] These relationships allow administration of high oxygen concentrations to the mother without exposing the fetus to the hazards of hyperoxia.

The oxygen hemoglobin dissociation curves of normal gravidae overlap the normal range,[120,121] but most lie to the right of their position when not pregnant.[120] P_{50} increases significantly during gestation, allowing more oxygen delivery at the tissue level.[122,123] The nonpregnant woman and first-, second-, and third-trimester values of P_{50} reflect the right-shifted oxygen hemoglobin dissociation curve (26.7, 27.8, 28.8, and 30.4, respectively).[124] The elevated P_{50} aids oxygen delivery to the uteroplacental unit.

The respiratory alkalosis of pregnancy pushes the oxygen hemoglobin dissociation curve to the left, serving as an impetus to increased 2,3 DPG production. Maternal 2,3 DPG levels rise by 30% above nonpregnant values.[125,126] However, some investigators report no change in 2,3 DPG.[122,127] The higher concentration of 2,3 DPG pushes the dissociation curve back to the right. Maternal 2,3 DPG concentration does not correlate with measured indices of iron metabolism in spite of the correlation with hemoglobin concentration in nonpregnant subjects.[125]

In sum, with pregnancy, the oxyhemoglobin dissociation curve moves slightly to the right but remains within the range of normal. This shift increases P_{50} and allows more oxygen delivery at the tissue level. This adaptation augments oxygen delivery to the uteroplacental unit. High-risk pregnancy also may alter these values. Preeclampsia shifts the oxygen hemoglobin dissociation curve to the left with a P_{50} of 25.1.[123]

Blood Gas Analysis

The hyperventilation of pregnancy decreases the Pa_{CO_2} to 26 to 32 mm Hg.[89,105,128–131] The supine position does not change Pa_{CO_2}.[96]

With pregnancy, Pa_{O_2} rises slightly to 92 to 106 mm Hg (mean oxygen saturation 97.2%).[89,96,98,128–130] The supine position impairs oxygen exchange and average Pa_{O_2} falls from 101.2 mm Hg to 94.6 mm Hg.[96] Capillary P_{O_2} also is higher (13 mm Hg) in the sitting versus the supine position.[132] This mild supine hypoxemia may relate to the increased volume of abdominal contents and elevated closing volume.[96] Aortocaval compression also could contribute by hindering venous return and widening the arteriovenous oxygen difference.

The metabolic compensation to this respiratory acidosis induces a fall in plasma bicarbonate concentration to 16 to 21 mEq/L, maintaining a near-normal or slightly elevated pH (7.405–7.42).[89,98,105,128–131,133,134] This adjustment begins early in pregnancy.[101,105] Acid–base values also change in high-risk pregnancies.[135]

Etiology

When significant respiratory changes arise, they usually begin early in gestation, before the uterus becomes an abdominal organ.[93] This trend suggests that hormonal or metabolic events, instead of mechanical developments, induce the transformation. Oxygen consumption escalates more gradually than cardiac output.[24] Unlike cardiac output, which probably rises in response to hormonal stimuli, oxygen consumption seems to increase in concert with the metabolic needs of the mother and her fetus.

Acid–base changes begin immediately after conception. They resemble acclimatization to high altitude.[101] A hormonal basis seems likely.[98,136] Both progesterone and estrogens may be involved. The production of various prostaglandins, cGMP, and cAMP increases during pregnancy. These compounds may ultimately demonstrate importance as mediators of some of the respiratory changes that accompany pregnancy.[98]

Progesterone augments the respiratory response to hypercarbia. Progesterone may modify the permeability of chemoreceptor cells or directly stimulate the central respiratory or hypothalamic neurons in contact with the blood.[137] When given to male volunteers, progesterone increases tidal volume, respiratory rate, and minute ventilation, with a resultant rise in pH and fall in $Paco_2$ and bicarbonate.[109]

Effects of Labor

Forced vital capacity, forced expiratory volume, and maximum voluntary ventilation do not change in labor.[138] Pain induces maternal hyperventilation. Uterine contractions increase oxygen consumption (63%) and minute ventilation (74%) during the first stage of labor.[139] Gravidae hyperventilate during early labor out of proportion to the increased metabolic demand.[140] Adequate analgesia eliminates these changes. Contractions do not significantly modify respiratory measurements in women receiving lumbar epidural analgesia.[139,140] Therefore, epidural block effectively decreases the work of breathing during labor. Even during expulsive efforts of the second stage, analgesia minimizes oxygen consumption and minute ventilation.[139]

Hypoxemia also may arise during labor. Oxygen saturation fell below 90% in 49% of laboring women. Systemic narcotics and inhalation analgesia increased the frequency of low oxygen saturations.[141]

In the first stage of labor, women hyperventilate during painful contractions and $Paco_2$ falls 6 to 7 mm Hg. This effect persists throughout parturition. In the second stage of labor, mean $Paco_2$ is 22.3 mm Hg between contractions and declines to 16.2 mm Hg during contractions. The pH and Pao_2 increase during the second stage.[142] Maternal hyperventilation can modify fetal acid–base status. The most alkalotic mothers ($Paco_2$ <17 mm Hg) deliver acidotic infants.[143] Uterine blood flow decreases if $Paco_2$ reaches a critical level.[143]

Effects of Delivery

Alveolar hyperventilation and sensitivity of respiratory centers to carbon dioxide suddenly decrease after delivery.[89] Carbon dioxide production and oxygen consumption approach normal 1 to 2 weeks postpartum.[106] Minute ventilation and oxygen uptake remain elevated for up to 2 weeks.[90,105,106] Vital capacity, total lung capacity and maximum breathing capacity fall markedly in the early postpartum period.[85,90] Tidal volume begins to decline within 5 days.[93,106] FRC and residual volume return to normal within 48 hours.[93]

Anesthetic Implications

The smaller FRC and increased oxygen consumption limit the gravida's oxygen reserve. With maternal apnea, Pao_2 falls rapidly (Fig. 1-13).[144] Critical hypoxemia can occur with alarming speed during induction of general anesthesia. Rapid intubation or oxygenation (by mask with cricoid pressure) by experienced personnel prevents disaster. Short-handled laryngoscopes and a range of sizes of endotracheal tubes may facilitate tracheal intubation.

Mechanical hyperventilation to a $Paco_2$ of 22 mm Hg in anesthetized gravid ewes lowers fetal carotid Po_2 by 8 mm Hg. Prolonged maternal hyperventilation may produce fetal asphyxia with severe hypoxia and

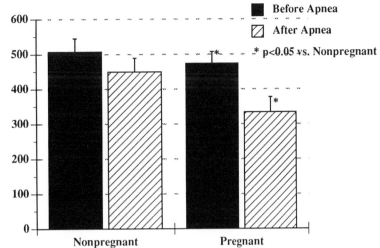

Figure 1–13. Fall in P_{O_2} after 60 seconds of apnea in 12 pregnant and 8 nonpregnant women. All patients were intubated and ventilated with 97.5% oxygen. The endotracheal tube was then disconnected from the anesthetic machine and exposed to room air. (Data from Archer GW Jr, Marx GF. Arterial oxygen tension during apnoea in parturient women. Br J Anaesth 1974;46:358)

metabolic acidosis.[145] Maintaining maternal arterial or end-tidal carbon dioxide near 30 mm Hg will avoid the deleterious effects of mechanical hyperventilation on fetal oxygenation. Mechanical hyperventilation also can worsen fetal acid–base status by limiting maternal cardiac output and therefore placental blood flow.[146] Although maternal hypercapnia may increase oxygen supply to the fetus above normal, it is not clinically indicated.[145]

Owing to the differences between fetal and maternal hemoglobin, raising maternal F_iO_2 from 50% to 100% elevates maternal Pao_2 but does not change fetal P_{O_2}.[118] High inspired concentrations of oxygen can safely maximize maternal oxygenation without compromising the fetus.

The sitting position minimizes the negative effects of pregnancy on the respiratory system. Gravidae with significant respiratory disease can best be evaluated and cared for when upright.

RENAL SYSTEM

Physical Changes

The gravid uterus or progesterone causes ureteral dilatation during pregnancy.[147–152]. The widening occurs above the pelvic brim.[153] Ureteral dilatation manifests early in pregnancy and may persist up to 12 weeks postpartum, making a solely mechanical explanation unlikely.[148,151,152] Postpartum intravenous pyelograms reveal a mean kidney length that is 1.5 cm greater than that measured in nonpregnant women.[147]

Glomerular Filtration

Glomerular filtration increases 50% during pregnancy,[147,151,152,154–157] lowering blood urea nitrogen and creatinine levels to 6 to 8 mg/100 mL and 0.4 to 0.6 mg/100 mL, respectively (Table 1-8, Fig. 1-14).[151,152] Effective renal plasma flow (ERPF) significantly increases during the first two trimesters.[154,156,158,159] The third trimester brings a fall in ERPF (as measured by para-aminohippurate clearance) but not in glomerular filtration rate (GFR).[157,160] Also, in the third trimester, creatinine production must increase. Serum creatinine concentration rises, but clearance does not change.[157]

Serial measurements of creatinine clearance reveal the early and progressive nature of the changes in GFR.[161] Creatinine clearance approximates GFR[162] and increases 25% by the fourth week of gestation.[161] By the ninth week, clearance rises 45%.[158,161]

Table 1–8

Renal Changes During Pregnancy*

	CHANGE AT TERM
Glomerular filtration rate	↑ 50%
Effective renal plasma flow	↑ 25%–90%
Blood urea nitrogen	↓ 40%
Serum creatinine	↓ 40%

*Data from references 157, 158, and 160.

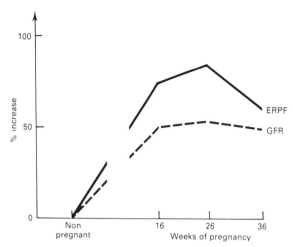

Figure 1–14. Relative changes in effective renal plasma flow (ERPF) and glomerular filtration rate (GFR) during pregnancy. (Hytten F, Chamberlain G, eds. Clinical physiology in obstetrics, 2nd ed. London: Blackwell Scientific Publications, 1991;249)

Elevated blood volume contributes to this augmented GFR.[155] However, the rise in plasma volume fails to explain the early changes in renal function.[161] A hormonal mechanism seems likely, because changes in creatinine clearance also occur during the normal menstrual cycle. In addition, women destined to have spontaneous abortions do not show sustained changes in creatinine clearance.[161]

Harder to explain is the third-trimester decrease in ERPF. Maternal position strongly influences renal blood flow.[24] Similar measurements of ERPF in the left lateral[160,163,164] or sitting[157,164] position make aortocaval compression an unlikely but still possible explanation. Prolonged measurement of ERPF in one position yields declining values.[164] Changes in plasma volume provide another possible explanation, but plasma volume continues to increase, albeit only minimally, in the third trimester.[74,75]

Tubular Function

Although pregnancy does not alter the tubular handling of some substances,[165] the ability to reabsorb glucose universally declines.[156,166–168] In women who develop minor degrees of glycosuria, tubular function returns to normal after delivery. Parturients who exhibit more glycosuria have postpartum evidence of tubular damage.[168] The mechanism of glycosuria is unclear. The presence of persistent tubular damage suggests involvement of more than just a larger filtered

glucose load presented to the tubules by volume expansion and elevated GFR. Glycosuria normally resolves within 1 week of delivery, faster than carbohydrate metabolism normalizes, suggesting a role for altered tubular function.[168]

To increase plasma volume, total body sodium also must rise. The body retains 500 to 850 mEq of sodium during pregnancy.[152] Increased renin and aldosterone contribute to sodium retention.[151] The uteroplacental unit contributes to elevated prorenin production.[51,169] Aldosterone secretion compensates for natriuretic effects of pregnancy.[170] Both the increased GFR and progesterone's competitive inhibition of aldosterone's action at distal tubular sites promote sodium loss.[170–173] Experimentally, the extent of natriuresis directly relates to dosage of exogenous progesterone.[174] Thus, aldosterone secretion must increase to maintain sodium and water balance.

Pregnant women retain a total of 300 mEq of potassium.[175] Progesterone inhibits potassium excretion by antagonizing aldosterone.[170,175] Plasma potassium concentration decreases by 10%.[159]

Bicarbonate reclamation remains normal during pregnancy in spite of lowered serum bicarbonate values. The gravida retains the normal renal acidifying mechanisms.[176]

Plasma osmolality decreases an average of 8 to 10 mOsm/kg by the tenth week of gestation.[158,177] The osmotic threshold for thirst declines, as does the threshold for arginine vasopressin (AVP) secretion. The parturient drinks more to maintain the lower osmolality.[158,177] Endorphins may alter AVP secretion.[177]

Renin activity remains elevated for 2 to 7 days after delivery. Umbilical venous blood contains high concentrations of prorenin.[169] Thus, the placenta may be the source of extra renin during gestation. However, the lack of change in renin activity with delivery casts doubt on this explanation.[178] At term, the gravida's position uniformly affects renin activity;[153] therefore, interpretation of renin data requires care.

Implications

Pregnancy modifies the interpretation of diagnostic studies that detect dilated ureters or increased kidney size. Ureteral dilatation contributes to frequent urinary tract infection. The risk of preterm labor increases with infection. A gravida with significant renal disease may maintain somewhat normal blood urea nitrogen and creatinine levels. Slight elevation of these values suggests a need for diagnostic evaluation. Glycosuria may be normal during pregnancy. Pregnancy modifies renal handling of drugs and may have significant effects on pharmacokinetics.

GASTROINTESTINAL SYSTEM

Progesterone, as a smooth muscle relaxant, decreases gastric motility during pregnancy. Male rats treated with progesterone have impaired esophageal, antral, and colonic contractile activity.[179] Progesterone and estradiol treatment inhibit the gastrointestinal contractile response elicited by acetylcholine and gastrin.[180]

Esophagus

At 16 weeks' EGA, pregnancy does not lower basal lower esophageal sphincter (LES) tone when measured by a three-lumen tube.[181] However, the response to agents that normally increase LES tone is attenuated.[181] The LES becomes progressively weaker during pregnancy.[182] The LES pressure reaches its nadir at 36 weeks.[183] Intragastric pressure rises during gestation, whereas lower intraesophageal pressure falls.[184,185] Thus, pregnancy narrows the pressure difference between the stomach and esophagus from 7 mm Hg in nonpregnant women to 3.4 mm Hg.[185] In addition, peristaltic speed and amplitude decline in the gravida. Elevated abdominal pressure and changes in the position of the stomach contribute to a higher incidence of hiatal hernia in parturients.[185] Heartburn and associated esophagitis become quite common (up to 70% of gravidae).[186] Esophagitis correlates with the lowest gradients across the LES[184] and pyloric sphincter relaxation.[187]

Stomach

Gastric Emptying

A variety of methods reveal conflicting results regarding gastric emptying. The first evaluations with barium meals[188] and induced vomiting[189] showed no delay in gastric emptying during labor without sedation. In contrast, a double-sampling technique revealed a longer total mean emptying time in term pregnant women than in nonpregnant subjects. However, the gastric volume present 30 minutes after a meal was *not* significantly different between the two groups.[190] As measured by this technique, labor (without analgesics or sedatives) further slows emptying of the final 100 to 200 mL of test solution. During labor, gastric volume at 30 minutes is greater than in nonpregnant women.[190]

Paracetamol absorption also measures gastric emptying. Paracetamol is absorbed only in the small bowel. Thus, the blood concentration of paracetamol correlates with gastric emptying.[191] Pregnancy at 12 to 14 weeks, but not 8 to 11 weeks, delays paracetamol absorption.[192] Studies during the third trimester and in the first 24 to 48 hours postpartum do not demonstrate delayed gastric emptying.[193] The use of systemic narcotics significantly slows paracetamol absorption in laboring patients.[194] Interestingly, although metoclopramide did not accelerate gastric emptying in nonpregnant patients given systemic narcotics,[194,195] it did increase emptying during pregnancy.[196] Ranitidine appears to decrease gastric volume whether or not narcotics have been given.[197] These studies have generated much debate without complete resolution.[198–200]

Technologic advances have provided another technique to evaluate gastric emptying. Noninvasive gastric impedance can measure gastric emptying in both pregnant and nonpregnant volunteers. Pregnancy alone, even in the third trimester, does not slow gastric emptying. Postpartum patients who had received opiate analgesia had significantly prolonged 70%, 50%, and 30% emptying times.[201] However, O'Sullivan *et al*[201] caution that the impedance technique does not always permit measurement of the final 20% to 30% of gastric fluid. That volume approximates the final 100- to 200-mL portion of the 750-mL test volume used in the double-sampling technique. Therefore, even this most recent report does not really disprove the possibility of rapid initial emptying followed by delayed complete emptying with pregnancy. Opiates significantly prolong both emptying phases in pregnant patients.[195,202]

Motilin stimulates gastrointestinal smooth muscle contraction. Pregnancy markedly decreases both fasting-and glucose-induced motilin secretion. Motilin may partially mediate the smooth muscle relaxation attributed to progesterone.[203]

Small bowel transit time, as measured by the lactulose hydrogen breath method, increases during pregnancy[204–206] and during the luteal phase of the menstrual cycle.[207] The greatest prolongation of in-transit time occurs while progesterone concentration rises from less than 1 ng/mL to 80 ng/mL.[206]

Gastric Secretions

The hormone gastrin partially controls secretion of gastric acid. Gastrin also tends to promote elevated tone of the LES and inhibit the pyloric sphincter.[208]

Early pregnancy does not modify serum gastrin concentration. The fetus, the placenta, or both produce gastrin, so gastrin production rises progressively throughout the second and third trimesters as well as during labor. The volume of acid secreted by the stomach, pancreas, and small intestine increases.[208] Pregnancy does not modify basal or pentagastrin-stimulated acid secretion.[183]

Postpartum Period

Administration of systemic opioids during the puerperium also delays gastric emptying after delivery.[201] Both paracetamol absorption[194] and the double-sampling technique[190] show normal emptying times by 4 to 5 days postpartum. However, these data should not suggest an absent risk of gastric acid aspiration. Postpartum studies of volume and pH suggest that 33% to 73% of patients undergoing postpartum tubal sterilization still meet "at-risk" criteria for aspiration pneumonitis.[209,210] (For a more detailed discussion of regurgitation and aspiration risk after delivery, see Chap. 25, "Anesthesia for Postpartum Tubal Ligation.")

Gallbladder

Progesterone inhibits cholecystokinin release from the intestinal mucosa.[211] In addition, the contractile response to cholecystokinin diminishes during pregnancy.[212] The gallbladder does not empty completely, particularly in the second and third trimesters.[211,213,214] These factors may contribute to the pathogenesis of cholesterol gallstones during pregnancy.[214]

Liver

Certain signs of pregnancy mimic liver disease. Spider angiomata and palmar erythema proliferate due to increased estrogens.[215] Eighty percent of normal parturients have prolonged retention of bromsulphalein.[216] The concentration of plasma proteins, particularly albumin, falls 20% to 30% and remains low for 6 to 7 weeks postpartum.[215,217] Still, the total amount of some proteins increases during pregnancy.[215,218]

Smooth endoplasmic reticulum proliferates, indicating a rise in hepatic microsomal activity.[219] Steroid hormones function as competitive inhibitors of enzymes involved in oxidative reactions but do not impair conjugation.[217] Certain liver enzymes show higher activities, particularly after the fifth month of gestation.[220] These include glucose-6-phosphate dehydrogenase and aminolevalinic acid synthetase.[217] Placental production raises the serum concentration of alkaline phosphatase by 200% to 400%.[215] Transferase (AST and ALT), lactic dehydrogenase, and gamma-glutamyl transpeptidase activity may rise.[215,221,220] Liver RNA content markedly increases.[217]

Implications

Increased gastric volume (due to delayed emptying and a larger volume of secretions), decreased LES tone, and elevated intragastric pressure require careful attention to acid aspiration prophylaxis. Avoidance of general anesthesia limits the population at risk for aspiration. Early institution of adequate regional anesthesia can help meet this goal. When general anesthesia is required, nonparticulate antacids, H_2-receptor antagonists, metoclopramide, and rapid sequence induction with cricoid pressure help to limit the risk of pulmonary damage.

Pregnancy complicates the diagnosis of hepatic disease by imitating certain signs. Although mild to moderate elevation of liver enzymes may be normal in pregnancy, they should not be overlooked. Protein drug binding may increase or decrease depending on specific drugs involved.

COAGULATION

Pregnancy activates the clotting system. All factors except XI and XIII increase during gestation.[222] The most significant elevations occur with factors VII, VIII, X, and fibrinogen.[215,217,223–226] Mean platelet volume rises, although platelet count either remains unchanged or falls due to hemodilution.[81,83,227–231] Platelet life span remains stable.[230] Pregnancy lowers plasma fibrinolytic activity,[223] although plasminogen concentration increases as early as 4 months' gestation.[224,225]

Recent evidence suggests that a compensated, accelerated state of fibrinolysis occurs during late pregnancy.[226,232] Such activity at the placental–uterine interface seems possible.[222,226] There, localized fibrin formation from platelet activation and coagulation occurs. Active fibrinolysis follows. Measuring indices of fibrinolysis in the peripheral blood may not detect uterine fibrinolysis.

Delivery accelerates platelet activation, coagulation, and fibrinolytic activity (Fig. 1-15).[233–235] Twenty-one percent of patients exhibit significant increases in fibrin degradation products during labor, with 32% showing the same immediately postpartum. Fibrin degradation remains elevated in only 10% of women 24 to 72 hours after delivery.[236] Platelet count also returns to normal 24 to 72 hours postpartum.[228] Fibrinolytic activity declines rapidly.[223,228,235,237] Placental separation activates the clotting mechanism.[235,238] Factor VIII activity transiently increases in uterine vein blood after delivery, shortening measured coagulation times.[235,238]

The coagulation system seems to prepare for the blood loss of delivery by increasing coagulation factors throughout pregnancy. At the same time, this hypercoagulable state complicates pregnancy and the immediate postpartum period with thromboembolic events. Regional anesthetic techniques that allow early ambulation (and thus limit venous stasis) minimize maternal morbidity and mortality.

ENDOCRINE

Glucose and Insulin

Pregnancy lowers fasting–glucose concentration.[239,240] Insulin secretion rises throughout gestation.[240–244] At the same time, the tissue sensitivity to insulin diminishes.[242–246] Insulin degradation does not vary.[247] Pregnancy-specific hormonal factors cause insulin resistance.[243,244,248] Human placental lactogen has anti-insulin activity.[239,246,248–250] Insulin secretion precipitously declines after delivery, suggesting that the placenta holds the stimulus for insulin release.[241] Speroff *et al*[246] describe human placental lactogen as a "major force in the diabetogenic effects of pregnancy." Progesterone alone does not cause the changes in glucose and insulin metabolism. In men, progesterone administration elevates fasting plasma insulin but does not lower fasting glucose as pregnancy does.[239] De-

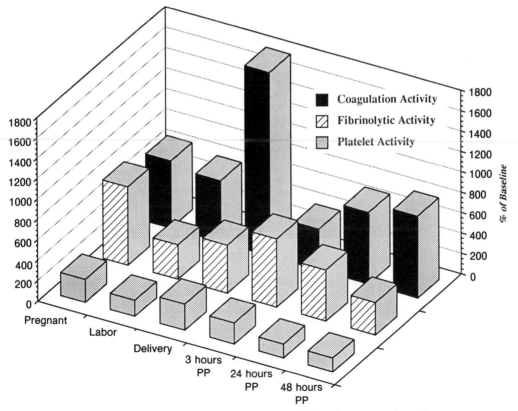

Figure 1–15. Relative changes in coagulation, platelet, and fibrinolytic activity during the puerperium. (Gerbasi FR, Bottoms S, Farag A, Mammen E. Increased intravascular coagulation associated with pregnancy. Obstet Gynecol 1990;75:385 and Gerbasi FR, Bottoms S, Farag A, Mammen EF. Changes in hemostasis activity during delivery and the immediate postpartum period. Am J Obstet Gynecol 1990;162:1158.)

creased buffering capacity predisposes the gravida to ketoacidosis.

Thyroid

Total serum thyroxine concentrations rise during gestation.[251] Thyroid-binding globulin concentration peaks in the third trimester.[217] The percentage of free thyroxine in the serum falls.[251] Progesterone administration replicates this situation.[251] Early in pregnancy, serum chorionic gonadotropin, with its intrinsic thyroid-stimulating activity, activates the thyroid gland.[251-253] Serum chorionic gonadotropin concentration peaks between 9 and 18 weeks of gestation. Thyroid-stimulating hormone (TSH) secretion then falls via a negative-feedback mechanism.[252] The thyroid gland grows larger.[254] Pituitary sensitivity to TSH remains constant.[254] In spite of elevated total serum thyroxine measurements, most parturients remain euthyroid. The patient should be evaluated carefully before beginning antithyroid treatment, perhaps unnecessarily.[251] Increased thyroid size may hinder rapid sequence induction.

Progesterone

Progesterone garners much interest as an explanation for various physiologic adaptations to pregnancy. Plasma progesterone concentration progressively rises throughout pregnancy[255,256] and abruptly declines after delivery of the placenta.[255,257] This time course alone makes progesterone a likely mediator in many physiologic alterations seen in pregnancy.

Prostaglandins

Peripheral concentrations of prostaglandins also increase during pregnancy. Prostaglandin A compounds multiply most dramatically. Early in gestation, Prostaglandin A–like material rises by 300%. Typical effects of prostaglandin A compounds include decreased systemic vascular resistance and increased cardiac output. Both changes occur early in pregnancy and correlate with the elevation in prostaglandin A activity.[258]

Prostaglandin E does not significantly increase until the third trimester.[258] Possible explanations include production in the peripheral arteriovenous system stimulated by angiotensin II. Prostaglandin E–induced vasodilation prevents angiotensin II from causing a hypertensive state.[258] Prostacyclin production also may mediate vasodilatation.[246]

MUSCULOSKELETAL

The corpus luteum initially secretes relaxin. During the first trimester, relaxin concentration rises dramatically. Then, the amount of relaxin declines to a stable level throughout the third trimester.[259] Relaxin softens the cervix, inhibits uterine contractions, and relaxes the pubic symphysis.[246] Peripheral joints become lax during the last trimester of pregnancy.[260] Ligamentous laxity may contribute to the high incidence of low back pain with pregnancy[261] and vulnerability to injury during the mechanical stress of labor.[262]

CENTRAL NERVOUS SYSTEM

The placenta produces endorphins and enkephalins that may function to provide a naturally occurring analgesia during pregnancy.[246,263] Pregnant animals are more tolerant to aversive stimuli.[264-266] The antinociceptive threshold abruptly rises 1 to 2 days before parturition.[264] Intrathecal or systemic opioid antagonists reverse this pregnancy-mediated analgesia.[264-266] Systemic beta-endorphin secretion increases during labor and correlates with the patient's perception of pain intensity.[267] However, beta-endorphin is a large molecule that does not cross the blood–brain barrier. If this compound is important in mediating the changes in pain sensitivity in pregnancy or labor, its cerebrospinal fluid concentrations also should rise. They do not.[268]

Cerebrospinal fluid 5-HIAA, a major metabolite of serotonin, increases with gestational age.[269] Plasma and cerebrospinal fluid concentrations of progesterone significantly rise with pregnancy.[270] An earlier report suggested an effective blood–brain barrier for progesterone.[271] Concentration of progesterone in cerebrospinal fluid falls rapidly in the postpartum period.[270]

Pregnant women require less local anesthetic per spinal segment blocked than nonpregnant controls.[272,273] This change arises early in gestation and persists into the postpartum period.[273] Although higher dermatomal levels develop as soon as 5 minutes after injection, pregnancy prolongs the time to complete epidural spread.[272] Pregnancy also increases the interpatient variation in the spread of caudal anesthesia.[274] Both mechanical and biochemical factors may have a role in producing this change.[272] Investigation of mechanical factors reveals conflicting data. Abdominal compression, which mimics the effects of the gravid uterus, increases IVC pressure to 25 cm H_2O. Intrathecal tetracaine, 4 mg, spreads further in women wearing an abdominal binder.[275] This dose of drug spreads further still in parturients. In addition, the gravid uterus elevates epidural but not cerebrospinal fluid pressure.[276,277] These data suggest that mechanical factors may explain some, but not all, of the altered sensitivity to local anesthetics seen in pregnancy.

Peripheral nerves also are more vulnerable to local anesthetics during pregnancy.[278] Pregnancy hastens the onset of 50% block with bupivacaine, 0.35 mmol, in A, B, and C vagal fibers.[279] This change relates to more than just altered diffusion of local anesthetic. The dose-response curve to conduction blockade in isolated A and C nerve fibers from pregnant animals also shifts to the left.[280] As with many other physiologic changes, progesterone's influence predominates. Prolonged (4 days), but not acute, exposure to progesterone makes nerve fibers more susceptible to local anesthetics.[281,282]

Pregnancy in ewes and exogenous progesterone in rabbits decrease the minimum alveolar concentration for halothane and isoflurane.[283,284] Pregnancy does not alter minimum alveolar concentration in rats and mice.[285]

Increased sensitivity to local and general anesthetics requires dosage adjustments for the gravida. Careful assessment of the patient's response allows one to minimize drug exposure and obtain the desired effects without excessive maternal or fetal side-effects.

PHARMACOKINETICS

Pregnancy alters drug binding and drug elimination. Albumin concentration falls, and hepatic microsomal activity rises. The larger plasma volume increases renal blood flow and augments glomerular filtration. Pharmacokinetic parameters do not show any consistent trend with pregnancy. The rate of elimination of various drugs can either rise or fall.[286] Gestation prolongs the elimination of bupivacaine, diazepam, thiopental, and theophylline.[219,286] The volume of distribution of thiopental and theophylline enlarges.[219,286] The unbound fraction of diazepam, phenytoin, phenobarbital, and lidocaine increases with pregnancy.[287]

Plasma pseudocholinesterase activity rapidly declines 24% during pregnancy and up to 60% after delivery.[288–293] Structural abnormality of pseudocholinesterase has not been found.[290] The augmented plasma volume inflates the volume of distribution of succinylcholine and counterbalances the fall in pseudocholinesterase activity. Postpartum, succinylcholine paralysis persists about 3 minutes longer than in nonpregnant patients.[294]

CONCLUSIONS

Adaptations to pregnancy manifest in every organ system, usually within several weeks of conception. These adaptations should be viewed as continually evolving from the first weeks after conception. Change continues during and after parturition.

The cardiovascular system must adapt to the increasing demands of the growing uterus and fetus. Increases in plasma volume and cardiac output alter the hemodynamic responses to anesthetic interventions. Beginning in the second trimester, aortocaval compression can hinder uterine blood flow and maternal cardiac output. The larger plasma volume allows the parturient to tolerate greater blood loss than her nonpregnant counterpart.

The changes in the respiratory system that accompany gestation significantly narrow the parturient's margin of safety during general anesthesia. A smaller FRC and a higher oxygen consumption render her more susceptible to hypoxemia during periods of apnea. Mechanical hyperventilation can lower uterine blood flow and incite fetal acidosis.

Gastric emptying slows while acid secretion increases. In combination with a higher intra-abdominal pressure, these changes place the parturient at greater risk of regurgitation and aspiration should her airway reflexes become impaired.

Pregnancy-induced alterations in the central nervous system increase the parturient's sensitivity to both local and general anesthetics. Understanding the extent and progressive nature of the body's response to pregnancy allows the anesthesiologist to approach any gravida with confidence.

REFERENCES

1. Cutforth R, MacDonald CB. Heart sounds and murmurs in pregnancy. Am Heart J 1966;71:741.
2. De Swiet M. The cardiovascular system. In: Hytten F, Chamberlain G, eds. Clinical physiology in obstetrics. 2nd ed. Oxford:Blackwell Scientific Publications, 1991:3.
3. Enein M, Zina AAA, Kassem M, El-Tabbakh G. Echocardiography of the pericardium in pregnancy. Obstet Gynecol 1987;69:851.

4. Clapp JF III, Seaward BL, Sleamaker RH, Hiser J. Maternal physiologic adaptations to early human pregnancy. Am J Obstet Gynecol 1988;159:1456.

5. Clapp JF III. Maternal heart rate in pregnancy. Am J Obstet Gynecol 1985;152:659.

6. Walters WA, MacGregor WG, Hills M. Cardiac output at rest during pregnancy and the puerperium. Clin Sci 1966;30:1.

7. Capeless EL, Clapp JE. Cardiovascular changes in early phase of pregnancy. Am J Obstet Gynecol 1989; 161:1449.

8. Lees MM, Taylor SH, Scott DB, Kerr MG. A study of cardiac output at rest throughout pregnancy. J Obstet Gynaecol Br Commonw 1967;74:319.

9. Bader RA, Bader ME, Rose DJ, Braunwald E. Hemodynamics at rest and during exercise in normal pregnancy as studied by cardiac catheterization. J Clin Invest 1955;34:1524.

10. McLennan FM, Haites NE, Rawles JM. Stroke and minute distance in pregnancy: A longitudinal study using Doppler ultrasound. Br J Obstet Gynaecol 1987; 94:499.

11. Ueland K, Novy MJ, Metcalfe J. Cardiorespiratory responses to pregnancy and exercise in normal women and patients with heart disease. Am J Obstet Gynecol 1973;115:4.

12. Ueland K, Novy MJ, Peterson EN, Metcalfe J. Maternal cardiovascular dynamics: IV. The influence of gestational age on the maternal cardiovascular response to posture and exercise. Am J Obstet Gynecol 1969;104:856.

13. Katz R, Karliner JS, Resnik R. Effects of a natural volume overload state (pregnancy) on left ventricular performance in normal human subjects. Circulation 1978;58:434.

14. Robson SC, Hunter S, Moore M, Dunlop W. Haemodynamic changes during the puerperium: A Doppler and M-mode echocardiographic study. Br J Obstet Gynaecol 1987;94:1028.

15. Elkayam U, Gleicher N. Cardiovascular physiology of pregnancy. In: Elkayam U, Gleicher N, eds. Cardiac problems in pregnancy diagnosis and management of maternal and fetal disease. New York: Alan R. Liss, 1982:5.

16. Lee W, Rokey R, Cotton DB. Noninvasive maternal stoke volume and cardiac output determinations by pulsed Doppler echocardiography. Am J Obstet Gynecol 1988;158:505.

17. Easterling TR, Carlson KL, Schmucker BC, Brateng DA, Benedetti TJ. Measurement of cardiac output in pregnancy by Doppler technique. Am J Perinatol 1990;7:220.

18. Kamal GD, Symreng T, Starr J. Inconsistent esophageal Doppler cardiac output during acute blood loss. Anesthesiology 1990;72:95.

19. Hart MV, Morton MJ, Hosenpud JD, Metcalfe J. Aortic function during normal human pregnancy. Am J Obstet Gynecol 1986;154:887.

20. Ihrman K. A clinical and physiological study of pregnancy in a material from Northern Sweden: VI. The arterial blood pressures at rest and in orthostatic test during and after pregnancy. Acta Soc Med Upsaliensis 1960;65:315.

21. MacGillivray I, Rose GA, Rowe B. Blood pressure survey in pregnancy. Clin Sci 1969;37:395.

22. Clark SL, Cotton DB, Lee W, et al. Central hemodynamic assessment of normal term pregnancy. Am J Obstet Gynecol 1989;161:1439.

23. Mashini IS, Albazzaz SJ, Fadel HE, et al. Serial noninvasive evaluation of cardiovascular hemodynamics during pregnancy. Am J Obstet Gynecol 1987;156:1208.

24. Ueland K, Metcalfe J. Circulatory changes in pregnancy. Clin Obstet Gynecol 1975;18:41.

25. Guzman CA, Caplan R. Cardiorespiratory response to exercise during pregnancy. Am J Obstet Gynecol 1970;108:600.

26. Ueland K, Parer JT. Effects of estrogens on the cardiovascular system of the ewe. Am J Obstet Gynecol 1966;96:400.

27. King TM, Whitehorn WV, Reeves B, Kubota R. Effects of estrogen on composition and function of cardiac muscle. Am J Physiol 1959;196:1282.

28. Rubler S, Damani PM, Pinto ER. Cardiac size and performance during pregnancy estimated with echocardiography. Am J Cardiol 1977;40:534.

29. Howard BK, Goodson JH, Mengert W. Supine hypotensive syndrome in late pregnancy. Obstet Gynecol 1953;1:371.

30. Vorys N, Ullery JC. The cardiac output changes in various positions in pregnancy. Am J Obstet Gynecol 1961;82:1312.

31. Milsom I, Forssman L. Factors influencing aortocaval compression in late pregnancy. Am J Obstet Gynecol 1984;148:764.

32. Lees MM, Scott DB, Kerr MG, Taylor SH. The circulatory effects of recumbent postural change in late pregnancy. Clin Sci 1967;32:453.

33. Calvin S, Jones OW III, Knieriem K, Weinstein L. Oxygen saturation in the supine hypotensive syndrome. Obstet Gynecol 1988;71:872.

34. Ellington C, Katz VL, Watson WJ, Spielman FJ. The effect of lateral tilt on maternal and fetal hemodynamic variables. Obstet Gynecol 1991;77:201.

35. Kerr MG, Scott DB, Samuel E. Studies of the inferior vena cava in late pregnancy. Br Med J 1964;1:532.

36. Wood CE, Keil LC, Rudolph AM. Hormonal and hemodynamic responses to vena caval obstruction in fetal sheep. Am J Physiol 1982;243:E278.

37. Lotgering FK, Wallenburg HCS. Hemodynamic effects of caval and uterine venous occlusion in pregnant sheep. Am J Obstet Gynecol 1986;155:1164.

38. Pirhonen JP, Erkkola RU. Uterine and umbilical flow velocity waveforms in the supine hypotensive syndrome. Obstet Gynecol 1990;76:176.

39. Marx GF, Husain FJ, Shiau HF. Brachial and femoral

blood pressures during the prenatal period. Am J Obstet Gynecol 1980;136:11.

40. Bieniarz J, Maqueda E, Caldeyro-Barcia R. Compression of aorta by the uterus in late human pregnancy: I. Variations between femoral and bracheal artery pressure with changes from hypertension to hypotension. Am J Obstet Gynecol 1966;95:795.

41. Bieniarz J, Crottogini JJ, Curuchet E, et al. Aortocaval compression by the uterus in late human pregnancy: II. An arteriographic study. Am J Obstet Gynecol 1968; 100:203.

42. Ohlson L. Effects of the pregnant uterus on the abdominal aorta and its branches. Acta Radiol Diagn 1978;19:369.

43. Kinsella SM, Spencer JAD, Whitwam JG. Use of digital arterial pressure to detect aortic compression during labour. Lancet 1989;2:714.

44. Janbu T. Blood velocities in the dorsal pedis and radial arteries during labour. Br J Obstet Gynaecol 1989;96:70.

45. Ueland K, Hansen JM. Maternal cardiovascular dynamics. II. Posture and uterine contractions. Am J Obstet Gynecol 1969;103:1.

46. Kinsella SM, Lee A, Spencer JAD. Maternal and fetal effects of the supine and pelvic tilt positions in late pregnancy. Eur J Obstet Gynecol Reprod Biol 1990;36:11.

47. Kasten GW, Martin ST. Resuscitation from bupivacaine-induced cardiovascular toxicity during partial inferior vena cava occlusion. Anesth Analg 1986;65:341.

48. DePace NL, Betesh JS, Kotler MN. 'Postmortem' cesarean section with recovery of both mother and offspring. JAMA 1982;248:971.

49. Nisell H, Hjemdahl P, Linde B. Cardiovascular responses to circulating catecholamines in normal pregnancy and in pregnancy-induced hypertension. Clin Physiol 1985;5:479.

50. Hardebo JE, Edvinsson L. Reduced sensitivity to alpha- and beta-adrenergic receptor agonists of intra- and extracranial vessels during pregnancy. Relevance to migraine. Acta Neurol Scand 1977;64:204.

51. Barron WM, Mujais SK, Zinaman M, Bravo EL, Lindheimer MD. Plasma catecholamine responses to physiologic stimuli in normal human pregnancy. Am J Obstet Gynecol 1986;154:80.

52. Nelson SH, Suresh MS. Comparison of nitroprusside and hydralazine in isolated uterine arteries from pregnant and nonpregnant patients. Anesthesiology 1988;68:541.

53. Suresh MS, Nelson SH, Nelson TE, Steinsland OS. Pregnancy: Increased effect of verapamil in human uterine arteries. Eur J Pharmacol 1985;112:387.

54. DeSimone CA, Leighton BL, Norris MC, Chayen B, Menduke H. The chronotropic effect of isoproterenol is reduced in term pregnant women. Anesthesiology 1988;69:626.

55. Leighton BL, Norris MC, Sosis M, Epstein R, Chayen B, Larijani GE. Limitations of epinephrine as a marker

of intravascular injection in laboring women. Anesthesiology 1987;66:688.

56. Carli A, Auclair MC, Bleichner G, Weber S, Monsallier JF, Lechat P. Inhibitory action of human serum on the isoprenaline-induced chronotropic effect in cultured rat heart cells. Influence of sex and pregnancy. Biomedicine 1977;27:166.

57. Dilts PV Jr, Brinkman CR III, Kirschbaum TH, Assali NS. Uterine and systemic hemodynamic interrelationships and their response to hypoxia. Am J Obstet Gynecol 1969;103:138.

58. Thaler I, Manor D, Itskovitz J, et al. Changes in uterine blood flow during human pregnancy. Am J Obstet Gynecol 1990;162:121.

59. McCall ML. Cerebral circulation and metabolism in toxemia of pregnancy. Observation on the effects of veratrum viride and apresoline (1-hydrazinophthalazine). Am J Obstet Gynecol 1953;66:1015.

60. Ikeda T, Mori N. Assessment of cerebral hemodynamics in pregnant women by internal carotid artery pulsed Doppler velocimetry. Am J Obstet Gynecol 1990; 163:494.

61. Sady SP, Carpenter MW, Thompson PD, Sady MA, Haydon B, Coustan DR. Cardiovascular response to cycle exercise during and after pregnancy. J Appl Physiol 1989;66:336.

62. Hendricks CH. The hemodynamics of a uterine contraction. Am J Obstet Gynecol 1958;76:969.

63. Ueland K, Hansen JM. Maternal cardiovascular dynamics. III. Labor and delivery under local and caudal analgesia. Am J Obstet Gynecol 1969;103:8.

64. Robson SC, Dunlop W, Boys RJ, Hunter S. Cardiac output during labour. Br Med J 1987;295:1169.

65. Maruta S. The observation of the maternal hemodynamics during labor and cesarean section. Acta Obst Gynaecol Jpn 1982;6:776.

66. Hendricks CH, Quilligan EJ. Cardiac output during labor. Am J Obstet Gynecol 1956;71:953.

67. Hansen JM, Ueland K. The influence of caudal analgesia on cardiovascular dynamics during normal labor and delivery. Acta Anaesthesiol Scand Suppl 1966; 23:449.

68. James CF, Banner T, Caton D. Cardiac output in women undergoing cesarean section with epidural or general anesthesia. Am J Obstet Gynecol 1989; 160:1178.

69. Robson SC, Boys RJ, Hunter S, Dunlop W. Maternal hemodynamics after normal delivery and delivery complicated by postpartum hemorrhage. Obstet Gynecol 1989;74:234.

70. Walters BNJ, Thompson ME, Lee A, DeSweit M. Blood pressure in the peurperium. Clin Sci 1986;71:589.

71. Brown E, Sampson JJ, Wheeler EO, Gundelfinger BF, Giansiracusa JE. Physiologic changes in the circulation during and after obstetric labor. Am Heart J 1947;34:311.

72. Newman B. Cardiac output changes during caesarean section. Anaesthesia 1982;37:270.

73. Lund CJ, Donovan JC. Blood volume during pregnancy. Am J Obstet Gynecol 1967;98:393.

74. Hytten FE, Paintin DB. Increase in plasma volume during normal pregnancy. J Obstet Gynaecol Br Commonw 1963;70:402.

75. Pritchard JA. Changes in the blood volume during pregnancy and delivery. Anesthesiology 1965;26:393.

76. Pirani BBK, Campbell DM. Plasma volume in normal first pregnancy. J Obstet Gynaecol Br Commonw 1973;80:884.

77. Hytten F. Blood volume changes in normal pregnancy. Clin Haematol 1985;14:601.

78. Chesley LC, Duffus GM. Posture and apparent plasma volume in late pregnancy. J Obstet Gynaecol Br Commonw 1971;78:406.

79. Longo LD. Maternal blood volume and cardiac output during pregnancy: A hypothesis of endocrinologic control. Am J Physiol 1983;14:R720.

80. Walters WAW, Lim YL. Cardiovascular dynamics in women receiving oral contraceptive therapy. Lancet 1969;2:879.

81. PR Sill, Lind T, Walker W. Platelet values during normal pregnancy. Br J Obstet Gynaecol 1985;92:480.

82. Jepson JH. Endocrine control of maternal and fetal erythropoiesis. Can Med Assoc J 1968;98:844.

83. Pitkin RM, Witte DL. Platelet and leukocyte counts in pregnancy. JAMA 1979;242:2696.

84. Pritchard JA, Baldwin RM, Dickey JC, Wiggins KM. Blood volume changes in pregnancy and the puerperium. II. Red blood cell loss and changes in apparent blood volume during and following vaginal delivery, cesarean section, and cesarean section plus total hysterectomy. Am J Obstet Gynecol 1962;84:1271.

85. Thomson KJ, Cohen ME. Studies on the circulation in pregnancy. II. Vital capacity observation in normal pregnant women. Surg Gynecol Obstet 1938;66:591.

86. Fabricant ND. Sexual functions and the nose. Am J Med Sci 1960;239:498.

87. Wong RC, Ellis CN. Physiologic skin changes in pregnancy. Semin Dermatol 1989;8:7.

88. Brock-Utne JG, Downing JW, Seedat F. Laryngeal oedema associated with pre-eclamptic toxaemia. Anaesthesia 1977;32:556.

89. Liberatore SM, Pistelli R, Potalano F, Moneta E, Incalzi RA, Ciappi G. Respiratory function during pregnancy. Respiration 1984;46:145.

90. Cugell DW, Frank NR, Gaensler EA, Badger TL. Pulmonary function in pregnancy.I. Serial observations in normal women. Am Rev Tuberc 1953;57:568.

91. Gee JBL, Packer BS, Millen JE, Robin ED. Pulmonary mechanics during pregnancy. J Clin Invest 1967;46:6.

92. Baldwin GR, Moorthi DS, Whelton JA, MacDonnell KF. New lung functions and pregnancy. Am J Obstet Gynecol 1977;127:235.

93. Alaily AB, Carrol KB. Pulmonary ventilation in pregnancy. Br J Obstet Gynaecol 1978;85:518.

94. Eng M, Butler J, Bonica JJ. Respiratory function in pregnant obese women. Am J Obstet Gynecol 1975;123:241.

95. Rubin A, Russo N, Goucher D. The effect of pregnancy upon pulmonary function in normal women. Am J Obstet Gynecol 1956;72:963.

96. Awe RJ, Nicotra MB, Newsom TD, Viles R. Arterial oxygenation and alveolar–arterial gradients in term pregnancy. Obstet Gynecol 1979;53:182.

97. Bevan DR, Holdcroft A, Loh L, MacGregor WG, O'Sullivan JC, Sykes MK. Closing volume and pregnancy. Br Med J 1974;1:13.

98. Weinberger SE, Weiss ST, Cohen WR, Weiss JW, Johnson TS. Pregnancy and the lung. Am Rev Respir Dis 1980;121:559.

99. Shankar KB, Moseley H, Vemula V, Kumar Y. Physiological dead space during general anaesthesia for caesarean section. Can J Anaesth 1987;34:373.

100. Lyons G, Tunstall ME. Maternal blood-gas tensions, (P_{AO_2}–P_{aO_2} physiological shunt and V_D/V_T during general anaesthesia for caesarean section. Br J Anaesth 1979;51:1059.

101. Prowse CM, Gaensler EA. Respiratory and acid–base changes during pregnancy. Anesthesiology 1965;26:381.

102. Knuttgen HG, Emerson K. Jr. Physiological response to pregnancy at rest and during exercise. J Appl Physiol 1974;36:549.

103. Milne JA, Mills RJ, Howie AD, Pack AI. Large airways function during normal pregnancy. Br J Obstet Gynaecol 1977;84:448.

104. Pernoll ML, Metcalfe J, Kovach PA, Wachtel R, Dunham MJ. Ventilation during rest and exercise in pregnancy and postpartum. Respir Physiol 1975;25:295.

105. MacRae DJ, Palavradji D. Maternal acid–base changes in pregnancy. J Obstet Gynaecol Br Commonw 1967;74:11.

106. Plass ED, Oberst FW. Respiration and pulmonary ventilation in normal nonpregnant, pregnant and puerperal women. Am J Obstet Gynecol 1938;35:441.

107. Pernoll ML, Metcalfe J, Schlenker TL, Welch E, Matsumoto JA. Oxygen consumption at rest and during exercise in pregnancy. Respir Physiol 1975;25:285.

108. Artal R, Wiswell R, Romem Y, Dorey F. Pulmonary responses to exercise in pregnancy. Am J Obstet Gynecol 1986;154:378.

109. Lyons HA, Antonio R. The sensitivity of the respiratory center in pregnancy and after the administration of progesterone. Trans Assoc Am Physicians 1959;72:173.

110. Byrne F, Oduro-Dominah A, Kipling R. The effect of pregnancy on pulmonary nitrogen washout: A study of pre-oxygenation. Anaesthesia 1987;42:148.

111. Norris MC, Kirkland MR, Torjman MC, Goldberg ME. Denitrogenation in pregnancy. Can J Anaesth 1989;5:523.

112. Norris MC, Dewan DM. Preoxygenation for cesarean section: A comparison of two techniques. Anesthesiology 1985;62:827.

113. De Swiet M. The respiratory system. In: Hytten F, Chamberlain G, eds. Clinical physiology in obstetrics. 2nd ed. Oxford: Blackwell Scientific Publications, 1991:83.

114. Gazioglu K, Kaltreider NL, Rosen M, Yu PN. Pulmonary function during pregnancy in normal women and in patients with cardiopulmonary disease. Thorax 1970;25:445.

115. Shankar KB, Moseley H, Ramasamy M. Arterial to end-tidal carbon dioxide tension difference during anaesthesia in early pregnancy. Can J Anaesth 1989;36:124.

116. Shankar KB, Moseley H, Kumar Y, Vemula V. Arterial to end tidal carbon dioxide tension difference during Caesarean section anaesthesia. Anaesthesia 1986; 41:698.

117. Shankar KB, Moseley H, Kumar Y, Vemula V, Krishnan A. Arterial to end-tidal carbon dioxide tension difference during anaesthesia for tubal ligation. Anaesthesia 1987;42:482.

118. Baraka A. Correlation between maternal and foetal Po_2 and Pco_2 during caesarean section. Br J Anaesth 1970;42:434.

119. Behrman RE, Peterson EN, De Lannoy CW. The supply of 0_2 to the primate fetus with two different O_2 tensions and anesthetics. Respir Physiol 1969;6:271.

120. Darling RC, Smith CA, Asmussen E, Cohen FM. Some properties of human fetal and maternal blood. J Clin Invest 1941;20:739.

121. Prystowsky H, Hellegers A, Bruns P. Fetal blood studies. XIV. A comparative study of the oxygen dissociation curve of nonpregnant, pregnant and fetal human blood. Am J Obstet Gynecol 1959;78:489.

122. Bauer C, Ludwig M, Ludwig I, Bartels H. Factors governing the oxygen affinity of human adult and foetal blood. Respir Physiol 1969;7:271.

123. Kambam JR, Handte RE, Brown WU, Smith BE. Effect of normal and preeclamptic pregnancies on the oxyhemoglobin dissociation curve. Anesthesiology 1986;65:426.

124. Leibson RG, Likhnitzky II Sax MG. Oxygen transport of the foetal and maternal blood during pregnancy. J Physiol 1936;87:97.

125. McCullogh JC, Kelly AM. Investigation of pregnancy-related changes in red cell 2,3-diphosphoglycerate. Clin Chim Acta 1979;98:235.

126. Hess W. Pregnancy and oxygen dissociation. Anesthesiology 1987;66:854.

127. Kambam JR. In reply. Anesthesiology 1988;69:801.

128. Blechner JN, Cotter JR, Stenger VG, Hinkley CM, Prystowsky H. Oxygen, carbon dioxide, and hydrogen ion concentrations in arterial blood during pregnancy. Am J Obstet Gynecol 1968;100:1.

129. Anderson GJ, James GB, Mathers NP, Smith EL, Walker J. The maternal oxygen tension and acid–base status during pregnancy. J Obstet Gynaecol Br Commonw 1969;76:16.

130. Lucius H, Gahlenbeck H, Kleine HO, Fabel H, Bartels H. Respiratory functions, buffer system, and electrolyte concentrations of blood during human pregnancy. Respir Physiol 1970;9:311.

131. Oberst FW, Plass ED. The acid-base balance in the plasma and blood cells of normal nonpregnant, pregnant and puerperal women. J Lab Clin Med 1940;26:513.

132. Ang CK, Tan TH, Walters WAW, Wood C. Postural influence on maternal capillary oxygen and carbon dioxide tension. Br Med J 1969;4:201.

133. Oard HC, Peters JP. The concentration of acid and base in the serum in normal pregnancy. J Biol Chem 1929;81:9.

134. Prystowsky H, Hellegers AE, Bruns PD. A comparative study of the alkali reserve of normal and pregnant women. Am J Obstet Gynecol 1961;82:1295.

135. Fadel HE, Northrop G, Misenhimer HR, Harp RJ. Acid–base balance in pre-eclamptic, hypertensive and diabetic pregnancies. Maternal blood and amniotic fluid studies. J Perinat Med 1979;7:202.

136. Tyler JM. The effect of progesterone on the respiration of patients with emphysema and hypercapnia. J Clin Invest 1960;39:34.

137. Novy MJ, Edwards MJ. Respiratory problems in pregnancy. Am J Obstet Gynecol 1967;99:1024.

138. Ramanathan J, Sibai BM, Duggirala V, Maduska AL. Pulmonary function in preeclamptic women receiving $MgS0_4$. J Reprod Med 1988;33:432.

139. Hagerdal M, Morgan CW, Sumner AE, Gutsche BB. Minute ventilation and oxygen consumption during labor with epidural analgesia. Anesthesiology 1983; 59:425.

140. Fisher A, Prys-Roberts C. Maternal pulmonary gas exchange. A study during normal labour and extradural blockade. Anaesthesia 1968;23:350.

141. Reed PN, Colquhoun AD, Hanning CD. Maternal oxygenation during normal labour. Br J Anaesth 1989;62:316.

142. Andersen GJ, Walker J. The effect of labour on the maternal blood–gas and acid–base status. J Obstet Gynaecol Br Commonw 1970;77:289.

143. Moya F, Morishima HO, Shnider SM, James LS. Influence of maternal hyperventilation on the newborn infant. Am J Obstet Gynecol 1965;91:76.

144. Archer GW Jr, Marx GF. Arterial oxygen tension during apnoea in parturient women. Br J Anaesth 1974; 46:358.

145. Motoyama EK, Rivard G, Acheson F, Cook CD. Adverse effect of maternal hyperventilation on the foetus. Lancet 1966;1:286.

146. Morishima HO, Moya F, Bossers AC, Daniel SS. Adverse effects of maternal hypocapnea on the newborn guinea pig. Am J Obstet Gynecol 1964;88:524.

147. Bailey RR, Rolleston GL. Kidney length and ureteric dilatation in the puerperium. J Obstet Gynecol Br Commonw 1971;78:55.

148. Dure-Smith P. Ureters in pregnancy. N Engl J Med 1971;284:395.

149. Rubi RA, Sala NL, Althabe O. Ureteral function in preg-

nant women. IV. Ureteral peristalsis during normal pregnancy, in patients with empty and physiologically refilled bladder. J Reprod Med 1972;8:29.

150. Katz AI, Lindheimer MD. Renal handling of acute sodium loads in pregnancy. Am J Physiol 1973;225:696.

151. Berman LB. The pregnant kidney. JAMA 1974; 230:111.

152. Lindheimer MD, Katz AI. Pregnancy and the kidney. J Reprod Med 1973;11:14.

153. Weinberger MH, Petersen LP, Herr MJ, Wade MB. The effect of supine and lateral recumbency on plasma renin activity during pregnancy. J Clin Endocrinol Metab 1973;36:991.

154. Rudolph JH, Wax SH. The ^{131}I renogram in pregnancy. II. Normal pregnancy. Obstet Gynecol 1967;3:386.

155. Shirley RL. The kidney in pregnancy. N Engl J Med 1970;284:107.

156. Davison JM, Dunlop W. Renal hemodynamics and tubular function in normal human pregnancy. Kidney Int 1980;18:152.

157. Dunlop W. Serial changes in renal haemodynamics during normal human pregnancy. Br J Obstet Gynaecol 1981;88:1.

158. Davison JM, Dunlop W. Changes in renal hemodynamics and tubular function induced by normal human pregnancy. Semin Nephrol 1984;4:198.

159. Brown MA, Sinosich MJ, Saunders DM, Gallery EDM. Potassium regulation and progesterone–aldosterone interrelationships in human pregnancy: A prospective study. Am J Obstet Gynecol 1986;155:349.

160. Ezimokhai M, Davison JM, Philips PR, Dunlop W. Non-postural serial changes in renal function during the third trimester of normal human pregnancy. Br J Obstet Gynaecol 1981;88:465.

161. Davison JM, Noble MCB. Serial changes in 24-hour creatinine clearance during normal menstrual cycles and the first trimester of pregnancy. Br J Obstet Gynaecol 1981;88:10.

162. Berliner RW, Grebisch G, eds. Body fluids and the excretion of urine. In: Brobeck JR, ed. Best and Taylor's physiological basis of medical practice. 10th ed. Baltimore: Williams & Wilkins, 1979:5-3.

163. Sims EAH, Krantz KE. Serial studies of renal function during pregnancy and the puerperium in normal women. J Clin Invest 1958;37:1764.

164. Dunlop W. Investigations into the influence of posture on renal plasma flow and glomerular filtration rate during late pregnancy. Br J Obstet Gynaecol 1976;83:17.

165. Kelly AM, McNay MB, McEwan HP. Renal tubular function in normal pregnancy. Br J Obstet Gynaecol 1978;85:190.

166. Lind T, Hytten FE. The excretion of glucose during normal pregnancy. J Obstet Gynaecol Br Commonw 1972;79:961.

167. Davison JM, Lovedale C. The excretion of glucose during normal pregnancy and after delivery. J Obstet Gyneacol Br Commonw 1974;81:30.

168. Davison JM, Hytten FE. The effect of pregnancy on the renal handling of glucose. Br J Obstet Gynaecol 1975;82:374.

169. Brar HS, Do YS, Tam HB, et al. Uteroplacental unit as a source of elevated circulating prorenin levels in normal pregnancy. Am J Obstet Gynecol 1986;155:1223.

170. Ehrlich EN, Lindheimer MD. Effect of administered mineralocorticoids or ACTH in pregnant women. J Clin Invest 1972;51:1301.

171. Landau RL, Bergenstal DM, Lugibihl K, Kascht ME. The metabolic effects of progesterone in man. J Clin Endocrinol Metab 1955;15:1194.

172. Landau RL, Lugibihl K. Inhibition of the sodium-retaining influence of aldosterone by progesterone. J Clin Endocrinol Metab 1958;18:1237.

173. Landau RL, Lugibihl K. The catabolic and natriuretic effects of progesterone in man. Recent Prog Horm 1961;17:249.

174. Landau RL, Lugibihl K, Bergenstal DM, Dimick DF. The metabolic effects of progesterone in man: Dose response relationships. J Lab Clin Med 1957;50:613.

175. Lindheimer MD, Richardson DA, Ehrlich EN, Katz AI. Potassium homeostasis in pregnancy. J Reprod Med 1987;32:517.

176. Lim VS, Katz AI, Lindheimer MD. Acid–base regulation in pregnancy. Am J Physiol 1976;231:1764.

177. Davison JM, Valotton MB, Lindheimer MD. Plasma osmolality and urinary concentration and dilution during and after pregnancy: Evidence that lateral recumbency inhibits maximal urinary concentrating ability. Br J Obstet Gynaecol 1981;88:472.

178. Geelhoed GW, Vander AJ. Plasma renin activities during pregnancy and parturition. J Clin Endocrinol 1968;28:412.

179. Bruce LA, Behsudi FM. Progesterone effects on three regional gastrointestinal tissues. Life Sci 1979;25:729.

180. Fisher RS, Roberts GS, Grabowski CJ, Cohen S. Inhibition of lower esophageal sphincter circular muscle by female sex hormones. Am J Physiol 1978;23:E243.

181. Fisher RS, Roberts GS, Grabowski CJ, Cohen S. Altered lower esophageal sphincter function during early pregnancy. Gastroenterology 1978;74:1233.

182. Nagler R, Spiro HM. Heartburn in late pregnancy. Manometric studies of esophageal motor function. J Clin Invest 1961;40:954.

183. Van Thiel DH, Gavaler JS, Joshi SN, Sara RK, Stremple J. Heartburn of pregnancy. Gastroenterology 1977; 72:666.

184. Lind JF, Smith AM, McIver DK, Coopland AT, Crispin JS. Heartburn in pregnancy. A manometric study. Can Med Assoc J 1968;98:571.

185. Ulmsten U, Sundstrom G. Esophageal manometry in pregnant and nonpregnant women. Am J Obstet Gynecol 1978;132:260.

186. Hart DM. Heartburn in pregnancy. J Int Med Res 1978;6:1.

187. Atlay RD, Gillison EW, Horton AL. A fresh look at

pregnancy heartburn. J Obstet Gynaecol Br Commonw 1973;80:63.

188. LaSalvia LA, Steffen EA. Delayed gastric emptying time in labor. Am J Obstet Gynecol 1950;59:1075.

189. Crawford JS. Some aspects of obstetric anaesthesia. Br J Anaesth 1956;28:201.

190. Davison JS, Davison MC, Hay DM. Gastric emptying time in late pregnancy and labour. J Obstet Gynecol Br Commonw 1970;77:37.

191. Nimmo WS. The measurement of gastric emptying during labour. J Int Med Res 1978;6:52.

192. Simpson KH, Stakes AF, Miller M. Pregnancy delays paracetamol absorption and gastric emptying in patients undergoing surgery. Br J Anaesth 1988;60:24.

193. Whitehead EM, Smith M, O'Sullivan G. An evaluation of gastric emptying times in pregnancy and the puerperium, [Abstract]. Soc Obstet Anesth Perinatol 1990;22:F1.

194. Nimmo WS, Wilson J, Prescott LF. Narcotic analgesics and delayed gastric emptying during labour. Lancet 1975;1:890.

195. Wilson J. Gastric emptying in labour: Some recent findings and their clinical significance. J Int Med Res 1978;6:54.

196. Howard FA, Sharp DS. Effect of metoclopramide on gastric emptying during labour. Br Med J 1973;1:446.

197. Colman RD, Frank M, Loughnan BA, Cohen DG, Cattermole R. Use of I.M. ranitidine for the prophylaxis of aspiration pneumonitis in obstetrics. Br J Anaesth 1988;61:720.

198. Dundee JW, Gamble JAS. Narcotic analgesics and delayed gastric emptying during labour. Lancet 1975;1:1032.

199. Davison JS. Gastric emptying in labour. Lancet 1975;2:227.

200. Davison JS. Gastric emptying in labour. Lancet 1975;2:930.

201. O'Sullivan GM, Sutton AJ, Thompson SA, Carrie LE, Bullingham RE. Noninvasive measurement of gastric emptying in obstetric patients. Anesth Analg 1987;66:505.

202. Holdsworth JD. Relationship between stomach contents and analgesia in labour. Br J Anaesth 1978;50:1145.

203. Christofides ND, Ghatei MA, Bloom SR, Borberg C, Gillmer MDG. Decreased plasma motilin concentrations in pregnancy. Br Med J 1982;285:1453.

204. Parry E, Shields R, Turnbull AC. Transit time in the small intestine in pregnancy. J Obstet Gynaecol Br Commonw 1970;77:900.

205. Wald A, Van Thiel DH, Hoechstetter L, et al. Effect of pregnancy on gastrointestinal transit. Dig Dis Sci 1982;27:1015.

206. Lawson M, Kern F Jr, Everson GT. Gastrointestinal transit time in human pregnancy: Prolongation in the second and third trimesters followed by postpartum normalization. Gastroenterology 1985;89:996.

207. Wald A, Van Thiel DH, Hoechstetter L, et al. Gastro-

intestinal transit: The effect of the menstrual cycle. Gastroenterology 1981;80:1497.

208. Attia RR, Ebeid AM, Fischer JE, Goudsouzian NG. Maternal fetal and placental gastrin communications. Anaesthesia 1982;37:18.

209. Blouw R, Scatliff J, Craig DB, et al. Gastric volume and pH in postpartum patients. Anesthesiology 1976; 45:456.

210. James CF, Gibbs CP, Banner T. Postpartum perioperative risk of aspiration pneumonia. Anesthesiology 1984;61:756.

211. Braverman DZ, Johnson ML, Kern F Jr. Effects of pregnancy and contraceptive steroids on gallbladder function. N Engl J Med 1980;302;362.

212. Ryan JP. Effect of pregnancy on gallbladder contractility in the guinea pig. Gastroenterology 1984;87:674.

213. Kern F Jr, Everson GT, DeMark B, et al. Biliary lipids, bile acids, and gallbladder function in the human female. J Clin Invest 1981;68:1229.

214. Everson GT, McKinley C, Lawson M, Johnson M, Kern F Jr. Gallbladder function in the human female: Effect of the ovulatory cycle, pregnancy, and contraceptive steroids. Gastroenterology 1982;82:711.

215. Cruikshank DP, Hays PM. Maternal physiology in pregnancy. In: Gabbe SG, Niebyl JR, Simpson JL, eds. Obstetrics normal and problem pregnancies. New York: Churchill Livingstone, 1986:137.

216. Smith B, Moya F, Shnider S. The effects of anesthesia on liver function during labor. Anesth Analg 1962;41:24.

217. Song CS, Kappas A. The influence of estrogens, progestins, and pregnancy on the liver. Vitam Horm 1968;26:147.

218. Flynn RJ, Moore J, Dwyer R, Duly E, Dundee JW. Changes in alpha$_1$ acid glycoprotein during labor. Anesth Analg 1988;67:S61.

219. Corke BC. Drugs and obstetric anesthesia. In: Wood M, Wood AJJ, eds. Drugs and anesthesia pharmacology: Pharmacology for the anesthetist. Baltimore: Williams & Wilkins, 1990:347.

220. Cerutti R, Ferrari S, Grella P, Castelli, GP, Rizzotti P. Behavior of serum enzymes in pregnancy. Clin Exp Obstet Gynecol 1976;3:22.

221. Walker FB IV, Hoblit DL, Cunningham FG, Combes B. Gamma glutamyl transpeptidase in normal pregnancy. Obstet Gynecol 1974;43:745.

222. Laros RK Jr, Alger LS. Thromboembolism and pregnancy. Clin Obstet Gynecol 1979;22:872.

223. Letsky E. The haematological system. In: Hytten F, Chamberlain G, eds. Clinical physiology in obstetrics. 2nd ed. Oxford: Blackwell Scientific Publications, 1991:39.

224. Bonnar J, McNicol GP, Douglas AS. Fibrinolytic enzyme system and pregnancy. Br Med J 1969;3:387.

225. Hellgren M, Blomback M. Studies on blood coagulation and fibrinolysis in pregnancy, during delivery and in the puerperium. 1. Normal condition. Gynecol Obstet Invest 1981;12:141.

226. Gerbasi FR, Bottoms S, Farag A, Mammen E. Increased

intravascular coagulation associated with pregnancy. Obstet Gynecol 1990;75:385.

227. Nilsson IM, Kullander S. Coagulation and fibrinolytic studies during pregnancy. Acta Obstet Gynecol Scand 1967;46:273.

228. Shaper AG, Kear J, Macintosh DM, Kyobe J, Njama D. The platelet count, platelet adhesiveness and aggregation and the mechanism of fibrinolytic inhibition in pregnancy and the puerperium. J Obstet Gynaecol Br Commonw 1968;75:433.

229. Sejeny SA, Eastham RD, Baker SR. Platelet counts during normal pregnancy. J Clin Pathol 1975;28:812.

230. Wallenburg HCS, Van Kessel PH. Platelet lifespan in normal pregnancy as determined by a nonradioisotpoic technique. Br J Obstet Gynaecol 1978;85:33.

231. Pekonen F, Rasi V, Ammala M, Viinikka L, Ylikorkala O. Platelet function and coagulation in normal and preeclamptic pregnancy. Thromb Res 1986;43:553

232. Woodfield DG, Cole SK, Allan AGE, Cash JD. Serum fibrin degradation products throughout normal pregnancy. Br Med J 1968;4:665.

233. Bonnar J, Davidson JF, Pidgeon CF, McNicols GP, Douglas AS. Fibrin degradation products in normal and abnormal pregnancy and parturition. Br Med J 1969;3:137.

234. Bonnar J, McNicol GP, Douglas AS. Coagulation and fibrinolytic mechanisms during and after normal childbirth. Br Med J 1970;2:200.

235. Gerbasi FR, Bottoms S, Farag A, Mammen EF. Changes in hemostasis activity during delivery and the immediate postpartum period. Am J Obstet Gynecol 1990;162:1158.

236. Stiehm ER, Kennan AL, Schelble DT. Split products of fibrin in maternal serum in the perinatal period. Am J Obstet Gynecol 1970;108:941.

237. Ygge J. Changes in blood coagulation and fibrinolysis during the puerperium. Am J Obstet Gynecol 1969;104:2.

238. Bonnar J, Prentice CRM, McNicol GP, Douglas AS. Haemostatic mechanism in the uterine circulation during placental separation. Br Med J 1970;2:564.

239. Kalkhoff RK, Jacobson M, Lemper D. Progesterone, pregnancy and the augmented plasma insulin response. J Clin Endocrinol 1970;31:24.

240. Buch I, Hornnes PJ, Kuhl C. Glucose tolerance in early pregnancy. Acta Endocrinol 1986;112:263.

241. Spellacy WN, Carlson KL, Birk SA. The fetus and the placenta as a source of insulin during pregnancy. Obstet Gynecol 1967;29:74.

242. Burt RL, Davidson IWF. Insulin half-life and utilization in normal pregnancy. Obstet Gynecol 1974;43:161.

243. Kuhl C. Glucose metabolism during and after pregnancy in normal and gestational diabetic women. Acta Endocrinol 1975;79:709.

244. Nordlander E, Hanson U, Persson B, Stangenberg M. Pancreatic B-cell function during normal pregnancy. Diabetes Res 1987;6:133.

245. Fisher PM, Sutherland HW, Bewsher PD. The insulin response to glucose infusion in normal human pregnancy. Diabetologia 1980;19:15.

246. Speroff L, Glass RH, Kase NG. Clinical gynecologic endocrinology and infertility. Baltimore: Williams & Williams, 1989:317.

247. Lind T, Bell S, Gilmore E, Huisjes HJ, Schally AV. Insulin disappearance rate in pregnant and in non-pregnant women given GHRIH. Eur J Clin Invest 1977;7:47.

248. Samaan N, Yen SCC, Gonzalez D, Pearson OH. Metabolic effects of placental lactogen (HPL) in man. J Clin Endocrinol 1968;28:485.

249. Beck P, Daughaday WH. Human placental lactogen: Studies of its acute metabolic effects and disposition in normal man. J Clin Invest 1978;46:103.

250. Kalkhoff RK, Richardson BL, Beck P. Relative effects of pregnancy, human placental lactogen and prednisolone on carbohydrate tolerance in normal and subclinical diabetic subjects. Diabetes 1969;18:153.

251. Malkasian GD, Mayberry WE. Serum total and free thyroxine and thyrotropin in normal and pregnant women, neonates, and women receiving progestogens. Am J Obstet Gynecol 1971;108:1234.

252. Harada A, Hershman JM, Reed AW, et al. Comparison of thyroid stimulators and thyroid hormone concentrations in the sera of pregnant women. J Clin Endocrol Metab 1979;48:793.

253. Kimura M, Amino N, Tamaki H, et al. Physiologic thyroid activation in normal early pregnancy is induced by circulating hCG. Obstet Gynecol 1990;75:775.

254. Kannan V, Sinha MK, Devi PK, Rastogi GK. Plasma thyrotropin and its response to thyrotropin-releasing hormone in normal pregnancy. Obstet Gynecol 1973;42:547.

255. Yannone ME, McCurdy JR, Goldfien A. Plasma progesterone levels in normal pregnancy, labor, and the puerperium. II. Clinical data. Am J Obstet Gynecol 1968;101:1058.

256. Greig M, Coyle MG, Cooper W, Walker J. Plasma progesterone in mother and foetus in the second half of human pregnancy. J Obstet Gynaecol 1962;69:772.

257. Deshpande GN, Turner AK, Sommerville IF. Plasma progesterone and pregnanediol in human pregnancy, during labour and post-partum. J Obstet Gynaecol Br Emp 1960;67:954.

258. Whalen JB, Clancey CJ, Farley DB, Van Orden DE. Plasma prostaglandins in pregnancy. Obstet Gynecol 1978;51:52.

259. Quagliarello J, Szlachter N, Steinetz BG, Goldsmith LT, Weiss G. Serial relaxin concentrations in human pregnancy. Am J Obstet Gynecol 1979;135:43.

260. Calguneri M, Bird HA, Wright V. Changes in joint laxity occurring during pregnancy. Ann Rheum Dis 1982;41:126.

261. Berg G, Hammar M, Moller-Nielsen J, Linden U, Thorblad J. Low back pain during pregnancy. Obstet Gynecol 1988;71:71.

262. O'Connell JEA. Lumbar disc protrusions in pregnancy. J Neurol Neurosurg Psychiatry 1960;23:138.

263. Akil H, Watson SJ, Barchas JD, Li CH. β-endorphin immunoreactivity in rat and human blood: Radioimmunoassay, comparative levels and physiological alterations. Life Sci 1979;24:1659.

264. Gintzler AR. Endorphin-mediated increases in pain threshold during pregnancy. Science 1980;210:193.

265. Sander HW, Gintzler AR. Spinal cord mediation of the opioid analgesia of pregnancy. Brain Res 1987; 408:389.

266. Sander HW, Portoghese PS, Gintzler AR. Spinal κ-opiate receptor involvement in the analgesia of pregnancy: Effects of intrathecal nor-binaltorphimine, a κ-selective antagonist. Brain Res 1988;474:343.

267. Bacigalupo G, Riese S, Rosendahl H, Saling E. Quantitative relationships between pain intensities during labor and beta-endorphin and cortisol concentrations in plasma. Decline of the hormone concentrations in the early postpartum period. J Perinat Med 1990;18:289.

268. Steinbrook RA, Carr DB, Datta S, Naulty JS, Lee C, Fisher J. Dissociation of plasma and cerebrospinal fluid beta-endorphin-like immunoactivity levels during pregnancy and parturition. Anesth Analg 1982;61:893.

269. Spielman FJ, Mueller RA, Corke BC. Cerebrospinal fluid concentration of 5-hydroxyindoleactic acid in pregnancy. Anesthesiology 1985;62:193.

270. Datta S, Hurley RJ, Naulty JS, et al. Plasma and cerebrospinal fluid progesterone concentrations in pregnant and nonpregnant women. Anesth Analg 1986;65:950.

271. Lurie AO, Weiss JB. Progesterone in cerebrospinal fluid during human pregnancy. Nature 1967;215:1178.

272. Fagraeus L, Urban BJ, Bromage PR. Spread of epidural analgesia in early pregnancy. Anesthesiology 1983; 58:184.

273. Abouleish EI. Postpartum tubal ligation requires more bupivacaine for spinal anesthesia than does cesarean section. Anesth Analg 1986;65:897.

274. Crawford OB, Chester RV. Caudal anesthesia in obstetrics: A combined procaine-pontocaine single injection technic. Anesthesiology 1949;10:473.

275. Barclay DL, Renegar OJ, Nelson EW Jr. The influence of inferior vena cava compression on the level of spinal anesthesia. Am J Obstet Gynecol 1968;101:792.

276. Marx GF, Zemaitis MT, Orkin LR. Cerebrospinal fluid pressure during labor and obstetrical anesthesia. Anesthesiology 1961;22:348.

277. Galbert MW, Marx GF. Extradural pressures in the parturient patient. Anesthesiology 1974;40:499.

278. Butterworth JF IV, Walker FO, Lysak SZ. Pregnancy increases median nerve susceptibility to lidocaine. Anesthesiology 1990;72:962.

279. Datta S, Lambert DH, Gregus J, Gissen AJ, Covino BG. Differential sensitivities of mammalian nerve fibers during pregnancy. Anesth Analg 1983;62:1070.

280. Flanagan HL, Datta S, Lambert DH, Gissen AJ, Covino BG. Effect of pregnancy on bupivacaine-induced conduction blockade in the isolated rabbit vagus nerve. Anesth Analg 1987;66:123.

281. Bader AM, Datta S, Moller RA, Covino BG. Acute progesterone treatment has no effect on bupivacaine-induced conduction blockade in the isolated rabbit vagus nerve. Anesth Analg 1990;71:545.

282. Flanagan HL, Datta S, Moller RA, Covino BG. Effect of exogenously administered progesterone on susceptibility of rabbit vagus nerves to bupivacaine. Anesthesiology 1988;69:A676.

283. Palahniuk RJ, Shnider SM, Eger EI II. Pregnancy decreases the requirement for inhaled anesthetic agents. Anesthesiology 1974;41:82.

284. Datta S, Migliozi RP, Flanagan HL, Krieger NR. Chronically administered progesterone decreases halothane requirements in rabbits. Anesth Analg 1989;68:46.

285. Mazze RI, Rice SA, Baden JM. Halothane, isoflurane, and enflurane MAC in pregnant and nonpregnant female and male mice and rats. Anesthesiology 1985;62:339.

286. Cummings AJ. A survey of pharmacokinetic data from pregnant women. Clin Pharmacokinet 1983;8:344.

287. Perucca E, Crema A. Plasma protein binding of drugs in pregnancy. Clin Pharmacokinet 1982;7:336.

288. Blitt CD, Petty WC, Alberternst EE, Wright BJ. Correlation of plasma cholinesterase activity and duration of action of succinylcholine during pregnancy. Anesth Analg 1977;56:78.

289. Shnider SM. Serum cholinesterase activity during pregnancy, labor and puerperium. Anesthesiology 1965; 36:335.

290. Hazel B, Monier D. Human serum cholinesterase: Variations during pregnancy and post-partum. Can Anaesth Soc J 1971;18:272.

291. Whittaker M. Plasma cholinesterase variants and the anaesthetist. Anaesthesia 1980;35:174.

292. Evans RT, Wroe JM. Plasma cholinesterase changes during pregnancy. Anaesthesia 1980;35:651.

293. Whittaker M, Crawford JS, Lewis M. Some observations of levels of plasma cholinesterase activity within an obstetric population. Anaesthesia 1988;43:42.

294. Leighton BL, Cheek TG, Gross JB, et al. Succinycholine pharmacodynamics in peripartum patients. Anesthesiology 1986;64:202.

CHAPTER 2

Preoperative Evaluation of the Parturient with Coexisting Disease

Part One
Diseases of the Cardiac, Renal, and Hematologic Systems

Raphael Y. Gershon

Major changes in physiology accompany pregnancy. The healthy parturient adapts well to these changes; yet, the additional stress of coexisting disease may contribute to significant maternal and fetal morbidity and mortality. To evaluate and treat these challenging patients, anesthesiologists must understand the normal, pregnancy-related alterations in physiology and the pathophysiologic changes related to the coexisting disease process. Ultimately, preoperative evaluation of pregnant patients with coexisting disease requires answers to these questions:

- How does the disease affect the pregnancy?
- How does the pregnancy affect the disease?

Only then can a safe anesthetic be planned and administered. The next four chapters of this book discuss the preoperative evaluation of parturients with a variety of medical and obstetric problems. They focus on the pathophysiology of the disease process and the management of these high-risk parturients before and during parturition. The goal of these chapters is to provide the anesthesiologist with the information needed for the initial evaluation of these women. With this background, the obstetric anesthesiologist can then formulate an appropriate anesthetic plan. Later chapters in this book will discuss specific anesthetic options and how to modify them for women with significant disease.

Disorders considered in this chapter involve the cardiac and renal systems. We also will discuss problems related to hematology and coagulation.

CARDIAC DISEASE

Diagnostic technology, medical and surgical management, and pharmacologic therapies of cardiac disease have advanced significantly over the past decades. Now many women with cardiac abnormalities not only survive to child-bearing age but successfully complete pregnancy.

Heart disease complicates 0.5% to 4.0% of pregnancies worldwide[1,2] and occurs in up to 2% of American women.[3] The incidence of rheumatic heart disease is falling, whereas increasing numbers of parturients have congenital heart disease.[4] Despite improved prognosis, normal hemodynamic changes associated with pregnancy may greatly increase the risk of morbidity and mortality in the parturient with cardiac disease. The maternal mortality associated with pregnancy approaches 50% in women with pulmonary hypertension, complicated coarctation of the aorta, and Marfan's syndrome with aortic involvement. However, uncomplicated atrial septal defect, ventricular septal defect or patent ductus arteriosus, corrected tetralogy of Fallot, porcine valve replacement, or mitral stenosis (New York Heart Association classes I or II) correlate with a maternal mortality risk of under 1%.[5]

Recognized risks for these parturients and their fetuses include the following:

- An inability of the mother to meet the physiologic demands of pregnancy
- An inadequate supply of well-oxygenated maternal blood for fetal nourishment
- A worsening of maternal disease
- Hereditary transmission to offspring from mothers with congenital heart disease
- Additional complications such as infection, hemorrhage, or thromboembolism[6]

Normal Physiologic Changes of Pregnancy

The normal changes of pregnancy have been discussed in Chapter 1. To review, a 35% increase in blood volume and a 45% increase in plasma volume generates the "physiologic anemia of pregnancy." A concomitant 30% rise in stroke volume and a 15% increase in heart rate augments cardiac output by 40%.[7] The great veins of the pelvis and lower extremities hold a large portion of this expanded blood volume. Aortocaval compression by the enlarging uterus can significantly impair venous return by the mid-second trimester. Total peripheral resistance decreases by 15%. Diastolic blood pressure declines by 10 to 20 mm Hg. Systolic blood pressure may decrease by up to 15 mm Hg, and mean arterial blood pressure drops by 15 mm Hg. Cardiac output progressively escalates until it peaks at 28 to 32 weeks' gestation and again in the third stage of labor with placental expulsion, uterine contraction, and autotransfusion. Because of the acute changes in blood volume, the reduction in aortocaval compression, and

the loss of progesterone and other hormones with fetal and placental expulsion, cardiac output remains elevated for several hours after delivery.

These normal changes in the cardiovascular system during pregnancy can simulate organic heart disease.[8] Fatiguability, dyspnea, orthopnea, chest discomfort, or palpitations are not uncommon (Table 2-1). However, paroxysmal nocturnal dyspnea, syncope with exertion, and activity-related chest pain need to be investigated (Table 2-2).[9]

One may appreciate a nonpathologic diastolic murmur in up to 10% of parturients. Higher blood flow across the atrioventricular valves during gestation probably causes this murmur. Bruits also may be normal variants if they originate from the internal mammary artery (the "mammary souffle"). Venous hums from increased flow, and the internal mammary bruit, both have diastolic components. One may mistake them for a diastolic murmur signifying cardiac pathology.

Table 2-1

Normal Physical Findings in Pregnancy

Signs
Peripheral edema (up to 80% of parturients)
Distended neck veins (not throughout cardiac cycle)
Laterally displaced point or maximum impulse

Symptoms
Dyspnea
Reduced exercise tolerance

Auscultation
Increased splitting of the first and second heart sounds
  S_3
Systolic ejection murmur (left sternal border, grades I and II)
Continuous venous murmur
Diastolic murmur (up to 10% of parturients nonpathologic flow-related)
Neck bruits (originating from the internal mammary artery)

Electrocardiogram
Left-axis deviation
Nonspecific ST- and T-wave changes

Chest Radiograph
Straightening of the left-heart border
Heart position more horizontal
Increased vascular markings

Table 2-2

Signs and Symptoms of Maternal Heart Disease

SIGNS	SYMPTOMS
Cyanosis	Severe dyspnea
Clubbing	Paroxysmal nocturnal
Persistent neck vein distention	dyspnea
Systolic murmur > grade II/VI	Hemoptysis
Diastolic murmur	Syncope with exertion
Cardiomegaly	Stress-related chest pain
Arrhythmia	
Loud P_2	

Cardiac Disease and Pregnancy

Successful management of pregnant patients with moderate to severe cardiac disease requires close cooperation between obstetrician, anesthesiologist, cardiologist, perinatologist, and nursing staff. Timely evaluation and frequent monitoring throughout pregnancy are needed to follow the mother's ability to adapt to the progressively increasing cardiac stresses of gestation. The personnel involved should meet early to discuss options and formulate plans to cope with a variety of clinical contingencies.

Classification

The New York Heart Association (NYHA) classification of functional impairment is a valuable way to assess severity and disability during pregnancy (Table 2-3). Approximately 5% to 10% of pregnant cardiac patients fall into NYHA class III or IV. These women have a 75% to 90% risk of maternal mortality and a high incidence of fetal loss.

Diagnosis and Management During Pregnancy

Relying solely on subjective signs and symptoms may lead one to make an erroneous diagnosis.[10] On serial measurement, a host of noninvasive, objective parameters can provide information about the ability of maternal cardiac function to cope with impending parturition. Intermittent measurements of peripheral oxygen saturation with a pulse oximeter may provide an early indication of maternal cardiac failure. Increases in cardiac volume and pulmonary vascular engorgement are detectable by measuring maternal vital capacity. Electrocardiograms (ECG) and Holter monitors aid in detecting ischemia, arrhythmias, conduction defects, and axis deviations.

Chest films, repeated as necessary, can diagnose or confirm progressive congestive heart failure, cardiomegaly, and pleural or pericardial effusions. A chest radiograph exposes the mother to a maximum of 80 mrad of radiation, with approximately 50 mrad to the chest and 5 mrad to the gonads.[11] A detailed analysis of prenatal radiation exposure and subsequent malformations or cancer suggests that fetal risk is very low. Fewer than 1 case of malformation or cancer is expected per 1000 patients irradiated by 1 rad in utero during the first 4 months of pregnancy.[12] So, no measurable risk is associated with a chest radiograph during pregnancy.

Radionuclide techniques expose the mother to 500 to 800 mrad,[13] and cardiac catheterization exposes the patient to as much as 28,000 mrad of radiation. Flow-directed right-heart and pulmonary artery catheterization without fluoroscopy can assess valvular function and chamber pressures. Two-dimensional contrast echocardiography can evaluate valve and ventricular function. Both alternatives help limit maternal and fetal exposure to radiation.

Echocardiography (two-dimensional and M-mode) generates high-frequency sound waves and records signals reflected from the blood–tissue interfaces. Assess-

Table 2-3

New York Heart Association Functional Classification

Class I	Asymptomatic
Class II	Slight limitation of physical activities; comfortable at rest
Class III	Marked limitation with less-than-ordinary activity causing fatigue, palpitation, dyspnea, or angina; remains comfortable at rest
Class IV	Symptomatic at rest

ment of cardiac chamber motion, myocardial contractility, and ejection fraction aid in patient evaluation. Doppler echocardiography detects the change in sound-wave frequency reflected from moving targets such as red blood cells. This technique can provide information about abnormal blood flow, transvalvular pressure gradients, valve area, and cardiac output.

Management at Term

Good communication between the obstetric anesthesiologist and the obstetrician facilitates the care of these high-risk parturients. Invasive monitoring, antibiotic regimens, anticoagulation, termination of pregnancy, the route of delivery, anesthetic management, maternal–fetal priorities, and the effects of various cardiac and uterine therapeutic modalities should all be discussed before parturition.

INVASIVE MONITORING. Clark *et al*[14] used the thermodilution method of cardiac output determination to assess ten primiparous volunteers. The women were studied at 36 to 38 weeks of gestation and again between 11 and 13 weeks postpartum. By late in the third trimester, parturients had significantly lower systemic vascular resistance, peripheral vascular resistance, and colloid osmotic pressure. Both cardiac output and heart rate were elevated. Left ventricular stroke work index remained unchanged. These investigators concluded that, in normal pregnancy, the third trimester of gestation is not associated with hyperdynamic left ventricular function. Lee and coworkers[15] prospectively compared pulsed-Doppler and thermodilution-derived estimates of left ventricular stroke volume and cardiac output in 16 gravidae. These women had undergone right-heart catheterization for several reasons (severe preeclampsia, eclampsia,

hemorrhagic shock, and renal failure). They found a good correlation between measurements of cardiac output made by pulsed Doppler and thermodilution via pulmonary artery catheter (Fig. 2-1).[15] These results should minimize the need for invasive modalities to measure maternal cardiac function.

There are few strict rules about when to insert a pulmonary catheter in the obstetric patient. Some physicians find them beneficial in pregnant women with NYHA class III and IV cardiac disease.[16] Such patients may have the following:

- Severe preeclampsia, eclampsia with oliguria or pulmonary edema
- Class III or IV rheumatic or congenital cardiac disease in labor
- Class II or III rheumatic or congenital cardiac disease with severe preeclampsia in labor
- Septic shock
- Adult Respiratory Distress Syndrome
- Amniotic fluid embolism
- Hypovolemic shock unresponsive to fluid replacement
- Thyroid storm

ENDOCARDITIS PROPHYLAXIS. Gravidae with prosthetic cardiac valves, most congenital cardiac malformations, surgically constructed shunts, rheumatic and other acquired valvular dysfunction, idiopathic hypertrophic subaortic stenosis (IHSS), previous history of potential endocarditis, and mitral valve prolapse should receive endocarditis prophylaxis during parturition. Renal dialysis patients with atrioventricular shunts or women with ventriculoatrial shunts, or transvenous pacemakers, also may need prophylaxis.[17,18]

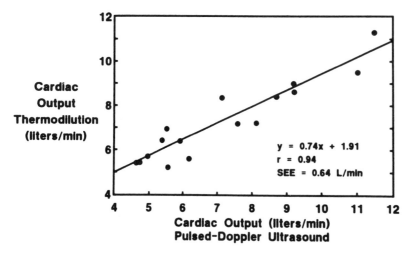

Figure 2–1. Correlation between pulsed Doppler and thermodilution cardiac output in parturients. (y = cardiac output, thermodilution technique; x = cardiac output, Doppler technique; r = slope-correlation between the techniques; SEE = standard error) (Lee W, Rokey R, Cotton DB. Noninvasive maternal stoke volume and cardiac output determinations by pulsed Doppler echocardiography. Am J Obstet Gynecol 1988;158:505)

Endocarditis prophylaxis during labor and delivery is the same as for genitourinary surgery or instrumentation. The American Heart Association recommends ampicillin, 2 g IM or IV, and gentamicin, 1.5 mg/kg IM (not to exceed 80 mg) 30 minutes before the procedure or at the start of labor. Repeat this dose once, 8 hours after the original dose. For patients allergic to penicillin, use vancomycin (1 g over 1 hour plus gentamicin 1.5 mg/kg IM (not to exceed 80 mg). Again, repeat the dose once, 8 hours later. Amoxicillin 3 g orally, 1 hour before the procedure and then 1.5 g, 6 hours later is an alternative in low-risk patients.

ANTICOAGULANTS. All patients with mechanical valve prostheses must receive anticoagulants. Those with cardiac valve disease and a history of systemic emboli also should take these drugs. Chronic atrial fibrillation, too, is an indication for prophylactic anticoagulation. Warfarin (coumarin) crosses the placenta and increases the danger of abnormal fetal development and congenital malformations, as well as abortion, stillbirth, and hemorrhage.[19] Heparin, the preferred anticoagulant during gestation, does not cross the placenta. Some begin heparin therapy after conception and through the first trimester and resume warfarin therapy in mid-pregnancy. Others believe that fetal bleeding may occur at all stages of development and so avoid warfarin throughout the pregnancy.[20] At term, most clinicians substitute heparin therapy until labor begins, when all anticoagulant therapy ceases until after delivery.

CHRONIC MEDICATIONS. Pregnant cardiac patients may arrive for delivery taking a host of medications. Digoxin appears safe during pregnancy, with therapeutic serum concentrations having no apparent toxic effects on the fetus. Lidocaine appears safe, whereas quinidine and procainamide may induce premature labor. Diuretics may reduce uteroplacental blood flow and yield fetal electrolyte imbalance, neonatal jaundice, thrombocytopenia, liver damage, and fetal death. Propranolol crosses the placenta and may cause fetal bradycardia, hypoglycemia, and intrauterine growth retardation. Beta-adrenergic blockers also may produce an oxytocic action. Short-term use of calcium channel blockers has not been associated with demonstrable adverse effects in the fetus or newborn infant. These drugs, however, can exert a tocolytic effect.[21,22]

Specific Lesions

Mitral Stenosis

The most common acquired valvular disease presenting in pregnancy is mitral valve stenosis of rheu- matic origin. The obstructing lesion usually develops 10 to 20 years after the initial infection. These women may have difficulty tolerating the normal cardiovascular alterations of pregnancy. Symptoms occur in as many as 25% of gravidae with mitral stenosis. Worsening dyspnea on exertion, fatigue, orthopnea, hemoptysis, recurrent bronchitis, and frank pulmonary edema may arise (Table 2-4).

In progressive mitral valve stenosis, a chronic decrease in left ventricular volume occurs, whereas the left atrium, pulmonic system, and right heart face an increase in both pressure and volume (Fig. 2-2). Normal adult mitral valve area varies from 4 to 6 cm². Stenotic lesions are graded as follows:

- Mild: 1.5–2.5 cm²
- Moderate: 1.0–1.5 cm²
- Severe: < 1 cm²

Distal to the valve, the left ventricle is small to normal in size. Left ventricular end-diastolic pressure is in the normal range. However, approximately one third of patients with mitral valve disease have a depressed ejection fraction. Either a chronic decrease in left ventricular volume or residual scarring from rheumatic myocarditis may be causative.[23] A dilated left atrium may predispose to left lower lobe pulmonary infections. Severe left atrial dilation can cause left recurrent laryngeal nerve paralysis and dysphagia.

On auscultation, classic findings include an accentuated first-heart sound, an "opening snap," an early diastolic sound heard best over the lower left sternal border, and a low-pitched apical diastolic "rumble" (Fig. 2-3).[9] Evidence of mitral regurgitation, as well as involvement of other valves, is not uncommon. Electrocardiogram and chest radiograph will detect signs of advanced disease, such as atrial fibrillation or right ventricular hypertrophy. Tachycardia, atrial fibrillation, or junctional rhythm may decrease stroke volume.

The Gorlin equation (equation 1) aids in the understanding of valvular disease hemodynamics. If valve area remains constant, the pressure gradient (equation 2) across the valve will increase by the square of any rise in flow rate (cardiac output). Left atrial pressure rises in relation to orifice size, atrial size, heart rate, cardiac compliance, and output.

During pregnancy, cardiac decompensation most likely occurs at 28 to 32 weeks' gestation, during the onset of labor, or early in the postpartum period. These are time periods of maximal increases in heart rate, systemic blood volume, cardiac output, and pulmonary blood volume. With a valvular pressure gradient greater than 25 mm Hg, acute cardiac decompensation

Table 2–4

Mitral Valve Disease: Severe Mitral Stenosis

Symptoms

Shortness of breath, dyspnea on exertion, orthopnea

Recurrent bronchitis

Hemoptysis

Systemic embolism

Acute pulmonary edema may occur with the onset of atrial fibrillation or acute pulmonary infection

Physical Findings

First heart sound and mitral opening snap are loud with pliable valve, faint with calcific valve

Diastolic murmur: Low-frequency apical murmur is longer with more severe stenosis; may be very faint in the elderly

Electrocardiogram: left atrial enlargement or atrial fibrillation; right-axis deviation; rarely, right ventricular hypertrophy

Chest radiograph: cardiac size, especially left atrium, calcification in mitral valve, pulmonary congestion

Echocardiogram: left atrial dilation, left ventricular performance, characteristic valve changes, whether pliable or rigid

Hemodynamic Findings

Diastolic gradient between the pulmonary wedge pressure and left ventricular diastolic pressure

(After Basta LL. Cardiovascular disease. New York: Medical Examination Publishing Co, 1983:276.)

---

may arise, accompanied by atrial fibrillation, paroxysmal tachycardia, pulmonary embolism, pulmonary vascular congestion, and infarction.[17] In late-stage mitral valve stenosis, elevations in pulmonary pressures lead to persistent pulmonary hypertension and irreversible pulmonary arterial hyperplasia. Right-heart failure, peripheral edema, hepatomegaly, ascites, and distended neck veins may occur. Ventilation–perfusion mismatching, which worsens in the Trendelenburg position, is not uncommon.

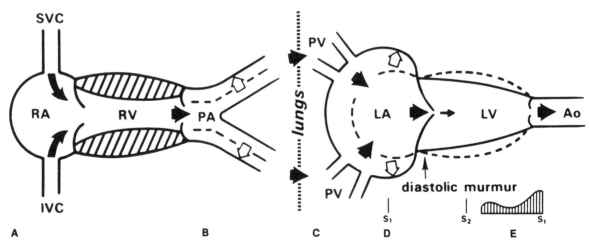

Figure 2–2. Pathophysiology of mitral stenosis. **(A)** Increased right atrial (RA) pressures reflect right-sided failure. **(B)** Degree of elevation in pulmonary artery (PA) pressure reflects the severity of increase in pulmonary venous (PV) pressure. **(C)** Increased PV pressure. **(D)** Enlarged left atrium (LA), increased LA pressure; diastolic gradient between LA and left ventricle (LV) reflects severity of stenosis. **(E)** Low cardiac output with severe stenosis. (Ao = aorta, IVC = inferior vena cava, SVC = superior vena cava.) (Basta LL. Cardiovascular disease. New York: Medical Examination Publishing Co, 1983:265)

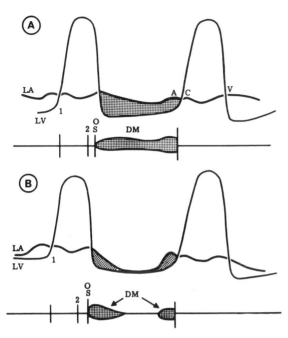

Figure 2–3. Schematic representation of the duration of the diastolic murmur (DM) of mitral stenosis and its relationship to intracardiac pressures. The DM persists as long as there is a significant diastolic pressure gradient across the mitral valve and is, therefore, longer in more severe grades of stenosis. (A, C, and V = central venous pulsation waves; OS = opening snap) **(A)** Severe stenosis. **(B)** Mild stenosis. (LA = left atrium, LV = left ventricle.) (Tavel ME. Clinical phonocardiography and external pulse recording, 4th ed. Chicago: Year Book Medical Publishers, 1985;169)

Equation 1. The Gorlin equation

$$\text{Valve area (cm}^2) = \frac{\text{Flow rate (mL/sec)}}{K \times \text{pressure gradient (mm Hg)}}$$

Equation 2. Pressure gradient, mitral valvular disease

$$\text{Pressure gradient} = \text{Left atrial pressure} - \text{left ventricular end-diastolic pressure}$$

$$\text{Pressure gradient} = \left[\frac{\text{Cardiac output}}{\text{Diastolic filling time}}\right]^2$$

Table 2–5

Etiology of Mitral Valve Insufficiency

Rheumatic fever
Mitral valve prolapse
Chordae tendineae dysfunction/rupture
Cardiac trauma
Endocarditis
Papillary muscle dysfunction/rupture
Cardiac trauma
Endocarditis
Spatial disorientation
Cardiomyopathy with left ventricular enlargement
Idiopathic hypertrophic subaortic stenosis

Mitral Insufficiency

Mitral insufficiency is often due to rheumatic fever and is usually associated with mitral stenosis.[24] However, there are other causes of regurgitant flow (Table 2-5).

Mitral insufficiency generally is better tolerated during pregnancy than mitral stenosis. Failure of valve closure permits left ventricular blood to flow into the left atrium during ventricular systole. Regurgitant flow depends on the ventriculoatrial pressure gradient, regurgitant orifice size, and heart rate. Heart rate affects both time for ventricular filling and duration of ventricular ejection. Regurgitant blood raises left atrial pressure and may produce pulmonary vascular congestion and pulmonary edema. The increased left ventricular diastolic volume is generally tolerated. As ventricular compliance increases, a larger left ventricular end-diastolic volume does not raise left ventricular end-diastolic pressure, and oxygen consumption is not initially prohibitive. When the regurgitant fraction is more than 60% of left ventricular volume, congestive heart failure develops. Left ventricular failure with reduced left ventricular output may cause pulmonary hypertension and ultimately right ventricular failure (Table 2-6).

When insufficiency of the mitral valve is combined with stenosis, both pressure and volume work increase. Symptoms are generally more severe and occur earlier than in pure insufficiency. Fatigue is the most typical early symptom. On physical examination, an apical holosystolic murmur radiating to the left axilla is common (Fig. 2-4). The ECG may show evidence of left atrial enlargement or fibrillation, and left ventricular hypertrophy. With significant insufficiency, chest

Table 2–6

Mitral Valve Insufficiency

	CHRONIC	ACUTE
Symptoms	Longstanding exertional dyspnea	Acute pulmonary edema, cardiogenic shock with papillary muscle rupture
Rhythm	Usually atrial fibrillation	Usually sinus rhythm
First heart sound	Faint	Faint
S_4 gallop	No	Very common
S_3	May be audible	May be audible
Heart size	Large	Normal or slightly enlarged
Left atrial size	Markedly increased	Slightly increased
Left ventricular hypertrophy on ECG	Common	Uncommon
Echocardiogram	Chamber size, valve characteristics depend on etiology	Chamber size, typical changes of flail valve leaflet
Left atrial pressure	Not considerably increased	Very prominent V wave may approach aortic diastolic pressure

(After Basta LL. Cardiovascular disease. New York: Medical Examination Publishing Co, 1983:278)

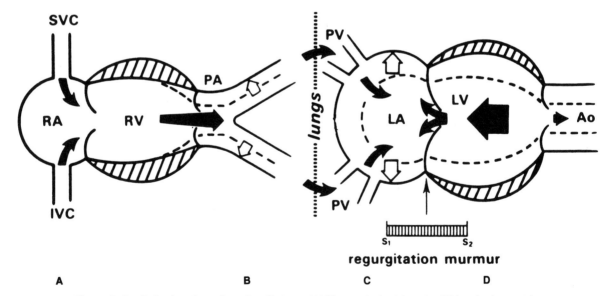

Figure 2–4. Pathophysiology of mitral insufficiency. **(A)** Changes in the right atrium (RA) and right ventricle (RV) depend on the degree of pulmonary hypertension. **(B)** Increased pulmonary artery (PA) pressure reflects the increased pulmonary venous (PV) pressure. **(C)** Dilation and increased pressure in left atrium (LA) reflect severity of the disease. Dilation is more pronounced in chronic insufficiency. Increased pressure is more pronounced in acute incompetence. **(D)** Degree of left ventricular (LV) dilation usually reflects the severity of the disease. (Ao = aorta, IVC = inferior vena cava, SVC = superior vena cava.) (Basta LL. Cardiovascular disease. New York: Medical Examination Publishing Co, 1983:279)

radiograph may show cardiomegaly and pulmonary vascular congestion.

The mild tachycardia of pregnancy may benefit the gravida with mitral regurgitation, as the area of the regurgitant orifice may decrease in the faster smaller heart. Mitral valve prolapse with regurgitation is the exception to this principle. Prolapse of redundant mitral leaflets worsens with a smaller ventricular valve orifice, as caused by tachycardia. The lower systemic vascular resistance of the gravida allows her to improve forward flow. Conversely, any increase in systemic vascular resistance may cause worsening regurgitation.

Mitral Valve Prolapse

Mitral valve prolapse affects 5% to 10% of young adults and is encountered mainly in women of childbearing age.[25] A mid- to late systolic click followed by a systolic murmur, heard best at the lower left sternal border or cardiac apex, is typical. The ECG and chest radiograph are generally nonspecific. Echocardiography reveals pathologic protrusion of the mitral leaflet into the left atrium during systole.[26] Symptoms range from atypical chest pain, dyspnea, fatigue, dizziness, palpitations, and anxiety, to syncope and sudden death. Structural abnormalities in primary mitral valve prolapse consist of elongated chordae tendineae with large redundant mitral leaflets. Histologically, the familial form of mitral valve prolapse shows myxomatous degenerative changes.

It appears that the valve in primary mitral valve prolapse is functionally too large for the ventricle. This mismatch causes the redundant leaflets to prolapse into the left atrium in mid- and late systole as the ventricular volume decreases. Severity of prolapse depends on ventricular volume. Increased myocardial contractility, decreased preload, tachycardia, straining, and excessive airway pressure decrease ventricular volume and worsen symptoms.

Pregnancy may change the physical signs of mitral valve prolapse, either enhancing or diminishing them, depending on changes in vascular resistance and blood volume.[27-29] One large series evaluated 3582 parturients. Forty-three patients had documented mitral valve prolapse (1.2%). All 43 had pregnancies complicated by cardiac compromise but with good fetal outcome. Neither spontaneous abortion nor premature delivery seemed higher in the women with mitral valve prolapse.[30]

Aortic Stenosis

The basic pathophysiology of aortic stenosis is the development of obstruction to left ventricular outflow.

Normal aortic valve area is approximately 2.5 to 3.5 cm^2. In advanced stages of aortic stenosis, when the valve area is less than 0.75 cm^2, stroke volume is decreased and fixed (Fig. 2-5). Concentric left ventricular hypertrophy and elevated left ventricular chamber pressure cause a reduction in subendocardial blood flow. Ischemia and ventricular failure follow. The increased oxygen required by the noncompliant, hypertrophied left ventricle, doing pressure work, combined with reduced coronary artery blood flow, caused by a decreased cardiac output, worsen the ischemia.

There is an increased reliance on atrial contraction. Normally, atrial contraction augments stroke volume by 20%. In women with aortic stenosis, atrial contraction may contribute as much as 40% of stroke volume.[31] Therefore, a loss of atrial function, whether through atrial fibrillation or junctional rhythms, may be lethal.

The classic physical finding of aortic stenosis is a harsh systolic ejection murmur heard at the base of the heart that radiates to the carotid arteries (Fig. 2-6). Other findings may include a slowly rising and prolonged arterial pulse, a fourth heart sound, or a paradoxically split second heart sound. History may reveal syncope, angina, or dyspnea on exertion (Table 2-7).

The increased oxygen requirements of pregnancy and labor make the parturient myocardium vulnerable to ischemic injury. The increased plasma volume of pregnancy may further exacerbate chamber pressure in the noncompliant left ventricle, elevating myocardial oxygen demand and encouraging pulmonary transudation of fluid. If hemodynamically severe aortic stenosis is diagnosed before pregnancy, surgical correction in advance is advisable. Parturients with aortic stenosis have reported mortality rates as high as 17%.[32] Diminished stroke volume and cardiac output may place uteroplacental blood flow at jeopardy, with possible intrauterine growth retardation and congenital anomalies. A fetal mortality rate of 32% has been reported in women with uncorrected aortic stenosis.[32] Correction of a maternal outflow obstruction before conception reduces the fetal mortality rate to about 12%.[33]

Aortic Insufficiency

Although more common than stenosis, aortic insufficiency remains uncommon in pregnant women. Regurgitation often develops as the result of rheumatic disease but also is found as a congenital abnormality, or in relationship with either rheumatoid arthritis or systemic lupus erythematosus. Marfan's syndrome causes aortic root dilatation and subsequent regurgitation. Acute regurgitation can succeed trauma and dissection.

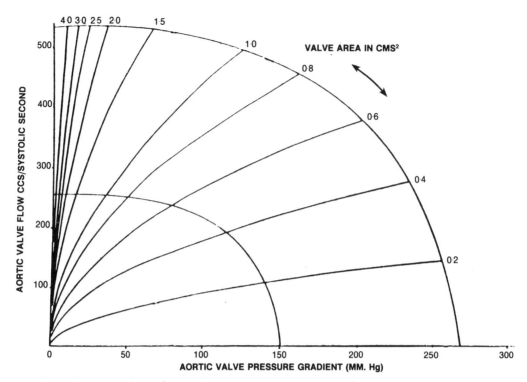

Figure 2–5. Interrelation of aortic valve pressure gradient, aortic valve flow, and aortic valve area. This diagram shows the theoretic pressure and flow curves for different aortic valve cross-sectional areas (in square centimeters). (Grossman W. Cardiac catheterization and angiography, 2nd ed. Philadelphia: Lea & Febiger, 1980:124)

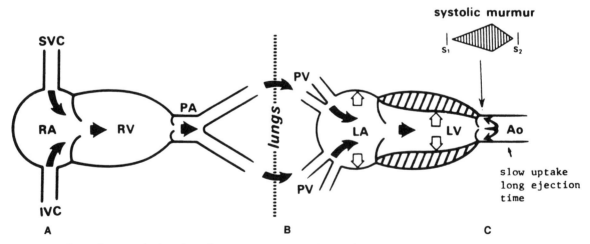

Figure 2–6. Pathophysiology of aortic stenosis. **(A)** The degree of right atrial (RA) and right ventricular (RV) pressure increase reflects the increase in left atrial (LA) pressure. **(B)** Degree of increase in pulmonary venous (PV) pressure reflects the degree of left ventricular (LV) failure or decreased left ventricular compliance. **(C)** Systolic pressure increases. Degree of increase reflects the severity of aortic stenosis. A systolic gradient greater than 50 mm Hg indicates severe stenosis. Diastolic pressure decreases. (Ao = aorta, IVC = inferior vena cava, PA = pulmonary artery, SVC = superior vena cava.) (Basta LL. Cardiovascular disease. New York: Medical Examination Publishing Co, 1983:298)

Table 2-7

Aortic Valve Disease

Severe Aortic Stenosis	
Symptoms	Angina; syncope; paroxysmal nocturnal dyspnea; congestive heart failure (rare)
Physical findings	Slow carotid upstroke; left ventricular enlargement, if marked signifies poor left ventricular performance; faint or absent aortic closure sound in calcific aortic stenosis; long ejection murmur that peaks in mid-systole heard maximally over the second space to the right of the sternum
Chest radiograph	Left ventricular enlargement; pulmonary congestion possible; aortic valve calcification
Electrocardiogram	Left ventricular hypertrophy and "stain"
Echocardiogram	Thickened valve with limited mobility; degree of left ventricular wall thickness and left ventricular performance
Cardiac catheterization	Large systolic gradient across aortic valve (> 50 mm Hg)
Severe Aortic Insufficiency	
Symptoms	Left ventricular failure; uncommonly angina or syncope
Physical findings	Wide pulse pressure; aortic diastolic pressure < 40 mm Hg; enlarged left ventricle; typical auscultatory findings
Chest radiograph	Left ventricular enlargement; pulmonary congestion possible
Electrocardiogram	Left ventricular hypertrophy with T-wave inversion in severe cases
Echocardiogram	Shows left ventricular dimensions; wall thickness and performance
Acute Aortic Insufficiency	
Symptoms	Recent history of pulmonary edema, features of low cardiac output
Physical findings	Frequently not prominent; aortic diastolic pressure is not considerably reduced, and the pulse pressure is not distinctly wide; left ventricular enlargement may not be impressive; aortic diastolic murmur may be short and faint; loud S_3 common
Chest radiograph	Pulmonary edema with only slightly enlarged heart
Electrocardiogram	May be normal
Echocardiogram	May provide important clues to the diagnosis; diastolic mitral valve closure; high-frequency diastolic vibrations of the mitral leaflet and hyperkinetic left ventricle

(After Basta LL: Cardiovascular Disease; New York: Medical Examination Publishing Co, 1983, 278)

With chronic insufficiency, symptoms follow a latent period of approximately 20 years. Fatigue and dyspnea may be worse at rest than during exercise. Pulse pressure may be increased with a rapid upstroke and rapid decline. The bisferious pulse, a double impulse during systole, may be seen. A high-pitched blowing diastolic decrescendo murmur along the sternal border is heard best with the patient sitting upright during end expiration. ECG, chest radiograph, and echocardiogram may help make the diagnosis (see Table 2-7).

An incompetent aortic valve allows regurgitation of blood into the left ventricle, causing ventricular strain, dilatation, and, ultimately, an abatement in contractile force and cardiac output (Fig. 2-7). The regurgitant blood adds to normal ventricular filling. The left ventricle sees a chronically elevated volume. A larger chamber size and eccentric wall thickening follow. As with all left-sided valvular lesions, in the most advanced state, pulmonary hypertension and right ventricular failure arise.

The changes wrought by aortic insufficiency are usually well tolerated in pregnancy. The parturient's increased plasma volume may help maintain cardiac output. A decreased maternal systemic vascular resistance and a faster pulse also encourage forward flow. Bradycardia incites ventricular distention and increased left atrial pressure and pulmonary congestion.[34]

Idiopathic Hypertrophic Subaortic Stenosis

Idiopathic hypertrophic subaortic stenosis (IHSS) is an uncommon autosomal dominant inherited disorder that causes disproportionate hypertrophy of the intraventricular septum. The abnormally large septum bulges into the left ventricular chamber and obstructs

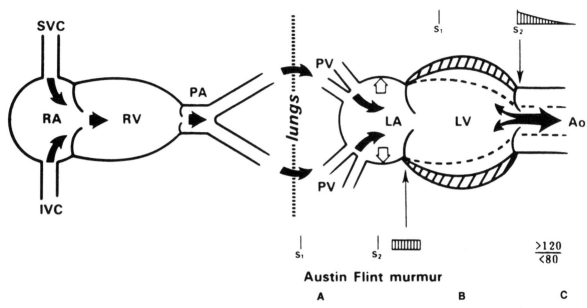

Figure 2–7. Pathophysiology of aortic insufficiency. **(A)** Pulmonary venous (PV) pressure increases only with left ventricular (LV) failure. **(B)** Dilated LV. Diastolic pressure increases with LV dysfunction or acute aortic incompetence. **(C)** Wide pulse pressure reflects the severity of aortic valve incompetence. Diastolic pressure less than 40 mm Hg usually means severe insufficiency. (Ao = aorta, IVC = inferior vena cava, LA = left atrium, PA = pulmonary artery, RA = right atrium, RV = right ventricle, SVC = superior vena cava.) (Basta LL. Cardiovascular disease. New York: Medical Examination Publishing Co, 1983:300)

the ventricular outflow tract in mid-to-late systole. Tachycardia, increased myocardial contractility, or hypovolemia increase the degree of outflow obstruction. A systolic ejection murmur is heard at the base of the heart. The murmur increases with maneuvers that lower left ventricular volume. The ECG may show left ventricular hypertrophy with large septal Q waves. The echocardiogram shows thickening of the ventricular septum and abnormal anterior movement of the mitral valve during systole. Symptoms include dyspnea, chest pain, and palpitations. Stress, exercise, excitement, or anxiety, all conditions that increase catecholamine secretions, worsen symptoms of IHSS. There is a 1% to 3% chance per year of sudden death.

Although a worsening of symptoms of IHSS has been reported during pregnancy (Table 2-8), the elevated plasma volume and autotransfusion of blood from the contracting uterus at placental delivery tend to maintain maternal blood pressure. Beta blockade, despite potential fetal hazards of intrauterine growth retardation and newborn bradycardia, usually is continued throughout gestation.[35,36]

Congenital Heart Disease

Congenital heart disease occurs in approximately 1% of live births in the United States.[37] Women with

Table 2-8

Pregnancy and IHSS: Symptom Exacerbation

Increase in contractility
Hypovolemia
Tachycardia
Decreased left ventricular end-diastolic volume
Decreased left atrial pressure
Increased left ventricular ejection velocity
Vasodilator agents
Decreased peripheral vascular resistance of pregnancy
Inferior vena caval obstruction
Increased catecholamine production with labor
Acute blood loss at delivery
Digitalis, ketamine, epinephrine, ephedrine, calcium chloride

congenital heart lesions are reaching child-bearing age in increasing numbers. Many have either a partially or fully corrected lesion. Corrective maternal cardiac surgery is most often done before conception to optimize the condition of both mother and fetus. The obstetric anesthesiologist needs to know both the medical and surgical history of the mother. Procure any other data to aid in understanding the pathophysiology of a parturient's particular lesion. These data may include ECG, chest radiograph, echocardiogram, or cardiac catheterization.

Left-to-Right Shunts

ATRIAL SEPTAL DEFECT. Atrial septal defects include ostium primum, ostium secundum, and sinus venosus. Ostium secundum, a defect located in the area of the foramen ovale and adjacent tissue occurs more often in women than men. Women are often asymptomatic unless pulmonary hypertension or a supraventricular arrythmia develops. A persistently split second heart sound associated with a systolic ejection murmur is best heard at the base of the heart (Fig. 2-8). The ECG shows right-axis deviation, and chest radiograph may show prominent pulmonary vasculature. Increases in systemic vascular resistance and decreases in

pulmonary vascular resistance allow worsening of the left-to-right shunt and hinder in cardiac output. A higher pulmonary vascular resistance may promote acute right-to-left shunting. In the absence of large left-to-right shunting or secondary pulmonary hypertension, parturients with this lesion tolerate pregnancy well.[33]

VENTRICULAR SEPTAL DEFECT. More common than atrial septal defects, ventricular septal defects occur as either membranous or muscular. They appear during embryogenesis and are of different sizes and multiple locations. Most close spontaneously in childhood. Remaining lesions are generally surgically corrected prior to conception. On physical examination, a loud holosystolic murmur is heard best along the left sternal border (Fig. 2-9). In the absence of symptomatic pulmonary congestion, a parturient with a ventricular septal defect may complain of fatigue and malaise but usually will tolerate pregnancy well. The predominant risk is endocarditis. Whittemore *et al*[38] reviewed 98 pregnancies in 50 women with ventricular septal defects.[38] Complications included congestive heart failure, arrhythmias, and hypertension. There were 78 live births, 15 spontaneous abortions or stillbirths, and 6 interrupted pregnancies.

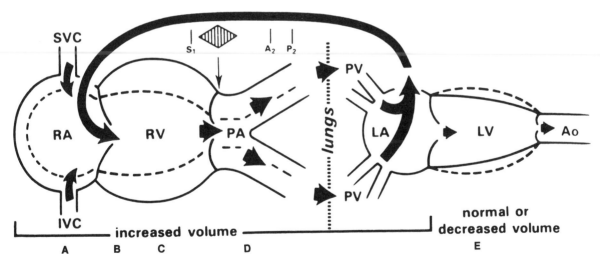

Figure 2–8. Hemodynamic characteristics of atrial septal defect and anomalous pulmonary venous drainage (pretricuspid shunt) **(E)**. The left ventricle (LV) and aorta (Ao) are small **(A)**. Pressures in left atrium (LA) and right atrium (RA) are equal **(B)**. There is increased diastolic flow through the tricuspid valve, often producing a diastolic tricuspid flow murmur **(C)**. The right ventricle (RV) is considerably dilated. **(D)** Pulmonary flow is increased, producing a short ejection systolic murmur and a wide split second sound. Pulmonary vasculature is exaggerated. *Solid arrow* indicates flow. (IVC = inferior vena cava, PA = pulmonary artery, PV = pulmonary vein, SVC = superior vena cava.) (Basta LL. Cardiovascular disease. New York: Medical Examination Publishing Co, 1983:324)

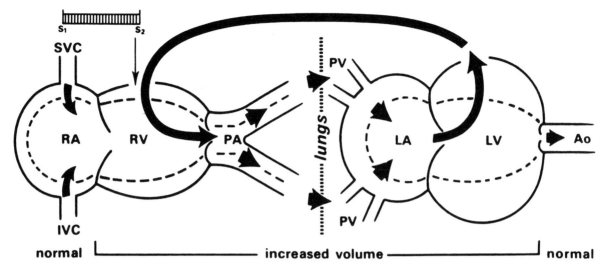

Figure 2–9. Hemodynamic characteristics of ventricular septal defect. Flow increases to right ventricle (RV, pulmonary artery (PA), left atrium (LA), and left ventricle (LV). With very large defects, the pressure in the two ventricles becomes equal, but in most cases, the pressure in the LV exceeds that in the RV. The shunt causes a holosystolic murmur, best heard over the third and fourth costal interspaces to the left of the sternum. Also, a mitral diastolic flow murmur may be audible. (Ao=aorta, IVC=inferior vena cava, PV=pulmonary vein, RA=right atrium, SVC=superior vena cava.) (Basta LL. Cardiovascular disease. New York: Medical Examination Publishing Co. 1983:330)

The parturient with an uncorrected ventricular septal defect does not tolerate large increases of systemic vascular resistance well. The subsequent increase in left-to-right shunting of blood will cause pulmonary hypertension and an increase in right ventricular work. An acute decrease in systemic vascular resistance also causes problems. With pulmonary hypertension, lower systemic vascular resistance may allow right-to-left shunting and both maternal and fetal hypoxemia. It is unclear whether the fall in both systemic and pulmonary vascular resistance and rise in cardiac output and blood volume during normal pregnancy worsen atrial and ventricular septal defect symptoms.

Hypoxia and hypercarbia increase pulmonary vascular resistance. Whether the typical Pao_2 of 105 mm Hg and $Paco_2$ of 33 mm Hg relieves pulmonary and right ventricular strain also is unclear.

Right-to-Left Shunts

TETRALOGY OF FALLOT. Tetralogy of Fallot is the most common cause of right-to-left shunt. Tetralogy of Fallot is anatomically characterized by the following:

- A ventricular septal defect
- An aorta that overrides the pulmonary outflow tract

- Infundibular pulmonary artery stenosis with obstruction to outflow from the right ventricle
- Right ventricular hypertrophy

Seventy percent of patients have a bicuspid aortic valve, and the distal pulmonary artery may be hypoplastic or absent (Fig. 2-10).

The predominant anatomic anomaly that determines the physiologic state is the degree of right ventricular and pulmonary artery hypoplasia. Right-to-left shunting occurs after pulmonary vascular resistance exceeds systemic vascular resistance. Blood following the path of least resistance is shunted through an atrial or septal defect before oxygenation in the lung. Cyanosis due to arterial hypoxemia is apparent by 6 months of age. Hypercyanotic attacks, or "tet spells," are classically treated with beta-adrenergic blockade to decrease spasm of the pathologic infundibular cardiac muscle. Recurrence of attacks is an indication for surgical correction. Survival to child-bearing age requires corrective surgery that usually includes closure of the ventricular septal defect and resection of the infundibular stenosis, or pulmonary valvulotomy.

In uncorrected tetralogy of Fallot, the most common auscultatory finding is an ejection murmur heard over the left sternal border resulting from blood

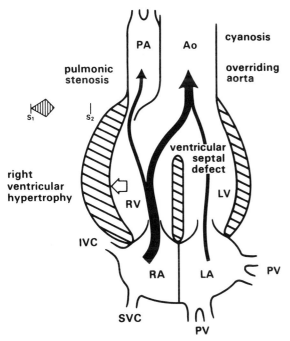

Figure 2–10. Hemodynamic characteristics of tetralogy of Fallot. Note that the four defects in this disease result from abnormal development of the pulmonary infundibulum. Right ventricular (RV) hypertrophy is due to the fact that pressures are equal in both ventricles. (Ao = aorta, IVC = inferior vena cava, LA = left atrium, LV = left ventricle, PA = pulmonary artery, PV = pulmonary vein, RA = right atrium, RV = right ventricle, SVC = superior vena cava.) (Basta LL. Cardiovascular disease. New York: Medical Examination Publishing Co, 1983:330)

flow across the infundibular pulmonary stenosis. One may appreciate a right ventricular heave. Chest radiograph shows a diminished pulmonary vasculature. The ECG shows right-axis deviation and right ventricular hypertrophy. Arterial blood gas determination usually reveals a normal pH and Pa_{CO_2}. In contrast, regardless of inspired oxygen tension, these women have a markedly reduced Pa_{O_2}. The echocardiogram reveals an aorta overriding the ventricular septum. There is a dynamic element to the right ventricular outflow obstruction. Depending on the inotropic state of the myocardium, the muscular infundibular area dilates or constricts.

The risk of fetal morbidity and mortality increases with the severity of maternal cyanosis. Congenital heart defects approach 15% to 20% in the offspring of mothers with tetralogy of Fallot who are cyanotic. Intrauterine growth retardation is common. Palliation or surgical correction improves outcome for both mother

and fetus.[39] In a series of 309 women who had surgical correction of tetralogy of Fallot, 40 pregnancies in 18 women resulted in 30 live-born children. Of the ten abortions, five were "therapeutic."[40]

A drop in peripheral vascular resistance and uterine compression of the vena cava decrease venous blood return to the heart. A subsequent decrease in pulmonary blood flow will increase the intracardiac shunt. Acute blood loss at delivery may have the same result. The autotransfusion with uterine contraction after delivery will increase venous blood return and may decrease the shunt.

EISENMENGER'S SYNDROME. The development of a pulmonary vascular resistance that exceeds systemic vascular resistance, reversing intracardiac shunt and producing cyanosis, is called Eisenmenger's syndrome (Fig. 2-11). This reversal may occur in up to 50% of untreated patients with a large ventricular septal defect and in 10% of patients with an atrial septal defect. A left-to-right intracardiac shunt initiates a progressive increase in right-heart volume. As the pulmonary vascular resistance and right-sided pressures increase over time, some bidirectional or right-to-left shunting begins.[41] Presence of this syndrome contraindicates surgical correction of the initiating congenital heart defect because pulmonary vascular resistance is irreversibly elevated.

The incidence of this syndrome during pregnancy in the patient with a long-standing ventricular septal defect is approximately 2% to 4%. Maternal and fetal mortality are 30% and 50%, respectively.[42] Prognosis is worse when advanced medial and intimal pulmonary vascular thickening is present.

Pregnancy aggravates Eisenmenger's syndrome. While systemic vascular resistance decreases, pulmonary vascular resistance remains fixed, progressively increasing the degree of right-to-left shunting, hypoxemia, and cyanosis throughout the course of gestation. The physiologic changes of pregnancy, including an increased cardiac output, heart rate, blood volume, and oxygen consumption, combined with the pain and stress of labor, acute blood loss at delivery, and autotransfusion of uterine blood in the third stage of labor, put these patients at very high risk. Expulsive efforts may overload the right heart and increase the right-to-left shunt, or cause complete right-heart failure.

Finger pulse oximetry may be an ideal noninvasive indicator of changes in shunt fraction and direction.[43] Reversibility of the shunt may be assessed with oxygen therapy. The pulmonary vasculature may respond to oxygen or be fixed irreversibly.[44] The time of greatest risk to the pregnant women with this syndrome is late

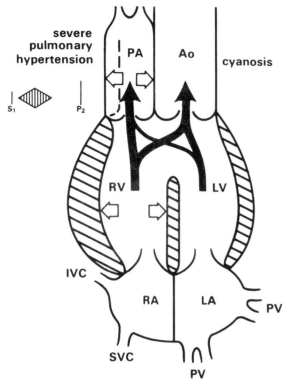

severe
pulmonary
hypertension

PA   Ao   cyanosis

S_1 P_2

RV   LV

IVC

RA   LA   PV

SVC

PV

Figure 2–11. Eisenmenger's syndrome. Note that Eisenmenger hemodynamics may result when severe pulmonary hypertension complicates any form of intracardiac shunt and produces shunt reversal. The defect itself does not produce a murmur. Only features of severe pulmonary hypertension and cyanosis are seen. (Ao = aorta, IVC = inferior vena cava, LV = left ventricle, PA = pulmonary artery, PV = pulmonary vein, RA = right atrium, RV = right ventricle, SVC = superior vena cava.) (Basta LL. Cardiovascular disease. New York: Medical Examination Publishing Co, 1983:338)

in pregnancy, when supine without uterine displacement, during labor and delivery or surgery, and in the early postpartum period. These women have little cardiac reserve. Sudden death may occur. Causes include embolism, arrhythmia, myocardial infarction, right-heart overload, and sudden drops in systemic vascular resistance. Emboli may affect both coronary or cerebral circulation.

Peripartum Cardiomyopathy

This uncommon phenomenon has a reported incidence of 1 in 3000 to 4000 pregnancies.[45] The overall mortality rate is between 30% and 60%.[46] Demakis[47] characterized peripartum cardiomyopathy as follows:

- Development of cardiac failure in the last month of pregnancy or within 5 months after delivery

- Absence of a defined etiology for the cardiac failure
- Absence of demonstrable heart disease before the last month of gestation

Patients whose ventricular failure does not resolve within 6 months have an especially poor prognosis.[48] The recurrence rate in subsequent pregnancies is at least 50%, with a mortality rate of 60%.

Signs and symptoms are of left ventricular failure. Early diagnosis is difficult because many women complain of fatigue, dyspnea on exertion, and edema while pregnant (see Table 2-1). The increased blood volume and cardiac output at term and in the peripartum period may raise pulmonary capillary pressure and incite congestive heart failure in women with cardiomyopathy and decreased ventricular function. The differential must include amniotic fluid or pulmonary embolisms, beta-mimetic tocolytic therapy, or preeclampsia. Central and systemic emboli occur in up to 25% of cases.[49] The final diagnosis is one of exclusion.

Echocardiography may show a dilated hypokinetic left ventricle.[50] Endomyocardial biopsy reveals fibrous deposition, mural thrombi, and generalized degenerative changes. Postulated etiologies of peripartum cardiomyopathy include: inadequate nutrition, viral agents, preeclampsia, immunologic disorders, advanced maternal age, multiple gestation, obesity and breastfeeding.

In 1986, O'Connel *et al*[51] published a review of 14 patients with peripartum cardiomyopathy who underwent right-heart catheterization, echocardiography, radionuclide ventriculography, and right ventricular endomyocardial biopsy 1 week after onset of symptoms. They found that women with postpartum cardiomyopathy are younger and have a shorter duration of symptoms than nonpregnant patients with idiopathic cardiomyopathy. Peripartum patients also have a higher incidence of myocarditis (29% vs. 9%). Still, these authors concluded that patients with peripartum cardiomyopathy do not have detectable differences in pathophysiology compared to those with non–pregnancy-related idiopathic cardiomyopathy and subsequent left ventricular failure.[51] Camann *et al*[52] reported a patient having undergone heart transplantation after an episode of severe peripartum cardiomyopathy who successfully delivered and survived without evidence of recurrent disease in a subsequent pregnancy.

Myocardial Infarction

The literature contains many reports of myocardial infarction during pregnancy. The relative incidence is approximately 1 in 10,000 deliveries.[53] The mortality rate is about 40% and approaches 45% if the initial infarction occurs in the third trimester.[54] It is difficult to pinpoint the etiology of myocardial infarction in the parturient, but coronary artery disease is involved in the vast majority of cases. Atherosclerosis, thrombosis, aneurysm, spasm, or obstruction of the coronary vasculature can occur.[55,56]

The increasing incidence of myocardial infarction in pregnancy may be related to advanced maternal age and smoking. The vasospastic effect of cocaine on the coronary vasculature[57] and its increasing usage in the general and maternal population[58] also may be a factor.

Diagnostic workup includes an extensive history. Elicit information regarding obesity, smoking, hypercholesterolemia, hypertension, arrhythmias, angina, heart disease, obstetric history, and drug usage. On physical examination, look for a carotid bruit, arrhythmia, extra heart sounds, or pulmonary congestion. Serial 12-lead ECG and cardiac isoenzymes are standard. Hematocrit, serum electrolytes, blood urea nitrogen and creatinine levels, coagulation profile, and baseline arterial blood gas will all provide relevant information. Echocardiography will evaluate left ventricular function.

The determinants of myocardial oxygen supply in pregnant woman are the same as in nonpregnant patients. Adequate coronary artery blood flow and oxygen content are required to avert myocardial injury. Mean aortic root diastolic pressure minus the left ventricular end-diastolic pressure determines coronary blood flow or perfusion pressure to the left ventricle. Many factors affect the oxygen content of blood perfusing the coronary arteries. Among them are hemoglobin, arterial oxygen saturation, pH, temperature, and 2,3-DPG. The major determinant of myocardial oxygen demand is heart rate. Other factors include preload, afterload, and contractility. The increased heart rate, stroke volume, plasma volume, metabolic rate, V/Q mismatching, and oxygen consumption of the term parturient allow her myocardium little reserve.

Primary Pulmonary Hypertension

Primary pulmonary hypertension is a very lethal, uncommon disorder that occurs most often in young women. Death often takes place within 2 years of onset of symptoms.[59] Pregnancy and primary pulmonary hypertension combined produce a maternal mortality rate of 50%.[60] In the later stages of the disease, a fixed, nonreactive pulmonary vasculature with a high resistance increases right ventricular work, which yields muscular hypertrophy. With a fixed, noncompliant right ventricle, the left heart eventually supplies an inadequate cardiac output. The end is cardiac failure. Signs and symptoms include syncope, hemoptysis, and chest pain. A right ventricular heave and a loud second heart are present. Peripheral cyanosis and clubbing are not uncommon.

As pregnancy progresses, plasma volume, cardiac output, and oxygen consumption rise, increasing the workload of the already strained right heart. Uterine compression of the vena cava and acute blood loss at delivery decrease venous return, left ventricular filling, and cardiac output.

RENAL DISEASE

Renal Function and Pregnancy

During pregnancy, the renal calyces, pelvis, and ureters dilate as ureteral smooth muscle hypertrophies.[61,62] These changes may allow stasis leading to bacteriuria and can make renal obstruction difficult to diagnose. Glomerular filtration rate and renal plasma flow increase 30% to 50% above nonpregnant levels (Fig. 2-12).[63] Creatinine and urea nitrogen production remain unchanged, so their serum concentrations fall in comparison to prepregnancy values.[64] Values considered normal in the nonpregnant state may suggest renal dysfunction in the parturient.

Osmoregulation is altered. There is an average 8 to 10 mOsm/kg decrease in plasma osmolality (P_{osm}) during gestation (Fig. 2-13).[65] This decrement in the nonparturient would produce a significant diuresis, yet the gravida appears to adjust both vasopressin secretion and thirst to maintain this lower osmolality.[66,67]

Water regulation also changes over the course of pregnancy. The gravida retains approximately 2 L of intravascular water, 290 mEq of sodium, and 155 mEq of potassium.[68] At term, there is 1.2 L of amniotic fluid, 700 mL of water in the uterus, 300 mL in the placenta, and 400 mL in the breasts. In all, the parturient retains 7 to 8 L of total body water. Water excretion is reduced in late gestation. This effect may relate to the hemodynamic effects of maternal posture.[69] The clinical usefulness of random specific gravity measurements in the supine third-trimester gravida is questionable.

Glucose

Glucosuria occurs frequently. The parturient cannot increase glucose reabsorption in parallel with the larger amount of filtered glucose. Over 30 years ago, Welsh and Sims[70] evaluated tubular maximum (T_m), a mea-

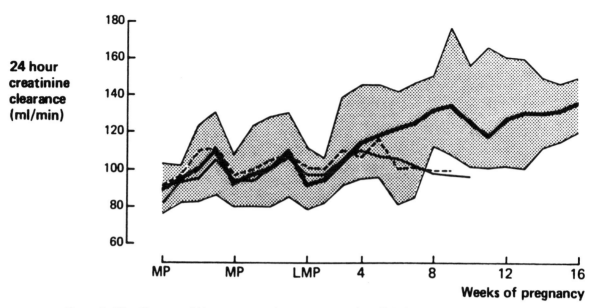

24 hour creatinine clearance (ml/min)

Weeks of pregnancy

Figure 2–12. Changes in 24-hour creatinine clearance measured weekly before conception and through to uncomplicated spontaneous abortion in two women (*solid* and *dashed lines*). *Thick solid line* represents the mean, and *stippled area* represents the range for nine women with successful obstetric outcome. (LMP = last menstrual period, MP = menstrual period. (Davison JM, Noble MCB. Serial changes in 24-hour creatinine clearance during normal menstrual cycles and the first trimester of pregnancy. Br J Obstet Gynaecol 1981;88:10)

sure of renal glucose handling, in normal nonpregnant women, as compared to nonglycosuric and normogly-cemic glycosuric pregnant patients. Tubular maximum was lower in the latter group of patients than in the nonglycosuric gravid patients. Therefore, urinary glucose sampling may be unreliable in evaluating pregnant diabetic patients. Also, changes in renal handling of glucose may not indicate renal pathology in the parturient.

Sodium

Sodium represents the principal determinant in volume homeostasis. Its reabsorption accounts for the largest major renal adjustment in pregnancy. Total body sodium increases by 1000 mEq, 60% of which remains maternal (Table 2-9).[67] Hormonal factors that increase sodium excretion generally work by competitive inhibition of aldosterone (Table 2-10).[68]

Acid–Base Balance

Plasma bicarbonate concentration decreases 4 mEq/L in response to maternal respiratory alkalosis. The average $Paco_2$ is 31 mm Hg; pH, 7.44; and serum bicarbonate, 20 mEq/L. The reduced total buffering capacity raises the risk of severe acidosis during pregnancy.

Evaluation

The initial workup for renal dysfunction includes history, physical examination, and laboratory data. Clues in the history may include hematuria, polyuria, nocturia, and enuresis. Symptoms of urinary tract infection include dysuria, urgency, and foul-smelling urine. Inquire about a history of hypertension, diabetes, gout, or renal disease in both the patient and her family. Electrolyte disturbances may present as weakness, paresthesia, and areflexia, or as cardiac manifestations.

The first voided urine in the morning is usually concentrated and requires careful examination. Proteinuria is an important sign of renal disease because it generally indicates a derangement in glomerular permeability. With pregnancy, daily protein excretion may reach 250 mg. Proteinuria between 150 mg and 2 g daily may signal chronic interstitial nephritis or nephrosclerosis, whereas heavy proteinuria, more than 2 g daily, may occur in chronic glomerulonephritis, diabetic nephrop-

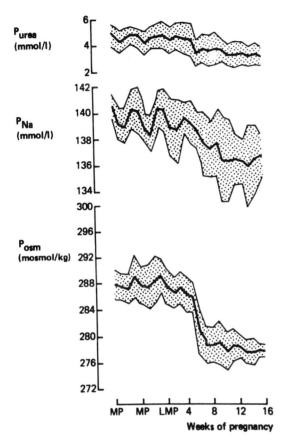

Figure 2–13. Plasma osmolality (O_{osm}), sodium (P_{Na}), and urea (P_{urea}) measured weekly from before conception through the first trimester in nine women who subsequently had successful obstetric outcomes. Solid line is mean, *stippled area* is ± 1 SD. (LMP = last menstrual period, MP = menstrual period.) (Davison JM, Volletton MB, Lindheimer MD. Plasma osmolality and urinary concentration and dilution during and after pregnancy. Br J Obstet Gynaecol 1981;88:472)

athy, systemic lupus erythematosus, membranous glomerulonephritis, lipoid nephrosis, and focal glomerulosclerosis.[71] Tubular epithelial cells are seen, particularly in tubular necrosis and nephrotoxic nephritis. The "Maltese Cross" of epithelial cells filled with lipid is typical of the nephrotic syndrome.

When red and white blood cell casts are found in the urinalysis, there is primary renal pathology. On the other hand, microscopic hematuria may be induced by exercise, acute febrile illness, or actual kidney trauma. Hematuria may suggest glomerulonephritis, systemic lupus erythematosus, and periarteritis. White blood cells and casts do not necessarily indicate an infectious process but simply an inflammatory response. Sterile

pyuria can accompany acute glomerulonephritis and chronic interstitial nephritis. Nonbacterial renal disease involving the interstitium may present with pyuria and white blood cell casts. Generally, a significant bacteriuria is necessary to diagnose pyelonephritis.[71]

Laboratory data should include hematocrit, serum blood urea nitrogen and creatinine levels, electrolytes, and uric acid as well as creatinine clearance. Both the serum blood urea nitrogen and creatinine concentrations of the parturient are lower than the nonparturient. "Normal" concentrations found in the parturient are suspicious. Abdominal radiographs are usually avoided, whereas an intravenous pyelogram is seldom needed. It is technically difficult to perform a renal biopsy in the pregnant patient, and the increase in renal blood flow presents a further risk.[72]

Uremia affects multiple organ systems. The uremic patient is immunologically compromised, and the obstetric anesthesiologist must treat her accordingly. Platelet function, determined by a prolonged Ivy bleeding time, may be depressed. Autonomic neuropathies and central nervous system irritability are not uncommon.[73] A uremic patient with erythropoetin-deficiency anemia has less 2,3-DPG than an otherwise normal anemic patient. Compromise of fetal oxygen delivery may subsequently occur. Uremia further prolongs gastric emptying times.[74]

Prognosis

The most important outcome determinants in both mother and child are the presence of either pre-existing chronic hypertension or onset of hypertension during pregnancy (Table 2-11). Outcome varies greatly according to the extent of the pre-existing renal disease and the etiology, type and severity of disease (Table 2-12).[75] Patients with glomerular disease may experience a worsening of their renal status with the increased glomerular filtration rate of pregnancy.[76] Uncontrolled hypertension concurrent with renal insufficiency during pregnancy can cause progression to end-stage renal disease.[77] The presence of hypertension before conception increases the risk of intrauterine growth retardation fivefold and doubles the premature delivery rate.[78]

Hematocrit affects oxygen delivery to the fetus. The anemia of renal disease, secondary to a depression in erythropoetin production, will decrease oxygen-carrying capacity. The incidence of infants with intrauterine growth retardation and infants who are small for their gestational age may increase.

Table 2-9

Storage of Minerals During Pregnancy

STORAGE SITE	SODIUM (mEq)	POTASSIUM (mEq)	CALCIUM (g)
Fetus	290	154	28.00
Placenta	57	42	0.65
Amniotic fluid	100	3	Negligible
Uterus	80	50	0.22
Breasts	35	35	0.06
Plasma	140	4	0.12
Red cells	5	8	0.25
Edema fluid	240	8	0.25
Total	**947**	**320**	**29.68**

(After Hytten FE, Leitch I. The physiology of pregnancy, 2nd ed. Oxford: Blackwell Scientific Publications, 1971)

Women with severe renal insufficiency (serum creatinine > 2.5 mg/dL or creatinine clearance < 50 mL/min) usually do not become pregnant. If they do conceive, 50% have poor fetal outcomes and will exhibit end-stage renal disease within 1 year.[79] Women with less depressed renal function have better fetal outcomes, and fewer advance to end-stage renal disease.

Pyelonephritis

If managed improperly, pyelonephritis, a common medical complication of pregnancy, may generate considerable morbidity in both mother and fetus. It is associated with low birth weight, increased perinatal mortality, anemia, preeclampsia, and premature rupture of membranes.[80] *Escherichia coli* is the predominant cause. Presentation is generally a combination of fever, chills, nausea, vomiting, costovertebral angle tenderness, and urinary symptoms. Untreated, pyelonephritis may lead to adult respiratory distress syndrome and death.

Glomerulonephritis

Gram-positive or gram-negative bacterial pathogens trigger the immune syndrome of glomerulonephritis. The condition may present as focal, diffuse, proliferative, or lupus type and may lead to the nephrotic syndrome in the presence of sufficient proteinuria. Edema and hypertension are not uncommon. Microscopic

Table 2-10

Sodium Excretion and Reabsorption: Hormonal Factors in Pregnancy

EXCRETION	REABSORPTION
Progesterone	Aldosterone
Vasopressin	Deoxycorticosterone
Natriuretic hormone	Renin
Vasodilating prostaglandins	Angiotensin
	Estrogen

Table 2–11

Chronic Renal Disease in Pregnancy: Effect of Level of Blood Pressure on Pregnancy Complication in 123 Pregnancies in 86 Women

	RENAL DETERIORATION	SMALL-FOR-DATE BABIES	PRETERM DELIVERY
Normotension	3.0%	2.3%	11.4%
Hypertension*	15.0%	15.6%	20.0%

(After Svrian M. Glomerular disease and pregnancy; a study of 123 pregnancies in patients with primary and secondary disease. Nephron 1984;36:101)
*Blood pressure consistently 140/90 mm Hg or greater.

hematuria with red blood cell casts, low serum complement, and a rising antistreptolysin titer suggest the diagnosis of acute post-streptococcal glomerulonephritis. Check for urine protein.

Berger's disease or IgA nephropathy also may present with hematuria but minimal proteinuria. Prognosis is generally good in these patients in the absence of hypertension.

The fetus seems protected from the maternal glomerulonephrites. Possible explanations of the phenomenon include the following:

- The antigen–antibody complexes are too large to cross the placental circulation.
- The fetal glomeruli do not react in the same manner to the complexes.
- The glomerular pressure (a possible factor in the development of this disease) is too low in the fetus.

Perinatal mortality may reach 18%, however.[81]

Systemic Lupus Erythematosus

Systemic lupus erythematosus complicates 1 in 1600 to 5000 pregnancies.[82] It is an autoimmune disorder in which antigen–antibody complexes form and deposit in tissues. It is of unknown etiology. In pregnancy, the most common clinical manifestations include arthralgias, fever, skin lesions, and renal disease.[83] Serum complement concentration falls, antibodies against DNA arise, and the lupus anticoagulant appears. Whether pregnancy exacerbates systemic lupus erythematosus is controversial. In a prospective case-controlled study, Lockshin *et al*[84] reported no significant increase in symptoms with pregnancy. On the other hand, Burkett[85] states that the disease will worsen in 50% of patients who experience exacerbations in the 6 months preceding conception.

The lupus anticoagulant might bind with platelet membranes, inciting aggregation and an increased inci-

Table 2–12

Pregnancy and Renal Disease: Functional Renal Status and Prospects*

PROSPECTS	SEVERITY OF RENAL DISEASE		
	Mild (%)	Moderate (%)	Severe (%)
Pregnancy complications	22	41	84
Successful obstetric outcome	95	90	47
Long-term sequelae	< 5	25	53

*Based on literature survey of 1162 pregnancies in 804 women in reports published between 1973 and 1987. These data to not include collagen diseases.
(After Lindheimer MD, Katz AI. The kidney and hypertension in pregnancy. In: Brenner BM, Rector FL, eds. The Kidney, 4th ed. Philadelphia: WB Saunders, 1991)

dence of thrombosis.[86] This thrombosis occurs in the deep veins, peripheral arteries, retinal vessels, placenta, pulmonary vessels, and brain.[87,88] The partial thromboplastin time, and rarely the prothrombin time, may be prolonged. Changes in these tests do not correlate with clinical hemorrhage. Furthermore, anticardiolipin antibodies may be detected, often with thrombocytopenia and thrombocytopathy. A bleeding time may help decide the clinical significance of these abnormalities (see Chap. 25).[89] Antibodies can make blood cross-matching difficult. A transient or permanent deterioration in renal function may occur. Proteinuria, hypertension, and reduced creatinine clearance correlate with a poor prognosis.

Immoglobulin-complement deposition in trophoblastic tissue may lead to fetal compromise. Congenital anomalies such as heart block and endocardial fibroelastosis are not infrequent. The risks of abortion, perinatal mortality, and premature delivery increase.[89] There are reports of infants of women with systemic lupus erythematosus born with congenital anomalies even though the maternal disease appeared quiescent for years before delivery.[90,91]

Diabetic Nephropathy

Glomerulosclerosis, or thickening of the glomerular basement membrane, whether localized nodular or diffuse, is the primary characteristic of diabetic nephropathy. Vascular disease of both large and small renal vessels can cause severe scarring of the renal interstitium. In the presence of proteinuria and diminished renal function, most parturients are hypertensive.[71] The hypertension associated with diabetic nephropathy is probably secondary to renal vascular disease. The incidence of bacteriuria increases. If allowed to progress to pyelonephritis, bacteriuria is hazardous to the parturient and her fetus. The prognosis of patients with diabetic nephropathy relates to the degree of proteinuria. Greater than 3 g in a 24-hour period correlates with a more rapid progression to renal insufficiency.[71] Preeclampsia occurs more often in these women, and when severe, perinatal mortality may approach 25%.[74]

Calculi

The incidence of renal calculi does not rise during pregnancy and remains between 0.1% and 1%.[92] This fact is remarkable considering the parturient anatomy, which encourages urinary stasis. Intestinal absorption of calcium increases during pregnancy, and urinary calcium excretion usually exceeds 250 mg in a 24-hour period. Hypercalciuria accounts for over 40% of calculi in the parturient. Urinary tract infections predispose to recurrent stone formation. Urease-containing organisms alkalinize the urine, allowing precipitation of calcium. Although incidence remains the same, dilatation of the gravida renal pelvis and ureter may ease passage of any calculi.

Nephrotic Syndrome

Proteinuria, hypoalbuminemia, hyperlipidemia, and edema characterize this syndrome. Normal physiologic changes of pregnancy may be confused with an exacerbation of the disease, which causes the nephrotic syndrome. Increases in urinary protein may simply be a consequence of the increments in renal hemodynamics, changes in the glomerular barrier, or rise in renal vein pressure. Serum albumin decreases 0.5 to 1.0 g/dL in normal gestation. Edema may follow. More cholesterol and other circulating lipids are found in both normal pregnancy and in nephrotic syndrome.

The most common cause of nephrotic syndrome in late gestation is preeclampsia. Additional etiologies include diabetic glomerulosclerosis, lupus nephritis, lipoid nephrosis, renal vein thrombosis, amyloidosis, and drug reaction. Edema results from the reduced plasma oncotic pressure. The patient may be effectively hypothyroid or immunodeficient with the total body protein loss. The parturient with nephrotic syndrome is intravascularly depleted. With uteroplacental blood flow at risk, patient positioning is crucial.

Hemodialysis

There are a few reports of conception and parturition with chronic maternal hemodialysis.[93,94] These women are at greater risk of spontaneous abortions, delivery of low-birth-weight infants, and premature labor and delivery. Risk of premature labor, vaginal bleeding, and systemic hypotension is greatest immediately at the cessation of dialysis. Ultrafiltration needs to be monitored carefully in the parturient. Dialysates containing both glucose and bicarbonate have been recommended for the gravida in renal failure. The pregnant patient may exhibit both hypoxemia and hypercarbia secondary to hypoventilation after excessive HCO_3 removal. Both intravascular volume depletion and acetate in the dialysate can cause hypotension. Bleeding may occur

Table 2-13

Causes of Acute Renal Failure in Obstetrics

ANTEPARTUM	POSTPARTUM
Abortion	Uterine atony
Placenta previa	Retained placenta
Placenta abruption	Amniotic fluid embolism
Hyperemesis gravidarum	Uterine rupture
Pregnancy induced hypertension	Vaginal/cervical tear
Preeclampsia	Hemolytic uremic syndrome
Chorioamnionitis	Septic abortion
Acute fatty liver	
Pyelonephritis	

from heparinization. Retention of platelets on the dialysis membrane increases the risk of thrombocytopenia and bleeding. Pseudocholinesterase levels and platelet function may be altered.[95] Premature contractions secondary to the depletion of progesterone by hemodialysis have been reported.[94]

Acute Renal Failure

Many complications may cause acute renal failure in the gravida (Table 2-13). Although acute renal failure in pregnancy reportedly accounts for 50% of cases of acute renal failure in young women,[96] this incidence may have fallen with the greater availability of therapeutic abortion and the decreased incidence of placental abruption.[97]

The most common etiology of acute renal failure is hypovolemia, renal hypoperfusion, and subsequent ischemia. With persistent hypovolemia, a reduced cortical blood flow and acute tubular necrosis may develop. Disseminated intravascular coagulation may result from amniotic fluid embolism, intrauterine fetal death, placental abruption, or major transfusion reaction and lead toward acute renal failure. The increased renal vascular resistance and decreased renal blood flow in preeclampsia coincides with a fall in urinary prostaglandin E_2 and may incite acute renal failure. Nephrotoxic renal failure may occur after the use of exogenous toxins, such as radiographic contrast media, antibiotics, and nonsteroidal anti-inflammatory drugs. Nephrotoxic renal failure, which is nonischemic in origin, may cause an interstitial nephritis as well. Endogenous toxins include hemoglobin, myoglobin, uric acid, oxalic acid, and myelomatous proteins from multiple myeloma. Urinary tract obstruction secondary to the gravid uterus, polyhydramnios, nephrolithiasis, pelvic and broad ligament hematoma, or surgically induced damage also can cause acute renal failure.

Table 2-14

Urinary Findings: Prerenal and Intrinsic Renal Disease

	PRERENAL	INTRINSIC RENAL
Urine sediment	Not remarkable	Renal epithelial cells and casts; granular, muddy, pigmented cells
Urine osmolality (mOsm/kg)	> 500	< 350
Urine sodium (mEq/L)	< 20	> 40
Urine specific gravity	> 1.020	< 1.015
Urine: plasma creatinine concentration ratio	> 40	< 20

Diagnosis needs to identify whether the problem is prerenal, intrinsic renal, or postrenal failure. History may reveal use of nephrotoxic agents. Elicitation of cardiac disease, hepatic disease, or recent muscle damage will aid in diagnosis. Physical examination should concentrate on signs and symptoms of dehydration and hypovolemia. Urinalysis, hematocrit, and serum blood urea nitrogen/creatinine ratio will aid in the diagnosis as well (Table 2-14).

The cortical necrosis that can follow acute renal failure in the gravida usually results from fibrin deposits in the renal vasculature. The outcome of acute tubular necrosis ranges from mild and short-lasting tubular damage to chronic renal failure from sclerosis of any remaining nephrons.

HEMATOLOGIC DISEASE

Anemia

The incidence of anemia during pregnancy ranges from 20% to 80%.[98] This risk is significantly greater than the 5% incidence in nonpregnant women of reproductive age. Data from the Center for Disease Control's Pregnancy Nutritional Surveillance System[98] suggest a prevalence of 20% to 40% in low-income women in the United States. The incidence is highest in the 15- to 19-year age group and in black women of all ages.

The medical evaluation of anemia in the pregnant patient is as per the nongravida. Anemia may present with fatigue and weakness, but often patients are asymptomatic. Patients may present with pallor or tachycardia, yet typically, physical examination does not detect anemia. The detection of anemia occurs most commonly during routine laboratory testing. The average red blood cell size (MCV) provides useful information regarding the mechanism of anemia. A macrocytosis coincides with both folate deficiency and vitamin B_{12}–deficiency anemia. A microcytosis occurs with iron deficiency, thalassemia, and lead poisoning. Hemoglobin content, red cell size distribution, reticulocyte count, and iron stores also may provide useful diagnostic information in determining the extent and possibly source of the anemia.

Physiology

Pregnancy is associated with several hematologic changes. Maternal blood volume begins to increase by the 6th to 10th week and peaks at the 32nd week, when it exceeds the nonpregnant level by 40%. Plasma volume increases by 50% to 55% and red cell mass by 20% to 30%. Because of these changes, a "physiologic anemia" of pregnancy occurs (hemoglobin < 11 g/dL in the first and third trimester, and a hemoglobin < 10.5 g/dL during the second trimester).[99–102] Erythropoietin secretion by the kidney controls the red blood cell production. Increased red cell mass occurs primarily in the latter half of pregnancy, in contrast with the increased plasma volume early in pregnancy. Progesterone, testosterone, and thyroxine stimulate erythropoietin production. Prolactin also may have a significant role in increasing the red cell mass.[100] It remains unclear the degree of maternal anemia that results in risk to the fetus or neonate. Although reports of decreased birth weight, prematurity, and perinatal death exist,[103] it is difficult to control for poor nutrition and low socioeconomic status. One report suggests a progressive increase in fetal risk as hemoglobin falls below 10 g/dL.[101] High-output congestive heart failure with intravascular volume overload is common in severe anemia. The gravida is therefore at an even greater risk of this complication.

Iron-deficiency Anemia

Approximately 1000 mg of additional iron are needed during pregnancy. Most adult women maintain a 500-mg iron storage pool. Furthermore, iron is preferentially delivered to the fetus secondary to the heavy concentration of transferrin receptors on the placental trophoblastic membranes.[104] Although the lack of bleeding due to amenorrhea during pregnancy saves approximately 200 mg of iron, there remains a maternal deficiency.

Iron-deficiency anemia may be difficult to diagnose during pregnancy. The characteristic microcytic, hypochromic red blood cell smear is a late finding (Fig. 2-14). The MCV typically increases during the first 2 months of gestation. Transferrin and total iron binding capacity rise during pregnancy, making the iron:transferrin ratio low, even in gravid women without iron deficiency. The most sensitive test in the pregnant patient for iron-deficiency anemia is measurement of serum ferritin.[102]

Oral iron replacement with 30 to 120 mg of elemental iron daily remains the treatment for iron-deficiency anemia. The rate of absorption varies and is reduced by 40% to 50% when iron is taken with meals. The most common untoward effect from oral iron preparations is gastrointestinal irritation. The reticulocyte count increases by the second week of treatment with iron supplementation. Iron replacement may be given parenterally, but the hematologic response is not improved; however, there are significant possible un-

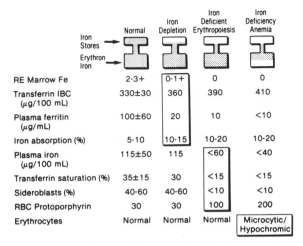

	Normal	Iron Depletion	Iron Deficient Erythropoiesis	Iron Deficiency Anemia
Iron Stores				
Erythron Iron				
RE Marrow Fe	2-3+	0-1+	0	0
Transferrin IBC (µg/100 mL)	330±30	360	390	410
Plasma ferritin (µg/mL)	100±60	20	10	<10
Iron absorption (%)	5-10	10-15	10-20	10-20
Plasma iron (µg/100 mL)	115±50	115	<60	<40
Transferrin saturation (%)	35±15	30	<15	<15
Sideroblasts (%)	40-60	40-60	<10	<10
RBC Protoporphyrin	30	30	100	200
Erythrocytes	Normal	Normal	Normal	Microcytic/ Hypochromic

Figure 2–14. Sequential changes in the development of iron deficiency. Indicators of iron store depletion include the visual inspection of marrow reticuloendothelial iron stores, the total iron-binding capacity, the plasma ferritin level, and the percent iron absorbed from an oral iron test dose. With the onset of iron-deficient erythropoiesis, the serum iron, percent saturation of transferrin, percent sideroblasts observed on the marrow stain, and the red cell protoporphyrin become abnormal. Then anemia appears. When anemia has been present for some time, red cells become microcytic/hypochromic. (Hillman RS, Finch CA. Red cell manual, 5th ed. Philadelphia: FA Davis Co. 1985:60)

toward reactions, such as anaphylaxis. Maternal and fetal effects of iron-deficiency anemia may include preeclampsia, low birth weight, premature labor, and stillbirth.[101,103]

Megaloblastic Anemia

Folic acid or vitamin B_{12} deficiency are the usual causes of megaloblastic anemia. The pregnant patient is unlikely to develop a vitamin B_{12} deficiency for two reasons. Vitamin B_{12} has an integral role in all DNA replication, and a significant deficiency should result in sterility. Furthermore, normally there are large stores of vitamin B_{12}, making this an unlikely source of anemia.

Folic acid, an essential cofactor in nucleic acid synthesis, is the most likely source of megaloblastic anemia in the gravida. During pregnancy, the growing fetus induces a 50% rise in folate requirements.[105] The main source of folate normally is leafy green vegetables. Excessive cooking of vegetables will decrease the available folate. Some drugs such as oral contraceptives and phenytoin will decrease the absorption of folic acid. The total body stores of this vitamin are small and short-lived. The nausea and vomiting of pregnancy may

significantly impair its intake. Unless the diet is supplemented, pregnancy is associated with a negative folate balance, which usually arises in the third trimester. Megaloblastic changes are most common in countries or socioeconomic groups with poor nutrition.

Definitive diagnosis frequently requires a bone marrow aspirate. Other findings may include sore tongue and mouth, purpura, hemolytic jaundice, thrombocytopenia, and bleeding diathesis. Pure folate deficiency results in a macrocytic anemia or may even cause pancytopenia. Iron-deficiency anemia frequently complicates folate deficiency, making examination of a peripheral smear difficult to interpret. Megaloblastic anemia has been linked to prematurity, low birth weights, preeclampsia, and abruptio placenta.

Thalassemias

Normal adult hemoglobin is 95% hemoglobin A and consists of two alpha and two beta chains that form a tetramine protein. Of the six different possible globin chains in the human genome, the alpha and beta chains are affected most in the thalassemias (Table 2-15). With suppression or absence of alpha- or beta-chain synthesis, hemoglobin precipitation and shortened red blood cell life span occur. The alpha-hemoglobin monomer is encoded on four genes. The absence of all four alpha globin chains is incompatible with life and results in hydrops fetalis (Fig. 2-15-**A**). The gamma tetramers

Table 2-15

Composition of Hemoglobins Found in Normal Human Development and Abnormal Hemoglobins Found in Thalassemia

GLOBIN CHAINS	HEMOGLOBIN	STATE
$\alpha_2\beta_2$	A	Adult
$\alpha_2\delta_2$	A_2	Adult
$\alpha_2{}^A\gamma_2$	F	Fetus
$\alpha_2{}^G\gamma_2$	F	Fetus
$\alpha_2\epsilon_2$	Gower 2	Embryo
$\zeta_2\epsilon_2$	Gower 1	Embryo
$\zeta_2\gamma_2$	Portland	Embryo
β_2	H	Alpha-thalassemia
γ_4	Bart's	Alpha-thalassemia
α_2 precipitate	—	Beta-thalassemia

that form have such high oxygen affinity that release to tissues does not occur effectively. High output congestive heart failure and end organ ischemia cause fetal death. In the absence of three alpha chains, Hgb H is formed (Fig. 2-15-**B**). The presence of two or more normal α chains results in alpha-thalassemia trait, which is generally asymptomatic. Patients with alpha-thalassemia trait and H disease have no increased incidence of fetal wastage with normal hemoglobin levels. However, maternal splenomegaly and bone marrow hyperplasia are not uncommon.

The beta chain is encoded by only two genes. Beta-thalassemia major is homozygous, whereas beta-thalassemia minor is heterozygous. Beta-thalassemia major is detected several months after birth as a severe anemia (Fig. 2-16). This condition results in infants who will require frequent transfusions. Complications of excessive iron may result in death by the second or third decade. Beta-thalassemia minor produces either a mild

anemia or a completely normal hemoglobin level. Few women with beta-thalassemia major reach reproductive age. At puberty, these women are frequently amenorrheic. Pregnancy is complicated by anemia, hepatosplenomegaly, bone deformities, and cardiomyopathy.[106]

Sickle Cell Anemia

Sickle cell anemia is the result of an error in the sixth position on the beta-globin chain, with valine substituted for glutamic acid. This change produces instability of the beta chain and decreased solubility of the hemoglobin molecule. When oxygen tension falls, the hemoglobin molecule will precipitate and produce the characteristic sickle-shaped red blood cells. Heterozygous sickle cell patients have 25% to 40% hemoglobin S. Patients with sickle cell trait are unlikely to have hemo-

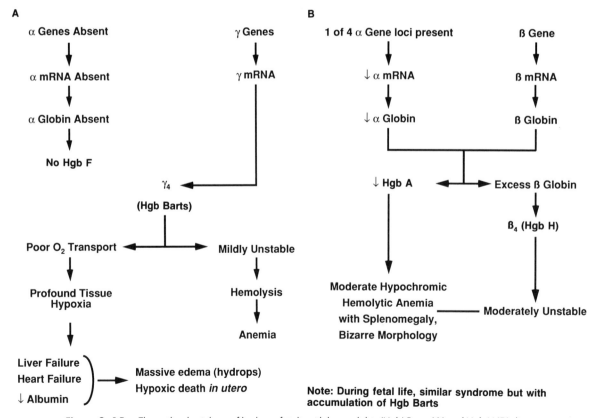

Figure 2–15. The pathophysiology of hydrops fetalis with hemoglobin (Hgb) Barts **(A)** and Hgb H **(B)** disease. (After Schwartz E, Benz EJ. The thalassemia syndromes. In: Hoffman R, Benz E, eds. Hematology: Basic principles and practice. London: Churchill Livingstone, 1991:386)

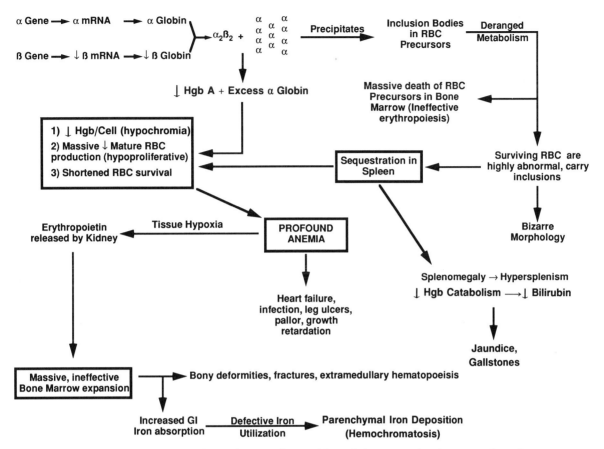

Figure 2-16. Pathophysiology of severe forms of beta-thalassemia. The diagram outlines the pathogenesis of clinical abnormalities from the primary defect in beta-globin synthesis. (GI = gastrointestinal, Hgb = hemoglobin, RBC = red blood cells.) (After Schwartz E, Benz EJ. The thalassemia syndromes. In: Hoffman R, Benz E, eds. Hematology: Basic principles and practice. London: Churchill Livingstone, 1991:381)

globin polymerize and precipitate unless hypoxia is severe (Pao_2 < 20 mm Hg). Homozygous patients may have 75% to 100% hemoglobin S. Patients with sickle cell anemia will develop sickling at a Pao_2 of 60 mm Hg. Acidosis, by shifting the oxyhemoglobin dissociation curve to the right, worsens sickling.

Parturients with sickle cell trait tend to have a benign course, and the disease poses little risk to mother or fetus.[107] The infant does not have an increased incidence of intrauterine growth retardation or low birth weight.[107] In contrast, a woman with homozygous sickle cell anemia is likely to have impaired fertility and limited survival. The mortality rate of the homozygous gravida has decreased in recent years with improved prenatal care. This patient population has a higher incidence of congestive heart failure, thrombotic events, infection, and preeclampsia. They also are at high risk for vaso-occlusive and aplastic crises (Fig. 2-17). Thrombotic events in the placenta may lead to fetal loss and intrauterine growth retardation.

Dysplasias

Leukemia, although rare, has been well described during pregnancy. Malignancy complicates 1 in 1000 pregnancies, but the incidence of leukemia is less than 1 in 75,000 pregnancies.[108,109] This low rate may reflect the relative infertility of women with leukemia. Pregnancy lacks effect on the course of chronic leukemia. Over 90% of women and 80% of fetuses will survive to delivery.[109] Acute leukemia presents a greater risk. The

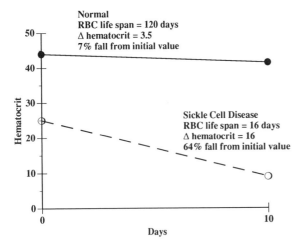

Figure 2–17. Aplastic crisis. Hemolysis in patients with sickle cell anemia results in a substantial fall in hematocrit when erythroid production is suppressed. In normal individuals, the decrease in hematocrit during a similar time interval is insignificant. (RBC = red blood cells.) (After Lubin B, Vichinsky F. Sickle cell disease. In: Hoffman R, Benz E, eds. Hematology: Basic principles and practice. London: Churchill Livingstone, 1991:459)

concurrent maternal treatment with toxic agents may have both cardiac and pulmonary sequelae, as well as induce anemia and thrombocytopenia.

The main defect in the leukemias is deregulation of precursor cell differentiation.[109] Subsequently, one cell line proliferates in the bone marrow at the expense of other cell lines.[110] Hemolysis, diminished red blood cell replacement, thrombocytopenia, and granulocytopenia cause maternal anemia, hemorrhage, and an increased susceptibility to infection. The gravida's liver, spleen, kidney, lymph node, skin, brain, and meninges may all be affected.

Thrombocytopenia

IDIOPATHIC THROMBOCYTOPENIA PURPURA. Idiopathic thrombocytopenia purpura is an autoimmune thrombocytopenia caused by an IgG antibody. Idiopathic thrombocytopenia purpura, most common in young women, is not uncommon in the parturient. The IgG antibody can cross the placenta and produce thrombocytopenia in the fetus. Placental receptors for the Fc portion of the IgG molecule allow the antibody to enter the fetal circulation. Maternal mortality may be as high as 5%, and a perinatal mortality ranges from 6% to 17%.[111,112] No strong correlation exists between maternal and infant platelet counts. Mothers with a previous splenectomy are at a reduced risk of having thrombocytopenic infants. The severity

of infant thrombocytopenia may be proportional to the amount of antiplatelet antibody that is transferred across the placenta.[112] A relationship between IgG antibody protein binding in the maternal serum and infant thrombocytopenia also may exist. Intracranial hemorrhage is a major risk for both mother and fetus.

Chronic idiopathic thrombocytopenia purpura may present with easy bruising and petechiae, menorrhagia, or epistaxis. If the diagnosis has been made, the parturient may present to the obstetric anesthesiologist already undergoing treatment. Therapy usually includes 1 to 2 mg/kg/day of oral prednisone for platelet counts below 50,000 μL. Because of concerns of hyperglycemia, increased blood pressure, and osteoporosis, medication is usually tapered when the platelet count begins to rise. In cases in which the parturient is resistant to steroids, intravenous IgG has been administered. The IgG raises the patient's serum IgG and impairs reticuloendothelial cell function, sparing the sensitized platelets from clearance.[113] The platelet-elevating effect generally lasts less than 3 weeks, and treatment is repeated several times throughout the pregnancy. With the availability of the preceding treatment modalities, splenectomy is usually avoided. Immunosuppressive therapy should be reserved for the most refractory cases, and administration should be limited to after fetal organogenesis. Platelet transfusions are only effective for several hours, and usage is reserved for severe bleeding or when surgery is planned.

To elevate both the maternal and fetal platelet counts, parturients with low platelet counts have their steroid regimens increased in the final weeks of gestation.[114] Because placental enzymes inactivate most of the administered prednisone, some substitute dexamethasone or betamethasone. Treatment is not without risk. Along with possible maternal hyperglycemia, hypertension, and postpartum psychosis, fetal adrenal suppression remains a concern. Platelet transfusion may place the parturient at risk for a transfusion-related complication. Splenectomy during pregnancy has a high risk of fetal loss.

Although platelet count falls in the face of autoimmune hyperdestruction, the platelets present are usually younger, larger and "superfunctional." Bleeding time in the parturient with idiopathic thrombocytopenia purpura may not rise above 10 minutes until the platelet count drops below 50,000/μL³.[115]

PREECLAMPSIA AND ECLAMPSIA. The most common cause of thrombocytopenia in pregnancy is preeclampsia.[116] Approximately 15% of parturients with preeclampsia will have some form of consumptive thrombocytopenia. The incidence is even greater in the patient with eclampsia. Patients with preeclampsia who have a platelet count less than 100,000 μL will probably have a prolonged bleeding time.[117] In addition, 25% of women with mild to severe preeclampsia, without thrombocytopenia, also may have prolonged bleeding times.[116]

DRUG-INDUCED THROMBOCYTOPENIA.
An extensive list of drugs can act as antigenic stimuli, resulting in an autoimmune thrombocytopenia. These purpura are indistinguishable from those in idiopathic thrombocytopenia. Resolution occurs with cessation of the offending agent. The typical drugs include aspirin, penicillin, streptomycin, sulfa drugs, phenobarbital, and isoniazid. Aspirin irreversibly acetylates cyclo-oxygenase, a thromboxane precursor, and impairs platelet function. Nonsteroidal anti-inflammatory agents competitively inhibit cyclo-oxygenase reversibly.

Hemophilias

VON WILLEBRAND'S DISEASE.
Von Willebrand's disease (VWD) is an autosomal dominant hemorrhagic disorder. It is characterized by abnormal platelet function and a decrease in all elements of the factor VIII complex. Factor VIII is a protein complex consisting of von Willebrand factor (VIII:vWF) and factor VIII:C. Factor VIII:C measures the biologic activity of factor VIII. This factor is part of the intrinsic coagulation cascade. It is needed for the formation of a definitive hemostatic plug. Factor VIII:vWF, a large glycoprotein, allows aggregation of platelets to proceed. It is essential for the formation of a primary hemostatic plug after injury. Factor VIII:vWF also regulates the production and release of factor VIII:C. Factor VIII–related antigen (VIII R:Ag) represents the antigenic determinants of von Willebrand factor.[118,119]

Although not a primary platelet disorder, because von Willebrand factor is essential for platelet aggregation, the pattern of bleeding is similar to that found in patients with dysfunctional platelets (Table 2-16). Patients with VWD may present with menorrhagia, epistaxis, and bleeding from mucous membranes or intravenous sites. Mildly afflicted patients may have no symptoms. The diagnosis is often made following excessive surgical bleeding after dental extractions or minor surgery. Patients have an abnormal partial thromboplastin time because of the decreased coagulant activity of factor VIII, and a prolonged bleeding time secondary to the decrease in factor VIII:vWF. Giving normal plasma with normal factor VIII:vWF activity corrects the platelet aggregation defect.

In normal pregnancy, factor VIII:C and factor VIII R:Ag increase 200% and 375%, respectively.[120] Parturients with VWD also show an increase in factor concentration, but by term, they attain only half the normal pregnant levels. Bleeding may range from moderate to severe, depending on the degree of factor deficiency. With mild (autosomal dominant) forms of the disease, bleeding time ranges from 12 to 24 minutes. Women with severe (autosomal recessive) VWD

Table 2–16

Comparison of Hemophilia A and Classic von Willebrand's disease

	HEMOPHILIA A	VON WILLEBRAND'S
Deficiency	VIII:C, VIII:AHF	VIII:vWF, VIII:R
Inheritance	Recessive, X-linked	Dominant, autosomal
Clinical bleeding	Hemarthrosis, muscle, soft tissue, viscera	Gums, gastrointestinal tract, mucous membranes
Bleeding disorder	Moderate to severe (60%–severe)	Mild to moderate
Laboratory tests		
Bleeding time	N	A
Clot retraction	N	N
Glass bead retraction	N	A
Platelet count	N	N
Ristocetin aggregation	N	A
Prothrombin times	N	N
Partial thromboplastin time	A	A
Factor VIII	A	A
vWF:Ag	N	A

may have bleeding times longer than 30 minutes. The increase in factor concentrations with gestation may improve bleeding time in these women.[121] There is no increase in maternal mortality or fetal loss. These women are at high risk for postpartum hemorrhage as factor VIII:C and factor VIIIR:Ag concentrations fall precipitously (within a few hours) to nonpregnant levels.

HEMOPHILIA. Hemophilia A has a sex-linked recessive inheritance pattern. It is characterized by a lack of procoagulant activity of factor VIII. Individuals with factor VIII levels of at least 25% of normal clot without difficulty. Patients with hemophilia A become symptomatic when factor VIII activity falls below 5%. Patients with less than 1% factor VIII activity have severe disease. They bleed frequently without evidence of trauma. Those with activity greater than 5% have mild disease. They bleed infrequently, most often after trauma. Hemophilic bleeding may occur up to days after injury, involve any organ, and, left untreated, may continue for days or weeks. Compartment syndromes, pseudophlebitis, or ischemic damage to compressed nerves may follow. Most often, these patients bleed into soft tissues, muscles, and weight-bearing joints.

Phenotypic hemophilia in women is extremely rare. Pregnancy produces an increase in the concentration of factor VIII:C. Carrier gravidae may reach normal levels by term.[122] With the rapid fall of factor VIII activity postpartum, abnormal bleeding following delivery may resume. Hemophiliacs may develop femoral neuropathy due to pressure from an unsuspected retroperitoneal hematoma. The parturient with symptomatic disease requires a careful preanesthetic neurologic assessment.

Autologous Blood Donation

In recent years, the increased risk of blood transfusion has led to a significantly increased use of autologous blood donation in the nonobstetric population. The relative anemia of pregnancy may result in a hemoglobin below the minimal concentration for nonobstetric autologous donation guidelines (12.5 g/dL).[123] A hemoglobin of 11 g/dL is a pre-donation level for inclusion in autologous donation.[123-125] With a pre-donation level higher than 11 g/dL, there have been no adverse effects reported to either mother or fetus.

REFERENCES

1. McFaul PB, Dorman JC, Lamki H, et al. Pregnancy complicated by maternal heart disease: A review of 519 women. Br J Obstet Gynaecol 1988;95:861.

2. Sullivan JM, Ramanathan KB. Management of medical problems in pregnancy: Severe cardiac disease. N Engl J Med 1985;313:304.

3. Mangano DT. Anesthesia for the Cardiac Patient. In: Shnider SM, Levinson G, eds. Anesthesia for Obstetrics. Baltimore:Williams & Wilkins, 1987:345.

4. Johnson MD, Saltzman DH. Cardiac disease. In: Datta S. ed. Anesthetic and obstetric management of high-risk pregnancy. St. Louis:Mosby Year Book. 1991:212.

5. Clark SL, Phelan JP, Cotton DB, eds. Critical Care Obstetrics. Oradell, NJ: Medical Economics Books, 1987:63.

6. Whittemore K. Congenital heart disease: Its impact on pregnancy. Hosp Pract 1983;18:65.

7. Cheek TG, Gutsche BB. Maternal physiologic alterations during pregnancy. In: Shnider SM, Levinson G, eds. Anesthesia for obstetrics. Baltimore:Williams & Wilkins, 1987:6.

8. Nolan TE, Hankins GD. Myocardial infarction in pregnancy. Clin Obstet Gynecol. 1989;32:68.

9. McAnulty JH, Metcalfe J, Cleland K. Cardiovascular disease. In: Burrow GN, Ferris TF, eds. Medical complications during pregnancy. Philadelphia:WB Saunders, 1988:185.

10. Rahimtoola SH. The need for cardiac catheterization and angiography in valvular heart disease is not disproven. Ann Intern Med. 1982;97:433.

11. Swartz HM, Reichling BA. Hazards of radiation exposure for pregnant women. JAMA 1978;239:1907.

12. Mole RH. Radiation effects on prenatal development and their radiological significance. Br J Radiol. 1979;52:89.

13. Elkayam U, Kawanishi D, Reid CL, et al. Contrast echocardiography to reduce ionizing radiation associated with cardiac catheterization during pregnancy. Am J Cardiol 1983;52:213.

14. Clark SL, Cotton, DB, Lee W et al. Central hemodynamic assessment of normal term pregnancy. Am J Obstet Gynecol 1989; 161:1439.

15. Lee W, Rokey R, Cotton DB. Noninvasive maternal stoke volume and cardiac output determinations by pulsed Doppler echocardiography. Am J Obstet Gynecol 1988;158:505.

16. Clark SL, Horenstein JM, Phelan JP. Experience with the pulmonary artery catheter in obstetrics and gynecology. Am J Obstet Gynecol 1985;152:374.

17. Joyce TH, Palacios Q. Cardiac disease. In: James FM III, Wheeler AS, Dewan DM, eds. Obstetric anesthesia: The complicated patient, 2nd ed. Philadelphia: FA Davis, 1988:163.

18. Dajani AS, Bisno AL, Chung KJ, et al. Prevention of bacterial endocarditis recommendation by the American Heart Association. JAMA 1990;264:2919.

19. Stevenson RE, Burton M, Ferlanto GJ, et al. Hazards of oral anticoagulants during pregnancy. JAMA 1980; 243:1549.

20. Iturbe-Alessio I, Inescio M, Mutchinik, O, et al. Risks of anticoagulant therapy in pregnant women with artificial heart valves. N Engl J Med 1986;315:1390.

21. Rotmensch HH, El Kayam U, Frishman W. Antiarrhythmic drug therapy during pregnancy. Ann Intern Med 1983;98:487.

22. Wolff F, Breuker KH, Schlensker KH, Bote A. Prenatal diagnosis and therapy of fetal heart rate anomalies: With a contribution on the placental transfer of verapamil. J Perinat Med 1980;8:203.

23. Jackson JM. Valvular heart disease. In: Thomas SJ, ed. Manual of cardiac anesthesia. New York: Churchill Livingstone, 1984:220.

24. Valvular heart disease. In: Stoelting RK, Dierdorf SF, McCamnon RL.. Anesthesia and coexisting disease, 2nd ed. New York: Churchill Livingstone, 1988:37.

25. Barlow JB, Polock WA. The problem of nonejection systolic clicks and associated mitral systolic murmurs: Emphasis on the billowing mitral leaflet syndrome. Am Heart J 1976;90:636.

26. Degani S, Abinader EG, Scharf M. MVP and pregnancy: A review. Obstet Gynecol Surv 1989;44:642.

27. Haas JM. The effect of pregnancy on the midsystolic click and murmurs of the prolapsing posterior leaflet of the mitral valve. Am Heart J 1976;407:92.

28. Cowles T, Gonik B. Mitral valve prolapse in pregnancy. Semin Perinatol 1990;14:34.

29. Shapiro EP, Trimble EL, Robinson JC. et al. Safety of labor and delivery in women with mitral valve prolapse. Am J Cardiol 1985;56:806.

30. Rayburn WF, Fontana ME. Mitral valve prolapse and pregnancy. Am J Obstet Gynecol 1981;141:9.

31. Kroetz FW, Leonard JJ, Shaver JA, et al. The effect of atrial contraction on left ventricular performance in valvular aortic stenosis. Circulation 1967;39:852.

32. Arias F, Pineda J. Aortic stenosis and pregnancy. J Reprod Med 1978;20:229.

33. Whittemore R, Hobbins JC, Engle MA. Pregnancy and its outcome in women with and without surgical treatment of congenital heart disease. Am J Cardiol 1982;50:641.

34. Thomas SJ. Anesthetic management of the patient with valve disease and other unusual cardiac problems. ASA refresher course lectures. Philadelphia: JB Lippincott, 1989;311.

35. Datta S, Ketzmuller JL, Ostheimer GW, Shoenbaum SC. Propranolol and parturition. Obstet Gynecol 1978;51:577.

36. Oakley GDG, McGarry K, Limb DG, et al. Management of pregnancy in patients with hypertrophic cardiomyopathy. Br Med J 1979;1:1749.

37. Hoffman JL, Christian SMR. Congenital heart disease in a cohort of 19,502 births with long-term follow-up. Am J Cardiol 1978;42:641.

38. Shime J, Molarsk EJM, Hasting D, et al. Congenital heart disease in pregnancy: short- and long-term implications. Am J Obstet Gynecol 1987;156:313.

39. Morris CD, Menashe VD. Recurrence of congenital heart disease in offspring of parents with surgical correction. Clin Res 1985;33:68A.

40. Singh H, Bolton PJ, Oakley CM. Pregnancy after surgical correction of tetralogy of Fallot. Br Med J 1982;285:168.

41. Alpert JS. Physiopathology of the cardiovascular system. Boston: Little, Brown & Co., 1984:122.

42. Gleicher R, Midwall J, Hochberger D, et al. Eisenmenger's syndrome and pregnancy. Obstet Gynecol Surv 1979;34:721.

43. Garber SZ, Choi HJ, Tremper KK, et al. Use of a pulse oximeter in the anesthesic management of a pregnant patient with Eisenmenger's syndrome. Anesthesiol Rev 1988;15:59.

44. Midwall J, Taffin H. Shunt flow and pulmonary hemodynamics during labor and delivery in the Eisenmenger syndrome. Am J Cardiol 1978;42:299.

45. Veille JC. Peripartum cardiomyopathies: A review. Am J Obstet Gynecol 148;805,1984.

46. Homans DC. Current concepts: Peripartum cardiomyopathy. N Engl J Med 1985,312:1432.

47. Demakis JG, Rahimtoola SH. Peripartum cardiomyopathy. Circulation 1971;44:964.

48. Demakis JG, Rahimtoola SH, Sutton GC, et al. Natural course of peripartum cardiomyopathy. Circulation 1971;44:1053.

49. Hodgman MT, Pessin MS, Homans DC, et al: Cerebral embolism as the manifestation of peripartum cardiomyopathy. Neurology 1982;32:668.

50. Silverman RI, Ribner II. Peripartum cardiomyopathy. Cardiac problems in pregnancy. In: Elkayam U, Gleicher N. eds. Diagnosis and management of maternal and fetal disease. New York: Alan R. Liss, 1982.

51. O'Connel JB, Constanzo-Nordu MR, Subramamian R, et al. Peripartum cardiomyopathy: Clinical, hemodynamic, histologic and prognostic characteristics. J Am Coll Cardiol 1986;8:52.

52. Camann W, Goldman G, Johnson M, et al. Cesarean delivery of a patient with a transplanted heart. Anesthesiology 1989;71:618.

53. Hankins GDV, Wendall GD, Leveno KJ, et al. Myocardial infarction during pregnancy: A review. Obstet Gynecol 1985;65:139.

54. Throuton TG, Sidhu H, Adgey AJ. Myocardial infarction in pregnancy. Int J Cardiol 1988;18:35.

55. Laughlin MP, From RP, Choi W. Recent myocardial infarction in a parturient. Anesthesiol Rev 1986;8:43.

56. Roberts SL, Chestnut DH. Anesthesia for the obstetric patient with cardiac disease. Clin Obstet Gynecol 1987;30:601.

57. Pasternack PF, Colvin SB, Bauman FG. Cocaine-induced angina pectoris and acute myocardial infarction in patients younger than 40 years. Am J Cardiol 1985;55:847.

58. Howard RE, Hueter DC, Davis GJ. Acute myocardial infarction following cocaine abuse in a young woman with normal coronary arteries. JAMA 1985;254:95.

59. Weir EK. Diagnosis and management of primary pulmonary hypertension. In: Weir EK, Reeves JT, eds. Pulmonary hypertension. New York: Futura, 1984.

60. Slomka F, Salmeron S, Zetaoni P, et al. Primary pulmo-

nary hypertension and pregnancy: Anesthetic management for delivery. Anesthesiology 1988;69:959.

61. Freidman AJ. The urinary tract in pregnancy. Am Urol-Gynecol Soc Rep 1987;7:1-3.

62. Beydoun SN. Morphologic changes in the renal tract in pregnancy. Clin Obstet Gynecol 1985;2:249.

63. Davison JM. Overview: Kidney function in pregnant women. Am J Kidney Dis 1987;9:248-252.

64. Marchant DJ. Alterations in anatomy and function of the urinary tract during pregnancy. Clin Obstet Gynecol. 1978;21:855.

65. Davison JM, Volletton MB, Lindheimer MD. Plasma osmolality and urinary concentration and dilution during and after pregnancy. Br J Obstet Gynaecol 1981;88:472.

66. Davison JM, Gilmore EA, Durr J, et al. Altered osmotic thresholds for vasopressin secretion and thirst in human pregnancy. Am J Physiol 1984;246:F105.

67. Lindheimer MD, Barron WM, Durr J, et al. Water homeostasis and vasopressin release during rodent and human gestation. Am J Kidney Dis. 1987;9:270-275.

68. Galley EDM, Brown MA. Control of sodium excretion in human pregnancy. Am J Kidney Dis 1987;9:290-295.

69. Weinberger MH, Kramer NJ, Petersen P, et al. Sequential changes in renin–angiotensin–aldosterone systems in normal and abnormal pregnancies. In: Lindheimer MD, Katz AI, Zuspan FP, eds. Hypertension in pregnancy. New York: John Wiley & Sons, 1976:264.

70. Welsh GW, Sims EAH. The mechanisms of renal glucosuria in pregnancy. Diabetes 1960;9:363.

71. Ferris TF. Renal disease. In: Burrow GN, Ferris TF, eds. Medical complications during pregnancy, 3rd edition, Philadelphia: WB Saunders, 1988:277.

72. Packham D, Fairley KF. Renal biopsy: Indications and complications in pregnancy. Br J Obstet Gynecol 1987;94:935.

73. Reese GN, Appel SH. Neurological complications of renal failure. Semin Nephrol 1981;1:137.

74. Zelnick EB, Goyal RK. Gastrointestinal manifestations of chronic renal failure. Semin Nephrol 1981;1:124.

75. Lindheimer MD, Katz AI. Gestation in women with kidney disease: Prognosis and management. Clin Obstet Gynecol 1987;1:921.

76. Katz AI, Lindheimer MD. Does pregnancy aggravate primary glomerular disease? Am J Kidney Dis 1985;6:261.

77. Jungers P, Forget D, Houillier P, et al. Chronic renal disease and pregnancy. Arch Nephrol 1986;15:103.

78. Davison JM, Katz AI, Lindheimer MD. Kidney disease and pregnancy: Obstetrics outcome and long-term renal prognosis. Clin Perinatol 1985;12:497.

79. Katz AI, Lindheimer MD. Effects of pregnancy upon the natural course of kidney disease. Semin Nephrol 1984;4:252.

80. Klein EA. Urologic problems of pregnancy. Obstet Gynecol Surv 1984;39:605.

81. Gabert HA, Miller JM Jr. Renal disease in pregnancy. Obstet Gynecol Surg 1985;40:449.

82. Estes D, Larson DC. Systemic lupus by erythematous and pregnancy. Clin Obstet Gynecol 1965;8:307.

83. Syrop CH, Varner MW. Systemic lupus erythematosus. Clin Obstet Gynecol 1983;26:547.

84. Lockshin MD, Reinitz E, Prozin ML, et al. Lupus pregnancy case control prospective study demonstrating absence of lupus exacerbation during or after pregnancy. Am J Med 1984;77:893.

85. Burkett G. Lupus nephropathy and pregnancy. Clin Obstet Gynecol 1985;28:311.

86. Malinow AM, Rickford WJK, Moriski BLK, et al. Lupus anticoagulant: Implications for obstetric anesthetists. Anesthesia 1987;42:1291.

87. Jungers P, Dougados M, Pelissier C, et al. Lupus nephropathy and pregnancy: Report of 104 cases in 36 patients. Am Med 1982;142:771.

88. Lubbe WF, Liggins GC. Lupus anticoagulant and pregnancy. Am J Obstet Gynecol 1985;153:322.

89. Gimovsky ML, Montoro M, Paul RH. Pregnancy outcome in women with systemic lupus erythematosus. Obstet Gynecol 1984;63:686.

90. McCune AB, Weston WL, Lee LA. Maternal and fetal outcome in neonatal lupus erythematosus. Ann Intern Med 1987;106:518.

91. Neonatal lupus syndrome. [editorial] Lancet 1987;ii:489.

92. Horowitz E, Schmidt JD. Renal calculi: Pregnancy. Clin Obstet Gynecol 1985;2:324.

93. Cameron JS, Hicks J. Pregnancy in patients with pre-existing glomerular diseases. Contrib Nephrol 1984;37:149.

94. Johnson TR, Lorenz RP, Menon KMJ. Successful outcome of a pregnancy requiring dialysis: Effects on serum progesterone and estrogens. J Reprod Med 1979;22:217.

95. Weir PHC, Chung FF. Anesthesia for patients with chronic renal disease. Can Anaesth Soc J 1984;31:468.

96. Knuppel RA, Montenegro R, O'Brien WF. Acute renal failure in pregnancy. Clin Obstet Gynecol 1985;28:288.

97. Pertuiset N, Ganeval D, Grunfeld JP. Acute renal failure in pregnancy: An update. Semin Nephrol 1984;4:232.

98. Anemia during pregnancy in low-income women. MMWR Atlanta: Centers for Disease Control 1987;39:73.

99. Goodlin RC. Maternal hematocrit and premature labor. Am J Obstet Gynecol 1989;161:1750.

100. Longo LD Maternal blood volume and cardiac output during pregnancy: A hypothesis of endocrinologic control. Am Physiol Soc 1983;83:R720.

101. Garn SM, Ridella SA, Petzold AS, Falkner F. Maternal hematologic levels and pregnancy outcomes. Semin Perinatol 1981;5:155.

102. Romslo I, Haram K, Sagen N, Avgensen K: Iron re-

quirement in normal pregnancy as assessed by serum ferritin, serum transferrin, saturation, and erythrocyte protoporphyin determinations. Br J Obstet Gynaecol 1983;90:101.

103. Murphy JF, Newcomber RG, O'Riordan J, et al. Relation of haemoglobin levels in first and second trimesters to outcome of pregnancy. Lancet 1986;i:992.

104. Okuyama T, Tawada T, Euruya H, Vinee CA. The role of transferrin and ferritin in the fetal-maternal placental unit. Am J Obstet Gynecol 1985, 152:344.

105. Taylor DJ. Prophylaxis and treatment of anemia during pregnancy. Clin Obstet Gynaecol 1981;8:297.

106. Alger LS, Golbus MS, Laros RK. Thalassemia and pregnancy: Results of an antenatal screening program. Am J Obstet Gynecol 1979;134:662.

107. Baill IC, Wither FR. Sickle cell trait and its association with birth weight and urinary tract infection in pregnancy. Int Fed Obstet Gynecol 1990;33:19.

108. McLain C. Leukemia in pregnancy. Clin Obstet Gynecol 1974;17:185.

109. Siddiqui T, Elfenbein GJ, Noyes WD, et al. Myelodysplastic syndromes presenting in pregnancy. Cancer 1990;66:377.

110. Aitchison RG, Marsh JCW, Hows JM, et al. Pregnancy-associated aplastic anemia: A report of 5 cases and review of current management. Br J Haematol 1989; 73:541.

111. Flessa H, Hemorrhagic disorders and pregnancy. Clin Obstet Gynecol 1974;17:237.

112. Kelton JG. Management of the pregnant patient with ITP. Ann Intern Med 1983;99:796.

113. Lavery JP. Immunologic thrombocytopenia in pregnancy: Use of antenatal immunoglobulin therapy. Case report and review. Obstet Gynecol 1985;66:415.

114. Hegde OM. Immune thrombocytopenia in pregnancy and the newborn. Br J Obstet Gynaecol 1985;92:657.

115. Thompson AR, Harker LA. Manual of hemostasis and thrombosis, 3rd ed. Philadelphia: FA Davis, 1983.

116. Kelton JG. A platelet function defect in preeclampia. Obstet Gynecol 1985;65:107.

117. Ramanathan J, Sibai BM. Correlation between bleeding times and platelet counts in women with preeclampsia undergoing cesarean section. Anesthesiology 1989; 71:188.

118. Writer WDR. Hematologic disease. In: James FM III, Wheeler AS, Dewan DM, eds. Obstetric anesthesia: The complicated patient, 2nd ed. Philadelphia: FA Davis, 1988:267.

119. Ellison N. Hemostasis and hemotherapy. In: Barash PG, Cullen BF, Stoelting RK, eds. Clinical Anesthesia. Philadelphia: JB Lippincott, 1989:707.

120. Hanna, W. Variant von Willebrand's disease and pregnancy. Blood. 1981;58:873.

121. Lipton RA, Ayromlooi J, Coller BS. Severe von Willebrand's disease during labor and delivery. JAMA 1982;248:1355.

122. Caldwell DC, Williamson RA, Goldsmith JG. Hereditary coagulopathies in pregnancy. Clin Obstet Gynecol 1985;28:53.

123. Kruskall MS, Leonard S, Klapholz H. Autologous blood donation during pregnancy: analysis of safety and blood use. Obstet Gynecol 1987;938:70.

124. McVay PA. Safety and use of autologous blood donation during the third trimester of pregnancy. Am J Obstet Gynecol 1989;160:1479.

125. Druzin ML, Wolf CFW, Edersheim TG, et al. Donation of blood by the pregnant patient for autologous transfusion. Am J Obstet Gynecol 1988;159:1023.

CHAPTER 3

Preoperative Evaluation of the Parturient with Coexisting Disease

Part Two
Pulmonary and Neuromuscular Disease, Acquired Immunodeficiency Syndrome, and Substance Abuse

Richard B. Becker
Marianne P. Matthews

This chapter explores the preanesthetic evaluation of pregnant patients who have common respiratory or neurologic diseases. We also examine, from a preanesthetic point of view, the more specific topic of substance abuse among pregnant patients and the increasingly prevalent human immunodeficiency virus (HIV)-positive parturient with acquired immunodeficiency syndrome (AIDS).

RESPIRATORY DISEASE

Changes in Respiratory Physiology in Pregnancy

Figure 3-1 reviews the major respiratory changes in pregnancy.[1-3]

Asthma

Asthma is the most common pulmonary disease in women of child-bearing age and complicates approximately 1% of pregnancies.[4] In asthmatic patients, the tracheobronchial tree becomes more sensitive to a variety of stimuli. In response to provocation, bronchospasm and the major symptoms of asthma—dyspnea, wheezing, and cough—occur. Asthmatic symptoms vary from mild and almost undetectable to the severe and unremitting syndrome of status asthmaticus. The primary physiologic manifestation of this hyperresponsiveness is intermittent small airway obstruction. Hypersecretion of mucus, mucosal edema, and smooth muscle hypercontractility also contribute to the obstructive physiology of this disease. Airway obstruction from smooth muscle contraction is most

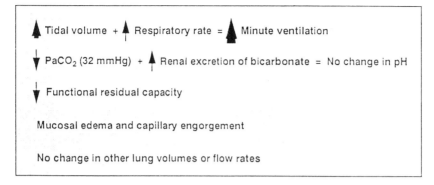

↑ Tidal volume + ↑ Respiratory rate = ↑ Minute ventilation

↓ $PaCO_2$ (32 mmHg) + ↑ Renal excretion of bicarbonate = No change in pH

↓ Functional residual capacity

Mucosal edema and capillary engorgement

No change in other lung volumes or flow rates

Figure 3–1. A review of major respiratory changes in pregnancy.

marked on expiration, creating air trapping with resultant hyperinflation.

Pathophysiology

Classically, asthma has two forms: intrinsic and extrinsic. Table 3-1 compares intrinsic and extrinsic asthma. Extrinsic asthma tends to be a seasonal allergic response to inhaled irritants. These patients usually have a lifelong history of allergies and have elevated blood and sputum eosinophils and increased serum immunoglobulin E (IgE) concentrations.[5] By contrast, patients with the intrinsic form are often older and may not have a seasonal allergic predisposition. These patients typically have normal serum IgE and eosinophils but may have increased sputum eosinophils. Because of the nonspecific nature of intrinsic asthma, it is usually more difficult to treat.[6] The distinction between the two forms may not be clear, and an individual may have elements of each. Common precipitating factors of an asthma attack include the following:

- IgE-mediated hypersensitivity to inhaled irritants
- Acute inflammatory disease
- Cold
- Exercise
- Aspirin

- Non–immune-mediated (direct) bronchoconstriction to inhaled substances (*e.g.*, animal dander, dust, and smoke)
- Emotional stress
- Mechanical stimulation (*e.g.*, intubation of the trachea)

Several theories attempt to explain the pathophysiology of an asthma attack. One hypothesis claims that asthma represents an imbalance between the sympathetic and parasympathetic nervous systems. Vagal tone and alpha-adrenergic action predominate over beta-adrenergic action.[7] Another theory suggests that asthma patients produce autoantibodies to beta-adrenergic receptors.[8] A final idea proposes that various stimuli produce inflammatory pulmonary changes in susceptible individuals.[9] Little definitive evidence supports most of these theories.[10] However, in inflammatory-mediated asthma, evidence suggests that the process proceeds in the following manner. Upon re-exposure of an individual to a particular allergen, an antigen–antibody complex forms and binds to specific mast cell receptors. This binding induces mast cell degranulation with release of vasoactive and cell-mediator biochemicals, including histamine, leukotrienes, prostaglandins, platelet-activating factor, and

Table 3–1

A Comparison of Intrinsic and Extrinsic Asthma

INTRINSIC	EXTRINSIC
Seasonal allergies	Lifelong allergies
Normal serum IgE and eosinophils	Increased blood and sputum eosinophils
Increased sputum eosinophils	Increased serum IgE concentration

cell chemotactic factors. These mediators produce vascular and airway changes, causing the symptoms seen during an asthma attack. They also attract increased numbers of inflammatory cells (macrophages and esosinophils) that cause further capillary endothelial and airway epithelial cell damage. This damage increases vascular permeability and incites airway hyperreactivity, resulting in further airway compromise from mucosal edema and bronchoconstriction.[10,11]

The mediators also may directly affect the autonomic control of airway tone.[10] Stimulation of parasympathetic airway fibers increases intracellular cyclic guanosine monophosphate (cGMP). This increase promotes bronchial smooth muscle contraction (bronchoconstriction) and airflow obstruction. Clinical evidence of obstruction includes wheezing, hyperinflated lung volumes, and decreased forced expiratory volume. The ultimate effects of obstruction are ventilation–perfusion abnormalities with resultant hypoxemia and hypercarbia. Bronchoconstriction reverses when sympathetic stimulation of beta$_2$ receptors increases intracellular cyclic adenosine monophosphate (cAMP). By interfering with bronchial smooth muscle actinomyosin activity, cAMP produces muscle relaxation and bronchodilation.[12] Figure 3-2 summarizes the pathophysiology of asthma.

Interaction with Pregnancy

EFFECT OF PREGNANCY ON ASTHMA.
Few studies show a consistent effect of pregnancy on pre-existing asthma. A review of 1054 pregnancies found that half of the parturients reported no change in the severity of asthma symptoms, 29% improved, and 21% got worse.[13] Recently, a small study found a strong overall decline in airway responsiveness in pregnancy. This improvement is greatest in those with the most hyperresponsive airways before pregnancy.[14] Asthma-related changes during gestation are difficult to study. It is hard to distinguish between the changes induced by the disease and those normally caused by pregnancy. Two things seem clear: Patients with severe asthma before pregnancy will have the most severe exacerbations during pregnancy, and the course of asthma in previous pregnancies is the best predictor of the course in future pregnancies.[15,16] The most common causes for exacerbation are respiratory tract infection (59%) and noncompliance with therapeutic regimens (27%).[17]

Specific pregnancy-related changes may worsen the course of asthma. Prostaglandin F$_{2\alpha}$ (a known bronchoconstrictor) increases.[18] Changes in cell-mediated immunity may increase the parturient's susceptibility

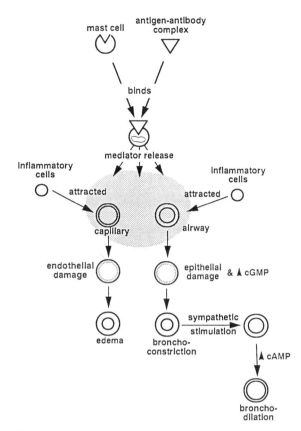

Figure 3–2. The asthma process.

to infection.[19] Plasma concentrations of cortisol and progesterone (which induces smooth muscle relaxation) rise during gestation and may improve asthma. Progesterone was formerly believed to be a major factor in the improvement of asthma during pregnancy. However, there is no statistically significant relationship between serum progesterone concentration and airway response. Therefore, if progesterone does improve asthma, it does not work alone.[20]

EFFECT OF ASTHMA ON PREGNANCY.
Asthma may complicate pregnancy in several ways.[21] One large study reported increases in hemorrhage, hyperemesis, and toxemia. This and other studies found an association between asthma and neonatal deaths, preterm deliveries, and low-birth-weight infants.[22,23] Table 3-2 summarizes the effects of asthma on pregnancy. During an acute asthma attack, maternal hypoxemia and respiratory alkalosis may severely compromise the fetus. Maternal–fetal oxygen exchange depends on, among other things, maternal arterial oxygen tension and the oxygen affinity of maternal blood.

Table 3–2

Asthma Complications of Pregnancy

Hemorrhage	Neonatal deaths
Hyperemesis	Preterm deliveries
Toxemia	Low-birth-weight infants

Maternal hypoxemia lessens the maternal–fetal oxygen diffusion gradient, hindering oxygen delivery to the fetus. Maternal alkalosis causes a leftward shift of the oxyhemoglobin dissociation curve, resulting in a greater affinity of maternal hemoglobin for oxygen and less exchange to the fetus. The fetus inhabits a relatively hypoxemic environment with an umbilical venous oxygen partial pressure of approximately 33 mm Hg.[24] Fetal hemoglobin has a greater affinity for oxygen than does maternal hemoglobin and can release oxygen more efficiently to the tissues at low oxygen saturations. In a state of maternal hypoxia with poor oxygen exchange, however, the fetus has very little oxygen reserve. As a consequence, the fetus rapidly develops hypoxemia and risks vital organ damage. A well-documented study of patients with severe asthma attempted to determine perinatal effects of uncontrolled asthma. It showed that "status asthmaticus during pregnancy may be deleterious to both the mother and the fetus, and management of asthma to prevent episodes of status asthmaticus may result in a favorable outcome."[25]

Pharmacotherapy

Management goals in treating asthma include the following:

- Identification and removal of precipitating factors
- Proper rest, nutrition, and hydration
- Aggressive antibiotic treatment of infection
- Pharmacotherapy where indicated

Strongly consider the risk–benefit ratios of therapeutic interventions. Avoid drugs that are teratogenic or otherwise harmful to the fetus. Pharmacotherapy for pregnant asthmatics differs very little from that used in the nonpregnant patient. Use the commonly employed agents. The available evidence suggests that they are safe for use in the pregnant patient. The benefits of avoiding uncontrolled asthma outweigh the risks of drug-induced fetal malformation. But, as it is impossible to eliminate all possibility of hazard to the fetus, avoid drug use in the first trimester if maternal condition allows.

Bronchodilator Agents

BETA-AGONISTS. Beta-adrenergic stimulation relaxes bronchial smooth muscle by increasing intracellular concentrations of cAMP. Figure 3-3 summarizes the mechanism of action of beta-adrenergic bronchodilators. Beta-agonist bronchodilators are safe for use throughout pregnancy and no known reports link their use with congenital defects.[26] However, use of beta-agonists may interfere with normal labor due to uterine relaxation and may contribute to postpartum

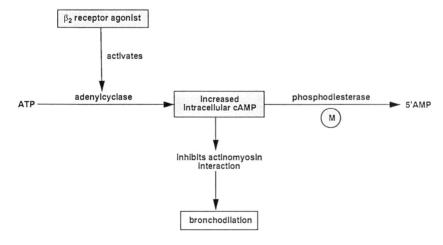

Figure 3–3. Mechanism of action of beta-adrenergic bronchodilators.

uterine atony and hemorrhage. Choose drugs and routes of administration to maximize beta$_2$ effects (bronchial dilation) and minimize beta$_1$ effects (tachycardia). Terbutaline, metaproterenol, and albuterol are the most beta$_2$-selective agents, and their administration by the aerosol route speeds onset, reduces the side-effects from systemic administration, and enhances beta$_2$ specificity.

Epinephrine has alpha-adrenergic (possible uteroplacental vasoconstriction) effects along with nonspecific beta-adrenergic activity. Some authors advocate its use during gestation to control acute asthma.[27] Others argue against its use because of possible fetal distress. In cases of life-threatening asthma refractory to other therapies, use epinephrine without hesitation because of the high risk of maternal and fetal complications resulting from respiratory failure.

PARASYMPATHOLYTICS. The anticholinergic agent ipratropium bromide relaxes bronchial smooth muscles by competitive inhibition of vagus-mediated bronchoconstriction. Aerosol administration minimizes systemic anticholinergic effects (*e.g.,* tachycardia, dry mouth). Because use of this agent in pregnancy has not been well studied, avoid it unless other agents have failed.

METHYLXANTHINES. Theophylline and its water-soluble salt aminophylline are methylxanthines. The exact mechanism of action of these agents is unknown. The most common theory is that they inhibit phosphodiesterase, the enzyme responsible for the breakdown of cAMP. This action increases intracellular cAMP (see Fig. 3-3). Other theories suggest that the methylxanthines modulate the interaction of actinomyosin and calcium, antagonize prostaglandins, or inhibit adenosine.[28–30] Inhibition of the effects of adenosine releases endogenous catecholamines, augmenting the bronchodilatory effects of cAMP. Adenosine antagonism also attenuates the release of mast-cell mediators.[29]

Methylxanthines have a long record of safe use in pregnancy and have traditionally been used as adjuvants to beta-agonist therapy. However, recent evidence suggests that aminophylline does not add significant improvement to the standard beta-agonist–steroid therapy in adult asthma exacerbations.[31] The most common dosing regimen advises an intravenous bolus of aminophylline (85% theophylline by weight) of 5 mg/kg, followed by a maintenance dose of 0.5 to 1.0 mg/kg/h to achieve a therapeutic plasma concentration between 10 and 20 µg/mL. Monitor theophylline levels closely in the last half of pregnancy. Some studies

have found significantly reduced theophylline clearance during the third trimester. Some patients develop signs of toxicity with their usual doses.[32] The most likely mechanisms include reduced hepatic metabolism and increased theophylline absorption from the gastrointestinal tract.[33] These findings contradict previous suggestions that higher theophylline doses may be needed to compensate for an increased volume of distribution in pregnancy.[34]

Anti-inflammatory Agents

STEROIDS. Glucocorticoids are potent anti-inflammatory agents that have proved beneficial in treating asthma.[35] They function by altering protein production, inhibiting mediator release, and suppressing inflammatory mediator action. During an acute asthma exacerbation, steroids increase the synthesis of proteins that inhibit the production of prostaglandins and platelet-activating factor. They also increase the synthesis of new beta$_2$-receptors.[36] Steroids regulate protein synthesis through gene induction. Glucocorticoids bind to and activate cell receptors. The activated receptor complex binds to the nucleus and then to gene regulators. The regulator then activates or inhibits gene transcription and ultimately increases or decreases protein production by that gene (Fig. 3-4).[37]

Steroids also suppress the symptoms of an asthma attack by mediating other processes (Table 3-3). They increase the responsiveness of beta-receptors to catecholamines, potentiate beta-agonist bronchodilation, and reverse beta-receptor fatigue from prolonged stimulation.[31] In addition, steroids reduce airway edema by inhibiting the release of chemical mediators and suppressing their adverse effect on microvascular permeability.[38] Finally, steroids inhibit the formation of inflammatory cell chemotactic mediators and inactivate inflammatory cells already involved in the asthma process.[39]

Steroid use in pregnant asthmatics is not greatly different from its use in treating nonpregnant asthmatics. Although high-dose systemic steroids may be lifesaving in treating acute asthma, some therapeutic actions have a lengthy period of onset. Use alternative therapies to medicate the attack until steroid onset. Steroid use in the chronic asthmatic is less well defined. Dunlap and Bailey[40] give the following recommendations:

- For chronic maintenance, use the lowest dose necessary to prevent bronchospasm.
- Aerosol administration may help eliminate or reduce systemic steroid use. It also localizes the action

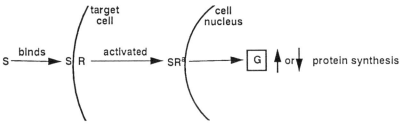

S   Steroid
R   Receptor
G   Gene Regulator
SR^a Activated Steroid-Receptor Complex

Figure 3–4. Steroid regulation of protein synthesis.

of steriods and reduces systemic side-effects, thereby minimizing the risk of adrenal suppression.

- If patients have used high-dose systemic steroids for a month or longer, adrenal suppression is possible. Taper doses when discontinuing the drug.
- During periods of increased physiologic stress, these patients may require steroid supplementation.

CROMOLYN SODIUM. Cromolyn sodium is an aerosol agent that prevents degranulation of mast cells by membrane stabilization. It is reasonably safe in pregnancy, but only as a prophylactic agent. Do not use it to treat acute bronchospasm because it cannot counter effects of previously released substances.

Evaluation

History is the most valuable tool in evaluating a stable asthmatic (Table 3-4). In an acute crisis, however, management of hypoxia and respiratory compromise take precedence over gathering history.[41] In addition, asking the patient how she rates her current ability to breathe provides a rough idea of the degree of bronchospasm.

Note the patient's general appearance. Marked tachypnea, cyanosis, and fatigue signal impending respiratory failure. Wheezing is evidence of diffuse bronchoconstriction and is a sign of air exchange; lack of wheezing is more serious and denotes inability to ventilate. Increasing use of accessory muscles and nostril flaring point to increasing distress. Note the patient's ability to converse. Someone who can speak in sentences is less ill than someone working so hard to breathe that she cannot speak at all. Additionally, note heart rate. Tachycardia is a compensatory response to stress and hypoxia; bradycardia may precede hypoxic cardiac arrest. Also, a decrease in heart rate of 15 beats/ minute or greater with inspiration (pulsus paradoxus) is a nonspecific indication of a severe attack. An elevated temperature may signal acute infection.

Other data can be helpful in evaluating an acute asthma attack. Obtain serum electrolytes, a complete

Table 3–3

Steroid Action

Alter protein production
New beta$_2$-receptors
Inhibit synthesis of prostaglandins and platelet-activating factor
Suppress biochemical mediator release
Augment function of beta$_2$-receptors
Reverse beta$_2$-receptor fatigue
Inhibit inflammatory cell function

Table 3–4

Pertinent History in Parturients with Acute Exacerbation of Asthma

Previous attacks
Number
Severity
Duration
Previous emergency room visits
Number
Most recent
Previous need for intubation and mechanical ventilation
Course of asthma in previous pregnancies
Current therapy
Medications
Compliance
Known precipitating factors
Environmental exposures
Recent or current upper respiratory infection
Coexisting pulmonary or cardiac problems

blood count, and Gram stain any sputum. Take a chest radiograph with abdominal shielding to protect the fetus. Evaluate the chest radiograph for an acute underlying infectious process, hyperinflation, pneumothorax, or pneumomediastinum. An arterial blood gas determination can be critical in evaluating severity. Remember that blood gas values normally change in pregnancy. The blood gas will uniformly show hypoxemia; therefore, this parameter is not as useful as pH and $Paco_2$. If the patient has alkalosis and lower-than-normal pregnancy $Paco_2$ (32 mm Hg), the attack is mild. If the observed pH and $Paco_2$ are normal for pregnancy, the attack is more severe. Acidosis and hypercapnia (pH 7.35 or below, $Paco_2$ 35–38 mm Hg or above) signal impending respiratory failure, especially combined with a Pao_2 below 60 mm Hg.[42] Spirometry can also provide useful information. A single set of values for forced expiratory volume in 1 second (FEV_1) and peak expiratory flow may not be significant because nomograms are not available for pregnant patients. However, a series of measurements taken before and at intervals after treatment can determine the efficacy of therapy.[41] For a summary of the treatment of acute asthma, refer to Table 3-5.

Differential Diagnosis

The initial reaction to acute respiratory distress may be to assume that its etiology is asthma. However, the following also cause respiratory distress and should be ruled out by differential diagnosis:

- Acute upper airway obstruction
- Pulmonary embolism, anaphylaxis
- Congestive heart failure
- Acute infection
- Chronic obstructive pulmonary disease
- Aspiration pneumonitis

Cystic Fibrosis

Cystic fibrosis (CF) is a multisystem, autosomal recessive disorder that occurs in approximately 1 in 1000 births. It is the most common lethal genetic disorder in the Caucasian population. The disease is one of chronic exocrine gland dysfunction, but the underlying defect is unknown. Cystic fibrosis shows itself through the dysfunction of several systems. These patients produce thick, tenacious mucus. They suffer pancreatic insufficiency with accompanying protein and fat malabsorption. Hepatobiliary disease with chronic cholestasis, fibrosis, and cirrhosis occurs. Lastly, abnormally high sweat duct excretion of sodium chloride is seen. The abnormal electrolyte content of sweat confirms the diagnosis in patients exhibiting symptoms of the disease. Patients typically are diagnosed early in childhood, but milder forms of the disease may not be recognized until much later.

The average survival of patients with CF is 20 to 30 years with death usually from respiratory failure. Patients have persistent bronchial infections, usually with *Pseudomonas aeruginosa*. Chronic infection generates

---

Table 3–5

Treatment of Acute Asthma

UNSTABLE ASTHMA	STABLE ASTHMA

Correct hypoxemia and acidosis
    Support ventilation, if necessary
    Give supplemental oxygen
    Give bronchodilators and steroids
Treat underlying cause
Proceed to **stable asthma** treatment when stable
	Obtain history
	Remove precipitating factors
	Hydrate
	Obtain clinical studies (labs, arterial blood gas, chest radiograph, spirometry, sputum stain)
	Initiate pharmacotherapy
	    Bronchodilators
	    Steroids
	    Consider aminophylline
	    Antibiotics for infection
	Repeat clinical studies to assess efficacy of therapy

airway fibrosis and, later, parenchymal fibrosis, ventilation–perfusion mismatching, and hypoxemia.

Improved survival of CF patients has allowed women to reach child-bearing age (Fig. 3-5).[43] The maternal outcome of pregnancy correlates with maternal condition before conception. Pregnant women with mild disease usually do well, whereas those with moderate or severe disease may deteriorate.[44] Pregnancy itself does not seem to influence the course of the disease. Patient deterioration in pregnancy stems from natural progression of the disease.[45] Maternal condition during gestation predicts perinatal outcome. Chronically, hypoxemic and malnourished mothers have increased perinatal morbidity and mortality, whereas well-managed mothers with mild disease have improved outcomes.[42]

Treatment of CF aims at the respiratory system. Advances in this area are responsible for the increased survival of patients. Aggressive antibiotic treatment of infection along with avid pharmacologic and physiotherapeutic measures to facilitate removal of secretions are the mainstays of management. Additionally, pancreatic enzyme replacement will decrease gastrointestinal malabsorption, and vitamin K supplementations can correct bleeding problems that arise from poor hepatic function or malabsorption of fat-soluble vitamins.

The preanesthetic evaluation of the pregnant patient with CF focuses on the degree of respiratory compromise. Ensure that the patient is in the best possible pulmonary condition. Hydrate the patient well to help her clear secretions. If there is any suspicion of a pulmonary infection, obtain a sputum Gram stain and initiate appropriate antibiotic therapy. Laboratory evaluation can detect electrolyte imbalance, acute infection, or

coagulation defect. Arterial blood gas tensions or pulse oximetry will detect hypoxemia, and the changes with time may help in assessing the degree of respiratory deterioration.

Cigarette Smoking

Smoking during pregnancy breeds many adverse maternal and fetal consequences. For the mother, smoking increases airway irritability and mucus production, and impairs respiratory tract mucocilliary function. The inhalation of carbon monoxide from smoke produces carboxyhemoglobin, shifting both maternal and fetal oxyhemoglobin dissociation curves leftward. This shift limits oxygen exchange between the mother and fetus and between the fetus and its vital organs. In addition, smoking is the leading risk factor for the development of pulmonary malignancies and chronic obstructive pulmonary disease (COPD).

Increased expiratory airway resistance with air trapping complicates both forms of COPD—emphysema and chronic bronchitis. Patients with emphysema have airflow obstruction because of loss of airway elasticity. Patients with chronic bronchitis have airflow obstruction because inflammation, edema, and excessive mucus secretion shrink airway diameter. These pathologic changes then produce ventilation and perfusion abnormalities that, in turn, cause hypoxemia and carbon dioxide retention. Dyspnea in patients with COPD reflects the increased work of breathing required to compensate for these changes.

Because older women, who may have longer smoking histories, are having babies, anesthesiologists are likely to encounter COPD in the pregnant population. Superimposing the normal respiratory changes of pregnancy upon the changes induced by COPD could produce so great an increase in the work of breathing that decompensation occurs. Fortunately, however, patients with COPD usually tolerate pregnancy.[46] Monitor such women closely. It may be difficult to distinguish between the pregnancy-related dyspnea and that caused by worsening pulmonary function.

Smoking can complicate pregnancy in several ways (Table 3-6). Smokers have a higher incidence of ectopic pregnancy[47] and placental complications, including abruption, previa, and premature calcification.[45,48] Fetal hazards include growth retardation, directly proportional to the numbers of cigarettes smoked,[49] prematurity, and spontaneous abortion.[50] The fetal effects relate chiefly to chronic fetal hypoxemia (secondary to increased fetal carboxyhemoglobin) and

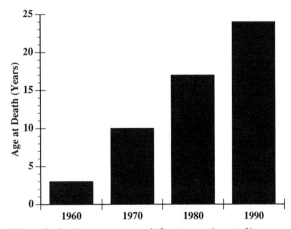

Figure 3–5. Increasing survival of patients with cystic fibrosis.

Table 3-6

Consequences of Smoking During Pregnancy

MATERNAL	FETAL
Increased airway irritability	Decreased oxygen exchange from mother
Increased mucous production	Growth retardation
Decreased mucocilliary function	Prematurity
Increased dyspnea	Spontaneous abortion
Increased risk of cancer and COPD	Uteroplacental hypoperfusion
Left shift of oxyhemoglobin dissociation curve	
Increased risk of ectopic pregnancy	
Increased placental abnormalities	

uteroplacental hypoperfusion (from nicotine-induced vasospasm). Studies have not consistently demonstrated a teratogenic effect of smoking.[49]

Treatment of pregnant smokers attempts to optimize pulmonary function. Cessation of smoking is paramount. In as little as 48 hours, the oxyhemoglobin dissociation curve resumes its normal configuration, increasing oxygen availability. In 2 to 3 months after stopping smoking, sputum production decreases and ciliary function improves. Acute respiratory infections occur frequently in patients with chronic bronchitis. Control such infection with antibiotics. Treat any bronchospastic component of airway disease with bronchodilators.

The anesthetic preoperative evaluation of the pregnant smoker should determine the presence and severity of pulmonary disease. A history of decreased exercise tolerance and increased cough, sputum production, and dyspnea requires further evaluation. In patients with COPD, pulmonary function testing shows a decrease in FEV_1 (and a consequent decrease in FEV_1:FVC ratio) as well as an increase in total lung capacity. The results of such testing predict the patient's ability to cough and clear her airway. Laboratory evidence may be helpful. An elevated leukocyte count may indicate respiratory infection, and an arterial blood gas analysis will show hypoxemia or hypercarbia.

Sarcoidosis

Sarcoidosis is a generalized granulomatous disease with a pulmonary predilection. Resulting fibrosis and a restrictive pattern of pulmonary disease can lead to hypoxemia, pulmonary hypertension, and cor pulmonale.

Steroids are often useful in the treatment of severe forms of sarcoidosis. Because of increased maternal serum cortisol levels, pregnant patients generally tolerate existing sarcoidosis well. Monitor oxygenation closely to prevent maternal and fetal hypoxemia. A small percentage of these patients have laryngeal involvement, so anticipate airway interference.

Pulmonary Infection

Pulmonary infections occur as commonly in pregnant women as in the general population. Like the general population, pregnant women tolerate these illnesses well unless immunocompromised or otherwise afflicted with chronic coexisting disease. Treatment in these special cases must be aggressive. Prophylaxis with immunizations or pharmacologic agents may be beneficial. The etiology of acute, community-acquired respiratory infection is most often viral (influenza). Such infections are rarely from varicella. Bacterial infections are uncommon unless the patient is debilitated. Isolate the infecting organism from blood or sputum, and tailor antibiotic therapy accordingly. Fungal pulmonary infections are rare in healthy patients. With the rising number of immunocompromised patients with AIDS, the incidence of fungal infections will likely increase.

NERVOUS SYSTEM DISEASE

Neurologic disease does not occur frequently in women of child-bearing age. Consequently, clinicians may be unfamiliar with the combined problems of pregnancy and neurologic disorders. Pregnant women are susceptible to the same neurologic illnesses as non-pregnant women. Because improved diagnosis and therapy allow women with neurologic disease to survive to reproductive age, and because older women are becoming pregnant, anesthesiologists will encounter more pregnant patients with neurologic disease and must prepare to care for them.

The gross neurologic examination of the healthy gravida is not greatly altered from that of the nonpregnant patient. Motor function, sensation, and reflexes are the same. Edema or a changed center of gravity from pregnancy may alter gait. Cranial nerves are grossly intact, although normal pregnancy-induced hypertrophy of the pituitary gland occasionally alters visual-field examination.

Seizure Disorders

Seizure disorders complicate approximately 0.5% of pregnancies and are the most common neurologic disorder encountered in pregnancy[51] Seizures are not themselves a disease but are the expression of an underlying neurologic dysfunction. Epilepsy is the ongoing tendency to have seizures. When excessive numbers of neurons discharge in a synchronous fashion, seizures result. This hyperexcitability can be focal or general or may begin in a localized fashion and spread to become generalized. The cerebral cortex, thalamus, and brain stem can all be involved. The most common etiology is idiopathic, but intracranial lesions, head trauma, metabolic derangement, hypoxia, cerebral inflammatory disease, and drug toxicity may all cause seizures. In pregnancy, eclampsia also may account for seizures.

Traditional classifications of seizure disorders have included the following categories:

- Tonic–clonic (grand mal) seizures involve generalized motor activity with loss of consciousness.
- Simple partial and complex partial seizures involve brief alterations in consciousness, behavior, and motor or sensory function.
- Absence seizures (petit mal) involve brief alterations in awareness with little or no change in motor function.

Epilepsy appears to increase the risk of maternal and fetal complications, particularly congenital malformations, prematurity, low birth weight, preeclampsia, stillbirth, hemorrhage, and obstetric intervention.[52,53] Although not all investigators have found evidence to support the theory that epilepsy predisposes women to purely obstetric complications,[54,55] most studies do

support this conclusion. Therefore, treat epileptic gravidas as a high-risk group. Indisputably, hypoxia and acidosis incurred during a prolonged seizure or status epilepticus can precipitate fetal distress and, if uncorrected, can lead to maternal and fetal demise.

Pregnancy has a variable effect on seizure frequency. In a review of 27 studies published between 1885 and 1980, Schmidt[56] found that of 2165 women, 24% experienced an increased frequency of seizures, 22% had fewer seizures, and in 53%, the frequency of seizures, did not change.[56] In an analysis of the effects of pregnancy on the frequency of seizures, Remillard *et al*[57] found that patients with secondary generalized and complex partial seizures were more likely than those with primary generalized epilepsy to experience an increase in seizure frequency. Seizure control before pregnancy seems to be the best predictor of seizure control during pregnancy. Although the most common reason for an increase in seizure frequency during pregnancy is poor compliance with anticonvulsant therapy, pregnancy-induced changes in drug levels also may account for some seizures.[58]

Treatment

Anticonvulsants appear to act by reducing the spread of activity from hyperexcitable neurons to normal neurons. They may be used singly or in combination. The simpler the regimen, the more likely the patient is to comply with it and the less likely are side-effects and adverse drug interactions. Because all anticonvulsants commonly used in pregnancy have been variably charged with being teratogens, it is vitally important to weigh the risks and benefits of pharmacologic therapy. The American Academy of Pediatrics Select Committee on Anticonvulsants in Pregnancy has made the recommendations shown in Table 3-7.[59]

Phenytoin (Dilantin) is the most commonly administered anti-epileptic drug. It is effective for most types of seizures except absence seizures. Its site of action is the motor cortex, where it may promote sodium efflux from neurons, thus stabilizing the membrane hyperexcitability threshold. Clearance is via the liver. Maternal side-effects include gastrointestinal distress, skin rash, pancytopenia, megaloblastic anemia, systemic lupus erythematosus, gingival hyperplasia, and peripheral polyneuropathy. Toxic manifestations include ataxia, nystagmus, and dysarthria progressing to respiratory and circulatory depression.

Phenytoin has been implicated as a causative factor in the increased incidence of congenital malformations in the offspring of epileptic women. In women taking anticonvulsants, however, it is difficult to determine

Table 3–7

Recommendations for Use of Anticonvulsants in Pregnancy

1. Before conception, withdraw anticonvulsant medication from women who have been seizure-free for many years.
2. A woman taking anticonvulsants should be told that if she becomes pregnant, she will have approximately a 90% chance of having a normal baby. However, the risk of having a baby with mental retardation or congenital malformations is two to three times greater than average.
3. There is no reason to switch a woman from well-known anticonvulsants, such as phenytoin or phenobarbital to less well known drugs.
4. Do not discontinue medication in women whose seizures are controlled by that medication because seizures may be deleterious to them and their fetuses.

(The American Academy of Pediatrics Select Committee on Anticonvulsants in Pregnancy, Pediatrics 1979;63:331)

the role of the drug in the increased incidence of birth defects because of the difficulties in collecting human data on drug teratogenicity. In addition, genetic factors in epileptic women may contribute more strongly to birth defects than any drug. Fetal malformations associated with phenytoin include craniofacial and limb malformations and fetal hydantoin syndrome. This syndrome is characterized by growth retardation, mental deficiency, and dysmorphic facial and limb features. Phenytoin may also cause deficiencies in folic acid and vitamin K–dependent clotting factors. Women should receive folic acid and vitamin K supplements during pregnancy to prevent megaloblastic anemia and hemorrhage.

Phenobarbital is a barbiturate with indications for use similar to phenytoin. Its major side effects are sedation, skin rash, and megaloblastic anemia. Toxic manifestations include nystagmus and ataxia. Phenobarbital is a potent inducer of hepatic microsomal enzymes and can enhance metabolism of other substances. Excretion is by the kidneys. In the past, because of lower suspected teratogenicity, many pregnant patients switched from phenytoin to phenobarbital. However, phenobarbital use now correlates with a syndrome similar to fetal hydantoin syndrome. Also, like phenytoin, phenobarbital may cause folate deficiency and coagulopathy. Unlike phenytoin, phenobarbital may cause neonatal depression and neonatal drug withdrawal. Primidone (Mysoline) is partly metabolized to phenobarbital, and its uses, side-effects, and cautions are similar to those for phenobarbital.

Some physicians believe that carbamazepine (Tegretal) is the safest and least teratogenic of the anticonvulsants and are using it more frequently as a primary agent in treating tonic–clonic and partial seizures.[60] Because much less is known about carbamazepine in pregnancy, use caution when considering prescribing it for a well-controlled pregnant epileptic who has been receiving phenytoin or phenobarbital. Side-effects include dizziness, drowsiness, skin rash, and bone marrow depression with aplastic anemia and congestive heart failure. Neuromuscular symptoms are prominent at toxic drug concentrations. Elimination is mainly by the renal route.

Ethosuximide, clonazepam, trimethadione, and valproic acid are all used to treat petit mal seizures. What little data exist for ethosuximide and clonazepam show few fetal effects and suggest that their use in pregnancy is relatively safe. Trimethadione is the most potent known teratogen among the anticonvulsants, and its use is contraindicated in women of reproductive age. Also avoid valproic acid in pregnancy. It is associated with craniofacial, limb, and heart malfunctions. Women using it also show a 1% incidence of neural tube defects.[61]

Anticonvulsant Pharmacokinetics in Pregnancy

Pregnancy induces several maternal pharmacokinetic changes that may significantly alter serum concentrations of anticonvulsants. In plasma, total protein and albumin content falls, whereas free fatty acids rise. Fewer proteins mean less drug–protein binding, whereas rising free fatty acids displace drugs from proteins. This combination allows a higher concentration of pharmacologically active free drug. Because protein binding is highly variable among individuals, the amount of free drug increase is unpredictable.

Despite the greater unbound fraction of drug, other pharmacologic changes combine to produce an overall reduction in the serum concentration of anticonvulsant drugs. Bowel absorption of phenytoin falls, probably as a result of decreased gastrointestinal motility and a change in gastric pH.[62] This impaired uptake may hold for other anticonvulsants as well. An increase in total body water, accumulation of fat mass, and the addition of fetal, placental, and uterine tissues produce a larger volume of distribution. The increased volume dilutes the drugs in the serum. Elevated estrogen and progesterone levels increase hepatic metabolism of anticonvulsant drugs, speeding their clearance from the body and lowering serum concentrations. In addition, the drugs themselves may induce liver enzymes to speed metabolism. Figure 3-6 summarizes the pregnancy-induced pharmacokinetic changes in anticonvulsant medications. These changes generally require increases in drug doses.

Monitor pregnant women taking anticonvulsants closely to ensure therapeutic drug concentrations. Estimate drug amounts from either plasma or saliva. Saliva drug concentration correlates well with plasma concentration of pharmacologically active drug. Measuring saliva concentrations is a simpler, less invasive, less expensive alternative to measuring plasma concentrations.[57] After delivery, because maternal physiology rapidly reverts to its prepregnancy state, decrease anticonvulsant doses to avoid toxicity.

Status Epilepticus and Pregnancy

Status epilepticus is the repetitive occurrence of grand mal seizures during which the patient does not regain consciousness. It is a medical emergency. Without treatment, hypoxia, acidosis, and death ensue. The prognosis depends on the promptness of therapy and the etiology of the seizure. Abruptly halting anticonvulsant medication is the most common reason for seizures. Treatment involves maintaining a patent airway and administering intravenous anticonvulsants. Because of the fatal nature of this condition if untreated, do not consider the teratogenicity of agents employed in arresting it. Initial therapy involves the administration of diazepam followed by loading and maintenance with phenytoin or phenobarbital. Ultimately, if these agents fail, induction of general anesthesia with an inhalation agent such as halothane and the use of a neuromuscular blocking agent may be necessary.

The anesthetic preoperative evaluation of the stable pregnant epileptic involves early recognition. To avoid the surprise, confusion, and misdiagnosis arising from

↑ Unbound drug fraction

↓ Bowel absorption

↑ Volume of distribution

+   ↑ Hepatic metabolism and clearance

↑ Dose requirement

Figure 3–6. Anticonvulsant pharmacokinetic changes in pregnancy.

unexpected convulsions, identify epileptic patients immediately on arrival. Determine the patient's seizure history and course during this and previous pregnancies along with anticonvulsant regimen and compliance with it. Measure serum or saliva concentrations of drugs and adjust to therapeutic ranges, if necessary. Finally, do a brief baseline neurologic examination to help assess subsequent changes.

Myasthenia Gravis

Myasthenia gravis (MG) is a chronic autoimmune neuromuscular disorder caused by a loss of functional acetylcholine receptors from the postsynaptic membrane of the neuromuscular junction. In about 85% of patients, autoantibodies against acetylcholine receptors cause this loss.[63] In the remaining patients, autoantibodies binding to non–acetylcholine receptor neuromuscular junction determinants induce the receptor loss.[64] Myasthenia gravis usually manifests in the third decade. Its incidence is approximately 1 in 15,000 to 20,000 adults. Myasthenia gravis affects women twice as often as men. Characteristically, the disease produces exacerbations and remissions of muscle weakness and fatigue, especially of oculomotor, facial, laryngeal, and respiratory muscles. Myasthenia gravis may be associated with cardiomegaly or other diseases of immune origin such as thyroid disease, lupus, or rheumatoid arthritis. Emotional or physiologic stress, infection, electrolyte imbalance, aminoglycoside antibiotics, magnesium sulfate, and neuromuscular blocking agents can precipitate or aggravate muscle weakness.

Interaction with Pregnancy

Pregnancy affects the disease process in unpredictable ways. In approximately equal numbers of patients, the disease stays the same, gets worse, or gets better during pregnancy. The course of MG in previous pregnancies does not predict the course in subsequent pregnancies. Respiratory difficulty and inadequate expulsive efforts from muscle fatigue during the second stage of labor are the only effects during labor and delivery. Stress or infection during labor may precipitate a myasthenic crisis. Crisis manifests as severe weakness with respiratory insufficiency. Cholinergic crisis also presents with severe weakness; however, these women also have evidence of muscarinic receptor stimulation with nausea, vomiting, lacrimation, and diarrhea. Because of transplacental transfer of antibodies, the newborn may show signs of neonatal MG. The symptoms may not appear for days, and although some infants require treatment, the condition is usually transient.

Treatment

The goal of treating MG is to increase the function of the acetylcholine receptors either by increasing the amount of endogenous acetylcholine or by decreasing the amount or function of acetylcholine receptor autoantibodies. The four methods of treatment are as follows:

- Administration of anticholinesterase drugs
- Immunosuppression
- Plasmapheresis
- Surgical thymectomy

The most common pharmacologic means of treatment is with anticholinesterase drugs such as edrophonium, neostigmine, and pyridostigmine. These drugs are quaternary ammonium structures that produce a reversible inhibition of acetylcholinesterase. By converting acetylcholine to acetic acid and choline, acetylcholinesterase terminates the action of acetylcholine. Acetylcholinesterase is found anywhere in the body there is acetylcholine. Inhibition of acetylcholinesterase increases the amount of acetylcholine available for neurotransmission and thereby augments the ability of skeletal muscle to respond to repetitive stimuli. Elevated acetylcholine levels in the vicinity of the uterus from anticholinesterase therapy theoretically increase uterine tone, resulting in spontaneous abortion or premature labor. In practice, however, this has not proved to be a great danger.

Edrophonium forms an electrostatic attachment to acetylcholinesterase, preventing the proper alignment of acetylcholine. Because the electrostatically bound complex is weak, acetylcholine can easily compete for binding sites, and the therapeutic effect of edrophonium is short-lived. The main use of edrophonium is in diagnosing MG and assessing the adequacy of anticholinesterase therapy. Give intravenous edrophonium in small (1 mg) doses every minute or two until weakness symptoms improve. In new-onset MG, this test is diagnostic. In treated patients, improvement in symptoms shows that current therapy is inadequate. In contrast, administering edrophonium to patients with weakness from cholinergic crisis (anticholinesterase overdose) will not improve symptoms.

The other commonly used anticholinesterase agents are neostigmine and pyridostigmine. These produce reversible carbamyl-ester complexes with acetylcho-

linesterase. Both competitively inhibit the enzyme interaction with acetylcholine and act longer than edrophonium. The longer duration of action is likely due to true chemical bonding instead of relatively weak electrostatic bonding.

The pharmacologic effect of anticholinesterase agents is present at both muscarinic and nicotinic receptors. Nicotinic receptors are responsible for effects at the neuromuscular junction, whereas muscarinic receptors effect such responses as bradycardia, salivation, and emesis. If necessary, control muscarinic side-effects with anticholinergic agents. When using anticholinesterase agents, consider that they impair the function of plasma cholinesterase, possibly prolonging the action of succinlycholine and ester local anesthetics.

During delivery, it is imperative that anticholinesterase therapy continue. Because gastric absorption of drugs during labor may be erratic, administer these agents by intravenous or intramuscular routes. In addition, to prevent further muscle weakness, judiciously avoid agents with muscle-relaxing properties such as neuromuscular blockers, magnesium sulfate, and certain antibiotics (*e.g.,* gentamicin and erythromycin).

When anticholinesterase drugs do not achieve adequate therapy, immunosuppression may prove beneficial. The common immunosuppressants (prednisone, azothioprine, and cyclophosphamide) prevent the production of, or reduce the circulating concentration of, acetylcholine receptor antibodies. No controlled data prove the efficacy of these agents in pregnancy. Because they are potentially teratogenic (especially azothioprine and cyclophosphamide), avoid their use during gestation.

Plasmapheresis is an uncommon therapy for MG that is aimed at reducing the circulating levels of autoantibodies. Consider its use when conventional therapeutic measures have failed. Plasmapheresis may benefit the acetylcholine receptor antibody-negative subset of MG patients by removing an unspecified pathogenic substance.[63]

Surgical thymectomy for the treatment of MG aims to remove the source of antibody production. Patients receiving this alternative treatment have favorable remission rates. It is not clear which patients benefit most from thymectomy. One review found that patients with moderate or advanced disease benefit more than do those with mild symptoms (27% improvement with mild disease vs 86% with moderate to advanced disease).[65] Another review found that the presence of acetylcholine receptor antibodies and thymic hyperplasia were the best indicators of a favorable response to thymectomy.[66] Table 3-8 provides a quick reference for MG.

Preoperative Evaluation

The anesthetic preoperative evaluation of patients with MG involves assessing the degree of neuromuscular weakness. Look closely for evidence of respiratory compromise. The evaluation should also catalogue the current drug regimen and previous therapies and their efficacies. Determine the ability of the patient to maintain a patent airway (*e.g.,* can she cough and clear secretions). Ask about coexisting major diseases. If a patient who is treated with an anticholinesterase agent exhibits weakness, a trial of edrophonium may help determine the adequacy of her current regimen. Conversely, consider anticholinergic crisis if edrophonium fails to alleviate symptoms. Finally, a brief baseline neurologic examination may prove helpful in determining subsequent deteriorations or improvements in neurologic status.

Multiple Sclerosis

Multiple sclerosis (MS) is a chronic, acquired disorder of the central nervous system characterized by multiple, random areas of axonal demyelination (plaques) in the brain and spinal cord. Multiple sclerosis occurs most frequently during the peak reproductive years (20y–40y). It affects women twice as often as men. Multiple sclerosis has a striking geographic distribution, with higher prevalence in temperate zones than in tropical or subtropical zones. Multiple sclerosis is most likely to affect affluent urban dwellers. First-degree relatives of those affected have a 12- to 15-fold increase in incidence, pointing to a genetic predisposition to the disease. Sixty percent of patients with MS have a common histocompatibility antigen (HLA-DW$_2$) compared to only 18% of controls.[67]

Although some patients suffer a chronic progressive course, most individuals with MS experience periods of exacerbation and remission throughout their disease. These episodes occur at unpredictable intervals over many years. Eventually, residual symptoms persist and the patient experiences disability. Typical symptoms include visual disturbances, spastic weakness, fatigue, bowel and bladder dysfunction, sexual dysfunction, gait disturbance, and incoordination. Less common symptoms include alterations in cognitive function and affective disorders. The symptomatology is a manifestation of the area of demyelination. For example, if demyelination occurs in the motor pathways, spastic weakness can result, whereas demyelination in frontal and periventricular areas correlates with psychologic disturbances.[68] Mastrostefano *et al*[69] report a case of partial seizures, headache, hemianopsia, apraxia, and aphasia in a woman with a focal parietal lobe mass ultimately diagnosed as MS. This presentation with intracranial symptoms and mass is rare.

Researchers have proposed several theories regarding the pathogenesis of MS. The most common theory suggests an infectious etiology. Although the identity of that agent is unknown, a virus seems the most likely culprit. Some viruses do cause human and animal demyelinating diseases. Presumably, the virus initiates an altered immune response in genetically susceptible individuals and autoimmune destruction of myelin follows. The viruses most often implicated are the measles virus and canine distemper virus.[70]

Evidence for the infectious agent theory seems strongest and best studied. Investigators have found a temporally related higher incidence of MS in previously low prevalence areas upon mass entry of people from high-prevalence areas, such as in times of war.[71] Also, increased blood and cerebrospinal fluid (CSF) titers of measles antibodies have been found in patients with MS when compared to controls; however, because antibody concentrations are low, the data are difficult to interpret. Furthermore, in two high-prevalence areas, there is no such measles antibody association.

Several factors relate MS and canine distemper virus. Canine distemper encephalitis, like MS, is a demyelinating disease.[72] Dogs with canine distemper encephalitis, as do patients with MS, have increased CSF gammaglobulin levels.[73] However, whereas dogs are common almost everywhere, MS is not, and even though vaccinations have caused a decline in canine distemper encephalitis, the incidence of MS has remained the same.

The remaining theories are more controversial and less well studied. A high-fat diet may be a risk factor for the development of MS.[74] The pathogenetic mechanism may relate in some way to the predominantly lipid composition of the myelin sheath. Geographic areas such as Norway and Switzerland and affluent urban areas with diets especially high in animal fat have higher rates of MS. In areas where dietary fats have become scarce, such as war-occupied countries, MS rates decline. People who migrate from areas of low-fat diets to ones of high-fat diets have higher rates of disease. However, certain populations with a low incidence of MS and high-fat diets contradict this theory.

Some researchers feel that trauma, especially of the head or spinal column, may also relate to the development of MS. Trauma alters the blood–brain barrier and

Table 3–8

Summary of Myesthenia Gravis in Pregnancy

Autoimmune	85% acetylcholine-receptor
	15% non–acetylcholine-receptor autoantibodies
Onset	Third decade
Epidemiology	Women two times the frequency of men
Characteristics	Exacerbations and remissions of muscle fatigue
Associated Diseases	Cardiomegaly
	Other autoimmune diseases
Precipitators	Stress
	Infection
	Electrolyte imbalance
	Neuromuscular blocking agents
Interaction with Pregnancy	Unpredictable
	Early second-stage fatigue
Interaction with Neonate	Transient MG syndrome
Diagnosis	Administer edrophonium until weakness improves
Treatment	Anticholinesterase
	Thymectomy
	Plasmapheresis
Cholinergic Crisis	
Symptoms	Weakness
	Diarrhea
	Excessive salivation
Treatment	Anticholinergics (atropine)

may lead to plaque formation in vulnerable individuals.[75] Other researchers find no evidence that trauma is a causative factor in MS.

Industrial workers exposed to zinc have an elevated incidence of MS.[76] This correlation suggests that exposure to heavy metals or other toxins may be a risk factor. One proposed mechanism is that a zinc imbalance causes an immunoregulatory defect. If this were the case, these same workers also should exhibit greater numbers of immunologically related diseases, but they do not.

Finally, Elias[77] hypothesizes that environmental exposure to an unknown agent in genetically predisposed individuals damages oligodendrocyte precursor cells. This damage prevents production of sufficient numbers of oligodendrocytes to maintain myelin.

Diagnosis

Diagnose MS by excluding other neurologic diseases with clinical findings and supporting laboratory data. In addition to exhibiting neurologic symptoms, the patient also may have evidence of demyelination with slowed nerve conduction on evoked potential testing. Computed tomography (CT) may reveal plaques

that are areas of demyelination. The majority of patients will have elevated CSF levels of immunoglobulin G (IgG) with mononuclear pleocytosis. This finding is not specific, however, and may occur with inflammatory or connective tissue diseases of the brain. Finally, elevated CSF levels of myelin basic protein signify myelin destruction.

Treatment

There is no known cure for MS. Treatment is supportive and aims to decrease the number and duration of exacerbations, decrease disability, and limit the progression of chronic disease. Because MS may involve immunologically mediated destruction of myelin, medical management of acute exacerbations centers around immunosuppressive therapy. The most commonly utilized agents are adrenocorticotropic hormone (ACTH) and corticosteroids. Adrenocorticotropic hormone stimulates the adrenal cortex to secrete cortisol, corticosteroid, and aldosterone. Adrenocorticotropic hormone decreases the duration of acute exacerbations but seems to have no long-term benefit.[78] Corticosteroids produce similar results more rapidly than ACTH. Both drugs decrease synthesis of CSF

IgG.[79] Adverse consequences of chronic steroid administration or adrenal stimulation include fluid and electrolyte disturbances, catabolism, hypertension, susceptibility to infection, poor wound healing, diabetes, peptic ulcer disease, hemorrhage, and secondary adrenocortical unresponsiveness.

Treatment of chronic progressive MS is controversial. Proposed therapies and therapies under investigation include azothioprine, cyclophosphamide, plasmapheresis, intrathecal interferon-β, total lymphoid irradiation, cyclosporin A, and monoclonal antibodies.

Interaction with Pregnancy

Women with MS are justly concerned about the consequences of MS for themselves and their babies. Multiple sclerosis does not seem to adversely affect the course of pregnancy[80] or the outcome of the fetus. There are no specific reports of MS-induced complications or malformations. Multiple sclerosis–related symptoms such as fatigue, weakness, and incoordination may influence pregnancy. These women may tire more readily during labor and may have weaker, less effective expulsive efforts. The choice of drugs used to treat MS may also affect pregnancy. Corticosteroids have proved safe for treating MS in pregnancy. Chronic steroid administration, on the other hand, may cause adverse affects such as hypertension, fluid and electrolyte imbalance, catabolism and muscle wasting, anemia from gastrointestinal bleeding, poor wound healing, and susceptibility to infection. Adrenocorticotropic hormone use in pregnancy has not undergone controlled testing and is embryocidal.[81] As with all drugs in pregnancy, use ACTH only if the potential benefits outweigh the risks. Do not use azothioprine, cyclophosphamide, and the agents under investigation because of the known or potential risk of teratogenesis. Khatri et al[82] report the successful use of plasmapheresis in a pregnant woman with severely progressive MS. They preferred plasmapheresis because of the potential teratogenicity of immunosuppressive therapy. The mother experienced rapid reversal of her neurologic decline and delivered a healthy term infant.

Unlike MG, there is no neonatal MS syndrome. Infants born to women with MS, as do other first-degree relatives, have an increased incidence of MS. This implies that even though the disease is not hereditary, there may be a genetic susceptibility.

Women with MS do not frequently experience neurologic deterioration during pregnancy. The normal, pregnancy-related hormonal changes such as elevated plasma cortisol may explain this phenomenon. The rate of exacerbation during the first 9 postpartum months, however, is up to 10 times the relapse rate during pregnancy. Many women deteriorate in the first 3 months after delivery.[79] This relapse rate may be related to the withdrawal of pregnancy-related hormones. Total numbers of pregnancies, exacerbation of MS in relation to pregnancy, and temporal relationship of the onset of MS to pregnancy do not influence long-term disability. Epidural or spinal anesthesia during parturition may correlate with exacerbation of MS. No study has fully elucidated the role of regional anesthesia in relapse, but a review of medical records supports this suggestion.[83] Table 3-9 provides a quick reference for MS.

Preoperative Evaluation

The anesthetic preoperative evaluation of patients with MS is similar to that for patients with myasthenia gravis. Assess the patient for degree of neuromuscular weakness and respiratory compromise. Obtain a history of concurrent major illness and current drug therapy. In those patients treated with chronic steroids, baseline blood chemistry data may be helpful in determining abnormalities. Perform a baseline neurologic examination to aid in assessing any later exacerbation.

Neurofibromatosis

Neurofibromatosis is a chronically progressive, autosomal dominant disorder of the supportive tissues of the nervous system. It occurs in approximately 1 in 3000 births and has diverse clinical expression. Classically, patients exhibit cutaneous pigmentary changes (*e.g.*, café au lait spots or axillary freckling) that are diagnostic. Neurofibromas are tumors that arise from the Schwann cell sheaths and fibroblasts of peripheral, cranial, or autonomic nerves. The tumors can be small, discrete masses or can be extensive. They usually involve the skin but can also occur in deeper nerves, blood vessels, or organs. Although usually a benign, cosmetic concern, they can undergo sarcomatous degeneration and cause major neurologic or obstructive symptoms. They can also be associated with physiologic derangement. Airway compromise can occur with neurofibromas of the oropharynx, larynx, or mediastinum. Neurofibromas are often very vascular and can cause severe hemorrhage. Some patients have intracranial or spinal cord tumors and may develop intracranial hypertension, neurologic compromise, or seizures according to the region of involvement. Cranial nerve involvement may lead to altered gag or swallowing reflexes. Disorders of bone growth are com-

Table 3-9

Summary of Multiple Sclerosis and Pregnancy

Pathology	Central nervous system demyelination
	Genetic predisposition (HLA-DW$_2$)
Onset	20–40 y
	Women affected two times more than men
Geographic distribution	Temperate zones
Pathogenic theories	Infectious agent (measles, canine distemper virus)
	High-fat diet
	Trauma
	Heavy metal exposure
	Oligodendrocyte precursor damage
Interaction with Pregnancy	Nonspecific, related to MS symptoms
	Higher risk of relapse postpartum
Interaction with Neonate	No immediate interaction
Diagnosis	Evoked potentials: slow nerve conduction
	Computed tomography evidence of plaques
	Increased CSF IgG
	Increased CSF myelin basic protein

mon. Cervical spine involvement is a major concern during positioning for laryngoscopy or surgery. Lumbar or thoracic spine involvement may make regional anesthesia impossible. Other organ involvement and associated diseases can include pulmonary parenchymal fibrosis leading to pulmonary hypertension, pheochromocytoma, hyperthyroidism, Wilm's tumor, neuroblastoma, and congenital heart lesions, especially pulmonary stenosis.

Treatment

The treatment of neurofibromatosis involves symptomatic drug therapy (*e.g.,* anticonvulsants for seizures) and surgical removal of selected neurofibromas. Reserve surgery for those tumors that are particularly disfiguring or associated with obstructive symptoms or neurologic compromise. Correlation or amelioration of associated symptoms such as orthopedic deformity, endocrine dysfunction, or cancer may also require surgery.

Interaction with Pregnancy

During pregnancy, neurofibromas often enlarge, creating the potential for hemorrhage, increased obstruction, and neurologic compromise. Laryngeal or pharyngeal tumors may obstruct the airway. Intracranial or spinal tumors may enlarge and create a mass effect or obstruct the flow of CSF. Pelvic neurofibromas may preclude vaginal delivery or create pressure symptoms. Pregnant women with neuro-

fibromatosis also can be hypertensive, probably due to renal artery stenosis from vascular changes associated with the disease.[84] Finally, patients may exhibit an altered response to muscle relaxants, resulting in prolonged paralysis with nondepolarizing neuromuscular blocking agents. The response to succinylcholine may be either exaggerated or diminished. Generalized neurofibromatosis may induce motor end-plate denervation. However, little evidence supports this hypothesis.[85,86]

Because neurofibromatosis is an autosomal dominant disorder, infants born to mothers with the disease have a 50% chance of developing the disease. Many of the signs and symptoms of this progressive disorder are absent at birth. Axillary freckling or the presence of five or more café au lait spots larger than 0.5 cm in diameter is diagnostic.

Preoperative Evaluation

The anesthetic preoperative evaluation of the pregnant patient with neurofibromatosis must include a careful history to alert the anesthesiologist to problematic manifestations of the disease. A history of strictly cutaneous disease is not alarming, whereas a history of voice changes, symptoms of increased intracranial pressure, or neurologic changes should cause concern. A history of significant cardiopulmonary disease, endocrine dysfunction, and orthopedic malformation is important. Assess the airway carefully for possible obstruction and cervical spine involvement.

Finally, as with all patients with neurologic disease, perform a baseline neurologic examination.

Paraplegia and Quadriplegia

Improved treatment of spinal cord injury victims has allowed more reproductive-aged women with these injuries to survive to bear children. Trauma, infection, tumors, and vascular lesions are the most common causes of spinal cord injury or transection. Paraplegia is paralysis of the lower extremities and quadriplegia is paralysis of all four extremities. The initial phase of an acute spinal cord transection is known as spinal shock. Characteristics of this period include flaccid paralysis and loss of sensation, temperature regulation, and spinal reflexes below the level of the lesion. Characteristically, patients experience hypotension, bradycardia, cardiac dysrhythmias (especially premature ventricular contractions), and electrocardiographic changes consistent with ischemia.[87] These symptoms usually resolve within 3 weeks. Women often have amenorrhea for 2 to 3 months following injury.

A lesion between C-2 and C-4 causing diaphragmatic denervation may require immediate and permanent ventilatory support. With lower lesions and intact diaphragmatic innervation, the patient can probably generate adequate tidal volumes but may not be able to cough and clear her airway. The mechanism behind this impairment is probably twofold. The first reason may be that paralysis of abdominal musculature does not allow the patient to generate the force required to cough. The second possibility is that abdominal muscle paralysis allows the intra-abdominal contents to shift, thus displacing the diaphragm. The result is altered lung volumes, particularly a decreased functional residual capacity and decreased expiratory reserve volume—the volume used to generate a cough. Another possible result of altered lung volumes is ventilation–perfusion mismatching, resulting in hypoxemia. Because of these overall respiratory changes, pulmonary aspiration and pneumonia are common.

Following the initial phase of injury, patients enter the chronic stage. During this stage, spinal cord reflexes gradually return and the patient experiences muscle spasm and sympathetic nervous system hyperactivity. Other findings associated with chronic spinal cord injury include chronic pulmonary and urinary tract infections, anemia, thermoregulatory dysfunction, and cardiovascular instability.

Respiratory changes during the chronic stage of spinal cord injury are not greatly different from those in the acute phase. Patients with high cervical transections and diaphragmatic paralysis will continue to require ventilatory support. Paralysis that spares the diaphragm, but affects the accessory respiratory muscles, may decrease ventilatory reserve and lead to alveolar hypoventilation. Impairment of the ability to cough and clear the airway along with atelectatis from hypoventilation makes these patients prone to chronic pulmonary infection.

Renal failure resulting from chronic urinary tract infection or renal calculi is a major cause of morbidity and mortality in patients with chronic spinal cord injuries. Spinal cord transection often disrupts the motor innervation of the bladder and ureters, causing urinary stasis, chronic bladder infection, and pyelonephritis. Also, chronic instrumentation for bladder elimination increases the risk of infection. Good perineal hygiene, routine bladder emptying, and chronic suppression therapy can lessen the risk of infection.

Spinal cord–injured patients often have anemia. Some of the most commonly proposed causes for this anemia are iron deficiency and renal failure from chronic infection, obstruction, or renal calculi. This anemia may also be an anemia of chronic disease from chronic infection, skin ulcer, or renal failure.

Sympathetic nervous system hyperactivity can result in cardiovascular instability following the return of spinal cord reflexes after spinal shock. This syndrome, known as autonomic hyperreflexia,[88] results from the dissociation of sympathetic spinal reflexes (below the level of the transection) from mechanisms controlling the central nervous system. Visceral or cutaneous stimulation, most commonly by distention of a hollow viscus such as the bowel, bladder, or uterus, initiates the reflex. In neurologically intact individuals, visceral stimulation sends afferent signals that enter the spinal cord and elicit a sympathetic nervous system response. Central nervous system centers normally regulate this response; however, spinal cord injury disrupts the descent of regulatory impulses, resulting in sympathetic hyperactivity. The level of the spinal cord lesion determines the incidence of autonomic hyperreflexia. Nearly all patients (85%) with transections above T-6 will experience the syndrome, whereas it is unlikely to occur in those with lesions below T-10. The most common manifestations are severe paroxysmal hypertension, tachycardia, bradycardia, headache, facial flushing, diaphoresis, piloerection, pupillary dilation, and nasal congestion.

Hyperreflexia requires immediate attention because severely elevated blood pressure can incite seizures and unconsciousness as well as retinal, cerebral, and subarachnoid hemorrhages.[89] The treatment of autonomic hyperreflexia involves rapid measures to control the blood pressure. Removal of the initiating stimulus is important (*e.g.*, empty a full bladder). Initiate pharmacologic therapy with peripheral vasodilators such as ganglionic blocking drugs, alpha-adrenergic agonists, direct vasodilators, or general or regional anesthesia. Because of the disruption of regulatory pathways, centrally acting agents are ineffective. Table 3-10 summarizes the consequences of spinal cord injury.

Spinal cord injury has several consequences for the pregnant patient. Women who suffer spinal cord injuries during pregnancy have a greater risk of stillbirth.[90] The level of the injury will determine the patient's response to labor pain. Women with lesions below T-11–L-1 will feel labor pain. Those with lesions from T-10 to T-5–6 will not have pain but can palpate contractions. Those with lesions above T-5–6 are at high risk for autonomic hyperreflexia. Because women in these last two groups may find labor painless, premature, unsupervised delivery may occur. Labor also tends to progress rapidly.[91] Additional problems related to pregnancy include possible respiratory embarrassment caused by the distended uterus, profound anemia, and urinary obstruction with increased incidence of distention, infection, and autonomic hyperreflexia.

The anesthetic preoperative evaluation of pregnant patients with spinal cord injuries focuses on the respiratory status of the patient. The level of the lesion will provide a clue to the likelihood of the need for ventilatory support. Other important points include assessing the patient's ability to clear her airway and considering the degree of respiratory compromise due to the gravid uterus. In any event, be prepared to lend ventilatory assistance. Knowing the level of transection will also alert the anesthesiologist to the possibility of autonomic hyperreflexia. Laboratory data can help detect severe anemia or pulmonary or urinary tract infection.

Central Nervous System Neoplasms

Central nervous system (CNS) neoplasms are uncommon in reproductive-aged women. Roelvink *et al*[92] reviewed 223 cases of primary brain and spinal cord tumors that became symptomatic during or immediately after pregnancy. The incidence of brain tumors that become symptomatic during pregnancy may be less than the incidence in nonpregnant women of the same age. This lowered risk may represent an artifact. Women with subclinical cancer may have more unnoticed, spontaneous early pregnancy losses.[93] Although CNS neoplasms are not more common in pregnancy, pregnancy can precipitate or aggravate the symptoms of

Table 3-10

Consequences of Spinal Cord Injury

ACUTE	CHRONIC
Neural	**Neural**
Flaccid paralysis	Muscle spasm
Loss of sensation, temperature regulation, and spinal reflexes	Altered thermoregulation
	Return of spinal reflexes
Cardiovascular	
Hypotension	**Cardiovascular**
Bradycardia	Autonomic hyperreflexia with lesions above T_6
Dysrhythmia	
ECG changes	**Respiratory**
	C_2–C_4 lesions require ventilatory support
Respiratory	Lower lesions alter lung volumes and may impair the ability to protect the airway
C-2–C-4 lesions require ventilatory support	
Lower lesions alter lung volumes and may impair the ability to protect the airway	**Renal**
	Failure from infection or calculi
Other	
Amenorrhea for 3 mo	**Other**
	Anemia

these lesions. The mechanism is unclear, but it is probably related to tumor enlargement due to water retention or increased vascularity.[94] Tumors may be either metastatic or primary. Metastatic tumors of particular importance to women in this age group are those from breast and lung cancer and from choriocarcinoma. Except for metastatic choriocarcinoma, there is no difference in the distribution of brain tumors whose symptoms first occur in pregnant women and in nonpregnant women in the same age group. Previous authors have suggested that meningiomas are particularly predisposed to manifest symptoms during pregnancy;[61,93,95] however, other evidence does not support this theory.[92]

Of spinal cord tumors, spinal hemangiomas seem to occur more frequently in the pregnant population. Certain tumors seem to manifest symptoms at different times during gestation. For example, spinal hemangiomas generally present in the third trimester, gliomas in the first trimester, and meningiomas progressively throughout pregnancy. Progesterone is positively apparently correlated to tumor symptoms. The role of progesterone in the etiology of CNS tumors is unknown.[91]

The diagnosis of CNS tumors in pregnant patients does not differ from their diagnosis in nonpregnant patients. Signs and symptoms suggestive of a CNS space-occupying lesion form the basis for diagnosis. Use CT and magnetic resonance imaging without hesitation.

Tumor-related symptoms may be difficult to distinguish from some pregnancy-related complaints. Typical symptoms of CNS tumors include nausea and vomiting, headache, visual changes, altered mental status, and convulsions. Other findings may include sensory or motor deficits. These symptoms can arise because of the anatomic location of the tumor, because they obstruct the flow of CSF, or because they produce an intracranial mass-effect with resultant intracranial hypertension.

Pregnancy should not alter or delay treatment of these tumors. Radiation treatment and chemotherapy (except for possible teratogens and surgery) should be used as indicated. If the mother's neurologic examination is stable and she shows no evidence of increased intracranial pressure, delay treatment until after delivery. A deteriorating status due to severe, uncontrolled intracranial hypertension signals the need for immediate therapy, with pregnancy termination and surgery as necessary. Some measures that may be necessary include the following:

- Intubation and hyperventilation
- Corticosteroids to reduce cerebral edema caused by the tumor

- Drainage of CSF via ventricular shunting or ventriculostomy
- The administration of barbiturates

If possible, avoid hyperosmotic drugs such as mannitol, which may shift water from the fetus to the mother.[96]

The anesthetic preoperative evaluation of the pregnant patient with known or suspected CNS lesions should focus on determining the patient's level of consciousness and assessing her ability to maintain and protect her airway. Also look for intracranial hypertension and initiate therapy as appropriate. To immediately appreciate changes in neurologic status, frequent neurologic examinations are essential.

Cerebrovascular Disease

Cerebrovascular disorders are uncommon in reproductive-aged women. But, when they do occur during pregnancy, they are a leading cause of maternal mortality.[97] Because these disorders are unusual in this age group, it is easy to attribute their symptoms to more common diseases such as eclampsia or seizure disorders. As a consequence, crucial delays in therapy may result. The cerebrovascular diseases most commonly seen in pregnancy include intracerebral hemorrhage and subarachnoid hemorrhage.

The etiologies of intracerebral hemorrhage include hypertension, eclampsia, and metastatic choriocarcinoma. Unless associated with a complication of gestation, pregnancy does not alter the incidence of intracerebral hemorrhage. Hemorrhage is rare except when due to eclampsia or preeclampsia. The presumed causes of bleeding in these instances are hypertension and vascular changes associated with preeclampsia. A review of 533 deaths due to eclampsia and preeclampsia found that cerebral dysfunction caused 180. Almost half of these had gross evidence of intracerebral hemorrhage.[98] Symptoms include headache, convulsions, changes in mental status, and focal neurologic findings depending on the location of the bleed.

Subarachnoid hemorrhage complicates fewer than 1 in 10,000 pregnancies.[99] The etiologies include cerebral aneurysm, ateriovenous malformation, metastatic choriocarcinoma, eclampsia, and disseminated intravascular coagulation. Aneurysm and arteriovenous malformation are the first and second most common causes, respectively.

Gravidas with aneurysms tend to be older (30 y–35 y) than those with arteriovenous malformations

(20 y–25 y). Aneurysms have a progressively increasing risk of rupture during the pregnancy, with the highest risk between 30 and 40 weeks of estimated gestational age. They rarely rupture during labor. By contrast, arteriovenous malformations may rupture at any time during pregnancy or labor or after delivery. Ruptured aneurysms are generally more fatal than ruptured arteriovenous malformations.[100,101]

Symptoms of subarachnoid hemorrhage include severe headache, nausea, vomiting, altered mental status, nuchal rigidity, and focal neurologic deficit. Distinguishing a ruptured aneurysm from a ruptured arteriovenous malformation by neurologic examination is difficult and may require specific testing such as CT and cerebral angiography. The anesthetic preoperative evaluation of the pregnant patient with cerebrovascular disorders is similar to that for a patient with CNS neoplasms.

HUMAN IMMUNODEFICIENCY VIRUS INFECTION

Epidemiology

Acquired immunodeficiency syndrome (AIDS) is a currently incurable disease complex that results from infection with the human immunodeficiency virus (HIV). There are at least 82,000 reported cases of AIDS and at least 1.5 million HIV-seropositive people in the United States.[102] The incidence among women has risen to approximately 10% of all HIV-positive persons.[103] This rise in risk shows no sign of slowing. In the United States, in areas with high prevalence, male-to-female HIV seropositive ratios approach 1:1.[104] Eighty percent of reported cases of AIDS in adult women occur among women of reproductive age.[105] A majority of these cases, 53% in one survey, occur in intravenous drug abusers, with another 27% resulting from heterosexual transmission.[106] Several studies of HIV seroprevalence in pregnant women re-

veal as many as 8 to 20/1000.[107,108] Although several prospective studies of HIV-infected pregnant women are under way, the interaction of pregnancy and HIV currently remains unclear. Based upon future projections of rising incidence of AIDS in women, the number of AIDS-related complications and deaths during pregnancy, now relatively low, will rise and become a significant problem.

Pathophysiology

The clinical AIDS syndrome results from immunosuppression by HIV-1, a large family of retroviruses that use host reverse transcriptase to produce, ultimately, more viral RNA. The virus replicates by binding to a receptor labeled CD4[109] on the cell membranes of T-cell lymphocytes, monocytes, macrophages, a small number of B-cell lymphocytes, glial cells, gut chromaffin cells, lymph nodes, skin, and rectal mucosal cells.[110] Once inside the cell, the viral RNA is converted to DNA, which either integrates into the DNA of the host cell (proviral DNA) or remains unintegrated. The proviral DNA may lie dormant indefinitely, but the cell is permanently infected and will reduplicate the viral DNA with each cell division. Cell-free virus is found in various body fluids—synovial, cerebrospinal, pleural, peritoneal—but the primary mode of transmission is via cells containing virus.

The HIV is detected either by culture or serology. Culturing the virus yields unreliable results.[111,112] Serologic tests for HIV antibodies prove reproducible, sensitive, and specific (Table 3-11).[113] The ELISA and rapid latex agglutination tests represent more sensitive, less specific tests for identifying HIV infection. The Western blot immunopheresis and cytoplasmic membrane immunofluorescence tests are very specific but more often require repeat testing to identify HIV antibodies.[113]

Identification of the pregnant woman with HIV infection requires a high degree of clinical suspicion.

Table 3-11

Sensitivity and Specificity of HIV Screening Tests

	SENSITIVITY	SPECIFICITY
ELISA	99.3%–100%	98.1%–99.5%
Western blot	97.1%–100%	97.8%–100%

Look for risk factors. Beware of the variable spectrum of disease. A history of intravenous drug abuse, a sexual partner who is either HIV-positive or an intravenous drug abuser, or the history of a blood transfusion since 1978 all are factors that heighten clinical suspicion of HIV seropositivity. Prevalence of this disease in women, as for men, peaks in lower socioeconomic class. Unlike men, in whom 63% of HIV infections are in whites, the racial distribution for women is such that 51% are black, 28% are white, and 20% are hispanic.[114] Initially, AIDS was recognized only in its end stages, when multiple opportunistic infections and unusual cancers occurred. Now, the disease is understood as a progression of various illness dependent upon a multitude of factors, including extent of initial exposure. Based on the correlation between quantity of virus in the blood and severity of illness, Redfield *et al*,[115] at Walter Reed Army Hospital, constructed a six-stage classification system. Stage 0 represents the initial exposure. Stage 6 is overt AIDS. This system also follows the T4 lymphocyte count. Fewer than 400 cells/mL coincides with most of the AIDS-related symptomatology.[116] Still, the progression of HIV-associated illness varies among individual patients. The patient's own immune response to the virus may slow the speed of viral replication. Ultimately, however, the virus multiplies to a degree sufficient to overpower the host immune system. Then T4 count becomes extremely low, and the patient develops frequent infections by opportunistic bacteria, fungi, viruses, and progression of various cancers. An in-depth discussion of AIDS and various organ systems is beyond the scope of this text, but AIDS-associated cardiomyopathy, nephropathy, and dementia may all complicate the course of this disease.

Despite relatively isolated success of therapy with various agents against the opportunistic infections of AIDS, pharmacologic therapy against the actual virus remains limited to azidothymidine (AZT, Retrovir).[117] In blocking the transcription of viral RNA, AZT improves survival, decreases the frequency and severity of opportunistic infections, and improves dementia.[118] Macrocytic anemia and neutropenia are side-effects of AZT therapy. Azidothymidine does not eliminate the macrophage reservoir of virions, thought to function as a store of virus for transmission.[110] The National Institute of Health is investigating several combinations of drugs for a synergistic approach in reducing this store of virus. Because the virus attacks the cells responsible for activating a cell-mediated immune response (T4 lymphocytes), and because there are many variants of the same HIV, production of an effective vaccine remains elusive.

Interaction with Pregnancy

There is no evidence that HIV infection or AIDS affects fertility. Although one of the primary goals in counseling this patient population is prevention of pregnancy, there is no irrefutable evidence that abortion, although frequently recommended, will alter the course of disease in these patients.

Cell-mediated immunity is depressed during pregnancy, especially in the second and third trimesters.[119,120] Some evidence supports the hypothesis that pregnancy accelerates the course of disease in HIV-infected women. Minkoff *et al*[121] and Scott *et al*,[122] in two separate studies, found that 45% to 75% of asymptomatic HIV-infected pregnant women developed symptoms of AIDS within 28 to 60 months of delivery. These studies, however, enrolled only a small number of patients and lacked controls. Other data suggest that pregnancy does not accelerate the occurrence of AIDS among HIV-positive women. Similarly, pregnancy may increase the death rate in women with AIDS. Koonin *et al*[105] examined mean survival from diagnosis of AIDS to death in New York City. They compared a population of pregnant women who were intravenous drug abusers and died of *Pneumocystis carinii* pneumonia to nonpregnant but otherwise identical controls. The parturients had a much shorter survival (59 d vs 187 d). Factors such as delayed diagnosis and access to health care may account for some of this difference. Other studies find no significant difference in survival among pregnant HIV-positive intravenous drug abusers versus their nonpregnant controls.[123,124] These data warrant further investigation to reach a definite conclusion on the true impact of pregnancy on the course of HIV infection.

Confusion also exists about the effect of HIV infection on pregnancy. Despite a much higher incidence of complications, including premature rupture of membranes, low birth weight, and preterm birth, patient populations with risk factors such as low socioeconomic status, drug abuse, poor nutritional status, and poor prenatal care show little difference in maternal risk and outcome between HIV-seropositive and HIV-seronegative mothers.[125] Drug-abusing women in general tend to have an increased incidence of complicated pregnancies (spontaneous abortion, preterm deliveries, and low-birth-weight infants).[126,127] Although the true effect of HIV infection on the course of pregnancy remains unclear, these patients should be approached as high-risk pregnancies.

With the implications on gestation of HIV seropositivity and even AIDS still unclear, the issue of screening for HIV in pregnant women remains in the foreground of debate. The arguments for screening include the following:

- Voluntary testing may miss a large percentage of positive individuals.
- Perinatal transmission of virus may be reduced.
- Health care workers may be better protected.

Those against screening point out the following:

- The high cost of an effective screening program
- The high false-positive rates in low-prevalence populations
- The likelihood of discouraging prenatal care with mandatory HIV screening.[128]

Instead of widespread testing, health care workers should rely on the concept of "universal precautions." Presuming that all patients are infected when handling blood or other body fluids should limit the risk of exposure and transmission of disease from patient to health care worker or vice versa. Testing for HIV should be limited to those patients at high risk for the disease.

The United States Public Health Service estimates that there will be approximately 3000 cases of pediatric AIDS by the end of 1991.[129] In most of these cases, infants will acquire the infection through vertical transmission from their mothers. Knowing that a pregnant woman is HIV-seropositive does not necessarily indicate that her fetus is or will be affected. Testing for HIV in newborns reveals only the presence or absence of maternal antibodies, establishing the presence of the virus in the mother but not the neonate. Current estimates are that 30% of HIV-positive mothers in the United States transmit HIV to their newborn infants.[103] Transmission may occur in utero, as virus has been isolated from an infant born by cesarean section.[130,131] Exposure to maternal blood and body fluids at time of birth is another possible route of HIV transmission. For this reason, scalp electrodes and fetal blood sampling should be avoided in the HIV-positive patient. Cesarean delivery does not appear to exert a protective effect.[131] Finally, HIV is present in breast milk, and there are several cases in which transmission is thought to have occurred during breast-feeding.[132–134]

Prenatal diagnosis of fetal HIV infection is currently not possible. Fetal dysmorphism, with characteristic findings that include "growth failure," microcephaly, oblique eyes, and a flattened forehead, appear to correlate in severity with age of the child at diagnosis of AIDS.[135] There is a great deal of overlap with other fetal dysmorphic syndromes attributable to other viruses or maternal substance abuse.

There is no association between risk of transmission and trimester during which exposure occurred. Absence of maternal symptoms does not appear protective,[136] although, following the birth of an affected child, an infected mother may give birth to an unaffected child.[137,138] The efficiency of sexual transmission varies in different risk groups. Similar stratification may exist with transmission of the virus to offspring.

SUBSTANCE ABUSE

Drug use constitutes a major public health problem in the United States today. Women of child-bearing age constitute a large portion of this population. Nicotine, alcohol, marijuana, and cocaine remain the most commonly abused substances. As many as 20% of pregnant women in the United States smoke cigarettes,[139] 12% abuse alcohol,[140] and 11% to 20% report regular use of cocaine or crack.[141] The proportion of birth certificates indicating use of illicit substances rose threefold between 1981 and 1987. Such evidence suggests a significant increase in this decade in maternal drug use during pregnancy.[142]

Drug use in various settings reflects factors varying from availability to social acceptance.[143] The maternal drug abuser stereotypically progresses from cigarettes to alcohol to marijuana and then on to cocaine and intravenous drugs.[144] With the rising prevalence of substance abuse, the anesthesiologist must understand and anticipate its various effects and consequences.

The physiologic changes of pregnancy alter pharmacokinetic and pharmacodynamic behavior and then amplify cardiovascular and respiratory depressant effects of many addictive drugs.[145] The placenta is similar to the liver in its ability to metabolize drugs, but environmental factors determine the quality and quantity of enzymes present. Drug abuse may decrease the number of placental neurotransmitter receptors and generate abnormal fetal and neonatal behavioral development.[146] Any substance that affects the vascular tone of the placenta may alter placental blood flow and ultimately result in placental infarction and fetal compromise.

Substances ingested, inhaled, or injected by the mother may cross the placenta and directly affect the fetus by one of several mechanisms. The drug or a metabolite may have direct fetal effects. Alternately, drugs can induce hepatic enzymes and affect development via altered synthetic and degradation pathways.[147] The risk of transmissible disease, as previously discussed in this chapter, is greatest for the fetus of a maternal substance abuser. The maternal malnutrition that so often accompanies substance abuse manifests not only as an increased incidence of neural tube defects but also in a host of peripartum complications.[148]

The course of gestation for substance abusers often depends upon their ability and willingness to participate in counseling and detoxification programs. Up to 25% of substance abusers who seek prenatal care deny drug use. Even so, a widely focused approach seems the best way to address the multiple problems of the pregnant substance abuser. Such a program might include the following:

- Counseling
- Detoxification and substitution therapy
- Education about nutrition, drug effects, maternal care, and HIV prophylaxis
- Screening for hepatitis, HIV, tuberculosis, and vaginal/cervical infections
- Evaluation of fetal growth with ultrasound, nonstress test, biophysical profile, and phosphatidyl glycerol.[149]

Central Nervous System

Ethanol

Ethanol, a CNS depressant, may induce behavioral stimulation by depressing inhibitory control mechanisms and allowing unrestrained activity of various parts of the brain. As intoxication advances, this initial excitatory phase is succeeded by a general impairment of nervous function. A condition of general anesthesia ultimately prevails. The effects of alcohol in the CNS are proportional to the concentration of alcohol in the blood. They are most marked in the face of a rising alcohol concentration.[150] The rate-limiting step in alcohol metabolism is the conversion of ethanol to acetaldehyde by alcohol dehydrogenase. This enzyme has variable activity. Multiple isoenzymes coded for by five genes exist.[151] Variable expression of these genes occurs between races and individuals.[152] Alcohol exhibits cross tolerance with most CNS depressant drugs. Acute intoxication increases the effects of cross-tolerant drugs. Chronic ingestion of alcohol decreases other drug effects. Tolerance on a metabolic basis does not alter the lethal blood concentration of alcohol.[153]

Acquired tolerance to and physical dependence on ethanol results from neurophysiologic changes that compensate for the depressant effect of alcohol on neuronal excitability, impulse conduction, and transmitter release. Abrupt cessation of alcohol ingestion incites hyperactivity of all sensory modalities: hyperreflexia, muscle tension and tremor, overalertness, anxiety, insomnia, and reduction of seizure threshold, once commonly known as the withdrawal syndrome.[154] Symptoms range from mild to severe and can appear as early as several hours after the last drink but more typically occur after 48 hours of abstinence. Delirium tremens is a medical emergency characterized by extreme autonomic hyperactivity and global confusion. If left untreated, it has a mortality rate greater than 40%. In contrast to opiate withdrawal, which responds immediately to administration of an opiate and is rarely fatal, delirium tremens, once established, cannot be rapidly reversed with alcohol.[155] Sedative therapy in withdrawal syndrome and delirium tremens involves replacement of alcohol with a cross-tolerant drug and calming of the anxious, hallucinating, or delirious patient. It is not currently known which sedative best achieves these goals. In the pregnant patient suffering withdrawal symptoms, pharmacologic substitution therapy is necessary despite the risk of further fetal drug exposure. Phenobarbital and clonidine are preferred. The teratogenicity of benzodiazepenes and the acidosis associated with paraldehyde have made these drugs less likely choices.[156]

The systemic effects of chronic alcohol abuse are well known and involve multiple organ systems. In addition to CNS symptoms, chronic myelopathy, polyneuropathy, and myopathy may be present. These problems can complicate anesthetic management of labor and delivery or cesarean section by altering recovery from muscle relaxants and regional or general anesthesia.

Acute cardiovascular effects of ethanol include myocardial depression and altered electrophysiology, leading to atrial and ventricular dysrhythmias. Chronic consumption results in cardiomyopathy and progressive myocardial dysfunction.[157] The increased cardiac demand of pregnancy may result in cardiac failure in the pregnant alcohol abuser with significant myocardial disease. Anesthetics that depress cardiac function may accelerate this process.

Respiratory complications are common among chronic alcohol abusers. These range from mild ventilation–perfusion mismatch and intrapulmonary shunting to chronic infection and aspiration pneumonia. Alcohol further compounds the already higher risk of aspiration in the term parturient because ethanol decreases gastric motility and lowers esophageal sphincter tone.

Liver disease is common after ethanol abuse. Fatty infiltration, cirrhosis, portal hypertension, and hepatic encephalopathy can occur. In addition, hepatocellular damage can yield hypoglycemia from impaired gluconeogenesis and induced glycogenolysis. Decreased drug metabolism and protein and coagulation factor synthesis may alter the anesthetic approach to the pregnant patient with alcoholic liver disease, either at term or upon earlier presentation.

Gastritis, esophagitis, bleeding varices, and pancreatitis are gastrointestinal manifestations of alcohol abuse and contribute to an increased risk of aspiration pneumonia either before, during, or after anesthesia. The stress response is altered. Cortisol, prolactin, epinephrine, norepinephrine, renin, angiotensin, and aldosterone rise while growth hormone decreases.[158] Electrolyte abnormalities such as hyponatremia, hypokalemia, and hypomagnesemia may require correction. Correct hyponatremia slowly to avoid overcorrection and central pontine myelinolysis.

Ethanol does not affect umbilical arterial tone, confirming the absence of a direct effect of alcohol on placental blood flow.[159] Alcohol consumption, however, blocks the placental transport of alpha-aminobutyric acid, implying that ethanol also inhibits transfer of other nutrients across the placenta.[160]

Alcohol works through several different mechanisms to cause fetal and subsequent neonatal morbidity. Fibrosis, cardiomyopathy, gastritis, and pancreatitis result in the mother. Alcohol increases the conversion of dihomogammalinolenic acid (DGLA) to prostaglandin E_1 (PGE$_1$) In addition, ethanol inhibits delta-6-desaturase, an enzyme essential for a continued supply of DGLA. As a result, these fetuses have low concentrations of PGE$_1$.[161] This deficiency may account for many of the changes noted with the fetal alcohol syndrome. This syndrome consists of growth deficiency, major and minor birth defects, abnormal mental and motor performance, and fetal or neonatal wastage, which are well-documented effects of alcohol abuse during pregnancy.[161]

Maternal alcoholism is not the only cause of fetal and neonatal morbidity from ethanol. Paternal exposure to ethanol also breeds fetal growth retardation and decreased DNA, RNA, and leucine synthesis.[162] Maternal consumption, however, relates to fetal and neonatal morbidity in a dose-dependent and temporal fashion. More than 90 g of alcohol per day produces developmental defects with first-trimester exposure. Exposure during the third trimester produces growth retardation and a delayed rise in the lecithin/sphingomyelin (L/S) ratio.[163]

Barbiturates

The barbiturates have both presynaptic and postsynaptic effects on the neurotransmitter gamma-aminobutyric acid (GABA) and its receptors. They reversibly depress the activity of all excitable tissues. The CNS is most sensitive. All degrees of depression of the CNS, from mild sedation to general anesthesia, are achievable with various doses of barbiturate. Mono- and polysynaptic responses are depressed by barbiturates. Only very large doses or doses of extended duration have clinically detectable direct effects on peripheral tissues. Pharmacodynamic and pharmacokinetic tolerance can occur, with the former more responsible for the decreased effect with repetitive dosing. Despite tolerance to mood-altering and other systemic effects, the lethal dose remains the same; thus, with continued use, the therapeutic index falls and the risk of lethal overdose rises. Barbiturates exhibit cross tolerance with ethanol. An abstinence syndrome similar to that occurring with ethanol can develop. The severity of withdrawal relates to the degree of tolerance and, therefore, the extent, duration, and continuity of abuse. Symptomatology is very similar to the alcohol abstinence syndrome, with a range of manifestations from tremors, insomnia, and irritability to seizures, delirium, and hallucinations. Convulsions are an ominous occurrence in barbiturate withdrawal. Administration of barbiturates does not acutely reverse this syndrome.

Compromise of uteroplacental blood flow may occur during maternal intoxication or withdrawal. Behavioral and morphologic features of the fetal alcohol syndrome also appear in children of barbiturate abusers, but there is no specific fetal defect attributable to barbiturates.[164] The induction of fetal hepatic enzymes tends to decrease neonatal bilirubin levels. Newborns of barbiturate abusers or even therapeutic users (*i.e.,* epileptics) may be dependent on barbiturates. Depending on the half-life of the barbiturate and the length of maternal use, withdrawal symptoms may arise up to a week after birth.

Benzodiazepenes

Benzodiazepenes also exert their CNS effects via the GABA receptor, although they are not general neuronal depressants like the barbiturates and ethanol. There are wide differences in selectivity among this group of drugs with varying clinical usefulness, but there is cross tolerance between benzodiazepenes and ethanol or barbiturates. Similarly, withdrawal syndromes do occur and are best managed with additional benzodiazepenes, as these drugs tend to lack cardiovascular or respiratory depressant effects when administered as single agents. Although physostigmine or naloxone partially antagonize the CNS effects of benzodiazepenes, flumazenil, a specific benzodiazepene antagonist, is currently under clinical trial.[165] Several studies attest to the teratogenicity of benzodiazepenes;[166,167] however, more recent studies contradict these data.[168] In the neonate, benzodiazepenes alter thermoregulation, resulting in hypothermia.

Cocaine

Cocaine alkaloid, an ester of benzoic acid, undergoes hydrolysis to become ecgonine, which is in turn benzoylated and methylated to the base cocaine.[169] The hydrochloride salt of this base is the commercial product that, when mixed with an alkali, produces cocaine freebase, or "crack." This illicit preparation is more stable on heating, vaporizes easily, and has a high bioavailability when smoked.[170] The bioavailability of topical intranasal cocaine is four to six times less than an equivalent intravenous dose, with peak plasma concentration proportional to the total dose administered.[171] Time to peak concentration, however, lengthens with increasing doses, as cocaine may limit its own absorption via potent vasoconstriction.[172]

The biologic half-life of cocaine is 0.5 to 1.5 hours. Metabolism occurs via plasma and liver esterases, with liver hydrolysis producing the only active metabolite, norcocaine.[173,174] Norcocaine has been detected in primate brain, where it inhibits the reuptake of norepinephrine more than cocaine.[175] Plasma from homozygotes for atypical cholinesterase have impaired in vitro decay of cocaine.[176] Acquired deficiencies of the enzyme (liver disease, malnutrition, plasmapheresis, anticholinesterase medications, and pregnancy) also result in impaired plasma hydrolysis.

Changes in cocaine metabolism, alterations in central or peripheral adrenergic receptor sensitivity to norepinephrine, or differences in cocaine-induced cardiac responsiveness, may individually or collectively account for the heightened sensitivity to cocaine seen in the pregnant ewe.[177] Liver cytochrome P_{450} concentrations fall by as much as 25%, and activity of glucuronyl transferase and monoxygenase declines in pregnant rats and rabbits in comparison with nonpregnant animals.[178,179] Progesterone treatment of nonpregnant rats increases N-demethylation of aminopyrine. This compound has almost identical kinetics as N-demethylation of cocaine to norcocaine.[180] Yet another recent study shows that high concentrations of progesterone in pregnant ewes can delay metabolism of cocaine or in-

crease its bioactivity. Progesterone may either increase N-demethylation to norcocaine or enhance alpha-adrenergic receptor sensitivity.[177] The fetus and newborn are also prone to altered metabolism and impaired clearance of cocaine and its metabolites. Esterase metabolites persist as long as 4 to 5 days in the neonate following maternal cocaine use.[181]

Cocaine's mechanism of action, although complex and not completely understood, is one of additive effects on many neurotransmitter systems, including nerve conduction, autonomic sympathetic, and CNS functions.[182] Several types of binding sites for cocaine exist in both central and peripheral nervous systems.[183] Although a subject's response to cocaine depends upon dosage, duration of exposure, mode of administration, concurrent medications, predisposition, and environmental setting, there are still predictable responses to a given dose of the drug.[184] The acute effects are brief and intense, resembling the neuropharmacologic and cardiovascular effects of amphetamines. Tachycardia, increased myocardial contractility, vasoconstriction, bronchodilation, pupillary dilation, muscle tremors, and an elevation in temperature are predictable even with low doses of intranasal or intravenous cocaine. Arousal and euphoria preceed dysphoria, anxiety, somnolence, and drug craving.[185] During gestation, cocaine may stimulate cardiac output to a greater degree than in the nonpregnant state. This effect may be mediated via a pregnancy-related increase in cardiac contractility, stroke volume, or both.[177] Additional data, from pregnant ewes, show elevated maternal and fetal mean arterial pressure and significantly reduced blood flow to the pregnant uterus, even with so-called "recreational" doses of cocaine.[186] Such changes can result in marked fetal hypoxemia, hypertension, and tachycardia secondary to reduced uterine blood flow, direct fetal effects of cocaine, and increased fetal catecholamine concentrations.[187]

Anyone using cocaine as a recreational drug may present with toxic manifestations regardless of dose or length of use. This toxicity may lead to sudden death and is characterized by its unpredictability and rapidity of onset.[188] Manifestations include overstimulation of respiratory, cardiovascular, and central nervous systems. Ultimately seizures, profound depression, and cardiovascular collapse appear. Because of the enhanced maternal sensitivity to the drug, one may hypothesize that the incidence of toxic effects is higher among pregnant cocaine users versus their nonpregnant counterparts, although currently no data confirm this theory. The syndrome of hypertension, altered mental status, and seizures may mimic preeclampsia or eclampsia and, in this case, history of cocaine use or urine and blood drug screening may be an important determinant of ensuing therapy and management.

Cocaine alkaloid, or "crack," is a highly potent, addictive, and relatively inexpensive form of cocaine that may prove to have more adverse perinatal effects than other forms of cocaine. Epidemic rates of maternal crack use bring national estimates of fetal cocaine exposure into the range of 91,500 to 240,000 children per year.[189-191] Maternal cocaine use increases the risk of a multitude of perinatal problems, such as the following:

- Congenital urogenital abnormalities
- Lower mean birth weight
- Lower mean gestational age at delivery
- Preterm labor and delivery
- Abruptio placentae
- Premature rupture of membranes
- Overall increased neonatal morbidity and mortality

The maternal "crack" user experiences increases in these complication rates above non-"crack" maternal cocaine users.[192-198]

Fetal cocaine exposure increases both the neonatal hospital costs and length of stay. "Crack" exposure increases these costs far beyond those incurred with other illicit drug or non-"crack" cocaine exposure. At a national level, these costs add up to almost $500 million/year.[199]

Opioids

The physiologic effects of narcotics in humans are well known. Except for a steeper dose–response curve, they are the same in the pregnant population. Most maternal effects of opioids occur secondary to narcotic-induced increases in carbon dioxide content and decreases in oxygen content of maternal blood. Maternal hypercarbia and hypoxemia impair uterine blood flow. During withdrawal, heightened sympathetic tone further lowers uterine blood flow. These physiologic changes result in a placental abruption rate of 25% among narcotic addicts.[200]

Neonatal effects of narcotics vary from an increased incidence of respiratory distress syndrome[201] and meconium aspiration to overt narcotic withdrawal syndrome.[202] Symptoms of withdrawal occur in up to 80% of (chronic) infants exposed to narcotics.[203] Maternal treatment, including prenatal care, through methadone clinics markedly lowers neonatal morbidity and morality.[200] Treatment, however, does not preclude an extremely high incidence of neonatal withdrawal syndrome among infants of methadone-dependent mothers.

For their first 2 years of life, infants exposed to narcotics are 250 to 500 g smaller and have a 1 cm smaller head circumference than controls.[204] After 2 years of age, there are no growth or developmental differences,[205] although an elevated incidence of central motor dysfunction persists until 5 years of age.[206]

REFERENCES

1. Prowse CM, Gaensler EA. Respiratory acid–base changes during pregnancy. Anesthesiology 1965;36:381
2. Cugell DW, Frank NR, Gaensler EA, et al. Pulmonary function in pregnancy: 1. Serial observations in normal women. Am Rev Tuberc Pulmon Dis 1953;67:568.
3. DiMarco AF. Asthma in the pregnant patient: a review. Ann Allergy 1989;62:527.
4. Schaefer G, Silverman F. Pregnancy complicated by asthma. Am J Obstet Gynecol 1961;82:182.
5. American Thoracic Society. Standards for the diagnosis and care of patients with chronic pulmonary obstructive disease (COPD) and asthma. Am Rev Respir Dis 1987;136:25.
6. Beck B. Pharmacologic approach to obstructed airway disease. Primary Care Clin 1985;12:239.
7. Szentivanyi A. The beta-adrenergic theory of the atopic abnormality in bronchial asthma. J Allergy 1968;42:203.
8. Ventner JC, Fraser CM, Harrison LC. Autoantibodies to β_2-adrenergic receptors: A possible cause of adrenergic hyporesponsiveness in allergic rhinitis and asthma. Science 1980;207:1361.
9. Holgate ST. Inflammatory cells and their mediators in the pathogenesis of asthma Postgrad Med J 1988;64(Suppl 4):82.
10. Insel PA, Wasserman SI. Asthma: A disorder of adrenergic receptors? FASEB 1990;4:2732.
11. George RB, Owens MW. Bronchial asthma. In: Bone RC, ed. Disease-a-Month. St. Louis: Mosby-Year Book, March 1991.
12. Popa V. Beta-adrenergic drugs. Clin Chest Med 1986;7:313.
13. Turner ES, Greenberger PA, Patterson R. Management of the pregnant asthmatic patient. Ann Intern Med 1980;6:105.
14. Juniper EF, Daniel EE, Roberts RS, et al. Effect of pregnancy on airway responsiveness and asthma severity. Relationship to serum progesterone. Am Rev Respir Dis 1991;143(suppl):78.
15. Schatz M, Harden K, Forsythe A, et al. The course of asthma during pregnancy postpartum and with successive pregnancies: A prospective analysis. J Allergy Clin Immunol 1988;81:509.

16. Gluck JC, Gluck PA. The effects of pregnancy on asthma: A prospective study. Ann Allergy 1976;37:164.

17. Apter AJ, Greenberger PA, Patterson R. Outcomes of pregnancy in adolescents with severe asthma. Arch Intern Med 1989;149:2571.

18. Mathe AA, Hedqvist P. Effect of prostaglandins $F_{2\alpha}$ and E_2 on airway conductance in healthy subjects and asthmatic patients. Am Rev Respir Dis 1975;111:313.

19. Jones E, Curzen P, Gaugas JM. Suppression activity of pregnancy plasma on mixed lymphocyte reaction. J Obstet Gynecol 1973;80:603.

20. Gee JBL, Packer BS, Millen JE, et al. Pulmonary mechanics during pregnancy. J Clin Invest 1967;46:945.

21. Barsky HE. Asthma and pregnancy. A challenge for everyone concerned. Postgrad Med 1991;89:125

22. Bahna SL, Bjerkdal T. The course and outcome of pregnancy in women with bronchial asthma. Acta Allergy 1972;27:397.

23. Schatz M, Zeiger RS, Hoffman CP. Intrauterine growth is related to gestational pulmonary function in pregnant asthmatic women. Chest 1990;98:389.

24. Wulf KH, Kunzel W, Lehmann V. Clinical aspects of placental gas exchange. In: Lango LD, Bartels H, eds. Respiratory gas exchange and blood flow in the placenta. Bethesda, MD: National Institutes of Health, Public Health Service, US Department of Health, Education, and Welfare, 1972:505.

25. Fitzsirnons R, Greenberger PA, Patterson R. Outcome of pregnancy in women requiring corticosteroids for severe asthma. J Allergy Clin Immunol 1986;78:349.

26. Schatz M, Zeiger RS, Harden KM, et al. The safety of inhaled β-agonist bronchodilators during pregnancy. J Allergy Clin Immunol 1988;82:686.

27. Greenberger PA, Patterson R. Management of asthma during pregnancy. N Engl J Med 1985;312:897.

28. Weinberger M. Pharmacology and therapeutic use of theophylline. J Allergy Clin Immunol 1984;73:525.

29. Ng WH, Polosa R, Church MK. Adenosine bronchoconstriction in asthma: Investigations into its possible mechanism of action. Br J Clin Pharmacol 1990;30(Suppl):89s.

30. Bukowsky M, Nakatsu K, Hunt BW. Theophylline reassessed. Ann Intern Med 1984;101:63.

31. Self TH, Aboul-Shalla N, Burns R, et al. Inhaled albuterol and oral prednisone therapy in hospitalized adult asthmatics. Does aminophylline add any benefit? Chest 1990;98:1317.

32. Gardner MJ, Schatz M, Cousins L, et al. Longitudinal effects of pregnancy on the pharmacokinetics of theophylline. Eur J Clin Pharmacol 1987;31:289.

33. Carter BL, Driscoll CE, Smith GD. Theophylline clearance during pregnancy. Obstet Gynecol 1986;68:555.

34. Sutton PL, Rose JQ, Goldstein S, et al. Theophylline pharmacokinetics during pregnancy and post partum. J Allergy Clin Immunol 1980;65:177.

35. Kelly HW, Murphy S. Corticosteroids for acute, severe asthma. DICP 1991;25:72.

36. Svedmyr N. Action of corticosteroids on β-adrenergic receptors. Am Rev Respir Dis 1990;141(Suppl):31.

37. Munck A, Mendel DB, Smith LI, Orti E. Glucocorticoid receptors and actions. Am Rev Respir Dis 1990;141(Suppl):2.

38. Williams TJ, Yarwood H. Effect of corticosteroids on microvascular permeability. Am Rev Respir Dis 1990;141(Suppl):39.

39. Schleimer RP. Effects of glucocorticoids on inflammatory cells relevant to their therapeutic applications in asthma. Am Rev Respir Dis 1990;141(Suppl):59.

40. Dunlap NE, Bailey WC. Corticosteroids in asthma. South Med J 1990;83:428.

41. McDonald AJ. Asthma. Emerg Med Clin North Am 1989;7:219.

42. Hernandez E, Angell CS, Johnson JWC. Asthma in pregnancy: Current concepts. Obstet Gynecol 1980;55:739.

43. Britton JR. Effects of social class, sex, and region of residence on age at death from cystic fibrosis. Br Med J 1989;298:483.

44. Cohen LF, di Sant'Agnese PA, Friedlander J. Cystic fibrosis and pregnancy: A national survey. Lancet 1980;2:842.

45. Pittard WB III, Sorensen RU, Schnatz PT. Pregnancy outcome in mothers with cystic fibrosis: Normal neonatal immune responses. South Med J 1987;80:347.

46. Longo LD. Some health consequences of maternal smoking: issues without answers. Birth Defects 1982;18:13.

47. Handler A, Davis F, Ferre C, Yeko T. The relationship of smoking and ectopic pregnancy. Am J Public Health 1989;79:1239.

48. Brown HL, Miller JM Jr, Knawli O, Gabert HA. Premature placental calcification in maternal cigarette smokers. Obstet Gynecol 1988;71:914.

49. Butler NR, Goldstein H, Ross EM. Cigarette smoking in pregnancy: Its influence on birth weight and perinatal mortality. Br Med J 1972;2:127.

50. Werler MM, Pober BR, Holmes LB. Smoking and pregnancy. In: Sever JL, Brent RL eds. Teratogen update: environmentally induced birth defects risks. New York: Alan R Liss, 1986:131.

51. Philbert H, Dam M. The epileptic mother and her child. Epilepsia 1982;23:85.

52. Bjerkdal T, Bahna SL. The occurrence and outcome of pregnancy in women with epilepsy. Acta Gynecol Scand 1976;55:187.

53. Niswander KR, Gordon M. The Collaborative Perinatal Study of the National Institute of Neurological Disease and Stroke. Washington, DC: Department of Health, Education, and Welfare publication number NIH-73-379, 1972.

54. Yerby MS. Problems and management of the pregnant woman with epilepsy. Epilepsia 1987;28(Suppl):529.

55. Hiilesmaa VK, Bardy A, Teram K. Obstetric outcome in women with epilepsy. Am J Obstet Gynecol 1985;152:499.

56. Schmidt D. The effect of pregnancy on the natural history of epilepsy: Review of the literature. In: Janz D, Dam M, Richens A, et al, eds. Epilepsy, pregnancy, and the child. New York: Raven Press, 1982:3.

57. Remillard G, Dansky L, Andermann E, Andermann F. Seizure frequency during pregnancy and the puerperium. In: Janz D, Dam M, Richens A, et al, eds. Epilepsy, pregnancy, and the child. New York: Raven Press, 1982:15.

58. Knott C, Williams CP, Reynolds F. Phenytoin kinetics during pregnancy and the puerperium. Br J Obstet Gynecol 1986;93:1030.

59. American Academy of Pediatrics Committee on Drugs. Anticonvulsants and pregnancy. Pediatrics 1979; 63:331.

60. Saunders M. Epilepsy in women of childbearing age. Br Med J 1989;299:581.

61. Fabra S ed. Valproic acid and birth defects. Reprod Toxicol Newsletter 1983;2:9.

62. Ramsay RE, Strauss RG, Wilder BJ, Willimore LJ. Status epilepticus in pregnancy: Effect of phenytoin malabsorption on seizure control. Neurology 1978; 28:85.

63. Vincent A. Immunology of acetylcholine receptor in relation to myasthenia gravis. Physiol Rev 1980;60:756.

64. Mossman S, Vincent A, Newsom-Davis J. Myasthenia gravis without acetylcholine–receptor antibody: A distinct disease entity. Lancet 1986;1:116.

65. Hatton PD, Diehl JT, Daly BDT, et al. Transsternal radical thymectomy for myasthenia gravis: A 15-year review. Ann Thorac Surg 1989;47:838.

66. Mulder DG, Graves M, Herrman C. Thymectomy for myasthenia gravis: Recent observations and comparisons with past experience. Ann Thorac Surg 1989;48:551.

67. Stoelting RK, Dierdorf SF, McCammon RL. Diseases of the nervous system. In: Stoelting RK, Dierdorf SF, McCammon RL, eds. Anesthesia and Co-existing Disease 2nd ed, New York: Churchill Livingstone, 1988:263.

68. Reischies FM, Baum K, Brau H, et al. Cerebral magnetic resonance imaging in multiple sclerosis. Arch Neurol 1988;45:1114.

69. Mastrostefano R, Occhipinti E, Bigotti G, Pompili A. Multiple sclerosis plaque-simulating cerebral tumor: Case report and review of the literature. Neurosurgery 1987;21:244.

70. Wynn DR, Rodriguez M, O'Fallon WM, Kurland LT. Update on the epidemiology of multiple sclerosis. Mayo Clin Proc 1989;64:808.

71. Kurtzke JF, Hyllested K. Multiple sclerosis in the Faroe islands. II. Clinical update, transmission, and the nature of MS. Neurology 1986;36:307.

72. McCullough B, Krakowka S, Koestner A. Experimental canine distemper virus–induced demyelination. Lab Invest 1974;31:216.

73. Cutler RWP, Averill DR Jr. Cerebrospinal fluid gamma globulins in canine distemper encephalitis. Neurology 1969;19:1111.

74. Swank RL. Multiple sclerosis: A correlation of its incidence with dietary fat. Am J Med Sci 1950;220:421.

75. Poser CM. Trauma and multiple sclerosis: An hypothesis. J Neurol 1987;234:155.

76. Stein EC, Schiffer RB, Hall WJ, Young N. Multiple sclerosis and the workplace: A report of an industry-based cluster. Neurology 1987;37:1672.

77. Elias SB. Oligodendrocyte development and the natural history of multiple sclerosis. Arch Neurol 1987; 44:1294.

78. Rose AS, Kuzma JW, Kurtzke JF, et al. Cooperative study in the evaluation of therapy in multiple sclerosis: ACTH vs. placebo: Final report. Neurology 1970;20:1.

79. Tourtellotte WW, Baumhefner RW, Pohin AR, et al. Multiple sclerosis de novo CSF IgG synthesis: Effect of ACTH and corticosteroids. Neurology 1980;30:1155.

80. Birk K, Ford C, Smeltzer S, et al. The clinical course of multiple sclerosis during pregnancy and the puerperium. Arch Neurol 1990;47:738.

81. Physician's Desk Reference, Oradell, NJ: Medical Economics Co. 1990;44:1860.

82. Khatri BO, D'Cruz O, Priesler G, et al. Plasmapheresis in a pregnant patient with multiple sclerosis. Arch Neurol 1990;47:11.

83. Birnbach DJ, Bader A, Ostheimer GW. Anesthesia and multiple sclerosis. JAMA 1988;260:2838.

84. Swapp GH, Main RA. Neurofibromatosis in pregnancy. Br J Dermatol 1973;80:431.

85. Magbagbeola JAO. Abnormal responses to muscle relaxants in a patient with von Recklinghausen's disease (multiple neurofibromatosis). Br J Anaesth 1970; 42:183.

86. Baraka A. Myasthenic response to muscle relaxants in von Recklinghausen's disease. Br J Anaesth 1974; 46:701.

87. Schonwald G, Fish KJ, Perkesh I. Cardiovascular complications during anesthesia in chronic spinal cord injured patients. Anesthesiology 1981;55:550.

88. Head H, Reddoch G. The autonomic bladder, excessive sweating and some other reflex conditions in gross injury of the spinal cord. Brain 1917;40:188.

89. Lambert DH, Deane RS, Mazuzan JE. Anesthesia and the control of blood pressure in patients with spinal cord injury. Anesth Analg 1982;61:344.

90. Goller H, Paeslack V. Our experiences about pregnancy and delivery of the paraplegic woman. Paraplegia 1970;8:161.

91. Greenspan JS, Paul RH. Paraplegia and quadriplegia: Special considerations during pregnancy and labor and delivery. Am J Obstet Gynecol 1986;155:738.

92. Roelvink NC, Kamphorst W, van Alphen HA, Rao BR. Pregnancy-related primary brain and spinal tumors. Arch Neurol 1987;44:209.

93. Choi NW. Epidemiology of primary central nervous system neoplasms. II. Case-controlled study. Am J Epidemlol 1970;91:467.

94. Weyand RD, MacCarty C, Wilson RB. The effect of pregnancy on intracranial meningiomas occurring about the optic chiasm. Surg Clin North Am 1951;31:1225.

95. Markwalder T. Estrogen and progesterone receptors in meningiomas in relation to clinical and pathologic features. Surg Neurol 1983;20:42.

96. Abouleish E. Neurologic disease. In: James FM, III, Wheeler S, Dewan D, eds. Obstetrical anesthesia: The complicated patient, 2nd ed., Philadelphia: FA Davis, 1988:133.

97. Biller J, Adams HP. Cerebrovascular disorders associated with pregnancy. Am Fam Physician 1986; 33:125.

98. Donnelly JF, Lock FR. Causes of death in 533 fatal cases of toxemia in pregnancy. Am J Obstet Gynecol 1954;68:184.

99. Reece EA, Chervenak FA, Coultrip L, Hobbins JC. The perinatal management of pregnancy complicated by massive intracerebral hemorrhage. Am J Perinatol 1984;1:266.

100. Robinson JL, Hall CJ, Sedizmir CB. Subarachnoid hemorrhage in pregnancy. J Neurosurg 1972;36:27.

101. Robinson JL, Hall CJ, Sedizmir CB. Arteriovenous malformations aneurysms and pregnancy. J Neurosurg 1974;41:63.

102. Centers for Disease Control: Quarterly report to the Domestic Policy Council on the prevalence and rate of spread of HIV and AIDS—United States. MMWR 1987;37:131.

103. Centers for Disease Control: HIV/AIDS Surveillance Report. Atlanta, GA: Centers for Disease Control; August, 1990:1.

104. Burke DS, Brundage JF, Herbold JR, et al: Human immunodeficiency virus infections among civilian applicants for United States military service: October, 1985–March, 1986. N Engl J Med 1987;317:131.

105. Koonin LM, Ellerbrock TV, Atrash HK, et al. Pregnancy-associated deaths due to AIDS in the United States. JAMA 1989;261:1306.

106. Centers for Disease Control: AIDS Weekly Surveillance Report—United States. Atlanta, GA: Centers for Disease Control, December 26, 1988:1.

107. Hoff R, Berardi VP, Weiblen BJ, et al. Seroprevalence of human immunodeficiency virus among childbearing women. N Engl J Med 1988;318:525.

108. Landesman S, Minkoff H, Holman S, et al. Serosurvey of human immunodeficiency virus infection in parturients. JAMA 1987;258:2701.

109. Ho DD, Pomerantz RJ, Kaplan JC. Pathogenesis of infection with human immunodeficiency virus. N Engl J Med 1987;317:278.

110. Boylston AW, Francis ND. Does it matter which cells are infected by the immunodeficiency virus type 1? J Pathol 1988;156:93.

111. Albert J, Gaines H, Sunnerborg A, et al. Isolation of human immunodeficiency virus from plasma during primary HIV infection. J Med Virol 1987;23:67.

112. Levy JA, Shimabukuro J. Recovery of AIDS-associated retroviruses from patients with AIDS-related conditions and from clinically healthy individuals. J Infect Dis 1985;152:734.

113. Schwartz JS, Dans PE, Kinosian BP. Human immunodeficiency virus test evaluation, performance, and use: Proposals to make good tests better. JAMA 1988; 259:2574.

114. Guinan ME, Hardy A. Epidemiology of AIDS in women in the United States. JAMA 1987;257:2039.

115. Redfield RR, Wright DC, Tramont EC. Special report: The Walter Reed staging classification for HTLV-III/LAV infection. N Engl J Med 1986;314:131.

116. Redfield RR, Burke DS. HIV infection: The clinical picture. Sci Am 1988;259:90-8.

117. Hirsch MS. The rocky road to effective treatment of HIV infection. Ann Intern Med 1987;317:278.

118. Creogh-Kirk T, Doi P, Andrews E, et al. Survival experience among patients with AIDS receiving zidovudine. Follow-up of patients in a compassionate plea program. JAMA 1988;260:3009.

119. Baines MG, Pross HF, Miller KG. Spontaneous human lymphocyte-mediated cytotoxicity against tumor target cells: IV. The suppressive effect of normal pregnancy. Am J Obstet Gynecol 1978;130:741.

120. Sridama V, Pacini F, Yang S, et al. Decreased levels of helper T cells: A possible cause of immunodeficiency in pregnancy. N Engl J Med 1982;307:352.

121. Minkoff HL, Nanda D, Menez R, et al. Follow up of mothers of children with AIDS. Obstet Gynecol 1987; 87:288.

122. Scott GB, Fischl MA, Klimas N, et al. Mothers of infants with the acquired immunodeficiency syndrome: Evidence for both symptomatic and asymptomatic carriers. JAMA 1985;253:363.

123. Schoenbaum EE, Selwyn PA, Feingold AR, et al. The effect of pregnancy on progression of HIV related disease. Abstracts of the 3rd International Conference on AIDS. Washington, DC, US Department of Health and Human Services and the World Health Organization, 1987.

124. The NYC Collaborative Study Group for Vertical Transmission of HIV. Human immunodeficiency virus infection during pregnancy: A longitudinal study. Abstracts of the 3rd International Conference on AIDS. Washington, DC, US Department of Health and Human Services and the World Health Organization, 1987.

125. Minkoff H, Nanda D, Menez R, et al. Pregnancies resulting in infants with acquired immunodeficiency syndrome or AIDS-related complex. Obstet Gynecol 1987;69:285.

126. Fricker HS, Segal S. Narcotic addiction, pregnancy, and the newborn. Am J Dis Child 1978;132:360.

127. MacGregor SW, Keith LG, Chasnoff IJ, et al. Cocaine use during pregnancy: Adverse perinatal outcome. Am J Obstet Gynecol 1987;157:686.

128. Dinsmoor MJ. HIV infection and pregnancy. Med Clin North Am 1989;73:701.

129. Coolfront Report: A PHS plan for prevention and control of AIDS and the AIDS virus. Public Health Rep. 1986;101:341.

130. Joviasas E, Koch MA, Schafer A, et al. LAV/HTLV-III in a 20-week fetus [letter]. Lancet 1985;2:1129.

131. Lapointe N, Michaud J, Pekovic D, et al. Transplacental transmission of HTLV-III virus [letter]. N Engl J Med 1985;312:1325.

132. Hino S, Yamaguchi K,Katamine S, et al. Mother-to-child transmission of human T-cell leukemia virus type 1. Jpn J Cancer Res 1985;76:474.

133. Thiry L, Sprecher-Goldberger S, Jonckheer T, et al. Isolation of AIDS virus from cell-free breast milk of three healthy virus carriers [letter]. Lancet 1985;2:891.

134. Ziegler JB, Johnson RO, Cooper, DA, et al. Postnatal transmission of AIDS-associated retrovirus from mother to infant. Lancet 1985;1:896.

135. Marion RW, Wiznia M, Hutcheon RG, et al. Fetal AIDS syndrome score. Arch Dis Child 1987;141:429.

136. Minkoff H, Nanda D, Menez R, Fikrig S. Pregnancies resulting in infants with AIDS or AIDS-related complex: Follow-up of mothers, children, and subsequently born siblings. Obstet Gynecol 1987;69:288.

137. Menez-Bautista R, Fikrig SM, Pahula S, et al. Monozygotic twins discordant for the acquired immunodeficiency syndrome. Arch Dis Child 1986;140:678.

138. Park CL, Streicher H, Rothberg R. Transmission of HIV from parents to only one dizygotic twin. J Clin Microbiol 1987;25:1119.

139. Williamson DF, Surdula JS, Kendrick NF, et al. Comparing the prevalence of smoking in pregnant and nonpregnant women, 1985–1986. JAMA 1989; 261:70.

140. Rubin PC, Craig GF, Gavin K, Sumner D. Prospective survey of use of therapeutic drugs, alcohol, and cigarettes during pregnancy. Br Med J 1986; January 11:292.

141. Valencia G, McCalla S, da Sllva M, et al. Epidemiology of cocaine use during pregnancy at Kings County Hospital Center [Abstract]. Am Pediatr Soc/Soc Pediatr Res 1989.

142. Chavkin W. Drug addiction and pregnancy—policy crossroads. Public health and the law. Am J Public Health 1990;80:483.

143. Kulberg A: Substane abuse: Clinical identification and management. Pediatr Clin North Am 1986;33:325.

144. Semlitz L, Gold MS. Adolescent drug abuse: Diagnosis, treatment, and prevention. Psychiatr Clin North Am 1986;9:455.

145. Mucklow JC. The fate of drugs in pregnancy. Clin Obstet Gynecol 1986;13:161.

146. Perry BD, Pesavento DJ, Kussie PH, et al. Prenatal exposure to drugs of abuse in humans: Effects on placental neurotransmitter receptors. Neurobehav Toxicol Teratol 1984;6:295.

147. Martin JC. Irreversible changes in mature and aging animals following intrauterine drug exposure. Neurobehav Toxicol Teratol 1986;8:335.

148. Milunsky A, Jick H, Jick SS, et al. Multivitamin/folic acid supplementation in early pregnancy reduces the prevalence of neural tube defects. JAMA 1989; 262:2847.

149. Zuckerman B, Frank DA, Hingson R, et al. Effects of maternal marijuana and cocaine use on fetal growth. N Engl J Med 1989;320:762.

150. Maling HM. Toxicology of single doses of ethyl alcohol. In: Trémolières J, ed. Alcohols and derivatives, vol 2. International Encyclopedia of Pharmacology and Therapeutics. Oxford: Pergamon Press, 1970:277.

151. Li TK, Bosron WF. Genetic variability of enzymes of alcohol metabolism in human beings. Ann Emerg Med 1986;15:997.

152. Chan AW. Racial differences in alcohol sensitivity. Alcohol 1986;21:93.

153. Erwin VG, McClearn GE. Genetic influences on alcohol consumption and action of alcohol. Curr Alcohol 1981;8:405.

154. Sellers EM, Kalant H. Alcohol intoxication and withdrawal. N Engl J Med 1976;294:757.

155. Thompson WL. Management of alcohol withdrawal syndromes. Arch Intern Med 1978;138:278.

156. Thompson WL, Johnson AD, Maddrey WL. Diazepam and paraldehyde for treatment of severe delirium tremens. A controlled trial. Arch Intern Med 1975;82:175.

157. Segel LD, Klausner SC, Gnadt JT, Amsterdam EA. Alcohol and the heart. Med Clin North Am 1984;68:147.

158. Ylikahari RH, Huttenen MU, Harkonen M. Hormonal changes during alcohol intoxication and withdrawal. Pharmacol Biochem Behav 1980;13:131.

159. Erskine RL, Ritchie JW. The effect of maternal consumption of alcohol on human umbilical artery blood flow. Am J Obstet Gynecol. 1986;154:318.

160. Fisher SE, Atkinson M, Van Thiel DH. Selective fetal malnutrition: The effect of nicotine, ethanol, and acetaldehyde upon in vitro uptake of alpha-aminobutyric acid by human term placental villous slices. Dev Pharmacol Ther 1984;7:229.

161. Horrobin DF. A biochemical basis for alcoholism and alcohol-induced damage including the fetal alcohol syndrome and cirrhosis: Interference with essential fatty acid and prostaglandin metabolism. Med Hypotheses 1980;6:929.

162. Tanaka H, Suzuki N, Arima M. Experimental studies on the influence of male alcoholism on fetal development. Brain Dev 1982;4:1.

163. Smith IE, Coles CD, Lancaster J, Fernhoff PM, Falek A. The effect of volume and duration of ethanol exposure on neonatal physical and behavioral development. Neurobehav Toxicol Teratol 1986;8:375.

164. Fishman RH, Yanai J. Long-lasting effects of early barbiturates on central nervous system and behavior. Neurosci Biobehav Rev 1983;7:19.

165. Ghoneim MM, Dembo JB, Block RI. Time course of an-

tagonism of sedative and amnesic effects of diazepam by flumazenil. Anesthesiology 1989;70:899.

166. Saxen I, Saxen L. Association between maternal intake of diazepam and oral clefts. Lancet 1975;2:498.

167. Safra MJ, Oakley GP. Association between cleft lip with or without cleft palate and prenatal exposure to diazepam. Lancet 1975;2:478.

168. Rice SA, Pelligrini M. Teratology of fixed agents. In: Baden JM, Brodsky JB, eds. The Pregnant Surgical Patient. Mt Kisco, NY:Futura Publishing Co, 1985:53.

169. Caldwell J, Sever PS. The biochemical pharmacology of abused drugs: 1. Amphetamines, cocaine, and LSD. Clin Pharmacol Ther 1974;116: 625.

170. Grabowski J, Dworkin SI. Cocaine: An overview of current issues. Int J Addict 1985;20: 1065.

171. VanDyke C, Barash PG, Jatlow P, Byck R. Cocaine: Plasma concentrations after intranasal application in man. Science 1976;191:859.

172. Wilkinson P, VanDyke C, Jatloow P, Barash PG, Byck R. Intranasal and oral cocaine kinetics. Clin Pharmacol Ther 1980;27:386.

173. Stewart DJ, Inaba T, Lucassen M, Kalow W. Cocaine metabolism: Cocaine and norcocaine hydrolysis by liver and serum esterases. Clin Pharmacol Ther 1979;25: 464.

174. Inaba T, Stewart DJ, Kalow W. Metabolism of cocaine in man. Clin Pharmacol Ther 1978;23:547.

175. Hawks RL, Kopin IJ, Colburn RW, Thoa NB. Norcocaine: A pharmacologically active metabolite of cocaine found in brain. Life Sci 1974;15: 2189.

176. Jatlow P, Barash PG, VanDyke C, Radding J, Byck R. Cocaine and succinylcholine sensitivity: A new caution. Anesth Analg 1979;58: 235.

177. Woods JR Jr, Plessinger MA. Pregnancy increases cardiovascular toxicity to cocaine. Am J Obstet Gynecol 1990;162:529.

178. Neale MG, Parke DV. Effects of pregnancy on the metabolism of drugs in the rat and rabbit. Biochem Pharmacol 1973;22: 1451.

179. Dean ME, Stock BH. Hepatic microsomal metabolism of drugs during pregnancy in the rat. Drug Metab Dispos 1973;3: 325.

180. Ochs H, Dusterberg B, Schulte-Hermann R. Induction of monooxygenases and growth in rat liver by progesterone. Arch Toxicol 1986;59: 146.

181. Chasnoff IJ, Lewis DE, Griffith DR, Willey S. Cocaine and pregnancy: Clinical and toxicological implications for the neonate. Clin Chem 1989;35: 1276.

182. Fleming JA, Byck R, Barash PG. Pharmacology and therapeutic applications of cocaine. Anesthesiology 1990;73: 518.

183. Reith MEA. Cocaine receptors on monoamine transporters and sodium channels. NIDA Res Monogr 1988;88: 23.

184. Adams EH, Kozel NJ. Cocaine use in America: Introduction and overview. NIDA Res Monogr 1985;61: 1.

185. Ritchie JM, Greene NM. Local anesthetics. In: Gilman AG, Goodman AF, Rall W, Murad F, eds. Goodman and Gilman's the pharmacological basis of therapeutics, 7th ed. New York: MacMillan, 1985:321.

186. Moore TR, Sorg J, Miller L, Key TC, Resnik R. Hemodynamic effects of intravenous cocaine on the pregnant ewe and fetus. Am J Obstet Gynecol 1986;155:883.

187. Woods JR, Plessinger MA Clark KE. Effect of cocaine on uterine blood flow and fetal oxygenation. JAMA 1987;257: 957.

188. Cregler LL, Mark H. Medical complications of cocaine abuse. N Engl J Med 1986;315:1495.

189. General Accounting Office. Drug-exposed infants: A generation at risk. Washington, DC: US General Accounting Office: Publication GAO/HRD-90-138, 1990.

190. Gomby D, Shiono PH. Estimating the number of substance-exposed infants. Future Child 1991;1:17.

191. Besharov DJ. The children of crack: Will we protect them? Public Welfare. Fall 1989:6.

192. MacGregor SN, Keith LLG, Bachicha JA, Chasnoff IJ. Cocaine abuse during pregnancy: Correlation between prenatal care and perinatal outcome. Obstet Gynecol 1989;74: 882.

193. Neerhof MG, MacGregor SN, Retzky SS, Sullivan TP. Cocaine abuse during pregnancy: Peripartum prevalence and perinatal outcome. Am J Obstet Gynecol 1989;161:633.

194. Chavez GF, Mulinaree J, Cordero JF. Maternal cocaine use during early pregnancy as a risk factor for congenital urogenital anomalies. JAMA 1989;262: 795.

195. Mitchell M, Sabbagha RE, Keith L, et al. Ultrasonic growth parameters in fetuses of mothers with primary addiction to cocaine. Am J Obstet Gynecol 1988;159: 1104.

196. Fulroth R, Phillips B, Durand DJ. Perinatal outcome of infants exposed to cocaine and/or heroin in utero. Am J Dis Child 1989;143: 905.

197. Cherukuri R, Minkoff H, Feldman J, Parekh A, Glass L. A cohort study of alkaloidal cocaine ("crack") in pregnancy. Obstet Gynecol 1988;72: 147.

198. Acker D, Saachs BP, Tracey KJ, et al. Abruptio placentae associated with cocaine use. Am J Obstet Gynecol 1983;146: 220.

199. Phibbs CS, Bateman DA, Schwartz RM. The neonatal costs of maternal cocaine use. JAMA 1991;266:1521.

200. Finnegan LP. Effects of maternal opiate abuse on the newborn. Fed Proc 1985;44: 2315.

201. Parekh A, Mukherjee TK, Jhaveri R, et al. Intrauterine exposure to narcotics and cord blood prolactin concentrations. Obstet Gynecol 1981;57: 477.

202. Panerai AE, Martini A, DiGiulio AM, et al. Plasma beta-endorphin, beta-lipotropin, and metenkephalin concentrations during pregnancy in normal and drug-addicted women and their newborn. J Clin Endocrinol Metab 1983;57: 537.

203. Edelin KC, Gurganious L, Golar K, et al. Methadone maintenance in pregnancy: Consequences to care and outcome. Obstet Gynecol 1988;71: 399.

204. Keith LG, MacGregor S, Friedell S, et al. Substance abuse in pregnant women: Recent experience at the perinatal center for chemical dependence of Northwestern Memorial Hospital. Obstet Gynecol 1989; 73:715.

205. Chasnoff IJ, Burns KA, Burns WJ, et al. Prenatal drug exposure and effects on neonatal and infant growth and development. Neurobehav Toxicol Teratol 1986;8: 357.

206. Dobercyzk TM, Kandall SR, Rongkapan O, et al. Peripheral nerve conduction studies in passively addicted neonates. Arch Phys Med Rehabil 1986;67:4.

CHAPTER 4

Diabetes Mellitus in Pregnancy: Pathophysiology and Obstetric Management

Jaya Ramanathan
George S. Allen III

Diabetes mellitus is a common cause of maternal and perinatal morbidity and mortality. In the United States, this disease afflicts approximately 1.5 million women of child-bearing age. In addition, transient disturbances in glucose tolerance occur in 1% to 3% of pregnancies.[1] Before the discovery of insulin, most diabetic pregnancies ended in abortion or premature labor. In those pregnancies that reached term, the incidence of maternal mortality and stillbirths reached or exceeded a staggering 50%.[2,3] The availability of insulin has allowed dramatic improvements in both the maternal and neonatal outcomes. A better understanding of the pathophysiology of the disease process and advances in fetal monitoring and obstetric management have also improved maternal and neonatal outcome in pregnant diabetic women.

Diabetes mellitus is a chronic metabolic disorder caused by an absolute or relative lack of insulin. This deficiency causes the following:

- Hyperglycemia
- Abnormal protein and lipid metabolism

- Microangiopathy involving the retinal and renal vessels
- Neuropathy affecting the peripheral nervous system[4]

Severe, uncontrolled diabetes culminates in catastrophic diabetic ketoacidosis, with a perinatal mortality rate of 50% to 90%.

White's classification of diabetes mellitus in pregnancy[5] (Table 4-1) is based upon the age of onset of diabetes, duration, severity, and the occurrence of related complications. Table 4-2 shows a newer classification, recently revised and adopted from the National Diabetes Data Group.[1] Type I diabetes accounts for approximately 10% of cases. The patients in this group are younger, usually of normal weight, dependent upon insulin, and prone to ketosis. Patients with type II diabetes are neither insulin-dependent nor ketosis-prone. They are usually obese, and although not insulin-dependent, may require insulin therapy during pregnancy. Type III diabetics are gestational diabetics diagnosed by screening tests such as the oral glucose

Table 4–1

Classification of Diabetes in Pregnancy

CLASS	DESCRIPTION
A	Gestational diabetes with normal fasting plasma glucose and postprandial plasma glucose $<$ 120 mg/100 mL
B_1	Gestational diabetes with fasting hyperglycemia and/or postprandial plasma glucose $>$ 120 mg/100 mL
B_2	Overt diabetes, onset after age 20, and duration less than 10 y
C	Overt diabetes, onset before age 20, or duration 10 to 20 y
D	Overt diabetes, duration more than 20 y or onset before age 10; benign retinopathy
E	Calcified pelvic vessels
F	Nephropathy (proteinuria, azotemia)
R	Malignant (proliferative) retinopathy (retinitis proliferans)

(After White P: Pregnancy and diabetes. In: Marble A, White P, Bradley RF, Krall LP, eds. Joslin's Diabetes Mellitus. 11th ed. Philadelphia: Lea & Febiger, 1971)

Table 4–2

Classification of Glucose Intolerance in Pregnant Women

NOMENCLATURE	OLD NAME(S)	CLINICAL CHARACTERISTICS OF CONDITION
Type I or insulin-dependent diabetes mellitus	Juvenile diabetes, Juvenile-onset diabetes, ketosis-prone diabetes	Ketosis-prone; insulin-deficient due to islet cell loss; often associated with specific HLA types with predisposition to viral insulitis or autoimmune (islet cell antibody phenomena); occurs at any age; common in youth; these women are usually of normal weight but may be obese
Type II or non–insulin-dependent diabetes mellitus, nonobese, obese	Adult-onset diabetes, maturity-onset diabetes, ketosis-resistant diabetes, stable diabetes	Ketosis-resistant; more frequent in adults but occurs at any age; majority are overweight; may be seen in family aggregates as an autosomal dominant genetic trait; *always* require insulin for hyperglycemia during pregnancy but not "insulin dependent"; previous history of "borderline diabetes," impaired glucose tolerance, or treatment with oral hypoglycemic agents; $HbA_{1c} >$ 8% during first 20 w of gestation
Type III or gestational carbohydrate intolerance, nonobese, obese	Gestational diabetes	Screening tests: all pregnant women; 50 g oral glucose given randomly (need not be fasting) at 24 to 28 w gestation; a plasma glucose 1 h later $\geq$ 140 g/100 mL (7.8 mmol) is an indication for an oral glucose tolerance test
Type IV or secondary diabetes	Conditions and syndromes associated with impaired glucose tolerance	Cystic fibrosis; endocrine disorders such as acromegaly, hyperprolactinemia, Cushing's syndrome, insulin receptor abnormalities, or aberrant forms of insulin, drugs or chemical agents, renal dialysis, organ transplantations, certain genetic syndromes

(Hollingsworth DR, Moore TR. Diabetes and pregnancy. In Creasy RK and Resnik R, eds. Maternal Fetal Medicine: Principles and Practice. Philadelphia: WB Saunders, 1989:925) tolerance test. Type IV, or secondary, diabetes affects 5% to 10% of pregnant women with conditions such as cystic fibrosis or endocrine disorders.

EFFECTS OF DIABETES ON THE MOTHER

Pregnancy is associated with major physiologic changes in glucose metabolism. Nonpregnant women, when fasted, maintain a basal concentration of plasma glucose by both the continuous release of glucose from hepatic glycogen stores and gluconeogenesis from amino acids and other glucose precursors. Insulin and circulating glucagon control plasma glucose concentrations. In healthy, pregnant women, fasting for a duration of 12 hours (overnight) can produce a rapid fall in plasma glucose concentration to as low as 40 to 45 mg/100 mL.[6] This rapid fall in plasma glucose results in a reduction in insulin secretion that in turn leads to ketosis.[7,8] Such exaggerated response to fasting during pregnancy is termed *accelerated starvation* of pregnancy. Increases in maternal and fetal glucose utilization and in the volume of distribution for glucose apparently cause this rapid lowering of maternal plasma glucose concentration during fasting.[9] Accelerated starvation and maternal hypoglycemia result in increased ketoacids that readily cross the placental barrier and accumulate in the fetus.

When healthy parturients eat, their plasma glucose concentration rises (Fig. 4-1).[10] This exaggerated hyperglycemic response to a carbohydrate load markedly increases insulin production (see Fig. 4-1).[10] Hypertrophy of the beta cells of the islets of Langerhans yields this hyperinsulinemic response. This effect is most evident during the third trimester.[11] Persistent hyperglycemia, despite the significant increase in insulin, signals the development of hepatic resistance to insulin. Earlier studies have shown that insulin resistance and decreased tissue sensitivity[12] to insulin during pregnancy result from the synergistic effects of placental hormones, human placental lactogen, estrogen, and progesterone.[4]

Diabetes during pregnancy exaggerates all these effects. In early pregnancy, maternal hypoglycemia frequently occurs and necessitates drastic reductions in insulin dose.[13,14] During the latter half of pregnancy, however, insulin resistance develops with a progressive increase in insulin requirements.[13,14] In addition, without tight metabolic control, these women are extremely prone to the development ketoacidosis.

The incidence of obstetric complications such as preeclampsia, hydramnios, and preterm labor is signifi-

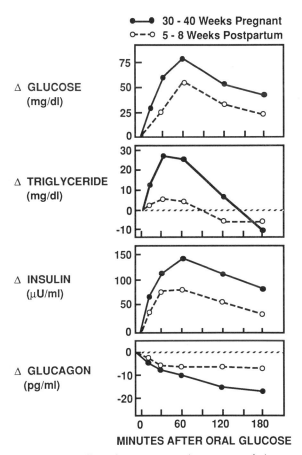

Figure 4–1. Effect of pregnancy on the response of plasma glucose, triglyceride, immunoreactive insulin, and glucagon to oral glucose. Values have been expressed as changes from basal concentrations after the administration of 100 mg of oral glucose after a 14-hour overnight fast. (Freinkel N. Of pregnancy and progeny. Diabetes 1980;29:1023)

cantly higher in pregnant women with diabetes. Other serious complications of severe diabetes mellitus during pregnancy include diabetic retinopathy, nephropathy, hypertension, and coronary insufficiency.

EFFECTS OF DIABETES ON THE FETUS

Congenital Anomalies

The coming of insulin therapy reduced perinatal mortality rates to less than 5%. Despite the general decline in perinatal morbidity and mortality, congenital anomalies continue to occur at a high rate of 6% to 12%.[1,4]

Inadequate control of diabetes during the early stages of pregnancy may at least partly explain the high incidence of anomalies.[15,16] Strict control of diabetes and maintenance of euglycemia beginning at conception or at very early gestation can significantly lower the incidence of congenital defects.[17] The following are some common congenital anomalies:

- Central nervous system defects such as spina bifida and hydrocephalus
- Cardiac defects such as atrial or ventricular septal defects and transposition of great vessels
- Renal anomalies such as renal agenesis and polycystic kidney

Macrosomia

Maternal hyperglycemia provides large quantities of glucose to the fetus. Glucose crosses the placenta by facilitated diffusion, a carrier-mediated and non-energy-dependent process. Hyperglycemia in the fetus stimulates increased insulin production and fuel utilization. So, increased fat deposition, hypertrophy of visceral organs, and increased growth of the skeletal system occur. During vaginal delivery, the large size of the fetus contributes to a high incidence of shoulder dystocia, facial nerve or brachial plexus injury, and asphyxia.[1] Studies have shown that despite good metabolic control, the incidence of macrosomia may be as high as 20% to 30% in the infants of diabetic women.

Neonatal Hypoglycemia

In infants of healthy, nondiabetic mothers, insulin concentration falls rapidly, with the separation of placenta at delivery, compensating for the sudden cessation of the fuel supply from the mother. Such rapid hormonal adaptation fails to occur in infants of diabetic women.[18,19] Hyperinsulinemia persists even after birth and often causes hypoglycemia, with blood sugar falling to less than 30 mg/100 mL.[4] Therefore, it is especially important to avoid giving these women bolus infusions of dextrose-containing solutions during labor.

Respiratory Distress Syndrome

Respiratory distress syndrome (RDS) is a common cause of neonatal morbidity and mortality. In recent years, with advances in the obstetric management, including frequent evaluations of fetal lung maturity, the incidence of RDS has decreased dramatically, from 30% to 3%.[20] Frequent estimations of lecithin–sphingomyelin ratio and phosphatidyl glycerol concentration enable the obstetrician to postpone delivery until the fetal lung matures. Fetal hyperinsulinemia may interfere with surfactant production, and delay pulmonic maturity,[21] another reason to maintain euglycemia during pregnancy.

Other neonatal complications in infants of diabetic mothers include polycythemia, hypocalcemia, hypomagnesemia, and hyperbilirubinemia.

CHANGES IN UTEROPLACENTAL CIRCULATION AND FETAL OXYGENATION

Several studies have shown that diabetes significantly impairs uteroplacental perfusion.[22,23] Either diminished uteroplacental blood supply[22] or a higher density placenta with limited intervillous space may cause this decrease.[23] The presence of increased maternal glycosylated hemoglobin (HbA_{1c}) also may compromise fetal oxygenation.[24] When glucose covalently binds to the two beta chains in the adult Hb (HbA), it creates HbA_{1c}, which interferes with oxygen uptake. Serial measurements of HbA_{1c} concentration provide valuable information regarding the quality of maternal blood sugar control and the effectiveness of therapy. In insulin-dependent diabetic women, HbA_{1c} interferes with hemoglobin oxygen transport and compromises fetal oxygenation.[25]

DIABETIC KETOACIDOSIS

Diabetic ketoacidosis remains a serious and often preventable cause of maternal and fetal morbidity and mortality. Perinatal mortality can be as high as 50%, especially in the third trimester of pregnancy. Maternal mortality rate is approximately 5%, the same as the mortality rate for ketoacidosis in the general population.

The primary cause of ketoacidosis in pregnancy is infection. Other predisposing factors include the use of beta-mimetic agents in the treatment of preterm labor in pregnant diabetics or the use of corticosteroids for fetal lung maturation.[26] Whatever the etiology, ketoacidosis occurs in gravid diabetics with a lesser degree of hyperglycemia (200–300 mg/100 mL) than in nongravid diabetics.[27]

The diagnosis of diabetic ketoacidosis is confirmed by the following:

- Plasma glucose > 300 mg/100 mL
- Plasma HCO_3 < 15 mEq/L

Table 4-3

Protocol for Management of Women with Insulin-Dependent Diabetes Mellitus Presenting for
Elective Cesarean Delivery

1. Administer the usual insulin dose on the evening before surgery.
2. Obtain a fasting glucose level on the morning of surgery.
3. If fasting glucose level is < 120 mg/100 mL, start intravenous fluids without dextrose. No insulin is given.
4. If fasting glucose level is > 120 mg/100 mL or if the surgery is delayed, start 5%–10% dextrose at a rate of 2.55 mg/kg/min and insulin at a rate of 1–5 units/h as needed to maintain blood sugar at 80–120 mg/100 mL.
5. If fasting glucose is > 120 mg/100 mL, delay surgery until plasma glucose has been less than 120 mg/100 mL for 4 h.

- pH < 7.30
- Serum acetone at 1:2 dilutions

Symptoms include nausea, vomiting, malaise, drowsiness, polydypsia, polyuria, and occasionally abdominal pain. Classic signs include hyperventilation (Kussmaul respirations), a fruity breath odor, dehydration, and, occasionally, hypotension.

Once a diagnosis is made, prompt treatment is imperative. Correct hyperglycemia with intravenous insulin infusion. Begin with a loading dose of 10 to 20 units of regular insulin. Follow this dose with a continuous infusion of 5 to 10 units of regular insulin per hour. These women may have a fluid deficit of 3L to 10L. Replace it with isotonic fluids (normal saline). Replete the typically deficient potassium and phosphate with potassium chloride and potassium phosphate as needed. Bicarbonate may cause a paradoxical intracerebral acidosis and may negatively affect oxygen delivery to tissues; therefore, do not give bicarbonate until the pH is less than 7.20. Limit the dosage to 89.2 mEq/L of intravenous fluid, and stop when the pH reaches 7.20. Any gravid patient in diabetic ketoacidosis during the third trimester also should undergo continuous fetal monitoring for signs of fetal distress. Still, if possible, correct the ketoacidosis and avoid a morbidly premature delivery.

INTRAPARTUM MANAGEMENT OF THE DIABETIC PARTURIENT

Hypoglycemia is the most common complication in neonates of diabetic mothers. Maintaining maternal plasma glucose at normal concentration during labor significantly reduces the incidence of neonatal hypoglycemia in infants of diabetic mothers. Therefore, intrapartum management of the diabetic parturient centers on maintaining maternal euglycemia. Simultaneous glucose and insulin infusions can maintain this strict metabolic control. Jovanovic and Peterson[28] noted that the glucose requirement during labor is constant at 2.55 mg/kg/min. Insulin requirements vary. Frequently, insulin is not required during the first stage of active labor.[28,29]

Monitor glucose concentration and insulin requirements in the following fashion. Measure plasma glucose concentration every hour using a capillary glucose reflectance meter. Infuse dextrose 5% to 10% at a constant rate of 2.55 mg/kg/min. Give insulin, also by infusion, as needed to maintain plasma glucose at 80 to 120 mg/dL. Usual insulin requirements range from 0 to 5 units of regular insulin per hour.

Patients with insulin-dependent diabetes presenting for elective cesarean delivery can receive their usual insulin dosage the evening before (Table 4-3). If possible, schedule surgery in the morning. Withhold both food and the usual insulin dosage. On the morning of surgery, check a fasting plasma glucose concentration. If it is less than 120 mg/100 mL, use intravenous solutions without dextrose. If surgery is delayed or if plasma glucose values are greater than 120 mg/100 mL, give combined glucose/insulin infusions as previously mentioned. Should plasma glucose be greater than 120 mg/100 mL, delivery should be delayed until the plasma glucose has remained less than 120 mg/100 mL for 4 hours. Management of diet-controlled, gestational diabetics is simpler. Usually, intravenous fluids without dextrose provide adequate control of maternal plasma glucose concentration.

REFERENCES

1. Hollingsworth DR, Moore TR. Diabetes and pregnancy. In: Creasy RK, Resnik R, eds. Maternal fetal medicine: Principles and practice. Philadelphia: WB Saunders, 1989:925.
2. Craigin EB, Ryder GH. Obstetrics. A practical textbook for students and practitioners. Philadelphia: Lea & Febiger, 1916.
3. Williams JW. Obstetrics. A textbook for the use of students and practitioners. New York: Appleton, 1925.
4. Coustan DR, Felig P. Diabetes mellitus. In: Burrow GN, Ferris TF, eds. Medical complications during pregnancy. Philadelphia: WB Saunders, 1988:34.
5. White P. Pregnancy and diabetes. In: Marble A, White P, Bradley RF, Krall LP, eds. Joslin's diabetes mellitus. 11th ed. Philadelphia: Lea & Febiger, 1971.
6. Felig P, Lynch V. Starvation in human pregnancy: Hypoglycemia, hypoinsulinemia, and hyperketonemia. Science 1970;170:990.
7. Kalhan SC, D'Angelo LJ, Savin SM, Adam PA. Glucose production in pregnant women at term gestation. Sources of glucose for human fetus. J Clin Invest 1979;63:388.
8. Buchanan TA, Unterman TG, Metzger BE. The medical management of diabetes in pregnancy. Clin Perinatol 1985;12:625.
9. Freinkel N. Effects of the conceptus on maternal metabolism during pregnancy. In: Leibel BS, Wrenshall GA, eds. On the nature and treatment of diabetes. Amsterdam: Excepta Medica 1964:679.
10. Freinkel N. Banting Lecture 1980. Of pregnancy and progeny. Diabetes 1980;29:1023.
11. Van Assche FA, Aerts L. Morphologic and ultrastructure modifications in the endocrine pancreas in pregnant rats. In: Camerini-Davalos RA, Cole HS, eds. Early diabetes in early life. New York: Academic Press, 1975.
12. Fisher PM, Sutherland HW, Bewsher PD. The insulin response to glucose infusion in normal human pregnancy. Diabetologia 1980;19:15.
13. Landon MB, Gabbe SG. Diabetes and pregnancy. Med Clin North Am 1988;72:1493.
14. Coustan DR, Berkowitz RL, Hobbins JC. Tight metabolic control of overt diabetes in pregnancy. Am J Med 1980;68:845.
15. Leslie RD, John PN, Pyke SA, White JM. Haemoglobin A_{1c} in diabetic pregnancy. Lancet 1978;2:958.
16. Miller E, Hare JW, Cloherty JP, et al. Elevated maternal hemoglobin A_1 in early pregnancy and major congenital anomalies in infants of diabetic mothers. N Engl J Med 1981;304:1331.
17. Fuhrmann K, Reiher H, Semmler K, Glockner E. The effect of intensified conventional insulin therapy before and during pregnancy on the malformation rate in offspring of diabetic mothers. Exp Clin Endocrinol 1984;83:173.
18. Sosenko IR, Kitzmiller JL, Loo SW, Blix P, Rubenstein AH, Gabbay KH. The infant of the diabetic mother: Correlation of increased cord C-peptide levels with macrosomia and hypoglycemia. N Engl J Med 1979;301:859.
19. Bloom SR, Johnston DI. Failure of glucagon release in infants of diabetic mothers. Br Med J 1972;4:453.
20. Frantz ID III, Epstein MF. Fetal lung development in pregnancies complicated by diabetes. In: Merkatz IR, Adam PA, eds. The diabetic pregnancy: A perinatal perspective. New York: Grune & Stratton, 1979.
21. Huffaker J. Fetal pulmonary maturation in the infant of the diabetic mother. In: Jovanovic L, Peterson CM, Fuhrmann K, eds. Diabetes and pregnancy: Teratology, toxicity and treatment. New York: Praeger, 1986:361.
22. Nylund L, Lunell NO, Lewander R, Persson B, Sarby B. Uteroplacental blood flow in diabetic pregnancy: Measurements with indium 113m and a computer-linked gamma camera. Am J Obstet Gynecol 1982;144:298.
23. Bjork O, Persson B. Placental changes in relation to the degree of metabolic control in diabetes mellitus. Placenta 1982;3:367.
24. Datta S. The diabetic parturient. In: James FM, Wheeler AS, Dewan DM, eds. Obstetric anesthesia. The complicated patient. Philadelphia: FA Davis, 1988:401.
25. Madsen H, Ditzel J. Changes in red blood cell oxygen transport in diabetic pregnancy. Am J Obstet Gynecol 1982;143:421.
26. Borberg C, Gillmer MD, Beard RW, Oakley NW. Metabolic effects of beta-sympathomimetic drugs and dexamethasone in normal and diabetic pregnancy. Br J Obstet Gynaecol 1978;85:184.
27. Pedersen J. The Pregnant Diabetic and Her Newborn. 2nd ed. Baltimore: Williams & Wilkins, 1977:22.
28. Jovanovic L, Peterson CM. Insulin and glucose requirements during the first stage of labor in insulin-dependent diabetic women. Am J Med 1983;75:607.
29. Golde SH, Good-Anderson B, Montoro M, Artal R. Insulin requirements during labor: A reappraisal. Am J Obstet Gynecol 1982;144:556.

CHAPTER 5

Pathophysiology and Obstetric Management of Preeclampsia

Jaya Ramanathan
Baha M. Sibai

Hypertension complicates 7% to 10% of all pregnancies and is a major cause of maternal morbidity and mortality worldwide.[1] Clinically, hypertension manifests as a wide spectrum of disorders. During pregnancy and parturition, these conditions range from mild elevations of blood pressures to severe disease involving all the major organ systems. The Committee on Terminology of the American College of Obstetricians and Gynecologists[2] has defined hypertension during pregnancy as an increase above baseline measurements obtained during the first trimester in

- Systolic pressure of 30 mm Hg
- Diastolic pressure of 15 mm Hg
- Mean arterial pressure of 20 mm Hg

In the absence of baseline measurements, the following measurements, on two occasions 6 hours apart, diagnose hypertension during pregnancy:

- A systolic pressure of 140 mm Hg or greater
- A diastolic pressure of 90 mm Hg or greater
- Mean arterial pressure of 105 mm Hg or greater

Table 5-1 shows a classification of the hypertensive disorders of pregnancy. Brief descriptions of the definitions are given in the following sections.

PREECLAMPSIA. Preeclampsia is the development of hypertension with proteinuria, generalized edema, or both after the 20th week of gestation. Preeclampsia can be mild or severe. Table 5-2 lists criteria for the diagnosis of severe preeclampsia. The presence of any one of these criteria diagnoses severe preeclampsia.

ECLAMPSIA. Eclampsia is defined as the development of convulsions or coma in women with preeclampsia without other precipitating causes of seizures.

CHRONIC HYPERTENSION OF PREGNANCY. Chronic hypertension of pregnancy is indicated by elevated blood pressure of any etiology that usually manifests before the 20th week of gestation and persists even after 6 weeks postpartum. The development of preeclampsia in pregnant women with chronic hypertension is classified as superimposed preeclampsia.

GESTATIONAL HYPERTENSION. Gestational hypertension develops in the second half of pregnancy or in the first 24 hours postpartum without evidence of edema or proteinuria. Blood pressure returns to normal within 10 days after delivery.

Table 5–1

Classification of Hypertensive Disorders in Pregnancy

> **I.** Pregnancy-induced hypertension
>   A. Preeclampsia
>   1. Mild
>   2. Severe
>   B. Eclampsia
> **II.** Chronic hypertension preceding pregnancy (any etiology)
> **III.** Chronic Hypertension with superimposed pregnancy-induced hypertension
> **IV.** Gestational hypertension
>
> (After Sibai BM. Preeclampsia–eclampsia. In: Beriberi RL, Berek SJ, Creasy RK, Decherney AH, Ryan KJ, eds. Current Problems in Obstetrics, Gynecology, and Fertility. Chicago: Year Book Medical Publishers, 1990:9)

Although the terminology and definitions are well described, diagnosis of the various forms of hypertension during pregnancy is often difficult. Lack of prenatal care, poor documentation of blood pressures, and inaccurate assessment of renal function during earlier visits can make differentiating preeclampsia from preexisting chronic hypertension and renal dysfunction an arduous task. In addition, the nonspecific signs (proteinuria and generalized edema) are often present in normal pregnancy. Lastly, there are no specific clinical markers for the positive diagnosis of preeclampsia.

INCIDENCE AND PREDISPOSING FACTORS

Preeclampsia is primarily a disease of the young primigravida. Preeclampsia also arises commonly among women over 35 years of age. This increased risk is presumably due to the higher incidence of chronic hypertension in this age group. Preeclampsia complicates 6% to 7% of pregnancies in the United States. The incidence among young, black primigravidae in inner-city hospitals is 19.6% to 20%.[1,2] Risk factors include preeclampsia during previous pregnancy, molar pregnancy, twin gestation, hydrops fetalis, and diabetes mellitus.[3,4] Other characteristic hazards include inadequate prenatal care, poor socioeconomic background, nutritional deficiencies, and ethnic origin.[5]

ETIOLOGY

Preeclampsia is a disease of unknown etiology. It occurs only in human pregnancy and has not yet been reproduced in animal models. Of the various theories regarding the etiology of preeclampsia, the following merit brief discussions.

Table 5–2

Criteria for the Diagnosis of Severe Preeclampsia

> **1.** Systolic pressure of 160 mm Hg or greater, or diastolic pressure 110 mm Hg or greater on two occasions at least 6 h apart
> **2.** Proteinuria of at least 5 g in 24-h urine collection (3+ or 4+ on semiquantitative assay)
> **3.** Oliguria of less than 400 mL in 24 h
> **4.** Cerebral or visual disturbances such as altered consciousness, headache, scotoma, or blurred vision
> **5.** Pulmonary edema or cyanosis
> **6.** Epigastric or right upper quadrant pain
> **7.** Impaired liver function of unclear etiology
> **8.** Thrombocytopenia
>
> (After American College of Obstetricians and Gynecologists: Preeclampsia. Tech Bull 91: February, 1986)

Abnormal Response to Placentation

In preeclampsia, the maternal vasculature does not respond adequately to the implantation and growth of placenta early in the first trimester. In normal pregnancy, endovascular trophoblasts initially invade the decidual segments of the spiral arteries. A second wave of trophoblast migration follows at the 16th week of gestation.[6–8] The second wave of migration invades the myometrial segments of the spiral arteries (Fig. 5-1). In preeclampsia, vascular changes arise only in the decidual segments of the spiral arteries. The musculoelastic portions of the myometrial segments of the spiral arteries remain intact. The myometrial portion of the spiral artery is small and narrow and responds readily to vasomotor stimuli with vasoconstriction. This narrowing decreases placental perfusion, produces areas of placental infarction, and predisposes to intrauterine growth retardation.[6–8] This abnormal maternal response to placentation is the earliest pathognomonic feature of preeclampsia; however, such changes are impossible to diagnose because the placenta is inaccessible during early pregnancy.

Thromboxane–Prostacyclin Imbalance

Thromboxane A_2, produced by the platelets, is a potent vasoconstrictor with a half-life of 30 seconds at 37°C. Prostacyclin, on the other hand, is a potent vasodilator and an inhibitor of platelet aggregation. Produced by the vascular endothelium and the renal cortex, it has a half-life of 3 minutes at 37°C. Many investigators have published conflicting reports about maternal serum and urinary concentrations of both these compounds in women with pregnancy-induced hypertension.[9–11]

In general, the ratio of thromboxane A_2 to prostacyclin levels in serum and urinary samples is consistently elevated in women with preeclampsia. Walsh *et al*[12,13] have shown that the ratio of placental thromboxane A_2 to prostacyclin is seven times higher in women with preeclampsia compared to normotensive pregnant women. Others have shown impaired production of prostacyclin in umbilical vessels and abnormal amounts in amniotic fluid in women with pregnancy-induced hypertension.[14,15] Results from these studies suggest that impaired production and metabolism of thromboxane A_2 and prostacyclin in umbilical and placental vasculature may have some role in causing the pathophysiologic changes of preeclampsia.

Altered Platelet Calcium Metabolism

Systemic vascular resistance is elevated in women with preeclampsia. A major determinant of vascular smooth muscle tone is the quantity of intracellular free calcium. Recent studies have shown increased intracellular calcium and altered calcium metabolism in preeclampsia and other hypertensive states.[16,17] Readily accessible platelets resemble vascular smooth muscle cells in having many similar anatomic and functional properties. In a recent study, Zemel *et al*[18] found an exaggerated response of platelet intracellular calcium to arginine vasopressin in women who subsequently developed preeclampsia. They also reported that this dramatic platelet response occurs early in pregnancy and so predicts subsequent preeclampsia. Others postulate that, in preeclampsia, the factors causing vascular smooth muscle constriction also may incite platelet activation.[19] Preeclampsia may be a trophoblast-dependent process mediated by platelet dysfunction and possibly prevented by antiplatelet therapy.

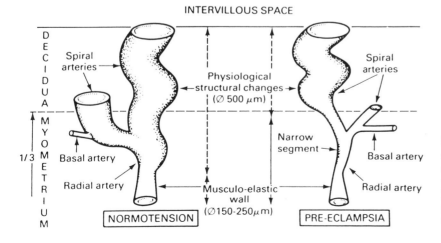

Figure 5–1. Diagrammatic representation of changes in decidual vessels in normal and preeclamptic pregnancies. (Brosens IA. Morphological changes in the uteroplacental bed in pregnancy hypertension. Clin Obstet Gynecol 1977;4:573)

Renin–Angiotensin–Aldosterone System

In women with a normal pregnancy, the plasma concentrations of renin, angiotensin II, and aldosterone are considerably higher than in nonpregnant controls.[20] In women with preeclampsia, however, the blood contains smaller amounts of these compounds.[21] In normal pregnancy, vascular response to pressors such as angiotensin II diminishes. In preeclampsia, despite the lower plasma concentrations, the pressor response to angiotensin II infusion increases significantly. This loss of refractoriness to angiotensin II infusions is an early finding in women with preeclampsia.[22]

Sympathoadrenal Activity

The many studies of adrenergic system activity, as measured by arterial and venous concentrations of epinephrine and norepinephrine, have reported conflicting results. Some investigators claim that there are higher plasma concentrations of both epinephrine and norepinephrine in women with pregnancy-induced hypertension compared to normotensive parturients.[23,24] In contrast, Pedersen *et al*[25] reported no differences in catecholamine concentrations in women with preeclampsia compared to control subjects. Nisell *et al*[26] found that women with preeclampsia had higher arterial epinephrine but unchanged norepinephrine concentrations at rest and under stress. Nisell postulates that, in women with preeclampsia, the autonomic nervous system fails to adapt to pregnancy. Adrenomedullary suppression fails to happen in parturients who develop preeclampsia.

Digoxine-like Immunoreactive Substance

Digoxine-like immunoreactive substance (DLIS) is a natriuretic and produces vasoconstriction. Several investigators have shown that the plasma concentration of DLIS rises in preeclampsia.[27] Others have found direct correlations between DLIS and diastolic pressures[28] reduced plasma volume.[29] These studies suggest that DLIS may produce the increased vascular tone and increased sensitivity to angiotensin infusion seen in preeclampsia. However, another study involving 41 women with preeclampsia found no differences in DLIS concentration between women with pregnancy-induced hypertension and normotensive controls.[30]

Atrial Natriuretic Peptides

Atrial natriuretic peptide (ANP) is a potent natriuretic, diuretic, and vascular smooth muscle relaxant; thus, the quantity of ANP affects volume status and vascular tone. During normal pregnancy, plasma ANP concentration can rise.[31,32] Atrial natriuretic peptide also increases, especially at midnight, in women with preeclampsia.[33,34] The significance of these changes remains a mystery.

Endothelin Levels

Endothelin, a vasoconstrictor ten times more potent than angiotensin II, is secreted in response to endothelial injury.[35,36] Endothelin concentrations rise in patients with acute myocardial infarction, severe hypertension, and acute and chronic renal failure.[37] A significant increase in plasma endothelin happens in women with preeclampsia and in patients with hemolysis, elevated liver enzymes, and low platelet counts (HELLP) syndrome.[38] Further studies should define the role of endothelial injury and endothelin syndrome production in the subsequent development of preeclampsia.

PATHOPHYSIOLOGY

Intense vasospasm is the single most important pathophysiologic change in women with pregnancy-induced hypertension. This process involves all major organs, including the uterus and placenta. Generalized vasospasm in turn decreases perfusion throughout the body, causing widespread organ dysfunction.

Blood Volume

In normal pregnancy, blood volume increases by 35%, plasma volume by 45%, and red cell volume by 20%.[39] In contrast, in mild preeclampsia, the plasma volume is approximately 9% lower than in normotensive pregnant women.[40] Plasma volume is 30% to 40% lower in women with severe preeclampsia than in normal parturients of similar gestational age.[40] It is unclear if this volume contraction causes or results from generalized vasoconstriction. Preeclamptic women with fetuses that are small for gestational age have less plasma volume expansion during pregnancy than other women.[41]

Despite decreased plasma volume, extravascular and interstitial volume markedly increase in these patients. Decreased plasma volume leads to hemoconcentration and increased whole blood viscosity. This change further reduces the already compromised uteroplacental perfusion, causing areas of placental infarction. Maternal hematocrit and hemoglobin concentrations correlate directly with the frequency of placental infarction and inversely with the weight percentile of the newborn.[42,43]

Hemodynamic Profile

Pregnancy, labor, and delivery cause major physiologic changes in the maternal cardiovascular system. Clark *et al*,[44] using a flow-directed pulmonary artery catheter, reported some of these changes in normotensive pregnant women (Table 5-3). These authors found the following at term:

- A 43% increase in cardiac output (17% increase in heart rate and 27% increase in stroke volume)
- A 21% decline in systemic vascular resistance (SVR)
- A 34% decrease in pulmonary vascular resistance (PVR)
- No significant changes in pulmonary capillary wedge pressure (PCWP), central venous pressure (CVP), and mean arterial pressure (MAP)
- Normal left ventricular function (Fig. 5-2)

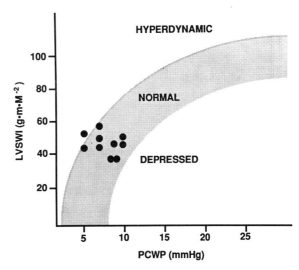

Figure 5–2. Left ventricular stroke work index (LVSWI) versus pulmonary capillary wedge pressure (PCWP) shows normal left ventricular function in healthy pregnant women. (Clark SL, Cotton DB, Lee W, et al. Central hemodynamic assessment of normal term pregnancy. Am J Obstet Gynecol 1989;161:1439)

The hemodynamic changes that accompany severe preeclampsia are much more complex and highly variable. Several investigators have attempted to explain the characteristic hemodynamic profile in severe preeclampsia. These studies are inconsistent and sometimes conflicting. The following list includes some of the confounding variables that complicate the interpretation of these studies.

Table 5–3

Hemodynamic Findings from Nonpregnant and Normal Term Pregnant Women*

HEMODYNAMIC VARIABLE	NONPREGNANT (n = 10)	PREGNANT (n = 10)
MAP (mm Hg)	86.4 ± 7.5	90.3 ± 5.8
Heart rate (beats/min)	71 ± 10	83 ± 10
Cardiac output (L/min)	4.3 ± 0.9	6.2 ± 1.0
SVR (dynes·sec·cm^{-5})	1530 ± 520	1210 ± 266
PCWP (mm Hg)	6.3 ± 2.1	7.5 ± 1.8
CVP (mm Hg)	3.7 ± 2.6	3.6 ± 2.5
LVSWI (g·m·m^2)	41 ± 8	48 ± 6
COP (mm Hg)	20.8 ± 1.0	18.0 ± 1.5

(After Clark SL, Cotton DB, Lee W *et al.* Central hemodynamic assessment of normal term pregnancy. Am J Obstet Gynecol 1989; 161:1439)
*Data are expressed as mean ± SEM.
Abbreviations: COP = colloid osmotic pressure, LVSWI = left ventricular stroke work index.

- Earlier administration of antihypertensive agents and fluids
- Presence of concurrent medical problems such as chronic hypertension
- Duration and severity of preeclampsia
- Effects of labor
- Mode of delivery
- Small number of patients in each study

Wallenburg *et al*[45] studied untreated preeclamptic women with no prior therapeutic interventions. Their patients had significantly lower cardiac output, stroke volume, and PCWP and higher SVR compared with normotensive pregnant women. These findings agree with the classic description of the hemodynamic profile in preeclampsia. Despite the low cardiac output, left ventricular function was hyperdynamic. In contrast, those women who had received various forms of treatment showed a wide range of values with no uniform pattern. More recently, two other groups have reported hemodynamic measurements made before major therapeutic interventions in women with severe preeclampsia.[46,47] Table 5-4 depicts some pertinent findings from these two studies. In general, women with severe preeclampsia have elevated cardiac output, normal to high PCWP, and a normal to elevated SVR. Most of these women also have hyperdynamic left ventricles (Fig. 5-3). Because preeclampsia is a disease process characterized by intense vasospasm involving all the major vascular beds, one would expect a significantly elevated SVR; however, because SVR is derived by dividing MAP by cardiac output, a high cardiac output can lower the calculated SVR to the normal range.[47]

Central Venous Pressure Versus Pulmonary Capillary Wedge Pressure

In the absence of valvular heart disease or left ventricular dysfunction, CVP correlates well with PCWP. In women with preeclampsia, however, changes in CVP often do not parallel changes in PCWP. Wallenburg[45] postulates that, in women with preeclampsia, a placid right atrium accommodates increased filling volume without simultaneous increases in pressure. This change would limit the sensitivity of CVP as a measure of intravascular volume. Cotton *et al*[46] speculate that, in severe preeclampsia, cardiac output remains high despite the increased left ventricular afterload. This effort leads to higher left-sided intracavitary pressures compared with normal or low pressures in the right heart. Mabie *et al*[47] suggest that the central redistribution of intravascular volume due to generalized vasospasm involving the capacitance vessels may produce the observed changes in severe preeclampsia.

Pulmonary Edema

A most serious complication of severe preeclampsia, pulmonary edema can be cardiogenic or noncardiogenic. Cardiogenic pulmonary edema results from left ventricular dysfunction in the face of severe increases in SVR, chronic hypertension, peripartum cardiomyopathy, and other conditions. Increased pulmonary capillary permeability, iatrogenic fluid overload, or a reduction in plasma oncotic pressure

Table 5-4

Hemodynamic Variables in Women with Severe Preeclampsia*

HEMODYNAMIC VARIABLE	MABIE *et al* [47] (n = 41)	COTTON *et al* [46] (n = 45)
Heart rate (beats/min)	94 ± 2	95 ± 2
MAP (mm Hg)	130 ± 2	138 ± 3
PCWP (mm Hg)	8.3 ± 0.3	10 ± 1
CVP (mm Hg)	4.8 ± 0.4	4 ± 1
Cardiac output (L/min)	8.4 ± 0.2	7.5 ± 0.2
SVR (dynes·sec·cm^{-5})	1226 ± 37	1496 ± 64
LVSWI (g·m·m^2)	84 ± 2	81 ± 2

(After Mabie WC, Ratts TE, Sibai BM. Central hemodynamics of severe preeclampsia. Am J Obstet Gynecol 1989;161:1443)
*Data are expressed as mean ± SEM.
Abbreviation: LVSWI = left ventricular stroke work index.

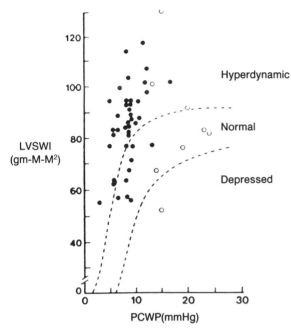

Figure 5-3. Left ventricular stroke work index (LVSWI) versus pulmonary capillary wedge pressure (PCWP) shows hyperdynamic left ventricular function in most women with severe preeclampsia. (Mabie WC, Ratts TE, Sibai BM. The central hemodynamics of severe preeclampsia. Am J Obstet Gynecol 1989;161:1443)

(POP)–PCWP gradient may cause noncardiogenic pulmonary edema.

The relationship between POP and PCWP is defined by the Starling's equation,[48] which follows:

$$Q = k(P_c - _i) - k (\pi_c - \pi_i),$$

where
Q is fluid flux, P is hydrostatic pressure in the capillaries (P_c) and interstitial space (P_i), π is osmotic pressure in the plasma (π_c) and interstitial space (π_i),

Clinically, PCWP reflects P_c. An oncometer will measure POP. Hydrostatic pressure in the capillaries facilitates outward movement of fluids from capillaries. Plasma oncotic pressure helps retain fluid and maintain intravascular volume. Approximately 70% of POP is exerted by plasma albumin and the remaining 30% by the globulin fraction. In nonpregnant state, POP averages 25.4 ± 2.3 mm Hg and PCWP varies from 8 to 12 mmHg, with a POP–PCWP gradient of about 12 mm Hg. In pregnancy, POP values range from 18 to 21 mm Hg and PCWP averages 7.5 ± 1.8 mm Hg. The POP–PCWP gradient remains similar to nonpregnant values.[44,49] Gonik *et al*[49] have shown that, in normal pregnancy, POP falls significantly after delivery. It

reaches its nadir 6 hours after delivery. This decline in POP presumably results from aggressive crystalloid therapy during the peripartum period.[49] Neither the type of anesthesia (epidural vs general), nor the mode of delivery (vaginal vs abdominal), significantly influenced the reduction in POP.[49,50]

Women with severe pregnancy-induced hypertension have lower than normal values for POP both before and after delivery. The lower POP in preeclampsia results from either renal loss of albumin or impaired synthesis of albumin (hepatic dysfunction). After delivery, POP falls from 17.9 ± 0.3 mm Hg to 13.7 ± 0.5 mm Hg.[51] Simultaneously, PCWP increases significantly owing to the mobilization of extravascular edema fluid, iatrogenic fluid overload, and diminished renal output. The lowering of POP with the simultaneous elevation of PCWP causes narrowing of the POP–PCWP gradient, risking noncardiogenic pulmonary edema.

Recently, Mabie *et al*[52] studied a subset of women with pulmonary edema probably of cardiac etiology. These women were markedly obese with chronic hypertension and superimposed preeclampsia. All had severe hypertension, elevated cardiac output, elevated PCWP, normal SVR, normal POP, and pulmonary edema. Echocardiography showed large chambers with thick walls, normal systolic function, and abnormal diastolic function. In these women, pulmonary edema resulted from intrinsic volume overloading in the presence of impaired left ventricular relaxation (diastolic dysfunction). Vasodilator therapy worsened the high-output state and pulmonary edema by further increasing cardiac output without lowering MAP. Then, reflex tachycardia associated with vasodilator therapy shortened the diastolic filling time, further impairing left ventricular filling. All patients in this study responded well to diuretic therapy. The authors still caution that diuretic therapy should be guided by invasive monitoring to keep PCWP and cardiac output within normal limits.

Coagulation Abnormalities

Preeclampsia is associated with microvascular endothelial damage and enhanced clotting. Levels of fibronectin, a marker of vascular endothelial damage, increase in preeclampsia.[53] Significant reductions in antithrombin III and alpha$_2$-antiplasmin signify enhanced clotting.[54] Platelet activation and platelet consumption with shortened platelet life span are characteristic features of preeclampsia. Serum levels of platelet-specific proteins such as beta-thromboglobulin and platelet factor 4 increase, suggesting ongoing platelet aggregation and degranulation.[55]

Thrombocytopenia occurs in 15% to 20% of women with preeclampsia. The incidence is as high as 50% in those with severe preeclampsia.[56] The exact mechanism of thrombocytopenia is uncertain. An earlier report suggested that thrombocytopenia occurred early in pregnancy and became evident even before the occurrence of renal dysfunction.[57] To investigate the causes of thrombocytopenia in women with preeclampsia, Burrows et al[58] did hemostatic and platelet function studies in 61 preeclamptic women and 24 healthy pregnant controls (Table 5-5). They found thrombocytopenia in 50% of their preeclamptic subjects. These women had a higher mean platelet volume (larger than normal platelets), which signified increased platelet destruction. They had normal prothrombin and partial thromboplastin times. These normal values showed that the increased platelet destruction was not related to increased thrombin activity (disseminated intravascular coagulation). In addition, a more sensitive indicator of thrombin activity, the protamine sulfate paracoagulation assay, also produced normal results. Platelet-associated immunoglobulin (IgG) concentrations increased in 35% of the preeclamptic patients and inversely correlated with severity of thrombocytopenia. These authors suggest that platelet-associated IgG suggests autoimmune-mediated platelet destruction as the cause of thrombocytopenia in preeclampsia.

Besides affecting the number of platelets, preeclampsia also alters their function. The template bleeding time, an in vivo platelet function test, is prolonged. Synthesis of platelet thromboxane A_2, an in vitro platelet function test, also falls.[58,59] Even in the presence of an adequate platelet count, women with preeclampsia may have a prolonged bleeding time (Fig. 5-4).[58,60]

Renal Changes

In normal pregnancy, both effective renal plasma flow and glomerular filtration rate increase by 30% to 50%.[61] In contrast, both glomerular filtration rate and renal plasma flow are significantly lower in women with preeclampsia.[62] In addition, certain intrinsic structural abnormalities arise. The changes include swelling of glomerular endothelial cells, deposition of fibrin along the basement membrane, and narrowing or complete obliteration of capillary lumen. Renal glomerular endotheliosis is the histopathologic marker for the diagnosis of preeclampsia.[63] Extent and severity of glomerular endotheliosis correlates with the amount of protein loss.[62] Significant urinary protein loss lowers POP. Diminishing the gradient between POP and capillary hydrostatic pressure leads to generalized edema. In addition, pregnancy-induced hypertension impairs renal excretion of sodium, increasing total body sodium. Clearance of urea, uric acid, and creatinine decline, which significantly increases their serum concentrations.

Table 5–5

Results of Hemostatic Assays Performed on 44 Nulliparous Preeclamptic Patients*

TEST	NON THROMBOCYTOPENIC (n = 22)	THROMBOCYTOPENIC (n = 22)
Platelet Count ($\times 10^3$/µL)	199.6 ± 34	79.4 ± 40.6*
Bleeding time (min)	7.6 ± 4.6	13.0 ± 8.3*
Platelet-associated IgG (fg per platelet)	3.9 ± 2.0	10.6 ± 12.2*
Mean platelet volume (fL)	11.5 ± 1.4	14.1 ± 6.4*
Prothrombin time (s)	10.9 ± 0.6	10.5 ± 0.6
Partial thromboplastin time (s)	30.4 ± 4.4	33.5 ± 4.3
Fibrinogen (mg/dL)	553.6 ± 199.0	452.8 ± 123
Beta-thromboglobulin (ng/mL)	5.0 ± 2.0	4.8 ± 2.9
Thromboxane B_2 (ng/mL)	120.4 ± 103.4	122.6 ± 94.3
Protamine sulfate paracoagulation assay	Negative	Negative

(After Burrows RF, Hunter DJS, Andrew M, Keltan J. A prospective study investigating the mechanism of thrombocytopenia in preeclampsia. Obstet Gynecol 1987;70:335)
*Data are expressed as mean ± SD.
†$P<0.05$.

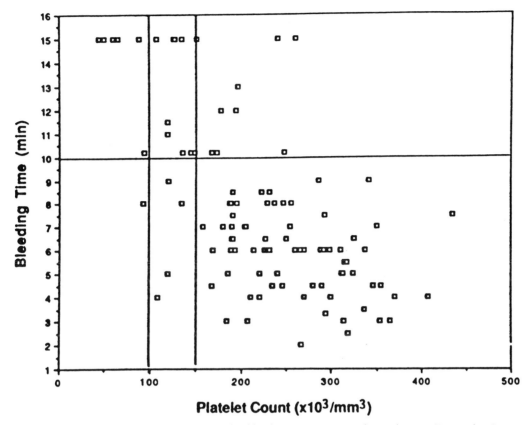

Figure 5–4. Platelet counts and corresponding bleeding times in women with preeclampsia. (Ramanathan J, Sibai BM, Vu T, Chauhan D. Correlation between bleeding times and platelet counts in women with preeclampsia undergoing cesarean section. Anesthesiology 1989;71:188)

Hepatic Changes

Intense vasospasm involving hepatic arteriolar bed can cause mid zonal necrosis and multiple areas of hepatic infarct. The epigastric or right upper quadrant pain in women with severe preeclampsia is symptomatic of small subcapsular hepatic hemorrhages. Rarely, severe spontaneous hepatic hemorrhage and rupture can occur with sudden cardiovascular collapse.[64] Hyperbilirubinemia and elevated liver enzymes, although frequently present, seldom persist after delivery.

Central Nervous System Changes

Cerebral hemorrhage is a common cause of maternal death in women with pregnancy-induced hypertension.[65] Eclamptic seizures may occur into the postpartum period. Sibai *et al*[66] showed that 75% of eclamptic women and 50% of preeclamptic women had abnormal electroencephalographic findings. Cerebral blood flow and oxygen consumption are usually within normal limits. Cerebral edema due to loss of cerebral autoregulation can occur because of sudden and severe increases in MAP. Such elevations of MAP are not uncommon during tracheal intubation in women with severe preeclampsia who are undergoing cesarean sections under general anesthesia.

OBSTETRIC MANAGEMENT OF PREECLAMPSIA

Because of the high risk of placental abruption and eclampsia, all women with mild preeclampsia at or near term require immediate hospitalization for further evaluation and treatment. Also, preeclampsia has reduced placental blood flow by 50% when clinical symptoms and signs become evident. Following hospitalization, most women with preeclampsia receive magnesium therapy and undergo induction of labor. Most obstetricians do not permit a preeclamptic pregnancy to continue beyond term (40 weeks' gestation).

Management of mild preeclampsia detected early in pregnancy is more controversial. Several prospective randomized clinical trials have examined the benefits of early and prolonged hospitalization versus ambulatory management.[67,68] At the University of Tennessee, all women with mild preeclampsia enter the hospital at the time of diagnosis. Figure 5-5 and Table 5-6 summarize our routine maternal and fetal evaluation and management. We advocate such detailed and frequent evaluations to detect quickly any thrombocytopenia or liver dysfunction that may occur. Spontaneous diuresis usually begins within 48 hours of hospitalization alone. As a result, body weight and blood pressure fall.[19] Those who become normotensive with this regimen then become candidates for home management. They must rest in bed, measure their urine protein daily by dipstick, count fetal movements, and have a visiting nurse check their blood pressures. They return to the hospital for antepartum evaluation twice a week. Any evidence of maternal or fetal deterioration results in immediate hospitalization for further evaluation and treatment.

Management of women with severe preeclampsia involves a more aggressive approach. All women with a diagnosis of severe preeclampsia are admitted to the labor and delivery floor for observation. All receive intravenous magnesium sulfate ($MgSO_4$) continuously as infusion, according to our standard protocol. In addition, we give hydralazine intravenously, in doses of 5 to 10 mg, to lower the diastolic pressure below 110 mm Hg. All women with persistent hypertension or maternal and fetal deterioration are delivered within 24 hours irrespective of gestational age and fetal lung maturity. In others who respond well to therapy (as evidenced by diuresis and diastolic pressures below 100 mm Hg), $MgSO_4$ and hydralazine therapy are stopped. Still, they are closely monitored until the fetal lungs mature. Patients at 33 to 35 weeks' gestation receive steroids to accelerate fetal lung maturity and are then delivered. Those women with gestational age beyond 35 weeks are delivered within 24 hours of admission.

TREATMENT

The major goals of therapy are as follows:

- Prevention of convulsions
- Control and stabilization of blood pressure
- Optimization of intravascular volume status

Attaining these goals will contribute to safe delivery of a viable baby.

Seizure Prophylaxis

Magnesium sulfate is the drug of choice in the United States for prevention of seizures. Earlier studies suggested that magnesium prevented convulsions by producing generalized depression of the central nervous system. However, animal studies have shown that magnesium ions specifically suppress experimentally induced electroencephalographic spike activity and neuronal burst response.[69] Magnesium also impairs neuromuscular function.[70] The extent of the effect on neuromuscular transmission correlates directly with the serum concentration of magnesium.[71] Infusion of $MgSO_4$ increases cardiac index by 12.5% and transiently lowers MAP without significantly changing other hemodynamic variables.[72] Magnesium rapidly crosses the placental barrier. With prolonged administration, fetal and maternal serum concentrations tend to equilibrate. Neonatal hypotonia and respiratory depression may follow. Therapeutic magnesium concentrations range from 5.0 to 7.0 mg/dL. Toxicity arises as the serum concentration approaches 9 mg/dL. Overdose, severely compromised renal function, or both can produce toxic serum concentrations of magnesium. Pulmonary function tests detect transient but mild deterioration at serum concentrations as low as 3.0 to 4.1 mg/dL.[73] Magnesium can cause respiratory arrest by impairing muscle strength and cardiac arrest by inducing a rapid decline in available calcium. Treatment usually involves cardiorespiratory support and administration of calcium chloride to counteract the cardiac effects of magnesium. Magnesium sulfate is a safe and effective agent for prevention of convulsions. Still, some patients can have eclamptic seizures while receiving magnesium infusion. In such cases, give further bolus doses of intravenous magnesium or small doses of a short-acting barbiturate. If convulsions persist, resort to tracheal intubation and artificial ventilation to prevent pulmonary aspiration of gastric contents.

Although intravenous magnesium is the standard therapy for preeclampsia in the United States, it is seldom used in the European countries. Instead, European obstetricians opt for anticonvulsants such as diazepam, barbiturates, and chlormethiazol. Although these agents are excellent anticonvulsants, their use may produce significant maternal and neonatal sedation and respiratory depression. Administration of

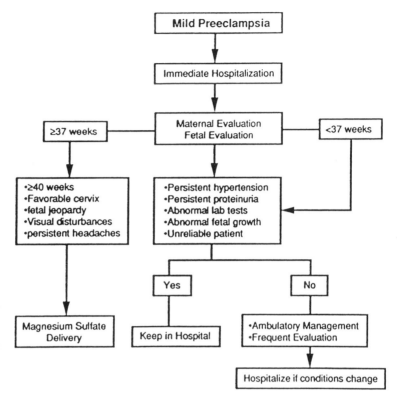

Figure 5–5. Management of women with mild preeclampsia. (Sibai BM. Preeclampsia-eclampsia. In: Beribri RL, Berek SJ, Creasy RK, Decherney AH, Ryan KJ, eds. Current problems in obstetrics, gynecology and fertility. Chicago: Year Book Medical Publishers, 1990:9)

Table 5–6

Maternal–Fetal Evaluation of Mild Preeclampsia

MATERNAL EVALUATION	FETAL EVALUATION
Blood pressure every 4 h	Daily fetal movements
Patellar reflexes daily	Non-stress tests twice a week
Presence of facial or abdominal edema	Biophysical profile; if nonreactive, non-stress test
Daily weight estimation	Ultrasound evaluation of fetal growth every 2 wk
Symptoms of impending eclampsia	
Occipital or frontal headaches	
Visual disturbances	
Right upper quadrant or epigastric pain	
Daily estimation of urine protein	
Hematocrit and platelet count every 2 wk	
Liver function tests 1–2 times/wk	
24-h urine collections twice/wk	

(After Sibai BM: Preeclampsia–eclampsia. In: Beriberi RL, Berek SJ, Creasy RK, Decherney AH, Ryan KJ, eds. Current Problems in Obstetrics, Gynecology, and Fertility. Chicago: Year Book Medical Publishers, 1990:9) large doses of diazepam to the mother correlates with neonatal hypothermia, jaundice, and respiratory depression.[74] Recent studies have reported that the anticonvulsant phenytoin can safely prevent and treat convulsions in preeclampsia without adverse maternal or neonatal effects.[75]

Treatment of Hypertension

Although MgSO$_4$ causes a transient reduction of maternal blood pressure, other potent antihypertensive agents often are needed to control hypertension in preeclampsia. Some commonly used agents are described in the following sections.

Hydralazine

Hydralazine is a commonly used antihypertensive agent. In pregnant ewes, hydralazine reduces blood pressure and uterine vascular resistance and increases uterine blood flow.[76] It has a slow onset of action, which, following intravenous administration, peaks in 20 minutes. In women with preeclampsia, hydralazine significantly increases maternal heart rate and cardiac index and reduces MAP and SVR without changing PCWP.[77] Hydralazine crosses the placental barrier with ease and in large doses causes hypotension and thrombocytopenia in the neonate. The slow onset, delayed peak effects, and compensatory tachycardia are some major disadvantages of this drug. At the University of Tennessee, we give hydralazine in bolus doses of 5 to 10 mg to lower diastolic pressure below 110 mm Hg. We adjust the dose to the maternal blood pressure response Both maternal electrocardiogram and blood pressure are continuously monitored during administration.

Labetalol

Labetalol is a combined alpha-and beta-adrenergic blocking agent with a beta–alpha blockade ratio of 3:1 after oral administration and 7:1 after intravenous use. In animals, intravenous labetalol ameliorates the effects of norepinephrine on maternal MAP, uterine blood flow, and fetal pH and P$_a$O$_2$.[83] The drug produces less adrenergic blockade in the fetus than in the mother. In women with preeclampsia, labetalol decreases SVR without altering cardiac output.[84] Compared with hydralazine, labetalol has a more rapid onset and produces a smoother reduction of blood pressure in women with preeclampsia. It crosses the placental barrier. The maternal:fetal ratio is 1:1. It does not cause

any adverse effects in the neonate. Infants have excellent Apgar scores and acid–base status. Hypotension and hypoglycemia do not occur.[84,85] Labetalol in doses of 1 mg/kg safely blunts the hypertensive response to endotracheal intubation during induction of general anesthesia in women with severe preeclampsia.[85] The major disadvantage of this drug is the widely varying dose requirement that cannot be predicted by any clinical criteria.

Other Drugs

Other drugs are undergoing clinical trials in patients with preeclampsia to establish the safety in mother and fetus. Some of these compounds include beta-adrenergic blocking drugs such as esmolol, metoprolol, and pindolol, and calcium-channel blocking agents such as nifedipine and verapamil.

We reserve other potent antihypertensive agents such as nitroglycerin, nitroprusside, and trimethaphan for specific treatment indications, such as the following:

- Acute hypertensive crisis
- Intractable hypertension unresponsive to conventional therapy
- Prevention of severe hypertensive response to tracheal intubation under general anesthesia

Administration of such potent antihypertensive agents requires continuous monitoring of maternal arterial pressure (via an indwelling radial artery catheter) and maternal electrocardiogram.

Sodium Nitroprusside

Sodium nitroprusside (SNP) is a potent arteriolar dilator with a rapid onset and short duration of action. Earlier animal studies showed that infusion of high doses of SNP caused fetal cyanide toxicity and death.[79] However, other studies have shown that SNP reverses the norepinephrine-induced reduction in uterine blood flow and normalizes maternal blood pressure without any evidence of accumulation of cyanide in the fetus.[80] Although fetal cyanide toxicity is a cause for concern, the use of low doses for a short period is probably safe. In women with pregnancy-induced hypertension, complicated by pulmonary congestion and heart failure, SNP dramatically decreases in PCWP and produces significant hemodynamic improvement.[78] No adverse maternal or fetal effects occurred. Significant amounts of cyanide were not detected in either maternal or umbilical cord blood.

Nitroglycerin

Nitroglycerin (NTG) is a venodilator that reduces cardiac filling pressures by acting mainly on capacitance vessels. Like SNP, NTG reverses the uterine vasoconstriction, restores uterine blood flow, and counteracts maternal hypertension caused by norepinephrine.[80] In women with severe preeclampsia, NTG produces smooth reductions of MAP (by 27.5%), PCWP, and cardiac index. Heart rate, stroke volume, and CVP do not change.[81] Volume expansion markedly impedes the hypotensive effects of the drug.[81] Nitroglycerin blunts the severe hypertensive response to tracheal intubation in women with severe preeclampsia undergoing cesarean delivery under general anesthesia.[82] Both SNP and NTG cross the blood–brain barrier with ease and increase cerebral blood flow and cerebrospinal fluid pressure.

Trimethaphan

Trimethaphan is an effective ganglionic blocking agent with limited placental transfer due to its high molecular weight. Still, compensatory tachycardia, tachyphylaxis, histamine release, and possible prolongation of the action of succinylcholine can complicate the use of this agent.

HELLP SYNDROME

First described by Weinstein in 1982,[86] the syndrome of hemolysis, elevated liver enzymes, and low platelet count (HELLP) is recognized as a complication of severe preeclampsia. The incidence varies from 2% to 12%. The HELLP syndrome can develop any time during pregnancy. Seventy percent of cases occur antepartum and 30% postpartum. The risk is highest among older (age > 25 years), white, multiparous women with poor obstetric history.[87]

The diagnosis of HELLP syndrome is somewhat easy at or near term; however, some patients present early in pregnancy with nonspecific symptoms such as malaise, nausea and vomiting, and right upper quadrant pain. Adding to difficulty of diagnosis, hypertension and proteinuria may not be present. In fact, many women are misdiagnosed as having conditions such as viral hepatitis, gastroenteritis, peptic ulcer, cholecystitis, fatty liver of pregnancy, idiopathic thrombocytopenia, or hemolytic uremic syndrome. Controversy still surrounds the definition and obstetric management of this syndrome. At the University of Tennessee, we use the following criteria for the diagnosis of HELLP syndrome:

- Hemolysis as evidenced by
  Abnormal peripheral smear
  Increased serum bilirubin (> 1.2 mg/dL)
  Increased lactic dehydrogenase levels (> 600 IU/L)
- Elevated liver enzymes:
  SGOT > 70 IU/L
  Increased lactic dehydrogenase levels
- Platelet count $< 100,000/$mm^3

All patients with a diagnosis of HELLP syndrome should be immediately transferred to a tertiary care center for further evaluation and treatment. Initial management resembles that for women with severe preeclampsia. First, stabilize the maternal condition, especially coagulation function. At our institution, we do not consider the presence of HELLP syndrome an indication for immediate cesarean delivery. We anticipate a vaginal delivery and begin oxytocin induction of labor in all women with gestational age of 32 weeks or more. Yet, we choose cesarean section in those women with gestational age of less than 32 weeks and an unripe cervix. Those developing laboratory evidence of dissemenated intravascular coagulation are delivered immediately, despite fetal gestational age. In these women, platelet function requires close monitoring as rapid deterioration often occurs.[88] Any deterioration in platelet function has significant implications for obstetric and anesthetic management.

CONCLUSION

The pathophysiologic changes of preeclampsia involve every major organ system. A thorough knowledge of these complex changes is essential for successful obstetric and anesthetic management of women with hypertensive disorders of pregnancy. The anesthesiologist, with his or her knowledge and expertise in critical care and invasive monitoring, can play a vital role in the peripartum management of these severely ill parturients.

REFERENCES

1. Roberts JM. Pregnancy-related hypertension. In: Creasy RK, Resnik R. eds. Maternal Fetal Medicine Principles and Practice. Philadelphia: WB Saunders, 1989;777.

2. Hughes HC, ed. Obstetric–Gynecologic Terminology. Philadelphia: FA Davis, 1972;422.

3. Long P, Oats J. Preeclampsia in twin pregnancy, severity and pathogenesis. Aust NZ J Obstet Gynæcol 1987;27:1.

4. Campbell DM, MacGillivray I, Carr-Hill R. Preeclampsia in second pregnancy. Br J Obstet Gynæcol 1985;92:131.

5. Sibai BM. Preeclampsia-eclampsia. In: Beribri RL, Berek SJ, Creasy RK, Decherney AH, Ryan KJ, eds. Current problems in obstetrics, gynecology and fertility. Chicago: Year Book Medical Publishers, 1990:9.

6. Brosens I, Robertson WB, Dixon G. The physiologic response of the vessels of the placental bed to normal pregnancy. J Pathol Bacteriol 1967;93:569.

7. Brosens IA. Morphological changes in the uteroplacental bed in pregnancy hypertension. Clin Obstet Gynaecol 1977;4:573.

8. Robertson WB, Brosens I, Dixon G. Uteroplacental vascular pathology. Eur J Obstet Gynaecol Reprod Biol 1975;5:47.

9. Koullapis EN, Nicolaides KH, Collins WP, Collins WP, Rodeck CH, Campbell S. Plasma prostanoids in pregnancy-induced hypertension. Br J Obstet Gynæcol 1982;89:617.

10. Lewis PJ. Does prostacyclin deficiency play a role in preeclampsia? In: Lewis PJ, Moncada S, O'Grady J, eds. Prostacyclin in pregnancy. New York: Raven Press, 1983:215.

11. Yamaguchi M, Mori N. 6-Keto prostaglandin F_{1a}, thromboxane B_2 and 13, 14-dihydro-15 keto prostaglandin F concentrations of normotensive and preeclamptic patients during pregnancy, delivery, and the postpartum period. Am J Obstet Gynecol 1985;151:121.

12. Walsh SW, Parisi VM. The role of arachidonic acid metabolites in preeclampsia. Semin Perinatol 1986;10:334.

13. Walsh SW: Preeclampsia: An imbalance in placental prostacyclin and thromboxane production. Am J Obstet Gynecol 1985;152:335.

14. Remuzzi G, Marchesi D, Zoja C, et al. Reduced umbilical and placental vascular prostacyclin in severe preeclampsia. Prostaglandins 1980;20:105.

15. Ylikorkala O, Makila UM, Viinikka L. Amniotic fluid prostacyclin and thromboxane in normal, preeclamptic, and some other complicated pregnancies. Am J Obstet Gynecol 1981;141:487.

16. Sowers JR, Zemel MB, Bronsteen RA, et al. Erythrocyte cation metabolism in preeclampsia. Am J Obstet Gynecol 1989;161:441.

17. Sowers JR, Zemel MB, Standley PR, Zemel PC. Calcium and hypertension. J Lab Clin Med 1989;114:338.

18. Zemel MB, Zemel PC, Berry S, et al. Altered platelet-calcium metabolism as an early predictor of increased peripheral vascular resistance and preeclampsia in urban black women. N Engl J Med 1990;323:434.

19. Redman CWG. Platelets and the beginnings of preeclampsia. N Engl J Med 1990;323:478.

20. Symonds EM. The renin-angiotensin system in pregnancy-induced hypertension. In: Sharp F, Symonds EM, eds. Hypertension in pregnancy. Ithaca, NY: Perinatology Press, 1987:91.

21. Broughton Pipkin F. The renin–angiotensin system in normal and hypertensive pregnancies. In: Rubin PL, ed. Handbook of hypertension, Vol 10, Hypertension in pregnancy. Amsterdam: Elsevier Science BV, 1988:118.

22. Gant NF, Daley GL, Chand S, Whalley PJ, MacDonald PC. A study of angiotensin II pressor response throughout primigravid pregnancy. J Clin Invest 1973;52:2682.

23. Oian P, Lande K, Kjeldsen SE, Aakesson I, Eide I, Maltau JM. Enhanced platelet release reaction related to arterial plasma adrenaline and blood pressure in preeclampsia. Br J Obstet Gynæcol 1986;93:548.

24. Davey DA, MacNab MF. Plasma adrenaline, noradrenaline and dopamine in pregnancy hypertension. Br J Obstet Gynæcol 1981;88:611.

25. Pedersen EB, Rasmussen AB, Christensen NJ, Johannesen P, Lauritsen JG, Kristensen S et al. Plasma noradrenaline and adrenaline in preeclampsia, essential hypertension in pregnancy and normotensive pregnant control subjects. Acta Endocrinol (Copenh) 1982;99:594.

26. Nisell H, Lunell NO, Hiendahl P, et al. Catecholamines in pregnancy-induced hypertension. In: Sharp F, Symonds EM, eds. Hypertension in pregnancy. Ithaca, NY: Perinatology Press, 1987:187.

27. Gudson JP, Buckalew VM, Henessy JF. A digoxin-like immunoreactive substance in preeclampsia. Am J Obstet Gynecol 1984;150:83.

28. Graves SW. The possible role of digitalis-like factors in pregnancy-induced hypertension. Hypertension 1987;10:84.

29. Goodlin RC. Expanded toxemia syndrome or gestosis. Am J Obstet Gynecol 1986;154:1227.

30. Gonzalez AR, Phelps SJ, Cochran EB, Sibai BM. Digoxin-like immunoreactive substance in pregnancy. Am J Obstet Gynecol 1987;157:660.

31. Steegers EA, Hein PB, Tan AC, Groeneveld EA, Jongsma HW, Benraad TJ. Plasma atrial natriuretic peptide (ANP) in late pregnancy and puerperium. Eur J Obstet Gynecol Reprod Biol 1987;26:213.

32. Kirai N, Yanaihara T, Nakayama T, Ishibashi M, Yamaji T. Plasma levels of atrial natriuretic peptide during normal pregnancy and in pregnancy complicated by hypertension. Am J Obstet Gynecol 1988;159:27.

33. Thomsen JK, Storm TJ, Thamsborg G, De Nully M, et al. Atrial natriuretic peptide concentrations in preeclampsia. Br Med J 1987;294:1508.

34. Miyamoto S, Shimokawa H, Sumioki H, Touno A, Nakano H. Circadian rhythm of plasma atrial natriuretic peptide, aldosterone and blood pressure during the third trimester in normal and preeclamptic pregnancies. Am J Obstet Gynecol 1988;158:393.

35. Yanagisawa M, Kuvishara H, Kimura S, Tombobe Y, Kobayashi M, Mitsui Y, et al. A novel potent vasoconstrictor peptide produced by vascular endothelial cells. Nature 1988;332:411.

36. Firth JD, Ratcliffe PJ, Raine AE, Ledingham JG. Endo-

thelin: An important factor in acute renal failure? Lancet 1988;2:1179.

37. Brenner BM, Troy JL, Ballermann BJ. Endothelium-dependent vascular responses: Mediators and mechanisms. J Clin Invest 1989;84:1373.

38. Nova A, Sibai BM, Barton JR, et al. Maternal plasma endothelin is increased in preeclampsia. Am J Obstet Gynecol 1991;165:724.

39. Gutsche BB, Cheek TG. Anesthetic considerations in preeclampsia–eclampsia. In: Shnider SM, Levinson G, eds. Anesthesia for obstetrics, 2nd ed. Baltimore: Williams & Wilkins, 1987:225.

40. Chesley LC. Plasma and red cell volumes during pregnancy. Am J Obstet Gynecol 1972;112:440.

41. MacGillivary I. Preeclampsia: The Hypertensive Disease of Pregnancy. Philadelphia: WB Saunders, 1983:62.

42. Koller O. The clinical significance of hemodilution during pregnancy. Obstet Gynecol Surv 1982;37:649.

43. Sagen N, Nilsen ST, Kim HC, Koller O, Bergsj P. The predictive value of total estriol, HPL and Hb on perinatal outcome in severe preeclampsia. Acta Obstet Gynæcol Scand 1984;63:603.

44. Clark SL, Cotton DB, Lee W et al. Central hemodynamic assessment of normal term pregnancy. Am J Obstet Gynecol 1989;161:1439.

45. Wallenburg HCS. Hemodynamics in hypertensive pregnancy. In: Rubin PC, ed. Hypertension in pregnancy. Amsterdam: Elsevier 1988:66.

46. Cotton DB, Lee W, Huhta JC, Dorman KF. Hemodynamic profile of severe pregnancy-induced hypertension. Am J Obstet Gynecol 1988;158:523.

47. Mabie WC, Ratts TE, Sibai BM. The central hemodynamics of severe preeclampsia. Am J Obstet Gynecol 1989;161:1443.

48. Gonik B. Intensive care monitoring of the critically ill pregnant patient. In Creasy RK, Resnik R, eds. Maternal fetal medicine: Principles and practice. Philadelphia: WB Saunders, 1989:845.

49. Gonik B, Cotton D, Spillman T, Abouleish E, Zavisca F. Peripartum colliod osmotic pressure changes. Effects of controlled fluid management. Am J Obstet Gynecol 1985;151:812.

50. Cotton DM, Gonik B, Spillman T, Dorman KF. Intrapartum to postpartum changes in colliod osmotic pressure. Am J Obstet Gynecol 1984;149:174.

51. Benedetti TJ, Carlson RW. Studies of colloid osmotic pressure in pregnancy-induced hypertension. Am J Obstet Gynecol 1979;135:308.

52. Mabie WC, Ratts TE, Ramanathan KB, Sibai BM. Circulatory congestion in obese hypertensive women: A subset of pulmonary edema in pregnancy. Obstet Gynecol 1988;72:553.

53. Stubbs TM, Lazarchick J, Horger EO III. Plasma fibronectin levels in preeclampsia: A possible biochemical marker for vascular endothelial damage. Am J Obstet Gynecol 1984;150:885.

54. Weiner CP, Brandt J. Plasma antithrombin III activity: An aid in the diagnosis of preeclampsia-eclampsia. Am J Obstet Gynecol 1982;142:275.

55. Socol ML, Weiner CP, Louis G, Rehnberg K, Rossi EC. Platelet activation in preeclampsia. Am J Obstet Gynecol 1985;151:494.

56. Giles C, Inglis TCM. Thrombocytopenia and macrothrombocytosis in gestational hypertension. Br J Obstet Gynæcol 1981;88:1115.

57. Redman CW, Bowman J, Berlin L. Early platelet consumption in preeclampsia. Br Med J 1978;1:467.

58. Burrows RF, Hunter DJ, Andrew M, Kelton J. A prospective study investigating the mechanism of thrombocytopenia in preeclampsia. Obstet Gynecol 1987; 70:334.

59. Kelton JG, Hunter DJ, Neame PB. A platelet function defect in preeclampsia. Obstet Gynecol 1985;65:107.

60. Ramanathan J, Sibai BM, Vu T, Chauhan D. Correlation between bleeding times and platelet counts in women with preeclampsia undergoing cesarean section. Anesthesiology 1989;71:118.

61. Lindheimer MD, Katz AL. The kidney in pregnancy. In: Brenner BM, Rector FC, eds. The kidney. Philadelphia: WB Saunders, 1986:1253.

62. James FM III. Pregnancy-induced hypertension. In: James FM, Wheeler AS, Dewan DM, eds. Obstetric anesthesia: The complicated patient. 2nd ed. Philadelphia: FA Davis, 1988:411.

63. McCartney CH. Acute hypertensive disorders of pregnancy, classified by renal histology. Gynæcologica 1969;167:214.

64. Dennis EJ, Hester LL, MacFarland K. The preeclampsia–eclampsia syndrome. In: Danforth DN, ed. Obstetrics and gynecology. New York: Harper & Row, 1982:455.

65. Donaldson JO. Neurologic emergencies during pregnancy. In: Berkowitz RL, ed. Critical care of the obstetric patient. New York: Churchill Livingstone, 1983:367.

66. Sibai BM, Spinnato JA, Watson DL, Lewis JA, Anderson GD. Effect of magnesium sulfate on electroencephalographic findings in preeclampsia–eclampsia. Obstet Gynecol 1984;64:261.

67. Gilstrap LC, Cunningham GF, Whalley PJ. Management of pregnancy-induced hypertension in the nulliparous patient remote from term. Semin Perinatol 1978;2:73.

68. Mathews DD. A randomized controlled trial of bed rest and sedation or normal activity and non-sedation in the management of non-albuminuric hypertension in late pregnancy. Br J Obstet Gynæcol 1977;84:108.

69. Borges LF, Gucer G. Effect of magnesium on epileptic foci. Epilepsia 1978;19:81.

70. Giesecke AH, Morris RE, Dalton MD, Dalton MD, Stephen CR. Of magnesium, muscle relaxants, toxemic parturients and cats. Anesth Analg 1968;47:689.

71. Ramanathan J, Sibai BM, Pillai R, Angel JJ. Neuromuscular transmission studies in preeclamptic women receiving magnesium sulfate. Am J Obstet Gynecol 1988;158:40.

72. Cotton DM, Gonik B, Dorman KF. Cardiovascular alterations in severe pregnancy-induced hypertension:

Acute effects of intravenous magnesium sulfate. Am J Obstet Gynecol 1984;148:162.

73. Ramanathan J, Sibai BM, Duggviala V, Maduska AL. Pulmonary function in preeclamptic women receiving MgSO₄. J Reprod Med 1988;33:432.

74. McAllister CB. Placental transfer and neonatal effects of diazepam when administered to women just before delivery. Br J Anæsth 1980;52:423.

75. Slater RM, Wilcox FL, Smith WD, et al: Phenytoin infusion in severe preeclampsia. Lancet 1987;1:1417.

76. Brinkman CR, Assali NS. Uteroplacental hemodynamic response to antihypertensive drugs in hypertensive pregnant sheep. In: Lindheimer MD, Katz AI, Zuspan FP, eds. Hypertension in pregnancy. New York: John Wiley & Sons, 1976;363.

77. Cotton DB, Gonik B, Dorman KF. Cardiovascular alterations in severe pregnancy-induced hypertension seen with an intravenously given hydralazine bolus. Surg Gynecol Obstet 1985;161:240.

78. Stempel JE, O'Grady JP, Morton MJ, Johnson KA. Use of sodium nitroprusside in complications and gestational hypertension. Obstet Gynecol 1982;60:533.

79. Naulty J, Cefalo RC, Lewis PE. Fetal toxicity of nitroprusside in the pregnant ewe. Am J Obstet Gynecol 1981;139:708.

80. Ellis SC, Wheeler AS, James FM III. Fetal and maternal effects of sodium nitroprusside used to counteract hypertension in gravid ewes. Am J Obstet Gynecol 1982;143:766.

81. Cotton DB, Longmire S, Jones MM, Dorman KF, Tessam J, Joyce TH. Cardiovascular alterations in severe pregnancy-induced hypertension: Effects of intravenous nitroglycerine coupled with blood volume expansion. Am J Obstet Gynecol 1986;154:1053.

82. Hood DD, Dewan DM, James FM III, Floyd HM, Bogard TD. The use of nitroglycerine in preventing the hypertensive response to tracheal intubation in severe preeclampsia. Anesthesiology 1985;63:329.

83. Eisenach JC, Mandell G, Dewan DM. Maternal and fetal effects of labetalol in pregnant ewes. Anesthesiology 1991;742:292.

84. Mabie WC, Gonzalez AR, Sibai BM, Amon E. A comparative trial of labetalol and hydralazine in the acute management of severe hypertension complicating pregnancy. Obstet Gynecol 1987;70:328.

85. Ramanathan J, Sibai BM, Mabie WC, Chauhan D, Ruiz AG. The use of labetalol for the attenuation of hypertensive response to endotracheal intubation in preeclampsia. Am J Obstet Gynecol 1988;159:650.

86. Weinstein L. Syndrome of hemolysis, elevated liver enzymes and low platelet count: Severe consequence of hypertension in pregnancy. Am J Obstet Gynecol 1982;142:159.

87. Sibai BM, Taslimi MM, El-Nazer A, Amon A, Mabie WC, Ryan GM. Maternal-perinatal outcome associated with the syndrome of hemolysis, elevated liver enzymes and low platelets in severe preeclampsia-eclampsia. Am J Obstet Gynecol 1986;155:501.

88. Ramanathan J, Khalil M, Sibai BM. Anesthetic management of the syndrome of hemolysis, elevated liver enzymes and low platelet count (HELLP) in severe preeclampsia. Reg Anaesth 1988;13:20.

CHAPTER 6

Perinatal Physiology and Pharmacology

M. Joanne Douglas

Of necessity, there is a close relationship between a mother and her fetus. The fetus receives all its nourishment and oxygen from the mother. In addition, this intimate connection exposes the fetus to almost any substance to which the mother is exposed. Any drug given during gestation can potentially affect the fetus and the newborn.

PLACENTA

Structure

The placenta is a unique disc-shaped organ that acts as an interface between the mother and her fetus. It performs as fetal lung, gastrointestinal system, and excretory system. It permits passage of some substances while acting as a barrier to others. During gestation, the placenta grows, offering an ever larger surface area for maternal–fetal exchange. At term, the placenta weighs about 500 g.

The basic structural unit of the placenta is the chorionic villus. The villi are highly vascular projections of fetal tissue surrounded by the chorion, the outermost layer of fetal tissue. The chorion has two layers, the syncytiotrophoblast and the cytotrophoblast. The syncytiotrophoblast lies in direct contact with maternal blood within the intervillous space (Fig. 6-1).[1] Substances that pass from mother to fetus travel in maternal blood to the intervillous space. There, they cross the two layers of trophoblast, some fetal connective tissue, and, finally, the fetal capillary wall into the fetal blood stream (Fig. 6-2). No continuous direct communication exists between maternal and fetal circulations. Occasionally, however, a delicate villus may break, allowing fetal cells to enter the intervillous space and the maternal circulation.[2,3] Maternal sensitization to fetal red blood cells (isoimmunization) may then occur.

Uteroplacental Circulation

The blood supply to the placenta is maternal in origin. Uteroplacental blood flow near term is approximately 600 mL/min. Maternal blood spurts into the intervillous space with each heart beat. This blood is then forced upwards and laterally, bathing the chorionic villi. Continued influx of blood pushes blood already within the intervillous space toward venous openings that ultimately drain through uterine and pelvic veins (see Fig. 6-1).[4,5]

The uteroplacental arteries have mostly alpha-adrenergic receptors.[6] Any event that lowers central ve-

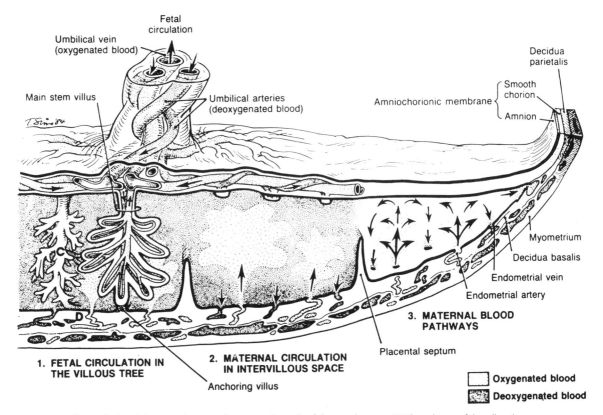

Figure 6–1. Schematic drawing of a section through a full-term placenta. (*1*) The relation of the villus chorion (*C*) to the decidua basalis (*D*) and the fetal–placental circulation. (*2*) The maternal placental circulation. Maternal blood flows into the intervillous spaces in funnel-shaped spurts, and exchanges occur with the fetal blood as the maternal blood flows around the villi. (*3*) The inflowing arterial blood pushes venous blood into the endometrial veins, which are scattered over the entire surface of the decidua basalis. Note that the umbilical arteries carry deoxygenated fetal blood to the placenta and that the umbilical vein carries oxygenated blood to the fetus. Note that the cotyledons are separated from each other by placenta (decidual) septa of the maternal portion of the placenta. Each cotyledon consists of two or more main-stem villi and their many branches. (Pritchard JA, MacDonald PC, Gant NF. Williams Obstetrics, 18th ed. Norwalk, CT: Appleton–Century–Crofts, 1989;60)

nous or systemic blood pressure (*i.e.*, aortocaval compression, hypovolemia, or drug-induced myocardial depression) may induce the release of catecholamines. Sympathetic stimulation then leads to uterine artery constriction, further decreasing blood supply to the placenta. Because of the vasoconstriction, placental blood flow can decrease even while maternal blood pressure remains stable. At term, the uteroplacental circulation appears maximally vasodilated. Flow, therefore, depends mostly on maternal blood pressure.[7] Changes in intrauterine pressure and the pattern of uterine contractions also can interfere with placental blood supply.

In summary, the basic site of exchange in the placenta is the intervillous space, where maternal blood contacts fetal tissue. Constant movement of blood through this space depends on the pressure of the blood entering the space. Vasoconstriction of the uterine vessels and changes in intrauterine pressure alter placental perfusion pressure.[8]

Function

Synthesis and Metabolism

The placenta contains enzyme systems that synthesize several hormones, including estrogen, progesterone, chorionic gonadotropin, and placental lac-

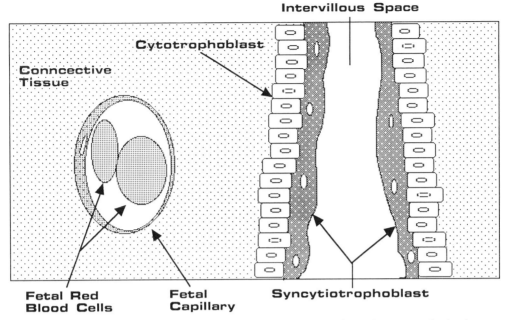

Figure 6–2. Schematic representation of a fetal villus, showing the tissue layers that separate fetal and maternal blood in the human placenta. The cytotrophoblast layer is much less distinct in the third trimester than depicted here. (Drawing courtesy of M Norris, MD)

togen.[9] Placental lactogen is abundant in the mother but not the fetus. It promotes insulin resistance in the mother by blocking the peripheral uptake and utilization of glucose. It also promotes maternal mobilization and use of free fatty acids. These effects ensure a ready supply of glucose for the fetus.

The placenta contains specialized cellular receptors and enzymes. These structures include insulin and beta-adrenergic receptors as well as the enzymes adenylate cyclase, alkaline phosphatase, and pseudocholinesterase. Two other enzymes, catechol-O-methyl transferase and monoamineoxidase, impede the passage of catecholamines across the placenta.

Immunology

The placental barrier allows the mother to accept the fetus (nonself). It also acts as a filter, permitting selective transport of maternal antibodies to the fetus. Some of these maternal antibodies help provide fetal immunity. Others, however can cause fetal disease. In Rh isoimmunization, maternal antibodies specific for fetal red blood cells cross the placenta and produce fetal hemolytic anemia. Antibodies producing maternal autoimmune disease (*i.e.*, thyrotoxicosis, idiopathic thrombocytopenic purpura, myasthenia gravis, and sys-

temic lupus erythematosus) also can attack fetal tissue.[10]

Placental Exchange

Functionally, the placenta is a complex organ of exchange. In this way, it is like the blood–brain barrier. A variety of nutrients, waste products, and toxins continuously cross this barrier. Most substances traverse the trophoblast by simple diffusion. Polar (hydrophilic) substances need special help to cross the lipid membranes of the placenta. Examples of such substances include metabolic wastes, nutrients, and some drugs. These processes include facilitated diffusion, active transport, endocytosis, and bulk flow. Unlike simple diffusion, these methods of transfer expend energy.[11] Table 6-1 lists the modes of placental exchanges and gives examples of compounds that use each approach.

Simple Diffusion

Most drugs and respiratory gases cross the placenta by simple diffusion, which uses no energy. The rate at which substances transfer from mother to fetus depends only on the difference in concentration of the

Table 6–1

Mechanisms of Placental Exchange

MECHANISM	EXAMPLE
Simple diffusion	Oxygen
	Carbon dioxide
	Sodium
	Chloride
	Fatty acids
Facilitated diffusion	Glucose
	Lactate
Active transport	Amino acids
	Calcium
	Phosphorous
	Iron
	Vitamins A and C
Endocytosis	IgG

substance in maternal and fetal blood. The Fick equation, which follows, describes the factors involved in this process:

$$Q/T = k \cdot A \frac{(C_m - C_f)}{X}$$

where
Q/T represents the quantity of a substance transferred per unit time;
k is the diffusion constant, which is determined by molecular weight, lipid solubility, degree of ionization, and spatial configuration;
A is the area available for diffusion;
C_m is the concentration in mother;
C_f is the concentration in fetus; and
X is the thickness of the membrane (placenta).

Facilitated Diffusion

As with simple diffusion, compounds that cross the placenta through facilitated diffusion travel down a concentration gradient. Here, however, the speed of transfer is faster than predicted by the Fick equation for simple diffusion. Substances occurring in low concentration in maternal plasma that are essential to the fetus (*i.e.,* glucose, lactate) traverse the placenta by facilitated diffusion.

Active Transport

This approach involves transferring compounds against a concentration gradient. Substances actively transported include some amino acids, calcium, phosphorous, iron, and vitamins A and C.

Endocytosis (Pinocytosis)

Some large molecules cross the placenta by being encircled in cellular membrane and are released into the fetal blood stream. For immunoglobin G (IgG), this is a receptor-specific process. There are specific receptors for immunoglobulins on the trophoblast. Small vacuoles then enclose bound IgG. These vacuoles then pinch off and cross to the fetal side of the trophoblast. There, they release their contents.[12]

Bulk Flow

Osmotic and hydrostatic forces are involved with the movement of water across the placenta. Bulk flow of water may carry some small molecules along.[1]

Respiratory Exchange

Transfer of respiratory gases to fetus occurs through simple diffusion. At the tissue level, respiratory exchange also depends upon the interaction of oxygen and carbon dioxide with hemoglobin and on the nature of blood flow in the maternal and umbilical circulations.[13]

Oxygen

Multiple factors enhance fetal oxygenation. Fetal hemoglobin binds oxygen tightly, favoring oxygen uptake from maternal blood. The high concentration of fetal hemoglobin and a cardiac output greater per unit of body weight than in the adult favor efficient uptake and distribution of oxygen within the fetus. Oxygen transfer across the placenta is blood flow–limited and not related to the thickness or surface area of the placenta.[14] The difference between the maternal and fetal partial pressures of oxygen determines the gradient for oxygen diffusion across the placenta.[15] Relative differences in the affinity of maternal and fetal hemoglobins for oxygen account for most of the difference between maternal and fetal P_{O_2}. The oxyhemoglobin dissociation curve of fetal hemoglobin lies to the left of the dissociation curve of adult hemoglobin. As a result, fetal blood binds oxygen more tightly and has a higher oxygen content at a given P_{O_2} than adult blood.[16]

Carbon Dioxide

Carbon dioxide diffuses readily across the placenta. The small difference between maternal and fetal P_{CO_2} may result from shunting or unequal distribution of maternal and fetal blood flow within the placental vasculature. Placental metabolism also may contribute carbon dioxide. Fetal hemoglobin has a lower affinity for carbon dioxide than does maternal hemoglobin. The hyperventilation of pregnancy leads to a lower maternal P_{CO_2}. Both factors favor transfer of carbon dioxide from fetus to mother. In addition, both oxygen and carbon dioxide influence the binding to the other to hemoglobin. Placental transfer of one gas enhances the exchange of the other.[13]

Fetal Oxygenation

The fetus obtains oxygenated blood from the mother by a unique arrangement.[17] The umbilical vein carries oxygenated blood to the fetus and empties into the portal sinus. From there, most of the blood bypasses the liver by flowing through the ductus venosus to the inferior vena cava. The remainder passes through the liver by way of the portal and hepatic veins. The oxygen-rich blood that skirts the liver enters the right atrium, and then passes through the foramen ovale and into the left atrium. It then mixes with pulmonary venous blood and travels through the left ventricle and into the aorta. This arrangement ensures a well-oxygenated blood supply for the coronary and cerebral circulations. Blood returning from the head, brain, and upper body via the superior vena cava enters the right atrium. There, with blood from the inferior vena cava, it flows into the right ventricle to the pulmonary artery. Most of the blood entering the pulmonary artery skips the lungs by flowing through the ductus directly into the descending aorta. The umbilical arteries, arising from the internal iliac arteries, carry desaturated blood out of the fetus and back to the placenta.

PHYSIOLOGIC CHANGES OF PREGNANCY THAT ALTER PHARMACOKINETICS

During pregnancy, the absorption, distribution, protein binding, and elimination of maternally administered drugs may change.[18] Maternal hyperventilation and a decreased functional residual capacity increase the uptake of inhalational anesthetics during pregnancy.[19] These changes, combined with an increase in cardiac output, speed anesthetic induction in the parturient. Progesterone and motilin concentrations increase during gestation. These compounds slow gastrointestinal motility, potentially altering the absorption of maternal oral medications.[20,21] Opiates administered for pain relief further delay gastric emptying.[22]

During pregnancy, total body water increases by up to 8 L and plasma volume increases by 50%.[23] This increase in body water expands the volume of drug distribution. Serum albumin concentration falls. Free fatty acids and acidic drugs (*i.e.,* salicylates, anticonvulsants, and benzodiazepines) compete for a reduced number of albumin binding sites. Affected drugs are less protein bound and may have a greater effect than in nonpregnant women. The serum concentration of alpha$_1$-acid glycoprotein remains stable.[24] The free fraction of basic drugs, including local anesthetics and opioids that bind primarily to alpha$_1$-acid glycoprotein, does not change during gestation.

Hepatic metabolism may increase during pregnancy, as enzyme induction by progesterone speeds elimination of some drugs. Renal plasma flow and glomerular filtration rise during gestation. Clearance of drugs that are primarily renally excreted, such as pancuronium, will increase.

Transfer of Drugs

Most drugs cross the placenta by simple diffusion. The ease of passage depends on their lipid solubility. Drugs that readily cross the blood–brain barrier also will cross the placenta with ease.[25] The concentration of drug on the maternal side of the placenta determines the degree of fetal exposure. Maternal drug delivery to the placenta depends on several of the following factors:

- Total dose and duration of administration
- Route of administration
- Rate of absorption
- Uteroplacental blood flow
- Maternal metabolism and excretion
- Maternal protein binding
- Maternal pH and the pK_a of the drug

Once the drug crosses the placental barrier, its concentration in fetal plasma depends on fetal protein binding, cardiac output, tissue uptake, metabolism, and excretion (Fig. 6-3).

FETAL PHYSIOLOGY AND PHARMACOKINETICS

Several aspects of the uptake, distribution, and elimination of drugs in the fetus and newborn differ from the adult. Uptake into the fetus begins as drugs pass through the placenta and flow by way of the umbilical vein into the fetal circulation. Once there, the extent of drug distribution depends on several factors. Drug may

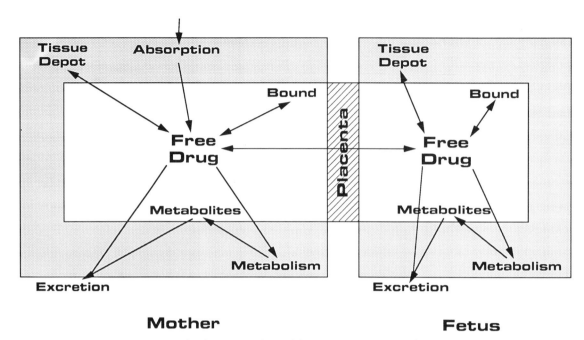

Figure 6–3. Drug distribution in mother and fetus. (Drawing courtesy of M Norris, MD)

undergo considerable metabolism within the liver or it may bypass the liver via the ductus venosus and directly enter the fetal arterial circulation. This "first-pass" metabolism by the fetal liver significantly lowers the amount of drug delivered to highly perfused organs such as the heart and the brain. Shunts within the fetal circulation (*i.e.,* foramen ovale, ductus arteriosus) also alter fetal drug distribution.

The concentration of drug in fetal blood depends on the dose administered to the mother and the placental transfer rate. The rate of transfer depends primarily on differences in maternal and fetal protein binding and acid–base status.[26–28] Maternal protein binding limits the amount of free (unbound) drug available for placental transport. This mechanism significantly limits fetal exposure to highly bound drugs (*i.e.,* bupivacaine) (Fig. 6-4).

The pH gradient between maternal and fetal blood also can influence the extent of placental transfer of weakly acidic or basic compounds. Normally, a slight (0.1) pH gradient exists between the maternal and fetal circulations. Only un-ionized drugs cross the lipid barrier of the placenta. With acidic drugs (salicylates, anticonvulsants, barbiturates), the pH gradient limits transfer. With basic drugs (local anesthetics and opiates), the lower fetal pH favors drug transfer to the fetus (Fig. 6-5A). "Ion trapping" of basic drugs can

occur if fetal pH falls. As un-ionized drug enters the fetal circulation, it becomes ionized and cannot diffuse back to the maternal circulation (Fig. 6-5B). Both local anesthetics and meperidine can become "trapped" in the fetus by this mechanism.[29–34]

The fetus and newborn have a larger total body water content and a higher extracellular-to-intracellular water ratio than adults. In relation to body weight, the fetus has a small muscle mass and a large liver and brain. In addition, the fetal brain has a low myelin content and a high cerebral blood flow.[35] The factors combine to increase the potential central nervous system effects of exogenous drugs.

Drugs are eliminated from the fetus by metabolism, urinary excretion, and diffusion back to the mother. By term, most hepatic microsomal enzyme systems are present. Still, these enzymes are often less able to metabolize drugs than adult enzymes.[35] As a result, although a newborn has a full compliment of hepatic enzymes, its ability to metabolize certain drugs is often limited. The premature infant has even lesser metabolic capabilities and experiences greater drug effects than the term infant. Drugs excreted in the urine in utero enter the amniotic fluid, where they may be swallowed by the fetus. Once re-ingested, drugs may enter the systemic circulation again after being absorbed by the gastrointestinal system.

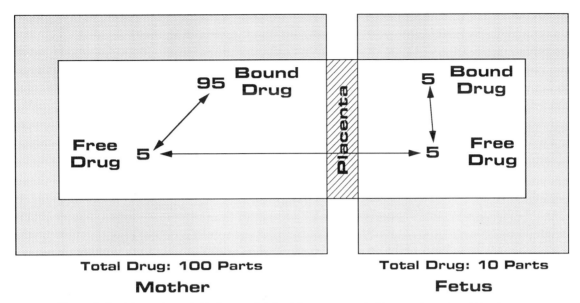

Figure 6–4. Maternal protein binding can limit fetal drug exposure. In this example, maternal blood contains 100 parts of drug. In maternal blood, the drug is highly protein bound (95%), so only 5 parts of drug are free (unbound) and able to diffuse across the placenta. At equilibrium, the concentration of free drug is the same (5) in maternal and fetal blood. In the fetus, however, the drug is only 50% protein bound. Because of these differences in protein binding, the total amount of drug in fetal blood is only 10% of the concentration of drug in maternal blood. (Drawing courtesy of M Norris, MD)

MEASURING FETAL DRUG EFFECT

Drug Measurement

To determine the effects of a drug on the fetus or newborn, one must know the plasma concentration of drug at the time the reputed drug effect occurs. It is hard to measure the fetal concentration of a drug directly. One can sample amniotic fluid or fetal scalp blood during labor, but the information derived from such sources is limited. Before birth, maternal plasma concentration of drug provides an indirect measurement of fetal plasma concentration.

Testing for Intrapartum Drug Effects

Early studies of intrapartum drug effects looked at changes in fetal heart rate pattern after maternal drug exposure.[36] More recently, investigators have studied the effects of anesthetic drugs and techniques on uterine, placental, and fetal blood flow (Table 6-2). Some techniques used include measuring uteroplacental blood flow with radioactive tracers (xenon[133] or indium[113])[37,38] and measuring fetal umbilical and aortic blood flow velocity with Doppler ultrasonography.[39,40]

Postpartum (Newborn) Testing

At birth, blood from maternal vein, umbilical vein, and umbilical artery can be analyzed for the presence of specific drugs and metabolites. These data can provide some information about the amount of drug transferred to the fetus and its uptake by fetal tissues. The umbilical venous concentration of drug represents drug delivered to the fetus via the placenta. The ratio of umbilical venous to maternal venous drug (UV/MV) reflects the rate and extent of placental transfer. Umbilical arterial concentration of drug is the portion of drug remaining after tissue uptake and metabolism. The ratio of drug concentration in the umbilical artery to the umbilical vein (UA/UV) shows the extent of drug uptake by fetal tissues (Table 6-3). These measurements do not, however, indicate the total amount of drug present in the infant. To quantitate fetal drug exposure accurately, one must sample and analyze neonatal blood and urine repeatedly.

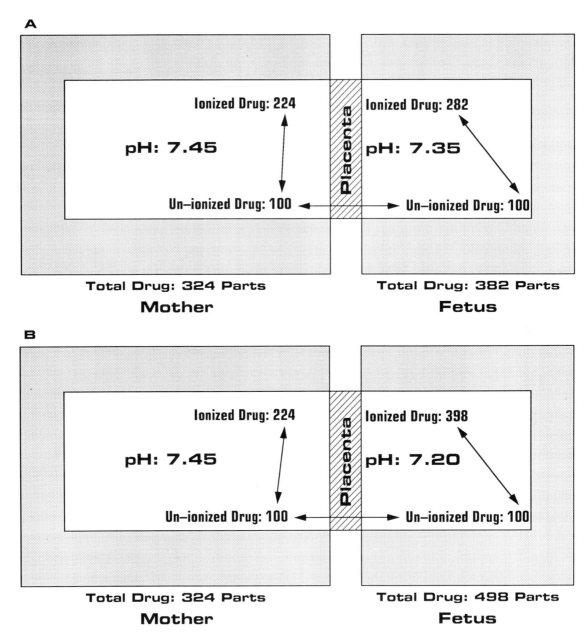

Figure 6–5. The pH gradient between mother and fetus affects the placental transfer of local anesthetic drugs. In this example, lidocaine exists in equilibrium between basic (un-ionized) and cationic (ionized) forms. The relative proportion of drug in each form is determined by the drug's pKa (7.8 for lidocaine) and the *p*H of the surrounding plasma (pH = pKa + log base/cation). Only un-ionized drug can cross the lipid membranes of the placenta. At equilibrium, the concentration of un-ionized drug is equal on both sides of the placenta. **(A)** The lower plasma pH in the fetus causes relatively more local anesthetic to be ionized in the fetal compared to maternal blood. **(B)** In fetal acidosis, the lower fetal pH creates more ionized drug that is "trapped" on the fetal side of the placenta. (Drawing courtesy of M Norris, MD)

Table 6–2

Testing for Fetal Drug Effects

Intrapartum

Maternal plasma drug concentration

Fetal heart rate changes
  Variability
  Decelerations

Blood flow studies
  Uteroplacental
  Fetal (umbilical and aortic)

Postpartum

Acid–base status

Apgar scores

Drug and metabolite concentrations
  Maternal vein
  Umbilical vein
  Umbilical artery
  Neonatal (blood and urine)

Neonatal neurobehavioral testing

Table 6–4

Neonatal Neurobehavioral Tests

Brazelton Neonatal Behavioral Assessment Scale

Most comprehensive

Forty-nine items

Reflects "mother–infant" interaction

Used mainly by developmental psychologists

Takes 30–45 min

Difficult to summarize for data analysis

Scanlon Early Neonatal Neurobehavioral Scale

Designed to examine newborn changes associated with anesthesia

Done 2–8 h after birth

Fifteen observations of primary reflexes, muscle tone, and response to repeated stimuli

Takes < 10 min

Neurologic and Adaptive Capacity Score

Designed to distinguish between drug effects and birth trauma

Twenty criteria in five areas
  Adaptive capacity
  Passive tone
  Active tone
  Primary reflexes
  General neurologic state

Takes < 5 min

Favored by anesthesiologists

Other methods of testing for neonatal drug effects include assigning Apgar scores and measuring acid–base status. Although sometimes useful, these tests are nonspecific and their results change in response to a multitude of variables.

Several investigators have developed tests designed to look for subtle behavioral effects of drugs (Table 6-4). These tests examine the neonate's muscle tone and his or her ability to do the following:

- Alter his or her state of arousal
- Suppress his or her responses to repetitive or intrusive stimuli
- Respond appropriately to external events
- Initiate complex motor acts and the appropriateness of reflex motor responses[41]

Table 6–3

Umbilical Artery: Umbilical Vein Ratios

UA/UV RATIO	EXTENT OF FETAL UPTAKE
1	Maternal/fetal equilibrium
<1	Continuing fetal tissue uptake
>1	Elimination of drug from fetus *via* diffusion into maternal blood

The Brazelton Neonatal Behavioral Assessment Scale (BNBAS), a test favored by developmental psychologists, looks explicitly at the mother–infant interaction.[42] It requires specific training and considerable time to perform.

In 1974, Scanlon designed the Early Neonatal Neurobehavioral Scale (ENNS) to examine the effect of anesthetic drugs.[43] It is done 2 to 8 hours after birth, a time that theoretically correlates with the maximum effect of prenatally administered drugs. It requires less time to perform than the BNBAS and focuses on muscle tone and the infant's response to repetitive stimuli.

Amiel–Tison *et al*[44] wanted to examine muscle tone more closely. They were especially interested in differences in tone between different muscle groups (*i.e.,* flexors and extensors of the neck). They believed that by examining these variables, they could distinguish between the effects of maternal drugs and birth trauma. The Neurologic and Adaptive Capacity Score (NACS) takes even less time to do than the ENNS and so has gained favor with many anesthesiologists.

The results obtained by all of these tests pose a dilemma for the obstetric anesthesiologist: "What do they mean?" If specifically sought, subtle neonatal effects result from most anesthetic agents and techniques. These tests offer an important tool when evaluating a new drug and its effects on the newborn. Many anesthesiologists, however, consider the subtle effects they detect to be clinically insignificant.[45]

Specific Drugs

Induction Agents

THIOPENTAL. Thiopental, a highly lipid soluble drug, passes readily from mother to fetus (Table 6-5). Equilibrium between maternal vein and umbilical vein occurs within 3 minutes (Fig. 6-6).[46] Pregnancy prolongs the half-life of thiopental, probably because of an increased volume of distribution.[47] Thiopental undergoes rapid distribution in the fetus. The UA/UV ratio is 0.46 by 4 to 7 minutes after induction and 0.87 after 8 to 22 minutes.[47-49] Some of the drug that crosses the placenta undergoes "first-pass" metabolism in the fetal liver. This effect decreases the amount of drug that reaches the fetal brain.[50] Thiopental appears to depress the neonate only when used in large doses (8 mg/kg).[49]

KETAMINE. Ketamine's ability to ablate awareness and provide profound analgesia has led to its use in obstetrics.[51,52] In a dose of 1 mg/kg, ketamine does not commonly cause maternal dreaming.[53,54] Ketamine does, however, cause maternal tachycardia and hypertension on induction. This property renders ketamine unsuitable for use in women with preeclampsia. Ketamine crosses the placenta rapidly. Umbilical cord drug concentrations exceed maternal blood ketamine concentration within 2 minutes.[55,56] Ketamine induction (1 mg/kg) of general anesthesia for cesarean delivery depresses neonatal neurobehavioral (ENNS) scores.[57] Epidural analgesia has less of an effect, whereas thiopental (4 mg/kg) has a greater depressant effect.

PROPOFOL. Propofol is a new intravenous induction agent. When used in a rapid-sequence induction for cesarean section, propofol is associated with less maternal hypertension than thiopental.[58] All studies show rapid placental transfer of this drug. The UV/MV ratio at delivery is about 0.65 (see Table 6-5).[59-61] A UA/UV ratio of 1.07 after a single maternal bolus of propofol suggests rapid fetal tissue uptake and equilibration.[62] Both fetal and maternal blood concentrations fall rapidly after induction (Fig. 6-7).[59] When using a continuous infusion of propofol to maintain anesthesia, UA/UV ratio is lower (0.70) than after a single bolus, suggesting continued fetal tissue uptake of drug.[59] Propofol is rapidly cleared from the fetal circulation. Fetal blood concentration falls to 0.078 ng/mL by 2 hours after birth. Little propofol can be detected in breast milk.

Table 6–5

Placental Transfer and Neonatal Elimination of Three Intravenous Induction Agents

	MV (µg/mL)	UV (µg/mL)	UV/MV	NEONATAL ELIMINATION HALF-LIFE
Thiopental (4 mg/kg)	4.31* (3.12–6.50)†	4.65 (3.25–5.69)	0.96 (0.79–1.15)	14.7 h
Propofol (2 mg/kg)	0.87 0.53–1.48	0.54 (0.39–1.40)	0.65 (0.31–0.97)	
Midazolam (0.3 mg/kg)	0.34 (0.23–0.62)	0.32 (0.19–0.41)	0.66 (0.5–1.05)	6.3 h

(Data from Bach V, Carl P, Ravlo O et al: A randomized comparison between midazolam and thiopental for elective cesarean section anesthesia. III. Placental transfer and elimination in neonates. Anesth Analg 68:238, 1989; and Gin T, Gregory MA, Chan K, Oh TE: Maternal and fetal levels of propofol at caesarean section. Anaesth Intensive Care 18:180, 1990)
*Mean
†Range

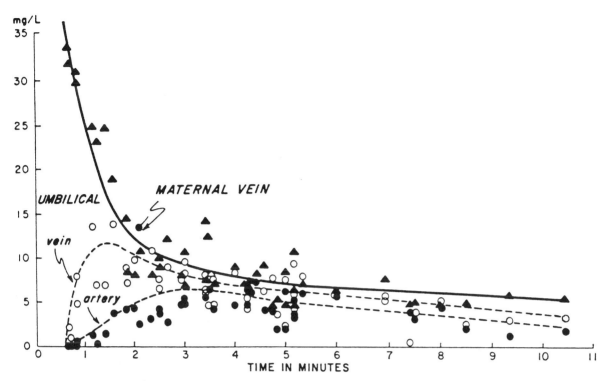

Figure 6–6. Thiopental concentration in maternal vein, umbilical vein, and umbilical artery after injection of a single 4 mg/kg dose for induction of general anesthesia. Note the rapid decay of maternal venous blood concentration and the rapid transfer to the fetus. (Kosaka Y, Yakahashi R, Mark LC. Intravenous thiobarbiturate anesthesia for cesarean section. Anesthesiology 1969;31:489)

Figure 6–7. Propofol concentrations at delivery versus induction to delivery interval during general anesthesia for cesarean section. Ten healthy term parturients received a single 2.5 mg/kg bolus of propofol for induction of anesthesia. The *solid regression line* describes the change in maternal venous (MV), the *dashed line* umbilical vein (UV), and the *dotted line* umbilical artery (UA) propofol concentrations. (Dailland P, Cockshott ID, Lirzin JD, et al. Intravenous propofol during cesarean section: Placental transfer, concentrations in breastmilk, and neonatal effects: A preliminary study. Anesthesiology 1989;71: 827)

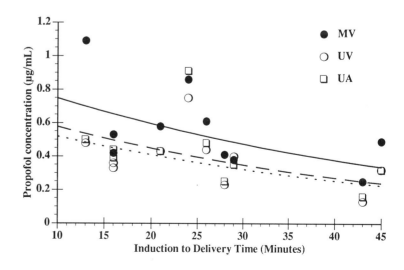

The neonatal effects of propofol are less clear. Dailland *et al*[59] induced general anesthesia for cesarean section with 2.5 mg/kg of propofol and maintained anesthesia with either 50% nitrous oxide or a 5 mg/kg/h propofol infusion. They found that Apgar scores correlated with neither the time from induction to delivery nor the umbilical venous concentration of propofol. Infants had good NACS scores by 2 hours with either anesthetic technique (Table 6-6).[59]

Another study, however, using only a slightly larger induction dose of propofol (2.8 mg/kg), reported different results.[63] This study compared infants whose mothers received propofol for induction of anesthesia for cesarean section to two other groups of infants. In one group, mothers who delivered abdominally under general anesthesia were induced with thiopental, 5 mg/kg. A third group consisted of infants born by uncomplicated and unmedicated vaginal delivery. Propofol significantly depressed Apgar scores at both 1 and 5 minutes (Table 6-7). Apgar scores in the propofol group were lower than those in both other groups. Five infants in the propofol group were severely hypotonic at birth. One baby was somnolent. The propofol infants had significantly lower ENNS scores at 1 hour. By 4 hours, their scores were normal.

BENZODIAZEPINES. Diazepam and midazolam are the two most thoroughly studied benzodiazepines. Both drugs are used for maternal sedation and to induce general anesthesia.[64,65] The pharmacokinetics of both drugs in pregnancy have been reported.[66,67]

Both drugs are highly protein bound but readily cross the placenta and induce neonatal effects. Oral administration produces poor suckling, whereas intravenous administration may yield hypotonia and hypothermia.[68,69]

Diazepam is highly lipid soluble and has a molecular weight of 285. In labor, it can decrease beat-to-beat fetal heart rate variability.[70,71] Maximum fetal blood concentrations occur 5 to 10 minutes after maternal administration. Neonatal plasma concentrations are higher than maternal concentrations at birth. This phenomenon may reflect more rapid distribution of the drug in the mother.[70]

Midazolam has a shorter half-life and produces less local irritation than diazepam. It is water-soluble in its injectable formulation. At physiologic pH, its structure changes and it becomes lipid-soluble.[72] Midazolam readily crosses the placenta,[73] and, like diazepam, can yield a depressed neonate. In pregnant sheep, less midazolam than diazepam crosses the placental barrier. Midazolam also produces lower maternal and fetal drug concentrations.[74] Ravlo *et al*[75] have compared midazolam to thiopental for induction of cesarean section anesthesia. Midazolam has a slower onset of action than thiopental (120 s vs 111 s). The neonates had lower ENNS scores for body temperature, general body tone, and arm recoil for the first 2 hours of life. Placental transfer was extensive with both drugs. The neonatal elimination half-life averaged 6.3 hours (see Table 6-5).[76]

In summary, all the intravenous induction agents

Table 6–6

NACS Scores in Infants Whose Mothers Received 2.5 mg/kg of Propofol to Induce and Either 50% Nitrous Oxide or a 5 mg/kg/h Propofol Infusion to Maintain Anesthesia*

TIME	NACS	INDUCTION ONLY (n = 10)	INDUCTION AND MAINTENANCE (n = 11)
30 min	Percentage of good scores	30%	55%
	NACS range	32–36	20–37
2 h	Percentage of good scores	90%	100%
	NACS range	34–38	35–39
24 h	Percentage of good scores	100%	100%
	NACS range	38–40	37–40

(Data from Dailland P, Cockshott ID, Lirzin JD, et al: Intravenous propofol during cesarean section: Placental transfer, concentrations in breastmilk, and neonatal effects. A preliminary study. Anesthesiology 71:827, 1989)
*A NACS score of > 35 was considered good (the maximum possible NACS score is 40).

Table 6–7

Apgar Scores at 1 and 5 Minutes after Vaginal Delivery Without Anesthesia or Cesarean Section Using Either Thiopental (5 mg/kg) or Propofol (2.8 mg/kg). (Scores in the propofol group are significantly different from those of the spontaneous delivery group at 1 (P<0.002) and 5 (P<0.02) minutes.)

APGAR SCORE	SPONTANEOUS DELIVERY (n = 20)	THIOPENTAL, 5 MG/KG (n = 20)	PROPOFOL, 2.5 MG/KG (n = 20)
1 min			
6	0	0	2*
7	0	5	8
8	0	6	7
9	20	9	3
10	0	0	0
5 min			
6	0	0	0*
7	0	0	1
8	0	3	3
9	0	6	10
10	20	11	6

(Data from Celleno D, Capogna G, Tomassetti M, Costantino P, Di Feo G, Nisini R: Neurobehavioral effects of propofol on the neonate following elective caesarean section. Br J Anaesth 62:649,1989)
*Scores in the propofol group are significantly different from those of the thiopental group at 1 and 5 minutes (P<0.05).

studied rapidly traverse the placental barrier. When reviewing these agents for cesarean section, Holdcroft and Morgan[77] commented that "No drug has been shown to offer sufficient advantages over thiopentone in obstetric anaesthesia to warrant its replacement."

Inhalation Agents and Muscle Relaxants

All the inhalational agents freely crisscross the placental barrier. The UV/MV ratio for nitrous oxide is 0.79 after 10 to 14 minutes of administration. Fetal uptake also occurs rapidly, with UA/UV ratio of 0.89 after an average of 36 minutes.[78] The halogenated agents are highly lipid soluble, un-ionized and low in molecular weight; thus, they cross the placenta rapidly. The UV/MV ratio for 0.65% halothane is 0.35; for 1% enflurane, it is 0.6.[79,80] The neonatal neurobehavioral effects of nitrous oxide, enflurane, and isoflurane are insignificant when used for cesarean section anesthesia.[81–83]

Muscle relaxants are highly polar compounds that do not cross the placenta easily. In monkeys, succinylcholine transfers rapidly to the fetus. However, the resulting fetal concentration is low.[84] Fetal blood concentrations of nondepolarizing muscle relaxants

are 5% to 20% of maternal blood concentrations (Table 6-8).[85–87]

Local Anesthetics

Local anesthetics are basic drugs that principally bind to alpha$_1$-acid glycoprotein. Placental transfer depends on the following factors:

- pKa (pH at which they are 50% unionized)
- Maternal and fetal pH
- The extent of protein binding

Fetal hypoxia and acidosis accentuate the transfer of these weak bases, yielding higher fetal:maternal ratios (Fig. 6-5B).[30–34] Acidosis also appears to intensify the toxic effects of local anesthetics on the fetus and newborn.[88] Neurobehavioral studies show varying results depending on the test used. Any effects found are subtle and must be sought diligently.

BUPIVACAINE. Bupivacaine is more than 80% bound to protein. As such, its placental transfer is limited more than lidocaine (70% protein bound).[89] Mean UV/MV ratio for bupivacaine is approximately

Table 6–8

Placental Transfer of Nondepolarizing Muscle Relaxants

	MV	UV	UV/MV
Atracurium (0.3 mg/kg)*	0.7–3.34 µg/mL	ND–0.23 µg/mL	0.05–0.2
Vecuronium (0.04 mg/kg)†	162.0 ± 10.0 ng/mL	17.9 ± 2.0 ng/mL	0.11 ± 0.22
Pancuronium (0.04 mg/kg)†	115.0 ± 10.5 ng/mL	21.6 ± 4.0 ng/mL	0.19 ± 0.03

(Data from Frank M, Flynn PJ, Hughes R: Atracurium in obstetric anaesthesia. Br J Anaesth 55:113S, 1983; and Dailey PA, Fisher DM, Shnider SM, et al: Pharmacokinetics placental transfer, and neonatal effects of vecuronium and pancuronium administered during cesarean section. Anesthesiology 60:569, 1984)
Abbreviation: ND = not detected.
* = range
† = mean ± SE

0.3.[90,91] These ratios are similar whether the drug is administered in the epidural or the subarachnoid space.[92] Bupivacaine's high lipid solubility encourages rapid uptake by fetal tissues. This property probably explains the increase in bupivacaine half-life of elimination seen in pregnancy. It is metabolized to an inactive metabolite 2,6-pipecolylxylidine. Both bupivacaine and 2,6-pipecolylxylidine can be detected in the newborn urine for at least 36 hours after delivery.

LIDOCAINE. Lidocaine is less highly protein bound than bupivacaine, resulting in higher UV/MV ratios (0.57) after epidural administration.[93] Unlike bupivacaine, the route of administration influences the UV/MV ratio of lidocaine. With local perineal infiltration, the ratio is higher (1.32) than after epidural administration.[94] Recent studies have not found any adverse neonatal neurobehavioral effects of lidocaine.[95–97]

2-CHLOROPROCAINE. 2-Chloroprocaine, an ester local anesthetic, is favored by many obstetric anesthesiologists because of its rapid hydrolysis by plasma cholinesterase. Also, its metabolites, 2-chloroaminobenzoic acid (CABA) and 2-diethylaminoethanol are allegedly pharmacologically inactive. The in vitro half-life of 2-chloroprocaine is measured in seconds. Its in vivo half-life after epidural anesthesia is measured in minutes.[98] Because of this rapid clearance from maternal plasma, only small amounts cross the placenta and appear in the fetal circulation.[99] In laboring parturients, 2-chloroprocaine has minimal effects on neuro-behavioral scores.[45] After cesarean section under epidural anesthesia, however, 2-chloroprocaine infants do less well on the BNBAS than bupivacaine infants.[100] Although very little 2-chloroprocaine remains in neonatal blood after delivery, significant amounts of metabolites do. These metabolites may induce the neurobehavioral effects seen. When choosing a drug for perineal infiltration, 2-chloroprocaine is a better option than lidocaine because little, if any, pharmacologically active drug reaches the fetus.[101]

Opioids

All narcotics administered to laboring women can potentially cause neonatal respiratory depression. The infant is more sensitive than the adult to the central nervous system effects of opioids. Neonates have lower brain myelin content, higher cerebral blood flow, altered protein binding, and different respiratory control mechanisms than adults.[35]

MEPERIDINE. Until recently, meperidine was the most widely used opioid for labor analgesia. Meperidine is less likely than morphine to induce neonatal respiratory depression. In newborns, compared to morphine, meperidine produces less depression of the respiratory response to carbon dioxide.[102,103]

Meperidine is very lipid soluble and readily crosses to the fetus. Pregnancy does not alter the maternal pharmacokinetics of meperidine.[104,105] Following intravenous injection, meperidine appears in fetal plasma within 2 minutes. Equilibrium with maternal blood develops by 6 minutes.[106–108] After intramuscular injection, UV/MV ratio rises as the time to delivery increases.[109] After 2 to 3 hours, the concentration of meperidine is higher in fetal than in maternal blood.[110–112] Larger maternal doses and repeated injections increase the fetal concentration of drug. With multiple doses, a concentration gradient persists between maternal and fetal blood, maximizing fetal exposure.[113,114]

The neonate can metabolize meperidine, although not as efficiently as the adult.[109] Normeperidine, the principle metabolite of meperidine, can be recovered from neonatal urine for 2 to 6 days after birth.[107,112,115,116] In animals, normeperidine depresses respiration as much as meperidine does.[117]

Like other opioids, meperidine decreases fetal heart rate variability during labor.[36] Most likely, this effect follows from central nervous system depression and does not warrant obstetric intervention.

Meperidine and probably normeperidine cause changes in neonatal electroencephalogram and neurobehavior.[118–121] Using the BNBAS, Kuhnert *et al*[122] reported that even low doses of meperidine (25 mg) depress scores. Infants exposed to meperidine in utero had more abnormal reflexes and altered regulation of state scores. The longer the drug-to-delivery interval, the greater the impact of meperidine on neurobehavior. Naloxone only partly reverses the neurobehavioral changes.[123,124] Naloxone does reverse meperidine-induced respiratory depression.[125] The prolonged half-life and pharmacologic actions of normeperidine in the neonate may explain the neurobehavioral changes seen after maternal meperidine administration.[41]

FENTANYL. Fentanyl is more lipophilic and more highly protein bound (69%) than meperidine. It provides excellent labor analgesia after intravenous, epidural or subarachnoid administration. After intravenous administration, rapid tissue uptake of fentanyl ensures a short plasma half-life. Fentanyl rapidly crosses the placenta and appears in fetal blood within 1 minute.[126] When given intravenously in labor, it provokes a brief decrease in fetal heart rate variability that lasts about 30 minutes.[127] Pain relief begins within 5 minutes and lasts less than 1 hour. When using 50 to 600 µg fentanyl during labor, UV/MV ratios range from 0.05 to 0.7.[127] Umbilical venous concentration correlates linearly with maternal fentanyl dose. In a nonrandomized, unblinded study, Apgar scores, incidence of respiratory depression, and NACS scores did not differ compared to unmedicated control infants.[128] When given intravenously within 10 minutes of deliv-

ery, fentanyl, 1 µg/kg, also produced no depression of Apgar scores, acid–base balance, or ENNS scores. The UV/MV ratio was 0.31.[129]

Despite the preceding results, fentanyl may still produce significant neonatal respiratory depression.[130] In an unblinded study comparing fentanyl and meperidine for labor analgesia, infants in both groups occasionally needed naloxone to treat respiratory depression.[127]

Adding fentanyl to epidural bupivacaine improves and prolongs labor analgesia.[131,132] When using epidural anesthesia for cesarean section, fentanyl improves the quality of lidocaine and bupivacaine analgesia without producing detectable changes in neonatal neurobehavior.[133–135] Giving fentanyl directly to the newborn for surgical analgesia does produce prolonged respiratory depression.[136] Maternal administration of epidural fentanyl during cesarean section produces no changes in neonatal respiratory rate, minute ventilation, or pulmonary compliance immediately after delivery. These authors still recommend caution when exposing premature or acidotic fetuses to fentanyl.[137]

ALFENTANIL. Alfentanil is a highly protein bound (88.7%), rapidly acting narcotic analgesic with a short elimination half-life. These properties suggest that alfentanil may be an ideal labor analgesic. The protein binding should limit transfer to the fetus. The rapid elimination should guard against long-term effects in the neonate. Unfortunately, animal and human studies have not confirmed these advantages. The pharmacokinetics of alfentanil are similar in pregnant and nonpregnant women.[138] After a 30 µg/kg dose, the UV/MV ratio of alfentanil is 0.31. Unbound alfentanil readily crosses the placenta. The fraction of unbound alfentanil is higher in the fetus than in the mother (fetuses have a lower serum concentration of alpha$_1$-acid glycoprotein, the main site of binding of basic drugs like alfentanil).[138] In newborn monkeys, alfentanil produces longer-lasting behavioral effects than does meperidine.[139] The NACS testing after an epidural infusion of alfentanil for maternal labor analgesia reveals neonatal hypotonia.[140]

BUTORPHANOL AND NALBUPHINE. Narcotic agonist-antagonist drugs often are used for maternal labor analgesia. These drugs may present less risk of respiratory depression than pure agonist agents. Both butorphanol and nalbuphine generate changes that are similar to those induced by meperidine in fetal heart rate pattern, Apgar scores, and neurobehavioral scores.[141–144] On the other hand, they cause fewer maternal side-effects. Epidural butorphanol prolongs the duration of local anesthetic analgesia. A dose of 3 mg, however, produces maternal sedation and a sinusoidal fetal heart rate pattern.[145]

Other Drugs

ANTICHOLINERGIC AGENTS. Atropine readily crosses the placenta and produces a fetal tachycardia.[146-149] A fetal:maternal ratio of 1.0 is seen 4 hours after injection.[146]

Glycopyrrolate, a quaternary ammonium compound, undergoes only limited placental transfer. In sheep, a peak UV/MV ratio of 0.13 arises 4 hours after injection.[146] In humans, glycopyrrolate, unlike atropine, produces no change in fetal heart rate.[150]

SYMPATHOMIMETIC AGENTS. Ephedrine crosses the placenta readily, increasing fetal heart rate and beat-to-beat variability.[151] Ephedrine has subtle effects on the newborn. Kangas-Saarela *et al*[152] compared ephedrine and fluid for prevention of maternal hypotension during spinal anesthesia for cesarean delivery. Neonates in both treatment groups scored similarly on ENNS testing; however, spectral electroencephalogram showed significant differences within the first 2 hours of life.[152]

ANTIHYPERTENSIVE AGENTS. Labetalol blocks both alpha- and beta-adrenoreceptors. It lowers blood pressure mostly through blockade of alpha-adrenoreceptors in peripheral arterioles. Reflex tachycardia does not occur because of labetalol's blockade of beta-adrenoreceptors. Labetalol is useful in the treatment of preeclampsia and in blunting the hypertensive response to endotracheal intubation.[153] Labetalol crosses the placenta with a UV/MV ratio of 0.5.[154] In mature newborns, maternal administration of labetalol produces no clinically significant sympathetic blockade.[155]

Esmolol, a water-soluble beta₁-adrenoreceptor antagonist, has a rapid onset of action and a short duration of action. Its distribution half-life is 2 minutes, and its elimination half-life averages 9 minutes in nonpregnant patients.[156] Because of its low lipid solubility and rapid metabolism, placental passage should be minimal. A study of esmolol in pregnant ewes found that the drug rapidly crossed the placenta and quickly left both maternal and fetal circulations.[157] Maternal and fetal heart rates decreased during the period of esmolol infusion. A further study by Eisenach *et al*[158] showed dose-dependent beta-adrenergic blockade in both ewe and fetus (Fig. 6-8). With prolonged administration, esmolol lowered fetal heart rate and

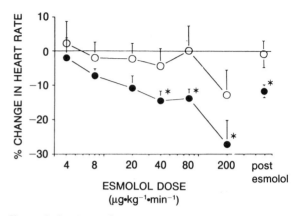

Figure 6–8. Resting heart rates in ewes (O) and fetuses (●) at the end of 4, 8, 20, 40, 80, and 200 μg/kg/min maternal esmolol infusions to the ewe and at 30 min after stopping maternal esmolol. All values are expressed as mean (± SEM) percent change from baseline (*p<0.05 versus baseline.) (Eisenach JC, Castro MI. Maternally administered esmolol produces fetal β-adrenergic blockade and hypoxemia in sheep. Anesthesiology 1989;71:718)

Pao₂. Until further studies elucidate the safety of this agent for the fetus, I urge using it with caution.

H₂-RECEPTOR AGONISTS. To reduce maternal morbidity and mortality from gastric acid aspiration, the H₂-receptor antagonists cimetidine and ranitidine have been used to reduce the volume and raise the pH of gastric secretion. Cimetidine has a low lipid solubility and a pKa of 6.8 and so might be expected to have limited placental transfer. However, when administered intravenously the UV/MV ratio is 0.84 at 90 to 120 minutes after injection.[159] Peak umbilical venous concentrations occur at 60 minutes. When given orally the night before cesarean section, and again intramuscularly one to three hours before surgery, cimetidine has a UV/MV ratio of 0.6.[160] Evaluation of the fetus using Apgar scores and ENNS testing revealed no significant differences compared to a group that did not receive cimetidine. Rapid renal excretion plays a role in elimination from the fetus.[159]

METOCLOPRAMIDE. Metoclopramide has a low molecular weight and high lipid solubility. Animal studies show rapid placental transfer (less than 1 min after intravenous injection).[161] The mean fetal to maternal ratio is 0.6 in humans.[162] Examination of the neonate using Apgar scores and NACS did not detect any observable effects.

CONCLUSION

All drugs administered to the mother cross the placenta into the fetal circulation. The extent to which passage occurs depends on the maternal–fetal concentration gradient, the lipid solubility of the drug, the amount of un-ionized drug, and the degree of protein binding. Effects on the fetus depend on the concentration of free drug present in the fetus and can only be measured indirectly. Current methods of testing the newborn (neonatal neurobehavior scores, Apgar scores, acid–base status) may not detect subtle changes. When drug effects are detected, it is difficult to assess their overall impact.

REFERENCES

1. Morriss FH, Boyd RDH. Placental transport. In: Knobil E, Neill JD, eds. The physiology of reproduction. New York: Raven Press, 1988;2043.
2. Beal RW. Non-rhesus (D) blood group isoimmunization in obstetrics. Clin Obstet Gynæcol 1979;6:493.
3. Cohen F, Zuelzer WW. The transplacental passage of maternal erythrocytes into the fetus. Am J Obstet Gynecol 1965;93:566.
4. Ramsey EM. Circulation in the intervillous space of the primate placenta. Am J Obstet Gynecol 1962;84:1649.
5. Ramsey EM. What we have learned about placental circulation. J Reprod Med 1985;30:312.
6. Adamsons K, Joelsson I. The placenta, II. Placental blood flow. In: Philipp E, Barnes J, Newton M, eds. Scientific foundations of obstetrics and gynecology, 3rd ed. Chicago: William Heinemann Medical Books, 1986.
7. Greiss FC. A clinical concept of uterine blood flow during pregnancy. Obstet Gynecol 1967;30:595.
8. Borell U, Fernstrom I, Ohlson L, Wiqvist N. Influence of uterine contractions on the uteroplacental blood flow at term. Am J Obstet Gynecol 1965;93:44.
9. Chard T. Placental synthesis. Clin Obstet Gynaecol 1986;12:447.
10. Redman CWG. Immunology of the placenta. Clin Obstet Gynaecol 1986;13:469.
11. Miller RK, Berndt WD. Mechanisms of transport across the placenta: An in vitro approach. Life Sci 1974;16:7.
12. Johnson PM, Brown PJ. Review article: Fcγ receptors in the human placenta. Placenta 1981;2:355.
13. Hill EP, Power GG, Longo LD. A mathematical model of carbon dioxide transfer in the placenta and its interaction with oxygen. Am J Physiol 1973;224:283.
14. Wilkening RB, Meschia G. Fetal oxygen uptake, oxygenation, and acid–base balance as a function of uterine blood flow. Am J Physiol 1983;244:H749.
15. Longo LD, Hill EP, Power GG. Theoretical analysis of factors affecting placenta O_2 transfer. Am J Physiol 1972;222:730.
16. Itskovitz J, Goetzman BW, Roman C, Rudolph AM. Effects of fetal–maternal exchange transfusion on fetal oxygenation and blood flow distribution. Am J Physiol 1984;247:H655.
17. Cunningham FG, MacDonald PC, Gant NF, eds. The morphological and functional development of the fetus. In: Williams Obstetrics. 18th ed. Norwalk, CT: Appleton & Lange, 1989:100.
18. Krauer B, Krauer F. Drug kinetics in pregnancy. Clin Pharmacokinet 1977;2:167.
19. Cohen SE. Physiological alterations of pregnancy. Clin Anaesthesiol 1986;4:33.
20. Wald A, Van Thiel DH, Hoechstetter L, et al. Effect of pregnancy on gastrointestinal transit. Dig Dis Sci 1982;27:1015.
21. Christofides ND, Ghatei MA, Bloom SR, Borberg C, Gillmer MDG. Decreased plasma motilin concentrations in pregnancy. Br Med J 1982;285:1453.
22. Nimmo WS, Wilson J, Prescott LF. Narcotic analgesics and delayed gastric emptying during labour. Lancet 1975;1:890.
23. Hytten FE, Thomson AM, Taggart N. Total body water in normal pregnancy. J Obstet Gynæcol Br Commonw 1966;73:553.
24. Krauer B, Dayer P, Anner R. Changes in serum albumin and α_1 acid glycoprotein concentrations during pregnancy: An analysis of fetal–maternal pairs. Br J Obstet Gynæcol 1984;91:875.
25. Reynolds F, Knott C. Pharmacokinetics in pregnancy and placental drug transfer. Oxf Rev Reprod Biol 1989;11:389.
26. Kennedy RL, Bell JU, Miller RP, et al. Uptake and distribution of lidocaine in fetal lambs. Anesthesiology 1990;72:483.
27. Hanshaw-Thomas A, Reynolds F. Placental transfer of bupivacaine, pethidine and lignocaine in the rabbit: Effect of umbilical flow rate and protein content. Br J Obstet Gynæcol 1985;92:706.
28. Hanshaw-Thomas A, Rogerson N, Reynolds F. Transfer of bupivacaine, lignocaine and pethidine across the rabbit placenta: Influence of maternal protein binding and fetal flow. Placenta 1984;5:61.
29. Finster M, Morishima HO, Boyes RN, Covino BG. The placental transfer of lidocaine and its uptake by fetal tissues. Anesthesiology 1972;36:159.
30. Datta S, Brown WU, Ostheimer GW, Weiss JB, Alper MH. Epidural anesthesia for cesarean section in diabetic parturients: Maternal and neonatal acid–base status and bupivacaine concentrations. Anesth Analg 1981; 60:574.
31. Gaylard DG, Carson RJ, Reynolds F. Effect of umbilical perfusate pH and controlled maternal hypotension on placental drug transfer in the rabbit. Anesth Analg 1990;71:42.
32. Kennedy RL, Erenberg A, Robillard JE, Merkow A,

Turner T. Effects of changes in maternal–fetal pH on the transplacental equilibrium of bupivacaine. Anesthesiology 1979;51:50.

33. Brown WU, Bell GC, Alper MH. Acidosis, local anesthetics and the newborn. Obstet Gynecol 1976;48:27.

34. Biehl D, Shnider SM, Levinson G, Callender K. Placental transfer of lidocaine: Effects of fetal acidosis. Anesthesiology 1978;48:409.

35. Morselli PL, Franco-Morselli R, Bossi L. Clinical pharmacokinetics in newborns and infants, age-related-differences and therapeutic implications. Clin Pharmacokinet 1980;5:485.

36. Petrie RH, Yeh S, Murata Y, et al. The effect of drugs on fetal heart rate variability. Am J Obstet Gynecol 1978;130:294.

37. Jouppila R, Jouppila P, Kuikka J, Hollmen A. Placental blood flow during Cæsarean section under lumbar extradural analgesia. Br J Anæsth 1978;50:275.

38. Skjoldebrand A, Eklund J, Lunnell NO, Nylund L, Sarby B, Thornstrom S. The effect on uteroplacental blood flow of epidural anæsthesia containing adrenaline for cæsarean section. Acta Anæsthesiol Scand 1990;34:85.

39. Baumann H, Alon E, Atanassoff P, Pasch T, Huch A, Huch R. Effect of epidural anesthesia for cesarean delivery on maternal femoral arterial and venous, uteroplacental, and umbilical blood flow velocities and waveforms. Obstet Gynecol 1990;75:194.

40. Lindblad A, Bernow J, Vernersson E, Marsal K. Effects of extradural anæsthesia on human fetal blood flow in utero: Comparison of three local anæsthetic solutions. Br J Anæsth 1987;59:1265.

41. Kuhnert BR, Linn PL, Kuhnert PM. Obstetric medication and neonatal behavior: Current controversies. Clin Perinatol 1985;12:423.

42. Brazelton TB. Neonatal Behavioral Assessment Scale, 2nd ed. Philadelphia: JB Lippincott, 1984.

43. Scanlon JW, Brown WU, Weiss JB, Alper MH. Neurobehavioral responses of newborn infants after maternal epidural anesthesia. Anesthesiology 1974;40:121.

44. Amiel-Tison C, Barrier G, Shnider SM, Levinson G, Hughes SC, Stefani SJ. A new neurologic and adaptive capacity scoring system for evaluating obstetric medications in full-term newborns. Anesthesiology 1982;56:340.

45. Kuhnert BR, Harrison MJ, Linn PL, Kuhnert PM. Effects of maternal epidural anesthesia on neonatal behavior. Anesth Analg 1984;63:301.

46. McKechnie FB, Converse JG. Placental transmission of thiopental. Am J Obstet Gynecol 1955;70:639.

47. Morgan DJ, Blackman GL, Paull JD, Wolf LJ. Pharmacokinetics and plasma binding of thiopental. II: Studies at cesarean section. Anesthesiology 1981;54:474.

48. Schepens P, Heyndrickx A. Placental transfer of thiopental. Eur J Toxicol 1975;8:87.

49. Kosaka Y, Takahashi T, Mark LC. Intravenous thiobarbiturate anesthesia for cesarean section. Anesthesiology 1969;31:489.

50. Finster M, Morishima HO, Mark LC, Perel JM, Dayton PG, James LS. Tissue thiopental concentrations in the fetus and newborn. Anesthesiology 1972;36:155.

51. Schultetus RR, Hill CR, Dharamraj CM, Banner TE, Berman LS. Wakefulness during cesarean section after anesthetic induction with ketamine, thiopental, or ketamine and thiopental combined. Anesth Analg 1986;65:723.

52. Baraka A, Louis F, Noueihid R, Diab M, Dabbous A, Sibai A. Awareness following different techniques of general anæsthesia for cæsarean section. Br J Anæsth 1989;62:645.

53. Meer FM, Downing JW, Coleman AG. An intravenous method of anæsthesia for cæsarean section. Part II: Ketamine. Br J Anæsth 1973;45:191.

54. Pelz B, Sinclair DM. Induction agents for cæsarean section: A comparison of thiopentone and ketamine. Anæsthesia 1973;28:37.

55. Ellingson A, Haram K, Sagen N, Solheim E. Transplacental passage of ketamine after intravenous administration. Acta Anæsthesiol Scand 1977;21:41.

56. Little B, Chang T, Chucot L et al. Study of ketamine as an obstetric anesthetic agent. Am J Obstet Gynecol 1972;113:247.

57. Hodgkinson R, Marx GF, Kim SS, Miclat NM. Neonatal neurobehavioral tests following vaginal delivery under ketamine, thiopental, and extradural anesthesia. Anesth Analg 1977;56:548.

58. Gin T, Gregory MA, Oh TE. The hæmodynamic effects of propofol and thiopentone for induction of cæsarean section. Anæsth Intensive Care 1990;18:175.

59. Dailland P, Cockshott ID, Lirzin JD et al. Intravenous propofol during cesarean section: Placental transfer, concentrations in breastmilk, and neonatal effects: A preliminary study. Anesthesiology 1989;71:827.

60. Moore J, Bill KM, Flynn RJ, McKeating KT, Howard PJ. A comparison between propofol and thiopentone as induction agents in obstetric anæsthesia. Anæsthesia 1989;44:753.

61. Valtonen M, Kanto J, Rosenberg P. Comparison of propofol and thiopentone for induction of anæsthesia for elective cæsarean section. Anæsthesia 1989;44:758.

62. Gin T, Gregory MA, Oh TE. Maternal and fetal levels of propofol at cæsarean section. Anæsth Intensive Care 1990;18:180.

63. Celleno D, Capogna G, Tomassetti AM, Costantino P, Di Feo G, Nisini R. Neurobehavioural effects of propofol on the neonate following elective cæsarean section. Br J Anæsth 1989;62:649.

64. Haram K, Lund T, Sagen N, Boe OE. Comparison of thiopentone and diazepam as induction agents of anæsthesia for cæsarean section. Acta Anæsthesiol Scand 1981;25:470.

65. Crawford ME, Carl P, Bach V, Ravlo O, Mikkelsen BO, Werner M. A randomized comparison between midazolam and thiopental for elective cesarean section anesthesia. I. Mothers. Anesth Analg 1989;68:229.

66. Gamble JAS, Moore J, Lamki H, Howard PJ. A study of

plasma diazepam levels in mother and infants. Br J Obstet Gynæcol 1977;84:588.

67. Wilson CM, Dundee JW, Moore J, Howard PJ, Collier PS. A comparison of the early pharmacokinetics of midazolam in pregnant and nonpregnant women. Anæsthesia 1987;42:1057.

68. Cree JE, Meyer J, Hailey DM. Diazepam in labour: Its metabolism and effect on the clinical condition and thermogenesis of the newborn. Br Med J 1973;4:251.

69. Owen JR, Irani SF, Blair AW. Effect of diazepam administered to mothers during labour on temperature regulation of neonate. Arch Dis Child 1972;47:107.

70. Scher J, Hailey DM, Beard RW. The effects of diazepam on the fetus. J Obstet Gynæcol Br Commonw 1972;79:635.

71. Yeh SY, Paul RH, Cordero L, Hon EH. A study of diazepam during labor. Obstet Gynecol 1974;43:363.

72. Greenblatt DJ, Arendt RM, Abernethy DR, Giles HG, Sellers EM, Shader RI. In vitro quantitation of benzodiazepine lipophilicity: Relation to in vivo distribution. Br J Anæsth 1983;55:985.

73. Vree TB, Reekers-Ketting JJ, Fragen RJ, Arts THM. Placental transfer of midazolam and its metabolite 1-hydroxymethylmidazolam in the pregnant ewe. Anesth Analg 1984;63:31.

74. Conklin KA, Graham CW, Murad S, et al. Midazolam and diazepam: Maternal and fetal effects in the pregnant ewe. Obstet Gynecol 1980;56:471.

75. Ravlo O, Carl P, Crawford ME, Bach V, Mikkelsen BO, Nielson HK. A randomized comparison between midazolam and thiopental for elective cesarean section anesthesia. II. Neonates. Anesth Analg 1989;68:234.

76. Bach V, Carl P, Ravlo O, et al. A randomized comparison between midazolam and thiopental for elective cesarean section anesthesia. III: Placental transfer and elimination in neonates. Anesth Analg 1989;68:238.

77. Holdcroft A, Morgan M. Intravenous induction agents for cæsarean section (editorial). Anæsthesia 1989;44:719.

78. Marx GF, Joshi CW, Orkin LR. Placental transmission of nitrous oxide. Anesthesiology 1970;32:429.

79. Latto IP, Waldron BA. Anæsthesia for cæsarean section: Analysis of blood concentrations of halothane using 0.2% or 0.65% halothane with 50% nitrous oxide in oxygen. Br J Anæsth 1977;49:371.

80. Coleman AJ, Downing JW. Enflurane anesthesia for cesarean section. Anesthesiology 1975;43:354.

81. Stefani SJ, Hughes SC, Shnider SM et al. Neonatal neurobehavioral effects of inhalation analgesia for vaginal delivery. Anesthesiology 1982;56:351.

82. Palahniuk RJ, Scatliff J, Biehl D, Wiebe H, Sankaran K. Maternal and neonatal effects of methoxyflurane, nitrous oxide and lumbar epidural anæsthesia for cæsarean section. Can Anæsth Soc J 1977;24:586.

83. Warren RM, Datta S, Ostheimer GW, Naulty JS, Weiss JB, Morrison JA. Comparison of the maternal and neonatal effects of halothane, enflurane, and isoflurane for cesarean delivery. Anesth Analg 1983;62:516.

84. Drabkova J, Crul JF, Van der Kleijn E. Placental transfer of ^{14}C labelled succinylcholine in near-term macaca mulatta monkeys. Br J Anæsth 1973;45:1087.

85. Frank M, Flynn PJ, Hughes R. Atracurium in obstetric anæsthesia. Br J Anæsth 1983;55:113S.

86. Dailey PA, Fisher DM, Shnider SM, et al. Pharmacokinetics, placental transfer, and neonatal effects of vecuronium and pancuronium administered during cesarean section. Anesthesiology 1984;60:569.

87. Duvaldestin P, Demetriou M, Henzel D, Desmonts JM. The placental transfer of pancuronium and its pharmacokinetics during cæsarean section. Acta Anæsthesiol Scand 1978;22:327.

88. Morishima HO, Heyman MA, Rudolph AM, Barrett CT. Toxicity of lidocaine in the fetal and newborn lamb and its relationship to asphyxia. Am J Obstet Gynecol 1972;112:72.

89. Tucker GT, Boyes RN, Bridenbaugh PO, Moore DC. Binding of anilide-type local anesthetics in plasma. II. Implications in vivo, with special reference to transplacental distribution. Anesthesiology 1970;33:304.

90. McGuinness GA, Merkow AJ, Kennedy RL, Erenberg A. Epidural anesthesia with bupivacaine for cesarean section: Neonatal blood levels and neurobehavioral responses. Anesthesiology 1978;49:270.

91. Scanlon JW, Ostheimer GW, Lurie AO, Brown WU, Weiss JB, Alper MH. Neurobehavioral responses and drug concentrations in newborns after maternal epidural anesthesia with bupivacaine. Anesthesiology 1976;45:400.

92. Kuhnert BR, Zuspan KJ, Kuhnert PM, Syracuse CD, Brown DE. Bupivacaine disposition in mother, fetus, and neonate after spinal anesthesia for cesarean section. Anesth Analg 1987;66:407.

93. Ralston DH, Shnider SM. The fetal and neonatal effects of regional anesthesia in obstetrics. Anesthesiology 1978;48:34.

94. Philipson EH, Kuhnert BR, Syracuse CD. Maternal, fetal and neonatal lidocaine levels following local perineal infiltration. Am J Obstet Gynecol 1984;149:403.

95. Abboud TK, Kim KC, Noueihed R, et al. Epidural bupivacaine, chloroprocaine, or lidocaine for cesarean section: Maternal and neonatal effects. Anesth Analg 1983;62:914.

96. Abboud TK, Sarkis F, Blikian A, Varakian L, Earl S, Henriksen E. Lack of adverse neonatal neuro-behavioral effects of lidocaine. Anesth Analg 1983;62:473.

97. Kileff ME, James FM, Dewan DM, Floyd HM. Neonatal neurobehavioral responses after epidural anesthesia for cesarean section using lidocaine and bupivacaine. Anesth Analg 1984;63:413.

98. Kuhnert BR, Kuhnert PM, Philipson EH, Syracuse CD, Kaine CJ, Changhyon Y. The half-life of 2-chloroprocaine. Anesth Analg 1986;65:273.

99. Kuhnert BR, Kuhnert PM, Prochaska AL, Gross TL. Plasma levels of 2-chloroprocaine in obstetric patients and their neonates after epidural anesthesia. Anesthesiology 1980;53:21.

100. Kuhnert BR, Kennard MJ, Linn PL. Neonatal neurobehavior after epidural anesthesia for cesarean section: A comparison of bupivacaine and chlorprocaine. Anesth Analg 1988;67:64.

101. Philipson EH, Kuhnert BR, Syracuse CD. 2-chloroprocaine for local perineal infiltration. Am J Obstet Gynecol 1987;157:1275.

102. Way WL, Costley EC, Way EL. Respiratory sensitivity of the newborn infant to meperidine and morphine. Clin Pharmacol Ther 1965;6:454.

103. Gerhardt R, Bancalari E, Cohen H, Macias-Loza M. Respiratory depression at birth-value of Apgar score and ventilatory measurements in its detection. J Pediatr 1977;90:971.

104. Kuhnert BR, Kuhnert PM, Tu AL, Lin DCK, Foltz RL. Meperidine and normeperidine levels following meperidine administration during labor. I. Mother. Am J Obstet Gynecol 1979;133:904.

105. Morgan D, Moore G, Thomas J, Triggs E. Disposition of meperidine in pregnancy. Clin Pharmacol Ther 1978;23:288.

106. Shnider SM, Way EL, Lord MJ. Rate of appearance and disappearance of meperidine in fetal blood after administration of narcotic to the mother. Anesthesiology 1966;27:227.

107. Crawford JS, Rudofsky S. The placental transmission of pethidine. Br J Anæsth 1965;37:929.

108. Szeto HH, Mann LI, Bhakthavathsalan A, Lui M, Inturrisi CE. Meperidine pharmacokinetics in the maternal-fetal unit. J Pharmacol Exp Ther 1978;206:448.

109. Caldwell J, Wakile LA, Notarianni LJ, et al. Maternal and neonatal disposition of pethidine in childbirth—a study using quantitative gas chromatography-mass spectrometry. Life Sci 1978;22:589.

110. Belfrage P, Boreus LO, Hartvig P, Irestedt L, Raabe N. Neonatal depression after obstetrical analgesia with pethidine: The role of the injection-delivery time interval and of the plasma concentrations of pethidine and norpethidine. Acta Obstet Gynæcol Scand 1981;60:43.

111. Shnider SM, Moya F. Effects of meperidine on the newborn infant. Am J Obstet Gynecol 1964;89:1009.

112. Kuhnert BR, Kuhnert PM, Tu AL, Lin DCK. Meperidine and normeperidine levels following meperidine administration during labor. II. Fetus and neonate. Am J Obstet Gynecol 1979;133:909.

113. Kuhnert BR, Philipson EH, Kuhnert PM, Syracuse CD. Disposition of meperidine and normeperidine following multiple doses during labor. I. Mother. Am J Obstet Gynecol 1985;151:406.

114. Kuhnert BR, Philipson EH, Kuhnert PM, Syracuse CD. Disposition of meperidine and normeperidine following multiple doses during labor. II. Fetus and neonate. Am J Obstet Gynecol 1985;151:410.

115. Hogg MIJ, Wiener PC, Rosen M, Mapleson WW. Urinary excretion and metabolism of pethidine and norpethidine in the newborn. Br J Anæsth 1977;49:891.

116. Cooper LV, Stephen GW, Aggett PJA. Elimination of pethidine and bupivacaine in the newborn. Arch Dis Child 1977;52:638.

117. Stephen GW, Cooper LV. The role of analgesics in respiratory depression: A rabbit model. Anæsthesia 1977;32:324.

118. Brower KR, Crowell DH, Leung P, Cashman TM. Neonatal electroencephalographic patterns as affected by maternal drugs administered during labor and delivery. Anesth Analg 1978;57:303.

119. Brackbill Y, Kane J, Manniello RL, Abramson D. Obstetric meperidine usage and assessment of neonatal status. Anesthesiology 1974;40:116.

120. Hodgkinson R, Husain FJ. The duration of effect of maternally administered meperidine on neonatal neurobehavior. Anesthesiology 1982;56:51.

121. Hodgkinson R, Bhatt M, Wang CN. Double-blind comparison of the neurobehaviour of neonates following the administration of different doses of meperidine to the mother. Can Anæsth Soc J 1978;25:405.

122. Kuhnert BR, Linn PL, Kennard MJ, Kuhnert PM. Effects of low doses of meperidine on neonatal behavior. Anesth Analg 1985;64:335.

123. Hodgkinson R, Batt M, Grewal G, Marx GF. Neonatal neurobehavior in the first 48 hours of life: Effect of the administration of meperidine with and without naloxone in the mother. Pediatrics 1978;62:294.

124. Wiener PC, Hogg MI, Rosen M. Neonatal respiration, feeding and neurobehavioural state. Anæsthesia 1979;34:996.

125. Gerhardt R, Bancalari E, Cohen H, Rocha LF. Use of naloxone to reverse narcotic respiratory depression in the newborn infant. J Pediatr 1977;90:1009.

126. Craft JB, Coaldrake LA, Bolan JC, et al. Placental passage and uterine effects fentanyl. Anesth Analg 1983;62:894.

127. Rayburn WF, Smith CV, Parriott JE, Woods RE. Randomized comparison of meperidine and fentanyl during labor. Obstet Gynecol 1989;74:604.

128. Rayburn W, Rathke A, Leuschen P, Chleborad J, Weidner W. Fentanyl citrate analgesia during labor. Am J Obstet Gynecol 1989;161:202.

129. Eisele JH, Wright R, Rogge P. Newborn and maternal fentanyl levels at cesarean section [Abstract] Anesth Analg 1982;61:179.

130. Gauntlett IS, Fisher DM, Hertzka RE, Kuhlis E, Spellman MJ, Rudolph C. Pharmacokinetics of fentanyl in neonatal humans and lambs: Effects of age. Anesthesiology 1988;69:683.

131. Justins DM, Knott C, Luthman J, Reynolds F. Epidural versus intramuscular fentanyl: Analgesia and pharmacokinetics in labour. Anæsthesia 1983;38:937.

132. Chestnut DH, Owen CL, Bates JN, Ostman LG, Choi WW, Geiger MW. Continuous infusion epidural analgesia during labor: A randomized, double-blind comparison of 0.0625% bupivacaine/0.0002% fentanyl versus 0.125% bupivacaine. Anesthesiology 1988;68:754.

133. Preston PG, Rosen MA, Hughes SC, et al. Epidural anesthesia with fentanyl and lidocaine for cesarean section: Maternal effects and neonatal outcome. Anesthesiology 1988;68:938.

134. Paech MJ, Westmore MD, Speirs HM. A double-blind comparison of epidural bupivacaine and bupivacaine-fentanyl for cæsarean section. Anæsth Intensive Care 1990;18:22.

135. Schlesinger TS, Miletich DJ. Epidural fentanyl and lidocaine during cesarean section: Maternal efficacy and neonatal safety using impedance monitoring [Abstract] Anesthesiology 1988;69:A649.

136. Koehntop DE, Rodman JH, Brundage DM, Hegland MG, Buckley JJ. Pharmacokinetics of fentanyl in neonates. Anesth Analg 1986;65:227.

137. Benlabed M, Dreizzen E, Ecoffey C, Escourrou P, Midgal M, Gaultier C. Neonatal pattern of breathing after cesarean section with or without epidural fentanyl. Anesthesiology 1990;73:1110.

138. Gepts E, Heytens L, Camu F. Pharmacokinetics and placental transfer of intravenous and epidural alfentanil in parturient women. Anesth Analg 1986;65:1155.

139. Golub MS, Eisele JH, Donald JM. Obstetric analgesia and infant outcome in monkeys: Infant development after intrapartum exposure to meperidine or alfentanil. Am J Obstet Gynecol 1988;159:1280.

140. Heytens L, Cammu H, Camu F. Extradural analgesia during labour using alfentanil. Br J Anæsth 1987; 59:331.

141. Maduska AL, Hajghassemali M. A double-blind comparison of butorphanol and meperidine in labour: Maternal pain relief and effect on the newborn. Can Anæsth Soc J 1978;25:398.

142. Hodgkinson R, Huff RW, Hayashi RH, Husain FJ. Double-blind comparison of maternal analgesia and neonatal neurobehaviour following intravenous butorphanol and meperidine. J Int Med Res 1979;7:224.

143. Hatjis CG, Meis PJ. Sinusoidal fetal heart rate pattern associated with butorphanol administration. Obstet Gynecol 1986;67:377.

144. Frank M, McAteer EJ, Cattermole R, Loughnan B, Stafford LB, Hitchcock AM. Nalbuphine for obstetric analgesia. Anæsthesia 1987;42:697.

145. Hunt CO, Naulty JS, Malinow AM, Datta S, Ostheimer GW. Epidural butorphanol-bupivacaine for analgesia during labor and delivery. Anesth Analg 1989;68:323.

146. Murad SHN, Conklin KA, Tabsh KMA, Brinkman CR, Erkkola R, Nuwayhid B. Atropine and glycopyrrolate: Hemodynamic effects and placental transfer in the pregnant ewe. Anesth Analg 1981;60:710.

147. Mendez-Bauer C, Poseiro JJ, Arellano-Hernandez G, Zambrana MA, Caldeyro-Barcia R. Effects of atropine on the heart rate of the human fetus during labor. Am J Obstet Gynecol 1963;85:1033.

148. Kivalo I, Saarikoski S. Placental transmission of atropine at full-term pregnancy. Br J Anæsth 1977;49:1017.

149. Kanto J, Virtanen R, Iisalo E, Maenpaa K, Liukko P. Placental transfer and pharmacokinetics of atropine after a single maternal intravenous and intramuscular administration. Acta Anæsthesiol Scand 1981;25:85.

150. Abboud TK, Read J, Miller F, Chen T, Valle R, Henriksen E. Use of glycopyrrolate in the parturient: Effect on the maternal and fetal heart and uterine activity. Obstet Gynecol 1981;57:224.

151. Hughes SC, Ward MG, Levinson G, et al. Placental transfer of ephedrine does not affect neonatal outcome. Anesthesiology 1985;63:217.

152. Kangas-Saarela T, Hollmen AI, Tolonen U, et al. Does ephedrine influence newborn neurobehavioural responses and spectral EEG when used to prevent maternal hypotension during cæsarean section? Acta Anæsthesiol Scand 1990;34:8.

153. Ramanathan J, Sibai BM, Mabie WC, Chauhan D, Ruiz AG. The use of labetalol for attenuation of the hypertensive response to endotracheal intubation in preeclampsia. Am J Obstet Gynecol 1988;159:650.

154. Michael CA. Use of labetalol in the treatment of severe hypertension during pregnancy. Br J Clin Pharmacol 1979;8:211S.

155. MacPherson M, Broughton Pipkin F, Rutter N. The effect of maternal labetalol on the newborn infants. Br J Obstet Gynæcol 1986;93:539.

156. Sun CY, Yacobi A, Kartzinel R, Stampfli H, Davis CS, Lai C. Kinetics of esmolol, an ultra–short-acting B-blocker, and of its major metabolite. Clin Pharmacol Ther 1983;34:427.

157. Ostman PL, Chestnut DH, Robillard JE, Weiner CP, Hdez MJ. Transplacental passage and hemodynamic effects of esmolol in the gravid ewe. Anesthesiology 1988;69:738.

158. Eisenach JC, Castro MI. Maternally administered esmolol produces fetal B-adrenergic blockade and hypoxemia in sheep. Anesthesiology 1989;71:718.

159. Howe SP, McGowan WAW, Moore J, McCaughey W, Dundee JW. The placental transfer of cimetidine. Anæsthesia 1981;36:371.

160. Hodgkinson R, Glassenberg R, Joyce TH, Coombs DW, Ostheimer GW, Gibbs CP. Comparison of cimetidine (Tagamet) with antacid for safety and effectiveness in reducing gastric acidity before elective cesarean section. Anesthesiology 1983;59:86.

161. Riggs KW, Axelson JE, Gruber NC, McErlane BA, McMorland GH, Rurak DW. Metoclopramide pharmacokinetics in pregnant and nonpregnant sheep. J Pharmacol Sci 1988;77:373.

162. Bylsma-Howell M, Riggs KW, McMorland GH, et al. Placental transport of metoclopramide: Assessment of maternal and neonatal effects. Can Anæsth Soc J 1983;30:487.

CHAPTER 7

Fetal Evaluation

Sheila L. Ronkin

INTRAPARTUM FETAL EVALUATION

During labor, monitoring fetal heart rate and uterine contraction patterns provides essential information about the status of the fetus and the progress of labor. Continuous electronic fetal monitoring (EFM) was introduced into clinical practice two decades ago to enable early recognition of fetal jeopardy and to prevent fetal and neonatal mortality. Its use and interpretation are based on experimental and clinical evidence that characteristics of the fetal heart rate pattern reflect the adequacy of fetal oxygenation and predict asphyxia.

Physiology

Fetal blood has a large capacity and a high affinity for oxygen. Fetal organs receive more blood than needed simply to meet their metabolic demands. These physiologic adaptations permit adequate tissue oxygenation despite the low fetal arterial Po_2 (20–25 mm Hg). Normal uterine contractions hinder blood flow to and from the placenta but leave flow within the intervillous space uninterrupted.[1] The normal fetus maintains its acid–base balance despite this alteration in blood flow. When oxygen delivery falls, the fetus initiates several compensatory responses:

- Fractional oxygen extraction increases[2–5]
- Oxygen carrying capacity of blood rises[6]

- Activity and the associated energy expense diminish[7–10]
- The distribution of blood flow changes to favor vital organs at the expense of nonvital organs[11,12]

With prolonged and severe hypoxia, these mechanisms fail. Anaerobic glycolysis begins, lactate and pyruvate accumulate, and metabolic acidosis results.

The fetal heart rate (FHR) is subject to several levels of control. Impulses from the sinoatrial node override the inherent rhythmicity of the myocardial cell. Sympathetic and parasympathetic input from the autonomic nervous system influence the depolarization rate of cells within the cardiac electrical conduction system. Mild sympathetic stimulation (epinephrine/norepinephrine) increases the baseline rate. Persistent sympathetic stimulation results in constriction of the peripheral circulation and bradycardia. Parasympathetic stimulation also slows the baseline heart rate. Alterations in intravascular pressure or blood oxygen content evoke these autonomic responses.

As hoped, intrapartum continuous EFM correlates with a decrease in intrapartum fetal wastage. Lee and Baggish[13] report a reduction in intrapartum fetal death from 3.7/1000 deliveries before the introduction of EFM to 0.3/1000 after incorporating universal EFM for intrapartum care. However, EFM has been unsuccessful in predicting or preventing long-term neurologic disorders, especially cerebral palsy.[14,15] Although asphyxia (hypoxemia plus acidemia) is associated with brain damage in monkey fetuses, it must be near lethal (reduction in oxygen content from 10 vol%–20 vol% to 0.8 vol%–1.5 vol%).[16] To experience and then survive such prolonged asphyxia is uncommon. Reports based on large databases show that perinatal asphyxia precedes fewer than 15% of cases of cerebral palsy.[17–19] Because perinatal asphyxia is implicated in only a fraction of cerebral palsy cases, it should not be surprising that EFM is a poor predictor of this disorder.

Currently, it is standard practice in high-risk obstetric patients to monitor, record, and evaluate the FHR at least every 15 minutes during the active phase of the first stage of labor. During the second stage of labor, the FHR is monitored, recorded, and evaluated every 5 minutes. The standard practice in low-risk patients is to monitor, record, and evaluate the FHR every 30 minutes in the active phase of the first stage of labor and every 15 minutes in the second stage.[20]

Intrapartum Record Interpretation

No universal language/system for intrapartum record interpretation currently exists. Viewing of records by several experts may result in subtle differences of opinion and diagnosis. The five components of the fetal heart rate tracing are (Figs. 7-1 to 7-6):

- Fetal heart baseline rate
- Fetal heart rate variability
- Accelerations of the fetal heart rate
- Decelerations of the fetal heart rate
- Uterine contraction pattern

Baseline

The normal FHR ranges between 120 and 160 beats/minute (bpm). An abnormal baseline rate alone does not predict acidosis. Chorioamnionitis, maternal fever, fetal movement, prematurity, or maternal medications can induce tachycardia. When seen in association with loss of FHR variability or FHR decelerations, tachycardia may represent fetal asphyxia.

Bradycardia, in the range of 100 to 120 bpm, is not associated with fetal acidosis when variability is normal and decelerations are absent. Sometimes post-term fetuses and normoxic fetuses during the second stage of labor exhibit this pattern. Congenital heart block due to maternal collagen vascular disease, congenital cardiac anomalies, or maternal hypothermia can cause baseline heart rates below 100 bpm. Sudden unremediable bradycardia often signals prolonged compression or prolapse of the umbilical cord, persistent compression of the fetal head, prolonged maternal hy-

potension, or placental abruption. Asphyxia is often present in these situations.

Variability

Fetal heart rate variability, or beat-to-beat variation, is the most significant prognosticator of fetal well-being. Beat-to-beat deflections represent the difference between each successive R-R interval of the fetal electrocardiogram (ECG). Normal FHR variability predicts normal neurologic function and Apgar score. Progressive loss of variability is a consistent feature preceding intrapartum fetal death.[21] Maternal administration of barbiturates, narcotics, local anesthetics or parasympathetic agents, or fetal sleep cycles may limit variability without producing hypoxia.

Accelerations

An acceleration is an increase in the FHR of at least 15 bpm that lasts at least 15 seconds. Accelerations occurring in the first 30 minutes and last 30 minutes of labor correlate well with positive neonatal outcome. They predict a 5-minute Apgar score greater than or equal to 7 and decreased perinatal mortality.[22]

Decelerations

Decelerations are periodic decreases of the baseline FHR of at least 15 bpm that last at least 15 seconds in relation to contractions. The most frequently observed FHR deceleration is the variable deceleration.[23] Variable decelerations vary in appearance, shape, onset, and duration from contraction to contraction. They may be sporadic or repetitive and typically show abrupt onset and recovery. These vagally induced decreases in heart rate are responses to fetal arterial pressure-induced baroreceptor discharge. They often occur during umbilical cord compression.

The normoxic fetus readily tolerates mild variable decelerations. Intervals of uterine relaxation with sufficient umbilical blood flow allow adequate oxygen and carbon dioxide exchange. Conversely, persistent or severe variables may lead to acidosis. Signs of compromise include the following:

- Absence of accelerations
- Decreased beat-to-beat variability
- Increased baseline heart rate
- Slow recovery to baseline following decelerations

Persistent variable decelerations correlate with decreased fetal scalp pH, low neonatal umbilical pH, and

(text continues on page 152)

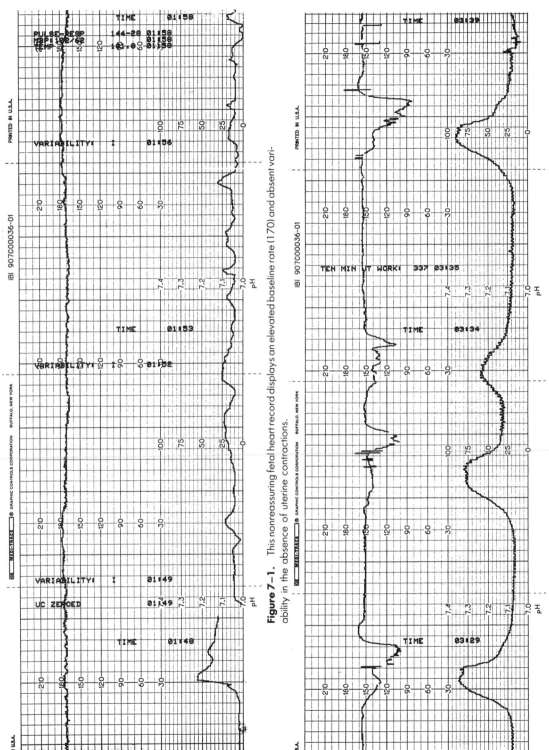

Figure 7–1. This nonreassuring fetal heart record displays an elevated baseline rate (170) and absent variability in the absence of uterine contractions.

Figure 7–2. This labor record demonstrates repetitive variable decelerations and absent variability. These findings should prompt prompt assessment of fetal acid–base status or delivery.

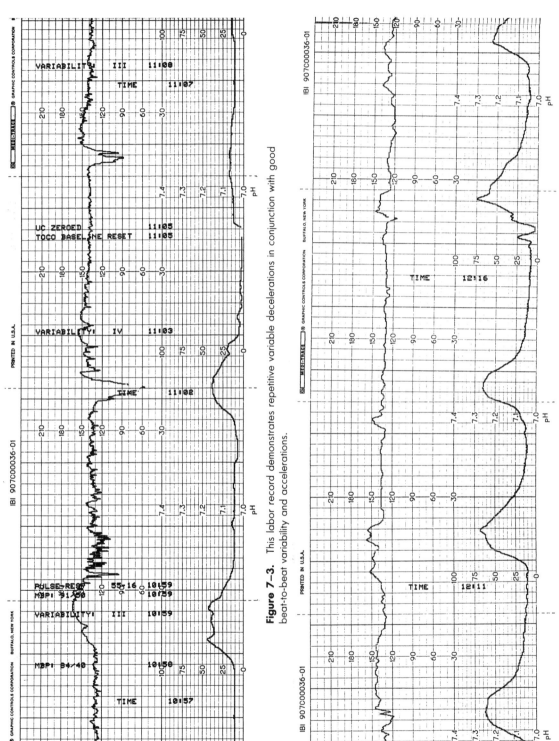

Figure 7–3. This labor record demonstrates repetitive variable decelerations in conjunction with good beat-to-beat variability and accelerations.

Figure 7–4. This reassuring labor record demonstrates a baseline heart rate of 130 bpm with accelerations. Contractions are occurring every 2 to 3 minutes.

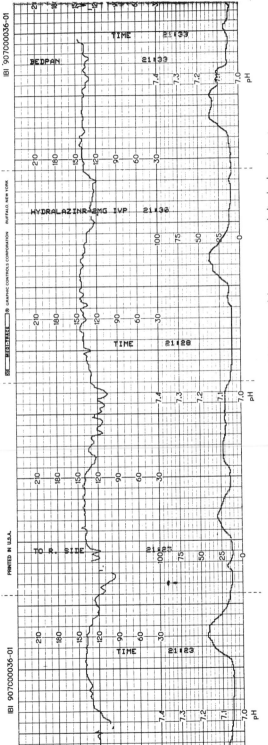

Figure 7–5. This labor record belongs to a 41-year-old G₆ P₅₀₀₅ with hypertension and oligohydramnios at 37 weeks. The external monitoring system reveals repetitive decelerations during the latent phase of labor. This record requires further assessment. The next step is placement of a fetal scalp electrode to better assess beat-to-beat variability and timing of decelerations in relation to contractions. Efforts at in utero resuscitation (as outlined in text) should follow.

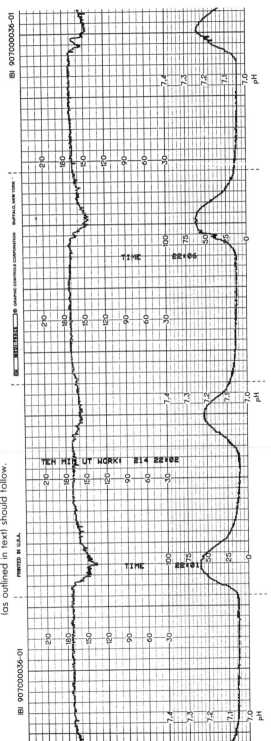

Figure 7–6. This nonreassuring labor record demonstrates a fetal tachycardia (baseline of 170 bpm) with absent variability and repetitive late decelerations. Contractions are occurring every 2 to 3 minutes. This tracing warrants prompt delivery.

low Apgar score.[24,25] So, this heart rate pattern merits intervention. Steps to take include the following:

1. Examine pelvis to search for cord presentation and to elevate the fetal presenting part.
2. Reposition mother to increase venous return to the heart, improve uterine blood flow, and alter the juxtaposition of the fetus and cord.
3. Confirm adequate maternal blood pressure and increase intravenous fluids if necessary to protect uterine blood flow.
4. Administer oxygen (8–10 L/min by face mask).
5. Initiate intrauterine saline infusion. (This procedure eliminates repetitive variable decelerations in 67.9% of cases.[26])
6. Finally, unremediable persistent variable decelerations in combination with other nonreassuring FHR changes (such as increased baseline or absent beat-to-beat variability) mandate acid–base assessment of the fetus or delivery.

Late decelerations are repetitive, symmetric, smooth decreases in the FHR. Their onset, nadir, and resolution occur 30 to 60 seconds after the onset, peak, and resolution of each uterine contraction. In the presence of normal beat-to-beat variability, late decelerations represent a vagally mediated chemoreceptor reflex and are remediable. In the absence of beat-to-beat variability, late decelerations signify hypoxic myocardial depression and are ominous.[27] Persistent late decelerations require intervention. Therapies include the following:

1. Treat maternal hypotension, if present, with intravenous fluid support and maternal repositioning.
2. Maximize oxygenation by administering oxygen by mask.
3. Discontinue exogenous uterine stimulation (oxytocin infusion).
4. Consider a tocolytic agent to relax uterine tetany.
5. Finally, unremediable late decelerations mandate clinical correlation and acid–base assessment of the fetus or delivery.

Uterine Contraction Pattern

A transducer, held in place on the maternal abdomen by a belt or elastic stocking, allows determination of the frequency and approximate duration of uterine contractions. The contracting uterus exerts pressure on the transducer. This pressure is translated electronically into a record of uterine activity. Both maternal and fetal movements interfere with these recordings.

An internal device, communicating with the intra-amniotic space at one end and a pressure transducer at the other, can measure the force of labor contractions. Placement of this intrauterine catheter requires rupture of the membranes. Normal resting uterine tone is 5 mm Hg or less in the latent phase of labor. Baseline tone increases to 10 to 12 mm Hg in the active phase. At the height of active phase, contraction force may reach 40 to 50 mm Hg, and contraction frequency may near four to five per 10-minute interval. During fetal descent, with maternal pushing effort, intrauterine pressures may rise even more (50–150 mm Hg).[28]

The Montevideo Unit was devised as an objective tool for quantifying the force of labor. The Montevideo Unit is the product of average contraction intensity and the frequency of contractions over a 10-minute interval. Adequate contractile activity is in the range of 250 Montevideo Units.[28]

In the setting of arrested labor progress, inadequate contractile activity may be hypotonic (synchronous contractions with normal basal tone) or hypertonic (elevated basal tone or distorted, asynchronous contractions). Etiologies include overdistention of the uterus, infection, drugs, cephalopelvic disproportion, and malpresentation of the fetus. Treatment of hypotonic dysfunction may include amniotomy, adequate hydration and pain relief, oxytocin augmentation of labor, treatment of underlying infection, or cesarean delivery. Hypertonic dysfunction is treated by morphine rest or cesarean delivery.

Fetal Acid–Base Assessment

The value of continuous electronic FHR monitoring is its ability to confirm fetal well-being, not its ability to identify fetal compromise. Low fetal pH rarely accompanies an innocuous fetal heart record, whereas deceleration patterns may coincide with normal fetal acid–base status.[29] Low fetal scalp pH correlates well with low Apgar scores.[30,31] (Stasis of blood in the scalp during late labor may produce local acidosis, leading to a low scalp pH that is not representative of the fetal central circulation.) Direct assessment of fetal acid–base status is indicated when the fetal heart tracing demonstrates a mixture of reassuring and nonreassuring features (*i.e.,* absent variability without periodic changes [accelerations or decelerations] or persistent late decelerations with adequate variability).

Fetal scalp blood sampling is possible only in laboring patients with ruptured membranes and with dilation of the cervix sufficient to allow access to the fetus (usually 2–3 cm). The obstetrician introduces a plastic cone with a light source through the vagina and cervix to the presenting fetal scalp or breech. The surface is cleaned and incised with a 2-mm long-handled blade. Beads of blood are collected into a heparinized capillary tube for assay. Pressure is applied to the scalp wound through two contractions, and hemostasis is visually confirmed by the operator. A pH greater than or equal to 7.25 is reassuring. A borderline pH of 7.20 to 7.24 requires repeating the technique immediately. A pH less than 7.20 mandates delivery.

ANTEPARTUM FETAL EVALUATION

Invasive Testing

Genetic Testing

Genetic evaluation of a pregnancy ideally begins before conception. Careful construction of a family pedigree is followed by confirmation or clarification of an inheritable diagnosis and education regarding various diseases and their antenatal and postnatal therapies. If available, carrier testing may be offered. The recurrence risk of a particular anomaly or disease is assessed and discussed. The risks, benefits, limitations, and utility of prenatal diagnosis are presented. Obstetric options (including termination of affected pregnancies, donor insemination, in vitro fertilization, embryo transfer, use of contraception in the hope that prenatal diagnosis or treatment will become available and reproductive sterilization) are presented as applicable to each patient's needs.

Invasive prenatal testing for genetic disorders is indicated for advanced maternal age (35 or older at the time of delivery), birth of a previous child with a chromosome abnormality, parental chromosomal translocation or inversion, parental aneuploidy, many Mendelian disorders, and abnormal maternal serum markers for Down syndrome (such as low alpha-fetoprotein). Also, invasive testing may be warranted in some cases of recurrent spontaneous abortion and many cases of antenatally diagnosed structural defects or growth abnormalities of the fetus.

Chorionic villus sampling is performed transcervically or transabdominally at 9 to 12 weeks of gestation. Amniocentesis is most often done at 15 to 17 weeks of gestation. (It is technically feasible at earlier gestational ages, but the risks have not been clearly established.) Both procedures are guided by sonar. Cho-

rionic villi or amniotic fluid is aspirated, fetal cells are cultured, and DNA is extracted for testing. Risks include bleeding, rupture of the fetal membranes, infection, and pregnancy loss. The accuracy and the risks of chorionic villus sampling are considered comparable to those of amniocentesis.[32]

Percutaneous Umbilical Blood Sampling

Percutaneous umbilical blood sampling (PUBS), or cordocentesis, is a sonar-guided transabdominal procedure for accessing the fetal circulation for diagnostic or therapeutic purposes. Indications include isoimmunization, alloimmune thrombocytopenia, sonar diagnosis of fetal structural abnormalities requiring cytogenetic, hematologic, biochemical, or virologic study, and some cases of intrauterine growth retardation with suspected placental failure. Risks include fetal hemorrhage, preterm labor, fetal bradycardia, rupture of the membranes, infection, isoimmunization, fetal trauma, and fetal death. The incidence of complications is related to the indication for sampling and the skills of the operator.[33]

Ultrasound

Detectable structural defects are present in 1% to 2% of human live births.[34] Prenatal recognition of anomalies allows parents and health care providers to prepare for the birth and care of a child who may require special obstetric, neonatal, surgical, rehabilitative, emotional, and financial resources.

Ultrasound has become an essential tool for fetal assessment. Uses include confirmation of fetal viability, diagnosis of fetal structural anomalies, evaluation of fetal growth, evaluation of fetal well-being (fetal activity, amniotic fluid volume, and Doppler blood flow), and guiding invasive diagnostic and therapeutic procedures. Sonar imaging techniques employ low-energy (less than 100 mw/cm^2), high-frequency (3.5–7.5 mHz) sound waves. Currently, no reproducible evidence indicates biologic adverse effects at approved power and frequency levels.[35] Obstetric ultrasound examination should include the following:

- Evaluation and detection of maternal pelvic masses
- Assessment of fetal number, presentation, and viability
- Gestational dating (by at least two parameters)
- Placental localization
- Estimation of amniotic fluid volume
- A basic survey of fetal anatomy

A basic anatomy survey includes examination of the fetal head, spine, four-chamber heart, gastrointestinal tract, kidneys, urinary bladder, umbilical cord insertion, extremities, and genitalia.[36] Maternal obesity, fetal positioning, fetal movement, or absent amniotic fluid may impair adequate visualization and preclude a complete survey. Normal ultrasound findings are 90% predictive of fetal structural integrity. Abnormal findings are 99% predictive of abnormal outcome.[37] Ultrasound has only limited ability to diagnose chromosome abnormalities or functional anomalies of the fetus. Disorders with childhood onset or adult onset are rarely, if ever, diagnosed antenatally.

Antepartum Surveillance of Fetal Well-Being

Antepartum fetal surveillance tests are noninvasive tools for evaluating the fetus before the onset of labor. The goal of testing is to predict fetal jeopardy and prevent antepartum and intrapartum fetal demise. The low false-negative rates of current testing modalities allow clinicians to postpone delivery and prevent the sequelae of preterm birth in selected complicated pregnancies. The value of antepartum testing is its ability to confirm fetal well-being rather than its ability to identify fetal compromise.

Indications for antepartum surveillance include post-term pregnancy, hypertensive disorders of pregnancy, gestational or pregestational diabetes, intrauterine growth retardation, previous stillbirth, maternal anemia, hemoglobinopathies, cyanotic heart disease, collagen vascular disease, preterm labor, preterm rupture of the membranes, decreased fetal movement, and other disorders associated with increased fetal loss. The risk of intrauterine fetal death and the chance of neonatal survival at a particular gestational age determines when antenatal surveillance begins.[38]

The Contraction Stress Test

The fetus with intact uteroplacental function does not demonstrate reflex heart rate decelerations in response to normal uterine contractions. In contrast, in the compromised fetus, the decrease in oxygen availability during transient decreases in blood flow stimulates a vascular chemoreceptor response, which produces periodic FHR depression. The contraction stress test (CST) evaluates the FHR response to uterine contractions.

The CST is performed in semi-Fowler's position (to minimize compression of the maternal vena cava by the pregnant uterus) using an external system to monitor uterine contractions and FHR. During an initial observation period of 15 to 20 minutes, FHR reactivity and contraction frequency are evaluated. In 10% to 15% of tests, adequate spontaneous uterine activity will obviate the need for uterine stimulation. Three contractions, lasting 40 to 60 seconds, within 10 minutes are necessary for an adequate CST. If spontaneous uterine activity is absent or inadequate, uterine stimulation is accomplished by nipple stimulation or intravenous oxytocin administration. Uterine stimulation is contraindicated in pregnancies complicated by previous vertical uterine incision, preterm labor, incompetent cervix, multiple gestation, placenta previa, preterm rupture of the membranes, or polyhydramnios.[39]

The CST is interpreted as negative (reassuring), positive (nonreassuring), or equivocal (Figs. 7-7 to 7-9) A negative CST shows adequate contraction duration and frequency with no late decelerations. Although reactivity of the FHR is often present, it is not necessary for a negative test. A positive CST shows late decelerations with at least one half of contractions. A positive CST implies compromise of baseline fetal oxygenation such that the decreased uterine perfusion common to normal uterine contractions results in transient fetal hypoxemia. A positive CST is an indication for delivery.

The equivocal CST represents 10% of tests.[39] Equivocal CSTs may be suspicious, hyperstimulated, or unsatisfactory. The suspicious CST shows an occasional late deceleration with an adequate contraction pattern. The hyperstimulated CST shows decelerations with excessive uterine activity (duration greater than 90 seconds or frequency greater than every 2 minutes). The hyperstimulated CST occurs with an incidence of 2% during artificial uterine stimulation.[39] The unsatisfactory CST shows inadequate uterine activity or inadequate quality of the FHR signal. In all cases, equivocal testing mandates clinical assessment and further testing. Repeating the CST within 24 hours or testing with an alternate surveillance tool is acceptable.

The Non-Stress Test

The non-stress test (NST) is an antepartum screening tool in which the FHR response to maternally perceived fetal movements is observed and recorded electronically. The test is done in semi-Fowler's position (to minimize compression of the maternal vena cava by the pregnant uterus) using an external system to monitor fetal movement, uterine contractions, and FHR. Interpretation of the NST is based on the premise that the normal fetus moves at

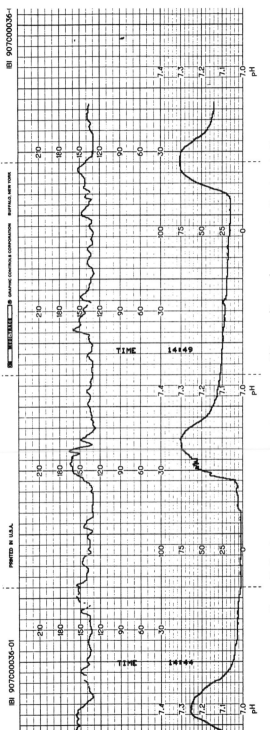

Figure 7–7. Reactive, negative contraction stress test. This record is an adequate contraction stress test in that it shows three contractions of greater than 40 seconds' duration within a 10-minute interval. The fetal heart tracing shows a baseline of 135, with four accelerations.

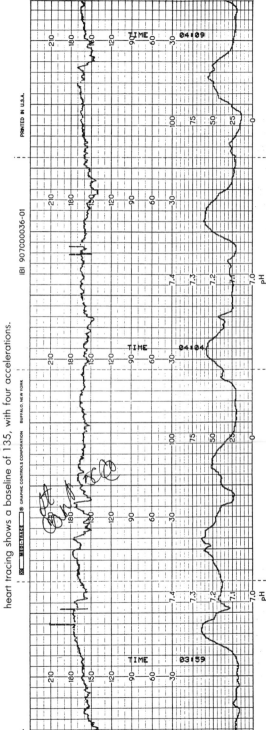

Figure 7–8. Hyperstimulated contraction stress test. This record shows greater than five contractions in 10 minutes with a nonreassuring fetal heart pattern (baseline decreases to 100 for 6 minutes).

varying intervals and that the normoxic fetal central nervous system and myocardium respond to movement by demonstrating a reflex increase (acceleration) of the heart rate. This reflex response depends on intact integration of peripheral receptors, spinal cord, brain, autonomic nervous system, and myocardium.[40] Absence of accelerations may be due to fetal rest cycles, maternally administered medications, congenital anomalies, hypoxia, or acidosis.[40]

Protocols for performing and interpreting the NST are not standardized and vary widely between institutions. Most protocols define an acceleration as an increase of the FHR of 15 bpm, lasting for 15 seconds. Reassuring or reactive tests require a "normal" baseline FHR (120 bpm–160 bpm), variability of 6 to 10 bpm or greater, absence of decelerations, and presence of accelerations with fetal movement (Figs. 7-10 and 7-11). Protocols vary with regard to observational period (10 min–40 min) and number of accelerations required to achieve a reassuring, or reactive, test (2–5).

The false-positive rate of the nonreactive NST may be as high as 80% (80% of nonreactive fetuses are, in fact, normoxic). Many authors have modified the NST in attempts to reduce the incidence of false-positive tests (nonreactive tests with normal perinatal outcomes). Simply extending the observational period reduces the number of nonreactive tests by 75%.[41] Acoustic stimulation of the fetus using various sound sources lowers the number of nonreactive tests by as much as 50%.[42] Acoustic stimulation also reduces testing time.[43] Fetal manipulation[44] and glucose loading[45] do not appear to alter consistently rates of reactivity or duration of testing.

Perinatal morbidity/mortality is a rare outcome within 1 week of a reactive NST. The fetal death rate with a reactive NST is less than 1% (1.9/1000–8.6/1000 depending on the protocol employed).[46] Twenty-four percent of fetal losses are associated with abruption, 21% with maternal diabetes, 17% with cord anomalies, 14% with postdate pregnancy, 14% with miscellaneous causes, and 10% with intrauterine growth retardation.[47] Twice-weekly testing is appropriate when these risk factors are identified.

Fetal Movement Counts

Clinical and experimental observations indicate that the compromised fetus reduces its oxygen expenditure by decreasing activity. Several authors have reported an association between reduced fetal activity and fetal compromise.[48–50] Maternal perception of fetal activity correlates well with sonar observations.[51] Maternally

perceived fetal movements remain constant from 24 weeks of gestation until term.[52] The highest incidence of movements occur in the late evening.[53,54] Most drugs, in therapeutic doses, do not reduce fetal activity.[55] Neither glucose loading[56] nor manual stimulation[57] influences movements. Fetuses with congenital anomalies show reduced activity.[58] Acoustic stimulation with an artificial larynx increases fetal movement.[59]

The unsupervised patient at home can count fetal movements without needing sophisticated equipment or personnel. Counting protocols involve (1) recording the number of movements in a fixed time period or (2) recording the time period required to count a fixed number of movements.

An active fetus predicts good outcome as reliably as a reactive NST, and reduced fetal activity predicts unfavorable perinatal outcome as reliably as a nonreactive NST.[51] As with the NST, the high false-positive rate should be respected. Obstetric intervention should not be based solely on fetal activity patterns. Decreased activity mandates further testing and clinical correlation.

The Biophysical Profile

In 1980, Manning *et al*[60] first described the biophysical profile, a fixed-interval sonar assessment of fetal activity. It combines the NST with a real-time assessment of fetal body movements, fetal breathing movements, fetal tone, and amniotic fluid volume. Original scoring criteria appear in Table 7-1. The biophysical profile combines variables to reduce the false-positive rate of each variable alone, and thereby improves the ability to identify accurately a compromised fetus.

Normal biophysical activity implies adequate oxygenation and intact functioning of the central nervous system center controlling a particular activity. Absence of a behavior may result from normal periodicity or hypoxia.[61,62]

Central nervous system centers may have varying sensitivities to hypoxia. Early developing areas may exhibit hypoxia-induced changes last, whereas late-developing areas are affected earliest. Progressing hypoxia results initially in a nonreactive NST and loss of fetal breathing, followed by loss of fetal movements and tone. Reduced amniotic fluid volume represents the decreased perfusion of fetal lungs and kidneys secondary to chronic hypoxia.[61]

An abnormal biophysical profile predicts low 5-minute Apgar scores, fetal distress in labor, and perinatal death.[60] Additional advantages of the biophysical profile include the following:

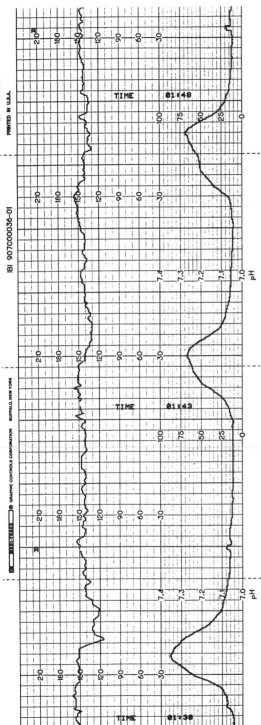

Figure 7-9. Positive contraction stress test. This nonreassuring record shows three 60-second contractions within 10 minutes, with late decelerations following the first two. Clinical management may depend upon fetal status (structural integrity, chromosome complement, growth curve, gestational age) and maternal condition. Generally, this finding warrants delivery.

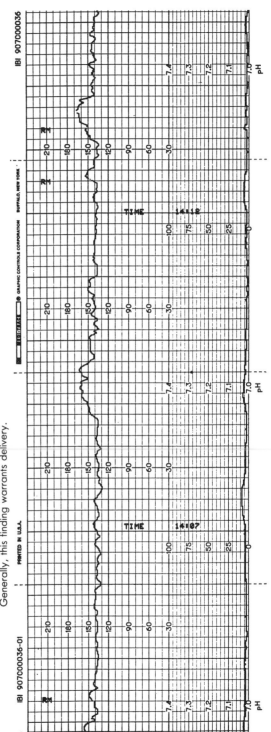

Figure 7-10. Reactive non-stress test. This fetal heart rate record shows a baseline of 140, two accelerations, and no decelerations.

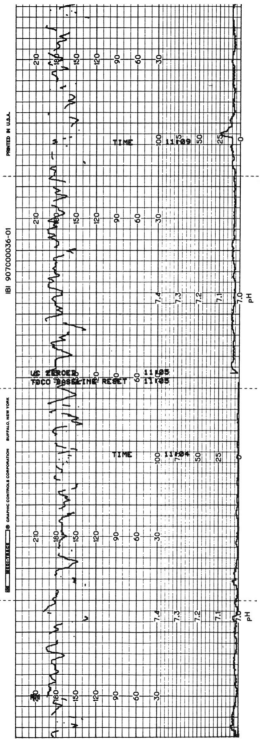

Figure 7–11. Uninterpretable non-stress test. The quality of this recording is too poor to interpret with certainty. The baseline is uncertain, and it is unclear whether decelerations are present in the last 2 minutes of strip.

Table 7–1

Scoring the Biophysical Profile

TEST	POINTS	CRITERIA
Non-stress Test		
Reactive	2	Two or more FHR accelerations of 15 bpm lasting 15 sec associated with fetal movement in a 40-min interval
Nonreactive	0	Fewer than two FHR accelerations in 40 min
Fetal Breathing Movements		
Present	2	Thirty sec of sustained breathing in a 30-min interval
Absent	0	Less than 30 sec in 30 min
Fetal Tone		
Present	2	One episode of motion of a limb from a position of flexion to extension with rapid return to flexion
Absent	0	No flexion–extension–flexion within 30 min
Fetal Movements		
Present	2	Three or more gross body movements in 30-min interval
Absent	0	Less than three movements in 30 min
Amniotic Fluid Volume		
Present	2	A pocket of amniotic fluid measuring at least 1 cm in two perpendicular planes
Absent	0	Largest fluid pocket measures less than 1 cm in two perpendicular planes

(After Manning FA, Morrision I, Lange IR. Fetal biophysical profile scoring: A prospective study of 1184 high-risk patients. Am J Obstet Gynecol 1981;140:289)

- The ability to identify 68% of major congenital anomalies before delivery[63]
- A decrease in cesarean sections for failed induction by allowing continued surveillance of postdate pregnancies[64]
- The ability to predict infection in patients with prematurely ruptured membranes[65]

REFERENCES

1. Reece EA, Antoine C, Montgomery J. The fetus as the final arbiter of intrauterine stress/distress. Clin Obstet and Gynecol 1986;29:23.
2. Richardson BS. Fetal adaptive responses to asphyxia. Clin Perinatol 1989;16:595.
3. Wilkening RB, Meschia G. Fetal oxygen uptake, oxygenation, and acid–base balance as a function of uterine blood flow. Am J Physiol 1983;244:H749.
4. Paulone ME, Edelstone DI, Shedd A. Effects of maternal anemia on uteroplacental and fetal oxidative metabolism in sheep. Am J Obstet Gynecol 1987;156:230.
5. Itskovitz J, La Gamma EF, Rudolph AM. The effect of reducing umbilical blood flow on fetal oxygenation. Am J Obstet Gynecol 1983;145:813.
6. Towell ME. Fetal respiratory physiology. In: Goodwin JW, Godden JO, Chance GW, eds. Perinatal Medicine. Toronto: Longman Canada Ltd, 1976:171.
7. Natale R, Clewlow F, Dawes GS. Measurement of fetal forelimb movements in the lamb in utero. Am J Obstet Gynecol 1981;140:545.
8. Boddy R, Dawes GS, Fisher R, et al. Fetal respiratory movements, electrocortical and cardiovascular responses to hypoxemia and hypercapnia in sheep. J Physiol 1974;243:599.
9. Richardson BS, Carmichael L, Homan J, et al. Electrocortical activity, electroocular activity and breathing movements in fetal sheep with prolonged, graded hypoxemia [Abstract 233]. Society for Gynecologic Investigation, Baltimore, MD, 1988.
10. Worthington D, Piercy WN, Smith BT. Effects of reduction of placental size in sheep. Obstet Gynecol 1981;58:215.
11. Itskovitz J, La Gamma EF, Rudolph AM. Effects of cord compression on fetal blood flow distribution and oxygen delivery. Am J Physiol 1987;252:H100.

12. Peeters LLH, Sheldon RE, Hones MD, et al. Blood flow to fetal organs as a function of arterial oxygen content. Am J Obstet Gynecol 1979;135:637.

13. Lee WK, Baggish MS. The effect of unselected intrapartum fetal monitoring. Obstet Gynecol 1976;47:516.

14. Stanley FJ, Watson L. The cerebral palsies in Western Australia. Trends, 1968–1981. Am J Obstet Gynecol 1988;158:89.

15. Hagberg B, Hagberg G, Olow I. The changing panorama of CP in Sweden. IV. Epidemiological trends 1959–78. Acta Paediatr Scand 1984;73:433.

16. Myers R. Two patterns of perinatal brain damage and their conditions of occurrence. Am J Obstet Gynecol 1972;112:246.

17. Nelson K, Ellenberg J. Antecedents of CP: Multivariate analysis of risk. N Engl J Med 1986;315:81.

18. Nelson K. What proportion of CP is related to birth asphyxia? J Pediatr 1988;112:572.

19. Blair E, Stanely F. Intrapartum asphyxia: A rare cause of CP. J Pediatr 1988;112:515.

20. American Academy of Pediatrics, American College of Obstetrics and Gynecology. Guidelines for perinatal care, 2nd ed. Washington, DC: American College of Obstetrics and Gynecology, 1988.

21. Quirk JG, Miller FC. Fetal heart rate tracing characteristics that jeopardize the diagnosis of fetal well-being. Clin Obstet Gynecol 1986;29:12.

22. Krebs HB, Petres RE, Dunn LJ, et al. Intrapartum fetal heart rate monitoring. VI. Prognostic significance of accelerations. Am J Obstet Gynecol 1982;142:297.

23. Schneider EP, Tropper PJ. The variable deceleration, prolonged deceleration and sinusoidal fetal heart rate. Clin Obstet Gynecol 1986;29:64.

24. Tejani N, Mann LI, Bhakthavathsalan A. Correlation of fetal heart rate patterns and fetal pH with neonatal outcome. Obstet Gynecol 1972;48:460.

25. Wood C, Newman W, Lumley J, Hammond J. Classification of fetal heart rate in relation to fetal scalp measurements and Apgar score. Am J Obstet Gynecol 1969;105:942.

26. Miyazaki FS, Taylor NA. Saline amnioinfusion for relief of variable or prolonged decelerations. Am J Obstet Gynecol 1983;146:670.

27. Harris JL, Krueger TR, Parer JT. Mechanisms of late decelerations of the fetal heart rate during hypoxia. Am J Obstet Gynecol 1982;144:491.

28. Silverman F, Hutson JM. The clinical and biological significance of the bottom line. Clin Obstet Gynecol 1986;29:43.

29. Kubli EW, Hon EH, Khazin AF, et al. Observations on heart rate and pH in the human fetus during labor. Am J Obstet Gynecol 1969;104:1190.

30. Hon EH, Khazin AF. Biochemical studies of the fetus. II. Fetal pH and Apgar scores. Obstet Gynecol 1969;33:237.

31. Modonlou H, Yeh SY, Hon H, et al. Fetal and neonatal biochemistry and Apgar scores. Am J Obstet Gynecol 1973;117:1942.

32. Visseler HC (ed). Precis IV. An update in obstetrics and gynecology. American College of Obstetrics and Gynecology, 1990:93.

33. Soothill PW. Cordocentesis: Role in assessment of fetal condition. Clin Perinatol 1989;16:755.

34. Visseler HC, ed. Precis IV. An update in obstetrics and gynecology. The American College of Obstetrics and Gynecologists, 1990:85.

35. Visseler HC, ed. Precis IV. An update in obstetrics and gynecology. The American College of Obstetricians and Gynecologists, 1990:84.

36. Ultrasound in pregnancy. ACOG Tech Bull 116. May 1988.

37. Sabbagha RE, Sheikh Z, Tamura RK, et al. Predictive value, sensitivity and specificity of ultrasonic targeted imaging for fetal anomalies in gravid women at high risk for birth defects. Am J Obstet Gynecol 1985;152:822.

38. Druzin ML. Antepartum fetal heart rate monitoring: State of the art. Clin Perinatol 1989;16:627.

39. Huddleston JF, Quinlan RW. Clinical utility of the contraction stress test. Clin Obstet Gynecol 1987;30:912.

40. Timor-Tritsch IE, Dieker LJ, Hertz RH, et al. Studies of antepartum behavioral state in the human fetus at term. Am J Obstet Gynecol 1978;132:524.

41. Keegan KA, Paul RH, Broussard PM, et al. Antepartum fetal heart rate testing. V. The nonstress test: An outpatient approach. Am J Obstet Gynecol 1980;136:81.

42. Smith CV, Phelan JP, Paul RH, et al. Fetal acoustic stimulation testing: A retrospective experience with the fetal acoustic stimulation test. Am J Obstet Gynecol 1985;153:567.

43. Smith CV, Phelan JP, Platt LD, et al. Fetal acoustic stimulation. II. A randomized clinical comparison with the nonstress test. Am J Obstet Gynecol 1986;155:131.

44. Druzin ML, Gratacos J, Paul Rh, et al. Antepartum fetal heart rate testing. XII. The effect of manual manipulation of the fetus on the nonstress test. Am J Obstet Gynecol 1985;151:61.

45. Druzin ML, Foodim J. Effect of maternal glucose ingestion compared with maternal water ingestion on the non-stress test. Obstet Gynecol 1986;67:4.

46. Devoe LD, Castillo RA, Sherline DM. The nonstress test as a diagnostic test: A critical reappraisal. Am J Obstet Gynecol 1985;152:1047.

47. Barret JM, Salyer SL, Boehm RH. The nonstress test: An evaluation of 1000 patients. Am J Obstet Gynecol 1981;141:153.

48. Sadovsky E, Yaffe H, Polishuk WZ. Fetal movement monitoring in normal and pathologic pregnancy. Int J Gynaecol Obstet 1974;12:75.

49. Leader LR. Baillie P, Van Scholkwyk DJ. Fetal movements and fetal prospective study. Obstet Gynecol 1981;57:431.

50. Pearson JF, Weaver JB. Fetal activity and fetal well-being: An evaluation. Br Med J 1976;1:1305.

51. Rayburn WF. Antepartum fetal assessment: Monitoring fetal activity. Clin Perinatol 1982;9:232.

52. Roberts AB, Little D, Cooper D, et al. Normal patterns of fetal activity in the third trimester. Br J Obstet Gynaecol 1979;86:4.

53. Connors G, Natale R, Nasello-Patterson C. Maternally perceived fetal activity from twenty-four weeks gestation to term in normal and at-risk pregnancies. Am J Obstet Gynecol 1988;158:294.

54. Patrick J, Campbell K, Carmichael L, et al. Patterns of gross fetal body movements over 24-hour observation intervals over the last 10 weeks of pregnancy. Am J Obstet Gynecol 1982;142:363.

55. Wood C, Gilbert M, O'Connor A, et al. Subjective recording of fetal movement. Br J Obstet Gynæcol 1979;86:836.

56. Zimmer EZ, Divon MY, Goldstein I, et al. Intrauterine fetal activity in at-term and prolonged pregnancy. J Perinat Med 1985;13:201.

57. Richardson B, Campbell K, Carmichael L, et al. Effect of external physical stimulation on fetuses near term. Am J Obstet Gynecol 1981;139:344.

58. Sadovsky E, Rabinowitz R, Yaffe H. Decreased fetal movements and fetal malformations. J Fetal Med 1981;1:62.

59. Gagnon R, Hunse C, Carmichael L, et al. Effects of vibratory acoustic stimulation on human fetal breathing and gross body movements near term. Am J Obstet Gynecol 1986;155:1227.

60. Manning FA, Platt LD, Sipos L. Antepartum fetal evaluation. Development of a fetal biophysical profile score. Am J Obstet Gynecol 1980;136:787.

61. Vintzileos AM, Campbell WA, Rodis JF. Fetal biophysical profile scoring: Current status. Clin Perinatol 1989;16:661.

62. Brar HS, Platt LD, Devore GR. The biophysical profile. Clin Obstet Gynecol 1987;30:936.

63. Johnson JM, Harman CR, Lange IR, et al. Biophysical profile scoring in the management of postterm pregnancy: An analysis of 307 patients. Am J Obstet Gynecol 1986;154:269.

64. Manning FA, Morrison I, Lange IR. Fetal biophysical profile scoring: A prospective study of 1184 high risk patients. Am J Obstet Gynecol 1981;140:289.

65. Vintzileos AM, Campbell WA, Nochimson DJ, et al. The fetal biophysical profile in patients with premature rupture of the membranes—an early predictor of fetal infection. Am J Obstet Gynecol 1985;152:510.

CHAPTER 8

Fetal Complications

Neil S. Silverman

This chapter considers fetal, rather than strictly maternal, conditions that predispose a pregnancy toward abnormal or adverse outcomes. Multiple gestations make up the largest single group of complicated pregnancies with normal fetuses. Complications unique to twin or higher-order pregnancies are addressed first. The remainder of the chapter covers true fetal abnormalities, both developmental and pathophysiologic. New and emerging modalities for approaching such pregnancies, including invasive fetal diagnostic procedures, are addressed. These deviations from "normal" gestation can result in an atypical prenatal course and have a significant impact on labor and delivery.

MULTIPLE GESTATIONS

Twins

Twin pregnancies account for just under 1% of births and yet are associated to a disproportionate degree with a variety of pregnancy complications. Some, like preterm labor, also occur in singleton gestations but have a markedly higher incidence in twin and higher-order gestations due to exaggerated maternal physiologic adaptations. The uterine overdistention produced by twins, for example, is thought to predispose to preterm labor.[1] Other complications, such as the twin–twin transfusion syndrome, are unique to twin

pregnancies. Problems seen in twin pregnancies significantly affect both antenatal and intrapartum courses.

As recently as 1980, published studies reported that one fourth of twin pregnancies remained undiagnosed before delivery.[2] The liberal use of ultrasound in antenatal management today has made this event increasingly uncommon; yet, in patient populations notable for late registration and poor prenatal care, undiagnosed twins can still produce unexpected delivery room emergencies. One recent study from an urban center reported 13% of patients with twins not identified until delivery. This group had a fetal death rate six times that of women registered for care.[3]

Earlier diagnosis of twins also allows for accurate dating of the pregnancy, because growth becomes difficult to assess by fundal height alone as a twin pregnancy progresses. Ultrasound (Fig. 8-1), used with more gross measures, can evaluate both overall and intertwin growth during the pregnancy. The definition of discordant growth in a twin pregnancy is controversial. At Thomas Jefferson University, we make the diagnosis if a 20% difference in estimated fetal weights arises. Discordant twins require closer antenatal surveillance. Their risk of adverse perinatal outcome increases compared to twins with concordant growth, especially if one twin is small for its gestational age.[4]

Experts disagree on the role of cesarean section in the management of twin deliveries. The nationwide rise in cesarean section rate has had little impact on the

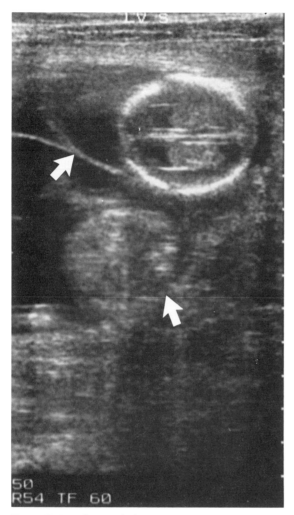

Figure 8–1. Ultrasound of twin gestation at 18 to 20 weeks. Head of fetus "A" is above, body of Fetus "B" below (*large arrow*). *Small arrow* indicates intertwin membrane.

perinatal mortality of twins.[5] Almost three fourths of adverse outcomes relate directly to prematurity.[6] Disagreements about the role of cesarean delivery surround even the management of low-birth-weight twins (less than 1500 g). Some authors have advocated abdominal delivery for all preterm twins.[7] Most series, however, support a conditional approach to the delivery of preterm twins, with fetal presentation (vertex vs breech or other) factoring strongly into a decision.[8] Cesarean section does not reduce the perinatal morbidity and mortality of vertex–vertex low-birth-weight infants.[8–10] In contrast, nonvertex presentation of one or both twins appears to increase the risk of adverse out-

come when delivered vaginally.[8,9] The retrospective nature of many of these studies makes evaluation of these data difficult. In addition, recent evidence suggests that abnormal neurologic development in preterm, particularly monochorionic, twins may occur long before the intrapartum period.[11]

Preventing preterm delivery in twin pregnancies will produce the largest impact on neonatal outcome. We do not advocate the prophylactic use of tocolytic agents but treat preterm labor early and aggressively upon its diagnosis. The early detection of twins does, still, allow for counseling regarding activity modification when needed. We also advocate periodic cervical examinations to detect subtle changes due to unnoticed contractions. Such an approach may predict labor without precipitating preterm labor.[12]

The outcome of a prematurely born twin is not innately worse than a premature singleton within a given birth-weight interval.[13] Second twins tend to do less well; however, this problem may relate to increased time to delivery. Some investigators have reported carbon dioxide retention in umbilical cord blood of second twins, but without differences in pH or bicarbonate values.[14]

Twin pregnancies have cesarean section rates that are higher than those for singleton pregnancies. These may occur either before or after delivery of the first twin. As with singleton pregnancies, however,[15] without coexisting medical or obstetric contraindications, a trial of labor for twin pregnancies, even with a history of a prior low-transverse cesarean section, will succeed 72% of the time.[16]

Antenatal complications unique to twin pregnancies relate mostly to abnormal vascular connections within the placental circulations. The twin–twin transfusion syndrome occurs almost exclusively between monochorionic–monozygotic twins. Hemodynamically "unbalanced" shunts develop between arterial and venous placental vessels.[17] The result is a set of discordant twins comprised of an anemic "donor" fetus and its polycythemic "recipient" co-twin. The recipient's hyperdynamic state results in hydramnios or, in severe cases, fetal hydrops. The large fluid shifts in this syndrome also affect fetal renal output. The donor twin becomes volume-contracted, with decreased urine output and resultant oligohydramnios.[18] Perinatal mortality is high in pregnancies complicated by twin–twin transfusion. Expectant management alone has been associated with loss rates as high as 100%.[19–21] More recently, Doppler velocimetry,[22–24] serial amniocentesis,[25–27] and placental laser surgery[28] have all been proposed as potentially useful adjuncts to more active management of this problem.

Higher-Order Gestations

Triplet gestations occur spontaneously at a rate of 1 in 6400 to 1 in 9520 pregnancies.[29] With the use of reproductive technologies such ovulation induction and gamete or embryo transfers, iatrogenic production of triplet and higher-order gestations (Fig. 8-2) is more common.

Aggressive antenatal care and, even more importantly, advances in neonatal intensive care have significantly improved outcomes for multifetal pregnancies. More favorable outcomes in recent series have supplanted earlier studies, with perinatal and early neonatal mortality rates of 130 to 240/1000 births for triplet and quadruplet pregnancies.[30-34] Still, prematurity accounts for the major morbidity and mortality compromising survival and development of these infants.

As with twin gestations, multifetal pregnancies increase the risk of maternal complications such as pregnancy-induced hypertension, postpartum hemorrhage, and gestational diabetes. Still, a matched series comparing twins to triplets for maternal morbidities showed a significant increase only for the occurrence of preterm labor (80% vs 40%).[35] Neonatal complications, however, were significantly more common, as shown by the following data:

- Lower mean gestational age at delivery (33 vs 37 wk)
- Lower mean birth weight (1720 vs 2475 g)
- Longer mean hospital stay (29 vs 8 days)
- Higher risk of intrauterine growth retardation and discordancy[35]

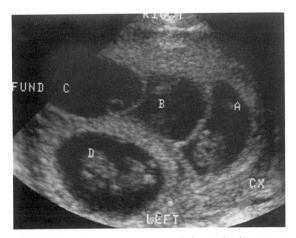

Figure 8–2. First-trimester ultrasound of a quadruplet pregnancy. Fetal parts are visible in all four sacs except (*C*), in which a yolk sac is seen.

The statistics for maternal complications persist for gestations of higher order than triplets. In recent series, preterm labor occurs in 98% to 100% of such pregnancies.[36-38] Even when they were managed at a tertiary perinatal referral center, no multifetal pregnancies reported by Gonen et al[36] reached term. Maternal hospitalization for antenatal management was required, on average, by 23 weeks' gestation for quadruplets. Lipitz et al[38] showed a total fetal loss rate of 23% in high-order pregnancies. In only three of seven sets of neonates followed for more than 2 years were all children developing normally. Thirty percent of survivors were developmentally handicapped.[38]

Multifetal Pregnancy Reduction

Because of the poor perinatal/neonatal outcome for higher-order pregnancies, investigators in a few centers have begun electively terminating one or more pregnancies in such gestations to achieve twin or triplet deliveries. This procedure was first used in twin pregnancies where prenatal diagnosis had detected a significant abnormality in one fetus. Such terminations were initially done in the second trimester, capitalizing on the refinement of ultrasound-directed skills. A variety of percutaneous techniques have been described, such as the following:

- Fetal cardiac puncture producing death via exsanguination[39-40]
- Air embolization via the fetal umbilical vessels[41]
- Cardiac puncture with intracardiac instillation of either calcium or potassium solutions[42,43]

In a large series of pregnancies, percutaneously introduced intracardiac potassium chloride was most effective. Using this technique, Chitkara et al[43] reported procedure-related complications in only one of ten terminations. That complication, uterine contractions, responded to short-term tocolysis. Eight of the ten remaining fetuses delivered at term; the other two delivered at 31 and 34 weeks of gestation. Maternal coagulation studies, followed serially, showed no abnormalities.[43]

Chorionic villus sampling, which took ultrasound-guided diagnostic procedures into the first trimester, coupled with experience with second-trimester selective abortions, led to the development of the technique currently termed *multifetal pregnancy reduction.* Berkowitz et al[44] reported the first small series of 12 cases of first-trimester multifetal pregnancy reduction. Their initial experience with pregnancy losses using a transcervical approach led them to prefer a transabdominal route.[44] A larger series from Thomas Jefferson University employed intracardiac potassium chloride injection, introduced transabdominally toward the end of the first trimester. Of 80 fetuses remaining after multifetal pregnancy reduction, 75 (94%) delivered at 32 weeks or greater and survived. Placental mapping or detectable malformations identified the pregnancy or pregnancies to be terminated. No short-term complications were encountered, but maternal serum alpha-fetoprotein values remained elevated well into the second trimester, rendering that test useless as a screen for neural tube defects.[45] Other centers have reported similar successes with multifetal pregnancy reduction for gestations of triplets or higher-order pregnancies.[46-48] Debate still centers on the optimal and ethically acceptable number of viable fetuses allowed to remain.[48] Still, reduction of high-order gestations increases the probability that two or three healthy infants will be born rather than four or more infants with significant prematurity-related problems.

FETAL INVASIVE DIAGNOSTICS

The refinement of real-time ultrasound has allowed for the development of many ultrasound-guided prenatal procedures. Multifetal pregnancy reduction represents the most recent of these techniques. Operator experience gained over time with second- and third-trimester amniocenteses has enabled the evolution of many new techniques.

Direct access to the fetus for purposes of diagnosis and therapy has obvious advantages. The difficulties encountered focus primarily on gaining such access without compromising the continuation of the pregnancy. The need to use a fetoscope, for example, limited attempts to sample fetal blood. A fetoscope is a rigid 14-gauge endoscope that is inserted through the mother's skin and uterus and provides direct visualization of the fetus, placenta, and umbilical cord. The procedure itself required considerable maternal premedication. Fetoscopic visualization did allow the operator to obtain pure fetal blood from placental vessels through a side-mounted 22-gauge aspiration needle. This technique produced no short- or long-term maternal complications. Increasing success rates in sampling fetal rather than maternal or mixed blood specimens developed as operator experience improved.[49] Although it is an unwieldy technique, especially in light of today's modifications, its success encouraged other investigators to explore simpler methods for making prenatal diagnoses (*e.g.,* of hemoglobinopathies)

through direct analysis of fetal blood. In addition, fetal loss rates as high as 3% to 4% occurred with fetoscopy, limiting the procedure to an extremely select population of highest-risk pregnancies.

The early 1980s saw the first reports of a major advance in prenatal diagnosis that was made possible by improvements in ultrasound resolution. Daffos *et al*[50] first reported in 1983 direct fetal blood sampling via ultrasound-guided percutaneous puncture of umbilical cord vessels with a 20-gauge needle alone. All procedures in pregnancies ranging from 17 to 32 weeks succeeded. No tocolytic agents were required before or after the procedure. In the pregnancies that continued, no short-term or long-term complications arose.[50] The same group subsequently reported repeating the procedure in the same pregnancy without adverse sequelae, including any demonstrable drop in fetal hematocrit from procedure to procedure.[51] Other groups next reported their experiences with the procedure.[52,53] Using ultrasonically visible 22- to 25-gauge needles decreased the amount of postprocedure bleeding from the puncture site.

Percutaneous umbilical blood sampling (PUBS) has drastically altered the antenatal management of a variety of fetal disorders. Sometimes fetal malformations are not detected until the third trimester (Fig. 8-3*A* and 8-3*B*). A fetus with a lethal chromosomal abnormality, such as trisomy 13 or 18, may be managed differently in labor than a chromosomally normal but structurally abnormal fetus. The 2- to 3-week wait for an amniocentesis-derived karyotype may be clinically unacceptable. Using PUBS, rapid fetal karyotyping usually can be obtained within 48 to 72 hours. A similar argument favors rapid karyotyping via PUBS-obtained blood when an anomaly is detected late enough in the second trimester that undue delay might preclude legal access to pregnancy termination.

Rh Isoimmunization

The availability of PUBS has radically changed the prenatal management of Rh isoimmunization. Traditionally, Rh-sensitized pregnancies have been managed by serial amniocenteses beginning at approximately 26 weeks. Spectrophotometric analysis of amniotic fluid concentrations of bilirubin provided an indirect measure of fetal hemolysis.[54] Steeply rising bilirubin titers or fetal hydrops (Fig. 8-4) in the face of significant fetal prematurity signaled the need for intervention. Intraperitoneal red blood cell transfusions were attempted, hoping to prolong the pregnancy until a

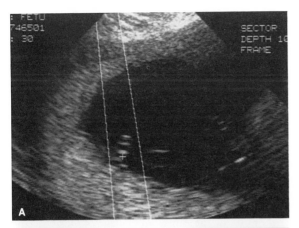

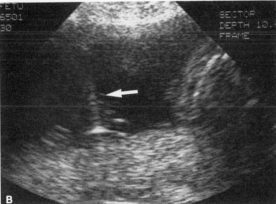

Figure 8–3. (A) Scan just prior to fetal blood sampling. Biopsy guidelines indicate path for needle. Cross-hatch is placed on umbilical vein. (B) Fetal umbilical blood sampling. *Arrow* shows needle, with tip in umbilical vein.

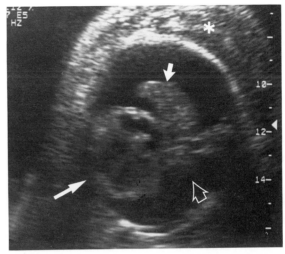

Figure 8–4. Fetal hydrops. Section through fetal thorax. Marked skin thickening as indicated by (`). Pleural effusions are indicated by *open arrow*. *Small arrows* point to fetal lung, and *large arrow* points to fetal heart.

gestational age consistent with viability. Mild-to-moderate rises in bilirubin titers were then an indication for preterm delivery. The affected child, although preterm, was thought to be better treated ex utero.

Using PUBS, fetal anemia can be diagnosed directly and appropriate therapy started before the development of fetal hydrops. We sample fetal umbilical venous blood using a stable transducer-supported biopsy guide. To make certain we have a pure fetal sample, we take the blood immediately to the hematology laboratory. Neonatal-range mean corpuscular volume (usually > 100) and lymphocyte predominance on an automated differential confirm a fetal source.[55,56] In the presence of significant anemia (hematocrit < 30) or of fetal hydrops, intravascular transfusion can be directly instituted via the umbilical vein.[57–60] Turbulent flow

within the intracord umbilical vein, even along its path of insertion into the fetal abdomen, provides reassurance of proper needle placement during the transfusion.[61] Intravascular transfusion requires a substantial period of fetal inactivity to avoid displacement of the needle. Therefore, we inject 0.1 mg/kg of pancuronium bromide directly into the fetal circulation after obtaining an initial blood sample for hematocrit determination.[62] We have encountered no adverse maternal effects, and fetal movement recommences within 2 to 3 hours, well after the average 15 to 30 minutes required for transfusion. Bolus transfusion, in our center's experience, is equally safe and effective as slower methods of red cell infusions.[60]

The safety and repeatability of PUBS and PUBS-directed transfusions in Rh-affected pregnancies currently allow the clinician to take a fetus close to term while forestalling or even reversing hydrops diagnosed in utero.[63] Although a definitive protocol is controversial,[64,65] we advocate management of sensitized pregnancies without fetal hydrops with serial amniocenteses. The risks associated with PUBS are, in our judgment, slightly higher than those associated with amniocentesis.[66] We reserve direct assessment of fetal hematocrit for suspiciously rising amniotic fluid bilirubin concentrations. Analysis of fetal red blood cells for Rh (or other) antigens also can then be done. Fetuses who are negative for the blood group antigen in question need no further invasive testing.

Maternal Idiopathic Thrombocytopenic Purpura

Percutaneous umbilical blood sampling also has changed the management of maternal idiopathic (autoimmune) thrombocytopenic purpura at term. The antibodies responsible for maternal idiopathic thrombocytopenic purpura can cross the placenta and cause fetal thrombocytopenia.[67] The true incidence of this occurrence is unknown. The major theoretical risk to the thrombocytopenic fetus is intracranial hemorrhage, presumably resulting from labor or delivery. No such sequela have been reported with a neonatal platelet count over 50,000/mm³.[68,69] This degree of fetal thrombocytopenia occurs in 37% to 70% of cases of maternal idiopathic thrombocytopenic purpura. The maternal platelet count is entirely nonpredictive of the newborn's platelet count.[70] Also, although intracranial hemorrhage happens in newborns with normal platelet counts, not all infants with thrombocytopenia will suffer this complication. Intracranial hemorrhage also has occurred in such infants delivered via cesarean section without labor. Fetal capillary scalp sampling in labor to count fetal platelets has been proposed as a way of avoiding vaginal delivery of severely thrombocytopenic infants. No thrombocytopenic infants had normal platelet counts in labor, although unnecessary cesarean sections have been done because of falsely low counts or technically unobtainable specimens.[71,72]

Percutaneous umbilical blood sampling provides an alternative to fetal scalp sampling to determine platelet counts.[73–75] It is done at term to avoid requiring the delivery of a preterm infant in the event of procedure-related distress, but before the onset of labor, to avoid the theoretical risks associated with uterine contractions themselves, separate from the birth process. The PUBS-obtained platelet counts correlate well with neonatal platelet counts determined after delivery.[73] We currently manage maternal idiopathic thrombocytopenic purpura with PUBS at 37 to 38 weeks of gestation. We coordinate the timing with both nursing and anesthesia staffs. We do the procedure on the labor floor, having a delivery room ready, should an emergency cesarean section be necessary. We allow vaginal delivery if the fetal platelet count is over 50,000/mm³.

Case reports also describe the use of PUBS in a variety of other maternal or fetal disorders. In hyperthyroidism, PUBS can assess fetal endocrine function and guide maternal therapy.[76,77] With intrauterine growth retardation, PUBS can evaluate fetal acid–base status.[78] As operator experience and enterprise grow, so will the list of potential indications for this procedure.

CONGENITAL MALFORMATIONS

Major congenital malformations, those that are either life-threatening or require surgical correction, occur in approximately 3% of live births.[79] Some influence the method of delivery for the affected infant if detected prenatally. Appropriate obstetric management can minimize potential trauma and maximize neonatal salvage. The increasing refinement of real-time ultrasound has permitted the antenatal diagnosis of still more congenital malformations.[80,81]

Most patients undergo an ultrasound examination at some point during pregnancy for a variety of indications. Routine testing is not currently considered standard of care by the American College of Obstetricians and Gynecologists. The American Institute of Ultrasound in Medicine, with the Roentgenologic Society of North America, have recommended that when an obstetric ultrasound is done, a fetal anatomic survey of major organ systems be included as part of the study.[82] Still, they also do not recommend routine ultrasound as part of prenatal care. A 1984 conference sponsored by the National Institutes of Health reached the same conclusion.[83]

If ultrasound becomes a standard prenatal test at least once during pregnancy, we would recommend doing it at 18 to 20 weeks of gestation. A scan then is accurate for dating purposes. It also allows an adequate systematic organ review even in low-risk patients. A survey at our center includes intracranial anatomy (particularly views of the lateral ventricles and cerebellum), spine, stomach, kidneys, bladder, umbilical cord insertion (a screen for abdominal wall defects), three-vessel cord, four-chamber heart, and, when possible, face and palate. Optimal cardiac studies are best done at 20 to 22 weeks. Examination at this time permits termination if major malformations are detected. In a recent retrospective study, only 34% of abnormal fetuses were detected before 23 weeks of gestation with an indication-based obstetric ultrasound system. Most defects eventually seen would have been apparent by ultrasound earlier in pregnancy.[84]

Antenatal detection of congenital malformations has significant impact on postnatal prognosis. Many neonates with significant anomalies may appear normal at birth and come to treatment only when a postnatal complication occurs. British workers have suggested that a scan done at 18 weeks of gestation could find 25% of congenital heart defects.[85] A study from Finland using routine ultrasound, also at 18 weeks, detected genitourinary abnormalities. Only 25% would have been suspected at birth.[81] In addition, over 90% of congenitally anomalous infants are the first to be affected in a family, removing family history as a possible screening indication for a survey ultrasound.[86]

Hydrocephalus

Commonly defined as increased intracerebral cerebrospinal fluid, hydrocephalus is congenital malformation that occurs in approximately 0.5/1000 births.[87] Most frequently, it results from an obstruction along the normal routes of cerebrospinal fluid circulation, either from atresia or postdevelopmental occlusion.

Prenatally, the diagnosis of hydrocephalus is usually made based on enlarged intracranial lateral ventricles (Fig. 8-5). Ultrasound criteria for the diagnosis vary from institution to institution. We rely on an abnormal ratio between distances from the intracranial midline to the outer border of the lateral ventricle and the lateral edge of the intracranial hemisphere, commonly called the lateral ventricle-to-intracranial hemispheric distance ratio. Deviations from normal measurements at the level of the intracranial atria are also useful in establishing a diagnosis, as is anterior displacement of the choroid plexus (Fig. 8-6).

The antenatal diagnosis of hydrocephalus in a fetus should trigger a survey for other major malformations. Other intracranial anomalies occur in 37% of cases with hydrocephalus. Sixty-three percent of cases have extra-

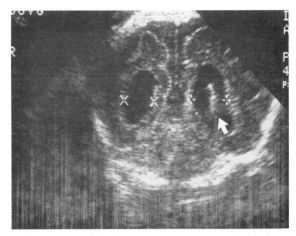

Figure 8–6. Fetal hydrocephalus, coronal view. Cursors mark the borders of both lateral ventricles, which are markedly dilated. Choroid plexus displacement is shown at the *arrow.*

cranial abnormalities. Furthermore, 11% of cases also have atypical karyotypes.[91,92]

Neonatal prognosis with hydrocephalus depends on the presence of associated anomalies and on the thickness of the remaining cortex before a postnatal shunting procedure can be done. Although not conclusive, one report suggested poorer outcome when the thickness of cortical mantle was less than 1 cm.[93]

Obstetrically, the antenatal diagnosis of fetal hydrocephalus should spark a search for other malformations. Amniocentesis is offered to detect chromosomal abnormalities. If the diagnosis is made later in the third trimester, placental biopsy or PUBS yields karyotype results more rapidly than amniocentesis.

At our institution, we do not plan elective cesarean delivery for hydrocephalus unless the head is massively enlarged (biparietal diameter >100 mm) or if the fetus is breech. If a concomitant lethal anomaly exists, we offer percutaneous cephalocentesis to avoid cesarean delivery of a nonviable fetus. Because this procedure has a perinatal mortality rate of over 90%, we restrict it to cases with uniformly poor prognoses.[94,95]

Neural Tube Defects

Neural tube defects (NTDs) result from a failure of the neural tube to close early in embryogenesis. They are classified as open or closed according to the underlying problem. Open defects are those that fail to become covered by skin, such as anencephaly (Fig. 8-7), men-

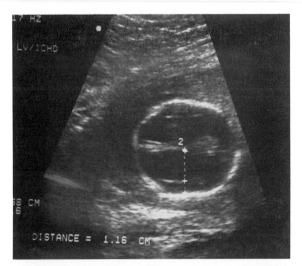

Figure 8–5. Fetal hydrocephalus. Cursors mark the distance from the midline to the lateral ventricle (LV) and to the cerebral hemisphere (ICHD). The ventricle in this view clearly makes up more than 75% of the total ICHD.

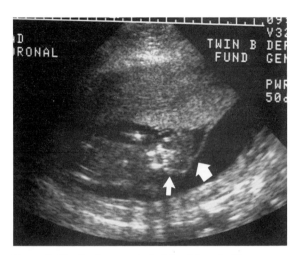

Figure 8–7. Fetal anencephaly, 13 to 14 weeks. The *arrow* indicates the area where fetal calvarium should normally be seen. The *small arrow* points to the fetal orbits and face.

ingomyelocele (Fig. 8-8), and complete rachischisis. These problems result from failure of the neural folds to fuse either rostrally (creating anencephaly) or caudally.

Neural tube defects are multifactorial in inheritance, with wide geographic variation. Prevalence varies from a high of 4 to 6/1000 live births in the British Isles, to a low of 0.1 to 0.6/1000 live births in Japan. In the United States, the prevalence is 1 to 2/1000 live births (Table 8-1).[96,97] Family history of NTD increases the risk to offspring (Table 8-2). Still, 90% to 95% of affected offspring are seen in families with negative NTD histories.[97]

Neural tube defects significantly increase perinatal and neonatal morbidity and mortality. Advances in screening techniques to identify at-risk pregnancies use detection of increased amounts of fetal-derived alpha-fetoprotein in maternal serum (MSAFP). The MSAFP concentrations are elevated in approximately 80% to 90% of pregnancies complicated by an open NTD. Closed defects are usually associated with normal values. Elevated values obtained at 16 to 18 weeks of gestation are repeated; 30 to 40 patients of 1000 tested will have persistently high values and require further evaluation. Ultrasound then will reveal inaccurate dates or unsuspected multiple gestation in one third of those patients to explain the elevation, and recalculation of MSAFP will yield a normal result. Ultrasound will detect a NTD in one or two of the remaining pregnancies with elevated values.[97]

The severity of the anomaly and the wishes of the parents guide the subsequent management of the pregnancy complicated by a NTD. Anencephaly and total

craniorachischisis are uniformly lethal anomalies. Pregnancy termination may be offered at any point in gestation when they are diagnosed. For the more common meningomyelocele, controversy still exists over the optimal route of delivery. As early as 1970, Stork and Drummond[98] suggested that vaginal delivery could compress exposed neural tissue and compromise neural function. Studies since then have supported both elective cesarean section and routine obstetric management in such cases. Avoiding labor may[99,100] or may not[101,102] benefit neonatal neurologic function. The most recent and possibly most convincing work comes from Luthy *et al*,[100] who showed a benefit to elective cesarean section before the onset of labor for infants with prenatally diagnosed meningomyelocele. They ensured an atraumatic delivery in a center where the infant could be expeditiously treated soon after delivery. These infants had better motor function at 2 years of age (by 3.3 spinal segments) than would be predicted by the anatomic level of the lesion alone. They had better motor function (by over two spinal segments) than infants who underwent any degree of labor and subsequently had either cesarean section or vaginal delivery.[100] Such reports will continue to shape our opinions about the optimal management of fetuses affected with meningomyelocele.

Abdominal Wall Defects

As with NTDs, the optimal route of delivery for fetuses diagnosed with abdominal wall defects remains controversial. Omphalocele, the more common of the two

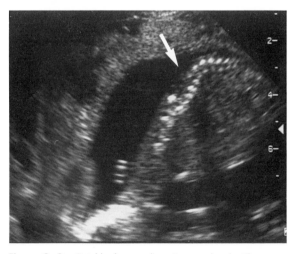

Figure 8–8. Fetal lumbosacral meningomyelocele. The *arrow* indicates the segment of spine with "dropout" of transverse processes in sagittal section.

Table 8–1

Incidence of Neurol Tube Defect in the United States (Approximately 6,000/y).

TYPE	INCIDENCE/ 1000 BIRTHS	NEONATAL DEATH (%)	LONG-TERM DISABILITY* (%)
Anencephaly	0.6–0.8	100	0
Spina bifida			
Open	0.5–0.8	33	65
Closed	0.1–0.14	7	10
Total	1.2–1.7	60	60

(After American College of Obstetricians and Gynecologists. Alpha-fetoprotein. Tech Bull 154, April 1991)
*Disability includes lower limb paralysis, sensory loss, chronic bladder or bowel problems, club foot, scoliosis, meningitis, hydrocephalus, and mental retardation.

major abdominal wall defects, complicates one in approximately 5500 live births. Gastroschisis occurs in about 1 in 10,000 to 15,000 live births.[103]

Omphalocele represents the persistence of the embryonic body stalk in an area of the ventral body wall normally replaced by a differentiated abdominal wall. Intra-abdominal contents herniate into the base of the umbilical cord. A membranous sac usually covers the herniated viscera. Omphalocele is a midline defect, and the umbilical cord inserts into the herniated sac itself. The size of the defect is extremely variable, with sacs containing anything from a few small loops of bowel to most of the abdominal organs, including the liver (Fig. 8-9). Thirty-five percent to 50% of babies with omphalocele also have chromosomal abnormalities, most commonly trisomies 13 and 18.[104–106] Up to 47% have other associated structural anomalies, most commonly cardiac, genitourinary, and neural tube defects.[107–109]

Gastroschisis is a sporadically occurring anomaly with only a rare risk of familial recurrence. Embryologically, it differs from omphalocele by being a postdevelopmental defect in an initially structurally normal fetus. Gastroschisis probably arises from compromise and subsequent ischemic changes along the distribution of the involuting omphalomesenteric arteries.[110–111] The left omphalomesenteric artery normally regresses, whereas the right develops into the superior mesenteric artery, whose terminal portion extends to the embryonic body stalk. Occlusion along that portion of the artery may result in right-sided ischemia lateral to the umbilicus with subsequent breakdown of that portion of the abdominal wall. The paramedian location of the abdominal defect in gastro-

Table 8–2

Relative Risks of Occurrence of Neurol Tube Defect in the United States

RISK FACTOR	RISK (INCIDENCE/1000 BIRTHS)
No family history of NTD	1
Positive family history	
Maternal	10
Paternal	5
One parent with NTD	30
One prior infant with NTD	20
Two prior infants with NTD	60
Insulin-dependent diabetes	20

(After American College of Obstetricians and Gynecologists. Alpha-fetoprotein. Tech Bull 154, April 1991)

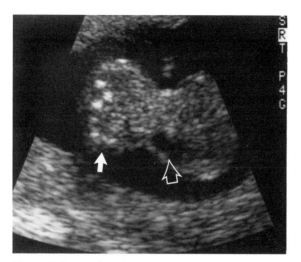

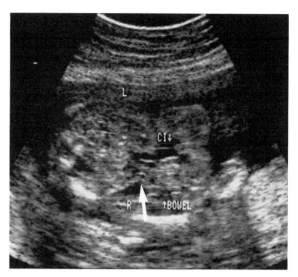

Figure 8–9. Fetal omphalocele. Fetal abdomen in transverse section is seen on the left (*closed arrow*); the omphalocele, within its sac, extrudes to the right. Fetal stomach (*open arrow*) can be seen within the sac.

Figure 8–10. Fetal gastroschisis. Fetal abdomen in transverse section is on the left. The umbilical cord insertion (CI) is seen separate from the point of extrusion (*arrow*) of abdominal contents (bowel), to the right of the CI.

schisis distinguishes it from an omphalocele. In addition, the extruded viscera float freely within the amniotic cavity without an investing peritoneal sac or membrane (Fig. 8-10).

Unlike omphalocele, gastroschisis does not carry a significantly increased risk of associated chromosomal abnormalities. Associated congenital anomalies per se are also low in incidence. Gastrointestinal complications from associated adhesions and vascular abnormalities within the displaced bowel do occur in up to 25% of cases.[112–114]

With antenatal detection of both omphalocele and gastroschisis, careful attention is also required to detect any other anomalies. Karyotyping is offered when an omphalocele is detected; a recent study suggests that the contents of the sac may help predict karyotypically abnormal fetuses. In their report, Benacerraf *et al*[115] described a series of 22 fetuses with sonographically apparent omphaloceles. The presence of bowel alone within the sac strongly correlated with an abnormal karyotype, whereas bowel and liver together in the herniation predicted a normal karyotype in 16 of 18 fetuses.[115] If no other anomalies are present with an omphalocele, a Canadian group, in a small series, showed a favorable outcome in 21 of 28 infants; the neonatal losses were all attributable to associated malformations.[116]

Debate surrounds the optimal method for delivery of an infant with a known abdominal wall defect. Arguments for elective cesarean section draw corol-

laries from the benefits shown by avoiding "birth trauma" with NTDs. Most studies have shown no change in either short- or long-term neonatal outcome after either cesarean or vaginal delivery.[107,114–120] All investigators still agree upon the need for a large randomized, prospective, multicenter study to address this issue. Our current management agrees with these findings, with one exception: We recommend abdominal delivery if there is an extremely large omphalocele with a large amount of hepatic tissue visible within the herniation.

REFERENCES

1. Quilligan EJ: Pathologic causes of preterm labor. In: Elder MG, Hendricks CH, eds. Preterm Labor. London: Butterworth, 1981;61-74.
2. Keith L, Ellis RE, Berger GS, et al. The Northwestern University multihospital twin study. I. A description of 588 twin pregnancies and associated pregnancy loss, 1971 to 1975. Am J Obstet Gynecol 1980;138:781.
3. Kovacs BW, Kirschbaum TH, Paul RH. Twin gestations. I. Antenatal care and complications. Obstet Gynecol 1989;74:313.
4. Blickstein I, Shoham-Schwartz Z, Lancet M. Growth discordancy in appropriate-for-gestational-age, term twins. Obstet Gynecol 1988;72:582.
5. Medearis AL, Jonas HS, Stockbauer JW, Domke HR. Perinatal deaths in twin pregnancy: A five-year analysis

of statewide statistics in Missouri. Am J Obstet Gynecol 1979;134:413.

6. Worthington D, Lowell ED, Grausz JP, Sobocinski K. Factors influencing survival with very low birth weight delivery. Obstet Gynecol 1983;62:550.

7. Barrett JM, Staggs SM, Van Hooydonk JE, Growdon JH, Killam AP, Boehm FH. The effect of type of delivery upon neonatal outcome in premature twins. Am J Obstet Gynecol 1982;143:360.

8. Chervenak FA, Johnson RE, Youcha S, Hobbins JC, Berkowitz RL. Intrapartum management of twin gestation. Obstet Gynecol 1985;65:119.

9. Morales WJ, O'Brien WF, Knuppel RA, Gaylord S, Hayes P. The effect of mode delivery on the risk of intraventricular hemorrhage in nondiscordant twin gestations under 1500 g. Obstet Gynecol 1989;73:107.

10. Rydhstrom H. Prognosis for twins with birth weight < 1500 gm: The impact of cesarean section in relation to fetal presentation. Am J Obstet Gynecol 1990;163:528.

11. Bejar R, Vigliocco G, Gramajo H, et al. Antenatal origin of neurologic damage in newborn infants. II. Multiple gestations. Am J Obstet Gynecol 1990;162:1230.

12. Neilson JP, Verkuyl DAA, Crowther CA, Bannerman C. Preterm labor in twin pregnancies: prediction by cervical assessment. Obstet Gynecol 1988;72:719.

13. Brown JE, Schloesser PT. Prepregnancy weight status, prenatal weight gain, and the outcome of term twin gestations. Am J Obstet Gynecol 1990;162:182.

14. Brown HL, Miller JM Jr, Neumann DE, Sarpong DF, Gabert HA. Umbilical cord blood gas assessment of twins. Obstet Gynecol 1990;75:826.

15. Phelan JP, Clark SL, Diaz F, Paul DH. Vaginal birth after cesarean. Am J Obstet Gynecol 1987;157:1510.

16. Strong TH Jr, Phelan JP, Ahn MO, Sarno AP Jr. Vaginal birth after cesarean delivery in the twin gestation. Am J Obstet Gynecol 1989;161:29.

17. Robertson EG, Neer KJ. Placental injections studies in twin gestation. Am J Obstet Gynecol 1983;147:170.

18. Blickstein I. The twin-twin transfusion syndrome. Obstet Gynecol 1990;76:714.

19. Weir PE. Ratten GJ, Beischer NA: Acute polyhydramnios—a condition of monozygous twin pregnancy. Br J Obstet Gynaecol 1979;86:849.

20. Mahony BS, Filly RA, Callen PW. Amnionicity and chorionicity in twin pregnancies: Prediction using ultrasound. Radiology 1985;155:205.

21. Patten RM, Mack LA, Harvey D, Cyr DR, Pretorius DH. Disparity of amniotic fluid volume and fetal size: Problem of the stuck twin—US studies. Radiology 1989;172:153.

22. Farmakides G, Schulman H, Saldana L, Bracero LA, Fleischer A, Rochelson B. Surveillance of twin pregnancy with umbilical arterial velocimetry. Am J Obstet Gynecol 1985;153:789.

23. Gerson AG, Wallace DM, Budgens NK, Ashmead GG, Weiner S, Bolognese RJ. Duplex Doppler ultrasound in evaluation of growth in twin pregnancies. Obstet Gynecol 1987;70:419.

24. Pretorius DH, Manchester D, Barkin S, Parker S, Nelson TR. Doppler ultrasound of twin transfusion syndrome. J Ultrasound Med 1988;7:117.

25. Mahony BS, Petty CN, Nyberg DA, Luthy DA, Hickok DE, Hirsch JH. The "stuck twin" phenomenon: Ultrasonographic findings, pregnancy outcome, and management with serial amniocenteses. Am J Obstet Gynecol 1990;163:1513.

26. Urig MA, Clewell WH, Elliott JP. Twin-twin transfusion syndrome. Am J Obstet Gynecol 1990;163:1522.

27. Elliott JP, Urig MA, Clewell WH. Aggressive therapeutic amniocentesis for treatment of twin-twin transfusion syndrome. Obstet Gynecol 1991;77:537.

28. DeLia JE, Cruikshank DP, Keye WR. Fetoscopic neodymium: YAG laser occlusion of placental vessels in severe twin transfusion syndrome. Obstet Gynecol 1990;75:1046.

29. Daw E. Triplet pregnancy. Br J Obstet Gynaecol 1978;85:505.

30. McFee JG, Lord EL, Jeffrey RL, et al. Multiple gestations of high fetal number. Obstet Gynecol 1974;44:99.

31. Itzkowic D. A survey of 59 triplet pregnancies. S Afr Med J 1984;66:92.

32. Ron-El R, Caspi E, Schreyer P, Weinraub Z, Arieli S, Goldberg MD. Triplet and quadruplet pregnancies and management. Obstet Gynecol 1981;57:458.

33. Holcberg G, Biale Y, Lewenthal H, Insler V. Outcome of pregnancy in 31 triplet gestations. Obstet Gynecol 1982;59:472.

34. Botting BJ, MacDonald Davies I, Macfarlane AJ. Recent trends in the incidence of multiple births and associated mortality. Arch Dis Child 1987;62:941.

35. Sassoon DA, Castro LC, Davis JL, Hobel CJ. Perinatal outcome in triplet versus twin gestations. Obstet Gynecol 1990;75:817.

36. Gonen R, Heyman E, Asztalos EV, et al. The outcome of triplet, quadruplet, and quintuplet pregnancies managed in a perinatal unit: Obstetric, neonatal, and follow-up data. Am J Obstet Gynecol 1990;162:454.

37. Collins MS, Bleyl JA. Seventy-one quadruplet pregnancies: Management and outcome. Am J Obstet Gynecol 1990;162:1384.

38. Lipitz S, Frenkel Y, Watts C, Ben-Rafael Z, Barkai G, Reichman B. High-order multifetal gestation-management and outcome. Obstet Gynecol 1990;76:215.

39. Aberg A, Miterian F, Cantz M, Geliler J. Cardiac puncture of fetus with Hurler's disease avoiding abortion of unaffected co-twin. Lancet 1978;2:990.

40. Kerenyi TD, Chitkara U. Selective birth in twin pregnancy with discordancy for Down's syndrome. N Engl J Med 1981;304:1525.

41. Rodeck CH, Mibashan RS, Abramowica T, et al. Selective feticide of the affected twin by fetoscopic air embolism. Prenat Diagn 1982;2:189.

42. Antsaklis A, Politis J, Karagiannopoulos C, Kaskarelis D. Selective survival of only the healthy fetus following prenatal diagnosis of thalassemia major in binovular twin gestation. Prenat Diagn 1984;4:289.

43. Chitkara U, Berkowitz RL, Wilkins IA, Lynch L, Mehalek KE, Alvarez M. Selective second-trimester termination of the anomalous fetus in twin pregnancies. Obstet Gynecol 1989;73:690.

44. Berkowitz RL, Lynch L, Chitkara U, et al. Selective reduction of multifetal pregnancies in the first-trimester. N Engl J Med 1988;318:1043.

45. Wapner RJ, Davis GH, Johnson A, et al. Selective reduction of multifetalpregnancies. Lancet 1990;335:90.

46. Lynch L, Berkowitz RL, Chitkara U, Alvarez M. First-trimester transabdominal multifetal pregnancy reduction: A report of 85 cases. Obstet Gynecol 1990; 75:735.

47. Tabsh KMA. Transabdominal multifetal pregnancy reduction: Report of 40 cases. Obstet Gynecol 1990;75:739.

48. Evans MI, May M, Drugan A, Fletcher JC, Johnson MP, Sokol RJ. Selective termination: Clinical experience and residual risks. Am J Obstet Gynecol 1990;162:1568.

49. MacKenzie IZ, Maclean DA. Pure fetal blood from the umbilical cord obtained at fetoscopy: Experience with 125 consecutive cases. Am J Obstet Gynecol 1980; 138:1214.

50. Daffos F, Capella-Pavlovsky M, Forestier F. A new procedure for fetal blood sampling in utero: Preliminary results of fifty-three cases. Am J Obstet Gynecol 1983;146:985.

51. Daffos F, Forestier F, Capella-Pavlovsky M. Fetal blood sampling during the third trimester of pregnancy. Br J Obstet Gynaecol 1984;91:118.

52. Hobbins JC, Grannum PA, Romero R, Reece EA, Mahoney MJ. Percutaneous umbilical blood sampling. Am J Obstet Gynecol 1985;152:1.

53. Benacerraf BA, Barss VA, Saltzman DH, et al. Fetal abnormalities: Diagnosis and treatment with percutaneous umbilical blood sampling under continuous ultrasound guidance. Radiology 1988;166:105.

54. Liley AW. Liquor amnii analysis in the management of isoimmunization. Am J Obstet Gynecol 1961;82:1359.

55. Forestier F, Cox WL, Daffos F, Rainaut M. The assessment of fetal blood samples. Am J Obstet Gynecol 1988;158:1184.

56. DeWaele M, Foulon W, Renmans W, et al. Hematologic values and lymphocyte subsets in fetal blood. Am J Clin Pathol 1988;89:742.

57. Barrs VA, Benacerraf BR, Frigoletto FD, et al. Management of isoimmunized pregnancy by use of intravascular techniques. Am J Obstet Gynecol 1988;159:932.

58. Berkowitz RL, Chitkara U, Wilkins IA, et al. Intravascular monitoring and management of erythroblastosis fetalis. Am J Obstet Gynecol 1988;158:783.

59. Grannum PA, Copel JA, Moya F, et al. The reversal of hydrops fetalis by intravascular intrauterine transfusion in severe isoimmune fetal anemia. Am J Obstet Gynecol 1988;158:914.

60. Ronkin S, Chayen B, Wapner RJ, et al. Intravascular exchange and bolus transfusion in the severely isoimmunized fetus. Am J Obstet Gynecol 1989;160:407.

61. Seeds JW, Bowes WA, Chescheir NC. Echogenic venous turbulence is a critical feature of successful intravascular transfusion. Obstet Gynecol 1989;73:488.

62. Copel JA, Grannum PA, Harrison D, Hobbins JC. The use of intravenous pancuronium bromide to produce fetal paralysis during intravascular transfusion. Am J Obstet Gynecol 1988;158:170.

63. Copel JA, Grannum PA, Hobbins JC. Interventional procedures in obstetrics. Semin Roentgenol 1991; 26:87.

64. Reece EA, Copel JA, Scioscia AL, Grannum PAT, De Gennaro N, Hobbins JC. Diagnostic fetal umbilical blood sampling in the management of isoimmunization. Am J Obstet Gynecol 1988;159:1057.

65. Parer JT. Severe Rh isoimmunization—current methods of in utero diagnosis and treatment. Am J Obstet Gynecol 1988;158:1323.

66. Benacerraf BR, Barss VA, Saltzman DH, et al. Acute fetal distress associated with percutaneous umbilical blood sampling. Am J Obstet Gynecol 1987;156:1218.

67. Aster RH. The immunologic thrombocytopenias. In: Kunicki TH, George E, eds. Platelet Immunology. Philadelphia: JB Lippincott, 1989;387.

68. Kelton JG. Management of the pregnant patient with idiopathic thrombocytopenic purpura. Ann Intern Med 1983;99:796.

69. Samuels P, Bussel JB, Braitman LE, et al. Estimation of the risk of thrombocytopenia in the offspring of pregnant women with presumed immune thrombocytopenic purpura. N Engl J Med 1990;323:229.

70. Cines DB, Dusak B, Tomaski A, et al. Immune thrombocytopenic purpura and pregnancy. N Engl J Med 1982;306:826.

71. Ayromlooi J. A new approach to the management of immunologic thrombocytopenic purpura in pregnancy. Am J Obstet Gynecol 1978;130:235.

72. Scott JR, Cruikshank DP, Kochenour NK, Pitkin RM, Warenski JC. Fetal platelet counts in the obstetric management of immunologic thrombocytopenic purpura. Am J Obstet Gynecol 1980;136:495.

73. Moise KJ Jr, Carpenter RJ Jr, Cotton DB, Wasserstrum N, Kirshon B, Cano L. Percutaneous umbilical cord blood sampling in the evaluation of fetal platelet counts in pregnant patients with autoimmune thrombocytopenic purpura. Obstet Gynecol 1988;72:346.

74. Scioscia AL, Grannum PA, Copel JA, Hobbins JC. The use of percutaneous umbilical blood sampling in immune thrombocytopenic purpura. Am J Obstet Gynecol 1988;72:346.

75. Kaplan C, Daffos F, Forestier F, et al. Fetal platelet counts in thrombocytopenic pregnancy. Lancet 1990;336:979.

76. Wenstrom KD, Weiner CP, Williamson RA, Grant SS. Prenatal diagnosis of fetal hyperthyroidism using funipuncture. Obstet Gynecol 1990;76:513.

77. Porreco RP, Bloch CA. Fetal blood sampling in the management of intrauterine thyrotoxicosis. Obstet Gynecol 1990;76:509.

78. Cox WL, Daffos F, Forestier F, et al. Physiology and management of intrauterine growth retardation. Am J Obstet Gynecol 1988;159:346.

79. Heinonen OP, Slone D, Shapiro S. Birth Defects and Drugs in Pregnancy. Littleton, MA: Publishing Sciences Group Inc., 1977.

80. Vintzileos AM, Campbell WA, Nochimson DJ. Antenatal evaluation and management of ultrasonically detected fetal anomalies. Obstet Gynecol 1987;69:640.

81. Rosendahl H, Kivinen S. Antenatal detection of congenital malformations by routine ultrasonography. Obstet Gynecol 1989;73:947.

82. Antepartum obstetrical ultrasound examination guidelines [Editorial]. J Ultrasound Med 1986;5:241.

83. Consensus Development Conference: Diagnostic ultrasound imaging in pregnancy. Washington, DC: United States Department of Health and Human Services (NIH publication 84-667), 1984.

84. Hegge FN, Franklin RW, Watson PT, Calhoun BC. An evaluation of the time of discovery of fetal malformations by an indication-based system for ordering obstetric ultrasound. Obstet Gynecol 1989;74:21.

85. Allan LD, Crawford DC, Chita SK, Tyman MJ. Screening for congenital heart disease. Br Med J 1986;292:1717.

86. Kurjak A, Kirkinen P, Latin V, Rajhvajn B. Diagnosis and assessment of fetal malformations and abnormalities by ultrasound. J Perinat Med 1980;8:219.

87. Habib Z. Genetics and genetic counseling in neonatal hydrocephalus. Obstet Gynecol Surv 1981;36:529.

88. Denkhaus H, Winsberg F. Ultrasonic measurement of the fetal ventricular system. Radiology 1979;131:781.

89. Campbell S, Pearce JM. Ultrasound visualization of congenital malformations. Br Med Bull 1983;39:322.

90. Chinn DH, Callen PW, Filly RA. The lateral cerebral ventricle in early second trimester. Radiology 1983:148:529.

91. Chervenak FA, Berkowitz RL, Romero R, et al. The diagnosis of fetal hydrocephalus. Am J Obstet Gynecol 1983;147:703.

92. Pilu G, Rizzo N, Orsini LF, et al. Antenatal detection of fetal cerebral anomalies. Ultrasound Med Biol 1986;12:319.

93. Vintzileos AM, Ingardia CJ, Nochimson DJ. Congenital hydrocephalus: A review and protocol for perinatal management. Obstet Gynecol 1983;62:529.

94. Chervenak FA, Berkowitz RL, Tortora M, et al. The management of fetal hydrocephalus. Am J Obstet Gynecol 1985;151:933.

95. Chervenak FA, Duncan C, Ment LR, et al. Outcome of fetal ventriculomegaly. Lancet 1984;2:179.

96. Cutler RWP. Neurology: Developmental anomalies. In: Rubenstein E, Federman DD, eds. Scientific American Medicine. New York: Scientific American, 1990:1(sec. 11).

97. American College of Obstetricians and Gynecologists: Alpha-fetoprotein. Tech Bull 154, April 1991.

98. Stark G, Drummond M. Spina bifida as an obstetric problem. Dev Med Child Neurol Suppl 1970;12:157.

99. Chervenak FA, Duncan C, Ment LR, Tortora M, McClure M, Hobbins JC. Perinatal management of meningomyelocele. Obstet Gynecol 1984;63:376.

100. Luthy DA, Wardinsky T, Shurtleff DB, et al. Cesarean section before the onset of labor and subsequent motor function in infants with meningomyelocele diagnosed antenatally. N Engl J Med 1991;324:662.

101. Bensen JT, Dillard RG, Burton BK. Open spina bifida: Does cesarean section delivery improve prognosis? Obstet Gynecol 1988;71:532.

102. Sakala EP, Andree I. Optimal route of delivery for meningomyelocele. Obstet Gynecol Surv 1990;45:209.

103. Baird PA, MacDonald EC. An epidemiologic study of congenital malformations of the anterior abdominal wall in more than half a million consecutive live births. Am J Hum Genet 1981;33:470.

104. Hauge M, Bugge M, Nielsen J. Early prenatal diagnosis of omphalocele constitutes indication for amniocenteses. Lancet 1983;2:507.

105. Mann L, Ferguson-Smith MA, Desai M, et al. Prenatal assessment of anterior abdominal wall defects and their prognosis. Prenat Diagn 1984;4:427.

106. Mayer T, Black R, Matlak ME, et al. Gastroschisis and omphalocele: An eight-year review. Ann Surg 1980;192:783.

107. Carpenter MW, Curci MR, Dibbins AW, et al. Perinatal management of ventral wall defects. Obstet Gynecol 1984;64:646.

108. Crawford DC, Chapman MG, Allan LD. Echocardiography in the investigation of anterior abdominal wall defects in the fetus. Br J Obstet Gynecol 1985;92:1034.

109. Greenwood RD, Rosenthal A, Nadas AS. Cardiovascular malformations associated with omphalocele. J Pediatr 1974;85:818.

110. Hoyme HE, Higginbotton MC, Jones KL. The vascular pathogenesis of gastroschisis: Intrauterine interruption of the omphalomesenteric artery. J Pediatr 1981;98:228.

111. Hoyme HE, Jones MC, Jones KL. Gastroschisis: Abdominal wall disruption secondary to early gestational interruption of the omphalomesenteric artery. Semin Perinatol 1983;7:294.

112. Grybowski J, Walker WA. Gastrointestinal Problems in the Infant. Philadelphia: WB Saunders, 1983:284.

113. deVries PA. The pathogenesis of gastroschisis and omphalocele. J Pediatr Surg 1980;3:245.

114. Lenke RR, Persutte WH, Nemes J. Ultrasonographic assessment of intestinal damage in fetuses with gastroschisis: Is it of clinical value? Am J Obstet Gynecol 1990;163:995.

115. Benacerraf BR, Saltzman DH, Estroff JA, Frigoletto FD Jr. Abnormal karyotype of fetuses with omphalocele: Prediction based on omphalocele contents. Obstet Gynecol 1990;75:317.

116. Tucci M, Bard H. The associated anomalies that determine prognosis in congenital omphaloceles. Am J Obstet Gynecol 1990;163:1646.

117. Kirk EP, Wah RM. Obstetric management of the fetus with omphalocele or gastroschisis: A review and report of one hundred twelve cases. Am J Obstet Gynecol 1983;146:512.

118. Sipes SL, Weiner CP, Sipes DR II, Grant SS, Williamson RA. Gastroschisis and omphalocele: Does either antenatal diagnosis or route of delivery make a difference in perinatal outcome? Obstet Gynecol 1990;76:195.

119. Lewis DF, Towers CV, Garite TJ, Jackson DN, Nageotte MP, Major CA. Fetal gastroschisis and omphalocele: Is cesarean section the best mode of delivery? Am J Obstet Gynecol 1990;163:773.

120. Moretti M, Khoury A, Rodriquez J, Lobe T, Shaver D, Sibai B. The effect of mode of delivery on the perinatal outcome in fetuses with abdominal wall defects. Am J Obstet Gynecol 1990;163:833.

SECTION

TWO

Intraoperative Management

CHAPTER 9

Anesthesia for Surgery During Pregnancy

James E. Honet

Elective surgery should be postponed until after delivery. During gestation, medical management is often preferable to surgery.[1] Nonetheless, urgent and emergent situations do arise that require surgical intervention. The goal of the next four chapters is to discuss theoretical and practical considerations surrounding surgery during pregnancy. This first chapter considers the changing issues the anesthesiologist faces throughout gestation. Early in pregnancy, concerns about altered maternal drug metabolism and the fetal developmental effects of maternally administered drugs predominate. Closer to term, the physical changes produced by the enlarging uterus and the direct effects of maternal drugs on fetal homeostasis prevail. Chapters 10 and 11 discuss the practical issues involved in providing safe anesthesia for gynecologic and other nonobstetric operations throughout gestation. The final chapter in this section covers the anesthetic concerns unique to intrauterine fetal surgery.

MATERNAL SAFETY

The key to maternal safety is understanding the physiologic changes that occur during pregnancy. Pregnancy is a dynamic physiologic event. The body is constantly evolving from the day a woman conceives until many weeks after delivery. All systems change. Many of these alterations place the parturient undergoing an anesthetic at increased risk for complications.

Physiologic Changes

Respiratory System

Both a smaller functional residual capacity and an elevated rate of oxygen consumption limit the parturient's tolerance for apnea. A well-oxygenated, nonpregnant woman will tolerate up to 5 minutes of apnea before oxygen saturation starts to fall. In contrast, in a parturient, oxygen saturation often starts declining within 90 seconds of the onset of apnea. Changes in plasma volume accompanying pregnancy produce significant peripheral edema. Swelling of the oropharynx and larynx combine to make endotracheal intubation a challenge. The smaller functional residual capacity with an increased minute ventilation, speeds the uptake of inhaled anesthetics. These changes rapidly expose gravidae to the hemodynamic and central nervous system effects of inhaled agents.

Cardiovascular System

Aortocaval compression induces significant hemodynamic changes as early as the 20th week of gestation.

Most pregnant women compensate for the effects of aortocaval compression. Induction of central neural blockade can worsen the hemodynamic effects of aortocaval compression and overwhelm a woman's compensatory mechanisms. Profound hypotension can follow. Hypotension causes not only maternal symptoms but lowers uterine blood flow and fetal oxygen delivery as well. In addition, increased plasma volume and aortocaval compression combine to yield engorgement of the vertebral venous plexus. These large, swollen blood vessels become prime targets when the anesthesiologist places a needle or catheter within the epidural space.

Gastrointestinal System

Gastric volume increases during pregnancy. Gastric pH falls. Intestinal tone and motility decrease. The lower esophageal sphincter weakens. These factors, taken together, raise the risk of active or passive regurgitation.

Pharmacokinetics and Pharmacodynamics

Changes in plasma volume, plasma proteins, red cell mass, cardiac output, hepatic and renal function, and end-organ sensitivity all combine to alter the response of the parturient to many anesthetic agents. The gravida's sensitivity to both regional and general anesthesia changes. Although some of these changes affect the uptake and metabolism of drugs, most influence their distribution and elimination.

General Anesthesia

Changes in protein binding, plasma volume, extracellular water, and adipose tissue mass alter the kinetics of intravenous anesthetic agents. Total circulating protein falls with pregnancy. At term, plasma albumin concentration is 30% below nonpregnant levels.[2] Fewer available protein binding sites increase the amount of free, active drug available.[3] As a result, the gravida may prove more sensitive to the actions of intravenous anesthetics. On the other hand, increases in plasma volume, extracellular water, and adipose tissue mass all provide a greater area for drug distribution. This effect can shorten the duration of drug effects. Changes in liver function and renal blood flow can prolong the elimination of many drugs.

Some of these changes prove beneficial. Pancuronium produces less tachycardia in pregnant women compared to nonpregnant women. For other drugs,

one change balances another. The volume of distribution of succinylcholine rises, whereas the rate it is metabolized falls. In all, its duration of action remains unchanged.[4,5] The changes in maternal physiology speed the clearance of propofol in parturients undergoing cesarean section.[6] Perhaps a rise in extrahepatic clearance is responsible for this effect.[6]

The increase in alveolar ventilation leads to a more rapid uptake and elimination of inhalational anesthetics in the parturient. Additionally, the decrease in functional residual capacity results in a more rapid equilibration of the partial pressure of alveolar gas and the partial pressure of arterial blood. These events result in a faster rise in brain concentration of inhaled anesthetic agents and a more rapid induction of anesthesia. The rise in cardiac output, however, antagonizes this rapid uptake and slows the rate of induction. Ultimately, the balance of the changes in pulmonary and cardiac physiology is a more rapid induction of inhalation anesthesia.

The hormonal changes that occur with pregnancy lower the minimum alveolar concentration of anesthetic needed to prevent movement to surgical stimulation. Increased production of progesterone probably produces this change.[7] By early in the second trimester, pregnancy lowers minimum alveolar concentration by as much as 40%.[8]

Regional Anesthesia

Pregnancy also alters the response to local anesthetic blockade. A given dose of local anesthetic produces a greater extent of block in the parturient than in the nonpregnant woman.[9] The action of both centrally and peripherally injected local anesthetics is augmented. Both mechanical and hormonal factors may contribute to the enhanced sensitivity to neuraxial blockade. Obstruction of venous return by the gravid uterus raises femoral venous pressure. Consequently, blood shunts to the azygous system, markedly engorging the epidural veins. In turn, the increased volume of epidural blood limits the size of the epidural space. Local anesthetics injected into the epidural space may then spread farther and produce higher levels of sensory block. Still, hormonal mechanisms also have a role. Even early in gestation (12–14 wk), epidural injection of local anesthetics produces wider sensory block than in nonpregnant women.[10] Animal studies of isolated nerves also show heighten sensitivity to the effects of local anesthetics with pregancy.[11,12] Pregnancy also potentiates lidocaine inhibition of impulse conduction in median nerve fibers in humans.[13] Progesterone may alter impulse conduction or raise the affinity of sodium channels for local anesthetic drugs.

Because of the changes in pharmacodynamics and pharmacokinetics, the gravida usually requires less drug for both regional and general anesthesia. Pregnancy speeds both the onset of and recovery from anesthesia. Safe care of the pregnant surgical patient demands an understanding of these effects.

FETAL SAFETY

For the purposes of the following discussion, I will divide gestation into two periods. In each period, specific fetal growth patterns occur. In early pregnancy, embryonic organs develop. In late pregnancy, these organs grow and mature. Although it appears that anesthetic concerns differ in early and late pregnancy, in reality, one must consider the same issues throughout gestation. However, I will present these potential problems as though they were separate and distinct.

Early Pregnancy

The foremost concern in the early stage of pregnancy is the fear that maternally administered drugs may alter the embryonic development of the fetus. The exact nature of this risk changes with increasing gestational age. In the early stages of pregnancy (before day 13), adverse drug reactions probably result in death of the fetus. Although no formal study documents this effect, death is most likely the result of the hostile environment inside the parturient's body. After day 13, unfavorable responses to particular medications result in teratogenicity (anomalies of formation). Organogenesis (formation of organs) occurs at various times for different organs. Most organs emerge from day 13 through day 55. Some organs continue to develop after delivery (*i.e.*, myelinization of central nervous system). After day 55, negative reactions to drugs will most likely lead to only minor morphologic changes or functional abnormalities.[14] Remember, there are other reasons for the fetus to develop abnormalities other than drug exposure. A few possibilities include genetic predisposition, an episode of hypoxia or changes in temperature. The mother may have been exposed to environmental hazards outside the operating room. Still, many drugs an anesthesiologist uses can lead to fetal compromise.

Many studies have looked at fetal drug exposure and teratogenicity. The Food and Drug Administration has devised a system of categories to help define risk to the fetus (Table 9-1). This information allows the clinician to balance the potential risk to the fetus against the hoped-for benefit to the mother. In the following pages, I will discuss the currently available information about the use of common anesthetic agents throughout pregnancy.

Table 9–1

FDA Classification System for Drug Use During Pregnancy

CATEGORY	INTERPRETATION
A	Controlled studies show no risk. Adequate, well-controlled studies in pregnant women have failed to demonstrate risk to the fetus.
B	No evidence of risk in humans. Either animal findings show risk, but human findings do not, or, if no adequate human studies have been done, animal findings are negative.
C	Risk cannot be ruled out. Human studies are lacking, and animal studies are either positive for fetal risk or lacking as well. However, potential benefits may justify the potential risk.
D	Positive evidence of risk. Investigational or postmarketing data show risk to the fetus. Nevertheless, potential benefits may outweigh the potential risk.
X	Contraindicated in pregnancy. Studies in animals or humans or investigational or postmarketing reports have shown fetal risk that clearly outweighs any possible benefit to the patient.

(Data from Physicians Desk Reference, 45th ed. Oradell, NJ: Medical Economics Company, 1991:2493)

Opioids

AGONISTS

MORPHINE *(CATEGORY C).* Morphine is used extensively in modern obstetric practice. Despite having a category C rating, the consensus is that morphine is a safe drug in the parturient for short-term use. The Collaborative Perinatal Project found a possible association between use of morphine at any time during pregnancy and inguinal hernia.[15] Recent animal studies suggest that morphine is not teratogenic. Instead, other fetal problems lead to the increase in postnatal mortality.[16] Maternal and fetal drug dependence are the primary problems associated with chronic exposure to morphine and other opioids during gestation. Infants of narcotic-addicted mothers will exhibit withdrawal symptoms soon after birth.

MEPERIDINE *(CATEGORY C).* No study has shown meperidine to cause major adverse fetal effects. The Collaborative Perinatal Project data suggested an association between first-trimester use of meperidine and inguinal hernia.[17] Widespread use of meperidine throughout gestation has not incited any noticeable complications. The limited use of meperidine in the operating room and postoperatively seems safe.

FENTANYL *(CATEGORY C).* In animals, fentanyl does not increase postnatal mortality.[16] Animal data suggest that this drug is without reproductive effects.[18] No reports of teratogenicity or reproductive repercussions in humans are available. Fentanyl given during general anesthesia may induce loss of fetal heart rate variability without causing fetal hypoxia.[19]

SUFENTANIL *(CATEGORY C).* Studies with sufentanil in animals reported embryocidal effects probably from maternal, not fetal, toxicity. These investigations found no evidence of teratogenicity.[20] Other animal studies showed no adverse reproductive or teratogenic effects.[21] There are no adequate human data concerning the use of sufentanil in pregnancy.[20]

ALFENTANIL *(CATEGORY C).* Alfentanil has an embryocidal effect in animals. Adverse maternal, not fetal, drug actions may explain these data. Other studies could not prove any adverse reproductive or teratogenic effects.[21] No adequate studies have been done in pregnant women.[22]

AGONIST–ANTAGONIST

NALBUPHINE *(CATEGORY B).* No congenital effects are reported in humans or in experimental animals.[23] Prolonged use during pregnancy theoretically could result in fetal addiction with subsequent withdrawal in the newborn.[24]

BUTORPHANOL *(CATEGORY B).* The safety of butorphanol before labor is not established. Use this drug in parturients only when it is deemed essential to the welfare of the patient.[25]

ANTAGONIST

NALOXONE *(CATEGORY B).* In mice and rats, at doses up to 1000 times the human dose, naloxone does not impair fertility or harm the fetus.[26] There are, however, no adequate and well-controlled studies in pregnant women.

Benzodiazepines

DIAZEPAM *(CATEGORY D).* Many studies through the years have postulated that diazepam increases the risk of congenital malformations, specifically cleft palate. One report claimed an association between cleft palate and exposure to diazepam in the first trimester.[27] Another group of investigators interviewed mothers of children with selected birth defects.[28] These women had all been exposed to a variety of drugs in the first trimester. Children whose mothers took diazepam had a four times more frequent incidence of cleft lip than did children with other defects; however, there are other large retrospective studies that show no association between diazepam and cleft lip/palate.[29–31] Other studies have suggested that diazepam exposure correlated with defects other than cleft palate. Some of these defects include inguinal hernia, cardiac defects,[32] absence of both thumbs, and spina bifida.[33]

Recent investigations, looking at primary cultures of cerebral cortex neurons, found that diazepam significantly inhibited cell proliferation. In this model, drugs that inhibited cell proliferation within twice their therapeutic concentration consistently correlated with major neural tube malformations.[34]

Ingestion of benzodiazepines at any time during pregnancy may result in visible malformations, functional deficits, or behavioral anomalies. Benzodiazepines may derange organogenesis. They may alter early differentiation of neural primordium. They also may incite aberrations after neural tube closure or during biochemical differentiation of the brain.[35] Some authorities, however, believe that physical development is disturbed only by extremely high doses of benzodiazepines.[36]

Recently, a study compared in utero and postnatal exposure to diazepam in rats. The results support the conclusion that diazepam is a behavioral teratogen. Neurochemical effects followed both pre- and post-natal diazepam exposure.[37]

All told, the currently available evidence supports avoiding diazepam during pregnancy. This recommendation apparently extends to all trimesters, not just the period of organogenesis.

MIDAZOLAM (CATEGORY D). Reproduction toxicology studies have shown that midazolam is neither embryotoxic nor teratogenic and that it lacks effect on the fertility and postnatal development of animals.[38,39] However, because midazolam is a benzodiazepine, it has been classified as a category D drug by the manufacturer.[38]

LORAZEPAM (CATEGORY C). No report linking the use of lorazepam with congenital defects has been located.

FLUMAZENIL (CATEGORY B). Reproductive toxicity studies revealed no drug-related embryotoxic or teratogenic effects of flumazenil. Additionally, these studies detected no adverse effects on either fertility or the peri- and postnatal development.[40]

Local Anesthetics

LIDOCAINE (CATEGORY B). In 1974 a study reported that epidural lidocaine during labor decreased neurobehavioral scores in the neonate.[41] Subsequent investigations could not confirm this finding.[42] In rats, even extremely large doses of lidocaine do not produce any teratogenic or adverse fetal effects.[43] Furthermore, doses up to 6.6 times the maximum safe dose for humans do not harm the fetus.[44] In contrast, later in pregnancy, lidocaine may act as a behavioral teratogen and alter a broad range of behaviors.[45] Potentially all local anesthetics may cause the same changes in behavior. Ultimately, lidocaine is probably safe in early pregnancy. The effects of lidocaine on infant behavior have yet to be completely clarified.

BUPIVACAINE (CATEGORY C). At five to nine times the maximum safe dose for humans, bupivacaine decreases pup survival and has embryocidal effects in rats and rabbits.[46] No adequate or well-controlled studies have been done in parturients. When used at delivery, bupivacaine yields no detectable neonatal neurobehavioral effects.[47]

2-CHLOROPROCAINE (CATEGORY C). Animal reproductive studies have not been conducted with 2-chloroprocaine.[48] It also is not known whether 2-chloroprocaine can affect reproductive capacity or harm the fetus if given to a pregnant woman. During labor and delivery, 2-chloroprocaine appears to induce no significant neonatal effects.[47]

Induction Agents

THIOPENTAL (CATEGORY C). There do not appear to be any studies specifically examining the effects of thiopental on pregnancy. Because of their use as antiseizure medications, there are many studies assessing the effects of other barbiturates. Studies examining the fetal effects of maternal barbiturate exposure have reported an increased incidence of fetal anomalies.[49,50] The incidence of cleft lip and cardiomyopathy may increase.[51] In contrast, another study reported no difference in the incidence of congenital malformations in infants born of treated and untreated women with seizure disorders.[52] If women taking antiepileptic medication seized during pregnancy, they had an elevated risk of giving birth to a child with a malformation. These reports investigated only the chronic use of barbiturates. The teratogenic effects of a single-induction dose of thiopental are unknown. The drug does, however, have a good safety record from many years of clinical use.

KETAMINE (CATEGORY B). Ketamine does not have an embryocidal effect in animals.[53,54] When used for cesarean section, however, it can depress Apgar scores.[55]

PROPOFOL (CATEGORY B). The manufacturer has done reproductive studies in animals.[56] These investigations found no evidence of impaired fertility or harm to the fetus. There are no adequate and well-controlled studies in humans during gestation. When used to induce general anesthesia for cesarean section, propofol compares favorably with other induction agents.[57–59] Infants born after propofol or thiopental induction have similar and satisfactory Apgar scores, Neurologic and Adaptive Capacity Scores (NACS), and umbilical cord blood gas values.[60] Propofol crosses the placenta rapidly. Prolonged fetal exposure immediately before birth may transiently lower NACS scores.[61]

In all, propofol has minimal effects on the fetus at delivery. Yet, there are no studies of its use during gestation. The Physicians Desk Reference recommends avoiding this drug unless specifically indicated.[56]

ETOMIDATE (CATEGORY B). Etomidate crosses the placenta to the fetus rapidly. It also can lower the plasma cortisol concentration in the neonate after cesarean delivery.[62] In animals, etomidate seems devoid of teratogenic effects.[63] It remains unknown what effect etomidate has on the fetus if used during gestation.

Inhalational Agents

ENFLURANE *(CATEGORY B)*. In most animal studies, enflurane neither impedes fertility and reproduction nor harms the fetus.[64] In mice, however, prolonged exposure to enflurane increases incidence of cleft palates and minor skeletal and visceral abnormalities.[65] In rats, shorter duration of exposure does not induce fetal morphologic abnormalities.[66] The finding of an elevated incidence of cleft palate in mice is probably a species-specific phenomenon. Other animal studies have shown a decrease in the number of progeny born after exposure to enflurane.[67] There are no adequate or well-controlled studies in humans.

ISOFLURANE *(CATEGORY C)*. Animal studies suggest that isoflurane might produce anesthetic-related fetotoxic effects in very large doses (six times the human dose);[68] others disagree. The use of nitrous oxide, a possible teratogen itself, complicates the interpretation of much of the animal data on isoflurane. A well-controlled animal study showed that isoflurane even prevented the adverse effects of nitrous oxide.[69] When compared with nitrous oxide, halothane, and enflurane in rats, isoflurane did not incite any adverse fetal effects.[66] No well-controlled studies have been done in humans.

HALOTHANE *(CATEGORY C)*. The manufacturer states that some animal studies have shown halothane is teratogenic, embryotoxic, and fetotoxic at both subanesthetic and anesthetic concentrations.[70] Other investigations have shown an embryocidal, but not a morphologic, effect.[67] Exposing mice to halothane for prolonged periods at high concentrations increases the risk of maternal and embryo death but does not produce morphologic changes.[71] Prolonged anesthetic exposure can yield maternal hypoxemia, hypercarbia, and other physiologic changes that could explain the high mortality risk. Giving mice subanesthetic doses of halothane before mating and then throughout gestation lacked adverse effects on reproduction.[72] At greater than anesthetic doses, pregnancy rate and litter size diminish. Postnatal survival does not change. In rats, exposure to three-fourths minimum alveolar concentration of halothane at different stages of pregnancy generated no major or minor teratologic effects.[66] There are no adequate studies in parturients.

NITROUS OXIDE *(CATEGORY ?)*. Few topics have generated as much recent controversy among anesthesiologists as the discussion of the possible teratogenic effects of nitrous oxide. In 1965 a study of chick embryos found that nitrous oxide by itself is not teratogenic, but when the embryos are made hypoxic with nitrous oxide, there is an increased number of anomalies.[73] Subsequent studies showed that nitrous oxide has a variety of metabolic effects. Because nitrous oxide rapidly crosses the human placenta and could interfere with development, some experts consider it unsafe for use during the first two trimesters of pregnancy.[74]

The most potentially significant metabolic action of nitrous oxide is its effect on B_{12} oxidation (Fig. 9-1). Vitamin B_{12} is a cofactor for methionine synthetase, an enzyme integral in the formation of thymidine. (Thymidine is a subunit of DNA.) In some animals, nitrous oxide does harm the fetus.[75] Nevertheless, the abnormalities seen in rats may not result simply from impairment of DNA synthesis.[76] The abnormalities in this study were blocked by halothane and not folinic acid. Additionally, other studies by the same group showed the same protective effect with isoflurane.[69]

Nitrous oxide was introduced into anesthesia in the late 19th century. Before 1985, no reports relating nitrous oxide to adverse fetal outcomes were published. In 1986, two retrospective studies could not document any adverse fetal outcomes associated with use of nitrous oxide during gestation.[77,78] Both articles stated that nitrous oxide yielded no increase in the incidence of low-birth-weight infants and cases of inevitable abortion when compared to regional anesthesia.

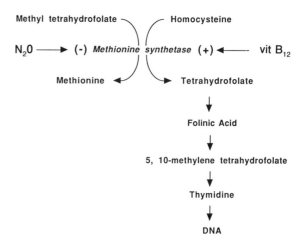

Figure 9–1. Nitrous oxide (N_2O) inhibits the enzyme methionine synthetase. This enzyme is necessary for DNA synthesis.

Many recent articles examining the effects of nitrous oxide in all patients undergoing anesthesia did not find any increase in adverse outcomes. A mild deficiency in folic acid after exposure to nitrous oxide was reported, but this was without clinical significance.[79] Eger, a participant in many of these studies, concluded that the use of nitrous oxide in typical patients is not dangerous. None of these studies examined the parturient.

Neuromuscular Blocking Drugs

SUCCINYLCHOLINE *(CATEGORY C)*. While succinylcholine is widely used to facilitate endotracheal intubation, there are no studies of its teratogenic effects in humans. Plasma cholinesterase concentration falls during pregnancy. Some investigators have reported a prolonged duration of action of succinylcholine in parturients.[80–82]

CURARE *(CATEGORY C)*. Curare was the first clinically used muscle relaxant. Before the introduction of other drugs, curare saw extensive use in obstetrics. When given directly to rat fetus for a prolonged time, curare can induce fetal anomalies.[83] This effect probably stems from the lack of movement, not an intrinsic action of the drug. There are no reports looking at teratogenicity in humans.

ATRACURIUM *(CATEGORY C)*. According to the manufacturer's tests, atracurium, when given in doses of approximately one half the human dose, is potentially teratogenic in rabbits.[84] Other animal studies have not found any specific adverse effects of atracurium, despite administration of supraparalyzing doses.[85] Atracurium, like all muscle relaxants, undergoes little placental transfer. Recently, this drug has been given directly to the fetus to inhibit movement during magnetic resonance imaging.[86] No adverse fetal effects were noted.

DOXACURIUM *(CATEGORY C)*. Teratology testing by the manufacturer revealed no maternal or fetal toxicity of teratogenic effects (package insert). There are no adequate and well-controlled studies in parturients. Doxacurium should be used only if the potential benefit justifies the potential risk to the fetus.

VECURONIUM *(CATEGORY C)*. Few data are available on this drug. Studies during cesarean delivery show placental uptake and rapid clearance of vecuronium.[87] No neonatal complications arose.

PANCURONIUM *(CATEGORY C)*. Pancuronium often is given directly to the fetus to produce immobility during magnetic resonance imaging and other in utero procedures. No adverse fetal sequelae have been reported.[86,88,89] Studies at the time of cesarean delivery report placental uptake, albeit small, and rapid placental clearance.[90]

PIPERCURONIUM *(CATEGORY C)*. The manufacturer did teratogenicity studies in animals (package insert). Pipercuronium produced no effects. In high doses, it did have an embryocidal effect secondary to maternal toxicity. Again, no adequate humans studies to recommend its use in parturients are available.

Anticholinesterase Agents

NEOSTIGMINE *(CATEGORY C)*. This drug is highly ionized at physiologic pH; therefore, it probably does not cross the placenta in significant amounts. Parturients with myasthenia gravis have taken neostigmine during pregnancy for many years. As a result, several studies of the effects of neostigmine and pregnancy have been published. One found no relationship to congenital defects when used in the first trimester.[91] Based on this and other studies, one group of authors stated that neostigmine is a drug of choice for pregnant patients with myasthenia gravis.[92] Why the drug is given a category C rating is unclear.

PYRIDOSTIGMINE *(CATEGORY C)*. This anticholinesterase also is used to treat myasthenia gravis in the parturient. It does not cause fetal malformations.[93] However, some experts caution against using this drug, particularly late in pregnancy, because it may cause premature labor.

Anticholinergic Drugs

ATROPINE *(CATEGORY C)*. This drug readily crosses the placenta. The Collaborative Perinatal Project did not find any association with malformations.[91] Additionally, atropine has no effect on uterine activity.[94]

GLYCOPYRROLATE *(CATEGORY B)*. In the Collaborative Perinatal Project, many women took anticholinergic drugs during the first trimester. Only four patients received glycopyrrolate.[91] Glycopyrrolate is a quaternary ammonium compound and does not cross the placenta. Its fetal effects are minimal. In parturients, glycopyrrolate does not alter fetal heart rate or variability.[94]

SCOPOLAMINE *(CATEGORY C)*. The Collaborative Perinatal Project found no evidence for fetal malformations.[91] However, this drug differs from the other anticholinergic drugs. It readily crosses the placenta[95,96] and has fetal effects. Fetal effects include tachycardia and decreased heart rate variability. Maternal tachycardia is equivalent to the other anticholinergics.[97] Because of its fetal effects, scopolamine is probably not the anticholinergic drug to choose when giving anesthesia to the parturient.

Miscellaneous Drugs

DROPERIDOL (*CATEGORY C*). Some authors have used droperidol as a continuous intravenous infusion for hyperemesis gravidarum during the second and third trimesters.[98] They did not note any apparent fetal harm, but experience with droperidol in gestation is limited.

EPHEDRINE (*CATEGORY C*). It is difficult to evaluate this drug. Ephedrine is used to alleviate problems (*e.g.,* hypotension) that cause fetal complications. Therefore, one cannot determine if a fetal complication stems from ephedrine or from the original problem. The Collaborative Perinatal Project found no evidence for fetal malformations.[91] Ephedrine, when used in treating maternal hypotension after spinal anesthesia, significantly increases fetal heart rate and beat-to-beat variability.[99]

EPINEPHRINE (*CATEGORY C*). As with ephedrine, this drug is difficult to evaluate. This drug is naturally occurring, which makes it even more difficult to study. Despite this, the Collaborative Perinatal Project found a significant association between first-trimester use and major and minor malformations.[91]

PHENYLEPHRINE (*CATEGORY C*). Animal reproductive studies have not been conducted.[100] It is also not known whether phenylephrine, when administered to a pregnant woman, can cause fetal harm or affect reproductive capacity.

Late Pregnancy

Late in gestation, the anesthesiologist has two main goals: (1) to avoid fetal asphyxia and (2) to avoid preterm labor.

Fetal Asphyxia

The uterine blood flow is a prime factor in the determination of fetal nutrition, oxygenation, and respiration. The fetus receives nutrients via the umbilical vessels. These vessels arise from the placenta. The placenta receives maternal blood through the uterine artery. Blood flow through the uterine artery changes during gestation. Uterine artery blood flow rises from 3.5% to 12% of cardiac output by term.[101] Importantly, the uterine vessels are almost maximally dilated, and their flow can only minimally increase. Uterine blood flow is affected by both changes in pressure and resistance. No autoregulation occurs. Any fall in blood pressure (uterine blood flow) can breed placental hypoperfusion and fetal asphyxia. Possible etiologies include hypotension and either endogenous or iatrogenic catecholamines.[102-104] Inferior vena cava compression, increased uterine tone, hypercarbia, and hypoxia also can all alter uterine blood flow. The effects of increased catecholamines on uterine blood flow are decreased with labetalol.[105]

Uterine blood flow is important for supporting the myometrium. Eighty percent of the uterine blood flow is to the placenta, and the remaining 20% goes to the myometrium. If the myometrium becomes ischemic, the fetus also is jeopardized secondary to hypoxemia and acidosis.[106]

Both regional and general anesthetics can have similar effects on uterine blood flow. Spinal or epidural anesthesia blocks conduction of sympathetic nerve impulses and can yield hypotension. Likewise, a fall in blood pressure during general anesthesia can lead to a decrease in uterine blood flow.[107]

Fetal oxygenation depends entirely on maternal oxygen delivery. The characteristics of oxygen delivery depend on the oxygen content of maternal blood and uterine perfusion. The placenta and uterine vessels constrict when exposed to high oxygen tensions;[108-110] however, this vasoconstriction is not enough to decrease fetal oxygenation. Instead the fetus' Po_2 increases in response to the rise in maternal Pao_2.[111] Placental oxygen-diffusing capacity is a limiting factor in placental oxygen transport.[122] The fetus is unable to achieve Po_2 above 45 to 60 mm Hg.[123] High placental oxygen consumption and maldistribution of maternal and fetal blood flow in the placenta explain this gap.

Another determinate of uterine blood flow is maternal $Paco_2$. Just as alkalosis decreases blood flow to the brain, so does it decrease uterine blood flow.[114] Vasoconstriction and the left shift in the oxyhemoglobin curve induced by alkalosis results in less oxygen availability for the fetus. Maternal acidosis also can lower fetal oxygen delivery. Acidosis is a myocardial depressant. Impaired cardiac output can limit uterine blood flow and increase the risk of fetal asphyxia. The fetus is able to compensate for asphyxia, yet its reserve is very small.[115,116]

Preterm Labor

Despite continued improvements in the care of the premature infant, a child's best hope for normal development is to remain in utero for the full 9 months of gestation. Both anesthesia and surgery could risk inducing preterm labor. Careful attention to maternal condition and anesthetic technique can help limit this risk.

Many investigators have attempted to define the fetal risk associated with anesthesia and surgery during pregnancy. Surgery within the first two trimesters of pregnancy may increase the risk of spontaneous abortion.[117] Almost 9% of parturients go into labor during the perioperative period.[118] In primates, surgical manipulation of the uterus did not result in uterine contractions while under halothane anesthesia, but during emergence, coordinated uterine contractions began.[119] Careful monitoring of uterine activity throughout surgery and recovery is important to allow early detection and treatment of preterm labor.

Fetal Monitoring

Doppler ultrasound can detect the fetal heart rate after the 16th week of development.[120] By the 25th or 27th week of gestation, significant beat-to-beat variability arises.[121] Fetal heart rate and uterine tone should be monitored whenever the site of surgery allows. Even for abdominal surgery, fetal and uterine monitoring should begin in the recovery room.

Anesthesia often eliminates fetal beat-to-beat variability. Hypothermia induces fetal bradycardia.[122] Other fetal heart rate changes may show a change in fetal status. Changes in baseline heart rate, prolonged tachycardia, or unexplained bradycardia may all herald fetal acidosis or hypoxemia. If these changes occur, make certain you have taken all possible steps to optimize fetal oxygen delivery.

SUMMARY AND CONCLUSIONS

During pregnancy, it is not unusual for a parturient to come to the operating room. The care that she receives is no different from the standard care any person coming to the operating room should receive (maintaining fetal and maternal homeostasis), with few exceptions. If a patient is having an entirely elective procedure, one should consider postponing the surgery until the parturient returns to her normal physiologic state. Of special import is aortocaval compression and maintenance of left uterine displacement after the 12th week of gestation. When administering anesthesia, consider the parturient at increased risk for aspiration. Although never proven, regional anesthesia is probably preferable, as there is less chance for fetal exposure to anesthetic drugs. Short-term opioid use should have no adverse sequelae. Avoid diazepam throughout pregnancy. Inhalational anesthetic agents should help preserve uterine relaxation (preventing uterine activity and preterm labor). Nitrous oxide probably should not exceed 50% to provide adequate fetal oxygenation. Avoid hypo- and hypercarbia (remember that $Paco_2$ changes as pregnancy progresses), as both will affect fetal oxygenation. Monitor the fetus and uterus (intraoperative and postoperative) after the 16th week; early diagnosis of complications may prevent disaster.

REFERENCES

1. Landers D, Carmona R, Crombleholme W, Lim R. Acute cholecystitis in pregnancy. Obstet Gynecol 1987;69:131.
2. Bletka M, Hlavaty V, Trnkova M, Bendl J, Bendova L, Chytil M. Volume decrease in whole blood and absolute amount of serum proteins in early stages of late toxemia of pregnancy. Am J Obstet Gynecol 106:10,1970.
3. Dean M, Stock B, Patterson RJ, Levy G. Serum protein binding of drugs during pregnancy in humans. Clin Pharmacol Ther 1980;28:253.
4. Blitt CD, Petty WC, Alberternst EE, Wright BJ. Correlations of plasma cholinesterase activity and duration of action of succinylcholine during pregnancy. Anesth Analg 1977;56:78.
5. Leighton BL, Cheek TG, Gross JB, et al. Succinylcholine pharmacodynamics in peripartum patients. Anesthesiology 1986;64:202.
6. Gin T, Gregory MA, Chan K, Buckley T, Oh TE. Pharmacokinetics of propofol in women undergoing elective caesarean section. Br J Anaesth. 1990;64:148.
7. Datta S, Migliozzi RP, Flanagan HL, Krieger NR. Chronically administered progesterone decreases halothane requirements in rabbits. Anesth Analg 1989;68:46.
8. Palahnuik RJ, Shnider SM, Eger EI II. Pregnancy decreases the requirement of inhaled anesthetic agents. Anesthesiology 1974;41:82.
9. Bromage PR. Continuous lumbar epidural analgesia for obstetrics. Can Med Assoc J 1961;85:1136.
10. Fragraeus L, Urban BJ, Bromage PR. Spread of epidural analgesia in early pregnancy. Anesthesiology 1983;58:184.
11. Datta S, Lambert DH, Gregus J, Gissen AJ, Covino BG. Differential sensitivities of mammalian nerve fibers during pregnancy. Anesth Analg 1983;62:1070.

12. Flanagan HL, Datta S, Lambert DH, Gissen AJ, Covino BG. Effects of pregnancy on bupivacaine-induced conduction blockade in the isolated rabbit vagus nerve. Anesth Analg 1987;66:123.

13. Butterworth JF IV, Wlaker FO, Lyzak SZ. Pregnancy increase median nerve susceptibility to lidocaine. Anesthesiology 1990;72:962.

14. Tuchmann-Duplessis H. The effects of teratogenic drugs. In: Phillipp E, Barnes J, Newton M, eds. Scientific foundations of obstetrics and gynaecology Philadelphia, FA Davis: 1970:636.

15. Heinen O, Slone D, Shapiro S. Birth defects in pregnancy. Littleton, CO: Publishing Science Group, 1977:287.

16. Fujinaga M, Mazze RI. Teratogenic and postnatal developmental studies of morphine in Sprague-Dawley rats. Teratology 1988;38:401.

17. Heinen O, Slone D, Shapiro S. Birth defects in pregnancy. Littleton, CO: Publishing Science Group, 1977:287.

18. Fujinaga M, Stevenson JB, Mazze RI. Reproductive and teratogenic effects of fentanyl in Sprague-Dawley rats. Teratology 1986;34:51.

19. Johnson ES, Colley PS. Effects of nitrous oxide and fentanyl anesthesia on fetal heart-rate variability intra- and postoperatively. Anesthesiology 1980;52:429.

20. Physicians Desk Reference, 45th ed. Oradell, NJ: Medical Economics Company, 1991:1121.

21. Fujinaga M, Mazze RI, Jackson EC, Baden JM. Reproductive and teratogenic effects of sufentanil and alfentanil in Sprague-Dawley rats. Anesth Analg 1988;67:166.

22. Physicians Desk Reference, 45th ed. Oradell, NJ: Medical Economics Company, 1991:1109.

23. Miller RR. Evaluation of nalbuphine hydrochloride. Am J Hosp Pharm 1980;37:942.

24. Briggs G. Drugs in pregnancy and lactation Baltimore: Williams & Wilkins, 1983:300.

25. Physicians Desk Reference, 45th ed. Oradell, NJ: Medical Economics Company, 1991:718.

26. Physicians Desk Reference, 45th ed. Oradell, NJ: Medical Economics Company, 1991:914.

27. Saxen I, Saxen L. Association between maternal intake of diazepam and cleft lip. Lancet 1975;2:498.

28. Safra MJ, Oakley GP. Association between cleft lip with or without cleft palate and prenatal exposure to diazepam. Lancet 1975;2:478.

29. Czeizel A. Diazepam, phenytoin and etiology of cleft lip and/or palate. Lancet 1976;1:810.

30. Rosenberg L, Mitchell AA, Parsells JL, et al. Lack of relation of oral clefts to diazepam use during pregnancy. N Engl J Med 1984;310:1121.

31. Shiono PH, Mills JL. Oral clefts and diazepam use during pregnancy. N Engl J Med 1984;311:919.

32. Bracken MB, Holford TR. Exposure to prescribed drugs in pregnancy and association with congenital malformations. Obstet Gynecol 1981;58:336.

33. Ringrose CAD. The hazards of neurotrophic drugs in the fertile years. Can Med Assoc J 1972;106:1058.

34. Regan CM, Gorman AM, Larsson OM, et al. In vitro screening for anticonvulsant-induced teratogenesis in neural primary cultures and cell lines. Int J Dev Neurosci 1990;8:143.

35. Weber LW. Benzodiazepines in pregnancy—academical debate or teratogenic risk? Biol Res Pregnancy Perinatol. 1985;6:151.

36. Tucker JC. Benzodiazepines and the developing rat: A critical review. Neurosci Biobehav Rev 1985;9:101.

37. Lauer JA, Adams PM, Johnson KM. Perinatal diazepam exposure: Behavioral and neurochemical consequences. Neurotoxicol Teratol 1987;9:213.

38. Physicians Desk Reference, 45th ed. Oradell, NJ: Medical Economics Company, 1991:1860.

39. Schlappi B. Safety aspects of midazolam. Br J Clin Pharmacol. 1983;16(Suppl)1:37.

40. Schlappi B, Bonetti EP, Burgin H, Strobel R. Toxicological investigations with the benzodiazepine antagonist flumazenil. Arzneimittelforschung. 1988; 38:247.

41. Scanlon JW, Brown WU, Weiss JB, Alper MH. Neurobehavioral response of newborn infants after maternal epidural anesthesia. Anesthesiology 1974;40:121.

42. Abboud TK, Sarkis F, Blikian A, Varakian L. Lack of adverse neurobehavioral effects of lidocaine. Anesthesiology 1982;57:A404.

43. Fujinaga M, Mazze RI. Reproductive and teratogenic effects of lidocaine in Sprague-Dawley rats. Anesthesiology 1986;65:626.

44. Physicians Desk Reference, 45th ed. Oradell, NJ: Medical Economics Company, 1991:622.

45. Smith RF, Kurkjian MF, Mattran KM, Kurtz SL. Behavioral effects of prenatal exposure to lidocaine in the rat: Effects of dosage and of gestational age at administration. Neurotoxicol Teratol 1989;11:395.

46. Physicians Desk Reference, 45th ed. Oradell, NJ: Medical Economics Company, 1991:619.

47. Abboud TK, Khoo SS, Miller F, Doan T, Henriksen EH. Maternal, fetal, and neonatal responses after epidural anesthesia with bupivacaine, 2-chloroprocaine, or lidocaine. Anesth Analg 1982;61:638.

48. Physicians Desk Reference, 45th ed. Oradell, NJ: Medical Economics Company, 1991:616.

49. Majewski F, Steger M, Richter B, et al. The teratogenicity of hydantoins and barbiturates in humans, with considerations on the etiology of malformations and cerebral disturbances in the children of epileptic parents. Int J Biol Res Pregnancy 1981;2:37.

50. Greenberg G, Inman WH, Weatherall JA, et al. Maternal drug histories and congenital abnormalities. Br Med J 1977;2:853.

51. Giraud JR, Hoppeler JM, Mettey R, et al. The teratogenic risks of anti-epileptic treatment. J Gynecol Obstet Biol Reprod 1982;11:385.

52. Majewski F, Raff W, Fischer P, et al. Teratogenicity of

anticonvulsant drugs. Dtsch Med Wochenschr 1980;105:719.

53. Kochhar MM, Aykac I, Davidson PP, Fraley ED. Teratologic effects of d,1-2-(o-chlorophenyl)-2-(methylamino) cyclohexanone hydrochloride (ketamine hydrochloride) in rats. Res Commun Chem Pathol Pharmacol 1986;54:413.

54. Physicians Desk Reference, 45th ed. Oradell, NJ: Medical Economics Company, 1991:1659.

55. Downing JW, Mahomedy MC, Jeal DE, Allen PJ. Anaesthesia for caesarean section with ketamine. Anaesthesia 1976;31:883.

56. Physicians Desk Reference, 45th ed. Oradell, NJ: Medical Economics Company, 1991:2169.

57. Dailland P, Jacquinot P, Lirzin JD, et al. Neonatal effects of propofol administered to the mother in anesthesia in cesarean section. Cah Anesthesiol 1989;37:429.

58. Moore J, Bill KM, Flynn RJ, et al. A comparison between propofol and thiopentone as induction agents in obstetric anaesthesia. Anaesthesia 1989;44:753.

59. Cortambert F, Marti-Flich J, Dasset MP, et al. The pharmacokinetics of propofol used in cesarean section: A preliminary study in the newborn infant. Cah Anesthesiol 1989;37:33.

60. Yau G, Gin T, Ewart MC, Kotur CF, Leung RK, Oh TE. Propofol for induction and maintenance of anaesthesia at caesarean section. A comparison with thiopentone/enflurane. Anaesthesia 1991;46:20.

61. Gin T, Yau G, Chan K, Gregory MA, Oh TE. Disposition of propofol infusions for caesarean section. Can J Anaesth 1991;38:31.

62. Reddy BK, Pizer B, Bull PT. Neonatal serum cortisol suppression by etomidate compared with thiopentone, for elective caesarean section. Eur J Anaesthesiol 1988;5:171.

63. Janssen PA, Niemegeers CJ, Marsboom RP. Etomidate, a potent non-barbiturate hypnotic. Intravenous etomidate in mice, rats, guinea-pigs, rabbits and dogs. Arch Int Pharmacodyn Ther 1975;214:92.

64. Green CJ, Monk SJ, Knight JF, Dore C, Luff NP, Halsey MJ. Chronic exposure of rats to enflurane 200 p.p.m.: No evidence of toxicity or teratogenicity. Br J Anaesth 1982;54:1097.

65. Wharton RS, Mazze RI, Wilson AI. Reproduction and fetal development in mice chronically exposed to enflurane. Anesthesiology 1981;54:505.

66. Mazze RI, Fujinaga M, Rice SA, et al. Reproductive and teratogenic effects of nitrous oxide, halothane, isoflurane and enflurane in Sprague-Dawley rats. Anesthesiology 1986;64:339.

67. Kundomal YR, Baden JM. Toxicity and teratogenicity of inhaled anesthetics in Drosophila melanogaster. Toxicol Lett. 1985;25:287.

68. Physicians Desk Reference, 45th ed. Oradell, NJ: Medical Economics Company, 1991:616.

69. Fujinaga M, Baden JM, Yhap EO, Mazze RI. Reproduc-

tive and teratogenic effects of nitrous oxide, isoflurane, and their combination in Sprague-Dawley rats. Anesthesiology 1987;67:960.

70. Physicians Desk Reference, 45th ed. Oradell, NJ: Medical Economics Company, 1991:2383.

71. Wharton RS, Wilson AI, Mazze RI, Baden JM, Rice SA. Fetal morphology in mice exposed to halothane. Anesthesiology 1979;51:532.

72. Wharton RS, Mazze RI, Baden JM, Hitt BA, Dooley JR. Fertility, reproduction and postnatal survival in mice chronically exposed to halothane. Anesthesiology 1978;48:67.

73. Smith BE, Gaub MI, Moya F. Teratogenic effects of anesthetic agents: Nitrous oxide. Anesth Analg 1965;44:726.

74. Nunn JF, Chanarin I. Nitrous oxide inactivates methionine synthetase. In: Eger EI II ed. Nitrous oxide/N_2O. New York: Elsevier, 1985:211.

75. Fujinaga M, Baden JM, Mazze RI. Susceptible period of nitrous oxide teratogenicity in Sprague-Dawley rats. Teratology 1989;40:439.

76. Mazze RI, Fujinaga M, Baden JM. Halothane prevents nitrous oxide teratogenicity in Sprague-Dawley rats; folinic acid does not. Teratology 1988;38:121.

77. Crawford JS, Lewis M. Nitrous oxide in early human pregnancy. Anaesthesia 1986;41:1900.

78. Aldridge IM, Tunstall ME. Nitrous oxide and the fetus. A review and the results of a retrospective study of 175 cases of anaesthesia for insertion of Shirodkar suture. Br J Anaesth 1986;58:1348.

79. Koblin DD, Tomerson BW, Waldman FM, et al. Effect of nitrous oxide on folate and vitamin B_{12} metabolism in patients. Anesth Analg 1990;71:610.

80. Kambam JR, Perry SM, Entman S, et al. Effect of magnesium on plasma cholinesterase activity. Am J Obstet Gynecol 1988;159:309.

81. Gyasi HK, Mohy O, Adu-Gyamfi Y, et al. Plasma cholinesterase in pregnancy—effect of enzyme activity on the duration of action of succinylcholine. Middle East J Anesthesiol 1986;8:379.

82. Baraka A, Wakid N, Noueihed R, et al. Pseudocholinesterase activity and atracurium v. suxamethonium block. Br J Anaesth 1986;58:91S.

83. Moessinger AC. Fetal akinesia deformation sequence: An animal model. Pediatrics 1983;72:857.

84. Physicians Desk Reference, 45th ed. Oradell, NJ: Medical Economics Company, 1991:804.

85. Skarpa M, Dayan AD, Follenfant M, et al. Toxicity testing of atracurium. Br J Anaesth 1983;55(Suppl 1):27S.

86. Fan SZ, Huang FY, Lin SY, et al. Intrauterine neuromuscular blockade in fetus. Ma Tsui Hsueh Tsa Chi 1990;28:31.

87. Dailey PA, Fisher DM, Shnider SM, et al. Pharmacokinetics, placental transfer, and neonatal effects of vecuronium and pancuronium administered during cesarean section. Anesthesiology 1984;60:569.

88. Wenstrom KD, Williamson RA, Weiner CP, Sipes SL,

Yuh WT. Magnetic resonance imaging of fetuses with intracranial defects. Obstet Gynecol 1991;77:529.

89. Moise KJ Jr, Carpenter RJ Jr, Deter RL, et al. The use of fetal neuromuscular blockade during intrauterine procedures. Am J Obstet Gynecol 1987;157:874.

90. Dailey PA, Fisher DM, Shnider SM, et al. Pharmacokinetics, placental transfer, and neonatal effects of vecuronium and pancuronium administered during cesarean section Anesthesiology 1984;60:560.

91. Heinen O, Slone D, Shapiro S. Birth defects in pregnancy. Littleton, CO: Publishing Science Group, 1977:345.

92. McNall PG, Jafarnia MR. Managment of myasthenia gravis on the obstetrical patient. Am J Obstet Gynecol 1965;92:518.

93. Foldes FF, McNall PG. Myasthenia gravis: A guide for anesthesiologists. Anesthesiology 1962;23:837.

94. Abboud T, Raya J, Sadri S, et al. Fetal and maternal cardiovascular effects of atropine and glycopyrrolate. Anesth Analg 1983;62:426.

95. Boehnn FH, Growdon JH Jr. The effect of scopolamine on fetal heart rate baseline variability. Am J Obstet Gynecol 1974;120:1099.

96. Ayromlooi J, Tobias M, Berg P. The effects of scopolamine and ancillary analgesics upon the fetal heart rate recording. J Reprod Med 1980;25:323.

97. Diaz DM, Diaz SF, Marx GF. Cardiovascular effects of glycopyrrolate and belladonna derivatives in the obstetric patients. Bull NY Acad Med 1980;56:245.

98. Briggs G. Drug effects in pregnancy and lactation, 2nd ed. Baltimore: Williams & Wilkins 1986:159.

99. Wright RG, Shnider SM, Levinson et al. The effect of maternal administration of ephedrine on fetal heart rate and variability. Obstet Gynecol 1981;57:734.

100. Physicians Desk Reference, 45th ed. Oradell, NJ: Medical Economics Company, 1991:2344.

101. Thaler I, Manor D, Itskovitz J, et al. Changes in uterine blood flow during human pregnancy. Am J Obstet Gynecol 1990;162:121.

102. James FM III, Griess FC Jr, Kemp RA. An evaluation of vasopressor therapy for maternal hypotension during spinal anesthesia. Anesthesiology 1970;33:22.

103. Ralston DH, Shnider SM, de Lorimier AA. Effects of equopotent ephedrine, metarminol, mephenteramine and methoxamine on uterine blood flow in the pregnant ewe. Anesthesiogy 1974;40:354.

104. Clark KE, Irion GL, Mack CE. Differential responses of uterine and umbilical vasculatures to angiotensin II and norepinephrine. Am J Physiol 1990;259:197.

105. Eisenach JC, Mandell G, Dewan DM. Maternal and fetal effects of labetalol in pregnant ewes. Anesthesiology 1991;74:292.

106. Calvert SA, Widness JA, Oh W, et al. The effects of acute uterine ischemia on fetal circulation. Pediatr Res 1990;27:552.

107. Brann AW, Myers RE. Central nervous system findings in the newborn monkeys following severe in utero partial asphyxia. Neurology 1975;25:327.

108. Nyburg R, Westin B. The influence of oxygen tension and some drugs on human placental vessels. Acta Physiol Scand 1957;9:216.

109. Panigel M. Placental perfusion experiments. Am J Obstet Gynecol 1962;84:1664.

110. Tomiga T, Page EW. Accomodation of the human placenta to hypoxia. Am J Obstet Gynecol 1966;94:679.

111. Khazin AF, Hon EH, Hahre FW. Effects of maternal hyperoxia on the fetus. I. Oxygen tension. Am J Obstet Gynecol 1971;109:628.

112. Wilkening RB, Meschia G. Effect of occluding one umbilical artery on placental oxygen transport. Am J Physiol 1991;260:1319.

113. Levinson G, Shnider SM. Anesthesia for surgery during pregnancy. In: Snider SM, Levinson G, ed. Anesthesia for obstetrics, 2nd ed. Baltimore: Williams & Wilkins, 1987:199.

114. Motoyama EK, Rivard G, Acheson F, et al. The effects of changes in maternal pH and P_{CO_2} on the P_{O_2} of fetal lambs. Anesthesiology 1967;28:891.

115. Block BS, Schlafer DH, Wentworth RA, et al. Intrauterine asphyxia and the breakdown of physiologic circulatory compensation in fetal sheep. Am J Obstet Gynecol 1990;162:1325.

116. Jensen A, Hohmann M, Kunzel W. Dynamic changes in organ blood flow and oxygen consumption during acute asphyxia in fetal sheep. J Dev Physiol 1987;9:543.

117. Duncan PG, Pope WD, Cohen MM, Greer N. Fetal risk of anesthesia and surgery during pregnancy. Anesthesiology 1986;64:790.

118. Shnider SM, Webster GM. Maternal and fetal hazards of surgery during pregnancy. Am J Obstet Gynecol 1965;92:891.

119. Nakayama DK, Harrison MR, Seron-Ferre M, Villa RL. Fetal surgery in the primate. II. Uterine electromyographic response to operative procedures and pharmacologic agents. J Pediatr Surg 1984;19:333.

120. Trimakas AP, Maxwell KD, Berkay S, Gardner TJ, Achuff SC. Fetal monitoring during cardiopulmonary bypass for removal of a left atrial myxoma during pregnancy. Johns Hopkins Med J 1979;144:156.

121. Steinberg ES, Santos AC. Surgical anesthesia during pregnancy. Int Anesthsiol Clin 1990;28:58.

122. Liu PL, Warren TM, Ostheimer GW, Weiss JB, Liu LM. Foetal monitoring in parturients undergoing surgery unrelated to pregnancy. Can Anaesth Soc J 1985;32:525.

CHAPTER 10

Gynecologic Surgery During Pregnancy

Norman L. Herman
Timothy J. Schlairet
Danny Bowen

At no other time is an anesthetist required to administer anesthesia to more than one patient simultaneously than in the pregnant women. This unique circumstance requires a thorough understanding of the anatomic and physiologic changes associated with pregnancy and the current developmental state of the embryo/fetus. More than 50,000 pregnant women undergo nonobstetric surgical procedures each year in the United States.[1] (An accurate count of surgery during pregnancy is difficult to obtain because of two factors. First, surgery may be done early in pregnancy before a woman knows that she is pregnant. Second, there is no nationwide reporting system to collect such data.) Estimates of the incidence of nonobstetric surgery during pregnancy range between 0.3% and 2.2%.[2]

PHYSIOLOGIC CHANGES OF PREGNANCY

Chapter 1 contains a thorough discussion of the physiologic changes of pregnancy. To provide anesthesia safely during pregnancy, one must know and understand not only these physiologic changes but the timing and anesthetic implications of each. To that end, we will reiterate a few of the adaptations to pregnancy.

Cardiovascular Changes

Beginning between the 6th and 12th week of gestation, maternal blood volume increases 25% to 40% by term.[3] Increments in plasma volume (50%) and red cell mass (15%) account for this expansion.[4] These changes in maternal blood volume have several important implications. The hemodilution that results from the unbalanced increase of plasma volume versus red cell mass leads to the physiologic anemia of pregnancy.[4] The rheologic changes produced by this relative anemia can cause a woman to exhibit heart murmurs not present in the nongravid state that may be indistinguishable from true pathologic conditions.[5] Hemodilution also accounts for the fall in total plasma protein concentration.[6] Fewer plasma proteins elevate the free fraction of highly protein-bound drugs. Augmented drug effect or toxicity at doses normally effective in nonpregnant patients may follow.[7,8] This reduction of plasma protein concentration also correlates with a decrease in pseudocholinesterase activity.[9] Prolonged neuromuscular blockade by succinylcholine has been reported.[10]

Compression of the great vessels by the gravid uterus when the pregnant patient assumes the supine position wreaks havoc on maternal hemodynamics. First, the caval obstruction and the resultant decrease in venous return from the lower extremities can produce maternal hypotension, tachycardia, pallor, and faintness. This *supine hypotension syndrome* occurs in up to 10% of pregnant women at term.[11] Supine hypotension may develop as early as the 27th week of gestation.[3] Even without symptoms of hypotension, 90% of parturients lying flat at term completely obstruct their inferior vena cava.[12] Venous blood must travel by alternative routes through the intervertebral venous plexus and azygous veins to reach the superior vena cava. The resulting engorgement of these vessels reduces the size of both the subarachnoid and epidural spaces and may contribute to smaller drug requirements for regional anesthesia.[13] Besides caval obstruction, the pregnant uterus can compress the abdominal aorta. Although measured brachial artery pressures remain unchanged, the aortic compression can profoundly alter both uteroplacental and renal blood flow.[14] This *occult supine hypotensive syndrome* can detrimentally affect both the mother and fetus.[15] For these reasons, second- and third-trimester parturients must avoid the supine position.

Respiratory Changes

The progressive upward growth of the pregnant uterus markedly reduces functional residual capacity. This change begins in the fifth month of gestation and reaches a maximum of 20% at term.[16,17] In addition, maternal basal metabolic rate and oxygen consumption increase by 15%. Because of these two factors, the parturient risks rapid and severe hypoxemia during periods of apnea.[18] Pay close attention to preoxygenation and denitrogenation before induction of general anesthesia. Give supplemental oxygen during regional anesthesia.

Capillary engorgement within the mucosa of the respiratory tract makes the upper airway more susceptible to bleeding with instrumentation. It also can distort or reduce the diameter of the glottic opening and make direct visualization and intubation difficult. Have an assortment of smaller endotracheal tubes and laryngoscope blades readily available.

Gastrointestinal Changes

Several changes occur in the gastrointestinal system during pregnancy. Placental gastrin release raises gastric volume and acidity. Progesterone inhibits gastrointestinal motility and delays gastric emptying. These changes begin as early as 8 to 10 weeks and become significant by 12 to 14 weeks of gestation.[19] Anatomic displacement of the stomach elevates gastric pressure. Mean barrier pressure (lower esophageal sphincter pressure minus intragastric pressure) falls.[19,20] These changes increase the risk of regurgitation and aspiration with the loss of airway reflexes. There is no consensus when and to what extent the risk of aspiration becomes significant. Our conservative recommendation is to give a nonparticulate antacid plus an H_2-receptor antagonist, and do a rapid-sequence induction/intubation with cricoid pressure when providing general anesthesia for any parturient.

Central Nervous System Changes

Pregnancy lowers the minimum alveolar concentration of inhalation anesthetic agents by 25% to 40%.[21] Progesterone, which has a sedating effect,[22] and endogenous opioids[23] may contribute to this change. Pregnancy, as early as the first trimester, also increases the susceptibility to local anesthetic action.[24] A progesterone-induced alteration on nerve cell membranes may lead to this heightened sensitivity.

CERVICAL CERCLAGE

Description

Cervical cerclage is the surgical intervention used to prevent recurrent second-trimester fetal loss from cervical incompetence. Classically, a diagnosis of incompetent cervix is made after repeated history of painless cervical dilatation in the second or early third trimester. Prolapse of the membranes through the cervix or spontaneous rupture of the membranes and expulsion of the fetus typically follow. An incompetent cervix seems to result from a weakness of the internal cervical os caused by trauma, congenital factors, or multiple pregnancies. When the fetus attains a critical weight, it overcomes the normal sphincteric resistance of the os and uterine contents begin to extrude. Premature contractions and delivery may follow this mechanical dilatation of the cervix.[25]

Making the diagnosis of cervical incompetence is often difficult. Painless cervical dilatation of 2 to 4 cm happens in 24% to 30% of otherwise asymptomatic gravid women who go on to deliver at term.[26,27] No single pathognomonic physical finding or test exists to confirm a precise diagnosis of incompetent cervix.[28] It is therefore a diagnosis of exclusion after the other causes of mid-trimester effacement (*e.g.*, preterm labor) have been ruled out.

Treatment

Once the diagnosis of incompetent cervix is made, the goal of therapy is to enhance the resistance of the cervix to effacement and dilatation and thereby prevent fetal loss. Vaginal pessary, progesterone therapy, and electrocautery of the cervix have all been investigated as treatments for incompetent cervix. Each has met with little success.[29] Surgery is the mainstay of therapy of incompetent cervix.

The surgical approach for cerclage is either vaginal or transabdominal. Several intravaginal methods have been described since the initial introduction of cerclage in 1950.[30] Shirodkar[31] was first to develop a method of encircling the internal cervical os for reinforcing a weakened cervix. The Shirodkar procedure involves the incision of the cervix at the level of the internal os, elevating the vaginal mucosa and bladder, and placing a ligature around the cervix at the level of the internal os. The complex nature of the Shirodkar method makes it difficult during pregnancy, especially with bulging membranes, and places the urinary tract at risk. The McDonald procedure uses a purse-string suture as high as possible around the exocervix, at approximately the level of the internal os.[32] With four to five bites, the suture is placed deeply into the muscle of the cervix and pulled tightly enough to close the cervical os completely. The McDonald method usually produces less blood loss and trauma to the cervix compared to the Shirodkar procedure. The McDonald procedure also induces less cervical scarring, resulting in a lower incidence of cervical dystocia.[33] A far less common method is the Wurm procedure, which was developed in Australia. This approach uses crisscrossing heavy double-mattress sutures across the cervical opening at the level of the internal os.[34] The Wurm procedure reportedly can delay delivery until at or near term.[34,35] It has been used in conjunction with amniocentesis to reduce bulging membranes[35] and as a method for repeat cerclage when either a Shirodkar or McDonald cerclage has failed.[36]

The transabdominal approach is by far the most complex and difficult procedure for the surgical treatment of cervical incompetence.[37] It involves the intra-abdominal placement of a ligature around the cervix above the cardinal and uterosacral ligaments. It is recommended for patients in whom the cervix is congenitally short, amputated, or scarred from unsuccessful prior cerclage, when the fornices are lacerated, or in the presence of subacute cervicitis.[29] Although this technique is effective, it has major disadvantages. It requires two abdominal procedures (the cerclage and then the subsequent cesarean section). It also has a higher complication rate, related to the high vascularity and proximity of ureters to the surgical site. This procedure is reserved for women in whom vaginal cerclage has either failed or is impossible to perform.

Cervical cerclage usually is done between 14 and 26 weeks of gestation. Cerclage done between the 16th and 19th weeks of gestation has the greatest chance of success.[38] Before 14 weeks, pregnancy losses frequently are due to genetic anomalies or imperfect implantation.[28] After 26 weeks, cerclage usually is avoided. The survival rates for a fetus of this gestational age in an American tertiary neonatal intensive care unit are good.

Indications, Contraindications, and Complications

Cervical cerclage is performed to treat cervical incompetence. As mentioned, however, this diagnosis can be a difficult one to make. Classically, patients have fallen into two categories. Either they have a history of repetitive late mid-trimester abortions, or they have a partially dilated cervix with intact membranes.[39]

Many reports of improved pregnancy outcomes in large series of patients with cerclage have bolstered the idea that cerclage prolongs pregnancy.[28] However, many cited series are not randomized prospective studies and do not exclude patients in preterm labor or with previous mid-trimester losses of unknown etiology. Cervical cerclage in patients with successive prior losses assumes a high recurrence rate and that any pregnancy salvage after cerclage is solely the result of the surgery. This conclusion may be erroneous. Factors predisposing a woman to preterm delivery may resolve spontaneously, independent of any therapy.[40] Two prospective randomized trials of women with prior preterm pregnancy losses compared cerclage with expectant management. In populations with multifactorial risks for preterm delivery, cerclage offered no benefit as either a therapy or prophylaxis for prolonging pregnancy.[41,42] Although the number of cerclages done over the past decade has fallen dramatically, these data do not dispel the need for cervical cerclage. They, instead, support the need for restricting cerclage to that subgroup of patients with a well-defined diagnosis of incompetent cervix as the etiology of their recurrent pregnancy losses.[40]

Contraindications to cervical cerclage include the following:[28,29]

- Bleeding
- Active labor or significant uterine contractions
- Ruptured membranes
- Cervical dilation greater than 4 cm
- Intrauterine infection
- Fetal abnormalities
- Abruptio placenta

Complications following cervical cerclage include rupture of membranes, chorioamnionitis, bleeding, cervical dystocia, placental abscess, uterine rupture, and maternal death.[29] The frequency and severity of these complications relate to the experience of the operator and rapidity of the intervention when they arise.

Prolapsing Fetal Membranes

A woman with bulging "hourglass" membranes prolapsing through an effaced and dilated cervix requires intervention because miscarriage is nearly inevitable. This situation carries a poorer prognosis than does cerclage in nonemergent circumstances. Many techniques have been used with varying success to reduce the protruding membranes back into the uterus before cerclage. Several small series have reported 44% to 100% viable births following emergent cerclage for prolapsing membranes.[35,36,43,44] Earlier series reported very low viability rates (13%–20%) in patients with prolapsed membranes without cervical cerclage.[39,43,45] Surgical intervention, therefore, appears beneficial in this population.

OTHER GYNECOLOGIC SURGERY

Laparoscopic Surgery

Laparoscopy is a common nonobstetric surgical procedure done during pregnancy.[46] As a diagnostic aid in ruling out ectopic pregnancy and ovarian cysts, laparoscopy boasts nearly 95% accuracy.[47] Success depends on optic equipment, distortion of the anatomy, and operator experience. If laparoscopy is inconclusive,

then laparotomy follows. Laparoscopy generally is bypassed in a woman with an obvious pelvic or abdominal process requiring immediate surgical intervention.

Exploratory Laparotomy

Surgery for ovarian cysts accounts for up to 39% of operations during pregnancy.[48] Two to five percent of these cysts are ovarian cancer.[49] Although no detrimental effects have been noted when an ovary with a corpus luteum is removed as early as 8 weeks of gestation,[50] most experts recommend deferring ovarian surgery at least until the 14th to 16th week of pregnancy. This delay allows generous time for the development of the endocrine function of the placenta before removing the corpus luteum.[51]

ANESTHETIC CONSIDERATIONS

Maternal Medical Condition

The preoperative assessment of the pregnant patient for nonobstetric surgery should incorporate all the aspects of a routine evaluation for a nonpregnant patient. The profound anatomic and physiologic changes of pregnancy strongly influence the medical condition of the parturient presenting for surgery. The duration of the pregnancy at the time of surgery determines the extent of these physiologic and anatomic influences on the patient.

Maternal and Fetal Monitoring

The presence and severity of preexisting maternal disorders help decide the extent of intraoperative maternal monitoring. An uncomplicated gravid patient requires the basic monitors recommended in the American Society of Anesthesiologists guidelines. Pulse oximetry and end-tidal capnography are especially important monitors in this population because they help detect hypoxemia and ensure proper endotracheal tube placement. The need for further invasive maternal monitoring depends on the extent of the proposed operation and the maternal condition.

Continuous fetal monitoring intraoperatively allows assessment of fetal well-being during anesthesia and surgery.[52] Fetal heart rate (FHR) is detectable transabdominally by ultrasonography after the 16th week of pregnancy.[53] An FHR transducer can be easily positioned and left in place (unless it would interfere with the sterile surgical field).[13] Between 25 and 27 weeks of gestation, FHR begins to exhibit fluctuations of 6 to 8 beats/minute. Changes in parasympathetic and sympathetic outflow from the fetal medulla produce FHR beat-to-beat variability. It is a good indicator of fetal well-being.[54] The FHR variability is best evaluated using a fetal scalp electrode, which gives sharp fetal electrocardiographic R waves for the cardiotocograph to calculate and plot.[55] External transducers have a poor signal-to-noise ratio when compared with the scalp electrode and do not allow assessment of subtle changes in beat-to-beat variability; however, because fetal scalp electrode monitoring is not an option in the majority of these surgical cases, the external transducer must be used. Gross alterations in FHR variability (*e.g.,* loss of beat-to-beat variability) give fairly reliable indications of changes in fetal status in these circumstances. Besides heart rate variability, changes in baseline FHR are an indicator of fetal condition. Moderate degrees of hypoxic insult can produce transient to prolonged fetal tachycardia (FHR > 160 beats/minute).[55] If fetal tachycardia does arise intraoperatively, search for maternal hypoxemia, hypovolemia, and any other factors that could interfere with gas exchange across the placenta.[56]

Any pregnant patient undergoing surgery may experience uterine contractions and even premature labor. A tocodynamometer can detect uterine contractions once the uterus rises above the pelvic brim. If possible, monitor uterine tone continuously with a tocodynamometer.[52] Data from this monitor help the obstetrician direct and assess tocolytic therapy. Continue checking uterine tone postoperatively as the uterine relaxing effects of inhalational anesthetic agents subside and regional analgesia or systemic medications blunt the patient's perception of premature contractions.[52]

Regional Versus General Anesthesia

Local, regional, and general anesthesia can all provide suitable surgical conditions in pregnant patients. The ultimate choice of the anesthetic technique should be based on maternal condition, extent and anatomic region of the surgery planned, and the expertise of the anesthetist.[53] Most obstetric anesthesiologists prefer regional anesthesia whenever possible. Regional anesthesia has the following advantages:

- Reduces the risk of maternal aspiration
- Decreases fetal drug exposure
- Uses local anesthetics (which, unlike inhalational agents, are not known teratogens[13])

- Allows the use of spinal or epidural opioids for intraoperative and postoperative pain relief
- Appears to carry a lower risk of spontaneous abortion than general anesthesia [57]

The aforementioned factors do not imply that general anesthesia is unsuitable. There are many situations in which regional and local anesthesia are not possible and general anesthesia is the only option. A carefully done general anesthetic presents no more maternal risk than local or regional anesthesia.

Anesthesia for Elective Cervical Cerclage

No consensus exists on the choice of anesthesia for vaginal cervical cerclage. This procedure requires adequate analgesia and relaxation of the vaginal canal. The surgeon must retract the vagina enough to expose the cervix for surgical manipulation.[40] Cerclage has been done under general (with and without potent inhalational agent), epidural, spinal, local (paracervical), and no anesthesia—all with equal success. The fear that uterine activity might commence with manipulation of the cervix during the procedure has led some to recommend general anesthesia with a potent agent.[25,58] However, no agent presently in use provides uterine relaxation effects much beyond the end of the anesthetic. In addition, retrospective comparisons of general and regional anesthesia have failed to show any difference in outcome (Fig. 10-1).[59,60]

Presently, most of the anesthesia literature recommends doing cervical cerclage under spinal anesthesia. The small drug dose needed to achieve adequate analgesia is the major advantage cited. Spinal anesthesia provides excellent operative conditions while minimizing fetal drug exposure.

Obstetric texts and reviews continue to espouse the need for deep general anesthesia for maximal uterine relaxation.[25,61,62] Other obstetric sources acknowledge regional anesthesia as a safe, reliable, and acceptable option for this procedure.[63–65]

As for any other surgical procedure, the best technique is the one with which the anesthetist has the most experience and feels most comfortable. No matter the anesthetic technique, anesthesia should not be considered a substitute for diligent intraoperative and postoperative monitoring of uterine activity and use of appropriate tocolytic agents if indicated.

Anesthesia for Emergent Cervical Cerclage

An even more controversial situation is the woman with bulging "hourglass" membranes who requires emergency reduction of the presenting part and

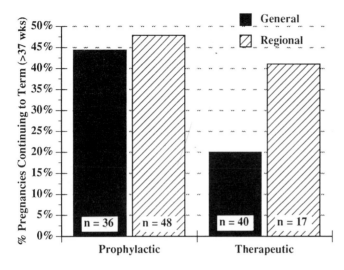

Figure 10–1. Success of cervical cerclage after general or regional anesthesia. Prophylactic cerclage was done in women less than 2 cm dilated (n = 84). Therapeutic cerclage was done if the cervix had dilated 2 cm or more (n = 57). Anesthetic technique did not make a statistically significant difference in outcome. (Engles ED. A retrospective study of regional vs general anesthesia for cervical cerclage and review of the literature. Anesthesiology 1989;71:A888)

cerclage. Obstetricians often recommend general endotracheal anesthesia in this situation for several reasons. Some fear that the requirement for steep Trendelenburg position to accomplish the return of membranes to the uterine cavity increases the risk of aspiration of stomach contents.[66] Others advocate the use of deep general anesthesia to provide uterine relaxation to allow return of the presenting parts to the uterus.[25,43,44,62] However, spinal anesthesia also has been used effectively for emergency cerclage with bulging membranes.[35,67]

No randomized study has investigated differences in outcome after emergent cerclage between general or regional anesthesia. Because ethically this may be a difficult study to do, we can offer only limited guidance about the most appropriate choice. Ultimately, the choice of anesthesia must be a personal decision forged between the patient and her anesthesiologist.

Risks and Complications

Premature Labor

Parturients undergoing anesthesia and surgery are at significant risk for premature labor and spontaneous abortion.[57,68,69] During the second trimester, the risk of spontaneous abortion after anesthesia and surgery is almost fivefold greater than in matched controls.[66] Whether this increased risk of abortion results from the surgery or the anesthesia remains highly controversial.[54,66] No matter what the etiology of premature labor following surgery, these data point to the neces-

sity for postoperative monitoring of uterine tone and aggressive tocolytic management if contractions are associated with cervical change.[5]

Fetal Drug Exposure

The effects of exposure of the fetus to anesthetic agents are extensively discussed in Chapter 9. If surgery is done during organogenesis, attempt to minimize the consequences of fetal drug exposure. Use regional or local anesthesia when possible. Avoid drugs with known or strongly suspected teratogenic effects.

Recommendations for Anesthesia for Gynecologic Surgery During Pregnancy

A preoperative visit is an important aspect of the anesthetic management of the pregnant patient for surgery. The anesthesiologist can allay the woman's concerns and fears for her unborn child and reduce her apprehension about the procedure by discussing the anesthetic plan and answering her questions. As with any other patient, a reassuring preoperative visit can reduce the need for premedication.[71]

Aspiration prophylaxis is an important consideration for any gravid patient undergoing surgery. All parturient's need prophylaxis after the gastrointestinal motility changes of pregnancy are well established (14–16 wk). Conservative management warrants prophylaxis for *all* pregnant patients. Give an H_2-receptor antagonist (cimetidine, ranitidine, or famotidine) the night before and the morning of surgery to reduce gastric acid secretion. A nonparticulate antacid (0.3 M sodium citrate, 30 mL) 15 to 30 minutes before induction will raise the pH of any existing gastric contents. Metoclopramide, 10 mg orally or intravenously, has been used to enhance gastric emptying in this patient population and could be part of an overall aspiration prophylaxis regimen.

To avoid supine and occult hypotensive syndrome, no women over 25 weeks of gestation should be transported to or placed on the operating room table in the supine position. If FHR and uterine contraction monitoring are feasible ($>$ 17 wk of gestation), place external transducers before induction to allow assessment of fetal well-being before, during, and after anesthesia and surgery. Because reading and interpreting FHR and uterine contraction patterns are not part of the usual day-to-day job of the anesthesiologist, close consultation with the obstetricians may be necessary if unusual changes occur intraoperatively.

We prefer regional or local anesthesia, if suitable and the patient consents. To avoid hypotension, infuse at least 1L of balanced salt solution before inducing either spinal or epidural anesthesia. Give more intravenous fluid if hypotension arises. If blood pressure falls below 15% of the preanesthetic level or the patient exhibits symptoms of cerebral hypoperfusion (*e.g.,* nausea, vomiting, altered level of consciousness), give ephedrine, 5 to 10 mg intravenously.

If general anesthesia is chosen, the following preventive measures must be observed:

- Carefully denitrogenate the patient with 100% oxygen by mask before induction to minimize the risk of maternal or fetal hypoxemia.
- Even with adequate gastric acid prophylaxis therapy, do not consider the patient to have an empty stomach. Do a rapid-sequence induction and intubation with a cuffed endotracheal tube with cricoid pressure. Oral or nasogastric suctioning after intubation can help to minimize the possibility of perioperative passive aspiration.
- Aspiration is as great a potential problem on extubation as it is on intubation. Delay extubation until you see objective signs of the return of airway reflexes (*e.g.,* train-of-four without decrement, tetany with 50 Hz without fade, head lift for 5 s).
- Proper ventilation is very important during general anesthesia in pregnancy. Mechanical hyperventilation markedly reduces uterine blood flow.[72] To avoid this peril, monitor end-tidal capnography or sample arterial blood gases to maintain arterial $Paco_2$ within normal pregnancy range (30–35 mm Hg).

REFERENCES

1. Brodsky JB. Anesthesia and the pregnant surgical patient. Regional Anesthesia 1984;9:119.
2. Diaz JH. Perioperative management of the pregnant patient undergoing nonobstetric surgery. Part I. Indications for surgery and direct and indirect effects of anesthesia on fetal well-being. Anesthesiol Rev 1991; 18:21.
3. Lees MM, Taylor SH, Scott DB, Kerr MG. A study of cardiac output at rest throughout pregnancy. J Obstet Gynaecol Br Common 1967;74:319.
4. Lund CJ, Donovan JC. Blood volume during pregnancy. Am J Obstet Gynecol 1967;98:393.
5. Leicht CH. Anesthesia for the pregnant patient undergoing nonobstetric surgery. Anesthesiol Clin North Am 1990;8:131.
6. Song CS, Merkatz IR, Rifkind AB, Gillette PN, Kappas A. The influence of pregnancy and oral contraceptive steroids on the concentration of plasma proteins. Studies with a quantitative immunodiffusion method. Am J Obstet Gynecol 1970;108:227.
7. Dean M, Stock B, Patterson RJ, Levy G. Serum protein binding of drugs during and after pregnancy in humans. Clin Pharmacol Ther 1980;28:257.
8. Santos AC, Pedersen H, Morishima HO, Finster M, Arthur GR, Covino BG. Pharmacokinetics of lidocaine in nonpregnant and pregnant ewes. Anesth Analg 1988;67:1154.
9. Shnider SM. Serum cholinesterase activity during pregnancy, labor, and puerperium. Anesthesiology 1965; 26:335.
10. Weissman DB, Ehrenwerth J. Prolonged neuromuscular blockade in parturient associated with succinylcholine. Anesth Analg 1983;62:444.
11. Howard BK, Goodson JH, Mengert WF. Supine hypotensive syndrome in late pregnancy. Obstet Gynecol 1953;1:371.
12. Kerr MG, Scott DB, Samuel E. Studies of the inferior vena cava in late pregnancy. Br Med J 1964;i:532.
13. Pedersen H, Finster M. Anesthetic risk in the pregnant surgical patient. Anesthesiology 1979;51:439.
14. Bieniarz J, Crottogini JJ, Curachet E, et al. Aortocaval compression by the uterus in late human pregnancy. II. An arteriographic study. Am J Obstet Gynecol 1968;100:203.
15. Malinow AM. Anesthesia for surgical operations during pregnancy. Anesthesiologist's view. In: Datta S, Ostheimer GW, eds. Common problems in obstetric anesthesia. Chicago: Year Book Medical Publishers, 1987:438.
16. Prowse CM, Gaensler EA. Respiratory and acid–base changes during pregnancy. Anesthesiology 1965;26:381.
17. Bonica JJ. Maternal respiratory changes during pregnancy and parturition. In: Marx G, ed. Parturition and perinatology. Clinical Anesthesia Series, Vol. 10. Philadelphia: FA Davis, 1973:9.

18. Archer GW, Marx GF. Arterial oxygenation during apnoea in parturient women. Br J Anaesth 1974;46:358.

19. Simpson KH, Stakes AF, Miller M. Pregnancy delays parcetamil absorption and gastric emptying in patients undergoing surgery. Br J Anaesth 1988;60:24.

20. Brock-Utne JG, Dow GB, Dimopoulos GE, Welman S, Downing JW, Moshal MG. Gastric and lower oesophageal sphincter (LOS) pressures in early pregnancy. Br J Anaesth 1981;53:381.

21. Palahniuk RJ, Shnider SM, Eger EI. Pregnancy decreases the requirement for inhaled anesthetic agents. Anesthesiology 1974;41:82.

22. Merryman W. "Progesterone" in human subjects. J Clin Endocrinol Metab 1954;14:1567.

23. Lyrenas S, Nyberg F, Linberg B, Terenius L. Cerebrospinal fluid activity of dynorphin-converting enzyme at term pregnancy. Obstet Gynecol 1988;72:54.

24. Butterworth JF IV, Walker FO, Lysak SZ. Pregnancy increases median nerve susceptibility to lidocaine. Anesthesiology 1990;72:962.

25. McDonald IA. Cervical cerclage. Clin Obstet Gynaecol 1980;7:461.

26. Floyd WS. Cervical dilatation in the mid-trimester of pregnancy. Obstet Gynecol 1961;18:380.

27. Schaffner F, Schanzer SN. Cervical dilatation in the early third trimester. Obstet Gynecol 1966;27:130.

28. Harger JH. Cervical cerclage: Patient selection, morbidity, and success rates. Clin Perinatol 1983;10:321.

29. Cousins L. Cervical incompetence, 1980: A time for reappraisal. Clin Obstet Gynecol 1980;23:467.

30. Lash AF, Lash FR. Habitual abortion: The incompetent internal os of the cervix. Am J Obstet Gynecol 1950;59:68.

31. Shirodkar VN. A method of operative treatment for habitual abortions in the second trimester of pregnancy. Antiseptic 1955;52:299.

32. McDonald IA. Suture of the cervix for inevitable miscarriage. J Obstet Gynaecol 1957;64:346.

33. Cuningham FG, MacDonald PC, Gant NF. Abortions. In: Williams Obstetrics, 18th ed. Norwalk, CT: Appleton & Lang, 1989:489.

34. Hefner JD, Patow WE, Ludwig JM. A new surgical procedure for the correction of the incompetent cervix during pregnancy. The Wurm procedure. Obstet Gynecol 1961;18:616.

35. Goodlin RC. Cervical incompetence, hourglass membranes, and amniocentesis. Obstet Gynecol 1979; 54:748.

36. McGahan JP, Hanson F. Prolapsing amniotic membranes: Detection, sonographic appearance, and management. J Perinatol 1987;7:204.

37. Benson RC, Durfee RB. Transabdominal cervicouterine cerclage during pregnancy for the treatment of cervical incompetency. Obstet Gynecol 1965;25:145.

38. Seppälä M, Vara P. Cervical cerclage in the treatment of incompetent cervix. Acta Obstet Gynecol Scand 1970;49:343.

39. Stromme WB, Wagner RM, Reed SC. Surgical management of the incompetent cervix. Obstet Gynecol 1960; 15:635.

40. Ayers JWT. Cervical incompetence: Diagnosis and management of preterm cervical effacement. In: Dilts PV, Sciarra JJ, eds. Gynecology and obstetrics, Vol. 2, chap. 46. Philadelphia: JB Lippincott, 1989:1.

41. Rush RW, Isaacs S, McPherson K, Jones L, Chalmers I, Grant A. A randomized controlled trial of cervical cerclage in women at high risk of spontaneous preterm delivery. Br J Obstet Gynaecol 1984;91:724.

42. Lazar P, Gueguen S, Dreyfus J, Renaud R, Pontonnier G, Papiernik E. Multicentred controlled trial of cervical cerclage in women at moderate risk of preterm delivery. Br J Obstet Gynaecol 1984;91:731.

43. Olatunbosun OA, Dyck F. Cervical cerclage operation for a dilated cervix. Obstet Gynecol 1981;57:166.

44. Scheerer LL, Lam F, Bartolucci L, Katz M. A new technique for reduction of prolapsed fetal membranes for emergency cervical cerclage. Obstet Gynecol 1989; 74:408.

45. Lauersen NH, Fuchs F. Experience with Shirodkar's operation and postoperative alcohol treatment. Acta Obstet Gynecol Scand 1973;52:77.

46. Mazze RI, Kallen B. Reproductive outcome after anesthesia and operation during pregnancy: A registry study of 5405 cases. Am J Obstet Gynecol 1989;161:1178.

47. Cunningham FG, MacDonald PC, Gant NF. Ectopic pregnancy. In: Williams Obstetrics. 18th ed. Norwalk, CT: Appleton & Lange, 1989:511.

48. Levine W, Diamond B. Surgical procedures during pregnancy. Am J Obstet Gynecol 1961;81:1046.

49. Stanhope CR. Management of the obstetric patient with malignancy. In: Dilts PV, Gerbie AB, Sciarra JJ, eds. Gynecology and obstetrics, Vol. 2, chap. 36. Philadelphia: JB Lippincott, 1989:1.

50. Bryan WM Jr. Surgical emergencies in pregnancies and the puerperium. Am J Obstet Gynecol 1955;70:1204.

51. McCorriston CC. Nonobstetrical abdominal surgery during pregnancy. Am J Obstet Gynecol 1963;86:593.

52. Liu PL, Warren TM, Ostheimer GW, Weiss JB, Liu LMP. Foetal monitoring in parturients undergoing surgery unrelated to pregnancy. Can Anaesth Soc J 1985;32:525.

53. Steinberg ES, Santos AC. Surgical anesthesia during pregnancy. Int Anesthesiol Clin 1990;28:58.

54. Paul RH, Suidan A, Yeh S-Y, Schifrin BS, Hon EH. Clinical fetal monitoring. VII. The evaluation and significance of intrapartum baseline FHR variability. Am J Obstet Gynecol 1975;123:206.

55. Petrie RH. Effect of drugs and anesthetics on fetal heart rate. Semin Perinatol 1978;2:147.

56. Ramanathan S. Anesthesia in nonobstetric situations. In: Obstetric anesthesia. Philadelphia: Lea & Febiger, 1988:296.

57. Duncan PG, Pope WDB, Cohen MM, Greer N. Fetal risks of anesthesia and surgery during pregnancy. Anesthesiology 1986;64:790.

58. Weingold AB, Palmer JJ, Stone ML. Cervical incompetency: A therapeutic enigma. Fertil Steril 1968; 19:244.

59. Peters WA III, Thiagarajah S, Harbert GM Jr. Cervical cerclage: Twenty years experience. South Med J 1979;72:933.

60. Engles ED. A retrospective study of regional vs general anesthesia for cervical cerclage and review of the literature. Anesthesiology 1989;71:A888.

61. Coutifaris B, Coutifaris C. Management of the incompetent uterine cervix: A modified technique. In: Hafez ESE, ed. Advances in reproductive health care: Spontaneous abortions. Boston: MTP Press Limited, 1984: 337.

62. McDonald IA. Cervical incompetence as a cause of spontaneous abortion. In: Bennett MJ, Edmonds DK, eds. Spontaneous and recurrent abortion. Oxford: Blackwell Scientific Publications, 1987:168.

63. Harger JH. Comparison of success and morbidity in cervical cerclage procedures. Obstet Gynecol 1980;56:543.

64. Ayers JWT, Peterson EP, Ansbacher R. Early therapy for the incompetent cervix in patients with habitual abortion. Fertil Steril 1982;38:177.

65. Cherry SH. The incompetent cervix. In: Cherry SH, Berkowitz RL, Kase NG, eds. Rovinsky and Guttmacher's medical, surgical, and gynecologic complications of pregnancy, 3rd ed. Baltimore: Williams & Wilkins, 1985:702.

66. Harger JH, Caritis SN. Preterm cervical dilation. In: Queenan JT, Gross EC, eds. Managing OB/GYN emergencies, 2nd ed. Oradell, NJ: Medical Economics Books, 1983:56.

67. Smith SG, Scragg WH. Premature cervical dilatation and the McDonald cerclage. Obstet Gynecol 1969;33:535.

68. Shnider SM, Webster G. Maternal and fetal hazards of surgery during pregnancy. Am J Obstet Gynecol 1965;92:891.

69. Brodsky JB, Cohen EN, Brown BW, Wu ML, Whitcher C. Surgery during pregnancy and fetal outcome. Am J Obstet Gynecol 1980;138:1165.

70. Cohen SE. Risk of abortion following general anesthesia for surgery during pregnancy: Anesthetic or surgical procedure? Anesthesiology 1986;65:706.

71. Egbert LD, Battit GE, Turndorf H, Beecher HK. The value of the preoperative visit by an anesthetist: A study of doctor patient rapport. JAMA 1963;185:553.

72. Levinson G, Shnider SM, deLorimier AA, Steffenson JL. Effects of maternal hyperventilation on uterine blood flow and fetal oxygenation and acid–base status. Anesthesiology 1974;40:340.

CHAPTER 11

Nongynecologic Surgery During Pregnancy

Jeffrey A. Weiss

Although the incidence of surgery unrelated to parturition in pregnant patients is low, it is not insignificant. The maternal and fetal morbidity related to these procedures may be profoundly influenced by anesthetic technique. Familiarity with the basic objectives involved in the care of these patients should optimize their outcome. This chapter focuses on the indications and anesthetic options for nongynecologic surgery in parturients. Chapter 1 examines the physiologic changes of pregnancy. Chapter 9 discusses the teratogenicity of anesthetics and related medications, and Chapter 10 considers gynecologic surgery in the gravid woman.

INCIDENCE

Current estimates of the incidence of nonobstetric surgery during pregnancy predominantly vary from 0.75% to 2.2%.[1-4] In the United States, approximately 50,000 women a year undergo surgery during gestation. Over the past 2 decades, the reported frequency of surgery has remained remarkably constant; however, the type of surgical procedures done has changed.

In the 1950s, the most common surgical conditions in the first and second trimesters, in descending order, were as follows:

1. Ovarian cysts
2. Acute appendicitis
3. Breast lesions
4. Laparotomy for missed diagnosis[5]

A recent study derived from three Swedish health care registries examined 720,000 pregnant patients for the years 1973 to 1981.[1] These women underwent 5045 operations (0.75% of all surgeries done during this time). The type of operation, reported by trimester, is shown in Table 11-1. Laparoscopy has become the most common operation in the first trimester, followed by abdominal, and genitourinary–gynecologic procedures. In the second trimester, intra-abdominal operations, followed by genitourinary–gynecologic and endoscopic procedures, become most common. These changes are not surprising considering the recent advent of laparoscopic procedures. This report does not state the indications for the laparoscopies, but probably the surgical conditions have not changed, just the surgical approach to their treatment. Surgeons undoubtedly will continue to do more laparoscopies and

Table 11-1

Type of Operation by Trimester

TYPE OF OPERATION	FIRST TRIMESTER (%)	SECOND TRIMESTER (%)	THIRD TRIMESTER (%)
Central nervous system	6.7	5.4	5.6
Eye–ear–nose–throat	7.6	6.4	9.5
Heart–lung	0.7	0.8	0.6
Abdominal	19.9	30.1	22.6
Genitourinary–gynecologic	10.6	23.3	24.3
Laparoscopy	34.1	1.5	5.6
Orthopedic	8.9	9.3	13.7
Endoscopy	3.6	11.0	8.6
Skin	3.8	3.2	4.1
Miscellaneous	4.0	4.2	5.5

(Data from Mazze RI, Källén B. Reproductive outcome after anesthesia and operation during pregnancy: A registry study of 5405 cases. Am J Obstet Gynecol 1989;161:1178)

fewer open laparotomies as the list of procedures done with the laparoscope continues to expand.

RISK AND OUTCOME

The risks presented by these operations, both surgical and anesthetic, can be broadly divided into maternal and fetal categories. This division is somewhat artificial, because both maternal and fetal risks are interrelated; however, this approach allows us to state clearly the following factors over which we have the most control.

- Timely diagnosis and appropriate treatment of the surgical condition
- Effective treatment of coexisting diseases
- Teratogenicity of administered drugs
- Changes in maternal homeostasis and their effects on the uteroplacental unit
- Potential for premature labor and fetal wastage

Multiple studies have attempted to assess the fetal risk of anesthesia and surgery during pregnancy. Four studies address the most clinically relevant points.[1–3,6] These reports have several common findings, which follow:

- There is an increased risk of fetal morbidity when an operation is done during pregnancy. The causes of this increased risk remain unclear.
- There is no association between anesthetic exposure and the incidence of congenital malformation.

In 1965, Shnider and Webster[3] reported a series of 9073 pregnant patients who delivered at their institution. Of these, 147 had operations during pregnancy (1.6%). In 8.8% of the women undergoing surgery, premature labor followed. Most women developing premature labor had surgery for an incompetent cervical os (*i.e.,* Shirodkar procedure). These operations also were associated with a high (33%) perinatal mortality rate. No anesthetic agent or technique correlated with a higher incidence of premature delivery after operation.

In 1980, Brodsky *et al*[2] reported a series of 12,929 pregnancies compiled from questionnaires sent to male dentists and female dental assistants. Of those who responded, 287 had operations requiring anesthesia during pregnancy. The patients undergoing anesthesia for surgery had a higher rate of fetal loss (8.0% first trimester, 6.9% second trimester) than the nonoperated control group (5.1% first trimester, 1.4% second trimester.) There were no differences between the two groups for incidence of congenital abnormalities

Another large study examined health insurance records from the entire province of Manitoba, Canada.[6] Here, 2565 patients underwent surgery during pregnancy. These women were matched with control patients having similar demographic characteristics. Surgery during both the first and second trimesters correlated with a higher incidence of spontaneous abortion but not congenital anomalies. Women who received general anesthesia appeared to have a higher incidence of abortion than their matched, nonanesthetized controls (Fig. 11-1). However, too few women had their operations under regional or local anesthesia to

Figure 11–1. Abortions by anesthetic type. Number of cases is the number of discordant pairs in which one member (either operated or nonoperated) had an abortion, and the matched subject did not. Stratification of women undergoing operative procedures, regardless of the procedure performed, revealed a significantly increased risk of abortion ($P \leq 0.05$) in those receiving general anesthesia when compared to their paired controls. A similar effect was not seen in those receiving no anesthetic (trauma), major regional, or local anesthetics for their procedures. (After Duncan PG, Pope WDB, Cohen MM, Greer N. Fetal risk of anesthesia and surgery during pregnancy. Anesthesiology 1986:64;790)

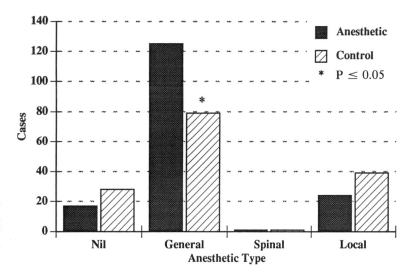

allow a valid comparison. The data appear to support the contentions of earlier studies that the surgical procedure itself most affects the risk for subsequent abortion (Fig. 11-2).

Most recently, data from three Swedish health care registries were analyzed with respect to reproductive outcomes after nonobstetric operations during pregnancy.[1] In a population of 720,000 parturients, 5405 operations were reported (0.75%). The incidence of congenital malformations was not increased in the group undergoing operation. However, surgery correlated with a significant increase in the incidence of very-low-and low-birth-weight infants. In addition, women undergoing surgery were more likely to deliver a live infant who died within 168 hours of birth (Fig.

11-3). None of these adverse outcomes could be associated with either a specific type of anesthesia or a specific category of operation. Although the study design did not allow the determination of the cause of the adverse outcomes, the authors concluded that "it is likely that the illness that necessitated the surgery played a significant role in determining the results."

GENERAL RECOMMENDATIONS

All elective surgical procedures should be postponed until after delivery. As a corollary, be certain that any woman of reproductive age about to receive an elective anesthetic is not pregnant. During pregnancy, surgery

Figure 11–2. Abortions by surgical site (general anesthetics). Number of cases is the number of discordant pairs in which one member (either operated or nonoperated) had an abortion and the matched subject did not. Stratification of women exposed to general anesthesia by operative site revealed a significantly increased risk ($P \leq 0.05$) compared with control subject when obstetric/gynecologic and "other" procedures were examined. The risk for abdominal surgery, while showing the same trend, was not statistically significant. (After Duncan PG, Pope WDB, Cohen MM, Greer N. Fetal risk of anesthesia and surgery during pregnancy. Anesthesiology 1986:64;790)

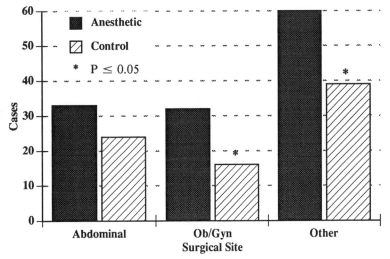

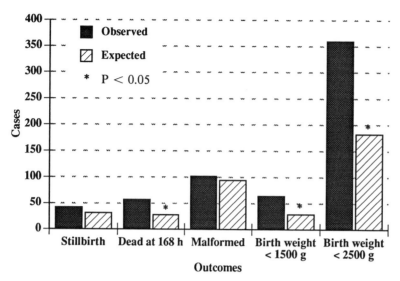

Figure 11–3. Total number of observed and expected adverse outcomes among 5405 women having nonobstetric operations during pregnancy. Incidences of low-birth-weight infants and death within 168 hours of birth were significantly increased. (Data from Mazze RI, Källén B. Reproductive outcome after anesthesia and operation during pregnancy: A registry study of 5405 cases. Am J Obstet Gynecol 1989;161:1178)

should only be entertained when the medical or surgical condition threatens maternal or fetal well-being. Because no anesthetic technique correlates with better outcome, the type of anesthesia administered should be dictated by the following factors:

- The physical and mental condition of the patient
- The extent of the planned procedure
- The clinical experience of the anesthesiologist

The quality, not the type, of anesthetic will predominantly affect outcome. The anesthesiologist should perform the technique with which he or she is most proficient and comfortable.

The single most important consideration in the treatment of these patients is maternal safety.[7-9] Take the steps described in the following sections to help ensure this goal.

Preoperative Treatment

As with all patients, do a thorough preoperative history and physical examination. This is an excellent time to establish a good rapport with the patient and alleviate maternal anxiety and minimize apprehension. Remember, the best preoperative anxiolytic is a good anesthesiologist–patient relationship. If further pharmacologic premedication is desired, no commonly used premedicant has been proven to be teratogenic in humans. I prefer to minimize maternal exposure to benzodiazepines and usually use barbiturates because of their proven safety record. Preoperative pain may be treated as necessary, most commonly with aceta-

minophen or narcotic analgesics. Avoid acetylsalicylic acid and nonsteroidal anti-inflammatory agents. They may stimulate in utero closure of the ductus arteriosus via inhibition of prostaglandin synthesis.[10-13] Glycopyrrolate, a quaternary ammonium compound with limited placental transfer, is a good choice as an anticholinergic–antisialagogue.

Whenever possible, obtain obstetric consultation before the surgical procedure. Complications such as preterm labor may require obstetric tocolytic intervention to avoid delivery of a preterm or nonviable fetus.

Gastric Contents

All parturients are at high risk for regurgitation and aspiration of gastric contents. Aspiration of gastric contents during anesthesia is a common cause of maternal anesthetic death.[14-18] Prophylactic treatment of gastric contents and rapid sequence induction with cricoid pressure may limit the risk and severity of maternal aspiration. Nonparticulate antacids, H_2-receptor blockers, and metoclopramide may be helpful in this respect.[19-26] Maintain cricoid pressure throughout the induction until proper placement of the endotracheal tube is confirmed.

Position

Beginning in the second trimester, no pregnant patient should undergo anesthesia in the supine position. Always maintain left uterine displacement to prevent aortocaval compression. This precaution applies to both regional or general anesthesia. Any anesthetic changes autonomic tone, venous return, and blood pressure. Left uterine displacement should aid in minimizing uterine hypoperfusion and fetal asphyxia.

Intravascular Volume Status

Attempt to maintain a normal or slightly elevated intravascular volume in these patients. Those patients who are to undergo major conduction blockade (*i.e.,* spinal or epidural) should receive a preinduction fluid load of at least 1 L of crystalloid solution. This preload will decrease the incidence of hypotension and may reduce the need for vasopressor support of systemic blood pressure.

Fetal Monitoring

Monitoring of fetal heart rate patterns by directional Doppler becomes practical at approximately the 16th week of gestation; however, to be clinically useful, this monitoring must fulfill the following conditions:

- Equipment and personnel must be available to record and interpret the heart rate patterns accurately.
- The transducer must not encroach on the surgical field.
- Therapeutic intervention should be possible if abnormalities arise.

Doppler monitoring of fetal heart rate patterns partially, although not completely, fulfills these criteria. It can prove extremely useful in parturients undergoing surgery unrelated to pregnancy.[27–30]

Monitoring of uterine tone intraoperatively also is possible through use of an external tocodynamometer once the fundus reaches the height of the umbilicus. This monitor may aid in the early diagnosis of uterine irritability. An external tocodynamometer may be difficult to place and maintain during surgery, but it should always be used in the immediate postoperative period. Should uterine contractions be detected, the obstetrician may elect to begin pharmacologic tocolysis. Prompt treatment of preterm labor may prevent premature delivery and fetal wastage.

Induction of General Anesthesia

To both assure maternal safety and prevent intrauterine fetal asphyxia, the foremost concern during induction of general anesthesia is maternal oxygenation. Do a

rapid sequence intravenous induction of anesthesia with cricoid pressure if the patient has normal airway anatomy and there is no reason to suspect difficulties with endotracheal intubation via direct laryngoscopy. However, if preoperative assessment suggests the potential for a difficult intubation, change the plan accordingly (see Chap. 32). I often opt to intubate the patient awake with a combination of intravenous sedation and topical anesthesia of the upper airway. Either direct laryngoscopy or fiberoptic bronchoscopy can guide attempts at intubation.[31] In the event that both ventilation and intubation prove impossible, rapid needle cricothyroidotomy will allow maternal oxygenation with a jet ventilator.[32]

CONSIDERATIONS FOR SPECIALIZED PROCEDURES

Cardiac Surgery

Reports in the medical literature of cardiac surgery during pregnancy are becoming more frequent. Although there are no large studies of cardiac surgery in parturients, there are many case reports and case series from which we may gain important clinical information.[33–47] From the reported cases, it appears that pregnancy does not increase maternal perioperative mortality. Early reports indicated a high fetal mortality rate, often 40% to 50%, whereas more recent reports suggest some improvement.

A detailed discussion of anesthetic considerations for cardiac surgery is beyond the scope of this chapter. Some points, however, do deserve mention because they relate to the pregnant patient.

Cardiopulmonary Bypass

The most appropriate approach to cardiopulmonary bypass in the parturient is unclear. Currently, unless circulatory arrest is required, most centers use full-flow bypass with moderate systemic hypothermia. Fetal heart rate will decrease during hypothermia, paralleling the change in maternal heart rate (Fig. 11-4).[48] Changes in fetal heart rate and rhythm (fetal bradycardia, loss of beat-to-beat variability, and, rarely, a sinusoidal heart rate pattern) commonly occur during this method of extracorporeal circulation.[49–52] These changes in heart rate are probably multifactorial in origin.

With the arrival of retrograde delivery of cardioplegia via the coronary sinus, more centers are doing valve replacement and aortocoronary bypass grafting under systemic normothermia with con-

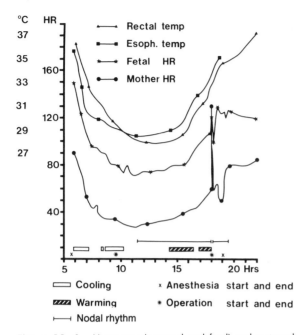

Figure 11-4. Heart rate (maternal and fetal) and maternal temperature (esophageal and rectal) during anesthesia with hypothermia. The time when cooling and warming of the mother was performed and the time during which the mother had nodal rhythm are indicated. (The hours indicate the time of the day.) (Stånge K, Halldin M. Hypothermia in pregnancy. Anesthesiology 1983;58:460)

tinuous delivery of normothermic cardioplegia.[53,54] To date, no reports of this technique in parturients have appeared in the literature; however, I believe this approach holds promise because it will not subject the fetus to hypothermia. Possible hazards of this technique may include maternal and fetal hyperglycemia, hyperkalemia, and hyponatremia. In addition, hypothermia has not proved uniformly detrimental to the fetus. Indeed, hypothermia may well protect the fetus by decreasing oxygen demand.

To limit the possible detrimental fetal effects of cardiopulmonary bypass and hypothermia, use cardiopulmonary bypass pump flows of at least 2.0 L/min/m² body surface area, if possible. To maintain placental perfusion, keep mean systemic blood pressure above 60 mm Hg, especially during normothermic periods.

Fetal Monitoring

Monitor fetal heart rate during cardiac operations. The appearance of unexpected abnormal fetal heart rate patterns should prompt a rapid search for any possible correctable causes. This includes the possibility of uterine irritability and contractions, which should be treated aggressively with tocolytics when present. More importantly, however, immediately correct any severe maternal impairment, even if the therapy may cause fetal morbidity.[55]

Vasopressors and Inotropes

Use vasopressors and inotropes during cardiac surgery in parturients to maintain maternal physiologic parameters at their normal pregnant level. Taking this step should help prevent fetal asphyxia. Pregnancy imposes some unique considerations when choosing a vasopressor or inotrope.

Ephedrine. This mixed alpha- and beta-agonist has a salutary effect on uterine blood flow when given during maternal hypotension.[56,57] Ephedrine has a proven maternal and fetal safety record, and it is my first choice as a therapeutic agent for the hypotensive gravida.

Epinephrine. The cardiovascular effects of epinephrine are similar to those of ephedrine, but they are more pronounced and of shorter duration.[58] In the parturient, however, epinephrine may markedly impair uterine blood flow.[59] Its effects on uterine contractility are dose-dependent. At low doses, it decreases uterine contractility, whereas at high doses, alpha-agonist effects prevail, stimulating uterine contractility.[60]

Norepinephrine. Like epinephrine, norepinephrine may profoundly decrease uterine blood flow despite markedly elevating maternal arterial pressure.[59,61] It also increases uterine tonus and frequency and intensity of uterine contractions.[62]

Dopamine. The effects of dopamine on uterine blood flow have differed in various reports.[63–65] The response of the uterine vasculature to dopamine likely depends on the dose administered. At low infusion rates, venoconstriction predominates.[66] At high doses, where vasoconstriction predominates, dopamine acts very much like norepinephrine.[67]

Dobutamine. As a synthetic catecholamine deriving its structure from isoproterenol, dobutamine acts directly on the beta-adrenergic receptor.[68] Although it has weak alpha properties, beta₂ effects predominate. For these reasons, dobutamine comes very close to being a "pure" inotrope. Although its use in pregnant patients has been extremely limited, it is intellectually attractive for that clinical purpose.

Amrinone. A member of a new class of drugs that acts primarily by inhibition of fraction III of the enzyme phosphodiesterase, amrinone is both a potent inotrope and vasodilator.[69] It has gained widespread acceptance in cardiac surgery, albeit primarily as a second-line drug for weaning from cardiopulmonary bypass. Although not yet widely tested in pregnant animal models, preliminary work shows that amrinone does not decrease uterine blood flow at clinically useful doses.[70] A recent case reported the clinical utility of amrinone in the gravid patient.[71] I feel this drug is an extremely promising agent for the parturient requiring inotropic support.

Phenylephrine. Considered a pure alpha-receptor agonist, phenylephrine elevates both arterial and venous tone.[72,73] In hypotensive ewes, phenylephrine returns maternal arterial pressure to normal, but it does not increase uterine blood flow.[74] In clinical studies, phenylephrine can effectively correct maternal hypotension associated with major conduction blockade without inciting fetal compromise.[75,76]

Sodium Nitroprusside. A balanced vasodilator with both rapid onset and short duration of clinical effects, nitroprusside is an extremely effective drug. Experienced personnel can easily titrate nitroprusside to the desired degree of vasodilation. In gravid ewes, it can diminish uterine blood flow and, in high doses, produce fetal cyanide toxicity.[77,78] Its clinical use in gravid humans has been reported without adverse consequences.[79-81] To prevent maternal or fetal cyanide toxicity, stop the drug if tachyphylaxis develops. Do not give more than 0.5 mg/kg/h.

Nitroglycerin. A venodilator, acting at the level of venules, nitroglycerin increases venous capacitance and decreases cardiac filling.[58] Its primary use is in the treatment of myocardial ischemia, but it also may be used to treat hypertension and to induce deliberate hypotension. In the parturient, nitroglycerin avoids some disadvantages of nitroprusside. There is no risk of cyanide toxicity. It is less potent and less likely to cause precipitous hypotension. Tachyphylaxis does not occur. It seems benign to the fetus.[82] Provided systemic normotension is maintained, nitroglycerin does not impair uterine perfusion.[83] Its ease of use clinically and its apparent lack of adverse side effects make nitroglycerin my vasodilator of choice in the pregnant patient.

NEUROSURGICAL PROCEDURES

Neurosurgical disorders during pregnancy produce a significant percentage of maternal and fetal deaths. Available estimates suggest that intracranial hemorrhage is responsible for 5% to 12% of maternal deaths during pregnancy.[84-87] Approximately 75% of these cases are caused by aneurysm, whereas arteriovenous malformation is liable for the remainder of cases.[88] Although the surgery for aneurysmal intracranial hemorrhage during pregnancy is well accepted,[89-95] the management of intracranial hemorrhage due to arteriovenous malformation is less clear.[88] For arteriovenous malformation, management decisions are based on neurosurgical, not obstetric, considerations.

The incidence of primary intracranial tumors is no different in pregnant and nonpregnant patients;[96] however, pregnancy may worsen the symptoms of many of these tumors.[97-102] Neurosurgical considerations again determine appropriate management.

Other neurosurgical conditions (*e.g.,* head trauma, spinal cord injury, peripheral neuropathies, lumbar disk disease, hydrocephalus, pseudotumor cerebri) will present less commonly. The management of these conditions should be based on the clinical presentation.

Anesthetic management of the parturient during neurosurgery will vary with the primary pathology and clinical severity. As always, meticulous attention to preservation of maternal and fetal homeostasis is paramount. Control of the maternal airway and maintenance of maternal ventilation and oxygenation are the primary concerns. Attempt fetal monitoring whenever possible.

Hyperventilation

Controlled hyperventilation is commonly used in the treatment of increased intracranial pressure. Hypocarbia decreases cerebral blood flow and intracranial blood volume. In the gravid patient, however, hyperventilation may do the following:

- Decrease uterine blood flow.
- Impair placental oxygen transfer by shift of the oxyhemoglobin dissociation curve.
- Decrease fetal oxygen tension.

These effects may put the fetus at risk. Most fetuses, however, will tolerate mild to moderate maternal hypocapnia. Fetal heart rate monitoring may aid in diagnosis of fetal compromise due to excessive maternal hyperventilation.

Hypothermia

Hypothermia does not seem to harm the fetus (Fig. 11-4). As with all other therapeutic options, it should only be used when its possible benefits outweigh its risks.

Deliberate Hypotension

In the past, neurosurgeons frequently requested deliberate hypotension to limit the risk of cerebral hemorrhage from vascular lesions. Although its use is diminishing, deliberate hypotension during gestation is safe for the mother,[92,95,103,104] but if uterine perfusion falls, hypotension can harm the fetus.[105,106] Use this technique only when absolutely necessary. I currently choose isoflurane as a primary agent for induction of deliberate hypotension. If needed, I add small doses of sodium nitroprusside. This combination yields an easily achieved and predictable hypotensive effect. It avoids excessively high doses of either the halogenated agent or nitroprusside.

Osmotic Diuretics

The most commonly used osmotic diuretic today is mannitol. Because of its ability to lower cerebral water content, it can help control elevated intracranial pressure and cerebral edema. Osmotic diuretics cross the placenta and increase fetal plasma osmolarity. As a result, fetal dehydration may result from a net flow of water to the mother.[107,108] Use these agents when absolutely necessary for maternal safety.

PHEOCHROMOCYTOMA

Pheochromocytomas are rare, usually benign, functionally active catecholamine-secreting tumors. They have their origin in chromaffin tissue and are most often located in the adrenal medulla, but they may occur elsewhere.[109-111] Pheochromocytomas that arise during pregnancy are potentially life-threatening to both mother and fetus. A review of 89 cases of pheochromocytoma in pregnancy published in 1971 revealed a maternal mortality rate of 18% and a fetal mortality rate of 50%.[112] If the diagnosis is first made at delivery, both maternal and fetal mortality were above 50%. In 1982, with the use of both alpha- and beta-adrenergic blocking agents, maternal and fetal mortality rates remained high (10.6% and 46%, respectively).[113]

In the past, suspected pheochromocytoma was diagnosed using provocative tests (*e.g.,* the regitine test). Today, measurement of urinary catecholamines and their metabolites is the most common diagnostic test. These assays are more sensitive and less dangerous than the provocative tests.[114,115] Another, recently added, analysis is the clonidine suppression test.[116-118]

As anesthesiologists, most of us will become involved in the care of these patients once a definitive diagnosis has been made. At that point, appropriate management requires input from all involved services. Controversy remains about the optimal management of these patients. Most authorities now recommend surgical intervention in the first two trimesters and medical management in the third trimester until fetal maturity. Then combined cesarean section and tumor removal should occur.[119-121]

The goals of medical management are control of hypertension and normalization of intravascular volume. Secondarily, once blood pressure is controlled, elevated heart rate may need treatment. Control of hypertension is possible with many agents. The most widely accepted method is the use of the alpha-blocker phenoxybenzamine.[110,122,123] Another approach involves inhibiting catecholamine synthesis with alpha-methyltyrosine.[124-128] This drug treats the primary pathology rather than its symptoms. Maternal sedation is the most common side effect of alpha-methyltyrosine therapy. Other reported regimens include the use of magnesium sulfate,[129-131] prazosin,[132] and (nicardipine intraoperatively).[133]

Assure adequate depth of anesthesia before endotracheal intubation to avoid catecholamine release. Be prepared to control intraoperative hypertension and maintain normovolemia at all times. Hypotension may occur following ligation of the venous drainage of the tumor. This event is most effectively treated with judicious intravascular volume expansion. Ventricular arrhythmias are not uncommon, and are usually treated effectively with lidocaine.

REFERENCES

1. Mazze RI, Källén B. Reproductive outcome after anesthesia and operation during pregnancy: A registry study of 5405 cases. Am J Obstet Gynecol 1989;161:1178.
2. Brodsky JB, Cohen EN, Brown BW, et al. Surgery during pregnancy and fetal outcome. Am J Obstet Gynecol 1980;138:1165.
3. Shnider SM, Webster GM. Maternal and fetal hazards of surgery during pregnancy. Am J Obstet Gynecol 1965;92:891.
4. Smith BE. Fetal prognosis after anesthesia during gestation. Anesth Analg 1963;42:521.
5. Levine W, Diamond B. Surgical procedures during pregnancy. Am J Obstet Gynecol 1961;81:1046.
6. Duncan PG, Pope WDB, Cohen MM, Greer N. Fetal

risk of anesthesia and surgery during pregnancy. Anesthesiology 1986;64:790.

7. Steinberg ES, Santos AC. Surgical anesthesia during pregnancy. Int Anesth Clin 1990;28:58.

8. James FM III. Anesthesia for nonobstetric surgery during pregnancy. Clin Obstet Gynecol 1987;30:621.

9. Shelley WC. Anesthetic considerations for nonobstetric surgery. Clin Perinatol 1982;9:135.

10. Coceani F, Olley PM. The response of the ductus arteriosus to prostaglandins. Can J Physiol Pharmacol 1973;51:220.

11. Starling MB, Elliott RB. The effects of prostaglandins, prostaglandin inhibitors, and oxygen on the closure of the ductus arteriosus, pulmonary arteries, and umbilical vessels in vitro. Prostaglandins 1974;8:187.

12. Heymann MA, Rudolph AM. Effects of acetylsalicylic acid on the ductus arteriosus and circulation in fetal lambs in utero. Circ Res 1976;38:418.

13. Arcilla RA, Thilenius OG, Ranniger K. Congestive heart failure from suspected ductal closure in utero. J Pediatr 1969;75:74.

14. Tompkinson J, Turnbull A, Robson G. Report on confidential inquiries into maternal deaths in England and Wales (1973–1975). Her Majesty's Stationary Office, London 1982:79.

15. Cohen SE. Aspiration syndromes in pregnancy. Anesthesiology 1979;5:375.

16. Moir D. Anaesthesia and maternal death. Scott Med J 1979;24:187.

17. Merrill RB, Hingson RA. Studies of the incidence of maternal mortality from the aspiration of vomitus during anesthesia occuring in major obstetric hospitals in the United States. Anesth Analg 1951;30:121.

18. Phillips OC, Frazier TM, Davis GH, et al. The role of anesthesia in obstetric mortality. Anesth Analg 1961;40:557.

19. Stock JGL, Sutherland AD. The role of H$_2$-receptor antagonist premedication in pregnant day care patients. Can Anaesth Soc J 1985;32:463.

20. Lahiri SK, Thomas TA, Hodgson RMH. Single-dose antacid therapy for the prevention of Mendelson's syndrome. Br J Anaesth 1973;45:1143.

21. Gibbs CP, Hempling RE, Wynne JW, et al. Antacid pulmonary aspiration. Anesthesiology 1979;51:S290.

22. Gibbs CP, Sophr L, Schmidt D. The effectiveness of sodium citrate as an antacid. Anesthesiology 1982;57:44.

23. Manchikanti L, Kraus JW, Edds SP. Cimetidine and related drugs in anesthesia. Anesth Analg 1982;61:595.

24. Hodgkinson R, Glassenberg R, Joyce TH III, et al. Comparison of cimetidine (Tagamet) with acidity before elective cesarian section. Anesthesiology 1983;59:86.

25. Wyner MB, Cohen SE. Gastric volume in early pregnancy. Anesthesiology 1982;57:209.

26. Cohen SC, Barrier G. Does metoclopramide decrease gastric volume in cesarian section patients? Anesthesiology 1983;59:A403.

27. Liu PL, Warren TM, Ostheimer GW, et al. Foetal monitoring in parturients undergoing surgery unrelated to pregnancy. Can Anaesth Soc J 1985;32:525.

28. Biehl DR. Foetal monitoring during surgery unrelated to pregnancy. Can Anaesth Soc J 1985;32:455.

29. Katz JD, Hook R, Barash PG. Fetal heart rate monitoring in pregnant patients undergoing surgery. Am J Obstet Gynecol 1976;125:267.

30. Douglas MJ. Foetal monitoring during general surgery: A case report. Can Anaesth Soc J 1979;26:220.

31. Benumof JL. Management of the difficult adult airway. Anesthesiology 1991;75:1087.

32. Benumof JL, Scheller MS. The importance of transtracheal jet ventilation in the management of the difficult airway. Anesthesiology 1989;71:769.

33. Strickland RA, Oliver WC, Chantigian RC, et al. Anesthesia, cardiopulmonary bypass and the pregnant patient. Mayo Clin Proc 1991;66:411.

34. Izquierdo LA, Kushnir O, Knieriem K, et al. Effect of mitral valve prosthetic surgery on the outcome of a growth retarded fetus: A case report. Obstet Gynecol 1990;163:584.

35. Conroy JM, Bailey MK, Hollon MF, et al. Anesthesia for open heart surgery in the pregnant patient. South Med J 1989;82:492.

36. Korsten HHM, Van Zundert AAJ, Mooij PNM, et al. Emergency aortic valve replacement in the 24th week of pregnancy. Acta Anaesth Belg 1989;40:201.

37. Vosa C, Renzulli A, Sante P, Micheletti E. Cardiac valve replacement during pregnancy. Report of two cases. Ital J Surg Sci 1988;18:175.

38. Mora CT, Grunewald KE. Reoperative aortic and mitral prosthetic valve replacement in the third trimester of pregnancy. J Cardiothorac Anesth 1987;1:313.

39. Cola LM, Lavin JP. Pregnancy complicated by Marfan's syndrome with aortic arch dissection, subsequent aortic ardch replacement and triple coronary artery bypass grafts. J Reprod Med 1985;30:685.

40. El-Maraghy M, Senna IA, El-Tehewy F, Bassiouni M, Ayoub A, El-Sayed H. Mitral valvotomy in pregnancy. Am J Obstet Gynecol 1983;145:708.

41. Becker RM. Intracardiac surgery in pregnant women. Ann Thorac Surg 1983;36:453.

42. Eilen B, Kaiser IH, Becker RM, et al. Aortic valve replacement in the third trimester of pregnancy: Case report and review of the literature. Obstet Gynecol 1981;57:119.

43. Estefanous FG, Buckley S. Management of anesthesia for open heart surgery during pregnancy. Cleve Clin Q 1976;43:121.

44. Zitnik RS, Brandenberg RO, Sheldon R, Wallace RB. Pregnancy and open-heart surgery. Circulation 1969;39:I257.

45. Harthorne JW, Buckley MJ, Grover JW, Austen WG. Valve replacement during pregnancy. Ann Intern Med 1967;67:1032.

46. Jacobs WM, Cooley D, Goen GP. Cardiac surgery with extracorporeal circulation during pregnancy. Obstet Gynecol 1965;25:167.

47. Leyse R, Ofstun M, Dillard DH, Merendino KA. Congenital aortic stenosis in pregnancy, corrected by extracorporeal circulation: Offering a viable male infant at term but with anomalies eventuating in his death at four months of age—report of a case. JAMA 1961;176:1009.

48. Stånge K, Halldin M. Hypothermia in pregnancy. Anesthesiology 1983;58:460.

49. Lamb MP, Ross K, Johnstone AM, Manners JM. Fetal heart monitoring during open heart surgery. Br J Obstet Gynaecol 1964;23:209.

50. Trimakas AP, Maxwell KD, Berkay S, et al. Fetal monitoring during cardiopulmonary bypass for removal of a left atrial myxoma during pregnancy. John Hopkins Med J 1979;144:156.

51. Bahary CM, Ninio A, Gorodesky IG, Neri A. Tococardiography in pregnancy during extracorporeal bypass for mitral valve replacement. Isr J Med Sci 1980;16:395.

52. Burke AB, Hur D, Bolan JC, et al. Sinusoidal fetal heart rate pattern during cardiopulmonary bypass. Am J Obstet Gynecol 1990;163:17.

53. Salerno TA, Houck JP, Barrozo CAM, et al. Retrograde continuous warm blood cardioplegia: A new concept in myocardial protection. Ann Thorac Surg 1991;51:245.

54. Engelman RM. Retrograde continuous warm blood cardioplegia. Ann Thorac Surg 1991;51:180.

55. Mangano DT. Anesthesia for the pregnant cardiac patient. In: Shnider SM, Levinson G, eds. Anesthesia for obstetrics. 2nd ed. Baltimore: Williams & Wilkins, 1984:348.

56. Conklin KA, Murad SHN. Pharmacology of drugs in obstetric anesthesia. Semin Anesth 1982;1:83.

57. James FM III, Greiss FC, Kemp RA. An evaluation of vasopressor therapy for maternal hypotension during spinal anesthesia. Anesthesiology 1970;33:25.

58. Durrett LR, Lawson NW. Autonomic nervous system physiology and pharmacology. In: Barash PG, Cullen BF, Stoelting RK, eds. Clinical anesthesia. Philadelphia: JB Lippincott, 1989:165.

59. Greiss FC, Crandell DL. The uterine vascular bed: Adrenergic receptors. Obstet Gynecol 1964;23:209.

60. Kaiser IH, Harris JS. The effect of adrenalin on the pregnant human uterus. Am J Obstet Gynecol 1950;59:775.

61. Greiss FC, Crandell DL. Therapy for hypotension induced by spinal anesthesia during pregnancy. JAMA 1965;191:793.

62. Cibils LA, Pose SV, Zuspan FP. Effect of 1-norepinephrine infusion on uterine contractility and the cardiovascular system. Am J Obstet Gynecol 1962;84:307.

63. Blanchard K, Dandavino A, Nuwayhid B, et al. Systemic and uterine hemodynamic responses to dopamine in pregnant and nonpregnant sheep. Am J Obstet Gynecol 1978;130:669.

64. Rolbin SH, Levinson G, Shnider SM, et al. Dopamine treatment of spinal hypotension decreases uterine blood flow in the pregnant ewe. Anesthesiology 1979;51:36.

65. Clark RB, Brunner JA. Dopamine as a vasopressor for the treatment of spinal hypotension during cesarian section. Anesthesiology 1980;53:514.

66. Marino RJ, Romagnoli A, Keats A. Selective venoconstriction by dopamine by dopamine in comparison with isoproterenol and phenylephrine. Anesthesiology 1975;43:570.

67. Rajfer SI, Goldberg LI. Sympathetic amines in the treatment of shock. In: Shoemaker WC, Thompson WL, Holbrook RP, eds: Textbook of critical care. Philadelphia: WB Saunders, 1984:490.

68. Leier CV, Unverferth DV. Dobutamine. Ann Intern Med 1983;99:490.

69. LeJemtel T, Keun E, Sonneblick E, et al. Amrinone: A new nonglycosidic, nonadrenergic cardiotonic agent effective in the treatment of intractable cardiac failure in man. Circulation 1979;59;1098.

70. Fishburne JI, Dormer KJ, Payne GG, et al. Effects of amrinone and dopamine on uterine blood flow and vascular responses in the gravid baboon. Am J Obstet Gynecol 1988;158:829.

71. Jelsma RD, Bhatia RK, Ganguly S. Use of intravenous amrinone in the short-term management of refractory heart failure in pregnancy. Obstet Gynecol 1992;78:935.

72. Marino RJ, Romagnoli A, Keats A. Selective venoconstriction by dopamine by dopamine in comparison with isoproterenol and phenylephrine. Anesthesiology 1975;43:570.

73. Schmid PG, Eckstein JW, Abboud FM. Comparison of the effects of several sympathomimetic amines on resistance and capacitance vessels in the forearm of man. Circulation 1966;34:209.

74. Levinson G, Shnider SM. Vasopressors in obstetrics. In: Zauder HL, ed. Clinical anesthesia. Philadelphia: FA Davis, 1973:77.

75. Moran DH, Perillo M, LaPorte RF. Phenylephrine in the prevention of hypotension following spinal anesthesia for cesarian delivery. J Clin Anesth 1991;3:301.

76. Ramanathan S, Grant GJ. Vasopressor therapy for hypotension due to epidural anesthesia for cesarian section. Acta Anesth Scand 1988;32:559.

77. Ring G, Krames E, Shnider SM, et al. Comparison of nitroprusside and hydralazine in hypertensive pregnant ewes. Obstet Gynecol 1977;51:598.

78. Naulty J, Cefalo RC, Lewis PE. Fetal toxicity of nitroprusside in the pregnant ewe. Am J Obstet Gynecol 1981;139:708.

79. Willoughby JS. Sodium nitroprusside, pregnancy, and multiple intracranial aneuryms. Anaesth Intensive Care 1984;12:358.

80. Rigg D, McDonogh A. Use of sodium nitroprusside for deliberate hypotension during pregnancy. Br J Anaesth 1981;53:985.

81. Donchin Y, Amirav B, Saher A, et al. Sodium nitroprus-

side for aneurysm surgery in pregnancy. Br J Anaesth 1978;50:849.

82. Hood DD, Dewan DM, James FM III, et al. The use of nitroglycerin in preventing the hypertensive response to tracheal intubation in severe preeclamptics. Anesthesiology 1985;63:329.

83. Wheeler AS, James FM III, Meis PJ, et al. Effects of nitroglycerin and nitroprusside on the uterine vasculature in gravid ewes. Anesthesiology 1980;52:390.

84. Barno A, Freeman DW. Maternal deaths due to spontaneous subarachnoid hemorrhage. Am J Obstet Gynecol 1976;125:384.

85. Hunt HR, Schifrin BS, Suzuli K. Ruptured berry aneurysms and pregnancy. Obstet Gynecol 1974;43:327.

86. Miller HJ, Hinckley CM. Berry aneurysms in pregnancy: A ten-year report. South Med J 1970;63:279.

87. Barnes JE, Abbott KH. Cerebral complications incurred during pregnancy and the puerperium. Am J Obstet Gynecol 1961;82:192.

88. Dias MS, Sekhar MN. Intracranial hemorrhage from aneurysms and arteriovenous malformations during pregnancy and the puerperium. Neurosurgery 1990;27:855.

89. Wiebers DO. Subarachnoid hemorrhage in pregnancy. Semin Neurol 1988;8:226.

90. Catanzarite VA, Ferguson JE II, Hensleigh P, et al. Management of pregnancy subsequent to rupture of an intracranial arterial aneurysm. Am J Perinatol 1984;1:174.

91. Barrett J, Van Hoovdonk J, Boehm F. Pregnancy-related rupture of arterial aneurysms. Obstet Gynecol Surv 1982;37:557.

92. Minielly R, Yuzpe AA, Drake CG. Subarachnoid hemorrhage secondary to ruptured cerebral aneurysm in pregnancy. Obstet Gynecol 1978;53:64.

93. Robinson JL, Hall CJ, Sedzimir CB. Subarachnoid hemorrhage in pregnancy. J Neurosurg 1972;36:27.

94. Amias AG. Cerebrovascular disease in pregnancy. I. Hemorrhage. J Obstet Gynaecol Br Commonwealth 1970;77:100.

95. Cannell DE, Botterell EH. Subarachnoid hemorrhage and pregnancy. Am J Obstet Gynecol 1956;72:844.

96. Haas JF, Jänisch W, Staneczek W. Newly diagnosed primary intracranial neoplasms in pregnant women: A population-based assessment. J Neurol Neurosurg Psychiatry 1986;49:874.

97. Wan WL, Geller JL, Feldon SE, et al. Visual loss caused by rapidly progressive intracranial meningiomas during pregnancy. Opthalmology 1990;97:18.

98. Kasarskis EJ, Tibbs PA, Lee C. Cerebellar hemangioblastoma symptomatic during pregnancy. Neurosurgery 1988;22:770.

99. Goldberg G, Rappaport ZH. Neurosurgical, obstetric and endocrine aspects of meningioma during pregnancy. Isr J Med Sci 1987;23:825.

100. Mills RP, Harris AB, Heinrichs L, et al. Pituitary tumor made symptomatic during hormone therapy and induced pregnancy. Ann Opthalmol 1979;11:1672.

101. Magyar DM, Marshall JR. Pituitary tumors and pregnancy. Am J Obstet Gynecol 1978;132:739.

102. Ehlers N, Malmros R. The suprasellar meningiomas. Acta Opthlmol 1973;121(Suppl):1.

103. Newman B, Lam AM. Induced hypotension for clipping of a cerebral aneurysm during pregnancy: A case report and brief review. Anesth Analg 1986;65:675.

104. Wilson F, Sedzmir CB. Hypothermia and hypotension during craniotomy in a pregnant woman. Lancet 1959;2:947.

105. Aitken RR, Drake CG. A technique of anesthesia with induced hypotension for surgical correction of intracranial hemorrhages. Clin Neurosurg 1974;21:107.

106. Pevehouse BC, Boldrey E. Hypothermia and hypotension for intracranial surgery during pregnancy. Am J Surg 1960;100:633.

107. Bruns PD, Linder RO, Drose VE, et al. The placental transfer of water from fetus to mother following the intravenous infusion of hypertonic mannitol to the maternal rabbit. Am J Obstet Gynecol 1963;86:160.

108. Battaglia F, Prystowsky H, Smisson H, et al. Fetal blood studies. XIII. The effect of the administration of fluids intravenously to mothers upon the concentrations of water and electrolytes in plasma of human fetuses. Pediatrics 1960;25:2.

109. Hull CJ. Phaeochromocytoma: Diagnosis, preoperative preparation, and anesthetic management. Br J Anaesth 1986;58:1453.

110. Pullerits J, Ein S, Balfe JW. Anaesthesia for phaeochromocytoma. Can J Anaesth 1988;35:526.

111. Gifford RW, Bravo EL, Manger WM. Diagnosis and management of pheochromocytoma. Cardiology 1985;72(Suppl 1):126.

112. Schenker JG, Cjowers I. Pheochromocytoma and pregnancy: Review of 89 cases. Obstet Gynecol Surv 1971;26:739.

113. Schenkar JG, Granat M. Phaeochromocytoma and pregnancy: An updated appraisal. Aust NZ J Obstet Gynaecol 1982;22:1.

114. Januszewicz W, Wocial B. Clinical and biochemical aspects of pheochromocytoma. Report of 110 cases. Cardiology 1985;72(Suppl 1):131.

115. Hengstmann JH. Evaluation of screening tests for pheochromocytoma. Cardiology 1985;72(Suppl 1):153.

116. Brandstetter K, Krause U, Beyer J. Preliminary results with the clonidine suppression test in the diagnosis of pheochromocytoma. Cardiology 1985;72(Suppl 1):157.

117. Bravo EL, Tarazi RC, Fouad FM, et al. Clonidine-suppression test: A useful aid in the diagnosis of pheochromocytoma. N Engl J Med 1981;305:623.

118. Bravo EL, Gifford RW Jr. Pheochromocytoma: Diagnosis, localization and management. N Engl J Med 1984;311:1298.

119. Chatterjee TK, Parekh U. Phaeochromocytoma in pregnancy. Aust NZ J Obstet Gynaecol 1985;25:290.

120. Geelhoed GW. Surgery of the endocrine glands in pregnancy. Clin Obstet Gynecol 1983;26:865.

121. Fudge TL, McKinnon WMP, Geary WL. Current surgical management of pheochromocytoma during pregnancy. Arch Surg 1980;115:1224.

122. Desmonts JM, Marty J. Anaesthetic management of patients with phaeochromocytoma. Br J Anaesth 1984;56:781.

123. Stenström G, Haljamäe H, Tisell LE. Influence of preoperative treatment with phenoxybenzamine on the incidence of adverse cardiovascular reactions during anaesthesia and surgery for phaeochromocytoma. Acta Anaesthiol Scand 1985;29:797.

124. Devoe LD, O'Dell BE, Castillo R, et al. Metastatic pheochromocytoma in pregnancy and fetal biophysical assessment after maternal administration of alpha-adrenergic, beta-adrenergic, and dopamine antagonists. Obstet Gynecol 1986;68:15S.

125. Triner L, Baer L, Gallagher R, et al. Use of metyrosine in the anaesthetic management of patients with catecholamine secreting tumors: A case report. Br J Anaesth 1982;54:1333.

126. Green KN, Larsson SK, Beevers DG, et al. Alpha-methyltyrosine in the management of phaeochromocytoma. Thorax 1982;37:632.

127. Brogden RN, Heel RC, Speight TM, et al. α-Methyl-p-tyrosine: A review of its pharmacology and clinical use. Drugs 1981;21:81.

128. Engelman K, Horwitz D, Jequier E. Biochemical and pharmacologic effects of α-methyltyrosine in man. J Clin Invest 1969;21:81.

129. James MFM. The use of magnesium sulfate in the anesthetic management of pheochromocytoma. Anesthesiology 1985;62:188.

130. James MFM, Huddle KRL, Owen AD, et al. Use of magnesium sulfate in the anaesthetic management of phaeochromocytoma in pregnancy. Can J Anaesth 1988;35:178.

131. James MFM. Use of magnesium sulphate in the anaesthetic management of pheochromocytoma: A review of 17 anaesthetics. Br J Anaesth 1989;62:616.

132. Miller D, Robblee JA. Perioperative management of a patient with a malignant pheochromocytoma. Can Anaesth Soc J 1985;32:278.

133. Arai T, Hatano Y, Ishida H, et al. Use of nicardipine in the anesthetic management of pheochromocytoma. Anesth Analg 1986;65:706.

CHAPTER 12

Anesthesia for Fetal Surgery

William M. Grieco

Congenital anomalies are the second most common cause of death in children below age 4 and the third most common cause up to age 19. Often, these children require repeated hospitalizations and multiple treatment procedures.

Traditionally, treatment for most congenital anomalies did not begin until after birth. However, with recent advances in prenatal diagnosis, these abnormalities are often detected early in gestation. Animal and human studies now suggest that some of these lesions even may be treated in utero.

These developments allow the medical community the opportunity to establish and perfect unique techniques for fetal anesthesia and surgery. The future holds promise as diagnostic and operative techniques continue to improve. Many abnormalities previously not seen until after birth may someday be treated in the once-hidden confines of the womb.

GENERAL CONSIDERATIONS

Diagnosis

Continued improvements in ultrasonography help make the diagnosis of potentially treatable or correctable fetal conditions possible. Ultrasound is a safe and reliable noninvasive tool.[1-3] Greater resolution and increasing specificity make early diagnosis of many le-

sions possible. Some recent developments in prenatal ultrasonography include the following:

- The development of a grading system for ventricular enlargement[3]
- The ability to visualize the fetal urinary tract and its components early to mid-gestation[6]
- Reliable detection and assessment of renal artery blood flow as early as 20 weeks' gestation[5]

Although ultrasound can alert an obstetrician to the presence of an abnormality, he or she often will need other diagnostic tools to define the problem clearly and decide its potential amenability to treatment. Fetoscopy, combined with real-time ultrasonography, allows direct visualization of the fetus;[6] however, fetoscopy does present some increased risk to both fetus and mother.[1,2,7] Amniography and amniocentesis provide useful tools for prenatal evaluation.[6] Fetal echocardiogram allows insight into the anatomy of the fetal heart.[8] Biochemical markers correlate with certain fetal conditions. For example, amniotic fluid concentrations of alpha-fetoprotein and acetylcholinesterase reliably indicate open neural tube defects.

Treatment

Once the diagnosis of a fetal anomaly is made, treatment options need to be considered (Table 12-1). Many conditions are best treated after term delivery.

Table 12-1

Management of Fetal Malformations

May Be Best Corrected After Term Delivery

Esophageal, duodenal, jejunoileal, and anorectal atresias

Meconium ileus

Omphaloceles and gastroshisis

Small intact meningocele, myelomenigocele, and spina bifida

Craniofacial, extremity, and chest wall deformities

Cystic hygroma and ovarian cysts

Amniotic band malformation complex

May Be Corrected Ex Utero or In Utero

Obstructive hydrocephalus

Obstructive hydronephrosis

Intestinal ischemia-necrosis secondary to volvulus

Hydrops fetalis

Intrauterine growth retardation

Can Be Treated In Utero

Deficient pulmonary surfactant

Anemia-erythroblastosis and hydrops

Hypothyroidism and goiter

Obstructive hydrocephalus?

Bilateral obstructive hydronephrosis

Diaphragmatic hernia

Sacral teratomas with hydropic changes

After Harrison MR, Golbus MS, Filly RA. Management of the fetus with a correctable congenital defect. JAMA 1981;246:774.

Other conditions may merit induction of labor or delivery by cesarean section before term to allow definitive treatment after birth. In these situations, transportation of the fetus in utero to a tertiary care facility is mandatory.

There also are some medical and surgical conditions for which correction in utero may offer the best treatment option. Substrate deficiency syndromes are medical conditions that can respond to in utero therapy. Examples of these syndromes include erythroblastosis fetalis, fetal hypothyroidism, and nutritional deficiencies. These syndromes require the return of that substrate to the fetus, either through the mother (*i.e.,* glucocorticoids to prevent respiratory distress syndrome) or directly into the fetus (*i.e.,* red blood cell transfusion in isoimmunization).[2] These procedures are technically simple and carry little risk to either mother or fetus.

Conditions that might respond to surgical treatment include obstructive hydrocephalus, bilateral

hydronephrosis, and congenital diaphragmatic hernia.[1,2] These conditions require technically more difficult intervention that can present significant maternal and fetal risk. The severity of functional damage to organs such as brain, lungs, and kidneys varies with the duration of the initial insult. For example, unrelieved obstructive hydronephrosis can produce both renal failure and pulmonary hypoplasia. The fetal surgeon must time the repair correctly to minimize functional damage.

The Society of Fetal Medicine, based in San Francisco, formed in 1983. This group, acting as an advisory body, has put together the following basic guidelines for fetal surgical intervention:

- The presence of a multidisciplinary treatment group
- A singleton pregnancy
- Absence of other significant anomalies
- Evidence for immature lungs
- Normal karyotype and negative viral studies
- Willingness of both parents and the treatment group to intervene[9]

There also is an International Fetal Registry, headquartered in Manitoba, Canada. This registry collects and coordinates information about experience with human in utero surgical procedures.

IN UTERO TREATMENT MODALITIES

History of In Utero Therapy

The first fetal surgery was essentially ablative.[9,10] Destructive operations date back hundreds of years, but they still have some use today.[9-11] Cephalocentesis can allow vaginal delivery of a dead fetus in parturients with dystocia.[6] Selective abortion of a nonviable twin has also been reported.[11]

Lilly, in 1963, using fluoroscopy, successfully transfused a fetus with erythroblastosis fetalis in utero. This event may be called the birth of modern fetal surgery. It showed that effective treatment is possible in humans without risking harm to either the mother or fetus.[12] Success with other percutaneous procedures soon followed. Researchers then directed their attention toward more complex maneuvers to repair various fetal anomalies. Several investigators developed animal models to simulate the occurrence and repair of a particular fetal defect. Successful models simulated the defect that occurred in humans, permitted quantitative assessment of the defect, and allowed for in utero repair. Investigators could then assess the effects of repair on subsequent fetal development.[9,13] Once they successfully repaired a defect in animals, fetal surgeons could begin work on human subjects.

Obstructive Hydrocephalus

Obstruction to drainage of cerebrospinal fluid (CSF) produces congenital hydrocephalus. This obstruction increases CSF pressure, which dilates the intracerebral ventricles and compresses the developing brain tissue. Compression, in turn, impairs neurologic function.[1] The resultant histologic changes increase in severity with the duration of obstruction.[4] Etiologies of obstructive hydrocephalus include the following:

- Stenosis of the aqueduct of Sylvius
- Dandy–Walker syndrome
- Chromosomal abnormalities such as trisomy 18 and 21
- Intrauterine viral infection[14]

Congenital hydrocephalus complicates approximately 2 in 1000 live deliveries. The total incidence of hydrocephalus is significantly higher because some stillborn fetuses also have this condition.[3] Up to 80% of affected fetuses have associated anomalies.[8] If left untreated, only 25% of liveborn hydrocephalic neonates survive infancy.[15] Of those infants that survive, 33% to 50% will be mentally retarded.[3]

The earliest attempts at in utero treatment of hydrocephalus involved serial cephalocentesis and percutaneous ventriculoamniotic shunts. Neither approach improved outcome.[3] Researchers then developed animal models to understand better the natural history of the disease and the effects of surgical correction. Harrison *et al,*[16] using fetal lambs, and Michejda *et al,*[17,18] using fetal monkeys, induced hydrocephalus in utero by injection of teratogens. Surgical shunting was done through an open hysterotomy. Survival and initial behavioral outcome improved, but white matter damage persisted.[3]

Work then proceeded to clinical trials in human fetuses. Initial projects yielded unfavorable results. Only a few isolated infants benefited. The fetal registry reveals that shunting may improve survival, but most of the time, functional and developmental outcome do not benefit.[3] The crude fetal mortality rate following the procedure approaches 10%. Follow-up studies on surviving infants show that only 33% are normal and over 50% have severe handicaps.[8] Currently, researchers feel that only in rare instances will a fetus benefit from in utero shunting.[19]

Obstructive Uropathy

Obstruction of the fetal urethra may cause hydronephrosis with dilation of the bladder, ureters, and renal collecting system.[20] Oligohydramnios, a decrease in amniotic fluid content, is usually present. Oligohydramnios is associated with abdominal wall defects and skeletal and facial deformities (Fig. 12-1).[1,3] Severe, untreated hydronephrosis can compress fetal lung tissue and lead to pulmonary hypoplasia. Urethral valves, either anterior or posterior, are the most common cause of fetal hydronephrosis.[20] Overall incidence of obstructive uropathy is unknown. There are many asymptomatic forms of this disease.[21] Oligohydramnios in mid- to late gestation should raise concern about the fetal renal system. Ultrasound may reveal a fluid-filled mass (the bladder) in the fetal abdomen. Obstruction will eventually produce functional renal impairment.

Fetal renal function can be measured in utero. Isothalamate clearance can determine glomerular filtration rate. The maternal and fetal blood concentrations of isothalamate are equal. Fetal clearance and glomerular filtration rate are determined by injecting isothalamate into the mother and obtaining maternal blood samples and fetal urine samples using a percutaneous catheter (Fig. 12-2).[22]

Harrison *et al*[23-25] simulated obstructive uropathy in fetal lambs by placing an ameroid constrictor around the fetal urethra. Subsequent ureteral shunting, if done early enough, resulted in marked histologic and functional improvement in both the kidneys and the lungs. The earlier the shunting was done, the more renal function improved.

Success with the animal models prompted attempts in humans. Fetal surgeons tried a variety of procedures, including a sophisticated repair using bilateral ureterostomies (Fig. 12-3).[26,27] Initial attempts at in utero repair in human fetuses met with mixed results. In a few cases, renal function improved significantly. Still, most infants did not benefit.[26]

Currently, clinical algorithms aid in choosing among treatment alternatives (Fig. 12-4). Open surgical correction through hysterotomy remains an option if certain criteria are met. Otherwise, less invasive treatments exist.[5,28]

Congenital Diaphragmatic Hernia

Congenital diaphragmatic hernia (CDH) results from a defect in the fetal diaphragm that allows herniation of abdominal contents into the thorax. The pleuroperitoneal canal fails to close when the intestines return to

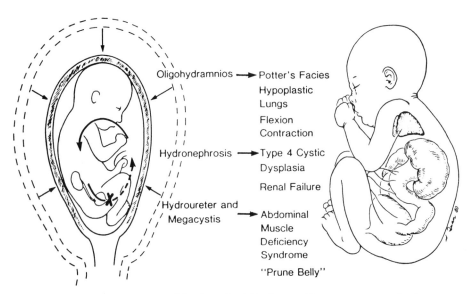

Figure 12–1. Consequences of fetal urethral blockage. Obstruction causes hydroureter, megacysitis, and hydronephrosis. Blockage of fetal urinary excretion alters normal amniotic fluid dynamics and produces oligohydramnios. Early decompression of an obstructed urinary tract may avoid sequela. (Bond SJ, Harrison MR. Obstructive uropathy—when to intervene. Contemp Obstet Gynecol (Special Issue) 1987:65)

the abdomen at 8 to 10 weeks' gestation. The most common site of herniation is through a posterolateral defect. The presence of abdominal contents within the chest compromises pulmonary development. In utero, the bronchial tree develops by the 16th week of gestation. Alveoli continue developing throughout gestation and, after birth, up to 8 years of age. The degree of pulmonary damage depends on when and how much of the viscera herniates into the chest. Earlier and larger herniation limits the number of bronchial divisions. Surgical correction decompresses the lung and allows resumption of normal pulmonary development. New alveoli can form, but no new airways can develop in affected hypoplastic lung.[29]

Congenital diaphragmatic hernia is usually an isolated finding in an otherwise normal fetus.[29] The incidence varies from 1 in 2200 to 1 in 5000 births. Mortality in liveborn infants, even with aggressive postnatal care is 50% to 75%.[29–32] Extracorporeal membrane oxygenation in the postnatal period has a limited effect on survival.[30]

Polyhydramnios, an increase in amniotic fluid content, is a risk factor for CDH. The fetus normally ingests amniotic fluid. Herniated abdominal contents prevent fetal swallowing, increasing amniotic fluid volume. Ultrasonography can detect the defect in utero.

Haller *et al*[33] first attempted to create an animal model of CDH. They placed a Silastic balloon in the thoracic cavity of fetal lambs.[33] The balloon was then completely inflated. Harrison *et al*[31,32] modified this approach by slowly inflating the balloon over time to simulate gradual herniation of viscera into the thorax. In utero repair, simulated by deflating the balloon, resulted in more normal lung tissue structure and function. In a further refinement, Harrison *et al*[32] simulated CDH by making a hole in the diaphragm of fetal lambs. Later, he repaired the hole through a subcostal incision. Pulmonary function again improved in the treated lambs.

Initial clinical experience in humans was disappointing. Return of the abdominal contents to the fetal peritoneal cavity produced a lethal increase in intraabdominal pressure. Harrison *et al*[3] overcame this problem by creating a Silastic omphalocele. This pouch increases the surface area of the abdominal wall, thus allowing easier return of abdominal contents to the peritoneal cavity. The fetal liver presents another technical problem in these repairs. When the surgeons attempt to replace the liver into the peritoneal cavity, it compresses the hepatic vein and severely impairs umbilical vein blood flow. This problem has not been solved.

There are some successful outcomes in recent re-

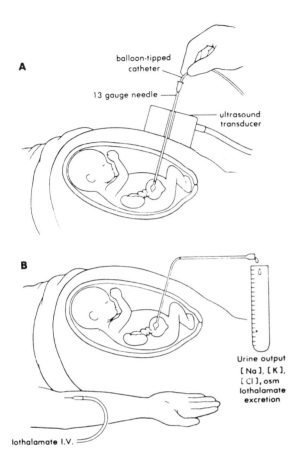

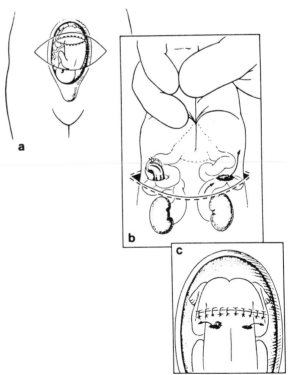

abnormalities,[7,8,10–12,20,39,40] cardiac abnormalities,[14,15] as well as the treatment of fetal neoplasm and organ transplantation.[26] New technologies, such as lasers, and continued improvement in surgical techniques promise more progress in this exciting field.[1,2,41]

OBSTETRIC CONSIDERATIONS

Premature Labor

The most common problem encountered after in utero surgery is the development of generalized uterine contractions. These contractions can both impede placental blood flow and progress to premature labor.[2,9] Prostaglandin synthetase inhibitors have a role in prevention of preterm labor.[42] If preterm labor occurs, several other drugs are useful. Beta-agonist tocolytic

Figure 12–2. Technique for diagnostic urinary catheterization. A balloon-tipped catheter is placed into the distended fetal bladder using ultrasound (*A*). An aliquot of fetal urine is sent for electrolyte concentration and osmolarity (*B*). After complete drainage of the fetal urinary tract is assured by ultrasound, isothalamate is given to the mother and hourly fetal urine output and isothalmate excretion are measured. (Glick PL, Harrison MR, Golbus MS. Management of the fetus with congenital hydronephrosis II: Prognostic criteria and selection for treatment. J Pediatr Surg 1985;20:376)

ported cases. One involves a 24-week-old fetus with repair through a subcostal incision (Fig. 12-5).[34] Researchers in this field believe that, with experience, successful in utero repair of CDH can be a realistic possibility in the future.

Other Lesions

Many other possible surgical interventions can be performed in utero. Experimental studies have begun that are aimed at the repair of spinal cord and neural tube defects,[35–37] skeletal malformations,[18,38] facial

Figure 12–3. Bilateral flank ureterostomies in a fetus with hydronephrosis. After hysterotomy incision (*A*), the surgeon performs the ureterostomies. (*B*) A silastic loop is placed around the right ureter to prevent retraction. The hysterotomy is closed (*C*), and the fetal urine is decompressed (*arrows*) into the amniotic fluid. (Harrison MR, Golbus MS, Filly RA. Fetal surgery for congenital hydronephrosis. N Engl J Med 1982;306:591)

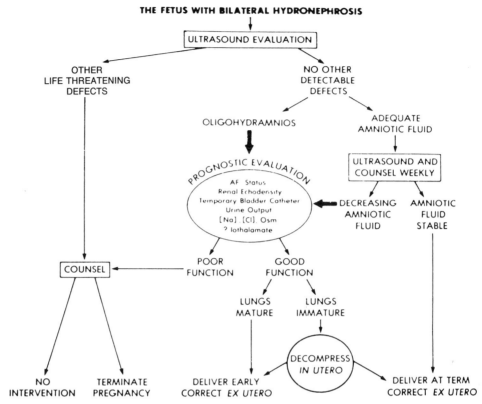

Figure 12.4 Algorithm showing possible treatment alternatives for fetal obstructive hydrocephalus. (Glick PL, Harrison MR, Golbus MS. Management of the fetus with congenital hydronephrosis II: Prognostic criteria and selection for treatment. J Pediatr Surg 1985;20:376)

drugs help prevent and treat preterm labor following all types of in utero therapy.[43] Bethamethasone may accelerate pulmonary maturity at 26 to 34 weeks' gestation.[44] However, both these drugs can produce severe side effects. Prostaglandin synthetase can induce in utero closure of the ductus arteriosis.[40] Beta-agonist drugs can cause pulmonary edema, myocardial ischemia, and cardiac dysrhythmias.[45] Researchers in the field do not stop preterm labor if it occurs after 32 to 36 weeks.

It is unclear what effect anesthetics have on endogenous hormones and substances promoting uterine contractions.[9] Several studies suggest that no single anesthetic technique predisposes to preterm labor.

Other Complications

For those patients who require an open hysterotomy, to avoid the placenta the most common location of the incision is in the upper segment of the fundus of the uterus. Because of the increased risk of uterine rupture with this scar, all subsequent deliveries must be by cesarean section. Fetal surgery appears to have no other effect on subsequent pregnancies.[46]

ANESTHETIC CONSIDERATIONS

Maternal Anesthesia

Many maternal physiologic changes that occur during pregnancy can affect mid-gestational surgical and anesthetic intervention. These changes involve cardiovascular, pulmonary, and gastrointestinal systems, as well as airway anatomy.

When anesthetizing a mother to allow fetal surgery, provide appropriate acid aspiration prophylaxis and do a rapid-sequence induction. Pay close attention to maternal positioning and ensure adequate left uterine displacement.

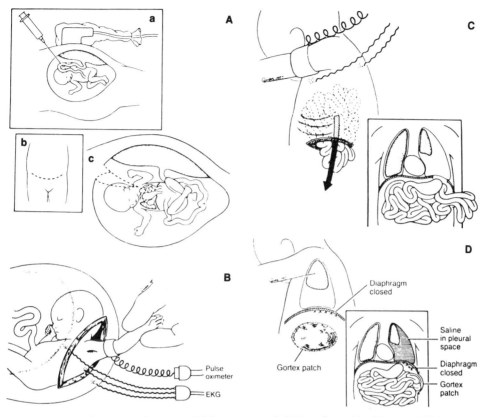

Figure 12–5. Illustration of a successful fetal repair of CDH performed by Harrison. *(A) (A inset)* Percutaneous umbilical cord sampling for preoperative fetal blood studies. *(B inset)* Low horizontal abdominal incision. *(C inset)* Because the placenta was located anteriorly, the hysterotomy was made in the posterior part of the uterus. *(B)* The left arm and chest are exposed, and the fetus continuously monitored by electrocardiogram (ECG), pulse oximetry, and sterile ultrasound. *(C)* The intestines and stomach are reduced through a subcostal incision. *(D)* The diaphragm is reconstructed, the chest filled with warm saline, and the abdomen enlarged with a patch. (Harrison MR, Langer JC, Adzick NS. Correction of congenital diaphragmatic hernia in utero. V. Initial clinical experience. J Pediatr Surg 1990;25:47)

Intraoperative uterine relaxation is an important consideration unique to fetal surgery. Good uterine relaxation allows optimal surgical exposure and helps maintain placental blood flow. The commonly used halogenated agents, at doses as low as 0.5 minimum alveolar concentration (MAC), significantly decrease contractile, but not resting, uterine tone. Higher doses of potent inhalational anesthetic further inhibit uterine contractility (Fig. 12-6). Only enflurane, at 1.5 MAC, significantly lowers resting uterine tension (Fig. 12-7).[47] Halothane, at low to moderate doses, also lowers uterine vascular resistance, helping to maintain uteroplacental blood flow. There is no particular advantage of any one halogenated agent, but halothane is most often chosen.

Many drugs can increase uterine tone. Alpha-adrenergic agonists, whether from endogenous or exogenous sources, cause uncoordinated uterine contractions that may lead to preterm labor.[48] Alpha-adrenergic agonists also directly increase uterine artery resistance, lowering placental blood flow. Ketamine, in doses greater than 1.1 mg/kg, and rapid intravenous injection of anticholinesterases, such as neostigmine, also can increase uterine tone. Toxic concentrations of local anesthetics may be direct uterine artery vasoconstrictors.[49]

Maternal anxiety, surgical stimulation, and postoperative pain can elevate plasma concentrations of endogenous catecholamines. These compounds can compromise the fetus by lowering placental blood flow

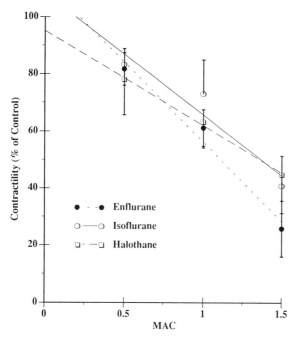

Figure 12–6. The effects of potent inhalation anesthetics on uterine contractility. All agents produce a significant, dose-related inhibition of contractility beginning at 0.5 MAC. Values are mean ± 2 SE. (After Munson ES, Embro WJ. Enflurane, isoflurane, and halothane and isolated human uterine muscle. Anesthesiology 1977;46:11)

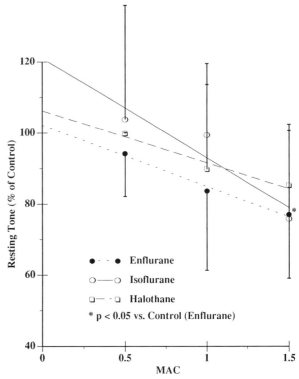

Figure 12–7. The effects of potent inhalation anesthetics on resting uterine tone. Only enflurane, at 1.5 MAC, significantly relaxes the resting uterus. Values are mean ± 2 SE. (Munson ES, Embro WJ. Enflurane, isoflurane, and halothane and isolated human uterine muscle. Anesthesiology 1977;46:11)

and predisposing to preterm labor. The anesthetic approach to these women strives to limit these events.

Fetal Anesthesia

Drugs may influence the fetus either directly or indirectly. Direct fetal effects occur after placental passage of a drug. Placental transfer and fetal drug concentration depend on lipid solubility, ionization, fetal pH, portal clearance, plasma protein binding, and metabolism. Anesthetic agents can act indirectly on the fetus through effects on maternal hemodynamics and respiratory physiology.

Anesthesia has three separate elements: loss of consciousness (amnesia), analgesia, and lack of movement.[50] Late in gestation, the fetus responds to stimuli such as noise, pressure, touch, cold, light, and music.[51] Surgical manipulation of an unanesthetized fetus increases hormonal and motor activity and results in varying degrees of autonomic nervous system stimulation. Intravenous, intramuscular, and inhalational anesthetics, given either directly to the fetus or via the mother clearly produce analgesia and lack of movement in response to surgical stimulation. Benzodiazepines may provide the fetus with amnesia and prevent dramatic swings in nervous system stimulation in response to fetal manipulation. Fetal amnesia may be of some importance in decreasing fetal response to subsequent stressful stimuli.[51,52]

Direct Drug Effects

LOCAL ANESTHETICS. All commonly used local anesthetics cross the placenta and diffuse into the fetal circulation. High plasma concentrations of local anesthetic after inadvertent intravenous injection may depress the fetal cardiovascular system. In fetal lambs, high concentrations of mepivacaine and lidocaine decrease heart rate.[52]

Local anesthetics also reach the fetal central nervous system. The blood–brain barrier is poorly developed in the fetus, predisposing to high central nervous system exposure to local anesthetics. Teramo *et al*,[53] using electroencephalogram, found that large doses of lidocaine induced seizure activity in fetal lambs.

INTRAVENOUS ANESTHETICS. Maternally administered intravenous agents also cross the placenta. Barbiturates can provide short-lasting fetal anesthesia. Barbiturates also may protect the fetal brain exposed to nonoxidative metabolism by decreasing oxygen consumption.[54] Barbiturate-induced maternal hypotension can produce fetal cerebral lactic acidosis and deplete cerebral energy stores (ATP and ADP). However, maternal administration of thiopental offers fetal cerebral protection by decreasing nonoxidative metabolism and $CMRO_2$ and by maintaining normal fetal cerebral energy stores. Maternally administered narcotics provide fetal analgesia and have no serious direct side-effects. Alfentanil accumulates on the fetal side of the placenta and may afford prolonged fetal pain relief.[55] Muscle relaxants are highly ionized but will slowly, and to a small extent, cross the placenta. Direct fetal intramuscular injection of pancuronium and d-tubocurare will help maintain fetal immobility.[55–58] Pancuronium is the better agent for two reasons: (1) it maintains hemodynamic stability, and (2) it has a more rapid onset of action.[55,57,58]

NITROUS OXIDE. Nitrous oxide concentrations above 60% correlate with fetal asphyxia.[59] Several studies and clinical trials show that nitrous oxide concentrations below 60% produce neither fetal asphyxia nor poor fetal outcome. Most authors agree that 50% to 60% nitrous oxide in oxygen is safe for both mother and fetus.[3,55,60] Maternal hyperoxia is not useful to the fetus. Maternal Pao_2 as high as 600 mm Hg will not increase fetal Po_2 above 60 mm Hg. Uneven distribution of placental blood flow and placental metabolism probably account for this large maternal–fetal oxygen gradient. At normal atmospheric pressures, maternal hyperoxia will not cause retrolental fibroplasia or premature closure of the ductus arteriosis.[61]

POTENT INHALATION AGENTS. Halogenated agents rapidly cross the placenta and appear in the fetal circulation within minutes. Equilibrium between the mother and the fetus does not occur for hours. The MAC of halothane in fetal lambs is about one half that of the adult sheep. Both a lower fetal metabolic rate and higher plasma concentrations of progesterone may contribute to the lower MAC in the fetus.[62] When the parturient is adequately anesthetized, the fetal anesthetic concentration is well above fetal MAC.[62,63]

Potent inhalation agents could produce significant fetal hemodynamic changes. These agents, however, have little effect on fetal blood pressure. When the fetus is exposed to maternal MAC, fetal blood pressure decreases by 7%. When the mother is exposed to maternal MAC, however, maternal blood pressure drops by 24% (Fig. 12-8).[62,64] Higher concentrations of halogenated anesthetics (above 1.5 maternal MAC) lower fetal heart rate, blood pressure, and cerebral blood flow.[65,66] Moderate concentrations of halogenated agents (below 1.5 maternal MAC) neither cause a significant decline in cerebral blood flow nor produce cerebral asphyxia in the normoxic fetus.[64,67]

Investigators also have studied the effects of potent agents on asphyxiated fetuses. Their results conflict. In one study, halothane aggravated fetal distress in a severely acidotic fetus by further lowering heart rate, blood pressure, and cerebral blood flow.[68] A different group of investigators saw no effect of halothane on the condition of the asphyxiated fetal lamb.[67] Isoflurane

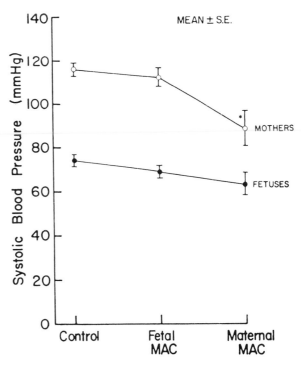

Figure 12–8. Systolic blood pressure to halothane in pregnant ewes and their fetuses. At maternal MAC, the ewe's blood pressure falls significantly, whereas the fetus' blood pressure remains unchanged. (Gregory GA, Wade JG, Beihl DR, Ong BY, Sitar DS. Fetal anesthetic requirement (MAC) for halothane. Anesth Analg 1983;62:9)

also has been reported to aggravate fetal distress in asphyxiated fetal lambs.[69]

Indirect Drug Effects

REGIONAL ANESTHESIA. Regional anesthesia can lower maternal blood pressure, decrease uterine blood flow, and lead to fetal asphixia.[55,70,71] If hypotension occurs, treat it with an indirect-acting agent such as ephedrine. This drug raises maternal blood pressure without impairing uterine blood flow.[49] High concentrations of local anesthetics can directly produce uterine vasoconstriction. Therefore, use regional techniques that produce high plasma concentrations of local anesthetics with caution.

INTRAVENOUS AGENTS. Maternally administered intravenous anesthetics also have indirect effects on the fetus. Maternal hypotension can follow thiopental induction. In sheep, thiopental produces a significant drop in uterine blood flow. There are also human data showing a 22% to 50% fall in intervillous blood flow following thiopental rapid sequence induction of anesthesia.[71] The two most likely causes of this phenomenon are (1) the vasodilating effect of thiopental and (2) release of endogenous catecholamines during airway instrumentation. Narcotics and benzodiazepines also can produce variations in maternal blood pressure and ventilation. Maternal hypoventilation can induce fetal hypoxemia and acidosis. Maternal hypercarbia also will raise maternal plasma catecholamine concentrations. These compounds, in turn, can constrict the uterine artery and impede blood supply to the fetus and placenta.

POTENT INHALATION AGENTS. The halogenated anesthetic agents also can affect the fetus by changing maternal hemodynamics. Low to moderate concentrations of halogenated compounds (1.0–1.5 MAC) may incite a small drop in maternal blood pressure, but this fall in blood pressure is offset by an increase in uterine blood flow secondary to uterine relaxation and a decrease in uterine vascular resistance.[62] At 2.0 MAC, halogenated agents significantly depress maternal cardiac output and blood pressure. The resultant fall in uterine blood flow diminishes fetal oxygen delivery. Changes in fetal heart rate, blood pressure, acid–base status, and oxygenation soon follow.[72] Both isoflurane and halothane are indistinguishable in their effects on fetal hemodynamics. Clinically, deep

---

Table 12–2

Anesthetic Recommendations for In Utero Treatment

Preoperative Evaluation
Preoperative visit with reassurance
Adequate premedication including a benzodiazepine
Sodium citrate, 30 mL, immediately before procedure
Metaclopromide, 10 mg, and ranitadine, 150 mg, if reflux symptoms exist

Intraoperative Management
Maintain lateral tilt
Noninvasive maternal monitoring
Fetal heart rate monitoring and, if possible, directly monitoring fetal electrocardigram and
   pulse oximetry
Treat maternal hypotension with ephedrine and fluids
Maintain normocapnic maternal ventilation and oxygenation

Regional Anesthesia	*General Anesthesia*
Prophylactic infusion of crystalloid, up to 1.5 L	Preoxygenation with rapid-sequence induction
Avoid intravascular injection	Use of halogenated agents, up to 1.5 MAC
	Nitrous oxide, up to 60%, in oxygen

Postoperatively
Cautious use of beta-tocolytics, if indicated
Adequate pain relief with either intravenous, intramuscular, or epidural narcotics

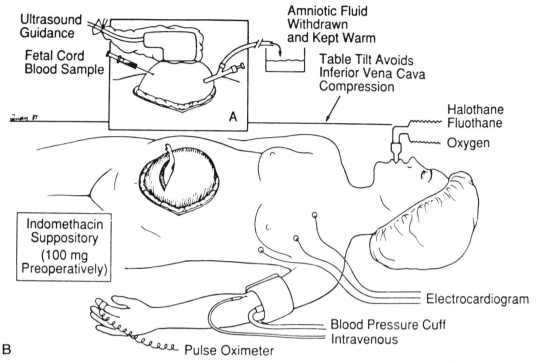

Figure 12–9. Diagram showing maternal positioning and monitoring during fetal surgery under general endotracheal anesthesia. (*A*) Following laparotomy and uterine exposure, the placenta is localized by ultrasound, fetal blood is withdrawn, and amniotic fluid is preserved. (*B*) Maternal positioning includes tilting to avoid aortocaval compression. Noninvasive maternal monitoring is shown. (Longaker MT, Golbus MS, Filly RA, Rosen MA, Chang SW, Harrison MR. Maternal outcome after open fetal surgery. JAMA 1991;265:737)

inhalational anesthesia is rarely required for adequate uterine relaxation or maternal anesthesia.

MATERNAL VENTILATION. Maternal ventilation can indirectly affect the fetus as well. Control ventilation to keep maternal $Paco_2$ in the physiologic range (30–35 mm Hg). Hypocarbia produces vasoconstriction, which impairs uterine blood flow. A leftward shift of the hemoglobin dissociation curve produced by respiratory alkalosis also will decrease oxygen availability for the fetus.[48] Positive-pressure ventilation can decrease venous return and cardiac output. In turn, uterine blood flow and fetal oxygen delivery fall. Hypoventilation can cause severe fetal cardiac depression secondary to maternal acidosis and hypoxia.[73]

CLINICAL RECOMMENDATIONS

Table 12-2 outlines several important considerations for the anesthetic management of a woman presenting for fetal surgery. An informative preoperative visit,

fully explaining all aspects and risks of the anesthesia, will help allay maternal anxiety. Premedication consisting of a benzodiazepine and possibly a narcotic also can help decrease maternal anxiety. Prophylactic indomethacin, 100 mg per rectum, may help prevent preterm labor.[46]

Appropriate intraoperative monitoring is essential. Maternal monitoring consists of pulse oximetry, blood pressure, precordial stethoscope, and electrocardiogram. Consider the use of invasive maternal pressure monitoring if large fluid shifts are expected. There are many newly developed fetal monitors including sterilizable Doppler probes and pulse oximeters for blood pressure and oxygen saturation determinations.[46] Special "screw in" fetal electrocardiogram electrodes are more accurate than standard electrocardiographic monitoring.[74] Systolic time interval monitoring will very accurately access the function of the fetal cardiovascular system.[75]

For percutaneous procedures, administration of local anesthetics by infiltration is the safest choice.[51,76] Maternally administered sedation helps provide fetal anesthesia. Pancuronium, 0.5 mg, injected into the fetal gluteal muscle will provide 2 to 3 hours of immobility.[56] Direct infiltration of small amounts of lidocaine into the fetal surgical site can provide additional fetal anesthesia.[77] Monitor maternal ventilation closely if using heavy maternal sedation.

In patients undergoing hysterectomy, general anesthesia is not only safe but preferable to regional anesthesia (Fig. 12-9).[34,55] General anesthesia allows more accurate control of uterine relaxation, ventilation, oxygenation, and maternal blood pressure.[44] Maternal anesthesia also will produce appropriate fetal anesthesia.

When inducing general anesthesia, observe the usual "full stomach" precautions, including a rapid-sequence induction with intubation of the trachea. Maintain left uterine tilt to limit maternal hypotension and ensure optimal uterine blood flow. Keep the mother normocapnic and avoid hypoxia. Nitrous oxide in oxygen and light-to-moderate amounts of halogenated agent are safe and adequate for maternal relaxation and fetal anesthesia. Intraoperative narcotics and benzodiazepines also may be used.

Use postoperative beta-tocolytics with caution. Pain relief with intravenous or neuraxial narcotics may help decrease maternal plasma catecholamines and help prevent the onset of preterm labor.[20,40,46]

SUMMARY

In utero diagnosis and treatment of anomalies such as congenital obstructive hydrocephalus, hydronephrosis, and diaphragmatic hernia have progressed to the point where clinical trials are currently in progress. Anesthesia for these procedures must be tailored to produce the least amount of risk to both mother and fetus. Regardless of anesthetic technique, carefully monitor the mother and fetus during and after the procedure. Percutaneous procedures frequently only require local anesthetic infiltration with sedation; however, local infiltration will not supply sufficient anesthesia for operations requiring hysterotomy. Regional anesthetics afford maternal comfort but may not provide adequate uterine relaxation or fetal anesthesia. A carefully conducted general anesthetic, using both nitrous oxide and low-to-moderate doses of halogenated agents, safely ensures good maternal and fetal operating conditions.

Preoperative prostaglandin synthetase inhibitors and beta-agonistas postoperatively help prevent the development of preterm labor after hysterotomy. Although helpful, these drugs must be used with caution.

Postoperative pain control, with systemic or epidural drugs, is also important in decreasing the risk of preterm labor.

REFERENCES

1. Harrison MR, Golbus MS, Filly RA, Nakayama DK, de Lorimier AA. Fetal surgical treatment. Pediatr Ann 1982;11:896.
2. Harrison MR, Golbus MS, Filly RA. Management of the fetus with a correctable congenital defect. JAMA 1981;246:774.
3. Pinckert TL, Golbus MR. Fetal surgery. Clin Perinatol 1988;15:943.
4. Colodny AH. Antenatal diagnosis and management of urinary abnormalities. Pediatr Clin North Am 1987;34:1365.
5. Manning FA. Fetal surgery for obstructive uropathy: Rational considerations. Am J Kid Dis 1987;10:259.
6. Redwine F, Petres RE. Fetal surgery—past, present, and future. Clin Perinatology 1983;10:399.
7. Levine MD, McNeil DE, Kaback MM, Frazer RE, Okada DM, Hobel CJ. Second-trimester fetoscopy and fetal blood sampling: Current limitations and problems. Am J Obstet Gynecol 1974;120:937.
8. Evans MI, Drugan A, Manning FA, Harrison MR. Fetal surgery in the 1990s. Am J Dis Child 1989;143:1431.
9. Pringle KC. In utero surgery. Adv Surg 1986;19:101.
10. Smale LE. Destructive operations on the fetus. Am J Obstet Gynecol 1974;119:369.
11. Robie GF, Payne GG Jr, Morgan MA. Selective delivery of an acardiac, acephalic twin. N Engl J Med 1989;320:512.
12. Liley AW. Intrauterine transfusion of foetus in haemolytic disease. Br Med J 1963;1107.
13. Harrison MR, Ross N, Noall R, De Lorimier AA. Correction of congenital hydronephrosis in utero. I. The model: Fetal urethral obstruction produces hydronephrosis and pumonary hypoplasis in fetal lambs. J Pediatr Surg 1983;18:247.
14. Clewell WH. Congenital hydrocephalus: Treatment in utero. Fetal Ther 1988;3:89.
15. Congenital hydrocephalus. In: Harrison MR, Golbus MS, Filly RA, eds. The unborn patient: Prenatal diagnosis and treatment. Orlando: Grune & Stratton, 1984:349.
16. Glick PL, Harrison MR, Halks-Miller M, et al. Correction of congenital hydrocephalus in utero. II. Efficacy of in utero shunting. J Pediatr Surg 1984;19:870.
17. Michejda M, Patronas N, Di Chir G, Hodgen GD. Fetal hydrocephalus. II. Amelioration of fetal porencephaly by in utero therapy in nonhuman primates. JAMA 1984;251:2548.
18. Michejda M, Hodgen GD. Antenatal treatment of induced congenital malformations. Prog Clin Biol Res 1985;163B:231.

19. Michejda M, Queenan JT, McCullough D. Present status of intrauterine treatment of hydrocephalus and its future. Am J Obstet Gynecol 1986;155:873.

20. Neal R, Andrassy R. Fetal surgery in utero. Texas Med 1984;80:40.

21. Johnston JH. Upper urinary tract obstruction. In: Williams DJ, Johnston JH, eds. Pediatric urology. 2nd ed. London: Butterworth Scientific 1982:189.

22. Adzick NS, Harrison MR, Glick PL, Flake AW. Fetal urinary tract obstruction: Experimental pathophysiology. Semin Perinatol 1985;9:79.

23. Harrison MR, Nakayama DK, Noall R, de Lorimier AA. Correction of congenital hydronephrosis in utero. II. Decompression reverses the effects of obstruction on the fetal lung and urinary tract. J Pediatr Surg 1982; 17:965.

24. Glick PL, Harrison MR, Noall RA, Villa RL. Correction of congenital hydronephrosis in utero. III. Early mid-trimester ureteral obstruction produces renal dysplasia. J Pediatr Surg 1983;18:681.

25. Glick PL, Harrison MR, Adzick NS, Noall RA, Villa RL. Correction of congenital hydronephosis in utero. IV. In utero decompression prevents renal dysplasia. J Pediatr Surg 1984;19:649.

26. Adamsons K Jr. Fetal surgery. N Engl J Med 1966;275:204.

27. Harrison MR, Golbus MS, et al. Fetal surgery for congenital hydronephrosis. N Engl J Med 1982;306:591.

28. Glick PL, Harrison MR, Golbus MS. Management of the fetus with congenital hydronephrosis. II. Prognostic criteria and selection for treatment. J Pediatr Surg 1985;20:376.

29. Harrison MR, de Lorimier AA. Congenital diaphragmatic hernia. Surg Clin North Am 1981;61:1023.

30. Pringle KC, Turner JW, Schofield JC, Soper RT. Creation and repair of diaphragmatic hernia in the fetal lamb: Lung development and morphology. J Pediatr Surg 1984;19:131.

31. Harrison MR, Jester JA, Ross NA. Correction of congenital diaphragmatic hernia in utero. I. The model: Intrathoracic balloon produces fatal pulmonary hypoplasia. Surgery 1980;88:174.

32. Harrison MR, Bressack MA, Churg AM, de Lorimier AA. Correction of congenital diaphragmatic hernia in utero. II. Simulated correction permits fetal lung growth with survival at birth. Surgery 1980;80:260.

33. Haller JA Jr, Signer RD, Golladar ES, et al. Pulmonary and ductal hemodynamics in studies of simulated diaphragmatic hernia of fetal and newborn lambs. J Pediatr Surg 1976;11:675.

34. Harrison MR, Adzick NS, Longaker MT, et al. Successful repair in utero of a fetal diaphragmatic hernia after removal of herniated viscera from the left thorax. N Engl J Med 1990;322:1582.

35. Pearson JF. Fetal surgery. Arch Dis Child 1983;58:324.

36. Harrison MR, Filly RA, Golbus MS, et al. Fetal treatment 1982. N Engl J Med 1982;307:1651.

37. Soper RT. The Pandora's box of antenatal surgery. Am Surg 1983;49:285.

38. Hutson J. Fetal surgery at the crossroads. Ind J Pediatr 1989;56:570.

39. Pringle KC. Fetal surgery: It has a past, has it a future? Fetal Ther 1986;1:23.

40. Harrison MR, Anderson J, Rosen, MA, Ross NA, Hendrickx AG. Fetal surgery in the primate. I. Anesthetic, surgical, and tocolytic management to maximize fetal–neonatal survival. J Pediatr Surg 1982;17:115.

41. Manning FA, Harrison MR, Roderk C, et al. Catheter shunts for fetal hydronephrosis and hydrocephalus. N Engl J Med 1986;315:336.

42. Nakayama DK, Harrison MR, Seron-Ferre M, Villa RL. Fetal surgery in the primate. II. Uterine electromyographic response to operative procedures and pharmacologic agents. J Pediatr Surg 1984;19:333.

43. Block BS, Parer JT, Llanos AJ, Court DJ. Effects of ritodrine and fetal oxygenation after in utero fetal surgery in sheep. Biol Neonate 1989;56:94.

44. Spielman FJ. Fetal surgery. In: James FM, Wheeler AS, Dewan DM, eds. Obstetric anesthesia: The complicated patient, 2nd ed. Philadelphia: FA Davis, Company, 1988:347.

45. Benedetti TJ. Maternal complications of parenteral beta-sympathomimetic therapy for premature labor. Am J Obstet Gynecol 1983;145:1.

46. Longaker MT, Golbus MS, Filly RA, Rosen MA, Chang SW, Harrison MR. Maternal outcome after open fetal surgery. JAMA 1991;265:737.

47. Munson ES, Embro WJ. Enflurane, isoflurane, and halothane and isolated human uterine muscle. Anesthesiology 1977;46:11.

48. Delaney AG. Anesthesia in the pregnant women. Clin Obstet Gynecol 1983;26:795.

49. Greiss FC Jr, Still J, Anderson SG. Effects of local anesthetic on the uterine vasculature and myometrium. Am J Obstet Gynecol 1976;124:889.

50. Hickle RS. Administration of general anesthesia. In: Firestone, LL, Lebowitz, PW, Cook, CE, eds. Clinical anesthesia procedures of the Massachusetts General Hospital, 3rd ed. Boston: Little, Brown, & Co. 1988:136.

51. Rosen MH. Anesthesia for fetal surgery. In: Shnider SM, Levinson G, eds. Anesthesia for obstetrics. 2nd ed. Baltimore: Williams & Wilkins, 1987:206.

52. Ralston DH, Shnider SM. The fetal and neonatal effects of regional anesthesia in obstetrics. Anesthesiology 1978;48:34.

53. Teramo K, Benowitz N, Heyman MA, et al. Effects of lidocaine on heart rate, blood pressure, and electrocorticogram in fetal sheep. Am J Obstet Gynecol 1974;118:935.

54. Vannucci RC, Wolf JW. Oxidative metabolism in fetal rat brain during maternal anesthesia. Anesthesiology 1978;48:238.

55. Johnson MD, Birnbach DJ, Burchman C, Greene MF,

Datta S, Ostheimer GW. Fetal surgery and general anesthesia: A case report and review. J Clin Anesth 1989;1:363.

56. Seeds JW, Corke BC, Spielman FJ. Prevention of fetal movement during invasive procedures with pancuronium bromide. Am J Obstet Gynecol 1986;128:818.

57. Chestnut DH, Weiner CP, Thompson CS, McLaughlin GL. Intravenous administration of d-tubocurarine and pancuronium in fetal lambs. Am J Obstet Gynecol 1989;160:510.

58. de Crespigny LC, Robinson HP, Ross AW, Quinn M. Curarisation of fetus for intrauterine procedures [letter]. Lancet 1985;1:1164.

59. Smith BE, Gaub ML, Moya F. Teratogenic effects of anesthetic agents: nitrous oxide. Anesth Analg 1968; 44:726.

60. Warren TM, Datta S, Ostheimer GW, Naulty JS, Weiss JB, Morrison JA. Comparison of the maternal and neonatal effects of halothane, enflurane, and isoflurane for cesarean delivery. Anesth Analg 1983;62:516.

61. Pederson H. Nonobstetric surgery in the pregnant patient. In: James FM, III, Wheeler AS, Dewan DM, eds. Obstetric anesthesia: The complicated patient 2nd ed. Philadelphia: FA Davis Company, 1988:531.

62. Gregory GA, Wade JG, Beihl DR, Ong BY, Sitar DS. Fetal anesthetic reqirement (MAC) for halothane. Anesth Analg 1983;62:9.

63. Norris MC, Joseph J, Leighton BL. Anesthesia for perinatal surgery. Am J Perinatology 1989;6:39.

64. Biehl DR, Tweed WA, Cote J, Wade JG, Sitar D. Effect of halothane on cardiac output and regional flow in the fetal lamb in utero. Anesth Analg 1983;62:489.

65. Biehl DR, Cote J, Wade JG, Gregory GA. Uptake of halothane by the foetal lamb in utero. Can Anaesth Soc J 1983;30:24.

66. Biehl DR, Yarnell R, Wade JG, Sitar D. The uptake of isoflurane by the foetal lamb in utero: Effect on regional blood flow. Can Anaesth Soc J 1983;30:581.

67. Yarnell R, Biehl DR, Tweed WA, Gregory GA, Sitar D. The effect of halothane anaesthesia on the asphyxiated foetal lamb in utero. Can Anaesth Soc J 1983;30:474.

68. Palahniuk RJ, Doig GA, Johnson GN, Pash MD. Maternal halothane anesthesia reduced cerebral blood flow in the acidotic sheep fetus. Anesth Analg 1980;59:35.

69. Baker BW, Hughes SC, Shnider SM, Field DR, Rosen MA. Maternal anesthesia and the stressed fetus: Effects of isoflurane on the asphyxiated fetal lamb. Anesthesiology 1990;72:65.

70. Wright RG, Shnider SM. Hypotension and regional anesthesia. In: Shnider SM, Levinson G, eds. Anesthesia for obstetrics. 2nd ed. Baltimore: Williams & Wilkins, 1987:293.

71. Jouppila P, Kuikka J, Jouppila R, Hollmen A. Effect of induction of general anesthesia for cesarean section on intervillous blood flow. Acta Obstet Gynaecol 1979; 58:249.

72. Palahniuk RJ, Shnider SM. Maternal and fetal cardiovascular and acid–base changes during halothane and isoflurane anesthesia in the pregnant ewe. Anesthesiology 1974;41:462.

73. Levinson G, Shnider SM. Anesthesia for surgery during pregnancy. In: Shnider SM, Levinson G, eds. Anesthesia for obstetrics. 2nd ed. Baltimore: Williams & Wilkins, 1987:188.

74. Harrison MR, Ross NA, de Lorimier AA. Correction of congenital diaphragmatic hernia in utero. III. Development of a successful surgical technique using abdominoplasty to avoid compromise of umbilical blood flow. J Pediatr Surg 1981;16:934.

75. De Muylder X, Fouron JC, Bard H, Urfer FN. Changes in the systolic time intervals of the fetal heart after surgical manipulation of the fetus. Am J Obstet Gynecol 1983;147:285.

76. Spielman FJ, Seeds JW, Corke BC. Anesthesia for fetal surgery. Anaesthesia 1984;39:756.

77. Brodner RA, Markowitz RS, Lantner HJ. Feasibility of intracranial surgery in the primate fetus. J Neurosurg 1987;66:276.

CHAPTER 13

Obstetric Management of Labor

Linda Chan
Ji-Bin Liu

EVENTS BEFORE PARTURITION

Definitions

The average duration of pregnancy in humans is 280 days (40 weeks) from the first day of the last menstrual period, or 267 days after ovulation. A fetus reaches term at 40 ± 2 weeks, is viable at 500 g, and is mature at 2500 g. Labor at 40 ± 2 weeks is labor at term. Preterm labor is labor between 20 to 37 completed weeks of pregnancy. A fetus born before 20 completed weeks of pregnancy is an abortus.

Preparatory Events

Before labor begins, several physiologic phenomena commonly occur. These events serve to ready the fetus and uterus for the onset of true labor.[1]

Lightening

Lightening is a subjective sensation felt by the mother as the baby settles into the brim of the pelvis. The abdominal shape changes. The fundal region flattens while the lower abdomen, just above the pubic bone, bulges. The uterus now compresses the bladder, inciting urinary frequency. In primigravid women, lightening (or engagement) commonly occurs 2 to 3 weeks before the onset of labor. Further descent of the fetus does not occur until late in labor. In most multigravid women, lightening does not take place until early in labor.

Cervical Ripening, Effacement, and "Bloody Show"

Before the onset of parturition, the cervix frequently softens and becomes increasingly flexible; this process is called *cervical ripening*. The softening of the cervix results from the following factors:

- A rise in its water content due to an increase in the relative amount of various glycosaminoglycans that have the capacity to retain water
- Collagen lysis and rearrangement of the collagen fibers

With cervical ripening, effacement (thinning or obliteration) of the cervix occurs as it is taken up into the lower uterine segment. Because of cervical effacement, the mucous plug (which often is blood-tinged) filling the cervical canal may break free. Labor usually begins several hours to a few days after this "bloody show." The average length of the unripe, uneffaced cervix is 2.5 cm. During labor, the cervix gradually thins until it is completely retracted and the cervicovaginal angle completely disappears (100% effaced). Figure 13-1 shows an example of the progression of cervical effacement and dilation during labor.

False Labor

During the later part of pregnancy, the uterus undergoes irregular, sporadic, brief contractions that produce neither progressive effacement and dilatation of the cervix nor descent of the presenting part. These contractions, so-called false labor or Braxton Hicks

contractions, may serve a physiologic role in preparing the uterus and cervix for true labor. Braxton Hicks contractions often are confined to the lower abdomen and groin and do not usually involve all the myometrium. The contractions of true labor usually originate in the fundal region and spread over the entire uterus and through to the lower back. False labor can be rhythmic and of mild intensity; however, these contractions may be painful and prevent the patient from sleeping and resting. The hazards of false labor include maternal physical and mental exhaustion, apprehension, and premature intervention by the obstetrician. The treatment for false labor is sedation and rest. When Braxton Hicks contractions occur before 37 completed weeks of pregnancy, it is important to distinguish them from true preterm labor.

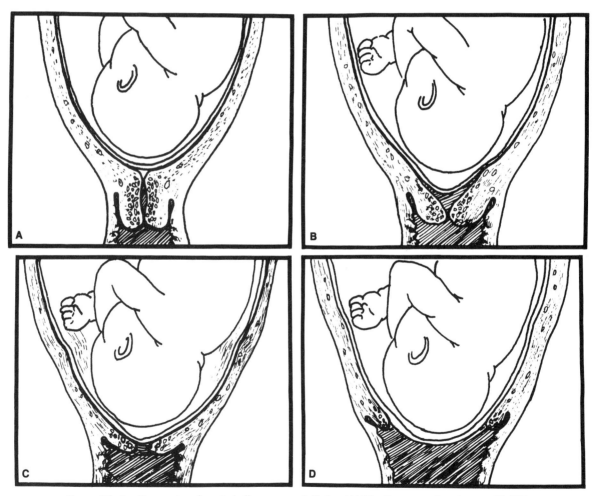

Figure 13–1. Progression of cervical effacement and dilation. (**A**) 0% effacement, closed cervix. (**B**) 50% effacement, closed cervix. (**C**) 100% effacement, 2–3 cm of cervical dilation. (**D**) 100% effacement, 9 cm of cervical dilation.

INITIATION OF PARTURITION

The exact mechanism of the initiation and progression of labor in the human is not entirely clear. Two schools of thought argue whether the fetus or the extrafetal tissues of the conceptus are the origins of the chain of events that begins parturition. A communication system exists between fetus and mother. It has two functional arms: the fetal–placental–maternal endocrine arm, and the fetal–decidual paracrine arm. Regardless of whether the chain begins within or outside the fetus, the signal is translated into the activation of the maternal myometrium and so labor.[2]

The uterine muscle cells undergo hypertrophy and hyperplasia up to the 20th week of gestation. After that, the predominant event is the marked distention and stretching of muscle fibers. Throughout most of gestation, the uterus rests in a somewhat quiescent state. Progressive increases in myometrial contractions antecede parturition. Possibly, labor begins when the myometrial fibers have stretched to their maximum (*i.e.,* pregnancy at term, polyhydramnios, multiple gestations).

Chemical Mediators

Oxytocin, an octapeptide hormone made by the posterior pituitary gland, induces uterine contractions and, during lactation, causes milk let-down. It was once thought to play a key role in the onset of labor. As parturition nears, the uterus becomes maximally sensitive to oxytocin as its oxytocin-receptor concentrations rise. However, an increase in circulating oxytocin concentration is difficult to prove, questioning the importance of oxytocin in the initiation of labor. Still, the elevation in oxytocin-receptor density may allow the myometrium to react to a small increase in circulating oxytocin. This change in the uterine sensitivity to endogenous oxytocin may play an adjuvant role in the initiation of partuition.[3,4] Oxytocin stimulates endometrial/decidual prostaglandin synthesis. In addition, prostaglandins make the myometrium more sensitive to oxytocin. It is possible that oxytocin may play a role in initiation of labor in conjunction with the prostaglandins.[3]

The decidua vera of pregnancy is macrophage-like and may play a role in the initiation and maintenance of labor. Its activation results in an outpouring of prostaglandins (prostaglandin [$PGF_{2\alpha}$] and prostaglandin [PGE_2]), arachidonic acid, platelet-activating factor, and selected cytokines, including interleukin-1. These factors, alone or in concert, can facilitate labor. Bac-

terial endotoxins or immunologic mechanisms may stimulate the decidua to synthesis and release the above compounds. The decidua vera may link infection in pregnancy with the onset of labor. The prevention of decidual activation may ensure myometrial quiescence and the maintenance of pregnancy.[1,2,5]

The fetal membranes, the amnion and chorion laeve, also may serve a pivotal role in the initiation of parturition. They are rich in arachidonic acid, the substrate for prostaglandin synthesis. The amnion and chorion laeve produce almost exclusively PGE_2, a potent uterotropin (serving to prepare the uterus for labor) that accumulates in the amniotic fluid. Early in labor, the amniotic fluid concentration of PGE_2, probably amnion origin, increases. As labor progresses, amniotic fluid $PGF_{2\alpha}$, preferentially synthesized by the decidua, and its metabolite, prostaglandin FM, increase.[1,6]

Progesterone and estrogen play only minor roles in the initiation of parturition in humans. The reduction of maternal plasma progesterone before labor commonly seen in sheep and other animal species does not play a role in the onset of labor in humans. Estrogen serves only a permissive function in parturition. Prolonged gestation or dysfunctional labor occasionally correlates with hypoestrogenism (fetal anencephaly, fetal adrenal hypoplasia, and placental sulfatase deficiency).[7]

Onset of Labor

Labor is characterized by regular, painful, progressive uterine contractions that cause dilation and effacement of the cervix, with descent of the presenting fetal part. The ultimate result is the delivery of the fetus and placenta through the birth canal.

The mechanism of labor comprises various movements of the fetus to enable its head to adapt to the bony maternal pelvic canal through which the fetus must pass during the birth process. Familiarity with the shape and size of the various types of pelves facilitates the understanding of normal and abnormal mechanisms of labor.

THE FEMALE PELVIS

Anatomy

The true pelvis is the only bony canal the fetus must pass through during its birth. This passageway lies beneath the pelvic brim, or linea terminalis. To describe the location of the fetus within the pelvis, it is divided into the following four imaginary planes (Figs. 13-2 and 13-3):

- The plane of pelvic inlet
- The plane of greatest dimensions
- The plane of the mid pelvis (least pelvic dimensions)
- The plane of pelvic outlet

The typical adult female pelvic inlet has an anteroposterior diameter of 10.5 cm (the obstetric conjugate) and a transverse diameter of 13.5 cm. The plane of least pelvic dimensions in the mid-pelvis has an anteroposterior diameter of 12 cm and a transverse or interspinous diameter (between the ischial spines) of greater than 10 cm (Fig. 13-4). This mid-pelvis plane is the most important because it has the least room; it is here where the arrest of labor progress often occurs. The plane of greatest dimensions lacks obstetric significance. If the areas of the pelvic inlet and mid-pelvis are adequate, the pelvic outlet will usually pose no problem to labor and delivery of the fetus.[8,9]

Classification

According to Caldwell and Moloy,[10] there are four pure types of pelves. They are named based on the shape of the inlet with mention of the nonconforming outlet. The four basic types of pelves are gynecoid, android, anthropoid, and platypelloid (Fig. 13-5). Many

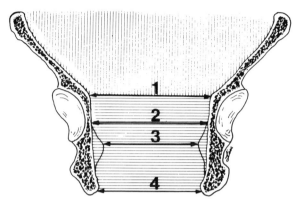

Figure 13.3. Coronal section of an adult female pelvis. (*1*) Plane of pelvic inlet. (*2*) Plane of greatest dimensions. (*3*) Plane of mid-pelvis (least pelvic dimensions). (*4*) Plane of pelvic outlet.

pelves are mixed with characteristics of more than one basic type. The gynecoid pelvis is the normal female pelvis with a round or transverse oval-shaped inlet. It is the most common type of pelvis, occurring in almost 50% of women. Approximately 20% of women have an android pelvis, a male-type pelvis with a heart- or wedge-shaped inlet. The extreme form of android pelvis frequently is associated with obstructed labor and difficult deliveries. The anthropoid pelvis has a long anteroposterior oval-shaped inlet. Twenty-five percent of women, commonly non-white, have this type of pelvis. The platypelloid pelvis, seen in only 3% to 5% of women, is flat with a flat transverse oval-shaped inlet. Labor in women with the platypelloid-type pelvis often ends with cesarean birth.[9,10]

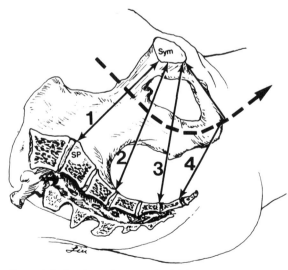

Figure 13–2. Sagittal section of adult female pelvis. (*1*) Plane of pelvic inlet. (*2*) Plane of greatest dimensions. (*3*) Plane of mid-pelvis (least pelvic dimensions). (*4*) Plane of pelvic outlet. (sym = symphysis pubis)

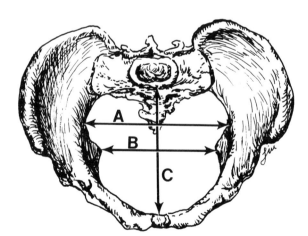

Figure 13–4. Anteroposterior view of the female pelvis. (*A*) Transverse diameter of pelvic inlet (13.5 cm). (*B*) Interspinous diameter of the mid pelvis (10 cm). (*C*) Anteroposterior diameter of the inlet, or the obstetric conjugate (10.5 cm).

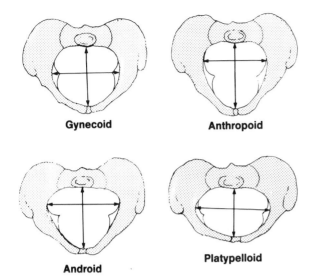

Figure 13–5. The Caldwell and Moloy classification of the four pure types of pelvis.

CHARACTERISTICS OF THE FETUS

Fetal Presentations

Presentation, or lie, is the relation of the long axis of the fetus to the long axis of the mother. It is the pole of the fetus that occupies the lower portion of the uterus.

The fetal lie may be either longitudinal or transverse. With a longitudinal lie, the presenting part is either the head (cephalic) or the breech. With a transverse lie, the shoulder presents. Oblique lie is in between the longitudinal and transverse presentations.

Cephalic presentations are classified according to the relation of the head to the body of the fetus (fetal attitude or habitus). Depending on the degree of flexion or extension of the fetal head, the occiput (vertex), face, mentum (chin), sinciput (large fontanelle), or brow may present (Fig. 13-6). Sinciput and brow presentations are considered intermediate conditions. They usually convert spontaneously to vertex or face presentations during labor.

Breech presentations are classified according to the flexion or extension of the thighs and knees (Fig. 13-7). If both thighs and knees are flexed, it is a complete breech. If the thighs are flexed with both knees extended, it is a frank breech. A single-footling breech has one leg extended at the thigh and knee, with the foot as the presenting part. The other leg is flexed at the thigh with either flexion or extension of the knee. A double-footling breech has both legs extended at the thigh and knee and both feet presenting.

Fetal Head

The fetal head is important from the obstetric viewpoint because it is the largest and the least compressible

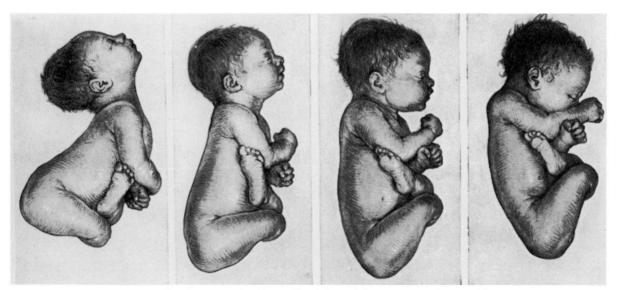

Figure 13–6. Differences in attitude of fetus in (from left to right) vertex, sinciput, brow, and face presentations. (Cunningham FG, MacDonald PC, Gant NF, eds. Williams Obstetrics, 18th ed. Norwalk, CT, Appleton & Lange, 1989:178)

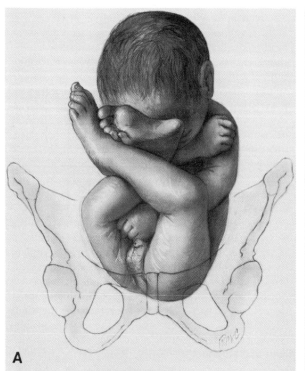

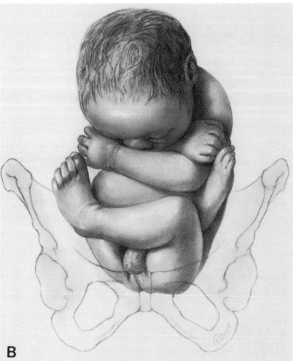

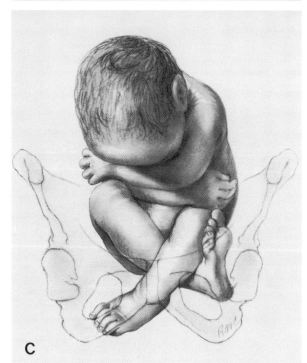

Figure 13–7. (**A**) Frank breech presentation. (**B**) Complete breech presentation. (**C**) Incomplete, or footling, breech presentation. (Cunningham FG, MacDonald PC, Gant NF, eds. Williams Obstetrics, 18th ed. Norwalk, CT: Appleton & Lange, 1989:178)

part of the fetus. In the cephalic presentation, the head must change its shape (molding) to adapt to the maternal pelvis. The force of uterine contractions, the resistance of the bony pelvis, and the loose connections between the bones of the fetal skull combine to mold the fetal head to the shape of the pelvis.

The anterior fontanelle (bregma) is the diamond-shaped junction of the parietal and frontal bones. The posterior fontanelle is the triangular junction of the two parietal bones and the occipital bone (Figs. 13-8 and 13-9). These landmarks and suture lines can be felt during a pelvic examination to confirm fetal position during labor. The average dimensions of the fetal-head diameters are listed in Table 13-1. Figure 13-10 shows some examples of fetal positions in the vertex presentation.

In prolonged labor, a caput succedaneum (edematous scalp swelling) may form before complete cervical dilatation in the portion of the fetal scalp immediately over the cervical os. Caput succedaneum can prevent the examiner from differentiating sutures and fontanelles.

Diagnosis of Fetal Presentation and Position

The diagnosis of fetal presentation and position is made by abdominal palpation, pelvic examination, and auscultation of the location of the fetal heart.

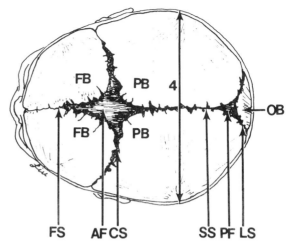

Figure 13–9. Common landmarks, suture lines, and diameter of the fetal head. (AF = anterior fontanelle; CS = coronal suture; FB = frontal bone; FS = frontal suture; line 4 = biparietal diameter; LS = lambdoid suture; OB = occipital bone; PB = parietal bone; PF = posterior fontanelle; SS = sagittal suture)

Ultrasonography helps to confirm fetal position in cases in which the physical examination may be difficult (*i.e.,* oligohydramnios or polyhydramnios, abnormal fetal lie, preterm pregnancies). In addition, sonography is valuable in placental localization, especially in cases with abnormal vaginal bleeding.

Fetal Station and Engagement

Station is the distance between the presenting fetal part to an imaginary line drawn between the maternal ischial spines. The leading bony portion of the fetal head (not the caput succedaneum) is used to estimate station in a cephalic presentation. In the breech presentation, the buttocks at the bitrochanteric diameter are used. By convention, station zero is when the presenting part is at the level of the ischial spines. Two systems exist for the designation of fetal stations, the three-level and the five-level classification. In the three-level system, the long axis of the birth canal is divided into thirds from the pelvic inlet to the ischial spines and again divided into thirds from the ischial spines to the pelvic outlet. When the presenting part is above the ischial spines, the station is designated with a minus sign (station −1, −2, −3). When the presenting part is below the ischial spines, a plus sign is given (station +1, +2, +3). In the five-level system, the station of the fetal head is estimated in centimeters away from the ischial spines. The fetus traverses the pelvis from about −5 sta-

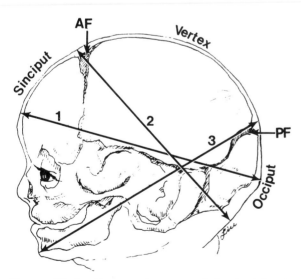

Figure 13-8. Common diameters of the fetal head. (AF = anterior fontanelle; PF = posterior fontanelle; line 1 = occipitofrontal diameter; line 2 = suboccipito-bregmatic diameter; line 3 = occipitomental diameter)

Table 13–1

Common Fetal Head Diameters

DIAMETER	AVERAGE DIMENSION (CM)	COMMENT
Occipitofrontal	11.0–11.5	Presents in military attitude
Biparietal	9.5	The greatest transverse diameter
Bitemporal	8.0	The shortest transverse diameter
Occipitomental	12.5–13.5	The longest anteroposterior diameter; presents in brow presentation
Suboccipitobregmatic	9.5	The anteroposterior diameter that presents in well-flexed head

(After Cunningham FG, MacDonald PC, Gant NF. The morphological and functional development of the fetus. In: Cunningham FG, MacDonald PC, Gant NF, eds. Williams Obstetrics, 18th ed. Norwalk, Connecticut: Appleton & Lange, 1989:87)

tion at the true pelvic inlet to +5 station at the outlet (bulging perineum). In Figure 13-3, line 1 represents −5 station, line 3 represents 0 station, and line 4 represents +5 station as the presenting part descends through the pelvis.[11,12]

In the vertex presentation, engagement occurs when the fetal biparietal diameter passes the plane of the pelvic inlet and the leading bony portion of the head is at or below the ischial spines (Fig. 11). Most heads engage in the occiput transverse position and deliver in the occiput anterior position. Engagement in the transverse position is common in gynecoid, android, and platypelloid pelves, whereas oblique engagement is more frequent in the anthropoid type pelvis.

STAGES OF LABOR

There are four stages of labor. The first stage of labor begins with the onset of true labor and ends with the complete dilation of the cervix (10 cm). The average duration of the first stage of labor is 8 hours in the primipara (or nullipara) and 5 hours in the multipara (range 6–18 h and 2–10 h, respectively). The second stage of labor extends from full dilation of the cervix to the birth of the fetus. The average duration of the second stage is 50 minutes in the primipara and 20 minutes in the multipara (range 30 min–3 h and 5–30 min, respectively). The third stage of labor begins with the birth of the fetus and ends with the complete expulsion or extraction of the placenta. The third stage is usually complete within 30 minutes of the delivery of the fetus

for both primipara and multipara. The fourth stage begins with the delivery of the placenta and ends at approximately 1 hour postpartum when the parturient is stabilized.[11,12]

The major difficulty in diagnosing labor is differentiating it from false labor. Unlike true labor, false labor is not accompanied by progressive cervical change or descent of the presenting fetal part.

First Stage of Labor

The first stage of labor must overcome cervical resistance. It is divided into latent and active phases. Early cervical effacement and softening may occur before true labor, but during the first stage of labor, the entire cervical length retracts into the lower uterine segment as the cervix progressively dilates.

The latent phase of labor is the time between the onset of regular uterine contractions to the beginning of the active phase (appreciable cervical effacement and more rapid cervical dilation). The duration of the latent phase varies. It can be differentiated from the active phase of labor with certainty only in retrospect. The average latent phase in nulliparas lasts 6.4 hours, with a standard deviation of 5.1 hours. By 20 hours, 95% of patients will complete the latent phase of labor. The latent phase is prolonged when it exceeds 20 hours in the nullipara and 14 hours in the multipara. The latent phase usually ends at 3 to 4 cm cervical dilation.[12,13] During the latent phase, contractions produce mild to moderate discomfort and may be irregular and infre-

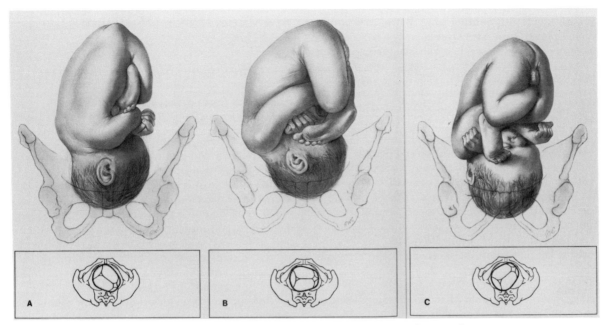

Figure 13–10. Vertex presentation. **(A)** Right occipitoanterior position. **(B)** Right occipital transverse position. **(C)** Right occipitoposterior position. (Cunningham FG, MacDonald PC, Gant NF, eds. Williams Obstetrics. 18th ed. Norwalk, CT: Appleton & Lange, 1989:180)

quent. Eventually, a regular pattern of painful contractions begins.

The active phase of labor usually begins when the cervix reaches 3 to 4 cm of dilation. The active phase of labor is subdivided into an acceleration phase, the phase of maximum slope, and the deceleration phase. The existence of a deceleration phase is not universally accepted. Its occurrence may be an artifact in clinical observation (*i.e.*, not an actual slowing down in cervical dilation, but the cervix being retracted cephalad

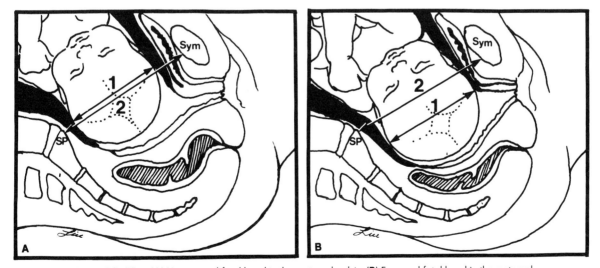

Figure 13–11. **(A)** Unengaged fetal head in the maternal pelvis. **(B)** Engaged fetal head in the maternal pelvis. (line 1 = biparietal diameter; line 2 = pelvic inlet; sym = symphysis pubis, sp = spine)

around the fetal presenting part). When cervical dilation is plotted against time, the curve typically takes on a sigmoid shape (Fig. 13-12). The fetal presenting part begins to descend in earnest during the phase of maximum slope. Descent then continues at its maximum rate through the second stage of labor. Most nulliparas have a maximum slope of cervical dilation in the active phase of at least 1.2 cm/h and a maximum slope of descent of 1.0 cm/h. In multiparas, the maximum rates of cervical dilation and descent are 1.5 cm/h and 2.0 cm/h in the phase of maximum slope and the deceleration phase, respectively.[12,13]

Friedman[12] divides the course of labor into three functional divisions. The first is the preparatory division. Here, there are changes in the ground substance and connective tissues in the cervix and possibly the uterus. The preparatory division includes the latent and the acceleration phases and is sensitive to sedation and analgesia. The second division is the dilatational division. It occurs during the phase of maximum slope in the active phase of labor. This division is predominantly involved with rapid cervical dilation and is usually not affected by sedation or analgesia. The third division is the pelvic division. It begins with the deceleration phase and continues through the second stage of labor simultaneously with the phase of maximum slope of descent. It is during the pelvic division of labor that the cardinal movements of the delivery of the fetus take place (refer to "Delivery of the Fetus").[1]

MANAGEMENT OF NORMAL LABOR

First and Second Stage of Labor

Patient Evaluation, Preparation, and Administration of Fluids

Maternal vital signs such as temperature, blood pressure, and pulse and respiratory rate are evaluated and recorded. Vital signs should be checked as clinically indicated but at least every 1 to 2 hours during the first and more frequently during the second stage of labor. Blood for hemoglobin and hematocrit, a blood group, rhesus type, and antibody screen is drawn upon admission. This blood later may be cross-matched if needed for transfusion in case of obstetric hemorrhage and emergencies. Additionally, a voided urine specimen should be examined for protein and glucose.

Obstetric experts no longer advocate the routine use of enema and perineal preparation (pubic and vulvar shaving). An enema may help minimize fecal contamination during labor and delivery in patients who are constipated or have large amounts of palpable stool. Enema should not be used to stimulate labor.

Because gastric emptying slows during labor, the patient should take nothing by mouth with the onset of labor. This precaution will hopefully lessen the risk of aspiration pneumonitis, especially if general anesthesia is required for an unforeseen emergent delivery.

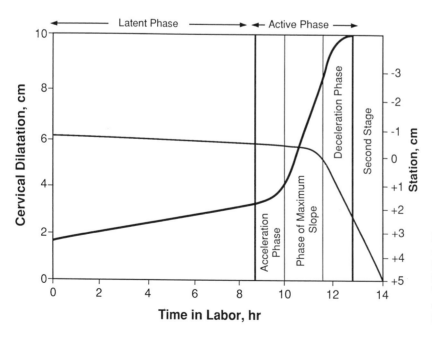

Figure 13–12. Composite of cervical dilation and fetal descent curves illustrating their interrelationship and their component phases. (After Cohen WR, Friedman EA, eds. Management of labor. Baltimore, MD: University Park Press, 1983:13)

An intravenous catheter with infusion of crystalloid solution should be established in active labor to prevent dehydration. Any patient needing analgesia for relief of labor pain especially requires an intravenous line. A large-bore (16- to 18-gauge) intravenous catheter should be used; these women may require transfusion for obstetric hemorrhage or need other medical treatments. Oxytocin, to facilitate uterine contraction before or after delivery, also may be given intravenously.

A careful record of fluid intake and urine output is necessary for the laboring patient. Oxytocin has considerable antidiuretic activity. Conduction analgesia can obliterate the urge to void. The bladder should be catheterized and emptied if the patient has difficulty voiding and the bladder is distended.

Diagnosis of Ruptured Membranes and Amniotomy

Spontaneous rupture of the amniotic membranes may occur anytime before (premature rupture of membranes) or during labor. The obstetrician may choose to rupture membranes artificially (amniotomy) during labor. Amniotomy may shorten the duration of labor slightly but increases the risk of chorioamnionitis if labor is prolonged. If the presenting part is not engaged, the umbilical cord may prolapse or become compressed between the presenting part and the pelvis after amniotomy. Immediately after rupture of the membranes, a vaginal examination should be done to evaluate cervical dilation and to detect prolapse of the umbilical cord. Amniotomy is not needed routinely unless internal monitoring is indicated. At the time of ruptured membranes, the volume of amniotic fluid and the presence or absence of meconium are noted.[11]

Vaginal Examinations and Evaluation of Labor Progress

The obstetrician should determine fetal presentation and position upon admission to the labor suite by abdominal and vaginal examination. If the patient presents with vaginal bleeding, the possibility of placenta previa or abruption must be eliminated before vaginal examination. At this time, station, cervical dilatation, and effacement also should be evaluated and recorded.

The vaginal examinations should be kept to a minimum and done under aseptic conditions to minimize bacterial contamination and decrease the risk of intrauterine infection. This precaution is especially important during the latent phase, or after the membranes rupture. Once in the active phase of labor, cervical examination approximately every 2 hours helps to follow the progress of labor. If the patient reports severe rectal pressure and the urge to push, vaginal examination will decide if full cervical dilatation and fetal descent have occurred (*i.e.,* imminent delivery of the fetus). If a significant fetal heart rate deceleration occurs, prompt vaginal examination is needed to rule out a prolapsed umbilical cord.

At the beginning of the second stage, the parturient usually has a desire to bear down with each contraction. It is important to instruct the patient not to bear down before complete cervical dilation.

Uterine Activity

Uterine contractility defines the power or adequacy of labor. The frequency and duration of uterine contractions may be palpated by an examiner or quantified by an external tocodynamometer. However, a pressure catheter in the amniotic cavity (intrauterine pressure catheter) is the only accurate way to measure the intensity or strength of uterine contractions. The use of an intrauterine pressure catheter is recommended during oxytocin augmentation of labor, or in patients undergoing a trial of labor after a previous cesarean delivery.

An effective uterine contraction reaches an intensity of 40 to 60 mm Hg. Uterine contractions of an intensity less than 25 mm Hg are ineffective and rarely produce cervical dilatation. In adequate labor, an average of three uterine contractions occurs every 10 minutes. Uterine work is measured in Montevideo units. This number represents the sum of the peak amplitude of all contractions within a 10-minute period. Adequate labors may have between 95 to 395 Montevideo units. Failure to progress or arrest of labor in the active phase is diagnosed when there are at least 200 Montevideo units per 10 minutes for at least 2 hours without cervical change.[13]

Maternal Position

During the first stage of labor, the parturient may ambulate, sit, or recline if intermittent monitoring confirms fetal well-being. In patients lying in bed, the lateral recumbent position, instead of the supine position, avoids aortocaval compression and helps assure adequate uteroplacental perfusion. To avoid prolapse of the umbilical cord, patients with ruptured membranes and an unengaged presenting fetal part should not ambulate. During the second stage, the mother may assume any comfortable position that allows effective bearing down.

Intrapartum Fetal Heart Rate Monitoring

During labor, the fetal heart rate may be counted intermittently with a fetal stethoscope or a Doppler ultrasonic device. Alternatively, continuous electronic monitoring of the fetal heart rate and uterine contractions may be used. Retrospective studies suggested that continuous electronic fetal monitoring detects fetal asphyxia in labor[14] and decreased the frequency of intrapartum stillbirth.[15] However, randomized prospective studies of low-risk and high-risk pregnancies have not confirmed this finding.[16–18] The perinatal mortality rate did not differ between those women monitored with auscultation and those monitored with electronic fetal monitoring.[17,19] Two studies suggest that continuous electronic fetal monitoring has the advantage over intermittent auscultation in lowering perinatal morbidity,[19,20] whereas six found no difference.[21] Most studies have found a significant increase in vaginal and abdominal operative deliveries in women receiving intrapartum continuous electronic fetal monitoring.

For low-risk patients, the American College of Obstetricians and Gynecologists and the American Academy of Pediatrics have recommended intermittent auscultation of the fetal heart every 30 minutes during the active phase of the first stage of labor, and at least every 15 minutes during the second stage. For higher-risk patients, they recommend listening every 15 minutes during active labor and every 5 minutes in the second stage of labor. Intermittent auscultation of the fetal heart requires a 1:1 nurse:patient ratio. It is done during a uterine contraction and for 30 seconds afterward. When using continuous electronic monitoring, the tracings should be evaluated at the same time intervals as those recommended for intermittent auscultation.[21]

Delivery of the Fetus

During labor in an occiput presentation, the baby undergoes a series of movements to adapt to the irregular shape of the maternal pelvic canal. These movements, the so-called cardinal movements of labor, are as follows:

1. Engagement
2. Descent
3. Flexion
4. Internal rotation
5. Extension
6. External rotation
7. Expulsion

In a typical occipitoanterior labor, the head delivers by extension over the perineum, followed by external rotation (or restitution) back to the transverse or anterior position. The anterior shoulder then delivers under the symphysis pubis, followed by the posterior shoulder over the perineal body. The rest of body follows quickly after the delivery of the posterior shoulder. Figure 13-13 illustrates the cardinal movements of labor and delivery in the left occiput anterior position.

The mechanism of labor in most occipitoposterior presentations is similar to that of the occipitoanterior presentation, except that the head has to rotate 135 degrees to the anterior before extension. Deviation from the normal mechanism of labor may occur if (1) the head does not completely rotate, resulting in transverse arrest, or (2) if ineffective contractions, large fetus, or inadequate flexion of the head lead to persistent occiput posterior position.

Forceps Delivery

Obstetric forceps are used for traction and rotation of the fetal head to hasten delivery of the fetus electively or for fetal or maternal indications (Table 13-2).[22] Forceps applications are classified as outlet, low, or mid depending on the station and position of the fetal head (Table 13-3). Mid-forceps deliveries are reserved for sudden severe fetal or maternal compromise. Simultaneous preparation for cesarean delivery must begin if forceps delivery fails. High-forceps (unengaged fetal head) and difficult mid-forceps deliveries have no place in modern obstetrics because of the associated maternal and fetal morbidity and mortality.

Episiotomy

Episiotomy is done as the head is crowning or distending the vulva and perineum to prevent perineal lacerations during delivery of the fetus. Episiotomy is routinely cut during forceps or vacuum delivery. It may be a midline incision, from the fourchette to middle of the perineum before the rectum, or it may be a mediolateral incision from the fourchette into the perineum approximately 45 degrees laterally and away from the rectum. Median episiotomy offers less blood loss, ease of repair, and less pain. The disadvantage of the median episiotomy is the risk of extension through the anal sphincter and into the rectum. The mediolateral episiotomy rarely extends through the anal sphincter and into the rectum. Disadvantages of the mediolateral episiotomy include greater blood loss, more difficult repair, more pain, and, occasionally, dyspareunia.

Theoretically, episiotomy prevents pelvic relaxation and the possible long-term consequences of childbirth, such as cystocele, urinary incontinence, rectocele, and the prolapse of the uterus; however, some argue against the use of routine prophylactic episiotomy because, by

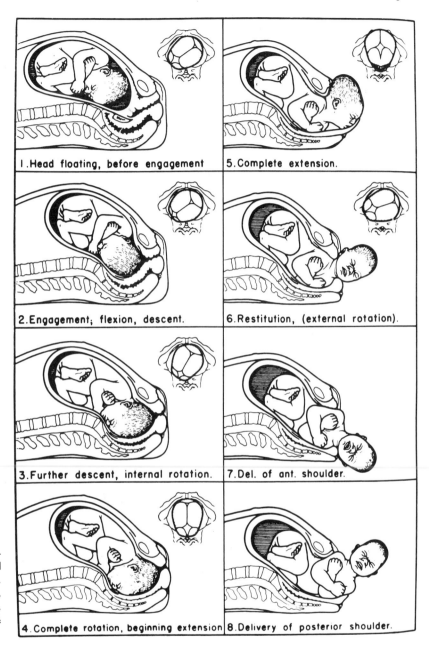

Figure 13–13. Cardinal movements in the mechanism of labor and delivery, left occiput anterior position. (Cunningham FG, MacDonald PC, Gant NF, eds. Williams Obstetrics, 18th ed, Norwalk, CT: Appleton & Lange, 1989:228)

1. Head floating, before engagement
2. Engagement; flexion, descent.
3. Further descent, internal rotation.
4. Complete rotation, beginning extension
5. Complete extension.
6. Restitution, (external rotation).
7. Del. of ant. shoulder.
8. Delivery of posterior shoulder.

the time the episiotomy is done, damage to the pelvic musculature has already occurred.[22] Nonetheless, episiotomy is indicated if the perineum is not adequately stretched and lacerations are anticipated, or when additional vaginal space is needed for operative delivery or for breech extractions.

A straight incision from an episiotomy is usually easier to repair than ragged lacerations. By definition, a first-degree perineal laceration involves only the vaginal mucosa or perineal skin. A second-degree laceration involves the submucosal tissue with or without damage to the perineal body. A third-degree laceration involves an extension into the body of the anal sphincter, and a fourth-degree laceration involves damage through the rectal mucosa.

Complications of inadequate repair of an episiotomy or perineal lacerations include infection, urinary retention, hematomas, and, occasionally, hemorrhagic

Table 13-2

Indications for Obstetric Forceps Delivery

Shortening the Second Stage by Outlet Forceps

Prolonged Second Stage	Definition
Nulliparous	> 3 h with regional anesthesia
	> 2 h without regional anesthesia
Multiparous	> 2 h with regional anesthesia
	> 1 h without regional anesthesia

Fetal Indications

Nonreassuring intrapartum surveillance ("fetal distress")

Maternal Indications

Cardiac disease

Exhaustion

Others

(After American College of Obstetricians and Gynecologists. Obstetric forceps. ACOG Committee Opinion 71. Washington, DC, 1989)

---

shock. A digital rectal examination, done after repair of the episiotomy or lacerations, ensures intact anal sphincter and rectum and should detect any sutures penetrating the rectal mucosa.

Table 13-3

Definitions of Obstetric Forceps

Outlet Forceps

Fetal scalp visible at the introitus without separating the labia

Fetal skull reached the pelvic floor

Fetal head at or on the perineum

Sagittal suture in the following positions:
  Anteroposterior diameter
  Right or left occiput anterior
  Right or left occiput posterior

Rotation cannot exceed 45 degrees

Low Forceps

Leading point of the fetal skull is at station +2 or more
  Rotation 45 degrees or less
  Rotation 45 degrees or more

Midforceps

Fetal head engaged

Leading point of the fetal skull above station +2

(After American College of Obstetricians and Gynecologists. Obstetric forceps. ACOG Committee Opinion 71. Washington, DC, 1989)

Analgesia

The method of pain control may affect the progress of labor. The preparatory division of labor (latent and acceleration phases) is sensitive to sedation and analgesia. The dilatational division of labor (phase of maximum slope) is not. The duration of the second stage also may vary depending on the type of analgesia.

The Third and Fourth Stages of Labor

Separation of the placenta generally occurs within 10 minutes of the end of the second stage. Signs of placental separation include the following:

- A sudden gush of blood from the vagina
- Lengthening of the umbilical cord
- The uterus becoming firm and globular in shape, with the fundal portion rising up in the abdomen

No traction should be applied to the umbilical cord until the placenta has separated. Forceful traction may invert the uterus, producing life-threatening hemorrhage and shock.[11]

Following its delivery, the placenta should be immediately inspected to assure its complete removal. If there is a torn vessel on the chorionic membrane or if there is a missing cotyledon, the uterus must be immediately explored for the removal of retained placental fragments. Retained placenta may incite immediate or delayed postpartum hemorrhage. The perineum, cervix, vagina, sphincter ani, and rectum should be examined for injuries, and surgical repair should be done if needed.

The uterus contracts dramatically after the delivery of the fetus and the placenta. Myometrial contractions occlude the open, bleeding sinuses and provide the primary mechanism of cessation of bleeding from the placental implantation site. Bimanual uterine massage can facilitate this process. Alternatively, when the placenta completely delivers, 10 to 20 units of oxytocin can be added to the intravenous infusion (at a rate of approximately 200 mU/min). Ergot derivatives such as methergine or ergotrate (0.2 mg IM) may be given instead of oxytocin immediately postpartum. Be careful to avoid ergot derivatives in hypertensive parturients. These compounds can elevate blood pressure themselves. The intramuscular route yields fewer hypertensive side effects.

Postpartum hemorrhage is defined as blood loss in excess of 500 mL during the first 24 hours after delivery. In the presence of excessive bleeding or if the placenta has not delivered after 30 minutes in the third stage, manual removal of the placenta under appropriate anesthesia will shorten the third stage and can limit blood loss.

The hour immediately following delivery is the fourth stage of labor. It is during this time that postpartum hemorrhage most commonly occurs. Vital signs and uterine blood loss should be monitored closely. Complaints of severe pelvic pain suggest significant pelvic or perineal trauma. The principal causes of postpartum hemorrhage are uterine atony, trauma to the genital tract, and retained placenta (Table 13-4).

The treatment of uterine atony includes bimanual uterine massage and the administration of oxytocin or ergot derivatives. Intramuscular injection of the 15-

Table 13–4

Predisposing Factors and Causes of Obstetric Hemorrhage

Trauma to the Genital Tract
Large episiotomy, including extensions
Perineal, cervical, or vaginal lacerations
Uterine rupture

Bleeding from Placental Implantation Site
Hypotonic myometrium/uterine atony
   Halogenated hydrocarbon anesthetics
   Conduction analgesia
   Poorly perfused uterus
      Hemorrhage
      Hypotension
   Overdistended uterus
      Large fetus
      Multiple gestation
      Hydramnios
   Exhausted uterus
      Prolonged labor
      Rapid or precipitous labor
      Oxytocin induction or augmentation of labor
   High parity
   Previous history of uterine atony
   Chorioamnionitis
Retained placental tissue
   Avulsed cotyledon
   Succenturiate or accessory lobe
   Abnormally adherent placenta
      Placenta accreta, increta, or percreta

Coagulation Defects

(After Cunningham FG, MacDonald PC, Gant NF. Obstetrical hemorrhage. In: Cunningham FG, MacDonald PC, Gant NF, eds. Williams Obstetrics, 18th ed, Norwalk, CT: Appleton & Lange, 1989:695) methyl derivative of $PGF_{2\alpha}$ at 15- to 90-minute intervals may help if the uterus does not respond to other physical and pharmacotherapy. If retained placental fragments are suspected, manual removal, manual exploration, and possibly curettage of the uterus may be necessary. The genital tract should be carefully inspected and any lacerations repaired. A blood sample can be drawn immediately for the observation of clot formation within 5 minutes to rule out clinical hypofibrinogenemia. In addition, blood tests (hemoglobin/hematocrit, platelet count, fibrinogen, fibrin-split products, prothrombin time, and partial prothrombin time) should be done to diagnose consumptive coal. Placenta accreta, incross, or percreta should be considered as a differential diagnosis in cases of postpartum hemorrhage unresponsive to conventional therapy. In cases in which conventional therapy fails, a laparotomy is indicated for possible bilateral hypogastric artery ligation or hysterectomy as a lifesaving procedure. The uterus generally should not be packed during the treatment of postpartum hemorrhage because one might mask excessive accumulation of blood behind the packing.

MANAGEMENT OF ABNORMAL LABOR

Dystocia

The following three main factors influence the course of labor:

- The powers (uterine contractions)
- The passage (bony pelvis and maternal soft tissues)
- The passenger (size and position of the fetus)[13]

The gradual descent, or change in station, of the presenting part in the pelvis determines the progress of labor. Determining the correct fetal station is important for the evaluation of labor progress. Molding, asynclitism (lateral flexion), deflexion, and caput succedaneum can lead to erroneous diagnosis of station because the head may feel lower than it is.

Dystocia, difficult labor or childbirth, may be caused by the following factors:

- Abnormal or inadequate uterine contractions (uterine dysfunction)
- Abnormalities of the maternal pelvic architecture or size
- Abnormalities in fetal size, presentation, or development

Any of the preceding factors may occur alone or in combination with others. For example, uterine dysfunction often accompanies a contracted pelvis.

Table 13-5 lists the definitions of the major disorders of abnormal labor, their diagnostic criteria, and treatment.[23] Figure 13-14 illustrates graphically some examples of the major labor aberrations.[24] The diagnosis of arrest of labor in the active phase cannot be made until the latent phase has been completed (cervical dilation of at least 3–4 cm) and adequate uterine contractions have been documented (at least 200 Montevideo units every 10 min for 2 h).[13] If using oxytocin to augment labor, the obstetrician should have a timetable in mind for the evaluation of labor progress. If cephalopelvic disproportion (*i.e.,* the fetus is large relative to the maternal bony pelvis) is suspected by abnormal progress of labor, the initiation or continuation of oxytocin stimulation is contraindicated and a cesarean section is indicated.

Shoulder Dystocia

Shoulder dystocia occurs if, after delivery of the fetal head, the delivery of the shoulders (and therefore the rest of the fetal body) arrests. Serious fetal consequences of shoulder dystocia are fractured humerus or clavicle, Erb's palsy secondary to brachial nerve damage, severe fetal asphyxia, possible neurologic damage, and death. Maternal consequences of shoulder dystocia are postpartum hemorrhage because of uterine atony or genital tract trauma, and infection.

If shoulder dystocia is suspected antepartum or intrapartum, a cesarean section is a reasonable and indicated alternative; however, the prediction of fetal shoulder dystocia by history and sonographic estimation of fetal biometry and weight is imprecise. There will always be unexpected cases. Fetal macrosomia with the fetal abdominal circumference larger than the fetal head circumference is a major predisposing factor. The fetal abdomen also may be enlarged because of fetal ascites, enlarged liver or kidneys, or marked bladder distention. Maternal obesity, diabetes mellitus, and post-term pregnancies also correlate with fetal macrosomia. Dysfunctional labor, such as arrest and protraction disorders, prolonged second stage, and mid-pelvic delivery, also increases the risk of shoulder dystocia.[25]

The management of shoulder dystocia requires the presence of a physician experienced in the maneuvers to deliver the fetal shoulders, adequate anesthesia, and a neonatal team for the resuscitation of the newborn.[26,26] If vaginal delivery does not succeed, the Zavanelli ma-

Table 13–5

Major Disorders of Labor

PHASE OF LABOR	NULLIPARA	MULTIPARA	TREATMENT
Latent Phase			
Prolonged latent phase	> 20 h	> 14 h	Rest or oxytocin
Active-phase Protraction Disorders			
Protracted dilatation	< 1.2 cm/h	< 1.5 cm/h	Oxytocin for inade-quate contractions
Protracted descent	< 1.0 cm/h	< 2.0 cm/h	
Active-phase Arrest Disorders			
Secondary arrest of dilatation	> 2 h	> 2 h	Oxytocin or forceps/vacuum delivery or cesarean section
Arrest of descent	> 1 h	> 1 h	
Prolonged deceleration phase	> 3 h	> 1 h	
Second Stage			
Failure to descend	No descent after complete dilatation		Oxytocin or cesarean section

(After Friedman EA. Dysfunctional labor. In Cohen WR, Friedman EA, eds. Management of Labor, 1st ed. Rockville, MD: Aspen Publishers, 1983:11)

neuver, pushing the fetal head back into the vagina and delivering the fetus by cesarean section, may be employed.[27]

Abnormal Intrapartum Fetal Monitoring

Fetal intolerance to labor, or fetal distress, occurs in 1% to 2% of most obstetric populations. Electronic fetal monitoring can prove a useful screening test for fetal acidosis. When electronic fetal monitoring shows a normal fetal heart rate pattern (120–160 beats/min, short-term variability greater than 6 beats/min, normal long-term variability, acceleration with fetal movements, and absence of decelerations), it is highly predictive of a nonacidotic fetus and normal outcome. Yet, an abnormal or nonreassuring electronic fetal monitoring test has poor specificity for detecting fetal compromise and little positive predictive value at forecasting subsequent neonatal morbidity or mortality.[28] Specific fetal heart rate patterns associated with increased incidence of fetal compromise are as follows:

- Severe bradycardia
- Repetitive late decelerations
- Undulating baseline alternating rapidly between tachycardia and bradycardia
- Any nonreassuring patterns associated with unexplained decreased or absent baseline variability[21]

In the presence of the preceding nonreassuring intrapartum fetal heart rate patterns, other tests help evaluate the well-being of the fetus before continued labor and delivery are allowed.

Intrapartum Assessment of Fetal Well-being

Some of the available modalities for the intrapartum evaluation of fetal well-being are fetal scalp blood sampling, fetal scalp stimulation, and vibroacoustic stimulation. In a healthy baby, the fetal heart rate should react by acceleration of at least 15 beats above the baseline from fetal scalp stimulation via digital pelvic examination or scalp puncture during fetal blood sampling,[29,30] or, alternatively, with transabdominal vibroacoustic stimulation via an artificial larynx.[31] A reactive fetal heart rate response after the preceding stimulations correlates with a nonacidotic fetus. In those fe-

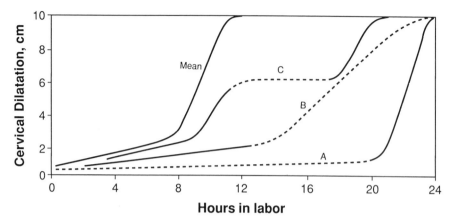

Figure 13–14. The major labor aberrations shown in comparison with the mean cervical dilatation–time curve for nulliparas. (*A*) Prolonged latent phase. (*B*) Protracted active-phase dilatation (primary dysfunctional labor). (*C*) Secondary arrest of dilatation. (After Friedman EA: Dysfunctional labor. In: Greenhill JP, ed. Obstetrics, 13th ed. Philadelphia: WB Saunders, 1965:833)

tuses with a nonreactive fetal heart response, acidosis is present in approximately 50%.[29]

Obtaining fetal blood for blood gas analysis via fetal scalp blood sampling (Fig. 13-15) confirms fetal acid–base status in the presence of nonreassuring fetal heart rate patterns. Fetal scalp blood sampling requires ruptured membranes and sufficient cervical dilation for the application of the endoscope to the presenting fetal part. The scalp is punctured with a 2-mm blade, and fetal blood is collected in a heparinized capillary tube for blood gas analysis. Some contraindications to fetal scalp blood sampling are maternal hemophilia carrier status with fetal status unknown, maternal acquired immunodeficiency syndrome, and active maternal genital infections.[32,33]

Fetal scalp blood pH of 7.25 is normal. Repeat blood sampling depends on the fetal heart rate pattern and progress of labor. Fetal pH between 7.20 and 7.25 is equivocal or suspicious for fetal metabolic compromise. In this setting, the procedure should be repeated in 15 to 30 minutes to detect a possible downward trend. A pH of less than 7.20 is abnormal, suggestive of significant asphyxia, and mandates rapid intervention.[33,34]

Intrapartum Resuscitation

Nonreassuring fetal heart rate patterns during labor require prompt action. Maximize uteroplacental perfusion by repositioning the mother to the lateral position. Improve placental intervillous space perfusion and correct maternal hypotension with rapid infusion of intravenous fluids. Oxygen by face mask at 8 to 10 L/min may improve fetal oxygenation. Intrauterine infusion of saline may diminish recurrent fetal variable decelerations. Amnioinfusion of saline probably works by reducing umbilical cord compression by expanding the intrauterine fluid volume (Fig. 13-16).[34,35] If these measures fail to improve the nonreassuring fetal heart rate pattern, expedient delivery, either vaginally or abdominally via a cesarean section, is indicated.[32]

In the presence of abnormal fetal heart rate patterns, uterine activity should be assessed. Uterine hyperactivity, or hyperstimulation, should be ruled out. If oxytocin is being used, it should be stopped. Some investigators advocate the use of tocolytic agents, such as beta-mimetics, to relax the uterus to resolve or temporize the abnormal heart rate pattern. This treatment al-

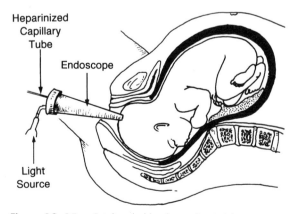

Figure 13–15. Fetal scalp blood sampling in labor.

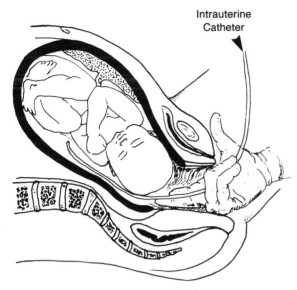

Intrauterine
Catheter

Figure 13–16. Application of an intrauterine water-pressure catheter. Amnioinfusion is performed with infusion of saline solution into the amniotic cavity via the catheter.

lows time for in utero fetal resuscitation (improvement in the fetal metabolic status) while awaiting continued progress in labor or expedient delivery[36–38] Assessment of umbilical cord gases for acid–base status at birth is important in further diagnosis and prompt treatment of the neonate.[21]

Induction and Augmentation of Labor

Induction of labor is the initiation of labor by artificial means. Both medical (oxytocin or PGE_2) or surgical (amniotomy) approaches are used. Augmentation of labor is the artificial stimulation, with oxytocic agents, of labor that has a spontaneous onset.

Labor is usually induced by combined amniotomy and oxytocin. Uterine contractions produced by oxytocin help apply the presenting part to the lower uterine segment. A well-applied presenting fetal part reduces the likelihood of prolapsed umbilical cord when the membranes are later ruptured. Amniotomy might increase uterine sensitivity and facilitate the progress of labor by reducing uterine volume. In patients with a favorable cervix, labor usually starts within 12 hours of amniotomy. However, the loss of amniotic fluid increases the risk of cord compression and consequent fetal intolerance to labor.

The Bishop score, which evaluates the station of the fetal head and the status of the cervix (Table 13-6), can help predict the likelihood of successful induction of labor in multiparous patients.[39] This score ranges from 0 to 13. A score of at least nine (a "ripened" or "favorable" cervix) suggests a very good chance of successful induction and vaginal delivery. A score below five (an "unripe" or "unfavorable" cervix) indicates a poor chance of success.

Indications and Contraindications

An obstetrician may decide to induce or augment labor for many reasons.[40] Elective induction of labor, for convenience alone, risks iatrogenic prematurity; uterine hyperstimulation, causing abnormal fetal heart rate; and fetal hypoxia, or failed induction requiring cesarean section. Assessing fetal maturity (Table 13-7) before elective induction of labor is important to decide the timing of induction.[41]

Therapeutic induction of labor may be needed for medical or obstetric reasons. Labor may be induced before term if the continuation of the pregnancy presents significant risks to the mother or fetus (Table 13-8). If an over-large fetus is mature, labor may be induced close to term to prevent the complications of macrosomia (shoulder dystocia, cesarean section).

The following are some contraindications to induction of labor:

- Absolute cephalopelvic disproportion (*i.e.,* contracted pelvis)
- Previous uterine surgery that involved the full thickness of the uterus (*i.e.,* classical cesarean section, myomectomy, or uterine reconstruction for congenital anomalies)
- Placenta previa or vasa previa
- Invasive cervical carcinoma
- Certain abnormal positions or presentations (*i.e.,* transverse lie, funic or umbilical cord presentation)
- Active genital herpes infection

Some of the aforementioned contraindications may not apply in certain clinical situations (*i.e.,* a dead fetus).

Augmentation of labor is indicated when labor is abnormal in the presence of inadequate uterine contractions (see Table 13-5). Contraindications to augmentation of labor are similar to those for induction of labor. Intrauterine pressure should be directly measured when augmenting labor, especially in a patient with previous low transverse cesarean section, to avoid hyperstimulation and possible uterine rupture.

Table 13–6

Bishop Scoring System

SCORE	0	1	2	3
Cervix				
Dilatation (cm)	0	1–2	3–4	≥ 5
Effacement (%)	0–30	40–50	60–70	≥ 80
Position	Posterior	Mid	Anterior	
Consistency	Firm	Medium	Soft	
Fetal Head				
Station	– 3	– 2	– 1/0	+1/+2

(After Bishop EN. Pelvic scoring for elective induction. Obstet Gynecol 1964;24:266)

Oxytocin

In the United States, oxytocin is the only drug approved for the purpose of induction and augmentation of labor. The uterine response to oxytocin varies with gestational age. The uterus is maximally sensitive to oxytocin close to term. It is somewhat unresponsive at the beginning of gestation and after parturition. As the sensitivity of the uterus changes, so does the oxytocin-receptor concentration in the myometrium.[3,4]

Although oxytocin has been used intravenously, intramuscularly, and transbuccally, the intravenous route is the only route used in pregnant women. Oxytocin has a half-life of 3 to 5 minutes. Plasma concentration stabilizes 40 to 60 minutes after beginning the infusion. The physiologic effects of oxytocin will abate within 30 minutes of stopping the infusion.

A maximum infusion rate of 2 to 8 mU of oxytocin per minute should provide adequate augmentation of labor at term.[42] Induction of labor usually requires more oxytocin than does augmentation of labor. Oxytocin may be infused at an initial rate of 0.5 to 1 mU/min. This rate is then increased every 40 to 60 minutes in increments of 1 to 2 mU/min.[43] Other experts advocate an initial infusion rate of 1 to 2 mU/min, increasing every 15 minutes in 1 mU/min increments.[44] Oxytocin must be discontinued in the presence of uterine hypertonus (> 60 mm Hg intrauterine pressure) or fetal intolerance to labor (abnormal fetal heart rate pattern or fetal distress).[41]

The major complications from the use of oxytocin are as follows:

- Uterine hyperstimulation causing fetal intolerance to labor
- Tetanic contractions leading to rupture of the uterus

- Possible water intoxication due to an intrinsic antidiuretic effect when high doses (> 40 mU/min) of oxytocin are employed[11]

Prolonged oxytocin infusion also may induce myometrial resistance to its effect. Postdelivery uterine atony and postpartum hemorrhage may follow.

Prostaglandins

Prostaglandins play a role in the initiation of labor and cause cervical ripening. None of the prostaglandins has been approved by the Food and Drug Administration for use in pregnancies with a viable fetus. The Food and Drug Administration has approved PGE$_2$, 20 mg, for use as an abortifacient in mid-trimester pregnancies. This compound, in lower doses (0.5 mg for intracervical use, and up to 5 mg for vaginal use), is currently undergoing clinical trials as a cervical ripening agent. Applications may be at 4- to 6-hour intervals, and usually no more than two to three times. For continued uterine stimulation, oxytocin infusion can begin 4 hours after the last dose of prostaglandin. Oxytocin given together with PGE$_2$ can cause uterine hyperstimulation.[41,45,46]

PRETERM LABOR

Definitions

The onset of labor is preterm or premature when it occurs before 36 completed weeks of gestation.[47] Low birth weight is when the fetus weighs less than 2500 g. Very low birth weight is when a fetus weighs less than 1500 g, and extremely low birth weight is birth weight less than 1000 g. A fetus that is born weighing less than 500 g, or less than 20 weeks, is an abortus.

Epidemiology and Neonatal Outcome of Preterm Birth

Neonatal survival and long-term cognitive, motor, or neurologic function depend on birth weight as a reflection of gestational age. With the advances in neonatal intensive care medicine, the developmental outcome for the group of infants with birth weight over 1000 g is approaching the expected outcome for term neonate. For the very immature infants (birth weight less than 1000 g), the risk of abnormal developmental outcome (cerebral palsy, blindness, bronchopulmonary dysplasia, sensorineural deficiencies, and developmental delay) remains significant.[47] Some common causes of preterm labor are listed in Table 13-9. Fifty percent of preterm births happen in women with no risk factors.[48]

Table 13–7

Fetal Maturity Assessment Prior to Elective Repeat Cesarean Delivery

Documentation of one of the following (no amniocentesis required):
Fetal heart tones for
20 wk by nonelectronic fetoscope, or
30 wk by Doppler
36 wk since a positive serum or urine human chorionic gonadotropin pregnancy test (performed by a reliable laboratory)
Ultrasound measurement of the crown–rump length, obtained at 6–11 wk, supports a gestational age ≥ 39 weeks.
Ultrasound examination at 12–20 wk confirms the gestational age of ≥ 39 wk determined by clinical history and physical examination.
These criteria are not intended to preclude the use of menstrual dating. If any one of the above criteria confirms gestational age determined from menstrual dates in a patient with normal menstrual cycles and no immediately antecedent use of oral contraceptives, it is appropriate to schedule delivery at ≥ 39 wk by the menstrual dates. Ultrasound may be considered confirmatory of menstrual dates if there is gestational age agreement within 1 wk by crown–rump measurement obtained at 6–11 wk or within 10 d by the average of multiple measurements at 12–20 wk.
Awaiting the onset of spontaneous labor is another option.
(After American College of Obstetricians and Gynecologists. Fetal maturity assessment prior to elective repeat cesareans delivery. ACOG Committee Opinion 98. Washington, DC, American College of Obstetricians and Gynecologists, 1991)

Table 13–8

Indications for Induction of Labor

Maternal
Diabetes
Preeclampsia/eclampsia
Cardiac disease
Renal disease
Pulmonary disease
Chorioamnionitis
Malignancy
History of rapid labor (distance from hospital)
Fetal
Intrauterine growth retardation
Premature rupture of membranes
Nonreassuring antepartum surveillance (abnormal biophysical profile or contraction stress test)
Postdate pregnancy
Fetal anomalies
Intrauterine fetal demise
Hemolytic diseases of the newborn (Rh isoimmunization, Kell sensitization, etc.)
(After American College of Obstetricians and Gynecologists. Induction and augmentation of labor. ACOG Technical Bulletin 157. Washington, DC, 1991)

In the United States, preterm delivery occurs in 8% to 10% of births. Prematurity is the leading cause of perinatal, neonatal, and infant mortality and morbidity. Pharmacologic inhibition of preterm labor has not convincingly reduced the rate of preterm birth or neonatal death. Still, until a more effective means of preventing preterm labor is identified, drug therapy remains the most effective way to delay premature delivery and improve neonatal outcome.[48]

Indications and Contraindications for the Use of Labor-Inhibiting (Tocolytic) Agents

The following are prerequisites for use of a labor-inhibiting (tocolytic) agent:

- The diagnosis of preterm labor
- A gestational age at which treatment will benefit the fetus
- The absence of medical or obstetric contraindications to the inhibition of labor or the tocolytic agent

Relative contraindications for tocolysis are eclampsia/severe preeclampsia, fetal demise, chorioamnionitis,

Table 13–9

Common Causes of Preterm Labor

Maternal Causes	**Uterine/Placental Causes**
Abdominal surgery	Overdistended uterus
Preeclampsia/eclampsia	Multiple gestations
Diabetic ketoacidosis	Polyhydramnios
Pyelonephritis	Abnormal placentation
Appendicitis	Placenta previa
Thyroid storm	Abruptio placentae
Systemic illness	Second trimester bleeding
Cervical incompetence	Chorioamnionitis
Prepregnancy weight < 45 kg	Spontaneous rupture of
Single parent	membranes
	Uterine or cervical anomalies
Fetal Causes	**Other**
Fetal demise	No prenatal care
Fetal anomalies	More than three first-trimester abortions
	Previous second-trimester abortion
	Prior preterm delivery

(After American College of Obstetricians and Gynecologists. Preterm labor. ACOG Technical Bulletin 133. Washington, DC, 1989)

advanced labor (> 5 cm cervical dilation), fetal maturity, acute fetal intolerance to labor (except in cases of intrauterine resuscitation), fetal anomalies incompatible with life, and maternal hemodynamic instability.

As with term labor, early differentiation between true and false preterm labor is difficult. Ideally, preterm labor is diagnosed by the presence of regular uterine contractions that produce progressive cervical dilatation or effacement after 20 but before 37 weeks of gestation. The success of tocolysis diminishes when advanced cervical dilatation or effacement has occurred. Most fetal mortality and serious morbidity occur before 34 weeks of gestation. The fetus most likely to benefit from labor inhibition is probably at a gestational age of less than 32 to 34 weeks. The upper gestational age limit for labor inhibition is determined on an individualized basis. Tocolysis may be of some value to prevent delivery during maternal transport to an appropriate medical facility.[50]

Treatment of Preterm Labor

Treatment of premature labor includes bed rest, mild sedation, hydration, and the use of tocolytic agents. Subclinical chorioamnionitis with bacterial coloniza-

tion decreases the effectiveness of tocolysis.[49] Preliminary reports suggest prolongation of pregnancy with the use of adjunctive antibiotics in the treatment of idiopathic preterm labor,[50,51] others did not confirm this finding.[52] Currently, a multicenter trial sponsored by the National Institutes of Health is evaluating the role of antibiotics in the treatment of preterm labor.

Ritodrine is the only drug approved by the Food and Drug Administration for the use as a tocolytic agent in the treatment of preterm labor; however, other drugs have also been used for tocolysis. The beta-adrenergic agonists, ritodrine and terbutaline, in addition to magnesium sulfate, are the most commonly used first-line intravenous tocolytic agents in the United States. (Some physicians prefer subcutaneous terbutaline instead of the intravenous agents as the initial tocolytic drug of choice). Once uterine contractions have stopped for 12 to 24 hours, tocolysis is usually maintained until 37 weeks of gestation with an oral agent such as ritodrine or terbutaline.[48,50] Oral magnesium produces subtherapeutic rises in the serum magnesium concentration[53] and may not be clinically effective as a tocolytic maintenance agent. In addition, oral magnesium is a potent cathartic agent.

Tocolytic agents are titrated aggressively until contractions stop (Table 13-10). Once labor is inhibited, infusion continues for 12 to 24 hours. Both ritodrine

Table 13–10

Protocol for Common Intravenous Tocolytic Agents

	RITODRINE	**MAGNESIUM**
Loading dose	100 μg/min	4 g over 20 min
Rate of infusion	50 μg/min, increase every 10 min until effective tocolysis, then reduce by 50 μg/min every 60 min to the lowest dose that sustains tocolysis	2 g/h with 0.5 g/h increase every 15–30 min until effective tocolysis, then reduce 0.5 g/h every 60 minutes to the lowest dose that sustains tocolysis
Maintenance	Minimum dose of 100 μg/min for 12–24 h	Minimum dose of 2 g/h for 12–24 h
Maximum dose	350 μg/min	Therapeutic serum level between 6–8 mg/dL

(After American College of Obstetricians and Gynecologists. Preterm labor. ACOG Technical Bulletin 133. Washington, DC, 1989)

and magnesium have significant maternal hemodynamic and metabolic effects (Table 13-11). These drugs should be stopped if significant maternal side effects, especially pulmonary edema, occur. The pulmonary edema is multifactorial; it is associated with fluid overload, chorioamnionitis, the use of steroids, prolonged tocolytic therapy, and multiple gestations. The toxic effects of magnesium, such as cardiac arrest and respiratory paralysis, are rarely seen below a serum concentration of 10 mg/dL.[48,50]

In a few medical centers, indomethacin has been used as the first-line tocolytic agent in the short-term treatment of selected cases of preterm labor with good clinical outcome. An initial dose of 50 to 100 mg can be given orally or as a rectal suppository, and followed by 25 mg every 4 to 6 hours for 24 to 48 hours. The major limitation of indomethacin is closure of the fetal ductus arteriosus. This drug should be avoided after 34 weeks of gestation, when this fetal risk is greatest. In addition, oligohydramnios may occur with its prolonged use. The contraindications to use are a history of gastric ulcer, renal disease, and known bleeding disorders.[50,54]

The calcium-channel blocking agents are being investigated for their safety and efficacy in the treatment of preterm labor. Clinical data are insufficient for their routine recommendation as tocolytic drugs.[50,55,56] The antihypertensive diazoxide is an effective tocolytic agent and has been used with success in some clinical studies. However, its potent vasodilating effects and its early misuse have limited its use as a tocolytic agent. Only very few medical centers in the United States continue to use diazoxide for the treatment of preterm labor.[57] Studies on the efficacy and safety of using multiple agents for labor inhibition are limited and conflicting.[50] Combination tocolytic therapy may be reserved for the selected high-risk patients who failed conventional single-agent therapy, but only after consultation with physicians familiar with the mechanism of actions and side effects of these agents.

Acceleration of Fetal Pulmonary Function

Various antenatal treatments have tried to speed the maturation of the fetal lungs in an attempt to decrease the development of severe respiratory distress syndrome. Maternal administration of glucocorticoids appears to reduce the incidence of neonatal respiratory distress syndrome when given to mothers between 27 and 34 weeks of gestation. Black female infants benefit most from this therapy. Glucocorticoids offer little to pregnancies complicated by premature rupture of the membranes, hypertension, or multiple gestation.[58,59] The use of glucocorticoids is not universally accepted, and there has been a recent trend toward not using them at all.[60]

The type and dosage of glucocorticoids vary among different medical centers. Some protocols give two doses of beta-methasone, 12 mg intramuscularly, 24 hours apart. Others give dexamethasone, 5 mg intramuscularly, twice daily for four doses. Hydrocortisone, 500 mg, also may be given intramuscularly every 6 hours for a total of four doses. The above agents may be repeated in 7 to 10 days if risks for preterm delivery still exist.[48]

Experience with preterm newborns of mothers with Graves' disease has suggested that thyroxine promotes

Table 13–11

Contraindications and Side Effects of Tocolytic Therapy

RITODRINE	MAGNESIUM
Relative Contraindications	
Maternal cardiac rhythm disturbance	Heart block
Other maternal cardiac disease	Myasthenia gravis
Pulmonary hypertension	Hypocalcemia
Severe anemia	Renal failure
Poorly controlled diabetes	Concurrent maternal sedatives or narcotics
Thyrotoxicosis	
Toxic Signs and Symptoms (Stop Drug)	
Severe palpitations	Chest pain
Tachycardia	Shortness of breath
Chest pain	Pulmonary edema
Shortness of breath	Respiratory arrest
Pulmonary edema	Cardiac arrest
Maternal Metabolic Effects	
Increased: glucose, insulin, lactate, free fatty acids, renin, arginine vasopressin	Hypermagnesemia
Hypokalemia	

(After American College of Obstetricians and Gynecologists. Preterm labor. ACOG Technical Bulletin 133. Washington, DC, 1989)

fetal lung maturity. Weekly intra-amniotic administration of 200 to 500 µg of thyroxine reportedly accelerates fetal maturation and reduces the incidence of respiratory distress syndrome.[61] The amniotic fluid lecithin to sphingomyelin (L/S) ratio increases after intra-amniotic injection of thyroxine.[62] This promising therapy requires further investigation before it sees routine clinical use in the United States.

Thyrotropin-releasing hormone also has been used in combination with corticosteroids for the purpose of accelerating fetal lung maturation. The thyrotropin-releasing appears to speed progression of L/S ratio. More data are needed to verify the safety and efficacy of this treatment.[63]

Preterm Rupture of the Membranes

Premature rupture of membranes is rupture anytime before the onset of labor regardless of the duration of gestation at the time of rupture. Preterm rupture is rupture of membranes before 38 weeks of gestation. Although premature rupture of the membranes may

occur at any stage of pregnancy, its incidence increases as term approaches. Premature rupture of membranes complicates approximately 10% of pregnancies. Preterm rupture of membranes happens in at least 30% of preterm deliveries. The time between rupture of the membranes and the onset of labor is inversely proportional to the gestational age at which rupture of membranes occurs. In preterm patients, labor occurs in 50% of women within 24 hours of ruptured membranes. At term, labor begins within 24 hours of membrane rupture in 90% of patients.[64]

The cause of premature rupture of membranes is unknown, but it is associated with premature delivery, maternal sepsis, and increased perinatal mortality and morbidity. Factors associated with premature rupture of membranes include hydramnios, multiple gestation, chorioamnionitis, incompetent cervix, abruptio placentae, and amniocentesis.

It is important to diagnose ruptured membranes promptly to allow appropriate management. Vaginal fluid should be sent for group B streptococcus, chlamydia, and gonococcus cultures. In addition, the L/S (lecithin to sphingomyelin) ratio and the presence of phosphatidyl glycerol, markers of fetal lung maturity, should be evaluated in the amniotic fluid.

If insufficient amniotic fluid is available from the vaginal pool for complete evaluation, amniocentesis may help clarify the pulmonary maturity status of the fetus. Additionally, the amniotic fluid obtained via amniocentesis also should be sent for Gram stain and cultures. Instillation of indigo carmine dye into the amniotic cavity before withdrawal of the amniocentesis needle may clarify questionable cases of rupture of the membranes.

The obstetric management of premature rupture of membranes is controversial. If membranes break after 36 weeks, or before 36 weeks with documented fetal lung maturity, delivery is recommended. If there are no signs of infection, it is reasonable to wait 12 to 24 hours for the onset of spontaneous labor before inducing labor. In the presence of chorioamnionitis at any gestational age, antibiotic therapy and prompt delivery are recommended. Chorioamnionitis in preterm rupture of membranes increases the risk of neonatal respiratory distress, intraventricular hemorrhage, sepsis, low 1-minute Apgar score, and mortality.[62,65]

Expectant management in cases of preterm rupture of membranes without obvious signs of chorioamnionitis allows continued fetal maturation and development. Treatment with appropriate antibiotics is reasonable for patients with cervical/vaginal or urinary infections as long as the antepartum surveillance of the fetus is reassuring. Follow-up cultures of cure should be obtained after completion of therapy.

In the management of preterm rupture of membranes, there is no consensus on the use of glucocorticoids for the acceleration of fetal lung maturity or the use of tocolytic therapy for the treatment of preterm labor. Current studies do not support the benefits of aggressive tocolysis, with or without steroid treatment, in these patients.[66,67]

REFERENCES

1. Cunningham FG, MacDonald PC, Gant NF. Parturition: Biomolecular and physiological processes. In: Cunningham FG, MacDonald PC, Gant NF, eds. Williams Obstetrics. 18th ed. Norwalk, CT: Appleton & Lange, 1989:187.

2. Casey ML, MacDonald PC. Decidual activation: The role of prostaglandins in labor. In: McNellis D, Challis JRG, MacDonald PC, Nathanielsz PW, Roberts JM, eds. The onset of labor: Cellular and integrative mechanisms. Reproductive and perinatal medicine. Vol. 9. Ithaca, NY: Perinatology Press, 1988:141.

3. Soloff MS. The role of oxytocin in the initiation of labor, and oxytocin–prostaglandin interactions. In: McNellis D, Challis JRG, MacDonald PC, Nathanielsz PW, Roberts JM, eds. The onset of labor: Cellular and integrative mechanisms. Reproductive and perinatal medicine. Vol. 9. Ithaca, NY: Perinatology Press, 1988:87.

4. Soloff MS. Oxytocin receptors and mechanism of oxytocin action. In: Amico JA, Robinson AG, eds. Oxytocin clinical and laboratory studies. Excerpta Medica ICS 666. New York: Elsevier Science Publishing, 1985:259.

5. Casey ML, MacDonald PC. Biomolecular processes in the initiation of parturition: Decidual activation. Clin Obstet Gynecol 1988;31:533.

6. Mitchell MD. Sources of eicosanoids within the uterus during pregnancy. In: McNellis D, Challis JRG, MacDonald PC, Nathanielsz PW, Roberts JM eds. The onset of labor: Cellular and integrative mechanisms. Reproductive and perinatal medicine. Vol. 9. Ithaca, NY: Perinatology Press, 1988:165.

7. Challis JRG. Steroid production by the fetal membranes in relation to the onset of parturition. In: McNellis D, Challis JRG, MacDonald PC, Nathanielsz PW, Roberts JM, eds. The onset of labor: Cellular and integrative mechanisms. Reproductive and perinatal medicine. Vol. 9. Ithaca, NY: Perinatology Press, 1988:233.

8. Oxorn H, Foote WR. Obstetric pelvis. In: Oxorn H, ed. Human Labor and Birth. 4th ed, New York: Appleton-Century-Crofts, 1980:22.

9. Cunningham FG, MacDonald PC, Gant NF. The normal pelvis. In: Cunningham FG, MacDonald PC, Gant NF, eds. Williams Obstetrics. 18th ed. Norwalk, CT: Appleton & Lange, 1989:163.

10. Steer CM, Moloy HC. General morphology of the pelvis. In: Steer CM, ed. Moloy's Evaluation of the Pelvis in Obstetrics, 3rd ed. New York: Plenum Medical Book Company, 1975:1.

11. Cunningham FG, MacDonald PC, Gant NF. Conduct of normal labor and delivery. In: Cunningham FG, MacDonald PC, Gant NF, eds. Williams Obstetrics. 18th ed. Norwalk, CT: Appleton & Lange, 1989:307.

12. Friedman EA. Normal and dysfunctional labor. In: Cohen WR, Acker DB, Friedman EA, eds. Management of Labor. 2nd ed, Rockville, MD: Aspen Publishers, 1989:1.

13. American College of Obstetricians and Gynecologists. Dystocia. ACOG Technical Bulletin 137. Washington, DC: American College of Obstetricians and Gynecologists, 1989.

14. Beard RW. The detection of fetal asphyxia in labor. Pediatrics 1974;53(2):157.

15. Paul RH, Huey JR Jr, Yaeger CF. Clinical fetal monitoring: Its effects on cesarean section rate and perinatal mortality: Five-year trends. Postgrad Med 1977;61(4):160.

16. Wood C, Renou P, Oats J, Farrell E, Beischer N, Anderson I. A controlled trial of fetal heart rate monitoring in a low-risk obstetric population. Am J Obstet Gynecol 1981;141:527.

17. Leveno KJ, Cunningham FG, Nelson S, et al. A prospective comparison of selective and universal electronic fetal monitoring in 34,995 pregnancies. N Engl J Med 1986;315:615.

18. Luthy DA, Shy KK, vanBelle G, et al. A randomized trial of electronic fetal heart monitoring in premature labor. Obstet Gynecol 1987;69:687.

19. MacDonald D, Grant A, Sheriden-Pereira M, Boylan P, Chalmers I. The Dublin randomized controlled trial of intrapartum fetal heart rate monitoring. Am J Obstet Gynecol 1985;152:524.

20. Renou P, Chang A, Anderson I, Wood C. Controlled trial of fetal intensive care. Am J Obstet Gynecol 1976;126:470.

21. American College of Obstetricians and Gynecologists. Intrapartum fetal heart rate monitoring. ACOG Technical Bulletin 132. Washington, DC: American College of Obstetricians and Gynecologists, 1989.

22. Thacker SB, Banta HD. Benefits and risks of episiotomy: An interpretative review of the English language literature, 1860–1980. Obstet Gynecol Surv 1983;38:322.

23. Friedman EA. Dysfunctional labor. In: Cohen WR, Friedman EA, eds. Management of labor. College Park, MD: University Park Press, 1983:11.

24. Friedman EA. Dysfunctional labor. In: Greenhill JP, ed. Obstetrics, 13th ed. Philadelphia: WB Saunders, 1965:831.

25. Cohen WR. The pelvic division of labor. In: Cohen WR, Acker DB, Friedman EA, eds. Management of labor, 2nd ed. Rockville, MD: Aspen Publishers, 1989:19.

26. Cunningham FG, MacDonald PC, Gant NF. Dystocia due to abnormalities in presentation, position, or development of the fetus. In: Cunningham FG, MacDonald PC, Gant NF, eds. Williams Obstetrics, 18th ed. Norwalk, CT: Appleton & Lange, 1989:349.

27. Sandberg EC. The Zavanelli maneuver: A potentially revolutionary method for the resolution of shoulder dystocia. Am J Obstet Gynecol 1985;152:479.

28. Smith CV. Fetal distress. In: Phelan JP, Clark SL, eds. Cesarean delivery. New York: Elsevier Science Publishing, 1988:70.

29. Clark SL, Gimovsky ML, Miller FC. The scalp stimulation test: A clinical alternative to fetal scalp blood sampling. Am J Obstet Gynecol 1984;148:274.

30. Clark SL, Gimovsky, Miller FC. Fetal heart rate response to scalp blood sampling. Am J Obstet Gynecol 1982;144:706.

31. Smith CV, Nguyen HN, Phelan JP, Paul RH. Intrapartum assessment of fetal well-being: A comparison of fetal acoustic stimulation with acid–base determinations. Am J Obstet Gynecol 1986;155:726.

32. Cohen WR, Schifrin BS. Clinical management of fetal hypoxemia. In: Cohen WR, Acker DB, Friedman EA, eds. Management of Labor, 2nd ed. Rockville, MD: Aspen Publishers, 1989:283.

33. American College of Obstetricians and Gynecologists. Assessment of fetal and newborn acid–base status. ACOG Technical Bulletin 127. Washington, DC: American College of Obstetricians and Gynecologists, 1989.

34. Owen J, Henson BV, Hauth JC. A prospective randomized study of saline solution amnioinfusion. Am J Obstet Gynecol 1990;162:1146.

35. Haubrich KL. Amnioinfusion: A technique for the relief of variable deceleration. J Obstet Gynecol Neonatal Nurs 1990;19:299.

36. Lipshitz J. Use of a β_2-sympathomimetic drug as a temporizing measure in the treatment of acute fetal distress. Am J Obstet Gynecol 1977;129:31.

37. Burke MS, Porreco RP, Day D, et al. Intrauterine resuscitation with tocolysis. An alternate-month clinical trial. J Perinatol 1989;9:296.

38. Shekarloo A, Mendez-Bauer C, Cook V, Freese U. Terbutaline (intravenous bolus) for the treatment of acute intrapartum fetal distress. Am J Obstet Gynecol 1989;160:615.

39. Bishop EN. Pelvic scoring for elective induction. Obstet Gynecol 1964;24:266.

40. American College of Obstetricians and Gynecologists. Induction and augmentation of labor. ACOG Technical Bulletin 157. Washington, DC: American College of Obstetricians and Gynecologists, 1991.

41. American College of Obstetricians and Gynecologists. Assessment of fetal maturity prior to repeat cesarean delivery or elective induction of labor. ACOG Committee Opinion 72. Washington, DC: American College of Obstetricians and Gynecologists, 1989.

42. Seitchik J, Castillo M. Oxytocin augmentation of dysfunctional labor. I. Clinical data. Am J Obstet Gynecol 1982;144:899.

43. Seitchik J, Castillo M. Oxytocin augmentation of dysfunctional labor. II. Uterine activity data. Am J Obstet Gynecol 1983;145:529.

44. Hauth JC, Hankins GDV, Gilstrap LC, Strickland DM, Vance P. Uterine contraction pressures with oxytocin induction/augmentation. Obstet Gynecol 1986;68:305.

45. Brindley BA, Sokol RJ. Induction and augmentation of labor: Basis and methods for current practice. Obstet Gynecol Surv 1988;43:730.

46. Rayburn WF. Prostaglandin E₂ gel for cervical ripening and induction of labor: Critical analysis. Am J Obstet Gynecol 1989;160:529.

47. Escobedo MB. Follow-up of prematurely born infants. Clin Obstet Gynecol 1988;31(3):662.

48. Caritis SN, Darby MJ, Chan L. Pharmacologic treatment of preterm labor. Clin Obstet Gynecol 1988;31(3):635.

49. Roberto R, Mazor M. Infection and preterm labor. Clin Obstet Gynecol 1988;31(3):553.

50. McGregor JA, French JI, Reller LB, Todd JK, Makowski EL. Adjunctive erythromycin treatment for idiopathic preterm labor: Results of a randomized, double-blinded, placebo-controlled trial. Am J Obstet Gynecol 1986;154:98.

51. Morales WJ, Angel JL, O'Brien WF, Knuppel RA,

Finazzo M. A randomized study of antibiotic therapy in idiopathic preterm labor. Obstet Gynecol 1988;72:829.

52. Newton ER, Dinsmoor MJ, Gibbs RS. A randomized, blinded, placebo-controlled trial of antibiotics in idiopathic preterm labor. Obstet Gynecol 1989; 74:562.

53. Martin RW, Gaddy DK, Martin JN, Lucas JA, Wiser WL, Morrison JC. Tocolysis with oral magnesium. Am J Obstet Gynecol 1987;156:433.

54. Niebyl JR, Witter FR. Neonatal outcome after indomethacin treatment for preterm labor. Am J Obstet Gynecol 1986;155:747.

55. Ulmsten U. Treatment of normotensive and hypertensive patients with preterm labor using oral nifedipine, a calcium antagonist. Arch Gynecol 1984;236:69.

56. Read MD, Wellby DE. The use of a calcium antagonist (nifedipine) to suppress preterm labour. Br J Obstet Gynaecol 1986;93:933.

57. Adamsons K, Wallach RC. Diazoxide and calcium antagonists in preterm labor. In: Fuchs FF, Stubblefield PG, eds. Preterm birth. Causes, prevention, and management. New York: Macmillan Publishing Company, 1984:249.

58. Collaborative group on antenatal steroid therapy: effects of antenatal dexamethasone administration on the prevention of respiratory distress syndrome. Am J Obstet Gynecol 1981;141:276.

59. Avery ME, Aylward G, Creasy R, Little AB, Stripp B. Update on prenatal steroids for prevention of respiratory distress: Report of a conference—September 26–28, 1985. Am J Obstet Gynecol 1986;155:2.

60. Cunningham FG, MacDonald PC, Gant NF. Preterm and post-term pregnancy and inappropriate fetal growth. In: Cunningham FG, MacDonald PC, Gant NF, eds. Williams Obstetrics. 18th ed. Norwalk, CT: Appleton & Lange, 1989:741.

61. Romaguera J, Reyes G, Caiseda D, Wallach RC, Adamsons K. Acceleration of fetal maturation with intra-amniotic thyroxine in the presence of maternal malignancy. Acta Obstet Gynecol Scand 1990;69:229.

62. Romaguera J, Zorrilla C, de la Vega A, Fromm R, Wallach RC, Rodriguez-Mariani A, et al. Responsiveness of L-S ratio of the amniotic fluid to intra-amniotic administration of thyroxine. Role of fetal age. Acta Obstet Gynecol Scand 1990;69:119.

63. Morales WJ, O'Brien WF, Angel JL, et al. Fetal lung maturation: The combined use of corticosteroids and thyrotropin-releasing hormone. Obstet Gynecol 1989; 73:111.

64. American College of Obstetricians and Gynecologists. Premature rupture of membranes. ACOG Technical Bulletin 115. Washington, DC: American College of Obstetricians and Gynecologists, 1988.

65. Morales WJ. The effect of chorioamnionitis on the developmental outcome of preterm infants at one year. Obstet Gynecol 1987;70:183.

66. Garite TJ, Keegan KA, Freeman RK, Nageotte MP. A randomized trial of ritodrine tocolysis versus expectant management in patients with premature rupture of membranes at 24 to 30 weeks of gestation. Am J Obstet Gynecol 1987;157:388.

67. Nelson LH, Meis PJ, Hatjis CG, Ernest JM, Dillard R, Schey HM. Premature rupture of membranes: A prospective, randomized evaluation of steroids, latent phase, and expectant management. Obstet Gynecol 1985;66:55.

BIBLIOGRAPHY

American College of Obstetricians and Gynecologists. Obstetric forceps. ACOG Committee Opinion 71. Washington, DC, American College of Obstetricians and Gynecologists, 1989.

American College of Obstetricians and Gynecologists. Fetal maturity assessment prior to elective repeat cesareans delivery. ACOG Committee Opinion 98. Washington, DC, American College of Obstetricians and Gynecologists, 1991.

American College of Obstetricians and Gynecologists. Premature rupture of membranes. ACOG Technical Bulletin 115. Washington, DC, American College of Obstetricians and Gynecologists, 1988.

American College of Obstetricians and Gynecologists. Assessment of fetal and newborn acid-base status. ACOG Technical Bulletin 127. Washington, DC, American College of Obstetricians and Gynecologists, 1989.

American College of Obstetricians and Gynecologists. Intrapartum fetal heart rate monitoring. ACOG Technical Bulletin 132. Washington, DC, American College of Obstetricians and Gynecologists, 1989.

American College of Obstetricians and Gynecologists. Preterm labor. ACOG Technical Bulletin 133. Washington, DC, American College of Obstetricians and Gynecologists, 1989.

American College of Obstetricians and Gynecologists. Dystocia. ACOG Technical Bulletin 137. Washington, DC, American College of Obstetricians and Gynecologists, 1989.

American College of Obstetricians and Gynecologists. Induction and augmentation of labor. ACOG Technical Bulletin 157. Washington, DC, American College of Obstetricians and Gynecologists, 1991.

American Academy of Pediatrics, American College of Obstetricians and Gynecologists: Guidelines for Perinatal Care, 2nd ed. Washington, DC, American Academy of Pediatrics, American College of Obstetricians and Gynecologists, 1988:67.

Amico JA, Robinson AG, eds. OXYTOCIN Clinical and Laboratory Studies. Excerpta Medica ICS 666. New York: Elsevier Science Publishing Company, 1985.

Cohen WR, Acker DB, Friedman EA, eds. Management of Labor, 2nd ed. Rockville, MD: Aspen Publishers, 1989.

Cunningham FG, MacDonald PC, Gant NF, eds. Williams Obstetrics, 18th ed. Norwalk, CT, Appleton & Lange, 1989.

Greenhill JP, ed. Obstetrics, 13th ed. Philadelphia, WB Saunders, 1965.

Jaffe RB, Dell'Acqua S, eds. The Endocrine Physiology of Pregnancy and the Peripartal Period, Vol 21. New York: Raven Press, 1985.

McNellis D, Challis JRG, MacDonald PC, Nathanielsz PW, Roberts JM, eds. The Onset of Labor: Cellular and Integrative Mechanisms. Reproductive and Perinatal Medicine. Vol. 9. New York: Perinatology Press, 1988.

Oxorn H, Foote WR, Oxorn H, eds. Human Labor and Birth, 4th ed. New York: Appleton-Century-Crofts, 1980.

Rosen MG, Rosen MG eds. Management of Labor. Physician Judgement and Patient Care. New York: Elsevier Science Publishing, 1990.

Steer CM, Moloy HC, Steer CM, eds. Moloy's Evaluation of the Pelvis in Obstetrics. 3rd ed. New York: Plenum Medical Book Company, 1975.

CHAPTER 14

Mechanisms of Labor Pain

Suzanne Huffnagle
H. Jane Huffnagle

Yahweh asked the woman, "What is this you have done?" The woman replied, "The serpent tempted me and I ate." Yahweh said to the women, "I will multiply your sorrows in childbearing. You shall give birth to your children in suffering."[1] Labor is very painful. The severity of labor pain compares to that of causalgia, cancer pain, and amputation of a digit.[2] Women describe it akin to amputation of a digit, similar to a kidney stone, or the worst pain ever experienced (Fig. 14-1). When asked during labor to describe their pain, women use the words "wrenching," "searing," scalding," "aching," "tearing," "torturing," "excruciating," and "unbearable."[3] This chapter discusses the anatomic, psychologic, and psychologic factors that are involved in creating and potentiating this "cramping," "agonizing" pain.

PAIN PATHWAYS

First Stage of Labor

Pain, under normal circumstances, results from activation of nociceptors in the periphery. Nociceptors are unencapsulated or free nerve endings that discharge in response to noxious levels of mechanical, thermal, or chemical stimulation. They are supplied by small-diameter myelinated Aδ and unmyelinated C nerve fibers that relay information to the spinal cord. Stimulation of Aδ fibers results in a short-lasting, pricking pain, whereas stimulation of only the C fibers induces a poorly localized burning sensation.

During the first stage of labor, pain starts in the uterus and its adnexa during contractions. This pain may have several sources:

- Pressure on nerve endings between the muscle fibers of the body and fundus of the uterus[4,5]
- Contraction of an ischemic myometrium and cervix[6]
- Vasoconstriction secondary to sympathetic hyperactivity[7]
- Inflammatory changes of the uterine muscle[5]
- Dilation of the cervix and lower uterine segment[4]

Most data suggest that the pain of the first stage of labor is primarily the result of dilation, distention, stretching, and tearing of the cervix and lower uterine segment during contractions. The force of the uterus contracting against the closed or dilating cervix and perineum also probably adds to the pain of contractions.[4]

Henry Head, in 1893, deduced that the pain of labor involved the T-11, T-12, and sometimes, T-10 and L-1 spinal segments.[8] He also believed the cervix was supplied by the second to fourth sacral segments. MacKenzie[9] observed that labor pain is felt between the umbilicus and pubes, across the back at the level of the

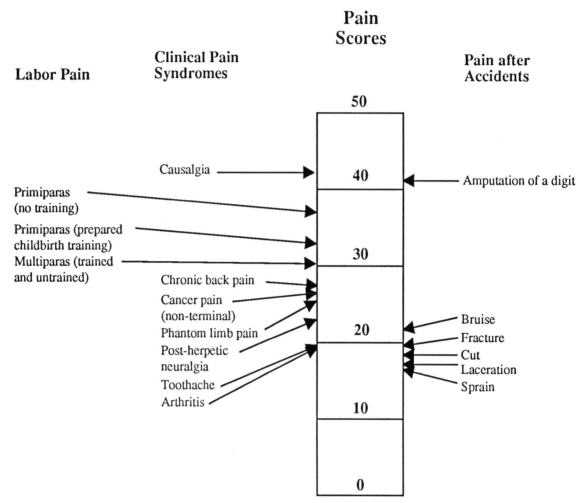

Figure 14–1. Pain scores derived from the McGill pain questionnaire. This graph compares the severity of labor pain to pain recorded in the emergency room after a variety of accidents. In addition, the graph depicts pain intensity as reported in a pain clinic for several clinical pain syndromes. (After Melzack R. The myths of painless childbirth [The John J. Bonica Lecture]). Pain 1984;19:321)

top of the sacrum. He suggested that the dermatomes involved extended from T-10 to L-3.[9] Extrapolating from animal data, Cleland[10] inferred that the uterine afferent roots in the human are T-11 and T-12. He also concluded that pain due to stretching of the birth canal is transmitted through certain undetermined sacral roots. Paravertebral block of the T-11 and T-12 roots blocked the pain of uterine contractions, whereas caudal block abolished the pain of dilatation of the birth canal. Without analgesia, painful impulses can spread in the spinal cord to produce pain in segments adjacent to those actually receiving nociceptive input.[10]

Bonica[11] studied 240 parturients and 35 gynecologic patients over a period of 22 years. He used paravertebral, segmental epidural, caudal, and transsacral blocks to delineate the peripheral nociceptive pathways of the uterus and cervix.

The pain of the first stage of labor is felt in the dermatomes supplied by the same spinal cord segments that receive input from the uterus and cervix. During the latent phase of the first stage, pain is experienced as an ache and is localized to the T-11 and T-12 dermatomes. In the active phase, the pain at T-11 and T-12 becomes more intense and spreads to the two adjacent dermatomes, T-10 and L-1. It becomes sharp and cramping. The surface distribution of the T-10 to L-1 dermatomes in the back overlies the lower three lumbar vertebrae and the upper half of the sacrum. Pain may be more severe in one or more parts of a dermatome (Fig. 14-2).[4]

Afferent Pathways

The afferent nerve fibers accompany the sympathetic nerves, first passing to the uterine and cervical plexus, then to the pelvic (inferior hypogastric) plexus, to the middle hypogastric plexus, and finally to the superior hypogastric and aortic plexus. The nociceptive afferents then pass to the lumbar sympathetic chain and run cephalad with the lower thoracic sympathetic nerves. They leave the sympathetic chain by way of the rami communicantes associated with the T-10, T-11, T-12, and L-1 spinal nerves. The cell bodies of these afferent fibers lie within the dorsal root ganglia. The afferent fibers pass through the posterior spinal nerve roots and make synaptic contact with interneurons in the dorsal horn of the spinal grey matter (Figs. 14-3 and 14-4).

The small primary afferents enter the spinal cord mainly in the lateral position of the dorsal root. They then bifurcate into both rostral and caudal branches. Injection of tracing agents into pain fibers originating in the skin, muscle, and viscera has shown projections into the ipsilateral spinal cord. A large concentration of nociceptive afferent projections terminate in Rexed's lamina I, II, and V, around the central canal as well as in contralateral lamina V.[13,14] There are differences in termination depending on the source (skin, muscle, viscera) and type (Aδ or C) of the fiber. Dendrites from visceral afferents extend the farthest longitudinally in the spinal cord. This phenomenon may explain the diffuse quality of visceral pain.

Spinal Cord

After entry into the spinal cord, the nociceptive signal is relayed, possibly through interneurons, to projection cells for transmission to the brain. Two main cate-

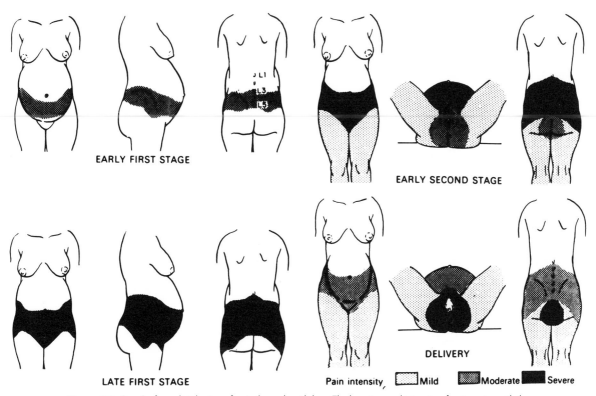

Figure 14–2. Surface distribution of pain throughout labor. The location and intensity of pain varies with the progress of labor. (Bonica JJ. Obstetric analgesia and anesthesia, 2nd ed. Seattle: University of Washington Press, 1980;46)

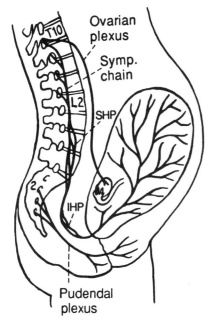

Figure 14–3. Line drawing showing the peripheral nociceptive pathways involved in the pain of parturition. The uterus, including the cervix and lower uterine segments, is supplied by afferents that accompany sympathetic nerves through the inferior hypogastric plexus (IHP), the hypogastric nerve, and the superior hypogastric plexus (SHP), to the lumbar and lower thoracic sympathetic chain. Then, they enter the spinal cord at T-10, T-11, T-12, and L-1. (Bonica JJ. The management of pain. 2nd ed. Philadelphia: Lea & Febiger, 1990;2:1327)

gories of projection cells exist in the dorsal horn of the spinal grey matter. Nociceptive specific cells respond to and project only noxious stimulation. Wide dynamic range cells respond to and project both noxious and innocuous stimuli. Significant concentrations of these two cell types are located in lamina I (mostly nociceptive specific) and lamina V (mostly wide dynamic range) of the spinal grey matter. The location of these cell bodies corresponds to the site of termination of dendrites from nociceptive afferent nerve fibers.[12]

Ventral Pathways

The spinothalamic, spinoreticular, and spinomesencephalic tracts or pathways carry nociceptive information rostrally to the brain (Fig. 14-5). Cells of the spinothalamic tract are located throughout the grey matter of the spinal cord. They cross the spinal cord very close to the cell body and then run to the contralateral thalamus through the ventrolateral funiculus.[14] Cells projecting laterally into the ventral posterior lateral nucleus of the thalamus are concentrated

in the dorsal horn in lamina V. Cells projecting medially end in the intralaminar complex, including the central lateral nucleus, and originate in laminae IV and VIII. The lateral projection relays information to the sensory cortex, whereas the medial projection relays information to the frontal, parietal, and limbic areas. The spinomesencephalic and spinoreticular tracts end in the midbrain and the more caudal reticular nuclei.

Dorsal Pathways

There are fiber tracts projecting through the dorsal half of the spinal cord that also probably contribute to the pain experience. In addition, they may take on some function of the ventral pathways after injury. These alternate dorsal pathways include the spinothalamic tract and spinomesencephalic projections from lamina I, the spinocervicothalamic pathway, and the postsynaptic dorsal column pathway (Fig. 14-6). The spinocervicothalamic pathway originates in lamina IV and projects to the ipsilateral lateral cervical nucleus. The postsynaptic dorsal column pathway synapses in the dorsal column nuclei. Both then continue to contralateral ventral posterior lateral nucleus of the thalamus.

Pain of the Second and Third Stages of Labor

Once the cervix is fully dilated, the nociceptive stimulation from it decreases. Uterine contraction and stretching of the lower uterine segment still cause pain as in the first stage of labor. The increasing pressure of the presenting part on pain-sensitive structures in the pelvis and perineum becomes an additional source of pain in the second stage of labor. Progressively greater distention causes stretching and tearing of fascia and subcutaneous tissues of the vagina. Some parturients also may develop aching, burning, or cramping in the thighs or legs. This additional pain seems to result from stimulation of pain-sensitive structures in the pelvic cavity, including the following:

- Traction on the pelvic parietal peritoneum and uterine ligaments
- Stretching and tension of the bladder, urethra, and rectum
- Stretching and tension of ligaments, fascia, and muscles in the pelvic cavity
- Pressure on one or more roots of the lumbosacral plexus[4]

These factors also cause mild to severe pain referred to the lower lumbar and sacral segments (see Fig. 14-2).

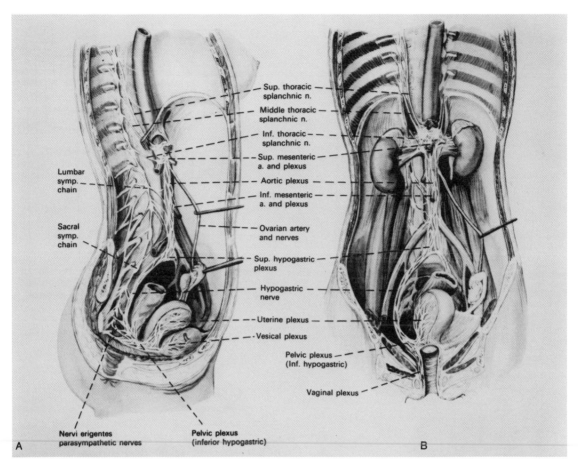

Figure 14–4. Gross anatomy of the nerve supply to the uterus. (**A**) Lateral view. (**B**) Anterior view. The uterus is shown in the nonpregnant state. The uterine and cervical plexuses are derived from the pelvic plexus, which contains parasympathetic and sympathetic efferents. The parasympathetic efferents have their cell bodies in the middle three sacral segments. Parasympathetic afferents pass through these segments and progress cephalad through the neuraxis. The sympathetic efferents and afferents pass through the hypogastric nerve, which in turn is a continuation of the superior hypogastric and aortic plexuses. Fibers from these latter two plexuses pass to the lumbar sympathetic chain. Afferents in the lumbar sympathetic chain mediate nociceptive impulses and accompany the sympathetic fibers. From the lumbar and lower thoracic sympathetic chain, the nociceptive afferents pass to the T-10, T-11, T-12, L-1 spinal nerves and reach the spinal cord via their posterior roots and rootlets. (Bonica JJ. Principles and practice of obstetric analgesia and anesthesia. Philadelphia: FA Davis, 1967:110)

FACTORS INFLUENCING THE SEVERITY OF LABOR PAIN

Although the preceding description outlines the source of the pain of labor, it does not consider its severity. The pain women feel during labor varies widely (Fig. 14-7).[2] Many factors, both intrinsic and extrinsic, can influence the parturient's level of pain. The following section will discuss the individual, environmental, and cultural factors that can alter the degree and intensity of pain felt with childbirth.

How does one reliably measure pain? Because pain is a purely subjective phenomenon, it cannot be quantitated easily. Ultimately, pain is as severe as the patient says it is. The McGill Pain Questionnaire has proved to be a reliable way to quantitate the pain of different syndromes, including labor and delivery. It consists of 20 sets of words describing sensory, affective, evaluative,

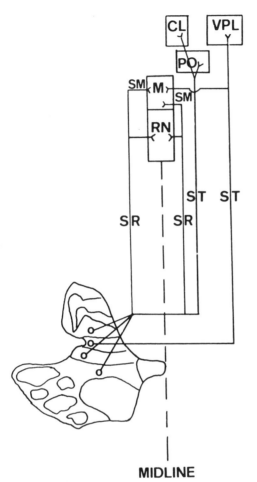

MIDLINE

Figure 14–5. Pain pathways in the ventrolateral white matter of the spinal cord. Spinothalamic tract (ST) terminations are shown in ventral posterior lateral (VPL), central (CL), and posterior (PO) thalamus. Spinomesencephalic (SM) and spinoreticular (SR) tracts end in the midbrain (M) and the more caudal reticular nuclei (RN), respectively. The SR and SM pathways are both bilateral, although the contralateral projection predominates. (Sorkin LS. Pain pathways and spinal modulation. Anesth Clinic North Am 1989;7:20)

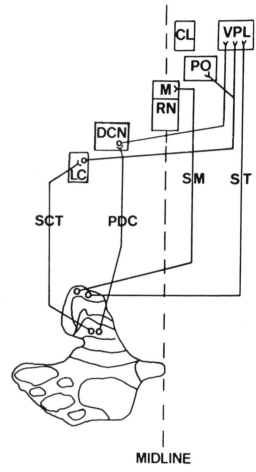

MIDLINE

Figure 14–6. Organization of pathways carrying nociceptive information in the dorsal spinal cord. Lamina I spinothalamic tract (ST) cells terminate in the ventral posterior lateral (VPL) and posterior (PO) thalamic nuclei. Other projections from VPL include the postsynaptic dorsal column (PDC) pathway, which synapses in the dorsal column nuclei (DCN), and the spinocervical tract (SCT), which synapses in the lateral cervical (LC) nucleus. A fourth dorsal tract, the spinomesencephalic tract (SM), goes from lamina I to the midbrain (M). (CL = central thalamus, RN = reticular nuclei) (Sorkin LS. Pain pathways and spinal modulation. Anesth Clinic North Am 1989;7:22)

and miscellaneous dimensions of the experience of pain (Fig. 14-8).[3] Linear visual analogue scales have also provided information about labor pain. Numerous studies have used these techniques to evaluate the pain of labor in many different patient groups. The results of these studies are often inconclusive or contradictory. As a whole, however, they do allow us to draw some conclusions about the severity of labor pain and to predict who might suffer more severe pain.

Obstetric Factors

Multiple obstetric factors seem to modify the severity of labor pain. Some of the variables studied include childbirth classes, parity, severity of menstrual pain, fetal position, and the use of oxytocin to stimulate uterine contractions. The severity of labor pain seems to be lower in women who received prepared childbirth training than in those who did not (Figs. 14-1 and 14-9).

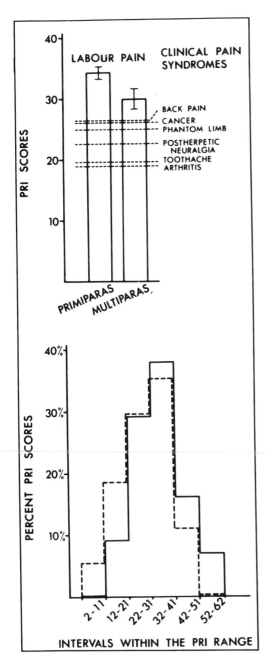

Figure 14–7. Variation in the severity of labor pain in primiparous (*solid line*) and multiparous (*dashed line*) women. (PRI = pain-rating index.) (Melzack R, Taenzer P, Feldman P, Kinch R. Labor is still painful after prepared childbirth training. Can Med Assoc J 1981;125:357)

McGILL PAIN QUESTIONNAIRE

Patient's Name_____

Date _____ Time _____

1 FLICKERING	11 TIRING
QUIVERING	EXHAUSTING
PULSING	12 SICKENING
THROBBING	SUFFOCATING
BEATING	13 FEARFUL
POUNDING	FRIGHTFUL
2 JUMPING	TERRIFYING
FLASHING	14 PUNISHING
SHOOTING	GRUELLING
3 PRICKING	CRUEL
BORING	VICIOUS
DRILLING	KILLING
STABBING	15 WRETCHED
LANCINATING	BLINDING
4 SHARP	16 ANNOYING
CUTTING	TROUBLESOME
LACERATING	MISERABLE
5 PINCHING	INTENSE
PRESSING	UNBEARABLE
GNAWING	17 SPREADING
CRAMPING	RADIATING
CRUSHING	PENETRATING
6 TUGGING	PIERCING
PULLING	18 TIGHT
WRENCHING	NUMB
7 HOT	DRAWING
BURNING	SQUEEZING
SCALDING	TEARING
SEARING	19 COOL
8 TINGLING	COLD
ITCHY	FREEZING
SMARTING	20 NAGGING
STINGING	NAUSEATING
9 DULL	AGONIZING
SORE	DREADFUL
HURTING	TORTURING
ACHING	PPI
HEAVY	0 No pain
10 TENDER	1 MILD
TAUT	2 DISCOMFORTING
RASPING	3 DISTRESSING
SPLITTING	4 HORRIBLE
	5 EXCRUCIATING

Figure 14–8. McGill pain questionnaire. Categories of pain: sensory, 1 to 10; affective, 11 to 15; evaluative, 16; and miscellaneous, 17 to 20. Rank value for each word based on position of word in category. Sum of rank values = pain-rating index (PRI). Index of present pain intensity (PPI) is based on scale of 0 to 5. (Melzack R, Kinch R, Dobkin P, Lebrun M, Taenzer P. Severity of labour pain: Influence of physical as well as psychologic variables. Can Med Assoc J 1984;130:579)

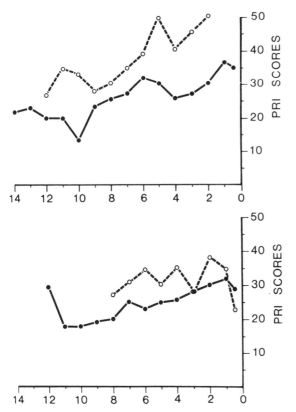

Figure 14–9. Average PRI scores reported hourly until delivery by primiparous women (*top*) and multiparous women (*bottom*). Women receiving prepared childbirth training (*dashed line*) reported less pain than those who did not (*solid line*). (Melzack R, Kinch R, Dobkin P, Lebrun M, Taenzer P. Severity of labour pain: Influence of physical as well as psychologic variables. Can Med Assoc J 1984;130:579)

Gaston–Johansson utilized the McGill Pain Questionnaire to compare pain in primiparous and multiparous women.[15] The primiparas reported more intense sensory pain, using words like "cramping," "aching," and "pressure," in the latent and transitional stages of labor, and more affective pain, assessed by the words "troublesome," "tiring," and "fearful," in all stages of labor, than the multiparas (Table 14-1). The primiparas also consumed significantly more pain medication than the multiparas. Corli *et al*[16] evaluated the characteristics of uterine contractions during labor using a visual analogue scale. The intensity of uterine pressure, or peak of the contraction, proved more important than the duration of the contraction in influencing perceived pain (Fig. 14-10).

Women often have less pain with their second or third labor than with their first (see Fig. 14-1). Labor is longer in primiparas than in multiparas, but the duration of labor does not correlate with pain scores. Lowe,[17] in a descriptive study, showed that primiparous women reported more severe pain than multiparous women during early labor but less severe pain during the second stage of labor. The frequency of contractions and the amount of cervical dilation significantly predicted pain for primiparous women, whereas only the amount of cervical dilation predicted pain for multiparas.[17] Multiparas reported less pain in early labor, but their pain dramatically increased in active and transitional labor. The transitional period of labor (8–10 cm) incites the greatest pain in both primiparas and multiparas.[18] More rapid and abrupt fetal descent accounts for the increased severity of pain reported by the multiparas in the later stages of labor. The more gradual descent of the fetus in the primiparous women allows more time for progressive distention of the pelvic structures and development of natural perineal anesthesia from prolonged pressure.

Primiparas and multiparas with histories of severe menstrual pain had significantly higher levels of labor pain.[3] Low back pain during menstruation also correlates with labor pain scores.[19] These women frequently complain of continuous low back pain in addition to the intermittent pain of contractions. Ten percent of laboring women felt that the continuous low back pain was worse than the labor contractions.[19]

A relationship between fetal position and maternal distress in latent labor has been reported.[20] Women with fetuses in the occiput posterior position displayed more distress-related thought than those with fetuses in the occiput transverse or occiput anterior positions. The author of this study has been unable to confirm this result.[21]

Does the use of oxytocin for induction or augmentation of labor cause the labor to be more painful? This question, although very relevant, does not have a definitive answer. Simpkin[22] conducted a survey of postpartum mothers, asking them to describe stressful events during their labor and delivery. These women rated oxytocin for induction or augmentation of labor as moderately to highly stressful. Excessive stress by producing anxiety and pain can raise plasma catecholamine concentrations.[23] However, pain scores in primiparous and multiparous women receiving oxytocin for induction or augmentation of labor did not differ from those not receiving oxytocin.[17] Prolactin concentration falls during labor, with or without oxytocin, while cortisol concentration rises.[24] Rising plasma cortisol levels reflect increased stress from both

Table 14–1

Number of Primiparas and Multiparas Choosing a Particular Word from the McGill Pain Questionnaire to Describe Labor Pain During Three Stages of Labor

WORDS		CERVICAL DILATION								
		Stage 1, 2–4 cm	P	M	Stage 2, 5–7 cm	P	M	Stage 3, 8–10 cm	P	M
Sensory		Cramping	16	20	Pressing	9	12	Pressing	11	16
		Aching	13	22	Cramping	8	10	Tearing	11	7
		Grinding	9	16	Aching	6	11	Cramping	11	7
		Pressing	8	13	Sore	6	5	Aching	6	8
		Cutting	6	7	Tearing	4	6	Cutting	5	6
		Sore	13	7				Pinching	4*	0
		Tearing	4*	1				Sore	4*	0
Affective		Troublesome	17*	16	Troublesome	10	12	Troublesome	16	17
		Tiring	18*	13	Tiring	7	11	Tiring	17*	10
		Happy	4	22*	Happy	6	7	Terrible	8	7
		Irritating	3	11				Fearful	7	3
		Worried	3	8						
		Fearful	6	4						

(After Gaston-Johansson F, Fridh G, Turner–Norvell K. Progression of labor pain in primiparas and multiparas. Nurs Res 1988;37:86.)
*P < 0.05 versus multiparas.
Abbreviations: P = primiparas (n = 30); M = multiparas (n = 54).

natural and oxytocin-induced labors. Relief of pain and anxiety with meperidine decreases the amount of cortisol released. If stress is greater, is pain more intense? Probably so, but there are no definitive studies linking oxytocin-induced or augmented labor to more painful uterine contractions.

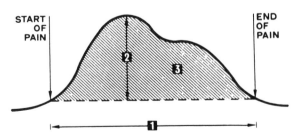

Figure 14–10. Diagrammatic representation of a tocographic curve showing the duration (1), peak (2), and area under the curve (3). Pain correlated most closely with the intensity (2), not the duration of the contraction. (Corli O, Grossi E, Roma G, Battagliarin G. Correlation between subjective labour pain and uterine contractions: A clinical study. Pain 1986;26:53)

Pain Tolerance

Pregnancy may change a woman's tolerance for pain. Animal studies have shown strong evidence for pregnancy-induced endogenous opiate antinociception.[25] Iwasaki *et al*[26] reported naloxone-reversible, pregnancy-induced analgesia in rats. They studied several forms of noxious stimuli, including colorectal distention, hypertonic saline-induced writhing, tail flick, and hot plate. Rats were tested when nonpregnant, during gestation, and postpartum. One group was also given naloxone and then tested. Pregnant and early postpartum rats had a higher pain threshold or a longer latency to response to some stimuli (Fig. 14-11). Naloxone reversed the elevation in pain threshold associated with pregnancy. Ginzler[27] also reported an increased pain threshold in rats as pregnancy progressed.

Do the results of these rat studies mean that the same processes are activated in human parturients? The subject is controversial. In one study, pregnancy did not induce any changes in response threshold to nox-

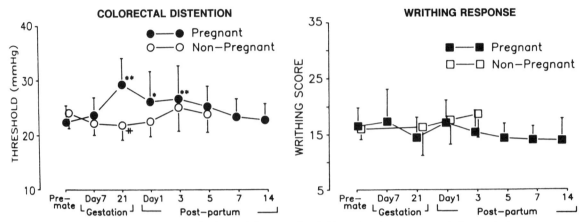

Figure 14–11. Comparison of colorectal distention thresholds and writing responses before and after parturition in pregnant and nonpregnant rats. On day 21 of gestation, mean colorectal distension thresholds in pregnant rats (n = 35) were significantly different from those observed in nonpregnant animals (n = 7). The prepregnant baseline thresholds in the two groups were not significantly different. Analgesia also was evident on postpartum days 1 and 3. In the writhing tests, no significant changes were observed. Each point represents mean ± SD. (** = P < 0.01, * = P < 0.05 versus prepregnant baseline, + + = P < 1970.05 versus pregnant animals.) (Iwasaki H, Collins JG, Saito Y, Kerman-Hinds A. Naloxone-sensitive pregnancy-induced changes in behavioral responses to colorectal distension: Pregnancy-induced analgesia to visceral stimulation. Anesthesiology 1991;74:927)

ious thermal stimuli.[28] Other investigators have reported elevated pain and discomfort thresholds during late gestation.[29] Tactile thresholds, however, have not been shown to change during pregnancy or in the postpartum period.[30] Parturients who exercise regularly have higher plasma beta-endorphin concentrations than those who do not.[31] The parturients who exercised also reported less pain during labor. During labor in humans, the noxious stimulus of uterine contractions may activate endogenous analgesic systems.[26] The concentration of endogenous plasma opioids falls in women who receive appropriate epidural anesthesia during labor, indirectly confirming this hypothesis. Plasma beta-endorphins may not totally eliminate pain, but they may blunt pain perception and increase tolerance to acute pain.[27]

Individual Factors

Several other factors may have some bearing upon how painful labor will be for a given parturient. The work of Melzack *et al*[2,3] shows that older women tend to have less painful labors than younger women. Other physical variables include the ratio of maternal prepregnancy weight to height, the weight of the baby, and the shape of the woman's pelvic brim.[3,33] The greater the

woman's weight per unit of height, the higher the woman's pain scores. Heavier women tended to have bigger babies and more painful labors.[3] A large baby or labor through an abnormally shaped pelvis may result in fetal and maternal distress.[33]

Psychological factors probably play the most important role in predicting labor pain. Does the parturient have realistic expectations of the labor experience? This question is very important. If she does not, then she may have higher levels of anxiety, less ability to cope with the labor pain, more fear, and more actual pain. Several studies have shown that most women do not have realistic expectations of labor.[34,35] Neither primiparas or multiparas can accurately predict the amount of labor pain they would experience. Despite previous labor experiences, the multiparous woman was no more realistic about the labor pain than the primipara. As a result, most women feel more pain during labor than they anticipated. Unexpected pain then incites anxiety and fear. Heightened anxiety in turn yields more painful uterine contractions and longer labor.[36,37] Confidence about one's ability to cope with labor pain can lower anxiety.[38,39] Childbirth classes provide factual information about labor and teach pain control strategies.[20,40] Women who received childbirth training had lower pain scores than those who had no training.[3,19,20,38] Prepared childbirth training gives the parturient a more realistic expectation of labor, lowering her anxiety level and decreasing labor pain.[41]

Women who believe they are in personal control of their lives (high internal locus of control) experienced shorter but more painful labors than those who believe in the uncontrollability of events.[42] A parturient's concerns for herself and the baby, and an acceptance of the pregnancy, predict pain and distress in active and transitional labor.[20,39] Finally, women of higher socioeconomic status usually have less painful labors, possibly due to an increased level of confidence in their coping abilities.[2]

Environmental Factors

The environment in which a woman gives birth may affect her perception of labor pain. The combination of crowded hospital conditions, the absence of prenatal preparatory classes, and the unfamiliar hospital environment may markedly increase maternal anxiety and, consequently, pain.[43] Out-of-hospital birth may lower maternal anxiety and pain. Home birth,[44] alternative birth centers,[45] single-unit delivery systems,[46] and water birth[47] are four alternatives to a traditional in-hospital birth. Although women may have more access to familiar support personnel and may feel less anxious in alternate birth sites, no studies have been done to show that these alternatives lessen the pain of labor.

Supportive Companion

Another factor that affects maternal pain in labor is the presence or absence of a support person, be it a nurse, husband, or duola. The Greek word *duola* refers to an experienced woman who guides and assists a new mother in her infant-care tasks. Kennell *et al*[48] use this term to describe a woman who provides continuous support during parturition. They studied 412 healthy nulliparous women in labor. The women were randomly assigned to a supported group (n=212) who received continuous support of a duola, or to an observed group (n=200) which was monitored by an inconspicuous observer. A control group (n=204) which was neither supported nor observed was added after the other two groups were assigned. Continuous labor support significantly reduced the rate of cesarean delivery and forceps delivery, the need for oxytocin, and the use of epidural anesthesia. The supported women also had the fastest labors (Tables 14-2 and 14-3).[48]

A supportive companion may relieve maternal anxiety and by that reduce catecholamine production and facilitate uterine contractile activity and uterine blood flow. The constant presence, physical touch, reassurance, explanations, and anticipatory guidance provided by a duola may all comfort the mother.

In a similar study, Sosa *et al*[43] examined the effects of a duola in healthy Guatemalan primigravidae. The presence of a supportive companion shortened labor and lowered the risk of certain complications (Table 14-4).

Women who have continuous supportive care during labor are less likely to need pain-relief medication.[49] The presence of a labor partner, usually the father of the child, reduces pain and anxiety, frequency of augmentation, anesthesia, and forceps delivery.[50,51] Cogan *et al*[18] reported that the experiences of women in labor depended on their confidence in their preparation and in the support of their partners. Copstick showed that support and encouragement in the use of pain-control techniques correlated with a lower frequency of epidural analgesia but not to a reduction in the intensity of labor pain.[52]

Male partners and duolas differ in the support that they provide to laboring women.[46] When all forms of touching (rubbing, stroking, clutching, and holding) by duolas and male partners were considered, on average, the duolas touched the laboring women more than 95% of the time compared with less than 20% by the male partners. Also, male partners chose to be present less often than duolas. Patricia Engle, as well, suggests that the male partner may not always be the most effective labor companion. She reports that, among Mexican women, support from the woman's family and friends relieved pre- and postnatal anxiety, whereas support from the baby's father did not. She feels that, for Latinas, family members might be equally or more valuable than the baby's father as labor coaches.[53]

Cultural Factors

Women of all cultures feel labor pain.[24] Different ethnic groups vary significantly in their outward indications of pain.[54] Attitudes, expectations, and appropriate emotional expressions are learned through observing the actions of others who are similar in identity to oneself.[55] Bus and Portnoy[56] showed that the stronger the identification a person has with his or her group, the more willing he or she is to tolerate the pain of an electric shock, just to conform to the group norm. Does this result mean that ethnic origin influences a parturient's response to the pain of labor? Are there any peculiarities associated with individual ethnic groups?

Table 14-2

The Effect of Continuous Labor Support (Duola) on the Need for Oxytocin Augmentation of Labor

TYPE OF DELIVERY	NO. OF PTS	OXYTOCIN USE BY GROUP (%)		
		Supported	Observed	Control
Total*	616	36/212 (17.9)	46/200 (23.0)	89/204 (43.6)
Spontaneous vaginal*	439	25/179 (14.0)	18/137 (13.1)	46/123 (37.4)
Forceps	97	6/16 (37.5)	12/37 (32.4)	20/44 (45.5)
Cesarean section†	80	5/17 (29.4)	16/26 (61.5)	23/27 (62.2)

(Data from Kennell J, Klaus M, McGrath S, Robertson S, Hinckley C: Continuous emotional support during labor in a US hospital. JAMA 1991;265:2197)
*$P < 0.0001$ supported group versus control and observed versus control.
†$P = 0.06$.

The literature contains only a few studies addressing these issues.

Pesce[54] studied Australian-born and Italian-born mothers, and mothers born in Australia of Italian parents. The nature, quality, and range of expressions used to describe the pain of labor did not differ between the groups.

Middle Eastern women have been compared to Western women during labor.[57] Middle Eastern women gave higher ratings of pain and showed more pain behavior during the labor than the Western women. Did they actually have more pain or did they simply express more pain? This study did not control for maternal age. Melzack *et al*[2,3] have shown that older women have less painful labors than younger women.

The Western women were significantly older than the Middle Eastern women.

A postpartum survey queried American and Dutch women about their expectations of labor pain and their use of analgesics.[58] American women expected labor to be more painful. Significantly more American than Dutch women received pain medications during labor. Again, this study did not control for maternal age, and the American women were significantly younger than the Dutch women. More of the Dutch women delivered at home, where pain medication may not have been as readily available. Almost all of the American women delivered in a hospital with ready availability of pain medication.

Mexican women giving birth in Los Angeles were

Table 14-3

The Effect of Continuous Labor Support (Duola) on the Duration of Labor

TYPE OF DELIVERY	DURATION OF LABOR BY GROUP (h)					
	Supported		Observed		Control	
	Mean ± SD	n	Mean ± SD	n	Mean ± SD	n
All deliveries*	7.4±3.8	212	8.4±4.2	200	9.4±4.2	204
Vaginal (no forceps)†	6.8±3.5	179	7.3±3.1	137	8.2±3.9	123
Spontaneous vaginal (no oxytocin)‡	6.1±3.0	154	7.1±3.1	119	6.8±3.3	77
Vaginal (no medications)	5.5±2.8	116	6.3±2.5	62	5.3±2.7	25

(Data from Kennell J, Klaus M, McGrath S, Robertson S. Hinckley C. Continuous emotional support during labor in a US hospital. JAMA 1991;265:2197)
*$P < 0.02$, supported group versus observed and control groups, and observed group versus control group.
†$P = 0.02$ supported group versus control group. $P = 0.03$ observed group versus control group.
‡$P = 0.01$ supported group versus observed group.

Table 14–4

Effect of Continuous Labor Support (Duola) on Labor Complications*

CHARACTERISTIC	CONTROL GROUP (n = 95) % (n)	SUPPORTED Group (n = 32) % (n)
No problems	21(20)	63(20)
Meconium staining	25(24)	9(3)
Depressed newborn	3(3)	0(0)
Stillbirth	2(2)	0(0)
Cesarean section	27(26)	19(6)
Oxytocin augmentation	17(16)	6(2)
Forceps	5(4)	3(1)
Total complications	79(75)	37(12)

(Data from Sosa R, Kennell J, Klaus M, Robertson S, Urrutia J. The effects of a supportive companion on perinatal problems, length of labor, and mother–infant interaction. N Engl J Med 1980;303:597)

*P < 0.001 for the association between group and the total number of complications.

studied for anxiety pre- and postnatally. No comparisons were made, but some preferences are worth noting. Latinas varied in their levels of anxiety and expectations of labor. Latino women also preferred female and Latino health care providers during their labors.[53]

Does religion have a major impact on the way women react to labor pain? In one study, Catholic women reported less pain during active labor than either Protestant or no-religion groups.[20] Other religions have not been extensively studied with regard to labor pain.

Rationale for Pain Relief

Is unrelieved labor pain harmful to mother or fetus? Conditions arousing maternal anxiety can prolong labor and have deleterious consequences for the fetus.[22,28] Morishima *et al*[59] studied anxiety in gravid monkeys. They found that maternal stress caused a fall in fetal oxygenation and an increase in acidosis. Maternal monkeys were frightened by shining a bright light into their faces. This stimulus incited fetal bradycardia. Bradycardia resolved after the investigators covered the mother's face, relieving her anxiety. Anxiety in the maternal monkeys produced an outpouring of catecholamines. Before this part of the study, several of the fetuses had been partially asphyxiated from induced placental insufficiency. Although all fetuses showed falls in pH and marked falls in oxygenation during ma-

ternal stress, the already compromised fetuses had a much greater response.

Lederman *et al*[23,37] investigated the effects of endogenous catecholamines on the duration of labor and fetal well-being in humans. During normal labor, epinephrine and norepinephrine concentrations increase. When parturients become anxious, catecholamines rise further. Norepinephrine, with its alpha-agonist effects, can increase the intensity of uterine contractions and decrease uterine blood flow.[37] More intense uterine contractions may lead to tetanic contractions, abruption, and even death of the fetus. Epinephrine has beta-agonist effects. During labor, it can reduce the number and strength of uterine contractions and predispose to dysfunctional and prolonged labor.[37] Fetal heart rate, beat-to-beat variability, and a greater number of variable decelerations correlate with increased plasma epinephrine during labor.[37] In animal studies, reducing catecholamine production beneficially affects the utero placental circulation.[60] This same beneficial effect may occur in human parturients.

Just as maternal anxiety may predispose to dysfunctional labor,[37] unrelieved pain may increase the incidence of instrumented and cesarean deliveries.[20] Wuitchick *et al*[20] found that 68.4% of the women who reported "horrible" or "excruciating" pain required instrumented delivery compared to only 29.6% of the women reporting "discomforting" pain. These same women with "excruciating" pain had a 26.3% incidence of cesarean delivery compared to 0% of the women with "discomforting" pain. Some evidence suggests that other labor disorders, including maternal hypertension, dystocia, meconium staining, and fetal distress, are stress-related.[20] If there is an iatrogenic element to these disorders, it should be minimized.

The obstetric anesthesiologist's goal is to relieve the parturient's pain and stress. Maternal pain relief benefits not only the parturient but her infant as well.[60] Shorter labors, less pain and stress, and fewer maternal and fetal complications may increase maternal satisfaction with labor and delivery as well as help ensure good neonatal outcome.

REFERENCES

1. Genesis 3:12–14,16.
2. Melzack R. The myths of painless childbirth (The John J. Bonica Lecture). Pain 1984;19:321.
3. Melzack R, Kinch R, Dobkin P, Lebrun M, Taenzer P. Severity of labour pain: Influence of physical as well as psychologic variables. Can Med Assoc J 1984;130:579.
4. Bonica JJ. The management of pain, 2nd ed. Philadelphia: Lea & Febiger, 1990;2:1326.
5. Reynolds SRM. Physiology of the uterus, 2nd ed. New York: Paul B. Hoeber, 1949.
6. Moir C. The nature of the pain of labor. J Obstet Gynecol 1939;46:409.
7. Dick-Read G. Childbirth without fear. New York: Harper, 1953.
8. Head H. On disturbances of sensation with special reference to the pain of visceral disease. Brain 1983;16:1
9. MacKenzie J. Symptoms and their interpretation. New York: Paul B. Hoeber, 1912.
12. Cleland JGP. Paravertebral anaesthesia in obstetrics. Surg Gynecol Obstet 1933;57:51.
11. Bonica JJ. The nature of pain in parturition. Clin Obstet Gynecol 1975;2:499.
12. Sorkin LS. Pain pathways and spinal modulation. Anesthesiol Clin North Am 1989;7:1.
13. Light AR, Perl ER. Spinal termination of functionally identified primary afferent neurons with slowly conducting fibers. J Comp Neurol 1979;186:133.
14. Willis WD, Kenshalo JR, Leonard RB. The cells of origin of the primate spinothalamic track. J Comp Neurol 1979;188:543.
15. Gaston-Johansson F, Fridh G, Turner-Norvell K. Progression of labor pain in primiparas and multiparas. Nurs Res 1988;37:86.
16. Corli O, Grossi E, Roma G, Battagliarin G. Correlation between subjective labour pain and uterine contractions: A clinical study. Pain 1986;26:53.
17. Lowe N. Parity and pain during parturition. J Obstet Gynecol Neonatal Nurs, 1987; September/October:340.
18. Cogan R, Hemeborn WJ, Klopfer F. Predictors of pain during prepared childbirth. J Psychosom Res 1976; 120:523.
19. Melzack R, Belonger E. Labour pain: Correlations with menstrual pain and acute low back pain before and during pregnancy. Pain 1989;36:225.
20. Wuitchick M, Hesson K, Bakal D. Perinatal predictors of pain and distress during labor. Birth 1990;17:186.
21. Wuitchick M, Bakal D, Lipshitz J. The clinical significance of pain and cognitive activity in latent labor. Obstet Gynecol 1989;73:35.
22. Simpkin P. Stress, pain, and catecholamines in labor. Part 2. Stress associated with childbirth events: A pilot survey of new mothers. Birth 1986;13:234.
23. Lederman RP, Lederman G, Work BA, McCann DS. The relationship of maternal anxiety, plasma catecholamines, and plasma cortisol to progress in labor. Am J Obstet Gynecol 1978;132:495.
24. Onur E, Ercal T, Karslioglu I. Prolactin and cortisol levels during spontaneous and oxytocin-induced labour and the effect of meperidine. Arch Gynecol Obstet 1989;244:227.
25. Cahil C. Beta-endorphin levels during pregnancy and labor: A role in pain modulation? Nurs Res 1989;38:200.
26. Iwasaki H, Collins JG, Saito Y, Kerman-Hinds A. Naloxone-sensitive pregnancy-induced changes in behavioral responses to colorectal distension: Pregnancy-induced analgesia to visceral stimulation. Anesthesiology 1991;74:927.
27. Ginzler A. Endorphin-mediated increase in pain threshold during pregnancy. Science 1980;210:193.
28. Dunbar AH, Price DD, Newton RA. An assessment of pain responses to thermal stimuli during stages of pregnancy. Pain 1988;35:265.
29. Cogan R, Spinnato JA. Pain and discomfort thresholds in late pregnancy. Pain 1986;27:63.
30. Whipple B, Josimovich JB, Kamisaruk BR. Sensory thresholds during the antepartum, intrapartum, and postpartum periods. Int J Nurs Stud 1990;27:213.
31. Varrassi G, Bazzano C, Edwards WT. Effects of physical activity on maternal plasma B-endorphin levels and perception of labor pain. Am J Obstet Gynecol 1989;160:707.
33. Beischer NA, Mackay EV. Obstetrics and the newborn. 2nd ed. Philadelphia: WB Saunders, 1986:457.
34. Fridh G, Gaston-Johansson F. Do primiparas and multiparas have realistic expectations of labor? Acta Obstet Gynecol Scand 1990;69:103.
35. Fridh G, Kopare T, Gaston-Johansson F, Novell K. Factors associated with more intense labor pain. Res Nurs Health 1988;11:117.
36. Reading AE, Cox DN. Psychosocial predictors of labor pain. Pain 1985;22:309.
37. Lederman RP, Lederman E, Work B, McCann DS. Anxiety and epinephrine in multiparous women in labor: Relationship to duration of labor and fetal heart rate pattern. Am J Obstet Gynecol 1985;53:870.
38. Crowe K, Hon BA, VonBaeyer C. Predictors of a positive childbirth experience. Birth 1989;16:59.
39. Lowe NK. Explaining the pain of active labor: The im-

portance of maternal conficence. Res Nurs Health 1989;12:237.

40. Leventhal EA, Levanthal H, Shacham S, Easterling DV. Active coping reduces reports of pain from childbirth. J Consult Clin Psychol 1989;57:365.

41. Price DD, Harkins SW, Baker C. Sensory-affective relationships among different types of clinical and experimental pain. Pain 1987;28:297.

42. Scott-Palmer J, Skevington SM. Pain during childbirth and menstruation: a study of locus of control. J Psychosom Res 1981:25:151.

43. Sosa R, Kennell J, Klaus M, Robertson S, Urrutia J. The effects of a supportive companion on perinatal problems, length of labor, and mother–infant interaction. N Engl J Med 1980;303:597.

44. Dixon RA. Review of maternity patients suitable for home delivery. Br Med J 1982;284:1753.

45. Allgarer A. Alternate birth centers offer family-centered care. J Am Hosp Assoc 1978;52:97.

46. Notelovitz M. The single-unit delivery system—a safe alternative to home deliveries. Am J Obstet Gynecol 1978;132:889.

47. Daniels K. Water birth: The newest form of safe, gentle, joyous birth. J Nurse-Midwifery 1989;34:198.

48. Kennell J, Klaus M, McGrath S, Robertson S, Hinckley C: Continuous emotional support during labor in a US hospital. JAMA 1991;265:2197.

49. Hodnett ED, Osborn RW. Effects of continuous intrapartum professional support on childbirth outcomes. Res Nurs Health 1989;12:289.

50. Niven C, Gijsbers K. Obstetric and nonobstetric factors related to labour pain. J Reprod Infant Psych 1984;2:61.

51. Hunter M, Philips C, Rachman S. Memory for pain. Pain 1979;6:35.

52. Copstick SM, Taylor KE, Hayes R, Morris N. Partner support and the use of coping techniques in labour. J Psychosom Res 1986;30:497.

53. Engle PL, Scrimshaw SC, Zambrana RE, Dunkel-Schetter C. Prenatal and postnatal anxiety in Mexican women giving birth in Los Angeles. Health Physiol 1990;9:285.

54. Pesce G. Measurement of reported pain of childbirth: A comparison between Australian and Italian subjects. Pain 1987;31:87.

55. Bates M. Ethnicity and pain: A biocultural model. Soc Sci Med 1987;24:1:47.

56. Buss AH, Portnoy NW. Pain tolerance and group identification. J Pers Soc Psychol 1967;6:106.

57. Weisenberg M, Caspi Z. cultural and educational influences on pain of childbirth. J Pain Symptom Manage 1989;4:13.

58. Senden IPM, Wetering MD, Eskes TKAB, Brerkens PB, Laube DW, Pitkin RM. Labor pain: A comparison of parturients in a Dutch and an American teaching hospital. Obstet Gynecol 1988;71:541.

59. Morrshima HO, Pederson H, Finster M. The influence of maternal psychological stress on the fetus. Am J Obstet Gynecol 1978;131:286.

60. Levinson G, Shnider SM. Catecholamines: The effect of maternal fear and its treatment on uterine function and arculation. Birth Fam J 1979;6:3:167.

61. Seguin L, Therrien R, Champagne F, Larouche D. The components of women's satisfaction with maternity care. Birth 1989;16:109.

CHAPTER 15

Nonpharmacologic Pain Relief

H. Jane Huffnagle

When the anesthetic effects of ether and chloroform were discovered in the mid-1800s, many members of the British clergy argued that human intervention in the miracle of birth was a sin against the Will of God. Following Queen Victoria's use of "blessed chloroform" during her eighth confinement, the practice of limiting the pain of labor gained wider acceptance.[1-3] As labor analgesia became more widely practiced, maternal and infant morbidity and mortality fell. Many attributed this improved outcome to the absence of pain that permitted the obstetrician to work unhindered in difficult labors.

Childbearing, viewed historically, has undergone several incarnations, which follow:

- A providentially appointed occasion to suffer
- A ritualized event in the female community
- A highly charged emotional and physical brush with death
- A pathology requiring medical intervention

A real concern for maternal–fetal safety and the desire for a satisfactory birth experience has fostered an "antianesthesia" atmosphere in some obstetric suites. Some claim that "intervention" is unnecessary in the natural process of parturition. To them, the use of anesthesia represents patient failure and risks disastrous fetal outcome. This sentiment has lead some patients and obstetricians to seek alternative methods of labor pain relief. These options include the following:

- Prepared childbirth, encompassing techniques of Grantly Dick-Read, Lamaze's psychoprophylaxis, and Leboyer's childbirth without violence
- Hypnosis
- Acupuncture
- Transcutaneous electrical nerve stimulation (TENS)
- Biofeedback techniques

Some women also consider nonhospital and often non-medical delivery (home delivery) options. Laboring women may use these techniques, in combination and with various modifications.

The purpose of this chapter is to review these alternative methods of labor pain control. It attempts to provide an understanding of how each is done and of the strengths and weaknesses of each approach. All these methods avoid exogenous drugs; however, most leave the parturient with considerable pain. The birth experience may still be unsatisfactory (or at least very painful).

PREPARED CHILDBIRTH

Natural Childbirth: The Dick-Read Method

During the past few decades, women in the United States have increasingly elected to have a "natural" childbirth. American culture defines natural childbirth in a variety of ways.[4] Some consider it the absence of analgesics during the first stage of labor. Others deem it the absence of monitoring, episiotomies, and all analgesic, anesthetic, and oxytocic medications.[4]

Grantly Dick-Read coined the term *natural childbirth*. He suggested that labor pain arose from socially induced expectations about parturition. He asserted that childbirth is not an inherently painful process. "There is no physiologic function in the body which gives rise to pain in the normal course of health."[5] He outlined a process called the fear–tension–pain syndrome. In this syndrome, fear incites tension in the circular muscle fibers of the lower part of the uterus. This tension produces pain perception. His prescription to eliminate labor pain rests upon correction of faulty expectations regarding parturition and on the provision of progressive muscle relaxation. He also introduced breathing exercises, advocating deep breathing during early stages of labor, more rapid breathing during contractions toward the end of the first stage, panting during a contraction if bearing down was undesirable, and breath-holding during the process of bearing down.[5,6] This method of natural childbirth does have its limitations. Even Dick-Read admitted that normal labor could involve some pain.

Figure 15–1. Fernand Lamaze. (Photo courtesy of Richard Clark, MD, and Patrick Sim [ASA Library])

Psychoprophylaxis

A second major theory of childbirth preparation was developed in the Soviet Union by A. Nikolayev in 1954. The technique, known as psychoprophylaxis, was presented to Western scientists by Velvovsky.[6-7] Velvovsky, like Dick-Read, postulated that labor was not an inherently painful experience. If a multipara felt pain, she was having "conditional reflex labor pain" because of an earlier exposure in labor to "cortical pain." Cortical pain resulted from neural impulses that arose during labor and were experienced as painful because of a disruption of excitatory–inhibitory processes in the cortex and subcortex. Psychoprophylaxis was supposed to prevent excitatory–inhibitory imbalance through the following methods:

- Deep breathing during each contraction
- Stroking of certain sections of the abdomen combined with deep breathing
- Pressure applied to certain "pain-prevention points" located along the small of the back and the medial surface of the anterior superior ilia[8]

Lamaze

A French obstetrician, Fernard Lamaze (Fig. 15-1), became acquainted with the teaching of Velvovsky in 1951 while touring Russia. Upon returning to France, he began using the techniques, with some of his own variations.[9] First, he modified the breathing techniques to include rapid breathing during the second stage of labor, and panting during crowning and delivery. Second, he advocated the use of controlled neuromuscular relaxation during labor, which "economizes on oxygen and reduces the production of waste products." Also, he deleted the use of stroking, pain-prevention points, and timing of contractions from Velvovsky's technique.[2]

Current approaches to prepared childbirth usually follow the techniques of Lamaze, although they include parts of the Dick-Read method as well. As Beck and Hall[16] indicate, there are differences in the preparatory techniques that reflect variance of trainers, treatment settings, and theoretical orientations. Most however, include three distinct components. The first consists of providing information concerning normal anatomy and physiology of pregnancy, labor, and delivery. The second consists of training in relaxation. The third presents breathing techniques that usually follow variations of the format outlined by Dick-Read. To these three components, many add husband participation. The husband takes an active role in timing contractions, delivering reminders about the use of breathing techniques, and providing moral support.

Natural childbirth techniques do seem to provide some degree of pain relief. In one study, primiparas who had completed antepartum Lamaze training were given narcotics less frequently during labor, received conduction anesthesia less often, and had a higher frequency of spontaneous vaginal deliveries compared to "matched" controls (Table 15-1).[8] Melzack and colleagues[10] report that primiparas who had prepared childbirth training reported lower pain scores than those with no training. However, 81% of the prepared childbirth patients still requested epidural anesthesia. Results of a study by Geden *et al*[11] indicated that relaxation training was the most therapeutically active component of the Lamaze regimen.

Duola

Reassurance and support during labor also seem to be important aspects of natural childbirth regimens. A "duola," or supportive lay companion, significantly improves labor outcome. One group of investigators studied the effects of a duola on the length of labor and on mother–infant interaction after delivery in healthy Guatemalan primigravid women.[12] They initially assigned women to a duola or no companion on a random basis. The control women had a significantly higher rate of subsequent perinatal problems (*i.e.,* cesarean section or meconium staining). The authors had to admit 103 mothers to the control group and 33 to the duola group to get 20 uncomplicated deliveries in each group. In the final sample, women having a duola delivered 8.8 hours after admission. Those laboring alone delivered 19.3 hours after admission to the hospital. Mothers who had a duola present during labor were awake more after delivery and stroked, smiled at, and talked to their babies more than the control mothers. This same group repeated their study in a US hospital and obtained similar results.[13] These observations suggest that constant human support during labor may offer substantial benefits. Lower maternal anxiety and, hence, decreased catecholamine concentrations may be the etiology of this benefit.

Many mothers who receive natural childbirth training will request additional analgesia, therefore, it is important that childbirth classes include reliable information about anesthetic options. Regional anesthesia can be offered as a reasonable compromise that minimizes stress but still allows participation of the mother and father in the birth of their infant.

Table 15–1

The Effect of Lamaze Preparation on Labor Pain and Obstetric Outcome in Primiparous Women

	LAMAZE GROUP	CONTROL GROUP	P VALUE
Number of patients	129	129	NS
Oxytocin induction or augmentation (n)	17	20	NS
Mean duration, first stage of labor (h ± SD)	8.98 ± 4.91	8.83 ± 4.34	NS
Mean duration, second stage of labor (min ± SD)	51.0 ± 35.4	56.9 ± 37.8	NS
Spontaneous vaginal delivery (%)	62.8	36.4	< 0.001
Low forceps (%)	24.8	53.5	< 0.001
Mid forceps (%)	6.2	5.4	NS
Cesarean section (%)	6.2	4.7	NS
No analgesia, first stage of labor (n)	36	9	< 0.001
Narcotics	84	109	< 0.001
Epidural or caudal	18	52	< 0.001
Pudendal block	83	59	< 0.001

(Data from Scott JR, Rose NB. Effect of psychoprophylaxis [Lamaze preparation] on labor and delivery in primiparas. N Engl J Med 1976;294:1205)

Leboyer

The French obstetrician Frederick Leboyer developed the concept of "childbirth without violence."[14] He believed that noise, bright lights, and other stimulation associated with a traditional delivery caused psychologic trauma to the newborn. He advocated delivery in semidarkness, with minimal noise to avoid disturbing the neonate. Immediately after delivery, the baby is lifted upwards onto the mother's abdomen. When the umbilical cord stops pulsating, the baby is lowered into a warm bath. Leboyer's methods have met with considerable controversy. Among the objections are the following:

- Subdued lighting may not be enough to see the condition and color of the baby.
- Hypothermia may develop after delivery while the baby is on the abdomen or in the bath.
- Placing the baby on the mother's abdomen, which is higher than the placenta, until the cord stops pulsating can allow a serious loss of blood from baby to placenta.

Henschel[15] tried to address these concerns by comparing the Leboyer technique to conventional delivery. That study reported the following results:

- Hypothermia did not occur in babies who had skin-to-skin contact with their mother at birth.
- Immersion in the water bath had no adverse effects
- No baby suffered from treatable jaundice.
- No baby suffered from anemia due to delayed clamping of the cord.
- The quiet and subdued lighting did not interfere with communication or observation of the mother's or baby's condition.

The Leboyer babies seemed to cry considerably less, and the mother's memories of the birth experience were positive in every case. On the other hand, a randomized clinical trial showed that the Leboyer procedure offers no advantage over a gentle, conventional delivery in infant and maternal outcomes.[16]

HYPNOSIS

Hypnosis has been used for many years to lessen or relieve the pain of labor and delivery. Hypnosis has the following advantages over other forms of pain relief:

- It does not result in obstruction of airway reflexes, impairment of sensorium, or hypoventilation as oversedation or narcotization can.[17]

- It does not produce hypotension or decreased uteroplacental perfusion as a rapidly dosed epidural can.
- It does not result in itching or nausea and vomiting as intrathecal narcotics can.
- It does not depress the neonate as can narcotics administered close to delivery.[18]

One study has suggested that hypnosis significantly shortened the first stage of labor.[19] Others, however, have found the opposite effect.[20] Moya and James[19] found better umbilical acid–base status after birth using hypnosis compared to general anesthesia. Also, infants recover more rapidly from birth asphyxia with hypnosis compared to either general or regional anesthesia.[18] A psychologist has described her experience with Lamaze and hypnosis for labor pain relief. She preferred hypnosis. The author states that Lamaze requires much more effort and causes anxiety in anticipation of contractions. She suggests that women can easily learn hypnosis during pregnancy and use it successfully in labor.[21] Maternity nurses or labor coaches could help with simple "deepening" techniques that would eliminate the need for constant physician attendance.

Harmon[22] studied the benefits of hypnotic analgesia as an adjunct to childbirth education in 60 nulliparous women. Hypnotic training significantly raised the pain threshold in susceptible parturients (Fig. 15-2A and B) Women who used hypnosis had a shorter first stage of labor, used less medication, and had more frequent spontaneous deliveries than controls (Table 15-2). Their infants had higher Apgar scores. Highly susceptible, hypnotically treated women had lower depression scores after birth as well. Superior outcomes in the hypnosis group may result from reduced pain perception as well as a higher tolerance to pain.[22] All the subjects in this study were highly motivated volunteers, willing to try hypnosis. They participated in twice the typical amount of childbirth training.

Women interested in hypnoanalgesia can be evaluated for suggestibility by using the eye roll test.[23] Preparation before labor consists of a series of conditioning sessions about 30 minutes in length. With each session, a greater degree of trance is obtained. One technique consists of an induction involving a counting down from 10 to 0 while descending a flight of stairs. The trance is deepened by imagining peaceful scenes, suggestions of arm levitation, glove anesthesia, and finally abdominal anesthesia.[22]

Hypnosis, however, is not for everyone. Of any random group of people, only 25% are easily hypnotized.[17] Reported complications range from acute anxi-

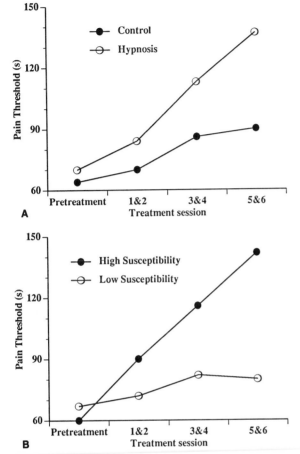

Figure 15–2. (A) Mean pain threshold scores for hypnosis and control subjects for the ischemic pain task (tourniquet-induced ischemia). **(B)** Mean pain threshold scores for high and low susceptibility to hypnosis for the ischemic pain task. (After Harmon TM, Hynan MT, Tyre TE. Improved obstetric outcomes using hypnotic analgesia and skill mastery combined with child-birth education. J Consult Psych 1990;58:525)

ety to frank psychosis. Whal[17] lists seven strong contraindications to the use of hypnosis:

- Evidence of psychosis
- Evidence of latent unconscious homosexuality
- Evidence of a strong unconscious wish to regress
- History of psychoneurotic hysterical conversion reactions
- Evidence of strong fear or ambivalence regarding birth or motherhood
- Hyperemesis gravidarum during the first trimester of pregnancy
- Nightmares in the last trimester

In addition to relieving the pain of labor, hypnosis has been used successfully as an adjunct to the medical treatment of premature labor,[24] and in the treatment of acute pregnancy-associated hypertension.[25] Although hypnosis may offer advantages over conventional methods of labor analgesia, it will not be effective with everyone and should be used only in carefully selected patients.

ACUPUNCTURE

Acupuncture has been used to help control labor pain in China and the Far East for many years. However, acupuncture can produce surgical analgesia in only 60% to 70% of patients, even in China.[26] It is least effective for pain in the lower part of the body.[27] The success of acupuncture seems to depend on careful patient selection, high patient motivation, and deeply embedded cultural conditioning. Depending on the pain threshold of the patient, a state of hypoalgesia is obtained with acupuncture, but complete pain relief is not. This hypoalgesic state may be mediated by endogenous opioids.[28]

Abouleish and Depp[29] studied electroacupuncture (the needles are electrically vibrated continuously after insertion) in 12 laboring women. Needles were inserted at selected points depending upon whether the patient was in stage 1 or stage 2 of labor (Fig. 15-3). The angle, depth, or site of insertion was changed until "Teh-Chi" (warmth, numbness, or tightness at the site of insertion, sometimes radiating along the corresponding meridian) was obtained. The needles were then vibrated at a frequency of 5 to 10 cps. The output from the machine was increased until the patient felt the needles vibrating but felt no associated discomfort. Four of these patients received no pain relief. Seven experienced a 66% reduction of pain. No patient was completely free of pain. Ten of the twelve patients studied required regional anesthesia for delivery; one delivered under acupuncture alone. Another group used only three acupuncture points, all located on one leg.[30] Of 85 patients in the acupuncture group, 37 required additional analgesia; however, the first stage of labor was 2.5 hours shorter for the primigravida in the acupuncture group as compared to the control group.

In a third study, patients used acupuncture repeatedly in the month before delivery.[31] Acupuncture did not improve the women's overall experience of labor and delivery. Still, 95% of the women in the acupuncture group stated that they would request this treatment before a future delivery. Acupuncture does not cloud the sensorium or depress airway reflexes. Women

Table 15–2

Obstetric Outcomes in Primiparous Women Using Hypnotic Analgesia and Skill Mastery Combined with Childbirth Education

	HYPNOSIS	**CONTROL**
Stage 1 (min)	78.9 ± 55.3*	247.9 ± 141.5
Stage 2 (min)	46.5 ± 27.0	63.5 ± 26.0
Spontaneous delivery	87%*	60%
Tranquilizer use	13%*	53%
Narcotic use	7%*	53%
Oxytocics	33%*	93%

*P < 0.01 versus control. All women listened to childbirth education tapes. Women in the hypnosis group also received instruction and practiced hypnotic induction. Women in both groups were initially determined to have "high susceptibility" to hypnosis.
(Data from Harmon TM, Hynan MT, Tyre TE. Improved obstetric outcomes using hypnotic analgesia and skill mastery combined with childbirth education. J Consult Clin Psych 1990;58:525)

who received acupuncture felt more in control of their labor and delivery.[30] However, acupuncture analgesia is incomplete, unpredictable, and inconsistent, and it is time-consuming. Needles may become dislodged. The patient's movements are restricted. Finally, electroacupuncture can cause interference with electronic monitoring of the mother and fetus.[29]

TRANSCUTANEOUS ELECTRICAL NERVE STIMULATION

Transcutaneous electrical nerve stimulation (TENS) techniques have been developed over the past decade for the relief of chronic pain of various etiologies. Electricity has been used in medicine since 46 AD, when Scribonius Largus, a Roman physician, used the torpedo fish for the treatment of headache and gout. The shock from the ray stimulated the area and relieved the pain.[32] The use of TENS in modern medicine derives from the gate-control theory of pain.[33] According to this hypothesis, cells in the posterior horn of the spinal grey matter have a gating function. Activity in low-threshold, large afferent fibers (not conducting pain) closes the gate to the central pain pathways. Increased activity in afferent pain fibers (Aδ and C fibers) opens the gate to the pain pathways. The pain experienced is controlled by the balance between the activity in the low-threshold, large afferent fibers, which have no pain function, and that in the afferent pain fibers.[34]

Dilation of the cervix and contraction of the uterus produce most of the pain of the first stage of labor. Visceral fibers of nerve roots T-10 to L-1 carry this information to the central nervous system. Distention of the pelvic outlet and perineum, and pressure on and stretching of other structures incites pain during the transitional and second stages of labor. This pain travels mostly in somatic fibers of the sacral plexus.[35]

The TENS stimulator is a dual-output device. Each output can be varied in both amplitude and rate. The amplitude varies from 0 to 220 volts, whereas frequency ranges from 40 to 150 Hz.[36] Two pairs of silicon electrodes are placed paravertebrally at the T-10 to L-1 and S-2–4 spinal levels (Fig. 15-4). The amplitude and frequency at the upper level is adjusted until the patient is aware of a tingling or tickling sensation. This stimulation is maintained continuously as background through labor. The amplitude and frequency at the lower level is set higher than the upper. When the patient begins a contraction, the lower-level electrodes are stimulated throughout the contraction until 30 seconds after its end.[36,37] As labor progresses, the frequency and amplitude of stimulation are varied to achieve the best results.

Usually, TENS provides some relief of pain during the first stage of labor. It seems less effective in the second stage.[32,36–38] Some patients find TENS especially helpful with "back labor."[35,37] Between 70.6% and 93% of parturients find TENS helpful enough to request its use again in subsequent labor.[32,39] Transcutaneous electrical nerve stimulation decreases the need

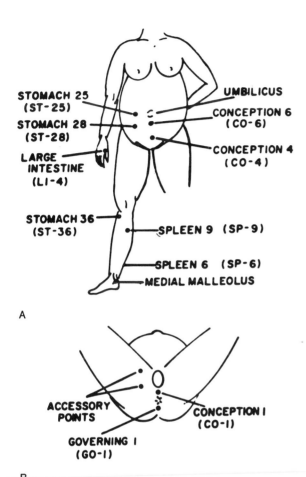

STOMACH 25
(ST-25)

STOMACH 28
(ST-28)

LARGE
INTESTINE
(LI-4)

STOMACH 36
(ST-36)

UMBILICUS

CONCEPTION 6
(CO-6)

CONCEPTION 4
(CO-4)

SPLEEN 9 (SP-9)

SPLEEN 6 (SP-6)

MEDIAL MALLEOLUS

A

ACCESSORY
POINTS

GOVERNING 1
(GO-1)

CONCEPTION 1
(CO-1)

B

Figure 15–3. Acupuncture meridians for pain relief during first stage (**A**) and second stage (**B**) of labor. (Abouleish E, Depp R. Acupuncture in obstetrics. Anesth Analg 1975;54:83)

for narcotic analgesics during labor and may shorten the first stage of labor.[32,34] A few cases of TENS interfering with the fetal heart trace have been reported.[34,39,40] The electrical stimulation from the TENS unit causes artifact on the cardiotocograph, which may produce a distorted reading. The TENS unit can be turned off momentarily to obtain a reading, or a filter that suppresses TENS interference can be applied.[40]

Transcutaneous electrical nerve stimulation has certain major advantages over other forms of analgesia in labor. It is safe for both mother and baby. It is noninvasive, instantly reversible, and can easily be administered by a trained midwife. Although TENS appears to be of minimal benefit in the second stage of labor, it can compliment conventional methods of analgesia.[38]

BIOFEEDBACK

Biofeedback has been used for over a decade to help patients cope with chronic pain.[41] It has recently been investigated for use during labor and delivery. St. James-Roberts and associates[42] studied two methods of biofeedback training: autonomic or skin conductance level (SCL) method, and voluntary-muscle relaxation or electromyographic (EMG) method. In the SCL method, electrodes are placed on the patient's second and third fingers of the left hand, and she wears an earphone. Skin conductance level is detected by the electrodes and is indicated to the patient by a series of clicks heard through the earphones. An increase in skin conductance level, heard as an increase in the rate of clicks, indicates an increase in arousal and a decrease in relaxation (Fig. 15-5). Using the EMG method, electrodes are applied 5 cm apart on the abdomen in the midline. The ground electrode is placed above the umbilicus and the two active electrodes are placed below (see Fig. 15-5). The patient also wears an earphone. As with the SCL method, increased electromyographic activity (decreased relaxation) is indicated by a faster rate of clicks through the earphones. By reducing tension of voluntary muscles, biofeedback may reduce some of the perineal trauma associated with delivery. Second, by concentrating and focusing on relaxation, the woman may be distracted from her pain. Hopefully, muscle relaxation will reduce perineal trauma and enhance descending modulatory pain pathways.[41]

The EMG method seems to be more effective than the SCL method.[42] Biofeedback helped in early labor but not once severely painful contractions had started. In another study, however, women using EMG biofeedback reported lower levels of pain both by visual analogue scale and by verbal descriptor scale than women who did not use biofeedback.[41] In addition,

Figure 15–4. TENS electrode placement. The wires connect to a nerve stimulator.

SCL

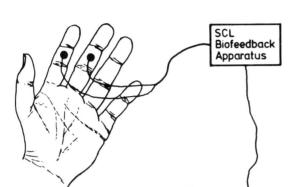

Subject's left hand

Personal Earphone
worn by subject

Relaxation=
Decreased skin conductance level=
Decreased rate of clicks

EMG

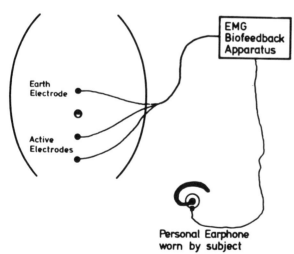

Earth
Electrode

Active
Electrodes

Personal Earphone
worn by subject

Relaxation=
Decreased electromyographic activity=
Decreased rate of clicks

Figure 15–5. Biofeedback electrode placement: skin conductance level (SCL) and electromyographic (EMG) methods. (St. James-Roberts I, Hutchinson C, Haran F, Chamberlain G. Biofeedback as an aid to childbirth. Br J Obstet Gynaecol 1983;90:56)

women in the biofeedback group labored an average of 2 hours less than the control group and used 30% fewer medications.[41]

Biofeedback is easily taught. Instruction can be given in group format, usually in four to six weekly training sessions followed by daily practice at home. It must be emphasized, however, that patients should receive this training before labor.

ALTERNATE BIRTH OPTIONS

Home Delivery

In the 1970s, demand for home deliveries in the United States increased. Some arguments in favor of home delivery are as follows:

- The individual woman should have the right to decide where she should have her baby.
- The environment of most institutions is very depersonalized.
- The cost of hospital deliveries continues to increase.[43]

Of 1015 parturients, however, only 278 were considered good candidates for home delivery.[44] Of these acceptable candidates, 41 (14.7%) had complications in the antenatal period, whereas 33 (13.9%) had difficulties during labor or up to the fifth postpartum day. Sixteen babies (6.8%) needed specialized pediatric care at or just after birth. In all, 31.3% of low-risk patients considered suitable for home delivery had complications that could make home delivery unsafe for either mother or baby.[44]

Alternate Birth Rooms

The safety problems related to home delivery have given rise to the concept of alternative birth centers, single-unit delivery systems, and hospital-based birthing rooms. Alternate birth centers have sprung up throughout the country. They provide one-room, homelike environments for labor, delivery, and recovery. Advantages include a Leboyer-like atmosphere, natural childbirth techniques, rooming in, and early discharge.[45] The single-unit delivery system allows for a natural and personalized childbirth experience within the confines of a modern obstetric unit. There is strict prenatal screening of patients into low- and high-risk categories, utilization of a single room for the entire labor process, and close supervision of women in labor by midwives and physicians.[43] The privacy of a single-unit delivery system unit allows the husband to be present without disrupting other patients. The hospital-based alternate birth room has become a popular alternative to the conventional labor and delivery room setting.[46] Alternate birth rooms provide a homelike atmosphere with a large clock, easy chairs, brightly colored curtains, television, radio, and so forth. All alternative birth rooms have oxygen and suction available as well as resuscitation equipment, which is usually kept concealed from sight but is readily available.

Water Birth

A gentle birth alternative developed by Soviet researcher Igor Charkovsky in the 1960s is birth in water.[47] Because warm fluid is the element most familiar and comfortable to the infant, water birth may be the smoothest possible birth transition. In a water birth, the mother-to-be is able to relax deeply during labor in a warm tub, her weight being supported by the water. The warmth of the bath relaxes her tension and eases her labor pains, and the water gives her the freedom to move into whatever position is most comfortable. The father might also be in the tub, holding or massaging the mother. After the infant has descended through the birth canal into the warm water, it is taken up to the mother's breast within the first minute of life. The cord is not cut for several minutes, and the baby stays with the parents so the important bonding processes can take place. In approximately 500 water births, more than 90% of mothers used no analgesic drugs during labor and delivery.[47] Risks of water birth include contaminated water (normal tap water is ideal) and oxygen deprivation if the baby is left under water after the cord stops providing oxygen (usually the baby is removed from the water within a minute following birth).

SUMMARY

This chapter has explored various nonpharmacologic methods of pain relief and coping available to the parturient. Not all methods are suitable for every patient. Most still leave the mother with a considerable amount of pain. Each labor is individualized, and regional anesthesia or systemic analgesia must not be withheld if the methods described here are unsuccessful or inappropriate for the patient.

REFERENCES

1. Crafter H. Pain-free labor. Nurs Times 1989;85:66.
2. Pitcock CDH, Clark RB. From Fanny to Fernand: The development of consumerism in pain control during the birth process. Am J Obstet Gynecol 1992 (in press).
3. Weintraub S. Queen Victoria: An intimate biography. New York: EP Dutton, 1987:224.
4. Stanton ME. The myth of "natural" childbirth. J Nurse-Midwife 1979;24:25.
5. Dick-Read G. Childbirth without fear, 2nd ed. New York: Harper and Row, 1959.
6. Beck NC, Geden EA, Brouder GT. Review article: Preparation for labor: a historical perspective. Psychosom Med 1979;41:243.
7. Beck NC, Hall D. Natural childbirth—a review and analysis. Obstet Gynecol 1978;52:371.
8. Scott JR, Rose NB. Effects of psychoprophylaxis (Lamaze preparation) on labor and delivery in primaparas. N Engl J Med 1976;294:1205.
9. Lamaze F. Painless childbirth (translated by LB Celestin). London: Burke, 1958.
10. Melzak R, Taenzer P, Feldman P, Kinch R. Labor is still painful after prepared childbirth training. Can Med Assoc J 1981;125:357.
11. Geden E. Beck N, Brouder G, Glaisler J, Pohlman S. Self-report and psychophysiological effects of Lamaze preparation: An analogue of labor pain. Res Nurs Health 1985;8:155.
12. Sosa R, Kennell J, Klaus M, Robertson S, Urrulia J. The effects of a supportive companion on perinatal problems, length of labor, and mother-infant interaction. N Engl J Med 1980;303:597.
13. Kennell J, Klaus M, McGrath S, Robertson S, Hinkley C. Continuous support during labor in a U.S. hospital. JAMA 1991;265:2197.
14. LeBoyer F. Birth without violence. New York: Alfred A. Knopf, 1975.
15. Henschel D. LeBoyer versus conventional care. Nurs Mirror 1982;September:38.
16. Nelson NM, Enkin NW, Saigal S, Bennett KJ, Milner R, Sackett DL. A randomized clinical trial of the LeBoyer approach to childbirth. N Engl J Med 1980;302:655.
17. Wahl CW. Contraindications and limitations of hypnosis in obstetric analgesia. Am J Obstet Gynecol 1962;84:1869.
18. Moya F, James LS. Medical hypnosis for obstetrics. JAMA 1960;174:2026.
19. Davidson JA. An assessment of the value of hypnosis in pregnancy and labour. Br Med J 1962;95:1.
20. Freeman RM, Macaulay AJ, Eve L, Chamberlain GV, Bhat AV. Randomized trial of self hypnosis for analgesia in labour. Br Med J 1986;292:657.
21. Weishaar BB. A comparison of Lamaze and hypnosis in the management of labor. Am J Clin Hypn 1986;28:214.
22. Harmon TM, Hynan MT, Tyre TE. Improved obstetric

outcomes using hypnotic analgesia and skill mastery combined with childbirth education. J Consult Clin Psych 1990;58:525.

23. Spiegel H. An eye-roll test for hypnotizability. Am J Clin Hypn 1972;15:25.

24. Omer H. A hypnotic relaxation technique for the treatment of premature labor. Am J Clin Hypn 1987;29:206.

25. Smith C. Acute pregnancy-associated hypertension treated with hypnosis: A case report. Am J Clin Hypn 1989;31:209.

26. Palahniuk RJ, Shnider SM, Wu SW. Acupuncture analgesia in obstetrics. ASA Sci Abstr: 1973;49.

27. McIntyre JWR. Observations on the practice of anesthesia in the People's Republic of China. Anesth Analg 1974;53:107.

28. Sjolund B, Teranius L, Erickson MBE. Increased cerebrospinal fluid levels of endorphins after electroacupuncture. Acta Physiol Scand 1977;100:382.

29. Abouleish E, Depp R. Acupuncture in obstetrics. Anesth Analg 1975;54:83.

30. Skelton IF, Flowerden MW. Acupuncture and labor—a summary of results. Midwives Chronical and Nursing Notes 1988;May:134.

31. Lyrenas S, Lutsch H. Hetta J, Nyberg F, Willdeck-Lundh G, Lindberg B. Acupuncture before delivery: Effect on pain perception and the need for analgesics. Gynecol Obstet Invest 1990;29:118.

32. Miller-Jones CMH. Transcutaneous nerve stimulation in labour (forum). Anaesthesia 1980;35:372.

33. Melzack R, Wall PD. Pain mechanism: A new thory. Science 1965;150:972.

34. Bundsen P, Peterson LE, Selstam U. Pain relief in labor by transcutaneous electrical nerve stimulation—a pro- spective matched study. Acta Obstet Gynecol Scand 1981;60:459.

35. Bonica JJ. The nature of pain of parturition. Clin Obstet Gynecol 1975;2:516.

36. Stewart P. Transcutaneous nerve stimulation as a method of analgesia in labour. Anaesthesia 1979;34:361.

37. Robson J. Transcutaneous nerve stimulation for pain relief in labour (forum). Anaesthesia 1979;34:357.

38. Lee ENC, Chung IWY, Lee JYL, Lam PNY, Chin RKH. The role of transcutaneous electrical nerve stimulation in management of labour in obstetric patients. Asia-Oceanis J Obstet Gynaecol 1990;16:247.

39. Hughes SC, Dailey PA, Partridge C. Transcutaneous electrical nerve stimulation for labor analgesia. Anesth Analg 1988;67:599.

40. Bundsen P, Erickson K. Pain relief in labor by transcutaneous electrical nerve stimulation safety aspects. Acta Obstet Gynecol Scand 1982;61:1.

41. Duchene P. Effects of biofeedback on childbirth pain. J Pain Symptom Management 1989;4:117.

42. St. James-Roberts I, Hutchinson C, Haran F, Chamberlain G. Biofeedback as an aid to childbirth. Br J Obstet Gynaecol 1983;90:56.

43. Nolelovitz M. The single-unit delivery system—a safe alternative to home deliveries. Am J Obstet Gynecol 1978;132:889.

44. Dixon EA. Review of maternity patients suitable for home delivery. Br Med J 1982;284:1753.

45. Allgarer A. Alternative birth centers offer family-centered care. J Am Hosp Assoc 1978;52:97.

46. Dobbs KB, Shy KK. Alternative birth rooms and birth options. Obstet Gynecol 1982;58:626.

47. Daniels K. Water birth: The newest form of safe, gentle, joyous birth. J Nurse-Midwifery 1989;34:198.

CHAPTER 16

Systemic Medications for Labor Analgesia

Stuart Bramwell

Childbirth can be the most painful event a woman will experience.[1] In North America, most women request some form of analgesia during parturition.[2,3] Qualitatively, only regional analgesia by selective denervation can provide complete pain relief. Often, regional block is not available, is not desired, or is contraindicated. In the United Kingdom, between 1982 and 1986, only 17% of parturients received epidural analgesia during labor.[4] This surprisingly low percentage implies that many women rely upon alternate methods of pain relief. Systemic opioids can relieve labor pain. In many hospitals, opioids and tranquilizers are the primary form of labor analgesia.[5] Despite allegations to the contrary,[6] the conservative use of opioid analgesics during labor leaves most neonates unaffected. However, giving excessive drug to improve maternal comfort may prove harmful. Overmedicating the mother can adversely affect the fetus by:

- Producing high blood concentrations of specific drugs
- Interfering with maternal/fetal homeostasis

To avoid compromise of mother and infant, the American Societies of Obstetrics and Pediatrics recommend judging the individual patient's needs and providing analgesia with the "minimal effective" dose of drug.[7] Although some argue against any use of opioids during labor, most experts agree that with appropriate monitoring these agents are safe.[8] This chapter attempts to evaluate the literature about systemic medication to challenge the bias against this form of analgesia.

SEDATION

Sedate, "from Latin, *sedare*—to settle, allay, make calm or quiet." Hence, sedation, the action of the above (Oxford English Dictionary).

Imprecise use of this word has expanded its meaning. Sedation has become synonymous with anxiolysis, analgesia, hypnosis, and relaxation (including paralysis). These misconceptions have led to serious mistakes in the management of patients. Some are undermedicated with homeopathic doses of analgesics, while others may receive muscle relaxants without ventilatory support. Mixtures of agents often attempt to provide an optimal combination of properties but may potentiate the risk of serious side effects.

PREGNANCY AND OPIOIDS

Placental Transport

The factors that affect the placental transport of opioids include:

- Molecular weight
- Protein binding
- Lipid solubility
- Ionization (pKa)
- Concentration gradient
- Placental factors
    Maturity
    Metabolism

The molecular weight of most opioids, 200–800 Daltons (Table 16-1), provides little restriction to simple diffusion. Protein binding in maternal blood is a more significant impediment to the passage of opioids across the placenta. The free (unbound) fraction of opioid in the maternal plasma and the resulting concentration gradient between mother and neonate predicts the extent of placental transfer. Agents that are highly protein bound in maternal blood cross the placenta in limited amounts. Pregnant mothers and neonates have reduced concentrations of plasma albumin. Because of the low concentration of albumin, plasma binding of many acidic drugs falls in late pregnancy. More of these agents can then pass to the neonate.[9] Binding of some drugs is reduced in the neonate. Low plasma albumin concentrations in the infant may explain this finding. However, neonatal albumin may also have less affinity for acidic drugs. The neonate has markedly less alpha$_1$-acid glycoprotein compared to the adult.[10] Meperidine, fentanyl, and alfentanil, which principally bind to alpha$_1$-acid glycoprotein, have a larger free fraction in the newborn.

While the placental passage of most opioids can be predicted from the physiochemical factors listed in Table 16-1, other effects also have a role. Lipid solubility predicts that fentanyl should cross the placenta more readily than meperidine, yet both have a fetomaternal ratio of 0.31. Placental uptake or metabolism might explain this discrepancy. Animal studies also suggest rapid fetal tissue uptake and distribution of fentanyl. Significant amounts of this drug accumulate in lung, kidney, and heart with resulting low plasma concentrations of drug.

The degree of ionization of a compound is an important factor in transmembrane flux. The pKa of a drug represents the pH of equilibrium between charged and uncharged forms. Most opioids have a pKa close to 8.0. At a physiologic pH of 7.4, much of the drug will be in the charged form and restricted in its passage across the placenta (see Chap. 6). The relative alkalosis of pregnancy increases the amount of uncharged drug. The unique exception is alfentanil, which, with a pKa of 6.5, is largely unionized at pH 7.4.

As the placenta matures, it becomes more efficient in allowing diffusion of drugs. The limited information about the opioid compounds in this context does not allow definitive statements of how this event might protect the premature infant from drug transmission.

Physiology of Pregnancy

Progesterone and Pregnanolone

The secretion of hormones sustains the developing pregnancy. Initially, placental chorionic gonadotropin prevents sloughing of the endometrium, maintaining the corpus luteum, the source of progesterone and estrogen, and enabling the endometrium to continue to grow. At approximately 12 weeks, the placenta takes over as a source of progesterone and estrogen (estriol). Progesterone production progressively rises until the third trimester.

The hormonal changes that accompany gestation alter the parturient's response to anesthetic and analgesic drugs. Pregnancy lowers the minimum alveolar concentration (MAC) of inhaled agents required to produce anesthesia.[11] The physiologic responses to hormones that may influence MAC include:

- Fifty percent increase of minute ventilation (progesterone)
- Pronounced sedative effect (progesterone)
- Changes in plasma volume/protein binding (estrogen)
- Inhibition of liver enzyme activity (estrogen)

The more than twentyfold increase in progesterone concentration at term may explain some of the increased sensitivity of the pregnant patient to both volatile anesthetics and sedative drugs. However, in pregnant rats, MAC does not correlate with progesterone concentration. Postpartum, MAC returns to normal, while in the rat, progesterone concentration remains elevated.[12]

Steroid compounds have anesthetic activity. In 1955, Laubach[13] introduced hydroxydione as an induction agent. In 1957, Figdor *et al*[14] reported a series of structurally related pregnanes with anesthetic activ-

Table 16–1

Physiochemical Properties of Commonly Used Opioids

	MOLECULAR WEIGHT	% PROTEIN BOUND		OCTANOL/WATER PARTITION COEFFICIENT (LIPID SOLUBILITY)	PKA	UV/MV
		Maternal	Fetal			
Morphine	285	20–40	NA	1.4	7.9	0.8–1.9
Meperidine	251	60–70	NA	3.9	8.5	0.31–1.0
Alfentanil	417	90	65	129	6.5	0.22–0.39
Fentanyl	336	69–81	NA	816	8.4	0.31 (0.05–0.7)
Sufentanil	387	92.5	NA	1757	8.0	0.45–1.4

NA: Not available
(Table prepared with assistance from L. Berman, M.D.)

ity in mice. The most potent agent was the naturally occurring metabolite of progesterone, pregnanolone.

Recently, Hogskilde *et al*[15] compared a pregnanolone emulsion with another steroidal induction agent, althesin (an aqueous suspension of alphaxolone and alphadolone) in mice. The mean anesthetic dose for the pregnanolone emulsion was 5.25 mg/kg, and for althesin was 2.8 mg/kg. These investigators then gave the emulsion, dissolved in soy bean oil, to six male volunteers. They found it to be a reliable induction agent at a dose of 0.6 mg/kg with loss of eyelid reflexes within 75 to 90 s and return to consciousness between 11 and 15 m.[16] Pregnanolone is a potent sedative, which may potentiate the effects of sedative or opioid drugs in the parturient.

Endorphins

Maternal beta endorphins also may alter the parturient's response to opioids. In rats, opioid antagonists can prevent the normal progressive rise in pain tolerance that accompanies gestation.[17]

Neurobehavioral Effects

Concern about the subtle effects of drugs upon the newborn led neonatologists to elaborate sophisticated neurologic tests to examine the infant soon after delivery. In 1964, Prechtl and Beintema[18] described one such examination. The results of this test, however, did not predict the tremendous variations of normal or abnormal development. Repetitive testing over the course of days or weeks could document the rate of change in results and proved more valuable than a single test. Subsequent neurobehavioral tests tried to provide better information about the state of the newborn when exposed to various drugs and stresses.

The Brazelton Behavioral Assessment Scale (BBAS) attempted to score interactive behavior. It evaluated the infant's available responses to the environment. The scale, developed over many years, consists of a chart with 27 behavioral items scored on a nine-point scale and 20 elicited responses rated on a three-point scale. Unlike many other assessment procedures, the BBAS often bases an infant's score on its best, not average performance.

The complexity of the BBAS and the necessary rigid training of the testers limited its practicality for non-psychiatrists or non-neonatologists. To appreciate a range of behaviors, examiners must complete a training procedure of first examining and scoring 30 "pilot" babies. Then, they complete a 2-day workshop with a qualified trainer. To achieve examiner reliability, the trainer judges the trainee's testing skills. The trainee must score within one point of the trainer on no less than 24 of 26 behavioral items and within two points on the remaining two items. The trainee also must score all 17 reflex items correctly.[19]

Scanlon developed the Early Neonatal Neurobehavioral Scale (ENNS). This test also emphasizes the ability of the infant to adapt to its environment. As with the BBAS, special training and reliability assessment are needed. The ENNS places greater emphasis on muscle tone. It also is a time-consuming test. The state of wakefulness must be assessed before each examination. The test uses noxious or aversive stimuli, which are unpleasant to both perform and observe.[20]

In 1982, Amiel Tison *et al*[21] introduced the Neurologic and Adaptive Capacity Scoring System (NACS). This test was designed primarily to look at the subtle effects of medications, perinatal asphyxia, and trauma. The NACS examines upper and lower body tone and central neurologic learning ability. In addition, it evaluates sucking, habituation to light and sound, and consolability. The test also looks at passive and active tone, reflexes (automatic walking, Moro, and sucking), and general state. The 20 criteria are rated as 0, 1, or 2. A score of 35–40 represents neurologically vigorous infants.

The NACS is rapid and reproducible. In one study, observers agreed on 92.8% of items compared to 88% for the ENNS.[21] The neurologic portion of the exam needs no equipment. An experienced examiner can do this part of the test within 60–90 seconds. The adaptive portion of the exam, requiring closer observation, takes longer. The NACS does have its critics. In an attempt to simplify the complexities of the Brazelton and ENNS examinations, the NACS fails to understand the capabilities of the neonate and the process of early development adequately. So, the NACS may not detect drug and other effects in neonatal performance.[22]

These tests and the studies that use them also suffer the following shortcomings:

- The NACS and ENNS both require subjective interpretations of the neonate.
- Many studies are poorly designed. They compare two or more drugs without including an unmedicated control group.
- The tests ignore birth trauma and acid–base status, both of which may strongly affect development.

These criticisms have not limited the use of these tests. Continued publication of the results of neurobehavioral testing often confuses more than illuminates the issue of neonatal drug effects. The significance of subtle drug effects detected at birth for emotional or learning development remains controversial. As yet, no long-term studies have examined this issue.

SYSTEMIC ANALGESICS IN OBSTETRICS

Table 16-2 lists some advantages and disadvantages of systemic opioids for labor analgesia.[23] These disadvantages, plus the persistent association with asphyxia neonatorum and the suggestion of an effect on intelligence, prompted the publication of guidelines for perinatal care by the American Academy of Pediatrics and the American College of Obstetrics and Gynecology.[24] These guidelines recommend using the least dosage to produce the desired effect. The following section reviews the current usage of opioid and nonopioid sedatives and analgesics in laboring women.

Morphine

Morphine, the progenitor of modern opioids, is no longer widely used in labor because of its association with profound respiratory depression in the newborn.[25] It remains in obstetric texts as a drug used to inhibit premature labor. The rationale for this use of mor-

Table 16–2

Advantages and Disadvantages of Systemic Analgesics for Labor Pain Relief

ADVANTAGES	DISADVANTAGES
Ease and simplicity	Inadequate pain relief
No anesthesia personnel	Dose-related sensory depression
Practical without IV fluids	Maternal/infant respiratory depression
Minimal monitoring	Delayed gastric emptying
Low incidence of complications	Nausea and vomiting
	Fetal neurobehavioral depression
	Loss of beat-to-beat variability
	Maternal hypotension
	Slowing of labor
	Necessity of bed rest
	Polypharmacy

phine has been ascribed to its central anxiolytic hypnotic effect. Also, morphine may produce hypotension, which can inhibit endogenous oxytocin secretion. There is, however, no documentation of a significant effect on labor by morphine in the recommended dose of 10 mg.

Infants are highly susceptible to the depressant effects of morphine. Newborn males between 12 and 60 hours old, scheduled for circumcision, are three times as sensitive to the respiratory effects of morphine as adults. Reportedly, morphine affects neonates more profoundly than meperidine.[25] Either greater permeability of the infant brain to morphine or altered biostransformation and excretion could be at fault.[26] Neonates excrete morphine more slowly than adults. Elimination half life is 6.8 h in the neonate vs 3.9 h in adults. Clearance is 6.3 mL/min/kg vs 23.8 mL/min/kg. Thus, some of the altered sensitivity of the newborn to morphine may reflect a higher blood concentration of drug for a longer time. Other evidence suggests heightened sensitivity of opioid receptors.[27]

Although morphine sulfate is still given to parturients because it is an effective and inexpensive sedative analgesic, its systemic use is undesirable in modern obstetric practice. Morphine's hypotensive properties compromise its use by the intravenous route. Its slow onset, a consequence of its hydrophilicity, makes effective titration difficult. The prolonged neonatal effects and unproved ability to inhibit premature labor further argue against its use.

Meperidine

Eisleb and Schaumann, seeking a new anticholinergic agent, developed meperidine in 1938. It was identified by chance when the Straub phenomenon (spasm of the perianal musculature leading to an erect tail) was noted in the recipient mice.[28] The combination of potent opioid activity, lipophilicity, and weak anticholinergic and local anesthetic properties made meperidine an apparently ideal agent for the parturient.

When given intravenously, meperidine produces a prompt, predictable effect. The drug appears in fetal blood within 90 s of maternal injection. Maternal and fetal blood concentrations equilibrate rapidly.[29] Early investigators noted many depressed infants following the use of meperidine. They correlated the respiratory depression with the time from drug injection.[30] Normeperidine, an active metabolite of meperidine, appears in fetal blood in steadily rising concentrations. Infants' scores worsen on neurobehavioral exams as drug-to-delivery interval increases. Changes attributed

to normeperidine persist for 72 h after birth.[31,32] In contrast, meperidine itself causes the respiratory depression seen at birth. Even low doses of meperidine (probably *via* normeperidine) influence neonatal behavior. Parturients metabolize meperidine to normeperidine in one of three distinct rates.[33] Knowledge of individual patterns could predict which patients might be least suited to this form of analgesia. Cost and time constraints have limited this approach.[34]

Fentanyl

A potent opioid with a rapid onset by virtue of its lipid solubility, fentanyl lacks active metabolites. A large volume of distribution renders the effects of a single dose evanescent. These properties have encouraged the use of fentanyl as a labor analgesic. In animals, fentanyl is more than 500 times as potent as meperidine (Table 16-3). In humans, however, fentanyl is only about 100 times as potent as meperidine. Fentanyl 100 µg provides analgesia comparable to meperidine 100–150 mg. In these doses, the two drugs also depress respiration to similar extents. A direct correlation exists between plasma fentanyl concentrations and analgesic and respiratory depressant effects. In parturients, a plasma fentanyl concentration of 1.5–3.0 ng/mL diminishes the ventilatory response to CO_2 by 50%.[35,36]

In gravid ewes, fentanyl 50–100 µg yields significant plasma concentrations of drug only briefly. By 10 minutes after injection, maternal blood concentration of fentanyl declines to 9% of its peak value.[37] Fentanyl appears in fetal blood within 1 minute after maternal injection. Fetal concentration peaks at 5 minutes. Maternal concentration of fentanyl was about 2.5 times the fetal concentration between 5 and 60 minutes. In sheep, fentanyl lacks deleterious effects on maternal or fetal cardiovascular systems. Uterine tone and blood flow also remain unchanged.

Vella *et al*[38] examined the transfer of fentanyl across the rabbit placenta. The ratio of umbilical vein concentration to maternal artery concentration (UV/MA) for fentanyl was 0.25, between that of meperidine (0.44) and bupivacaine (0.11). In humans, the feto-maternal ratio averages 0.31.[39] In rabbits, fentanyl is cleared from maternal plasma more rapidly than either meperidine or bupivacaine. In adult humans, plasma elimination of a single dose of fentanyl is 98.6% complete within 60 minutes.[40] In the neonate, the clearance of fentanyl is prolonged, variable, and unpredictable, but seems related to hepatic enzyme activity.[41,42]

Intravenous fentanyl has been studied as a labor analgesic. Parturients in active labor received 50–100 µg

Table 16–3

Efficacy and Safety of Opioid Compounds*

DRUG	LOWEST ED$_{50}$ (MG/KG)	LD$_{50}$ (MG/KG)	SAFETY MARGIN	POTENCY RATIO	PEAK EFFECT (MIN)
Meperidine	6.2	29	4.8	1	4
Morphine	3.2	223	71	1.9	30
Piritramide	1.3	13	10	4.9	7
Methadone	0.8	9.4	12	7.9	6
Dextromoramide	0.1	10	105	65	6
Phenoperidine	0.1	4.7	39	51	8
Alfentanil	0.04	48	1080	140	1
Fentanyl	0.01	3.1	277	560	4
Sufentanil	0.0007	18	26,716	9200	8
Lofentanil	0.0006	0.07	112	10,400	8
Carfentanil	0.0004	3.1	8460	16,600	10

*Lowest LD$_{50}$ values in the tail withdrawal test in rats, LD$_{50}$ values, safety margins, and potency ratio of different drugs after IV administration. (Estsphanous FG. Opioids in anesthesia. Boston: Butterworth Publishers 1984:104)

doses of fentanyl at hourly intervals.[43] The total dose of drug ranged from 50–600 µg. At delivery, umbilical blood fentanyl concentrations were below 0.4 ng/mL. Maternal blood concentrations did not exceed 0.5 ng/mL (Fig. 16-1). The mothers only complained of mild sedation. Respiration, CO_2 and oxygen saturation were not continuously monitored. Newborns were assessed at 1 and 24 hours with the Amiel Tison neurobehavioral scale. Infants exposed to fentanyl citrate scored the same as unmedicated controls.[43]

A subsequent unblinded study compared fentanyl given at hourly intervals to meperidine 25–50 mg every 2 to 3 hours. Hourly visual analog pain scores did not differ between groups. In neither group was pain relief complete. Women in both groups reported moderately severe pain during active labor (4–7 cm).[44] By complete cervical dilation, analgesia was inadequate in both groups (Fig. 16-2). The major difference between the two groups was the incidence of side effects. None of the parturients in the fentanyl group suffered nausea, vomiting, or sedation. Up to 20% of those in the meperidine group experienced side effects. The newborn neurobehavioral scores were comparable for each group. However, 13% of babies in the meperidine group received naloxone at birth compared to 2% (one infant) in the fentanyl group.

In summary, fentanyl rapidly crosses the placenta to the fetus. It lacks active metabolites. Despite a slower metabolism, a function of hepatic development, mater-nally administered fentanyl only minimally affects the neonate.

Newer Opioids

Pharmaceutical research has attempted to defeat the limitations of fentanyl by synthesizing derivatives with greater potency, faster onset, and shorter duration of action.[45,46] Two fentanyl derivatives, alfentanil and sufentanil, are available for clinical use.

Sufentanil

This drug is twice as lipophilic as fentanyl (Table 16-4). The greater lipophilicity of sufentanil has encouraged its use alone, and with local anesthetics for conduction labor analgesia. The potency of sufentanil (10 times that of fentanyl) has inhibited its use systemically. Here, a slightly faster onset does not seem a significant advantage over fentanyl. Neonates metabolize sufentanil more slowly than infants or older children (Table 16-5).[47] To avoid unanticipated fetal depression, use sufentanil with caution, particularly if the fetus is premature. When injected into the epidural space, sufentanil, in doses up to 50 µg, does not depress Apgar scores.[48] Following epidural injection, maternal blood concentration of sufentanil falls rapidly. By 15 minutes, venous concentration is below 0.1 ng/mL.[48]

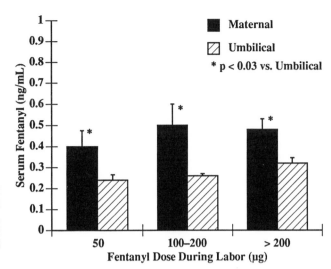

Figure 16–1. Maternal and umbilical cord serum fentanyl citrate concentrations at delivery according to maternal dose during labor. Values are mean ± SEM. (Rayburn W, Rathke A, Leuschen MP, Chleborad J, Weidner W. Fentanyl citrate analgesia during labor. Am J Obstet Gynecol 1989;161:202)

Alfentanil

Alfentanil has 80 times the analgesic potency of morphine.[49] Alfentanil is approximately one third as potent as fentanyl and lasts 30% as long. Compared to fentanyl and sufentanil, this drug has a small volume of distribution. Alfentanil's high degree of protein binding and low lipid solubility account for this difference (Tables 16-1 and 16-4). The small volume of distribution keeps more drug in the circulation, where it is metabolized and excreted. Blood concentration falls rapidly, yielding a shorter duration of action than fentanyl. Terminal elimination half-life, volume of dis-

tribution at steady state, and total plasma clearance of alfentanil are similar in pregnant and nonpregnant women.[50] The fetal–maternal ratio of alfentanil is 0.3. Due to differences in protein binding, the free fraction of alfentanil is much higher in the neonate than in the mother (Table 16-6).

Golub *et al*[51] studied the neonatal effects of intravenous meperidine 2 mg/kg and alfentanil 100 μg/kg during labor in rhesus monkeys. The feto-maternal ratio of alfentanil at birth was 0.2. However, in the first 2 hours after birth, neonatal alfentanil concentration remained unchanged or increased. Three of five monkeys treated with meperidine and three of six treated

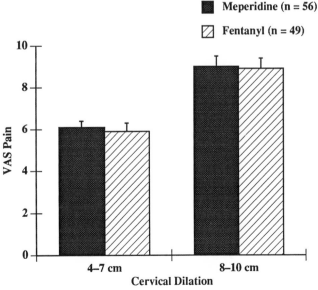

Figure 16–2. Visual analog pain scores in laboring parturients receiving systemic opioids for labor analgesia. Women in the meperidine group received IV meperidine 25–50 mg every 2 to 3 hours. In the fentanyl group, women receive fentanyl 50–100 μg, IV every hour. Patients rated their pain on 10-cm visual analog scales. Data are mean ± SD. Pain scores did not differ between groups. More women in the meperidine group needed antiemetic therapy or were sedated for a prolonged time. (Rayburn WF, Smith CV, Parriott JE, Woods RE. Randomized comparison of meperidine and fentanyl during labor. Obstet Gynecol 1989;4:604)

Table 16–4

Physiochemical Factors Affecting the Disposition of Opioid Analgesics

FACTOR	Morphine	Alfentanil	Meperidine	Sufentanil	Fentanyl	Lofentanil
Ionization (pKa) constant	7.9	6.5	8.5	8.0	8.4	7.8
Percent un-ionized at pH 7.4	23	89	7.4	24.5	8.5	28
Octanol-water partition coefficients						
Un-ionized base	6	145	525	8913	9550	16,596
Ionized form		0.07		1.0	0.5	0.26
Apparent at pH 7.4	1.4	129	39	1757	816	5571
Ratio to morphine	1	89	128	1241	676	3265
Free fraction in human plasma (%) at pH 7.4	70	7.9	30	7.5	16	6.4
Relative potency for entering CNS[†]	1	10	12	133	133	299

[†]Apparent partition coefficient at pH 7.4 multiplied by the free fraction of drug in the plasma and divided by the value for morphine (Estaphanous FG. Opioids in anesthesia. Boston: Butterworth Publishers 1984:52)

Table 16–5

Sufentanil Pharmacokinetics in Neonates and Children

AGE	$T_{1/2\alpha}$ (MIN)	$T_{1/2\beta}$ (MIN)	Cl (ML/KG/MIN)	VD_{ss} (L/KG)
Neonates (0–8 days)	20.5	635	4.2	2.7
Neonates 20–28 days)	8.8	217	17.3	3.4
0–1 month	23.4	737	6.7	4.15
1 month–2 years	15.8	214	18.1	3.09
2–12 years	19.6	140	16.9	2.73
12–16 years	20.4	209	13.1	2.75

$T_{1/2\alpha}$: redistribution half-life, $T_{1/2\beta}$: elimination half-life, Cl: clearance, VD_{ss}: volume of distribution at steady state. (Greeley WJ, De Bruijn NP, Davis DP. Sufentanil pharmacokinetics in pediatric cardiovascular patients. Anesth Analg 1987;66:1067)

Table 16–6

Alfentanil Protein Binding in Mother and Fetus

	MOTHER	NEONATE
Protein binding capacity %	90.01 ± 1.45	64.68 ± 5.41
Ratio of bound to unbound alfentanil	12:1	2.3:1
Alpha₁ acid glycoprotein (mg/100 mL)	55.10 ± 12.97	21.64 ± 6.95

(Gepts E, Heytens L, Camu F. Pharmacokinetics and placental transfer of intravenous and epidural alfentanil in parturient women. Anesth Analg 1986;65:1155)

with alfentanil had respiratory depression. Infant Macaco mulatto monkeys exposed during labor to alfentanil 100 µg/kg had a higher incidence of infections and depressed neurobehavioral scores compared to unmedicated controls. Compared to control and meperidine monkeys, cognitive testing was impaired for several months.[52] These results suggest that alfentanil is not an appropriate systemic analgesic for labor. Smaller doses of alfentanil (10–30 µg/kg) have been used safely in combination with local anesthetics for labor epidural analgesia.[53] Even in this setting, some experts recommend using alfentanil only when delivery is remote.[54]

Agonist/Antagonist Agents

Nalbuphine

A synthetic analgesic of the phenanthrene series, nalbuphine is often touted as producing comparable analgesia to morphine, but with a ceiling effect for respiratory depression. In male volunteers, nalbuphine 0.15 mg/kg increased pain tolerance by 40%. Further increments did not yield additional analgesia. Nalbuphine produced similar effects on respiratory function. These authors suggested that any correlation between morphine and nalbuphine at low doses does not apply at higher drug doses.[55] In dogs, nalbuphine had only an 8% enflurane sparing effect at up to 40 times the minimally effective dose. In contrast, pure opioid agonists reduce the MAC of enflurane by up to 70%.[56]

In spite of its limited potency, nalbuphine is used as a labor analgesic. One double-blind study compared nalbuphine and meperidine by patient-controlled analgesia (PCA) in laboring women. Women in the nalbuphine group reported significantly lower pain scores, but they also used more nitrous oxide than women in the meperidine group.[57] Sedation, progress of labor, and cardioventilatory charges did not differ significantly between the two groups. Fetal effects such as fetal heart rate, Apgar score, need for resuscitation, or neurobehavioral assessment (modified NACS, evaluating, arousability, visual and aural stimuli, and habituation) also did not differ between drugs. Nalbuphine produced less nausea and vomiting. Another double-blind comparison of nalbuphine and meperidine for labor analgesia found no significant differences in pain relief or neurobehavioral effects (NACS) (Bramwell S, unpublished data). Nalbuphine has been given during labor both by intermittent intravenous bolus (10–20 mg, every 4–6 h) and by PCA (2–4 mg loading dose

and 1 mg on demand at 6- to 10-minute intervals). PCA lowers drug consumption compared to intravenous use. Less sedation and less frequent need for antiemetics are other advantages of PCA administration.[58]

Nalbuphine rapidly crosses the placenta. At delivery, fetal blood concentrations are 30% to 60% of maternal concentrations. Even with high fetal blood concentrations, nalbuphine reportedly has no adverse neonatal effects.[59] The pKa of nalbuphine (8.7) increases the risk of ion trapping, particularly in the acidotic fetus (see Chap. 6). However, the ceiling effect for respiratory depression makes it less likely that the newborn will develop bradypnea with nalbuphine than with other opioids.

Shortcomings of nalbuphine include increased sedation (related to Kappa agonist activity) and limited (ceiling) analgesia.[60] PCA administration may help overcome these limitations.

The mu-receptor antagonist properties of nalbuphine have led to its use in managing the side effects of neuraxial opioids. Nalbuphine has been used to treat opioid-induced respiratory depression[61] and pruritus.[62] Relief of itching begins within 15 minutes and persists for up to 2 hours. Prophylactic nalbuphine, however, seems unable to prevent pruritus.[63]

Butorphanol

A derivative of levorphanol tartrate structurally similar to pentazocine, butorphanol is 3.5 to 7 times more potent than morphine and 30 to 40 times more potent than meperidine. Butorphanol 2 mg is as effective as meperidine 80 mg for relieving labor pain. After intramuscular injection, maximum analgesia develops within 30 minutes.[64] In the above doses, both drugs have comparable respiratory and newborn effects. Babies exposed to butorphanol recovered more rapidly. Psychomimetic effects were not observed.[64] Neither drug influenced the progress of labor. Both drugs provided adequate pain relief with few side effects. With multiple administrations of butorphanol, only 2% of laboring parturients reported side effects.[65]

Sinusoidal fetal heart rate pattern can occur after maternal butorphanol administration. This effect, of unknown mechanism, occurs in conjunction with severe Rh sensitization, fetal anemia, severe hypoxia, and maternal alphaprodine administration. While not associated with a significant incidence of fetal mortality, it is an ominous sign that may complicate assessment of the unborn child.[65] A retrospective review of 51 laboring parturients who received butorphanol 1 mg found a 75% incidence of transient sinusoidal fetal heart rate pattern. In contrast, only 13% of 55 fetuses whose mothers did not receive any opioid developed this pattern. In addition, the duration of sinusoidal pattern was significantly shorter in the unmedicated group. No short-term maternal or fetal sequelae arose in either group. If there are no other signs of fetal distress, a sinusoidal fetal heart rate pattern does not indicate hypoxia.[66]

As with nalbuphine, this drug produces only a limited amount of respiratory depression.[67] In nonpregnant patients, doses as high as 0.15–0.3 mg/kg do not yield excessive sedation or somnolence. Psychomimetic side effects do increase with higher doses.

Avoid both butorphanol and nalbuphine in opioid addicted patients. Their mu-receptor antagonism could precipitate an acute withdrawal syndrome.[68]

Buprenorphine

A highly lipid soluble, synthetic thebane derivative, buprenorphine is an agonist/antagonist analgesic. Like nalbuphine and butorphanol, its pain relieving and repiratory depressant effects have a "ceiling." Buprenorphine 0.3 mg is as strong an analgesic as morphine 10 mg. It does, however, produce slightly more nausea than morphine (27% vs 13%). Buprenorphine binds very strongly to the kappa receptor. This property ensures a long duration of action, but makes the drug almost irreversible by naloxone. Because of this intense receptor binding, buprenorphine is rarely used in obstetrics.[69]

Naloxone

A pure narcotic antagonist, naloxone remains the treatment of choice for opioid agonist- or agonist/antagonist-induced central nervous system and cardiorespiratory depression. Naloxone can be given to the baby after birth to reverse depression caused by analgesics given to the mother. The practice of giving naloxone to the mother just before delivery may have limited neonatal depression, but it exposed the mother to the pain of delivery unprotected by opioids or endogenous endorphins.

The therapeutically effective serum concentration of naloxone is unknown. No data relate serum concentration to neonatal effect. Maternal blood naloxone concentration exceeds 2.5 μg/mL for 30 minutes after a 400-μg intravenous bolus.[70] In nonpregnant patients,

this dose yields naloxone concentrations greater than 3 μg/mL. In both populations, this dose of intravenous naloxone rapidly reverses opioid analgesic and respiratory effects.

Naloxone rapidly crosses the placenta. Umbilical vein concentration varies widely but often equals maternal venous concentration. Elimination from the neonate is prolonged ($T_{1/2\beta}$ 3 h).[71] Individual neonatal blood naloxone concentrations cannot be predicted. To insure a therapeutic effect in the infant, some experts recommend a 600-μg maternal dose.[70] The practice of routine administration of naloxone, however, remains an affront to the careful practitioner. Also, removing the protection of endorphins at delivery possibly exposes the fetus to unnecessary stress.[72]

TRANQUILIZERS

Modern obstetric practice encourages the participation of the mother in the birth of newborn. Unlike the practice of "twilight sleep" with scopolamine, it does not set out to ablate the memory of the birth process. Animal work in the 1930s and 1940s correlated apnea neonatorum with tranquilizing and sedative drugs. Later workers illustrated the protective powers of barbiturates to reduce cerebral metabolic disturbances and improve the outcome of the asphyxiated the newborn.[73] In 1979, Myers and Myers[74] even suggested using barbiturates as prophylaxis against the damaging effects of fetal asphyxia in high risk pregnancies. They gave four mechanisms for improvement in fetal outcome:

1. High doses of barbiturates depress fetal brain metabolism and extend the brain's tolerance of asphyxia.
2. Barbiturates and other sedatives decrease maternal sympathetic nervous system activity, improve uterine blood flow, and increase oxygen delivery to the fetus.
3. Barbiturates diminish the forces of labor and, consequently, augment oxygen delivery to the fetus.
4. Barbiturates modify hyperglycemia caused by maternal stress by reducing catecholamine release.

These authors suggest that using barbiturates and sedatives would reduce the use of cesarean delivery. Reservations about using barbiturates persist because of associated prolonged neurobehavioral depression. Barbiturates are most commonly used as a sedative hypnotic during the early latent phase of labor, when delivery is remote.

Phenothiazines

This group of drugs may help calm patients during labor. Chlorpromazine, promazine, and prochlorperazine possess significant alpha-adrenergic blocking ability. In combination with meperidine, they can produce profound postural hypotension. Chlorpromazine induces the metabolism of meperidine leading to increased normeperidine production and sedation.[75] Promethazine possesses potent antiemetic effects that are a component of its properties as an H_2-receptor antagonist. Other properties include a marked anticholinergic action and a duration of up to 24 hours. The drug's potent sedative properties appear to potentiate opioid effects; however, the existence and extent of this effect are debatable.[76] Promethazine also is a mild respiratory stimulant.[77]

Rapid placental transfer of phenothiazines leads to a reduction of fetal heart rate beat-to-beat variability. Neurobehavioral depression is absent with up to 50 mg of intramuscular propiomazine.[78] The neonatal effects of intravenously administered phenothiazines, which can induce hypotension and depress uterine contractility, have not been studied.

Phenothiazines have a long history of use without long-term confirmed detrimental effects.[79] While many prefer a single drug, such as nalbuphine, which combines analgesia, sedation, and reduced emetic properties, conservative use of phenothiazines is an acceptable alternative.

Benzodiazepines

This group of drugs acts primarily by binding to specific postsynaptic benzodiazepine receptors in the central nervous system. At the receptor (a protein complex containing a chloride channel), benzodiazepines increase the efficacy or availability of glycine, an inhibitory compound. Benzodiazepines also increase the effect of gamma amino butyric acid (GABA), an inhibitory neurotransmitter. These effects yield anxiolysis, sedation, and muscle relaxation. Benzodiazepines also have anticonvulsant properties.

Diazepam

The pronounced lipid solubility of diazepam allows the drug to cross the placenta rapidly. Equilibrium between maternal and fetal blood occurs within minutes. Fetal blood concentration may exceed maternal concentration.[80,81] In healthy volunteers, the elimination half-life of diazepam is 21 to 37 hours.[82]

Metabolism in the liver yields active metabolites. These compounds, desmethyldiazepam and oxazepam, are further metabolized, more slowly. Their elimination half-life exceeds 48 hours. These metabolites are as potent as the parent compound, diazepam. Rebound sedation may develop 6 to 8 hours after the initial dose of drug.[83] Diazepam, in doses of 10–30 mg, is used in some countries to treat preeclampsia. Complications of this therapy include:

- Loss of fetal heart rate beat-to-beat variability
- Neonatal hypotonia
- Neonatal hypothermia (impaired thermogenesis)
- A decrease in respiratory quotient
- Kernicterus (an effect of the sodium benzoate buffer)

In small doses (< 5 mg) diazepam still depresses fetal heart rate variability. However, newborn motor tone is only transiently diminished.[84]

Diazepam can induce the activity of the microsomal enzymes responsible for its metabolism. Cimetidine inhibits the microsomal enzyme system and prolongs the effect of diazepam by delaying its hepatic clearance.[85]

The development of a specific benzodiazepine antagonist flumazenil has simplified management of accidental overdose. Titrate the dose of this drug to obtain the desired effect without precipitating an anxiety response.[86]

Midazolam

Unlike diazepam, midazolam is water soluble. It is rapidly metabolized to minimally active compounds, limiting its duration of action. Midazolam is 2 to 3 times as potent as diazepam due to a greater affinity for the benzodiazepine receptor. Midazolam yields higher blood concentrations in laboring women than in nonlaboring parturients before cesarean delivery or gynecologic patients.[87] These data suggest that uterine contractions interfere with hepatic blood flow, altering the rate of midazolam metabolism. Despite the rapid placental transmission (less than diazepam), adverse neonatal effects have not been noted.

Many have expressed concern about the pronounced amnestic quality of this drug. If used during cesarean delivery under regional anesthesia, mothers may not recall the birth of their child.[88-91] Fortunately, delivery is rarely a time of anxiety. However, in rare circumstances the drug may prove a useful anesthetic adjuvant.

Midazolam is comparable to diazepam as an anticonvulsant, but it reportedly induces seizures in intravenous doses as low as 2 mg.[92] The mechanism for this effect is unclear.

Midazolam may be used with an opioid. However, subanesthetic doses of opioid markedly potentiate the hypnotic effect of midazolam (Fig. 16-3).[93] In parturients, this combination could lead to unexpected loss of consciousness, increasing the risk of maternal regurgitation and aspiration.

Droperidol

A butyrophenone that acts at postsynaptic receptors to inhibit the action of dopamine, droperidol has antipsychotic activity and some sedative properties. It is a poor anxiolytic. Central activity at dopaminergic receptors in the medulla makes droperidol an effective antiemetic. Droperidol does not enhance analgesia with short-acting opioids. It does, however, prolong their duration. In anesthetized patients, the elimination half-life is 104 minutes. Total body clearance is similar to hepatic blood flow.[94]

Droperidol produces cerebral vasoconstriction, reducing cerebral blood flow, contraindicating its use in the severely preeclamptic patient. It is not associated with amnesia and is not an anticonvulsant. Extrapyramidal effects occur in 1% of patients receiving large doses with neuroleptanalgesia.[95] More ominously, in one study, droperidol 1.25 mg intravenously incited delayed dysophoric reactions in 23% of ambulatory surgery patients.[96]

Although droperidol is an effective antiemetic in some patient populations, not all studies have found this effect.[97] There is a paucity of literature on the use of droperidol as an antiemetic in pregnancy. Since the antiemetic effect of droperidol appears limited in some patient groups and even modest doses may produce anxiety and restlessness, I urge caution if considering its use in the laboring woman.

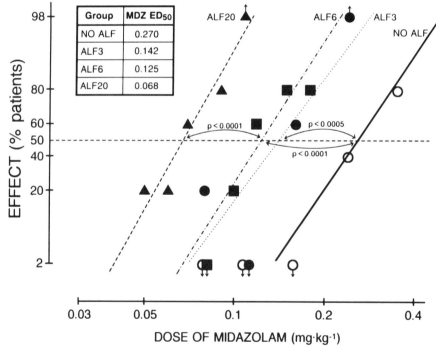

Figure 16–3. The effect of alfentanil (ALF) on the midazolam dose-response curves for induction of anesthesia. NO ALF (O)—the midazolam dose-response curve without the addition of alfentanil. ALF 3 (●), ALF 6(■), and ALF 20 (▲)—the midazolam dose-response curves with the addition of alfentanil in the doses 3, 6, 20 μg/kg, respectively. Each point represents the effect in a subgroup of five patients at the indicated dose. *Arrow* superimposed on symbols indicates that their actual locations are higher or lower. The *inset* shows the midazolam ED_{50} values for the four dose-response curves. (Kissin I, Vinik HR, Castillo R, Bradley EL, Jr. Alfentanil potentiates midazolam-induced unconsciousness in subanalgesic doses. Anesth Analg 1990;71:65)

ANTICHOLINERGICS

Atropine

A naturally occurring, lipid-soluble tertiary amine, atropine structurally resembles cocaine and has very weak analgesic properties. A racemic mixture, its activity is primarily associated with the levorotatory form. Atropine is usually given to the mother to counter the cardiac effects of vagal over-activity or as an antisialagogue. The drug crosses the placenta. The literature about its effect on fetal heart rate conflicts. Abboud *et al*[98] gave atropine and glycopyrrolate intravenously to mothers in comparable doses and did not see any significant change in fetal heart rate with either drug. In pregnant sheep, atropine also induces no change in fetal heart rate.[99] In contrast, Kanto *et al*[100] found significant fetal tachycardia after intravenous and intramuscular injection of atropine. The difference in effect may be related to dose. Injecting small doses of atropine can produce a bradycardia even in the presence of bilateral vagotomy.[101]

Scopolamine

Similar in structure to atropine, scopolamine has a more pronounced antisialogogue effect, but a lesser cardiac chronotropic action. Scopolamine is 100 times as potent as atropine as a depressant of the reticular activating system.[102] Scopolamine potentiates many sedative medications, including opioids and benzodiazepines. It has a pronounced amnestic effect. The marked central nervous system effects reflect the ease with which scopolamine crosses the blood brain barrier. The fetus is equally susceptible to this penetrance. Fetal tachycardia develops with loss of beat-to-beat variability after 10 to 20 minutes. This effect can persist for up to 90 minutes.[103]

The sedative and dysphoric side effects of scopolamine can be reversed with physostigmine. The need for scopolamine, once used to ablate the memory of the traumatic and horrifying labors of the era of twilight sleep, has, I hope, passed.

Glycopyrrolate

This quaternary ammonium compound has little placental penetrance and induces little sedation because of its inability to cross the blood brain barrier. Effective when administered to the mother, it produces minimal effects on the fetal heart or uterine activity.[104] Glycopyrrolate has twice the potency of atropine as an antisialogogue.[102]

CONCLUSION

In a recent survey of women in the early postpartum period, overall satisfaction with childbirth correlated more closely with the quality of pain relief than with obstetric care.[105] The lack of labor epidural analgesia has necessitated the use of some medication during parturition for many women.

In anesthetic practice, we strive to manipulate pharmacologically active drugs to produce desired effects while avoiding undesirable side effects or toxicity. In the obstetric setting, understanding the subtle influences of the physiologic changes of pregnancy is obligatory to avoid compounded effects. Experience with medication in pregnancy has allowed more effective dosage and revealed undesirable features of some popular drugs.

There are demonstrable physiologic and neurobehavioral effects of many sedative and analgesic drugs used in pregnancy. These effects are a function of dose. Most experts now agree that a single maternal dose of any analgesic agent lacks long-term consequences on the newborn. The subtle neurobehavioral changes that may develop are of minimal clinical significance. Long-term studies attempting to correlate these changes with outcome are still inconclusive.[106]

REFERENCES

1. Melzack R. The myth of painless childbirth. Pain 1984;19:321.
2. Scott JR, Rose NB. The effect of psychoprophylaxis (Lamaze preparation) on labor and delivery in primiparas. N Engl J Med 1976;294:1205.
3. Hew EM, Rolbin SH, Cole AFD, Virgint S. Obstetrical anaesthesia practice in the University of Toronto affiliated hospitals and some randomly selected community hospitals. Can Anaesth Soc J 1981;28:158.
4. Scott H. The availability of epidural anaesthesia and analgesia in obstetrics. Br J Obstet Gynaecol 1990;97:402.
5. Gibbs CP, Krischer J, Peckham BM, Sharp H, Kirschbaum TH. Obstetric anesthesia: A national survey. Anesthesiology 1986;65:298.
6. Brackbill Y, Kane J, Manniello RL, Abramson D. Obstetrical premedication and infant outcome. Am J Obst Gynecol 1974;118:337.
7. American Academy of Pediatrics Committee on Drugs. Effect of medication during labor and delivery on infant outcome. Pediatrics 1978;62:402.

8. Porter KB, Goldhamer R, Mankad A, Peevy K, Gaddy J, Spinnato JA. Evaluation of arterial oxygen saturation in pregnant patients and their newborns. Obstet Gynecol 1988;71:354.

9. Perucca E, Crema A. Plasma protein binding of drugs in pregnancy. Clin Pharm 1982;7:336.

10. Wood M, Wood AJJ. Changes in plasma drug binding and alpha-1-acid glycoprotein in mother and newborn infant. Clin Pharmacol Ther 1981;29:522.

11. Palahniuk RJ, Shnider SM, Eger EI. Pregnancy decreases the requirement for inhaled anesthetic agents. Anesthesiology 1974;41:82.

12. Strout CD, Nahrwold ML, Halothane. Requirements during pregnancy and lactation in rats. Anesthesiology 1981;55:322.

13. Laubach GD, P'An SY, Rudel HW. Steroid anesthetic agent [letter]. Science 1955,122:78.

14. Figdor SK, Kodet MJ, Bloom BM, Agnello EJ, P'An SY, Lauback GD. Central activity and structure in a series of water soluble steroids. J Pharmacol Exper Ther 1957;119:299.

15. Hogskilde S, Nielsen JW, Carl P, Sorensen MB. Pregnanolone emulsion. Anaesthesia 1987;42:586.

16. Carl P, Hogskilde S, Nielsen JW, et al. Pregnanolone emulsion: A preliminary pharmacokinetic and pharmacodynamic study of a new intravenous anaesthetic agent. Anaesthesia 1990;45:189.

17. Gintzler AR. Endorphin mediated increases in pain threshold during pregnancy. Science 1980;210:193.

18. Prechtl H, Beintema D. The neurological examination of the full-term newborn infant. Little Club Clinics in Developmental Medicine No. 12, London: William Heinemann Medical Books, 1964.

19. Brazelton, TB. Neonatal behavioral assessment scale. Clinics in Developmental Medicine No. 50, Spastics. International Medical Publications, London: William Heinemann Medical Books, 1973.

20. Scanlon JW, Brown WU Jr, Weiss JB, et al. Neurobehavioral responses of newborn infants after maternal epidural anesthesia. Anesthesiology 1974;40:121.

21. Amiel-Tison C, Barrier G, Shnider SM, Levinson G, Hughes SC, Stefani SJ. A new neurologic and adaptive capacity scoring system for evaluating obstetric medications in full term newborns. Anesthesiology 1982;56:340.

22. Tronick E. A critique of the neonatal neurologic and adaptive capacity score (NACS). Anesthesiology 1982;56:338.

23. Petrie RH, Yeh SY, Murata Y, et al. The effect of drugs on fetal heart rate variability. Am J Obstet Gynecol 1978;130:294.

24. Guidelines for perinatal care. American Academy of Pediatrics. Washington, DC: American College of Obstetricians and Gynecologists, 2nd ed. 1988:63.

25. Way WL, Costley EC, Way EL. Respiratory sensitivity of the newborn infant to meperidine and morphine. Clin Pharmacol Ther 1965;6:451.

26. Kupferberg HJ, Leong E, Way J. Pharmacological basis for the increased sensitivity of the newborn rat to morphine. J Pharmacol Exper Ther 1963;141:105.

27. Lynn AM, Slattery JJ. Morphine pharmacokinetics in early infancy. Anesthesiology 1987;66:136.

28. Eisleb O, Schaumann O. Dolantin ein neurartiges spasmolyticum und analgetikum (chemisches und pharmakologisches). Deutsche Med Izinische Wochenschift 1939;65:967.

29. Crawford JS, Rudofsky S. The placental transmission of pethidine. Br J Anaesth 1965;37:929.

30. Shnider SM, Moya F. Effects of meperidine on the newborn infant. Am J Obstet Gynecol 1964;89:1009.

31. Kuhnert BR, Kuhnert PM, Tu Al, Lin DCK. Meperidine and normeperidine levels following meperidine administration during labor. Am J Obstet Gynecol 1979;133:904.

32. Kuhert BR, Linn PL, Kennard MJ, Kuhnert PM. Effect of low dose meperidine on neonatal behavior. Anesth Analg 1985;64:335.

33. Morrison JC, Whybrew WD, Rosser Sl, Bucovaz ET, Wiser WL, Fish SA. Metabolites of meperidine in fetal and maternal serum. Am J Obstet Gynecol 1976;126:997.

34. Morrison JC, Davie SG, Rhodes PG, Christie RJ, Bucovaz ET, Wiser WL. Meperidine and normeperidine metabolism in the rhesus monkey. Int J Gynecol Obstet 1984;22:345.

35. Cartwright P, Prys-Roberts C, Gill K, Dye A, Stafford M, Gray A. Ventilatory depression related to plasma fentanyl concentrations during and after anesthesia in humans. Anesth Analg 1983;62:966.

36. Wynands EJ, Wong P, Townsend GE, Sprigge JS, Whalley DG. Narcotic requirements for intravenous anesthesia. Anesth Analg 1984;63:101.

37. Craft JB, Coaldrake LA, Bolan JC, et al. Placental passage and uterine effects of fentanyl. Anesth Analg 1983;62:894.

38. Vella LM, Knott C, Reynolds F. Transfer of fentanyl across the rabbit placenta, effect of umbilical flow and concurrent drug administration. Br J Anaesth 1986;58:49.

39. Estaphanous FG. Opioids in anesthesia. Boston: Butterworth Publishers, 1984:104.

40. McClain DA, Hug CC. Intravenous fentanyl kinetics. Clin Pharmacol Ther 1980;28:106.

41. Johnson KL, Endson JP, Holly FO, Scott JC. Fentanyl pharmacokinetics of fentanyl in the pediatric population. Anesthesiology 1984;61:A441.

42. Koehntop DE, Rodman JH, Brundage DM, Hodgkins MG, Buckby JJ. Pharmacokinetics of fentanyl in the neonate. Anesth Analg 1986;65:227.

43. Rayburn W, Rathke A, Leuschen MP, Chleborad J, Weidner W. Fentanyl citrate analgesia during labor. Am J Obstet Gynecol 1989;161:202.

44. Rayburn WF, Smith CV, Parriott JE, Woods RE. Ran-

domized comparison of meperidine and fentanyl during labor. Obstet Gynecol 1989;74:604.

45. Hug CC Jr. Pharmacokinetics and dynamics of narcotic analgesics. In: Prys-Roberts C, Hug CC Jr, eds. Pharmacokinetics of anaesthesia. London: Blackwell Scientific 1984:187.

46. Moldenhauer CC, Hug CC. Use of narcotic analgesics as anaesthetics. Clinical Anesthesia, 1984;2:107.

47. Greeley WJ, De Bruijn NP, Davis DP. Sufentanil pharmacokinetics in pediatric cardiovascular patients. Anesth Analg 1987;66:1067.

48. Steinberg RB, Powell G, Hu X, Dunn SM. Epidural sufentanil for analgesia for labor and delivery. Reg Anesth 1989;14:225.

49. Spierdijk J, Van Kleef J, Nante J, Stanley TH, De Lange S. Alfentanil: A new narcotic anesthetic induction agent. Anesthesiology 1980;53:S32.

50. Gepts E, Heytens L, Camu F. Pharmacokinetics and placental transfer of intravenous and epidural alfentanil in parturient women. Anesth Analg 1986;65:1155.

51. Golub MS, Eisele JH Jr, Kuhnert BR. Disposition of intrapartum narcotic analgesics in monkeys. Anesth Analg 1988;67:637.

52. Golub MS, Eisele JH, Donald JM. Obstetric analgesia and infant outcome in monkeys: Infant development after intrapartum exposure to meperidine of alfentanil. Am J Obstet Gynecol 1988;159:1280.

53. Palot M, Visseaux H, Levron JC, Lemoins JP, Rendoins J. The pharmacokinectics in mothers and neonates of fentanyl, alfentanil and sufentanil administered by epidural continuous infusion during labor. Anesthesiology 1990;73:A1002.

54. De Sousa H, Kennedy R, Stiller R, Cook R, Kuzior K. Quantitative placental transfer of fentanyl and alfentanil in the gravid ewe. Reg Anesth 1988;13:16.

55. Gal TJ, DiFazio CA, Moscicki J. Analgesic and respiratory depressant activity of nalbuphine: A comparison with morphine. Anesthesiology, 1982;57:367.

56. Murphy MR, Hug CC. The enflurane sparing effect of morphine, butorphanol, and nalbuphine. Anesthesiology 1982;57:489.

57. Frank EJ, McAteer R, Cattermole B, Loughnan, Stafford LB, Hitchcock AM. Nalbuphine for obstetric analgesia. Anaesthesia, 1987;42:697.

58. Podlas J, Breland ABD. Patient-controlled analgesia with nalbuphine during labor. Obstet Gynecol 1987;70:202.

59. Wilson SJ, Errick JF, Balkon J. Pharmacokinetics of nalbuphine during parturition. Am J Obstet Gynecol 1986;155:340.

60. Lewis JR. Evaluation of new analgesics, butorphanol and nalbuphine. JAMA 1980;243:1465.

61. Moldenhauer CC, Roach GW, Finlayson DC, et al. Nalbuphine antagonism of respiratory depression following high dose fentanyl anesthesia. Anesthesiology 1985;62:647.

62. Davies, GG, From R. A blinded study using nalbuphine

63. Morgan, PJ, Melito, S, Rapake, DM. Nalbuphine pretreatment in cesarean section patients receiving epidural morphine. Reg Anesth 1991;16:84.

64. Maduska AL, Hajghassemali M.A Double-blind comparison of butorphanol and meperidine in labour: Maternal pain relief and effect on the newborn. Can Anaesth Soc J 1978;25:398.

65. Hodgkinson R. Double-blind comparison of maternal analgesia and neonatal neurobehaviour following intravenous butorphanol and meperidine. J Int Med Res 1979;7:224.

66. Hatjis CG, Meis PJ. Sinusoidal fetal heart rate pattern associated with butorphanol administration. Obstet Gynecol 1986;67:377.

67. Kallos T, Caruso FS. Respiratory effects of butorphanol and pethidine. Anaesthesia, 1979;34:633.

68. Hug CC. New narcotic analgesics and antagonists in anesthesia. Semin Anesth 1982;1:14.

69. Tigerstedt I, Tammisto T. Double-blind, multiple-dose comparison of buprenorphine and morphine in postoperative pain. Acta Anaesth Scand 1980;24:462.

70. Hibbard BM, Rosen M, Davies D. Placental transfer of naloxone. Br J Anaesth 1986;58:45.

71. Moreland TA, Brice JEH, Walker CHM, Panja AE. Naloxone pharmacokinetics in the newborn. Br J Clin Pharmacol 1980;9:609.

72. Goodlin RC. Naloxone and its possible relationship to fetal endorphin levels and fetal distress. Obstet Gynecol 1981;139:16.

73. Goodlin RC. Fetal medication in high risk pregnancies. Obstet Gynecol 1969;34:109.

74. Myers RE, Myers SE. Use of sedative, analgesic, and anesthetic drugs during labor and delivery: Bane or boon? Am J Obstet Gynecol 1979;133:83.

75. Stainbaugh JE, Wainer IW. Drug interaction. Meperidine and chlorpromazine: A toxic combination. J Clin Pharmacol 1981;21:140.

76. Keats AS, Telford J, Jurosa Y. Potentiation of meperidine by promethazine. Anesthesiology 1961;22:34.

77. Clark RB, Seifen AB. Systemic medication during labor and delivery. Obstet Gynecol Ann 1983;12:165.

78. Powe CE, Kiern IM, Fromhagen C, Cavanagh D. Propiomazine hydrochloride in obstetrical anesthesia. JAMA 1962;181:280.

79. Slone D, Siskind V, Heinonen OP, Monson RR, Kaufman DW, Shapiro S. Antenatal exposure to the phenothiazines in relation to congenital malformations, perinatal mortality rate, birth weight and intelligence quotient score. Am J Obstet Gynecol 1977;128:486.

80. Dawes JA. The distribution and action of drugs on the fetus in utero. Br J Anaesth 1973;45:766.

81. Desilva JAF, D'Anconte L, Kaplan J. The determination of blood levels and the placental transfer of diazepam in humans. Curr Ther Res 1964;6:121.

82. Kaplan SA, Jack ML, Alexander K, Weinfeld RE.

Pharmacokinetic profile of diazepam in man following single intravenous and oral and chronic oral administrations. J Pharm Sci 1973;62:1789.

83. McAllister CB. Placental transfer and neonatal effects of diazepam when administered to women just before delivery. Br J Anaesth 1980;52:423.

84. Rolbin SH, Wright PG, Shnider SM, Roizen LG, Johnson JJ. Diazepam during cesarean section: Effects on neonatal Apgar scores, acid base status, neurobehavioral assessment and maternal fetal plasma norepinephrine levels. Anesthesiology 1977;49:S449.

85. Greenblatt DJ, Abernathy DR, Mose DS, Harmat JS, Shader RL. Clinical importance of the interaction of diazepam and cimetidine. N Engl J Med 1984;310:1639.

86. White PF, Shafer A, Boyle WA, Doze VA, Duncan S. Benzodiazepine antagonism does not provoke a stress response. Anesthesiology 1989;70:636.

87. Wilson CM, Dundee JW, Moore J. Plasma midazolam levels in non-pregnant and parturient women. Anesthesiology 1986;65:A167.

88. Camann WC, Cohen MB, Ostheimer GW. Is midazolam desirable for sedation in parturients? Anesthesiology, 1986;65:441.

89. Heyman HJ, Salem MR. Is midazolam desirable for sedation in parturients? [reply]. Anesthesiology 1987; 66:577.

90. Seidman SF, Marx GF. Midazolam in obstetric anesthesia. Anesthesiology 1987;67:443.

91. Ginsberg FB, Bell SN. Midazolam in obstetric anesthesia [reply]. Anesthesiology 1988;68:296.

92. Engstrom RH, Cohen SE. A complication associated with the use of midazolam. Anesthesiology 1989; 70:719.

93. Kissin I, Vinik HR, Castillo R, Bradley EL Jr. Alfentanil potentiates midazolam-induced unconsciousness in subanalgesic doses. Anesth Analg 1990;71:65.

94. Fischler M, Bonnet F, Trang H. The pharmacokinetics of droperidol in anesthesized patients. Anesthesiology 1986;64:486.

95. Rivera VM, Keichian AH, Oliver RE. Persistent Parkinsonism following neuroleptanalgesia. Anesthesiology 1975;42:635.

96. Melnick B, Sawyer R, Karambelkar D, Phitayakorn P, Uy NTL, Patel R. Delayed side effects of droperidol after ambulatory general anesthesia. Anesth Analg 1989;69:748.

97. Cohen SE, Woods WA, Wyne J. Antiemetic efficacy of droperidol and metoclopramide. Anesthesiology 1984; 60:67.

98. Abboud T, Raya J, Sadi S, Grobler N, Stine L, Miller F. Fetal and maternal cardiovascular effects of atropine and glycopyrrolate. Anesth Analg 1983;62:426.

99. Murad SHN, Conklin KA, Tabsh KMA, Brinkman CR, Erkkola R, Nuwayhid B. Atropine and glycopyrrolate: Hemodynamic effects and placental transfer in the pregnant ewe. Anesth Analg 1981;60:710.

100. Kanto J, Virtanen R, Lisalo E. Placental transfer and pharmacokinetics of atropine after a single maternal intravenous and intramuscular administration. Acta Anesth Scand 1981;25:85.

101. Flacke JW, Flacke WE. Cholinergic and anticholinergic agents. In: Smith NT, Corbascio AN, eds. Drug interactions in anesthesia. Philadelphia: Lea & Febiger 1986:160.

102. Anticholinergic drugs. In: Stoelting RK. Pharmacology and physiology in anesthetic practice. Philadelphia: JB Lippincott 1987:232.

103. Moya F, Thorndike V. The effects of drugs used in labor on the fetus and newborn. Clin Pharmacol Ther 1963;4:628.

104. Abboud JK, Read J, Miller J. Use of glycopyrrolate in the parturient. Effect on the maternal and fetal heart and uterine activity. Obstet Gynecol 1981;57:224.

105. Paech, MJ. The King Edward Memorial Hospital 1000 mother survey of methods of pain relief in labour. Anaesth Intensive Care 1991;19:393.

106. Kanto J. Obstetric analgesia: Clinical pharmacokinetic considerations. Clin Pharmacokinet 1986;11:283.

CHAPTER 17

Peripheral Nerve Blocks for Labor and Delivery

Doris Costello

Lumbar epidural anesthesia can provide analgesia for labor and delivery for most patients. If anesthesia personnel are not available or a contraindication to epidural placement exists, other nerve blocks can provide pain relief for labor and delivery. Paracervical and lumbar sympathetic blocks can relieve the pain of the first stage of labor. Pudendal block provides comfort during the second stage of labor.

During the first stage of labor, dilatation of the cervix and distention of the lower uterine segment stimulate small unmyelinated nerve fibers. These afferent visceral nerve fibers converge in the paracervical plexus. These high-frequency impulses travel to the sympathetic chain at L-2–L-3 and then join the somatic nerves of the spinal cord at T-10–L-1.[1,2] When this neural signal reaches the cortex, the patient experiences pain. Regional anesthetic techniques used to relieve labor pain aim toward interrupting these neural impulses before they reach the central nervous system.

PARACERVICAL BLOCK

The paracervical block alleviates pain during the first stage of labor by blocking the afferent nerves at the paracervical or Frankenhauser's plexus. This plexus lies lateral and posterior to the junction of the uterus and cervix at the base of the broad ligament.

Technique

As with the performance of any regional technique, establish intravenous access before the procedure. Have resuscitative equipment available and know how to give emergency treatment.

The patient assumes the lithotomy position to ease cervical examination. A 12- to 14-cm, 22-gauge needle with a guide is used most commonly. The guide serves to protect the vaginal mucosa and fetal parts from the needle tip and limits the depth of injection. A needle guide ("trumpet") and long needle are commonly used for this block (Fig. 17-1).[2] Hold the needle guide between the middle and index fingers of the right hand to block the right side of the cervix.[3] Direct the fingers into the lateral fornix of the cervix (Fig. 17-2). This technique helps prevent intrafetal and intramyometrial injection. The uterine vessels lie near the paracervical plexus. Injecting too deeply risks high maternal uptake of local anesthetic (Fig. 17-3). Excessive pressure also will decrease the distance to the uterine vessels.[3] Jagerhorn[4] found that injecting at a depth less than 3 mm

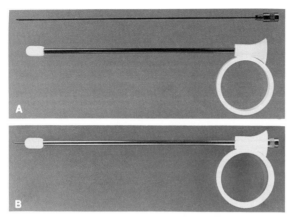

Figure 17–1. **(A)** Needle guide and needle for paracervical and pudendal block. **(B)** Note that guide prevents needle from passing deeply into tissues.

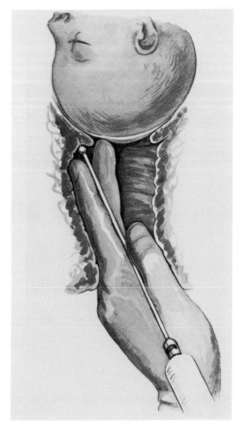

Figure 17–2. Paracervical nerve block. Direct the needle through the vagina and into the lateral fornix of the cervix. (John J. Bonica, M.D.)

decreased the speed of intravascular uptake. Inject the local anesthetic in incremental doses with frequent aspirations to rule out intravascular injection.

Several techniques for local anesthetic injection have been advocated. Originally, two injections were made with half the drug in the 3 o'clock cervical position and the other half in the 9 o'clock cervical position. Subsequently, some authors recommended injecting the local anesthetic in the 4 and 8 o'clock positions, thereby placing the needle further from the uterine vessels. King and Sherline[2] have proposed injecting equal amounts of drug at four sites around the cervix (4 and 8 o'clock, 5 and 7 o'clock) to further decrease the chance of injecting a large amount of local anesthetic near a vessel. Radiologic studies have shown that despite varying injection sites, local anesthetic spreads uniformly around the uterus.[5]

In the past, experts have recommended waiting 10 to 15 minutes before blocking the other side of the cervix.[6] A more recent study, however, found no increase in complications when injecting the contralateral side immediately. These authors emphasized that uterine displacement is the most important factor in preventing problems while doing the block.[7]

Pain relief begins within 2 to 5 minutes. The success of the technique varies with the operator's experience. Complete relief develops in 80% of patients, partial relief in 10% to 15%, and no relief in 5% to 10%. The block can be repeated in 30 minutes if the patient is still not comfortable.[1]

The limited duration of the analgesic effect of the paracervical block is a major shortcoming of this technique (Table 17-1). Epinephrine has little effect on the duration of bupivacaine and mepivacaine but does prolong the analgesic effect of lidocaine and 2-chloroprocaine.[8] Adding epinephrine to the local anesthetic may cause uterine vasocontriction or decrease uterine activity. A continuous catheter technique has been used successfully by some to avoid repeat paracervical injections.[9]

Effect on Labor

Use paracervical block only after the active phase of labor begins. Never do this block at 8 cm of cervical dilatation, as the risk of intrafetal injection increases greatly.[1]

The effect of the paracervical block on the progression of labor is unknown. Many authors suggest that the block can enhance cervical dilation by softening the cervix or by relaxing the lower uterine segment. Some

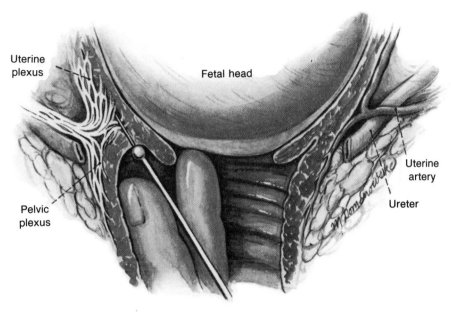

Figure 17–3. Paracervical nerve block. Note that, in addition to the pelvic plexus, the needle lies close to the uterine artery and vein and the fetal head. (John J. Bonica, M.D.)

have even advocated paracervical block to treat patients with cervical dystocia.[10,11] Others have found no change in the rate of cervical dilation.[6] Uterine activity may increase after paracervical block,[12] but, in most studies, paracervical block has little effect on the duration of labor.[6,8,11,13]

Complications

The most serious complication of the paracervical block is fetal bradycardia. The reported incidence of this event is extremely variable (2%–70%). Reasons for this variablity include the following:

- Inconsistent definitions of bradycardia
- Intermittent versus continuous fetal monitoring
- Patient selection

Shnider *et al*[14] defined bradycardia as a fetal heart less than 120 beats per minute (bpm) or a decrease of 20 bpm from baseline. They reviewed 845 paracervical blocks and reported a 30% incidence of fetal bradycardia. Bradycardia begins 2 to 10 minutes after injection and usually resolves within 20 minutes.[15]

The mechanism of the fetal bradycardia associated with the paracervical block is a mystery. One theory suggests that local anesthetic passes rapidly across the

intervillous space and has a direct toxic effect on the fetal central nervous system and myocardium.[16] Asling *et al*[17] reported higher mepivacaine concentrations in the blood of bradycardic fetuses than in their mother's blood after paracervical block,[17] but many other investigators have found no correlation between fetal local anesthetic concentration and bradycardia.[13,18,19] In addition, Freeman *et al*[20] reported a case of direct fetal injection of mepivacaine, 375 mg, without any fetal bradycardia. He suggests that the electrocardiographic changes usually associated with postparacervical block bradycardia—a short PR interval and normal QRS duration—resemble those seen with fetal hypoxia. When bradycardia results from a large intra-

Table 17–1

The Duration of Pain Relief After Paracervical Block

DRUG	DURATION
Lidocaine, 1%	45–90 min
Chloroprocaine, 2%	30–45 min
Mepivicaine, 1%	45–90 min
Prilocaine, 1%	60–90 min
Bupivicaine, 0.25%	90–120 min

fetal injection, a wide QRS complex and increased QT interval develop, as in adult local toxicity.[20]

Decreased uteroplacental perfusion that produces fetal hypoxia is another possible mechanism for fetal bradycardia. Uterine activity can increase after paracervical block. (Uterine contractions decrease uterine blood flow.) Still, there are many reports of fetal bradycardia without change in uterine activity.[12,21]

Currently available evidence strongly supports the existence of local anesthetic-induced vasoconstriction that significantly decreases uterine blood flow. Cibils[22] and Gibbs and Noel[23] have shown, in vitro, a direct, nonadrenergic, vasoconstrictive effect of local anesthetic (Fig. 17-4). Others have reported significant decreases in uterine blood flow at local anesthetic concentrations comparable to those arising during paracervical blockade.[21,24,25]

Significant clinical data exists to support the theory that decreased uteroplacental perfusion and fetal hypoxia cause post paracervical block bradycardia. Le Fevre[18] found a fivefold increase in fetal bradycardia in patients with evidence of preexisting uteroplacental insufficiency.[18] Baxi *et al*[26] found decreased PO$_2$ in ten fetuses monitored with a transcutaneous electrode after paracervical block. He attributed this change to a decrease in fetal perfusion.

The significance of the fetal bradycardia varies. Only when the bradycardia lasts longer than 10 minutes does the fetus develop a transient metabolic acidosis.[20] The neonatal effects of a transient bradycardia are directly related to the time available for in utero recovery of the fetus. Apgar scores are better in those fetuses that delivered more that 30 minutes after their bradycardic episode.[27] Shnider *et al*[14] found depressed 1-minute Apgar scores in fetuses experiencing bradycardia, but all had normal scores by 5 minutes. Jensen *et al*[28] reported less neonatal depression in the postparacervical fetus than in those exposed to meperidine, 75 mg, during labor. Neurobehavioral testing on neonates exposed to the paracervical block did not reveal significant long-term effects when compared to unmedicated controls.[29]

If bradycardia occurs, treatment aims at optimizing uteroplacental perfusion. Maintain uterine displacement. Assure that maternal blood pressure is adequate. Give supplemental oxygen.[3] Avoid immediate delivery to allow time for intrauterine resuscitation. If bradycardia persists for more 10 minutes, scalp pH determinations should be made to help decide the need for immediate delivery.[30] Intrauterine deaths from severe fetal hypoxia have occurred when bradycardia persisted for longer than 45 and 80 minutes.[31] When immediate delivery is required, postnatal exchange transfusion may be needed to treat local anesthetic toxicity.[3]

Maternal Complications

Maternal complications of the paracervical block are rare. Local anesthetic systemic toxicity usually presents as central nervous system irritability. These symptoms are usually transient, but one must be prepared to provide ventilatory or circulatory support if needed. Paracervical hematomas or vaginal lacerations can occur but are usually of little consequence.

Subgluteal and retropsoal abscesses after paracervical block also have been reported.[32] These can pre-

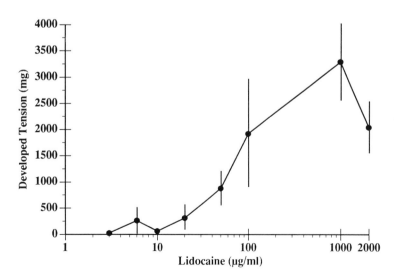

Figure 17–4. Dose–response curve of pregnant human uterine artery to lidocaine (n = 9). (After Gibbs CP, Noel SC. Response of arterial segments from gravid uterus to multiple concentrations of lignocaine. Br J Anaesth 1977;49:409)

sent a few hours to several days after the block. The chief complaint is usually severe hip pain and limitation of hip motion with fever. Initial treatment consists of antibiotics directed at gram-negative or anaerobic organisms. If the diagnosis is delayed and a large abscess has formed, surgical debridement may be required.

Neuropathy also has developed after paracervical block in 1 in 2000 patients. The symptoms can occur in 12 hours or up to 10 days after the block. Most likely, the injury results from direct trauma to the sacral plexus or to hematoma formation around the plexus. Patients complain of severe buttock pain on the affected side with radiation down the posterior surface of the leg and inability to ambulate. Infection may cause similar symptoms. A mass can commonly be palpated over the sacroiliac area. Treatment consists of analgesics and early ambulation. Resolution can take weeks to months.[33]

Choice of Local Anesthetic

Many investigators have advocated the use of ester local anesthetics instead of amides for the paracervical block because of their rapid metabolism and low potential for toxicity. Some investigators have reported lower rates of post-block bradycardia with the use of chloroprocaine.[12,34] Only trace amounts of chloroprocaine persist in fetal blood at delivery.[12] In contrast, significant concentrations of unmetabolized lidocaine remain in neonates receiving that drug.[12] Even with repeated injections of chloroprocaine, fetal drug accumulation does not occur. The major disadvantage of chloroprocaine is its short duration of action, approximately 40 minutes.

Cibils[22] reported that each amide correlated with a different rate of bradycardia: lidocaine, 4% to 22%; mepivacaine, 10% to 45%; and bupivacaine, 10% to 56%. Shnider *et al*[35] found prilocaine produced bradycardia in 10% of patients. This incidence was half that he reported after mepivacaine and lidocaine, but prilocaine causes methemoglobinemia. Fetal cyanosis has occurred after paracervical block with this drug.[35] Bupivacaine is not approved for use in the paracervical block in the United States.

Summary

Although the paracervical block may seem obsolete to the academic anesthesiologist, community use of the paracervical block is significant. In 1989, Day[36] reported that two thirds of the laboring patients in his community hospital received a paracervical block. He reported, with careful patient selection, a success rate for pain relief of 75%, with a 6% incidence of bradycardia.

Based on review of the literature, the following recommendations can be made regarding paracervical block for labor analgesia:

- Avoid this block in high-risk patients (*i.e.,* premature, stressed fetuses or those with suspected uteroplacental insufficiency).
- Avoid the block in complicated deliveries such as breech and multiple gestations.
- Do not place the block when the cervix is more than 8 cm dilated.
- Maintain uterine displacement during and after the block.
- Monitor the fetal heart rate continuously after the block.
- Have resuscitative equipment available.

LUMBAR SYMPATHETIC BLOCK

Lumbar sympathetic block can provide adequate analgesia during the first stage of labor. It is particularly useful in the parturient with previous back surgery in whom epidural anesthesia can be difficult, if not impossible. Lumbar sympathetic block provides labor analgesia by blocking the transmission of pain from the cervix and lower uterine segments at the sympathetic chain before the nerves enter the spinal cord.[1,30]

Technique

The patient sits to provide maximal flexion of the spine, facilitating identification of the spinous process of L-2 (Fig. 17-5A). After sterile preparation, locate the midpoint of the L-2 spinous process and inject a wheal of local anesthetic 4 to 5 cm laterally on each side of the back. Introduce a 10-cm, 22-gauge needle at a 20-degree angle cephalad, and attempt to contact the transverse process of L-2 (Fig. 17-5B, C, and D) Then, withdraw the needle to the skin and redirect it to pass below the transverse process. At this point, the needle will be directed medially. At approximately 4.5 cm depth, it will contact the vertebral body. After touching the vertebral body, withdraw the needle again and redirect it laterally 5 to 10 degrees to "walk off" the vertebral body. The needle will then be located on the anterolateral surface of the vertebral body, just anterior to the medial attachment of the psoas muscle (Fig. 17-

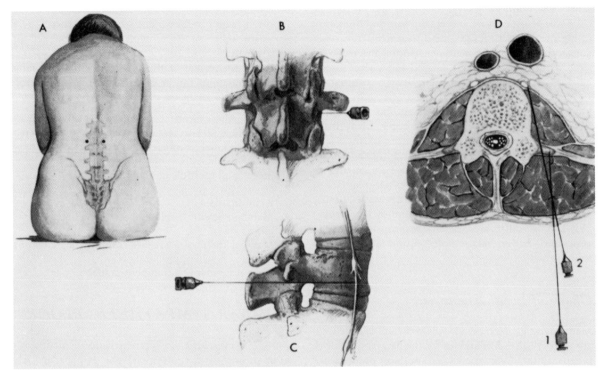

Figure 17–5. Technique of lumbar sympathetic block. (**A**) Patient in sitting position with spine flexed. Note that the two skin wheals are opposite the mid-portion of the spinous process of the second lumbar vertebra. (**B**) Enlarged posterior view of the vertebral column with details of these landmarks. (**C**) Side view showing relation of needle to the bones. (**D**) Cross section showing two of the steps used in inserting the needle (see text). (John J. Bonica, M.D.)

5D).[1,3,30] Carefully inject the local anesthetic, aspirating frequently to avoid intravascular injection. The needle also will be close to the subarachnoid and epidural spaces. One must therefore aspirate for cerebrospinal fluid and question the patient to elicit signs of spinal blockade. Repeat the procedure on the contralateral side to provide complete analgesia. Catheters can be passed through the needles to allow repeated injections (Fig. 17-6).

Lumbar sympathetic block does not interfere with the progress of labor. Some evidence suggests that it may even accelerate labor. A study by Hunter[37] of 39 patients found 5 to 15 minutes of uterine hypertonus after block in 20 patients. The other 19 patients showed no change in their labor patterns. Another study noted rapid progression of labor after the block, with an average time of 158 minutes from block placement to complete cervical dilatation.[38] Because no motor block develops, this technique does not affect the second stage of labor.

The duration of analgesia after lumbar sympathetic block varies with the choice of local anesthetic. Lidocaine, 1%, without epinephrine provides pain relief for 60 to 90 minutes, and lidocaine with epinephrine provides pain relief for approximately 120 minutes. Tetracaine, 0.5%, lasts for up to 4 hours.[38] Meguiar and Wheeler[38] used 20 mL of bupivacaine, 0.5%, with epinephrine, 1:200,000, for bilateral lumbar sympathetic block. They obtained good analgesia in 38 of their 40 patients. Most patients delivered before the regression of the block; 12 required a second procedure. The mean duration of the analgesia was 283 minutes.[38]

Maternal Complications

The most common side effect produced by the lumbar sympathetic block, hypotension, occurs 15% to 20% of the time. Spread of local anesthetic to the celiac and splanchnic plexi increases the sympathectomy pro-

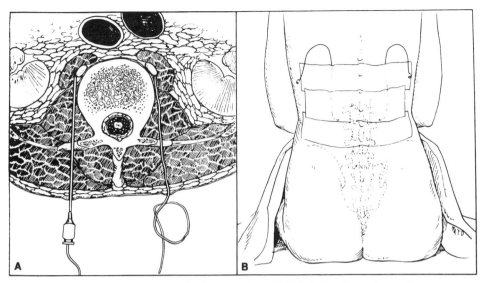

Figure 17–6. Technique of continuous lumbar sympathetic block. **(A)** After placing the needle in proper position, pass a catheter to just beyond its tip, then remove the needle. **(B)** The catheters are then secured in place. (John J. Bonica, M.D.)

duced by lumbar sympathetic block, leading to vasodilation and hypotension.[1] Using a smaller volume of drug may decrease the magnitude of the hemodynamic changes. Meguiar and Wheeler[38] reported only a 5% decrease in blood pressure. They routinely administered a 500 mL bolus of Ringer's lactate.

Other complications related to this block include systemic toxic reaction and subarachnoid or epidural blockade. In an early review of 1200 patients, 3 patients experienced convulsions, 4 had minor systemic symptoms, 2 had subarachnoid injections, and 5 patients had epidural injection with sensory blockade up to T-6.[1] Three patients suffered retroperitoneal hemorrhage after inadvertent penetration into this space during the block.[1] Meguiar and Wheeler[38] noted a 2% incidence of intravascular needle placement but saw no resultant complications. Another report described total spinal anesthesia in two patients after the lumbar sympathetic block.[39] One must be prepared for these possible complications when performing this block.

Fetal Complications

There are no direct fetal complications reported with the lumbar sympathetic block.[1] The fetus may suffer from significant maternal hypotension. Use caution if contemplating this block in situations of fetal distress

and uteroplacental insufficiency.[38] Increased uterine activity after the block also could affect the fetus. Still, there are no reports of fetal distress related to uterine tetany.

Summary

Lumbar sympathetic block is used infrequently in labor and delivery. It is technically difficult to place. Patients are more uncomfortable during placement than they are during induction of epidural analgesia. This technique also offers only a limited duration of action and does not relieve pain during the second stage of labor, but it does have the advantage of not producing motor blockade. Consider lumbar sympathetic block in patients who cannot have a lumbar epidural because of back problems or other contraindications.[30]

PUDENDAL BLOCK

Distention of the lower vagina, vulva, and perineum produces pain during the second stage of labor. The pudendal nerve is the major source of sensation in this area. This nerve carries somatic nerves from the anterior primary divisions of the second, third and fourth sacral nerves. The pudendal nerve also provides the motor innervation of the perineal muscles.

The pudendal nerve travels through the lower part of the greater sciatic foramen and enters the gluteal region. The nerve then passes posterior to the ischial spine and continues into the lesser sciatic foramen. It enters Alcock's canal, where it lies along the lateral border of the ischiorectal fossa. The pudendal nerve then divides into the perineal nerve, dorsal nerve to the clitoris, and the inferior hemorrhoidal nerve (Fig. 17-7).

The success of the pudendal block requires blocking the nerve after the formation of the anterior divisions of S-2–S-4 but before the division into the three terminal branches. To accomplish this end, block the nerve between the sacrotuberous and sacrospinous ligament.

Technique

The block can be done either transvaginally or through the perineum. The most commonly used approach in labor is the transvaginal. As with the paracervical block, use a needle with a guide to protect the vaginal mucosa and the fetal parts from the needle tip.[1,4,30]

Place the patient in the lithotomy position. Hold the needle between the middle and index fingers of the right hand to block the right pudendal nerve. Palpate the ischial spine. The sacrospinous ligament lies 1 cm medial and posterior to the spine. Direct the needle through the sacrospinous ligament to a depth of about 1 cm. You should appreciate loss of resistance as the needle pierces the ligament into the area of the pudendal nerve (Fig. 17-8). The pudendal nerve lies in proximity to the pudendal vessels. Carefully aspirate during injection. Inject a total volume of 10 mL of local anesthetic on each side. Alternatively, inject 7 mL of local anesthetic in the location already described and an additional 3 mL 1 cm distal to the spine to block any aberrant nerve branches.[3]

This block may be done immediately before delivery. If done at the completion of cervical dilatation, it will provide relief of pain during the second stage of labor. One study reports that doing the pudendal block at the time of complete cervical dilation prolongs the second stage of labor. By eliminating the urge to bear down, pudendal block may impair the parturient's ability to push. The block appears to have little effect on uterine activity.[40]

As with other regional blocks for labor, concern about which local anesthetic to use exists. The drug is injected near blood vessels and either intravascular or rapid systemic uptake could occur. In addition, most fetuses deliver shortly after the block; therefore, they

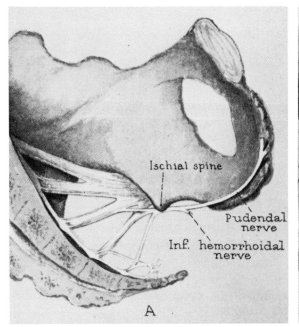
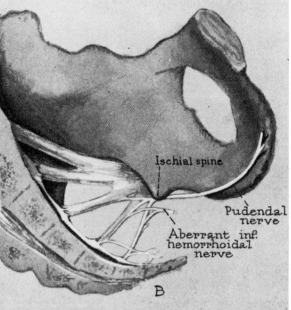

Figure 17–7. Origin and course of the pudendal nerve in relation to the bones of the pelvis. Note particularly its relations to the ischial spine. (John J. Bonica, M.D.)

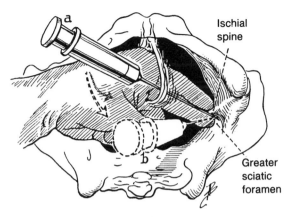

Figure 17–8. Transvaginal pudendal block. **(A)** The position of the syringe directed downward and laterally to pierce the vagina just below the projection of the ischial spine. **(B)** The redirection of the needle to make it parallel with the longitudinal axis of the mother is indicated by the *arrows*. (Kobak AJ, Evans FE, Johnson GR. Transvaginal pudendal nerve block: A simple procedure for effective anesthesia in operative vaginal delivery. Am J Obstet Gynecol 1956;71:981)

do not have the benefits of placental clearance if exposed to large amounts of local anesthetic. Lidocaine, 1%, is most commonly used for this block. Lidocaine appears in maternal and fetal blood within 5 minutes of the block; peak concentrations arise within 10 to 20 minutes.[40] The maternal plasma concentrations of lidocaine that develop after pudendal block are much lower than those reported after epidural or paracervical blockade with the same dose of local anesthetic. Others have recommended 2-chloroprocaine because of its rapid metabolism and low toxicity.[41] Merkow *et al*[42] compared the neonatal neurobehavioral effects of bupivacaine, mepivacaine, and 2-chloroprocaine for pudendal block. The groups did not differ at 4 and 24 hours after delivery. Adding epinephrine to the local anesthetic for pudendal block prolongs both the duration of pain relief and the second stage of labor.[41]

Maternal Complications

The most common problem associated with this block is failure to provide adequate analgesia for delivery because of doing the block too late. As with other regional blocks, the patient may experience symptoms of systemic toxic reaction from intravascular injection, rapid absorption, or administration of a large amount of local anesthetic.

Hematoma formation also can occur, but this rarely requires intervention. Retropsoal or subgluteal abscesses have been reported for pudendal as well as paracervical blocks.[40]

Fetal Complications

It is rare to see fetal problems associate with this block. Remember to limit the dose of drug injected to avoid fetal exposure to toxic amounts of drug. No maternal hemodynamic effects occur with this block that could effect the fetus.

Summary

Pudendal block provides analgesia during the second stage of labor and for delivery. It is useful in patients who do not have a functioning epidural catheter in place. This technique also may be used for operative vaginal deliveries (vacuum or outlet forceps). Vaginal and perineal damage can be repaired using pudendal block; however, this block is not adequate for repair of deep vaginal or cervical lacerations. It also is not effective for midforceps deliveries or uterine manipulations.[2]

REFERENCES

1. Bonica JJ. Principles and practice of obstetrical anesthesia, Philadelphia: FA Davis, 1967:520.
2. King JC, Sherline DM. Paracervical and pudendal block. Clin Obstet Gynecol 1981;24:587.
3. Abouleish E. Pain control in obstetrics, Philadelphia: JB Lippincott, 1977.
4. Jagerhorn M. Paracervical block in obstetrics: An improved injection method. Acta Obstet Gynecol Scand 1975;54:9.
5. Kobak AJ, Sadove MS. Anatomic studies of transvaginal regional anesthesia. Obstet Gynecol 1962;19:302.
6. Thiery M, Vroman S. Paracervical block analgesia during labor. Am J Obstet Gynecol 1972;113:988.
7. Van Dorsten JP, Miller FC, Yeh SY. Spacing the injection interval with the paracervical block: A randomized study. Obstet Gynecol 1981;58:696.
8. Nesheim BI. Which local is best for the paracervical block? Acta Obstet Gynecol Scand 1983;62:261.
9. Tafeen CH, Freeman HL, Harris H. A system of continuous paracervical block anesthesia. Am J Obstet Gynecol 1966;94:854.
10. Jenssen H. The effect of the paracervical block on cervical dilatation and uterine activity. Acta Obstet Gynecol Scand 1973;52:13.

11. Read JA, Miller FC. The bupivicaine paracervical block in labor and its effect on quantitative uterine activity. Obstet Gynecol 1979;53:166.

12. Weiss RR, Halevy S, Almonte RO, Gunderson K, Hinsvark ON, O'Brien JE. Comparison of lidocaine and 2-chloroprocaine in paracervical block. Anesth Analg 1983;62:168.

13. Miller FC, Quesnel G, Petrie RH, Paul RH, Hon Ett. The effect of paracervical block on uterine activity and beat-to-beat variability of fetal heart rate. Am J Obstet Gynecol 1978;130:284.

14. Shnider SM, Asling JH, Holl JW, Margolis AJ. Paracervical block anesthesia in obstetrics. Part I. Am J Obstet Gynecol 1970;107:619.

15. Paul RH, Freeman RK. Fetal cardiac response to paracervical block anesthesia. Part II. Am J Obstet Gynecol 1972;113:592.

16. Teramo K. Effect of the obstetrical paracervical block on the fetus. Acta Obstet Gynecol Scand (Suppl) 1971;16:1.

17. Asling JH, Shnider SM, Margolis AJ, Wilkinson GL, Way EL. Paracervical block anesthesia in obstetrics. Part II. Am J Obstet Gynecol 1970;107:626.

18. Le Fevre ML. Fetal heart rate pattern and postparacervical block fetal bradycardia. Obstet Gynecol 1984;64:343.

19. Gordon HR. Fetal bradycardia after paracervical block : correlations with maternal blood levels of local anesthetics. N Engl J Med 1968;279:911.

20. Freeman RK, Gutierrez NA, Roy ML, Stovall D, Paul RH, Hon EH. Fetal cardiac response to paracervical block anesthesia. Part I. Am J Obstet Gynecol 1972;113:583.

21. Fishburne JI, Greiss FC, Hopkinson R, Rhyne AL. Response of the gravid uterine vasculature to arterial levels of local anesthetic agents. Am J Obstet Gynecol 1979;133:753.

22. Cibils LA. Response of human uterine arteries to local anesthetics. Am J Obstet Gynecol 1976;126:202.

23. Gibbs CP, Noel SC. Response of arterial segments from gravid uterus to multiple concentrations of lignocaine. Br J Anæsth 1977;49:409.

24. Greiss FC, Still JG, Anderson SG. Effects of local anesthetic agents on uterine vasculature and myometruim. Am J Obstet Gynecol 1976;124:889.

25. Van Dorsten JP, Miller FC. Fetal heart rate changes after accidental intrauterine lidocaine. Obstet Gynecol 1981;57:257.

26. Baxi LV, Petrie RH, James LS. Human fetal oxygenation following paracervical block. Am J Obstet Gynecol 1979;135:1109.

27. Teramo K. Studies on foetal acid–base values after para-cervical block during labor. Acta Obstet Gynecol Scand (Suppl) 1969;48:80.

28. Jensen F, Qvist I, Brocks V, Secher NJ, Westergaard LG. Submucous paracervical block compared to IM meperidine during labor: A double-blind study. Obstet Gynecol 1984;64:724.

29. Kangas-Saarela T, Jouppila R, Puolakka J, Jouppila P, Hollmen A, Puukka M. The effect of bupivicaine paracervical block on the neurobehavioral responses of new born infants. Acta Anæsth Scand, 1988;32:566.

30. Chestnut DH. Regional anesthesia, other than epidural, for labor and vaginal delivery. Clin Obstet Gynecol 1987;30:530.

31. Rosefsky JB, Petersiel ME. Perinatal deaths associated with mepivacaine paracervical block in labor. N Engl J Med 1968;278:530.

32. Hibbard LT, Snyder EN, McVann RM. Subgluteal and retropsoal infection in obstetrical practice. Obstet Gynecol 1972;39:137.

33. Gaylord TG, Pearson JW. Neuropathy following paracervical block in the obstetric population. Obstet Gynecol 1982;60:521.

34. Philipson EH, Kuhnert BR, Syracuse CB, Reese AL, Rosen MG. Intrapartum paracervical block anesthesia with 2-chloroprocaine. Am J Obstet Gynecol 1983;146:16.

35. Shnider SM, Gildea J. Paracervical block in obstetrics, Am J Obstet Gynecol 1973;116:320.

36. Day TW. Community use of the paracervical block in labor. J Fam Pract 1989;28:545.

37. Hunter CA. Uterine motility studies during labor. Observations on bilateral sympathetic nerve block in normal and abnormal first stage labor. Am J Obstet Gynecol 1963;85:681.

38. Meguiar RV, Wheeler AS. Lumbar sympathetic block with bupivacaine: Analgesia for labor. Anesth Analg 1978;57:486.

39. Gay GR, Evans JA. Total spinal anesthesia following lumbar paravertebral block: A potentially lethal complication. Anesth Analg 1971;50:344.

40. Zador G, Lindmark G, Nilsson, BA. Pudendal block in normal vaginal deliveries. Acta Obstet Gynecol Scand (suppl) 1974;34:51.

41. Schierup L, Schmidt JF, Jensen AT, Rye BA. Pudendal block in vaginal deliveries. Acta Obstet Gynecol Scand 1988;67:195.

42. Merkow AJ, McGuinness GA, Erenberg A, Kennedy RL. The neonatal neurobehavioral effects of bupivicaine, mepivicaine and 2-chloroprocaine used for pudendal block. Anesthesiology 1980;52:309.

CHAPTER 18

Identifying the Epidural Space

Felicity Reynolds

With a sound knowledge of anatomy and careful teaching, safe and successful identification of the epidural space can be easy. What has turned out to be probably the most reliable approach was first described in 1921. This technique consists of loss of resistance (LOR) using continuous pressure on the plunger of a liquid-filled syringe.[1] This method has since been described repeatedly in standard textbooks,[2,3] and even re-invented.[4]

Despite decades of research, controversy remains about many aspects of the technique for epidural insertion. These questions include the following:

- Does the operator wear a mask or even a sterile gown, or only sterile gloves?
- Does the patient sit or lie?
- Does the operator sit or stand?
- Does the operator use the midline or the paramedian approach?
- Does the operator use LOR or some other technique?
- Should air or liquid be used for LOR?
- Is a glass or a plastic syringe best?
- What size of needle is best, and should the bevel be horizontal or vertical?
- Should the catheter have a stylet, and should it have a single end-hole or three-sided holes?

Even the anatomy of the epidural space is a subject of controversy; therefore, this subject will be addressed first.

ANATOMY

Bones

The aspiring epiduralist first must become familiar with the lumbar vertebrae (Figs. 18-1 and 18-2). Have access to a skeleton to study these bones in the articulated state. In particular, examine their spinous processes and laminae. The spinous processes (except that of the fifth lumbar vertebra) are hatchet-shaped. The important fact to grasp is that their shape is roughly rhomboid and their height is considerably greater than the gaps between them (Fig. 18-3). Thus, if the needle is inserted in the midline, but because of obesity an interspace cannot be felt, the odds favor the needle's hitting a spinous process rather than a gap. The size of the interspace also depends on the degree of lordosis and the amount of flexion that the patient can achieve (Fig. 18-4). Flattening out a lumbar lordosis is possible even in the presence of a large gravid uterus. Many women do not have sufficient control over their bodies to do so, thus their interspinous distances may remain exceedingly small. The distance from the posterior border of a spinous process to the inner aspect of the laminae is 2 to 3 cm in most women. The variability in the depth of the epidural space from the skin depends largely on the amount of subcutaneous tissue.

The vertebral arch consists of the pedicles and, posteriorly, the laminae that meet in the midline. The laminae bones form a gentle arch in the upper lumbar re-

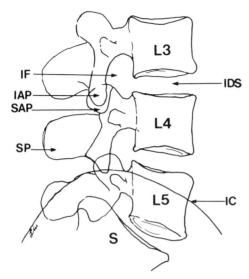

Figure 18–1. Lateral view of the lumbar vertebrae. Note the shape and size of the spinous processes of L-3 and L-4. (IAP = inferior articular process; IC = iliac crest; IDS = intervertebral disc space; IF = intervertebral foramina; S = sacrum; SAP = superior articular process; SP = spinous process)

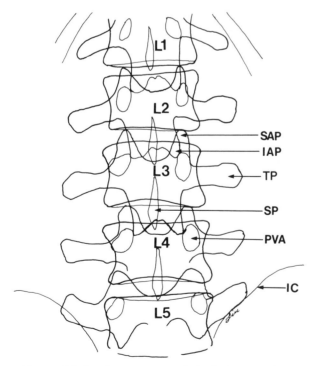

Figure 18–2. Posterior view of the lumbar vertebrae. (TP = transverse process, IAP = inferior articular process; IC = iliac crest; PVA = pedicle of vertebral arch; SAP = superior articular process; SP = spinous process)

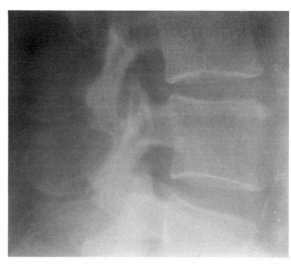

Figure 18–3. Radiograph of the lumbar spine in extension. The spaces between the spinous processes are considerably smaller than the processes themselves. Refer to Figure 18-1 to identify the structures.

gion and meet at an angle of 90 degrees in the fifth lumbar vertebra. A gradual change transpires between the two extremes. When viewed from behind, the vertebral arches form an impenetrable slab; hence, if the interspinous space is missed, the needle meets what appears to be ubiquitous bone. The epidural space is approached, however, through one of the interlaminar foramina, which appear between the spinous pro-

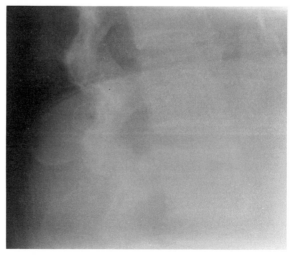

Figure 18–4. Radiograph of the lumbar spine in flexion. Flattening the lumbar lordosis widens the gaps between the spinous processes. Refer to Figure 18-1 to identify the structures.

cesses on an anteroposterior radiograph (Fig. 18-5), and the interspinous spaces lead inexorably toward them. Because the lumbar interspinous spaces do not slope so steeply downwards and backward as those in the thoracic region, a needle approaching the epidural space in the midline of necessity must do so at a near right angle to the coronal plane. By contrast, when using the paramedian approach, the needle may pass into the epidural space at a much more acute angle, making passage of an epidural catheter easier.

Ligaments

The supraspinous ligament unites and covers the posterior borders of the spinous processes. Interspinous ligaments join the spines throughout their length. These tissues are tough and dense. At their anterior ends, they split to form the ligamenta flava (Fig. 18-6). The ligamenta flava are so called because they contain yellow elastic tissue. They fill the inter laminar foramina. Each unites the anterior, or inner, surface of the lower border of the lamina above with the outer surface of the upper border of the lamina below. Laterally, they

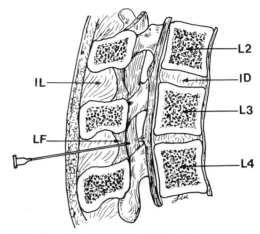

Figure 18–6. Ligaments of the lumber vertebrae. (ID = intervertebral disc; IL = interspinous ligament; LF = ligamentum flavum)

merge with the capsules of the facet joints. Each ligamentum flavum is between 13 and 20 mm high, 12 and 20 mm wide, and 3 and 5 mm thick.[5] Each pair of ligaments meets at an angle of between 70 degrees and 90 degrees. They may unite in the midline, or there may be a small gap between them. A needle reaches the epidural space in the midline either by emerging from the interspinous ligament and passing between the two ligamenta flava, or by passing through a united ligament.[6] If the needle is not exactly in the midline, or if the paramedian approach is used, it must pass through the ligamentum flavum.

The Epidural Space

The laminae are in direct contact with the dura beneath. Between each vertebral arch, the ligamenta flava form a much deeper sulcus between the two laminae, creating a series of midline fat-filled spaces. These spaces are essentially the shape of flattened cones (the posterior cones) (Figs. 18-7 to 18-9). Thus, the epidural space is deepest (about 4–6 mm) in the midline at a point midway between two vertebral arches. It narrows down to merely a potential space opposite each pair of laminae. It also widens out laterally within each intervertebral foramen to communicate with the paravertebral spaces, in a series of lateral cones (Fig. 18-9).

The Epidural Space Depth

The distance of the epidural space from the skin is a subject that has interested many anesthesiologists.

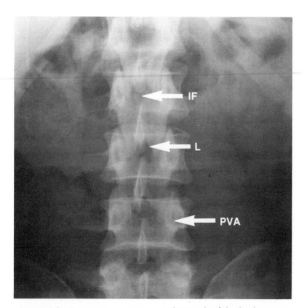

Figure 18–5. Anteroposterior radiograph of the lumbar spine shows the interlaminar foraminae as radiolucent spaces opposite the bodies of the vertebrae and between spinous processes. The epidural space is entered through the interlaminar foraminae. Such radiographs can be of value to show the rotation in patients with scoliosis. (IF = interlaminar foramina; L = lamina; PVA = pedicle of vertebral arch)

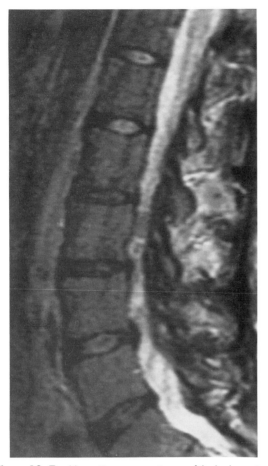

Figure 18–7. Magnetic resonance image of the lumbar spine. Sagittal view.

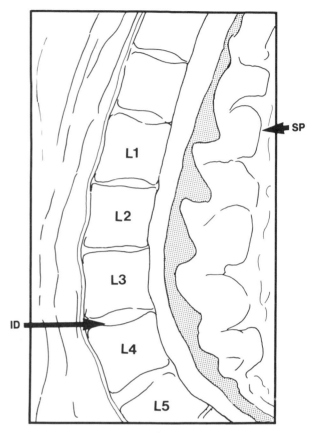

Figure 18–8. Line drawing of image shown in Figure 18-7. Gray area represents epidural space. (ID = intervertebral disc; SP = spinous process)

Measurement of this depth has been reported in hundreds[7] and even thousands[3] of individuals. It varies between 2.5 and 9 cm in the usual obstetric population (mode 4–5 cm).[8] The depth correlates best with body weight and body mass index or ponderal index.[7,9] Unfortunately, the degree of correlation is insufficient to be of any predictive value when inserting an epidural needle (Fig. 18-10). The depth of the epidural space also can be assessed using ultrasound with a high degree of accuracy.[9,10] One cannot but think, however, that gauging it with the LOR technique is quicker and simpler.

The Contents of the Epidural Space

The posterior cones of the epidural space are essentially fat-filled. The lateral cones contain the nerve roots. Blood vessels (the epidural plexus of veins) are also largely confined to the lateral cones. Keeping the needle carefully in the midline, and gentle insertion of a soft catheter, can minimize the incidence of blood vessel puncture during epidural placement.

A median septum or midline dural fold has been postulated as a cause of unilateral block. This structure has been demonstrated only by methods that distort the anatomy (*i.e.,* by injecting contrast medium[11] or polyester resin,[12] or by epiduraloscopy[13]). In contrast, when the anatomy is left undisturbed, this fold is not seen.[6] Indeed, Asato and colleagues[14] pointed out that, were a median septum a common cause of unilateral block, sensory blockade would rise higher than normal when confined to one side. They found, on the contrary, that unilateral blocks were lower than expected. Catheter reinsertion was, in their series, universally successful at alleviating unilateral block.[14] Catheters in-

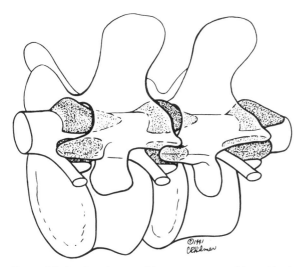

Figure 18–9. Line drawing of the compartments of the epidural space (*stippled areas*). The epidural contents are discontinuous circumferentially and repeat segmentally. Where no contents are represented, the dura is in contact with the spinal canal wall. Lateral cones communicate with the paravertebral spaces. (Hogan QH. Lumbar epidural anatomy: A new look by cryomicrotome section. Anesthesiology 1991;75:767)

serted in the midline may diverge from it,[6] and passage of a catheter into a lateral cone is a potential cause of unilateral block. This problem can commonly be corrected by either catheter withdrawal or appropriate repositioning of the patient. Subdural catheter placement is a more plausible explanation for an obstinate unilateral block.[15]

The dura mater is a tough membrane that cannot be penetrated by a sensibly designed epidural catheter,[16] but a catheter can easily tear through the arachnoid mater. So-called "catheter migration" cannot therefore be evoked as an excuse for an unexpected total spinal block after a negative test dose or earlier normal response to a full dose of local anesthetic.

The subdural (extra-arachnoid) space is a potential space of variable distensibility.[17] Insertion of needle tip or catheter into this space is not as infrequent as many suppose.[18] Subdural injection can explain several perplexing phenomena. Subdural block is characteristically of slow onset, extensive, and, occasionally, unilateral. If the delicate arachnoid mater later tears, a positive test dose can occur after a negative aspiration test; total spinal may develop after a negative test dose. The same development can lead to a delayed total spinal after a previous normal response to a top-up and an "unexplained" spinal headache after an apparently normal epidural.[15]

DOES THE OPERATOR WEAR MASK AND STERILE GOWN?

Although masks are out of fashion and are of little value, I dislike the idea that bacteria might alight by droplet infection onto a catheter that is about to become an indwelling foreign body. I therefore recommend that a mask be worn.

It is interesting that, in the United Kingdom, it is common practice to wear both sterile gloves and gown to place an epidural catheter. In contrast, in North America, despite a higher level of litigation, a sterile gown is not usually worn. In either case, epidural insertion as a cause of infection has been reported rarely on both sides of the Atlantic. Epidural abscesses generally result from blood-borne infection, not from local introduction of bacteria. Recently, however, bacterial meningitis has occurred in previously uninfected women following spinal anesthesia[19] and accidental dural puncture.[20] I myself have encountered two cases in which an abscess occurred along the tract of an epidural catheter. I prefer to wear a mask, scrub to the elbow, and don sterile gown and gloves before siting an epidural catheter.

DOES THE PATIENT SIT OR LIE?

If using the sitting position, have the patient hang her legs over the side of the bed (while sitting as far from the edge as the length of her thighs will allow). Place a pillow on her lap, and encourage her to slouch forward at the waist, not the hips, with her arms folded in front of her on the pillow. An attendant or her partner should stand in front of her supporting her shoulders. Employing the partner frees the attendant but puts the partner in a position from which he or she may observe the epidural insertion. This maneuver does place the partner at risk of fainting, thus producing three patients instead of two.

If the mother is to lie, she should be in the precise lateral position, with a pillow supporting her head but not beneath her shoulder. Her arms should be in front of her and she should flex her lumbar spine as much as possible. Most women are unable to comply with this request unless they bend their knees up and head down. Neither move is strictly necessary except as an aid to lumbar flexion. The partner can sit in front of the patient, where he or she is unlikely to faint.

Anesthesiologists vary in their preference for the sitting or lateral position. They tend to prefer and to perform better using the position they learned in training.

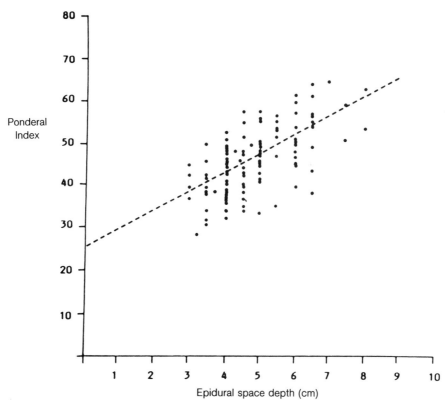

Figure 18–10. Correlation between epidural space depth and patient weight. This graph demonstrates that, despite a highly significant correlation between ponderal index and epidural space depth, this relationship is of no predictive value. For a given ponderal index, epidural depth varies by 4 or even more cm. (r = 0.618 [P < 0.001]; ponderal index = weight/height.) (Meiklejohn BH. Distance from the skin to the lumbar epidural space in an obstetric population. Reg Anesth 1990;15:134)

As more anesthesiologists learn to use the sitting position, use of this posture propagates itself. Those trained to use the lateral position, however, can more readily adapt to the sitting than vice versa.[21] If the women themselves express a preference, more obese women prefer to sit for epidural insertion, usually because they find breathing easier in this position, whereas leaner women and those in labor prefer to lie (Fig. 18-11).[22]

The midline is easier to identify in the sitting position, particularly in the obese parturient. On the other hand, in the sitting position, hydrostatic pressure is higher in the epidural space,[23] the lumbar dural sac, and the epidural veins. This increased pressure augments the theoretical risk of dural and venous puncture. Some studies have reported slight, but insignificant, increases in the incidence of venous puncture in the sitting position.[21,24]

Caudal spread of analgesia does *not* increase with injection of local anesthetic in the sitting position.[25] In fact, the reverse occurs. In the sitting position, there is more cerebrospinal fluid in the lumbar region to occupy the space available in the vertebral canal. So, epidurally injected local anesthetics flow more readily upward than downward.

Taking all factors into consideration, there would appear to be an advantage in placing obese patients in the sitting position. Nevertheless, train residents to use the lateral position, because they will find it easier to change if the need arises.

DOES THE OPERATOR SIT OR STAND?

Many epiduralists, who were trained to do dural punctures by internists and neurologists, probably sit to site an epidural. This habit particularly applies to those who have their patients sit. Yet two great teachers of the art of epidural insertion[2,26] advocate that the operator stand. Bromage[2] suggests that the standing position of-

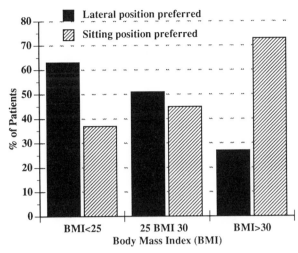

Figure 18–11. Patient position preference versus body mass index (wt/ht²). (After Vincent RD, Chestnut DH. Which position is more comfortable for the parturient during identification of the epidural space? Int J Obstet Anesth 1991;1:9)

fers better control and places the hand and eye over the work rather than behind it. A good view of the epidural needle is not provided by seeing it foreshortened. Besides, the best control over the hands is obtained when they are operating at waist level. This question, however, has not been the subject of research, and each operator probably acquires a personal preference at an early stage in his or her training.

THE PROCEDURE

Prepare the sterile work surface carefully *before* starting the procedure. Neatly lay out all the necessary equipment. This step minimizes the time the patient must spend in an uncomfortable position. Prep the skin at the back widely. Place a sterile towel beneath the patient. If you use an O-towel, anchor it firmly in place over the back. I feel, however, that a perforated drape serves mainly to obscure the surface landmarks.

During the procedure, absolute quiet and stillness must be ensured. The patient must not laugh or cry (as this will increase dural pressure). Conversation should be limited to that necessary for the conduct of the epidural, to avoid distracting the operator.

The L-2–3 or L-3–4 interspace is usually chosen. These levels are relatively safe but provide ready access to the T-11 and T-12 segments for uterine analgesia. In the presence of a marked lumbar lordosis, the approach is generally easier in the upper rather than the lower lumbar region.

The Midline Approach

Raise a skin wheal over the chosen interspace and infiltrate the subcutaneous layers with about 2 mL of local anesthetic. Use less local anesthetic for thin and more for fat people. Use an introducer first to remove a small core of skin. This step allows smooth passage of the needle (for discussion of needles, see below). Insert the epidural needle in the same hole. The needle then passes through skin, subcutaneous tissue, supraspinous and interspinous ligaments, and probably ligamentum flavum. Keep the needle in the midline and in the sagittal plane, but angle it slightly cephalad. Once the tip of the needle enters the ligaments, painful sensation is least unless it strays from the midline. The tissues (especially the ligamentum flavum) exert significant resistance both to advance of the needle and to injection of fluid. Carefully avoid any sudden advances (see following section on the LOR technique).

The Paramedian Approach

Raise a skin wheal 1.5 cm from the midline, opposite the spinous process (whether the center,[27] the cephalad,[6] or the caudal[28] end matters little). Infiltrate the subcutaneous tissues, paravertebral muscles, and periosteum of the lamina (the latter is particularly sensitive) with local anesthetic. In all, use about 5 mL of dilute solution. Break the skin with an introducer. Next, insert the epidural needle, initially perpendicular to the skin, until it reaches lamina (ouch!). Then, withdraw the needle 1 to 2 cm and, with its tip directed cephalad, reinsert it until it reaches either upper border of lamina or ligamentum flavum. Saw the needle to and fro as often as needed until the tip finds the ligamentum flavum, which it then strikes at an angle. Alternatively, Bonica[28] recommends inserting the needle at an angle of 15 degrees to the sagittal plane and 135 degrees to the long axis of the patient. This method requires less sawing to and fro but requires a better understanding of spatial geometry.

Which Approach?

Although the midline approach may be more widely used (again, probably because of early training), several writers[6,27–30] strongly advocate the paramedian. This approach does not require significant back flexion and presents no problems when the spinous processes are close together. Another advantage is the very oblique angle at which the needle attains the epidural space. This angle eases passage of the catheter, which then passes smoothly up the epidural space in the midline. In contrast, when using the midline approach, the catheter is more likely to be deflected off center.[6] Also, the oblique entry of the needle with the paramedian approach should, in theory, minimize the chance of dural puncture. Experience suggests, however, that this is not so. Also, Carrie[27] claims that teaching the technique is easier because the ligamentum flavum is the same depth as the lamina. Estimating when the oblique needle will strike the lamina, however, requires instant trigonometry. Bromage[2] also points out that the periosteum is sensitive and should not be "struck," as this technique often requires.[27] Furthermore, a number of anesthesiologists have found teaching the midline approach to many trainees a relatively simple and trouble-free process.[28,31,32] Moreover, Griffin and Scott,[33] in a randomized trial, found no significant difference in success or complication rate between the two approaches. They did report that the paramedian approach was more painful. Also, when several attempts were necessary, the midline approach was more likely to succeed when the paramedian had failed.[33]

Reportedly, when using the midline approach, cavitation in interspinous ligaments may cause false LOR.[34] Such degenerative changes are, however, expected only in the older age group. False LOR in the obstetric population is more likely to occur because the needle tip strays from the midline. To invoke ligamentous cavitation is to seek an excuse for poor technique. The boggy LOR produced by entry into the paravertebral muscles is unlike the clear-cut sign of entry into the epidural space (vide infra).

METHODS OF IDENTIFYING THE EPIDURAL SPACE

The Negative-Pressure Sign

Negative pressure develops in most individuals on first entry into the epidural space. This finding has been ascribed to

- Negative pressure transmitted from the pleural cavity
- Flexion of the spine, stretching the epidural space
- Indenting the dura with the needle tip

Although the latter phenomenon has been seen in the dog,[35] knowledge of human anatomy (Fig. 18-7 and 18-8) suggests that such indenting could only result

from poor technique. The following methods of identifying the space make use of negative pressure:

- *The Hanging Drop Sign.* First described by Gutierrez,[36] a drop of liquid is placed on the open end of the epidural needle. Upon entry into the epidural space, the drop is sucked in.
- *Odom's Indicator.* This is a glass tube containing liquid, with or without an air bubble. On entry into the epidural space, the contents of the tube move inwards.
- *The Macintosh Balloon.* An air-filled balloon is attached to the epidural needle. The balloon deflates upon entry into the epidural space.

More detailed description of these and other gadgets may be found in textbooks.[2] I do not advocate their use for several reasons. First, the negative-pressure sign is unreliable. Second, they are far too fiddly to be appropriate for what should be a quick and simple procedure. Third, any gadget may fail for technical reasons; simplicity is the hallmark of success.

Loss of Resistance

There is almost complete resistance to injection of fluid through an epidural needle as it passes through the interspinous and flaval ligaments. As the needle tip emerges in the epidural space, the resistance to injection disappears abruptly.

Using the midline approach, insert the epidural needle, with its stylet in place, until its tip lodges firmly in the interspinous ligament. (When using the paramedian approach, advance the needle until it reaches the ligamentum flavum.) Then remove the stylet and attach a fluid-filled syringe. The syringe used can be 5 to 20 mL in size (but see section on choice of syringe). It should be free from leaks, and its plunger *must* run freely within the barrel. This end is best achieved by using a high-quality product; if using a glass syringe, the barrel and plunger must be perfectly clean, and, if necessary, polished with a lint-free swab before use.

Loss of Resistance May Be Detected Using Saline or Air in the Syringe

Loss of Resistance Using Physiologic Saline

Using a liquid-filled syringe, the epidural needle may be advanced solely by pressure on the plunger of the syringe.[1] This approach works best with either a

20-mL glass syringe containing 10 mL of saline or a 10-mL plastic syringe filled with saline. The smaller the syringe, the easier it is to inject fluid against the resistance of the ligaments. Advance the syringe slowly and steadily by pushing on the plunger. Apply an inertia or breaking force by bracing the nondominant hand against the patient's back while holding the hub of the needle. The dominant hand provides forward movement by pressure on the plunger of the syringe. Once you reach the epidural space, injection of fluid becomes possible and forward movement of barrel and needle stop automatically. As soon as LOR occurs, release the pressure on the plunger so that you inject only a minimal amount of saline. Detach the syringe; any drip back of saline is transient and readily distinguished from cerebrospinal fluid. Once in the space, disturb the epidural needle as little as possible to minimize trauma to the dura.

A modification of this technique may be necessary in the occasional patient whose ligaments do not provide absolute resistance to injection of saline. As before, the nondominant hand prevents sudden movement. Now, however, provide forward motion using the fingertips of the dominant hand on the barrel of the syringe. Simultaneously, use the palm of that hand to apply more modest pressure to the plunger. You will feel and see the plunger move forward on entry into the epidural space. This, the true Doughty technique,[32] also prevents the inappropriate injection of saline into ligaments and paravertebral muscles.

If unsure whether LOR has occurred, use a small air-filled syringe. Pressure on the plunger will elicit bounce if the needle tip is in ligament or muscle.

Loss of Resistance Using Air

This technique is commonly practiced using a winged needle, and both the patient and operator are in the sitting position. Attach an air-filled syringe to the needle hub. Brace both hands against the patient's back. Hold the wings of the needle and advance it in a series of quantal steps. Pause between each step to apply pressure on the plunger. If the plunger bounces, advance the needle another step before testing again for LOR.

Some anesthesiologists use a hybrid technique in which they hold and advance the needle using one hand and hold the syringe in the other. This is slightly less tedious, because bounce may be elicited repeatedly without having to pause between advances. Alternately, apply continuous pressure to the plunger of the syringe while advancing the needle with the nondominant hand.[2]

Air or Saline?

Protagonists for air claim that the endpoint is clear and that confusion does not arise when cerebrospinal fluid drips back. Regrettably, however, the technique is tedious for the novice; he or she may become impatient. As the epidural space approaches, each successive advance, instead of becoming smaller and more cautious, becomes greater. Eventually the needle passes from ligament to subarachnoid space in a single quantal leap! Not surprisingly, proponents of LOR with air regard dural puncture as inevitable during the learning process. Not so the devotees of the saline technique, who detect LOR using *continuous* steady pressure on the plunger. In practice, the endpoint using LOR with the saline is easily recognized and taught to the novice. The difference between a few drops of saline and a steady drip of cerebrospinal fluid is readily distinguished. A novice who has made several attempts at catheter insertion may, it is true, have injected a fair amount of saline. This fluid can then be distinguished from cerebrospinal fluid by testing for sugar.

The use of air for LOR has several more serious drawbacks, which follow:

- Accidental intravenous injection of air may occur.[37] This event, although rarely dangerous, is certainly less safe than intravenous saline injection.
- Air injected into the epidural space with the patient in the sitting position may cause severe pain in the neck and shoulders.[38,39]
- Injected air may cause subcutaneous emphysema.[40,41]
- Large amounts of epidural air may cause symptomatic nerve root compression.[42]
- Epidural bubbles may cause incomplete analgesia.[43–45] Dalens[44] points out that air is 80% nitrogen, which is markedly insoluble in all compartments of the body. Furthermore, he has shown that, in children, the position of air bubbles localized using contrast medium, coincides with areas of poor analgesia.[43] This problem is not confined to children. Unblocked segments are significantly more common in parturients when using air instead of saline for LOR.[45] These unblocked segments persist on the uppermost side, suggesting an effect of gravity on the air bubbles.

The Syringe

Many operators prefer glass to plastic syringes because resistance to movement between plunger and barrel is less with the former. Sticking, however, sometimes occurs with glass syringes.[46] Clearly, the saline LOR technique falls down with a sticky syringe. Because of this danger, Bromage[2] suggests that glass syringes may be suitable for LOR with air. A sticking plunger would be detected when bounce was attempted. He feels that plastic syringes, however, may be preferable for LOR with saline. A glass syringe can, nevertheless, be rendered as proof against this risk. The syringe should be of high quality and either new, as in a commercial epidural set, or properly cleaned, free of "lubricant" and sterilized with plunger and barrel separate. Immediately before use, test it carefully for both absence of leak and smooth running. If necessary, polish it with a lint-free gauze swab. Both dryness and polishing can improve the free running of a glass syringe.[47] In the United States, several companies manufacture silicone-treated plastic syringes usable for LOR with air or saline. The barrel of these syringes produces very little drag on the plunger. In clinical use, they perform very much like glass syringes. They require no special attention or preparation before use.

The larger the syringe, the clearer the endpoint of LOR with saline. Smaller syringes are more likely to allow injection of fluid against the resistance of the ligaments. An ideal method may be to use a 20-mL syringe containing 10 mL of saline. The plunger thereby protrudes a comfortable and safe distance beyond the barrel. This technique has been popularized in the United Kingdom by Doughty.

The Needle

A Tuohy (or Hustead) needle is used. These needles possess curved and fairly blunt tips. The curve assists the passage of the catheter around the corner into the epidural space. Both curve and bluntness reduce the chance of dural puncture. The bluntness also lessens the chance of shearing off the catheter tip in the space. A 16- to 18-gauge needle commonly is used, with the wider bore being most popular in the United Kingdom. Recognition of the epidural space and passage of the catheter are easier with the larger needles. Set against these advantages, headache following accidental dural puncture will be more severe with the larger needle. Using the larger needle, which greatly facilitates the procedure, requires employing a technique that minimizes the frequency of dural puncture. Like epidural catheters, Tuohy needles used in the United Kingdom are graduated in centimeters so that the depth of the epidural space and, hence, the length of the catheter in the space can be measured with precision.

Should the Needle Bevel Be in the Transverse or the Sagittal Plane?

When using the paramedian approach, the needle normally passes through the ligamentum flavum with the hole facing cephalad and, when angled sharply, posteriorly. When using the midline approach, however, the question arises whether the bevel of the needle should be perpendicular or parallel to the long axis of the spine. This choice makes no difference to the occurrence of backache following a normal epidural. Inserting the needle bevel parallel, then rotating it after entry into the epidural space to allow cephalad passage of the catheter, may increase trauma to the dura.[48] This maneuver, in theory, might increase the chance that the catheter will penetrate the dura. A delayed total spinal or arachnoid tear and subsequent "unexplained" headache[15] might occur. Bromage[2] suggests that rotating the needle in the epidural space is unnecessarily traumatic. However, experience with spinal anesthesia, and the findings of Norris *et al*[49] show that headaches are more frequent and more severe when the needle pierces the dura with the bevel perpendicular to its longitudinal fibres. The dural puncture hole is smaller when splitting, not cutting, the dural fibres. Thus, inserting the needle with the hole facing cephalad may be simplest and, in some respects, most satisfactory, but it requires a technique that minimizes the risk of dural puncture.

The Catheter

The catheter needs to contain a stylet only if it is unmanageably fine. It must be soft to minimize trauma to the epidural veins, but not so soft that it will not travel easily up the epidural space. A relatively large catheter, such as can pass through a 16-gauge needle, can hold a steady course without the aid of a stylet. By itself, however, such a catheter cannot penetrate the dura.[16]

Should an Epidural Catheter Have a Single End-hole or Three Helical Holes and a Smooth Tip?

Three-holed catheters have been criticized because they may be partially in a blood vessel or in the subarachnoid space.[50] Accidental intravenous or intrathecal injection of local anesthetic is not, however, reported more frequently with these than with single end-holed catheters. Aspiration down a three-holed catheter is very much less likely to give rise to a false-negative test of intravascular or intrathecal placement than a single-holed catheter.[51] Indeed, some claim that intravascular placement will never be unnoticed using three-holed catheters.[52,53] By contrast, false-negative aspiration is not uncommon with single end-holed catheters. Intravascular placement of these catheters is reliably detected only by using air injection and precordial Doppler ultrasound.[54,55] Helical-holed catheters were designed to allow local anesthetic to spread evenly in the epidural space. Unilateral block and missed segments occur more commonly using single end-holed catheters.[53] In addition, end-holed catheters are more likely to cause pain on insertion than side-holed catheters.[53]

OTHER COMPLICATIONS THAT MAY BE RELATED TO TECHNIQUE

Unblocked Segments

Missed segments have been reported to occur with a frequency of 6.7% when administering epidural analgesia in labor.[56] Unilateral or inadequate block may occur more frequently. Unsatisfactory analgesia develops more than twice as often when using single end-holed catheters compared with three-holed catheters.[52] This problem seems largely overcome when using saline as opposed to air for LOR.[45] Indeed, when using three-holed catheters and saline consistently over many thousands of blocks, I cannot recall a true missed segment. Because of the normal site of labor pain over dermatomes T-11 and T-12, a block that fails to rise sufficiently high on one side may be misinterpreted as a missed segment, and the catheter should be resited in a higher space.

Dural Puncture

A high incidence of accidental dural puncture is sometimes accepted as inevitable in inexperienced hands. Doughty,[57] however, suggests that this view is unjustifiable. He has reported a frequency of unintended dural puncture of 0.4% over nearly 5000 blocks, while instructing carefully a new trainee every 2 weeks.[26] He taught the midline approach with a 16-gauge Tuohy needle. He directed the hole of the needle cephalad. His trainees applied LOR by exerting continuous pressure on the plunger of a 20-mL syringe containing 10 mL of saline. His patients were recumbent, and the operator stood. Using the same technique, Reynolds[32] reported a dural puncture rate of 1 in 500 over 8000 epidurals carried out by all

grades of staff, with no particular grade overrepresented. Macdonald[31] reported a dural tap rate among her trainees of 0.276% using LOR with saline compared to 1.6% when using LOR with air. By contrast, using the lateral or sitting position, a 17- or 18-gauge Hustead needle, and air or saline for LOR, a 2.6% dural puncture rate has been reported among first-year residents.[49] In the past, others have admitted an initial rate of 7.6%, with 3.2% in the second thousand and 0.9% thereafter.[26]

Accidental dural puncture is highly undesirable in the parturient and should be regarded as an avoidable event.[26] There is no doubt that with good technique and early, close supervision of trainees, it can be extremely rare. Whenever it occurs, the perpetrator should be asked to try to work out the cause, and his or her technique should be reviewed carefully.

REFERENCES

1. Sicard JA, Forestier J. Radiographic method for exploration of the extradural space using lipiodol. Revue Neurologique 1921;28:1264.
2. Bromage P. Epidural analgesia, 2nd ed. Philadelphia: WB Saunders, 1978.
3. Reynolds F. Spinal and epidural block. In: Churchill Davidson HC, ed. A practice of anæsthesia, 5th ed. London: Lloyd Luke, 1984:856.
4. Galea PJ. Avoiding accidental dural punctures. Br J Anaesth 1988;60:347.
5. Zarzur E. Anatomic studies of the human lumbar ligamentum flavum. Anesth Analg 1984;63:499.
6. Gaynor PA. The lumbar epidural region: Anatomy and approach. In: Reynolds F, ed. Epidural and spinal blockade in obstetrics. London: Bailliere Tindall, 1990:3.
7. Meiklejohn BH. Distance from the skin to the lumbar epidural space in an obstetric population. Reg Anesth 1990;15:134.
8. Sutton DN, Linter SPK. Depth of extradural space and dural puncture. Anaesthesia 1991;46:97.
9. Cork RC, Kryc JJ, Vaughan RW. Ultrasonic localization of the lumbar epidural space. Anesthesiology 1980;52:513.
10. Currie JM. Measurement of the depth to the extradural space using ultrasound. Br J Anaesth 1984;56:345.
11. Savolaine ER, Pandya JB, Greenblatt SH, et al. Anatomy of the human lumbar epidural space: New insights using CT epidurography. Anesthesiology 1988;68:217.
12. Husemeyer RP, White DC. Topography of the lumbar epidural space. A study in cadavers using injected polyester resin. Anaesthesia 1980;35:7.
13. Blomberg RG, Olsson SS. The lumbar epidural space in patients examined with epiduroscopy. Anesth Analg 1989;68:157.
14. Asato F, Hirakawa N, Oda M, et al. A median epidural

septum is not a common cause of unilateral epidural blockade. Anesth Analg 1990;71:427.

15. Reynolds F, Speedy H. The subdural space: The third place to go astray. Anæsthesia 1990;45:120.

16. Hardy PAJ. Can epidural catheters penetrate dura mater? An anatomical study. Anaesthesia 1986;41:1146.

17. Blomberg RG. The lumbar subdural extra-arachnoid space of humans: An anatomical study using spinaloscopy in autopsy cases. Anesth Analg 1987;66:177.

18. Lubenow T, Keh-Wong E Kristof K, et al. Inadvertent subdural injection: A complication of an epidural block. Anesth Analg 1988;67:175.

19. Lee JJ, Parry H. Bacterial meningitis following spinal anaesthesia for caesarean section. Br J Anaesth 1991; 66:383.

20. Sansome AJT, Barnes GR, Barrett RF. An unusual presentation of meningitis as a consequence of inadvertent dural puncture. Int J Obstet Anesth 1991;1:35.

21. Stone PA, Kilpatrick AWA, Thorburn J. Posture and epidural catheter insertion. Anaesthesia 1990;45:920.

22. Vincent RD, Chestnut DH. Which position is more comfortable for the parturient during identification of the epidural space? Int J Obstet Anesth 1991;1:9.

23. Messih MNA. Epidural space pressures during pregnancy. Anaesthesia 1981;36:775.

24. Shearer ES. Trauma to epidural veins: the role of posture [letter]. Anaesthesia 1990;45:788.

25. Merry AF, Cross JA, Mayadeo SV, et al. Posture and the spread of extradural analgesia in labour. Br J Anaesth 1983;55:303.

26. Doughty A. Epidural analgesia in labour: The past, the present and the future. J R Soc Med 1978;71:879.

27. Carrie LES. The approach to the epidural space [letter]. Anaesthesia 1971;26:252.

28. Bonica J. Continuous peridural block. Anesthesiology 1956;17:626.

29. Carrie LES. The paramedian approach to the epidural space. Technique and choice of needle [letter]. Anaesthesia 1977;32:670.

30. Blomberg RG, Jaanivald A, Walthers S. Advantages of the paramedian approach for lumbar epidural analgesia with catheter technique. A clinical trial between midline and paramedian approaches. Anaesthesia 1989;44:742.

31. Macdonald R. Dr Doughty's technique for the location of the epidural space [letter]. Anaesthesia 1983;38:71.

32. Reynolds F. Avoiding accidental dural puncture [letter]. Br J Anaesth 1988;61:515.

33. Griffin RM, Scott RPF. A comparison between the midline and paramedian approaches to the extradural space. Anaesthesia 1984;39:584.

34. Sharrock NE. Recordings of, and an anatomical explanation for, false-positive loss of resistance during lumbar extradural analgesia. Br J Anaesth 1979;51:253.

35. Aitkenhead AR, Hothersall AP, Gilmour DG, et al. Dural dimpling in the dog. Anaesthesia 1979;34:14.

36. Gutierrez A. Valor de la aspiracion liquida en el espacio peridural en la anestesia peridural. Rev Cirug 1933;12:225.

37. Naulty JS, Ostheimer GW, Datta S. et al. Incidence of venous air embolism during epidural catheter insertion. Anesthesiology 1982;57:410.

38. Heggie NW. Unexplained pain during epidural anaesthesia. Anaesthesia 1984;39:609.

39. Munro HM. Pain in the neck [letter]. Anaesthesia 1990;45:173.

40. Laman EN, McLeskey CH. Supraclavicular subcutaneous emphysema following lumbar epidural anesthesia. Anesthesiology 1978;48:219.

41. Thomas JE, Schachner S, Reynolds A. Subcutaneous emphysema as a result of loss-of-resistance identification of the epidural space. Reg Anesth 1982;7:44.

42. Kennedy TM, Ullman DA, Harte FA, et al. Lumbar root compression secondary to epidural air. Anesth Analg 1988;67:1184.

43. Dalens B, Bazin J-E, Haberer J-P. Epidural bubbles as a cause of incomplete analgesia during epidural analgesia. Anesth Analg 1987;66:679.

44. Dalens B. Gone with the wind—the fate of epidural air. Reg Anesth 1990;15:150.

45. Valentine SJ, Jarvis AP, Shutt LE. Comparative study of the effects of air or saline to identify the extradural space. Br J Anaesth 1991;66:224.

46. Butler BD, Warters RD, Elk JR, et al. Loss-of-resistance technique for locating the epidural space: Evaluation of glass and plastic syringes. Can J Anaesth 1990;37:438.

47. Leiman BC, Katz J, Salzarulo H, et al. A comparison of different methods of lubrication of glass syringes used to identify the epidural space. Anaesthesia 1988;43:397.

48. Meiklejohn BH. The effect of rotation of an epidural needle. Anaesthesia 1987;42:1180.

49. Norris MC, Leighton BL, DeSimone CA. Needle bevel direction and headache after inadvertent dural puncture. Anesthesiology 1989;70:729.

50. Beck H, Brassow F, Doehn M, et al. Epidural catheters of the multi-orifice type: Dangers and complications. Acta Anaesthesiol Scand 1986;30:549.

51. Morrison LMM, Buchan AS. Comparison of complications associated with single-holed and multi-holed extradural catheters. Br J Anaesth 1990;64:183.

52. Reynolds F. Epidural catheter migration during labour [letter]. Anaesthesia 1988;43:69.

53. Michael S, Richmond MN, Birks RJS. A comparison between open-end (single-holed) and closed-end (three lateral holes) epidural catheters. Complications and quality of sensory blockade. Anaesthesia 1989;44:578.

54. Leighton BL, Gross JB. Air: An effective indicator of intravenously located epidural catheters. Anesthesiology 1989;71:848.

55. Leighton BL, Norris MC, DeSimone CA, et al. The air test as a clinically useful indicator of intravenously placed epidural catheters. Anesthesiology 1990;73:610.

56. Ducrow M. The occurrence of unblocked segments during continuous lumbar epidural analgesia for pain relief in labour. Br J Anaesth 1971;43:1172.

57. Doughty A. Inadvertent dural puncture—an avoidable accident. Anaesthesia 1979;34:116.

CHAPTER 19

Epidural Analgesia for Labor

J. Steven Naulty

Analgesia for labor, since its inception, has been a controversial subject. In 1849, one year after the introduction of inhalation anesthesia, Channing clearly stated the dilemma that still confounds obstetric anesthesiologists today. He wondered whether or not it is "reasonable to provide analgesia for a process which is not always painful and which can come to a successful conclusion (delivery) in the absence of analgesia."[1] Lumbar epidural anesthesia and analgesia have become commonly employed methods of labor pain relief. The frequent and widespread use of this technique has increased the controversy surrounding the use of major regional anesthesia during labor.

An analgesic technique used in these circumstances must, above all, be safe. In this context, "safe" implies a minimum of maternal and fetal toxic potential, combined with the least possible effect on the forces of labor and the normal process of parturition. In addition, the ideal analgesic technique will be sufficiently flexible to allow for the variability in the process of labor and delivery. Any labor may end with an instrumental or cesarean delivery. Lumbar epidural analgesia has the potential to be such a technique, but this potential has only recently been realized.

On first inspection, lumbar epidural anesthesia offers many advantages for labor analgesia. The patient remains "awake" throughout labor. She avoids the potential risks associated with the somnolence that can accompany the use of powerful systemic analgesics such as narcotics and inhalation anesthetics. These risks include excessive sedation with loss of consciousness, hypoxemia and hypercapnia, and aspiration of gastric contents.

Another advantage of lumbar epidural anesthesia is its ability to be a continuous technique. The insertion of a catheter into the epidural space allows the careful titration of analgesic effect. This property allows the analgesia provided to be truly regional. Ideally, one strives to provide the minimum amount of analgesia needed to produce comfort during labor. Changing the local anesthetic and dosing regimen alters the onset and intensity of blockade. Depending on the clinical situation, epidural analgesia can provide rapid, profound, or gradual, muted pain relief. The presence of a catheter allows analgesia to be maintained for as long as needed. This flexibility is ideal for a dynamic situation like labor. Here, analgesic requirements can change drastically within a few fetal heartbeats. Unfortunately, clinicians have not always used this potential to its fullest extent.

However, the advantages of epidural block are offset by some potential disadvantages. Epidural analgesia can adversely affect both mother and fetus. Concerns include effects on labor itself and changes in maternal hemodynamics. The absorption of local anesthetics by the fetus may produce observable and occasionally deleterious changes in the newborn. These potential problems are often overestimated in frequency and severity. The existence and significance of the disadvantages of epidural analgesia have produced a sometimes acrimonious controversy. The public (our patients) has received a distorted image of these issues. I occasionally even hear obstetricians telling women: "I had to do a cesarean delivery because you had an epidural."

Much of this misunderstanding comes from the use of large doses of epidural local anesthetics to produce anesthesia (that is, the total absence of sensation and the presence of significant motor block) during labor, which until recently has been common practice. These complications and misunderstandings can be minimized by the appropriate use of epidural analgesia (the relief only of pain, with as little sensory and motor block as possible) in the laboring parturient. This distinction is important. The following sections discuss how the use of epidural analgesia can minimize the incidence of these potential complications.

LABOR PAIN

To provide only pain relief, one must understand the pain process and the role of epidural injections of analgesic drugs in modulating this process. Stimulation of nerve receptors by tissue trauma eventually produces the sensation of pain. Stimulation of each type of receptor causes a characteristic pattern of impulses. The nature and intensity of the initiating stimulus further modulate this pattern. Nervous impulses arising from these receptors travel as "packets" of neural firings, which are conducted primarily in small myelinated and unmyelinated nerves. These packets have a frequency and duration specific for the type of pain experienced, not unlike the digital "words" that form the basis of computer architecture.

Afferent somatic and visceral sensory nerve fibers carry the "encoded" information that arises from noxious stimuli. The nerves enter the spinal cord primarily through the dorsal roots corresponding to the embryonic dermatomes from which the involved tissues developed. The afferent nerve fibers from the uterus and cervix include somatic and visceral sensory fibers that travel with the sympathetic nervous supply to the uterus. These fibers pass through the paracervical tissue, along the uterine artery, and then through the inferior, middle, and superior hypogastric plexuses to the sympathetic chain. These impulses then enter the spinal cord through the 10th, 11th, and 12th thoracic nerves.

Somatic impulses have a different "word structure" and speed of conduction than visceral impulses. These different syntaxes and pathways produce two very different types of pain sensation. Uterine contractions and cervical dilation, in the first stage of labor, produce visceral pain that has unique characteristics. Visceral pain is:

- Poorly localized
- Described as "dull and aching"
- Carried by slow conducting fibers
- Associated with low frequency firing of both conducting and internuncial neurons

Second-stage labor pain (somatic pain) is:

- Well localized
- Described as "sharp"
- Carried by rapidly conducting fibers
- Associated typically with high rates of firing of the conducting neurons

These two types of pain-information–bearing impulses also differ in their neuropharmacology. Different analgesics control these two types of pain.

Central Nervous System

Upon entering the central nervous system, pain-information–bearing nervous impulses undergo a complex modulatory process in the posterior horn of the spinal cord. Many neurotransmitters,[2] notably enkephalins, polypeptides (substance P), serotonin, gamma-aminobutyric acid (GABA), dopamine, and epinephrine, participate in the processing of pain impulses. The interaction between these neurotransmitters determines if a painful stimulus will ultimately produce the sensation of pain. If sufficient inhibitory modulation takes place, the sensation will be perceived as something other than pain (*i.e.*, pressure or pruritus). Excitatory modulation produces disproportionate responses to otherwise ordinary stimuli, as found in causalgia and similar hyperesthetic syndromes.

If this polysynaptic modulation in the dorsal horn permits upward transmission of impulses whose information content is "pain," these impulses then exit from the dorsal horn and travel rostrally, primarily via the neo-and paleo-spinothalamic tracts. These impulses can then stimulate the reticular formation and tegmental tract in the brain stem, where they will evoke the typical physiologic responses to pain (*i.e.*, tachycardia, hyperventilation, increased blood pressure, release of catecholamines and hypothalamic hormones). The nervous impulses continue upward to the ventral posterolateral nucleus of the thalamus. From there, fibers project to the sensory cortex for localization and discrimination of pain. Importantly, nerve fibers also *arise* from the medulla, thalamus, and cortex and project to the dorsal horn of the spinal cord, where they release modulatory neurotransmitters. This descending input creates a feedback loop by which pain may provide analgesia for itself. This feedback loop system seems particularly effective during pregnancy. Measured pain thresholds are two to three times higher for pregnant than for nonpregnant subjects.[3] Increased concentrations of either progesterone or its metabolites may contribute to this elevation of pain tolerance.[4] In addition, pregnancy may alter the production of, or sensitivity to, cerebrospinal fluid (CSF) and spinal cord inhibitory neurotransmitters.[5] These compounds can induce down modulation of the response to noxious impulses received in the dorsal horn.

Applying local anesthetics, inhibitory neurotransmitters or their analogues (*i.e.,* opioids), or antagonists of excitatory neurotransmitters (clonidine) to the spinal cord by epidural injection can diminish the transmission of pain to consciousness. This action forms the physiologic and pharmacologic basis for the use of opioids and other drugs in the central nervous system to produce analgesia, especially the spinal cord.

TECHNIQUE

Many methods have been described to identify and cannulate the epidural space (see Chap. 18). Only details of technique unique to labor analgesia are presented here. These include the choice of drugs and dosing techniques to optimize labor analgesia and minimize side effects.

Catheter Location

The first task after successful identification and cannulation of the epidural space is the confirmation of proper placement of the epidural catheter. Improper placement of an epidural catheter may produce severe, life-threatening complications. For example, epidural doses of local anesthetics in the subarachnoid space may lead to rapid, total spinal anesthesia. Intravascular injections may result in complications ranging from inadequate analgesia to lethal cardiovascular collapse. Placement outside the epidural space provides no analgesia at all. Many techniques have been advocated for identification of these potential problems, but most, if not all, share a common feature. The development of expected symptoms or signs of improper placement has considerable positive predictive value. A negative test

may mean that the catheter is properly placed, but it also can mean that the test merely failed to provoke a positive result (a false–negative response). Therefore, a useful test for proper epidural placement should have as low an incidence of these false–negative results as possible. The remainder of the technique should minimize the likelihood and severity of complications, should they occur.

Aspiration

To detect subarachnoid or intravascular catheter placement, aspirate the catheter with a syringe before every injection. This task is best done with gentle negative pressure, using a small (2–3 mL) syringe. Allow adequate time for blood or cerebrospinal fluid to traverse the catheter, a process that may take 30 seconds.[6] If blood returns into the syringe, remove and replace the catheter.

Cerebrospinal fluid is more difficult to detect. It may be confused with local anesthetic present in the epidural space from previous injections. Two easy methods are available to decide, bedside, the nature of the aspirate:

1. Cerebrospinal fluid contains glucose. If the aspirate is placed on a blood–glucose test strip and the characteristic blue color develops, the catheter is in the subarachnoid space. (Editor's Note: Aspirate from more than 50% of appropriately placed epidural catheters may test positive for glucose. Based on its protein content, this glucose may originate in the CSF. This CSF may enter the subarachnoid space from subarachnoid villi that protrude into the epidural space.)[7]
2. Local anesthetics precipitate at high pH. When placed in thiopental solution or sodium bicarbonate, a white precipitate forms if the aspirate is local anesthetic, while CSF remains in solution.

Remember, an aspiration that does not result in the return of fluid is merely a negative aspiration. It does not mean that the catheter is properly located in the epidural space. After aspiration, test doses of local anesthetic or other substances further help to confirm proper catheter placement.

Test Dose

The idea of test dosing an epidural catheter is a simple one. A substance is injected that will produce one physiologic effect when placed into the epidural space and a different effect when injected into CSF or a blood vessel.

DETECTION OF SUBARACHNOID INJECTION

Local anesthetics are most often used to detect subarachnoid catheter placement (following negative aspiration). The dose of local anesthetic injected should produce the signs and symptoms of subarachnoid block (Table 19-1), but not a life-threatening high spinal. Isobaric local anesthetic 1–2 mL is an effective test (Fig. 19-1).[8] However, careful attention to detail is vitally important. First, allow sufficient time to elapse for the development of subarachnoid blockade. Let at least 2 to 3 minutes pass after the injection before testing for block. Second, the commonly used doses and concentrations of local anesthetic test solutions may never produce signs and symptoms of motor blockade. Observe the patient carefully for subtle signs and symptoms of sensory blockade. In laboring women, the rapid (within one contraction) relief of labor pain after test dose injection suggests subarachnoid injection. Also, observe the patient for changes in temperature sensation in the dermatome where the catheter lies (most often L-1–2). Allow a few drops of local anesthetic solution to fall on the involved dermatome and ask whether or not the liquid feels cool to the patient.

DETECTION OF INTRAVASCULAR INJECTION

Detection an intravascular catheter can prove much more difficult than diagnosing a subarachnoid catheter. First, the consequences of the intravascular injection of large amounts of local anesthetic are truly severe and, especially in pregnancy, are occasionally lethal. Intravenous injection of as little as 20–25 mg of bupivacaine has been reported to induce fatal cardiovascular collapse.[9] Local anesthetics themselves, catecholamines, and most recently, air, have all been proposed as intravenous epidural test doses.

Local Anesthetics. The intravascular injection of local anesthetics leads to a dose-related spectrum of signs and symptoms (Fig. 19-2), ranging from tinnitus and excitement to seizures and cardiovascular collapse. 2-Chloroprocaine, prilocaine, and lidocaine most reliably produce symptoms of systemic injection.[10] Bupivacaine can yield an undependable prodrome, and seizures are not infrequently the presenting symptom of intravascular injection.[11] After each injection of any local anesthetic, observe the patient carefully for subtle signs of systemic toxicity (giddiness, shivering, drowsiness) for at least 2 to 3 minutes

Remember, a lack of response to a small dose of local anesthetic is not a guarantee of proper catheter placement.[6] As with aspiration, a negative response merely means that the patient did not respond, not that the catheter is properly located. Each injection of local anesthetic is a test dose. Never give a dose of drug that could produce a seizure. Fractionated doses allow titration of the amount of drug for the desired effect. Divided doses do not provide any less effective analgesia or anesthesia than that produced by large boluses of drug.[12]

Catecholamines. Many experts recommend using catecholamines, most commonly epinephrine, as indicators of an intravascular catheter.[13] However, chronotropic test doses have many limitations in laboring women. Catecholamines do not produce a predictable tachycardia in parturients. During gestation, the chronotropic response to β-receptor stimulation declines (Fig. 19-3).[14] In painful labor, spontaneously occurring heart rate changes may completely obscure any tachycardia induced by epinephrine.[15] In addition, intravenous epinephrine may reduce uterine blood flow.[16] I find epinephrine or isopoterenol to be useful markers of intravascular injection in the operating suite or at elective cesarean delivery. However, these drugs are useless in laboring parturients. Just as with local anesthetic test doses, a negative response after epinephrine injection does not guarantee that the epidural catheter is not in a blood vessel. All subsequent drug injections should still be fractionated.

Air. Epidural injection of 5 mL of air will produce precordial Doppler detectable air emboli in 40% of women.[17] Recently Leighton *et al*[18] have observed that injection of 1 mL of air into an epidural catheter is a highly specific and sensitive marker of intravascular catheter location (see Chap. 32).

Regardless of the results of any test dose, if a catheter does not yield signs of appropriate epidural blockade, do not continue to inject more drug. Instead, remove and replace the epidural catheter.

Table 19-1

Signs and Symptoms Suggesting Subarachnoid Local Anesthetic Injection*

SIGN	SYMPTOM
Objective sensory block	Sensation of warmth in buttocks, legs, toes
Motor weakness	Relief of labor pain
Hypotension	Numbness in buttocks, legs, toes

*If any of the above arise within 5 minutes of local anesthetic injection, strongly suspect subarachnoid catheter location.

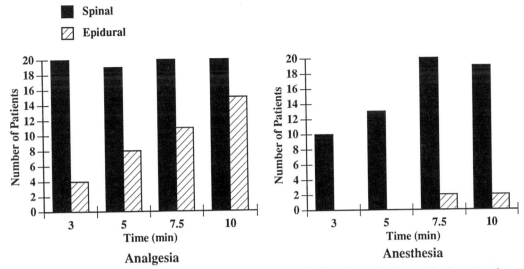

Figure 19–1. Sensory analgesia and anesthesia (to pinprick) after subarachnoid or epidural injection of 1.6 mL of 0.5% bupivacaine in term parturients. Sensory block after subarachnoid injection ranged from T-11 to C-4. (After Prince GD, Shetty GR, Miles M. Safety and efficacy of a low volume extradural test dose of bupivacaine in labour. Br J Anaesth 1989;62:503)

Methods of Administration

Until recently, intermittent bolus injection of local anesthetics was the most common way of providing labor analgesia (Table 19-2). An increasing realization of the hazards of this method of administration, plus the development of reliable and inexpensive infusion pumps, has produced widespread interest in continuous epidural infusion techniques for the relief of labor pain (Table 19-3). The use of continuous infusions of local anesthetics can produce reliable pain relief with similar or lower blood concentrations of local anesthetics than intermittent bolus injections of these drugs.[19] Infusion techniques also allow the intensity and extent of sensory block to be adjusted in promptly. Most importantly, continuous infusion reduces the possibility of sudden disastrous complications (total spinal anesthesia, massive intravascular injection with cardiovascular collapse) that can follow injections of large doses of local anesthetics outside the epidural space. If an epidural catheter enters a vein during a continuous infusion, the analgesia merely ceases, without producing central, nervous, or cardiovascular toxicity.[20] If the catheter enters the subarachnoid space, the level of sensory and motor blockade slowly rises without the sudden onset of complete subarachnoid blockade, as may occur when using bolus techniques.[21] This technique is safe and simple, but continuous monitoring of the patient for improper catheter place-

ment or pump malfunctions is essential. I highly recommend using a different type or model of pump than that used for magnesium or oxytocin infusions in the parturient. This precaution will minimize the dangers of someone adjusting the wrong pump.

The choice of drug for continuous infusion remains controversial. Solutions of lidocaine, bupivacaine, and 2-chloroprocaine all produce adequate labor analgesia.[22,23] In addition, experts differ on the concentration and volume of drug required to induce analgesia

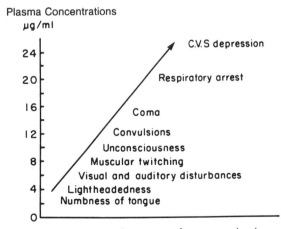

Figure 19–2. Signs and symptoms of intravenous local anesthetic toxicity.

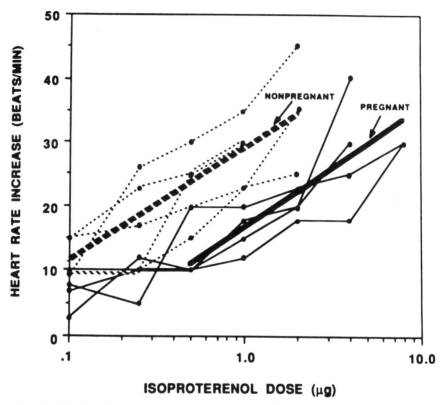

Figure 19–3. The chronotropic response to isoproterenol in term pregnant and nonpregnant women. The graph shows individual dose–response curves. Mean regression lines for pregnant and nonpregnant women were interpolated from the individual curves. The dose of isoproterenol needed to induce a 25 beat/min increase in heart rate was significantly greater in term parturients (3.6 μg) than in nonpregnant women (0.7 μg); the slopes of the mean regression lines do not differ. (After De Simone CA, Leighton BL, Norris MC, Chayen B, Menduke H. The chronotropic effect of isoproterenol is reduced in term pregnant women. Anesthesiology 1988;69:626)

before beginning the infusion. Inducing epidural blockade with 10–12 mL of a high concentration of local anesthetic (*e.g.*, 0.5% bupivacaine) is no more effective than injecting a slightly larger volume of a lower concentration of local anesthetic (*e.g.*, 0.125% bupivacaine) (Table 19-4).[24] The higher concentration of drug sometimes may provide a slightly faster onset of analgesia.[23]

The volume of local anesthetic required for continuous infusion may be less than that currently recommended. When women self-administer local anesthetic using a patient-controlled analgesia (PCA) pump (2–4 mL of 0.125% bupivacaine, every 5 to 20 minutes),

they use 6–10 mL of drug per hour. In contrast, women receiving continuous infusions managed by anesthesiologists receive 12–15 mL/h.[25] The final dose required varies widely from patient to patient.

The need to use concentrations and volumes of drug that eventually induce significant motor blockade ultimately limits the usefulness of continuous infusions of local anesthetics alone for labor analgesia.[24] An epidural technique that does not induce significant motor blockade would be a major improvement in the management of the pain of labor. Epidural opiate injections appear to offer this possibility.

Table 19-2

Local Anesthetics and Opioids Commonly Used for Intermittent Bolus Injection Labor Epidural Analgesia

CONCENTRATION	TOTAL DOSE	OPIOID	RESULT	INDICATIONS
Bupivacaine				
0.5%	5–10 mL	None	Profound sensory block Profound analgesia Good motor block	Painful labors "Trial of forceps" Midforceps rotation
0.25%	10–15 mL	None	Good sensory block Good analgesia Some motor block	Painful labors Malrotations
0.25%	5–10 mL	Fentanyl 1–3 μg/mL, Sufentanil 0.1–0.5 μg/mL	Profound sensory block Profound analgesia Some motor block	Painful labors "Trial of forceps" Midforceps rotation
0.125%	10–15 mL	Fentanyl 1–3 μg/mL	Good sensory block Good analgesia Some motor block	Normal labors Outlet forceps
0.03–0.06%	10–15 mL	Sufentanil 0.1–0.5 μg/mL	Little sensory block Good analgesia No motor block	Normal labors Outlet forceps
Lidocaine				
1–2%	10–20 mL	None (usually), may add fentanyl or sufentanil	Profound sensory block Profound analgesia, Good motor block	Painful labors "Trial of forceps" Midforceps rotation Postpartum procedures
2-Chloroprocaine				
2–3%	10–20 mL	None	Profound sensory block Profound analgesia, Good motor block	Fetal distress "Trial of forceps" Midforceps rotation

DRUGS

Local Anesthetics

Epidural injection of local anesthetics is widely used for the relief of labor pain. The exact mechanism by which epidural injections of local anesthetics produce analgesia is only poorly understood. They decrease both the number and frequency of afferent nerve firings in the vicinity of the spinal cord. These drugs most effectively reduce or eliminate somatic pain. A consequence of their action is a decrease in efferent nerve activity, leading to motor blockade. The ideal local anesthetic for labor then would reliably produce analgesia and sensory blockade while preserving motor function. In addition, minimal uptake into the maternal and fetal circulation is highly desirable.

Successful epidural analgesia for labor requires sensory blockade to at least the tenth thoracic dermatome.

Inducing this type of block with local anesthetics alone requires the administration of 10–15 mL of potent local anesthetics.[26] These large doses can lead to both maternal and fetal local anesthetic toxicity. For any given patient, the obstetric anesthesiologist strives to choose the least toxic drug that will yield effective analgesia with minimal maternal and fetal side effects.

Bupivacaine

Bupivacaine is an extremely useful local anesthetic in labor, but several concerns exist regarding its safety. Intravenous injection of bupivacaine may incite seizures, ventricular arrhythmias, and death (see Chap. 19-32). In one parturient, cardiac arrest followed intravenous injection of 25 mg of bupivacaine.[27] To ensure maternal safety, never give more than 20 mg of bupivacaine as a single bolus. Inject all local anesthetics as fractionated doses. Injection of an initial large bolus

Table 19-3

Local Anesthetics and Opioids Commonly Used for Continuous Infusion Labor Epidural Analgesia

CONCENTRATION	TOTAL DOSE	OPIOID	RESULT	INDICATIONS
Bupivacaine				
0.5%	5–10 mL/h	None	Profound sensory block Profound analgesia Good motor block	Extremely painful labor Planned instrumental delivery
0.25%	10–15 mL/h	None	Good sensory block Good analgesia Some motor block	Painful labors ? Instrumental delivery ? Preeclampsia
0.25%	5–10 mL/h	Fentanyl 1–3 µg/mL, Sufentanil 0.1–0.5 µg/mL	Profound sensory block Profound analgesia Some motor block	Painful labors ? Instrumental delivery ? Preeclampsia
0.125%	10–15 mL/h	Fentanyl 1–3 µg/mL Some motor block	Good sensory block Good analgesia	Normal labors ? Instrumental delivery
0.03–0.06%	10–15 mL/h	Sufentanil 0.1–0.5 µg/mL	Little sensory block Good analgesia No motor block	Normal labors Early labor
Lidocaine				
0.25–0.5%	7–15 mL/h	None (usually), may add fentanyl or sufentanil	Profound sensory block Profound analgesia Good motor block	Painful labors Planned instrumental delivery Postpartum procedures
2-Chloroprocaine				
0.5–1.0%	7–15 mL/h	None	Profound sensory block Profound analgesia Good motor block	Fetal distress "Trial of forceps" Midforceps rotation

does not speed onset or improve the quality of pain relief. A slow, controlled induction of epidural anesthesia can greatly reduce the risk of local anesthetic toxicity and is an essential element of safe practice.

Despite these safety concerns, bupivacaine is an excellent local anesthetic for labor analgesia. It produces relatively greater sensory block than motor block. This difference becomes more evident with more dilute concentrations of bupivacaine.[28] Several strategies help minimize the dose and, therefore, limit the potential toxicity of epidural bupivacaine:

- Fractionate doses. Give no more than 20 mg of bupivacaine at one time.
- Use the most dilute concentration of bupivacaine that provides adequate analgesia for a given patient. Recognize that each labor is different. Adjust the concentration and dose of local anesthetic to meet the analgesic requirements of a given patient (see Table 19-2).

- Use combinations of bupivacaine and opioids to lower the requirements for local anesthetic (*vide infra*).

Ropivacaine

Ropivacaine is a local anesthetic with structure and properties similar to bupivacaine. However, in animals, ropivacaine appears less toxic than bupivacaine, while retaining many of the latter drug's desirable characteristics. Limited experience is available with ropivacaine in pregnancy.[29] It appears to be a promising drug that soon may supplant bupivacaine.[30]

Lidocaine

Lidocaine provides a more rapid onset of analgesia (approximately 12 minutes) than bupivacaine. It has been extensively employed for labor analgesia (see Tables 19-2, 19-3).[31] When given by bolus administra-

Table 19–4

Onset of Blockade and Incidence of Hypotension With Equal Volumes of Concentrated or Dilute Bupivacaine

GROUP	ONSET (MIN)	TIME TO HIGHEST LEVEL	INCIDENCE HYPOTENSION (%)
0.5% Bupivacaine 3 mL + 0.08% Bupivacaine 8 mL	13.6 ± 1.8*	143.0 ± 23.1*	7
0.5% Bupivacaine 11 mL	9.1 ± 0.9	44.0 ± 5.5	37

(After MacLeod DM, Tey HK, Byers GF, Dollery WD, Tunstall ME. The loading dose for continuous infusion epidural analgesia. A technique to reduce the incidence of hypotension. Anaesthesia 1987;42:277)
Data are mean ± SE.
*$p < 0.05$ vs. 0.5% bupivacaine 11 mL

tion, significant motor block develops quickly. Continuous infusions of lidocaine also produce motor block, though at a slower rate.[32] I use lidocaine for the following:

- To provide profound motor and sensory block (*i.e.,* emergency forceps deliveries)
- To induce analgesia rapidly (*i.e.,* the multipara with tumultuous labor)
- To supply blockade of short duration (*i.e.,* patients with persistent occiput posterior presentation, to facilitate rotation of the fetal head)

2-Chloroprocaine

2-Chloroprocaine is an ester local anesthetic that produces intense motor and sensory blockade rapidly. This drug also undergoes rapid hydrolysis in plasma, with a half-life of approximately 40 seconds.[33] These properties make 2-chloroprocaine unique, because even with large, rapidly administered boluses of the drug, placental transfer is small and maternal systemic toxicity is unlikely. However, 2-chloroprocaine has several undesirable characteristics that preclude its routine use. Motor block develops rapidly, even with dilute infusions.[32] Several authors have reported a high incidence of severe back spasm following the epidural injection of 2-chloroprocaine.[34,35] Tissue toxicity, including nerve and muscle tissue lysis may be a problem, especially when large doses are given over a prolonged period.[36] Finally, 2-chloroprocaine antagonizes the action of epidural opiates.[37]

2-Chloroprocaine is useful in situations similar to those in which lidocaine is employed (see Table 19-2,19-3). If fetal acidosis or distress appears likely, the lack of apparent fetal effects of 2-chloroprocaine may be an advantage.[38]

Catecholamines

The catecholamine epinephrine often is added to local anesthetics to potentiate and prolong their effects.[39] Recently, catecholamines also have been shown to potentiate epidural opioid analgesia.[40] The action of catecholamines has long been attributed to their ability to decrease uptake of local anesthetics into the systemic circulation. However, at least some of their action comes from analgesia produced by spinal cord alpha-receptor activation. Other alpha agonists, most notably clonidine, are powerful neuraxial analgesics themselves.[41] The role of these drugs as labor analgesics is unclear. Their hemodynamic and uterine muscular effects may limit their usefulness in this setting.[42]

Opiates

Large doses of epidural morphine (7.5 mg) provide satisfactory analgesia for about 6 hours during the first stage of labor (Fig. 19-4).[43] Morphine 2–5 mg yields satisfactory analgesia in less than 50% of patients (Fig. 19-5).[44] In some reports, even the larger doses of morphine did not provide significantly better pain relief than natural childbirth techniques.[45] The long latency of morphine also is a significant problem. Studies with epidural fentanyl alone have yielded similar results.[46] In all, epidural opioids (even rapidly acting ones like fentanyl and meperidine) as sole analgesic drugs are inferior to dilute concentrations of local anesthetics.[47] Adding epinephrine to the opioid appears to increase the incidence of satisfactory analgesia slightly but not sufficiently enough to make this technique reliable.[48] Epidural opioids reduce but do not eliminate visceral pain (first stage of labor). They have no significant ef-

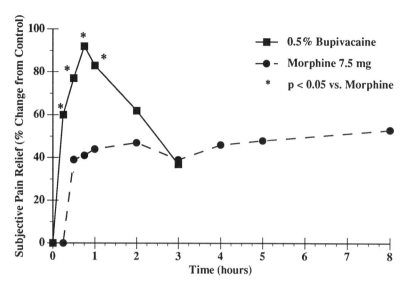

Figure 19–4. Subjective pain relief after epidural injection of either 0.5% bupivacaine 10 mL (n = 10) or morphine 7.5 mg (n = 11) in healthy laboring women. (After Hughes SC, Rosen MA, Shnider SM, Abboud TK, Stefani SJ, Norton M. Maternal and neonatal effects of epidural morphine for labor and delivery. Anesth Analg 1984;63:319)

fect in the treatment of somatic pain (second and third stages of labor). In contrast, local anesthetics produce better somatic than visceral analgesia. The combination of these two effects should provide better analgesia than either separately.

Opiate–Local Anesthetic Combinations

This combination of dilute epidural local anesthetics and opioids can produce profound analgesia. Epidural injection of a local anesthetic combined with an opioid generates a more rapid onset of more profound analgesia with little motor blockade. Pain relief then lasts

longer than after either drug alone.[49] A combination of dilute concentrations of bupivacaine and opioids significantly lowers the risk of systemic local anesthetic toxicity. Using this method, one can induce analgesia with less than 20 mg of bupivacaine. Maintaining pain relief with a continuous infusion limits the bupivacaine dose to 10–15 mg per hour. This approach seems considerably safer than bolus injections of the larger doses of local anesthetic required in the absence of opioids.

The disadvantages of this technique include the possibility of adverse maternal and fetal effects of epidural opioids. The most serious risk is the chance of maternal and fetal respiratory depression. In addition, many of these drugs are used in humans before careful animal

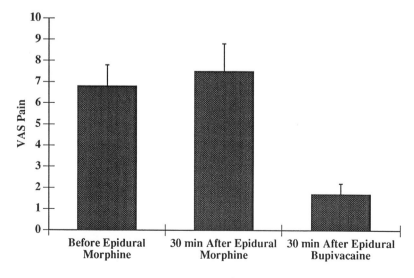

Figure 19–5. Mean ± SD pain scores of patients in labor before and after epidural injections of morphine 2 mg and 0.375% bupivacaine 8 mL. (Husmeyer RP O'Connor MC, Davenport HT, Cummings AJ, Rosankiewicz JR. Failure of epidural morphine to relieve pain in labor. Anaesthesia 1980;35:161)

toxicity studies are published. Recently, Rawal *et al* presented evidence in sheep of histopathologic toxicity and agitation, rigidity, vocalization, and restlessness, as well as one case of irreversible respiratory depression following subarachnoid of high but clinically relevant doses of butorphanol.[50]

Further study and evaluation of large numbers of mothers and neonates can prove if the advantages of this technique outweigh the potential risks. To date, several apparently safe epidural local anesthetic/opiate regimens have been described and used in thousands of women.

Specific Drug Combinations

FENTANYL–BUPIVACAINE

Fentanyl was the first opioid widely employed as an adjunct to local anesthetics for labor analgesia.[51] Early investigators postulated that fentanyl and bupivacaine had a synergistic interaction specifically at the level of the spinal cord.[52] Others, however, challenged this conclusion. They argued that any additional analgesia produced by epidural fentanyl arose from the drug's systemic, not neuraxial, effects.[53] In one study, bupivacaine 0.25% with fentanyl 5 µg/mL produced the same degree of pain relief as 0.25% bupivacaine alone (Fig. 19-6).[54] Since 0.25% bupivacaine alone can provide excellent labor analgesia, however, this study could not detect any improvement related to the epidural fentanyl.

In a cleverly designed clinical study, Reynolds *et al*[47] attempted to elucidate the site of action of fentanyl injected into the epidural space. Parturients who received epidural fentanyl 80 µg with the initial dose of 0.25%

bupivacaine had more rapid and longer-lasting analgesia than patients who received intravenous fentanyl 80 µg at the time of epidural injection of local anesthetic (Fig. 19-7). They concluded that epidural fentanyl has a specific spinal effect; it does not merely produce systemic analgesia.

Recently, the use of increasingly dilute local anesthetic/opiate solutions has become popular. Investigators have attempted to determine the minimum amount of bupivacaine and fentanyl necessary to produce satisfactory analgesia.[19,55] One study compared continuous epidural infusion of 0.0625% (1/16%) bupivacaine with fentanyl 2 µg/mL to an infusion of 0.125% (1/8%) bupivacaine alone (Fig. 19-8). During the first stage of labor, 88% of the women in the bupivacaine–fentanyl group and 95% of the women in the bupivacaine-only group had excellent or good analgesia (p = NS). During the second stage, 59% of the women in the bupivacaine–fentanyl group and 66% of the women in the bupivacaine group rated their analgesia as excellent or good (p = NS). However, women who received bupivacaine alone were much more likely to have significant motor block at full cervical dilatation (p < 0.001). The groups did not differ in duration of the second stage of labor, duration of pushing, position of the vertex before delivery, method of delivery, Apgar scores, or umbilical cord blood–gas and acid–base values. Other investigators have reported similar results (Table 19-5).[55] The addition of fentanyl roughly doubles the analgesic efficacy of continuously infused bupivacaine (*i.e.*, 0.0625% bupivacaine with fentanyl is as potent as 0.125% bupivacaine).

An initial dose of fentanyl 50 µg combined with 0.25% or 0.125% bupivacaine can produce good initial

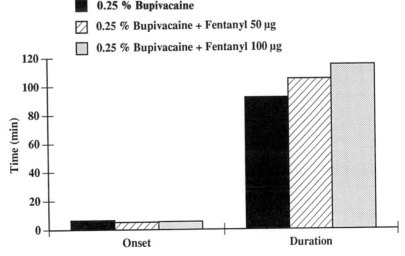

Figure 19–6. Onset and duration of labor analgesia in term parturients receiving epidural injection of 0.25% bupivacaine 9 mL with 0, 50, or 100 µg fentanyl. Neither dose of fentanyl significantly shortened the latency or prolonged the duration of 0.25% bupivacaine. (Cohen SE, Tan S. Albright GA, Halpern J. Epidural fentanyl/bupivacaine mixtures for obstetric analgesia. Anesthesiology 1987;67:403)

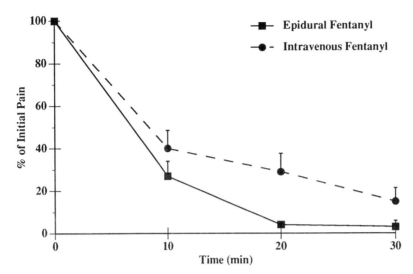

Figure 19–7. Reduction in labor pain following epidural or intravenous injection of fentanyl 80 μg. All woman also received an epidural injection of bupivacaine 12 mg. Women in the epidural group had significantly better pain relief despite lower blood concentrations of fentanyl. These data strongly suggest that epidural fentanyl has a direct spinal action. (After Vella LM, Willatts DG, Knott C, Lintin DJ, Justins DM, Reynolds F. Epidural fentanyl in labor. An evaluation of the systemic contribution to analgesia. Anaesthesia 1985;40:741)

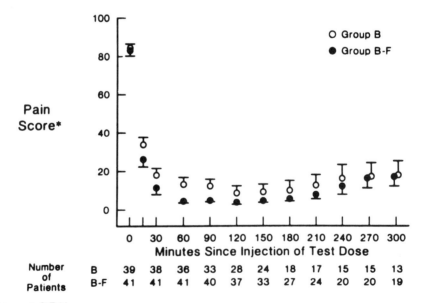

Figure 19–8. Mean (± SE) pain scores during labor in women receiving continuous infusion epidural analgesia for labor. Group B women received 0.125% bupivacaine at 12.5 mL/h. Group B-F women received 0.0625% bupivacaine with 2 μg/mL fentanyl at 12.5 mL/h. Both groups had similar degrees of pain relief. Group B women had significantly more motor block at complete cervical dilation. (After Chestnut DH, Owen CL, Bates JN, Östman LG, Choi WW, Geiger MW. Continuous infusion epidural analgesia during labor: A randomized, double-blind comparison of 0.0625% bupivacaine/0.0002% fentanyl versus 0.125% bupivacaine. Anesthesiology 1988;68:754)

Table 19–5

Effects of the Addition of Fentanyl on the Quality and Duration of Epidural Bupivacaine Labor Analgesia

QUALITY OF ANALGESIA (%)	0.125% BUPIVACAINE + 1:800,000 EPINEPHRINE	0.125% BUPIVACAINE + 1:800,000 EPINEPHRINE + FENTANYL 50 µg	0.125% BUPIVACAINE + 1:800,000 EPINEPHRINE + FENTANYL 100 µg
Excellent	5.7	6.6	43.3*
Good	65.7	66.6	46.6
Incomplete	22.8	13.3†	3.3†
Duration of analgesia (min)	55.0 ± 7.0	93.0 ± 9.0*	106.0 ± 8.0*
Number of redoses	7.3 ± 0.15	4.3 ± 0.02†	3.7 ± 0.15
Total bupivacaine dose (mg)	109.5 ± 1.3	64.0 ± 0.1	55.0 ± 1.5

(After Celleno D, Capogna G. Epidural fentanyl plus bupivacaine 0.125 per cent for labour: Analgesic effects. Can J Anaesth 1988;35:375)
*p < 0.05 versus bupivacaine alone and bupivacaine + fentanyl 50 µg
†p < 0.05 versus bupivacaine alone

analgesia in most laboring parturients. A continuous infusion of 0.125% bupivacaine with 1–2µg/mL fentanyl at 10–15 mL/h will maintain good pain relief throughout parturition (see Table 19-3). Further lowering the fentanyl dose or concentration of local anesthetic may not produce completely reliable analgesia. No adverse effects on either the mother or neonate have been attributed to this technique. (Editor's Note: I find a combination of 0.05% bupivacaine with 1.5 µ/mL fentanyl and 1:800,000 epinephrine very effective for continuous epidural infusions.)

SUFENTANIL–BUPIVACAINE

Epidural sufentanil combined with 0.25% bupivacaine also provides good labor analgesia.[56] Patients given sufentanil 20–30 µg combined with 10 mL 0.25% bupivacaine had a faster onset of more profound, longer lasting analgesia than those who received lower doses or no sufentanil. Sufentanil 50 µg also improves the analgesic efficacy of 0.125% bupivacaine.[57] Women who received epidural sufentanil had significantly better pain relief with less motor block than those who received bupivacaine alone.

Van Steenberge *et al*[58] have attempted to identify the optimum dosage of sufentanil for use with bupivacaine for labor analgesia. They investigated the use of epidural sufentanil with bupivacaine and epinephrine (1:200,000) during labor in 120 patients who were randomly allocated into three groups. Each woman received an epidural injection of 0.125% bupivacaine with epinephrine 10 mL with sufentanil 0, 7.5, or 15 µg. A second injection, given upon request, was identical with the first. Then, patients received a further 10-mL injection of bupivacaine and epinephrine, if required. The addition of sufentanil significantly shortened the onset and increased the duration and intensity of analgesia (Fig. 19-9,19-10). Women receiving sufentanil needed less bupivacaine and had less motor blockade at delivery. There were no differences in Apgar scores among the three groups. Others, however, have reported changes in neonatal neurobehavioral scores in infants whose mothers received larger doses of sufenantil (30–80 µg).[59] Use caution when using large doses of sufentanil for labor analgesia until the neonatal effects are clearly understood.

Such large doses of sufentanil are unnecessary.[60] Patients who received sufentanil 5 µg with 10 mL of either 0.125%, 0.0625%, or 0.0312% bupivacaine had a significantly faster onset and longer duration of complete analgesia (a pain score of 0) than the patients receiving either 0.25% or 0.125% bupivacaine alone (Fig. 19-11). Five patients who received 0.25% bupivacaine became hypotensive and required treatment with intravenous ephedrine. No patients who received 0.0625% or 0.0312% bupivacaine with sufentanil developed hypotension. Patients in each sufentanil-containing group required approximately half the total amount of local anesthetic as in the next larger dosage group. This reduction correlated with a significant decrease in motor block. Patients who re-

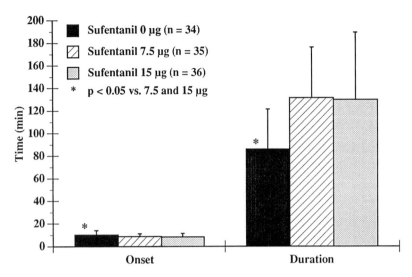

Figure 19–9. Onset and duration of pain relief after epidural injection of 12.5 mg bupivacaine (0.125%) and 0, 7.5, or 15 μg of sufentanil in 120 laboring parturients. Women receiving epidural sufentanil had significantly faster and longer-lasting analgesia. (After Van Steenberge A, Debroux HC, Noorduin H. Extradural bupivacaine with sufentanil for vaginal delivery. A double-blind trial. Br J Anaesth 1987;59:1518)

ceived 0.0312% bupivacaine with 0.5 μg/mL sufentanil exhibited no observable motor block and could ambulate without assistance (Table 19-6).

Epidural injection of sufentanil 5 μg plus bupivacaine provides safe, excellent analgesia with extremely low concentrations of bupivacaine (Table 19-7). I think epidural sufentanil 0.3–0.5 μg/mL provides more profound potentiation of bupivacaine than that observed with epidural fentanyl 30–100 μg. Extraordinarily low concentrations of bupivacaine (0.0625-0.0312%) will produce superb analgesia in more than 95% of parturients with sufentanil, but not with fentanyl.

ALFENTANIL–BUPIVACAINE

Alfentanil, with its short duration and low systemic toxic potential, offers potential advantages over longer-lasting drugs for epidural infusion during labor. However, this promise may prove false. A preliminary report described 16 laboring patients who received a continuous epidural infusion of alfentanil 30 μg/kg/h.[61] Supplementary bolus doses of alfentanil were given when needed. All patients in early labor obtained excellent pain relief rapidly. However, in five of the 16 patients, analgesia proved inadequate in the latter part of stage 1 and during the second stage. The only serious

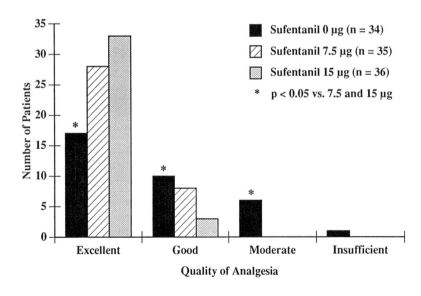

Figure 19–10. Quality of pain relief after epidural injection of 12.5 mg bupivacaine (0.125%) and 0, 7.5, or 15 μg of sufentanil in 120 laboring parturients. Women receiving epidural sufentanil had significantly better analgesia. (Van Steenberge A, Debroux HC, Noorduin H. Extradural bupivacaine with sufentanil for vaginal delivery. A double-blind trial. Br J Anaesth 1987;59:1518)

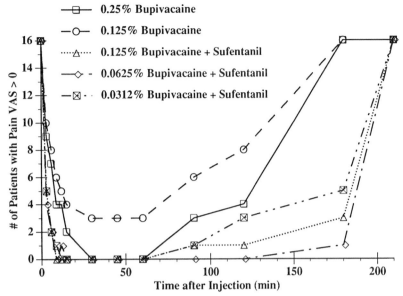

Figure 19–11. Sufentanil/bupivacaine labor analgesia. Eighty laboring multiparae received an epidural injection of 10 mL of either 0.25% or 0.125% bupivacaine alone or sufentanil 5 μg with 0.125%, 0.0625%, or 0.0312% bupivacaine. Women receiving sufentanil had faster onset of more profound analgesia than those receiving only bupivacaine. (Naulty JS, Ross R, Bergen W. Epidural sufentanil-bupivacaine for analgesia during labor and delivery. Anesthesiology 1989; 71:A842)

Table 19–6

Side Effects During Labor Analgesia With Intermittent Epidural Injection of 10 mL Bupivacaine With or Without Sufentanil 0.5 μg/mL

	0.25% BUPIVACAINE	0.125% BUPIVACAINE	0.125% BUPIVACAINE + SUFENTANIL	0.0625% BUPIVACAINE + SUFENTANIL	0.0312% BUPIVACAINE + SUFENTANIL
Systolic BP < 100 mm Hg	5/16 (31%)	1/16 (6%)[†]	1/16[†]	0/16[†]	0/16[†]
Ephedrine*	18 ± 6.7 mg	10.0 mg	—[†]	—[†]	—[†]
VAMB at Delivery*	6.5 ± 3.3	3.4 ± 2.1	2.2 ± 1.8	0.5 ± 0.8[†]	0.1 ± 0.3[†]
No. Pts with No Motor Block at Delivery	0	0	0	11[†]	15[†]
Total Dose Bupivacaine (mg)*	81.3 ± 11.8	85.2 ± 8.9	42.5 ± 6.5[†]	26.4 ± 8.1[§]	21.8 ± 6.1[§]
Total Dose Sufentanil (μg)*	0	0	17.1 ± 4.1[†]	21.3 ± 3.2[†]	19.6 ± 4.9[†]

(After Naulty JS, Ross R, Bergen W. Epidural sufentanil–bupivacaine for analgesia during labor and delivery. Anesthesiology 1989;71:A842)
*Mean ± SD
[†]p < 0.05 versus 0.25% bupivacaine
[‡]p < 0.05 versus 0.25% and 0.125% bupivacaine alone
[§]p < 0.05 versus 0.25% and 0.125% bupivacaine groups

Table 19–7

Suggested Technique for Continuous Infusion of Bupivacaine–Sufentanil for Labor Epidural Analgesia

> 1. Epidural catherization in normal fashion.
> 2. Drug solution
>   Bupivacaine 25 mg
>   Sufentanil 6–10 μg
>   Final volume 20 mL
> 3. Inject 10–12 mL of drug solution in divided doses as needed for initial pain relief.
> 4. Wait 30 minutes, if block satisfactory, begin infusion of 0.0312–0.0625% bupivacaine with 1–2 μg/mL sufentanil at 10–15 mL/h.
> 5. Continue infusion until delivery is imminent.
> 6. Stop infusion at delivery, give additional local anesthetic, if needed, for delivery and repair.
> 7. Remove catheter after delivery.

maternal side effect was nausea. Although all neonatal Apgar scores were between 7 and 10, Amiel-Tison neonatal neurobehavioral assessment detected neonatal hypotonia. In addition, others have reported significant, albeit short-lived (100 minutes), decreases in the ventilatory response to carbon dioxide following the epidural injection of alfentanil 15 μg/kg (Fig. 19-12).[62] Finally, Golub and Kuhnert[63] examined maternal–fetal disposition and neonatal respiratory effects of meperidine (2 mg/kg, IV) or alfentanil (IV infusion, 0.1 mg/kg total dose) during labor in rhesus monkeys. Fe-

tal–maternal plasma ratios were lower for alfentanil, the more highly protein-bound drug (fetal–maternal ratio 0.20 at birth versus 0.46 for meperidine). However, they found delayed elimination of alfentanil in the neonate. Neonatal plasma concentrations of alfentanil actually increased during the first 2 postnatal hours, indicating a shift from tissues to circulation. Six of 10 alfentanil-treated monkeys had suboptimal (less than 60 breath/min) respiratory rates at birth.

BUTORPHANOL–BUPIVACAINE

With our expanding knowledge of opiate receptor pharmacology, interest in the use of non–mu-receptor agonists to produce spinal analgesia also has increased.[64,65] Kappa-opiate receptors exist in the dorsal horn of the spinal cord. Epidural administration of kappa-receptor agonists can produce significant analgesia, particularly for visceral pain.

Butorphanol is an analgesic with significant kappa-receptor agonist activity. Epidural butorphanol potentiates analgesia produced by 0.25% bupivacaine.[66] The addition of butorphanol 0.2–0.3 mg/mL to 0.25% bupivacaine 10 mL significantly hastened the onset and doubled the duration of labor analgesia compared to 0.25% bupivacaine alone. Transient, low-amplitude sinusoidal fetal heart rate patterns occurred after epidural injection of butorphanol 30 mg. No adverse neonatal effects were detected. However, this study consisted of only 40 patients.

Subsequent patients have complained of somnolence and occasional dysphoria, two side effects of kappa-receptor agonism. In sheep, there is evidence of histopathologic toxicity produced by intrathecal doses

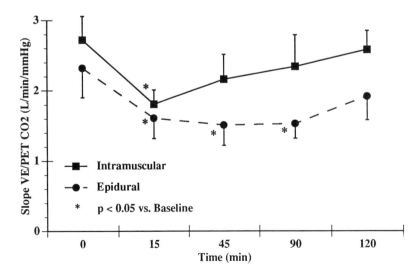

Figure 19–12. Change in ventilatory response to inhaled CO_2 after epidural and intramuscular alfentanil. Healthy males received epidural or intramuscular injections of alfentanil 15 μg/kg. The slope of the CO_2 response curve remained significantly depressed for up to 90 minutes after epidural administration. (VE/PET$_{CO_2}$ = minute ventilation/end-tidal CO_2 tension) (Penon C, Negre I, Ecoffey C, Gross JB, Levron JC, Samii K. Analgesia and ventilatory response to carbon dioxide after intramuscular and epidural alfentanil. Anesth Analg 1988;67:313)

of as little as 0.075 mg/kg butorphanol.[50] These doses also were associated with agitation, rigidity, vocalization, and restlessness, as well as one case of irreversible respiratory depression. In this model, small doses of sufentanil and nalbuphine did not produce these adverse effects. I feel that further study of this class of drugs, with particular emphasis on psychotomimetic side effects and a more careful assessment of fetal/neonatal outcome, is necessary before their widespread use for labor epidural analgesia.

EFFECTS OF EPIDURAL ANALGESIA ON LABOR AND HEMODYNAMICS

The effect of anesthesia during labor on labor itself has been a controversial subject since the very inception of obstetric anesthesia, in 1849. Channing, in his "treatise on etherization," took great pains to proclaim that etherization lacked discernible effects on the process of parturition, but merely suspended pain. This statement was quickly contradicted by objective measurements of duration of labor with and without etherization, and the controversy, which continues to this day, began.

Potential Interaction between Anesthesia and Labor

The ways in which anesthesia and labor can interact are many, but they can be initially divided into *direct* and *indirect* effects. Direct effects are those produced by anesthetic drugs on the forces of labor and include the following:

- Drug effects on uterine muscle itself
- Changes in catecholamine release
- Impairment of the expulsive forces produced by voluntary and involuntary skeletal muscular activities in the second stage of labor

Indirect effects are those induced by the impact of anesthetic drugs and techniques on the physiology of the parturient that secondarily impair labor. Such actions include the following:

- Decreased uteroplacental perfusion, produced by maternal hypotension secondary to sympathetic blockade during epidural analgesia
- Alterations in oxytocin metabolism
- Impaired reflex activity (bearing down)

Direct Effects

UTERINE MUSCLE

Inhalation anesthetics such as halothane, enflurane, and isoflurane relax uterine smooth muscle. They are employed when uterine relaxation is desired (*e.g.*, for entrapped heads during vaginal breech extraction). In contrast, the local anesthetic agents commonly employed in obstetrics produce constriction of uterine muscle. With the blood concentrations of local anesthetic normally achieved during lumbar epidural anesthesia, this effect is not noticeable. However, a direct intravenous injection will elevate uterine baseline tone and the force of contractions. This rise may be of a magnitude and duration that could produce fetal distress.

The direct effects of neural blockade on uterine smooth muscle, however, are noticeable. Uterine innervation, both sympathetic and parasympathetic, does not initiate contractions. It merely serves to regulate the intensity and duration of contraction. Sympathetic stimulation decreases, while parasympathetic stimulation increases, the force and duration of uterine contraction. Therefore, the effects of neural blockade depend on the balance of sympathetic to parasympathetic blockade produced. During modern epidural analgesia for labor, more sympathetic blockade is produced than parasympathetic (the converse is true for caudal blockade). Therefore, the overall direct effect of modern segmental epidural blockade is to increase the force and duration of uterine contractions.

SKELETAL MUSCLE

The most controversial area of interaction between obstetric anesthesia and labor involves the potential effects of reductions in skeletal muscle strength. Local anesthetics can produce significant motor blockade. The potential effects of motor impairment include the following:

- Decrease in expulsive forces generated by maternal valsalva maneuvers
- Inability of the mother to alter her position with intense motor blockade
- Reduced pelvic floor muscle tone

In the last 12 years, journals have published more than 90 papers that attempt to quantitate the significance of these effects. These studies measure forceps delivery rates, cesarean delivery rates, length of the second stage, and fetal and neonatal assessments. They describe widely varying results, ranging from no perceptible effects to tremendous impact. How can any sense be made of this information?

The reported incidence of operative delivery in patients receiving epidural analgesia varies from less than 10% to over 93%. Depending on the bias of the investigators, these results have been credited to or blamed on labor epidural analgesia. Variations in practice patterns and obstetric variables greatly increase the difficulty in controlling the many factors that determine whether an obstetrician will choose forceps or cesarean delivery. Additionally, patients who are more likely to require operative delivery also may be more likely to request epidural block for relief of labor pain. In contrast, patients with adequate pelvic dimensions who experience short, painless labors are the least likely to receive epidural analgesia. A recent, widely quoted study shows this phenomenon well. The authors found an "increase in the cesarean section rate for dystocia" in a "randomly" selected group of women who "elected" labor epidural anesthesia.[67] But, both birth weights and incidence of oxytocin induction were higher in the epidural group. Although neither factor alone correlated with the increased cesarean rate observed in the epidural group, analysis of covariance reveals that these two factors together would account for a cesarean delivery rate greater than that observed.

Anesthesia is necessary for forceps and cesarean delivery. Several studies have cited a high forceps or cesarean rate following epidural anesthesia, when, in fact, the anesthetics were administered to facilitate such deliveries![68,69] Also, the presence of adequate anesthesia allows operative delivery. In this setting, the obstetrician may be more likely to elect forceps delivery than in a woman with no anesthesia.

Some recent studies have attempted to control these and other confounding variables (*i.e.,* the indications for forceps delivery; the experience, skill, and philosophy of the obstetrician; and the acceptable duration of the second stage of labor). Various investigators have studied the effects of continuous epidural analgesia using a variety of infusion techniques under well-controlled conditions.[70–73] These authors report that infusions of dilute concentrations of local anesthetics are associated with minimal, if any, significant motor blockade in the second stage of labor. However, these studies contain too few patients to draw meaningful conclusions about the effects of these newer techniques of analgesia on labor outcome. Retrospective data supports the contention that alterations in anesthetic practice may influence the outcome of labor. At George Washington University, we have examined labor outcome following several abrupt changes in anesthetic practice.[70] Initially, a high-dose pure local anesthetic epidural technique was used. Then, our anesthesiologists changed to a low-concentration (0.125%) bupivacaine–fentanyl technique. A year later, a second change occurred. Now, we use an even lower concentration (0.0615%) bupivacaine–sufentanil technique. The incidence of both cesarean and outlet- and mid-forceps delivery declined after both changes in practice (Fig. 19-13).

Indirect Effects

DECREASED UTEROPLACENTAL PERFUSION

The most commonly observed effect of obstetric analgesia/anesthesia on labor and delivery is a transient de-

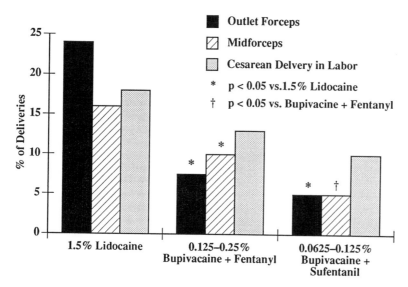

Figure 19–13. Percent of patients undergoing forceps and cesarean deliveries using three different anesthetic techniques (Naulty JS. Unpublished data.)

crease in uterine contractility secondary to decreased uterine perfusion. This change may occur without hypotension and is thought to be secondary to a decrease in cardiac output, which, in turn, is secondary to decreased preload and contractility.[73] It may, if placental perfusion is sufficiently impaired, be sufficient to produce transient fetal distress. Blockade of sympathetic nerve conduction produces vasodilation and lowers cardiac preload. The fall in myocardial contractility, in contrast, seems due to a direct action of the local anesthetics on the myocardium. This effect is most pronounced with bupivacaine,[75] and less with lidocaine and 2-chloroprocaine.[76] Small doses of ephedrine (5–10 mg, IV) will easily reverse the decreases in both preload and contractility. If fetal "stress" is evident, this treatment will quickly restore fetal condition.[77]

INTRAPARTUM MANAGEMENT

The successful insertion of an epidural catheter and the injection or infusion of analgesic drugs is frequently the easiest part of the technique. Often, the successful management of epidural analgesia for labor and its complications requires considerably more effort. The truly skilled anesthesiologist can manage these problems and make the technique work even in the most difficult situations. The most common of these problems are atypical blocks.

The Atypical Block

I apply this term to any lumbar epidural that does not yield the expected results (analgesia of an appropriate degree and location). These atypical blocks can be inadequate or too extensive.

Inadequate Analgesia

The primary cause of inadequate analgesia following insertion of a lumbar epidural catheter and the injection of an appropriate amount of drug is improper placement of the epidural catheter. There are several types of improper placement. If 2–3 mL of drug is injected into the epidural space via the epidural needle, labor pain may be partially or completely relieved. Thus, if the epidural catheter is misplaced, analgesia may still develop briefly.[78] Because the initial dose is small and subsequent injections or infusions through the catheter do not deliver drug into the epidural space, the analgesia regresses after 45 to 60 minutes. If ade-

quate doses of drug (see Table 19-2) have been injected through the catheter, but the expected degree of comfort has not developed, promptly remove and replace the catheter. This is the only reliable and uniformly successful remedy for the "epidural was working for a while, but now she's not comfortable" problem. Injection of larger than necessary doses of analgesic drugs in high concentrations in an attempt to "make the catheter work" is doomed to failure and is fraught with hazard.

The usual reason for failure of an epidural catheter to provide adequate pain relief is unrecognized intravascular catheter placement.[79] With the analgesic techniques discussed previously, the only reliable sign of intravascular catheter placement is the failure to develop the expected analgesia. The doses of local anesthetic are so small that they fail to produce reliable symptoms of intravascular injection.[6] A misguided attempt to produce analgesia with inappropriately high doses of local anesthetic can lead to significant systemic toxicity, including seizures and cardiac arrest. If you suspect intravascular placement, inject 1–2 mL of air through the catheter, while listening to maternal heart sounds with a Doppler device.[80] If you hear a distinct change in maternal heart sounds after injecting the air, the catheter is in a blood vessel (see Chap. 32). If the catheter is intravascular, remove and replace it. If the Doppler test is negative and you think the catheter is in the epidural space, carefully inject small doses of drug (0.125–0.25% bupivacaine 5–10 mL) to intensify the block.

Patients whose fetus presents in the occiput posterior location or who progress rapidly to the second stage of labor frequently require extra local anesthetic to obtain adequate pain relief. If, however, reasonable doses of local anesthetic fail to relieve the pain, replace the catheter. At best, it will be an unreliable anesthetic for further possible emergency surgical manipulations.

Excessive or Unusual Blockade

RECOGNIZED DURAL PUNCTURE

The incidence of placement of an epidural needle into the subarachnoid space (the "wet tap") varies with the facility, technique, and experience of the person performing the anesthetic. When this complication arises, there are several options. A catheter can be reinserted in the epidural space at another interspace and used successfully. However, local anesthetic may pass from the epidural space through the dural puncture into the subarachnoid space, producing greater than expected blockade. I prefer to place a subarachnoid catheter deliberately. The location of the catheter is certain. I then use reduced doses of local anesthetic and opiates to provide labor analgesia.

UNRECOGNIZED DURAL PUNCTURE

Not all subarachnoid catheters are immediately evident. If doses of local anesthetics and opiates appropriate for epidural use are accidentally introduced into the subarachnoid space, then high or total spinal anesthesia may develop. This phenomenon seems more common with continuous infusions than with bolus techniques. Aspiration of the catheter for CSF is rarely done during continuous infusions, and significant amounts of local anesthetic may be accidentally infused into the CSF. Gradually, intense and extensive sensory block develops. Significant, refractory hypotension also may arise. Dilute bupivacaine/opiate infusions rarely induce significant motor weakness. Therefore, a lack of motor block does not rule out intrathecal catheter placement. If such placement is suspected, aspirate the catheter. If CSF is present, manage the block as a subarachnoid catheter (see Chap. 20). If no CSF can be aspirated, the catheter may lie in the subdural (epiarachnoid) space. Subdural placement produces asymmetric, abnormally distributed blocks, with unusually extensive sensory analgesia for the dose of drug administered.[81] I find this type of catheter placement difficult to manage. Often, further attempts at either epidural or spinal anesthesia lead to the rapid development of total spinal anesthesia. For this reason, if I suspect a subdural catheter, I do not perform a repeat lumbar puncture until all signs of the previous block have dissipated (see Chap. 32).

SUMMARY

Epidural injections of local anesthetics with or without the addition of opiates can produce excellent, safe analgesia for labor pain. Details of technique and management are vitally important to maximize the safety and efficacy of epidural anesthesia. The most significant advantage of epidural analgesia over other techniques is its flexibility and adaptability to the dynamics of labor and labor pain. To maximize this flexibility, it is important to understand the nature of labor pain and the variety of drugs available to manage its constantly varying causes and severity. Currently, continuous infusions of dilute local anesthetics and opiates provide good labor analgesia and limit the risk of complications. As our knowledge of the neuropharmacology of pain expands, other analgesic drugs may be included in our armamentarium of epidural analgesics, but the essentials of the technique will remain the same.

REFERENCES

1. Channing W. A treatise on etherization in childbirth. Boston: William D. Ticknor and Company 1849:2.
2. Otsuka M, Yanagisawa M. Pain and neurotransmitters. Cell Mol Neurobiol 1990;10:293.
3. Gintzler AR. Activation of opioid-containing systems during gestation. Ann N Y Acad Sci 1982;398:302.
4. Ratka A, Simpkins JW. A modulatory role for luteinizing hormone-releasing hormone in nociceptive responses of female rats. Endocrinology 1990;127:667.
5. Sander HW, Gintzler AR. Spinal cord mediation of the opioid analgesia of pregnancy. Brain Res 1987;408:389.
6. McLean BY, Rottman RL, Kotelko DM. Failure of multple test doses and techniques to detect intravascular migration of an epidural catheter. Anesth Analg 1992; 74:454.
7. Waters J, Chuba JV, Ramanathan S, Turndorf H. Epidural catheter aspirate. Anesthesiology 1990;73: A959.
8. Prince GD, Shetty GR, Miles M. Safety and efficacy of a low volume extradural test dose of bupivacaine in labour. Br J Anaesth 1989;62:503.
9. Van Zundert A. Is there a need for chloroprocaine 3% and bupivacaine 0.75%? Acta Anaesthesiol Belg 1988; 39:151.
10. Grice SC, Eisenach JC, Dewan DM, Mendell G. Evaluation of 2-chloroprocaine as an effective test dose for epidural analgesia. Anesthesiology 1987;67:A627.
11. Eldor J, Frankel DZ, Olshwang D, Davsion JT. Tinnitus as an early diagnostic sign of inadvertent intravenous injection of bupivacaine epidural test dose. Resuscitation 1988;16:303.
12. Chan VW, Morely FP, Vosu FP. Predictability of spread of epidural anesthesia for cesarean section using incremental doses of lidocaine hydrocarbonate with epinephrine. Reg Anesth 1989;14:133.
13. Albright GA. Epinephrine should be used with the theraputic dose of bupivacaine in obstetrics. Anesthesiology 1984;61:217.
14. De Simone CA, Leighton BL, Norris MC, Chayen B, Menduke H. The chronotropic effect of isoproterenol is reduced in term pregnant women. Anesthesiology 1988;69:626.
15. Chestnut DH, Owen CL, Brown CK, Vandewalker GE, Weiner CP. Does labor affect the variability of maternal heart rate during induction of epidural anesthesia? Anesthesiology 1988;68:622.
16. Hood DD, Dewan DM, James FM III. Maternal and fetal effects of epinephrine in gravid ewes. Anesthesiology 1986;64:610.
17. Naulty JS, Ostheimer GW, Datta S, Knapp R, Weiss JB. Incidence of venous air embolism during epidural catheter insertion. Anesthesiology 1982;57:410.
18. Leighton BL, Norris MC, De Simone CA, Rosko T, Gross JB. Air as a clinically useful indicator of intravenously place epidural catheters. Anesthesiology 1990;73:610.
19. Chestnut DH, Owen CL, Bates JN, Ostman LG, Choi

WW, Geiger MW. Continuous infusion epidural analgesia during labor: A randomized, double-blind comparison of 0.0625% bupivacaine/0.0002% fentanyl versus 0.125% bupivacaine. Anesthesiology 1988;68:754.

20. D'Athis F, Macheboeuf M, Thomas H, et al. A comparative study of continuous and intermittent epidural analgesia for labour and delivery. Can J Anesth 1988;35:234.

21. Daley MD, Rolbin MB, Hew E, Morningstar B. Continuous epidural anaesthesia for obstetrics after major spinal surgery. Can J Anaesth 1990;37:S112.

22. Chestnut DH, Bates JN, Choi WW. Continuous infusion epidural anaglesia with lidocaine: Efficacy and influence during the second stage of labor. Obstet Gynecol 1987;69:323.

23. Naulty JS. Continuous infusions of local anesthetics and narcotics for epidural analgesia in the management of labor. Int Anesthesiol Clin 1990;28:17.

24. MacLeod DM, Tey HK, Byers GF, Dollery WD, Tunstall ME. The loading dose for continuous infusion epidural analgesia. A technique to reduce the incidence of hypotension. Anaesthesia 1987;42:277.

25. Grambling DR, Yu P, Cole C, McMorland GH, Palmer L. A comparative study of patient controlled epidural analgesia (PCEA) and continuous infusion epidural analgesia (CEIA) during labor. Can J Anaesth 1988;35:249.

26. Shnider SM, Levinson G. Anesthesia for obstetrics. In: Miller RD, ed. Anesthesia. 3rd ed. New York: Churchill Livingston 1990:1855.

27. Albright GA. Cardiac arrest following regional anesthesia with etidocaine or bupivacaine. Anesthesiology 1979; 51:285.

28. Flynn RJ, McMurray TJ, Dwyer R. Comparison of plasma bupivacaine concentrations during continuous extradural infusions for labor. Br. J Anaesth 1988;61:382.

29. Santos AC, Pederson H, Sallusto JA, et al. Pharmacokinetics of ropivacaine in nonpregnant and pregnant ewes. Anesth Analg 1990;70:262.

30. Concepcion M, Arthur GR, Steele SM, Bader AM, Covino BG. A new local anesthetic, ropivacaine: Its epidural effects in humans. Anesth Analg 1990;70:80.

31. Chan R. Epidural block for caesarean section and circulatory changes. Lancet 1989;2:1076.

32. Abboud TK, Afrasiabi A, Sarkis F, et al. Continuous infusion epidural analgesia in parturients receiving bupivacaine, chloroprocaine or lidocaine—maternal, fetal and neonatal effects. Anesth Analg 1984;63:421.

33. Phillipson EH, Kuhnert BR, Syracuse CD. Fetal acidosis, 2-chloroprocaine, and epidural anesthesia for cesarean section. Am J Obstet Gynecol 1985;151:322.

34. MacArthur C, Lewis M, Knox EG, Crawford JS. Epidural anaesthesia and long-term backache after childbirth. BMJ 1990;301:9.

35. Hynson JM, Sessler DI, Glosten B. Back pain in volunteers after epidural anesthesia with chloroprocaine. Anesth Analg 1991;72:253.

36. de Jong R. The chloroprocaine controversy. Am J Obstet Gynecol 1981;140:237.

37. Malinow AM, Mokriski BLK, Wakefield ML, et al. Anesthetic choice affects postcesarean epidural fentanyl analgesia. Anesth Analg 1988;67:138.

38. Kuhnert BR, Kennard MJ, Linn PL. Neonatal neurobehavior after epidural anesthesia for cesarean section: A comparison of bupivacaine and chloroprocaine Anesth Analg 1988;67:64.

39. Brose WG, Cohen SE. Epidural lidocaine for cesarean section: Effect of varying epinephrine concentration. Anesthesiology 1988;69:936.

40. Madsen KE, Stowe DF, McDonald DJ, Ebert TJ, Kampine JP. A comparison of epidural narcotics, with and without a test dose, to epidural lidocaine for extracorporeal shock wave lithotripsy. Reg Anesth 1990; 15:288.

41. Huntoon M, Eisenach JC, Boese P. Epidural clonidine after cesarean section. Appropriate dose and effect of prior local anesthetic. Anesthesiology 1992;76:187.

42. Nishikawa T, Haruhuni I, Asakura N, Hamaya Y. Effects of epidural clonidine added to lidocaine solution upon the requirements of sedatives during epidural anesthesia. Masui 1991;40:717.

43. Hughes SC, Rosen MA, Shnider SM, Abboud TK, Stefani SJ, Norton M. Maternal and neonatal effects of epidural morphine for labor and delivery. Anesth Analg 1984;63:319.

44. Husmeyer RP, O'Connor MC, Davenport HT, Cummings AJ, Rosankiewicz JR. Failure of epidural morphine to relieve pain in labor. Anaesthesia 1980;35:161.

45. Scott DB. Effect of psychoprophylaxia (Lamaze preparation) on labor and delivery in primiparas. N Engl J Med 1976;294:1205.

46. Cousin MT, Maneglia R, Bahno M, et al. Fentanyl with or without adrenaline in peridural administration in obstetrics: Plama analysis and analgesic effects. Ann Fr Anesth Reanim 1989;8:R62.

47. Vella LM, Willatts DG, Knott C, Lintin DJ, Justins DM, Reynolds F. Epidural fentanyl in labor. An evaluation of the systemic contribution to analgesia. Anaesthesia 1985;40:741.

48. Skjolderbrand A, Garle M, Gustaffson LL, Johansson H, Lunnell N-O, Rane A. Extradural pethidine with and without adrenaline during labor: Wide variation in effect. Br J Anesth 1982;54:415.

49. Naulty JS. Obstetrical analgesia. Problems in Anesthesia 1988;2:408.

50. Rawal N, Nuutinen L, Raj PP, et al. Behavioral and histopathological effects following intrathecal administration of butorphanol, sufentanil, and naluphine in sheep. Anesthesiology 1991;75:1025.

51. Justins DM, Francis D, Houlton PG, Reynolds F. A controlled trial of extradural fentanyl in labour. Br. J Anaesth 1982;54:409.

52. Robinson DE, Leicht CH. Epidural analgesia with low-dose bupivacaine and fentanyl for labor and delivery in a parturient with severe pumonary hypertension. Anesthesiology 1988;687:285.

53. Ross BK, Hughes SC. Epidural and spinal narcotic analgesia. Clin Obstet Gynecol 1987;30:552.

54. Cohen SE, Tan S, Albright GA, Halpern J. Epidural fentanyl/bupivacaine mixtures for obstetric analgesia. Anesthesiology 1987;67:403.

55. Celleno D, Capogna G. Epidural fentanyl plus bupivacaine 0.125 percent for labor: Analgesic effects. Can J Anaesth 1988;35:375.

56. Phillips GH. Epidural sufentanil/bupivacaine combinations for analgesia during labor: Effect of varying sufentanil doses. Anesthesiology 1987;67:835.

57. Phillips G. Continuous infusion epidural analgesia in labor: The effect of adding sufentanil to 0.125% bupivacaine. Anesth Analg 1988;67:462.

58. Van Steenberge A, Debroux HC, Noorduin H. Extradural bupivacaine with sufentanil for vaginal delivery. A double-blind trial. Br J Anaesth 1987;59:1518.

59. Capogna G, Celleno D, Tomassetti M. Maternal analgesia and neonatal effects of epidural sufentanil for cesarean section. Reg Anesth 1989;14:282.

60. Naulty JS, Griffith W, Barnes D, Becker RB, Pate A. Epidural PCA vs. continuous infusion of sufentanil-bupivacaine for analgesia during labor and delivery. Anesthesiology 1990;73:A963.

61. Heytens L, Cammu H, Camu F. Extradural analgesia during labor using alfentanil. Br J Anaesth 1987;59:331.

62. Penon C, Negre I, Ecoffey C, Gross JB, Levron JC, Samii K. Analgesia and ventilatory response to carbon dioxide after intramuscular and epidural alfentanil. Anesth Analg 1988;67:313.

63. Golub MS, Eisele JH Jr, Kuhnert BR. Disposition of intrapartum narcotic analgesics in monkeys. Anesth Analg 1988;67:637.

64. Carr DB, Murphy MT. Operation, anesthesia, and the endorphin system. Int Anesthesiol Clin 1988;26:199.

65. Yaksh TL. Opioid receptor systems and the endorphins: A review of their spinal organization. J Neurosurg 1987;67:157.

66. Hunt CO, Naulty JS, Malinow AM, Datta S, Ostheimer GW. Epidural butorphanol-bupivacaine for analgesia during labor and delivery. Anesth Analg 1989;68:32.

67. Thorp JA, Parisi VM, Boylan PC, Johnston DA. The effect of continuous epidural analgesia on cesarean section for dystocia in nulliparous women. Am J Obstet Gynecol 1989;161:670.

68. Shane JA. Forceps—use and abuse. Clin Perinatol 1981;8:63.

69. Neuhoff D, Burke MS, Porreco RP. Cesarean birth for failed progress in labor. Obstet Gynecol 1989;73:915.

70. Naulty JS, Ross R, Smith RH. Effect of changes in labor analgesic practice on labor outcome. Anesthesiology 1988;69:A213.

71. Phillips KC, Thomas TA. Second stage of labour with or without extradural analgesia. Anaesthesia 1983;38:972.

72. Vertommen JD, Vandermeulen E, VanAken H, et al. The effects of the addition of sufentanil to 0.125% bupivacaine on the quality of analgesia during labor and on the incidence of instrumental deliveries. Anesthesiology 1991;74:809.

73. Chestnut DH, Laszewski LJ, Pollack KL, Bates JN, Manago NK, Choi WW. Continuous epidural infusion of 0.0625% bupivacaine-0.0002% fentanyl during the second stage of labor. Anesthesiology 1990;72:613.

74. Ramos-Santos E, Devoe LD, Wakefield ML, Sherline DM, Metheny WP. The effects of epidural anesthesia on the Doppler velocimetry of umbilical and uterine arteries in normal and hypertensive patients during active term labor. Obstet Gynecol 1991;77:20.

75. Lynch C. Depression of myocardial contractility in vitro by bupivacaine, etidocaine and lidocaine. Anesth Analg 1986;65:551.

76. Buffington CW. The magnitude and duration of direct myocardial depression following intracoronary local anesthetics: A comparison of lidocaine and bupivacaine. Anesthesiology 1989;70:280.

77. Bader AM, Wojtowicz S, Naulty JS, Datta S, Ostheimer GW. Effects of epidural anesthesia on maternal cardiac output during labor. Abstracts of Scientific Papers. Meeting of Society of Obstetric Anesthesia and Perinatolgy, Halifax, Nova Scotia, May 30, 1987:65.

78. Hollmen A, Jouppilia R, Pihlajaniemi R, Karvonen P, Sjostedt E. Selective lumbar epidural block in labour. A clinical analysis. Acta Anaesthiol Scand 1977;21:174.

79. Ravindran R, Albrecht W, McKay M. Apparent intravascular migration of epidural catheter. Anesth Analg 1979;58:252.

80. Leighton BL, Gross JG. Air: An effective indicator of intravenously located epidural catheters. Anesthesiology 1989;71:848.

81. Reynolds F, Speedy FM. The subdural space: The third place to go astray. Anaesthesia 1990;45:120.

CHAPTER 20

Spinal Analgesia for Labor

Valerie A. Arkoosh

The search for a completely safe and totally effective method of labor analgesia goes on. The ideal labor analgesic should have the following attributes:

- A localized site of action
- No effects on motor function or the progress of labor
- A small dose requirement
- Low maternal and fetal drug exposure
- Minimal maternal and fetal side effects
- Reversibility

The use of subarachnoid injection of opioids alone or in combination with small doses of local anesthetics fulfills many of these criteria. The purpose of this chapter is to review the development of intrathecal labor analgesics and introduce the reader to new applications of both intrathecal opioids and local anesthetics for labor analgesia.

RATIONALE FOR SPINAL ANALGESIA IN OBSTETRICS

With the introduction of small-gauge spinal catheters, the options for intrathecal labor analgesia are increasing. The many advantages of the intrathecal approach include reliable identification of the subarachnoid space, a small drug dose requirement that greatly decreases the chance of systemic drug toxicity, and rapid, bilateral analgesia. A continuous spinal technique allows incremental drug injection to achieve a specific endpoint. Depending upon patient characteristics and the chosen technique of administration, one may use intrathecal opioids or local anesthetics alone or in combination.

Intrathecal opioids are a particularly attractive analgesic choice for the obstetric anesthesiologist. In parturients, intrathecal opioids produce dose-dependent analgesia without significant changes in autonomic function, voluntary motor function, or response to innocuous stimuli. In gravid rats and rabbits, intrathecal morphine lacks effect on the onset of labor, maternal or fetal respiratory rate, or fetal viability.[1] Naloxone antagonizes subarachnoid opioid analgesia in a dose-dependent fashion.

Small doses of intrathecal isobaric local anesthetics provide adequate but brief labor analgesia with little hypotension or motor blockade.[2,3] Intrathecal local anesthetics are best used for pain relief in the second stage of labor or in combination with intrathecal opioids for the first stage of labor.

MECHANISM OF SPINAL OPIOID ANALGESIA

There is a growing appreciation that multiple spinal receptor systems are involved in nociceptive processing. These include opioid, alpha-adrenergic, gamma-aminobutyric acid (GABA), and adenosine receptor systems. Acetylcholine, calcitonin, neurotensin, serotonin, somatostatin, and neuropeptide Y have all produced antinociceptive effects after intrathecal administration in animals.[4] Because most work to date in obstetric anesthesia describes the use of intrathecal opioids to provide pain relief, the following discussion will concentrate on the opioid receptor system.

Identification of opiate receptors in the central nervous system[5] and their subsequent localization in the substantia gelatinosa of the dorsal horn of the spinal cord[6] initiated the study of regional analgesia using intraspinal opioids. Several classes of opioid receptors with differing pharmacologic profiles exist. Martin and colleagues,[7] in a chronic spinal dog model, originally proposed the μ, κ, and σ opioid-receptor classes. Subsequent reports have described δ and ε opioid receptors as well as subclasses of some receptor types.[8]

Stimulation of peripheral nociceptors activates thinly myelinated (Aδ) and unmyelinated (C) afferent nerve fibers. These primary afferents enter the spinal cord in the lateral portion of the dorsal root and bifurcate into both rostral and caudal branches (Fig. 20-1). They synapse with both second-order neurons in the substantia gelatinosa of the dorsal horn and dendrites of more deeply lying cells. These second-order neurons process and transmit the nociceptive message to supraspinal centers.[8] Modulation of the synapse between the primary afferent and the second-order neuron can alter the central passage of painful information. This control can be exercised at several points, including the following:

- Inhibiting afferent neurotransmitter release
- Antagonizing the effector mechanism by which the neurotransmitters released from primary afferents act
- Altering the excitability of the second-order link

Intrathecal opioids appear to act at sites both before and after the synapse between the primary afferent and the second-order neuron. Aδ- and C-fiber stimulation releases substance P, a putative nociceptive neurotransmitter. Presynaptic actions of intrathecal opioids inhibit the release of substance P.[9] Intrathecal opioids also hyperpolarize the postsynaptic cell membrane by increasing potassium conductance and decreasing the excitability of the neuron. This effect appears mediated by the G-protein that couples the opioid receptor directly to the potassium channel (see Fig. 20-1).

Other mechanisms also may be involved in opioid modulation of nociceptive impulse transmission. Recent work suggests that morphine stimulates the release of adenosine from primary afferent nerves.[10,11] Occupation of adenosine receptors produces mild analgesia.[12]

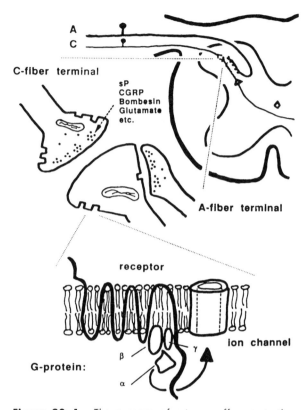

Figure 20–1. The synapse of primary afferents in the substantia gelatinosa of the dorsal horn. The C-fiber, but not the A-fiber, terminals have opioid receptors. Opioids also bind postsynaptically on the dendrites of neurons receiving A-fiber and C-fiber excitatory input. Agonist occupation of the presynaptic opioid receptor reduces the release of neurotransmitters from the C-terminal and postsynaptically decreases the excitability of the neuron. At the membrane level, agonist–receptor binding activates the G-protein. The alpha subunit, which contains the guanine nucleotide binding site, dissociates from the beta and gamma subunits, increasing potassium permeability. (Sosnowski M, Yaksh TL. Spinal administration of receptor-selective drugs as analgesics: New horizons. Pain Symptom Management 1990;5:191)

Additionally, high concentrations of morphine, fentanyl, meperidine, and sufentanil produce a weak local anesthetic effect on isolated nerves.[13–15] Recorded A- and C-fiber action potential amplitude decreases following opioid administration.

In sum, intrathecally administered opioids suppress the processing of nociceptive stimuli via several mechanisms, culminating in depressed neuronal excitability and decreased secretion of nociceptive transmitters.[9] Through these mechanisms, intrathecal opioids alter rostral transmission of nociceptive information and, ultimately, a patient's perception of pain.

PHARMACOKINETICS

Once injected into the subarachnoid space, opioid and local anesthetic drugs undergo redistribution via three mechanisms—diffusion, vascular transport, and bulk flow within the cerebrospinal fluid (CSF).[8,16] Initially, the drug moves by diffusion into the spinal cord, nerve roots, and perineural fat, and across the dura into the epidural space. The drug is absorbed from these areas into the systemic vasculature. Depending upon the lipid solubility of the drug, it also may undergo rostro-caudal movement within the CSF. The predominant mechanism of redistribution for each drug depends upon the lipid solubility, ionization, and molecular weight of that drug.

Lipid Solubility

Lipid solubility is the most important characteristic of a drug. It affects uptake, clearance, and likelihood of rostral spread of both opioids and local anesthetics. Increasing opioid lipid solubility permits rapid uptake into the spinal cord, resulting in a faster analgesic onset. A somewhat lipid-insoluble drug such as morphine has an analgesic latency ranging from 15 to 60 minutes. The more lipid-soluble opioids, such as fentanyl or sufentanil, begin to produce analgesia within 5 to 10 minutes. High lipid solubility also results in rapid clearance through systemic vascular absorption. Rapid clearance reduces the duration of action of the drug. Rostral spread of lipid-soluble intrathecal opioids, with resultant respiratory depression, is less likely.

After systemic administration of opioids, potency correlates directly with lipid solubility. More lipid-soluble drugs (*i.e.*, sufentanil) are more potent than a hydrophilic drug such as morphine. For drugs given intrathecally, however, lipid solubility relates inversely to opioid potency. McQuay *et al*[17] showed that, when given intrathecally, two poorly lipid-soluble opioids, morphine and normorphine, are more potent than two highly soluble opioids, meperidine and methadone.[17] McQuay *et al* hypothesize that significant nonspecific tissue binding of highly lipid-soluble opioids within the spinal cord limits the amount of drug available for binding at specific opioid receptors.

Clinically, this idea is important when determining equianalgesic intrathecal opioid doses. Many investigators use systemic opioid potency ratios to estimate equipotent intrathecal opioid doses, however, the ability of a drug to cross the blood–brain barrier and gain access to opioid receptors influences its systemic potency. Because intrathecally administered drugs avoid the blood–brain barrier, the intrathecal potency ratio of two drugs may not correlate with the systemic potency ratio. Indeed, high lipid solubility, which implies high systemic potency, results in a less potent intrathecal drug. McQuay *et al* extrapolate that achieving the analgesia produced by morphine, 0.5 mg intrathecally, would require 5 mg of intrathecal meperidine or 8.5 mg of intrathecal methadone (Table 20-1).

Ionization and Molecular Weight

Opioids and local anesthetics cross membranes and interact with specific receptors in the nonionized form.[8,16] Commonly used opioids and local anesthetics have a pKa of 7.5 or greater; therefore, these drugs will exist mainly in the ionized form within the CSF.

Movement of molecules across the dura and into tissues is inversely related to the molecular weight and molecular configuration. Opioids and local anesthetics used for labor analgesia have similar molecular weights but different molecular configurations. Both types of drugs readily cross dural and tissue membranes.

Table 20-1

Opioid Lipid Solubility and Potency

DRUG	OCTANOL/WATER PARTITION COEFFICIENT	SYSTEMIC EQUI-ANALGESIC DOSE (MG)	INTRATHECAL EQUI-ANALGESIC DOSE (MG)
Morphine	1.4	10–15	0.5
Meperidine	39	75–100	5
Methadone	116	8–10	8.5

(Data from McQuay HJ, Sullivan AF, Smallman K, Dickenson AH. Intrathecal opioids, potency and lipophilicity. Pain 1989;36:111)

PHYSIOLOGIC EFFECTS

Opioids

Besides analgesia, stimulation of intrathecal opioid receptors also can affect bladder, motor, gastrointestinal, and respiratory function and cause pruritus. Animal studies and clinical reports provide evidence for a receptor-specific suppression of the micturition reflex, which involves both bladder contractility and sphincter tone.[18,19] High doses of μ-receptor agonists can induce skeletal muscle rigidity due to a receptor-specific interaction in brain-stem centers.[20] In the presence of spinal spasticity, low doses of spinally administered morphine can reduce motor tone.[21] The mechanism for nausea and vomiting is most likely related to an action on the chemoemetic trigger zone in the dorsal medulla.[22] Potential respiratory effects of spinally administered opioids include a decrease in minute ventilation due to decreased respiratory rate and tidal volume, a shift in the carbon dioxide response curve down and to the right, and an impaired response to hypoxia.[23,24] Systemic vascular uptake and redistribution of drug produce early respiratory effects. Delayed effects are due to rostral spread of morphine in the CSF, causing respiratory depression by an action on the chemosensitive anterolateral surface of the medulla.[24] Pruritus occurs frequently after intrathecal opioid administration. Pruritus is a rare side effect after systemic administration, which strongly suggests a spinal mechanism for the occurrence of itching.[25]

Local Anesthetics

The physiologic effects of local anesthetics are well known to most practitioners. Besides inhibiting pain pathways, local anesthetics also block sympathetic, sensory, and motor pathways. Effects at these sites of action result in a greater incidence of maternal hypotension, urinary retention, and sensory and motor blockade when compared with administration of intrathecal opioids. The occurrence of the above effects depends upon the amount and concentration of local anesthetic injected. Small intrathecal doses of dilute local anesthetic solutions block mainly the small $A\delta$- and C-fibers, resulting in decreased pain perception but little motor blockade or hypotension.

PATIENT SELECTION

Patients who are candidates for neuraxial labor analgesia are candidates for intrathecal opioid administra-

tion. Additionally, intrathecal opioids have proved effective in a subset of patients who, because of coexisting disease, might not tolerate the hemodynamic changes induced by lumbar epidural local anesthetic blockade. This list includes patients with severe pulmonary hypertension,[26] Wolff-Parkinson-White syndrome,[27] and a single ventricle.[28] Also, a patient allergic to local anesthetics obtained adequate analgesia with continuous administration of intrathecal meperidine.[29]

In our practice at Thomas Jefferson University Hospital, we consider most parturients potential candidates for intrathecal opioids. In particular, patients in early labor(< 3–4 cm), those whose fetus is high in the pelvis, those who say they do not like "feeling numb," or patients who wish to deliver their baby with minimal analgesic intervention are offered this technique. Additionally, we offer this technique to any parturient whose medical condition is such that it would be difficult for her to tolerate significant sympathetic blockade.

Patients who are suboptimal candidates for intrathecal opioid administration include those receiving intravenous agonist–antagonist drugs immediately before intrathecal opioid administration and patients known to abuse narcotics. The reliability of intrathecal opioids is poor in these patient groups. Contraindications to this technique include patient refusal, infection at the puncture site, and coagulation defects (some authors consider this a relative contraindication).

CHOICE OF AGENT

Available research supports the use of several opioids for intrathecal labor analgesia. These include morphine, fentanyl, sufentanil, and meperidine. Much less published information is available on the use of intrathecal local anesthetic solutions for labor analgesia. This section will review published data as well as our experience with both opioids and local anesthetics for intrathecal labor analgesia.

Opioids

Morphine

Scott *et al*,[30] in 1980, first described the use of 1.5 mg of intrathecal morphine, in 12 parturients. This dose abolished pain in the first stage of labor in all patients. Second-stage pain was relieved in four patients and lessened in three. Scott *et al* noted no change in hemodynamic or respiratory parameters and no evidence of motor weakness. All women experienced facial itching. Nine parturients felt nauseated, and five vomited. Four subjects required catheterization for urinary retention. All infants did well.

Baraka and colleagues[31] administered either 1 or 2 mg of intrathecal morphine to 20 primiparous patients in active labor. All reported relief within 15 to 60 minutes. Time from intrathecal injection to delivery ranged from 2.0 to 10.5 hours in the 1-mg group and 3.0 to 14.5 hours in the 2-mg group. All parturients, except three in the 2-mg group, were pain-free until delivery. The three women experiencing pain did so after 8 hours. Patients in the 2-mg group required more use of oxytocin. At delivery, all parturients received supplemental analgesia via either local infiltration, pudendal block, or epidural block. Equally high percentages of patients in each group experienced itching, nausea, vomiting, and somnolence. All fetuses exhibited normal neurobehavioral responses when tested during the first 24 hours postpartum.

Mok and Tsai[32] described seven parturients who obtained 75% to 90% relief of labor pain that lasted 20 to 36 hours after 2 mg of intrathecal morphine in 4 mL of 0.9% saline solution. These authors, however, chose not to pursue this technique because of the high incidence of pruritus (73%), vomiting (66%), somnolence (60%), and urinary retention (40%).

Although pleased with the analgesic effects of intrathecal morphine, most investigators are unhappy with the high incidence of side effects. To lessen the side effects, Abboud *et al*[33] studied smaller doses of morphine. Intrathecal morphine, 0.5 mg, or 1.0 mg in hyperbaric solution, produced analgesia beginning 15 to 60 minutes after injection and maximum pain relief by 90 to 120 minutes after injection. Analgesia lasted 6 to 8 hours (Fig. 20-2). Mild or moderate pruritus occurred in 80% of patients, nausea or vomiting in 53%, drowsiness or dizziness in 43%, and urinary retention in 43%. The two doses produced analgesia of similar duration. The lower, 0.5-mg dose caused less pruritus.

Morphine–Phenylpiperidine Combinations

Besides the high incidence of side effects produced by intrathecal morphine, this drug has a long analgesic latency. Many parturients are not comfortable for up to an hour after intrathecal administration. To bridge the latency gap, a more lipid-soluble opioid can be given in combination with morphine. In a study of 15 healthy parturients, Leighton *et al*[34] injected 25 μg fentanyl with 0.25 mg of morphine in 2 mL of normal saline intrathecally. All patients had significant pain relief within 5 minutes of opioid injection (Fig. 20-3). Nine patients delivered vaginally with supplemental pu-

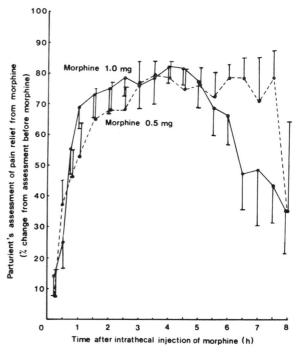

Figure 20–2. Maternal pain relief after intrathecal administration of morphine 0.5 mg or 1 mg. (Abboud TK, Shnider SM, Dailey PA, et al. Intrathecal administration of hyperbaric morphine for the relief of pain in labour. Br J Anaesth 1984;56:1351)

dendal block anesthesia at a mean of approximately 200 minutes after intrathecal injection. Six patients had lumbar epidural analgesia induced 140 ± 51 minutes after opioid injection. Moderate to severe postpartum itching and vomiting occurred in seven of eight patients given either no prophylactic opioid antagonists or 12.5 mg of oral naltrexone after delivery. Three of five patients given a continuous infusion of naloxone, 0.2 mg/h, had mild postpartum itching or nausea. Two patients given 25 mg of oral naltrexone had no postpartum side effects.

Sharkey and coworkers[35] compared either sufentanil, 10 μg, or fentanyl, 25 μg, as adjuncts to intrathecal morphine 0.25 mg. These parturients underwent simultaneous epidural catheter placement. At patient request for additional analgesia, the investigators injected local anesthetic through the epidural catheter. Mean time to epidural local anesthetic injection in the sufentanil group was 162 minutes versus 130 minutes in the fentanyl group (not significant, Fig. 20-4). The patients in the sufentanil group had a significantly higher incidence of pruritus (Fig. 20-5). These authors conclude that, clinically, there is little difference between these two drug combinations.

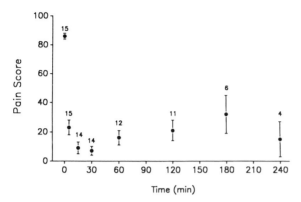

Figure 20–3. Mean ± SEM pain scores after intrathecal injection of fentanyl, 25 μg, and morphine, 0.25 mg. The number of patients still laboring under intrathecal narcotic analgesia appears above each value. (Leighton BL, DeSimone CA, Norris MC, Ben-David B. Intrathecal narcotics for labor revisited: The combination of fentanyl and morphine provides onset of profound, prolonged analgesia. Anesth Analg 1989;69:123)

Mankad and colleagues[36] reported a mean duration of analgesia of 98 to 162 minutes after spinal injection of fentanyl, 25 μg, with morphine, 0.5, 0.75, or 1.0 mg. The larger doses of morphine did not significantly prolong pain relief.[36] Naltrexone, 5 mg orally, given immediately after intrathecal opioid injection appeared to have no effect upon the incidence of mild pruritus (24 of 30 patients).

Fentanyl

Few investigators have reported the use of intrathecal fentanyl alone. Zakowski and associates[37] obtained an 80-minute mean duration of analgesia after 25 μg of fentanyl was administered via an intrathecal catheter. No patient experienced nausea, and most reported moderate pruritus. The third dose of intrathecal fentanyl produced analgesia for a significantly shorter duration than the first dose.

Sufentanil

Sufentanil in doses ranging from 3 to 15 μg intrathecally provides labor analgesia of rapid onset and moderate duration.[38,39] No significant changes in maternal hemodynamics or fetal heart rate arise following these doses. The mild maternal side effects that occur rarely require treatment.

Meperidine

Meperidine, 10 to 20 mg, provides adequate labor analgesia with a duration between 83 and 136 minutes.[40,41] Meperidine has weak local anesthetic effects and does produce sympathetic blockade. Occasional patients require ephedrine for hypotension.[41]

Which Opioid?

Only a few studies comparing the lipid-soluble opioids currently exist. Leicht *et al*[42] contrasted 25 μg of intrathecal fentanyl and 10 μg of sufentanil. This dose of sufentanil relieved labor pain faster and better than fentanyl. Honet and associates[43] compared fentanyl, meperidine, and sufentanil as continuous spinal labor analgesics. The 65 laboring patients required an average dose of fentanyl (15.5 μg), meperidine (10.5 mg), and sufentanil (6.5 μg) for initial pain relief. The onset of analgesia, the duration of initial analgesia, or the duration of effective opioid analgesia did not differ

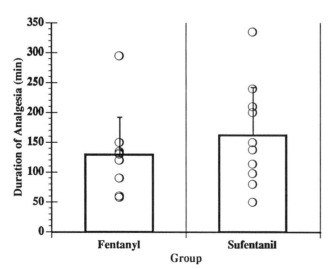

Figure 20–4. Time (minutes) ± SEM from intrathecal opioid injection to epidural injection of local anesthetic. Each point represents one patient. (Data from Sharkey SJ, Arkoosh VA, Norris MC, Honet JE, Leighton BL. Comparison between intrathecal sufentanil and fentanyl for labor analgesia. Anesthesiology 1991;75:A841)

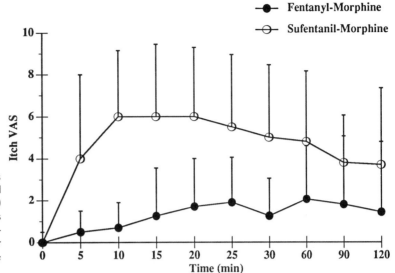

Figure 20–5. Mean ± SEM pruritus scores versus time after intrathecal opioid injection. (VAS = visual analog scores) (Data from Sharkey SJ, Arkoosh VA, Norris MC, Honet JE, Leighton BL. Comparison between intrathecal sufentanil and fentanyl for labor analgesia. Anesthesiology 1991; 75:A841)

among the groups (Table 20-2). Meperidine provided significantly better pain relief once cervical dilation passed 6 cm (Fig. 20-6). Patients in the meperidine group experienced more nausea. All three patient groups had slight decreases in blood pressure but none greater than 15% of baseline. Patients in all groups experienced segmental loss of temperature discrimination (Fig. 20-7). No woman showed any evidence of motor blockade. Intrathecal fentanyl and meperidine correlated with an increase in variable decelerations. Neonates in all groups had good Apgar scores. Although still an evolving area, it appears that among the

lipid-soluble opioids, meperidine and sufentanil will prove superior to fentanyl for providing intrathecal labor analgesia.

Local Anesthetics

Bupivacaine

After injection of 2.5 mg of bupivacaine (1 mL of 0.25% solution) through a spinal catheter, our patients had adequate labor analgesia for a mean of 51.7 ± 25.5

Table 20–2

Intrathecal Opioids for Labor Analgesia

DRUG	n	MEDIAN (MIN)	MEAN ± SE (MIN)	RANGE (MIN)
Duration of First-Dose Intrathecal Opioid				
Fentanyl	20	70.0	81.6 ± 8.9	0–150
Meperidine	20	98.7	103.5 ± 10.6	35–205
Sufentanil	21	95.0	103.9 ± 8.7	0–210
Total Duration of Effective Opioid Analgesia				
Fentanyl	20	227.1	216.9 ± 30.9	0–380*
Meperidine	20	301.0	267.5 ± 23.9	35–710*
Sufentanil	21	250.7	266.7 ± 31.9	0–545*

(Data from Honet JE, Arkoosh VA, Huffnagle HJ, Norris MC, Leighton BL. Comparison of fentanyl, meperidine and sufentanil for intrathecal labor analgesia. Anesthesiology 1991;75(3A):A839)
*Potential range of effective analgesia unknown because some patients delivered while still comfortable with opioid.

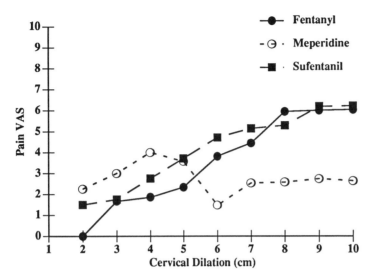

Figure 20–6. Mean pain scores versus cervical dilation. (VAS = visual analog scores) (Data from Honet JE, Arkoosh VA, Huffnagle HJ, Norris MC, Leighton BL. Comparison of fentanyl, meperidine and sufentanil for intrathecal labor analgesia. Anesthesiology 1991;75:A839)

minutes.[2] Two of six patients experienced partial motor blockade that resolved in 15 minutes. Benedetti and Tiengo[3] reported 48 minutes of analgesia (range: 16–98 min) after a mean dose of 2.45 mg of intrathecal bupivacaine. Although the resulting analgesia is adequate and the motor blockade minimal, the short duration of action of small doses of intrathecal bupivacaine makes intermittent bolus injection of this drug impractical.

Lidocaine

Huckaby and colleagues[44] described the successful use of intermittent injections of lidocaine 1% through a 32-gauge spinal catheter. They noted few hemodynamic effects, partial motor block in some patients, and the need for frequent reinjections of drug.

Because of the short duration of low-dose local anesthetics, there is little place for single or intermittent bolus use of these drugs to provide first-stage labor analgesia. A continuous-infusion technique, however, could make their use practical.

TECHNIQUES

Labor Analgesia

Single Injection

A single subarachnoid injection of opioid can be given at almost any point in labor. Intrathecal opioids are particularly effective analgesics in the early stages of labor but are less so near delivery. Advantages include reliability and speed of placement and the rapid onset

of analgesia with lipid-soluble agents. The major disadvantage of this technique is the lack of an alternative analgesic method if the duration or effectiveness of the opioid is inadequate.

Double Needle

A double-needle technique allows injection of subarachnoid opioids and insertion of an epidural catheter with one skin puncture. Without any additional discomfort to the patient, simultaneous epidural catheter placement provides a secondary method of analgesia should the intrathecal opioids prove inadequate for the duration of labor. Identify the epidural space with a 17- or 18-gauge epidural needle. Then, pass a small-gauge 120-mm needle through the epidural needle (Fig. 20-8) into the subarachnoid space (Fig. 20-9). Inject opioid and withdraw the spinal needle. Next, thread a catheter through the epidural needle into the epidural space and tape it in place. When the patient requests additional analgesia, test and dose the epidural catheter in the standard fashion.

Spinal Catheter

With a single dural puncture, a spinal catheter allows the anesthesiologist to administer repeated injections of subarachnoid opioids or local anesthetic as required for patient comfort or type of delivery.[3,43,44] Several microcatheter and needle systems are currently in use. In choosing a system, one must consider the size and tensile strength of the catheter and the size and type of spinal needle through which the catheter will thread. The original 32-gauge microspinal catheter described by Hurley and Lambert can prove very difficult

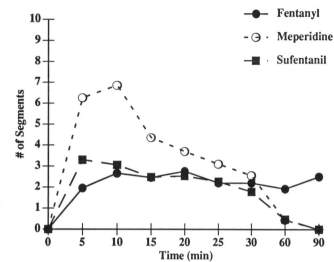

Figure 20–7. Sensory change to temperature versus time after intrathecal opioid injection. (Data from Honet JE, Arkoosh VA, Huffnagle HJ, Norris MC, Leighton BL. Comparison of fentanyl, meperidine and sufentanil for intrathecal labor analgesia. Anesthesiology 1991;75:A839)

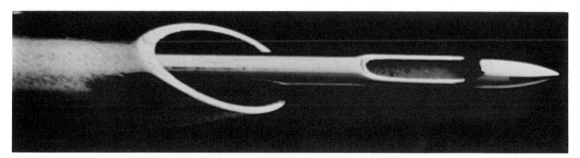

Figure 20–8. Sprotte spinal needle (24 gauge × 120 mm) through an 18-gauge Hustead epidural needle.

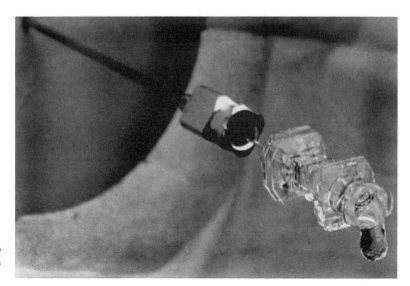

Figure 20–9. Sprotte spinal needle placed into cerebrospinal fluid through epidural needle.

to insert.[44,45] Another system uses a 28-gauge polyurethane catheter with a removable stylet and a 22-gauge pencil-point needle. The needle has a ramp built into the tip that aids in guiding the catheter out of the needle (Fig. 20-10). Other manufacturers produce similar polyamide catheters. In our practice, we have found this needle and catheter combination easy to use.

Advantages of continuous spinal analgesia include the following:

- Rapid onset of pain relief
- Bilateral analgesia
- The ability to use intrathecal opioids, with their lack of motor blockade and minimal hemodynamic effects, for most of labor
- The ability to provide surgical anesthesia rapidly if urgent delivery is necessary

Table 20-3 describes our current approach to continuous spinal analgesia for labor.

Although this technique is widely accepted by patients, obstetricians, and nursing staff at our institution, we experience two somewhat interrelated disadvantages. One is the development of clinically apparent tachyphylaxis to both opioid and local anesthetic drugs. This problem may relate to the changing nature of labor pain as parturition progresses or true tachyphylaxis. The second issue is the short duration of pain relief following intrathecal injection of currently available drugs. Intermittent dosing of these catheters can be very labor-intensive. We are currently developing a system using a patient-controlled analgesia device with the ability to administer a basal infusion of drug. At this writing, although very promising, continuous spinal analgesia for labor requires further research and refinement before becoming a widely recommended technique.

Analgesia for Vaginal Delivery

Single Injection

Occasionally, a parturient may present for delivery, and time or other circumstances do not allow for establishment of continuous-catheter analgesia. A single subarachnoid injection technique, using either opioids or local anesthetics, can provide analgesia for delivery. Of the opioid drug choices, meperidine, 20 to 25 mg, provides adequate analgesia for spontaneous or instrumented deliveries with little or no motor blockade. This dose is adequate for episiotomy and repair as well. A traditional "saddle block" with 25 to 30 mg of lidocaine 5% also provides adequate analgesia for delivery but with a higher incidence of motor blockade.[46]

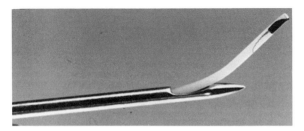

Figure 20–10. Preferred Medical Products 28-gauge spinal catheter through a 22-gauge ramped Sprotte spinal needle.

Double Needle

We often use the double-needle technique with meperidine, 20 to 25 mg, to provide second-stage analgesia. Should delivery outlast the meperidine or should the obstetrician elect cesarean delivery, we use the in situ epidural catheter.

AFFECT ON PROGRESS OF LABOR

Opioids

Although this question has not been studied directly, information is emerging that intrathecal morphine may have an effect upon the progress of labor. In a randomized study, Abouleish *et al*[47] compared three groups of patients receiving either 0.2 mg of intrathecal morphine, epidural bupivacaine 0.125%, or both.[47] Only the patients in the combined intrathecal morphine and epidural bupivacaine group initially become comfortable. Forty minutes after the initial injection, women still in pain received bupivacaine, 0.125%, in 10 mL-increments as needed. All women received repeat injections of bupivacaine, 0.125% for analgesia throughout the remainder of labor and delivery. Oxytocin use was similar among the three groups. The patients in the epidural-only group had a significantly shorter duration of first stage of labor than either group receiving morphine. The duration of stage 2 was unaffected (Table 20-4). Abouleish *et al*[47] hypothesized that a morphine action on the spinal cord or hypothalamus may depress uterine contractions. Intrathecal morphine labor analgesia has a long latency, up to 1 hour. By treating uncomfortable patients after only 40 minutes, not enough time may have passed for the intrathecal morphine to have begun working. If the morphine subsequently did begin to contribute analgesia, the morphine/bupivacaine patients may have experienced a greater level of pain relief than the epidural-only group. This additional degree of analgesia, not the morphine, may have prolonged the first stage of labor.

Table 20–3

Suggestions for Managing a Spinal Catheter

Preparation

1. Prepare intravenous fluid, 250 mL (most important if administering meperidine or local anesthetics).
2. Dilute drugs with preservative-free saline.

Induction

1. Insert at most 2–3 cm of catheter of choice, 28 or 32 gauge. (Paramedian placement allows easier catheter removal.)
2. Inject drug of choice with 1-mL luer lock syringe. (One may use 3-mL luer lock syringe with very slow injection rate.)
3. Position patient with left uterine displacement, and monitor blood pressure every 2–3 min for 15 min.
4. Treat inadequate opioid analgesia with a second dose of the opioid.
5. If analgesia is still inadequate, locate the discomfort in the following manner:
   a. Abdominal: Inject 1 mL of bupivacaine 0.25%.
   b. Lower abdominal/perineal: Check bladder, inject 0.5 mL of bupivacaine 0.75% with dextrose with patient sitting.
   c. If no relief achieved with above maneuvers, consider misplaced catheter.
   d. If partial relief achieved, repeat local anesthetic dose.

Note: Bupivacaine 0.25% is hypobaric (important for patient positioning).

Vaginal Delivery

If additional analgesia is necessary, administer bupivacaine 0.75% with dextrose in 3.75-mg increments or lidocaine 5% with dextrose in 10-mg increments with patient sitting (maximum dose: 0.75% bupivacaine, 7.5 mg, or 5% lidocaine, 50 mg).

Cesarean Section

1. Prehydrate as needed.
2. Inject hyperbaric local anesthetic of choice in incremental doses to achieve T-4 level (maximum dose: 0.75% bupivacaine, 15 mg; 1% tetracaine, 15 mg; and 5% lidocaine, 100 mg).
3. If inadequate level is present with normal dose, consider manipulating patient position, as drug may be pooling in the lumbosacral area.
4. If still inadequate, administer bupivacaine 0.5% (isobaric) in 1-mL increments.
5. Consider alternative technique.

Catheter Removal

1. Place patient in lateral decubitus position.
2. Polyurethane and polyamide catheters stretch before breaking. Make sure catheter is actually coming out and not just stretching. Distance between the 1-cm marks on the catheters should remain constant.
3. If difficult, do the following:
   a. Have patient extend her back. This maneuver relaxes the ligamentum flavum.
   b. Have patient bend laterally to each side.
   c. If these maneuvers fail, leave the catheter in place until the patient is able to stand upright and completely extend her back. Catheters are easily withdrawn in this position.

Morphine also can have direct depressant effects on the uterus. In an in vitro study, Sivalingam *et al*[48] described the effects of morphine, meperidine, and pentazocine on uteri from 22-day pregnant rats or nonpregnant rats in estrus. In this study, meperidine and pentazocine enhanced contraction rate in both pregnant and nonpregnant preparations. Conversely, morphine had a negligible effect on the pregnant rat uterus but caused significant reductions in contractile activity in nonpregnant uterine tissue. Naloxone, in concentrations between 1 and 100 ng/mL, did not antagonize these effects. Because of species variation, the relevance

Table 20–4

The Effect of Intrathecal Morphine, 0.2 mg, on the Duration of Labor*

GROUP	DURATION OF FIRST STAGE (H)	DURATION OF SECOND STAGE (H)
Intrathecal Morphine		
Nullipara (n = 9)	10.5 ± 1.3[†]	1.3 ± 0.4
Multipara (n = 7)	11.3 ± 3.1[†]	0.6 ± 0.2
Epidural bupivacaine		
Nullipara (n = 9)	6.5 ± 0.8	0.5 ± 0.1
Multipara (n = 9)	5.2 ± 0.6	0.3 ± 0.03
Both		
Nullipara (n = 9)	11.1 ± 0.2[†]	1.1 ± 0.3
Multipara (n = 6)	9.4 ± 0.8	0.6 ± 0.2

(Data from Abouleish E, Rawal N, Shaw J, Lorenz T, Rashad MN. Intrathecal morphine, 0.2 mg, versus epidural bupivacaine 0.125% or their combination: effects on parturients. Anesthesiology 1991;74:711)
*Data are mean ± SEM.
†P < 0.05 versus epidural bupivacaine.

of this study to the use of opioids in human labor is uncertain. However, given some clinical evidence that intrathecal morphine may affect the duration of the first stage of labor, further study is needed in this area.

Local Anesthetics

There is no information available on the effect that low-dose subarachnoid local anesthetics may have on the progress of labor. Concerning epidural use, Epstein and colleagues[49] found no correlation between the concentration of local anesthetic and its blood concentration on the force of uterine contractions as measured by external tocography or the rate of dilation of the cervix.[49] It is unlikely, therefore, that subarachnoid local anesthetics, administered in small doses, would have any appreciable direct effect upon uterine contractions. It is possible that a simultaneously administered intravenous fluid bolus or an untreated maternal hypotension could affect the progress of labor.

SOME CLINICAL ISSUES

Managing Intrathecal Opioid Side Effects

Most side effects resulting from the use of intrathecal morphine are more of an annoyance to the patient than a serious consequence. Nausea and vomiting can be readily treated by intravenous administration of metoclopramide, 10 mg, or nalbuphine, 5 to 10 mg. Pruritus, which can be severe, usually responds to intravenous nalbuphine, 5–10 mg, diphenhydramine, 25 mg, ranitidine, 50 mg, or a naloxone infusion (200–250 µg/h). Urinary retention frequently requires intermittent or continuous bladder catheterization. Reactivation of herpes labialis cold sores is associated with administration of epidural morphine in some populations of cesarean section patients.[50] At our institution, we followed a total of 203 cesarean section patients, 105 of whom received either intrathecal (n=81) or epidural (n=24) morphine.[51] Oral lesions developed in 6 of 105 patients receiving neuraxial morphine and 4 of 98 patients who received no morphine (p=NS). There is no clear evidence that practitioners should avoid intrathecal morphine in patients with a history of cold sores.

More serious and potentially life-threatening to the parturient is the occurrence of delayed respiratory depression.[52] Lipid-insoluble morphine undergoes slow rostral spread within the CSF. Upon reaching the respiratory centers in the medulla, morphine can cause a direct depressant effect.[24] One recent survey of surgical pain management in Sweden found a 1:275 (0.36%) incidence of delayed ventilatory depression occurring between 7 and 9 hours after intrathecal morphine (0.3–0.75 mg) injection.[53] Respiratory depression also can occur early during treatment with intrathecal opioids. Palmer[54] reported a case of early respiratory depression occurring 25 minutes after the injection of morphine, 0.2 mg, with fentanyl, 15 μg, and lidocaine, 100 mg, in 5% dextrose for cesarean section. This patient responded to naloxone, in a total dose of 0.24 mg.

Currently, most authors recommend close supervision and monitoring of parturients for the first 12 hours after receiving intrathecal morphine.[53] At our institution, any woman receiving intrathecal morphine is discharged from the delivery suite with a special set of orders. If a parturient delivers vaginally within 12 hours of intrathecal morphine administration, she receives 25 mg of naltrexone by mouth on admission to the recovery room.[34] She is monitored with continuous pulse oximetry and a count of respirations every hour for the remainder of the 12-hour period. An ampule of naloxone remains at the bedside, and the patient's room and nursing care sheets are specially marked. For the first 12 hours the patient is not allowed to receive any other opioids or sedatives without approval of an anesthesiologist. We also include standing orders for the treatment of nausea and vomiting, pruritus, pain, and urinary retention.

Other Complications

When using the 24-gauge pencil-point spinal needle, the occurrence of postdural puncture headache after the double-needle technique is a rare complication at our institution. Following insertion of a spinal catheter with a 22-gauge pencil-point needle, we experience approximately a 3% incidence of moderate to severe headache. Using a 26-gauge spinal needle and 32-gauge catheter, Benedetti[55] reports an 11% incidence of mild to moderate positional headache.

As with epidural catheters, catheter breakage can occur with microspinal catheters.[45,56] Most authors recommend informing the patient and following a course of expectant management. Great care should be exercised when removing these catheters (see Table 20-3). Gravenstein et al[57] recommend placing patients in the lateral decubitus position to decrease the axial loading of the vertebral interspaces that occurs when a patient is sitting.

Following a greater-than-usual dose of hyperbaric local anesthetic solution, four cases of cauda equina syndrome have been reported in association with the continuous spinal technique.[58] Most likely, this is a result of maldistribution of large doses of hyperbaric local anesthetic in the sacral area.[59,60] There have not been any reports of neurologic injury following the injection of opioid solutions. Most authors believe that if adequate anesthesia is not achieved with a normal dose of local anesthetic, the patient or catheter position should be manipulated and drugs of differing baricity should be used in an attempt to reach unblocked segments.[61–63] Under no circumstance should one inject larger-than-normal doses of hyperbaric local anesthetic solution through a microspinal catheter.

Which Technique?

There is no single answer to this question. Once the decision is made to administer spinal opioids in our practice, we use either the double-needle or continuous spinal technique. Approximately 40% to 60% of our laboring patients receive spinal opioids as part of their labor analgesia. Most of these women have an epidural catheter placed simultaneously. Most receive only a lipid-soluble opioid, usually meperidine or sufentanil. Because of the many side effects, we do not routinely administer intrathecal morphine for labor. If a parturient presents with a medical problem that could be aggravated by sympathetic blockade or is uncomfortable with the type of analgesia resulting from local anesthetic injection, the continuous spinal technique is very useful. Because of the ability to achieve surgical levels of anesthesia quickly, we frequently place spinal catheters in parturients with multiple gestations or those attempting vaginal breech delivery. As in all areas of obstetric anesthesia, treatment choices must be made on an individual basis.

SUMMARY AND CONCLUSIONS

Spinal labor analgesia is a rapidly expanding area of great interest to the obstetric anesthesiologist. Spinal administration of opioid analgesics, in particular, fulfills many of the desiderata of labor analgesia. The list includes bilateral analgesia of rapid onset, low risk of systemic drug toxicity, minimal effect upon maternal expulsive efforts, no appreciable effect upon the neonate, and reversibility. Options for administration range from a single injection to a continuous spinal technique.

Areas for further study include the effect of intrathecal opioids and low-dose local anesthetics on the progress of labor, a comparison of intraspinal techniques with lumbar epidural analgesia, and further refinement of drug doses and combinations to maximize the duration of a single dose of analgesia. Additionally, a continuous spinal technique using an infusion of opioid analgesics for the duration of labor is particularly appealing. Intrathecal analgesia for labor gives the obstetric anesthesiologist many interesting and exciting options.

REFERENCES

1. Yaksh TL, Wilson PR, Kaiko RF, Inturrisi CE. Analgesia produced by a spinal action of morphine and effects upon parturition in the rat. Anesthesiology 1979;51:386.
2. Arkoosh VA, Leighton BL, Norris MC. Continuous spinal analgesia for labor. Society of Obstetric Anesthesia and Perinatology, Abstracts of Scientific Papers. 1990.
3. Benedetti C, Tiengo M. Continuous subarachnoid analgesia in labour. Lancet 1990;335:225.
4. Sosnowski M, Yaksh TL. Spinal administration of receptor-selective drugs as analgesics: New horizons. J Pain Symptom Management 1990;5:204.
5. Pert CB, Snyder SH. Opiate receptor: demonstration in nervous tissue. Science 1973;179:1011.
6. Atweh SF, Kuhar MJ. Autoradiographic localization of opiate receptors in rat brain. I. Spinal cord and lower medulla. Brain Res 1977;124:53.
7. Martin WR, Eades CG, Thompson JA, Huppler RE, Gilbert PE. The effects of morphine- and nalorphine-like drugs in the non-dependent and morphine-dependent chronic spinal dog. J Pharmacol Exp Ther 1976;198:66.
8. Sabbe MB, Yaksh TL. Pharmacology of spinal opioids. J Pain Symptom Management 1990;5:191.
9. Yaksh TL, Noueihed R. The physiology and pharmacology of spinal opiates. Ann Rev Pharmacol Toxicol 1985;25:433.
10. Sweeney MI, White TD, Sawynok J. Involvement of adenosine in the spinal antinociceptive effects of morphine and noradrenaline. J Pharmacol Exp Ther 1987;243(2):657.
11. Sawynok J, Sweeney MI, White TD. Adenosine release may mediate spinal analgesia by morphine. Trends in Pharmacological Sciences 1989;10:186.
12. Sosnowski M, Stevens CW, Yaksh TL. Assessment of the role of A1/A2 adenosine receptors mediating the purine antinociception, motor and autonomic function in the rat spinal cord. J Pharmacol Exp Ther 1989;250(3):915.
13. Power I, Brown DT, Wildsmith JAW. The effect of fentanyl, meperidine and diamorphine on nerve conduction in vitro. Reg Anesth 1991;16:204.
14. Gissen AJ, Gugino LD, Datta S, Miller J, Covino BG. Effects of fentanyl and sufentanil on peripheral mammalian nerves. Anesth Analg 1987;66:1272.
15. Shefner SA, North RA, Zukin RS. Opiate effects on rabbit vagus nerve: Electrophysiology and radioligand binding. Brain Res 1981;221:109.
16. Greene N. Uptake and elimination of local anesthetics during spinal anesthesia. Anesth Analg 1983;62:1013.
17. McQuay HJ, Sullivan AF, Smallman K, Dickenson AH. Intrathecal opioids: Potency and lipophilicity. Pain 1989;36:111.
18. Durant PAC, Yaksh TL. Drug effects on urinary bladder tone during spinal morphine-induced inhibition of the micturition reflex in unanesthetized rats. Anesthesiology 1988;68:325.
19. Rawal N, Mollefors K, Axelsson K, Lingårdh G, Widman B. An experimental study of urodynamic effects of epidural morphine and of naloxone reversal. Anesth Analg 1983;62:641.
20. Havemann U, Lechoslaw T, Kuschinsky K. Role of opioid receptors in the substantia nigra in morphine-induced muscular rigidity. Life Sci 1982;31:2319.
21. Erickson DL, Blacklock JB, Michaelson M, Sperling KB, Lo JN. Control of spasticity by implantable continuous flow morphine pump. Neurosurgery 1985;16:215.
22. Costello DJ, Borison HL. Naloxone antagonizes narcotic self-blockade of emesis in the cat. J Pharmacol Exp Ther 1977;203:222.
23. Atchison SR, Durant PA, Yaksh TL. Cardiorespiratory effects and kinetics of intrathecally injected d-ala-d-leu-enkephalin and morphine in unanesthetized dogs. Anesthesiology 1986;65:609.
24. Etches RC, Sandler AN, Daley MD. Respiratory depression and spinal opioids. Can J Anaesth 1989;36:165.
25. Ballantyne JC, Loach AB, Carr DB. Itching after epidural and spinal opiates. Pain 1988;33:149.
26. Abboud TK, Raya J, Noueihed R, Daniel J. Intrathecal morphine for relief of labor pain in a parturient with severe pulmonary hypertension. Anesthesiology 1983;59:477.
27. Brizgys RV, Shnider SM. Hyperbaric intrathecal morphine analgesia during labor in a patient with Wolff-Parkinson-White syndrome. Obstet Gynecol 1984;64:44S.
28. Copel JA, Harrison D, Whittemore R, Hobbins JC. Intrathecal morphine analgesia for vaginal delivery in a women with a single ventricle. J Reprod Med 1986;31:274.
29. Johnson MD, Hurley RJ, Gilbertson LI, Datta S. Continuous microcatheter spinal anesthesia with subarachnoid meperidine for labor and delivery. Anesth Analg 1190;70:658.
30. Scott PV, Bowen FE, Cartwright P, et al. Intrathecal morphine as sole analgesic during labor. Br Med J 1980;281:351
31. Baraka A, Noueihid R, Hajj S. Intrathecal injection of morphine for obstetric analgesia. Anesthesiology 1981;54:136.
32. Mok MS, Tsai SK. More experience with intrathecal morphine for obstetric analgesia [letter]. Anesthesiology 1981;55:481.
33. Abboud TK, Shnider SM, Dailey PA, et al. Intrathecal administration of hyperbaric morphine for the relief of pain in labour. Br J Anaesth 1984;56:1351.

34. Leighton BL, DeSimone CA, Norris MC, Ben-David B. Intrathecal narcotics for labor revisited: The combination of fentanyl and morphine intrathecally provides rapid onset of profound, prolonged analgeisa. Anesth Analg 1989;69:122.

35. Sharkey SJ, Arkoosh VA, Norris MC, Honet JE, Leighton BL. Comparison between intrathecal sufentanil and fentanyl for labor analgesia. Anesthesiology 1991; 75:A841.

36. Mankad AV, Segers LM, Pickard PW, Dark-Mezick DL, Shah AK. Intrathecal narcotics for labor: Efficacy of morphine, 0.5 mg, 0.75 mg, 1.0 mg, combined with fentanyl, 25 µg. Anesthesiology 1990;73:A1001.

37. Zakowski MI, Goldstein MJ, Ramanathan S, Turndorf H. Intrathecal fentanyl for labor analgesia. Anesthesiology 1991;75:A840.

38. Leicht CH, Evans DE, Durkan WJ. Intrathecal sufentanil for labor analgesia: Results of a pilot study. Anesthesiology 1990;73:A981.

39. Naulty JS, Barnes D, Becker R, Pate A. Continuous subarachnoid sufentanil for labor analgesia. Anesthesiology 1990;73:A964.

40. Swayze CR, Sholte FG, Walker EB, Skerman JH. Efficacy of intrathecal meperidine for labor analgesia. Anesth Analg 1991;72:S287.

41. Norris MC, Boreen S, Leighton BL, Mingey D, Kent H. Intrathecal meperidine for labor analgesia. Anesthesiology 1990;73:A983.

42. Leicht CH, Evans DE, Durkan WJ, Noltner S. Sufentanil versus fentanyl intrathecally for labor analgesia. Anesth Analg 1991;72:S159.

43. Honet JE, Arkoosh VA, Huffnagle HJ, Norris MC, Leighton BL. Comparison of fentanyl, meperdine and sufentanil for intrathecal labor analgesia. Anesthesiology 1991;75:A839.

44. Huckaby T, Skerman JH, Hurley RJ, Lambert DH. Sensory analgesia for vaginal deliveries: A preliminary report of continuous spinal anesthesia with a 32-gauge catheter. Reg Anesth 1991;16:150.

45. Hurley RJ, Lambert DH. Continuous spinal anesthesia with a microcatheter technique: Preliminary experience. Anesth Analg 1990;70:97.

46. Phillips OC, Nelson AT, Lyons WB, Graff TD, Harris LC, Frazier TM. Spinal anesthesia for vaginal delivery. Obstet Gynecol 1959;13:437.

47. Abouleish E, Rawal N, Shaw J, Lorenz T, Rashad MN. Intrathecal morphine 0.2 mg versus epidural bupivacaine 0.125% or their combination: Effects on parturients. Anesthesiology 1991;74:711.

48. Sivalingam T, Pleuvry BJ. Actions of morphine, pethidine and pentazocine on the oestrus and pregnant rat uterus in vitro. Br J Anaesth 1985;57:430.

49. Epstein BS, Banerjee S, Chamberlain G, Coakley CS. The effect of the concentration of local anesthetic during epidural anesthesia on the forces of labor. Anesthesiology 1968;29:187.

50. Crone LL, Conly JM, Storgard C, et al. Herpes labialis in parturients receiving epidural morphine following cesarean section. Anesthesiology 1990;73:208.

51. Weiss JH, Carney MD, Norris MC, Leighton BL, Torjman M. Incidence of recurrent herpes simplex virus labialis after cesarean section. Anesthesiology 1990; 73:A951.

52. Abouleish E. Apnoea associated with the intrathecal administration of morphine in obstetrics. Br J Anaesth 1988;60:592.

53. Rawal N, Arner S, Gustafsson LL, Allvin R. Present state of extradural and intrathecal opioid analgesia in Sweden. Br J Anaesth 1987;59:791.

54. Palmer CM. Early respiratory depression following intrathecal fentanyl–morphine combination. Anesthesiology 1991;74:1153.

55. Benedetti C, Chadwick HS, Mancuso JJ, Ross BK, Tiengo M. Incidence of postspinal headache after continuous subarachnoid analgesia for labor using a 32-gauge microcatheter. Anesthesiology 1990;73:A922.

56. Baxter AD. Microcatheters for continuous spinal anesthesia. Anesth Analg 1990;71:200.

57. Gravenstein N, Blackshear RH, Wissler RN. An approach to spinal or epidural catheters that are difficult to remove [letter]. Anesthesiology 1991;75:544.

58. Rigler ML, Drasner K, Krejcie TC, et al. Cauda equina syndrome after continuous spinal anesthesia. Anesth Analg 1991;72:275.

59. Lambert DH, Hurley RJ. Cauda equina syndrome and continuous spinal anesthesia. Anesth Analg 1991; 72:817.

60. Rigler ML, Drasner K. Distribution of catheter-injected local anesthetic in a model of the subarachnoid space. Anesthesiology 1991;75:684.

61. Bevacqua BK, Cleary WF, Slucky AV. Catheter spinal anesthesia and cauda equina syndrome: An alternative view [letter]. Anesth Analg 1991;73:367.

62. Rosenberg AL, Gold MI. Catheter spinal anesthesia and cauda equina syndrome: An alternative view [letter]. Anesth Analg 1991;73:368.

63. Wildsmith JAW. Catheter spinal anesthesia and cauda equina syndrome: An alternative view [letter]. Anesth Analg 1991;73:368.

CHAPTER 21

Cesarean Delivery: Obstetric Implications in the 1990s

Marilyn J. Darby-Gage
Richard Depp

TRENDS IN THE CESAREAN DELIVERY RATE

Cesarean birth has become the most common inpatient operative procedure in the United States and is the method of delivery of more than 25% of all live births.[1,2] Over the past 2 decades, the incidence of cesarean delivery has risen fivefold (Fig. 21-1).[3] Factors contributing to this increased rate are many and include the following:

- A broader definition of labor abnormalities proceeding to cesarean delivery
- Increasing fetal indications
- More women delaying childbearing into their thirties and beyond
- Concerns regarding medical–legal issues
- A resultant secondary increase in repeat cesarean births because of a rising number of previous primary cesarean deliveries

Although controversy regarding the proper role of cesarean birth has become a common topic of both medical and lay literature, the debate is not a new one. By the mid 1930s, Goldston suggested that "cesarean section was practiced by some as if it were merely an alternate method to normal delivery."[4] Advances in surgical and perioperative care that have reduced the morbidity and mortality of the procedure have simultaneously allowed a liberalization of the indications of cesarean birth with relative safety. The maternal mortality rate for cesarean delivery, however, remains several times higher than the mortality rate for obstetric patients undergoing vaginal delivery.[5] Major sources of morbidity and mortality relate directly to the operative procedure, including sepsis, anesthetic complications, and thromboembolic disease. A portion of the increased morbidity and mortality also relates to pre-existing risk factors that increase the need for cesarean delivery. Nonetheless, even when excluding the morbidity and mortality arising from the indications leading to cesarean delivery, maternal complications remain several-fold higher for cesarean compared to vaginal delivery.[6] These considerations also do not include any assessment of long-term morbidity such as transfusion-

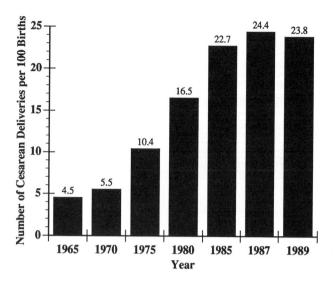

Figure 21–1. Cesarean delivery rate from 1965 to 1989. (Data from National Center for Health Statistics)

related complications or subsequent surgical complications related to the previous surgery.

The likelihood of cesarean delivery varies substantially among developed countries (Fig. 21-2).[7] The United States currently has one of the highest rates of delivery occurring by cesarean section in the industrialized world. Compared to other industrialized nations, it has had only modest success in reducing the perinatal mortality rate. From Dublin, Ireland, O'Driscoll *et al*[8] reported a stable cesarean section rate of 5% over the years of 1965 to 1980. Concom-

itantly, the perinatal mortality rate at that institution fell from 42.1 to 16.8/1000 births. Other factors also may influence the ultimate rate of cesarean delivery, making comparison of these results to American women difficult. These issues include the following:

- Differences in perinatal morbidity not conclusively evaluated

- The homogeneous nature of the Dublin patient population (including more multiparous patients who have a lower cesarean delivery rate)

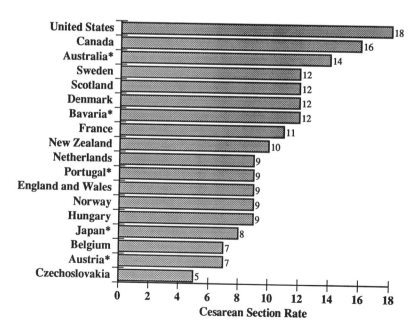

Figure 21–2. Cesarean delivery rates per 100 hospital deliveries in selected countries for 1981. (*=incomplete coverage.) (After Notzon FC, Placek PJ, Taffell SM. Comparisons of national cesarean-section rates. N Engl J Med 1987; 316:386)

- Differing styles in delivery room management, such as the use of one-to-one midwifery

Improvement in perinatal outcome cannot be clearly related to the observed increase in cesarean delivery rate. Factors unrelated to the mode of delivery itself, including early gestational age at delivery, fetal growth abnormalities, and congenital anomalies, lead to most perinatal deaths. More likely, the improvement in perinatal mortality stems from improvement in perinatal care rather than an increased rate of cesarean delivery (Fig. 21-3).[9]

Several studies also have addressed the cesarean section rate in university versus community hospital settings.[10,11] The data conflict. Both differing degrees of antecedent risk factors in patients delivering at these institutions and different practice styles influence the findings. The studies available to date do not support any consistent trends affecting the cesarean delivery rate. Two studies have, however, suggested that style of practice of individual physicians is an important determinant of the likelihood of cesarean delivery.[12,13]

In all but the smallest obstetric services in this country, anesthetic services are readily available and have little impact on the decision of whether or not cesarean delivery should be chosen. The recognized "standard of care" includes the ability to effect delivery within 30 minutes of the time of such a decision. Still, the availability and use of epidural anesthesia during labor may indirectly affect the intrapartum course. Some studies have shown a prolongation of the second stage of labor and an increase in instrumented deliveries. Still, no one has documented a clear increase in the cesarean delivery rate because of failure to progress or relative cephalopelvic disproportion coincident with the use of epidural anesthesia.[14,15]

INDICATIONS FOR CESAREAN DELIVERY

Cesarean delivery may be done either for the sole benefit of the fetus or the mother or for the combined benefit of both parties. Many indications for cesarean delivery are more relative than absolute. They also include a substantial component of subjective interpretation that remains controversial. Table 21-1 summarizes the common indications for cesarean delivery and their relative acceptance in the obstetric community.

Congenital Anomalies

Improved prenatal diagnosis over the past several years has led to the antenatal detection of fetal congenital anomalies, which allows for predelivery planning. The superiority of cesarean delivery over vaginal delivery with some specific congenital anomalies has been evaluated. Most of these studies have been retrospective, with possible biases in other confounding factors. Preliminary evidence supports a role of elective cesarean delivery in infants with a known meningomyelocele.[16] Cesarean delivery has no clear benefit for infants with omphalocele or gastroschisis,[17-19] despite the prior suggestion that this approach would decrease morbidity related to possible delivery trauma. Cesarean delivery also may permit a fetal/neonatal advantage with other anomalies, such as osteogenesis imperfecta, although objective data to support this opinion are lacking. Cesarean delivery seems not to offer any benefit for the majority of other congenital anomalies; however, these fetuses may be less tolerant of labor and therefore be indirectly more likely to undergo cesarean delivery. Occasionally, a fetal anomaly may be associated with risk to both mother and fetus. Significant fetal hydrocephalus with macrocephaly or all but the most immature conjoined twins may require cesarean delivery because of fetopelvic disproportion and its attendant risk of uterine rupture.

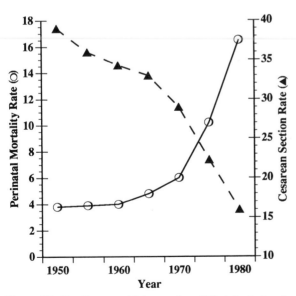

Figure 21–3. Cesarean birth rates (per 100 deliveries) and perinatal mortality rates (per 1000 deliveries) in the United States from 1950 to 1980. Note that much of the fall in perinatal mortality occurred before the cesarean section rate began to rise. (After Bottoms SF, Rosen MG, Sokol RJ. Current concepts: The increase in the cesarean birth rate. N Engl J Med 1980;302:559)

Table 21–1

Commonly Reported Indications for Cesarean Delivery

	SELECTIVE	SUBJECTIVE	CONTROVERSIAL*	UNIVERSALLY ACCEPTED†
Fetal Indications				
Nonreassuring fetal heart rate	✔	✔		✔
Breech, frank	✔		✔	
Breech, nonfrank	✔		✔	
Breech, preterm	✔		✔	
Very low birth weight (<1500 g)	✔		✔	
Herpes simplex virus	✔			
Immune thrombocytopenia purpura	✔			
Congenital anomalies, major	✔		✔	
Maternal Fetal Indications				
Cephalopelvic disproportion (relative)	✔	✔		✔
Failure to progress	✔	✔		✔
Placental abruption	✔	✔		✔
Placental previa				✔
Absolute pelvic disproportion		✔		✔
Maternal Indications				
Obstructive tumors	✔	✔		✔
Large vulvar condyloma	✔	✔		
Cervical cerclage (abdominal)	✔			
Prior vaginal colporrhaphy	✔			
Conjoined twins				✔

*Controversy regarding need to universal application.
†Universally accepted if selective/subjective criteria present.

Prematurity

Whether cesarean delivery affords any intrinsic benefit to the very-low-birthweight fetus (< 1500 g) has been widely debated. Hypothesized benefits include diminished risk of asphyxia in the immature brain, intracranial trauma, and intraventricular hemorrhage.

Most of the available data are of a descriptive nature from retrospective studies in which a multitude of confounding factors may have significantly affected the neonatal outcome. Foremost among these is the impact of physician and patient expectation regarding outcome on the likelihood of cesarean delivery. The net outcome in the vaginal delivery group was very likely adversely affected by inclusion of those fetuses in whom an inappropriate nonintervention approach was taken because of the a priori expectation of poor prognosis. It is also important to recognize that cesarean delivery by itself does not guarantee an atraumatic delivery. To date, there are insufficient data to suggest that universal cesarean delivery in the very-low-birthweight fetus improves survival or long-term outcome, particularly neurologic impairment,[20–22] but two recent studies have again suggested that cesarean delivery may reduce the risk of intraventricular hemorrhage.[23,24] The very-low-birthweight fetus presenting as a breech for delivery is an especially controversial aspect of the importance of delivery route on ultimate outcome in this group of infants. Again, nearly all studies are retrospective and have considerable potential study design flaws that substantially limit their generalizability. Although there is more similarity of opinion and practice for the low birthweight fetus presenting as a breech rather than vertex,[25,26] objective data to support a clear benefit of cesarean delivery remain elusive.[27]

Medicolegal

Medicolegal pressures also have had an impact on the liberalization of indications for cesarean delivery. Concern regarding potential malpractice action for failure to intervene in a timely fashion has increased dramatically during the last decade. One study has shown that private nulliparous patients are more likely than indigent patients cared for in a teaching hospital to undergo cesarean delivery if dystocia, malpresentation, or "fetal distress" are diagnosed.[10] The practice of obstetrics has become more defense-oriented since many obstetricians have concluded that they are less likely to be sued for unnecessary cesarean section than for failure to proceed with cesarean delivery in a timely manner. Hindsight, especially with a known adverse outcome, often suggests the need for earlier intervention.

Vaginal Birth After Cesarean Section

Approximately 10% of parturients will have had a prior cesarean delivery. As late as 1987, more than 90% of these women delivered by repeat cesarean delivery, most without an attempt at vaginal delivery.[3] If these women attempted a trial of labor, conservatively, 50% or more would have a successful vaginal delivery. This approach would reduce the overall cesarean delivery rate by a full 5%.

A trial of labor is now considered safe in women with a single lower-segment transverse uterine incision.[28–30] The primary maternal and fetal risk, scar separation, results in either dehiscence or frank uterine rupture. A distinction between uterine dehiscence and rupture is useful in consideration of the relative risk of labor after a prior cesarean delivery. Uterine dehiscence is a uterine scar separation that does not penetrate the uterine serosa, does not cause hemorrhage, and causes no major clinical problem.[31] This complication is no more likely to occur in patients who attempt a trial of labor than in those who undergo elective repeat cesarean delivery.[31,32] Dehiscence develops in approximately 0.5% to 5% of patients delivering after a previous cesarean delivery. The somewhat broad range of incidences probably reflects differing degrees of diagnostic certainty, particularly in an asymptomatic patient who delivers vaginally. Maternal mortality and intrapartum fetal death because of dehiscence of a low transverse uterine incision is rare, particularly when using continuous fetal monitoring. Most fetal deaths arising from uterine dehiscence occurred either before admission or before the advent of widespread use of continuous electronic fetal monitoring. Data for multiple prior lower-segment transverse scars and vertical lower-segment incisions also are accumulating. Preliminary results suggest that these circumstances, negligibly, if at all, increase the risk of uterine rupture or dehiscence.[33,34] The safety of vaginal delivery after an incision in the uterine fundus is less optimistic, and a known "classical" uterine incision generally remains a contraindication to an attempt at subsequent vaginal delivery.

Despite theoretic concerns, neither artificial stimulation of the uterus with oxytocin to induce or augment labor nor low-dose prostaglandin gel to attempt cervical softening increase the risk of scar separation or rupture.[31–37] Similarly, hypothetical concerns that epidural anesthesia may mask signs and symptoms of uterine scar separation have not been realized.[38–41]

There is little doubt that vaginal delivery following a prior cesarean birth can be effected in most patients in whom it is seriously attempted. Those women who have had a cesarean delivery for a nonrecurring indication (*e.g.,* malpresentation, "fetal distress") will successfully deliver vaginally in upwards of 80% of attempts. Even in those women with potentially recurring indications, such as dystocia or cephalopelvic disproportion, as many as 70% also will successfully deliver vaginally.[42]

Implementation of more widespread acceptance of vaginal birth after cesarean delivery is progressing, albeit slowly. Physician and patient reluctance are gradually dissipating. Younger obstetricians have more direct familiarity with the idea and its safety and success. Patients are beginning to both passively accept and actively pursue vaginal birth after cesarean section. The American College of Obstetricians and Gynecologists has formulated and proposed guidelines that unequivocally support vaginal birth after cesarean section in women with one prior low transverse cesarean delivery, in most instances.[43] The potential economic impact of this change is substantial. In 1985, Flamm[28] estimated a potential savings of one-half billion dollars, assuming a repeat cesarean section rate of 6% instead of 10% and 3.4 million births per year in the United States.

SUMMARY

The proper role of cesarean delivery in obstetric care in the 1990s will generate much discussion among both obstetricians and the patients and families whom they care for. The incidence of cesarean delivery has increased dramatically over the past 2 decades. How much of that increase is truly justified is open to question. Although some believe that the increase in cesarean deliveries is certainly medically justified, it is also likely that both the primary and repeat cesarean section rates may be selectively decreased. Strategies to reduce the cesarean delivery rate will involve a concerted effort on the parts of both physicians and patients and their families. How the rate of cesarean delivery can be reduced without imposing unnecessary risk on either the mother or the fetus is the challenge of the present decade.

REFERENCES

1. Rutkow I. Obstetric and gynecologic operations in the United States, 1979 to 1984. Obstet Gynecol 1986; 67:755.

2. Taffel SM, Placek PJ, Liss T. Trends in the United States cesarean section rate for the 1980–1985 rise. Am J Public Health 1987;77:955.

3. Shiono PA, McNellis D, Rhoads GS. Reasons for the rising cesarean delivery rates, 1978–1984. Obstet Gynecol 1987;69:696.

4. Goldston I. Maternal death and ways to prevention. New York: Commonwealth Fund. 1937:47.

5. Petitti DB. Maternal mortality and morbidity in cesarean section. Clin Obstet Gynecol 1985;28:763.

6. Rubin GL, Peterson HB, Rochat RW, McCarthy BJ, Terry JS. Maternal death after cesarean section in Georgia. Am J Obstet Gynecol 1981;139:681.

7. Notzon FC, Placek PJ, Taffel SM. Comparisons of national cesarean-section rates. N Engl J Med 1987; 316:386.

8. O'Driscoll K, Foley M. Correlation of decrease in perinatal mortality and increase in cesarean section rate. Obstet Gynecol 1983;61:1.

9. Williams RL, Hawes WE. Cesarean section, fetal monitoring, and perinatal mortality in California. Am J Public Health 1979;69:864.

10. Blumenthal NJ, Harris RS, O'Connor MC, et al. Changing cesarean section rates experience at a Sydney obstetric teaching hospital. Aust NZ J Obstet Gynaecol 1984;24:246.

11. Haynes de Regt RH, Minkoff HL, Feldman J, Schwarz RH. Relation of private or clinic care to the cesarean birth rate. N Engl J Med 1986;315:619.

12. Phillips RN, Thornton J, Gleicher N. Physician bias in cesarean section. JAMA 1982;248:1082.

13. Goyert GL, Bottoms SI, Treadwell MC, Nehra PC. The physician factor in cesarean birth rates. N Engl J Med 1989;320:706.

14. Kaminski HM, Stafl A, Aiman J. The effect of epidural analgesia on the frequency of instrumental obstetric delivery. Obstet Gynecol 1987;69:770.

15. Chestnut DH, Vahdewallch GE, Oven CL, Bates JN, Chsi WW. The influence of continuous epidural and bupivacaine analgesia on the second stage of labor and method of deliveries in nulliparous women. Anesthesiology 1987;66:774.

16. Luthy DA, Wardinsky T, Shurtleff DB, et al. Cesarean section before the onset of labor and subsequent motor function in infants with meningomyelocele diagnosed antenatally. N Engl J Med 1991;324:662.

17. Morett M, Khourg A, Rodriquez J, Lobe T, et al. The effect of mode of delivery on the perinatal outcome in fetuses with abdominal wall defects. Am J Obstet Gynecol 1990;163:833.

18. Lewis DF, Towers CV, Garite TJ, Jackson DN, et al. Fetal gastroschisis and omphalocele: Is cesarean section the best mode of delivery? Am J Obstet Gynecol 1990; 163:773.

19. Bethel CA, Seashore JH, Touloukian RJ. Cesarean section does not improve outcome in gastroschesis. J Pediatr Surg 1989;24:1.

20. Malloy MH, Onstad L, Wright E. The effect of cesarean delivery on birth outcome in very low birthweight infants. Obstet Gynecol 1991;77:498.

21. Vu VY, Bajuk B, Cutting D, Orgill AA, Astbury J. Effect of mode of delivery on outcome of very-low-birthweight infants. Br J Obstet Gynecol 1984;91:633.

22. Barrett JM, Boehm FH, Vaughn WK. The effect of type of delivery on neonatal outcome in singleton infants of birthweight of 1000 g or less. JAMA 1983;250:625.

23. Leviton A, Tenton T, Kuban KC, Pagano M. Labor and delivery characteristics and the risk of germinal matrix hemorrhage in low birthweight infants. J Child Neurol 1991;6:35.

24. Phillip AG, Allen WC. Does cesarean section protect against intraventricular hemorrhage in preterm infants? J Perinatol 1991;11:3.

25. Main DM, Main EK, Maurer MM. Cesarean section versus vaginal delivery for the breech fetus weighing less than 1500 grams. Am J Obstet Gynecol 1983;146:580.

26. Doyle LW, Richards AL, Ford GW, Pepperell RJ, Kitchen W. Outcome for the very low birth-weight (500–1499 g) singleton breech: Benefit of cesarean section. Aust NZJ Obst Gynaecol 1985;25:259.

27. Socol ML, Cohen L, Depp R, Dooley SL, Tamura RK: Apgar scores and umbilical cord arterial pH in the breech neonate. Int J Gynaecol Obstet 1988;27:37.

28. Flamm BL. Vaginal birth after cesarean section: Controversies old and new. Clin Obstet Gynecol 1985;28:735.

29. Lavin JP, Stephens RJ, Miodovnik M, et al. Vaginal delivery in patients with a prior cesarean section. Obstet Gynecol 1982;59:135.

30. Tahilramaney MP, Boucher M, Eglinton GS, et al. Previous cesarean section and trial of labor: Factors related to uterine dehiscene. J Reprod Med 1984;29:17.

31. Phelan JP, Clark SL, Diaz F, et al. Vaginal birth after cesarean. Am J Obstet Gynecol 1987;157:1510.

32. Paul RH, Phelan JP, Yeh S. Trial of labor in the patient with a prior cesarean birth. Am J Obstet Gynecol 1985;151:297.

33. Martin JN, Harris BA, Huddleston JF, et al. Vaginal delivery following previous cesarean birth. Am J Obstet Gynecol 1983;146:255.

34. Porreco RP, Meier PR. Trial of labor in patients with multiple previous cesarean section. J Reprod Med 1983; 28:770.

35. Horenstein JP, Phelan JP. Previous cesarean section: The risks and benefits of oxytocin usage in a trial of labor. Am J Obstet Gynecol 1985;151:564.

36. Horenstein J, Phelan JP. Vaginal birth after cesarean: The role of oxytocin. In: Phelan JP, Clark SL, eds. Cesarean delivery. New York: Elsevier, 1988.

37. Mackenzie IZ, Bradley S, Embrey MP. Vaginal protaglandins and labor induction for patients previously delivered by cesarean section. Br J Obstet Gynecol 1984;91:7.

38. Flamm BL, Dunnett C, Fischermann E, et al. Vaginal delivery following cesarean section: Use of oxytocin augmentation and epidural anesthesia with internal tocodynamic and internal fetal monitoring. Am J Obstet Gynecol 1984;148:759.

39. Carlson C, Lybell-Lindahl G, Ingemarsson I. Extradural block in patients who have previously undergone cesarean section. Br J Anaesth 1980;52:827.

40. Crawford JS. The epidural sieve and MBC (minimal blocking concentration): A hypothesis. Anaesthesia 1976;31:1278.

41. Uppington J. Epidural analgesia and previous caesarean section. Anaesthesia 1983;38:336.

42. Eglinton GS. Effect of previous indications for cesarean on subsequent outcome. In Phelan JP, Clark SL, eds. Cesarean delivery. New York: Elsevier, 1988.

43. American College of Obstetricians and Gynecologists Committee on Maternal and Fetal Medicine: Guidelines for vaginal delivery after a previous cesarean birth. October, 1988.

CHAPTER 22

General Anesthesia for Cesarean Delivery

Andrew M. Malinow

In North America, 20% to 40% of cesarean deliveries are accomplished under general anesthesia.[1,2] The frequency of general anesthesia for cesarean delivery varies greatly between individual hospitals. Several factors influence the use of general anesthesia. These issues include the following:

- Patterns of labor analgesia (a higher use of epidural analgesia for labor increases the use of epidural anesthesia for cesarean delivery)
- Patient populations (high-risk obstetric centers with more stressed and distressed fetuses needing immediate termination of labor may use general anesthesia more commonly)
- Obstetrician and anesthesiologist practice patterns (the diagnosis of fetal distress and therefore the need for emergency delivery vary from institution to institution)

INDICATIONS

Although the use of general anesthesia for elective cesarean delivery is no longer routine, the technique must be available at any time to facilitate obstetric intervention. In modern practice, general anesthesia for cesarean delivery is reserved for limited situations (Table 22-1). Coexisting maternal disease that contraindicates

regional anesthesia and rapid deterioration of fetal well-being are the most common of these indications. In addition, not every regional anesthetic proves adequate for the entire surgical procedure. Oversedation, resulting in loss of maternal airway reflexes, may lead to disaster. In the face of inadequate regional anesthesia, I prefer intraoperative induction of general anesthesia with tracheal intubation.

ADVANTAGES

General anesthesia produces rapid, reproducible conditions for cesarean delivery. General anesthesia has a long record of fetal and relative maternal safety. Success of general anesthesia is independent of a patient's anxiety about remaining "awake." Stoicism is not a factor in the patient under general anesthesia.

DISADVANTAGES

Disadvantages of general anesthesia center on airway management (Table 22-2). Anatomic and physiologic changes of pregnancy increase the risk of failed intubation. Parturients are at high risk for aspiration of gastric contents. The often hectic and tumultuous conditions surrounding emergent cesarean delivery may compromise preoperative evaluation of the parturient with a potentially difficult airway.

Today, an anesthesiologist routinely uses a multitude of drugs during a general anesthetic. The obstetric suite is an ideal site for drug substitution or other misuse. Anesthetic medications often are prepared, labeled, and left unattended on an operating room anesthesia cart. Later, they may be used immediately to induce general anesthesia. Owing to the frequent use of regional anesthesia in the labor and delivery suite, anesthesia machines are used less often than in the general surgical suite. These anesthesia machines may receive less frequent routine maintenance. The possibility of undetected machine malfunction increases. All anesthetic machines in the labor and delivery suite should be checked out daily and after every use in anticipation of emergency induction of general anesthesia. Finally, the physiologic consequences of the induction of general anesthesia and tracheal intubation may prove deleterious to the mother with coexisting medical conditions (*e.g.*, cardiac or neurologic).

PREPARATION FOR GENERAL ANESTHESIA

Airway Assessment

Preoperative evaluation begins with a thorough evaluation of the airway. The following factors contribute to difficulties with tracheal intubation of the parturient:

- The often emergent nature of cesarean delivery that limits the time available for preanesthetic evaluation and preparation
- The relative scarcity of medical personnel who can help with a difficult airway
- The anatomic changes in the airway of the gravida, perhaps exacerbated by obesity or preeclampsia/eclampsia
- The inexperience of anesthesiology personnel often assigned to the labor and delivery suite

Importance of Airway Assessment

INCIDENCE. In the United States, anesthetic-related maternal mortality is now almost exclusively due to airway problems at the time of general anesthesia for cesarean delivery.[3] The incidence of failed intubation in the obstetric population is 1/280, eight times more frequent than in the general surgical patient population.[4]

Table 22-1

Indications for General Anesthesia for Cesarean Delivery

Acute Severe Fetal Distress
Epidural catheter *not* in situ
Relative and Absolute Contraindications to Regional Anesthesia
Maternal hemodynamic instability
Severe maternal hemorrhage
Coexisting maternal cardiac disease (*e.g.*, severe right-to-left shunt, fixed primary pulmonary hypertension, severe aortic stenosis)
Maternal coagulopathy
Maternal infection
Superficial to the lumbosacral spine
Sepsis
Patient Refusal of Regional Anesthesia
Regional Anesthesia Inadequate for Surgery

IDENTIFYING THE PATIENT "AT-RISK." The Confidential Enquiry into Perioperative Death (1987) found that important preanesthetic assessment did not occur in 10% of the mortalities reviewed.[5] Regular review of patients admitted to the labor and delivery suite can anticipate 87% of urgent or emergent cesarean deliveries.[5] The anesthesiologist must identify the parturient with a potentially difficult airway soon

Table 22-2

Disadvantages of General Anesthesia for Cesarean Delivery

Maternal airway management
Failed intubation
Trauma
Increased number of anesthetic drugs needed (drug substitution)
Anesthesia machine failure
Physiologic consequences of general anesthesia
Stress response and coexisting disease (*i.e.*, increase intracranial pressure), at induction, tracheal intubation, emergence, tracheal extubation
Pharmacologic response to general anesthesia
Anesthetic agents desired effects (*i.e.*, intraoperative amnesia), undesired effects (*i.e.*, hyperkalemic response to succinylcholine in patient with paraplegia)

after her admission to the labor and delivery suite. Look for the presence of the many different indicators of difficult airway (*i.e.,* ability to open the mouth, mandibular length, loose dentition). Attempt to visualize the normal oropharyngeal anatomy (soft palate, uvula, and tonsillar fossae).

Factors Associated with Difficult Airway

ANATOMIC ABNORMALITIES. Samsoon and Young[4] reported retrospectively a group of seven parturients who previously experienced failed intubation. At the first post-discharge visit, they confirmed the immediate antepartum conclusion that external examination of the head and neck would not hint at difficult tracheal intubation. However, visual inspection of the oropharynx in six of these seven women revealed partial or total obliteration of anatomic detail (the seventh women had normal structure but was already diagnosed with tracheal stenosis). On laryngoscopy, the glottic aperture and posterior arytenoid cartilage were not visualized in five of these six women.[4] The relative absence of normal anatomic detail (soft palate, uvula, and tonsillar fossae) upon visual inspection of the oropharynx therefore correlates with possible difficult intubation in obstetric as well as nonobstetric patients (see Chap. 32).[6]

OBESITY. In one recent review, obesity complicated 80% of anesthetic-related maternal deaths. Forty-seven percent of the cases involved general anesthesia for cesarean delivery. One half of the deaths were directly due to failure to establish an adequate airway.[7] Obesity (BMI > 23) doubles the incidence of partially obliterated oropharyngeal anatomy.[8] The cesarean delivery rate and, therefore, incidence of anesthetic intervention also increases from 18% to 30%. In the morbidly obese parturient (> 300 lb), the cesarean delivery rate exceeds 50%. Half these operations are done during labor.[9] In one series, 24% of cesarean deliveries were accomplished under general anesthesia. One third of the intubations were difficult, with a failed intubation rate of 6% (1 patient of 17).[9]

PREGNANCY-INDUCED HYPERTENSION. Pregnancy-induced hypertension also may predispose to difficult intubation. Women with pregnancy-induced hypertension (a population with a high cesarean delivery rate) are twice as likely as normotensive parturients to have poorly visible oropharyngeal structures.[10]

Avoiding Trouble with the Difficult Airway

EARLY INDUCTION OF EPIDURAL ANALGESIA. Early induction of labor analgesia precludes the need for general anesthesia in most parturients should cesarean delivery later become necessary; however, not every epidural anesthetic proves adequate for cesarean delivery. Intraoperative induction of general anesthesia may be required should unanticipated intraoperative events delay closure of the abdomen and create distress in the awake (and aware) parturient. For example, massive hemorrhage (with possible hemodynamic instability), unplanned uterine repair, or hysterectomy occur in 1.3% to 1.6% of repeat cesarean deliveries in women given a trial of labor.[11] In addition, labor epidural analgesia cannot always be converted to adequate anesthesia for emergent cesarean delivery. Morgan *et al*[5] had to convert 14% of already established epidural anesthetics to general anesthesia before emergent cesarean delivery of the fetus. When the decision to delivery time was less than 10 minutes, the incidence of an epidural anesthetic being converted to general anesthesia was 50%.[5] Although these clinicians used 50% nitrous oxide to supplement inadequate epidural anesthesia, they did not use rapidly acting 3% 2-chloroprocaine. At the University of Maryland, for comparison, the anesthesiologist uses 3% 2-chloroprocaine to extend and intensify epidural anesthesia for emergent cesarean delivery. Inadequate regional anesthesia requires general anesthesia via tracheal tube. We do not use supplemental inhalation or intravenous ketamine analgesia. Using this protocol, approximately 8% of epidural anesthetics for cesarean delivery are converted to general anesthesia at some time during the surgery, usually under conditions of emergent cesarean delivery for fetal distress.

DEVELOPING A PLAN. Identification of the parturient with a potentially difficult airway helps ensure adequate time to plan and to communicate with the obstetrician before the need for general anesthesia. Appropriate planning may include such possibilities as awake intubation, fiberoptic bronchoscopy–assisted intubation, surgical control of the airway, or retrograde intubation. Such intention requires time to collect personnel and equipment.

EXPERIENCED PERSONNEL. Finally, the experience of the anesthesiologist plays an important role in the incidence of anesthetic-related maternal mortality.[12] Experience, especially as it relates to the prediction and management of the difficult airway, is acquired during training and is not innate to the unsupervised junior trainee.

Acid-Aspiration Prophylaxis

Pharmacologic methods of acid-aspiration prophylaxis are part of the planning for every general anesthetic for cesarean delivery. Drug trials in humans provide conflicting data on which regimen is best. No one agent (or combination of agents) will ensure a nonfatal aspiration. Even the accepted criteria of critical intragastric volume (0.4 mL/kg) and acidity (pH > 2.5)[13] have not been rigorously developed. Acidity of the aspirate may be more crucial than volume.[14] This fact is important, especially in pharmacologic preparation of the nonfasted parturient whose labor is being terminated with an urgent or emergent cesarean delivery. Obstetric practices about the ingestion of food (*i.e.,* clear liquids) vary greatly, particularly in the latent phase of labor. In addition, labor analgesia practices using parenteral (and epidural ?) narcotics, known inhibitors of gastric motility, also vary greatly. Applying study data to the clinical situation requires careful interpretation. The urgency of the clinical situation often precludes certain agents. Clinicians use antacids, H_2-receptor antagonists, and metoclopramide in varying combinations in a search for the optimally prepared "full stomach."

Urgent or Emergent Cesarean Delivery

Adequate preparation of gastric contents in the laboring patient differs somewhat from that of the fasted parturient presenting for elective delivery. Women may eat just before admission. Labor significantly slows or eliminates physiologic gastric emptying, resulting in a true "full stomach." No acid-aspiration prophylaxis regimen reliably reduces the volume and raises the acidity of gastric contents in the laboring patient. Mechanically emptying the stomach before induction of anesthesia for cesarean delivery is no better than a single dose of sodium citrate at decreasing the number of patients at risk for aspiration pneumonitis.[15] This cruel punishment, awake passage of a gastric tube, has, I hope, been abandoned in the modern practice of obstetric anesthesia.

Antacid

Administration of 0.3 M of sodium citrate quickly and reliably increases the pH of intragastric contents (Figs. 22-1 and 22-2B).[16-18] There is mild controversy over the dose (15 mL or 30 mL) of sodium citrate. In some studies, the larger dose produces a greater rise in pH (5.7 ± 0.8 vs 4.6 ± 1.1).[18] In addition, 30 mL maintains pH above 2.5 for a longer time[19] without significantly increasing intragastric volume[18] as compared to the smaller dose (Table 22-3). Sodium bicarbonate has been used as a single-dose antacid in parturients with questionable efficacy.[20]

Ranitidine

The co-administration of single-dose ranitidine (50 mg) intravenously and sodium citrate (0.3 M) orally maintains intragastric alkalinization longer than the

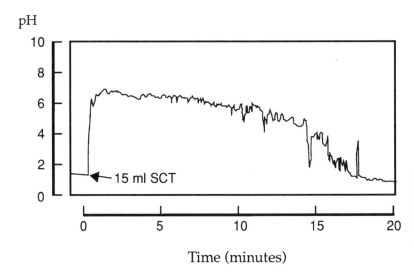

Figure 22–1. Intragastric pH change after the administration of 15 mL of 0.3 M sodium citrate (SCT) to a woman in labor. (O'Sullivan GM, Bullingham RE. Noninvasive assessment by radiotelemetry of antacid effect during labor. Anesth Analg 1985;64:95)

ingestion of antacid alone;[15] however, this effect becomes significant only 2 hours after treatment. Ranitidine does not reduce intragastric volume;[15] therefore, the co-administration of single-dose intravenous ranitidine and oral antacid is of little practical use in the parturient presenting for emergent or urgent cesarean delivery under general anesthesia. Regularly scheduled parenteral ranitidine doses during labor do not adequately prepare the gastric contents of the laboring parturient presenting for emergent or urgent cesarean delivery under general anesthesia (Fig. 22-2C).[18] Therefore, at the very least, give an oral antacid before inducing general anesthesia for urgent or emergent cesarean delivery (Table 22-4).[18,21]

Effervescent Cimetidine/Sodium Citrate

Effervescent cimetidine/sodium citrate (400 mg/ 0.9 M, respectively, in 15 mL of water) effectively alkalinizes intragastric contents.[22] This combination will maintain intragastric pH significantly higher than antacid alone at 1 hour after treatment and beyond. In addition, fewer patients have gastric aspirates with pH less than 2.5 at 20 minutes (1.6%) and at 60 minutes (1.6%) as compared to antacid treatment alone (14% and 10% at 20 min and 60 min, respectively). These results are similar to those seen after the coadministration of intravenous ranitidine and oral sodium citrate (Fig. 22-2D). Additional studies may confirm that this promising oral combination drug is superior to oral antacid alone.

Metoclopramide

Metoclopramide often is given before the induction of general anesthesia for urgent cesarean delivery. It will increase lower esophageal sphincter tone within 2 to 5 minutes of parenteral administration.[23] As compared to placebo, intravenous metoclopramide (10 mg) decreases mean residual intragastric volume (59.5 ± 61 mL vs 19.0 ± 13 mL). In addition, fewer patients have volumes greater than 25 mL (75% vs 36%).[24]

Narcotic administration inhibits the effects of metoclopramide.[25] A dose of metoclopramide at induction or during general anesthesia in hope of emptying the stomach before extubation is therefore of questionable value. In addition, the use of metoclopramide is not without risk.[26–28] Therefore, I give metoclopramide only to parturients who present for urgent or emergent cesarean delivery soon after eating (see Table 22-4).

Elective Cesarean Delivery

The patient scheduled for cesarean delivery should routinely fast for at least 8 hours before induction of general anesthesia. Feeding women clear liquids just before a 4-hour fast doubles the volume of gastric aspirate compared to those patients conventionally fasted (65 ± 21 mL vs 33 ± 22 mL, respectively).[29] Antacid ingestion adequately alkalinized gastric aspirates in all patients.[29] In the conventionally fasted patient presenting for elective cesarean delivery, two doses of ranitidine (150 mg PO then 50 mg IM) or cimetidine (400 mg PO then 200 mg IM) over 6 to 8 hours will decrease intragastric volume (to 9 ± 7.2 mL) and increase pH (to 6.2 ± 0.8).[13,30] In these studies, no patient had a gastric aspirate volume greater than 25 mL or pH less than 2.5. Further alkalinization of the stomach (at the expense of increased intragastric volume) increases the risk in an already acceptably "prepared" patient. The use of a double-dose (orally, then intramuscularly) H_2-receptor antagonist regimen therefore avoids the need for routine use of oral antacid (or intravenous metoclopramide). Single-dose oral ranitidine (150 mg) regimens yield statistically similar mean intragastric volume and pH as a double-dose oral regimen in women presenting for cesarean delivery.[21,31] However, the incidence of "treatment failures" (or those patients exceeding acceptable intragastric volume or acidity criteria) is increased with a single- or double-dose oral ranitidine regimen (3%) as compared to a double-dose (orally, then intramuscularly) ranitidine regimen (0%). Parenteral metoclopramide eliminated treatment failures in patients given double-dose oral ranitidine.[31] If a double-dose H_2-receptor antagonist regimen has not been followed or if there is suspicion over the fasted status of the patient, then intragastric volume reduction with parenteral metoclopramide[31] as well as ingestion of oral antacid[32] seems justified before induction of anesthesia (see Table 22-4).

Omeprazole

Preliminary work has shown that omeprazole (which blocks the proton pump in the parietal cell) is effective in reducing both intragastric volume and acidity after a double-dose oral (40 mg at night and early morning) regimen in women fasted before elective cesarean section.[33] Double-dose omeprazole yields intragastric volumes and acidity that are similar to those yielded by double-dose oral ranitidine (150 mg). However, the incidence of treatment failures was nil compared to 6% for the parturients receiving ranitidine.[33] Omeprazole seems a promising oral alternative to oral

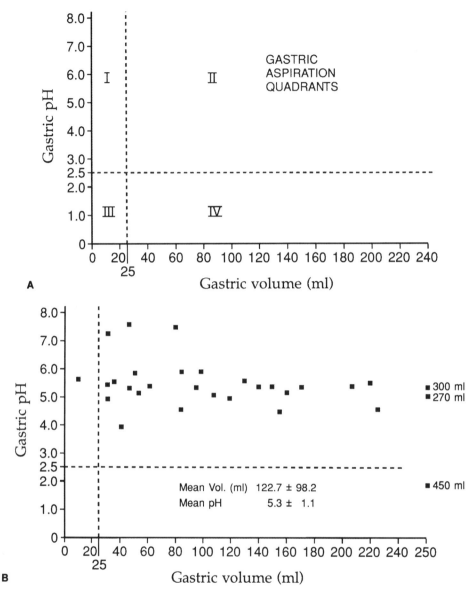

Figure 22–2. **(A)** Division of gastric pH and volume coordinates into four quadrants indicating risk level. Patients in quadrant IV (pH < 2.5, and volume > 25 mL) should be at greatest risk for the development of acid pneumonitis after aspiration of gastric contents. **(B)** Gastric volume and pH in laboring parturients receiving only 0.3 M sodium citrate before emergency cesarean delivery. Fifteen received 15 mL of sodium citrate and 15 received 30 mL. **(C)** Gastric volume and pH at cesarean delivery in laboring parturients receiving ranitidine, 50 mg IM, every 6 hours during labor. **(D)** Gastric volume and pH at cesarean delivery in laboring parturients receiving ranitidine, 50 mg IM, every 6 hours during labor and one dose of 0.3 M sodium citrate, 15 mL, immediately before the induction of anesthesia. (Colman RD, Frank M, Loughnan BA, Cohen DG, Cattermole R. Use of IM ranitidine for the prophylaxis of aspiration pneumonitis in obstetrics. Br J Anaesth 1988;61:720)

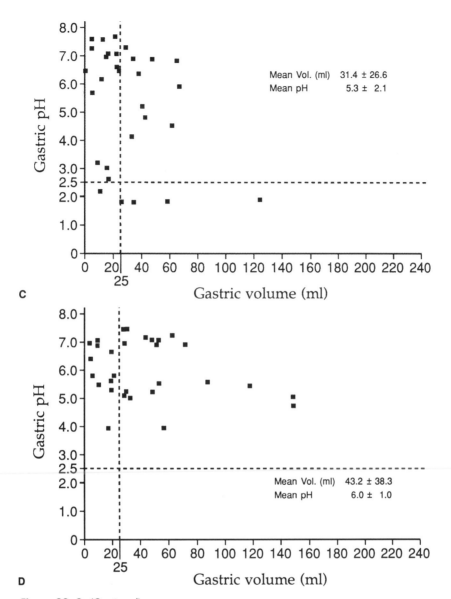

Figure 22–2. *(Continued)*

and parenteral combinations. Single-dose omeprazole provides inadequate preparation of gastric contents.[34]

Cost-effectiveness

The cost-effectiveness of acid-aspiration prophylaxis is often questioned in the modern practice of obstetric anesthesia; there are few answers. An abstract presented at the 1985 Annual Meeting of the Society of Obstetric Anesthesia and Perinatology statistically modeled the cost-effectiveness of three acid-aspiration prophylaxis regimens (0.3 M sodium citrate, double-dose parenteral cimetidine, and the combination of these two drugs) in a parturient population.[35] For elective cesarean deliveries, the combination of antacid and H_2-receptor antagonist reduced mortality to almost nil, with an incremental cost of $130,000/life saved as compared to antacid alone. In the laboring parturient, antacid was both more effective and less costly than cimetidine. Antacid therapy reduced mortality by al-

Table 22-3

Alkalinization of Gastric Contents by 0.3 M Sodium Citrate, as Measured by Noninvasive Radiotelemetry

	MEDIAN BASAL pH (RANGE)	MEDIAN MAXIMUM pH (RANGE)	MEAN TIME TO PEAK pH (RANGE)*	MEAN TIME pH > 3.0 (RANGE)*
15 mL Sodium citrate (in labor)	2 (1.4–2.5)	6.8 (5.4–7.9)	1.0 (0.6–2.8)	84† (11.8–195.8)§
15 mL Sodium citrate (term but not in labor)	1.4 (1.3–2.8)	6.8 (5.9–7.5)		26.6 (17.8–104.3)§
30 mL Sodium citrate (term but not in labor)	2 (1.6–2.5)	6.8 (5.8–8.3)		42.1 (6.6–97.5)§

(Data from O'Sullivan GM, Bullingham RE. Non-invasive assessment by radiotelemetry of antacid effect during labor. Anesth Analg 1985;64:95; and O'Sullivan GM, Bullingham RE. Does twice the volume of antacid have twice the effect in pregnant women at term? Anesth Analg 1984;63:752)

*Minutes

†Prolonged duration patients in labor; probably due to effects of labor decreasing gastrointestinal motility.

§Note wide range of duration of action.

most 90% when compared to no intervention, at a cost of $57,000/life saved. Combination therapy further reduced mortality at the great incremental cost of $40,000,000/life saved. Results from this model support the routine use of H_2-receptor antagonist therapy before elective cesarean delivery. Results from this model cast added doubt (about cost efficacy) to my skepticism about the routine use of H_2-receptor antagonist therapy during labor.

Positioning

Uterine Displacement

All parturients placed on an operating room table in anticipation of cesarean delivery should have uterine displacement assured to avoid supine hypotension. Methods of uterine displacement are not as important as their routine and vigilant practice.

Table 22-4

Suggested Acid-aspiration Prophylaxis

Scheduled Elective Cesarean Delivery	
(Assuming a fasted patient for scheduled 7:30 AM delivery)	
Ranitidine	150 mg PO at 10 PM, 50 mg IV at 6 AM
Urgent Cesarean Delivery	
(Patient may or may not be in labor; at least 5 min available before induction of anesthesia)	
Metoclopramide	10 mg slow IV
0.3 M Sodium citrate	30 mL PO before moving to operating room table
Ranitidine	Consider 50 mg IV if there are 30–60 min until need for induction of anesthesia
Emergent Cesarean Delivery	
(Less than 5 min until needed induction of anesthesia)	
0.3 M Sodium citrate	30 mL PO before moving to operating room table

Operating Table Position

Venous air emboli occur commonly during cesarean delivery (44%–62%)[36-38] and are unrelated to the type of anesthesia.[37] Venous air emboli at cesarean delivery are only rarely hemodynamically significant, although their occurrence has been associated with cardiorespiratory collapse.[39] Positioning the table in a 5-degrees reverse Trendelenburg's position decreases the incidence of venous air emboli to less than 8%.[37] I routinely place the patient in a slight head-up position at the start of surgery and avoid Trendelenburg's position during cesarean delivery.

Optimal Airway Management

No matter how emergent the need for delivery, take time before the induction of general anesthesia to ensure optimal alignment of the shoulders, neck, and head ("sniffing" position). This step will maximize the chances of successful intubation and help emergency airway management, should it become necessary. Blankets are ubiquitous in the delivery suite. Even the extremely obese parturient can be optimally positioned using folded and stacked blankets to support the upper back and maternal occiput (see Chap. 26).

Monitoring and Equipment

The parturient undergoing cesarean section requires the same types of intraoperative monitoring as any patient undergoing emergency intra-abdominal surgery.

Airway/Breathing

End-tidal gas analysis is essential in the management of the patient under general anesthesia. Measurement of end-tidal nitrogen can document adequate denitrogenation before rapid sequence induction of anesthesia. Capnography helps ensure proper position of the tracheal tube. Intraoperative capnometry aids in monitoring maternal ventilation. Although the short interval between intubation and delivery of the fetus may not be clinically similar to the animal model; in the gravid ewe, intermittent positive-pressure hyperventilation decreases uteroplacental perfusion in the gravid ewe. The resultant hypocapnia may hinder placental exchange of oxygen and carbon dioxide owing to a shift in oxyhemoglobin affinity.[40] In the term gravida, a decrease in the alveolar dead space relative to increased alveolar ventilation[41] lowers the end-tidal/arterial carbon dioxide gradient toward zero.[42,43] A tidal volume of 10 mL/kg at 10 breaths/minute using a semiclosed circle system will provide the least change in fetal acid–base balance, will not increase the incidence of low Apgar score, and will provide maternal normocapnia.[44] Monitoring maternal exhaled carbon dioxide with capnometry will document normocapnia.

Circulation

Establish sufficient intravenous access to allow rapid replacement of large fluid volumes. A free-flowing, securely fastened, large-bore (at least 18-gauge) peripheral intravenous catheter should be in situ before induction of general anesthesia for anticipated routine cesarean delivery. Certain high-risk conditions as well as changing intraoperative surgical conditions may demand additional intravenous access to allow rapid transfusion (vide infra). Have equipment available to allow rapid infusion of warmed, intravenous fluids in the hemorrhaging parturient.

Today, the anesthesiologist is encountering, with increasing frequency, the parturient with peripheral intravenous access made difficult (or impossible) from a long history of drug use. Keep an adequate supply of disposable central venous access kits immediately available. Sonography can help locate the internal jugular vein. Such equipment is available in almost every labor and delivery suite, and I have, on occasion, used this approach. Sometimes, however, the anesthesiologist is faced with the need to provide general anesthesia immediately in a parturient without obvious venous access. In such dire emergencies, I have found that cannulation of the femoral vein is relatively easy to do with a catheter of proper length. Difficulty in securing the catheter and infectious complications are drawbacks to this approach. Later, alternate routes of venous access can be obtained at a (hopefully) less harried pace.

The ability to transduce intra-arterial and central venous pressures, as well as to measure cardiac output, is vital in the management of certain obstetric or coexisting medical disease.

Temperature

I have incorporated the use of forced hot air circulation blankets into my routine anesthetic practice at cesarean delivery. I have found these devices useful in maintaining intraoperative maternal body temperature. Besides obvious intraoperative benefit, normothermia enhances maternal "bonding" in the postanesthesia care unit.

Fetus

I monitor fetal heart rate electronically until surgical preparation of the abdomen or even induction of anesthesia (if an internal scalp electrode is already in place) in the parturient presenting for cesarean delivery. Any alteration in fetal heart rate can be evaluated by the perinatal team and perhaps can lead to increased urgency to deliver a fetus with signs of rapid intrauterine deterioration. Conversely, there have been times when the diagnosis of acute fetal distress has been obstetrically reevaluated on arrival in the operating room, eliminating the need for immediate termination of labor.

Preoxygenation and Denitrogenation

Pregnancy-related alterations in respiratory physiology greatly influence anesthetic technique in the parturient about to undergo induction of general anesthesia. Filling the lungs with oxygen prolongs the interval from onset of apnea to hypoxemia and is of primary importance in the rapid sequence induction of any emergent surgical patient, especially the parturient.

The gravida has multiple reasons for a decreased apnea to hypoxemia time.[45] At term, the gravida has a 20% to 30% increase in oxygen consumption.[46] In labor, oxygen consumption may increase by 80%.[47] Especially in the supine position, airway closure may occur during tidal breathing,[48] thereby increasing shunt fraction and producing hypoxemia.

Functional residual capacity is smaller in parturients,[49–51] whereas minute ventilation rises.[52] These alterations speed nitrogen washout and oxygenation as compared to nonpregnant women.

Two methods of preoxygenation and denitrogenation are commonly employed in the operating room: four vital capacity breath hyperventilation and 3-minute tidal volume breathing of 100% oxygen. The breathing circuit on the anesthesia machine influences the efficiency of each of these methods. Using a Magill apparatus (common to the United Kingdom) with an 8 L/min oxygen flow and at tidal volume breathing, Byrne *et al*[52] found a decrease in the time to denitrogenation (end-tidal nitrogen less than 2%) in gravidae at term (80 s) as compared to nonpregnant controls (130 s). Russell *et al*,[53] using similar methodology, also found more rapid preoxygenation in nonlaboring term gravidae (90 s) as compared to nonpregnant controls (124 s). Giving 100% oxygen via a nonrebreathing apparatus in parturients during rapid sequence induction of general anesthesia, Bone and May[54] found that either 3-minute tidal volume breathing or four vital capacity breath hyperventilation produced a similar degree of arterial desaturation during apnea (an average duration of 50 s). However, unless a tight mask fit is ensured, hyperventilation predisposes to room air (and, therefore, nitrogen) entrainment. Alveolar oxygen levels then become unpredictable.[53]

Using a circle system (common in the United States) and oxygen flows of 5 to 6 L/min, Norris and Dewan[55] showed that four vital capacity breath hyperventilation and 3-minute tidal volume breathing produced similar levels of arterial oxygenation during rapid sequence induction of general anesthesia. In a follow-up study, Norris *et al*[56] showed that parturients needed a mean 55 seconds to reach a level of 5% end-tidal nitrogen, as compared to 111 seconds for nonpregnant women. Four vital capacity breath hyperventilation does not wash out nitrogen as effectively as 3-minute tidal volume breathing (5% end-tidal nitrogen as compared to 1%, respectively) (Fig. 22-3).

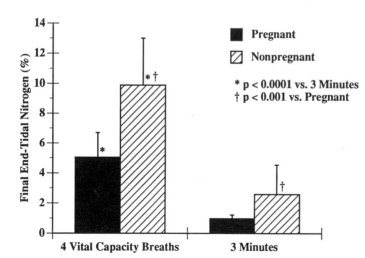

Figure 22–3. Final end-tidal nitrogen concentration (%) following 3 minutes of tidal breathing or four deep breaths of 100% oxygen in 10 healthy parturients and 9 healthy nonpregnant women. (After Norris, MC, Kirkland MR, Torjman M, Goldberg ME. Denitrogenation during pregnancy. Can J Anaesth 1989;36:523)

The extra margin of safety (10–15 additional seconds of apnea) provided before hypoxemia, however, is clinically insignificant.[56]

From these studies, it becomes evident that in the nonemergent situation, the additional 2.5-minute wait for tidal volume breathing preoxygenation may give added, although slight, benefit. In the emergent situation, four vital capacity breath hyperventilation of high-flow oxygen will safely suffice if proper attention is given to mask fit and patient instruction.

Pretreatment/Defasiculation

Fasiculation

The need for a defasiculating (or pretreatment) dose of nondepolarizing neuromuscular relaxant before the intubating dose of succinylcholine is questionable. Between 68% and 100% of nonpregnant surgical patients experience vigorous fasiculation in response to succinylcholine.[57-60] However, pregnancy, as early as in the first trimester, decreases the incidence and severity of fasiculation.[57] At term, the incidence of fasiculation decreases to 9%.[61] Pretreatment with d-tubocurarine (0.05 mg/kg) does not further reduce this incidence.[61]

Myalgia

The incidence of postoperative myalgia is 20% in first-trimester patients as compared to 30% to 40% of nonpregnant controls.[57,62] At term, 7.5% to 13% of women report postoperative myalgia.[61-63] Pretreatment with d-tubocurarine does not decrease the incidence of postoperative myalgia.[61-63] Hormonal effects on skeletal muscle may explain this low risk of myalgia during gestation.[62,63]

Action of Succinylcholine

In term parturients, pretreatment with d-tubocurarine does not alter the onset time of neuromuscular blockade after succinylcholine as measured by time to 100% twitch depression.[61] However, paralysis lasts 120 to 150 s longer (increasing from 7–9 min) in term parturients not pretreated with d-tubocurarine.[61] This prolongation of neuromuscular paralysis is of questionable clinical significance. The time to recovery is short enough to have the patient begin spontaneous (or assisted) ventilation before the end of surgery, but it is still far longer than a patient could tolerate failed airway management. Interestingly, decreasing the dose of succinylcholine by 30% in non-pretreated parturients decreases the recovery time toward the duration found in pretreated parturients but does not prolong the onset time to neuromuscular blockade as compared to 1 mg/kg succinylcholine.[61] I perceive no benefit to pretreatment with regard to incidence of postoperative myalgia or fasiculation (especially in the term parturient receiving 1 mg/kg succinylcholine). Therefore, I routinely omit pretreatment during induction of general anesthesia for cesarean delivery.

INTRAVENOUS INDUCTION AGENTS

Many induction agents used for cesarean delivery were studied in an era when maintenance techniques of general anesthesia (*i.e.,* predelivery maternal inspired oxygen concentrations of 30%–100%, with or without the use of a volatile agent) were very different from today. Comparison of two or more studies of neonatal outcome after maternal induction with one of these agents requires caution.

Thiopental/Thiamylal

In the United States, thiopental (or its analog, thiamylal) is the drug most frequently used to induce general anesthesia for cesarean delivery (Table 22-5). In the parturient, the mean dose of thiopental needed to induce general anesthesia (3.5 mg/kg pregnant body weight) is 35% less than the mean induction dose needed in nonpregnant patients.[64-66] Thiopental appears in fetal blood within 45 s of maternal administration. Fetal drug concentrations peak 1.5 to 3.0 minutes after induction.[66-69]

Rapid maternal redistribution and nonuniform intervillous blood flow lead to a wide variability in measured umbilical venous (UV) and maternal venous (MV) blood thiopental concentration ratios (UV/MV).[70] At delivery, neither UV nor MV thiopental concentrations correlate with induction-to-delivery times.[67] However, UV and MV thiopental concentrations closely correlate with each other, and the UV/MV ratio is usually below 1.[67] Uptake by the fetal liver and dilution with systemic venous blood lead to even further decreases in fetal arterial blood thiopental concentration.[66]

Varying a single bolus of thiobarbiturate from 4 to 7 mg/kg does not affect Apgar scores.[67,69] A maternal induction dose of 8 mg/kg will increase the number of

Apgar scores less than 7 (40%) as compared to lower doses of thiobarbiturate (10%).[69]

In my practice, 4 mg/kg of thiopental/thiamylal is the standard induction dose for general anesthesia for cesarean delivery. I sometimes increase the dose by 25% to 50% (or supplement it with adjuvant agents) when inducing general anesthesia for parturients who may be compromised by the stress response to induction or intubation.

Methohexital

Methohexital is 2.5 to 3 times as potent as thiopental.[66] An induction dose of methohexital greater than 1 mg/kg has been associated with an increased number of low Apgar scores and a delayed time to sustained respiration (see Table 22-5).[71]

Ketamine

Many anesthesiologists use intravenous ketamine (1 mg/kg) to induce general anesthesia in the following clinical situations:

- In the face of maternal hemorrhage
- In parturients with asthma (potential salutary effects of peripheral catecholamine release on bronchospasm)
- For cesarean delivery for fetal distress

Some anesthesiologists use ketamine as their routine induction agent (see Table 22-5). This drug appears to lower the incidence of intraoperative maternal awareness (vide infra).[72]

Dose-dependent maternal hypertension after induction with ketamine occurs in humans[73] and animals.[74] Although perhaps best avoided in parturients who may not tolerate hypertension at induction (*i.e.*, preeclampsia or coexisting neurosurgical disease), in elective cesarean delivery, 1 mg/kg of ketamine does not increase maternal blood pressure at induction/intubation any higher than does 4 mg/kg of thiopental.[75]

Ketamine concentrations in umbilical blood peak 1 to 2 minutes after maternal intravenous administration.[66,76] Apgar scores are similar in neonates delivered abdominally after induction of anesthesia with 1 mg/kg of ketamine or 3 mg/kg of thiopental.[72] Induction of general anesthesia with 2 mg/kg of ketamine is associated with neonatal depression.[66] Some experts

Table 22-5

General Anesthesia for Cesarean Delivery: Induction Agents

DRUGS	DOSE	MATERNAL EFFECTS	NEONATAL EFFECTS
Thiopental/thiamylal	4 mg/kg		Increased low Apgar scores with dose > 7 mg/kg
Methohexital	1 mg/kg		Increased incidence of low Apgar scores*
			Prolonged time to sustained respiration*
Ketamine	1–1.5 mg/kg	Possibly augmented hypertensive response*	> 2 mg/kg increased neonatal depression
		Decreased recall	
		Increased dreaming	
Etomidate	0.3 mg/kg	Pain on injection	Slight increase in UV base deficit*
		Myoclonus	Possible neonatal adrenal suppression
Midazolam	0.2–0.3 mg/kg	0 (%) recall	± Increased incidence of low 1-min Apgar scores*
		Slight hypotensive effect*	Transient postdelivery hypotonus
Propofol	2.0–2.8 mg/kg	Cutaneous rash	Increased incidence of low 1-min Apgar scores*
		Pain on injection	± Transient neurobehavioral changes
		Slight decrease in heart rate*	

*As compared to thiopental/thiamylal, 3 to 4 mg/kg.

advocate ketamine as the anesthetic-induction drug of choice for cesarean delivery of the distressed fetus. In the gravid ewe, ketamine maintains uteroplacental blood flow without deleterious effects on fetal cardiovascular or blood acid–base measurements.[77] In sheep with induced fetal asphyxia, neither cerebral and myocardial blood flow nor blood acid–base measurements deteriorate after ketamine.[78] In a similar model, induction of anesthesia with ketamine better preserved fetal blood pressure and cerebral blood flow than did thiopental.[74]

Etomidate

Etomidate has been subjected to limited study as an induction drug for general anesthesia at cesarean delivery. Etomidate, which rapidly induces anesthesia, is also quickly hydrolyzed to an inactive substance, limiting its duration of action.[79] In addition, etomidate produces little cardiorespiratory change.

Etomidate is effective at inducing anesthesia for cesarean delivery (see Table 22-5);[79–81] however, it frequently produces pain on injection and myoclonus.[80] The incidence of myoclonus may be reduced in the parturient undergoing rapid sequence induction due to the rapid paralysis seen with succinylcholine.[79]

Placental transfer has been shown after induction of general anesthesia with etomidate.[80] As compared to thiopental (3.5 mg/kg), etomidate (0.3 mg/kg) produces a questionably significant decrease in the time to sustained respiration of the neonate (27.3–10.8 s).[81] There is a slight increase in base deficit in the umbilical vein blood of neonates delivered after etomidate induction as compared to thiopental (−6.5 vs −4.7, respectively).[79] The greater degree of neonatal acidosis is also of questionable clinical significance. Early neonatal adrenal suppression also has been shown in a preliminary study.[82] Because of reports of bothersome maternal side effects, possible neonatal effects, and its expense as compared to thiopental and ketamine, I use etomidate only as the induction agent at cesarean delivery in the occasional patient with coexisting maternal cardiac disease.

Midazolam

Studies of midazolam, a water-soluble benzodiazepine with a short elimination half life, as an induction agent for cesarean delivery have yielded mixed results (see Table 22-5).[67,83–85]

Midazolam, 0.2 to 0.3 mg/kg, is an effective induction agent for cesarean delivery.[83,85] A slight (8 mm Hg) increase in maternal diastolic blood pressure during induction[83] is the only hemodynamic difference seen when comparing midazolam, 0.2 to 0.3 mg/kg, to thiopental, 3.5 to 4.0 mg/kg, for induction of general anesthesia for cesarean delivery.[85] Neither induction time (time to loss of maternal lid reflex after injection of midazolam) nor the duration of postanesthetic recovery differed from thiopental.[83]

Midazolam crosses the placenta less rapidly than thiopental.[67] The UV/MV ratio for midazolam is 0.66.[67] One study reported lower 1-minute Apgar scores in neonates delivered abdominally after midazolam compared to those delivered after thiopental induction. Twenty percent (5/26) of neonates delivered after induction of general anesthesia with midazolam had low Apgar scores (and three of the five needed tracheal intubation and intermittent positive-pressure ventilation) as compared to 4% after thiopental.[85] This difference in 1-minute Apgar score was not seen in another comprehensive study of midazolam, although predelivery anesthetic maintenance was different.[84] Funic blood acid–base analysis was similar in neonates delivered after induction of general anesthesia with either drug.[85] Time to sustained neonatal respiration was similarly independent of the drug used for maternal induction.[85] There was a significant interaction seen between body temperature, general body tone, and arm recoil in neonates delivered abdominally to mothers who had received midazolam induction.[84] This alteration in neurobehavioral scores disappeared within 4 hours of delivery.[84,85] The average elimination half-life in neonates is shorter for midazolam than for thiopental (6.3 and 14.7 h, respectively).[67]

Midazolam is safe for induction of general anesthesia for cesarean delivery, although maternal hemodynamic changes are very similar to those seen with thiopental. The high incidence of low 1-minute Apgar scores (although funic blood acid–base values are similar with thiopental) and the transient neonatal hypotonus are troublesome. I therefore see no place for midazolam induction of general anesthesia in my routine practice of obstetric anesthesia.

Propofol

Intravenous propofol rapidly induces general anesthesia and provides quick recovery owing to its rapid metabolism to inactive substances. Propofol, 2.0 to 2.8 mg/kg, has been compared to thiopental, 4.0 to 5.0

mg/kg, for induction of general anesthesia for cesarean delivery (Table 22-5).[86-94]

Blood pressure tends to fall more after induction of general anesthesia with thiopental as compared to propofol.[87,88] This hypotension corrects with intubation. Following intubation, maternal systolic arterial blood pressure rises higher and returns to baseline more slowly after thiopental compared to propofol induction (32 mm Hg vs 17 mm Hg, respectively) (Fig. 22-4A).[87,91] With propofol induction, maternal blood pressure then remains 10 to 12 mm Hg below baseline during the remainder of the predelivery period (see Fig. 22-4A).[87,89,91] The maternal heart rate after induction of general anesthesia with propofol is similar[88] or lower[89] than after thiopental (see Fig. 22-4B). The decrease in maternal heart rate seen after induction of general anesthesia with propofol is evident only after 3 to 4 minutes.[89,91] Response to surgical manipulation or hemorrhage may account for the variability in reported heart rate.

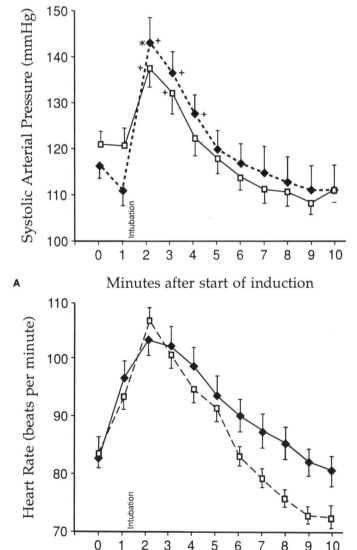

A Minutes after start of induction

B Minutes after start of induction

Figure 22–4. (**A**) Systolic arterial blood pressure (mean ± SEM) after induction of general anesthesia with propofol, 2 mg/kg (n = 20, *open boxes*), or thiopental, 4 mg/kg (n = 20, *solid diamonds*), for elective cesarean delivery. (*P < 0.05 vs propofol, +P < 0.01 vs baseline.) (**B**) Maternal heart rate (mean ± SEM) after induction of general anesthesia with propofol, 2 mg/kg (n = 20, *open boxes*), or thiopental, 4 mg/kg (n = 20, *solid diamonds*), for elective cesarean delivery. There are no statistically significant differences between the two groups. (Gin T, Gregory MA, Oh TE. The haemodynamic effects of propofol and thiopental for induction of caesarean section. Anesth Intensive Care 1990;18:175)

Up to 37% of parturients complain of pain on injection of propofol[89] and 7% exhibit a cutaneous rash.[88] Propofol does not significantly shorten post-anesthetic recovery time in parturients compared to thiopental.[89]

Propofol readily crosses the placenta. The UV/MV ratio for propofol as calculated from four studies is approximately 0.75.[86,87,89,92] Propofol is rapidly cleared from the neonatal circulation.[86] Although not seen in all studies, the number of neonates with low 1-minute Apgar scores (< 7) is as high as 57% after induction of general anesthesia with propofol compared to 11% after thiopental.[86–91,94] Funic blood acid–base analysis is similar in neonates after induction of general anesthesia with propofol or thiopental.[87–89,94] Some investigators have reported mildly depressed 1-hour neurobehavioral scores in neonates delivered after induction of general anesthesia with propofol.[90] However, others find no neurobehavioral changes,[86] and the findings are transient (not seen at 4 h of life).[90]

In my practice, induction of general anesthesia with propofol offers no advantages over thiopental. Unpredictability in maternal hemodynamics is troubling. Currently, the price of propofol does not justify its routine use for an inpatient procedure.

Propofol infusions have been used to maintain general anesthesia with or without nitrous oxide.[85,94] This technique seems to have no significant advantage over traditional methods of anesthetic maintenance.

NEUROMUSCULAR RELAXANTS

All neuromuscular relaxants used today cross the placenta. Their highly ionized, hydrophilic state greatly limits placental transfer. Therefore, only under aberrant conditions is the neonate clinically affected.

Succinylcholine

Succinylcholine, 1.0 to 1.5 mg/kg, is the most commonly used drug to facilitate tracheal intubation in a rapid sequence induction of general anesthesia for cesarean delivery. The estimated UV/MV ratio of succinylcholine is 0.04.[95] Although detectable neonatal concentrations of succinylcholine are possible after routine clinical maternal administration, neonatal paralysis has been reported only in an infant homozygous for atypical serum cholinesterase.[96]

Nondepolarizing Neuromuscular Relaxants

Common obstetric practice attempts to limit induction to delivery time. This practice usually obviates the need for additional predelivery muscle paralysis after the intubating dose of succinylcholine. On occasion, additional muscle paralysis can be provided by using a succinylcholine infusion or the administration of a small dose of nondepolarizing neuromuscular relaxant. Only trace concentrations of d-tubocurarine have been found in the neonate after routine maternal dose.[97] The UV/MV ratio of vecuronium is approximately 0.14;[98,99] the UV/MV ratio of atracurium is 0.08.[100] The UV/MV ratio of pancuronium is 0.22 but rises with increasing induction to delivery intervals.[101] The small doses of nondepolarizing muscle relaxants needed during maintenance of anesthesia for cesarean delivery yield no detectable neonatal effects.

After delivery of the fetus, any of the muscle relaxants already mentioned can be used to maintain paralysis. A peripheral nerve stimulator helps to manage paralysis and neuromuscular relaxant reversal and tracheal extubation.

Under certain conditions (*i.e.,* malignant hyperthermia, cholinesterase deficiency, neurologic disease with upper motor neuron paresis), the use of succinylcholine to facilitate tracheal intubation is contraindicated. Awake intubation without sedation can be difficult, unpleasant for both patient and anesthesiologist, and potentially deleterious in certain coexisting disease states. Superior laryngeal nerve blocks are relatively contraindicated because they leave the patient with an unprotected airway. Injection of high-dose vecuronium has been used to facilitate tracheal intubation at cesarean delivery. Vecuronium, 0.2 mg/kg, given in a rapid sequence before thiopental, will provide intubating conditions in 156 seconds. Use of a priming technique to lower the total dose of vecuronium by 45% does not hasten the onset of paralysis. Intubating conditions were judged good or excellent in all parturients given the high-dose vecuronium. Only two patients recalled paresis before loss of consciousness. Paralysis lasted almost 2 hours,[98] and postoperative sedation and ventilation need to be anticipated by the perinatal team. Skilled assistance in maintaining cricoid pressure during the interval until intubation is required. As always, the possibility of failed intubation and difficult or impossible mask ventilation under cricoid pressure remains a specter in the mind of the anesthesiologist.

MAINTENANCE OF ANESTHESIA

Volatile Agent

The choice of a volatile anesthetic agent to maintain anesthesia before delivery has little or no effect on mother or fetus. The placental transfer of halothane and enflurane is similar (UV/MA ratios are 0.54 and 0.64, respectively).[102] The UA/UV ratios for halothane and enflurane are both less than 0.5.[102] Substitution of isoflurane, enflurane, or halothane as the volatile agent for general anesthesia for elective cesarean delivery does not alter behavioral or biochemical markers of neonatal outcome.[102-104] Giving two thirds of the minimum alveolar capacity (MAC) of the volatile agent limits the maternal stress response better than lesser concentrations of anesthetic.[103]

There is little information about the effects of general anesthetic agents on fetal environment during acute fetal distress. In the acidotic fetus, cerebral vasodilation and a decrease in cerebral metabolic oxygen consumption in the face of a fall in cardiac output help maintain cerebral blood flow. Maternal administration of low-dose halothane supports cerebral blood flow, cerebral oxygen supply, and lowered cerebral metabolic oxygen consumption during the first 15 minutes of asphyxia.[105] In animal models subjected to longer periods of fetal asphyxia, halogenated agents sometimes produce decreases in fetal cerebral blood flow.[106,107] Conflicting results may be due to slight differences in protocol to produce and maintain fetal acidosis. In the clinical situation of general anesthesia for cesarean delivery of the distressed fetus, maternal administration of 2/3 MAC isoflurane or halothane in 50% nitrous oxide/oxygen does not alter neonatal outcome as measured by Apgar score or funic blood acid–base analysis.[108]

Oxygen Concentration

General anesthesia for cesarean delivery usually includes 50% nitrous oxide in oxygen plus 2/3 MAC volatile agent before delivery of the fetus. Increasing maternal Pa_{O_2} above 280 to 300 mm Hg (corresponding to an $F_{I_{O_2}}$ of 0.5–0.6) fails to increase umbilical vein blood oxygen tension during general anesthesia for cesarean delivery.[109-111] In these studies, however, the inspired maternal concentration of volatile agent was not varied to maintain the same total MAC of anesthetic given (deletion of nitrous oxide from the anesthetic was not accompanied by an increase in the inspired volatile anesthetic concentra-

tion). Therefore, an increase in stress-related catecholamines from "lighter" anesthesia could have decreased uteroplacental blood flow.

More recent studies have addressed the effect of both inspired maternal oxygen concentration and total MAC of the anesthetic on fetal outcome. A study of 35 parturients (mixed obstetric diagnoses, some patients in labor but none with fetal distress) for cesarean delivery under general anesthesia with 2/3 MAC isoflurane has shown that a decrease of maternal $F_{I_{O_2}}$ from 0.5 to 0.33 does not produce significant change in funic blood acid–base analysis.[112]

In another study, 200 patients presenting for elective or emergent cesarean delivery under general anesthesia were randomly assigned to receive either 100% inspired maternal oxygen or 50% inspired maternal oxygen in nitrous oxide.[113] Isoflurane, 1.5 MAC, was given for 5 minutes and then decreased to 1 MAC and continued until delivery in parturients who were not receiving nitrous oxide. Induction-to-delivery times were 10 to 12 minutes, even for emergent deliveries! There was no difference in umbilical vein or artery blood carbon dioxide tension, pH, or base deficit between the group of women who inspired 100% oxygen or 50% oxygen.[113] There was no difference between patient groups in umbilical artery blood oxygen tension.[113] However, there was a mean increase (to 28–35 mm Hg) in umbilical vein blood oxygen tension in the group of parturients receiving 100% inspired maternal oxygen being delivered emergently (42% for fetal distress).[113] There were no differences in need for ventilation or intubation, or in Apgar scores in neonates with the statistically lower umbilical vein oxygen tension.[113] Substitution of enflurane or halothane for isoflurane in 100% oxygen in a similar protocol (but now comparing neonatal outcome to a group of parturients receiving 2/3 MAC halothane in 50% nitrous oxide in oxygen) showed no difference in funic blood carbon dioxide tension or pH, Apgar score, or need for resuscitation.[114] Umbilical vein blood oxygen tension was not significantly or consistently higher in any one comparison group, although when all (three) patient groups receiving 100% inspired maternal oxygen were combined, there was a statistically significant increase in umbilical vein oxygen tension from 33.4 to 39.7 mm Hg.[114] The clinical significance of this increase remains obscure. It is therefore of questionable neonatal benefit to increase inspired maternal oxygen concentrations above 50% to 60%. In addition, the use of 100% inspired maternal oxygen may increase the incidence of maternal awareness (vide infra).

See Table 22-6 for a suggested method of general anesthesia for cesarean delivery.

Table 22–6

A Suggested Technique for General Anesthesia

Premedication

Elective delivery: two doses of H_2-receptor antagonist (*e.g.,* ranitidine, 150 mg PO at bedtime; ranitidine, 50 mg IV in morning)

Nonelective delivery or if patient is in labor: 30 mL of 0.3 M sodium citrate (or its equivalent) PO; metoclopramide, 10 mg IV slow push optimally 30 min before delivery

Positioning

Uterine displacement

Arrange shoulders and neck to optimize "sniffing" position

Monitors and Special Equipment

Continuous electrocardiography

Noninvasive oscillometric blood pressure monitor

Pulse oximetry

Temperature monitor

Peripheral nerve stimulator

Oxygen analyzer

Mass spectrometer or capnograph

Orogastric tube

Bladder catheter

Forced warm air warming blanket

Induction

(in delivery room after surgeon ready to make incision)

Preoxygenation (High-flow 100% oxygen, tight-fitting anesthesia mask)

Elective delivery: 3-min tidal volume breathing

Emergency delivery: four vital capacity breath hyperventilation

Rapid sequence intravenous induction with cricoid pressure

Thiopental, 4 mg/kg IV pregnant body weight (PBW)

Succinylcholine, 1.5 mg/kg PBW, to facilitate intubation

Tracheal intubation and inflation of cuff; check breath sounds, and check for capnographic evidence of expired carbon dioxide

Begin surgery

Maintenance

Before delivery

High-flow nitrous oxide:oxygen 50:50 with up to 0.67 MAC volatile agent

Succinylcholine, 0.1% infusion, as necessary to maintain muscle relaxation

After delivery of neonate

Decrease gas flows; nitrous oxide:oxygen 70:30

Intravenous narcotic (*i.e.,* morphine sulfate, 0.2 mg/kg, as tolerated according to maternal hemodynamic status)

Intravenous amnestic agent (*i.e.,* diazepam 2.5–5 mg or midazolam 1–2 mg)

Succinylcholine infusion continued as needed

Extubation

Fully reactive and awake

5-sec tetanus without fade elicited by peripheral nerve stimulator

Emergence and Recovery

Supplemental oxygen

Monitoring

Pulse oximetry

Continuous electrocardiography

Continual blood pressure

Titrate intravenous analgesic to patient comfort, begin intravenous patient-controlled analgesia (PCA) infusion (*i.e.,* morphine sulfate, 2 mg PRN q 10 min; 10-min lockout; 1-h maximum of 10 mg); PCA protocol orders

Discharge from recovery room by usual criteria

Patient discharge instructions

Follow-up note the next day and thereafter as indicated

BLOOD LOSS

Mild controversy exists regarding the effects of general anesthesia on blood loss at cesarean delivery. The dispute focuses on potential uterine muscle relaxation caused by volatile anesthetics, which may lead to relative uterine inertia and hemorrhage. The parturient given low-dose volatile anesthetic (halothane or enflurane) and stimulated with oxytocin will have contractions sufficient to prevent hemorrhage.[115] This conclusion is based on data obtained using intrauterine balloons in women who had delivered vaginally. Clinically, the supplemental use of low-dose halothane, enflurane, or isoflurane to help ensure amnesia, especially when administered over the short periods before delivery and then discontinued, does not increase intraoperative blood loss.[116–119]

Gilstrap *et al*[120] reviewed 239 cesarean deliveries in which the type of anesthesia (regional or general) was not controlled. General anesthesia was maintained with a halogenated agent (up to 1.0% halothane for greater than 10 min) in most patients. There was no difference in pre- and postdelivery hematocrit change in either group of women (Table 22-7), but 35% of women receiving the halogenated agent had a drop in hematocrit greater than 8 vol %, and one half of these women received a transfusion as compared to only 1% of women receiving regional anesthesia. Therefore, average blood loss at delivery was not affected by technique of maternal anesthesia, although these authors suggested an interesting association between the incidence of hemorrhage necessitating transfusion and general anesthesia.[120]

Consider these data with caution. Transfusion therapy has evolved as physicians (and the public) focus on the transmission of blood-borne pathogens. Camann and Datta reported a series of 9596 cesarean deliveries of which 336 were complicated by a need for red cell transfusion. During the 4-year study period (1984–1987), the need for transfusion was halved to an incidence of 3.2%/year. The need for massive transfusion (8% of transfusions were more than 5 U of packed red cells) was usually complicated by a coexisting obstetric condition associated with hemorrhage, including abnormality of placentation, coagulopathy after abruption or with preeclampsia, and emergency surgery. Of high-risk parturients needing transfusion at cesarean delivery, almost 70% received general anesthesia. Of low-risk parturients (including elective cesarean delivery, breech, and nonobstetric reasons for cesarean delivery) needing transfusion at cesarean delivery, only 31% received general anesthesia. There was no increase in blood requirements with regard to the type of anesthesia in this low-risk population, although the incidence of transfusion in these low-risk patients was low (0.53%).[121]

AWARENESS

Doses of general anesthetics for cesarean delivery are chosen to decrease potential neonatal drug effects. In addition, the short induction-to-incision time often leaves the anesthesiologist with a "lightly" anesthetized mother. Maternal awareness and, more importantly, post-cesarean recall is possible in parturients under general anesthesia. Awareness, dreaming, and recall have all been described in the parturient under general anesthesia. The anesthesiologist must differentiate between these entities. Carefully distinguish between dreaming and recall when dealing with complaints in the postpartum period. The incidence of these potentially unpleasant effects varies greatly between reports. The following factors seem to influence the reported incidence of unpleasant effects:

- Choice of induction agent
- Technique for anesthetic maintenance before delivery of the fetus
- Time from anesthetic induction to delivery
- The possible emergency nature of delivery

Table 22–7

Effects of General Anesthesia for Cesarean Delivery on Blood Loss

	REGIONAL ANESTHESIA (n = 150)	GENERAL ANESTHESIA (WITH HALOGENATED AGENT)(n = 114*)	STATISTICAL SIGNIFICANCE
Hematocrit			
Predelivery	37.1	37.3	NS
Postdelivery	33.4	30.8	NS
Percentage of patients with hematocrit decreased ≥ 8 vol %	10%	35%	$P < 0.05$
Percentage of patients receiving red blood cells	1%	18%†	$P < 0.05$

(Data from Gilstrap LC, Howth JC, Hankins GDV, Patterson AR. Effect of type of anesthesia in blood loss at cesarean section. Obstet Gynecol 1987;69:328)
*Fifty-nine percent of patients exposed to halogenated agent more than 11 minutes. Eighty-five percent of patients received halothane 0.5% to 1%.
†Sixty-seven percent of the patients received halogenated agent for more than 15 minutes.
Abbreviation: NS = not significant.

- The method of detection of intraoperative awareness

Thiopental and Ketamine

The use of 0.67 MAC volatile agent to supplement 50% nitrous oxide/oxygen or 100% oxygen general anesthesia before delivery of the fetus is associated with an incidence of maternal awareness as high as 60% after an induction with thiopental, 4 mg/kg, as detected by purposeful movements of an isolated limb.[122,123] The addition of ketamine, 0.5 mg/kg, to a 2 mg/kg dose of thiopental for induction of general anesthesia reduces the incidence of awareness by half. Ketamine, 1.5 mg/kg, induction of general anesthesia reduces the incidence of awareness to 0 to 10%.[122–124]

The reported incidence of dreaming varies between 0% and 25%.[124,125] The incidence of dreaming seems to depend on the emergent nature of the delivery and perhaps the emotional state of the mother before induction of general anesthesia.

Maternal recall is potentially damaging to both the mother (psychologically) and the anesthesiologist (medicolegally as well as psychologically). The incidence of recall is reported to be 0% to 18%.[122–128] The incidence of recall is seemingly unaffected by the choice of ketamine or thiopental as the induction agent but again may be increased after the induction of general anesthesia for emergency cesarean delivery.

Propofol

Induction with propofol (2.3 to 2.5 mg/kg) followed by anesthetic maintenance with low-dose halothane in 50% nitrous oxide/oxygen is associated with a 40% incidence of intraoperative awareness.[86] This rate may have been affected by discontinuation of all anesthetic agents between uterine incision and delivery. There was a 0% to 20% incidence of recall after induction of general anesthesia with propofol (2.1–2.3 mg/kg) followed by 50% nitrous oxide/oxygen and low-dose isoflurane, as compared to 0% to 5% after induction with thiopental (4–5 mg/kg).[86–89]

Midazolam

The incidence of recall is 0% after induction of general anesthesia with midazolam, 0.2 mg/kg, followed by maintenance of anesthesia with low-dose halothane and 50% nitrous oxide/oxygen.[129]

Practical Considerations

Isolated limb techniques and lower esophageal contractility monitors may reveal awareness or "light" anesthesia but are poor predictors of maternal recall.[125] If "light" anesthesia is detected, there may not be any pharmacologic intervention that can "erase" the event. It would therefore seem prudent to consider all parturients at least aware of the auditory environment in the operating room. Limit casual conversation in the operating room. Quiet verbal reassurance of the parturient by the anesthesiologist is perhaps justified until delivery of the baby, and the opportunity to "deepen" the anesthetic.

NEONATAL EFFECTS OF GENERAL ANESTHESIA

Many variables confound the study of neonatal effects of general anesthesia, including the method of neonatal evaluation used, surgical technique and timing, and pre-existing fetal condition. Most studies only include neonates born at elective cesarean deliveries.

Neonatal Evaluation

In many prospective studies (with relatively small numbers of patients enrolled), general anesthesia produces a similar incidence of depressed neonates (reflected by low 1- and 5-minute Apgar scores) as regional anesthesia.[130–133]

Amiel–Tyson/Barrier/Shnider Neurological and Adaptive Capacity Scores (NACS) have been performed on neonates born to mothers under general anesthesia. Analysis reveals lower scores on test items for adaptive capacity, passive tone, active tone, primary reflexes, and total scores at 15 minutes and 2 hours of life but not beyond, compared to neonates born under regional anesthesia.[133] Using Scanlon Early Neonatal Neurobehavioral Score (ENNS), neonates born to mothers under general anesthesia scored lower on habituation and orientation items at 3 hours but were similar at 24 hours of life and beyond compared to neonates born under regional anesthesia.[131]

Pre-existing Fetal Condition

Neonatal outcome of 3940 elective and nonelective cesarean deliveries has been studied using multivariate regression analysis (Table 22-8). Compared to those in-

Table 22–8

Neonatal Outcome After Cesarean Section by Anesthetic Technique

INDICATIONS FOR CESAREAN SECTION	ANESTHETIC TECHNIQUE	INFANTS WITH 1-MIN APGAR SCORES 0 to 4 (%)	INFANTS WITH 5-MIN APGAR SCORES 0 to 4 (%)	NEONATES REQUIRING OXYGEN BY MASK (%)	NEONATES REQUIRING INTUBATION AND VENTILATION (%)	NEONATAL DEATHS
Elective	Regional	2.0	0.2	10.1	1.7	0.5
	General	6.5*	0.4	16.3†	0.8	1.2
Fetal distress	Regional	18.5	2.8	19.7	19.0	3.3
	General	43.5†	8.3†	18.0	42.5‡	6.5
Cephalopelvic disproportion	Regional	9.1	0.5	14.5	10.4	0.7
	General	23.0†	3.4†	24.0†	19.6‡	1.4

(Data from Ong BY, Cohen MM, Palahniuk RJ. Anesthesia for cesarean section: Effects on neonates. Anesth Analg 1989;68:270)
*P ≤ 0.05 vs regional anesthesia.
†P ≤ 0.01 vs regional anesthesia.
‡P ≤ 0.001 vs regional anesthesia.

fants born under regional anesthesia, neonates born under general anesthesia had a greater incidence of low (< 4) 1-minute Apgar scores after elective cesarean deliveries, cesarean deliveries with a diagnosis of cephalopelvic disproportion (CPD), and cesarean deliveries with a diagnosis of fetal distress.[134]

Neonates born under general anesthesia have a higher incidence of low (<4) 5-minute Apgar scores after cesarean deliveries with a diagnosis of cephalopelvic disproportion or fetal distress. Neonates born under general anesthesia after nonelective cesarean delivery also were more likely to need oxygen and intubation. However, anesthetic technique did not correlate with neonatal mortality.[134]

Timing of Delivery

There is a difference of opinion about the optimal time for delivery of the fetus after induction of general anesthesia. Traditionally, minimizing induction–to–delivery (I–D) intervals has been stressed in all patients undergoing general anesthesia for cesarean delivery.[135] However, no correlation of clinical or biochemical indices of fetal outcome and I–D interval has been reported.[135,136]

Datta *et al*[135] have suggested that long uterine incision–to–delivery (U–D) intervals also influence neonatal outcome. Reasons for deterioration in neonatal status with increasing U–D interval include the following:

- An acute decrease in uteroplacental perfusion due to uterine artery spasm or venocaval compression during uterine manipulation
- Inhalation of amniotic fluid by the fetus during prolonged delivery
- Fetal head compression during difficult delivery

The data, however, are confusing. An I–D interval longer than 8 minutes with a U–D interval longer than 3 minutes is associated with a significant decrease in funic blood pH.[135,136] The values for the mean umbilical artery pH (7.22 ± 0.01), and mean umbilical vein pH (7.30 ± 0.01), however, are not considered acidotic. In one study, maternal vein–to–umbilical vein pH gradient increased significantly in the long I–D, long U–D interval patients. This finding suggests decreased uteroplacental oxygen delivery and resultant fetal acidosis perhaps from maternal hyperventilation during this time.[135] A U–D interval longer than 3 minutes also correlates with a greater incidence of low 1-minute Apgar scores.[124,135,136] There is no difference, however, in funic blood oxygen tensions with prolonged I–D and U–D intervals.[135]

A recent study has challenged the importance of U–D intervals.[137] Multivariate regression analysis of a group of 204 parturients delivered abdominally relates low (1 and 5 min) Apgar scores to the presence of fetal distress and preeclampsia.[137] The presence of meconium-stained amniotic fluid also correlated with low 1-minute Apgar scores. This finding may be due to neonatal cardiorespiratory response to tracheal suction.[137] These investigators found no relationship of I–D interval or U–D interval to Apgar scores or umbilical vein blood pH despite the type of maternal anesthesia.[137]

Controversy still exists over the proper timing of delivery of the neonate under general anesthesia. In our institution, we routinely induce general anesthesia after surgical preparation and draping of the patient is complete. Sacrifice of surgical technique for speed of delivery has occasionally led to unexpected maternal and even fetal trauma. Our obstetricians attempt to minimize both I–D and U–D intervals after induction of general anesthesia, but not at the sacrifice of surgical technique. Pediatricians are present at all cesarean deliveries to provide prompt attention to the neonate. Time of induction of general anesthesia, skin incision, uterine incision, and delivery as well as Apgar scores and results of funic blood acid–base analysis are all recorded in the anesthesia record.

SUMMARY

The scientific basis of the practice of general anesthesia for cesarean delivery is based on human and animal data, but routine practice is more often dictated by tradition, cost, or the choice of the individual anesthesiologist. Choice of induction agent probably is based on cost and tradition. Thiopental and ketamine are inexpensive and have a long record of safety. Development of newer drugs to induce general anesthesia has had little practical application in obstetric anesthesia. There is no alternative at present to the use of succinylcholine to facilitate rapid sequence induction and tracheal intubation. The three volatile agents in routine use today are interchangeable. Within the guidelines of routine anesthetic care, fetal outcome may depend mostly on pre-existing fetal status at the time of cesarean delivery, that is, a healthy term fetus can withstand anesthesia and delivery better than a distressed, preterm fetus.

Techniques of general anesthesia have long proved safe for the mother; however, prevention of anesthetic-related maternal morbidity and mortality today centers on management of the difficult or impossible airway. Many investigators are attempting to prevent maternal hypoxemia and the sequelae of acid aspiration. There will always be a need for general anesthesia in the delivery suite, and there will always be "difficult" airways, which may lead to failed intubation. However, one must continue to focus on increasing the margin of safety at the time of induction of general anesthesia. The methods of prediction, identification, and management of the difficult airway must improve. Better methods of acid-aspiration prophylaxis also might have considerable impact in reducing maternal morbidity and mortality. Continuing education of anesthesia personnel (as well as our obstetric and nursing colleagues) in the safe practice of obstetric anesthesia is mandatory.

REFERENCES

1. Gibbs CP, Krischer J, Peckham BP, Sharp H, Kirschbaum TH. Obstetric anesthesia: A national survey. Anesthesiology 1986;65:298.
2. Ong B, Cohen MM, Cumming M, Palahniuk R. Obstetrical anaesthesia at Winnepeg Women's Hospital 1975-83: Anaesthetic techniques and complications. Can J Anaesth 1987;34:294.
3. Sachs BP, Oriol NE, Ostheimer GW, et al. Anesthetic-related maternal mortality: 1984–1985. J Clin Anesth 1989;1:333.
4. Samsoon GLT, Young RB. Difficult tracheal intubation: A retrospective study. Anaesthesia 1987;42:487.
5. Morgan BM, Magni V, Goroszeniuk T. Anaesthesia for emergency caesarean section. Br J Obstet Gynecol 1990;97:420.
6. Mallampati SR, Gatt P, Gugino LD, et al. A clinical sign to predict difficult intubation: A prospective study. Can Anaesth Soc J 1985;32:429.
7. Endler GC, Mariona FG, Sokal RJ, Stevenson LB. Anesthetic-related maternal mortality in Michigan, 1972-1984. Am J Obstet Gynecol 1988;159:187.
8. Dupont X, Hamza J, Jullien P, Narchi P. Risk factors associated with difficult airways in normotensive parturients [Abstract]. Anesthesiology 1990;73:A999.
9. Hood DD, Dewan DM, Ashten K. Anesthesia in the morbidly obese parturient [Abstract]. Anesthesiology 1990;73:A952.
10. Dupont X, Hamza J, Jullien P, Narchi P. Is pregnancy induced hypertension a risk factor for difficult intubation? [Abstract] Anesthesiology 1990;73:A985.
11. Chazotte C, Cohen WR. Catastrophic complications of previous cesarean section. Am J Obstet Gynecol 1990;738:163.
12. Morgan M. Anaesthetic contribution to maternal mortality. Br J Anaesth 1987;59:842.
13. Roberts B, Shirley A. Reducing the risk of acid aspiration at cesarean section. Anesth Analg 1974;53:859.
14. James CF, Modell JH, Gibbs CP, Kuck EJ, Ruiz C. Pul-
monary aspiration—effects of volume and pH in the rat. Anesth Analg 1984;63:665.
15. Brock-Utne JG, Rout C, Moodley J, Mayat N. Influence of perioperative gastric aspiration on the volume and pH of gastric contents on obstetric patients undergoing cesarean section. Br J Anaesth 1989;62:397.
16. Gibbs CP, Spohr L, Schmidt D. The effectiveness of sodium citrate as an antacid. Anesthesiology 1982;57:44.
17. O'Sullivan GM, Bullingham RE. Non-invasive assessment by radiotelemetry of antacid effect during labor. Anesth Analg 1985;64:95.
18. Colman RD, Frank M, Loughran BA, Cohen DG, Cattermole R. Use of IM ranitidine for the prophylaxis of aspiration pneumonitis in obstetrics. Br J Anaesth 1988;61:720.
19. O'Sullivan GM, Bullingham RES. Does twice the volume of antacid have twice the effect in pregnant women at term? Anesth Analg 1984;63:752.
20. Matthews ML, Moore J. Sodium bicarbonate as a single dose antacid in obstetric anaesthesia. Anaesthesia 1989;44:590.
21. Thompson M, Loughran PG, McAuley DM, Wilson CM, Moore J. Combined treatment with ranitidine and saline antacids prior to obstetric anaesthesia. Anaesthesia 1984;39:1086.
22. Ormezano X, Francois TP, Viaud J-Y, et al. Aspiration pneumonitis prophylaxis in obstetric anaesthesia: A comparison of effervescent cimetidine-sodium citrate mixtures and sodium citrate. Br J Anaesth 1990;64:503.
23. Cohen S, Morris DW, Schoen HG, Dimarino AJ. The effects of oral and intravenous metoclopramide on human lower esophageal pressure. Gastroenterology 1976;70:484.
24. Bylsma-Howell M, Riggs KW, McMorland GH, et al. Placental transfer of metoclopramide: assessment of maternal and neonatal effects. Can Anaesth Soc J 1983;30:487.
25. Nimmo WS, Wilson J, Prescott F. Narcotic analgesia and delayed gastric emptying during labour. Lancet 1975;1:890.
26. Manchikanti L. Metoclopramide's role in anesthetic practice. Anesthesiol Rev 1984;17:8.
27. Caldwell C, Rains G, McKiterick K. An unusual reaction to preoperative metoclopramide. Anesthesiology 1987;67:854.
28. Bevacqua A. Supraventricular tachycardia associated with postpartum metoclopramide administration. Anesthesiology 1988;68:124.
29. Lewis M, Crawford JS. Can one risk fasting the obstetric patient for less than 4 hours? Br J Anaesth 1987;59:312.
30. Frank M, Evans M, Flynn P, Aun C. Comparison of the prophylactic use of magnesium trisilicate mixture B.P.C., sodium citrate mixture or cimetidine in obstetrics. Br J Anaesth 1984;56:355.
31. O'Sullivan GM, Sear W, Bullingham RE, Carrie LES. The effect of magnesium trisilicate mixture, metoclo-

pramide and ranitidine on gastric pH, volume and serum gastrin. Anaesthesia 1985;40:246.

32. Dewan DM, Floyd HM, Thistlewood JM, et al. Sodium citrate pretreatment in elective cesarean section patients. Anesth Analg 1985;64:34.

33. Ewart MC, Yau G, Gin T, Kotur CF, Oh TE. A comparison of the effects of omeprazole and ranitidine on gastric secretion in women undergoing elective cesarean section. Anaesthesia 1990;45:527.

34. Moore J, Flynn RJ, Sampaio M, Wilson CN, Gillon KRW. Effect of single-dose omeprazole on intragastric acidity and volume during obstetric anaesthesia. Anaesthesia 1989;44:559.

35. Koren MJ, Freiberg HV, Ostheimer GW. Prophylaxis against acid aspiration during general anesthesia in obstetric patients: a cost-effectiveness analysis. Proceedings of the Annual Meeting of the Society of Obstetric Anesthesia and Perinatology. 1985:96.

36. Malinow AM, Naulty JS, Hunt CO, Datta S, Ostheimer GW. Venous air emboli at cesarean delivery. Anesthesiology 1987;66:816.

37. Fong J, Gadalla F, Druzin M. Venous air emboli occurring during cesarean section: The effect of patient position. Can J Anaesth 1991;38:191.

38. Vartikar JV, Johnson MD, Datta S. Precordial Doppler monitoring and pulse oximetry during cesarean delivery with detection of venous air embolism. Reg Anesth 1989;14:145.

39. Robinson DA, Albin M. Venous air embolism and cesarean sections [letter]. Anesthesiology 1987;66:93.

40. Levinson G, Shnider SM, de Lorimier M, et al. Effects of maternal hyperventilation on uterine blood flow and fetal oxygenation and acid–base status. Anesthesiology 1974;40:340.

41. Shankar KB, Mosely H, Vemula V, Kumar Y. Physiologic dead space during general anaesthesia for cesarean section. Can J Anaesth 1987;34:373.

42. Shankar B, Mosely H, Kumar Y, Vemula V. Arterial to end-tidal carbon dioxide tension difference during caesarean section anaesthesia. Anaesthesia 1986;41:698.

43. Rampton AJ, Mallaiah S, Garrett P. Increased ventilation requirements during obstetric general anaesthesia. Br J Anaesth 1988;61:730.

44. Burger GA, Datta S, Chantigian C, et al. Optimal ventilation in general anesthesia for cesarean delivery [Abstract]. Anesthesiology 1983;59:A420.

45. Archer GW, Marx GF. Arterial oxygen tension during apnoea in parturient women. Br J Anaesth 1974; 46:358.

46. Pernoll MC, Metcalfe J, Schlenker TL, Welch JE, Matsumoto JA. Oxygen consumption at rest and during exercise in pregnancy. Respir Physiol 1975;25:285.

47. Hagerdal M, Morgan CW, Sumner AE, Gutsche BB. Minute ventilation and oxygen consumption during labor with epidural analgesia. Anesthesiology 1983; 59:425.

48. Awe RJ, Nicotra MB, Newsom TD, Viles R. Arterial

oxygenation and alveolar-arterial gradients in term pregnancy. Obstet Gynecol 1979;53:182.

49. Baldwin GR, Moorthi DS, Welton A, Macdonald KF. New lung functions and pregnancy. Am J Obstet Gynecol 1977;127:235.

50. Cugell DW, Frank NR, Grensler ER, Badger TL. Pulmonary function in pregnancy I. Serial observations in normal women. Am Rev Tuberc 1953;67:568.

51. Gee JBL, Packer BS, Millen JE, Robin ED. Pulmonary mechanics during pregnancy. 1967;46:945.

52. Byrne F, Odeno-Dominah A, Kipling R. The effect of pregnancy on pulmonary nitrogen washout: A study of preoxygenation. Anaesthesia 1987;42:148.

52. Russell GN, Smith CL, Snowden SL, Bryson THL. Preoxygenation and the parturient patient. Anaesthesia 1987;42:346.

54. Bone ME, May AE. Preoxygenation techniques in the obstetric patient. Anesthesiol Rev 1987;15:37.

55. Norris MC, Dewan DM. Preoxygenation for cesarean section: A comparison of two techniques. Anesthesiology 1985;67:827.

56. Norris MC, Kirkland R, Torjman MC, Goldberg ME. Denitrogenation in pregnancy. Can J Anaesth 1989;36:523.

57. Datta S, Crocker J, Alper MH. Muscle pain following administration of suxamethonium to pregnant and nonpregnant patients undergoing tubal ligation. Br J Anaesth 1977;49:625.

58. Cullen DJ. The effect of pretreatment with nondepolarizing muscle relaxants on the neuromuscular blocking action of succinylcholine. Anesthesiology 1971;35:572.

59. Blitt CD, Carlson GL, Rolling GD, Hameroff R, Otto CW. A comparative evaluation of the pretreatment with nondepolarizing neuromuscular blockers prior to the administration of succinylcholine. Anesthesiology 1981;55:687.

60. Manchikanti L. Diazepam does not prevent succinylcholine-induced fasiculations and myalgia-a comparative evaluation of the effect of diazepam and d-tubocurarine pretreatments. Acta Anesthesiol Scand 1984;28:523.

61. Cook WF, Schultetus RR, Caton D. A comparison of d-tubocurarine pretreatment and no pretreatment in obstetric patients. Anesth Analg 1987;66:756.

62. Thind GS, Bryson THL. Single-dose suxamethonium and muscle pain in pregnancy. Br J Anaesth 1983; 55:745.

63. Crawford JS. Suxamethonium muscle pains and pregnancy. Br J Anaesth 1971;43:677.

64. Christensen JH, Andreasen F, Jansen JA. Pharmacokinetics of thiopentone in cesarean section. Acta Anaesth Scand 1981;25:174.

65. Christensen JH, Andreasen F, Jansen JA. Pharmacokinetics of thiopentone in a group of young women and a group of young men. Br J Anaesth 1980;52:913.

66. Chantigian RC, Ostheimer GW. Effects of maternally

administered drugs in the fetus and newborn. In: Friedman E, ed. Advances in perinatal medicine. Vol 5. New York: Plenum, 1986:181.

67. Bach V, Carl P, Ravlo O, et al. A randomized comparison between midazolam and thiopental for elective cesarean section anesthesia. III. Placental transfer and elimination in neonates. Anesth Analg 1989;68:238.

68. McKechnie FB, Converse G. Placental transmission of thiopental. Am J Obstet Gynecol 1955;70:369.

69. Kosaka Y, Takahashi T, Mark LC. Intravenous thiobarbituate anesthesia for cesarean section. Anesthesiology 1969;31:489.

70. Datta S, Alper MH. Anesthesia for cesarean section. Anesthesiology 1980;53:142.

71. Holdcroft A, Robinson MT, Gordon H, Whitman JG. Comparison of effect of two induction doses of methohexitone on infants delivered by elective caesarean section. Br Med J 1974;2:472.

72. Pelk B, Sinclair DM. Induction agents for caesarean section—a comparison of thiopentone and ketamine. Anaesthesia 1973;28:37.

73. Meer FM, Downing W, Coleman AJ. An intravenous method of anaesthesia for caesarean section. Part II. Ketamine. Br J Anaesth 1973;45:191.

74. Pickering BG, Palahniuk RJ, Cote J, Wade JG, Pash MG. Cerebral vascular response to ketamine and thiopentone during foetal acidosis. Can Anaesth Soc J 1982;29:463.

75. Schultetus RR, Paulus DA, Spohr GL. Hemodynamic effects of ketamine and thiopental during anesthetic induction for caesarean section. Can Anaesth Soc J 1982;32:592.

76. Haram K, Sagen A, Solheim E. Transplacental passage of ketamine after intravenous administration. Acta Anesth Scand 1977;21:41.

77. Levinson G, Shnider SM, Gildea E, deLorimier M. Maternal and foetal cardiovascular and acid–base changes during ketamine anaesthesia in pregnant ewes. Br J Anaesth 1973;45:1111.

78. Swartz J, Cumming M, Biehl D. The effect of ketamine anaesthesia in the acidotic foetal lamb. Can J Anaesth 1987;34:233.

79. Downing JW, Bailey RJR, Brock-Utne JG, Boulton JG. Etomidate for induction of anesthesia at cesarean section: Comparison with thiopentone. Br J Anaesth 1979;51:135.

80. Suresh MS, Solanaki R, Andrews JJ, et al. Comparison of etomidate with thiopental for induction of anesthesia at cesarean section [Abstract]. Anesthesiology 1986; 65:A400.

81. Houlton PJ, Downing JW, Buley RJ, Brock-Utne JG. Anaesthetic induction for caesarean section with etomidate compared with thiopentone. S Afr Med J 1978;54:773.

82. Reddy BK, Pizer B, Bull PT. Neonatal serum cortisol suppression by etomidate. Eur J Anesth 1988;5:171.

83. Crawford ME, Carl P, Bach V, Ravlo O, Mikkelsen BO, Werner M. A randomized comparison between midazolam and thiopental for elective cesarean section. I. Mothers. Anesth Analg 1989;68:229.

84. Ravlo O, Carl P, Crawford ME, Bach V, Mikkelsen BO, Nielsen HK. A randomized comparison between midazolam and thiopental for elective cesarean section anesthesia. II. Neonates. Anesth Analg 1989;68:234.

85. Bland BAR, Lawes EG, Duncan PW, Warnell I, Downing JW. Comparison of midazolam and thiopental for rapid sequence induction for elective cesarean section. Anesth Analg 1987;66:1165.

86. Dailland P, Cockshott ID, Lirzin JD, et al. Intravenous propofol during cesarean section: Placental transfer, concentrations in breast milk, and neonatal effects. A preliminary study. Anesthesiology, 1989;71:827.

87. Moore J, Bill KM, Flynn RJ, McKeating KT, Howard PJ. A comparison between propofol and thiopentone as induction agents in obstetric anaesthesia. Anaesthesia 1989;44:753.

88. Capogna G, Celleno D, Sebastiani M, et al. Propofol and thiopentone for caesarean section revisited: Maternal effects and neonatal outcome. Int J Obstet Anaesth 1991;1:19.

89. Valtonen M, Kanto J, Rosenberg P. Comparison of propofol and thiopentone for induction of anaesthesia for elective caesarean section. Anaesthesia 1989; 44:758.

90. Celleno D, Capogna G, Tomassetti M, Constantino P, Di Feo G, Nisini R. Neurobehavioral effects of propofol on the neonate following elective cesarean section. Br J Anaesth 1989;62:649.

91. Gin T, Gregory MA, Oh TE. The haemodynamic effects of propofol and thiopentone for the induction of caesarean section. Anaesth Intensive Care 1990;18:175.

92. Gin T, Gregory MA, Chan K, Oh TE. Maternal and fetal levels of propofol at caesarean section. Anaesth Intensive Care 1990;18:180.

93. Gin T, Gregory MA, Chan K, Buckley T, Oh TE. Pharmacokinetics of propofol in women undergoing elective caesarean section. Br J Anaesth 1990;64:148.

94. Gregory MA, Gin T, Yaw G, Leung RKW, Chan K, Oh TE. Propofol infusion for caesarean section. Anaesthesia 1990;37:514.

95. Drabkhova J, Crul JF, van der Kleijn E. Placental transfer of ^{14}C-labelled succinylcholine in near term macaca mulatta monkeys. Br J Anaesth 1973;45:1087.

96. Baraka A, Haroun S, Bassili M, et al. Response of the newborn to succinylcholine injection in homozygotic atypical mothers. Anesthesiology 1975;43:115.

97. Cohen EN, Paulson WJ, Wall J, et al. Thiopental, curare and nitrous oxide anesthesia for cesarean section with studies on placental transmission. Surg Obstet Gynecol 1953;97:456.

98. Hawkins J, Johnson TD, Kubicek MA, Skjonsby BS, Morrow DH, Joyce TH. Vecuronium for rapid-sequence intubation for cesarean section. Anesth Analg 1990;71:185.

99. Demtriou M, Depoix JP, Diakite B, Fromartin M, Duvaldstein P. ORG N 45 in women undergoing cesarean section. Br J Anaesth 1982;54:643.

100. Flynn RJ, Frank M, Hughes R. The use of atracurium in caesarean section. Br J Anaesth 1984;56:599.

101. Duvaldestin P, Demtriou M, Henzel D, et al. The placental transfer of pancuronium and its pharmacokinetics during caesarian section. Acta Anaesthesiol Scand 1978;22:327.

102. Abboud TK, Kim SH, Henriksen EH, et al. Comparative maternal and neonatal effects of halothane and enflurane for cesarean section. Acta Anaesthesiol Scand 1985;29:663.

103. Abboud TK, D'Onofrio L, Reyes A, et al. Isoflurane or halothane for cesarean section: Comparative maternal and neonatal effects. Acta Anaesthesiol Scand 1989; 33:578.

104. Tunstall ME, Sheikh A. Comparison of 1.5% enflurane with 1.25% isoflurane in oxygen for cesarean section: avoidance of awareness without nitrous oxide. Br J Anaesth 1989;62:138.

105. Cheek DBC, Hughes SC, Dailey PA, et al. Effect of halothane on regional cerebral blood flow and cerebral metabolic oxygen consumption in the fetal lamb in utero. Anesthesiology 1987;67:361.

106. Palahniuk RJ, Doig GA, Johnson GN, Pash MP. Maternal halothane anesthesia reduces cerebral blood flow in the acidotic sheep fetus. Anesth Analg 1980;59:35.

107. Yarnell R, Biehl DR, Tweed WA, Gregory GA, Siter D. The effect of halothane anaesthesia on the asphyxiated foetal lamb in utero. Can Anaesth Soc J 1983;30:474.

108. Mokriski BLK, Malinow AM. Neonatal acid–base status following general anesthesia with halothane or isoflurane for emergent abdominal delivery. J Clin Anesth 1992;4:97.

109. Marx GF, Mateo CV. Effects of different oxygen concentrations during general anaesthesia during caesarean section. Can Anaesth Soc J 1971;18:587.

110. Baraka A. Correlation between maternal and foetal P_{O_2} and P_{CO_2} during caesarean section. Br J Anaesth 1970;42:434.

111. Rorke NJ, Davey DA, DuToit HJ. Foetal oxygenation during caesarean section. Anaesthesia 1968;23:585.

112. Lawes EG, Newman B, Campbell MJ, Irwin M, Durenska S, Thomas TA. Maternal inspired oxygen concentration and neonatal status for caesarean section under general anaesthesia: a comparison of effects of 33% or 50% oxygen in nitrous oxide. Br J Anaesth 1988;61:250.

113. Piggott SE, Bogod DG, Rosen M, Rees GAD. Isoflurane with either 100% oxygen or 50% nitrous oxide in oxygen for caesarean section. Br J Anaesth 1990;65:325.

114. Bogod DG, Rosen M, Rees GAD. Maximum F_{IO_2} during caesarean section. Br J Anaesth 1988;61:255.

115. Marx GF, Young IK, Lin CC, et al. Postpartum uterine pressure under halothane or enflurane anesthesia. Obstet Gynecol 1978;57:695.

116. Moir DD. Anaesthesia for caesarean section. Br J Anaesthesia 1970;42:136.

117. Coleman AJ, Downing JW. Enflurane anesthesia for cesarean section. Anesthesiology 1975;42:354.

118. Abboud TK, Kim SH, Henriksen EH, et al. Comparative maternal and neonatal effects of halothane and enflurane for cesarean section. Acta Anesth Scand 1985;29:663.

119. Warren TM, Datta S, Ostheimer GW, et al. Comparison of the maternal and neonatal effects of halothane, enflurane and isoflurane for cesarean delivery. Anesth Analg 1983;62:516.

120. Gilstrap LC, Hauth JC, Hankins DV, Patterson AR. Effect of the type of anesthesia on blood loss at cesarean section. Obstet Gynecol 1987;69:328.

121. Camann WR, Datta S. Red cell use during cesarean delivery. Transfusion 1991;31:12.

122. Schultetus RR, Hill CR, Dharamaj CM, Banner TE, Berman J. Wakefulness during cesarean section after anesthetic induction with ketamine, thiopental, or ketamine and thiopental combined. Anesth Analg 1986;65:723.

123. Baraka, A, Louis F, Nouehid R, Diab M, Dabbous A, Sibai A. Awareness following different techniques of general anesthesia for cesarean section. Br J Anaesth 1989;62:645.

124. Baraka A, Faek L, Dalleh R. Maternal awareness and neonatal outcome after ketamine anaesthesia for caesarean section. Can J Anaesth 1990;37:641.

125. Bogood DG, Orton K, Yaw HM, Oh TE. Detecting awareness during general anaesthetic caesarean section: A comparison of two methods. Anaesthesia 1990; 45:279.

126. Warren TM, Datta S, Ostheimer GW, Naulty S, Weiss JB, Morrison JA. Comparison of the maternal and neonatal effects of halothane, enflurane and isoflurane for cesarean delivery. Anesth Analg 1983;62:516.

127. Moir DD. Anaesthesia for caesarean section. An evaluation of a method using low flow concentrations of halothane and 50% oxygen. Br J Anaesth 1970;42:136.

128. Morgan BM, Aulakh JM, Barker JP, Goroszeniuk T, Trojanowski A. Anaesthesia for cesarean section. A medical audit of junior anaesthetic staff practice. Br J Anaesth 1983;55:885.

129. Bland BAR, Lawes EG, Duncan PW, Warnell L, Downing JW. Comparison of midazolam and thiopental for rapid sequence anesthetic induction for elective cesarean section. Anesth Analg 1987;66:1165.

130. Zagorzycki MT, Brinkman CR. The effect of general and epidural anesthesia upon neonatal Apgar scores in repeat cesarean section. Surg Gynecol Obstet 1982;155:641.

131. Kangos-Saarela T, Koivisto M, Joupilla R, Joupilla P, Hollmen A. Comparison of the effect of general and epidural anesthesia for cesarean section on the neurobehavioral responses of newborn infants. Acta Anaesth Scand 1989;33:313.

132. Downing JW, Houlton PC, Barclay A. Extradural analgesia for cesarean section: A comparison with general anaesthesia. Br J Anaesth 1979;51:367.

133. Abboud TK, Naggappala S, Murakawa K, et al. Comparison of the effect of general and regional anesthesia for cesarean section on neonatal neurologic and adaptive scores. Anesth Analg 1985;64:996.

134. Ong BY, Cohen MM, Palahniuk RJ. Anesthesia for cesarean section: Effects on neonates. Anesth Analg 1989;68:270.

135. Datta S, Ostheimer GW, Weiss JB, Brown WU, Alper MH. Neonatal effect of prolonged anesthetic induction for cesarean section. Obstet Gynecol 1981;58:331.

136. Crawford JS, James FM, Crawley. A further study of general anesthesia for cesarean section. Br J Anaesth 1976;48:661.

137. Andersen HF, Auster GH, Marx GF, Merkatz IR. Neonatal status in relation to incision intervals, obstetric factors and anesthesia at cesarean delivery. Am J Perinatol 1987;4:279.

CHAPTER 23

Epidural Anesthesia for Cesarean Section

Richard Flynn

Epidural anesthesia is a more versatile option for cesarean section than either spinal or general anesthesia. Its benefits extend not only throughout the intraoperative period but also well into the recovery phase.

Epidural analgesia for operative delivery has achieved great popularity. In 1971, Moir[1] stated that cesarean section under regional anesthesia could be a satisfying experience for women of the right temperament but few were willing to undergo the experience. Fifteen years later, the same author reported that over 70% of elective cesarean sections in his hospital were done under epidural block.[2]

Epidural anesthesia poses major challenges to the anesthesiologist. Unlike subarachnoid block, epidural anesthesia requires drug dosages large enough to produce appreciable transfer of local anesthetic across the placenta. Both the dosage of local anesthetic and the method of administration can influence maternal and fetal safety. The maternal cardiovascular responses can be profound and potentially hazardous to both mother and fetus. Intraoperative discomfort can complicate inadequate epidural blockade.

This chapter provides the reader with the information needed to provide safe and successful epidural anesthesia for cesarean section. It will consider the following issues:

- The choice of local anesthetic and its effect on the neonate
- Other drugs that may be used in association with local anesthetics
- Inadequate intraoperative analgesia
- Some points about technique

INCREASING INCIDENCE OF CESAREAN SECTION

There is a remarkable worldwide increase in the cesarean section rate, and, in the present medicolegal climate, this trend seems unlikely to reverse.[4] In the United States, the cesarean rate is approximately 25%. Figure 23-1 shows the increasing trend toward cesarean delivery in England and Wales from 1970 to 1984.[5] There, the rate now approximates 15%. Fortunately, this increase has not correlated with a rise in maternal mortality. The growing popularity of regional anesthetic techniques may be responsible. In the United States, despite the sharply rising cesarean birth rate, perinatal and maternal mortality rates have continuously declined, illustrating the increasing safety of abdominal delivery.[5]

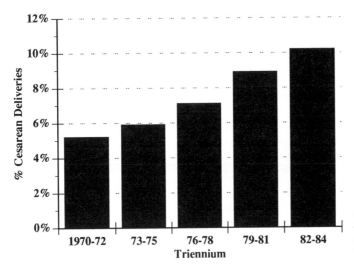

Figure 23–1. Percentage of deliveries performed by cesarean section in England and Wales. (Data from Report on Confidential Enquiries into Maternal Deaths in the United Kingdom [1985-87]. London HMSO DHSS, 1991)

MORTALITY ASSOCIATED WITH EPIDURAL ANESTHESIA

Since 1952 detailed accounts of maternal deaths in England and Wales have been reviewed. The results are published every 3 years by the Department of Health and Social Security as the *Report on Confidential Enquiries into Maternal Deaths in England and Wales.* These reports have identified anesthesia as a leading cause of maternal mortality.

During the 35-year period from 1952 to 1987, the maternal mortality rate in England and Wales fell by approximately 90%. There were 98.9 deaths per 100,000 live births in the first report but only 7.6 per 100,000 live births in the 1985-to-1987 report. Although the maternal mortality rate steadily declined, anesthetic deaths did not. Only the latest report shows a significant fall in the number of deaths directly attributed to anesthesia (Fig. 23-2).

Apart from the latest report, anesthesia was consistently the third most common cause of maternal death. Pulmonary embolism and hypertensive disease ranked higher. Gastric aspiration and failed intubation remain the major causes of anesthetic-related maternal death. In the last six reports, difficult intubation or aspiration of gastric contents accounted for 107 deaths (79%). During the last seven reports (1967–1987), 234 anesthetic deaths have been recorded. Only 11 have been associated with regional techniques. Four of these 11 mothers received general anesthesia as well. The remaining deaths resulted from either direct toxic effects of the local anesthetic or the indirect effects of regional anesthesia on the cardiovascular system. The most compelling argument for performing cesarean section under regional anesthesia is the virtual elimination of the risk of pulmonary aspiration of stomach contents.[6]

ADVANTAGES OF EPIDURAL ANESTHESIA FOR CESAREAN SECTION

Epidural versus General Anesthesia

Epidural anesthesia for cesarean delivery offers many advantages to both mother and infant (Table 23-1). The risks associated with general anesthesia, namely failed intubation and aspiration pneumonitis, are virtually eliminated. An awake mother can take a more active role in the delivery of her infant. In most hospitals, she can share the joy of the delivery with her partner in the operating room. The mother can establish breastfeeding when she pleases and begin bonding with her infant immediately. Postnatal depression seems to occur less commonly following cesarean delivery with epidural compared to general anesthesia.[7]

Regional anesthesia may have several hematologic advantages over general anesthesia. Women lose less blood during cesarean section under epidural compared to general anesthesia.[1] Significantly better fibrinolytic function and a lower tendency toward clotting follow epidural anesthesia.[8] These women then have a lower risk of deep venous thrombosis.[9] In addition, epidural blockade prevents lymphopenia and re-

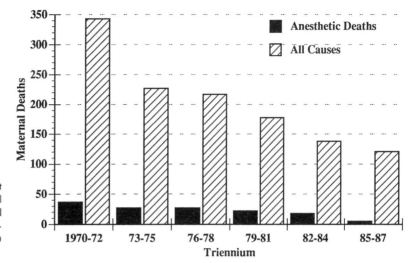

Figure 23–2. A comparison of direct anesthetic deaths and direct maternal deaths. (Data from Report on Confidential Enquiries into Maternal Deaths in the United Kingdom [1985-87]. London HMSO DHSS, 1991)

duces the granulocytosis often seen following general anesthesia.[10]

Regional techniques also reduce the stress response to surgery. Abboud *et al*[11] found that plasma beta-endorphin concentrations rose during general anesthesia but not under epidural anesthesia.[11] Loughran *et al*[12] reported that epidural blockade to the T-6 dermatome can obtund the maternal stress response to cesarean delivery. Xenon-clearance techniques have shown that intervillous blood flow does not fall during epidural anesthesia but may wane under general anesthesia.[13] This difference in response may relate to the high plasma catecholamine concentrations that arise under light general anesthesia.

General anesthesia exposes both mother and fetus to many different drugs, most of which cross the placental barrier and appear in breast milk. Epidural anesthesia limits fetal drug exposure and may lower the incidence of neonatal depression. The frequency and duration of early breast-feeding is significantly higher after epidural compared to general anesthesia.[14]

Comparisons of Apgar scores[15–19] and maternal arterial and umbilical venous pH values[16,17,20,21] usually show little or no differences between epidural and general anesthesia. Neurobehavioral examination, however, reveals some dissimilarities. After cesarean delivery, neonates score lower with general anesthesia compared to epidural anesthesia.[22] In fact, some investigators have detected no neurobehavioral effects of epidural bupivacaine for epidural cesarean section.[23] If time to delivery is long, less neonatal acidosis develops with epidural blockade.[24]

Epidural versus Spinal Anesthesia

Hypotension occurs less rapidly with the gradual onset of sympathetic blockade following epidural anesthesia compared to the rapid effect of spinal anesthesia. Also, the level of sensory block may be more easily titrated under epidural anesthesia. In addition, the risk of postdural puncture headache should be zero compared to the potential for headache following spinal anesthesia. After cesarean section, the epidural catheter provides many options for providing postoperative analgesia.

DISADVANTAGES

Epidural anesthesia for cesarean delivery also has some perceived disadvantages. The time required to induce

Table 23–1

Advantages of Epidural Anesthesia Compared to General Anesthesia for Cesarean Delivery

MATERNAL	PHYSIOLOGIC
Awake	Decreased stress response
Rapid bonding	Less blood loss
Early breast-feeding	Lower risk of deep venous thrombosis
Decreased morbidity and mortality	

adequate epidural blockade safely, especially in the patient without any pre-existing block, may obviate the use of this technique in an emergency. However, some experts argue that, in most emergency cases, infants are delivered no quicker with general anesthesia than with rapidly established epidural anesthesia.[25] Nonetheless, subarachnoid block is probably the regional anesthetic of choice for emergency situations. Another disadvantage is the frequent occurrence of intraoperative discomfort. This problem may require adjunctive measures depending on the severity of the pain and occasionally general anesthesia becomes necessary. Lastly, establishing adequate epidural sensory blockade often requires considerable quantities of local anesthetic, risking possible systemic toxicity.

INDICATIONS AND CONTRAINDICATIONS

With the growing popularity of epidural blockade in obstetric practice, our knowledge of who cannot receive this method of anesthesia has improved. Research and case reports help identify those patients in whom it may or may not be desirable. Contraindications to epidural anesthesia traditionally have been divided into absolute and relative and remain controversial.

Absolute Contraindications

Patient Refusal

We cannot insert an epidural catheter against a patient's wishes. Discuss the advantages and disadvantages of anesthetic techniques in detail during a preoperative consultation. Document the conclusion of the conversation in the chart with a note explaining the risks and complications discussed with and accepted by the patient. Fortunately, most patients understand a calm and thorough discussion of anesthetic choices. Few persist in refusing regional block simply out of fear or prejudice.

Coagulopathy

Significant clotting abnormalities preclude epidural anesthesia. Patients with severe preeclampsia should be evaluated carefully for signs and symptoms of coagulopathy. Most patients on subcutaneous heparin do not appear to be at risk of bleeding, because this therapy should not interfere with hemostatic mechanisms or platelet function.[26]

Local Sepsis

Do not insert an epidural needle through an area of infected skin.

Uncorrected Hypovolemia

Epidural blockade is dangerous in the presence of uncorrected hypovolemia. If considering epidural anesthesia, complete appropriate fluid resuscitation before beginning blockade. Placenta previa, without active bleeding or hemodynamic instability, does not contraindicate epidural anesthesia.[27]

Relative Contraindications

Some anesthesiologists also avoid epidural block in a variety of other clinical situations. Relative contraindications can include the following:

- Patients on aspirin therapy
- Those with neuromuscular diseases such as multiple sclerosis
- Patients with either spinal deformity or those who have had previous spinal surgery
- Systemic infection

Always make the decision only following a detailed explanation and discussion of the benefits and risks of the procedure and the alternatives with the patient.

INDICATIONS FOR EPIDURAL ANESTHESIA

Although epidural anesthesia can be used in most routine clinical situations, it can prove especially beneficial in women who present significant anesthetic risks. This technique is an obvious choice in women with suspected difficult intubation. (It is absurd to suggest that the remote possibility of a high block requiring emergency intubation precludes this approach.) Patients with diseases of the respiratory system, most notably asthma but also bronchitis, bronchiectasis, and cystic fibrosis, often are encountered in the delivery room. For cesarean delivery, these women may benefit significantly from a regional anesthetic. Carefully conducted epidural blockade is the anesthetic method of choice for parturients with some cardiac conditions. The gradual onset of block obtained by the slow administration of local anesthetic through an epidural catheter helps avoid hypotension, an advantage over spinal anesthesia. Epidural anesthesia is acceptable in patients with most forms of neuromuscular disease, including multiple sclerosis, providing the patients understands the pros and cons of this approach. Epidural anesthesia is especially beneficial in women with spinal cord injuries who are at risk for autonomic hyperreflexia. Patients with lesions above T-7 may have no sensation of pain in the operative field but have extreme surges in blood pressure both during surgery and the early postoperative period. Epidural local anesthetic blockade prevents these hemodynamic swings. (See Chaps. 25 and 26 for a complete discussion of anesthesia for the patient with coexisting medical disease.)

CHOICE OF LOCAL ANESTHETIC

Analgesic requirements for cesarean delivery are very different from those of vaginal delivery. This operation requires more extensive and profound blockade to abolish perception of operative stimuli. In addition, preservation of motor power is not necessary for delivery of the fetus.

What's Available?

Although many local anesthetics are available for epidural blockade, few have proved suitable for obstetric use (Table 23-2). Some, like procaine and tetracaine, are rarely used for clinical reasons. Procaine has a slow onset, low potency, and a short duration of action. Tetracaine has a very slow onset of action and a narrow safety margin. Other drugs, such as mepivacaine and prilocaine, see little use because of concerns about fetal toxicity. Mepivacaine has a similar anesthetic profile to

lidocaine, but its metabolism is considerably prolonged in the infant, making it unsuitable for obstetric use. Prilocaine, with its rapid breakdown and low toxicity, would appear to be a useful drug for obstetrics. Unfortunately, its breakdown product, alpha-orthotoluidine, causes methemoglobinemia, which rules out its use in pregnancy. Etidocaine, a long-acting drug, has a rapid onset of action but causes profound, prolonged motor blockade when administered epidurally. This lengthy postoperative immobility has limited its popularity in obstetrics.

2-Chloroprocaine

2-Chloroprocaine has proved popular for obstetric use owing to its rapid onset of action, its good quality of sensory blockade, and its very low risk of systemic toxicity. However, it does have a short duration of action, and additional doses often are required during surgery. As an amino ester agent, it is rapidly metabolized in the blood by plasma pseudocholinesterase. The in vitro half-life in maternal plasma is 21 seconds; in umbilical cord plasma, it is 43 seconds.[28] Appreciable accumulation of drug in either maternal or fetal blood is unlikely. (Atypical pseudocholinesterase can markedly prolong its duration of action.[29]) Although its metabolite, chlorobenzoic acid, crosses the placenta, it does not appear to cause appreciable fetal depression. 2-Chloroprocaine comes in several concentrations; use the 3% solution to produce sensory blockade for cesarean section.

Two issues have diminished the popularity of 2-chloroprocaine in the United States: (1) concern over reports of neurologic damage following 2-chloropro-

Table 23-2

Agents for Epidural Blockade

AGENT	ONSET	DURATION	CLINICAL USE
2-Chloroprocaine	Rapid	Short	Obstetrics and surgery
Procaine	Slow	Short	Surgery
Tetracaine	Very slow	Long	
Lidocaine	Rapid	Moderate	Obstetrics and surgery
Etidocaine	Rapid	Long	Surgery
Mepivacaine	Rapid	Moderate	Surgery
Bupivacaine	Moderate	Long	Obstetrics and surgery
Prilocaine	Rapid	Moderate	Surgery

caine administration (which precluded its use in some countries) and (2) its inhibition of the action of other epidurally administered drugs.

Neurotoxicity

Around the time reports of bupivacaine toxicity appeared in the literature, case reports on neurotoxicity after 2-chloroprocaine usage also were published. These articles described prolonged or persistent neurologic deficits after apparently uneventful epidural anesthesia.[30] Deficits also followed accidental spinal anesthesia with large volumes of 2-chloroprocaine.[31,32] Animal studies attempted to elucidate the cause of these reactions. Dogs[33] and rabbits[34] showed signs of neurotoxicity, whereas sheep and monkeys did not.[35] These conflicting results underlined the problems of species difference and the difficulties in applying animal findings to humans.

Wang *et al*[34] showed that neurotoxicity correlated with the antioxidant sodium bisulfite. Until recently, the commercial preparation of 2-chloroprocaine contained a higher concentration of sodium bisulfite (0.2%) than other local anesthetic solutions (less than 0.05% bisulfite). In addition, it had pH of approximately 3, considerably less than other local anesthetic solutions. Gissen *et al*[36] found that 2-chloroprocaine, at low pH, when combined with sodium bisulfite, produced irreversible conduction blockade in isolated nerve fibres. 2-Chloroprocaine alone or sodium bisulfite 0.2% at physiologic pH produced no signs of irreversible toxicity. They suggested that sulphur dioxide liberated from the bisulfite at a low pH diffused into the nerve membrane and formed sulphurous acid, which caused the damage. The same workers also reported that the rapid administration of large volumes of fluid into the subarachnoid space, in the presence of systemic hypotension, decreased spinal cord perfusion and produced signs of cord ischemia.

In response to this controversy, the commercial preparation of 2-chloroprocaine has been changed. It no longer contains sodium bisulfite, although it still has a low pH. To date, no reports have appeared of neurologic damage using this new preparation.

Interactions with Other Drugs

There is some evidence to suggest that 2-chloroprocaine antagonizes the analgesic effect of subsequently administered epidural morphine. Following 2-chloroprocaine administration, Kotelko *et al*[37] reported that epidural morphine, 5 mg, provided analgesia lasting approximately 2 hours, whereas analgesia lasted up to 20 hours after either bupivacaine or lidocaine. On the other hand, Youngstrom *et al*[38] reported long-lasting analgesia following epidural morphine in parturients who received 2-chloroprocaine anesthesia for cesarean delivery.

Recent evidence also suggests that 2-chloroprocaine adversely affects the action of epidural fentanyl.[39–41] Camann *et al*[39] studied 60 patients who received either lidocaine or 2-chloroprocaine for elective cesarean section. Postoperatively, when they needed analgesia, the women randomly received either fentanyl, 50 µg, or butorphanol, 2 mg, epidurally in a double-blinded fashion. Butorphanol produced good postoperative analgesia after either local anesthetic. Fentanyl produced good-quality analgesia in those patients who received lidocaine but only brief pain relief after 2-chloroprocaine (Fig. 23-3). In addition, 2-chloroprocaine inhibits the action of subsequently epidurally injected alpha$_2$-agonists.[42]

The mechanism of these interactions is unclear. Kotelko *et al*[37] postulated that the acidic 2-chloroprocaine solution lowers the pH within the epidural space. Then, more morphine remains ionized, thus delaying its onset and reducing its potency. However, Malinow *et al*[43] found that alkalinization of 2-chloroprocaine did not reverse its antagonism of epidural fentanyl. Others suggested that the rapid regression of 2-chloroprocaine anesthesia, combined with the slow onset of epidural morphine, results in a "window" when pain is felt.[44] These workers showed that small doses of intravenous opioid administered during this time produced satisfactory analgesia for up to 18 hours. Fentanyl has a rapid onset when given epidurally. Its antagonism by 2-chloroprocaine suggests more than a "window" of pain.

Butorphanol has kappa-receptor effects, whereas morphine and fentanyl are pure mu-receptor agonists. Perhaps 2-chloroprocaine or its metabolite, 4-amino-2-chlorobenzoic acid, has a direct antagonistic effect on mu opiate receptors.

2-Chloroprocaine also reportedly impairs the action of bupivacaine if the two agents are used together or sequentially. Cohen and Thurlow[45] reported that a mixture of 2-chloroprocaine and bupivacaine produced shorter-acting epidural analgesia than did bupivacaine alone. Other groups found that 2-chloroprocaine affected the onset, quality, and duration of subsequently administered epidural bupivacaine.[46,47]

Galindo and Witcher[48] showed, in vitro, that a mixture of bupivacaine and 2-chloroprocaine produced neural blockade of similar duration to 2-chloroprocaine alone. Interestingly, they found that increasing the pH of the mixture from 3.60 to 5.56 produced neural blockade similar to that of bupivacaine. They

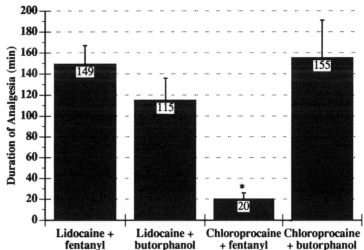

Figure 23–3. The effect of 2-chloroprocaine on subsequent fentanyl administration. Parturients received either fentanyl, 50 μg, or butorphanol, 2 mg, by epidural injection after cesarean section under epidural anesthesia. The *bars* represent the mean time (± SEM) until the women requested additional analgesia. (*P < 0.05 *vs.* other groups.) (Data from Camann WR, Hartigan PM, Gilbertson LI, Johnson MD, Datta S. Chloroprocaine antagonism of epidural opioid analgesia: A receptor-specific phenomenon. Anesthesiology 1990;73:860)

suggested that the low pH of 2-chloroprocaine may decrease the amount of diffusible free bupivacaine base, thus inhibiting its activity.

Lidocaine

Lidocaine is a safe, reliable agent that can provide excellent analgesia for cesarean delivery. For many years, it was the most popular local anesthetic for epidural cesarean section. It fell into disrepute when a report appeared suggesting that it caused neurobehavioral changes in the newborn.[49] More recently, these findings have been challenged, and lidocaine has regained its popularity; however, it does require added epinephrine. Epidural injection of lidocaine alone frequently provides inadequate surgical analgesia.[50,51] One group investigating maternal and neonatal effects of lidocaine and other local anesthetics had to abandon their lidocaine-without-epinephrine group because of the high incidence of unsatisfactory anesthesia.[50]

Placental transfer of lidocaine is considerable. The ratio of umbilical venous to maternal venous plasma concentrations at delivery approximate 0.5 (compared to approximately 0.3 with bupivacaine). Despite this substantial placental transfer, neonatal outcome is good.

Bupivacaine

Bupivacaine has a long duration of action and produces good operative analgesia. Its main disadvantage is the long time required to produce surgical anesthesia for cesarean delivery.

Low concentrations of bupivacaine provide pain relief during labor but do not deliver adequate surgical anesthesia. Bupivacaine 0.5% produces good operating conditions for cesarean section. For many years, the 0.75% concentration of bupivacaine enjoyed widespread popularity as a local anesthetic agent for cesarean section. It offered prompt onset of action, profound sensory blockade, and excellent neonatal outcome. Fatal cardiovascular collapse stemming from misuse of the drug led to its demise in obstetric anesthesia.

Which Drug?

The advantages and disadvantages of the three local anesthetics suitable for cesarean section are shown in Table 23-3. A comparative study of bupivacaine, lidocaine, and 2-chloroprocaine concluded that no drug produced adverse neonatal effects nor was there any difference in the incidence of hypotension among groups.[50] Another study also reported no difference in the incidence of hypotension between bupivacaine and chloroprocaine.[52] The differences in onset time can be altered by pH adjustment of solutions. 2-Chloroprocaine has the advantage of rapid metabolism with little placental transfer, but its interaction with other drugs may affect its popularity. Lidocaine is very suitable but requires the addition of epinephrine. Adding drugs then introduces the risk of error. In the end, the choice among these three agents rests mostly on personal preference.

Table 23-3

Advantages and Disadvantages of Various Local Anesthetics for Cesarean Section

	CHLOROPROCAINE	BUPIVACAINE	LIDOCAINE
Onset	Fastest (10–15 min)	Slowest (20–30 min)	Intermediate (15–20 min)
Duration	Short (< 60 min)	Long (> 90 min)	Intermediate (60–90 min)
	Advantages		
	Rapid metabolism	Long duration of action	Safety
	Low risk of toxicity	Good neonatal outcome	Reliability
	Minimal placental transfer	Good operative analgesia	
	Disadvantages		
	Additional doses often required	Toxicity	Appreciable placental transfer
	Interactions with other epidurally administered drugs		Needs epinephrine

ADRENERGIC AGONISTS

Epinephrine

Adrenergic agonists, specifically epinephrine, frequently are added to local anesthetic solutions for several reasons. They may improve the quality of sensory blockade, prolong analgesia, and reduce systemic absorption of the local anesthetic. Epinephrine also can alter the cardiovascular changes that accompany epidural anesthesia. In healthy parturients, 40 to 100 μg of epidural epinephrine does not affect uteroplacental blood flow.[53,54]

Bupivacaine

Studies of the effect of epinephrine conflict. Wilson et al[55] studied the effects of adding epinephrine 1:200,000 to 0.5% bupivacaine for elective cesarean section. They reported that epinephrine did not change the onset of blockade. It did prolong analgesia (time from maximum sensory blockade until subsequent analgesia was required) from 187 to 321 minutes. Mean arterial blood pressure fell significantly less in the epinephrine group. The incidence of side effects and the quality of blockade were similar in both groups. Plasma bupivacaine concentrations were consistently higher in those patients who received plain bupivacaine, but this difference was only statistically significant at 10 minutes (Fig. 23-4).

Laishley et al[56] compared the effect of epinephrine on bupivacaine in both elective (n=40) and emergency

(n=40) cesarean sections. They also found that epinephrine did not alter the onset time of satisfactory anesthesia. They found that patients undergoing elective cesarean section with plain bupivacaine needed significantly more supplementary analgesia than did those who received bupivacaine with epinephrine 1:200,000. This result suggested that added epinephrine prolonged and improved the quality of anesthesia provided by 0.5% bupivacaine. No differences in pulse rates or blood pressure occurred. These investigators also found slightly lower plasma bupivacaine concentrations in elective patients receiving bupivacaine with epinephrine. They concluded, however, that epinephrine does not usefully reduce bupivacaine absorption.

Reynolds et al[57] studied the addition of 1:200,000 epinephrine to bupivacaine in laboring women. Epinephrine lacked effect on the duration of sensory blockade but significantly reduced the mean maternal and umbilical venous plasma concentrations of local anesthetic. Abboud et al[58] showed that adding 1:300,000 epinephrine to bupivacaine during epidural analgesia in labor significantly prolonged sensory blockade and decreased the incidence of maternal hypotension. Epinephrine lacked adverse effects on uterine activity and fetal heart rate and did not significantly alter maternal or fetal plasma concentrations of bupivacaine.

These latter two studies were carried out in laboring patients. The difference in effect of epinephrine on plasma bupivacaine concentrations may reflect variations in uptake, distribution, and elimination of the drugs with the stages of parturition.

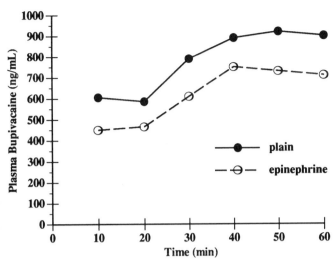

Figure 23–4. The effect of epinephrine on plasma bupivacaine concentration. Only at 10 minutes does epinephrine significantly lower plasma bupivacaine concentration. (After Wilson CM, Moore J, Ghaly RG, Flynn RJ, Dundee JW. Plasma concentrations of bupivacaine during extradural anaesthesia for Caesarean section: The effect of adrenaline. Anaesthesia 1988;43:12)

Adding epinephrine to the local anesthetic also may help detect intravascular drug injection.[59] In addition, Moore and Schurlock[60] suggested that epinephrine may have a role in the prevention or amelioration of myocardial depression associated with an accidental intravenous injection of bupivacaine. However, a recent study in rats suggests that epinephrine increases the cardiorespiratory toxicity of intravenously administered bupivacaine.[61]

Lidocaine

Adding epinephrine to lidocaine enhances the quality of the epidural blockade.[50,51] Brose and Cohen[51] investigated the effect of different concentrations of epinephrine when added to 2% lidocaine for cesarean section. Four groups of 10 patients received 20 mL of 2% lidocaine with epinephrine 1:400,000, 1:300,000, 1:200,000, or no epinephrine. No significant differences in onset time were found between groups. Hypotension occurred in two, four, three, and six patients, respectively, but the differences were not significant. Plasma lidocaine concentrations were only slightly lower in the epinephrine groups. The plain lidocaine group frequently experienced intraoperative pain and required significantly more additional analgesia. The epinephrine groups did not differ in the quality of analgesia.

Based on the preceding studies, it appears that the routine addition of epinephrine to 0.5% bupivacaine for epidural cesarean section is not warranted. However, the addition of epinephrine to lidocaine improves the quality of block sufficiently to recommend its use.

Other Adrenergic Agonists

Other adrenergic agonists also have been employed to prolong anesthesia and reduce systemic absorption. These drugs include phenylephrine and felypressin. Stanton-Hicks *et al*[62] found that adding 50 μg/mL of phenylephrine to epidurally administered lidocaine was less effective than epinephrine, 5 μg/mL, at reducing plasma lidocaine concentrations. The synthetic agent felypressin (0.03 U/mL) is an effective adjuvant to local anesthetics, but its use in obstetrics has not been fully evaluated.

Alpha₂-Adrenergic Agonists

Recently, there has been great interest in the use of epidurally administered alpha₂-adrenergic agonists. Despite their potential advantages, they do have limitations that may restrict their use in obstetric anesthesia.

Clonidine, the only agent available for epidural use in clinical practice, has been shown to provide good postoperative analgesia when given in doses of 300 to 800 μg following cesarean section.[63] In addition, clonidine may prolong the action of epidurally administered local anesthetics.[63] Unfortunately, clonidine causes bradycardia and sedation in nonobstetric patients.[61,64] The systemic effects of clonidine will require careful evaluation in mothers and neonates. As yet, there have been no clinical trials of clonidine in parturients. Animal studies reveal many alpha₂-receptors in the uterus. The functional role of these receptors remains unclear.[65] Epinephrine, by a direct action on alpha$_2$-receptors in the spinal cord, may itself produce some degree of analgesia.

RATE OF ONSET OF EPIDURAL ANESTHESIA

Spinal anesthesia usually produces more rapid blockade than does epidural anesthesia. In an attempt to accelerate epidural blockade, various adjustments to local anesthetic solutions have been tried. These measures include pH adjustment, warming local anesthetic solutions, and carbonation.

pH Adjustment

The onset of neural blockade can be affected by adjusting the pH of the local anesthetic solution. Local anesthetics are weak bases that exist in solution as both ionized and nonionized (free base) forms. Raising the pH of the solution (alkalinization) can increase the amount of diffusible free base. Adding sodium bicar-bonate to the local anesthetic solution immediately before administration will achieve this end. Several clinical studies have shown that pH adjustment significantly reduces the onset time for bupivacaine,[66,67] lidocaine,[68] and chloroprocaine (Fig. 23-5).[69–71]

Beware—the literature regarding the effect of alkalinization on onset of blockade is somewhat muddled. Different studies use differing methods of local anesthetic dosing. Varying endpoints and dermatome levels have been used to decide onset, and different criteria (pin prick, temperature, tetanic nerve stimulation) have been measured. Variance in initial solution pH will affect the degree of alkalinization occurring after the addition of a standard amount of bicarbonate.[72] These factors must be considered when evaluating the reports of alkalinization. Differences among them may explain some of the discrepant results.

Difazio *et al*[68] compared various pH-adjusted lidocaine solutions for epidural anesthesia. They used loss of discomfort following tetanic nerve stimulation applied to skin at the L-2 dermatome as the endpoint. The time from completion of injection to loss of dis-

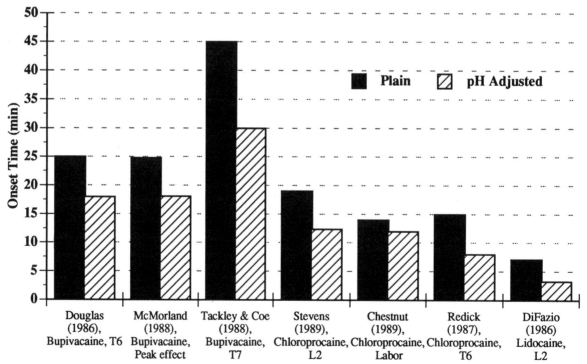

Figure 23–5. Reduction in onset times provided by pH adjustment. X-axis labels show study (year), local anesthetic used, and the endpoint measured.

comfort was significantly shorter with the pH-adjusted solutions. The pH-adjusted lidocaine also produced greater spread of sensory blockade 5, 10, and 15 minutes after injection. Both solutions produced comparable levels of sensory blockade at 30 minutes. The groups did not differ regarding maternal or umbilical vein plasma lidocaine concentrations, nor did they differ with respect to Apgar scores. One interesting point to emerge from this study was the comparison of onset times between commercially prepared lidocaine with epinephrine and lidocaine to which epinephrine was freshly added (7.11 min vs 4.27 min). The faster onset associated with pH-adjusted lidocaine can increase the incidence of hypotension.[73]

McMorland *et al*[67] studied the effects of pH adjustment on bupivacaine. Elevating the pH significantly hastened the onset and reduced the time to peak effect from 25 to 18 minutes. Again, pH adjustment did not alter maternal and umbilical vein plasma concentrations of bupivacaine. The quality of block was similar in both groups. Tackley and Coe[74] also reported significantly faster onset with pH-adjusted bupivacaine. They also found less need for supplementary analgesia with alkalinized bupivacaine. Apgar scores were similar for both groups.

Others have examined 2-chloroprocaine. Here, pH adjustment also accelerated the onset of epidural blockade.[70] Onset of surgical anesthesia at L-2 was reduced from 19 to 12 minutes. When using 2-chloro-procaine for labor analgesia, alkalinization reduced the median onset time from 14 to 12 minutes. The pH-adjusted solution also yielded a better-quality block.[71]

The amount of bicarbonate required to shorten the onset of blockade varies among the different local anesthetics. In addition, the starting pH of the local anesthetic solution varies depending on the drug and its source (Table 23-4). The pH values of commercially manufactured solutions of the same drug can vary widely from one lot to another.[75] The standard error of the mean pH of bupivacaine is 1.00.[67,72] Commercial solutions containing epinephrine have a lower pH owing to the addition of preservatives.[76] The amount of bicarbonate that can be added differs with each local anesthetic. Precipitation of free base occurs when the pH reaches approximately 7 (Table 23-5).[77]

Finally, pH adjustment does speed the onset of local anesthetic blockade. This effect has obvious implications for the clinical situation when we want to establish epidural blockade for cesarean delivery rapidly. However, remember that the faster the onset, the greater the chance of hypotension.

Warming Local Anesthetic Solutions

Mehta *et al*[78] reported that warming 0.5% bupivacaine to 38°C decreased the onset time of epidural anesthesia to the T-6 dermatome by 21% (approximately 5 min).

Table 23–4

pH of Local Anesthetic Solutions

AGENT	pH	REFERENCE
2-Chloroprocaine	3.27	Stevens et al[70]
2-Chloroprocaine	3.35	Chestnut et al[71]
2-Chloroprocaine	4.40	Hughes et al[43]
Lidocaine plain	6.43	Zahl et al[75]
Lidocaine and epinephrine (commercial)	3.84	Zahl et al[75]
Lidocaine and epinephrine (commercial)	4.55	Difazio et al[68]
Lidocaine and epinephrine (freshly added)	6.35	Difazio et al[68]
Lidocaine and epinephrine (freshly added)	4.81	Howell et al[76]
Bupivacaine plain	5.38	Bonhomme et al[72]
Bupivacaine plain	5.49	McMorland et al[67]
Bupivacaine plain	5.66	Howell et al[76]
Bupivacaine and epinephrine (commercial)	4.08	Bonhomme et al[72]
Bupivacaine and epinephrine (commercial)	3.16	Howell et al[76]
Bupivacaine and epinephrine (freshly added)	5.41	Howell et al[76]

Table 23–5

Recommended Amounts of Bicarbonate for pH Adjustment of Commonly Used Local Anesthetics

AGENT	BICARBONATE (1 mL = 1 mEq)	pH CHANGE
2-Chloroprocaine 3%	1 mL/30 mL	3.35 → 7.04[71]
Bupivacaine 0.5%	0.1 mL/20 mL	5.49 → 7.04[67]
Lidocaine 2%	1 mL/10 mL	4.60 → 7.15[68]

Carbonation

In vitro experiments have shown that carbon dioxide enhances the diffusion of local anesthetics through the nerve sheath. In isolated nerves, carbonated 0.5% bupivacaine has a more rapid onset of action than does plain bupivacaine.[79] Carbonation also lowers the minimal effective concentration of bupivacaine.[80] Clinical studies have produced conflicting results. Bromage[81] first showed that carbonated lidocaine shortened the onset of epidural block by 33%. In contrast, Morrison,[82] in a double-blind study, did not detect a significant reduction in onset time with carbonated lidocaine. In another double-blind study of cesarean delivery patients, Cole et al[83] also could not show any significant advantage of carbonated lidocaine over lidocaine hydrochloride. In addition, a recent randomized, double-blind study by Liepert et al[84] compared the clinical effects of carbonated lidocaine, pH-adjusted 2% lidocaine, and plain 2% lidocaine for cesarean section. They found no differences between the groups in onset, quality, or duration of sensory blockade. Carbonation does not shorten the onset of epidural bupivacaine.[85]

Plasma concentrations of both bupivacaine[86] and lidocaine[87] appear to be higher with carbonated agents. The greater availability of free drug base and the vasodilator properties of carbon dioxide may both contribute to this effect. Clinical studies have not supported laboratory findings that carbonation produces a faster block. Possibly, carbon dioxide is buffered rapidly in vivo, and intracellular pH does not change significantly. It appears that carbonation of lidocaine and bupivacaine does not offer any clinical advantage.

EPIDURAL OPIOIDS

Perhaps the biggest change in obstetric anesthesia during the last decade has been the growing use of epidural opioids. Besides providing postoperative analgesia, epidural opioids can improve intraoperative patient comfort as well. They also may shorten the latency of epidural local anesthetics. Epidurally injected opioids act both locally, at the level of the spinal cord, and centrally after being absorbed into the systemic circulation.[88] Pharmacokinetic studies of epidural opioids have shown good pain relief with plasma concentrations below normal therapeutic levels. There is no relationship between plasma concentration of epidural opioid and analgesic effect.[89-91] The idea of good analgesia with minimal systemic drug exposure appealed to obstetric anesthesiologists. A survey of the members of the Society of Obstetric Anesthesia and Perinatology revealed that about 60% used epidural opioids, especially fentanyl, during cesarean delivery.[92]

Epidural opioids may hasten the onset of local anesthetic blockade. In a randomized, double-blind study of 14 patients undergoing elective cesarean delivery, Johnson et al[93] compared the onset time to T-4 between bupivacaine 0.5% and bupivacaine 0.5% with fentanyl, 75 µg. The mean onset time was 19.3 ± 4.9 and 12.7 ± 2.0 minutes, respectively, a significant (P < 0.0001) 35% reduction of mean onset time. They also reported no adverse effects on the neonate or clinically important changes in maternal hemodynamics.[93] On the other hand, a larger randomized, double-blind investigation found no difference in onset time between parturients given bupivacaine 0.5% and those given bupivacaine 0.5% with fentanyl, 100 µg.[94] Women in the fentanyl group did have better intraoperative analgesia. No adverse maternal side effects were detected apart from mild pruritus. Epidural fentanyl did not impair neonatal outcome.

Epidural opioids improve the quality of intraoperative analgesia. Schlesinger and Miletich,[95] in a randomized, double-blind study, investigated maternal efficacy and neonatal safety of 100 µg of epidural fentanyl in combination with pH-adjusted 2% lidocaine (with 1:200,000 epinephrine) for cesarean section.[95] The lidocaine with fentanyl group reported significantly less intraoperative pain compared to lidocaine alone. The women receiving fentanyl noted feeling pleasantly drugged, relaxed, or drowsy. Otherwise, no adverse maternal effects occurred. The neonates did not differ in respiratory rates in the first 15 minutes of life or Newborn Neurologic and Adaptive Capacity Scores (NACS) at 15 minutes and 12 hours. Monitoring during the first 5 hours of life found no difference in apneic or bradycardic episodes; the fentanyl neonates tended to sleep more. The impression that epidural fentanyl improves the quality of intraoperative analgesia also was supported by Gaffud *et al*.[96] In a randomized study, 7 of 10 women receiving plain 0.5% bupivacaine felt intraoperative pain. Only 2 of 10 subjects who received 0.5% bupivacaine with fentanyl suffered pain. A similar study of 30 parturients by King and coworkers[97] also found better intraoperative analgesia when adding fentanyl to epidural bupivacaine.

Studies of the effects of epidural fentanyl on the neonate are encouraging. Labor studies also have not shown any difference in Apgar and neurobehavioral scores with bupivacaine–fentanyl combinations.[98] Maternal administration of epidural fentanyl, 100 μg, for cesarean delivery incites neither abnormal neonatal breathing pattern nor impaired lung mechanics in healthy full-term infants.[99]

ANXIOLYTICS

Occasional patients may be so apprehensive that they would benefit from an anxiolytic agent. Midazolam, a short-acting benzodiazepine, is sometimes used for this purpose. Sedative doses of midazolam range from 2 to 7 mg intravenously.[100] One of the effects of midazolam is amnesia. In obstetric anesthesia, most mothers want to remember their delivery. Heymann and Salem[101] advise avoiding midazolam until after delivery of the baby to stave off maternal amnesia. Ginsberg and Bell[102] reported that 2 to 4 mg of midazolam did not produce any adverse maternal amnesic effects. They advocated its use as an adjuvant for increasing maternal comfort during epidural anesthesia. However, Seidman and Marx[103] counseled limiting midazolam administration, as uncomfortable moments can be remedied by conversation, music, or a sedative without amnesic properties.

THE TECHNIQUE OF EPIDURAL ANESTHESIA FOR CESAREAN DELIVERY

The success of epidural anesthesia for cesarean section depends on avoiding pain and discomfort during surgery and preventing hypotension. Anesthesiologists doing epidural anesthesia should be aware of the dangerous, potentially fatal complications, namely acute hypotension, total spinal anesthesia, and local anesthetic toxicity, that may occur. Careful attention to technique (Table 23-6) can increase the chances of providing good surgical anesthesia while minimizing maternal and fetal risks.

Positioning

The dangers of aortocaval compression by the pregnant uterus are well known. In the supine position, the uterus compresses the inferior vena cava, reducing venous return to the heart and compromising both mother and fetus. Always position parturients in a lateral tilt position.

Monitoring

Surgery under epidural anesthesia with the patient awake requires the same standards of monitoring as surgery with general anesthesia. Electrocardiogram, automatic blood pressure recording, and pulse oximetry are obligatory. Full resuscitative facilities must be immediately available to treat any possible complication that could arise.

Fluid

Why?

Maternal hypotension, caused by sympathetic blockade, remains a major complication of obstetric epidural anesthesia. Although transient hypotension does not appear to influence the neonate, prolonged episodes may cause hypoxia, acidosis, and neurologic damage.[104–106] Additionally, the duration of hypotension may be more critical than its severity.[107] Intravenous fluid administration during epidural anesthesia expands intravascular volume and minimizes the changes in uteroplacental blood flow.

Marx *et al*[108] first described the use of "fluid preloading" as a preventive measure against hypotension

Table 23-6

Epidural Anesthesia for Elective Cesarean Delivery: Suggested Technique

---

Antacid

0.3 M sodium citrate, 30 mL, on admission to the operating room or an oral H_2-receptor antagonist 2 h before induction

Monitoring

Electrocardiogram, automatic blood pressure, and pulse oximetry

Position

Ensure uterine displacement.

Fluids

1–2 L nonglucose-containing crystalloid. Give at least 1 L before beginning to inject local anesthetic.

Drug Preparation

Add 0.1 mL (0.1 mEq) of $NaHCO_3$ to 20 mL 0.5% bupivacaine.

Test Dose Drug Injection

Inject 10–15 mL 0.5% bupivacaine in 5-mL increments. Wait at least 5 min between doses.

Wait 20 min.

Check level of analgesia.

Give additional drug to obtain T-4 to S-5 sensory blockade.

Supplementary Oxygen

At least 50% by face mask until delivery, then, as needed to keep maternal $S_aO_2 > 95\%$.

Treat Anxiety

Reassurance, midazolam, 1–2 mg IV (rarely needed)

Treat Pain

Epidural fentanyl, 50–100 µg

50% N_2O

Ketamine, 5 mg IV boluses

General anesthesia (last resort)

---

during induction of regional block. Since then, many investigations have looked at various solutions and volumes as prophylaxis against maternal hypotension.

What Solution?

Although all agree that preloading the circulation is a good idea, the question of which solution is most ap-

propriate has caused vociferous debate. Experts have advocated both crystalloid and colloid solutions. Giving colloid before the induction of lumbar epidural blockade limits the fall in mean arterial blood pressure and possibly protects placental intervillous blood flow.[109] Both crystalloid and colloid infusion produce equally satisfactory maternal and fetal outcomes.[110] Murray *et al*[111] compared infusion of 2 L of crystalloid to 1 L of colloid (hydroxyethyl starch) in 60 parturients receiving epidural anesthesia for cesarean delivery. No differences arose between the two groups in the incidence of hypotension, the degree of hemodilution, umbilical blood gas tensions, or umbilical blood osmolalities. In all, colloid solutions appear to offer no advantage in these patients.

Which Crystalloid?

Some important aspects have to be considered about crystalloid solutions. Philipson *et al*[112] studied the effects of circulatory preload before elective cesarean section with 1000 mL of either 5% dextrose, Ringer's lactate, or isotonic saline solution. They showed that rapid glucose infusion resulted in maternal hyperglycemia, hyperinsulinemia, and an increase in blood lactate. Neonatal hyperglycemia and then hypoglycemia followed. Glucose-containing solutions also lowered the pH in the umbilical cord vein and artery when compared to the nonglucose infusion groups. Therefore, rapid infusion of dextrose-containing solutions may cause fetal hyperglycemia, metabolic acidosis, and neonatal hypoglycemia.

Thomas *et al*[113] did serial blood glucose estimations in 30 women who had received a rapid infusion of 2 L of Ringer's lactate before undergoing elective epidural cesarean section. Neonatal blood glucose measurements were made on cord blood at birth and then 1 and 2 hours after delivery. A small, statistically insignificant, rise in maternal blood glucose occurred during the period of fluid infusion and before delivery. No biochemical or clinical evidence of neonatal hypoglycemia was detected. They concluded that, following rapid infusion of nondextrose crystalloid solution, there is no danger of a relative maternal hypoglycemia in fasted mothers, nor is there a risk of neonatal hypoglycemia. Even small amounts of dextrose in any preloading mixture seem unnecessary.

What Volume?

Crawford *et al*,[114] reviewing the frequency of hypotension during epidural cesarean section, reported a 50% reduction in the latter part of their study (1978–1985 as opposed to 1971–1977). They attributed this improvement to two changes in their practice. First, they infused a larger volume of fluid before induction of blockade (Fig. 23-6). Second, they increased the interval between successive doses of local anesthetic. Lewis *et al*[115] noted a similar trend. They reported that the incidence of hypotension fell from 45% to 7% by increasing the crystalloid preload from one to two liters.

Factors besides the amount of fluid infused alter the risk of maternal hypotension. Injecting the local anesthetic as a single bolus instead of in small increments increases the risk of hypotension. Drugs with a rapid onset of action (*i.e.,* 2-chloroprocaine or pH-adjusted anesthetics) induce a more rapid fall in maternal blood pressure.

The question of how much fluid should be given before local anesthetic administration begins has not been answered. I recommend infusing 1 L rapidly just before beginning to inject the local anesthetic. I then continue to infuse fluids while dosing the epidural catheter. Remember that all the fluid in the world will not prevent hypotension in the presence of significant aortocaval compression.

Antacid

The importance of administering an antacid cannot be overemphasized; 3% to 5% of these patients may require general anesthesia. Therefore, the risk of gastric acid aspiration has to be addressed. A nonparticulate antacid such as a 0.3 mol of sodium citrate, 30 mL, given on admission to the operating room or an oral H_2-receptor antagonist given 2 hours before

institution of blockade provide some measure of protection.[116,117]

Oxygen

Give oxygen to the mother via nasal prongs or clear plastic face mask. Ramanathan *et al*[118] showed a progressive rise in umbilical venous and arterial PaO_2 as maternal inspired oxygen concentration rose from 21% to 100%. Young *et al*,[119] in a randomized, double-blind study, gave 32 parturients undergoing elective cesarean section either room air or oxygen by face mask. Oxygenation significantly increased maternal PaO_2 and umbilical venous and arterial PO_2. Fears that a high maternal PaO_2 may cause uterine vasoconstriction, thus affecting fetal acid–base status, have not been authenticated.

Level of Analgesia

The sensory nerve supply of the uterus extends no higher than the 10th thoracic nerve root. Sensory nerves stimulated by surgery through skin, muscle, and peritoneum are confined to upper lumbar and lower thoracic nerve roots. Both Thorburn and Moir[19] and Crawford[120] recommended anesthesia to the level of the T-6 dermatome for cesarean delivery. Other authorities advocate extending sensory blockade to the level of T-4 to include those afferent fibers running in the greater splanchnic nerves. Most experts now agree that T-4 is the target. Although much attention is directed at the upper level of blockade, the lower level of anes-

Figure 23–6. Mean volumes of fluid infused into mothers for epidural cesarean section. (Data from Crawford JS, Davies P, Lewis M. Some aspects of epidural block provided for elective caesarean section. Anaesthesia 1986;41:1039)

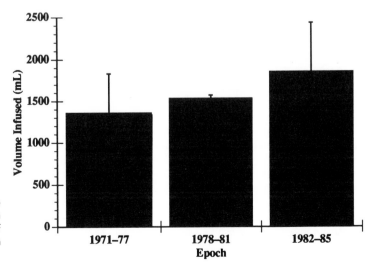

thesia often is ignored. The birth canal is supplied by the second to fourth sacral nerve roots, and these nerves should be checked and adequately anesthetized before surgery begins. In addition, pain from traction of the uterosacral ligaments transmitted via S-1 may be a common cause of intraoperative distress.

Another common source of intraoperative discomfort is the diaphragm. Either blood or amniotic fluid may pool beneath this structure during surgery. Patients may complain of chest pain or shoulder tip pain; however, the nerve supply of the diaphragm is from the phrenic nerve (C-3–5) and cannot be blocked safely. If shoulder pain is problem, try a slight head-up tilt to reduce the cephalad spread of fluid.

Test Dose

Inadvertent intravascular or intrathecal administration of local anesthetic may have disastrous consequences. One must exercise extreme caution to avoid this catastrophe. Aspiration with a syringe may discover intravascular or intrathecal catheter placement. Unfortunately, failure to aspirate either blood or cerebrospinal fluid does not guarantee safe placement of the epidural catheter. Injection of a test does containing a small amount of local anesthetic should detect intrathecal catheter placement. Intravascular catheter placement can prove more difficult to recognize. The first indication of systemic toxicity may be a convulsion or cardiac arrest. For this reason, a test dose also should reliably identify intravascular catheter placement. Many experts recommend epinephrine for this task.

Moore and Batra[121] first studied epinephrine as an epidural test dose. They gave 175 adults an intravenous injection of 15 μg of epinephrine in 3 mL of local anesthetic. Mean heart rate rose from 79 to 111 beats per minute within 23 seconds of epinephrine injection. Pulse rate returned to baseline within 1 minute. Their findings led many experts to recommend epinephrine-containing test doses in obstetric anesthesia strongly.

However, the epinephrine test dose can yield both false-positive and false-negative results. Cartwright *et al*[122] gave 100 laboring patients 3 mL of bupivacaine *without* epinephrine and reported an increase in heart rate of more than 30 beats per minute in 12 patients.[122] Leighton *et al*[123] recorded a heart rate increase of greater than 25 beats per minute in 2 of 10 laboring women given 3 mL of saline intravenously. Heart rate increased more than 25 beats per minute in only 5 of 10 laboring patients given 15 μg of epinephrine intravenously. Based on the latter two studies, using an epi-

nephrine-containing test dose in laboring women may mislead the practitioner. False-positive results occur in 12% to 20% of cases, whereas false-negative results arise in 50% of patients. No test dose can substitute for careful clinical practice (see Chap. 32).

Factors Affecting the Spread of Local Anesthetic Within the Epidural Space

The spread of local anesthetic inside the epidural space can be unpredictable. Various studies have attempted to investigate factors that may influence the spread of drug within this space.

Anatomy

The epidural space contains many sites where local anesthetic can leak out. Most of these are found laterally in the intervertebral foramina. Some drug also exits through the anterior sacral foramina.[124] Therefore, once a solution is injected, it not only spreads within the epidural space but also escapes through these openings. In addition, the capacity of epidural space varies greatly at different levels along the spine. Therefore, the site of injection of local anesthetic also will significantly sway its subsequent spread.

Height

The size of the epidural space is related to the length of the back. In adults, individual differences in the length of the back are small compared to differences in height.[125] Therefore, height can be ignored except in very short or very tall patients.

Weight

Body weight correlates poorly with local anesthetic spread in most patients.[126] However, epidural block extends significantly higher in obese compared to nonobese parturients.[127] The spread of neural blockade produced by injection of a standard volume of local anesthetic solution also correlates with the mother's body-mass index (BMI = weight [kg] divided by the square of the height [m²]).

Patient Positioning

Norris and Dewan[128] studied the effect of gravity on the spread of epidural anesthesia in 50 patients undergoing elective cesarean delivery. Half the patients received local anesthetic in a 30-degree to 40-degree head-up position, whereas the other half received the same dose of drug in the supine position. Neither the extent of sacral block nor the spread of sensory analgesia differed between the two groups. Other workers also have reported that maternal posture does not influence the spread of sensory blockade in lean subjects. In contrast, in obese subjects, blockade extends significantly higher in those who assume the lateral position compared to those who remain sitting during the period of fixation of the drug.[127]

Site of Injection

Sensory blockade is most rapid and intense near the site of injection. In addition, cephalad spread is greater than caudal spread.[129]

Administration of the Local Anesthetic

Following selection of a suitable local anesthetic agent, our concerns focus on how much drug should be given and how fast it should be injected. Larger doses of drug produce better blockade more often. Increasing the dose of local anesthetic also quickens the onset of blockade. In laboring patients, increasing the concentration and dose of bupivacaine from 10 mL of 0.125% to 10 mL of 0.5% decreases latency, improves the incidence of satisfactory analgesia, and prolongs duration of sensory blockade.[130] Unfortunately, there is also a direct relationship between the total dose of drug administered and peak plasma concentration of local anesthetic.

How Much Drug?

A compromise must be reached between dose and safety. The margin of safety of a local anesthetic lies in the difference between the maximum effective dose and the minimum toxic dose.[131] Toxicity relates directly to plasma drug concentration, which in turn depends on the rates of systemic absorption, distribution, and metabolism. Although maximum doses of local anesthetic have been recommended, it is unrealistic to define a maximum dose without due regard for the factors that influence plasma concentration.

DOSE OF LOCAL ANESTHETIC. The dose of local anesthetic required to produce a given level of surgical anesthesia is a product of volume and concentration. Bromage[132] showed that 20 mL of 2% lidocaine blocked the same number of spinal segments as did 8 mL of 5% lidocaine. He concluded that neither volume

nor concentration alone, but, instead, the total dose of drug determined the extent of epidural blockade. Other studies have contradicted these findings. Erdemir *et al*[133] reported that 30 mL of 1% lidocaine produced sensory blockade four segments higher compared to 10 mL of 3% lidocaine. Burn *et al*,[134] by epidurogram, showed that 40 mL of contrast media injected into the epidural space was more likely to spread into the cervical area than 20 mL of a more concentrated solution.

Greater volumes of local anesthetic do increase the spread of sensory blockade. Still, this relationship is not a linear one. Increasing the volume of local anesthetic from 10 mL to 20 mL increases sensory blockade by only three to four spinal segments, about one quarter that predicted by a direct linear relationship.[135,136]

There have been very few randomized, double-blind studies on the effects of dose, concentration, and volume of solution on sensory blockade. One such study by Duggan *et al*[137] compared these variables using bupivacaine (Fig. 23-7). Thirty nonobstetric patients aged 20 to 50 years were studied. The subjects received 0.5% or 0.75% bupivacaine. In two groups, they injected a total of 75 mg of drug. The third group received 112.5 mg. The larger dose produced the quickest onset and had a longer duration of action. The 0.75% solution produced a more rapid onset than the 0.5% solution, although this difference was not statistically significant. Neither volume nor dose altered the extent of sensory blockade.[137]

VOLUME OF LOCAL ANESTHETIC. Clinical studies investigating epidural anesthesia for cesarean delivery have used many different volumes of solutions to get satisfactory anesthesia. This reflects the great variation in the level of sensory blockade produced by a given volume of local anesthetic solution. It is impossible to know in advance the minimum volume of solution needed to provide satisfactory analgesia for cesarean section in a given patient.

Crawford,[120] in a series of 70 elective cesarean deliveries, used a mean dose of 27.2 mL of 0.5% bupivacaine. He admitted giving more than 40 mL (200 mg) by incremental administration, without maternal complications. (The highest dose reported was 55 mL.) Thorburn and Moir[19] consider 18 to 26 mL of 0.5% bupivacaine as usual for elective cesarean section.

Techniques

Much controversy exists regarding the best method of local anesthetic administration (Table 23-7). Should it be injected as a bolus dose or in increments? Should it

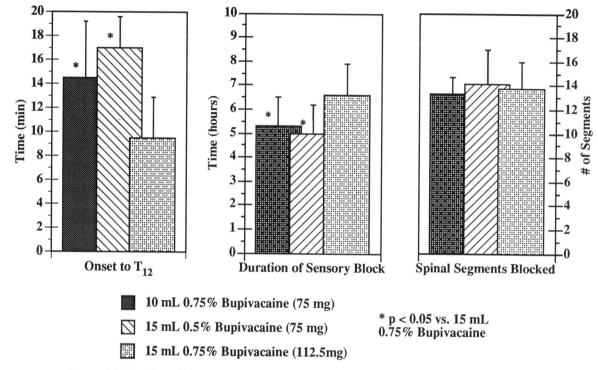

Figure 23–7. Effect of dose, volume, and concentration of bupivacaine on epidural blockade in 30 nonpregnant subjects. The largest total dose of drug had the fastest onset and the longest duration. Doses of 75 mg and 112.5 mg bupivacaine blocked the same number of spinal segments. Values are mean ± SD. (Data from Duggan J, Bowler GMR, McClure JH, Wildsmith JAW. Extradural block with bupivacaine: Influence of dose, volume, concentration and patient characteristics. Br J Anaesth 1988;61:324)

be administered through the needle or through the catheter?

NEEDLE. Some advocate injecting a bolus dose of local anesthetic slowly through a Tuohy needle. In expert hands, this approach may be as safe as injecting through a catheter. Its main advantage is a reduction in onset time by more than 50%.[56] This approach also may produce superior analgesia with less anesthetic than injection via a catheter.[56] A drawback with this technique is the risk of dural puncture while the needle remains in the epidural space. Catastrophe will follow

Table 23–7

Advantages and Disadvantages of Bolus and Incremental Administration of Local Anesthetic

ADVANTAGES	DISADVANTAGES
Bolus Dose	
Quicker onset	More hypotension
Smaller doses required	Higher blood concentrations of local anesthetic
Incremental Dose	
Less risk with intravenous or subarachnoid administration	Slow onset
	Larger drug doses required

accidental injection of this large dose of drug into an epidural vein. All agree that doses through the needle should be given slowly. One group administered the test dose, waited 5 minutes, and then administered the bolus dose over another 5 minutes.[138]

CATHETER. Some experts believe that incremental drug injection through a catheter is safer than bolus injection directly into the epidural needle. Small volumes of local anesthetic are administered at various intervals until adequate surgical anesthesia develops. Even if these small doses of drug are injected intravenously, maternal cardiovascular collapse is unlikely to occur. Accidental intravascular injection of local anesthetic can occur via either needle or catheter. Regardless of the technique chosen, the anesthesiologist must take all possible steps to minimize the frequency and consequences of this complication.

HOW FAST? The speed of local anesthetic injection may affect the rate of systemic absorption, which in turn has implications for local anesthetic toxicity. Scott *et al*[139] compared maximum plasma concentrations (C_{max}) following administration of a fixed dose of lidocaine given over 15 seconds and given over 1 minute. They found that C_{max} was 16% higher with the more rapid injection rate. On the other hand, Rosenberg and Heinonen[140] reported that increasing the speed of epidural injection from 20 to 100 seconds did not alter plasma bupivacaine concentrations.[140]

INCREMENTAL TECHNIQUE. Two respected experts recommend incremental administration of local anesthetic.[19,120] Unfortunately, they give no fixed guidelines about what time interval should elapse between increments. Thompson *et al*[141] first addressed this important issue. They measured plasma concentrations of bupivacaine following bolus and incremental administration at different time intervals. They showed that those patients who had a 20-minute interval between increments developed significantly lower plasma bupivacaine concentrations than did those with a 10-minute interval. Hypotension occurred in 33% and 24% of patients, respectively, considerably less than the 65% reported for their bolus technique. Although incremental administration of local anesthetic does require more time, it significantly reduces plasma drug concentrations and the incidence of hypotension compared to the bolus technique.

Thorburn and Moir[19] advocate giving 10 mL of 0.5% bupivacaine followed 20 minutes later by a second dose calculated based on 1.5 mL of bupivacaine per unblocked segment from the existing level of block to the level of the T-6. The extent of anesthesia is then reassessed 20 minutes later, with further increments given, if necessary, using the same formula. Most patients achieve satisfactory block with a total dose of 18 to 26 mL (90–130 mg) of bupivacaine. They report a 16% incidence of hypotension. Crawford,[142] another exponent of incremental administration, recommended a 10-mL dose of bupivacaine 0.5% with further increments, based on the above formula, at 10-to-15 minute intervals until sensory blockade reached T-6.

BOLUS DOSE. Bolus administration offers a more rapid onset of more effective blockade. Its advocates also claim less risk of intravenous or intrathecal administration; however, studies using bolus administration of bupivacaine report a higher incidence of hypotension than those using incremental dosing.

Various methods of bolus administration have been described. Laishley *et al*[56] administered a 20-mL dose of 0.5% bupivacaine through a Tuohy needle. Following a 2-mL test dose, they gave 18 mL slowly over 5 minutes before inserting a catheter. If needed, further increments were given through the catheter. Most of their patients (65%) required no more than 100 mg of bupivacaine. The dose of drug needed ranged between 100 and 150 mg in 39 out of 40 patients. One woman required 275 mg over 2 hours. The onset time was 20 minutes following drug injection, and hypotension occurred in 27.5% of patients. They concluded that the bolus-dose method decreased onset time, used lower doses, and was more effective than comparable studies reporting incremental administration. Thompson *et al*[141] administered 100 mg of bupivacaine over 20 seconds through a Tuohy needle, with further increments given as necessary. Their mean total dose was 127 ± 5 mg, with a mean onset time of 40 min.[141] Hypotension occurred in 65% of patients.

Crochetiere *et al*[143] compared two techniques of lidocaine administration in a series of 45 patients undergoing elective cesarean section. All received 20 mL of 2% lidocaine with epinephrine. One group had a bolus dose injected through the needle over 2 minutes. In the other group, 5-mL increments were given over 1 minute, with 2-minute intervals between doses. Both groups received additional drug as needed to establish a T-4 sensory level. The mean total dose in both groups was 540 mg (with an upper range of 720 mg). Onset occurred in 43 versus 44 minutes, and hypotension developed in 52% versus 14% of patients, respectively. Maternal and umbilical vein plasma lidocaine concentrations did not differ between groups. Peak plasma lidocaine concentration did not differ between the two groups. The highest plasma concentration reported in their study was 4.4 µg/mL. Another group of investigators gave 6 mg/kg lidocaine through a catheter in two increments, 5 minutes apart.[144] All patients developed sensory analgesia to T-6 with the initial dose of lidocaine. The average onset time was 12 minutes, and 40% of the women experienced transient hypotension. Plasma concentrations, estimated at 5-minute intervals, were well below toxic levels (C_{max} 2.7 ± 0.8 µg/mL).

Inadequate Analgesia

Occasionally, we face the problem of inadequate anesthesia, a situation that can prove distressing for patient and anesthesiologist alike. Many remedies have been tried to "wallpaper over the cracks." These countermeasures include nitrous oxide, intravenous ketamine, and opioids.

Nitrous oxide and oxygen in a 50% mixture can provide effective supplementary analgesia. The patient breathes this mixture through either a well-fitting face mask or a disposable mouth piece. Encourage the patient to breathe slowly and deeply. Nitrous oxide does not accumulate in either the mother or the fetus, and continuous use for 5 minutes does not depress laryngeal reflexes.[145] Labor studies have shown nitrous oxide to be twice as effective as meperidine at relieving the pain of uterine contractions.[146] Concentrations of nitrous oxide above 50% provide only marginally more analgesia and may obtund airway reflexes.[147]

Intravenous ketamine in doses of 0.2 to 0.4 mg/kg can supply good additional analgesia without depressing the neonate.[148] Titrate the dose of ketamine carefully to ensure that the mother remains awake and maintains her laryngeal reflexes.

Fentanyl, either intravenously or epidurally, can be an effective adjuvant for inadequate epidural analgesia. Intravenous fentanyl, 1 µg/kg, appears to have no adverse effect on the neonate. Eisele *et al*[149] found no significant differences in neonatal neurobehavior when examining infants whose mothers received fentanyl, 1 µg/kg, intravenously immediately before cesarean delivery compared to those whose mothers received no opioid.

Epidural fentanyl, in a dose of at least 50 µg, also can relieve intraoperative pain.[150] Smaller amounts of fentanyl are proved ineffective. A higher dose (100 µg) had a more rapid onset of action (3.4 vs 9 min). Both 50 and 100 µg of epidural fentanyl provide the same degree of pain relief. Epidural fentanyl, 100 µg, furnishes better perioperative analgesia than either 20 or 30 µg of sufentanil.[151] Sufentanil, 50 µg, produces an unacceptably high incidence of side effects (sedation, pruritus, and nausea).

A recent communication reported a case of respiratory depression arising 100 minutes after the epidural administration of 75 µg of fentanyl.[152] A continuous lumbar epidural catheter had been used to provide labor analgesia. The parturient then received fentanyl with bupivacaine for cesarean delivery. Earlier, she also had been given intravenous diamorphine. The authors concluded that patients should be monitored carefully following epidural fentanyl.

If a parturient still complains of pain despite your best efforts to make her comfortable, the option of general anesthesia should be offered. All patients should be forewarned of this possibility before embarking on epidural anesthesia for cesarean delivery.

Shivering: Prevention and Treatment

Shivering remains a common side effect associated with epidural anesthesia. Although it appears innocuous, it does generate patient complaints. Approximately 30% of women shiver during cesarean section with epidural anesthesia.[153] Current work suggests that shivering arises as part of the normal thermoregulatory response to cooling. Warming the intravenous fluids infused before elective cesarean delivery significantly reduces the incidence of shivering from 64% to 14%.[154]

CONDITION OF THE NEWBORN

Neonatal Responses to Local Anesthetics

Epidural anesthesia for cesarean delivery requires the use of large doses of local anesthetic. These drugs readily cross the placenta and could yield significant side effects in the newborn. The neonatal effects of local anesthetics and other drugs can be evaluated using Apgar scores, umbilical cord blood–gas analysis, and neurobehavioral examinations.

Apgar Scores

Many anesthesiologists believe that babies whose mothers receive epidural anesthesia have better Apgar scores than babies whose mothers undergo a general anesthetic. Marx *et al*,[155] in a series of 126 babies born by emergency cesarean delivery for fetal distress, reported significantly better Apgar scores under regional compared to general anesthesia. In a retrospective study of 610 patients having elective cesarean delivery under either epidural or general anesthesia, Evans *et al*[156] evaluated neonatal condition at birth. When babies were delivered under general anesthesia, 6% had Apgar scores below 4 at 1 minute and below 7 at 5 minutes. All babies in the epidural group had higher Apgar scores. Interestingly, this study found no difference in umbilical artery pH (7.28) between the two groups. These authors concluded that general anesthesia, not asphyxia or aortocaval compression, induced most low Apgar scores. Ong *et al*[157] compared the effects of regional and general anesthesia on neonates in a large retrospective chart review of 3940 cesarean deliveries. They reported better Apgar scores and less need for active resuscitation in babies born under epidural anesthesia.

On the other hand, Abboud *et al*[22] prospectively compared general and regional anesthesia. They reported no difference in 1-minute Apgar scores: All 52 babies scored more than 7 at both 1 and 5 minutes. Other prospective, randomized studies also report no difference in Apgar scores in babies born under either general or epidural anesthesia.[158,159]

Blood-Gas Analysis

Many obstetricians commonly sample umbilical cord blood at delivery for evaluation of acid–base parameters. Various workers have reported differing results when attempting to correlate Apgar scores with acid–base status.[160-162] Most studies of acid–base values after epidural or general anesthesia for elective cesarean delivery show no clinically significant differences between the two techniques.[16,17,22,158]

Neurobehavioral Effects

Although maternal drug administration may result in good Apgar scores, it can produce subtle changes in newborn behavior. In 1961, Brazelton[163] noted that maternal medication affected newborn behavior following normal delivery. He then devised a method of detecting these changes during the first week of life. This test became known as the Brazelton Neonatal Behavioral Assessment Scale (NBAS). The examination has 49 parameters and is thorough, exhaustive, and time-consuming (approximately 45 min). Like all neurobehavioral tests, it must be performed by an appropriately trained observer.

Another method of neurobehavioral assessment is the Early Neonatal Neurobehavioral Scale (ENNS). This test, devised by Scanlon *et al*,[49] evaluates babies during the first 8 to 12 hours of life. The ENNS is easy to do and yields an excellent level of reproducibility between observers. Subsequently, other neurobehavioral examinations have been devised. Amiel-Tison *et al*[164,165] developed the Neurologic and Adaptive Capacity Score (NACS). This test, which has 20 parameters, was created to detect drug-induced central nervous system depression instead of that caused by asphyxia or trauma. It requires no special equipment, takes less than 5 minutes to perform, has a high degree of reproducibility, and provides easily analyzed data. At present, it is the most popular test for assessing neonatal neurobehavioral status.

Several studies have compared neurobehavioral scores in babies delivered by cesarean section under either general or epidural anesthesia. Most report better scores for infants born with epidural anesthesia.[22,23,166] Most of these differences disappear by 24 hours.[22] Maternal hypotension complicating epidural anesthesia can yield depressed neurobehavioral scores.[159] In a series of 41 patients receiving appropriate doses of bupivacaine, Jani *et al*[167] reported no difference in NCAS scores between epidural and spinal anesthesia for cesarean section.

In 1974, Scanlon *et al*[49] published an article on the effect of epidural analgesia on neonatal neurobehavioral responses. They reported that infants whose mothers received continuous epidural block during labor had a significant reduction in muscle power and tone compared to those whose mothers received meperidine for pain relief. They concluded that lidocaine and mepivacaine produced adverse neurobehavioral effects in neonates. In a series of 28 patients, 11 receiving lidocaine and 17 receiving mepivacaine, umbilical venous plasma concentrations of mepivacaine were at least three times higher than those of lidocaine. The same workers subsequently examined infants of mothers given epidural analgesia with bupivacaine and 2-chloroprocaine.[168,169] Comparing these infants with the control group from the original study, they found no differences in neurobehavioral responses and concluded that bupivacaine and 2-chloroprocaine offered advantages over lidocaine for epidural analgesia for labor. Further support for this hypothesis was provided by Higuchi and Takeuchi.[170] They determined the ENNS of infants delivered by cesarean section with epidural anesthesia using a variety of agents. They concluded that babies exposed to lidocaine and mepivacaine did more poorly than those exposed to bupivacaine, 2-chloroprocaine, or spinal anesthesia.

Many subsequent studies, however, have not demonstrated any adverse neonatal effects of lidocaine. Abboud *et al*[50,171] compared babies whose mothers received epidural anesthesia with lidocaine, bupivacaine, and 2-chloroprocaine to a control group of neonates whose mothers received no analgesia.[50,171] The ENNS scores did not differ between the three different groups, nor did any of the groups score below the control group. Kileff *et al*[172] compared infants after epidural cesarean delivery with either 2% lidocaine or 0.5% bupivacaine. Both groups had similar ENNS scores. Kuhnert *et al*,[173] using a different behavioral assessment scale, found only clinically insignificant differences between lidocaine and 2-chloroprocaine.

Most anesthesiologists now accept that epidural lidocaine does not cause significant neurobehavioral changes in the neonate; therefore, this drug is regaining popularity in obstetric anesthesia.

CONCLUSIONS

Properly conducted epidural anesthesia is safe for both mother and baby. It avoids the major life-threatening risks of failed intubation and acid aspiration. One disadvantage associated with this technique is the slow onset of action, but bolus administration and pH adjustment of local anesthetic solutions can reduce this time considerably. [Editor's Note: I do not feel that the few minutes saved by bolus injection are worth the risk of accidental intravenous injection of a large dose of local anesthetic. I do not think that any test dose can *completely* rule out intravenous catheter location.] Hypotension must be avoided, and the dangers of local anesthetic toxicity fully understood. Epidural opioids have been one of the main advances over the last decade and in combination with alpha$_2$-agonists may provide fresh approaches in the next decade.

REFERENCES

1. Moir DD. Recent advances in pain relief in childbirth: Regional anaesthesia. Br J Anaesth 1971;43:849.
2. Moir DD, Thorburn J. Obstetric anaesthesia and analgesia. 3rd ed. London: Bailliere Tindall, 1986.
3. Lomas J. Holding back the tide of caesareans. Br Med J 1988;297:569.
4. Report on Confidential Enquiries into Maternal Deaths in the United Kingdom (1985-87). London HMSO DHSS, 1991.
5. Bottoms SF, Rosen MG, Sokol RJ. The increase in the cesarean birth rate. N Engl J Med 1980;302:559.
6. Moir DD. Local anaesthetic techniques in obstetrics. Br J Anaesth 1986;58:747.
7. Morgan BM, Barker JP, Goroszeniuk T, Aulakh JM, Reginald PW, Trojanowski A. Anaesthetic morbidity following caesarean section under epidural or general anaesthesia. Lancet 1984;1:328.
8. Modig J, Borg T, Bagge L, Saldeen T. Role of extradural and of general anaesthesia in fibrinolysis and coagulation after total hip replacement. Br J Anaesth 1983;55:625.
9. Cousins MJ, Wright CJ. Graft, muscle and skin blood flow after epidural block in vascular surgical procedures. Surg Gynecol Obstet 1971;133:59.
10. Rem J, Brandt MR, Kehlet H. Prevention of postoperative lymphopenia and granulocytosis by epidural analgesia. Lancet 1980;1:283.
11. Abboud TK, Noueihed R, Khoo S, et al. Effects of induction of general and regional anaesthesia for cesarean section on maternal plasma β-endorphin levels. Am J Obstet Gynecol 1983;146:927.
12. Loughran PG, Moore J, Dundee JW. Maternal stress response associated with caesarean delivery under general and epidural delivery. Br J Obstet Gynaecol 1986;93:943.
13. Jouppila R, Jouppila P, Kuikka J, Hollmen E. Placental blood flow during Caesarean section under lumbar extradural analgesia. Br J Anaesth 1978;50:275.
14. Lie B, Juul J. Effect of epidural vs. general anesthesia on breastfeeding. Acta Obstet Gynaecol Scand 1988;67:207.
15. Palahniuk RJ, Scatliff J, Biehl D, Wiebe H, Sankaran K. Maternal and neonatal effects of methoxyflurane, nitrous oxide and lumbar epidural anaesthesia for caesarean section. Can Anaesth Soc J 1977;24:586.
16. James FM, Crawford JS, Hopkinson R, Davies P, Naiem H. A comparison of general anesthesia and lumbar epidural analgesia for elective cesarean section. Anesth Analg 1977;56:228.
17. Fox GS, Smith JB, Namba Y, Johnston RC. Anesthesia for cesarean section: Further studies. Am J Obstet Gynecol 1979;133:15.
18. Crawford JS. Experiences with lumbar extradural analgesia for caesarean section. Br J Anaesth 1980;52:821.
19. Thorburn J, Moir DD. Epidural anaesthesia for elective caesarean section. Anaesthesia 1980;35:3.
20. Crawford JS, James FM, Davies P, Crawley M. A further study of general anaesthesia for caesarean section. Br J Anaesth 1976;48:661.
21. Downing JW, Houlton PC, Barclay A. Epidural anaesthesia for caesarean section: A comparison with general anaesthesia. Br J Anaesth 1979;51:367.
22. Abboud TK, Nagappala S, Murakawa K, et al. Comparison of the effects of general and regional anesthesia for cesarean section on neonatal neurologic and adaptive capacity scores. Anesth Analg 1985;64:996.
23. McGuinness GA, Merkow AJ, Kennedy RL, Erenberg A. Epidural anesthesia with bupivacaine for cesarean section: Neonatal blood levels and neurobehavioral responses. Anesthesiology 1978;49:270.
24. Crawford JS, Davis P. Status of neonates delivered by elective caesarean section. Br J Anaesth 1982;54:1015.

25. Davis AG. Anaesthesia for caesarean section: The potential for regional block. Anaesthesia 1982;37:748.

26. Letsky E. Haemostasis in pregnancy. In: Morgan B, ed. Foundations of obstetric anaesthesia. London: Farrand Press, 1987:189.

27. Chestnut DH, Dewan DM, Redick LF, Caton D, Spielman FJ. Anesthetic management for obstetric hysterectomy: A multi-institutional study. Anesthesiology 1989;70:607.

28. O'Brien JE, Abbey V, Hinsvark O, et al. Metabolism and measurement of 2-chloroprocaine, an ester type anesthetic. J Pharm Sci 1979;68:75.

29. Kuhnert BR, Philipson EH, Pimental R, et al. A prolonged chloroprocaine epidural block in a post-partum patient with abnormal pseudocholinesterase. Anesthesiology 1982;56:478.

30. Ravindran RS, Bond VK, Tasch MD, Gupta CD, Luerssen TG. Prolonged neural blockade following regional analgesia with 2-chloroprocaine. Anesth Analg 1980;59:447.

31. Resiner LS, Hochman BN, Plumer MH. Persistant neurologic deficit and adhesive arachnoiditis following intrathecal 2-chloroprocaine injection. Anesth Analg 1980;59:452.

32. Moore DC, Spierdijk J, Van Kleef JD, Coleman RL, Love GF. Chloroprocaine neurotoxicity: Four additional cases. Anesth Analg 1982;61:155.

33. Ravindran RS, Turner M, Muller J. Neurological effects of subarachnoid administration of 2-chloroprocaine-CE, bupivacaine and low pH normal saline in dogs. Anesth Analg 1982;61:279.

34. Wang BC, Hillman DE, Spielholz NI, Turndoff H. Chronic neurological deficits and Nesacaine-CE. An effect of the anesthetic, 2-chloroprocaine, or the anti-oxidant, sodium bisulphite? Anesth Analg 1984;63:445.

35. Rosen MA, Curtis CL, Schnider SM, et al. Evaluation of neurotoxicity after subarachnoid injection of large volumes of local anesthetic solutions. Anesth Analg 1983;62:802.

36. Gissen AJ, Datta S, Lambert D. The chloroprocaine controversy. II. Is chloroprocaine neurotoxic? Reg Anesth 1984;9:135.

37. Kotelko DM, Dailey PA, Shnider SM, Rosen MA, Hughes SC, Brizgys RV. Epidural morphine analgesia after cesarean delivery. Obstet Gynecol 1984;63:409.

38. Youngstrom PC, Cowan RI, Sutheimer C, Eastwood DW, Yu JCM. Pain relief and plasma concentrations from epidural and intramuscular morphine in post cesarean patients. Anesthesiology 1982;57:404.

39. Camann WR, Hartigan PM, Gilbertson LI, Johnson MD, Datta S. Chloroprocaine antagonism of epidural opiod analgesia: A receptor-specific phenomenon. Anesthesiology 1990;73:860.

40. Ackerman WE, Juneja MM. 2-chloroprocaine decreases the duration of analgesia of epidural fentanyl [Abstract]. Anesth Analg 1989;68:S2.

41. Grice SC, Eisenach JC, Dewan DM. Labor analgesia with epidural bupivacaine plus fentanyl: Enhancement with epinephrine and inhibition with 2-chloroprocaine. Anesthesiology 1990;72:623.

42. Huntoon M, Eisenach JC, Boese P. Epidural clonidine after cesarean section. Appropriate dose and effect of prior local anesthetic. Anesthesiology 1992;76:187.

43. Malinow AM, Mokriski BLK, Wakefield MI, et al. Does pH adjustment reverse nesacaine antagonism of postcesarean epidural fentanyl analgesia [Abstract]? Anesth Analg 1988;68:S137.

44. Hughes SC, Wright RG, Murphy D, et al. The effect of pH adjusting 3% 2-chloroprocaine on the quality of post cesarean section analgesia with epidural morphine [Abstract]. Anesthesiology 1988;69:A689.

45. Cohen SE, Thurlow A. Comparison of a chloroprocaine-bupivacaine mixture with chloroprocaine and bupivacaine used individually for obstetric epidural analgesia. Anesthesiology 1979;51:288.

46. Hodgkinson R, Husain FJ, Bluhm C. Reduced effectiveness of bupivacaine 0.5% to relieve labor pain after prior injection of chloroprocaine 2% [Abstract]. Anesthesiology 1982;57:A201.

47. Corke BC, Carlson CG, Dettbarn WD. The influence of 2 chloroprocaine on the subsequent analgesic potency of bupivacaine. Anesthesiology 1984;60:25.

48. Galindo A, Witcher T. Mixtures of local anesthetic: Bupivacaine-chloroprocaine. Anesth Analg 1980;59:683.

49. Scanlon JW, Brown WU, Weiss JB, Alper MH. Neurobehavioral responses of newborn infants after maternal epidural anesthesia. Anesthesiology 1974;40:121.

50. Abboud TK, Kyung CK, Noueihed R, et al. Epidural bupivacaine, chloroprocaine or lidocaine for cesarean section–maternal and neonatal effects. Anesth Analg 1983;62:914.

51. Brose WG, Cohen SE. Epidural lidocaine for cesarean section: Effect of varying epinephrine concentration. Anesthesiology 1988;69:936.

52. Datta S, Corke BC, Alper MH, et al. Epidural anesthesia for cesarean section: A comparison between bupivacaine, chloroprocaine and etidocaine. Anesthesiology 1980;52:48.

53. Jouppila R, Jouppila P, Kuikka J, Hollmen E. Placental blood flow during Caesarean section under lumbar extradural analgesia. Br J Anaesth 1978;50:275.

54. Albright GA, Jouppila R, Holleman AI, et al. Epinephrine does not alter intervillous blood flow during epidural anesthesia. Anesthesiology 1981;54:131.

55. Wilson CM, Moore J, Ghaly RG, Flynn RJ, Dundee JW. Plasma concentrations of bupivacaine during extradural anaesthesia for Caesarean section: The effect of adrenaline. Anaesthesia 1988;43:12.

56. Laishley RS, Morgan BM, Reynolds F. Effect of adrenaline on extradural anaesthesia and plasma bupivacaine concentrations during caesarean section. Br J Anaesth 1988;60:180.

57. Reynolds F, Hargrove RL, Wyman JB. Maternal and foetal plasma concentrations of bupivacaine after epidural block. Br J Anaesth 1973;45:1049.

58. Abboud TK, Sheikh-ol-Eslam A, Yanagi T, et al. Safety and efficacy of epinephrine added to bupivacaine for lumbar epidural analgesia in obstetrics. Anesth Analg 1985;64:585.

59. Marx GF. Cardiotoxicity of local anesthetics—the plot thickens. Anesthesiology 1984;60:3.

60. Moore DC, Scurlock JE. Possible role of epinephrine in prevention or correction of myocardial depression associated with bupivacaine. Anesth Analg 1983;62:450.

61. Kamban JR, Kinney WW, Matsuda F, Wright W, Holaday D. Epinephrine and phenylephrine increase cardiorespiratory toxicity of intravenously administered bupivacaine in rats. Anesth Analg 1990;70:543.

62. Stanton-Hicks MD'A, Berges PU, Bonica J. Circulatory effects of peridural block. IV. Comparison of the effects of epinephrine and phenylephrine. Anesthesiology 1973;39:308.

63. Mendez R, Eisenbach JC, Kashtan K. Epidural clonidine analgesia after cesarean section. Anesthesiology 1990;73:848.

64. Nishikawa T, Dohi S. Clinical evaluation of clonidine added to lidocaine solution for epidural anesthesia. Anesthesiology 1990;73:853.

65. Hoffman BB, Lavin TN, Lefkowitz RJ, Ruffolo RR. Alpha-adrenergic receptor subtypes in rabbit uterus: Mediation of myometrial contraction and regulation by estrogens. J Pharmacol Exp Ther 1981;219:290.

66. Douglas MJ, McMorland GH, Jeffery WK, et al. The effect of pH adjustment of bupivacaine on epidural anesthesia for cesarean section [Abstract]. Anesthesiology 1986;65:A380.

67. McMorland GH, Douglas MJ, Axelson JE, et al. The effect of pH adjustment of bupivacaine on onset and duration of epidural anaesthesia for caesarean section. Can J Anaesth 1988;35:457.

68. DiFazio CA, Carron H, Grosslight KR, Moscicki JC, Bolding WR, Johns RA. Comparison of pH-adjusted lidocaine solutions for epidural anesthesia. Anesth Analg 1986;65:760.

69. Redick LF. pH adjustments of chloroprocaine solutions. Anesth Analg 1987;66:286.

70. Stevens RA, Chester WL, Grueter JA, Zumrick J, Schubert A. pH adjustment of 2-chloroprocaine quickens the onset of epidural anesthesia. Anesth Analg 1989;68:S279.

71. Chestnut DH, Geiger M, Bates JN, Choi WW. The influence of pH adjusted 2-chloroprocaine on the quality and duration of subsequent epidural bupivacaine analgesia during labor: A randomized, double-blind study. Anesthesiology 1989;70:437.

72. Bonhomme L, Benhamou D, Jebri M, et al. Chemical stability of bupivacaine in pH-adjusted solutions. Anesthesiology 1988;69:754.

73. Parnass SM, Curran MJ, Becker GL. Incidence of hypotension associated with epidural anesthesia using alkalinized and nonalkalinized lidocaine for cesarean section. Anesth Analg 1987;66:1148.

74. Tackley RM, Coe AJ. Alkalinized bupivacaine and adrenaline for epidural caesarean section. A comparison with 0.5% bupivacaine. Anaesthesia 1988;43:1019.

75. Zahl K, Jordan A, Sorenson B, Gotta AW. pH-adjusted lidocaine bupivacaine mixtures are superior for peribulbar anesthesia. Anesthesiology 1988;69:A368.

76. Howell P, Davies W, Wrigley M, Tan P, Morgan B. Comparison of four local extradural anaesthetic solutions for elective caesarean section. Br J Anaesth 1990;65:648.

77. Ikuta PT, Vasireddy AR, Raza SM, Winnie AP, Durrani Z, Masters RW. pH adjustment schedule for the amide local anesthetics. Reg Anesth 1989;14:229.

78. Mehta PM, Theriot E, Mehrotra D, Patel K, Kimball BG. A simple technique to make bupivacaine a rapid acting epidural anesthetic. Reg Anesth 1987;12:135.

79. Catchlove RFH. The influence of CO_2 and pH on local anesthetic action. J Pharmacol Exp Ther 1972;181:291.

80. Gissen AJ, Covino BG, Gregus J. Differential sensitivities of fast and slow fibres in mammalian nerve. IV. Effect of carbonation of local anaesthetics. Reg Anesth 1985;10:68.

81. Bromage PR. A comparison of the hydrochloride and carbondioxide salts of lidocaine and prilocaine in epidural analgesia. Acta Anaesthesiol Scand. (Suppl) 1965;16:55.

82. Morison DH. A double-blind comparison of carbonated lidocaine and lidocaine hydrochloride in epidural anaesthesia Can Anaesth Soc J 1981;28:387.

83. Cole CP, McMorland GH, Axelson JE, Jenkins LC. Epidural blockade for cesarean section comparing lidocaine hydrocarbonate and lidocaine hydrochloride. Anesthesiology 1985;62:348.

84. Liepert DJ, Douglas MJ, McMorland GH, Gambling DR, Kim JH, Ross PL. Comparison of lidocaine CO_2, two percent lidocaine hydrochloride and pH adjusted lidocaine hydrochloride for caesarean section anesthesia. Can J Anaesth 1990;37:333.

85. Brown DT, Morrison DH, Covino BG, Scott DB. Comparison of carbonated bupivacaine and bupivacaine hydrochloride for extradural anaesthesia. Br J Anaesth 1980;52:419.

86. Appleyard TN, Witt A, Atkinson RE, Nicholas RDG. Bupivacaine carbonate and bupivacaine hydrochloride: A comparison of blood concentrations during epidural blockade for vaginal surgery. Br J Anaesth 1974;46:530.

87. Martin R, Lamarche Y, Tetreault L. Comparison of the clinical effectiveness of lidocaine hydrocarbonate and lidocaine hydrochloride with and without epinephrine in epidural anaesthesia. Can Anaesth Soc J 1981; 28:217.

88. Morgan M. The rational use of intrathecal and extradural opioids. Br J Anaesth 1989;63:165.

89. Nordberg G, Hedner T, Mellstrand T, Borg L. Pharmacokinetics of epidural morphine in man. Eur J Clin Pharmacol 1984;26:233.

90. Weddel SJ, Ritter RR. Serum levels following epidural morphine and correlation with relief of post surgical pain. Anesthesiology 1981;54:210.

91. Youngstrom PC, Cowan RI, Sutheimer C, Eastwood DW, Yu JCM. Pain relief and plasma concentrations from epidural and intramuscular morphine in post cesarean patients. Anesthesiology 1982;57:404.

92. Knapp RM, Writer WDR. Epidural narcotics in obstetrics. Survey of SOAP members. Abstracts of the Society for Obstetric Anesthesia and Perinatology. San Francisco, 1988:66.

93. Johnson C, Oriol N, Feinstein D, Ransil BJ. Onset of action between bupivacaine 0.5% and bupivacaine 0.5% plus fentanyl 75 μg. J Clin Anesth 1989;1:440.

94. Paech MJ, Westmore MD, Speirs HM. A double-blind comparison of epidural bupivacaine and bupivacaine-fentanyl for caesarean section. Anaesth Intensive Care 1990;18:22.

95. Schlesinger TS, Miletich DJ. Epidural fentanyl and lidocaine during cesarean section: Maternal efficacy and neonatal safety using impedence monitoring. Anesthesiology 1988;69:A649.

96. Gaffud MP, Bansal P, Lawton C, Velasquez N, Watson WA. Surgical analgesia for cesarean delivery with epidural bupivacaine and fentanyl. Anesthesiology 1986;65:331.

97. King MJ, Bowden MI, Cooper GM. Epidural fentanyl and 0.5% bupivacaine for elective caesarean section. Anaesthesia 1990;45:285.

98. Cohen SE, Tan S, Albright GA, Halpen J. Epidural fentanyl/bupivacaine mixtures for obstetric analgesia. Anesthesiology 1987;67:403.

99. Benlabed M, Midgal M, Dreizzen E, et al. Neonatal patterns of breathing after cesarean section with and without epidural fentanyl. Anesthesiology 1990;73:1110.

100. Camann W, Cohen MB, Ostheimer GW. Is midazolam desirable for sedation in parturients? Anesthesiology 1986;65:441.

101. Heymann HJ, Salem MR. Is midazolam desirable for sedation in parturients? Reply. Anesthesiology 1987;66:577.

102. Ginsberg FB, Bell SN. Midazolam in obstetric anesthesia. A reply. Anesthesiology 1988;68:296.

103. Seidman SF, Marx GF. Midazolam in obstetric anesthesia. Anesthesiology 1987;67:443.

104. Antoine C, Young BK. Fetal lactic acidosis with epidural anesthesia. Am J Obstet Gynecol 1982;142:55.

105. Brizgys RV, Dailey PA, Shnider SM, Kotelko DM, Levinson G. The incidence of neonatal effects of maternal hypotension during epidural anesthesia for cesarean section. Anesthesiology 1987;67:782.

106. Corke BC, Datta S, Ostheimer GW, Weiss JB, Alper MH. Spinal anesthesia for cesarean section. Anaesthesia 1982;37:658.

107. Ramanathan S, Grant GJ. Vasopressor therapy for hypotension due to epidural anesthesia for cesarean section. Acta Anaesthesiol Scand 1988;32:559.

108. Marx GF, Cosmi EV, Wollman SB. Biochemical status and clinical condition of mother and infant at cesarean section. Anesth Analg 1969;48:986.

109. Houvinen K, Lehtovirta P, Forss M, Kivalo I, Termao K. Changes in placental intervillous blood flow measured by the ^{133}xenon method during lumbar epidural block for elective caesarean section. Acta Anaesth Scand 1979;23:529.

110. Ramanathan S, Masih A, Rock FI, Chalon J, Turndorf H. Maternal and fetal effects of prophylactic hydration with crystalloids or colloids before epidural anesthesia. Anesth Analg 1983;62:673.

111. Murray AM, Morgan M, Whitwam JG. Crystalloid versus colloid for circulatory preload for epidural caesarean section. Anaesthesia 1989;44:463.

112. Philipson EH, Kalhan SC, Riha MM, Pimentel R. Effects of maternal glucose infusion on fetal acid–base status in human pregnancy. Am J Obstet Gynecol 1987;157:866.

113. Thomas P, Buckley P, Fox M. Maternal and neonatal blood glucose after crystalloid loading for epidural caesarean section. Anaesthesia 1984;39:1240.

114. Crawford JS, Davies P, Lewis M Some aspects of epidural block provided for elective caesarean section. Anaesthesia 1986;41:1039.

115. Lewis M, Thomas P, Wilkes RG. Hypotension during epidural analgesia for cesarean section: Arterial and central venous pressure changes after acute intravenous loading with two litres of Hartmann's solution. Anaesthesia 1983;38:250.

116. McAuley DM, Moore J, McCaughey W, Donnelly PB, Dundee JW. Ranitidine as an antacid before elective Caesarean section. Anaesthesia 1983;38:108.

117. Johnston JR, McCaughey W, Moore J, Dundee JW. Cimetidine as an oral antacid before elective Caesarean section. Anaesthesia 1982;37:26.

118. Ramanathan S, Gandhi S, Arismendy J, Chalon J, Turndorf H. Oxygen transfer from mother to fetus during cesarean section under epidural anesthesia. Anesth Analg 1982;61:576.

119. Young DC, Popat R, Luther ER, Scott KE, Writer WD. Influence of maternal oxygen administration on the term fetus before labor. Am J Obstet Gynecol 1980;136:321.

120. Crawford JS. Experiences with lumbar extradural analgesia for caesarean section. Br J Anaesth 1980;52:821.

121. Moore DC, Batra MS. the components of an effective test dose prior to epidural block. Anesthesiology 1981;55:693.

122. Cartwright PD, McCarroll SM, Antzaka C. Maternal heart rate changes with a plain epidural test dose. Anesthesiology 1986;65:226.

123. Leighton BL, Norris MC, Sosis M, Epstein R, Larijani GE. Limitations of an epinephrine epidural test dose in laboring patients. Anesthesiology 1987;66:688.

124. Southworth JL, Hingson RA. Pitkin's conduction anesthesia. Philadelphia:JB Lippincott, 1946:671.

125. Park WY. Factors influencing distribution of local anesthetics in the epidural space. Reg Anesth 1988;39:49.

126. Erdemir HA, Sopper LE, Sweet RB. Studies of factors affecting peridural anesthesia. Anesth Analg 1965; 44:400.

127. Hodgkinson R, Husain FJ. Obesity, gravity and spread of epidural anesthesia. Anesth Analg 1981;60:421.

128. Norris MC, Dewan DM. Effect of gravity on the spread of extradural anesthesia for caesarean section. Br J Anaesth 1987;59:338.

129. Bromage PR. Epidural analgesia. Philadelphia:WB Saunders, 1978:133.

130. Littlewood DG, Buckley P, Covino BG, Scott DB, Wilson J. Comparative study of various local anaesthetic solutions in extradural block in labour. Br J Anaesth 1979;51:47S.

131. Reynolds F. Adverse effects of local anesthetic agents. Br J Anaesth 1987;59:78.

132. Bromage PR. Mechanism of action of extradural analgesia. Br J Anaesth 1975;47:199.

133. Erdemir HA, Sopper LE, Sweet RB. Studies of factors affecting peridural anesthesia. Anesth Analg 1965; 44:400.

134. Burn JM, Guyer PB, Langdon L. The spread of solutions injected into the epidural space. A study using epidurograms in patients with the lumbosciatic syndrome. Br J Anaesth 1973;45:338.

135. Grundy EM, Ramamurthy S, Patel KP, et al. Extradural anesthesia revisited: Statistical study. Br J Anaesth 1978;50:805.

136. Park WY, Massengale MD, Kim SI, et al. Age and epidural dose response in adult men. Anesthesiology 1982;56:318.

137. Duggan J, Bowler GMR, McClure JH, Wildsmith JAW. Extradural block with bupivacaine: Influence of dose, volume, concentration and patient characteristics. Br J Anaesth 1988;61:324.

138. Laishley RS, Morgan BM. A single-dose epidural technique for cesarean section. Anaesthesia 1988;43:100.

139. Scott DB, Jebson PJR, Braid DP, Ortengren B, Frisch P. Factors affecting plasma levels of lignocaine and prilocaine. Br J Anaesth 1972:44:1040.

140. Rosenberg PH, Heinonen E. Differential sensitivity of A and C nerve fibres to long acting amide local anesthetics. Br J Anaesth 1983;55:143.

141. Thompson EM, Wilson CM, Moore J, McClean E. Plasma bupivacaine levels associated with extradural anaesthesia for caesarean section. Anaesthesia 1985; 40:426.

142. Crawford JS. Caesarean section. In: Obstetric analgesia and anaesthesia (Current reviews in obstetrics and gynaecology). London:Churchill Livingstone, 1984: 105.

143. Crochetiere CT, Trepanier CA, Cote JJ. Epidural anaesthesia for cesarean section: Comparison of two injection techniques. Can J Anaesth 1989;36:133.

144. Flynn RJ, Moore J, Collier PS, Howard PJ. Effect of intravenous cimetidine during extradural caesarean section. Anesthesia 1989;44:739.

145. Cleaton-Jones P. The laryngeal closure reflex and nitrous oxide—oxygen analgesia. Anesthesiology 1976; 45:569.

146. Holdcroft A, Morgan M. An assessment of the analgesic effect in labour of pethidine and 50% nitrous oxide in oxygen. J Obstet Gynaecol Br Commonwealth 1974;81:603.

147. Cole PV Crawford JS, Doughty AG, et al. Specifications and recommendations for nitrous oxide–oxygen apparatus to be used in obstetric anaesthesia. Anaesthesia 1970;25:317.

148. Akamatsu TJ, Bonica JJ, Rehmet R, Eng M, Ueland K. experiences with the use of ketamine for parturition. I. Primary anesthetic for vaginal delivery. Anesth Analg 1974;53:284.

149. Eisele JH, Wright R, Rogge P. Newborn and maternal fentanyl levels at cesarean section [Abstract]. Anesth Analg 1982;61:179.

150. Naulty JS, Datta S, Ostheimer GW, Johnson MD, Burger GA. Epidural fentanyl for post cesarean delivery pain management. Anesthesiology 1985;63:694.

151. Madej TH, Strunin L. Comparison of epidural fentanyl with sufentanil. Analgesia and side effects after a single bolus dose during elective caesarean section. Anaesthesia 1987;42:1156.

152. Brockway MS, Noble DW, Sharwood-Smith GH, McClure JH. Profound respiratory depression after extradural fentanyl. Br J Anaesth 1990;64:243.

153. Sessler DI, Ponte J. Shivering during epidural anesthesia. Anesthesiology 1990;72:816.

154. Workhoven MN. Intravenous fluid temperature, shivering, and the parturient. Anesth Analg 1986;65:496.

155. Marx GF, Luykx WM, Cohen S. Fetal–neonatal status following caesarean section for fetal distress. Br J Anaesth 1984;56:1009.

156. Evans CM, Murphy JF, Gray OP, Rosen M. Epidural versus general anaesthesia for elective caesarean section. Effect on Apgar score and acid–base status of the newborn. Anaesthesia 1989;44:778.

157. Ong BY, Cohen M, Palahniuk RJ. Anesthesia for cesrean section—effects on neonates. Anesth Analg 1989; 68:270.

158. Palahniuk RJ, Scatliff J, Biehl D, Wiebe H, Sankaran K. Maternal and neonatal effects of methoxyflurane, nitrous oxide and lumbar epidural anaesthesia for caesarean section. Can Anaesth Soc J 1977;24:586.

159. Hollmén AI, Jouppila R, Koivisto M, et al. Neurologic activity of infants following anesthesia for cesarean section. Anesthesiology 1978;48:350.

160. Crawford JS, Davies P, Pearson JE. Significance of the individual components of the Apgar score. Br J Anesth 1973;45:148.

161. Marx GF, Mahajan S, Miclat MN. Correlation of biochemical data with Apgar scores at birth and at one minute. Br J Anaesth 1977;49:831.

162. Sykes GS, Molloy PM, Johnson PM, et al. Do Apgar scores indicate asphyxia? Lancet 1982;494.

163. Brazelton TB. Psychophysiologic reactions in the neonate. II. Effect of maternal medication on the neonate and his behavior. J Pediatr 1961;58:513.

164. Amiel-Tison C, Barrier G, Shnider SM, Levinson G, Hughes SC, Stephani SJ. A new neurologic and adaptive capacity scoring system for evaluating obstetric medications in full-term newborns. Anesthesiology 1982; 56:340.

165. Amiel-Tison C. A method for neurological evaluation within the first year of life. Experience with full-term newborns. In: Major Mental Handicap: Methods and Costs of prevention. Ciba Foundation Symposium No 59. Amsterdam:Elsevier/Excerpta Medica/North Holland, 1978:107.

166. Hodgkinson R, Bhatt M, Kim SS, Grewal G, Marx GF. Neonatal neurobehavioral tests following cesarean section under general and spinal anesthesia. Am J Obstet Gynecol 1978;132:670.

167. Jani K, McEvedy B, Harris S, Samaan A. Maternal and neonatal bupivacaine concentrations after spinal and epidural anesthesia for caesarean section. Br J Anaesth 1989;62:226.

168. Scanlon JW, Ostheimer GW, Lurie AO, Brown WU, Weiss JB, Alper MH. Neurobehavioral responses and drug concentrations in newborns after maternal epidural anesthesia with bupivacaine. Anesthesiology 1976;45:400.

169. Brown WU. Guest discussion: Neonatal neurobehavioral tests following vaginal delivery under ketamine, thiopental and extradural anesthesia. Anesth Analg 1977;56:548.

170. Higuchi M, Takeuchi S. Studies on the neurobehavioral response (Scanlon test) in newborns after epidural anesthesia with various anesthetic agents for cesarean section. Acta Obstet Gynaecol Jpn 1982;4:2143.

171. Abboud TK, Khoo SS, Miller F, Doan T, Henricksen EH. Maternal, fetal and neonatal responses after epidural anesthesia with bupivacaine, 2-chloroprocaine or lidocaine. Anesth Analg 1982;61:638.

172. Kileff ME, James FM III, Dewan DM, Floyd HM. Neonatal neurobehavioral responses after epidural anesthesia for cesarean section using lidocaine and bupivacaine. Anesth Analg 1984;63:413.

173. Kuhnert BR, Harrison MJ, Linn PL, Kuhnert PM. Effect of maternal epidural anesthesia on neonatal behavior. Anesth Analg 1984;63:301.

CHAPTER 24

Spinal Anesthesia for Cesarean Section

Mark C. Norris

"Cesarean section in an awake patient is undoubtedly a major test of regional anesthesia. The operation may be lengthy, profound blockade of many nerves is required, strong visceral stimulation is present, sudden cardiovascular changes are compounded by posture, and fetal well-being may be influenced by several physiologic variables and drugs."[1] Spinal anesthesia represents perhaps the most elegant approach to this challenge. With one small needle, and an almost homeopathic amount of drug, the anesthesiologist can readily provide profound anesthesia and excellent operating conditions for major intra-abdominal surgery.

Historically, spinal anesthesia has seen intermittent use in obstetrics since 1900.[2] In the past, a high incidence of hypotension and the risk of headache limited the application of this technique.[3] By the early 1980s, most experts recommended epidural rather than spinal blockade as the regional anesthetic of choice for cesarean section.[4] Currently, spinal anesthesia is regaining popularity. Obstetric anesthesiologists now have a better understanding of ways to prevent and treat hypotension. Manufacturers have made smaller-gauge spinal needles that limit the risk of postdural puncture headache. In many institutions, spinal blockade is the most commonly used anesthetic for elective cesarean delivery.

This chapter reviews the present-day role of spinal blockade for cesarean delivery. It examines closely the maternal and fetal hemodynamic effects of spinal anesthesia. Then, it discusses ways to minimize the incidence and impact of maternal hypotension. Finally, this chapter considers issues surrounding drug selection and drug dosage.

ADVANTAGES AND DISADVANTAGES

Advantages

Spinal anesthesia offers several advantages over epidural blockade for cesarean section.[5] It offers simplicity and speed. Once you have located the subarachnoid space and injected an appropriate amount of local anesthetic, you are virtually assured of good, dense, bilateral sensory blockade. The operation can begin within 10 minutes.[6] In contrast, epidural anesthesia is a technically complex procedure, which places the woman at risk of dural puncture with a large-gauge needle. Epidural blockade also is time-consuming; safe induction for cesarean section requires 30 to 45 minutes

Spinal anesthesia offers more than convenience. It offers safety. Epidural anesthesia for cesarean section requires injection of nearly toxic amounts of local anesthetic. Accidental injection of all or part of this drug dose into the mother's vascular system or subarachnoid space can be lethal. In contrast, spinal blockade produces extensive anesthesia with only a tiny amount of drug. Spinal anesthesia requires only 5% to 10% as much drug as epidural anesthesia. Maternal systemic absorption produces blood drug concentrations of about 5% of those developing after epidural blockade (Fig. 24-1). Both mother and fetus therefore are exposed to only minute amounts of drug.[7]

Disadvantages

Although I find spinal anesthesia to be a safe, reliable anesthetic technique for cesarean section, others express a variety of concerns. Sensory blockade occasionally may ascend into the cervical region. These high levels of block could impair maternal respiration; most often, however, diaphragmatic function remains intact, and only minor changes in respiratory capability develop.[8] Rarely, sensory block extends high enough that endotracheal intubation is warranted to limit the risk of maternal aspiration. At Thomas Jefferson University Hospital, this event occurs less than once in every 500 cesarean deliveries under spinal anesthesia.

The risk of spinal headache seems inseparable from this anesthetic technique. Fortunately, preliminary experience with small-gauge, atraumatic spinal needles is promising (Arkoosh VA, unpublished data). These needles may succeed in almost eliminating headache as a complication of intended dural puncture.

Maternal hypotension frequently follows subarachnoid injection of local anesthetics. Profound, prolonged hypotension can harm both mother and infant. Fortunately, both the severity and the consequences of maternal hypotension can be limited. Adequate prehydration, careful attention to left uterine displacement, and the judicious use of ephedrine can all minimize this problem.

Finally, a single subarachnoid injection provides only a finite period of anesthesia. One must always consider the possibility that surgery may outlast the anesthetic. Careful selection of drug and dosage can reliably provide 2 hours of good surgical conditions. Continuous spinal anesthesia provides a reasonable alternative for procedures that may possibly be prolonged.

INDICATIONS AND CONTRAINDICATIONS

There are few absolute contraindications to spinal anesthesia (Table 24-1). Some of these include maternal refusal, uncorrected hypovolemia, coagulopathy, and infection at the site of needle puncture. Many also hesitate to induce spinal anesthesia in a variety of other situations (see Table 24-1). Other chapters in this book will discuss these issues.

Significant controversy also surrounds the use of spinal anesthesia in the presence of a nonreassuring fetal heart rate tracing. Although some argue for the rapid induction of general anesthesia in this setting, several pieces of evidence suggest that spinal anesthesia may be a safe alternative in some situations. Induction of spinal anesthesia in laboring patients decreases maternal circulating catecholamine concentration.[9] This

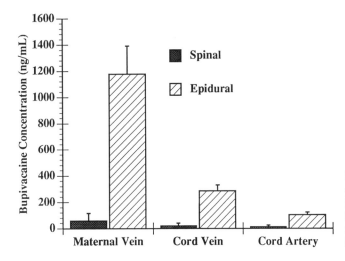

Figure 24–1. Comparison of plasma bupivacaine concentrations at delivery after spinal or epidural anesthesia for cesarean section. (After Kuhnert BR, Zuspan KJ, Kuhnert PM, Syracuse CD, Brown DE. Bupivacaine disposition in mother, fetus and neonate after spinal anesthesia for cesarean section. Anesth Analg 1987;66:407)

Table 24–1

Contraindications to Spinal Anesthesia for Cesarean Section

Absolute Contraindications

Maternal refusal

Uncorrected hypovolemia

Clinically apparent coagulopathy

Infection at the site of needle insertion

Relative Contraindications

Potential hypovolemia (placenta previa/accreta)

Laboratory coagulopathy

Systemic infection

Neurologic disease

Back pain

Fetal distress

Severe preeclampsia

effect may help relieve any existing uterine artery spasm and improve fetal oxygen supply. In contrast, induction of general anesthesia increases maternal serum catecholamine concentration and decreases uterine blood flow.[10] Maternal hypotension brought on by spinal blockade can worsen fetal condition. In laboring women, however, this complication is less likely to develop. One group of investigators reported a 50% incidence of hypotension during induction of spinal blockade in nonlaboring women. In contrast, none of their laboring patients (n=14) experienced a significant drop in blood pressure.[9]

Fetal catecholamine secretion plays an important role in the adaptation to extrauterine life. Infants born by cesarean section have lower plasma catecholamine concentrations than do infants delivered vaginally. However, infants whose mothers receive regional anesthesia for cesarean section have higher plasma catecholamine concentrations than do infants whose mothers receive general anesthesia.[11]

Marx *et al*[12] compared regional and general anesthesia in 126 parturients undergoing emergency cesarean section. All women carried acutely distressed fetuses (persistent, severe, late fetal heart rate decelerations, scalp pH < 7.20 or falling steadily) (Table 24-2). In all cases, surgery began within 20 minutes of the last scalp pH. The women selected either general or regional anesthesia. Those choosing general anesthesia received either ketamine or thiopental followed by 40% nitrous oxide in oxygen. Fifty-five parturients picked regional anesthesia. In the 22 with indwelling epidural catheters, the investigators extended sensory block with 3% 2-chloroprocaine. Thirty-three women received a tetracaine spinal anesthetic. All spinal injections were done by the most senior person available using a 22-gauge needle. All women in the regional group received at least 800 mL of crystalloid during induction of anesthesia and 6 L/min of oxygen, until delivery. No women in the regional group developed a blood pressure below 100 mm Hg. Infants in both groups had similar umbilical blood gas values. Infants in the regional group had better 1-minute Apgar scores (Table 24-3). The authors suggested that the beneficial effects of regional anesthesia on maternal catecholamine secretion and uterine blood flow explained their results.

Table 24–2

Indications for Delivery in 168 Parturients Presenting for Emergent Cesarean Section

ETIOLOGY	GENERAL ANESTHESIA (n = 71) (%)	REGIONAL ANESTHESIA (n = 55) (%)
Late decelerations	26	29
Variable decelerations	9	12
Persistent bradycardia	34	31
Persistent tachycardia	7	8
Acidosis	14	8
Thick meconium, first stage of labor	10	12

(Data from Marx GF, Luykx WM, Cohen S. Fetal–neonatal status following caesarean section for fetal distress. Br J Anaesth 56:1009, 1984)

Table 24-3

Outcome: Induction-to-Delivery Intervals, Fetal and Neonatal Data in 126 Cases of Cesarean Section for Fetal Distress with Either General or Regional Anesthesia

PARAMETER	GENERAL ANESTHESIA (n = 71)	REGIONAL ANESTHESIA (n = 55)
Scalp pH	7.204 ± 0.053	7.198 ± 0.043
Induction to skin incision	67.0 ± 12.0	5.3 ± 0.5
Skin incision to delivery	7.0 ± 2.8	7.8 ± 2.9
Uterine incision to delivery	68.3 ± 42.7	74.0 ± 40.3
Umbilical venous pH	7.286 ± 0.050	7.282 ± 0.054
Umbilical artery pH	7.221 ± 0.057	7.220 ± 0.053
Apgar score > 7 (%)		
1 min	51	78
5 min	85	98

(Data from Marx GF, Luykx WM, Cohen S. Fetal-neonatal status following caesarean section for fetal distress. Br J Anaesth 56:1009, 1984)

In summary, in experienced hands, rapidly induced spinal anesthesia for cesarean section does not harm, and may help, the distressed fetus. I favor spinal anesthesia in most urgent and emergent clinical situations. Continuous fetal heart rate monitoring can provide reassuring information during induction of spinal anesthesia in these circumstances. I do *not* attempt spinal anesthesia in extremely urgent clinical situations. These settings include prolapsed cord, significant bleeding, and severe, nonrecovering fetal bradycardia.

HEMODYNAMIC EFFECTS OF SPINAL ANESTHESIA

Providing the extensive sensory blockade required for cesarean section has discernible effects on both mother and fetus. Profound maternal hypotension can occur rapidly. This section of the chapter reviews the significance and etiology of maternal hypotension. It also discusses strategies for minimizing the impact of spinal anesthesia on maternal blood pressure. Finally, this section considers the influence of spinal anesthesia on uterine and fetal blood flow.

Maternal

Hypotension is the most clinically significant hemodynamic effect of spinal anesthesia. In the untreated parturient, hypotension can be especially severe and harm both mother and infant (Fig. 24-2).[13] In supine parturients who are not receiving intravenous fluids, maternal blood pressure falls by an average of **44%** after subarachnoid injection of local anesthetics (Fig. 24-3).[14]

Etiology

Maternal hypotension develops in proportion to the extent of sympathetic blockade (Fig. 24-4). Blockade of sympathetic nerve conduction extends several spinal segments higher than blockade of sensory nerves. Greene[15] has extensively described this "zone of differential blockade." Small, thinly myelinated, preganglionic sympathetic nerve fibers are more susceptible to local anesthetic blockade than are larger, more heavily myelinated sensory fibers. In the cephalad regions of blockade, low concentrations of local anesthetic may therefore block conduction of sympathetic but not sensory impulses. Alternatively, "frequency-dependent" or "use-dependent" blockade may explain the "zone." Tonically active sympathetic fibers may be more easily blocked than phasically active sensory nerves. Sodium channels may remain open for a proportionally longer period in tonically active nerve fibers, increasing their susceptibility to local anesthetic blockade.[16]

Some experts disagree on the extent of the "zone of differential blockade." Studies measuring differences in the loss of ability to detect light touch, pin prick, and temperature find a one- to two-segment "zone." In one such study by Greene, loss of sensation of sharpness to pin prick stopped at T-4–T-5. Loss of ability to perceive warm or cold extended to T-3–T-4.[15,17] In contrast, in-

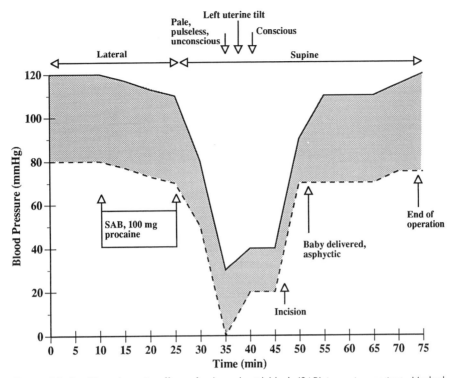

Figure 24–2. Hemodynamic effect of subarachnoid block (SAB) in supine patient. Marked hypotension caused loss of consciousness. Patient regained consciousness with left uterine tilt. Blood pressure did not recover fully until delivery. Note that the infant was born markedly depressed. (After Holmes F. The supine hypotension syndrome: Its importance to the anaesthetist. Anaesthesia 1960; 15:298)

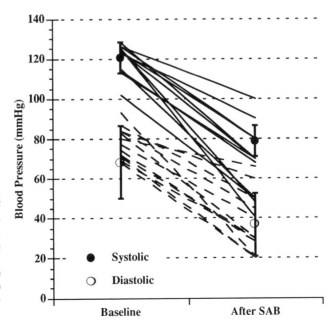

Figure 24–3. Change in blood pressure in 12 healthy term parturients following subarachnoid injection (SAB) of 0.2% procaine. All women lay supine, and none received intravenous fluids. Systolic pressure fell by 44 ± 14%, whereas diastolic pressure fell by 54 ± 18%. (Data from Assali NS, Prystowsky H. Studies on autonomic blockade. I. Comparison between the effects of tetraethylammonium chloride (TEAC) and high selective spinal anesthesia on blood pressure of normal and toxemic pregnancy. J Clin Invest 1950;29:1354)

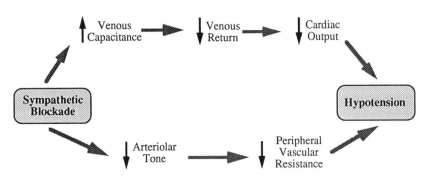

Figure 24–4. Mechanism of hypotension during spinal anesthesia.

vestigators using thermography to measure temperature elevation as a sign of sympathetic blockade find a much wider "zone."[18] These authors found a 6- to 10-segment difference between the upper limit of sensory block and the upper limit of temperature elevation. This second study may have measured incomplete sympathetic blockade, whereas the Greene study measured complete blockade. However, Greene's patients experienced a fall in blood pressure with no compensatory tachycardia. This response suggests that blockade of cardioaccelerator fibers (T-1–T-4) had developed. Although these patients had some sympathetic function above T-3 (temperature discrimination), they also showed signs (absent tachycardia) that blockade of other sympathetic functions extended to higher spinal levels. Therefore, any level of sensory blockade above T-6–T-8 probably will produce signs of total sympathectomy with at least partial blockade of cardioaccelerator fibers.

The hemodynamic effects of spinal blockade for cesarean section also suggest that complete sympathetic blockade routinely develops. Heart rate may increase little, if at all, as blood pressure falls.[19] More commonly, heart rate decreases as blood pressure falls.[20]

During the onset of spinal anesthesia, sympathetic blockade causes an acute increase in venous capacitance with an accompanying fall in central venous pressure (CVP). After CVP falls, cardiac output, stroke volume, and, therefore, blood pressure also fall (Fig. 24-4).[19,21] All these effects are more pronounced if the mother lies supine without left uterine displacement (Fig. 24-5).

Incidence

The incidence of maternal hypotension varies according to definition, frequency of measurement, method of measurement (manual vs automatic cuff), and prophylactic therapy (if any). In addition, hypotension develops less often in laboring compared to nonlaboring women.[9]

Fetal Effects of Maternal Hypotension

The effect of maternal hypotension on the fetus or neonate varies with the severity and duration of hypoperfusion. In addition, maternal position, volume status, and drug therapy also alter the fetal consequences of hypotension.

If prolonged, the type of severe hypotension that occurs in poorly hydrated, supine parturients can harm the fetus. Ebner[3] reported that when maternal systolic pressure fell below 50 mm Hg for more than 12 minutes, fetal bradycardia followed. A follow-up study investigated further the relationship between maternal hypotension and fetal bradycardia. Twenty-nine women received a spinal anesthetic for elective cesarean delivery. The investigators monitored maternal blood pressure and fetal electrocardiogram for 15 minutes after induction of blockade. No fetal bradycardia transpired in the 13 women whose systolic blood pressure remained above 70 mm Hg. Among women experiencing a systolic blood pressure below 70 mm Hg, a statistically significant correlation existed between both the severity and the duration of maternal hypotension and the incidence of fetal bradycardia (Table 24-4).[22] Thus, severe, prolonged maternal hypotension can cause significant fetal bradycardia. Nonetheless, these authors concluded that promptly recognized and treated maternal hypotension poses no threat to the fetus. Prolonged hypotension also can lead to abnormal neurobehavioral tests lasting 2 to 7 days after birth.[23]

Marx *et al*[24] reported that maternal hypotension (systolic blood pressure < 96 mm Hg, duration undefined) also may cause prolonged time to sustained respiration. Infants of nonhypotensive mothers developed sustained respirations in 20.0 seconds. Babies born of hypotensive mothers did not breath consistently until 48.8 seconds after delivery. Babies in the hypotensive group also had lower umbilical artery pH values. The women in this study received only a small

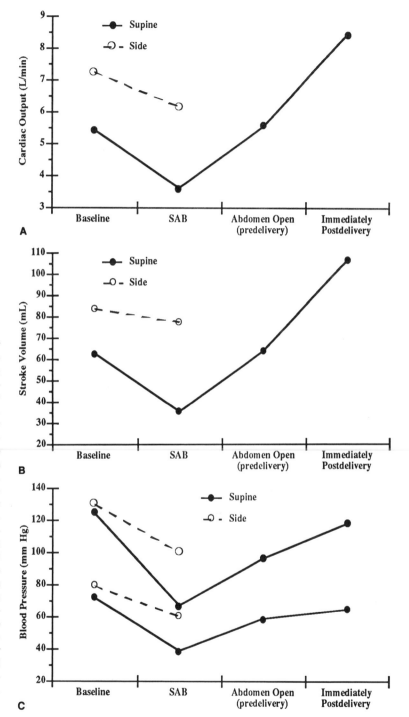

Figure 24–5. (**A**) Cardiac output after spinal blockade in 12 term parturients undergoing cesarean section. Relieving aortocaval compression by turning the patient to her side or with delivery significantly ameliorates the effects of spinal anesthesia. Note that cardiac output is significantly lower in the supine position even before induction of spinal anesthesia. (**B**) Stroke volume after spinal blockade in 12 term parturients undergoing cesarean section. Relieving aortocaval compression by turning the patient to her side or with delivery significantly eases the effects of spinal anesthesia. Note that stroke volume is significantly lower in the supine position even before induction of spinal anesthesia. (**C**) Blood pressure falls precipitously after spinal blockade when term parturients remain supine. Relieving aortocaval compression by turning the patient to her side or by delivering the infant significantly alters the hemodynamic response to spinal anesthesia. (SAB = subarachnoid block.) (After Ueland K, Gills, RE, Hansen JM. Maternal cardiovascular dynamics. I. Cesarean section under subarachnoid block anesthesia. Am J Obstet Gynecol 1968;100:42)

Table 24–4

Relation Between Severity and Duration of Maternal Hypotension Following Induction of Spinal Anesthesia and the Incidence of Fetal Bradycardia

	NO. OF PATIENTS	INCIDENCE OF FETAL BRADYCARDIA (%)
Minimal Maternal Systolic Blood Pressure After Spinal Anesthesia (mm Hg)		
> 100	9	0
90–99	1	0
80–89	0	0
70–79	3	0
60–69	5	20
50–59	8	38
< 50	3	67
Duration of Maternal Systolic Blood Pressure < 80 mm Hg (min)		
0–1.9	8	0
2–3.9	8	0
4–5.9	3	33
> 6	9	44

(Data from Ebner H, Barcohana J, Bartoshuk AK. Influence of postspinal hypotension on the fetal electrocardiogram. Am J Obstet Gynecol 80:569, 1960)

volume of prehydration (≤ 1 L) and a limited amount of ephedrine. When hypotension occurred, it was probably significant and prolonged.

Even transient maternal hypotension can cause fetal acidosis. Datta and Brown[25] reported a study of 15 healthy term parturients. All received 1 L of crystalloid before induction of anesthesia. All were placed supine with left uterine displacement and received oxygen by face mask. The investigators defined hypotension as a systolic blood pressure below 100 mm Hg or a fall of more than 30 mm Hg from base line. If hypotension developed, they treated it promptly with ephedrine as needed to keep the systolic blood pressure above 100 mm Hg. Hypotension arose in 8 of the 15 women. In all cases, hypotension lasted less than 3 minutes. Even with this brief duration of hypotension, uterine artery pH was 7.26 in neonates of hypotensive mothers but was 7.30 in babies of normotensive mothers.

This same group did a follow-up study using a similar protocol. These mothers received slightly more fluid (1–1.5 L), and the investigators evaluated neonatal neurobehavioral status. They found that "Babies born to mothers with hypotension were significantly more acidotic than controls, although acid–base levels were still within normal limits." Neurobehavioral studies were normal in both groups.[26]

Not all investigators have found this correlation between transient, promptly treated maternal hypotension and neonatal acidosis. In one such study, parturients received 1 L of crystalloid before induction of spinal anesthesia for cesarean section. Those who experienced hypotension (systolic blood pressure < 100 mm Hg) received 10-mg increments of ephedrine. These authors found no difference between infants of hypotensive and normotensive mothers in uterine artery or uterine vein pH values.[27]

Prevention and Treatment of Maternal Hypotension

Anesthesiologists have used a variety of strategies to lower the incidence and impact of maternal hypotension. Some investigators have tried giving larger amounts of fluid. Others have tried to minimize the size of the maternal circulation with leg-compression devices. Vasopressors have been used in attempts to both prevent and treat changes in maternal blood pressure.

VOLUME. Many studies have investigated the role of maternal prehydration in the genesis of hypotension. Early studies examined the maternal safety of a rapidly infused fluid bolus. Wollman and Marx[21] addressed this issue in a study of 19 term parturients. All had CVP catheters inserted before the induction of spinal anesthesia. Fourteen of the women received a rapid infusion of 1 L of crystalloid before induction of anesthesia. Hydration caused a slight increase in CVP but markedly decreased the incidence of hypotension after induction of spinal anesthesia. After delivery, CVP was the same whether or not the women received the fluid bolus (Fig. 24-6).

Interestingly, in the aforementioned study, the uterus was not displaced until *after* hypotension developed. It remained for subsequent investigators to show that left uterine displacement also can prevent maternal hypotension. Clark *et al*[28] did so in a large study of 247 parturients. Hypotension (systolic blood pressure < 100 mm Hg) developed less often with left uterine displacement plus fluid prehydration than with fluid administration alone (Fig. 24-7).

Increasing the volume of fluid infused diminishes both the frequency and the repercussions of maternal hypotension. An interesting study by Caritis et al[29] found that increasing the volume of prehydration did not alter incidence or severity of hypotension but did decrease the incidence of umbilical acidemia (uterine vein pH < 7.20)(Table 24-5). They allocated 64 term

parturients to one of two groups. One group received 500 to 999 mL of crystalloid before the induction of spinal anesthesia. The other group received 1000 to 1500 mL. Maternal hypotension, as defined by a systolic pressure below 80% of base line, occurred with equal frequency in both groups. In the less-hydrated group, the lower the maternal pressure, the lower the uterine vein pH and the greater the uterine vein base deficit. In contrast, maternal hypotension did not correlate with umbilical acid–base status in the better-hydrated group. In the less-hydrated group, 20% of the neonates were acidotic. Only 8% of the babies in the better-hydrated group were acidotic (see Table 24-5). Severe hypotension (systolic blood pressure < 70 mm Hg) also developed with equal frequency in both groups, but its gravity and duration were less in the better-hydrated group. In addition, less neonatal acidemia followed severe hypotension in the better-hydrated group (Table 24-6). These authors concluded that although larger volumes of prehydration may not prevent postspinal hypotension, they do improve its fetal biochemical consequences.[29]

In women receiving epidural anesthesia for cesarean section, even more crystalloid (2.0 L) continues to decrease the incidence and severity of hypotension. None of the women receiving 2 L of crystalloid experienced a decrease in systolic blood pressure of more than 30% of base line. In contrast, 25% of women receiving just 1 L of crystalloid had significant hypotension. No woman

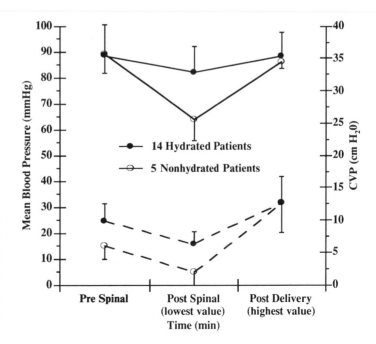

Figure 24–6. Changes in mean arterial pressure (*solid line*) and central venous pressure (*dashed line*) following induction of spinal anesthesia for cesarean section with 8 mg tetracaine in hydrated (1000 mL D$_5$RL) and nonhydrated parturients. After hypotension developed the nonhydrated women also received 1000 mL D$_5$RL. (Data from Wollman SB, Marx GF. Acute hydration for prevention of hypotension of spinal anesthesia in parturients. Anesthesiology 1968;29:374)

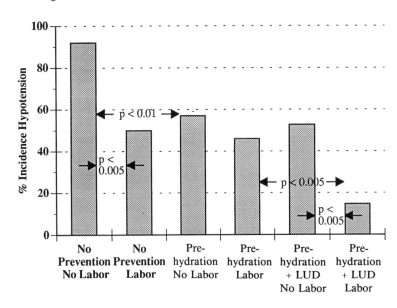

Figure 24–7. Incidence of hypotension in laboring and nonlaboring parturients receiving spinal anesthesia for cesarean section. Women had either no preventive measures, prehydration with 1 L of D_5RL only, or prehydration with 1 L of D_5RL plus mechanical left uterine displacement (LUD). (Data from Clark RB, Thompson DS, Thompson CH. Prevention of spinal hypotension associated with cesarean section. Anesthesiology 1976;45:670)

had any signs or symptoms of fluid overload (Fig. 24-8).[30]

Another recent study also examined the effects of large volumes of prehydration on neonatal outcome. Thirty-five parturients received 1.5 to 2.0 L of crystalloid before induction of spinal anesthesia. They continued to receive rapidly administered fluids until blood pressure stabilized (3.3 L by delivery). Over half the women in this study experienced transient hypotension (systolic blood pressure<100 mm Hg). Neither mild nor moderate maternal hypotension adversely affected neonatal acid–base status (Fig. 24-9).[31]

Table 24–5

Effects of Volume of Crystalloid Prehydration on Maternal Blood Pressure and Neonatal Acid–Base Status*

VOLUME OF PREHYDRATION	**500–999 mL (n = 40)**	**1000–1500 mL (n = 24)**
Maximum decrease		
Systolic blood pressure (mm Hg)	25 ± 16	28 ± 11
Diastolic blood pressure (mm Hg)	11 ± 10	16 ± 13
$\Sigma\Delta S$† (mm Hg)	79 ± 54	70 ± 38
Maximum decrease systolic blood pressure (% of cases)		
> 20 mm Hg	69	74
> 30 mm Hg	18	29
Percentage requiring vasopressor	62	71
Dose of vasopressor (mg)	12 ± 12	12 ± 10
Umbilical venous pH	7.32 ± 0.06	7.32 ± 0.03
Umbilical artery pH	7.24 ± 0.05	7.25 ± 0.04
Percentage with umbilical acidemia	20	8†

(After Caritis SN, Abouleish E, Edelstone DI, et al. Fetal acid–base state following spinal or epidural anesthesia for cesarean section. Obstet Gynecol 1980;56:610)
*All values are Mean ± SD.
†$\Sigma\Delta S$ = Summed decrease blood pressure.
†P less than 0.05 versus 500 to 999 mL.

Table 24-6

Maternal Blood Pressure and Neonatal Acid–Base Status in Cases of Severe Hypotension (Systolic Blood Pressure < 70 mm Hg) Following Spinal Anesthesia*

VOLUME OF PREHYDRATION	500–999 mL (n = 7)	1000–1500 mL (n = 7)
Maximum decrease in systolic blood pressure (mm Hg)	49 ± 10	43 ± 5
ΣΔS† (mm Hg)	164 ± 53	91 ± 22†
Dose of vasopressor (mg)	21 ± 7	13 ± 3†
Umbilical venous pH	7.28 ± 0.07	7.31 ± 0.04
Base deficit (mEq/L)	10.5 ± 2.6	6.4 ± 1.5†
Umbilical artery pH	7.19 ± 0.08	7.25 ± 0.04
Base deficit (mEq/L)	11.5 ± 2.6	8.0 ± 2.6†

(After Caritis SN, Abouleish E, Edelstone DI, et al. Fetal acid–base state following spinal or epidural anesthesia for cesarean section. Obstet Gynecol 1980;56:610)
*Increased fluid prehydration limits the duration and impact of severe maternal hypotension. All values are mean ± SD.
†ΣΔS = Summed decrease blood pressure.
‡P less than 0.05 versus 500 to 999 mL.

The preceding studies suggest that generous maternal hydration benefits both mother and infant. In the mother, it decreases the incidence and severity of hypotension.[28–30] In the infant, maternal hydration also blunts or eliminates the deleterious effects of transient hypotension.[29,31]

Some anesthesiologists advocate using colloid rather than crystalloid solutions for maternal hydration. One study compared equal volumes of albumin and crystalloid. None of the mothers in the albumin group (n=24) developed hypotension. In contrast, 25% of the women in the crystalloid group developed

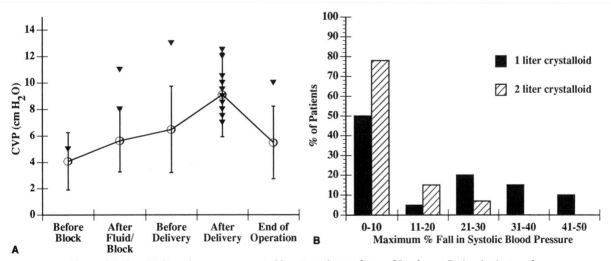

Figure 24-8. (**A**) Central venous pressure in 20 patients during infusion of 2 L of crystalloid and induction of epidural analgesia for cesarean section. (O = mean CVP ± SD, ▼ = highest CVP recorded in each patient.) (**B**) Incidence and severity of hypotension following prehydration with 1 L and 2 L of crystalloid solution and induction of epidural analgesia for cesarean section. (Data from Lewis M, Thomas P, Wilkes RG. Hypotension during epidural analgesia for caesarean section. Arterial and central venous pressure changes after acute intravenous loading with two litres Hartmann's solution. Anaesthesia 1983;38:250)

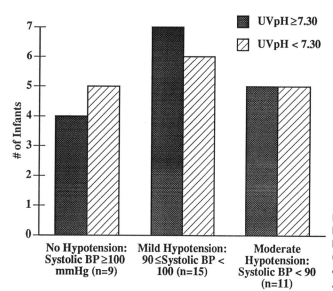

Figure 24–9. Number of infants with UVpH above and below 7.30 after no, mild, or moderate maternal hypotension. (BP = blood pressure, UV = umbilical vein.) (After Norris MC. Hypotension during spinal anesthesia for cesarean section: Does it affect neonatal outcome? Reg Anesth 1987;12:191)

hypotension (systolic blood pressure < 100 mm Hg). In addition, these investigators reported significantly better Apgar scores in the albumin group.[32] On the other hand, Gibbs *et al*[33] could show no benefit to prehydration with albumin. They compared women receiving 15 mL/kg of 1.2% albumin in crystalloid (50 mL of 50% albumin added to 1.0 L Ringer's lactate) to those receiving 15 or 30 mL/kg of crystalloid alone. The incidence and severity of hypotension was similar in the two groups receiving 15 mL/kg of fluid. Infusion of 30 mL/kg of crystalloid alone was most effective at maintaining maternal hemodynamic stability. Given that albumin is expensive and that generous crystalloid administration seems just as effective, I do not see the need to use colloid solutions for maternal hydration before spinal anesthesia.

LABOR. Clark *et al*[28] noted that laboring patients were less inclined to develop hypotension than nonlaboring women. Other groups of investigators have confirmed this observation.[9,34] There are several possible explanations for this phenomenon. Laboring women usually receive intravenous fluids while hospitalized; thus, these patients may simply be better hydrated than are those who present for elective cesarean delivery.[34] Fluids may not be the only explanation, however. The laboring, hydrated patients in the study by Clark *et al*[28] probably received more total fluid than their nonlaboring, hydrated patients. Despite this extra fluid, these two groups still had a similar incidence of hypotension (see Fig. 24-7).

The protective effect of labor is most marked in conjunction with left uterine displacement. Descent of the fetal head into the pelvis lessens aorto–caval compression. This development may improve the subsequent efficacy of left uterine displacement. In addition, left uterine displacement allows the blood (300 mL) squeezed from the uterus with each contraction to reach the maternal central circulation and help support maternal blood pressure.

LEG COMPRESSION. Several groups have investigated the efficacy of leg compression as a way to lower the incidence of maternal hypotension during spinal anesthesia. Compressing the venous system in the legs should transfuse about 500 mL of blood back into the central circulation. This "autotransfusion" could then help support maternal blood pressure in the face of systemic vasodilation.

One group studied inflatable boots. They inflated toe-to-thigh boots to 90 mm Hg immediately after injecting tetracaine into the subarachnoid space. Unfortunately, 60% of the women in both groups developed hypotension.[35]

Another group used "inflatable splints" to provide leg compression. Although this approach did reduce by half the incidence of hypotension, 48% of the parturients in the study group still experienced a significant fall in blood pressure.[36]

Recently, a third group of investigators used Esmarch bandages for this purpose. They wrapped the patient's legs tightly with the bandages immediately after blockade. Hypotension developed in 83% of the control women but in only 17% of the bandaged women.[37]

VASOPRESSORS. Ephedrine is the vasopressor of choice in obstetrics. This drug has been used both to treat and to prevent maternal hypotension. Several studies have been conducted to find the optimal timing and route of ephedrine administration.

Prophylactic intramuscular ephedrine does not reliably prevent maternal hypotension. Moya and Smith[38] reviewed their clinical experience with prophylactic ephedrine. Their patients received an intramuscular injection of ephedrine, 50 mg, about 10 minutes before induction of spinal anesthesia. Nonetheless, 46% of their parturients had a decline in blood pressure exceeding 20% of base line (Fig. 24-10). This study was done before benefits of prehydration and left uterine displacement became widely appreciated. More recent investigators, who paid attention to these issues, still found that prophylactic intramuscular injection of ephedrine 25 mg failed to reliably prevent hypotension.[32,34]

On the other hand, prophylactic intravenous ephedrine does prevent both maternal hypotension and neonatal acidosis. Datta *et al*[39] recommend giving 10 to 30 mg of intravenous ephedrine "as soon as any fall from base line pressure" arises. This technique "virtually eliminates hypotension." These authors compared this prophylactic ephedrine therapy to giving therapeutic ephedrine only after blood pressure fell by more than 30 mm Hg or to less than 100 mm Hg. Women in the prophylactic group experienced less nausea and vomit-

ing. Neonates in the prophylactic group had significantly better Apgar scores and acid–base parameters than those in the therapeutic group.

Unfortunately, these two groups are not strictly comparable. They were studied in sequence, not as a part of a randomized, blinded protocol. Other concurrent changes in clinical practice may have occurred to induce the observed differences. The prophylactic group includes patients whose blood pressure fell slightly but who would not have become significantly hypotensive. The therapeutic group, in contrast, consists only of women who actually developed hypotension.

In addition, the infants in this study seemed especially sensitive to maternal hypotension. In the therapeutic group, 83% of the neonates had 1-minute Apgar scores below 7. Other studies have not found any effect of transient maternal hypotension on 1-minute Apgar scores.[24,40] Although prophylactic ephedrine seems to limit maternal side effects, the need to use it to ensure a good neonatal outcome remains unclear.

Although most anesthesiologists administer ephedrine by intravenous bolus, some use ephedrine infusions. Kang *et al*[40] mixed 50 mg of ephedrine with 500 mL of crystalloid. They infused this solution at 50 mL/min for the first 2 minutes after induction of spinal blockade. After that, they adjusted the infusion rate as needed to maintain maternal blood pressure above 100 mm Hg. When blood pressure stabilized, they stopped the infusion. They compared this infusion group to a control group of women who received 20-mg boluses of ephedrine if their blood pressure fell below 80% of baseline. Maternal hypotension, nausea,

Figure 24–10. Incidence of hypotension following spinal anesthesia in 1141 parturients who received 50 mg of ephedrine intramuscularly within 10 minutes of spinal blockade. Note that all patients were probably supine and received little intravenous fluids. (After Moya F, Smith B. Spinal anesthesia for cesarean section: Clinical and biochemical studies of effects on maternal physiology. JAMA 1962;179:115)

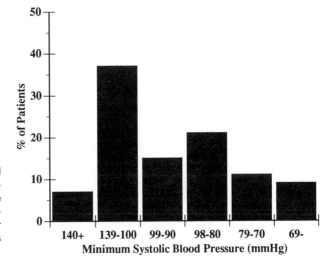

and vomiting occurred less often in the infusion group. Neonates in both groups had good Apgar scores and acid–base values.[40]

Ephedrine, although effective and seemingly safe, does cross the placenta. It causes fetal tachycardia. It raises fetal catecholamine concentrations, and, in the neonate, it transiently increases electroencephalographic delta wave activity.[41]

Uterine and Placental Blood Flow

Because of the potential for significant maternal hypotension, we must be concerned with the effects of spinal anesthesia on uterine and placental blood flow. Although these parameters cannot be measured directly in humans, they can be evaluated indirectly using radioactive tracers or ultrasound.

Investigators in Sweden have examined intervillous blood flow (IVBF) during spinal anesthesia using xenon.[133] Their patients received 1.5 to 2.0 L of crystalloid before spinal anesthesia. The investigators treated "incipient" hypotension with an ephedrine infusion. In only one of their nine patients did blood pressure fall more than 30 mm Hg. The IVBF did not change significantly in seven of their parturients (Fig. 24-11). In one woman with preeclampsia, IVBF increased by 193%. In another woman, who had diabetes, it fell 72%. The investigators found no correlation between the change in IVBF and the change in maternal blood pressure. They suggested that, in their well-hydrated parturients, the increased maternal blood volume compensated for small changes in blood pressure. Without this volume load, spinal blockade may

induce relative maternal hypovolemia and decrease IVBF.[42]

Fetal Blood Flow

The maternal hemodynamic response to subarachnoid anesthesia also could indirectly affect fetal blood flow. Using ultrasound and pulsed Doppler measurements, Lindblad et al[43] measured vessel diameter and blood flow velocity in the descending fetal aorta and umbilical artery and vein. They made these measurements before and 15 and 30 minutes after induction of spinal anesthesia in 15 term parturients. All women received 2.0 L of crystalloid before blockade. In addition, an ephedrine infusion maintained blood pressure. Maternal spinal anesthesia produced no changes in fetal aortic or umbilical blood flows. The rising slope, a measure of myocardial contractility, also did not change. At 30 minutes, a moderate decrease in umbilical pulsatility index developed. The pulsatility index reflects peripheral and, possibly, placental resistance. These results suggest that slight placental vasodilation develops after maternal spinal anesthesia. Because this change occurred late (30 minutes after induction), these authors postulate that it reflected an effect of the ephedrine.[43] Another study looking at umbilical artery flow velocity waveforms reported no significant changes 15 minutes after spinal blockade.[44]

Conclusions

Spinal anesthesia can present significant threats to maternal and fetal well-being. A high level of sensory

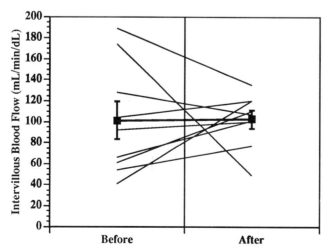

Figure 24–11. Intervillous blood flow as measured by xenon-133 isotope clearance in nine term parturients before and after the induction of spinal anesthesia for cesarean section. All women received 1500 to 2000 mL of lactated Ringer's solution before subarachnoid injection of isobaric 0.5% bupivacaine. The greatest decrease (72%) in flow occurred in a parturient with diabetes mellitus. A women with mild preeclampsia had the greatest increase (193%). The changes in blood flow did not correlate with changes in maternal blood pressure. (Data from Jouppila P. Jouppila R, Barinoff T, Koivula A. Placental blood flow during caesarean section performed under subarachnoid blockade. Br J Anaesth 1984;56:1379)

blockade, headache, and hypotension are significant risks, but these threats can be readily avoided. The chapters on intraoperative and postoperative complications discuss high block and postdural puncture headache. Generous hydration, careful attention to left uterine displacement, and judicious use of ephedrine can limit the incidence and repercussions of hypotension. By understanding the potential hemodynamic consequences of subarachnoid blockade in parturients and by careful attention to preventive and therapeutic measures, the obstetric anesthesiologist can safely use this reliable technique.

SOME TECHNICAL ISSUES

This section discusses in detail how to provide spinal anesthesia for cesarean section. It focuses primarily on four issues. First, we consider the choice of crystalloid solution for prehydration. Second, we examine how high a level of sensory blockade is required. This issue addresses both patient comfort and hemodynamic response. Third, a discussion of drug choice follows. Questions addressed in this section include the following:

- Which drug?
- How much drug?
- What other drugs might be added to improve the quality of sensory blockade?

Fourth, we briefly consider what position the patient should assume during induction of blockade.

Patient Preparation

Venous Access

Patients presenting for cesarean section should have a well-functioning large-bore intravenous catheter in place. Although 18-gauge catheters are probably adequate, I prefer inserting a 16-gauge catheter. Remember, a cesarean section is a major intra-abdominal operation with the potential for significant and rapid blood loss. Women undergoing even routine, elective cesarean delivery lose, on average, 1000 mL of blood. A large-bore intravenous catheter is essential to allow rapid response to changing clinical situations.

Aspiration Prophylaxis

These women should receive some type of acid-aspiration prophylaxis. I give them 30 mL of sodium citrate by mouth on the way to the operating suite.

Prehydration

Adequate prehydration plays a primary role in minimizing the hemodynamic consequences of spinal blockade. All nonlaboring women should receive 1.5 to 2.0 L of crystalloid within 15 minutes of induction of blockade. A pressurized bag or infusion device can help deliver this fluid as rapidly as possible. The choice of crystalloid to be infused can have significant impact on neonatal outcome.

Acute maternal infusion of as little as 10 g of glucose causes significant maternal and, consequently, fetal hyperglycemia. The fetus secretes insulin in response to this hyperglycemia. After delivery, with insulin but not glucose still present, fetal hypoglycemia can occur (Fig. 24-12).[45,46] Some authors express concern that maternal hypoglycemia might develop if the fasted parturient receives no glucose.[47] At Jefferson, maternal fasting glucose concentrations range from 60 to 100 mg/dL (mean ± SD: 80.5 ± 13.1).[48] I rarely give glucose to healthy parturients during cesarean section.

Even without sugar, the choice of crystalloid solution can still affect neonatal outcome. Sodium chloride, although free of glucose, contains a large amount of unbuffered chloride ion. Acute infusion of large volumes of 0.9% sodium chloride induces a maternal hyperchloremic metabolic acidosis and increases the risk of neonatal acidosis.[49] Other available crystalloid solutions contain lactate and acetate as buffers (lactated Ringer's, Plasmalyte). Kenepp[50] has voiced concern that these compounds might upset maternal and fetal carbohydrate metabolism, increasing the risk of neonatal hypoglycemia, but a clinical comparison of Plasmalyte and 0.9% sodium chloride as fluid therapy before and during cesarean section revealed no differences in maternal or neonatal glucose concentrations.[48]

How High a Level?

A level of sensory blockade above T-10 will block the somatic sensations of cesarean section. Eliminating visceral pain resulting from peritoneal stimulation and manipulation of the uterus requires more extensive blockade. In some reports, more than 70% of women undergoing cesarean section under spinal anesthesia report some painful sensations.[51] Patients often will tolerate the procedure with a T-6–T-8 level of sensory blockade, but they will more likely need supplemental systemic analgesics than will those patients who have a higher level of block.[52] Although most experts recommend at least a T-4 level of sensory blockade for cesarean section,[53] even with this level of blockade, over

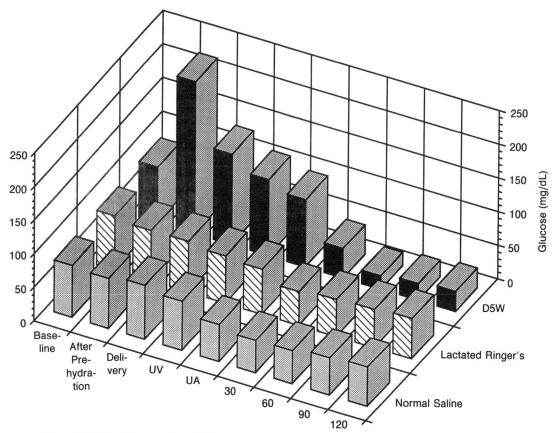

Figure 24–12. Changes in blood glucose concentration in mother and infant after intravenous fluid administration (UA = umbilical artery, UV = umbilical vein.) (Data from Philipson EH, Kalhan SC, Riha MM. Effects of maternal glucose infusion on fetal acid–base status in human pregnancy. Am J Obstet Gynecol 1987;157:866)

50% of patients may feel pain.[54] Higher levels of sensory blockade (T-1) do not increase the risk of hypotension (these women already have complete sympathetic blockade with a sensory level to T-4) but do improve patient comfort.[6,55] I strive for a level of sensory blockade between T-4 and T-1. I prefer having the block spread a little too high than not high enough. Occasionally, the level of sensory blockade creeps up into the cervical dermatomes. I then place an extra pillow under the woman's head in an attempt to limit further cephalad spread. I also assess motor function by checking grip strength and respiratory function by asking her to speak and breath deeply. If the block extends so high that the patient cannot phonate or maintain her oxygen saturation above 95%, I apply cricoid pressure and secure the airway to protect against possible aspiration. Fortunately, this complication occurs only rarely (< 1/100 spinal anesthetics).

Drugs

Which Drug?

Tetracaine has long been the most commonly used drug for spinal anesthesia for cesarean section. This agent often fails to provide good maternal sensory blockade. In one report, 228 patients received tetracaine spinal anesthesia for emergent and elective cesarean section. Less than 40% of these women were comfortable with the spinal anesthetic alone. In 4% the block failed completely. An additional 6% needed general anesthesia because of inadequate blockade, and 65% required some analgesic supplementation.[51]

Recently, bupivacaine has gained popularity in obstetric anesthesia, but an early study of hyperbaric 0.5% bupivacaine did not report promising results. Twenty-two term parturients received 7.5 to 10 mg of drug.

Two patients never developed an adequate level of block. Eighteen required 20 degrees of head-down tilt to raise the level of blockade above T-8. All but one woman needed supplemental intravenous meperidine because of intraoperative pain.[56] On the other hand, hyperbaric 0.75% bupivacaine works much better. In doses of 12 to 15 mg, most patients develop good sensory blockade to at least the T-6 dermatome. Sensory change begins within 4 to 6 minutes and peaks between 15 and 20 minutes.[6] The drug provides good maternal comfort for 60 to 120 minutes of intra-abdominal surgery.

Hyperbaric bupivacaine offers two significant advantages over tetracaine. In commonly used doses, it provides better intraoperative analgesia. In addition, motor blockade regresses much more rapidly than with tetracaine (Table 24-7).[57] Moore[58] first observed these differences when he compared hyperbaric solutions of tetracaine and bupivacaine in nonpregnant patients. Patients undergoing vaginal hysterectomy with tetracaine anesthesia experienced more intraoperative pain than did those receiving bupivacaine. At equal doses, tetracaine produced more profound and prolonged motor blockade.

Another study, also in nonpregnant patients, again reported better analgesia with bupivacaine. Concepcion *et al*[59] compared equal doses tetracaine and bupivacaine in 40 patients undergoing knee surgery with a tourniquet. Tetracaine produced longer-lasting sensory and motor blockade, but 60% of the patients in the tetracaine group complained of tourniquet pain compared to only 25% in the bupivacaine group.[59] These authors postulate that high-frequency impulses carried by unmyelinated, slowly conducting C-fibers cause tourniquet (and visceral) pain. These fibers may recover more rapidly from tetracaine than bupivacaine blockade. Indeed, in vitro, bupivacaine delays the recovery of high-frequency impulses for a longer time than tetracaine.[60]

Lidocaine also can produce good operating conditions for cesarean section. The major limitation of this drug is its short duration of action. Sensory blockade begins regressing within 60 minutes of injection. I use this drug only with surgeons who routinely complete their operations within 30 minutes. Because of its short duration of action, few academic institutions can study lidocaine for cesarean section. The literature does contain one clinical study of 30 parturients who received 65 to 75 mg of 5% lidocaine in 7.5% dextrose for cesarean section. A T-10 level of sensory blockade developed 3 to 6 minutes after injection. Maximum spread occurred by 11 to 15 minutes. Numbness receded to

Table 24–7

Onset, Duration and Quality of Blockade at Cesarean Section*

	TETRACAINE (n = 20)	**BUPIVACAINE** (n = 20)
Onset and Duration		
Onset	8.95 ± 4.74	6.65 ± 2.83[†]
Duration of blockade		
Sensory	180 ± 80	117 ± 38[†]
Motor	372 ± 140	201 ± 64[†]
Quality of Intraoperative Analgesia		
Category		
A (painless)	11	20*
B (discomfort, no analgesia)	4	0
C (discomfort/pain, analgesia required)	3	0
D (general anesthesia after surgery begun)	1	0
E (general anesthesia before surgery)	1	0

(Data from Michie AR, Freeman RM, Dutton DA, Howie HB: Subarachnoid anaesthesia for elective caesarean section: a comparison of two hyperbaric solutions. Anaesthesia 1988;43:96)
*Parturients received either 10 mg of hyperbaric tetracaine or 12.5 mg of hyperbaric bupivacaine.
All values are mean (minutes) ± SD.
[†]P less than 0.01.

T-10 by 1 hour. These authors complained of the unpredictable spread of lidocaine. Four of their patients developed high cervical levels of sensory blockade.[61]

How Much Drug?

In the past, "common sense" and "clinical experience" implied to many anesthesiologists that a given dose of local anesthetic would produce a higher level of sensory blockade in a shorter patient compared to a taller patient.[62] This line of thought reasons that a bolus of hyperbaric local anesthetic flows a certain distance from the site of subarachnoid injection. If two patients receive the same dose of local anesthetic, and, in both, the drug travels the same distance along the spinal canal, then the shorter patient should develop a higher dermatomal level of sensory blockade. Many authors therefore recommend varying the dose of local anesthetic according to the height of the patient.[63,64] However, several recent studies in parturients, have shown, no correlation between the height of the patient and the spread of sensory blockade (Fig. 24-13).[65-67]

If the distance the local anesthetic flows is the important variable, then vertebral column length instead of height should predict the ultimate dermatomal spread of sensory block. Two studies of term parturients have compared the spread of spinal anesthesia to vertebral column length. One study of 52 term parturients receiving 15 mg of hyperbaric bupivacaine found no correlation between the loss of sensation to pin prick and vertebral column length (Fig. 24-14).[66] Another study found a weak correlation between "sensory anesthesia to pin prick" and vertebral column length

(Fig. 24-15).[67] Even in this latter study, differences in the length of the patient's spine predicted only 14% of the variation in the spread of sensory block. Vertebral column length therefore accounts for very little, if any, of the variation in the spread of sensory blockade. Thus, there is no need to adjust the dose of local anesthetic in response to this variable.

An important limitation to these studies is the somewhat narrow range of patient heights and vertebral column lengths included. A patient shorter than 147 cm (4'10") or taller than 174 cm (5'8") might develop too high or too low a level of block. I have given 15 mg of hyperbaric bupivacaine to women as short as 145 cm without complications.

An explanation of this phenomenon may lie with the physical properties of the injected local anesthetic and the anatomic shape of the spinal column. Using glass tubes and methyl violet dye, Barker[68] demonstrated that hyperbaric solutions of local anesthetic will pool in dependent regions of the spinal column. Kitahara *et al*[69] measured the spread of radioactivity after injecting local anesthetic plus iodine. Radioactivity was greatest in the dependent regions of the spinal column and correlated with the spread of sensory blockade (Fig. 24-16).[131] When the patient lies supine, the thoracolumbar spine slopes 8 to 12° in the cephalad direction. Hyperbaric solutions pool in the lowest part of the thoracic curvature (T-5–T-6). They produce sensory blockade into the upper thoracic dermatomes regardless of the distance between the site of injection and the base of the thoracic curve.[70]

Within the range of doses of hyperbaric drug commonly used in clinical situations (7.5–12 mg of hyper-

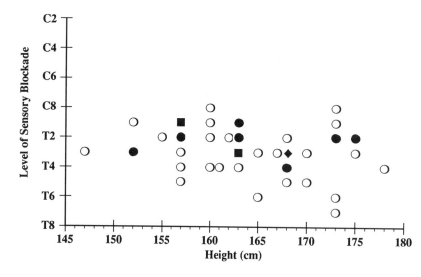

Figure 24–13. Sensory blockade after subarachnoid injection of 12 mg of hyperbaric bupivacaine in 50 term parturients. Sensory blockade develops independently of patient height. (O = one patient, ● = two patients, ■ = three patients, ◆ = four patients.) (After Norris MC. Height, weight and the spread of subarachnoid hyperbaric bupivacaine in the term parturient. Anesth Analg 1988;67:555)

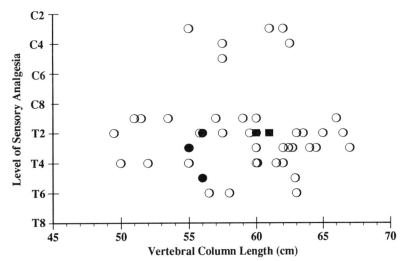

Figure 24-14. Maximum level of sensory analgesia to pinprick, measured 15 minutes after subarachnoid injection of 15 mg of hyperbaric bupivacaine in 52 term parturients. Sensory blockade develops independently of vertebral column length. (O = one patient, ● = two patients, ■ = three patients.) (After Norris MC. Patient variables and the subarachnoid spread of hyperbaric bupivacaine in the term parturient. Anesthesiology 1990; 72:478)

baric bupivacaine or 7–15 mg of hyperbaric tetracaine), similar levels of sensory blockade develop despite varying doses of drug injected (Fig. 24-17A).[55,71] Baricity, not the amount of drug injected, primarily determines the spread of subarachnoid local anesthetics. When the dose of local anesthetic increases further (15 mg of bupivacaine or 18 mg of tetracaine), it exceeds the capacity of the upper thoracic curvature, and greater dermatomal spread can follow (Figs. 24-17B and 24-18; Table 24-8).[6,55]

Although large enough doses of local anesthetic do alter the spread of blockade, the volume in which the drug is diluted appears to have no effect. Van Zundert

et al[20] injected 10 mL of 0.125% bupivacaine with 1:800,000 epinephrine (12.5 mg of bupivacaine). As happens when 0.5% bupivacaine is injected in the usual 2.5 mL volume (12.5 mg), a T-2 level of sensory blockade developed.[20] In term parturients, Russell[72] injected 15 mg of bupivacaine mixed to progressively greater dilutions (Table 24-9). All solutions of drug behaved as if hypobaric. During drug injection, most women developed unilateral sensory blockade on the nondependent side. When they were placed supine, the distribution of block equalized. The volume of injected drug did not alter the final level of sensory block attained (median T-2).

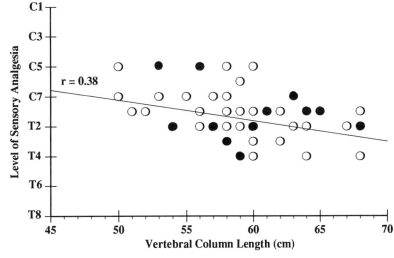

Figure 24-15. Maximum level of sensory analgesia to pinprick after subarachnoid injection of 12 mg of hyperbaric bupivacaine in 50 term parturients. Vertebral column length predicts 14% (r^2) of the variation in level of sensory blockade. (O = one patient, ● = two patients.) (After Hartwell BL, Aglio LS, Hauch MA, et al. Vertebral column length and spread of hyperbaric subarachnoid bupivacaine in the term parturient. Reg Anesth 1991; 16:17)

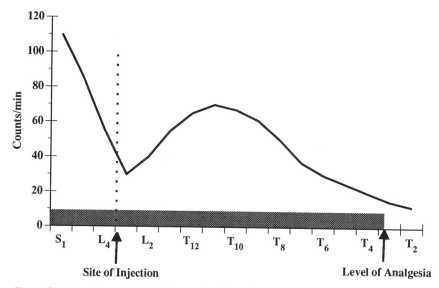

Figure 24–16. Spread of iodine[131], mixed with hyperbaric tetracaine, 30 minutes after injection into the subarachnoid space at L-3–4 with the patient supine. The hyperbaric solution flows with gravity to the dependent regions of the spinal column. (After Kitahara T, Kuri S, Yoshida J. The spread of drugs used for spinal anesthesia. Anesthesiology 1956;17:205)

Improving the Quality of Block

Many investigators, dissatisfied with the degree of patient comfort they obtain with their usual technique, have tried a variety of ways to improve the quality of anesthesia during cesarean section. Tetracaine and dextrose alone often prove inadequate for cesarean section.[51] Mixing the tetracaine with an equal volume of 10% procaine instead of dextrose increases the level of sensory blockade and improves the quality of analgesia (Table 24-10).[73] The authors of this study suggested that procaine produced better sensory blockade than did tetracaine, improving patient comfort. However, the tetracaine–procaine group received more local anesthetic than the tetracaine–dextrose group. Would simply injecting more tetracaine, rather than adding a second local anesthetic, have the same effect? Pan *et al*[55] answered this question by injecting 9, 12, 15, or 18 mg of hyperbaric tetracaine in a series of parturients. They noted steadily increasing patient comfort with each larger dose of tetracaine (Table 24-8).

Other investigators have looked at ways to improve patient comfort when using hyperbaric bupivacaine. Abouleish *et al*[74] reported that hyperbaric bupivacaine alone often fails to eliminate visceral pain sensations. The addition of either epinephrine or morphine improves the quality of

bupivacaine intraoperative analgesia. Adding 0.2 mg of epinephrine to 9.3 ± 0.1 mg of hyperbaric bupivacaine does not affect the level of sensory blockade. It does cause slightly more dense motor blockade and a slightly longer two-segment regression time. The added epinephrine also provides significantly better intraoperative analgesia (Fig. 24-19). Epinephrine probably improves the quality of sensory block, not by inhibiting the absorption of local anesthetic from the subarachnoid space, but by potentiating local anesthetic effect via an alpha-adrenergic–mediated action in the spinal cord.[64] Similarly, Abouleish *et al*[74] reported that intrathecal morphine, 0.2 mg, not only provides excellent postoperative pain relief but also improves intraoperative analgesia (see Fig. 24-19).

Another group of investigators showed that adding fentanyl to hyperbaric bupivacaine also makes patients more comfortable. Hunt *et al*[75] injected at least 7.5 mg of hyperbaric bupivacaine into the subarachnoid space of 56 term parturients. In addition, these women received 0, 2.5, 5.0, 6.25, 12.5, 25, 37.5, or 50 µg of intrathecal fentanyl. Sixty-seven percent of the women in the control group, 50% in the 2.5-µg group, and 25% in the 5.0-µg group needed supplemental intravenous opioids during surgery. No patient receiving at least 6.25 µg of intrathecal fentanyl required supplemental analgesics. Women receiving at least 25 µg of fentanyl

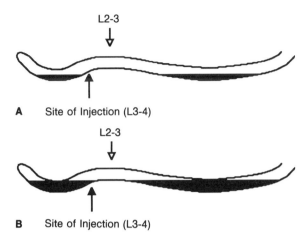

A   Site of Injection (L3-4)

L2-3

B   Site of Injection (L3-4)

Figure 24–17. (**A**) Hyperbaric local anesthetics in moderate doses (7.5–12 mg of 0.75% bupivacaine in 8.25% dextrose or 9–15 mg of 0.5% tetracaine in 5% dextrose) pool in the lowest region of the thoracic spine. In term parturients, these doses of drug produce mid- to upper thoracic levels of sensory blockade (median T-3) regardless of the height of the patient or the dose of drug injected. (**B**) When larger doses of drug are injected (15 mg of 0.75% bupivacaine in 8.25% dextrose or 18 mg of 0.5% tetracaine in 5% dextrose), the capacity of this upper thoracic pool is exceeded and higher levels (median T-1) of sensory blockade occur.

complained of itching.[75] The small number of patients in each group (n=5–9) limits the interpretation of these data.

As with tetracaine, simply injecting a larger dose of bupivacaine can improve the quality of blockade. Pederson *et al*[71] studied the incidence of visceral pain

during cesarean section in two groups of parturients. One group of 17 women received 7.5 to 10 mg of hyperbaric bupivacaine. Another group of 19 women received 10 to 12.5 mg of drug. (These authors varied the dose of bupivacaine according to the patient's height.) Two women in the low-dose group needed a general anesthetic because of inadequate sensory blockade. Otherwise, both groups exhibited similar sensory and hemodynamic changes. Even though the high-dose group received 25% more bupivacaine, the two groups developed similar levels of sensory block. Sensory blockade lasted longer in the high-dose group. Twelve of the 17 women in the low-dose group experienced moderate to severe pain after delivery. In contrast, only 6 of the 19 subjects in the high-dose group suffered pain. All but one patient had a level of sensory block above T-4 at the time they felt pain. These findings suggest that larger doses of drug, pooling in the upper thoracic curve, produce denser but not higher sensory blockade. In this dosage range, baricity, not the dose of drug injected, determines the ultimate spread of blockade (see Fig. 24-17A).

Increasing the dose of bupivacaine further continues to improve patient comfort, but if the amount of drug injected exceeds the capacity of the upper thoracic curvature, a higher level of sensory blockade can result (Figs. 24-17B and 24-20). De Simone *et al*[6] administered spinal anesthesia to 28 term parturients. They injected 12 mg of hyperbaric bupivacaine in 16 patients, and 15 mg in 12 patients. Sensory block developed in more dermatomes and lasted longer after 15 mg of bupivacaine. Thirteen of the 16 patients in the 12-mg group reported good-to-excellent intraoperative pain

Figure 24–18. Maximum level of sensory analgesia to pinprick, measured 15 minutes after subarachnoid injection of 12 or 15 mg of hyperbaric bupivacaine in term parturients. The mode shifts from T-3 to T-2 with the larger dose of drug. (Data from Norris MC. Height, weight and the spread of subarachnoid hyperbaric bupivacaine in the term parturient. Anesth Analg 1988;67:555, and Norris MC. Patient variables and the subarachnoid spread of hyperbaric bupivacaine in the term parturient. Anesthesiology 1990;72:478)

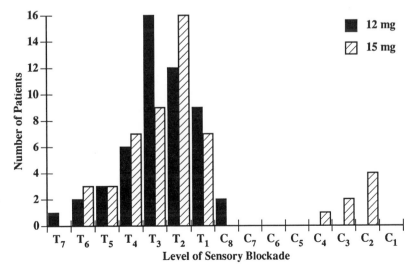

Table 24-8

Spread of Sensory Blockade and the Quality of Analgesia in 88 Term Parturients

DOSE OF TETRACAINE	9 MG	12 MG	15 MG	18 MG
Number of patients	20	27	25	16
Maximal level of analgesia	T-4	T-4	T-3	C-7†
Quality of analgesia (% good)	67	81	96	100

Data from Pan PM, Lin Z-F, Lim J, Tung M-C, Wei T-T. The optimal dose of hyperbaric tetracaine spinal anesthesia for cesarean section. Anaesth Sinica 27:349–52, 1989)
*Analgesia was rated as good if patients required less than 100 µg of fentanyl and 50 mg of meperidine after delivery.
†P less than 0.05.

Table 24-9

Dilutions of Bupivacaine

GROUP	VOLUME (mL)	DRUG DILUTION
0.5%	3	Plain 0.5% bupivacaine
0.25%	6	Plain 0.25% bupivacaine
0.125%	12	Equal volumes 0.25% bupivacaine and 0.9% sodium chloride
0.083%	18	0.25% bupivacaine and 0.9% sodium chloride mixed in 1:2 ratio

(After Russell IF. Spinal anesthesia for cesarean delivery with dilute solutions of plain bupivacaine: The relationship between infused volume and spread. Reg Anesth 1991;15:130)

Table 24-10

Quality of Intraoperative Analgesia After Tetracaine–Dextrose and Tetracaine–Procaine Mixtures for Spinal Anesthesia for Cesarean Section

	TETRACAINE–DEXTROSE (n = 10)	TETRACAINE–PROCAINE (n = 11)
Narcotics		
None	1	7
≤ 5 mg morphine	1	3
> 5 mg morphine	8	1
Tranquilizers		
None	1	3
≤ 5 mg diazepam	3	5
> 5 mg diazepam	6	3

(Data from Chantigian RC, Datta S, Burger GA, Naulty JS, Lambert DH, Ostheimer GW. Anesthesia for cesarean delivery utilizing spinal anesthesia. Tetracaine versus tetracaine and procaine. Reg Anesth 1984;9:195)

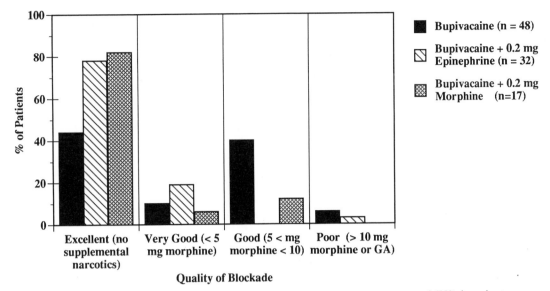

Figure 24–19. Quality of intraoperative analgesia in term parturients receiving 0.75% hyperbaric bupivacaine, average dose 9.3 mg, with or without epinephrine or morphine. Adding either drug significantly improves patient comfort. Onset and extent of sensory blockade were similar in all groups. Epinephrine slightly prolonged the duration of sensory blockade. (Data from Abouleish EI. Epinephrine improves the quality of spinal hyperbaric bupivacaine for cesarean section. Anesth Analg 1987;66:395, and Abouleish E, Rawal N. Fallon K, Hernandez D. Combined intrathecal morphine and bupivacaine for cesarean section. Anesth Analg 1988;67:370)

relief. All the women in the 15-mg group had good or excellent blocks.[6]

Although 15 mg of hyperbaric bupivacaine produces a slightly higher level of block, it offers several advantages. The longer duration of sensory blockade provides good operating condition for up to 2 hours. With 12 mg of bupivacaine, patients begin to get uncomfortable between 60 and 90 minutes after induction. In addition, the intraoperative analgesia produced by 15 mg of bupivacaine eliminates the need for adjuvant drugs. At Thomas Jefferson University, we routinely use hyperbaric bupivacaine, 15 mg, for cesarean section

Figure 24–20. Onset and duration of sensory blockade in term parturients after subarachnoid injection of either 12 or 15 mg of 0.75% bupivacaine with 8.25% bupivacaine. The higher dose of drug blocks significantly more spinal segments for a significantly longer time. Sensory block regressed to T-10 in 140.6 ± 16.5 min (mean ± SD) after 12 mg and in 162.1 ± 33.8 min after 15 mg. (Data from De Simone CA, Norris MC, Leighton BL, et al. Spinal anesthesia with hyperbaric bupivacaine for cesarean section: A comparison of two doses. Anesthesiology 1988;69:A670)

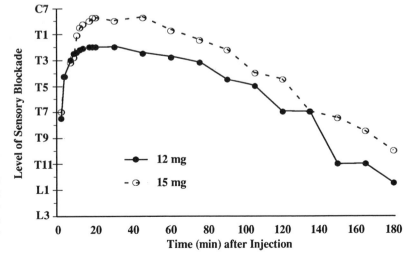

anesthesia. In addition, many women receive 0.15 mg of intrathecal morphine for postoperative analgesia. The morphine is given at the discretion of the resident or staff anesthesiologist administering the anesthetic. A recent retrospective review of 103 randomly selected anesthetic records revealed no differences in the need for intraoperative supplemental medication between women who did or did not receive intrathecal morphine (Fig. 24-21).

Conclusion

Any of the three local anesthetics mentioned can, if given in high enough doses, provide good maternal comfort during cesarean delivery. Because it provides better sensory blockade at commonly used doses and produces shorter duration of motor block, I prefer hyperbaric bupivacaine for most cesarean sections. I routinely use 15 mg of 0.75% bupivacaine with 8.25% dextrose. Those who wish to use smaller doses of local anesthetic should consider adding opioid or epinephrine to improve the quality of their blocks. Lidocaine can prove an effective alternative if one is working with a reliably fast surgeon.

Maternal Position

Neither the sitting nor the lateral decubitus position offers any clear advantage during induction of spinal anesthesia. When inducing blockade in the lateral decubitus position, the side on which the patient lies does matter. If the patient assumes the *left* lateral position for induction and then lies supine with *left* tilt for uterine displacement, blockade on the *right* side may not extend high enough for surgery.[76] In contrast, inducing anesthesia with the patient in the *right* lateral position and then placing her supine with *left* tilt for uterine displacement helps assure good bilateral blockade.

A similar phenomenon occurs when using isobaric bupivacaine. Here, however, the greater extent of blockade develops on the nondependent side (0.5% bupivacaine is slightly hypobaric).[77] Should this problem arise, rolling the patient from side to side reportedly evens the spread of analgesia.[78]

NEONATAL OUTCOME

For the infant, spinal anesthesia offers advantages over both general and epidural anesthesia. Babies born under general anesthesia often have lower Apgar scores than those delivered with regional anesthesia.[12,79] They also score lower on neurobehavioral examination. Hodgkinson *et al*[80] examined neonatal neurobehavior during the first 2 days of life. The infants studied were delivered by cesarean section using either general or spinal anesthesia. The infants in the spinal group scored much better at all times on all tests than the infants in the general anesthesia group.[80] Abboud *et al*[81]

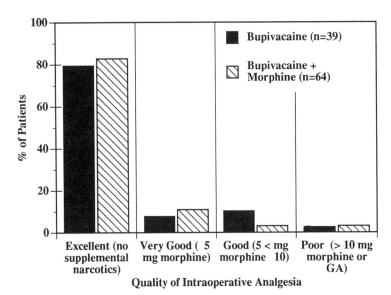

Figure 24–21. Quality of intraoperative analgesia in term parturients receiving 15 mg of hyperbaric 0.75% bupivacaine, with or without 0.15 mg of morphine, for spinal anesthesia for cesarean section. Adding intrathecal morphine does not improve the quality of analgesia. Most patients in both groups had excellent sensory blockade. (Norris MC. Unpublished data.)

Preparation:	Large-bore peripheral IV
Premedication:	30 mL sodium citrate within 15 minutes of induction
Prehydration:	1.5 to 2.0 L balanced saline solution (*i.e.,* Plasmalyte) within 15 to 30 minutes of induction. Infuse under pressure if necessary. Give less fluid if mother is actively laboring.
Positioning:	Sitting or right lateral decubitus

Induction:	Identify the subarachnoid space:
	    Small-gauge needle ($\leq$ 24 gauge)
	    L-2–3 interspace or lower
	    Midline or paramedian approach (paramedian approach often easier when patient is in the lateral decubitus position)
	Inject local anesthetic:
	    15 mg 0.75% bupivacaine with 8.25% dextrose
	    80 mg 5% lidocaine with 7.5% dextrose if surgical time less than 30 minutes
	    Add morphine, if desired, for postoperative analgesia

Maintenance:	Position patient supine with 10 to 15 degrees of left uterine tilt. Administer at least 50% oxygen by face mask. Monitor maternal blood pressure every minute for 20 minutes, then every 2 to 3 minutes. Continue rapid infusion of fluids until maternal blood pressure stabilizes.
Hypotension:	Well hydrated: 5 to 10 mg ephedrine when blood pressure is less than 90 mm Hg or mother is symptomatic Poorly hydrated: 10 mg ephedrine when blood pressure begins to fall

Figure 24–22. A suggested technique for spinal anesthesia for cesarean section.

also examined this issue. They obtained neurologic and adaptive capacity scores (Newborn Neurologic and Adaptive Capacity Scores) in infants delivered by cesarean section under general, epidural, or spinal anesthesia. As in the study by Hodgkinson *et al,*[80] the babies in the general anesthesia group had overall lower scores than the infants in the regional groups. Even epidural anesthesia, however, depressed some scores at the 2-hour measurement compared to spinal anesthesia. All infants scored equally as well by 24 hours of life. These authors postulated that the large dose of local anesthetic required for epidural blockade produced these differences.[81]

Maternal hypotension, besides risking umbilical acidosis, can depress neurobehavioral scores. Infants whose mothers experienced 4 to 8 minutes of hypotension during the induction of epidural anesthesia for cesarean section had abnormal neurobehavioral tests for 2 to 7 days.[23] Still, with good maternal hydration and careful blood pressure monitoring, brief episodes of maternal hypotension do not adversely effect neurobehavioral scores.[26]

CONCLUSION

This chapter has reviewed spinal anesthesia for cesarean section. I hope the reader now understands the practical and theoretic issues surrounding its safe use (Fig. 24-22) and the reasons behind its use. With proper attention to maternal hydration and to drug selection and dosage, spinal blockade provides profound, reliable, and safe anesthesia for both mother and fetus.

REFERENCES

1. Brownridge P. Central neural blockade and caesarean section. Part 1. Review and case series. Anaesth Intensive Care 1979;7:33.
2. Greene NM. Physiology of spinal anesthesia. 3rd ed. Baltimore: Williams & Wilkins, 1981:247.
3. Ebner H. An evaluation of spinal anesthesia in obstetrics. Anesth Analg 1959;38:378.
4. Shnider SM, Levinson G. Anesthesia for cesarean section. In: Shnider SM, Levinson G, eds. Anesthesia for ob-

stetrics. 2nd ed. Baltimore: Williams & Wilkins, 1987:159.

5. Carrie LES. Debate on use of spinal anesthesia in obstetrics: Spinal anesthesia has definite indications in obstetrics. Acta Anaesth Belg 1988;39:177.

6. DeSimone CA, Norris MC, Leighton BL, et al. Spinal anesthesia with hyperbaric bupivacaine for cesarean section: A comparison of two doses. Anesthesiology 1988;69:A670.

7. Kuhnert BR, Zuspan KJ, Kuhnert PM, Syracuse CD, Brown DE. Bupivacaine disposition in mother, fetus and neonate after spinal anesthesia for cesarean section. Anesth Analg 1987;66:407.

8. Norris MC, Torjman M, Leighton BL, DeSimone CA. Respiratory and motor function during bupivacaine spinal anesthesia for cesarean section. Anesth Analg 1990;70:S283.

9. Abboud TK, Artal R, Henriksen EH, Earl S, Kammula RK. Effects of spinal anesthesia on maternal circulating catecholamines. Am J Obstet Gynecol 1982;142:252.

10. Jouppila P, Kuikka J, Jouppila R, Hollmén A. Effect of general anesthesia for cesareans section on intervillous blood flow. Acta Obstet Gynecol Scand 1979;58:249.

11. Irestedt L, Lagercrantz H, Hjemdahl P, Hägnevik K, Belfrage P. Fetal and maternal plasma catecholamine levels at elective cesarean section under general or epidural anesthesia versus vaginal delivery. Am J Obstet Gynecol 1982;142:1004.

12. Marx GF, Luykx WM, Cohen S. Fetal–neonatal status following caesarean section for fetal distress. Br J Anaesth 1984;56:1009.

13. Holmes F. The supine hypotensive syndrome: Its importance to the anaesthetist. Anaesthesia 1960;15:298.

14. Assali NS, Prystowsky H. Studies on autonomic blockade. I. Comparison between the effects of tetraethylammonium chloride (TEAC) and high selective spinal anesthesia on blood pressure of normal and toxemic pregnancy. J Clin Invest 1950;29:1354.

15. Greene NM. Area of differential block in spinal anesthesia with hyperbaric tetracaine. Anesthesiology 1958;19:45.

16. Courtney KR, Kendig JJ, Cohen EN. Frequency-dependent conduction block: The role of nerve impulse pattern in local anesthetic potency. Anesthesiology 1978;48:111.

17. Brull SJ, Greene NM. Time-courses of zones of differential sensory blockade during spinal anesthesia with hyperbaric tetracaine or bupivacaine. Anesth Analg 1989;69:342.

18. Chamberlain DP, Chamberlain BDL. Changes in the skin temperature of the trunk and their relationship to sympathetic blockade during spinal anesthesia. Anesthesiology 1986;65:139.

19. Ueland K, Gills RE, Hansen JM. Maternal cardiovascular dynamics. I. Cesarean section under subarachnoid block anesthesia. Am J Obstet Gynecol. 1968;100:42.

20. Van Zundert AA, DeWolf AM, Vaes L, Soetens M. High-volume spinal anesthesia with bupivacaine 0.125% for cesarean section. Anesthesiology 1988;69:998.

21. Wollman SB, Marx GF. Acute hydration for prevention of hypotension of spinal anesthesia in parturients. Anesthesiology 1968;29:374.

22. Ebner H, Barcohana J, Bartoshuk AK. Influence of postspinal hypotension on the fetal electrocardiogram. Am J Obstet Gynecol 1960;80:569.

23. Hollmen AI, Jouppila R, Koivisto M, et al. Neurologic activity of infants following anesthesia for cesarean section. Anesthesiology 1978;48:350.

24. Marx GF, Cosmi EV, Wollman SB. Biochemical status and clinical condition of mother and infant at cesarean section. Anesth Analg 1969;48:986.

25. Datta SJ, Brown WU Jr. Acid–base status in diabetic mothers and their infants following general or spinal anesthesia for cesarean section. Anesthesiology 1977;47:272.

26. Corke BC, Datta S, Ostheimer GW, Weiss JB, Alper MH. Spinal anaesthesia for caesarean section: The influence of hypotension on neonatal outcome. Anaesthesia 1982;37:658.

27. Clark RB, Brunner JA III. Dopamine for the treatment of spinal hypotension during cesarean section. Anesthesiology 1980;53:514.

28. Clark RB, Thompson DS, Thompson CH. Prevention of spinal hypotension associated with cesarean section. Anesthesiology 1976;45:670.

29. Caritis SN, Abouleish E, Edelstone DI, Mueller-Heubach E. Fetal acid–base state following spinal or epidural anesthesia for cesarean section. Obstet Gynecol 1980;56:610.

30. Lewis M, Thomas P, Wilkes RG. Hypotension during epidural analgesia for caesarean section. Arterial and central venous pressure changes after acute intravenous loading with two litres Hartmann's solution. Anaesthesia 1983;38:250.

31. Norris MC. Hypotension during spinal anesthesia for cesarean section: Does it affect neonatal outcome? Reg Anesth 1987;12:191.

32. Mathru M, Rao TKL, Kartha RK, Shanmugham M, Jacobs HK. Intravenous albumin administration for prevention of spinal hypotension during cesarean section. Anesth Analg 1980;59:655.

33. Gibbs CP, Spohr L, Petrakis J, Paulus D, Schultetus R. Prevention of hypotension with hydration. Anesthesiology 1981;55:A308.

34. Brizgys RV, Dailey PA, Shnider SM, Kotelko DM, Levinson G. The incidence and neonatal effects of maternal hypotension during epidural anesthesia for cesarean section. Anesthesiology 1987;67:782.

35. James FM III, Greiss FC Jr. The use of inflatable boots to prevent hypotension during spinal anesthesia for cesarean section. Anesth Analg 1973;52:246.

36. Goudie TA, Winter AW, Ferguson DJM. Lower limb compression using inflatable splints to prevent hypotension during spinal anaesthesia for cæsarean section. Acta Anaesthesiol Scand 1988;32:541.

37. Bhagwanjee S, Rocke DA, Rout CC, Koovargee RV, Brijball R. Prevention of hypotension following spinal Anaesthesia for elective caesarean section by wrapping of the legs. Br J Anaesth 1990;65:819.

38. Moya F, Smith B. Spinal anesthesia for cesarean section. Clinical and biochemical studies of effects on maternal physiology. JAMA 1962;179:115.

39. Datta S, Alper MH, Ostheimer GW, Weiss JB. Method of ephedrine administration and nausea and hypotension during spinal anesthesia for cesarean section. Anesthesiology 1982;56:68.

40. Kang YG, Abouleish E, Caritis S. Prophylactic intravenous ephedrine infusion during spinal anesthesia for cesarean section. Anesth Analg 1982;61:839.

41. Kangas-Saarela T, Hollmén AI, Tolonen U, et al. Does ephedrine influence newborn neurobehavioral responses and spectral EEG when used to prevent maternal hypotension during caesarean section? Acta Anaesthesiol Scand 1990;34:8.

42. Jouppila P, Jouppila R, Barinoff T, Koivula A. Placental blood flow during cæsarean section performed under subarachnoid blockade. Br J Anaesth 1984;56:1379.

43. Lindblad A, Bernow J, Marsál K. Fetal blood flow during intrathecal anaesthesia for elective caesarean section. Br J Anaesth 1988;61:376.

44. Fairlie FM, Kirkwood I, Lang GD, Sheldon CD. Umbilical artery flow velocity waveforms during spinal anesthesia. Eur J Obstet Gynecol Reprod Biol 1990;38:3.

45. Knepp NB, Shelley WC, Gabbe SG, Kumar S, Stanley CA, Gutsche BB. Fetal and neonatal hazards of maternal hydration with 5% dextrose before caesarean. section. Lancet 1982;1:1150.

46. Philipson EH, Kalhan SC, Riha MM, Pimentel R. Effects of maternal glucose infusion on fetal acid–base status in human pregnancy. Am J Obstet Gynecol 1987;157:866.

47. Peng ATC, Shamsi HH, Blancato LS, Shulman SM, Chervenak FA, Castro JL. Euglycemic hydration with dextrose 1% in lactated Ringer's solution during epidural anesthesia for cesarean section. Reg Anesth 1987; 12:184.

48. Norris MC, Leighton BL, De Simone CA, Palmer CM. Does the choice of crystalloid affect maternal and neonatal glucose homeostasis at cesarean section? Anesth Analg 1989;68:S212.

49. Norris, MC, Leighton BL, De Simone CA, Goodman DA, Gorman RM. Influence of the choice of crystalloid solution on neonatal acid-base status at cesarean section. Anesthesiology 1987;67:A458.

50. Kenepp NB. Intravenous fluid during labor for patients undergoing cesarean section. In: Datta S, Ostheimer GW, eds. Common problems in obstetric anesthesia. Chicago: Yearbook Medical Publishers, 1987:44.

51. Shnider SM. Anesthesia for elective cesarean section. In: Shnider SM, ed. Obstetrical anesthesia. Baltimore: Williams & Wilkins, 1970:94.

52. Craft JB Jr, Roizen MF, Dao SD, Edwards M, Gilman R. A comparison of T_4 and T_7 dermatomal levels of analgesia for caesarean section using the lumbar epidural technique. Can Anaesth Soc J 1982;29:264.

53. Pederson H, Santos AC, Finster M. Obstetric anesthesia. In: Barash PG, Cullen BF, Stoelting RK, eds. Clinical anesthesia. Philadelphia: JB Lippincott, 1989:1215.

54. Alahuhta S, Kangas-Saarela R, Hollmén AI, Edström HH. Visceral pain during caesarean section under spinal and epidural anaesthesia with bupivacaine. Acta Anaesthsiol Scand 1990;34:95.

55. Pan PM, Lin Z-F, Lim J, Tung M-C, Wei T-T. The optimal dose of hyperbaric tetracaine spinal anesthesia for cesarean section. Anaesthe Sinica 1989;27:349.

56. Santos A, Pederson H, Finster M, Edström H. Hyperbaric bupivacaine for spinal anesthesia in cesarean section. Anesth Analg 1984;63:1009.

57. Michie AR, Freeman RM, Dutton DA, Howie HB. Subarachnoid anaesthesia for elective caesarean section. A comparison of two hyperbaric solutions. Anaesthesia 1988;43:96.

58. Moore DC. Spinal anesthesia: Bupivacaine compared with tetracaine. Anesth Analg 1980;59:743.

59. Concepcion MA, Lambert DH, Welch KA, Covino BG. Tourniquet pain during spinal anesthesia: A comparison of plain solutions of tetracaine and bupivacaine. Anesth Analg 1988;67:828.

60. Stewart A, Lambert DH, Concepcion MA, et al. Decreased incidence of tourniquet pain during spinal anesthesia with bupivacaine: A possible explanation. Anesth Analg 1988;67:833.

61. Bembridge M, MacDonald R, Lyons G. Spinal anæsthesia with hyperbaric lignocaine for elective cæsarean section. Anaesthesia 1986;41:906.

62. Greene NM. Distribution of local anesthetic solutions within the subarachnoid space. Anesth Analg 1985; 64:715.

63. Shnider SM, Levinson G. Anesthesia for cesarean section. In: Shnider SM, Levinson G, eds. Anesthesia for obstetrics. 2nd ed. Baltimore: Williams & Wilkins, 1987:183.

64. Abouleish EI. Epinephrine improves the quality of spinal hyperbaric bupivacaine for cesarean section. Anesth Analg 1987;66:395.

65. Norris MC. Height, weight and the spread of subarachnoid hyperbaric bupivacaine in the term parturient. Anesth Analg 1988;67:555.

66. Norris MC. Patient variables and the subarachnoid spread of hyperbaric bupivacaine in the term parturient. Anesthesiology 1990;72:478.

67. Hartwell BL, Aglio LS, Hauch MA, Datta S. Vertebral column length and the spread of hyperbaric subarachnoid bupivacaine in the term parturient. Reg Anesth 1991;16:17.

68. Barker AE. A report of clinical experiences with spinal analgesia in 100 cases and some reflections on the procedure. Br Med J 1907;1:655.

69. Kitahara T, Kuri S, Yoshida J. The spread of drugs used for spinal anesthesia. Anesthesiology 1956;17:205.

70. Smith TC. The lumbar spine and subarachnoid block. Anesthesiology 1968;29:60.

71. Pedersen H, Santos AC, Steinberg ES, Schapiro HM, Harmon TW, Finster M. Incidence of visceral pain during cesarean section: The effect of varying doses of spinal bupivacaine. Anesth Analg 1989;69:46.

72. Russell IF. Spinal anesthesia for cesarean delivery with dilute solutions of plain bupivacaine: The relationship between infused volume and spread. Reg Anesth 1991;16:130.

73. Chantigian RC, Datta S, Burger GA, Naulty JS, Lambert DH, Ostheimer GW. Anesthesia for cesarean delivery utilizing spinal anesthesia. Tetracaine versus tetracaine and procaine. Reg Anesth 1984;9:195.

74. Abouleish E, Rawal N, Fallon K, Hernandez D. Combined intrathecal morphine and bupivacaine for cesarean section. Anesth Analg 1988;67:370.

75. Hunt CO, Naulty JS, Bader AM, et al. Perioperative analgesia with subarachnoid fentanyl-bupivacaine for cesarean delivery. Anesthesiology 1989:71:535.

76. Sprague DH. Effects of position and uterine displacement on spinal anesthesia for cesarean section. Anesthesiology 1976;44:164.

77. Carrie LES, O'Sullivan G. Subarachnoid bupivacaine 0.5% for caesarean section. Eur J Anaesth 1984;1:275.

78. Russell IF. Effect of posture during the induction of subarachnoid analgesia for caesarean section. Br J Aesth 1987;59:342.

79. James FM III, Crawford JS, Hopkinson R, Davies P, Naiem H. A comparison of general anesthesia and lumbar epidural analgesia for cesarean section. Anesth Analg 1977;56:228.

80. Hodgkinson R, Bhatt M, Kim SS, Grewal G, Marx GF. Neonatal neurobehavioural tests following cesarean section under general and spinal anesthesia. Am J Obstet Gynecol 1978:132:670.

81. Abboud TK, Nagappala S, Murakawa K, et al. Comparison of the effects of general and regional anesthesia for cesarean section on neonatal neurologic and adaptive capacity scores. Anesth Analg 1985;64:996.

CHAPTER 25

Anesthesia and Coexisting Maternal Disease

Part One
Cardiac and Hematologic Disease

D.A. Rocke
C.C. Rout
Christopher Ernest Peter Orlikowski

CARDIAC DISEASE

Maternal cardiac disease complicates 1% to 2% of pregnancies and is a significant cause of maternal mortality.[1] The additional cardiac work demanded by the physiologic changes of pregnancy (see Chap. 1) and the hemodynamic instability of labor and delivery increase the maternal risk from anesthetic intervention. The obstetric anesthesiologist faces two principal concerns:

- Can epidural analgesia be safely used for labor and delivery?
- What is the safest method of providing anesthesia for cesarean section? (A debate that usually devolves to a choice between epidural and general anesthesia.)

Regional Anesthesia

Women with most cardiac lesions withstand the hemodynamic effects of a carefully conducted epidural block to T-12 better than the hemodynamic effects of a labor and delivery without the benefit of effective analgesia.

Patients with valvular stenosis or right-to-left intracardiac shunts may not tolerate the high sympathetic block associated with epidural anesthesia for cesarean delivery. Even women with regurgitant valvular lesions that normally improve with epidural analgesia may not withstand a poorly conducted block.[2] Whatever the circumstances, induce epidural blockade using incremental doses of drug. Follow the hemodynamic response to block closely. Epidural or spinal opiates can provide excellent analgesia for the first stage of labor and avoid the deleterious effects of sympathetic blockade; however, neuraxial opioids alone rarely provide adequate analgesia for the second stage of labor. They also do not ensure sufficient pain relief for operative delivery. Saddle block (single injection spinal or via intrathecal catheter) or a caudal/epidural can be effective for second stage analgesia.

Systemic Analgesia for Labor

The most common contraindication to epidural anesthesia in the parturient with cardiac disease is anticoagulant therapy. Maternal anticoagulation precludes major conduction analgesia. In these cases, if the patient cannot withstand the hemodynamic effects of labor and delivery without epidural analgesia, it is best to proceed to elective cesarean section under general anesthesia. If the patient is going to labor, the standard regimen of intermittent intramuscular meperidine provides neither adequate analgesia nor cardiovascular stability. In this circumstance, we recommend a continuous intravenous infusion of alfentanil. Start the drug in early labor with a loading dose of 30 µg/kg over 10 minutes. Then, begin an infusion of 1 µg/kg/min. This technique can provide excellent analgesia for the first stage of labor. Additional bolus doses may be required for the second stage. The neonate should receive intravenous naloxone if necessary upon delivery and be observed closely in a neonatal unit for the first 12 hours of life.

General Anesthesia

An important consideration when planning a general anesthetic is maternal cardiovascular stability. The rapid sequence induction recommended in obstetric anesthesia induces a profound adrenergic response; however, this reaction can be modified without compromising maternal safety. We find that giving alfentanil, 30 µg/kg, then etomidate, 0.3 mg/kg, and succinylcholine, 1 mg/kg, usually obtunds the pressor response to intubation. Following delivery, most infants have respiratory depression with this dose of alfentanil. They respond promptly to intravenous naloxone. The infant should be observed closely in the neonatal unit and further naloxone given if necessary. Use the inhalational agent most appropriate to the patient's cardiac lesion for maintenance of anesthesia. Avoid nitrous oxide because it increases pulmonary vascular resistance. After delivery, supplemental opiates safely deepen maternal anesthesia. Vecuronium is an appropriate nondepolarizing muscle relaxant.

Monitoring

Take maximum advantage of noninvasive methods of cardiovascular monitoring. In addition, we recommend central venous pressure monitoring in all but the most trivial cases. In the more severe lesions, we use systemic and pulmonary artery catheters. Continue monitoring into the postdelivery period, if necessary in an intensive care unit. The greatest risk of circulatory overload arises just after delivery as the contracted uterus displaces blood into the systemic circulation. If using epidural anesthesia, continue injecting local anesthetics so that the receding sympathetic block does not compound the increase in blood volume.

Vasoactive Drugs

Exercise caution in the use of vasopressors and oxytocic agents. Consider using a pure constrictor, such as phenylephrine, in patients with stenotic valvular lesions. Patients with regurgitant valvular lesions or poor left ventricular function should respond better to an agent with inotropic activity, such as ephedrine. If an oxytocic agent is necessary, then an infusion of synthetic oxytocin is best. Avoid bolus doses because significant, albeit transient, systemic hypotension can occur. Ergometrine causes a sustained increase in systemic vascular resistance.

Beta-blockers are increasingly used in pregnancy, particularly in the management of mitral stenosis. These drugs may cause intrauterine growth retardation and loss of beat-to-beat variability in the fetus, and bradycardia and hypoglycemia in the neonate.[3] However, their use undoubtedly causes symptomatic improvement and decreases the need for closed mitral valvotomy during pregnancy.[4] Beta-blockers do not contraindicate incremental epidural anesthesia; however, be careful with the high block required for cesarean delivery. Significant bradycardia is possible, and the heart's ability to respond to decreased afterload is impaired.

Antibiotic Prophylaxis.

Antibiotic prophylaxis against bacterial endocarditis is necessary for both vaginal and operative deliveries in all patients with valvular or congenital lesions or previous cardiac surgery. The appropriate agents should provide gram-positive and gram-negative coverage (see Chap. 2).

Other Considerations

Patients with cardiac disease are more vulnerable to the effects of obstetric complications should they occur. Pay particular attention to avoiding aortocaval compression. Give an effective antacid before general anesthesia.

Valvular Heart Disease

Mitral Stenosis

Of the isolated valvular lesions seen in pregnancy, mitral stenosis is the most common. It also is the dominant lesion in most cases of mixed mitral valve disease. Hemodynamically, it should be regarded as a fixed obstruction to left ventricular filling. Although the maternal mortality in pregnancy is 1%, this risk may rise to 14% to 17% in patients who develop atrial fibrillation.[5]

EVALUATION. On examination, determine the NYHA functional classification (see Chap. 2) and exclude remediable exacerbating features such as anemia, infection, and tachycardia. Make a thorough record of the patient's medications. Examine the patient while looking for features of severe disease (*i.e.,* an opening snap within 80 ms of the second heart sound and features of pulmonary hypertension). The electrocardiogram may show atrial fibrillation or, if sinus rhythm, a broad notched P wave in lead II (P mitrale). Evidence of right ventricular hypertrophy on electrocardiogram suggests pulmonary hypertension. Radiographic findings in the chest include a straight left-heart border, left atrial enlargement, and Kerley's B lines. Upper lobe blood diversion is a common finding in pregnancy and is not a helpful sign. Echocardiography will exclude other valvular lesions and allow assessment of left ventricular function (invariably good in isolated mitral stenosis, but may be decreased in a few patients with mixed valvular lesions). Direct measurement or Doppler flow studies across the valve can provide objective assessment of mitral valve area.

ANESTHESIA AND ANALGESIA. Avoid maternal tachycardia. The pressure gradient across the valve is inversely proportional to the square of the diastolic filling time.[6] A small increase in heart rate (decreased diastolic filling time) will therefore cause a marked increase in left atrial pressure. Beta-blockers can control heart rate. Consider starting this therapy in patients with good left ventricular function who are not taking beta-blockers chronically.

Use epidural block for labor analgesia unless it is specifically contraindicated. The venous dilation caused by the epidural helps attenuate the effects of increased venous volume associated with the contracting uterus. Do not give extra fluid before the epidural anesthetic. Instead, infuse fluid as indicated by central volume status. Use at least a central venous catheter to assess volume status. Strongly consider pulmonary arterial catheterization in NYHA functional classes III and IV.

If epidural analgesia is contraindicated, NYHA functional classes I and II manage well with intermittent parenteral analgesia, provided maternal heart rate is kept under control. Meperidine is not the ideal agent because it may cause a tachycardia (see Chap. 16). For NYHA grades III and IV, intermittent analgesia is insufficient. In these cases, we recommend alfentanil by infusion.

For cesarean section, NYHA class I and II patients tolerate the higher epidural block required for operative delivery. Monitor cardiac preload and adjust as necessary. However, NYHA grades III and IV may fare better with general anesthesia. These patients do not tolerate any reduction in cardiac afterload. Epidural anesthesia is possible in severe stenosis. In this setting, monitor pulmonary artery pressure. Maintain adequate left ventricular preload during the onset of sympathetic blockade. Carefully avoid fluid overload.

If using a general anesthetic, obtund the adrenergic response to intubation with beta-blockers, alfentanil, or a combination of both. Etomidate and succinylcholine are the most suitable intravenous induction agents. Maintain anesthesia with halothane or enflurane in air and oxygen. Avoid isoflurane, as it reduces systemic vascular resistance. Nitrous oxide can raise pulmonary artery pressure. Following delivery, give a long-acting opiate.

The immediate postpartum period is when the patient has the greatest risk of developing pulmonary edema. Blood volume expands as the uterus contracts and the vasodilator effects of regional blockade wear off. Because of the high incidence of pulmonary edema in the early postpartum period, we always give furosemide, 20 to 40 mg, intravenously with delivery of the placenta. Then, we closely monitor the patient's volume status for the next 24 to 48 hours.

Mitral Regurgitation

Mitral regurgitation usually improves during pregnancy owing to the decreased systemic vascular resistance and increased blood volume. The key to anesthetic management is to encourage forward flow of blood. Lowering systemic vascular resistance, maintaining left ventricular filling pressure, and avoiding bradycardia help achieve this goal. Epidural anesthesia, with fluid preloading, provides these conditions. It is the preferred anesthetic technique for both labor with vaginal delivery and for cesarean section. Atrial fibrillation, requiring anticoagulant therapy, is comparatively common. If general anesthesia is required, try to avoid the pressor response to intubation and any myocardial depression. A vasodilator infusion may be a useful adjunct to anesthesia. In severe cases, an inotrope may be necessary. The usual monitoring considerations apply.

Mitral Valve Prolapse

The vast majority of patients with this common congenital lesion are asymptomatic and have trivial regurgitation. Decreases in left ventricular volume increase the degree of prolapse. Avoid volume depletion and tachycardia. Patients with significant or symptomatic regurgitation should be managed as for mitral regurgitation.

Mixed Mitral Valve Disease

Manage these patients according to the dominant lesion as assessed by echocardiography. The combination of both significant stenosis and regurgitation may impair left ventricular function, and the patient will not tolerate beta-blockade. Here, keep the heart rate between 80 and 100 beats/minute using digoxin.

Aortic Stenosis

EVALUATION. This lesion is uncommon in pregnancy. Most patients develop symptoms beyond child-bearing age. Patients with aortic stenosis poorly tolerate any decrease in afterload or diastolic filling time; however, they also do not endure bradycardia well. (The stenotic valve limits stroke volume.) Unlike mitral stenosis, absence of symptoms does not necessarily suggest mild disease. All patients with aortic valve disease must have echocardiographic evaluation before delivery to assess the pressure gradient across the valve, valve area, and ventricular performance. A pressure gradient of less than 50 mm Hg (as assessed by Doppler) usually implies mild disease. Pressure gradient, however, depends on flow. The valve area and systolic ejection time also should be considered (valve area < 1 cm² implies severe disease).

ANESTHESIA AND ANALGESIA. In mild cases, epidural conduction blockade can be used for both vaginal and abdominal delivery. A continuous-infusion technique minimizes the hemodynamic changes associated with local anesthetic blockade. For severe cases, we recommend avoiding local anesthetic-induced sympathectomy. Neuraxial opioids or intravenous analgesia can be used for labor and delivery. General anesthesia is the safest method for cesarean section in severe cases. Easterling *et al*[7] reported the successful use of epidural conduction blockade in four patients with varied degrees of aortic stenosis. Only one

of these patients had isolated aortic stenosis. The other three had associated moderate aortic regurgitation.

Noninvasive monitoring is sufficient in mild cases, but for severe cases, we strongly recommend direct arterial pressure monitoring and a pulmonary artery catheter for perioperative fluid management.

Avoid bolus injections of synthetic oxytocin. Use phenylephrine rather than ephedrine to treat hypotension that does not respond readily to volume.

Aortic Regurgitation

Any reduction in heart rate or increase in systemic vascular resistance can cause acute volume overload in a chronically distended left ventricle. The sympathetic block associated with epidural anesthesia reduces systemic vascular resistance and improves cardiac output. We recommend this technique for labor and cesarean delivery. If general anesthesia has to be used, consider a continuous vasodilator infusion. Avoid myocardial depression and attempt to suppress the intubation response. Pulmonary artery catheters are not particularly useful for routine use because a rise in left atrial pressure occurs late in the disease process.

Hypertrophic Obstructive Cardiomyopathy (Idiopathic Subaortic Stenosis)

This uncommon condition occurs in young people and may complicate pregnancy. Although it is hemodynamically and symptomatically similar to valvular aortic stenosis, the management is sufficiently different to warrant separate consideration. Like aortic stenosis, decreases in systemic vascular resistance are tolerated poorly. However, adrenergic stimulation (increased inotropy) and the Valsalva maneuver significantly increase the subvalvular obstruction. Pay close attention to maternal volume status. Use fluids to avoid decreases in left ventricular volume. Injudicious fluid therapy, however, may precipitate pulmonary edema. Tachycardia, which increases the obstruction, raises the risk of decompensation.[8,9] If hypotension develops, use a vasoconstrictor without inotropic activity (phenylephrine). As the obstruction to left ventricular outflow can increase rapidly, all patients should be monitored invasively, even if asymptomatic, with systemic and pulmonary artery catheters.

These patients benefit significantly from effective epidural analgesia for labor and delivery.[10] Epidural block can prevent the effects of stress and pain on the outflow obstruction. Still, the extensive sympathetic block associated with epidural anesthesia for cesarean section is likely to prove hazardous. We prefer general anesthesia for abdominal delivery. Because most of these patients already will be receiving beta-blockers, the addition of alfentanil to the induction sequence should successfully obtund the intubation response. Halothane is the most appropriate inhalational agent for maintenance of anesthesia. If the left ventricle fails, treat hypotension and tachycardia using a vasopressor and propranolol. Inotropic therapy worsens the obstruction and is contraindicated.

Peripartum Cardiomyopathy

Although peripartum cardiomyopathy most commonly presents in the second postpartum month, it may arise during cesarean section[11] or any time in the last trimester or first 6 months postpartum. Epidural analgesia is strongly indicated for labor and delivery. Decreased systemic vascular resistance improves cardiac output. For cesarean delivery, we also choose epidural anesthesia. These women need little or no additional volume before induction of regional block. If asymptomatic, a central venous pressure catheter is adequate with noninvasive blood pressure monitoring, but we suggest using a percutaneous catheter introducer to allow rapid insertion of a pulmonary artery catheter if needed.[12] If symptomatic or echocardiographic findings show severe left ventricular dysfunction, then a pulmonary artery catheter and arterial line should be inserted. Some patients are on anticoagulants because of the possibility of mural thrombosis. For general anesthesia, avoid increases in afterload and negative inotropic agents. Use invasive monitors. Isoflurane is the inhalational agent of choice. Consider the use of a vasodilator infusion, and have inotropic support available.

Arrhythmias

Any disturbance of cardiac rhythm should be treated promptly. Supraventricular arrhythmias are particularly problematical in patients with rheumatic heart disease and commonly occur in mitral valve disease. Atrial fibrillation occurring during pregnancy may increase the maternal mortality rate to as high as 19%.[13] Patients with chronic atrial fibrillation should be taking digoxin or propranolol to control ventricular rate. They also may be using anticoagulants to prevent thromboembolic complications.

Sudden onset of atrial fibrillation or supraventricular tachycardia with severe cardiac compromise should be treated by direct-current cardioversion. This therapy often is best done in the operating room under general anesthesia, with the usual precautions. Energy discharges of approximately 1 watt·sec/kg usually suffice. Although transient fetal arrhythmias may occur, cardioversion

during pregnancy does not adversely affect mother or child.[14]

Previous Valve Replacement

Increasing numbers of patients are presenting in pregnancy with a history of previous valve replacement. Usually, these patients are hemodynamically corrected and do not cause many problems if the valve prosthesis is working properly. However, pulmonary hypertension and atrial fibrillation may persist following mitral valve replacement. Stenosis of tissue valves and perivalvular regurgitation should be excluded, and ventricular function should be assessed before anesthesia.

The most common problem is the use of anticoagulants in patients with mechanical prostheses, which may contraindicate epidural anesthesia. The practice in our unit is to use subcutaneous or intravenous heparin during the first trimester (when possible) and during the 2 weeks before delivery, with oral warfarin during the intervening weeks. Planned vaginal or operative delivery allows heparin therapy to be stopped the evening before and recommenced 3 to 24 hours following delivery.[15,16] A 12-hour delay after the last heparin dose usually ensures normal coagulation. Even so, check partial thromboplastin time and platelet count before beginning a major conduction anesthetic. Antiplatelet agents are ineffective when used alone,[17] but they are occasionally used as an adjunct to subcutaneous heparin. If this is the case, platelet function also should be assessed. Although the exact safety margin is uncertain, the epidural catheter should be removed as soon as it is no longer needed and well before restarting the anticoagulant therapy. Epidural hematoma has been described following catheter removal in a patient receiving anticoagulant therapy.[18]

If a patient presents in labor while on anticoagulant therapy, protamine can reverse the effects of heparin. The patient on warfarin should receive fresh frozen plasma to prevent hemorrhagic complications. However, the baby will remain anticoagulated and often is delivered by urgent cesarean section to avoid the trauma of vaginal delivery. This operation should be done under general anesthesia if time does not permit confirmation of anticoagulant reversal in the mother and induction of regional block.

Primary Pulmonary Hypertension

Primary pulmonary hypertension in combination with pregnancy carries an extremely high mortality rate of 60%.[19] Wherever possible, these patients should be advised not to become pregnant. Management includes early admission and hospitalization beginning around 28 weeks of gestation. A team approach is essential.

Evaluation

Assessment of the severity of the disease includes a history, clinical examination, electrocardiogram, and chest radiograph to determine the presence of right ventricular dysfunction. Definitive assessment must be made by pulmonary artery catheter. A cardiac index less than 4.0 L/min/m², right atrial pressure greater than 10 mm Hg, or pulmonary vascular resistance greater than 1000 dynes·s·cm⁻⁵ suggest an extremely poor prognosis. At the time of pulmonary artery catheterization, estimate the pharmacologic reversibility of the increased pulmonary vascular resistance.[20,21] Drugs used to assess pulmonary vascular reactivity include prostacyclin, (10 ng/kg/h), diltiazem (20 mg/h) and isoproterenol (0.4 mg/h). These drugs may decrease pulmonary vascular resistance and pulmonary artery pressure and increase cardiac output.[21] However, a marked reduction in pulmonary vascular resistance is not the most common response, and the efficacy of pulmonary vasodilation appears to decrease as the pregnancy progresses.

Following the initial hemodynamic assessment, the echocardiogram provides an ongoing estimate of systolic pulmonary artery pressure and atrial and ventricular size. Increasing right ventricular failure must be managed by bed rest, digitalis, and diuretics. Avoid hypoxia by the continuous administration of oxygen. Prophylactic low-dose heparin, 10,000 units twice a day, should be administered in the face of low cardiac output and bed rest.

Labor and Delivery

Vaginal delivery is preferable to cesarean section because the latter appears to lead to a poorer maternal outcome. Despite the mode of delivery, these women require intense monitoring. Systemic and pulmonary artery catheters and continuous estimation of oxygen delivery by oximetry are essential. Associated tricuspid incompetence may make insertion of the pulmonary artery catheter difficult. Anticipate the potential for severe bradycardia. Have atropine, isoproterenol, and transvenous pacing facilities available. Pay meticulous attention to blood loss to avoid hypovolemia. Any decrease in venous return to the heart aggravates the reduced right ventricular output owing to the obstruction presented by the pulmonary circulation. A fall in right ventricular output, in turn, leads to hypoxia, which further raises pulmonary vascular resistance, cre-

ating a vicious cycle. Unless broken, this cycle leads to progressive ventricular failure, hypoxemia, and acidosis in both mother and fetus. Death ultimately follows.

LABOR ANALGESIA. Epidural block, using reduced doses of 3 to 5 mL 0.25% bupivacaine, provides first-stage analgesia. Using 5 mL of 0.5% bupivacaine in the sitting position ensures perineal second-stage analgesia. Alternate techniques include the sole use of intrathecal morphine,[22] however, such a technique may not be suitable for primiparae or oxytocin-augmented labor. (Oxytocin causes severe increases in pulmonary vascular resistance and should be avoided, if possible.) Other techniques used include low-dose epidural bupivacaine and fentanyl.[23] Caudal analgesia, pudendal blocks, and dual epidural catheter techniques with one catheter directed caudally also have been used to provide second-stage analgesia.[21]

CESAREAN DELIVERY. For operative delivery, the balance of risk lies between the extensive sympathetic blockade associated with the higher sensory block required with epidural block versus the marked increase in pulmonary vascular resistance associated with laryngoscopy and tracheal intubation. Epidural anesthesia has been used successfully for cesarean section.[24] The alternative would be balanced anesthesia using etomidate for induction, vecuronium for muscle relaxation, and early intubation with fentanyl, 10 µg/kg, to modify the intubation response. Isoflurane is the volatile agent of choice because it is associated with the least myocardial depression. Avoid hypoxia, hypercarbia, high intrathoracic pressures, and acidosis. Maintain maternal hypocapnia. Patients should be ventilated postoperatively with continued invasive monitoring.

Drugs to be avoided include ergometrine, oxytocin, prostaglandin F₂ₐ, ketamine, and nitrous oxide. If needed, use pulmonary vasodilators (sodium nitroprusside, nitroglycerin, prostaglandin-E, isoproterenol), but monitor for systemic hypotension and arterial hypoxemia, negative inotropism, and fetal and uterine side effects. Use oxygen delivery as the therapeutic endpoint. Inotropic support (dopamine, up to 10 µg/kg/min, or dobutamine) may be required to improve right ventricular function. Increasing preload with volume loading is usually unsuccessful and may precipitate right ventricular ischemia.

Myocardial Infarction

Myocardial infarction during pregnancy is rare, with an estimated incidence of 1 in 10,000. The greatest frequency is in the third trimester in women more than 35 years old.[25] Overall maternal mortality approximates 35%. Normal electrocardiographic findings in pregnancy include reversible ST-, T-, and Q-wave changes. These aberrations can be differentiated from those indicating heart disease by echocardiographic assessment of ventricular wall motion.

A recent review found no convincing support for either cesarean or vaginal delivery in parturients with recent myocardial infarction.[26] Vaginal delivery with epidural analgesia eliminates stress, reduces blood loss, provides hemodynamic stability, and allows early ambulation; however, one has to deal with the unpredictable course of labor and delivery. Cesarean delivery under epidural eliminates the capriciousness of vaginal delivery, yet may be associated with increased blood loss and increased cardiorespiratory and metabolic demands. We recommend a two-catheter epidural technique for labor and vaginal delivery.[27] Use the upper catheter for the first stage of labor and the lower catheter for second-stage pain.

Predelivery assessment of the patient with previous or recent myocardial infarction should include Holter monitoring and exercise testing, if appropriate. In addition, two-dimensional echocardiography and radionuclide ventriculography can assess left ventricular function.

Patients with poor ventricular function require insertion of a pulmonary artery catheter to monitor cardiac function during labor and delivery. Nitroglycerin (0.5 µg/kg/min) may help provide coronary artery vasodilation. Carefully maintain diastolic pressure to allow subendocardial perfusion.

Use phenylephrine to treat hypotension associated with regional block. Ephedrine increases myocardial work owing to beta-stimulation, and metaraminol is a potent coronary vasoconstrictor. Keep these patients in the lateral position. The reduction in uterine blood flow associated with any degree of aortocaval compression may release uterine renin. The subsequent production of angiotensin can yield coronary artery spasm.[28]

Congenital Heart Disease

Left-to-Right Shunt

ATRIAL SEPTAL DEFECT. Serious clinical manifestations do not usually occur until the fourth or fifth decade. Patients with an atrial septal defect who become pregnant and are asymptomatic without evidence of pulmonary hypertension or right ventricular failure require little additional management.

Use epidural analgesia for labor, vaginal delivery, and cesarean section. This technique avoids increases in systemic vascular resistance, which could induce left-to-right shunting. If a general anesthetic is required, take care to avoid exacerbating preexisting pulmonary hypertension. Patients with atrial septal defect are prone to supraventricular arrhythmias, which are poorly tolerated. Acute onset of supraventricular tachycardia in association with either hypotension or right ventricular failure should be managed with direct-current cardioversion or intravenous beta-blockade. In less-acute situations, patients should be digitalized.

VENTRICULAR SEPTAL DEFECT. Patients with a small ventricular septal defect, no evidence of pulmonary hypertension, and who are asymptomatic tolerate pregnancy well and require no intervention. Examine those with a large ventricular septal defect to exclude respiratory infection, pulmonary hypertension, bacterial endocarditis and left or right ventricular failure. Continuous lumbar epidural analgesia prevents marked increases in systemic vascular resistance due to pain. This technique is optimal for labor and vaginal delivery. Epidural anesthesia also is preferred for operative delivery. These patients do not tolerate increases in heart rate associated with endotracheal intubation. If using general anesthesia, we favor a balanced technique using narcotics and inhalation agents.

Marked increases in systemic vascular resistance may require low-dose vasodilator therapy with either sodium nitroprusside or phentolamine. To counteract the development of a right-to-left shunt and hypoxemia, treat significant decreases in systemic vascular resistance with small doses of vasopressor.

Either of two mechanisms may incite peripheral cyanosis. An increase in the left-to-right shunt (due to increased systemic vascular resistance) may cause pulmonary edema. Volume overload, however, is an uncommon cause of pulmonary edema in the adult. More likely, the increased right ventricular work load leads to right ventricular failure and, ultimately, biventricular failure and pulmonary edema with a low cardiac output. Alternatively, a rise in pulmonary vascular resistance or a fall in systemic vascular resistance may reverse interventricular flow (right-to-left shunt), increasing left ventricular output. Therefore, if the patient becomes hypotensive and cyanosed with signs of increased cardiac output (warm peripheries, full pulse), she should be managed with 100% oxygen, lightening of depth of anesthesia, and small doses of a vasopressor until the blood pressure increases and the shunt reverts to left-to-right. Cyanosis accompanied by low cardiac output (poor peripheral perfusion, decreased urine output, elevated central venous pressure) should be treated with 100% oxygen, inotropic support, and vasodilation.

PATENT DUCTUS ARTERIOSUS. This lesion is only serious if the patent ductus arteriosus is large and surgically uncorrected. Look for signs and symptoms of left or right ventricular failure, pulmonary hypertension, and shunt reversal. Treat asymptomatic patients with no evidence of ventricular dysfunction as normal. Use continuous epidural analgesia for labor and vaginal and operative delivery, but take care to avoid excessive reduction of systemic vascular resistance. When using general anesthesia, avoid increases or decreases in systemic vascular resistance and myocardial depressants.

Right-to-Left Shunt

TETRALOGY OF FALLOT. Uncorrected tetralogy is associated with high maternal and fetal mortality. Following surgical correction, only fetal mortality remains increased. For uncorrected women, the immediate postpartum period has the greatest risk of complications. Anesthesia should avoid decreases in systemic vascular resistance, blood volume, venous return, and myocardial depression. If possible, avoid epidural and spinal conduction blockade. However, epidural or spinal narcotics may be useful. Alternatively, use a low-dose intravenous infusion of narcotic. Manage any decline in systemic vascular resistance that exacerbates the right-to-left shunt with increased left lateral tilt and fluids. Vasopressors that increase pulmonary vascular resistance should be used judiciously.

General anesthesia is recommended for cesarean section. Maintain a slightly elevated central venous pressure. A narcotic-based technique avoids the myocardial depression caused by volatile agents. Patients with infundibular obstruction may decompensate in response to a fall in right ventricular filling, a faster heart rate, or depressed myocardial contractility. Increased peripheral cyanosis usually indicates right ventricular outflow obstruction with increased right-to-left shunt. Give 100% oxygen and fluids, deepen the anesthetic, and eliminate any tachycardia with beta blockade.

EISENMENGER'S SYNDROME. Maternal and fetal progress depend upon the severity of the pulmonary hypertension. Maternal mortality ranges between 12% and 33%. The right-to-left shunt may be at the atrial, ventricular, or aortopulmonary level. Increases in pulmonary vascular resistance must be avoided (see section on primary pulmonary hypertension). Oxygen may reduce the peripheral vascular resistance and the right-to-left shunt. Assess oxygen saturation both before and after oxygen therapy.

Decreases in systemic vascular resistance will result in marked increases in right-to-left shunt and must be avoided. Sympathetic blockade with local anesthetics is contraindicated; however, first-stage analgesia can be provided by neuraxial opioids. Pollack used 1.5 mg of subarachnoid morphine and carefully monitored for respiratory depression and apnea.[29] Pudendal block provided second-stage analgesia. Because of the high incidence of thromboembolism, some patients may require a low-dose (45 IU/h) intravenous infusion of heparin throughout labor, precluding use of an epidural catheter.

Monitoring should include electrocardiogram, Sao[2], and central venous pressure. Avoid decreases in central venous pressure by administering fluids. Give supplementary oxygen. The use of a pulmonary artery catheter is controversial. The high risk of arrythmias, thrombi, paradoxical emboli, pulmonary artery rupture, patent ductus arteriosus occlusion, and misleading data contraindicate its use. A fall in oxygen saturation equates with a rise in right-to-left shunt. In the presence of a patent ductus arteriosus, right hand and foot saturations can be used simultaneously to monitor the degree of shunt, because blood flow to the right arm is predominantly preductal.[29] Increases in heart rate and stroke volume elevate right ventricular oxygen consumption. Right ventricular failure should be treated with inotropic support.

Coarctation of the Aorta

Following surgical correction, maternal and fetal mortality and morbidity are not increased. Asymptomatic patients require no additional care. In uncorrected patients, avoid decreases in systemic vascular resistance, heart rate, and left ventricular filling. Epidural anesthesia also is not recommended because of the potential for bleeding into the epidural space secondary to enlarged collaterals. Neuraxial opioids can provide adequate analgesia and allow rapid detection of any compromise from an expanding hematoma. Alternatives include intravenous narcotic infusion or inhalation analgesia. For cesarean section, we recommend general anesthesia. Maintain heart rate, myocardial contractility, and vascular resistance. Manage maternal bradycardia by removing the precipitating cause and giving atropine or isoproterenol.

Congenital Aortic Stenosis

Anesthetic considerations are similar to those for acquired aortic stenosis.

Congenital Pulmonary Stenosis

Asymptomatic patients with little right ventricular dysfunction require no additional intervention. In other women, avoid changes in right ventricular filling pressure, decreased heart rate, decreased systemic vascular resistance, and myocardial depressants. Epidural analgesia with local anesthetic agents should be used cautiously. Neuraxial opioids, systemic narcotics, inhalation agents, and pudendal blocks can be used for labor and vaginal delivery. If using epidural local anesthetics, carefully monitor central venous pressure and maintain systemic vascular resistance with ephedrine. General anesthesia is recommended for cesarean section. Sustain vascular resistance, heart rate, and myocardial contractility. Withdraw volatile agents, and give inotropic support for any evidence of right ventricular failure.

HEMATOLOGIC DISEASE

Hematologic problems facing the obstetric anesthesiologist are most commonly those of anemia and coagulation defects. In the woman with anemia, one must understand the physiologic consequences of decreased oxygen delivery and the effects of her underlying disease. As the risks of transfusion are increasingly being recognized, blood must only be offered following careful consideration of the needs of the individual, rather than based solely on laboratory values.

Problems of coagulation usually involve the amount or function of platelets and clotting factors. The greatest, and yet unresolved, problem is that level at which regional anesthesia can be safely practiced. The purpose of this section is to try to provide some guidelines for the clinician faced with providing optimal anesthetic care for these complicated obstetric patients.

Anemia

Anemia, defined as a hemoglobin concentration less than 11.0 g/dL by the World Health Organization, is very common in pregnancy and may be acute or chronic. There is no set minimum hemoglobin concentration for labor, vaginal delivery, or cesarean section. The decision to transfuse must weigh the risks and benefits to both mother and fetus. Transfusion of blood and blood products carries a small but definite risk of disease transmission. One in 153,000 units transfused contain human immunodeficiency virus.[30] Seven percent to 10% of transfused patients will be in-fected with non-A, non-B viral hepatitis. Half these patients will develop chronic active hepatitis, and 10% to 20% will develop cirrhosis.[31] Recent development of a serologic assay (anti HCV) should diminish this risk.[32] In addition, nonhemolytic transfusion reactions can occur but vary in severity. Minor episodes often are not recognized.[33] Hemolytic transfusion reactions are very rare, varying between 1 in 4000 and 15,000.[34] Finally, the incidence of ABO incompatibility varies from 1 in 5000 recipients[35] to 1 in 22,000.*

Factors to consider before transfusion include the following:

- Duration and degree of anemia
- Extent of surgery
- Probability of blood loss
- Presence of underlying cardiorespiratory disease

Symptoms of the latter may be confused with those of a normal pregnancy. Clinically, chronic anemia is well tolerated up to a 50% reduction in red blood cell mass in the absence of any complicating factors.[36,37] These patients sustain tissue oxygen delivery by increasing cardiac output and decreasing peripheral resistance because of increased sympathetic activity. We would not transfuse patients with a hemoglobin concentration greater than 8.0 g/dL without cardiorespiratory symptoms. This hemoglobin concentration easily provides the oxygen needs of the body.[38] If blood loss is below 500 mL, these patients are at little perioperative risk.[39] There is no link between anemia and postoperative infection, bleeding, or delayed wound healing.[40] Preeclamptic parturients, in whom oxygen dissociation curves shift to the left,[41] may require higher hemoglobin concentrations to maintain oxygen delivery to the tissues.

During anesthesia, always maintain plasma volume. Regional anesthesia is associated with sympathetic blockade and vasodilation. Epidural block, with a more gradual onset of sympathetic blockade than spinal anesthesia, allows easier control of blood pressure with fluids and vasopressors. For general anesthesia, chronically anemic dogs (mean hemoglobin of 3.4) tolerate halothane anesthesia.[42] Isoflurane, which is associated with less myocardial depression, may be a better choice. Monitor both end-tidal carbon dioxide, to prevent respiratory alkalosis, and temperature, to avoid hypothermia.

Data from University of Natal during a 2-year period involving almost 400,000 transfusions.

Postoperative management includes oxygen and prevention of shivering (increase in oxygen consumption by 35%–40%).[43] Also, follow hemoglobin concentration after surgery. Provided that adequate volume replacement is undertaken, very low values of hemoglobin can be tolerated.[44]

Sickle Cell Disease

Homozygous sickle cell anemia has an incidence of 0.3% to 1.0% in blacks in the United States. These severely symptomatic patients have more than 70% hemoglobin S.[45] Sickle cell hemoglobin C disease (HbSC) and sickle thalassemia (β Thal) are both heterozygous diseases and may present with severe symptoms. In sickle cell trait, the heterozygous manifestation (HbAS), erythrocytes contain 20% to 40% HbS, with the remainder being HbA. Ten percent of blacks in the United States carry sickle cell trait. Most of these individuals are asymptomatic.[45] Rarely, sickle cell trait patients have more than 50% HbS. These people are then designated HbSA.[46]

In pregnancy, the most common maternal complication is vasoocclusive sickle cell crisis (VSCC), which occurs most commonly in HbSS.[47] The symptoms of VSCC often mimic other obstetric or medical problems. In one third of cases, infection also is present. Management of VSCC is supportive and symptomatic. Intravenous fluids correct dehydration and reduce viscosity. Avoid central venous and urinary catheters to reduce the risk of infection. Use systemic opioids, if necessary. Partial exchange transfusions are the most important therapeutic maneuver.[47] Automated erythrocytapheresis using a cell separator is quicker than manual methods and allows the return of the patient's plasma, platelets, and leukocytes. Leukocyte-poor, washed red blood cells that are less than 5 days old should be used to achieve an HbA greater than 40%.

Hematologic crises are rare in pregnancy. At-risk patients should be screened, and, if positive, hemoglobin electrophoresis should be performed to identify the hemoglobins.

Although many patients with HbS will be anemic, oxygen delivery by HbS remains efficient owing to a right-shifted dissociation curve. Symptomatic anemic patients require transfusion and, if time allows, preoperative exchange transfusion with continuous-flow erythrocytapheresis.[48] Patients also should be examined for cor pulmonale secondary to repeated pulmonary emboli, an increased A–ao$_2$ gradient, decreased vital capacity, and renal damage.

Patients with sickle cell trait also may sickle if stressed.[49–51] Hypoxia, cold, acidosis, and dehydration all may precipitate sickling. Rigorously avoid these stresses in both homozygous and heterozygous parturients. Regional analgesia and anesthesia, although not contraindicated, are not recommended during a vaso-occlusive sickle cell crisis.[47] However, one report describes a good outcome using epidural analgesia for labor pain in a patient in crisis.[52] Choice of anesthetic technique is less important than avoidance of precipitating factors.[53,54] Details to attend to include the following:

- A warm operating suite (or labor room)
- Warming blanket
- Humidified inspired gases
- Avoidance of hypoventilation
- Measurement of arterial blood gases for evidence of metabolic acidosis.[55]

Wrap the legs in elasticized bandages to reduce stasis in the lower extremities.[56] Use lateral tilt and avoid aortocaval compression because massive sickling can occur in the lower limbs, even in those with sickle cell trait.[50] Monitor lower limb oxygen saturation with a pulse oximeter on the foot. Use the plethysmographic trace and the percentage saturation to monitor peripheral perfusion, and assess the adequacy of uterine displacement.

We recommend epidural blockade, with careful attention to proper preloading and gradual onset of sensory blockade for these women. We avoid spinal anesthesia because of the risks of sudden, marked hypotension and the subsequent need for vasopressors. Treat hypotension during regional anesthesia with fluids, not vasopressors. If a vasopressor is essential, use ephedrine instead of phenylephrine.

Complications can continue to arise postoperatively. Pay persistent attention to a warm environment, fluid intake, oxygen, and analgesia. Epidural opioid analgesia, with careful monitoring for respiratory depression, is ideal. Encourage early mobilization and vigorous chest physiotherapy.

Thalassemia

A reduced or absent synthesis of structurally normal hemoglobin characterizes thalassemia.[45] Two linked genes on chromosome 16 control alpha-chain production. The normal genotype is written as αα/αα. The most severe form of alpha-thalassemia is Bart's hemoglobinopathy (—/—), or homozygous alpha-thalassemia. This disease is incompatible with life. Hemoglobin H occurs with three deleted genes (-α/—), alpha-thal minor (α°-thal) with 2, and α⁺-thal with a single gene deletion. Mothers carrying infants with Bart's hemoglobinopathy have an increased incidence of anemia, pregnancy-induced hypertension, antepartum and postpartum hemorrhage, and retained placenta.[57] The major consideration in parturients with alpha-thalassemia is the degree of anemia.[58] Hgb-H has a high oxygen affinity, reducing oxygen delivery to the tissues.

Beta-thalassemia is due to a relative or absolute lack of formation of the beta-globulin chains of hemoglobin. As a result, normal adult hemoglobin is not formed. Beta-thalassemia is categorized as minor, intermedia, or major (Cooley's anemia). Patients with beta-thalassemia intermedia may have increased hemolysis. If hemolysis induces significant anemia, these women may need preoperative transfusion. Patients with thalassemia major will have severe anemia, and the frequent transfusions will result in tissue hemosiderosis.[59,60]

Thalassemia minor and intermedia do not present many peripartum anesthetic problems.[61] Women with thalassemia major rarely become pregnant. If they do, they may require up to 6 L of washed packed cells during the antenatal period to maintain an adequate hemoglobin.[59] Some experts advocate "supertransfusion" with young red cells (neocytes) for these women.[62] Women with hemosiderosis may have significant hepatic damage and lack clotting factors. Splenomegaly may lead to increased hemolysis and thrombocytopenia.[45]

With severe beta-thalassemia and chronic iron overload, cardiac hemosiderosis leads to left ventricular mechanical dysfunction and, eventually, arrhythmias.[63] Use cardiac glycosides carefully. Sensitivity to their effects relates to the degree of cardiac dysfunction. Evaluate cardiac function with electrocardiogram and echocardiography.

Examine the airway closely. Maxillary overgrowth secondary to extramedullary erythropoiesis can make visualization of the glottis difficult.

During labor, correct severe anemia early. Monitor volume status carefully. Women with severe left ventricular dysfunction will need a pulmonary artery catheter. For pain relief, we advocate continuous-infusion epidural analgesia. Induce blockade slowly. Pay careful attention to fluids and blood pressure. Treat hypotension with phenylephrine, 20 to 40 μg, intravenously. This drug corrects hypotension more readily than ephedrine without increasing the heart rate. For cesarean section, we prefer epidural anesthesia. Provide postoperative analgesia with epidural opiates. We avoid spinal anesthesia because these patients with potentially significant myocardial compromise may not tolerate the acute hemodynamic changes associated with this technique. In the presence of severe cardiac compromise with pulmonary edema, thrombocytopenia, or skeletal abnormalities that may make the epidural block technically difficult, we choose general anesthesia.

Aplastic Anemia

Patients presenting with profound pancytopenia in pregnancy have a high mortality (33%) and a poor prognosis.[64] Others, with less cell depression, recover between pregnancies. Women with only red cell aplasia usually revert to normal postpartum. Early pregnancy termination is controversial.[64–66] Steroids often are used. Treatment with antilymphocyte globulin also has been reported.[65] At term, transfuse the symptomatic, severely anemic parturient. If the platelet count is adequate, major conduction anesthesia is safe. Avoid unnecessary urinary and central venous catheters because of risk of infection. For cesarean section, we prefer epidural or spinal to general anesthesia. For the latter, meticulous attention is necessary to prevent infection. Avoid trauma by using well-lubricated endotracheal tubes. Continue steroids and give prophylactic antibiotics.

Hemolytic Anemia

Patients with hereditary spherocytosis and hereditary elliptocytosis usually have a mild anemia.[45] In patients with glucose-6 phosphate dehydrogenase deficiency, drugs such as aspirin, penicillin, sulfonamides, antimalarials, vitamin K, and methylene blue can induce intravascular hemolysis.[45] This hemolysis primarily affects only older red cells, limiting its severity. Treatment is supportive, but blood transfusion may be required and maintenance of good urine output is essential.

Hematologic Malignancies

Although neoplasms do not directly interfere with pregnancy, indirect effects may be important. A comparison of pregnancy outcome in a group of 56 pregnancies in 48 women with leukemia or lymphoma revealed a similar incidence of complications, term pregnancies, spontaneous abortions, and premature births to healthy pregnancies. Cytostatic treatment should not be postponed because of pregnancy, but antifolic or alkylating agents and radiotherapy should be avoided.[67]

Obtain a full history of disease including current mediation. Measure hemoglobin and hematocrit platelets, blood urea nitrogen electrolytes, and clotting factors. Consider a bleeding time, if suggested by a low platelet count. If coagulation status is satisfactory, use regional anesthesia for labor and cesarean section.

Fanconi's Anemia

Pregnancy is rare and usually happens only in women with mild disease.[68] Regional analgesia is contraindicated owing to thrombocytopenia. Platelet transfusion is usually required at delivery. These patients have an increased incidence of hypertensive disorders. Significant bleeding, very low platelet counts, and the need for blood and platelet transfusion may complicate the postoperative course.[69]

COAGULATION DISORDERS

Anesthetic Alternatives

If regional anesthesia is contraindicated because of coagulopathy, alternate methods of labor analgesia are required.[70] Psychoprophylaxis,[71] transcutaneous electrical nerve stimulation,[72] and systemic opioids all have a role (see Chaps. 15 and 16). Intramuscular meperidine has been the most frequently used opiate. Unfortunately, this drug carries a high incidence of side effects (nausea, vomiting, drowsiness, and potential for neonatal respiratory depression). Fentanyl given intravenously in doses of 50 or 100 μg/h is effective and safe to mother and infant.[73] Patient-controlled analgesia with fentanyl also has been reported.[74] Intermittent inhalation of 50% nitrous oxide in oxygen is useful in the first stage of labor. Low-dose ketamine (0.2–0.4 mg/kg IV) provides some analgesia for vaginal delivery with no significant maternal or newborn complications.[75] Local infiltration of perineum with local anesthetics is safe in the presence of coagulopathy. Pudendal nerve block should be avoided because the artery and vein are too close to the site of injection.

Vascular Purpuras

Systemic Lupus Erythematosus

Thrombocytopenia may be present in up to one third of patients with systemic lupus erythematosus (SLE); however, platelet count is rarely less than $100,000/mm^3$.[76] Vasculitis may lead to purpurae. Circulating lupus anticoagulant occurs in 5% to 37% of affected women. Still, half the patients with lupus anticoagulant do not have SLE. The presence of anticoagulant increases the risk of maternal thrombosis and fetal wastage.[77] Some experts doubt that either lupus anticoagulant or IgG anticardiolipins are risk factors for fetal loss.[78] Lupus anticoagulant is associated with a prolonged activated partial thromboplastia time (aPTT); rarely, a prolonged prothrombin time (PT); and, paradoxically, thrombosis in 28% of cases.[79] Antepartum treatment with low-dose aspirin and prednisone shortens the aPTT and reduces the rate of pregnancy loss.[80] Either heparin or coumarin prevent further episodes of venous thrombosis.[81]

Avoid regional anesthesia in anticoagulated patients. In patients with lupus anticoagulant, balance the risks of regional block against those of a general anesthetic.[82]

Henoch–Schonlein Purpura

Despite purpura, PT, aPTT, platelets, and bleeding time are often normal, and regional anesthesia is not contraindicated.[83]

Platelet Disorders

Idiopathic Thrombocytopenic Purpura

Idiopathic thrombocytopenic purpura (ITP), characterized by the presence of an IgG antibody directed against the platelet, decreases platelet survival to less than 10% of normal.[84] In some women, ITP may be an incidental finding, with a platelet count less than $150,000/mm^3$. These patients have no symptoms but have shortened platelet survival and increased platelet turnover by the marrow. In the antenatal period, patients with milder forms (platelets $>50,000/mm^3$) are either monitored or started on prednisone, 20 mg/d. In severe disease, prednisone, 1 mg/kg, is tried initially, and then splenectomy may be considered if steroids fail.[85] High-dose intravenous immunoglobulin, by blocking macrophage-related platelet destruction, raises platelet counts for a few weeks only. This therapy may have a place in the preparation of patients for splenectomy or cesarean section.[86]

As IgG crosses the placenta, the fetus also may be affected. Infants with low platelet counts are at high risk of intracranial hemorrhage if delivered vaginally. Not all infants are affected, however, and routine cesarean delivery would needlessly induce excess morbidity in many mothers and infants. Therefore, the obstetrician attempts to determine which infants are at risk of thrombocytopenia before delivery.

Maternal platelet count, steroid therapy, or previous splenectomy are of no use in predicting neonatal thrombocytopenia. The place of maternal bound or unbound IgG in the prediction of neonatal thrombocytopenia is uncertain.[85,87,88] The only reliable predictor is a fetal platelet count, which can be obtained from a percutaneous umbilical blood sample before labor (see Chap. 8) or a scalp sample early in labor.[88] Low fetal platelet count is an indication for cesarean section.

Even if disease is mild (platelet count > 100,000/mm³) and the patient lacks symptoms, a modified Ivy bleeding time should be performed. Occasionally, patients with platelet-associated antibody may present with a qualitative defect.[84] If the bleeding time is less than 10 minutes, regional anesthesia is safe. If platelet count is 50 to 100,000/mm³, check the bleeding time. Megathrombocytes, a feature of ITP, are more efficient, and bleeding time may be normal. Again, if the bleeding time is less than 10 minutes, regional anesthesia is probably safe. We avoid regional block if the platelet count is less than 50,000/mm³ or the bleeding time is greater than 10 minutes. [Editor's Note: I have safely used spinal anesthesia in asymptomatic women with fewer than 50,000 platelets/mm³ and a bleeding time less than 10 minutes.] Thromboelastography may have a place in the assessment of the overall clotting status (Fig. 25-1). Platelet transfusion to cover regional techniques is not recommended, because the life span of the transfused platelet is indeterminable and may be very short.

General anesthesia, especially intubation, also requires care. At cesarean section, give platelets if the count is less than 50,000/mm³. If the count is more than 50,000/mm³, have platelets available and transfuse if clinically indicated at time of surgery. Transfusion of platelets present an increased risk of disease transmission because they are pooled from six to eight donors.

Postoperatively, patients should be nursed in a high-care area and watched carefully. They may bleed or develop respiratory obstruction secondary to airway trauma following intubation. Neonatal platelet counts

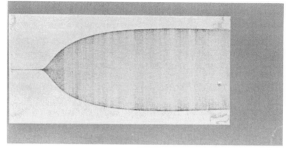

Figure 25–1. Thromboelastogram from an 18-year-old parturient with idiopathic thrombocytopenic purpura in early labor. Platelet count is 53,000/mm³, bleeding time is 13 minutes, time to initial fibrin formation is 8 minutes, time of rapid fibrin buildup and cross-linking is 5 minutes, maximum clot strength is 44 mm. The maximum clot strength is reduced compared to normal pregnancy values (see Fig. 25-4).

should be done daily for at least 7 days, because they may fall over the first week of life to less than 50,000/mm³.

Thrombotic Thrombocytopenic Purpura

Thrombotic thrombocytopenia purpura (TTP) is a rare severe disease characterized by thrombocytopenia, microangiopathic hemolytic anemia, transient neurologic abnormalities, fever, and renal failure.[89,90] Diffuse intravascular thrombosis occludes capillaries and arterioles throughout the body. Prognosis of TTP in pregnancy is poor for mother and fetus. Unlike ITP, damage to maternal organs and placenta indirectly injures the fetus. In the acute phase, plasma infusion or plasma-exchange therapy results in improvement in 90% of cases. This treatment may enhance maternal and fetal survival.[89,91] Platelet transfusions may exacerbate maternal symptoms.[92]

Steroids, aspirin, and dipyridamole are commonly used in the treatment of TTP. High-dose intravenous gamma globulin therapy may raise platelet counts and should be started 10 to 15 days before delivery.[76]

Measure hemoglobin and hematocrit, platelets, bleeding time, blood urea nitrogen, and electrolytes, and perform liver function tests. Transfuse blood only for severe, symptomatic anemia. Note patient's medication, especially antiplatelet drugs, and stop these 7 days before delivery. If bleeding time is normal and platelet count is greater than 100,000/mm³, regional anesthesia can be used for labor or cesarean section; otherwise, use systemic opioids or general anesthesia. In the face of a bleeding diathesis or a falling platelet count, give fresh frozen plasma and consider exchange transfusion. Intraoperatively, maintain adequate volume status and good urine output, and avoid anemia and hypotension. Postoperatively, nurse in an intensive care unit.

Postpartum Hemolytic Uremic Syndrome

This syndrome resembles TTP, but it is characterized by acute renal failure associated with microangiopathic hemolytic anemia. It is not uncommon to find a platelet count greater than 100,000/mm³. However, in all well-documented cases with hemolysis, there is severe thrombocytopenia and markedly shortened platelet survival time. Other clotting tests are normal. Diagnosis is made postpartum in 94% of cases. Mean symptom-free interval is 27 to 35 days. The mortality rate exceeds 50%.[91] Treatment is as for TTP in combination with dialysis.

Incidental Thrombocytopenia

The incidence of thrombocytopenia (platelet count < 150,000/mm³) in term parturients is 7.6%. Sixty-five percent of these women are otherwise normal.[93] In another series of 1621 healthy parturients, 6.4% had platelet counts less than 150,000/mm³.[94] The lower limit for safe practice of regional anesthesia remains unknown. Uneventful epidural anesthesia followed by vacuum-assisted vaginal delivery has been reported in a patient with a platelet count of 2000 to 4000/mm³.[95] Another large retrospective study identified 24 patients with platelet counts less than 100,000/mm³. Four of the seven patients without an obvious cause and 10 of the 17 patients with thrombocytopenia associated with a medical or obstetric problem underwent uncomplicated regional anesthesia.[96]

Rolbin *et al*[94] reported the outcome of more than 50,000 regional anesthetics over 18 years. They did not measure the platelet count, but they estimated that more than 300 women had platelet counts less than 100000/mm³. They saw no cases of spinal or epidural hematoma.[94] Sixty-one thrombocytopenic parturients (33 with platelet counts of 50,000–99,000/mm³ and 58 with 100,000–150,000/mm³ platelets) underwent epidural analgesia without neurologic complications.[94] Our management of the normal gravida is outlined in Figure 25-2.

Drug-Induced Platelet Disorders

A full drug history is essential before any anesthetic intervention in a patient with a low platelet count or bleeding tendency.

THROMBOCYTOPENIA. Many drugs can induce thrombocytopenia. The most common pathway is through the formation of an immune complex. This mechanism often involves IgG, which can cross the placenta and affect the fetus. Generalized bone marrow depression (*e.g.,* chloramphenicol) or a selective effect involving only the megakaryocytes (*e.g.,* thiazides, tolbutamide) may occur.

THROMBOPATHY. Many commonly used drugs can inhibit platelet life span and function. A comprehensive review is available.[97] Aspirin and other nonsteroidal anti-inflammatory drugs impair platelet aggregation. They inhibit the formation of thromboxane by binding irreversibly with cyclo-oxygenase. Dipyridamole inhibits primary aggregation.[98] Penicillin, in high doses, but more commonly ticarcillin and carbenicillin, epsilon aminocaproic acid, in high doses, and ethanol can interfere with platelet function.[99] Heparin-associated thrombocytopenia occurs in 5% of patients on heparin therapy. This problem usually arises after 6 to 12 days.[100] Diazepam, chlordiazepoxide, propranolol, and phentolamine also may decrease platelet function. Phenothiazines may alter platelet numbers and function.[83] Ticlodipine prolongs the bleeding time and reduces platelet aggregation.[101] After stopping the offending drug, platelets should recover within 1 to 2 weeks. Recovery may take longer if the marrow was depressed.

Aspirin poses a particular problem for the obstetric anesthesiologist. Low-dose aspirin reduces the incidence of pregnancy-induced hypertension in high-risk patients.[102] A single dose of aspirin prolongs the bleeding time for 48 to 72 hours. Platelet aggregation may be affected for longer.[103] The risk of epidural hematoma following regional anesthesia in patients on aspirin is unknown. The incidence of paraplegia following extradural analgesia is less than 1: 10,000.[104] An important risk factor for developing this complication is extradural bleeding and hematoma formation.[105] A retrospective review of 1013 spinal or epidural anesthetics for orthopedic procedures revealed that, although 39% of patients were on antiplatelet medications, none developed a spinal hematoma.[106] Benzon[107] reported 239 epidural and 7 spinal anesthetics in patients receiving aspirin without neurologic complications. The risk of vessel damage during insertion of an epidural catheter in the parturient is higher than the 12% incidence reported in surgical patients.[108] When using either 16- or 18-gauge Tuohy needles, 18% of parturients had detectable bleeding.[109] Some experts rely heavily on the bleeding time in this situa-

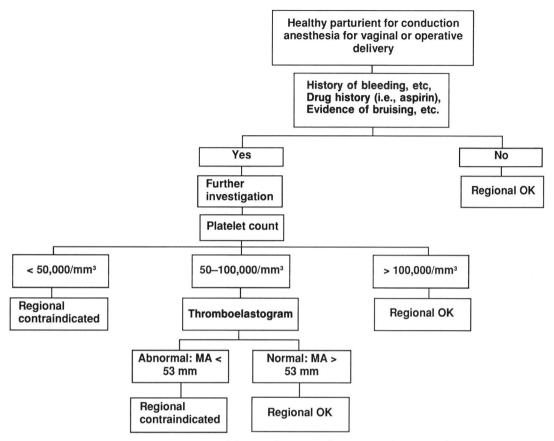

Figure 25–2. Assessment of the normal parturient for major conduction anesthesia.

tion. They advocate having a bleeding time kit available in all clinical areas where conduction anesthetics may be done.[104] We measure the template bleeding time (Simplate II) in any pregnant patient who has taken aspirin within the last 72 hours (Fig. 25-3). [Editor's Note: I do not measure bleeding time in patients taking low-dose aspirin during pregnancy.]*

PREECLAMPSIA AND ECLAMPSIA. Thrombocytopenia, probably due to increased platelet consumption,[110] commonly complicates preeclampsia. Thirty-four percent of parturients with this diagnosis

have fewer than 150,000 platelets/mm^3,[111] and 7.5% have platelet counts less than 100,000/mm^3.[112] Also, a platelet function defect may occur despite adequate platelet count. Prolonged bleeding time (modified Ivy) may be present in 34% of patients with severe and 13% of patients with mild disease, with platelet counts greater than 100,000/mm^3.[112] A 25% incidence of prolonged bleeding time has been reported with platelet counts greater than 150000/mm^3.[111] Using the Duke method, Schindler *et al*[113] found no prolonged bleeding times with platelet counts greater than 100,000/mm^3.[113] The Duke method is less sensitive than the modified Ivy methods.[114] This difference may account for some discrepancies in the literature.

In preeclampsia, thrombin time has been reported to be prolonged in 50% to 97%, prothrombin time prolonged in 4% to 13%, and partial thromboplastin time either prolonged in 37% or shortened in 25% of cases.[115] However, a recent retrospective review found coagulation abnormalities only in severe preeclampsia.

The authors have also abandoned use of the bleeding time in patients receiving aspirin, following a study of the thromboelastogram in pregnant patients receiving aspirin. (Orlikowski CEP, Payne AJ, Moodly J, Rocke DA. Thromboelastography following aspirin ingestion in pregnant and non-pregnant subjects. Br J Anaesth [in press]).

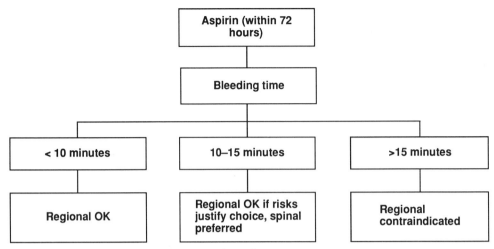

Figure 25–3. Regional anesthesia in parturients on aspirin.

The coagulation abnormality was always associated with reduced platelet count.[116] A similar study confirmed that no preeclamptic patient with platelet count greater than 150000/mm³ had abnormal coagulation.[117]

A unique group of preeclamptic patients may present with the associated findings of hemolysis, elevated liver enzymes, and low platelets (HELLP syndrome).[118] This syndrome is associated with poor maternal and perinatal outcome.[119] Although hypertension is not always severe,[120] regional anesthesia has many advantages for mother and fetus in this condition.[121]

Regional Anesthesia in the Presence of Coagulopathy or Platelet Dysfunction

Regional anesthesia is contraindicated in the presence of thrombocytopenia or coagulopathy as manifested by prolonged laboratory tests of coagulation (*e.g.,* PT, aPTT). A major controversy is the assessment of the risks of regional anesthesia in the presence of a platelet dysfunction. In practice, this issue most commonly arises in association with preeclampsia or aspirin therapy. At present, there is no single, reliable, rapid monitor of platelet dysfunction that also can predict risk of bleeding. Our measures are limited to the history, examination, platelet aggregation tests, bleeding time, and thromboelastograph.

History

Take a thorough history to determine if any bleeding problems are present in the patient or her family. Pay particular attention to medications taken within the last 10 days. Stop any antiplatelet medications at least 1 week before delivery and attempt to postpone the procedure.[104]

Examination

Look for any signs of bruising, bleeding from mucous membranes, or venipuncture sites.

Platelet Aggregation Tests

Platelets of women with preeclampsia are less responsive to collagen and vasopressin.[122] Aspirin therapy impairs platelet aggregation in response to adenosine diphosphate.[123] However, platelet aggregation studies take several hours to perform, are expensive, and are only available in the larger centers. Their ability to predict increased risk of bleeding is unknown.[124]

Bleeding Time

The bleeding time, which is measured by pricking the earlobe[125] and has been modified by using a sphygmomanometer to elevate capillary pressure,[126] a template device to standardize depth of the incision,[127] and development of disposable devices,[128] is still a controversial investigation. A very extensive review of the bleeding time concluded that it is not a specific in vivo indicator of platelet function. In addition, there is no evidence that the bleeding time can predict the risk of hemorrhage.[129] Also, the degree of bleeding from the skin may not accurately reflect the risk of bleeding elsewhere in the body. In a group of volunteers and patients on aspirin, prolongation of the bleeding time did

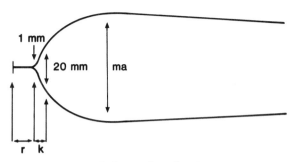

Normal thromboelastogram

Figure 25–4. Normal thromboelastogram tracing showing the measurement of r, k, and ma. In the term parturient, normal mean (± SD) values include r = 7.6 ± 0.9 minutes; k = 3.4 ± 0.7 minutes; and ma = 59.7 ± 3.5 minutes.

not correlate with any increase in mean gastric bleeding time following biopsy at gastroscopy.[130] Others also have expressed qualms about the bleeding time.[131,132] [Editor's Note: I have abandoned the bleeding time altogether. I rely on history and physical examination to decide if a parturient at risk for platelet dysfunction can have a regional anesthetic.]

Thromboelastograph

Unlike laboratory tests of coagulation, the thromboelastograph examines whole blood coagulation and the interaction of the protein coagulation cascade, fibrinogen, and the platelet surface, as a whole.[133] Only loose correlations exist between standard coagulation tests and various thromboelastograph parameters as they measure different processes.[134,135]

Recently, we have begun to use the thromboelastograph in parturients. The following variables are useful:

- **r** (time to initial fibrin formation)
- **k** (time reflecting period of rapid fibrin build-up and cross-linking)

- **ma** (measure of maximum clot strength and dependent on fibrinogen level, platelet numbers, and function) (Fig. 25-4)

During normal pregnancy, the thromboelastograph trace becomes hypercoagulable (Table 25-1, Fig. 25-5).

Our initial observations in severe preeclampsia found no correlation between the ma and the bleeding time. The ma correlates more closely with the platelet count with platelets less than 150,000/mm³ than does the bleeding time. We have observed normal thromboelastograph tracings with prolonged bleeding time (Fig. 25-6) and have also documented an abnormal thromboelastograph despite normal bleeding time in a patient with a platelet count of 30,000/mm³ (Fig. 25-7). Figure 25-8 shows the improvement in the thromboelastograph following platelet transfusion.

Aspirin does not alter the thromboelastograph in healthy volunteers.[136] We have measured the thromboelastograph 17 times in nine pregnant (> 18 wk) patients taking aspirin, 75 mg daily, and compared our results to a control group of 41 normal healthy antenatal patients (Table 25-2).[137]

From these initial results, we conclude that the thromboelastograph is not as sensitive as the bleeding time in detecting the platelet dysfunction of aspirin or preeclampsia. However, the thromboelastograph provides a global view of coagulation that may more closely reflect the clinical response to bleeding. Further work is necessary to establish whether or not the thromboelastograph is a useful predictor of risk of bleeding.

Clinical Guidelines

We attempt to balance risks in individual cases. Patients with mild pregnancy-induced hypertension are not at increased risk of bleeding. No neurologic sequelae were seen in 156 patients with mild disease following epidural anesthesia.[138] In our practice, we rely on history, physical examination, severity of dis-

Table 25–1

Thromboelastographic Parameters (r, k, ma) at Different Stages of Pregnancy*

	R (MIN)	K (MIN)	MA (MM)
Nonpregnant	6–12	3–6	40–60
First trimester (n = 25)	7.8 ± 0.9	3.6 ± 0.8	56.1 ± 3.9
Second trimester (n = 28)	7.4 ± 1.4	3.3 ± 0.5	58.1 ± 4.1
Third trimester (n = 23)	7.8 ± 0.9	3.2 ± 0.7	59.7 ± 3.5

*Data are mean ± SD.

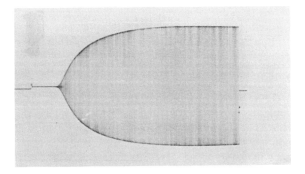

Figure 25–5. Hypercoagulable thromboelastogram tracing from a healthy third-trimester parturient (r = 6 min, k = 3 min, ma = 64 mm).

ease, and, despite its limitations, bleeding time (Figs. 25-3 and 25-9). Thromboelastography is being increasingly used in our institution in an attempt to establish the coagulation status more accurately.

Other principles include the following:

- Spinal instead of epidural block
- The left lateral position (less epidural vein distention)
- The midline approach (less risk of vessel puncture)
- An experienced operator

Although some anesthesiologists consider bleeding at the time of catheter insertion an indication for abandoning the procedure, there is no evidence to support this practice.[139] We use low-dose bupivacaine infusions in labor in combination with fentanyl. Dense motor block secondary to cord compression will be more likely to be noticed. Use only opiates via the extradural route in the postoperative period and actively watch for symptoms or signs of cord compression.

Primary Thrombocythemia

This disease is a rare myeloproliferative disorder with elevated platelet counts and increased marrow megakaryocytes.[140,141] Symptoms may relate to either thrombosis or hemorrhage. Platelet aggregation studies, bleeding time, and clinical symptoms do not correlate.[142] Treatment may include aspirin, low-dose subcutaneous heparin, plateletpheresis, and, rarely, antiproliferative drugs (*i.e.,* busulfan). Regional anesthetics are contraindicated, and antithrombotic therapy should be continued.

CLOTTING DISORDERS

von Willebrand's Disease

Von Willebrand's disease is a disorder of the von Willebrand factor portion of the factor VIII complex. This complex consists of factor VIII:C, linked by noncovalent bonds to the larger von Willebrand factor molecule. Von Willebrand factor is responsible for platelet adhesion to exposed collagen in injured vessels. The most sensitive test for von Willebrand's disease is ristocetin cofactor assay, which measures the ability of plasma to agglutinate normal platelets in the presence of ristocetin.[143] Type 1 (80% of cases) is usually mild and is characterized by a prolonged bleeding time, low levels of factor VIII:C, von Willebrand factor, and ristocetin cofactor.[144] Type 2 involves a dysfunctional von Willebrand factor.

Von Willebrand factor and factor VIII:C increase during normal pregnancy.[145] Rises in von Willebrand factor depend on the severity of the disease. Bleeding time often may stay prolonged.[146] Preoperative evaluation should include hemoglobin/hematocrit, PT, aPTT, bleeding time, and, if possible, factor VIII:C, von Willebrand factor, and ristocetin cofactor activity.

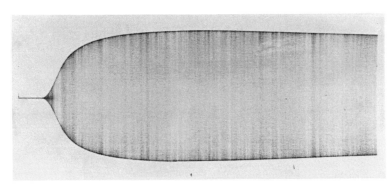

Figure 25–6. Thromboelastogram of a patient with severe preeclampsia. Platelet count was 219,000/mm³, and bleeding time was 13 minutes. This thromboelastogram is normal for pregnancy.

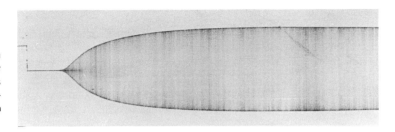

Figure 25–7. Thromboelastogram from a patient with severe preeclampsia. Platelet count was 30,000/mm³, and bleeding time was 7 minutes. On thromboelastogram the ma is reduced to 43 mm. Other thromboelastogram measurements are r (7.0 min) and k (6.0 min).

Anesthetic management is guided by the preceding results. Regional anesthesia is safe in mild type 1 disease with a normal bleeding time.[147] Predictors of bleeding include factor VIII:C activity, ristocetin cofactor activity (< 50%), and prolonged bleeding time.[144,148] Commercial preparations of factor VIII concentrates remove ristocetin cofactor activity.[143] These preparations, then, have no use in the management of women with von Willebrand's disease. Factor VIII:C and von Willebrand factor levels fall after delivery, and bleeding may occur. Arginine vasopressin, by releasing von Willebrand factor from endothelial cells, may then be useful.[144]

made by history, prolonged aPTT, normal PT and low factor VIII:C activity.

Regional anesthesia is contraindicated.[86] Thirty percent of factor VIII activity is generally sufficient for hemostasis. Should bleeding occur, factor VIII levels must be increased to 80% to 100% for 3 to 5 days and maintained at 30% to 40% for an additional 10 to 14 days.[146] Cryoprecipitate (100 units of factor VIII:C/bag), Factor VIII concentrate (200–400 units of factor VIII:C/vial) or fresh frozen plasma (100–200 units of factor VIII:C/200–250 mL plasma) can be used.[86] Postoperatively, factor VIII:C levels will fall, and close monitoring is needed. DDAVP infusion may be useful if bleeding occurs at this time.

Hemophilia A
(Classical Hemophilia)

Hemophilia A is usually only a carrier state in women, but homozygous hemophilia rarely occurs. Factor VIII:C activity increases in pregnancy.[145] Diagnosis is

Hemophilia B
(Christmas Disease)

This condition is diagnosed by low factor IX and prolonged aPTT in the presence of normal factor VIII activity. Manage as for hemophilia A.

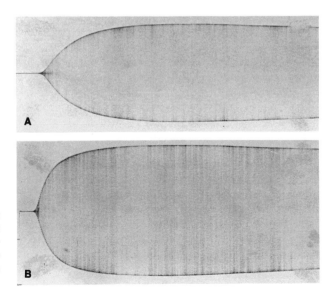

Figure 25–8. (A) An 18-year-old parturient with eclampsia. Platelet count was 59,000/mm³, the r was 7.0 minutes, k was 4.0 minutes, and ma was 49 mm. (B) Same patient following transfusion of 10 units of platelets. The thromboelastogram has improved. (r = 4.0 min, k = 2.0 min and ma = 66 mm.)

Table 25–2

The Effects of Aspirin, 75 mg/day, on Thromboelastographic Parameters (r, k, ma) in Parturients*

	R (MIN)	K (MIN)	MA (MM)
Control (n = 41)	7.6 ± 1.1	3.2 ± 0.6	59.6 ± 3.5
Post-aspirin (n = 17)	7.7 ± 1.7	2.9 ± 0.8	60.6 ± 3.5

*Data are mean ± SD. There are no significant differences between the two groups.

Factor VII deficiency

A prolonged PT with a normal aPTT makes the diagnosis. Pregnancy will elevate factor VII to a variable degree. Correct any deficiency with fresh frozen plasma.[149]

Factor XI deficiency

This problem occasionally is encountered in pregnancy as a mild defect. Treat with fresh frozen plasma, if necessary.[86]

Fibrinogen

Congenital abnormalities of fibrinogen include afibrinogenemia, dysfibrinogenemia, and hypofibrinogenemia.[150] Dysfibrinogenemia is less severe, and many patients are asymptomatic. Only 7 of 83 reported cases were complicated by mild to moderate bleeding.[151] Management depends on the degree of fibrinogen depletion. If bleeding is a problem or if levels are very low, give cryoprecipitate[152] or fresh frozen plasma. The PT and aPTT may be normal, with low concentrations of fibrinogen, but thrombin and reptilase times will be prolonged.[150]

Antithrombin III Deficiency

Antithrombin III (AT III) is the major inhibitor of thrombin Xa and other serine proteases. Deficiency of AT III is associated with a high risk of venous thrombosis (40% to 70%) and pulmonary embolism. Risk of these complications are markedly increased in pregnancy.[146] Measuring low plasma AT III activity makes the diagnosis.

Heparin therapy will lower the risk of thrombosis. High doses may be required because AT III levels are low. (Heparin exerts its anticoagulant effect by binding and activating AT III.) Try to prolong the aPTT by 5 to 10 seconds. Before delivery, heparin can be reduced and AT III infusions used.[153] Continue heparin into the postpartum period.

Anticoagulants in Pregnancy

Major indications for anticoagulant therapy during gestation include the following:

- Prophylaxis against venous thrombosis in patients with a positive history
- Treatment of acute thromboembolic disease
- Patients with prosthetic heart valves
- A variety of at-risk patients (obesity, immobilization, etc.)

Heparin and oral anticoagulants should be used with extreme care during pregnancy because both can have adverse effects on mother and fetus.[154] Oral anticoagulants are associated with an increased incidence of fetal wastage and congenital malformations. Previous reports of the high frequency of adverse effects of heparin[154] are now explained by maternal disease. Many experts encourage the exclusive use of heparin.[155]

Regional techniques are contraindicated in patients who are anticoagulated on heparin (*i.e.*, aPTT 1.5–2.0 times normal) or on oral anticoagulants. The thromboelastograph is useful alternative method of monitoring heparin therapy (Fig. 25-10). More controversial is the risk of regional anesthesia in patients on prophylactic subcutaneous doses of heparin.

A questionnaire survey of anesthetic departments in Denmark, a country where prophylactic anticoagulant therapy and regional anesthesia are widely practiced, showed that 60% of departments used spinal and epidural techniques and no side effects were reported.[156] On the other hand, 5000 units of heparin given subcutaneously every 12 hours may be associated with

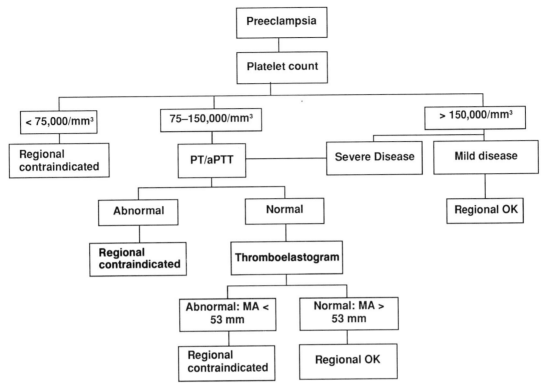

Figure 25–9. An approach to regional anesthesia in patients with preeclampsia. (aPTT = activated partial thromboplastin time, PTT = partial thromboplastin time.)

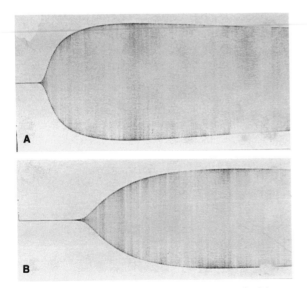

Figure 25–10. (*A*) Thromboelectrogram tracing of a 24-year-old parturient with deep vein thrombosis of leg. Note that r = 6.5 min, k = 2.5 min, and ma = 60 mm. (*B*) Thromboelectrogram after heparin infusion at 1750 μ/h. The r and k times are now prolonged. (r = 17.0 min, k = 6.0 min, and ma = 52 mm).

therapeutic heparin blood concentrations for up to 4 hours in 50% of patients.[157]

Most patients who are on heparin prophylaxis would benefit from epidural anesthesia. Therefore, assess the risks and benefits in each patient individually. Wait at least 6 hours from the last dose of heparin. Measure aPTT at the time of planning the block. If the aPTT is within normal limits, proceed with care.

REFERENCES

1. Mangano DT. Anesthesia for the pregnant cardiac patient. In: Shnider SM, Levinson G, eds. Anesthesia for obstetrics. 2nd ed. Baltimore: Williams & Wilkins, 1987:345.
2. Alderson JD. Cardiovascular collapse following epidural anaesthesia for caesarean section in a patient with aortic incompetence. Anaesthesia 1987;42:643.
3. Renou P, Newman W, Wood C. Autonomic control of fetal heart rate. Am J Obstet Gynecol 1969;105:949.
4. Al Kasab SM, Sabag T, Al Zaibag M, et al. β-Adrenergic receptor blockade in the management of pregnant women with mitral stenosis. Am J Obstet Gynecol 1990;163:37.

5. Szekely PI, Snaith L. Atrial fibrillation and pregnancy. Br Med J 1961;1:1407.

6. Gorlin R, Gorlin SG. Hydraulic formula for calculation of the area of the stenotic mitral valve, other cardiac valves and central circulatory shunts. Am Heart J 1951;41:1.

7. Easterling TR, Chadwick HS, Otto CM, Benedetti TJ. Aortic stenosis in pregnancy. Obstet Gynecol 1988; 72:113.

8. Tessler MJ, Hudson R, Naughler-Colville MA, Biehl DR. Pulmonary oedema in two parturients with hypertrophic obstructive cardiomyopathy (HOCM). Can J Anaesth 1990;37:469.

9. Boccio RV, Chung JH, Harrison DM. Anesthetic management of cesarean section in a patient with idiopathic hypertrophic subaortic stenosis. Anesthesiology 1986; 65:663

10. Minnich ME, Quirk JG, Clark RB. Epidural anaesthesia for vaginal delivery in a patient with idiopathic hypertrophic subaortic stenosis. Anesthesiology 1987; 67:590.

11. Malinow AM, Butterworth JF, Johnson MD, et al. Peripartum cardiomyopathy presenting at cesarean delivery. Anesthesiology 1985;63:545.

12. Gambling DR, Flanagan ML, Huckell VF, Lucas SB, Kim JHK. Anaesthetic management and non-invasive monitoring for caesarean section in a patient with cardiomyopathy. Can J Anaesth 1987;34:505.

13. Mendelson CL. Disorders of the heartbeat during pregnancy. Am J Obstet Gynecol 1956;72:1268.

14. Klepper I. Cardioversion in late pregnancy. Anaesthesia 1981;36:611.

15. Gothard JWW. Heart disease in pregnancy. Anaesthesia 1978;33:523.

16. Saka DM, Marx GF. Management of a parturient with cardiac valve prosthesis. Anesth Analg 1976;55:214.

17. Oakley C. Valve prostheses and pregnancy. Br Heart J 1987;58:303.

18. Varkey GP, Brindle GF. Peridural anaesthesia and anticoagulant therapy. Can Anaesth Soc J 1974;21:106.

19. Roberts NV, Keast PJ. Pulmonary hypertension and pregnancy—a lethal combination. Anaesth Intensive Care 1990;18:366.

20. Simonneau G, Herve P, Escouttou P, Baudruin C, Nebout T, Durouz P. Short- and long-term effects of vasodilators in primary pulmonary hypertension: Predictive value of prostacyclin acute infusion [Abstract]. J Crit Care 1986;1:117.

21. Slomka F, Salmeron S, Zetlaoui P, Cohen H, Simonneau G, Samii K. Primary pulmonary hypertension and pregnancy: anesthetic management for delivery. Anesthesiology 1988;69:959.

22. Abboud TK, Raya J, Noueihed R, Daniel J. Intrathecal morphine for relief of labor pain in a parturient with severe pulmonary hypertension. Anesthesiology 1983; 59:477.

23. Robinson DE, Leicht CH. Epidural analgesia with low-dose bupivacaine and fentanyl for labor and delivery in a parturient with severe pulmonary hypertension. Anesthesiology 1988;68:285.

24. Roessler P, Lambert TF. Anaesthesia for caesarean section in the presence of primary pulmonary hypertension. Anaesth Intensive Care 1986;14:317.

25. Hankins GDV, Wendel GD, Leveno KJ, Stoneham J. Myocardial infarction during pregnancy. A review. Obstet Gynecol 1985;65:139.

26. Aglio LS, Johnson MD. Anaesthetic management of myocardial infarction in a parturient. Br J Anaesth 1990;65:258

27. Laughlin MP, From RF, Choi W. Recent myocardial infarction in a parturient: Discussion of risk, delivery alternative, and choice of anesthesia. Anesthesiol Rev 1986;13:43.

28. Sasse L, Wagner R, Murray FE. Transmural myocardial infarction during pregnancy. Am J Cardiol 1975; 35:448.

29. Pollack KL, Chestnut DH, Wenstrom KD. Anesthetic management of a parturient with Eisenmenger's syndrome. Anesth Analg 1990;70:212.

30. Cumming PD, Wallance EL, Schorr JB, Dodd RY. Exposure of patients to human immunodeficiency virus through the transfusion of blood components that test antibody-negative. N Engl J Med 1989;321:941.

31. Haljamae H, Rosenberg PH. Present and future concepts in transfusion practice. Acta Anaesthesiol Scand 1988; 32, Suppl 89:1.

32. Alter HJ, Purcell RH, Shih JW, et al. Detection of antibody to hepatitis C virus in prospectively followed transfusion recipients with acute and chronic non-A, non-B hepatitis. N Engl J Med 1989;321:1494.

33. Rush B, Lee NLY. Clinical presentation of non-haemolytic transfusion reactions. Anaesth Intensive Care 1980;8:125.

34. Webster BH. Clinical presentation of haemolytic transfusion reactions. Anaesth Intensive Care 1980; 8:115.

35. Mollison PL. Some clinical consequences of red cell incompatibility. J R Coll Physicians Lond 1979;13:15.

36. Linman JW. Physiologic and pathophysiologic effects of anemia. N Engl J Med 1968;279:812.

37. Czer LSC, Shoemaker WC. Optimal hematocrit value in critically ill postoperative patients. Surg Gynecol Obstet 1978;147:363.

38. Kowalyshyn TJ, Prager D, Young J. A review of the present status of preoperative hemoglobin requirements. Anesth Analg 1972;51:75.

39. Carson JL, Spence RK, Poses RM, Bonavita G. Severity of anaemia and operative mortality and morbidity. Lancet 1988;2:727.

40. Consensus Conference. Perioperative red blood cell transfusion. JAMA 1988;260:2700.

41. Kambam JR, Handte RE, Brown WU, Smith BE. Effect of normal and preeclamptic pregnancies on the oxyhemoglobin dissociation curve. Anesthesiology 1986;65:426.

42. Barrera M, Miletich DJ, Albrecht RF, Hoffman WE.

Hemodynamic consequences of halothane anesthesia during chronic anemia. Anesthesiology 1984;61:36.

43. Lichtenstein A, Eckhart WF, Swanson KJ, Vacanti CA, Zapol WM. Unplanned intraoperative and postoperative hemodilution: Oxygen transport and consumption during severe anemia. Anesthesiology 1988;69:119.

44. Rabinowitz M, Gilibert JE, Lenes BA. Avoiding blood transfusion. A report of two cases. J Reprod Med 1990;35:569.

45. Stoelting RK, Dierdorf SF, McCammon RL. Anesthesia and co-existing disease. 2nd ed. New York: Churchill Livingstone, 1988:557.

46. Foster HW Jr. Maternal death associated with sickle cell trait. Am J Obstet Gynecol 1985;153:346.

47. Martin JN Jr, Martin RW, Morrison JC. Acute management of sickle cell crisis in pregnancy. Clin Perinatol 1986;13:853.

48. Jacobs P, Wood L, Elliott T. General anaesthesia in sickle cell disease. South Africa Med J 1989;76:124.

49. van Dinh T, Boor PJ, Garza JR. Massive pulmonary embolism following delivery of a patient with sickle cell trait. Am J Obstet Gynecol 1982;143:722.

50. Dunn A, Davies A, Eckert G, et al. Intraoperative death during caesarian section in a patient with sickle-cell trait. Can J Anaesth 1987;34:67.

51. Pastorek JG, Seiler B. Maternal death associated with sickle cell trait. Am J Obstet Gynecol 1985;151:295.

52. Finer P, Blair J, Rowe P. Epidural analgesia in the management of labor pain and sickle cell crises—a case report. Anesthesiology 1988;68:799.

53. Maduska AL, Guinee WS, Heaton JA, North WC, Barreras LM. Sickling dynamics of red blood cells and other physiologic studies during anesthesia. Anesth Analg 1975;54:361.

54. Holzmann L, Finn H, Lichtman HC, Harmel MH. Anesthesia in patients with sickle cell disease: A review of 112 cases. Anesth Analg 1969;48:566.

55. Esseltine DW, Baxter MRN, Bevan JC. Sickle cell states and the anaesthetist. Can J Anaesth 1988;35:385.

56. Charache S, Niebyl JR. Pregnancy in sickle cell disease. Baillieres Clin Haematol 1985;14:729.

57. Liang ST, Wong VC, So WW, Ma HK, Chan V, Todd D. Homozygous α thalassaemia: Clinical presentation, diagnosis and management. A review of 46 cases. Br J Obstet Gynaecol 1985;92:680.

58. Miller JM Jr. Alpha-thalassemia minor in pregnancy. J Reprod Med 1982;27:207.

59. Mordel N, Birkenfeld A, Goldfarb AN, Rachmilewitz EA. Successful full-term pregnancy in homozygous, β-thalassemia major: Case report and review of the literature. Obstet Gynecol 1989;73:837.

60. Fosburg MT, Nathan DG. Treatment of Cooley's anemia. Blood 1990;76:435.

61. Fleming AF, Lynch W. Beta-thalassaemia minor during pregnancy, with particular reference to iron status. J Obstet Gynaec Br Commwealth 1969;76:451.

62. Propper RD, Button LN, Nathan DG. New approaches to the transfusion management of thalassemia. Blood 1980;55:55.

63. Leon MB, Borer JS, Bacharach SL, et al. Detection of early cardiac dysfunction in patients with severe beta-thalassemia and chronic iron overload. N Engl J Med 1979;301:1143.

64. Snyder TE, Lee LP, Lynch S. Pregnancy-associated hypoplastic anemia: A review. Obstet Gynecol Surv 1991;46:264.

65. Aitchison RGM, Marsh JCW, Hows JM, Russell NH, Gordon-Smith EC. Pregnancy associated aplastic anaemia: A report of five cases and review of current management. Br J Haematol 1989;73:541.

66. Knispel JW, Lynch VA, Viele BD. Aplastic anemia in pregnancy: A case report, review of the literature, and a re-evaluation of management. Obstet Gynecol 1976; 31:523.

67. Zuazu J, Julia A, Sierra J, et al. Pregnancy outcome in hematologic malignancies. Cancer 1991;67:703.

68. Alter BP, Frissora CL, Halperin DS, et al. Fanconi's anaemia and pregnancy. Br J Haematol 1991;77:410.

69. Seaward PGR, Setzen R, Guidozzi F. Fanconi's anaemia in pregnancy. A case report. South Africa Med J 1990;78:691.

70. Douglas MJ. Alternatives to epidural analgesia during labour. Can J Anaesth 1991;38:421.

71. Melzack R. The myth of painless childbirth. Pain 1984;19:321.

72. Harrison RF, Woods T, Shore M, Mathews G, Unwin A. Pain relief in labour using transcutaneous electrical nerve stimulation (TENS). A TENS/TENS placebo-controlled study in two parity groups. Br J Obstet Gynaecol 1986;93:739.

73. Rayburn W, Rathke A, Leuschen MP, Chleborad J, Weidner W. Fentanyl citrate analgesia during labor. Am J Obstet Gynecol 1989;161:202.

74. Kleiman SJ, Wiesel S, Tessler MJ. Patient-controlled analgesia (PCA) using fentanyl in a parturient with a platelet function abnormality. Can J Anaesth 1991;38:489.

75. Akamatsu TJ, Bonica JJ, Rehmet R, Eng M, Ueland K. Experiences with the use of ketamine for parturition. I. Primary anesthetic for vaginal delivery. Anesth Analg 1974;53:284.

76. Colvin BT. Thrombocytopenia. In: Letsky EA, ed. Haematological disorders in pregnancy. Clin Haematol 1985;14:661.

77. Malinow AM, Rickford WJK, Mokriski BLK, Saller DN, McGuinn WJ. Lupus anticoagulant. Implications for obstetric anaesthetists. Anaesthesia 1987;42:1291.

78. Infante-Rivard C, David M, Gauthier R, Rivard GE. Lupus anticoagulants, anticardiolipin antibodies, and fetal loss. N Engl J Med 1991;325:1063.

79. Gastineau DA, Kazmier FJ, Nichols WL, Bowie EJ. Lupus anticoagulant: An analysis of the clinical and laboratory features of 219 cases. Am J Hematol 1985;19:265.

80. Branch DW, Scott JR, Kochenour NK, Hershgold E.

Obstetric complications associated with the lupus anticoagulant. N Engl J Med 1985;313:1322.

81. Mueh JR, Herbst KD, Rapaport SI. Thrombosis in patients with the lupus anticoagulant. Ann Intern Med 1980;92:156.

82. Lowson SM. Lupus anticoagulant—implications for the obstetric anaesthetist. Anaesthesia 1988;43:508.

83. Writer WDR. Hematologic disease. In: James FM III, Wheeler AS, Dewan DM, eds. Obstetric anesthesia: The complicated patient. 2nd ed. Philadelphia: FA Davis, 1988:267.

84. Karpatkin S. Autoimmune thrombocytopenic purpura. Blood 1980;56:329.

85. Kelton JG. Management of the pregnant patient with idiopathic thrombocytopenic purpura. Ann Intern Med 1983;99:796.

86. Gatt S. Haematological disorders responsible for maternal bleeding in late pregnancy. Anaesth Intensive Care 1990;18:335.

87. Cines DB, Dusak B, Tomaski A, Mennuti M, Schreiber AD. Immune thrombocytopenic purpura and pregnancy. N Engl J Med 1982;306:826.

88. Scott JR, Rote NS, Cruikshank DP. Antiplatelet antibodies and platelet counts in pregnancies complicated by autoimmune thrombocytopenic purpura. Am J Obstet Gynecol 1983;145:932.

89. Maina A, Donvito V, Giachino O, Stratta P, Camaschella C. Thrombotic thrombocytopenic purpura in pregnancy with maternal and fetal survival. Case report. Br J Obstet Gynaecol 1990;97:443.

90. Kwaan HC. Thrombotic thrombocytopenic purpura and hemolytic uremic syndrome in pregnancy. Clin Obstet Gynecol 1985;28:101.

91. Weiner CP. Thrombotic microangiopathy in pregnancy and the postpartum period. Semin Hematol 1987;24:119.

92. Harkness DR, Byrnes JJ, Lian EC-Y, Williams WD, Hensley GT. Hazard of platelet transfusion in thrombotic thrombocytopenic purpura. JAMA 1981;246:1931.

93. Burrows RF, Kelton JG. Thrombocytopenia at delivery: A prospective survey of 6715 deliveries. Am J Obstet Gynecol 1990;162:713.

94. Rolbin SH, Abbott D, Musclow E, Papsin F, Lie LM, Freedman J. Epidural anesthesia in pregnant patients with low platelet counts. Obstet Gynecol 1988;71:918.

95. Hew-Wing P, Rolbin SH, Hew E, Amato D. Epidural anaesthesia and thrombocytopenia. Anaesthesia 1989;44:775.

96. Rasmus KT, Rottman RL, Kotelko DM, Wright WC, Stone JJ, Rosenblatt RM. Unrecognized thrombocytopenia and regional anesthesia in parturients: A retrospective review. Obstet Gynecol 1989;73:943.

97. George JN, Shattil SJ. The clinical importance of acquired abnormalities of platelet function. N Engl J Med 1991;324:27.

98. Barrer MJ, Ellison N. Platelet function. Anesthesiology 1977;46:202.

99. Lind SE. Prolonged bleeding time. Am J Med 1984;77:305.

100. King DJ, Kelton JG. Heparin-associated thrombocytopenia. Ann Intern Med 1984;100:535.

101. Vermylen J, Blockmans D. Acquired disorders of platelet function. Bailliere's Clin Haematol 1989;2:729.

102. Schiff E, Peleg E, Goldenberg M, et al. The use of aspirin to prevent pregnancy-induced hypertension and lower the ratio of thromboxane A_2 to prostacyclin in relatively high-risk pregnancies. N Engl J Med 1989;321:351.

103. Ferraris VA, Swanson E. Aspirin usage and perioperative blood loss in patients undergoing unexpected operations. Surg Gynecol Obstet 1983;156:439.

104. Macdonald R. Aspirin and extradural blocks. Br J Anaesth 1991;66:1.

105. Kane RE. Neurologic deficits following epidural or spinal anesthesia. Anesth Analg 1981;60:150.

106. Horlocker TT, Wedel DJ, Offord KP. Does preoperative antiplatelet therapy increase the risk of hemorrhagic complications associated with regional anesthesia? Anesth Analg 1990;70:631.

107. Benzon HT, Brunner EA, Vaisrub N. Bleeding time and nerve blocks after aspirin. Reg Anesth 1983;9:86.

108. Beck H, Brassow F, Doehn M, et al. Epidural catheters of the multi-orifice type: dangers and complications. Acta Anaesthesiol Scand 1986;30:549.

109. McNeil MJ, Thorburn J. Cannulation of the epidural space. A comparison of 18- and 16-gauge needles. Anaesthesia 1988;43:154.

110. Redman CWG, Bonnar J, Beilin L. Early platelet consumption in preeclampsia. Br Med J 1978;1:467.

111. Kelton JG, Hunter DJ, Neame PB. A platelet function defect in preeclampsia. Obstet Gynecol 1985;65:107.

112. Ramanathan J, Sibai BM, Vu T, Chauhan D. Correlation between bleeding times and platelet counts in women with preeclampsia undergoing cesarean section. Anesthesiology 1989;71:188.

113. Schindler M, Gatt S, Isert P, Morgans D, Cheung A. Thrombocytopenia and platelet functional defects in pre-eclampsia: Implications for regional anaesthesia. Anaesth Intensive Care 1990;18:169.

114. Harker LA, Slichter SJ. The bleeding time as a screening test for evaluation of platelet function. N Engl J Med 1972;287:155.

115. Wright JP. Anesthetic considerations in preeclampsia-eclampsia. Anesth Analg 1983;62:590.

116. Barker P, Callander CC. Coagulation screening before epidural analgesia in pre-eclampsia. Anaesthesia 1991;46:64.

117. Trotter TN, Wood JK, Armstrong AL, May AE. Coagulation screening before epidural analgesia in pre-eclampsia. Anaesthesia 1991;46:596.

118. Weinstein L. Syndrome of hemolysis, elevated liver enzymes, and low platelet count: A severe consequence of hypertension in pregnancy. Am J Obstet Gynecol 1982;142:159.

119. Sibai BM, Taslimi MM, El-Nazer A, Amon E, Mabie

BC, Ryan GM. Maternal-perinatal outcome associated with the syndrome of hemolysis, elevated liver enzymes, and low platelets in severe preeclampsia-eclampsia. Am J Obstet Gynecol 1986;155:501.

120. Duffy BL. HELLP syndrome and the anaesthetist. Anaesthesia 1988;43:223.

121. Douglas MJ. Coagulation abnormalities and obstetric anaesthesia. Can J Anaesth 1991;38:R17.

122. Whigham KAE, Howie PW, Drummond AH, Prentice CRM. Abnormal platelet function in pre-eclampsia. Br J Obstet Gynaecol 1978;85:28.

123. de Swiet M. The use of aspirin in pregnancy. Obstet Gynecol 1990;10:467.

124. Cross MH, Haxby EJ, Robinson PN. Bleeding time. Lancet 1991;338:187.

125. Duke WW. The relation of blood platelets to hemorrhagic disease. JAMA 1910;55:1 185.

126. Ivy AC, Nelson D, Bucher G. The standardization of certain factors in the cutaneous "venostasis" bleeding time technique. J Lab Clin Med 1941;26:1812.

127. Mielke CH Jr, Kaneshiro MM, Maher IA, Weiner JM, Rapaport SI. The standardized normal Ivy bleeding time and its prolongation by aspirin. Blood 1969;34:204.

128. Babson SR, Babson AL. Development and evaluation of a disposable device for performing simultaneous duplicate bleeding time determinations. Am J Clin Pathol 1978;70:406.

129. Channing-Rogers RP, Levin J. A critical reappraisal of the bleeding time. Semin Thromb Hemost 1990;16:1.

130. O'Laughlin JC, Hoftiezer JW, Mahoney JP, Ivey KJ. Does aspirin prolong bleeding from gastric biopsies in man? Gastrointest Endosc 1981;27:1.

131. The bleeding time [Editorial]. Lancet 1991;337:1447.

132. Triplett DA. The bleeding time: Neither pariah nor panacea. Arch Pathol Lab Med 1989;113:1207.

133. Franz RC, Coetzee WJC. The thrombelastographic diagnosis of hemostatic defects. Surg Annu 1981;13:75.

134. Spies BD, Tuman KJ, McCarthy RJ, Ivankovich AD. Thrombelastopgraphy as an indicator of post-cardiopulmonary bypass coagulopathies. J Clin Monit 1987;3:25.

135. Zuckerman L, Cohen E, Vagher JP, Woodward E, Caprini JA. Comparison of thrombelastography with common coagulation tests. Thromb Haesmost 1981;46:752.

136. Mallet SV, Platt M. Role of thromboelastography in bleeding diatheses and regional anaesthesia. Lancet 1991;338:765.

137. Orlikowski CEP, Moodley J, Rocke DA. Thrombo-elastography in pregnant patients on low-dose aspirin. Lancet 1991;338:1276.

138. Troché G, Hamza J, Narchi P, Lecoq G. Pregnancy-induced hypertension and bleeding in parturients under epidural anesthesia [Abstract]. Anesthesiology 1990;73(3A):A998.

139. Wildsmith JAW, McClure JH. Anticoagulant drugs and central nerve blockade. Anaesthesia 1991;46:613.

140. Mercer B, Drouin J, Jolly E, d'Anjou G. Primary thrombocythemia in pregnancy: A report of two cases. Am J Obstet Gynecol 1988;159;127.

141. Jones EC, Mosesson MW, Thomason JL, Jackson TC. Essential thrombocythemia in pregnancy. Obstet Gynecol 1988;71:501.

142. Beard J, Hillmen P, Anderson CC, Lewis SM, Pearson TC. Primary thrombocythaemia in pregnancy. Br J Haematol 1991;77:371.

143. Letsky EA. Coagulation defects. In: de Swiet M, ed. Medical disorders in obstetric practice. 2nd ed. Oxford: Blackwell Scientific Publications, 1989.

144. Conti M, Mari D, Conti E, Muggiasca ML, Mannuccio PM. Pregnancy in women with different types of von Willebrand disease. Obstet Gynecol 1986;68:282.

145. Stirling Y, Woolf L, North WRS, Seghatchian MJ, Meade TW. Haemostasis in normal pregnancy. Thromb Haemost 1984;52:176

146. Caldwell DC, Williamson RA, Goldsmith JC. Hereditary coagulopathies in pregnancy. Clin Obstet Gynaecol 1985;28:53.

147. Milaskiewicz RM, Holdcroft A, Letsky E. Epidural anaesthesia and von Willebrand's disease. Anaesthesia 1990;45:462.

148. Lipton RA, Ayromlooi J, Coller BS. Severe von Willebrand disease. JAMA 1982;248:1355.

149. Fadel HE, Krauss JS. Factor VII deficiency and pregnancy. Obstet Gynecol 1989;73:453.

150. Goodwin TM. Congenital hypofibrinogenemia in pregnancy. Obstet Gynecol Surv 1989;44:157.

151. Mammen EF. Fibrinogen abnormalities. Semin Thromb Hemost 1983;9:1.

152. Ness JM, Perkins HA. Cryoprecipitate as a reliable source of fibrinogen replacement. JAMA 1979;241:1690.

153. Owen J. Antithrombin III replacement therapy in pregnancy. Semin Hematol 1991;28:46.

154. Ginsberg JS, Hirsh J. Anticoagulants during pregnancy. Annu Rev Med 1989;40:79.

155. Ginsberg JS, Hirsh J, Turner DC, Levine MN, Burrows R. Risks to the fetus of anticoagulant therapy during pregnancy. Thromb Haemost 1989;61:197.

156. Willie-Jorgensen P, Jorgensen LN, Rasmussen LS. Lumbar regional anaesthesia and prophylactic anticoagulant therapy. Is the combination safe? Anaesthesia 1991;46:623.

157. Cooke ED, Lloyd MJ, Bowcock SA, Pilcher MF. Monitoring during low-dose heparin prophylaxis. N Engl J Med 1976;294:1066.

CHAPTER 26

Anesthesia and Coexisting Maternal Disease

Part Two
Diabetes Mellitus, Obesity, and Pulmonary and Neurologic Disease

Beth Glosten

Anesthesiologists often assist with the management of labor and delivery or cesarean section in parturients with significant medical problems. These medical conditions impact both the maternal and fetal/neonatal response to anesthetics. This chapter reviews how some common maternal medical problems influence anesthetic management. Some relatively uncommon medical problems that significantly alter anesthetic care also are discussed. Specific problems covered include diabetes mellitus, obesity, pulmonary disease (asthma, cigarette use), and neurologic problems (seizure disorders, multiple sclerosis, myasthenia gravis, and intracranial vascular abnormalities).

ANESTHETIC MANAGEMENT OF THE DIABETIC PARTURIENT

General Considerations

Maternal glucose homeostasis, the potential for impaired uteroplacental perfusion, and the high likelihood of the need for cesarean delivery are all important features for the anesthesiologist to consider when caring for the diabetic parturient. Preoperative evaluation of the diabetic parturient includes assessment of the severity of maternal diabetes. In addition, watch for renal or vascular disease or preeclampsia (Table 26-1). Evaluation of the fetus includes looking for evidence of fetal distress, assessment of fetal lung maturity, and estimated fetal weight. Review the obstetric chart to determine maternal insulin requirements during pregnancy. Know what insulin has been given and the subsequent glucose response.

Maintaining normal maternal glucose concentrations is very important throughout gestation. The anesthesiologist is often involved with this task in the peripartum period. Patients in labor can be managed with slow infusions of glucose and either intermittent or continuous insulin injections.[1] Monitor blood glucose closely, and adjust glucose and insulin infusions accordingly. Most obstetricians try to keep maternal glucose less than 110 mg/dL, and, hopefully, less than 90 mg/dL.

Avoid maternal hyperglycemia (Fig. 26-1). Do not use glucose-containing solutions for prehydration be-

Table 26–1

The Diabetic Parturient and Anesthesia

MATERNAL CONSIDERATIONS	FETAL/NEONATAL CONSIDERATIONS
Glucose control	Lung maturity
Coexisting diseases:	Uteroplacental insufficiency
Renal	Macrosomia
Cardiovascular	Acidosis
Preeclampsia	Hypoglycemia after birth
Need for operative delivery	Birth trauma
Cesarean section	
Forceps delivery	
Shoulder dystocia	

fore inducing regional anesthesia.[2] Studies in animals and humans show that maternal hyperglycemia contributes to neonatal hypercarbia and acidemia.[3–5] Increased hydrogen ion concentration displaces oxygen from hemoglobin, thereby decreasing the oxygen-carrying capacity of the fetal blood and decreasing blood oxygen content (Haldane effect). The fetus of the diabetic mother often is chronically hypoxemic. In this setting, the stresses imposed by maternal hyperglycemia only worsen the situation. The placenta metabolizes maternal glucose to lactate,[6] further contributing to neonatal acidosis. Glucose crosses the placenta via facilitated diffusion. Fetal hyperglycemia stimulates fetal insulin secretion. In animals, fetal insulin increases glucose uptake and reduces oxygen content, presumably by increasing fetal oxygen consumption.[7]

Maternal hyperglycemia shortly before delivery also can cause neonatal hypoglycemia. High maternal serum glucose just before delivery causes high umbilical venous concentrations of glucose (Fig. 26-2).[8] As before, this hyperglycemia stimulates fetal hyperinsulinemia. After delivery and loss of the maternal source of glucose, however, this hyperinsulinemia leads to neonatal hypoglycemia (Fig. 26-3). The neonate cannot mobilize its own glucose stores to maintain a normal serum glucose. The higher the umbilical cord glucose concentration at birth, the more likely neonatal hypoglycemia will occur.[8]

Diabetes further worsens fetal condition by hindering placental function and uteroplacental perfusion. Pathologic examinations of the diabetic placenta reveal enlarged villi that reduce the surface area over which gas exchange can occur.[9] Maternal vascular dis-

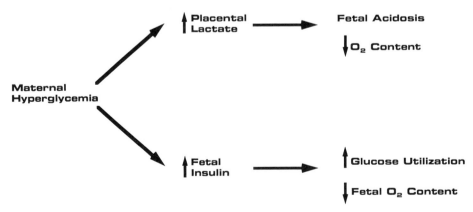

Figure 26–1. Maternal hyperglycemia contributes to fetal acidosis and reduced fetal oxygen (O_2) content.

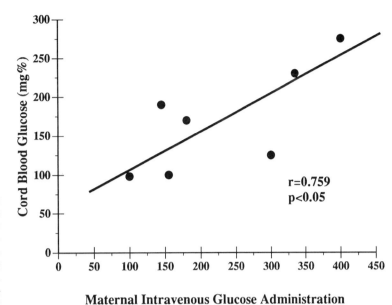

Figure 26–2. Intravenous glucose infusion can cause maternal hyperglycemia. Glucose equilibrates rapidly across the placenta. At birth, umbilical cord blood glucose concentrations reflect the maternal glucose concentrations. (After Light IJ, Keenan WJ, Sutherland JM. Maternal intravenous glucose administration as a cause of hypoglycemia in the infant of the diabetic mother. Am J Obstet Gynecol 1972;113:345)

ease can further impede gas exchange. These changes result in a growth-retarded fetus or a fetus unable to tolerate uterine contractions during labor.

For both placental and metabolic reasons, the fetus of a diabetic parturient has less reserve than the fetus of a normal gestation. Fetal distress occurs frequently in diabetic pregnancies, often necessitating operative delivery. The anesthesiologist must recognize the potentially limited fetal reserve and exercise care when inducing anesthesia in these patients.

Often, the fetus of a diabetic mother suffers from macrosomia. Large fetal size increases the likelihood of cephalopelvic disproportion and the need for cesarean delivery.[10] Furthermore, vaginal delivery of a macrosomic fetus may require the use of forceps or result in shoulder dystocia. The large, overdistended uterus of a diabetic parturient may not contract well after delivery, resulting in uterine atony and postpartum hemorrhage. Again, preoperative evaluation of the diabetic parturient can help foresee these conditions. Formulate an anesthetic plan for use in the event these emergencies arise.

Analgesia for Labor and Delivery

Systemic narcotics and sedatives can provide analgesia during early labor in the diabetic patient. Just as in other patients, consider the effects of placental transfer of these medications. Should birth occur shortly after their administration, the neonate of the diabetic patient may be particularly sensitive to depression from sedatives.

Epidural analgesia is a very useful and effective technique of providing pain relief for labor and delivery in diabetic parturients. In nondiabetic laboring parturients, epidural analgesia reduces circulating maternal plasma concentrations of catecholamines and 11-hydroxycorticosteroids.[11,12] This effect has two potential benefits for diabetic patients. First, epinephrine and cortisol stimulate hyperglycemia and may contribute to difficulties with maternal glucose control. Second, reducing circulating maternal plasma concentrations of catecholamines may improve placental perfusion.

Before inducing regional analgesia in diabetic parturients, establish normovolemia with a non–glucose-containing solution to prevent maternal hypotension. Remember the potential for impaired uteroplacental perfusion in these patients. Pay close attention to fetal monitoring and proper maternal positioning. Avoid aortocaval compression.

Parturients with juvenile-onset diabetes may have lower epidural local anesthetic dose requirements. For unclear reasons, these patients respond as if they are older than their chronological age.[13] Therefore, dose their epidural catheters judiciously.

Spinal anesthesia can be used for vaginal delivery, especially if forceps delivery is necessary in a patient

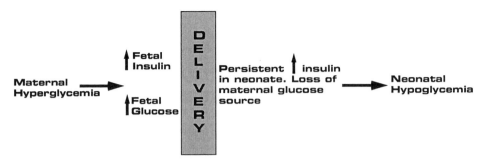

Figure 26–3. Maternal hyperglycemia results in neonatal hypoglycemia.

without a functioning epidural catheter. As mentioned previously, take care with prehydration, maternal positioning, and monitoring the fetus.

Anesthesia for Cesarean Section

As with laboring parturients, do not use glucose-containing fluids for prehydration or volume replacement during cesarean section in diabetic parturients. Patients receiving insulin need a maintenance infusion of glucose. It is often best to place two intravenous catheters in these women—one for glucose infusion and one for prehydration and volume replacement. Insulin and glucose therapy following the NPO period before elective cesarean delivery depends on the severity of the patient's disease. Gestational diabetics may not need insulin on the morning of surgery; however, patients who have diabetes when not pregnant may receive one third or one half of their prepregnant insulin dose before surgery. Parturients receiving insulin must have a functioning intravenous line with a glucose infusion. To minimize the impact on diabetic management, these patients should have their surgery early in the day. As with all diabetic patients, measure blood glucose frequently.

Following delivery, maternal insulin requirements fall rapidly, often to below prepregnant requirements.[14] The loss of insulin resistance conferred by the placenta stimulates this change in insulin sensitivity. Patients receiving insulin before delivery may develop hypoglycemia at this time. Carefully monitor maternal plasma glucose after delivery and adjust glucose/insulin therapy as indicated.

The specific anesthetic technique chosen depends on the patient's preference and the clinical situation. Good maternal and fetal outcome follows a carefully performed regional or general anesthetic.

Clinical studies evaluating the acid–base status of neonates born of normal or diabetic parturients who re- ceived general anesthesia for cesarean section have shown no differences between the two patient groups;[15] however, neonatal depression (defined as Apgar scores < 7 at 1 min) occurs more commonly in the infants of diabetic mothers. The increased likelihood of prematurity in neonates of diabetic mothers may explain this higher risk of depression.

To safely use spinal anesthesia for cesarean delivery, one must ensure adequate maternal hydration and strive to prevent hypotension. Early studies suggested that infants of diabetic pregnancies developed more severe acidosis after spinal anesthesia–induced hypotension than did infants of normal pregnancies.[15] However, these patients received glucose-containing solutions for prehydration; therefore, maternal hyperglycemia likely contributed to the fetal acidosis. Later studies found that avoiding maternal hyperglycemia and treating hypotension aggressively (ephedrine, 10–20 mg IV when systolic blood pressure falls 10 mm Hg) ensures comparable neonatal outcome in normal and diabetic women receiving spinal anesthesia for cesarean delivery.[16]

Epidural anesthesia is another good choice of anesthesia for cesarean section in diabetic patients. As with spinal anesthesia, maternal hypotension may cause neonatal acidosis, particularly if the maternal diabetes is severe.[17] Use care when giving large doses of epidural local anesthetics to a diabetic parturient with a potentially acidotic fetus. Local anesthetic ion-trapping may occur in these fetuses, resulting in accumulation of the anesthetic in the neonate.[17] The rapid metabolism of 2-chloroprocaine may make it useful in this setting. Still, its rapid onset of action, greater incidence of hypotension,[18] and short duration of action also must be considered.

Be certain that the person responsible for neonatal resuscitation is aware that he or she is receiving an infant of a diabetic mother. Measure glucose in the neonate after delivery, and watch for signs of hypoglycemia (lethargy, hypothermia, seizures).

ANESTHETIC MANAGEMENT OF THE OBESE PARTURIENT

The obese parturient (> 90 kg) can pose considerable physiologic and technical challenges to the anesthesiologist (Table 26-2). Obesity complicates 6% to 10% of pregnancies and occurs more commonly in older women of greater parity.[19,20] The literature concerning maternal complications associated with obesity reports varying results because of differing definitions of obesity and poor control for other medical problems associated with obesity. Obese parturients develop preeclampsia, hypertension, and diabetes more commonly than nonobese parturients,[19,21-24] and these diseases affect obstetric care. These women also may have hypertriglyceridemia and coronary artery disease. Obesity is a risk factor for a long and difficult labor and often correlates with a high cesarean delivery rate.[19-23] Associated fetal problems include macrosomia, shoulder dystocia, and birth trauma.

Of particular importance to anesthesiologists are the effects of obesity on pulmonary (Table 26-3) and cardiac function. During normal pregnancy, functional residual capacity diminishes (due to a reduction in expiratory reserve volume) and oxygen consumption increases.[25] Pulmonary changes from obesity include decreased lung and chest wall compliance due to chest wall and abdominal fat, increased work of breathing, increased minute ventilation, and, possibly, even a further reduction in total lung capacity and functional residual capacity.[24,26,27]

Pulmonary function studies in obese nonpregnant patients show a restrictive ventilatory defect. Obese volunteers exhibit a diminished ventilatory response to hypercarbia when compared to nonobese volunteers.[27] The combined pulmonary changes of pregnancy and obesity make hypoventilation of some lung units very likely. Closing capacity may fall within the range of tidal ventilation in obese parturients, particularly if they assume the supine position. Airway closure then causes ventilation/perfusion defects that contribute to hypoxemia. Hypoventilation from sedatives or residual anesthetics further increases the risk of hypoxemia in these patients.

The cardiovascular system is stressed during obesity and pregnancy; both conditions contribute to increased cardiac work. This combination may lead to symptoms of myocardial failure during pregnancy. If a patient gives a history of orthopnea or severe dyspnea on exertion, cardiac evaluation should be done to clar-

Table 26-2

The Obese Parturient and Anesthesia

MATERNAL CONSIDERATIONS	FETAL CONSIDERATIONS
Concomitant medical problems 　Pulmonary dysfunction 　Hypertension 　Diabetes 　Cardiovascular disease Monitoring and intravenous access problematic	Macrosomia Abnormal presentation

ANESTHETIC CONSIDERATIONS

Regional Anesthesia	General Anesthesia
Landmarks difficult to palpate Gravid uterus and abdominal fat pad contribute to hypotension Epidural/spinal local anesthetic dose requirements reduced/unpredictable	Difficult intubation Pulmonary aspiration of gastric contents Hypoxia Unpredictable drug dose requirements

POSTOPERATIVE PROBLEMS

Hypoxemia, hypoventilation
Thromboembolism

Table 26–3

Pulmonary Changes in the Obese Parturient

Decreased functional residual capacity
Decreased chest wall compliance
Small airway closure
Ventilation/perfusion mismatch
Decreased ventilatory response to carbon dioxide
Increased minute ventilation
Increased work of breathing

ify cardiac function. Furthermore, obstructive sleep apnea can occur in obese patients, causing right-heart failure and cor pulmonale. Hypertensive disorders of pregnancy are also common in these patients.

Obese parturients are apt to require anesthetic care because of the likelihood of having a long labor or needing operative vaginal or cesarean delivery. Preanesthetic evaluation must include careful assessment of the patient's cardiac and pulmonary function. Evaluate the patient for evidence of preeclampsia and diabetes. Check that intravenous access is adequate. Know the obstetric plan and develop a corresponding anesthetic plan. Pay close attention to the airway. Assess jaw and neck mobility. The Mallampati scale[28] (Table 26-4 and Fig. 26-4) or awake laryngoscopy will help determine which patients will need awake intubation should general anesthesia be necessary.

Analgesia for Labor and Delivery

Use systemic medications with caution. The sedative effects of narcotics can contribute to hypoventilation and hypoxemia. Because of the variable response to narcotics in the obese patient, give them in small incremental doses, titrating to the desired effect. Should somnolence occur, use a pulse oximeter to assess adequacy of oxygenation and to guide treatment with supplemental oxygen.

Epidural blockade can very effectively provide labor analgesia in obese parturients. Beyond pain relief, epidural block offers significant additional benefits for these women. Adequate epidural analgesia will help diminish ventilatory requirements during labor, a beneficial effect in these women with already stressed cardiopulmonary systems.[29] Furthermore, adequate epidural analgesia prevents the hyperventilation with painful contractions and the resultant hyperventilation in the rest period between contractions.[30] Hypoxemia may occur while the parturient hypoventilates because of airway closure, high oxygen consumption, and altered ventilatory drive. In addition to helping maintain good oxygenation, epidural blockade also provides a means of anesthetizing the patient should cesarean or operative vaginal delivery become necessary.

Identifying the epidural space, inserting a catheter, and successfully providing labor analgesia can prove a daunting task in obese parturients.[21] Not uncommonly, the epidural catheter needs replacement or repositioning to achieve and maintain continuous pain relief (Table 26-5).[21] By inserting an epidural catheter

Table 26–4

A Clinical Sign to Predict Difficult Intubation

VISIBILITY OF STRUCTURES	NO. OF PATIENTS	LARYNGOSCOPY GRADE			
		Grade 1[§]	Grade 2[‖]	Grade 3[¶]	Grade 4[**]
Class 1*	155	125	30		
Class 2†	40	12	14	10	4
Class 3‡	15		2	9	5

(Data from Mallampati SR, Gatt SP, Gugino LD, et al. A clinical sign to predict difficult tracheal intubation: A prospective study. Can Anaesth Soc J 1985;34:429)
*Class 1: Faucial pillars, soft palate, and uvula visualized (Figure 26-4*A*).
†Class 2: Faucial pillars and soft palate visualized, uvula masked by base of tongue.
‡Class 3: Only soft palate seen (Figure 26-4*B*).
§Grade 1: Glottis fully exposed.
‖Grade 2: Glottis partly exposed.
¶Grade 3: Glottis not exposed (corniculate cartilages only seen).
**Grade 4: Glottis, including corniculate cartilages, not exposed.

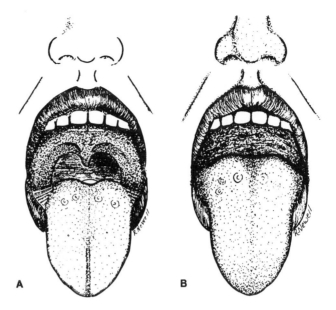

Figure 26–4. A clinical sign to predict difficult intubation. (**A**) A patient in whom faucial pillars, soft palate, and uvula are visible. (**B**) A patient in whom none of the three structures are visible. (Mallampati SR, Gatt SP, Gugino LD, et al. A clinical sign to predict difficult tracheal intubation: A prospective study. Can Anaesth Soc J 1985;34:429)

early in labor, one has more time to optimize the anesthetic. In addition, the patient may be more cooperative in early labor than later in the more painful active phase. Feeling landmarks for epidural needle placement is often not possible in obese patients. It helps to place the epidural catheter with the patient in the sitting position. Recent clinical studies suggest that this position is more comfortable for these patients.[31] The sitting position allows one to estimate the location of the vertebral column in the midline of the patient by drawing a line between the often easily palpated spinous process of the C-7 vertebra in the neck and the gluteal fold.[32] Marks at the waist from undergarments or the fetal heart rate monitor belt can approximate the

Table 26–5

Anesthesia for the Obese (> 300 lb) Parturient (n = 117)

	n	**PERCENT**
Epidural Analgesia for Labor (n = 85)		
Successful epidural placement	80/85	94
Epidural catheters needed replacement	37/80	44
Epidural catheters needed replacement > 2 times	17/80	20
Accidental dural puncture	3/80	4
	72/117	**62**
Anesthesia for Cesarean Section		
General anesthesia	17/72	24
Difficult intubation	6/17	35
Epidural anesthesia	51/72	71
Spinal anesthesia	4/72	5

(After Hood DD, Dewan DM, Kashtan K. Anesthesia outcome in the morbidly obese parturient. Anesthesiology 1990;73:A952)

level of the L-3–4 or L-4–5 interspaces (Fig. 26-5). The spinous processes above and below the interspace used can be identified, after local infiltration, by probing with a long 26-gauge spinal needle. An extra-long epidural needle may be necessary to reach the epidural space. If reaching the epidural space necessitates indenting the skin or subcutaneous tissue of the back, be sure the needle stays in a stable position while inserting the epidural catheter to prevent the indented skin from pushing the needle out.

Monitoring both mother and fetus can prove difficult in obese parturients. The fetal heart rate may be difficult to trace with an external monitor. If a fetal scalp electrode is not being used for fetal heart rate monitoring, having the patient sit up for epidural placement can exacerbate this problem. Nonetheless, do your best to monitor fetal heart rate continuously, particularly when dosing the epidural catheter. Accurately measuring maternal blood pressure is another challenge. An appropriately sized blood pressure cuff should be 20% to 30% as wide as the arm circumfer-

ence. You may need to use a thigh cuff on the upper arm or a large blood pressure cuff on the forearm. Pulse oximetry can be very helpful in guiding the use of supplemental oxygen in these patients with potentially reduced pulmonary reserve.

Exercise caution when dosing the epidural catheter for labor analgesia. Both the gravid uterus and the large obese abdomen contribute to aortocaval compression. Dose the catheter slowly to avoid sudden hypotension, which could precipitate fetal distress and the need for an emergent delivery. In addition, epidural local anesthetics seem to spread farther in obese parturients, increasing the level of sensory blockade in response to a given dose of local anesthetic (Fig. 26-6).[33,34]

If dural puncture occurs while attempting to identify the epidural space, consider taking advantage of the situation by threading a catheter into the intrathecal space and conducting a continuous spinal anesthetic. Dose this spinal catheter slowly, since local anesthetic dose requirements are quite low (see Chap. 20). Again, watch for hypotension vigilantly and maintain proper patient position to minimize caval compression.

Anesthesia for Cesarean Section

The obese patient also presents some unique challenges to the anesthesiologist in the event of operative delivery. These patients may develop subjective symptoms of shortness of breath when adopting the supine position. In addition, the supine position may exacerbate airway closure and inadequate alveolar ventilation, leading to hypoxemia and hypercarbia. Proper patient position will help ventilation (Fig. 26-7). The type of skin incision used for cesarean delivery can affect the patient's ventilatory status. Some recommend the Pfannenstiel incision in these women to lower postoperative pain and favor earlier ambulation.[24,35,36] The abdominal fat pad needs to be displaced cephalad to provide good surgical exposure; doing so, however, may further compromise the patient's pulmonary status and worsen aortocaval compression. Hodgkinson[37] described an obese parturient undergoing cesarean section with epidural anesthesia and a Pfannenstiel incision who had refractory hypotension due to cephalad retraction of the panniculus, which resulted in fetal death. The anesthesiologist needs to know the obstetric surgical plan and watch for hemodynamic and pulmonary effects of the patient's position.

Again, monitoring of the mother may prove difficult during cesarean section. Use properly sized blood pressure cuffs. In extreme cases, consider placing an arterial catheter for monitoring blood pressure and ma-

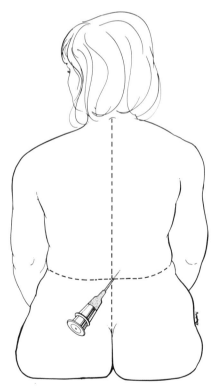

Figure 26–5. Landmarks for regional anesthesia in the obese patient. Midline is estimated by drawing a line from the prominence of the C-7 vertebra to the gluteal fold. The lower lumbar interspaces are estimated from skin creases left by undergarments or the fetal heart rate monitor belt.

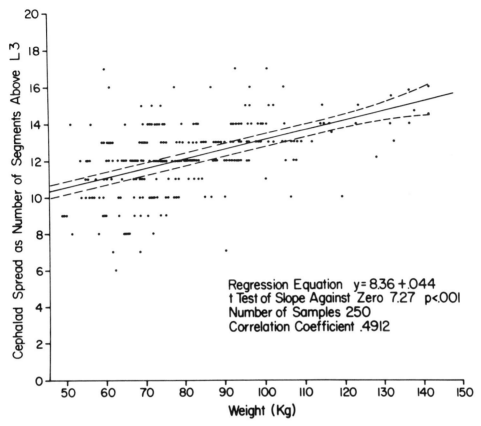

Figure 26–6. Relationship of parturient's weight to highest point of cephalad spread of epidural analgesia as determined by pinprick following single injection at L-3–4 of 20 mL of 0.75% bupivacaine. The three lines on the graph represent the regression line, with the 95% confidence limits drawn on either side. (Hodgkinson R, Husain FJ. Obesity, gravity, and spread of epidural anesthesia. Anesth Analg 1981;60:421)

ternal blood gas tensions. Older obese parturients or those with pre-existing hypertension or cardiac disease may require hemodynamic monitoring with central venous or pulmonary artery catheters.[22] Pulse oximetry is necessary to assess maternal oxygenation. In this group of patients, the ability to measure end-tidal carbon dioxide is crucial should placement of an endotracheal be necessary. If possible, monitor the fetus during positioning and induction of anesthesia.

If the patient can breathe when lying fairly flat and positioned for cesarean section, regional anesthesia has significant advantages over general anesthesia. Epidural anesthesia can be titrated to effect. It also offers a slower onset of sympathetic blockade than spinal anesthesia. Because of the risk of aortocaval compression by the uterus and the fat pad, the slower onset of sympathetic blockade will allow the anesthesiologist time to alter maternal position and volume status should the

blood pressure start to fall. Remember, these patients may require a smaller dose of epidural local anesthetic to achieve surgical anesthesia.[33,34] Inject local anesthetic in small (5 mL) increments until an adequate level of sensory blockade develops.

Spinal anesthesia also can prove useful in the obese parturient; however, one must pay close attention to prehydration and positioning to prevent maternal hypotension. Norris[38] studied the effect of patient weight on the spread of 12 mg of intrathecal hyperbaric bupivacaine and did not find any correlation between increased maternal weight and the level of sensory blockade (Fig. 26-8). The patients studied weighed between 57 and 94 kg. The obese population per se has not been carefully evaluated. Most likely, the spread of spinal anesthesia in obese parturients, like all parturients, is unpredictable. The anesthesiologist must be prepared to manage a total spinal anesthetic.

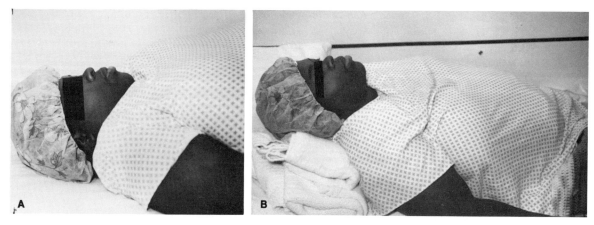

Figure 26–7. **(A)** An obese pregnant woman in the supine position. Large breasts limit access to the airway with the laryngoscope, and the inability to extend the head on the atlanto-occipital joint prevents alignment of oral, pharyngeal, and laryngeal axes. **(B)** Proper positioning with elevation of the shoulders, flexion of the cervical spine, and extension of the head on the atlanto-occipital joint (the "sniffing position"). The breasts fall forward and allow improved access to the airway. The sniffing position helps align the oral, pharyngeal, and laryngeal axes. This position will also aid resting ventilation in the awake parturient. (Photographs courtesy of Dr. B. Leighton, Philadelphia, PA)

One other disadvantage of single-injection spinal anesthesia is its finite duration of action. In obese patients, surgery may be technically difficult and its duration unpredictable. The spinal anesthetic may wear off before the end of surgery. This drawback can be overcome with a continuous spinal technique. As with a continuous epidural blockade, local anesthetic can be titrated to effect, and the duration of anesthesia can be extended rather than having to resort to a general anesthetic technique.

General anesthesia presents significant risks to the obese parturient. The inability to secure an airway is a leading cause of maternal mortality.[39] Obesity is an important risk factor for difficult intubation.[40] Hood *et al*[21] reviewed the anesthetic course of 117 parturients weighing at least 300 pounds. Six of the 17 patients who required general anesthesia for cesarean section were difficult to intubate (see Table 26-5).

Preoperatively, one must carefully evaluate the airway of these women. The Mallampati scale can help

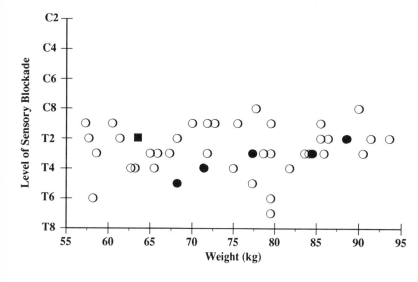

Figure 26–8. Sensory blockade after subarachnoid injection of 12 mg of hyperbaric bupivacaine in 50 term parturients. Sensory blockade develops independently of patient weight. (O = one patient, ● = two patients, ■ = three patients.) (After Norris MC. Height, weight, and the spread of subarachnoid hyperbaric bupivacaine in the term parturient. Anesth Analg 1988;67:555)

predict the ease of intubation (see Table 26-4 and Fig. 26-4). Awake laryngoscopy is another option, but even if you see airway structures with awake laryngoscopy, the induction of general anesthesia and muscle relaxation can change the position of the larynx. Subsequent laryngoscopy may not reveal any identifiable structures.[41] If you see the larynx during awake laryngoscopy, you may wish to pass the endotracheal tube at that time. Fiberoptic laryngoscopy is another option for awake intubation in these patients.

Other factors contribute to the difficult airway in the obese parturient. Large breasts make placement of the laryngoscope in the mouth quite difficult. A short-handled laryngoscope blade can help in this situation.[42] Redundant tissue in the airway may be difficult to displace with any laryngoscope blade. To optimize the chances of a successful intubation, pay close attention to maternal position before inducing anesthesia. Have the patient in the "sniffing position." This position includes flexion of the cervical spine with extension of the head on the atlanto-occipital joint. Because of the generous fat pad behind the shoulders, many obese parturients have difficulty assuming this position with only a small pillow under their heads. Prop up the patient's shoulders on blankets and further support the base of her skull with additional towels (see Fig. 26-7). This positioning helps the breasts fall forward and increases the space between the neck and the chest, allowing easier manipulation of the laryngoscope and proper alignment of the oral, pharyngeal, and laryngeal axes.

One must have appropriate equipment available to detect successful tracheal intubation. Because breath sounds can be distant and difficult to hear, auscultation is not the best way to confirm proper placement of an endotracheal tube. In contrast, detection of exhaled carbon dioxide conclusively confirms the correct placement of the endotracheal tube.

Even with the best of preoperative evaluations, impediments to intubation may arise.[43] For this reason, the obstetric anesthesiologist always must be prepared for the difficult airway. One should have appropriate equipment available and have practiced a "failed intubation drill." As soon as you identify a difficult airway, call for help. Have small endotracheal tubes and a variety of laryngoscope blades at hand. Most importantly, set your priorities in advance. Know ahead of time how you will manage a patient should intubation prove difficult or impossible (see Chap. 32).

Pulmonary aspiration of gastric contents is another significant risk of general anesthesia. The physiologic changes associated with pregnancy place all obstetric patients at increased risk for gastric acid aspiration.

However, obese patients tend to have even larger gastric volumes and lower gastric pHs.[44] Furthermore, difficulties with intubation and the potential for multiple manipulations of the airway may further increase the risk of regurgitation in these patients. For these reasons, use a rapid sequence induction with cricoid pressure and endotracheal intubation when providing general anesthesia. In addition, before anesthesia, use pharmacologic measures to reduce intragastric volume and raise intragastric pH in these patients. Give clear antacids within 30 minutes of the planned surgery. H_2 antagonists will also raise intragastric pH.[45,46] Metoclopramide also may help reduce gastric volume in these patients. Because of their increased risk, I recommend using several pharmacologic measures to help minimize the chances of pulmonary damage should aspiration occur in obese patients.

Obese parturients are at high risk for developing hypoxia during the induction of anesthesia. Nonobese parturients have a more rapid fall in Pa_{O_2} during apnea than nonpregnant patients (Fig. 26-9).[47] They have both a reduced FRC[25] and a higher oxygen consumption than nonpregnant women. Obesity further reduces functional residual capacity. Significant airway closure occurs during tidal ventilation in the supine position.[27,48] General anesthesia exacerbates this problem by further mismatching ventilation and perfusion and increasing the risk of hypoxemia.[48,49] Obese parturients also consume more oxygen than nonobese parturients.[24,27] Consequently, these patients deplete their already low oxygen stores rapidly. Preoxygenation, therefore, is essential in these patients before the induction of anesthesia. In nonobese parturients, clinical studies have shown that either 3 to 5 minutes of tidal breathing or four deep breaths of 100% oxygen provide adequate preoxygenation before the induction of anesthesia.[50] Both techniques also provide effective preoxygenation in nonpregnant obese patients.[51] In addition, obese patients taking four deep breaths do not experience the same rise in Pa_{CO_2} as when they breathe quietly into a face mask for 3 minutes. This factor may help avoid hypercarbia during a difficult intubation. Remember, with any technique of preoxygenation, use high fresh gas flows (8–10 L/min) to prevent rebreathing of exhaled nitrogen, and maintain a tight mask fit to avoid entrainment of room air.

Intraoperatively, pulse oximetry and capnometry provide important information. Capnometry will help guide mechanical ventilation to maintain a normal maternal Pa_{CO_2}. Pulse oximetry assesses the adequacy of maternal oxygenation. Because of the changes in pulmonary function during general anesthesia, obese patients may need a high F_{IO_2} to maintain adequate ma-

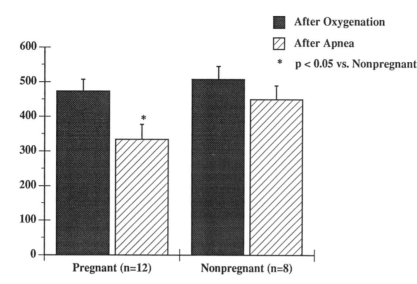

Figure 26–9. The fall in PaO_2 after 60 seconds of apnea is greater in pregnant women than in nonpregnant women. (After Archer GW, Marx GF. Arterial oxygen tension during apnoea in parturient women. Br J Anaesth 1974;46:358)

ternal oxygenation. If the mother cannot tolerate nitrous oxide, low levels of volatile anesthetics can provide maternal anesthesia and amnesia. Large tidal volumes or positive end-expiratory pressure will help maintain maternal oxygenation. If using positive end-expiratory pressure, however, watch for adverse effects on cardiac output and blood pressure.[52]

Obese parturients have altered pharmacokinetics. Obese nonpregnant patients demonstrate greater biotransformation of halothane than do nonobese patients.[53] You may want to avoid this agent in obese parturients and use the lesser metabolized anesthetics enflurane or isoflurane. These patients also may respond unpredictably to muscle relaxants. Weinstein *et al*[54] studied the pharmacodynamics of vecuronium and atracurium in nonpregnant surgical patients and found prolonged recovery times for vecuronium in obese patients. They concluded that obesity most likely alters hepatic clearance. Therefore, carefully titrate vecuronium and other drugs dependent upon hepatic metabolism in obese patients.

Significant hypertension may occur in obese parturients during the induction of general anesthesia and airway manipulation. These patients often have pre-existing hypertensive disorders that further exacerbate the catecholamine response to laryngoscopy and intubation. Control of blood pressure can be achieved by judicious use of additional anesthetics (such as small doses of fentanyl or high doses of volatile anesthetics for a short period of time) or administration of antihypertensive agents (*e.g.,* hydralazine, labetalol).

After completion of surgery, carefully evaluate the adequacy of ventilation, oxygenation, and airway reflexes before extubating the trachea. Assist ventilation in the early postoperative period as needed to provide adequate oxygenation and ventilation.

Neonatal Risks

Cesarean delivery in the obese parturient also can pose significant risks for the neonate. Because of technical difficulties during surgery, the time from induction of anesthesia to delivery of the infant may be prolonged.[22] With general anesthesia, placental passage of anesthetic drugs for a long time (greater than 15 min) can contribute to neonatal depression. The time from uterine incision to delivery also may be protracted in the obese patient; when this time exceeds 3 minutes, fetal acidosis can develop.[55] Diabetes is common in the obese parturient, and these infants may become hypoglycemic after delivery.[19] The person responsible for resuscitation of the newborn should be aware of these additional risk factors.

Postoperative Care

Significant problems continue to occur after cesarean section in obese patients. Pulmonary function abnormalities persist. In nonpregnant obese patients undergoing abdominal surgery, oxygenation remains poor up to the fourth postoperative day (Fig. 26-10).[56] Possible etiologies for this hypoxemia include pain and inadequate ventilation, excessive sedation from analgesics, and diaphragmatic dysfunction. In obese pa-

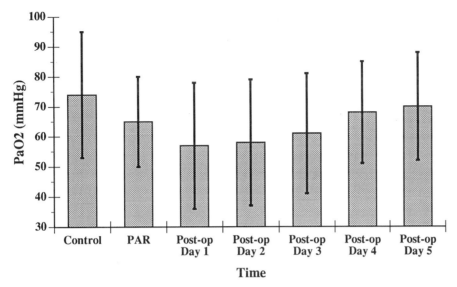

Figure 26–10. Graphic representation of the fall in PaO$_2$ (mm Hg) with time postoperatively in obese patients who have undergone major abdominal surgery. (After Vaughan RW, Englehardt RC, Wise L. Postoperative hypoxemia in obese patients. Ann Surg 1974;180:877)

tients, good postoperative analgesia promotes early ambulation and good pulmonary toilet. Spinal narcotics can prove helpful by providing good analgesia without excessive maternal sedation. In nonobstetric obese patients, the use of spinal narcotics for postoperative pain relief after abdominal surgery improves pulmonary function in the early postoperative period (Fig. 26-11).[57] They can help promote early ambulation, coughing, and deep breathing and good alveolar ventilation.

Cardiac function may be stressed in the early postoperative period. Cardiac demands are highest in the period shortly after birth. Delivery of the placenta eliminates the low-resistance placental bed, raising resistance to ejection. Autotransfusion of blood from the contracted uterus increases end-diastolic volume. Patients with borderline cardiac function may show signs of decompensation at this time. Both resolution of sympathetic blockade from regional anesthesia and mobilization of interstitial edema will contribute to this volume load. The obese parturient with hypertension, preeclampsia, or other evidence of myocardial dysfunction must be monitored carefully after delivery.

Obese patients are at risk for venous stasis and thrombosis in the postoperative period. Thromboembolic disease is a leading cause of mortality in obese parturients (Table 26-6).[58] Early ambulation, compression stockings, and subcutaneous heparin may help prevent venous thrombosis.

ANESTHETIC MANAGEMENT OF THE PATIENT WITH PULMONARY DISEASE

Asthma

Preoperative evaluation of the patient with asthma includes assessment of the severity of asthma during pregnancy, the medications taken by the patient (beta-sympathomimetics, theophylline, steroids, inhaled agents), and events that precipitate asthma. Examine the patient for evidence of bronchospasm. Recognize, however, that bronchospasm alone may not accurately reflect the severity of disease.[59] Spirometry and, if necessary, arterial blood gases provide more information when evaluating the current status of the asthmatic patient (Table 26-7).[59,60] When interpreting arterial blood gases, remember that a normal Paco$_2$ during pregnancy ranges from 32 to 34 mm Hg.[61] Try to optimize maternal pulmonary status before induction of labor or cesarean section.

Important goals for the anesthesiologist caring for the parturient with asthma include avoiding events or agents that would precipitate bronchoconstriction and minimizing the work of breathing during labor or cesarean section. Optimize bronchodilation and continue bronchodilator therapy throughout labor.

Acute asthma occurs uncommonly during labor and delivery. Schatz *et al*[62] studied 336 pregnancies in asth-

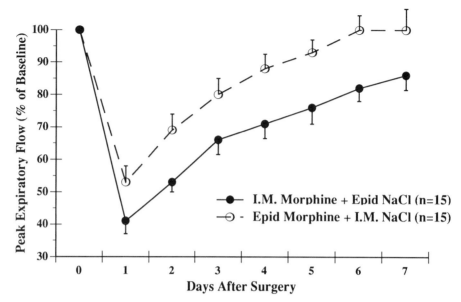

Figure 26-11. Peak expiratory flow values pre- and postoperatively in obese patients who received either intramuscular (IM) or epidural (Epid) morphine for postoperative analgesia. (After Rawal N. Sjöstrand U, Christoffersson E, Dahlström B, Arvill A, Rydman H. Comparison of intramuscular and epidural morphine for postoperative analgesia in the grossly obese: Influence on postoperative ambulation and pulmonary function. Anesth Analg 1984;63:583)

matic patients. Only 10% of these women had symptomatic wheezing during parturition.[62] If acute asthma occurs during labor and delivery, give supplemental oxygen, make sure the patient is well hydrated, and look for an inciting cause (such as pneumonia). Treat the bronchospasm initially with inhaled beta$_2$-adrenergic agonists such as metoproterenol, terbutaline, or albuterol.[59,63-65] Either metered inhaler and nebulized doses can be used during labor and delivery or cesarean section (Table 26-8).

Corticosteroid therapy may be necessary if inhaled beta-agonists do not relieve bronchospasm.[64] Use either beclomethasone, an inhaled steroid, or parenteral corticosteroids. Patients who have taken oral steroids to manage asthma during the previous year should receive steroid coverage during labor and delivery with intravenous hydrocortisone, 100 mg, every 6 hours.[59]

Intravenous aminophylline can also be given in the acute situation; however, recent data suggest that theophylline added to beta-agonist therapy does not improve pulmonary status in the treatment of acute asthma.[64,65] Therefore, the role of this drug in the therapy of acute asthma is unclear. If using intravenous aminophylline, determine the bolus dose based on the patient's current oral theophylline therapy, the pre-existing serum theophylline concentration, and the presence of any other diseases. In patients not taking theophylline, give a loading dose of 5.6 mg/kg (lean body weight) followed by an infusion of 0.5 mg/kg/min.[66] If the patient takes theophylline but has inadequate serum concentrations (therapeutic: 10-20 μg/mL), give 2.5 mg/kg as a loading dose. If the patient already has a therapeutic serum concentration, omit the loading dose. Patients who smoke may need higher infusion rates than other patients. Patients who are on cimetidine or who have cardiac or liver disease will need a lower infusion rate. Toxicity from theophylline produces tachycardia, restlessness, and convulsions. Serum concentrations must be monitored to prevent toxicity.

When treating the asthmatic patient during parturition, bear in mind the potential effects of the bronchodilator agents on uterine tone. Beta-sympathomimetic drugs have similar effects on uterine smooth muscle as on bronchial smooth muscle and cause uterine relaxation. Oxytocin infusions may be needed to continue labor in patients receiving these bronchodilators. Postpartum uterine atony and hemorrhage also may occur. This risk seems minimal in patients receiving inhaled bronchodilators, presumably because of their limited systemic absorption.[63]

Table 26–6

Causes of Death in Obstetric Patients Weighing More than 175 Pounds

CAUSE	NUMBER
Pulmonary embolism	7
Hemorrhage	6
Infection (obstetric)	2
Meningitis	1
Toxemia	1
Amniotic fluid embolism	1
Anesthesia	1
Intracranial hemorrhage	1
Pneumonia	1
Hemorrhagic pancreatitis	1
Acute fatty metamorphosis of liver	1
TOTAL	**23**

(After Maeder EC, Barno A, Mecklenburg F. Obesity: A maternal high-risk factor. Obstet Gynecol 1975;45:669)

Analgesia for Labor and Delivery

Table 26-9 summarizes the issues to consider when providing anesthesia for the asthmatic parturient. Systemic medications can provide analgesia and sedation in the early phases of labor. In more active and painful labor, however, epidural analgesia has distinct advantages. In patients without analgesia, the pain of active

Table 26–7

Clinical Classification of Impairment of Pulmonary Function in Asthma (Percent of Predicted)

	VC, FVC, FEV$_1$, MVV	FEF 25%–75%
Normal	< 80	> 75
Mild	65–80	60–75
Moderate	50–64	45–59
Severe	35–49	30–44
Very severe	< 35	< 30

(Kingston HGG, Hirshman CA. Perioperative management of the patient with asthma. Anesth Analg 1984;63:844) (VC = vital capacity; FVC = forced vital capacity; FEV$_1$ = forced expiratory volume in one second; MVV = maximum voluntary ventilation; FEF = forced expiratory flow)

Table 26–8

Treatment of Peripartum Bronchospasm

Oxygen
Hydration
Treat inciting event (such as pneumonia)
Inhaled bronchodilators
Metoproterenol
Terbutaline
Albuterol
Subcutaneous terbutaline
Intravenous corticosteroids
Aminophylline infusion

labor increases minute ventilation and oxygen consumption.[29] In the asthmatic patient, this hyperventilation and hypocarbia may precipitate bronchospasm. Epidural analgesia blunts these effects.[29] For patients who do not receive epidural analgesia for labor, low levels of spinal anesthesia may be used for vaginal or forceps delivery.

Anesthesia for Cesarean Delivery

If at all possible, optimize a patient's pulmonary status before surgery begins. Continue asthma medications up to the time of surgery. Monitor pulmonary status during surgery. In some patients, this task may require only verbal communication, pulse oximetry, and chest auscultation. In unstable patients, sample arterial blood gases as needed.

Regional anesthesia offers significant advantages in these women. By avoiding airway manipulation, one can markedly diminish the risk of inciting bronchospasm. In an awake patient, one can maintain con-

Table 26–9

The Asthmatic Parturient and Anesthesia

Optimize pulmonary status before delivery, if possible.
Avoid events that precipitate asthma (hyperventilation, hypocarbia, airway manipulation).
Continue bronchodilator therapy during labor and delivery or perioperative period.
Regional analgesia for labor diminishes ventilatory work.
General anesthesia via endotracheal tube may precipitate bronchospasm.
Avoid 15-methyl prostaglandin F$_{2\alpha}$.

tinuous verbal contact and readily elicit and assess subjective signs of respiratory difficulty.

EPIDURAL ANESTHESIA. Epidural anesthesia is a very good choice for these women. A continuous epidural catheter technique allows careful titration of the level of sensory blockade. Epinephrine (1:200,000) in epidural local anesthetics improves sensory block and may aid in bronchodilation; however, no documentation exists that this small amount of absorbed epinephrine produces significant bronchial relaxation. During epidural anesthesia, the level of motor block is usually four to five spinal segments below the level of sensory block. While the level of sensory block required for cesarean section does not affect resting pulmonary ventilation,[67] this level of blockade does reduce forced expiratory flow rates. The patient with pre-existing pulmonary disease may have difficulty coughing in this situation.[68] Assess the patient's ventilatory function continuously. Reassure the patient should the loss of sensation in the chest wall contribute to a feeling of shortness of breath. If the woman cannot cough, avoid sedatives that further suppress coughing and watch for problems with oral secretions or regurgitation.

SPINAL ANESTHESIA. Spinal anesthesia can also be used for these women. In one report, however, intraoperative bronchospasm developed in an asthmatic patient with a T-5 level of sensory blockade. The author of that report hypothesized that loss of circulating epinephrine from the sympathetic blockade precipitated the bronchospasm.[69] This single case of bronchospasm with spinal anesthesia should not label this anesthetic technique as contraindicated in the asthmatic parturient. Be aware that bronchospasm can occur during any regional anesthetic.

GENERAL ANESTHESIA. General anesthesia carries significant risks for the parturient with asthma. In addition to the usual concerns about general anesthesia in parturients, the rapid sequence induction and intubation for cesarean section may precipitate bronchospasm.[70] Try to establish an adequate depth of anesthesia to help avoid intubation-induced bronchospasm. Ketamine, even in low doses (0.5 mg/kg, or less), causes bronchodilation in nonpregnant patients with pulmonary disorders.[71] Bronchodilation begins within 1.5 minutes, and lasts 6 to 8 minutes.[71] Animal studies have confirmed the bronchodilator characteristics of ketamine.[72] This feature makes ketamine the best induction agent in asthmatic parturients. Minimal neonatal depression occurs if the induction dose remains below 1.5 mg/kg.[73,74] At this dose, however, ketamine

transiently increases uterine tone.[75] Consider this side effect when using ketamine as an induction agent for cesarean section in situations in which increased uterine tone would be harmful (abruptio placenta, cord prolapse). Ketamine also causes sympathetic stimulation increasing maternal blood pressure and heart rate.[74] This effect makes ketamine a less favorable induction agent in hypertensive parturients.

An alternative to ketamine is thiopental, 4 to 5 mg/kg, in rapid sequence with succinylcholine, 1.5 mg/kg. Small doses of narcotic can help assure deeper anesthesia for intubation. This generous dose of succinylcholine helps achieve a rapid onset of dense neuromuscular blockade, preventing coughing and straining with intubation. If endotracheal intubation is complicated by severe bronchospasm or if bronchospasm occurs any time during general anesthesia, give high concentrations of oxygen. Administer inhaled bronchodilators via the endotracheal tube. Volatile anesthetics are potent bronchodilators. Use them to maintain anesthesia and promote bronchodilation in these patients.[76-78] If used in high concentrations before delivery of the fetus, however, potent agents will contribute to neonatal depression. Alert the physician responsible for newborn resuscitation to this potential. High concentrations of these anesthetics also may contribute to uterine atony and increased blood loss after delivery.

Ventricular dysrhythmias have been reported when patients receiving theophylline are exposed to halothane.[79] Animal studies suggest that halothane, unlike enflurane or isoflurane, sensitizes the myocardium to the arrythmogenic effects of theophylline.[80,81] Avoid this volatile anesthetic in patients receiving theophylline.

As in all parturients, the usual precautions to minimize the chance of pulmonary aspiration of gastric contents should be performed in these patients. Asthmatic patients tolerate irritation of the airways and any intrapulmonary process very poorly.

Extubation is a tricky time in asthmatic parturients. An awake extubation is important to minimize the chance of pulmonary aspiration of gastric contents. However, the endotracheal tube may prompt bronchospasm as the level of anesthesia lightens. Inhaled bronchodilators can be used during this time, and small doses of fentanyl or lidocaine given before emergence also can help minimize airway reactivity during extubation.

Asthmatic patients are exquisitely sensitive to the bronchoconstrictor effects of prostaglandin $F_{2\alpha}$.[82] Therefore, do not use the synthetic analogue of this prostaglandin, 15-methyl prostaglandin$_{2\alpha}$, carboprosttromethamine (Prostin-15 M, Hemabate), to treat uterine atony in asthmatic patients. To control uterine bleeding, continue vigorous uterine massage and use intravenous infusions of oxytocin or intramuscular ergot derivatives.

Cigarette Use

Cigarette use during pregnancy is a common problem, with significant effects on pregnancy outcome. In a dose-dependent fashion, cigarette use decreases birth weight and increases perinatal mortality.[83] It also increases the risks of abruptio placenta, placenta previa, and bleeding during pregnancy.[84] Premature and prolonged rupture of membranes also occurs more commonly in smokers.[84] Cigarette smoking contributes to fetal hypoxia by increasing maternal carbon monoxide levels. Carbon monoxide competes with oxygen for binding sites on hemoglobin in both the mother and the fetus. Elevated carbon monoxide levels decrease fetal oxygen content. This chronic hypoxemia alters both fetal and placental development. The fetus redirects perfusion to priority organs (brain, heart, and adrenal glands) at the expense of overall growth. The placenta increases in size, surface area, and vascularity to optimize fetal oxygenation. These changes predispose the mother to hemorrhagic complications.

Analgesia for Labor and Delivery

Regional anesthetic techniques can provide excellent labor, delivery, or cesarean section analgesia in these women. During the induction of either spinal or epidural anesthesia, however, take care to avoid hypotension with adequate maternal prehydration, left uterine displacement, and careful monitoring of blood pressure. Monitor the fetus during the induction of anesthesia to assess any potential effects of the anesthetic on placental perfusion.

Anesthesia for Cesarean Delivery

General anesthesia for cesarean section has significant disadvantages for parturients who smoke. Airway reactivity increases in patients who smoke regularly.[85] Therefore, the induction of general anesthesia may provoke bronchospasm. The same induction techniques and treatments for intraoperative bronchospasm described in the section on patients with asthma are appropriate. General anesthesia also has adverse effects on mucociliary clearance and macrophage function in patients who smoke cigarettes.[86] This action may increase the risk of postoperative pulmonary problems.

Regional anesthesia, in contrast, avoids airway manipulation and suppression of mucociliary clearance. However, the motor blockade that accompanies the high level of sensory block necessary for cesarean section may interfere with the ability of the some parturients to cough during and immediately after surgery.[87]

Cigarette smokers produce more airway secretions than nonsmokers. Encourage aggressive postoperative pulmonary toilet with incentive spirometry and deep breathing and coughing. Avoid drugs that cause cough suppression (systemic narcotics and sedatives) as much as possible. Postoperative analgesia with intraspinal narcotics can minimize cough suppression and help maintain optimal pulmonary function.

ANESTHETIC MANAGEMENT OF THE PARTURIENT WITH NEUROLOGIC DISEASE

Anesthetic care of the parturient with pre-existing neurologic disease must be individualized. It should take into consideration the natural history of the patient's disease and the likelihood that a specific anesthetic technique or drug will alter the course of that disease. Some anesthesiologists hesitate, for example, to do a regional anesthetic in a patient with a neuropathy. If the patient's condition worsens after the anesthetic, they fear their anesthetic will be blamed for the problem. Others believe it is unfair to consider all patients with neurologic disease ineligible for the potential benefits of regional anesthesia for labor, delivery, or cesarean section.[87,88] Consider each case individually in consultation with the patient, her neurologist, and her obstetrician to design a reasonable and safe anesthetic plan. Understand the pathophysiology of the neurologic problem, and consider the potential effects of anesthesia on the disease. Come to an agreement with the patient regarding anesthetic management before labor begins. The following sections outline the information available concerning the effects of anesthetics on patients with seizure disorders, multiple sclerosis, myasthenia gravis, paraplegia, and intracranial vascular abnormalities.

Seizure Disorder

Possible causes of seizures during pregnancy include eclampsia, intracranial tumor or vascular abnormality, subarachnoid hemorrhage, metabolic disturbances, drug or alcohol withdrawal, and trauma. Be aware of the etiology of seizures in a given parturient. Review the medications used by the patient with a pre-existing seizure disorder. Check the serum concentration of the patient's medication, and give supplemental medication if needed. Avoid situations that could lower seizure threshold.

Epidural analgesia provides significant benefits to these patients during labor. Hypocarbia, which develops when labor pain causes maternal hyperventilation, lowers seizure threshold. Epidural analgesia limits this maternal hyperventilation in response to pain.[29] Similarly, regional anesthesia is suitable for anesthesia for cesarean section.

Two anesthetic agents, enflurane and ketamine, can potentially cause seizures. High concentrations (2.5%–3%) of enflurane in the presence of hypocarbia lower the seizure threshold and cause convulsions.[89] At lower doses and with normocarbia, however, Oshima *et al*[90] found enflurane to have anticonvulsant properties in cats. These authors conclude that enflurane carries little risk of exacerbating a pre-existing epileptic focus. The presence of a seizure disorder probably does not contraindicate the use of enflurane in low doses during cesarean section. Ketamine incites electroencephalographic seizure activity when given to patients with preexisting seizure disorders.[91,92] Ferrer-Allado[92] studied the effects of ketamine on patients with epilepsy and found electrical seizure activity in all six patients who received 2 or 4 mg/kg ketamine intravenously. Do not use ketamine as an induction agent in parturients with epilepsy.

Some seizure medications may alter anesthetic requirements. Phenytoin and carbamazepine reportedly antagonize the action of nondepolarizing muscle relaxants.[93,94] Monitor neuromuscular function carefully in patients receiving these medications. Phenobarbital increases hepatic metabolism of anesthetics by inducing hepatic enzyme function. I suggest using only the minimally metabolized volatile anesthetics enflurane or isoflurane.

Multiple Sclerosis

Multiple sclerosis is a neurologic disease characterized by nerve demyelination with intermittent exacerbations and improvements in symptoms (muscle weakness, neurogenic bladder, visual problems, paraplegia, emotional lability). Infections, exhaustion, and emotional trauma can worsen symptoms. Parturients with multiple sclerosis who relapse tend to do so in the 3 months after delivery instead of during pregnancy.

There are theoretic concerns about the use of regional anesthesia in patients with multiple sclerosis. Given the waxing and waning nature of the disease, the timing and exacerbation of the disease may coincide with the use of a regional anesthetic. In addition, local anesthetics may be neurotoxic when injected close to these demyelinated nerves and could contribute directly to worsening of the disease. Still, individual case reports[88,95] and a recent case series document safe use of epidural block for labor analgesia and cesarean delivery.[96] There is, however, an association between the use of high concentrations of local anesthetics in the epidural space and the incidence of relapse of multiple sclerosis after delivery (Table 26-10).[96] The number of patients in the case series was small. Other factors (long difficult labor, fetal malpresentation, difficult delivery, etc.) may both fuel the need for high concentrations of local anesthetics and magnify the risk of relapse of multiple sclerosis. Nevertheless, in light of the aforementioned findings, one should probably use as little local anesthetic as possible in patients with multiple sclerosis. In addition, discuss the possibility of relapse with the parturient preoperatively. No data exist concerning the use of spinal anesthesia in these women. Most experts do not recommend spinal block because of the theoretic concern of neurotoxicity from injecting the local anesthetic close to demyelinated nerves.

General anesthesia with a variety of different agents has been used in nonpregnant patients with multiple sclerosis without consistent alterations in relapse rate.[97] There is one case report of hyperkalemia following succinylcholine administration in a patient with multiple sclerosis.[98] However, the absence of other reports suggests a low incidence of this problem in these

Table 26-10

Relapse of Multiple Sclerosis in the First 3 Months Postpartum

TYPE OF ANESTHETIC	CESAREAN DELIVERY	RELAPSE NUMBER
Epidural	5	1
General	3	1
VAGINAL DELIVERY		
Epidural	9	4
Local	13	2
General	2	1

(After Bader AM, Hunt CO, Datta S, Naulty JS, Ostheimer GW. Anesthesia for the obstetric patient with multiple sclerosis. J Clin Anesth 1988;1:21)

patients.[99] Routine techniques of giving general anesthesia to parturients is probably appropriate.

Myasthenia Gravis

Myasthenia gravis is a disease characterized by the lack of response of the postsynaptic acetylcholine receptor to acetylcholine, probably due to antibodies to that receptor. Symptoms include weakness and easy fatigability of voluntary muscles. Anticholinesterase therapy usually produces significant improvement.[100] This disease affects mostly women and often becomes symptomatic by age 20. Pregnancy has a variable effect on the course of this disease. Exacerbations can arise postpartum.[101] Preoperative evaluation of the parturient with myasthenia gravis must include knowing the muscles involved (respiratory, bulbar), current symptoms, ventilatory status assessed by serial spirometric measurements, and status of anticholinesterase therapy. Continue anticholinesterase medications throughout the peripartum period to allow preservation of adequate muscle strength during the work of labor and delivery (Table 26-11).

Systemic medications can provide labor analgesia for myasthenic patients, but give only small doses to avoid ventilatory depression.[100] Epidural analgesia will reduce the ventilatory work in response to the pain of labor without interfering with the muscles of respiration.[67] This effect makes segmental epidural blockade potentially beneficial in these women, who may have limited muscle strength and ventilatory capacity.

Parturients with myasthenia gravis present a more difficult anesthetic challenge should they require cesarean delivery. Anesthetic choice depends upon the patient's ventilatory status and muscle strength. Although regional anesthesia has advantages, high levels of sensory and motor block with spinal anesthesia can worsen ventilatory function. An epidural anesthetic may prove more advantageous. In contrast to spinal anesthesia, the anesthetic level can be carefully titrated. Motor blockade is lower and less profound than that seen with a comparable sensory level of spinal anesthesia.[67] These effects minimize the interference of epidural anesthesia with ventilatory function.[67] If one chooses a regional anesthetic technique, one should be prepared to intubate and ventilate should muscle weakness and respiratory failure develop. A regional anesthetic technique does offer the option of using spinal or epidural narcotics for postoperative pain relief, therefore minimizing the need for sedating systemic narcotics after surgery. Anticholinesterase medications may impede the metabolism of ester local anesthetics (*i.e.*, 2-chloroprocaine). Use amide-type local anesthetics only in women taking these drugs.

Because of either maternal or fetal concerns, one also may choose general anesthesia for a patient with myasthenia gravis. Parturients unable to maintain satisfactory ventilation during labor are unlikely to tolerate the stress of surgery under regional anesthesia. However, when contemplating general anesthesia for such a patient, consider her unpredictable response to muscle relaxants.[99,100] Patients taking anticholinesterase medications respond erratically to succinylcholine. In nonpregnant patients without the risk of pulmonary aspiration of gastric contents or neonatal depression, one can obtain adequate conditions for tracheal intubation with volatile anesthetics alone or with small doses of nondepolarizing muscle relaxants.[99] Baraka and Tabbouch[102] reported the response to 1.5 mg/kg of succinylcholine in three myasthenic patients (two had their anticholinesterase medications discontinued the evening prior to surgery, one did not). Complete neuromuscular blockade occurred in 60 seconds and lasted 10 to 15 minutes. In pregnancy, when aspiration is a risk, I recommend either awake intubation with topical anesthesia or a rapid sequence induction of anesthesia using 1.5 mg/kg of succinylcholine. Closely monitor neuromuscular function and prepare for the possibility of postoperative mechanical ventilation.

Paraplegia and Quadriplegia

Proper anesthetic management is crucial to the safe conduct of labor and delivery in the patient with paraplegia or quadriplegia. Although patients with spinal

Table 26-11

Anesthesia and Myasthenia Gravis

Preoperative Evaluation

Determine muscles involved.

Assess ventilatory status, serial spirometry.

Administer anticholinesterase medications.

Anesthetic Issues

Avoid fatigue.

Continue anticholinesterase medications.

Use minimal systemic sedatives.

Avoid aminoglycoside antibiotics and magnesium therapy.

Keep in mind that response to muscle relaxants is unpredictable.

Avoid ester local anesthetics in patients receiving anticholinesterase medications.

cord injury above T-10 may not perceive pain during labor, sympathetic discharge can incite dangerous autonomic hyperreflexia. Preoperative evaluation of these patients must include assessment of the level spinal cord injury, symptoms of autonomic hyperreflexia, and ventilatory function.

Autonomic hyperreflexia is a syndrome seen in 85% of patients with spinal cord lesions at or above T-6.[103] It involves flushing, sweating, severe hypertension, and bradycardia. Distention or contraction of a viscus below the level of spinal cord injury can trigger autonomic hyperreflexia. Reflex sympathetic discharge, not modified or inhibited by supraspinal centers, follows. The vasculature in the region below the spinal cord level, very sensitive to catecholamines, responds with pronounced vasoconstriction. The resulting very severe hypertension can lead to convulsions or cerebral hemorrhage. Hypertension, via afferents from the carotid and aortic arch baroreceptors, then stimulates vagally mediated bradycardia (Fig. 26-12). Uterine contractions can initiate autonomic hyperreflexia,[104-108] and paroxysmal hypertension may be the only sign of labor in patients with complete spinal cord transection.

Measure blood pressure and heart rate frequently in patients at risk for autonomic hyperreflexia. Undiag-

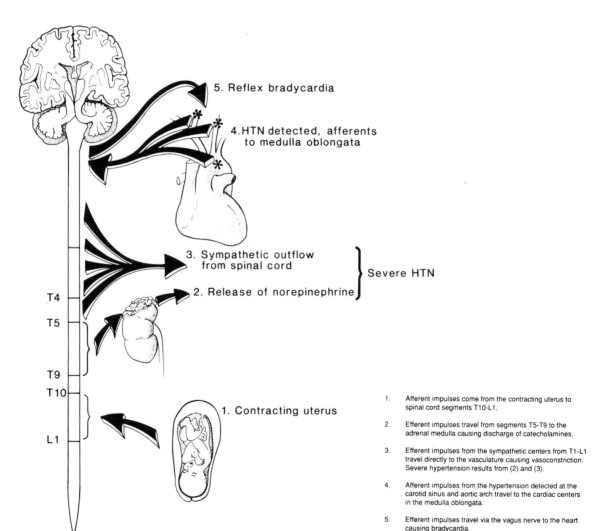

Figure 26–12. Mechanism of cardiovascular changes in autonomic hyperreflexia. (HTN = hypertension.) (After Abouleish EI, Hanley ES, Palmer SM. Can epidural fentanyl control autonomic hyperreflexia in a quadriplegic parturient? Anesth Analg 1989;68:523)

nosed severe hypertension during labor has caused intracerebral hemorrhage and death.[109,110] Consider invasive monitoring of blood pressure with a radial artery catheter.

Epidural analgesia can block autonomic hyperreflexia. Several case reports describe the safe and effective use of epidural blockade for labor analgesia in patients with symptoms of autonomic hyperreflexia (Fig. 26-13).[105–108] One problem with epidural anesthesia in a patient with complete spinal cord transection is the inability to diagnose intrathecal injection of local anesthetic; therefore, proceed cautiously with initial dosing. Epidural fentanyl alone does not block autonomic hyperreflexia.[107] In contrast, epidural meperidine, probably because of its local anesthetic effect, can.[102] An epidural anesthetic allows continuous administration of local anesthetic throughout labor with supplementation for delivery. In patients with reduced motor strength and the inability to push, epidural analgesia also will permit forceps delivery without risking autonomic hyperreflexia. Epidural anesthesia also should work nicely for cesarean section.

If general anesthesia becomes necessary in the paraplegic parturient, using succinylcholine may cause severe hyperkalemia.[98,111] This problem occurs up to a

year after the injury. If the paralysis is progressive, hyperkalemia continues to be a risk.[98] Alternatives to succinylcholine do exist. Intubate the trachea either with the patient awake or following a large dose of a short-acting nondepolarizing muscle relaxant. In nonpregnant patients, adequate intubating conditions develop 60 seconds after vecuronium, 0.25 mg/kg, or atracurium, 1.5 mg/kg.[112] At these doses, however, muscle relaxation lasts 70 to 80 minutes. Less hypotension transpires following this large dose of vecuronium compared to atracurium. Alternatively, one may give these drugs in divided doses. Tessum *et al*[113] studied the onset of vecuronium given in divided doses (0.01 mg/kg followed in 4–6 min by 0.1 mg/kg) to parturients. Adequate intubating conditions developed in all patients by 2.7 minutes. Paralysis persisted for 71 minutes.

Once you have secured the airway, maintain an adequate depth of general anesthesia to prevent autonomic hyperreflexia during surgery.[103] Again, monitor blood pressure carefully. Autonomic hyperreflexia can also occur postoperatively. Adequate postoperative analgesia is important. Epidural (and presumably spinal morphine) appears to help limit postoperative sympathetic discharge due to pain.[114]

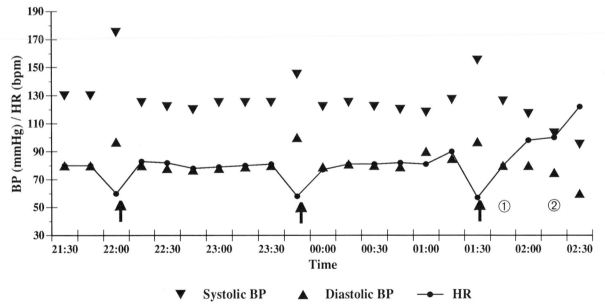

Figure 26–13. Vital signs in a paraplegic parturient with twin gestation during labor. Autonomic hyperreflexia was managed with epidural anesthesia. Note the severe hypertension responsive to repeat administration of the epidural catheter with bupivacaine (arrows). (BP = blood pressure, HR = heart rate, 1 = delivery of first twin, 2 = delivery of second twin.) (After Watson DW, Downey GO. Epidural anesthesia for labor and delivery of twins of a paraplegic mother. Anesthesiology 1980;52:259)

Intracranial Vascular Lesions

Subarachnoid hemorrhage may happen in women of child-bearing age. Most intracranial bleeding follows rupture of either a berry (saccular) aneurysm or an arteriovenous malformation. The timing of bleeding from these two lesions varies, but events that likely increase the risk of subarachnoid hemorrhage include coughing, straining, emotional stress, and lifting. Therefore, anesthetic management of these patients must limit those situations that might magnify the risk of hemorrhage while preserving a healthy environment for the fetus.

Preoperative evaluation of patients with intracranial vascular lesions must examine several factors. What is the intracranial pathology? What surgical intervention, if any, has been performed? Has she bled in the past? Does she currently have symptoms attributable to intracranial blood (meningismus, headache) or increased intracranial pressure (headache, nausea, vomiting, altered sensorium)? Also, one must know the contemplated obstetric plan (induction of labor vs cesarean delivery). Patients with acute symptoms may need invasive arterial blood pressure or central venous pressure monitoring to guide therapy directed at blood pressure control and maintenance of normal intravascular volume.

Anesthesia for Labor and Delivery

Continuous lumbar epidural or caudal anesthesia has been used in patients with intracranial vascular lesions for both labor and vaginal delivery and for cesarean section. This type of anesthesia can limit the hyper-tensive response to the pain of uterine contractions, prevent "bearing down" during the later stages of labor, and provide anesthesia for forceps delivery.[115-118] All of these effects potentially benefit the patient with intracranial vascular lesions. Direct measurements of cerebrospinal fluid (CSF) pressure in normal parturients have shown that it increases markedly during a painful uterine contraction associated with maternal pushing efforts.[120] Then, when the "pushing" or Valsalva maneuver is released, CSF pressure falls quickly. At the same time, blood pressure rises as venous return improves after the Valsalva maneuver. This reaction places extra stress on intracranial vessels (Fig. 26-14). The risk of rupture at this time is greater for an arteriovenous malformation than for an aneurysm. Therefore, avoiding pain and "bearing down" is a priority in these patients.

Anesthetic management differs when an acute intracerebral hemorrhage has occurred and the patient has increased intracranial pressure. When elevated intracranial pressure is suspected, careful neurologic examination must be performed. As in the patient with an intact lesion, avoid events that can increase intracranial pressure. In these women, however, epidural anesthesia may not offer the best choice to accomplish this end. First, if accidental dural puncture occurs in a patient with high intracranial pressure, the cerebellum may herniate. Injecting fluid into the epidural space also may increase CSF pressure. In patients with abnormal intracranial compliance (after head trauma), Hilt *et al*[120] demonstrated marked increases in intracranial pressure when injecting lumbar epidural catheters with 10 mL of bupivacaine or saline (Fig. 26-15). These in-

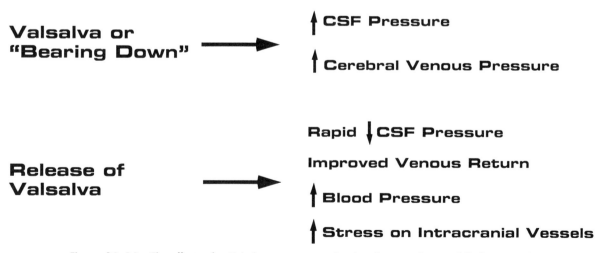

Figure 26–14. The effects of a Valsalva manuever, or "pushing," on cerebrospinal fluid (CSF) and intravascular pressures.

creases in intracranial pressure lasted a few minutes. Smaller increments in intracranial pressure followed injection of 5 mL of fluid. This report underscores the need for care when injecting an epidural catheter in someone who may have reduced intracranial compliance.

Systemic medications may be used if the clinical situation contraindicates regional anesthesia.[121] Use narcotics sparingly to avoid hypoventilation, hypercarbia, and cerebral venodilation. Nitrous oxide and oxygen analgesia may help during labor and avoid the ventilatory depressant effects of systemic medications. Paracervical block also may be used in these patients. Although effective for the mother, this technique may cause fetal bradycardia. Avoid it in patients in whom fetal acidosis is suspected. Minimize the hemodynamic effects of uterine contractions (hypertension, tachycardia) in these patients with appropriate antihypertensive therapy. Pudendal block and inhalation analgesia can provide pain relief during delivery.

Anesthesia for Cesarean Section

Epidural anesthesia has been used safely for cesarean section in patients with intracranial vascular abnormalities.[122] Dose the epidural catheter slowly while observing the patient for any symptoms of increased intracranial pressure or falling blood pressure. Prophylactic antiemetic drugs, such as metoclopramide or droperidol, can limit nausea and vomiting.

Certain situations (coma, high intracranial pressure, emergency surgery) may necessitate general anesthesia for cesarean delivery.[123,124] The goals of minimizing hemodynamic perturbations, preventing elevations of intracranial pressure, hypoxia, and pulmonary aspiration of gastric contents, and avoiding neonatal depression persist.

Maternal hypertension develops commonly during the usual rapid sequence induction of general anesthesia. This hypertension can cause rupture of an aneurysm or arteriovenous malformation and will contribute to increases in intracranial pressure. Deep anesthesia is essential before endotracheal intubation. Small doses of fentanyl before induction with a generous dose of thiopental, 4 to 6 mg/kg, can accomplish the goal. Intravenous lidocaine and voluntary hyperventilation before the induction of anesthesia also will help blunt changes in intracranial pressure. Pretreat with a small dose of nondepolarizing muscle relaxant to blunt fasciculations due to succinylcholine. Avoid airway manipulation until anesthesia and complete muscle relaxation have developed. Treat any elevations in blood pressure aggressively. Infusions of nitroprusside or trimethaphan help. To limit the risk of precipitous hypotension, use nitroprusside only with direct arterial pressure monitoring.

An alternate approach to giving general anesthesia to the parturient with intracranial vascular abnormalities is to avoid the risk of inadequate anesthesia and hypertension with laryngoscopy by performing a slower

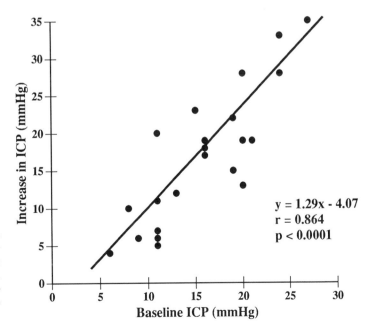

Figure 26–15. Increases in intracranial pressure (ICP) seen after injection of 10 mL of bupivacaine or saline into the lumbar epidural space of two patients with abnormal intracranial compliance. (After Hilt H, Gramm HJ, Link J. Changes in intracranial pressure associated with extradural anaesthesia. Br J Anaesth 1986;58:676)

$$y = 1.29x - 4.07$$
$$r = 0.864$$
$$p < 0.0001$$

induction of anesthesia. After preoxygenation, apply cricoid pressure and induce anesthesia with barbiturate and narcotic slowly. Control blood pressure with antihypertensive medications or additional anesthesia. Secure the airway after complete paralysis with a nondepolarizing muscle relaxant. This technique risks pulmonary aspiration of gastric contents during mask ventilation and neonatal depression. Reserve this technique for those clinical situations in which the risk of hemodynamic perturbations from a rapid sequence induction outweigh the likelihood of aspiration. The parturient with acutely elevated intracranial pressure or recent bleed from an aneurysm would probably fall into this category.[123,124] This technique also will anesthetize the neonate. Be prepared to resuscitate the newborn appropriately.

With any technique, consider the potential for adverse effects on uteroplacental perfusion and the fetus. Maternal positioning must avoid aortocaval compression so that when blood pressure does fall, adequate venous return will help maintain a normal cardiac output. Hyperventilation may decrease intracranial pressure in the mother but has adverse effects on the fetus. Positive-pressure ventilation reduces uterine blood flow, and hypocarbia reduces fetal blood oxygen content.[125]

After delivery, do not use ergot derivatives to treat uterine atony; they cause hypertension via alpha-receptor stimulation. Oxytocin poses no problem.

SUMMARY AND CONCLUSION

Proper anesthetic management of the parturient with medical problems demands knowledge of the following:

- The patient's disease
- The impact of her pregnancy on her disease
- The impact of her disease on the pregnancy and fetus
- The impact of the planned anesthetic on both patient and fetus

Consult the patient's internist, endocrinologist, pulmonologist, or neurologist, and learn the current extent and management of her medical problem. Consult the patient's obstetrician about the delivery plan. Consider the side effects of the available anesthetic techniques and what specific agents are best used or avoided. Finally, spend time discussing these concerns with the patient. This discussion is not always possible in the labor and delivery suite, where management plans change frequently. Seeing these patients in advance of parturition will allow gathering of information from the patient's primary physicians, discussing anesthetic options with the patient, and formulating an anesthetic plan.

REFERENCES

1. West TET, Lowy C. Control of blood glucose during labour in diabetic women with combined glucose and low-dose insulin infusion. Br Med J 1977;1:1252.
2. Kenepp NB, Shelley WC, Kumar S, Gutsche BB, Gabbe S, Delivoria–Papadopoulos M. Effects on newborn of hydration with glucose in patients undergoing caesarean section with regional anesthesia. Lancet 1980;1:645.
3. Robillard JE, Sessions C, Kennedy RL, Smith FG Jr. Metabolic effects of constant hypertonic glucose infusion in well-oxygenated fetuses. Am J Obstet Gynecol 1978;130:199.
4. Kitzmiller JL, Phillipe M, Von Oeyen P, Datta S, Brouilard E. Hyperglycemia, hypoxia and fetal acidosis in rhesus monkey [Abstract]. Proc Soc Gynecol Invest 1981:98.
5. Lawrence GF, Brown VA, Parsons RJ, Cooke ID. Fetal–maternal consequences of high-dose glucose infusion during labour. Br J Obstet Gynaecol 1982;89:27.
6. Hauguel S, Desmaizieres V, Challier JC. Glucose uptake, utilization, and transfer by the human placenta as functions of maternal glucose concentration. Pediatr Res 1986;20:269.
7. Carson BS, Phillips AF, Simmons MA, Battaglia FC, Meschia G. Effects of a sustained insulin infusion upon glucose uptake and oxygenation of the ovine fetus. Pediatr Res 1980;14:147.
8. Light IJ, Keenan WJ, Sutherland JM. Maternal intravenous glucose administration as a cause of hypoglycemia in the infant of the diabetic mother. Am J Obstet Gynecol 1972;113:345.
9. Jones CJP, Fox H. Placental changes in gestational diabetes. Obstet Gynecol 1976;48:274.
10. Cousins L. Pregnancy complications among diabetic women: Review 1965–1985. Obstet Gynecol Surv 1987;42:140.
11. Shnider SM, Abboud TK, Artal R, Henriksen EH, Stefani SJ, Levinson G. Maternal catecholamines decrease during labor after lumbar epidural anesthesia. Am J Obstet Gynecol 1983;147:13.
12. Buchan PC, Milne MK, Browning MCK. The effect of continuous epidural blockade on plasma 11-hydroxycorticosteroid concentrations in labour. Obstet Gynecol Br Commonwealth 1973;80:974.
13. Bromage PR. Physiology and pharmacology of epidural analgesia. Anesthesiology 1967;28:592.
14. Lev-Ran A. Sharp temporary drop in insulin requirement after cesarean section in diabetic patients. Am J Obstet Gynecol 1974;120:905.

15. Datta S, Brown Jr., WJ. Acid–base status in diabetic mothers and their infants following general or spinal anesthesia for cesarean section. Anesthesiology 1977;47:272.

16. Datta S, Kitzmiller JL, Naulty JS, Ostheimer GW, Weiss JB. Acid–base status of diabetic mothers and their infants following spinal anesthesia for cesarean section. Anesth Analg 1982;61:662.

17. Datta S, Brown Jr., WU, Ostheimer GW, Weiss JB, Alper MH. Epidural anesthesia for cesarean section in diabetic parturients: Maternal and neonatal acid–base status and bupivacaine concentration. Anesth Analg 1981;60:574.

18. James FM III, Dewan DM, Floyd HM, et al. Chloroprocaine vs. bupivacaine for lumbar epidural analgesia for elective cesarean section. Anesthesiology 1980;52:488.

19. Kliegman RM, Gross T. Perinatal problems of the obese mother and her infant. Obstet Gynecol 1985;66:299.

20. Thomson M, Hanley J. Factors predisposing to difficult labor in primiparas. Am J Obstet Gynecol 1988;158:1074.

21. Hood DD, Dewan DM, Kashtan K. Anesthesia outcome in the morbidly obese parturient. Anesthesiology 1990;73:A952.

22. El-Naggar M, Mehta K, Kartha RK. Morbid obesity in the parturient patients. Anesthesiology 1990;73:A1000.

23. Garbaciak JA, Richter M, Miller S, Barton JJ. Maternal weight and pregnancy complications. Am J Obstet Gynecol 1985;152:238.

24. Molitch ME. Obesity—maternal risks associated with obesity. In Barron WM, Lindheimer MD, eds. Medical disorders during pregnancy. St. Louis: Mosby–Year Book, 1991:136.

25. Bevan DR, Holdcroft A, Loh L, MacGregor WG, O'Sullivan JC, Sykes MK. Closing volume and pregnancy. Br Med J 1974;1:13.

26. Eng M, Butler J, Bonica JJ. Respiratory function in pregnant obese women. Am J Obstet Gynecol 1975;123:241.

27. Burki NK, Baker RW. Ventilatory regulation in eucapnic morbid obesity. Am Rev Respir Dis 1984;129:538.

28. Mallampati SR, Gatt SP, Gugino LD, et al. A clinical sign to predict difficult tracheal intubation: A prospective study. Can Anaesth Soc J 1985;34:429.

29. Hagerdal M, Morgan CW, Sumner AE, Gutsche BB. Minute ventilation and oxygen consumption during labor with epidural analgesia. Anesthesiology 1983;59.425.

30. Peabody JL. Transcutaneous oxygen measurement to evaluate drug effects. Clin in Perinatol 1979;6:109.

31. Vincent RD, Chestnut DH, Russell PK, Walker BJ, Östman LP. What position is more comfortable for the parturient during induction of epidural anesthesia? Anesthesiology 1990;73:A978.

32. Maitra AM, Palmer SK, Bachhuber SR, Abram SE. Continuous epidural analgesia for cesarean section in a patient with morbid obesity. Anesth Analg 1979;58:348.

33. Hodgkinson R, Husain FJ. Obesity and the cephalad spread of analgesia following epidural administration of bupivacaine for cesarean section. Anesth Analg 1980;59:89.

34. Hodgkinson R, Husain FJ. Obesity, gravity, and spread of epidural anesthesia. Anesth Analg 1981;60:421.

35. Ahern JK, Goodlin RC. Cesarean section in the massively obese. Obstet Gynecol 1978;51:509.

36. Wolfe HM, Gross TL, Sokol RJ, Bottoms SF, Thompson KL. Determinants of morbidity in obese women delivered by cesarean. Obstet Gynecol 1988;71:691.

37. Hodgkinson R, Husain FJ. Caesarean section associated with gross obesity. Br J Anaesth 1980;52:919.

38. Norris MC. Height, weight, and the spread of subarachnoid hyperbaric bupivacaine in the term parturient. Anesth Analg 1988;67:555.

39. Turnbull A, Tindall VR, Beard RW, et al. Report on confidential enquiries into maternal deaths in England and Wales, 1982–1984. Report on Health and Social Subjects, Department of Health: London, 96.

40. Endler GC, Mariona FG, Sokol RJ, Stevenson LB. Anesthesia-related maternal mortality in Michigan, 1972 to 1984. Am J Obstet Gynecol 1988;159:187.

41. Sivarajan M, Fink BR. The position and the state of the larynx during general anesthesia and muscle paralysis. Anesthesiology 1990;72:439.

42. Datta S, Briwa J. Modified laryngoscope for endotracheal intubation of obese patients. Anesth Analg 1981;60:120.

43. Glassenberg R, Vaisrub N, Albright G. The incidence of failed intubation in obstetrics—is there an irreducible minimum? Anesthesiology 1990;73:A1062.

44. Vaughan RW, Bauer S, Wise L. Volume and pH of gastric juice in obese patients. Anesthesiology 1975;43:686.

45. Colman RD, Frank M, Loughnan BA, Cohen DG, Cattermole R. Use of i.m. ranitidine for the prophylaxis of aspiration pneumonitis in obstetrics. Br J Anaesth 1988;61:720.

46. Hodgkinson R, Glassenberg R, Joyce TH, Coombs DW, Ostheimer GW, Gibbs CP. Comparison of cimetidine (Tagamet) with antacid for safety and effectiveness in reducing gastric acidity before elective cesarean section. Anesthesiology 1983;59:86.

47. Archer GW Jr., Marx GF. Arterial oxygen tension during apnœa in parturient women. Br J Anæsth 1974;46:358.

48. Hedenstierna G, Santesson J, Norlander O. Airway closure and distribution of inspired gas in the extremely obese, breathing spontaneously and during anæsthesia with intermittent positive pressure ventilation. Acta Anæsth Scand 1976;20:334.

49. Vaughan RW, Wise L. Intraoperative arterial oxygenation in obese patients. Ann Surg 1976;184:35.

50. Norris MC, Dewan DM. Preoxygenation for cesarean section: A comparison of two techniques. Anesthesiology 1985;62:827.

51. Goldberg ME, Norris MC, Larijani GE, Marr AT, Seltzer JL. Preoxygenation in the morbidly obese: A comparison of two techniques. Anesth Analg 1989;68:520.

52. Eriksen J, Andersen J, Rasmussen JP, Sorensen B. Effects of ventilation with large tidal volumes or positive end-expiratory pressure on cardiorespiratory function in anesthetized obese patients. Acta Anaesth Scand 1978;22:241.

53. Bentley JB, Vaughan RW, Gandolfi AJ, Cork RC. Halothane biotransformation in obese and nonobese patients. Anesthesiology 1982;57:94.

54. Weinstein JA, Matteo RS, Ornstein E, Schwartz AE, Goldstoff M, Thal G. Pharmacodynamics of vecuronium and atracurium in the obese surgical patient. Anesth Analg 1988;67:1149.

55. Datta S, Ostheimer GW, Weiss JB, Brown WU Jr, Alper MH. Neonatal effect of prolonged anesthetic induction for cesarean section. Obstet Gynecol 1981;58:331.

56. Vaughan RW, Englehardt RC, Wise L. Postoperative hypoxemia in obese patients. Ann Surg 1974;180:877.

57. Rawal N, Sjöstrand U, Christoffersson E, Dahlström B, Arvill A, Rydman H. Comparison of intramuscular and epidural morphine for postoperative analgesia in the grossly obese: Influence on postoperative ambulation and pulmonary function. Anesth Analg 1984;63:583.

58. Maeder EC, Barno A, Mecklenburg F. Obesity: A maternal high-risk factor. Obstet Gynecol 1975;45:669.

59. Schmidt GA, Hall JB. Pulmonary disease. In: Barron WM, Lindheimer MD, eds. Medical disorders during pregnancy. St. Louis: Mosby–Year Book, 1991:197.

60. Kingston HGG, Hirshman CA. Perioperative management of the patient with asthma. Anesth Analg 1984;63:844.

61. Prowse CM, Gaensler EA. Respiratory and acid–base changes during pregnancy. Anesthesiology 1965;26:381.

62. Schatz M, Harden K, Forsythe A, et al. The course of asthma during pregnancy, postpartum, and with successive pregnancies: A prospective analysis. J Allergy Clin Immunol 1988;81:509.

63. Schatz M, Zeiger RS, Harden KM, et al. The safety of inhaled β-agonist bronchodilators during pregnancy. J Allergy Clin Immunol 1988;82:686.

64. Barnes PJ. A new approach to the treatment of asthma. N Engl J Med 1989;321:1517.

65. Siegel D, Sheppard D, Gelb A, Weinberg PF. Aminophylline increases the toxicity but not the efficacy of an inhaled beta-adrenergic agonist in the treatment of acute exacerbations of asthma. Am Rev Respir Dis 1985;132:283.

66. Mitenko PA, Ogilvie RI. Rational intravenous doses of theophylline. N Engl J Med 1973;289:600.

67. Freund FG, Bonica JJ, Ward RJ, Akamatsu TJ, Kennedy WF Jr. Ventilatory reserve and level of motor block during high spinal and epidural anesthesia. Anesthesiology 1967;28:834.

68. Gamil M. Serial peak expiratory flow rates in mothers during cæsarean section under extradural anæsthesia. Br J Anæsth 1989;62:415.

69. Mallampati SR. Bronchospasm during spinal anesthesia. Anesth Analg 1981;60:839.

70. Gal TJ. Pulmonary mechanics in normal subjects following endotracheal intubation. Anesthesiology 1980;52:27.

71. Huber FC Jr, Reves JG, Gutierrez J, Corssen G. Ketamine: Its effect on airway resistance in man. South Med J 1972;65:1176.

72. Hirshman CA, Downes H, Farbood A, Bergman NA. Ketamine block of bronchospasm in experimental canine asthma. Br J Anæsth 1979;51:713.

73. Little B, Chang T, Chugot L, et al. Study of ketamine as an obstetric anesthetic agent. Am J Obstet Gynecol 1972;113:247.

74. Dich-Nielsen J, Holasek J. Ketamine as induction agent for cæsarean section. Acta Anaesth Scand 1982;26:139.

75. Marx GF, Hwang HS, Chandra P. Postpartum uterine pressures with different doses of ketamine. Anesthesiology 1979;50:163.

76. Hirshman CA. Halothane and enflurane protect against bronchospasm in an asthma dog model. Anesth Analg 1978;57:629.

77. Hirshman CA, Edelstein G, Peetz S, Wayne R, Downes H. Mechanism of action of inhalational anesthesia on airways. Anesthesiology 1982;56:107.

78. Shah MV, Hirshman CA. Mode of action of halothane on histamine-induced airway constriction in dogs with reactive airways. Anesthesiology 1986;65:170.

79. Roizen MF, Stevens WC. Multiform ventricular tachycardia due to the interaction of aminophylline and halothane. Anesth Analg 1978;57:738.

80. Stirt JA, Berger JM, Sullivan SF. Lack of arrhythmogenicity of isoflurane following administration of aminophylline in dogs. Anesth Analg 1983;62:568.

81. Stirt JA, Berger JM, Roe SD, Ricker SM, Sullivan SF. Safety of enflurane following administration of aminophylline in experimental animals. Anesth Analg 1981;60:871.

82. Mathe AA, Hedqvist P, Holmgren A, Svanborg N. Bronchial hyperreactivity to prostaglandin $F_{2\alpha}$ and histamine in patients with asthma. Br Med J 1973;193:January 27.

83. Kleinman JC, Pierre MB Jr, Madans JH, Land GH, Schramm WF. The effects of maternal smoking on fetal and infant mortality. Am J Epidemiol 1988;127:274.

84. Meyer MB, Tonascia JA. Maternal smoking, pregnancy complications, and perinatal mortality. Am J Obstet Gynecol 1977;128:494.

85. Gerrard JW, Cockcroft DW, Mink JT, Cotton DJ, Poonawala R, Dosman JA. Increased nonspecific bronchial reactivity in cigarette smokers with normal lung function. Am Rev Respir Dis 1980;122:577.

86. Hegab ES, Matulionis DH. Pulmonary macrophage mobilization in cigarette smoke–exposed mice after halothane anesthesia. Anesth Analg 1986;65:37.

87. Crawford JS, James FM, Nolte H, Van Steenberge A, Shah JL. Regional analgesia for patients with chronic neurological disease and similar conditions. Anæsthesia 1981;36:821.

88. Crawford JS. Epidural analgesia for patients with chronic neurological disease. Anesth Analg 1983; 62:620.

89. Neigh JL, Garman JK, Harp JR. The electroencephalographic pattern during anesthesia with ethrane: Effects of depth of anesthesia, $Paco_2$, and nitrous oxide. Anesthesiology 1971;35:482.

90. Oshima E, Urabe N, Shingu K, Mori K. Anticonvulsant actions of enflurane on epilepsy models in cats. Anesthesiology 1985;63:29.

91. Bennett DR, Madsen JA, Jordan WS, Wiser WC. Ketamine anesthesia in brain-damaged epileptics. Neurology 1973;23:449.

92. Ferrer-Allado T, Brechner VL, Dymond A, Cozen H, Crandall P. Ketamine-induced electroconvulsive phenomena in the human limbic and thalamic regions. Anesthesiology 1973;38:333.

93. Ornstein E, Matteo RS, Young WL, Diaz J. Resistance to metocurine-induced neuromuscular blockade in patients receiving phenytoin. Anesthesiology 1985; 63:294.

94. Roth S, Ebrahim ZY. Resistance to pancuronium in patients receiving carbamazepine. Anesthesiology 1987; 66:691.

95. Warren TM, Datta S, Ostheimer GW. Lumbar epidural anesthesia in a patient with multiple sclerosis. Anesth Analg 1982;61:1022.

96. Bader AM, Hunt CO, Datta S, Naulty JS, Ostheimer GW. Anesthesia for the obstetric patient with multiple sclerosis. J Clin Anesth 1988;1:21.

97. Bamford C, Sibley CBW, Laguna J. Anesthesia in multiple sclerosis. Cana Sci Neurol 1978;5:41.

98. Cooperman LH. Succinylcholine-induced hyperkalemia in neuromuscular disease. JAMA 1970;213:1867.

99. Azar I. The response of patients with neuromuscular disorders to muscle relaxants: A review. Anesthesiology 1984;61:173

100. Foldes FF, McNall PG. Myasthenia gravis: A guide for anesthesiologists. Anesthesiology 1962;23:837.

101. Rolbin SH, Levinson G, Shnider SM, Wright RG. Anesthetic considerations for myasthenia gravis and pregnancy. Anesth Analg 1978;57:441.

102. Baraka A, Tabboush Z. Neuromuscular response to succinylcholine-vecuronium sequence in three myasthenic patients undergoing thymectomy. Anesth Analg 1991;72:827.

103. Schonwald G, Fish KJ, Perkash I. Cardiovascular complications during anesthesia in chronic spinal cord–injured patients. Anesthesiology 1981;55:550.

104. Baraka A. Epidural meperidine for control of autonomic hyperreflexia in a paraplegic parturient. Anesthesiology 1985;62:688.

105. Watson DW, Downey GO. Epidural anesthesia for labor and delivery of twins of a paraplegic mother. Anesthesiology 1980;52:259.

106. Katz VL, Thorp JM Jr, Cefalo RC. Epidural analgesia and autonomic hyperreflexia: A case report. Am J Obstet Gynecol 1990;162:471.

107. Abouleish EI, Hanley ES, Palmer SM. Can epidural fentanyl control autonomic hyperreflexia in a quadriplegic parturient? Anesth Analg 1989;68:523.

108. Stirt JA, Marco A, Conklin KA. Obstetric anesthesia for a quadriplegic patient with autonomic hyperreflexia. Anesthesiology 1979;51:560.

109. McGregor JA, Meeuwsen J. Autonomic hyperreflexia: A mortal danger for spinal cord–damaged women in labor. Am J Obstet Gynecol 1985;151:330.

110. Abouleish E. Hypertension in a paraplegic parturient. Anesthesiology 1980;53:348.

111. Cooperman LH, Stroebel GE Jr, Kennell EM. Massive hyperkalemia after administration of succinylcholine. Anesthesiology 1970;32:161.

112. Lennon RL. Atracurium or vecuronium for rapid sequence endotracheal intubation. Anesthesiology 1986;64:510.

113. Tessem JH, Johnson TD, Skjonsby RN, Kubicek MF, Joyce TH. Evaluation of vecuronium for rapid sequence induction in patients undergoing cesarean section. Anesthesiology 1987;67:A452.

114. Breslow MJ, Jordan DA, Christopherson R, et al. Epidural morphine decreases postoperative hypertension by attenuating sympathetic nervous system hyperactivity. JAMA 1989;261:3577.

115. Dunn JM, Raskind R. Rupture of a cerebral arteriovenous malformation during pregnancy. Obstet Gynecol 1967;30:423.

116. Tuttleman RM, Gleicher N. Central nervous system hemorrhage complicating pregnancy. Obstet Gynecol 1981;58:651.

117. Young DC, Leveno KJ, Whalley PJ. Induced delivery prior to surgery for ruptured cerebral aneurysm. Obstet Gynecol 1983;61:749.

118. Hunt HB, Schifrin BS, Suzuki K. Ruptured berry aneurysms and pregnancy. Obstet Gynecol 1974;43:827.

119. Marx GF, Zemaitis MT, Orkin LR. Cerebrospinal fluid pressures during labor and obstetrical anesthesia. Anesthesiology 1961;22:348.

120. Hilt H, Gramm HJ, Link J. Changes in intracranial pressure associated with extradural anæsthesia. Br J Anæsth 1986;58:676.

121. Baker JW. Subarachnoid hæmorrhage associated with pregnancy. Aust N Z J Obstet Gynæcol 1969;9:12.

122. Laidler JA, Jackson IJ, Redfern N. The management of cæsarean section in a patient with an intracranial arteriovenous malformation. Anaesthesia 1989;44:490.

123. Kofke WA, Wuest HP, McGinnis LA. Cesarean section following ruptured cerebral aneurysm and neuroresuscitation. Anesthesiology 1984;60:242.

124. Lennon RL, Sundt TM Jr., Gronert GA. Combined cesarean section and clipping of intracerebral aneurysm. Anesthesiology 1984;60:240.

125. Levinson G, Shnider SM, deLorimier AA, Steffenson JL. Effects of maternal hyperventilation on uterine blood flow and fetal oxygenation and acid–base status. Anesthesiology 1974;40:340.

CHAPTER 27

Anesthesia and Preeclampsia/Eclampsia

Joy L. Hawkins

Pregnancy-induced hypertension, or preeclampsia, alters function in many organ systems. The physiologic alterations of a preeclamptic pregnancy also may be markedly different from those of a healthy gestation. Recognition of these differences allows anesthesiologists to modify their routine anesthetic practice to provide optimum care for these high-risk parturients. Preoperative evaluation requires additional and more frequent laboratory evaluation. These women may need invasive hemodynamic monitoring. Control of blood pressure assumes a high priority. A safe anesthetic requires careful planning.

The anesthesiologist must understand the pathophysiology of preeclampsia. He or she must assess the extent of the disease process in the patient in question. Then, the anesthetic must be tailored to the needs of the patient and the obstetric situation. In obstetric anesthesia, several anesthetic plans must be developed for each patient. Even though the obstetrician may initially plan a trial of labor and vaginal delivery, he or she may eventually decide that cesarean section is a better choice. Although some indications for cesarean delivery can be managed semi-electively, others may be true emergencies; therefore, the anesthetic plan should cover all of these possibilities. The anesthesiologist must be flexible, plan ahead, and communicate actively with the obstetrician at all times. The obstetrician may also need help placing and interpreting invasive hemodynamic monitors.

PREOPERATIVE ASSESSMENT

The parturient with preeclampsia requires extensive evaluation to assess the extent of organ system involvement. Every patient should have a complete blood count, platelet count, fibrinogen, prothrombin time/partial thromboplastin time, blood urea nitrogen, creatinine, liver function tests, and serum magnesium concentration measured every 6 to 8 hours while in labor and immediately postpartum.

Hemoglobin and Hematocrit

The hematocrit provides an initial estimation of volume status. The "physiologic anemia of pregnancy" normally permits a hematocrit no greater than 36%; attribute values above that number to intravascular volume contraction. In 10% of patients with severe preeclampsia, a microangiopathic hemolytic anemia associated with thrombocytopenia and elevated liver enzymes—the HELLP syndrome—may develop.

Even in milder forms of preeclampsia, endothelial cell damage and vasospasm cause destruction of red cells. Increased heme catabolism increases production of carboxyhemoglobin and causes a leftward shift of the oxy-hemoglobin dissociation curve.[1] Normally, pregnancy shifts P_{50} rightward to approximately 30 mm Hg. In preeclampsia, it is 24.4 mm Hg, to the left of even the nonpregnant value (Fig. 27-1). This leftward shift decreases the release of oxygen to the fetus at the placenta, perhaps increasing the risk of fetal distress and intrauterine growth retardation.

Coagulation

Laboratory Evaluation

Fibrinogen should be evaluated as an index of intravascular coagulation, but disseminated intravascular coagulation is rare. This complication arises in association with placental abruption or fetal demise. A recently developed test, the D-dimer assay, utilizes monoclonal anti-D dimer antibody to detect degradation products of stable (cross-linked) fibrin rather than fibrinogen.[2] The test specifically detects in vivo clot dissolution. Presence of the D-dimer in preeclamptic women correlates consistently with elevated fibrin

degradation products and platelet count less than 100,000/mm³. This test may help define a subset of patients with severe disease. When compared to preeclamptic women who were negative for the D-dimer, positive women had higher blood pressures, greater proteinuria, higher serum creatinine levels, and more abnormal liver function tests. They also had a higher incidence of cesarean and premature delivery. Their infants often had low birth weights and Apgar scores.

Thrombocytopenia is the most common coagulopathy in preeclampsia; it occurs in about 20% of cases.[3] Preeclampsia also may impair platelet function. Two studies have documented platelet abnormalities in patients with preeclampsia despite platelet counts above 100,000/mm³. Kelton *et al*[4] reported that 25% of preeclamptic patients with a platelet count greater than 150,000/mm³ had a bleeding time longer than 10 minutes. Likewise, Ramanathan *et al*[5] found that 34% of patients with severe preeclampsia and 13% of those with mild preeclampsia had prolonged bleeding times despite platelet counts above 100,000/mm³. Of note, 2% of normotensive parturients, with normal platelet counts, also had abnormal bleeding times. Overall, patients with preeclampsia had lower platelet counts and longer bleeding times than healthy controls. In contrast, a more recent study failed to show platelet dysfunction in any patient with a platelet count greater

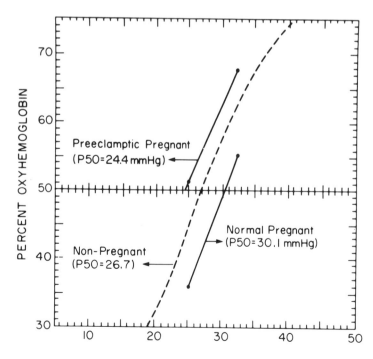

Figure 27–1. Effect of normal and preeclamptic pregnancies on P_{50}. The rightward shift in normal pregnancy encourages oxygen release to the fetus. The leftward shift in preeclamptic pregnancies inhibits oxygen release and contributes to fetal hypoxemia. (Kambam JR, Entman S, Mouton S, Smith BE. Effect of preeclampsia on carboxyhemoglobin levels. Anesthesiology 1988;68:434)

than 100,000/mm³.⁶ These authors suggested checking a bleeding time if the screening platelet count was between 50,000/mm³ and 100,000/mm³. Below 50,000 platelets/mm³, thrombocytopenia alone will prolong the bleeding time. These studies have caused tremendous controversy among obstetric anesthesiologists. Must we measure bleeding time in some or all women with preeclampsia before inducing regional anesthesia?

There are no reported cases of epidural hematoma in preeclamptic patients after epidural anesthesia. Indeed, several anesthesiologists have reported performing epidural anesthesia in parturients with unrecognized thrombocytopenia without complications.⁷⁻⁹ Given a 6% to 8% incidence of thrombocytopenia in normal parturients,¹⁰ many patients have probably received regional anesthesia while thrombocytopenic without incident.

Clinical Evaluation

Routine use of bleeding time to make clinical judgments is, at best, inconvenient. Laboratory personnel are usually available to perform the test only from 8 AM to 5 PM. Although anesthesia residents can be trained to perform accurate and reproducible bleeding times,¹¹ the test may provide little useful information. A recent extensive review of the literature on the bleeding time test concluded that no existing data support the use the bleeding time to predict adequacy of hemostasis, nor do any data show that bleeding from the skin can predict bleeding elsewhere in the body. In addition, there is no evidence that the bleeding time will prolong sufficiently in advance of serious bleeding to allow intervention or a change in management.¹²

Aspirin

Recently, obstetricians have begun giving aspirin to prevent and treat preeclampsia. Aspirin inhibits thromboxane synthesis and corrects the imbalance of thromboxane and prostacyclin production seen in preeclampsia. Because aspirin impairs platelet function, anesthesiologists have voiced concern about the use of regional anesthesia in these patients. Benigni *et al*¹³ reported that the ingestion of 60 mg of aspirin per day from 12 weeks of gestation until term did not prolong bleeding times performed at 28 weeks. In the absence of other indications of a coagulopathy, bleeding times do not seem to be necessary in these patients.

Guidelines

What then should we use as criteria for performing regional anesthesia in these patients? A recent survey of anesthesiology training programs explored the laboratory tests required before induction of regional anesthesia in parturients with preeclampsia.¹⁴ For the patient with mild preeclampsia, 20% of programs obtained a bleeding time in the elective setting, but only 15% obtained one in an urgent setting. For patients with severe preeclampsia, 65% required a bleeding time before an elective procedure and 45% before an urgent procedure (Fig. 27-2). Likewise, a survey of British obstetric units found widely varying use of

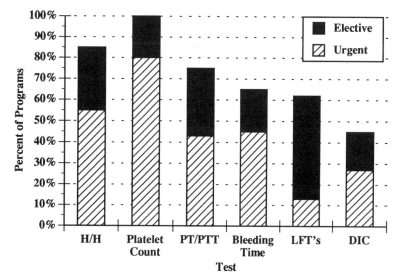

Figure 27–2. Percentage of programs ordering specific laboratory tests before inducing regional anesthesia in parturients with severe preeclampsia. There is no consensus concerning which tests are appropriate. The tests required also vary considerably with the urgency of the situation. (DIC = disseminated intravascular coagulation, H/H = hemoglobin/hematocrit, LFT = liver function tests, PT = prothrombin time, PTT = partial thromboplastin time.) (Data from Voulgaropoulos DS, Palmer CM. Coagulation studies in the parturient: How do we practice? Anesthesiology 1991:75: A1073)

the bleeding time.[15] Only 9% of hospitals routinely obtained bleeding times in all preeclamptic patients. Eighteen percent used the test in severe preeclamptics, and 55% rarely or never used the bleeding time. At our institution, we require a routine screening platelet count on all preeclamptic patients. If the initial value is greater than 150,000/mm³, we do no further testing. If the value is less than 150,000/mm³, we repeat the value while looking for a rapid downward trend, which is indicative of a worsening of the disease process. If the platelet count is less than 100,000/mm³, we usually avoid regional anesthesia. A platelet count of 100,000/mm³ is an arbitrary cut-off; the true safe lower limit for platelet count before epidural placement is unknown. If regional anesthesia, in preference to parenteral medications or general anesthesia, offers an overwhelming therapeutic advantage to the parturient (*e.g.,* suspected inability to intubate, prolonged induction of labor), we may check a bleeding time and proceed with the regional anesthetic if it is not prolonged. Ultimately, the individual anesthesiologist must make a decision based on the facts of the case at hand and his or her own clinical judgment.

What about the patient who develops thrombocytopenia or other coagulopathy with an epidural catheter in place? There are no definite guidelines in the literature. It seems prudent to allow the platelet count to normalize before removing the catheter in case a blood vessel has been punctured; however, the longer a catheter is left in place, the greater the chance that the catheter will migrate into a blood vessel. In patients with HELLP syndrome, the nadir of the platelet count occurs 1 to 3 days after delivery. Recovery to a concentration above 100,000/mm³ does not happen until 5 to 6 days postpartum.[16] Few practitioners would transfuse patients to correct thrombocytopenia for catheter removal, but few are comfortable leaving an epidural catheter in place for 3 to 6 days. Again, the individual anesthesiologist must use his or her clinical judgment. If one removes the catheter while the patient is thrombocytopenic, one should perform frequent neurologic examinations to detect spinal cord compression if epidural hematoma formation occurs.

Renal Function

Intravascular volume depletion and renal artery vasospasm can cause a decrease in creatinine clearance and oliguria. Maternal urine output is probably the best way to assess volume status in the absence of invasive hemodynamic monitoring. When creatinine values exceed 1 mg/dL, significant renal dysfunction is pres-

ent, compromising the excretion of drugs such as magnesium sulfate. To prevent toxicity, reduce the dose of magnesium if creatinine is elevated. Check deep tendon reflexes and serum magnesium concentrations frequently.

Liver Function

Laboratory examination may reveal elevated liver enzymes. Patients with preeclampsia may complain of right upper quadrant or epigastric pain perhaps due to stretching of the liver capsule. Subcapsular hemorrhage, hematoma, or liver rupture can occur. This event is characterized by acute maternal and fetal deterioration and requires immediate cesarean section and exploratory laparotomy.[17] Maternal mortality approaches 75%. When associated with the HELLP syndrome, coagulopathy and hemolysis increase maternal morbidity. Assure large-bore intravenous access and blood, fresh frozen plasma, and platelet availability if hepatic involvement is suspected.

Nervous System

Complete a careful neurologic examination before any anesthetic intervention. Deficits due to cerebral edema, cerebral hemorrhage, or a post-ictal state already may exist. Headaches, visual disturbances including cortical blindness, and, ultimately, seizures characterize central nervous system involvement. Although the etiology of eclampsia is unknown, pathologic examination of the brain reveals numerous hemorrhages, capillary thrombi, and small infarcts. Eclamptic patients have lower arterial blood pressure, systemic vascular resistance (SVR), and colloid osmotic pressure than parturients with severe preeclampsia who have not had seizures.[18,19] Computed tomography in the eclamptic patient with recurrent seizures may reveal structural lesions. Changes seen are similar to those found in hypertensive encephalopathy in nonpregnant patients—cerebral edema, cerebral vein thrombosis, and low-density white matter.[20] The indications for computed tomography in the eclamptic patient are controversial. Patients who present with focal signs, decreasing level of consciousness, or recurrent seizures despite therapeutic levels of magnesium or phenytoin need further evaluation.

Evaluation of the Fetus

In addition to fetal heart rate monitoring, other parameters of fetal well-being help predict type of delivery that may occur and the risk of fetal distress. Intra-uterine growth retardation, oligohydramnios, extreme prematurity, and uteroplacental insufficiency can all contribute to fetal distress. Evaluation of the fetus includes documentation of fetal presentation, estimated weight, biophysical profile, and oxytocin contraction test. Hypertensive parturients are much more likely than normotensive women to develop ominous intrapartum fetal heart rate patterns during labor (20.5% vs 7.6%).[21] Therefore, early and continuous fetal monitoring is a necessity.

Other preoperative preparation should include separate large-bore intravenous access should rapid infusion of fluid or blood products be needed. I recommend early and aggressive aspiration prophylaxis with some combination of a histamine-2 blocking agent, metoclopramide, or a nonparticulate antacid. This approach helps assure a therapeutic effect should seizures occur or operative delivery be required.

MONITORING

Basic intrapartum monitoring of a parturient with preeclampsia should include the following:

- Automated noninvasive blood pressure
- Accurate intake and output measurements (usually requiring a urinary bladder catheter)
- Hourly examination of deep tendon reflexes
- Fetal scalp electrode as soon as the cervix is adequately dilated
- An intrauterine pressure catheter to monitor strength and frequency of contractions and timing of decelerations

I do not continuously monitor the maternal electrocardiogram (ECG) unless I am also monitoring cardiac filling pressures; however, continuous ECG monitoring of 21 patients with hypertensive crises during pregnancy found that 13 had episodes of ventricular tachycardia during a 24-hour period.[22] These women had central venous catheters in place and were screened to assure normal serum potassium levels. The authors suggested dysrhythmias might play a role in the pathogenesis of pulmonary edema and sudden death in these patients.

Invasive Hemodynamic Monitoring

General Considerations

Considerable controversy surrounds the issue of when and how to use invasive monitoring in the parturient with preeclampsia. Yet, as we understand more about the pathophysiology of preeclampsia, the more hemodynamic data we need to guide our management decisions.

Obstetric patients are generally a young and healthy group. Many hospitals hesitate to supply the expertise and equipment for labor and delivery units to care for critically ill parturients. Nursing issues are a primary concern. Without nurses trained in critical care and comfortable with invasive monitoring, attempts to treat these patients aggressively in the labor unit will not succeed and could be dangerous. Likewise, placing a laboring patient with a fetal monitor in a medical or surgical intensive care unit does not allow for optimal monitoring of the fetus and disrupts the normal intensive care unit routine. Ideally, the labor and delivery unit should have an intensive care unit bed staffed by nurses comfortable with the parturient and knowledgeable in critical care issues. The anesthesiologist becomes an important and necessary source of information and support for the nursing service in this situation.

Arterial Catheter

The following are potential indications for continuous arterial blood pressure monitoring:

- Sustained diastolic blood pressure greater than 90 mm Hg
- Beat-to-beat monitoring during use of parenteral vasodilators such as nitroprusside or nitroglycerin
- Induction of regional or general anesthesia with the potential for rapid changes in blood pressure
- Inability to obtain accurate blood pressure measurements by cuff in the morbidly obese patient
- The need for repeated sampling for arterial blood gas tensions or other laboratory studies (especially if the patient is a difficult "stick" because of edema, obesity, or intravenous drug abuse)
- The patient with a coagulopathy (avoids repeated venipuncture)

Pulmonary Artery Catheter

Patients with severe preeclampsia may present with profound hemodynamic derangements and may benefit from placement of a pulmonary artery catheter. Presently accepted indications for use of a pulmonary artery catheter in the parturient with severe preeclampsia include the following:

- Severe hypertension unresponsive to conventional antihypertensive therapy
- Pulmonary edema
- Persistent oliguria unresponsive to fluid challenge

- Occasionally, induction of conduction or general anesthesia.[23]

A report of 56 obstetric patients managed with pulmonary artery catheterization in the labor and delivery suite documented the safety and advantages of this approach.[24] Advantages included consolidation of care for pathophysiology unique to pregnancy (such as severe preeclampsia), fetal monitoring, and the ability to provide immediate medical and surgical management. However, these authors emphasize that "establishment of such a service requires an intensive care unit with properly trained nurses, appropriate equipment, and physicians with the necessary clinical skill to place and troubleshoot central lines." Certainly, the obstetric anesthesiologist can have a major role in this area.

Central Venous Pressure or Pulmonary Artery Catheter?

The choice of a central venous pressure (CVP) catheter versus a pulmonary artery (PA) catheter has been controversial.[25] The CVP alone may provide misleading information. Several studies have shown that CVP cannot reliably predict pulmonary capillary wedge pressure (PCWP).[26–28] Cotton *et al*[26] compared 208 CVP and PCWP measurements in 18 patients with severe preeclampsia. They found no linear relationship between the CVP and PCWP in 39% of their patients. In the 56% of women in whom the two measures correlated, the gradient between PCWP and CVP varied so widely as to preclude any predictive value. This lack of linearity occurs when SVR rises and increases left ventricular afterload. Shifting blood from the systemic to the pulmonary circulations elevates left ventricular filling pressures and maintains cardiac output; thus, the filling pressures on the right and left sides of the heart are not similar. The CVP may be the more accurate index of true intravascular volume, especially when the value is low. The PCWP reflects the risk of pulmonary edema and the amount of left ventricular dysfunction. Although a low CVP value rarely indicates an elevated PCWP, higher CVP values do not always imply elevated left-sided filling pressures.

The PA catheter provides far more than information about volume status. The CVP gives no indication of cardiac output, and unfortunately, there is no good noninvasive substitute for thermodilution techniques. The impedance cardiography technique is inaccurate in pregnancy when compared with thermodilution (r=0.17),[29] and although the Doppler technique correlates well with thermodilution

(r=0.91),[30] it provides no assessment of filling pressures.

Colloid osmotic pressure (COP) is lower in patients with preeclampsia than in normal pregnant patients, perhaps due to proteinuria. One of the mechanisms responsible for development of pulmonary edema in severe preeclampsia is an imbalance of Starling forces across the pulmonary capillary membrane. A PCWP/COP gradient of less than 4 mm Hg may allow excessive fluid flux out of the pulmonary vascualture.[18,31] The COP falls to its lowest level in the postpartum period, whereas filling pressures often rise before the onset of normal postpartum diuresis. Cotton *et al*[32] noted that the two women they saw with pulmonary edema were also the only two with a negative COP/PCWP gradient.[32] If COP measurements are used, they can be combined with PCWP measurements to guide fluid therapy and use of diuretics. Again, this information is not available with only a CVP catheter.

Finally, there is the issue of the risks of placing a PA catheter versus a CVP catheter. Most of the risks of central monitoring, such as carotid or subclavian artery puncture, pneumothorax, dysrhythmias, hematoma, or infection, are related to obtaining central venous access, and are common to both CVP and PA catheter placement. The additional risks of placing the PA catheter, such as pulmonary infarction and rupture of the PA, are very rare in this patient population. Because the risks of access are the same, the more comprehensive information obtained from the PA catheter provides a favorable risk/benefit ratio. If concerned about central venous access in a patient with abnormal coagulation studies, you can insert the CVP catheter or PA catheter sheath through the antecubital basilic vein or external jugular vein. If needed, you can easily apply pressure to bleeding at these sites. Also consider peripheral access via an antecubital vein in the postictal, uncooperative, or actively laboring patient. Contemplate too this approach in the obese or edematous patient with obscure landmarks.

Hemodynamic Profile

There is now more than a decade's worth of literature on hemodynamic findings in severe preeclampsia. Early studies revealed a hyperdynamic state with elevated cardiac output and low-to-normal filling pressures in the face of high SVR.[33–35] Others, however, found a depressed cardiac index with low filling pressures and high vascular resistance.[36] In a group of 45 women with severe preeclampsia or eclampsia, Cotton *et al*[18] found a wide range of hemodynamic patterns that could not be easily classified (Fig. 27-3). When investigating persistent oliguria in severe preeclampsia, Clark *et al*[37] described three distinct hemodynamic subsets requiring markedly different therapies. Thus, no single hemodynamic profile describes all parturients with preeclampsia. Recently, Easterling and Benedetti[38] followed 120 women throughout their pregnancies and measured cardiac output using a Doppler technique. Women destined to develop preeclampsia had significantly higher cardiac outputs and lower SVR from early in gestation when compared to parturients who remained normotensive (Fig. 27-4). These differences remained postpartum. The authors suggest vasodilation of terminal arterioles predispose to end-organ damage by exposing these capillary beds, especially the renal glomeruli, to systemic pressures.[39] The resultant endothelial damage incites platelet adherence, vasospasm, and the clinically overt disease we see in patients with severe preeclampsia. Thus, depending on when a patient presents in the course of her disease, there may be a spectrum of hemodynamic patterns reflecting the extent of endothelial and end-organ damage.

PERIOPERATIVE MANAGEMENT OF SPECIAL PROBLEMS

Eclampsia

Convulsions occur antepartum or intrapartum in 63% of cases of eclampsia;[40] therefore, the obstetric anesthesiologist may have to evaluate or manage the seizing or post-ictal parturient. Manage the eclamptic woman initially with airway support, oxygen by mask, left uterine displacement, and cricoid pressure. Do not force an oral airway or tongue blade into her mouth; this action may cause vomiting or break teeth. A simple jaw lift should suffice. Intubate if the seizure is prolonged, regurgitation occurs, or ventilation cannot be maintained. If necessary, treat the seizure with thiopental, 75 mg, instead of a long-acting sedative such as diazepam. This choice will rapidly end the seizure yet

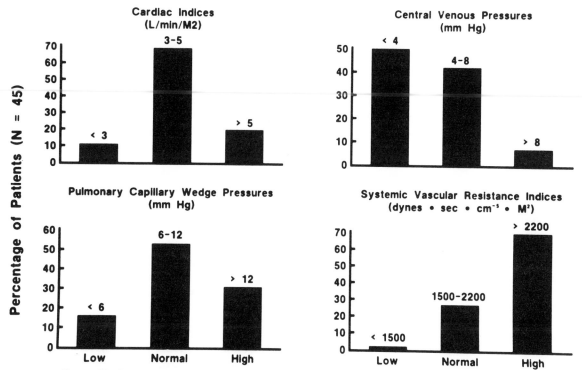

Figure 27–3. Hemodynamic subsets associated with severe pregnancy-induced hypertension. These women present with a wide range of initial findings. (Cotton DB, Lee W, Huhta JC, Dorman KF. Hemodynamic profile of severe pregnancy-induced hypertension. Am J Obstet Gynecol 1988;158:523)

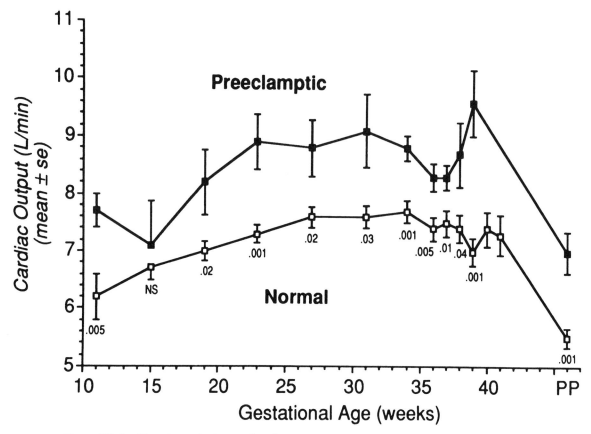

Figure 27–4. Mean ± standard error of cardiac output in normotensive (normal) and preeclamptic patients throughout pregnancy. (NS = not significant, PP = postpartum.) (Easterling TR, Benedetti TJ, Schmucker BC, Millard SP. Maternal hemodynamics in normal and preeclamptic pregnancies: A longitudinal study. Obstet Gynecol 1990;76:1061)

allow faster awakening for neurologic assessment. Magnesium is the treatment of choice for prevention of seizures in preeclampsia. A nontherapeutic serum concentration may allow recurrent seizures. Infuse magnesium sulfate as a bolus dose of 4 to 6 g over 20 minutes; repeat once if seizures recur. Focal seizures, or seizures in the presence of a therapeutic magnesium concentration, should raise the suspicion of a structural lesion or intracerebral hemorrhage. Give an additional parenteral anticonvulsant such as phenytoin. At this point, consider further neurologic work-up such as computed tomography.

A large series of eclamptic patients has shown that magnesium sulfate successfully prevents recurrent seizures.[41] It remains the anticonvulsant of choice for preeclampsia in North America.[42] Its mechanism of action is unclear; however, magnesium enhances production of prostacyclin by vascular endothelium, thereby promoting vasodilation and inhibiting platelet aggregation. This effect on the cerebral vasculature may account for its antiseizure effects.[43] Unfortunately, when compared with phenytoin, magnesium, because of its tocolytic effects, also slows cervical dilation and increases blood loss at delivery.[44]

Eclampsia is rarely an indication for immediate delivery. Give stabilization, monitoring, and neurologic evaluation precedence to avoid unnecessary maternal obstetric and anesthetic risks. Once seizure activity stops, continue to give the mother supplemental oxygen. Fetal decelerations occur commonly during a seizure because of maternal hypoxia and acidosis. Unless placental abruption has occurred, fetal acidosis will improve more quickly in utero than if delivery occurs during or immediately following the seizure. Induction of labor should be attempted if the cervix is favorable. Begin aspiration prophylaxis early in labor because seizures may recur and these women are likely to need urgent or emergent cesarean delivery.

Oliguria

Oliguria is a common complication of severe preeclampsia. Although postpartum renal failure rarely occurs, most physicians become anxious when urine output falls below 0.5 mL/kg/h for several hours. Because magnesium sulfate is cleared only by glomerular filtration, oliguria may also increase the risk of magnesium toxicity. Begin treating oliguria with a fluid challenge of 500 mL of crystalloid over 20 minutes. If urine output remains unchanged or declines, I recommend pulmonary artery catheterization before further fluid therapy. Clark *et al*[37] found three distinctly different hemodynamic profiles in parturients with persistent oliguria (Table 27-1). Most commonly, patients had low filling pressures, hyperdynamic ventricular function, and moderate elevation of vascular resistance, reflecting intravascular volume depletion. These women responded to further volume infusion with an increase in PCWP, a fall in SVR, and no change in

blood pressure. Patients in the second group also had hyperdynamic ventricular function, but with higher filling pressures (9–18 mm Hg) and normal SVR. In these women, the authors suspected renal artery vasospasm as the cause of oliguria. Women with preeclampsia may have selective vasospasm (*i.e.*, normal pulmonary vascular resistance in the face of elevated SVR). Selective renal artery spasm would decrease renal blood flow in the presence of normal filling pressures and cardiac output. In this group of patients, urine production increased after vasodilator therapy with hydralazine and cautious fluid administration. A single patient had depressed left ventricular function, elevated PCWP, and marked elevation of SVR. She responded to afterload reduction and fluid restriction to relieve vasospasm and improve cardiac output. Again, this report underscores the importance of evaluating the patient's hemodynamic status to avoid overly aggressive and inappropriate use of fluid or diuretic therapy.

Kirshon *et al*[45] used another approach to the possibility of renal artery vasospasm. They gave low-dose dopamine (1–5 µg/kg/min) to patients who were oliguric with PCWP greater than 8 mm Hg (see Table

Table 27-1

Hemodynamic Subsets Associated with Oliguria in Preeclampsia and Their Therapy

	Therapy	GROUP 1 (CLARK) Volume	GROUP 2 (CLARK) Vasodilator and Volume	GROUP 3 (CLARK) Vasodilator and Fluid Restriction	KIRSHON Dopamine (1–5 µg/kg/h)
Before Therapy	MAP (mm Hg)	111	125	140	114
	CVP (mm Hg)	2	8	3	6
	PCWP (mm Hg)	4	12	18	12
	CI (l/min/m²)	3.9	5.4	2.6	4.0 (estimated)
	SVR*	1330	1019	2790	1371
After Therapy	MAP (mm Hg)	115	107	104	116
	CVP (mm Hg)	7	9	—	8
	PCWP (mm Hg)	10	9	8	11
	CI (l/min/m²)	4.5	5.4	4.0	4.7 (estimated)
	SVR*	1150	879	1867	1157

(Data from Clark SL, Greenspoon JS, Aldahl D, Phelan JP. Severe preeclampsia with persistent oliguria: management of hemodynamic subsets. Am J Obstet Gynecol 1986;154:4; and Kirshon B, Lee W, Mauer MB, Cotton DB. Effects of low-dose dopamine therapy in the oliguric patient with preeclampsia. Am J Obstet Gynecol 1988;159:604)
Abbreviation: CI = cardiac index.
*dynes = sec•cm^{-5}

27-1). Dopamine selectively dilates splanchnic vessels and increases renal blood flow, sodium excretion, and glomerular filtration rate. Without changing blood pressure, PCWP, or CVP, dopamine caused a significant increase in urine production and cardiac output. Fractional excretion of sodium and osmolar clearance also tended to rise. No fetal distress occurred, implying that dopamine did not compromise placental perfusion.

Pulmonary Edema

Pulmonary edema is a significant cause of maternal and perinatal morbidity and mortality. In one large series, 70% of cases occurred postpartum.[46] Most patients had a medical, surgical, or obstetric complication that required large volumes of crystalloid and colloid infusions. These complications included sepsis, abruption, disseminated intravascular coagulation, aspiration, and ruptured liver. The incidence of pulmonary edema was also higher in older multigravidae and in those with chronic hypertension. Volume infusion for regional anesthesia did not contribute to pulmonary edema in any case. These authors emphasized the need to monitor severely preeclamptic patients for 72 hours postpartum.

Pulmonary edema normally occurs at a PCWP of 20 to 25 mm Hg, but if the patient also has a low COP, clinical symptoms may manifest earlier. Preeclampsia lowers COP, but correction of COP with albumin antepartum produces much higher filling pressures after delivery. These women then often need diuretic therapy.[47]

Pulmonary artery catheterization helps to determine the cause of the pulmonary edema and to optimize filling pressures and cardiac function. In addition to oxygen therapy and diuresis, nitroglycerin has been shown to reduce preload and correct the hemodynamic derangements associated with pulmonary edema.[48] Nitroglycerin inhibits hypoxic pulmonary vasoconstriction, and, in preeclampsia, hypoxemia does not improve with this therapy.

ANTIHYPERTENSIVE THERAPY

Antihypertensive therapy aims to prevent cerebral hemorrhage, pulmonary edema, and other complications of acute hypertension in the mother while preserving or improving placental circulation. To this end, strive to lower mean maternal blood pressure to 105 to 110 mm Hg, or by no more than 30% from baseline. The fetus with uteroplacental insufficiency is an exquisitely sensitive monitor of placental perfusion when lowering maternal blood pressure. Fetal decelerations may limit the degree of blood pressure reduction. If hemodynamic monitoring is available, use these values to guide your choice of antihypertensive therapy. For example, the parturient with hyperdynamic left ventricular function and normal SVR may respond well to a negative inotrope (*i.e.,* labetalol), whereas a vasodilating agent would best correct an elevated vascular resistance in the presence of high filling pressures.

Although each has its pros and cons, a number of antihypertensive agents can be used in obstetrics. The anesthesiologist should be aware of the safety and potential harmful effects of the drugs chosen to control blood pressure (Table 27-2). These agents can be divided into the following classes based on their mechanism of action:

- Direct-acting vasodilators
- Ganglionic blocking drugs
- Competitive beta-receptor blocking agents
- Sympatholytic agents
- Calcium channel blocking drugs
- Angiotensin-converting enzyme inhibitors

Table 27-2

Reported Adverse Effects of Antihypertensive Therapy During Pregnancy

DRUG	ADVERSE EFFECT
Esmolol (Brevibloc)	Decrease in fetal arterial PO_2
	Equivalent maternal and fetal beta-blockade
	Prolonged fetal beta-blockade
	? Decreased fetal tolerance to asphyxia
Clonidine (Catapres)	Fetal hypoxemia
	Increased uterine tone
	Decreased uterine blood flow
Nifedipine (Adalat, Procardia)	Tocolysis
	Additive myocardial depression with magnesium
	Additive neuromuscular blockade with magnesium
	? Fetal hypoxemia with nicardipine infusion
Angiotensin-converting enzyme inhibitors (Enalapril)	Neonatal hypotension
	Neonatal renal failure
	Teratogenicity

Magnesium sulfate is not an antihypertensive agent. Although SVR and blood pressure decrease for about 30 minutes following a loading dose, the effect is transient.[49]

Direct-Acting Vasodilators

Hydralazine

Hydralazine remains a popular drug for use in preeclampsia. It causes direct vasodilation of arteriolar smooth muscle while improving renal and uterine blood flow.[50] Its onset is relatively slow (15–20 min); its effects last hours. Parturients given a bolus dose of 10 mg of hydralazine while monitored with a PA catheter had a significant increase in heart rate and cardiac index and a fall in SVR. The peak effect and duration of action varied considerably.[51] In the presence of unrecognized hypovolemia, hydralazine can produce acute hypotension, eliciting fetal distress. Its unpredictable onset and effect make dose titration difficult.

Nitroprusside

Nitroprusside causes arterial and venous dilation. Its fast onset, short duration, and rapid metabolism (plasma half-life of 12 s) make it titratable as an infusion. Patients are rarely resistant to its effect, and it preserves uterine blood flow.[52] Like all vasodilators, it can cause severe hypotension when the patient is hypovolemic, and heart rate increases in response to the fall in SVR. Concern about its use in obstetrics arose when Naulty *et al*[53] reported extensive placental transfer of nitroprusside in pregnant ewes. In addition, when ewes exhibited tachyphylaxis to the drug, fetuses died of cyanide toxicity; however, these sheep had two different responses to the drug. When infusion rates required to control blood pressure were low (less than 1 μg/kg/min), mothers and fetuses did well. When animals exhibited tachyphylaxis to nitroprusside and required a mean dose of 25 μg/kg/min to control blood pressure, all fetuses died. In both groups, uterine blood flow did not change. Cyanide caused all toxicity seen. Keep in mind, however, that the maximum acceptable dose of nitroprusside is 8.0 μg/kg/min or 0.5 mg/kg/h. If exceeding this dose to achieve adequate blood pressure control, use another hypotensive agent. Many obstetricians and obstetric anesthesiologists have used nitroprusside safely and effectively within these guidelines.[54] Nitroprusside is a cerebral and pulmonary vasodilator. Potential increases in intracranial pressure (ICP) may be detrimental when a patient is post-ictal, neurologic exam is equivocal, or a structural intracerebral lesion is suspected. Pulmonary vasodilation decreases hypoxic pulmonary vasoconstriction and could cause hypoxemia.

Nitroglycerin

Nitroglycerin has venous and arterial vasodilating properties. Its short duration of action makes it easily titrated. In animals, it partially restores uterine blood flow diminished by phenylephrine infusion.[55] Its low molecular weight allows rapid placental transfer. In untreated preeclamptics, nitroglycerin lowers blood pressure, PCWP, and cardiac output. Volume expansion prevents the fall in filling pressures and cardiac index. After volume expansion, however, patients can develop a marked resistance to nitroglycerin's hypotensive effects.[56] Fetal heart rate variability also diminishes, possibly as a result of loss of cerebral autoregulation and elevated ICP in the fetus. The fall in filling pressures may help correct the hemodynamic abnormalities associated with pulmonary edema. Increased ICP and decreased hypoxic pulmonary vasoconstriction are concerns. Oxygenation does not improve with nitroglycerin infusion in women with pulmonary edema.

Ganglionic Blocking Agents

Trimethaphan exerts its hypotensive effect by ganglionic blockade of sympathetic nerve impulses. It can be used as an infusion or in bolus doses without causing reflex tachycardia. However, tachyphylaxis can develop during prolonged infusion. Of the vasodilating agents, it has the largest molecular weight (597 Dalton), which should limit its placental transfer. Although not a direct cerebral vasodilator, animal work has shown a transient increase in intracranial pressure during the induction stage of hypotension.[57] Increases in ICP can occur during its use, but the risk seems greatest when blood pressure falls rapidly (< 1 min) to a mean pressure below 60 mm Hg or in patients who already have critically elevated ICP.[58] Pupillary dilation due to ganglionic blockade can be expected and should not cause concern. Trimethaphan inhibits plasma cholinesterase,[59] and can prolong the duration of action of succinylcholine.[60] However, the patient reported in that case had received 1700 mg of trimethaphan over a 2-hour period, suggesting that tachyphylaxis had developed. In the usual clinical doses, trimethaphan might double the normal duration of succinylcholine.

Beta-receptor Blocking Agents

Labetalol

Labetalol is a relatively new drug that is achieving great popularity in obstetrics. It has nonselective beta- and alpha$_1$-blocking properties in a ratio of about 7:1 when given intravenously. It decreases SVR and blood pressure without changing heart rate or cardiac index.[61] Despite this fall in maternal blood pressure, uteroplacental flow does not change, suggesting that labetalol lowers placental vascular resistance.[62,63] In pregnant ewes, labetalol can completely reverse norepinephrine-induced hypertension. At the same time, uterine blood flow, markedly diminished by the norepinephrine, returns toward normal.[64] Labetalol does not produce significant adrenergic blockade in the fetus or newborn,[65] an important finding because cardiac output in the newborn is heart-rate dependent. The peak onset during parenteral use occurs within 10 minutes, but the dose response is variable. A study comparing labetalol and hydralazine for control of hypertension in pregnancy-induced hypertension found that labetalol acted more rapidly but failed to lower blood pressure in 10% of patients. The dose of intravenous labetalol required varied considerably from patient to patient, ranging from 20 mg to 300 mg.[66] Those women requiring the largest doses also had the shortest duration of effect.

Esmolol

Esmolol is an ultra–short-acting beta$_1$ selective blocking agent with an elimination half-life of 9 minutes. Metabolism occurs by hydrolysis by red blood cell esterases. Initial animal studies showed rapid maternal and fetal elimination, with minimal placental transfer or effect on fetal hemodynamics (maximal decrease in fetal mean arterial pressure [MAP] and heart rate were 7% and 12%).[67] However, further animal studies found adverse fetal effects. Fetal arterial Po_2 decreased significantly, and isoproterenol challenge testing revealed fetal beta-blockade that persisted for 30 minutes after completion of the esmolol infusion.[68] In contrast to labetalol, which produced minimal fetal adrenergic blockade, esmolol produced equivalent degrees of beta-blockade in the fetus and ewe. Other animal work showed that maternal beta$_1$-blockade with metoprolol reduced fetal tolerance to asphyxia. In addition, fetal neural function, as assessed by somatosensory evoked potentials, recovered more slowly than in the control group.[69] These studies suggest that the fetus requires intact adrenergic function to respond to stress. There are no human studies on the use of esmolol in pregnancy. When given to a parturient at 22 weeks of gestation undergoing resection of a cerebral arteriovenous malformation, esmolol infusion (50 µg/kg/min) produced no significant effect on fetal heart rate.[70] However, when used in a similar situation in a woman at 30 weeks of gestation, esmolol administration (100 µg) was associated with a 30 beat/minute fall in fetal heart rate.[71] Both women later delivered healthy babies.

Sympatholytic Agents

Sympatholytic drugs produce a gradual reduction of maternal blood pressure without reflex tachycardia. Alpha-methyldopa is a centrally acting alpha$_2$-receptor agonist with a long history of safe use in obstetrics. It provides a peripheral sympathectomy and has both parenteral and oral forms. Its main drawbacks are a slow onset of action (6 h) and only moderate efficacy. Additionally, it is contraindicated in patients with liver dysfunction, something not uncommon in severe pregnancy-induced hypertension.

Clonidine acts by the same mechanism as alpha-methyldopa, but it is not available in a parenteral form. Although it seems to be safe in long-term use in parturients with chronic hypertension,[72] intravenous use in animals causes fetal hypoxemia, increased uterine tone, and decreased uterine blood flow.[73] At our institution, we have used the patch formulation for postpartum control of blood pressure. Several hypertensive crises precipitated by noncompliant patients removing the patch and developing rebound hypertension caused us to discontinue the practice.

Calcium Channel Blocking Drugs

Calcium antagonist drugs exert their hypotensive effects mostly by vasodilation. Verapamil is available in oral and intravenous forms, whereas nifedipine can be given orally or sublingually. Animal studies showed verapamil and nifedipine to be effective antihypertensive agents in pregnancy, although neither improved the decrease in uterine blood flow induced by norepinephrine.[74] Unlike nifedipine, verapamil does not produce a maternal tachycardia. In severely preeclamptic parturients, verapamil infusion following volume expansion with colloid allowed effective control of maternal blood pressure. Cardiac index increased significantly, whereas SVR fell.[75] Doppler ultrasound studies found no change in impedance in the uterine or umbilical arteries and no change in uteroplacental blood flow.[76] Other studies, however, have raised concern about the use of calcium channel blocking drugs in pregnancy. Infusion of nicardipine in pregnant monkeys produced progressive fetal acidosis and hypoxemia.[77] In addition, these agents all produce significant uterine relaxation. Still, these adverse effects have not been reported in human pregnancies. Oral nifedipine can treat acute hypertensive episodes during and immediately after pregnancy.[78,79] Postpartum, nifedipine also correlated with significantly higher urine output than in control patients who were receiving placebo. At present, it is unclear whether the antepartum use of these "tocolytic" drugs will slow the progress of labor or increase the risk of postpartum hemorrhage.

Another problem with calcium channel blocking drugs is the potential interaction with magnesium, another calcium channel blocking agent. This combination could increase the risk of cardiac or respiratory toxicity. In isolated, perfused hearts, the combination of magnesium sulfate and nifedipine produces additive myocardial depression and decreases heart rate, left ventricular contractility, and left ventricular systolic pressure.[80] Progressive degrees of heart block and even asystole occur with increasing doses of nifedipine. A patient receiving nifedipine for tocolysis who also got a small dose of magnesium developed acute respiratory insufficiency.[81] The combination of these two drugs may potentiate the neuromuscular effects of magnesium.

Angiotensin-Converting Enzyme Inhibitors

There are numerous case reports in the literature associating angiotensin-converting enzyme inhibitors during pregnancy with neonatal hypotension, neonatal renal failure, and teratogenicity.[82] These agents should be avoided in the parturient.

ANALGESIA FOR LABOR AND VAGINAL DELIVERY

After initial stabilization of the mother and fetus, the obstetrician must decide on the most appropriate mode of delivery. The anesthesiologist needs time for thorough preoperative preparation of these high-risk patients. Obstetricians must understand that these women deserve no less attention than a seriously ill patient having surgery in the main operating suite. Lack

of sufficient time to prepare the patient is almost always due to a failure in communication.

Epidural Analgesia

Advantages and Disadvantages

Pritchard *et al*[41] report excellent maternal outcome in a large series of eclamptic patients. Pritchard advocates magnesium sulfate by intramuscular injection, hydralazine to lower diastolic blood pressures to less than 110 mm Hg, fluid restriction, and rapid delivery (usually by vaginal delivery) after convulsions have stopped. He does not use invasive monitors. He avoids regional anesthesia for fear of inducing precipitous maternal hypotension. Because the maternal and perinatal results are very good despite the serious nature of the disease, Pritchard's regimen is the standard to which others will be compared. However, the strong bias against fluid administration and regional anesthesia has led to conflicts between anesthesiologists and their obstetric colleagues.

Most other centers consider epidural blockade for labor and vaginal delivery or cesarean section the best anesthetic for parturients with preeclampsia.[83] Besides providing better patient comfort than the alternatives, epidural analgesia offers numerous other benefits to the woman with preeclampsia. The preeclamptic patient is more sensitive to catecholamines than is the healthy parturient. Catecholamines, secreted in response to pain and stress, can raise blood pressure and compromise uteroplacental blood flow. Epidural analgesia during labor lowers circulating catecholamine concentrations. Preeclamptic parturients have higher baseline serum concentration of epinephrine than normal parturients. The serum concentration of epinephrine falls significantly after induction of epidural anesthesia (Fig. 27-5).[84] The resultant potential improvement in uteroplacental blood flow might benefit the fetus with uteroplacental insufficiency.

Other investigators have shown that epidural blockade does indeed improve intervillous blood flow during labor in women with severe preeclampsia. Jouppila *et al*[85] have published the results of two studies on this issue. They gave epidural local anesthetics to laboring women with preeclampsia. All of their patients received 500 mL of crystalloid before blockade and were lying in a 15-degree left lateral tilt position. Providing a narrow band of analgesia, between T-10 and T-12, produced a small but insignificant 34% rise in intervillous blood flow.[85] Providing a wider band of

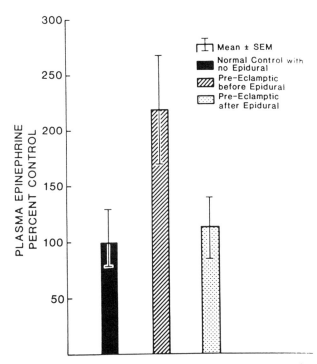

Figure 27–5. Plasma concentration of epinephrine in normal and preeclamptic parturients. Epinephrine concentration falls significantly after induction of epidural anesthesia in preeclamptic women. (Abboud T, Artal R, Sarkis F, Henriksen EH, Kammula RK. Sympathoadrenal activity, maternal, fetal, and neonatal responses after epidural anesthesia in the preeclamptic patient. Am J Obstet Gynecol 1982;144:915)

sympathetic blockade with 10 mL of 0.25% bupivacaine, significantly increased intervillous blood flow by 77%.[86] No patient in either series became hypotensive.

Epidural analgesia also furnishes the obstetrician and anesthesiologist with considerable flexibility. Once in place, the epidural catheter can provide effective anesthesia for labor and vaginal or cesarean delivery as the situation demands. If the need arises for extensive episiotomy and repair or cesarean section, epidurally administered opioids can assure excellent postoperative analgesia. Finally, sympathectomy can be maintained in the postpartum period if desired to buffer intravascular volume changes during fluid mobilization.

Hemodynamic Effects

A retrospective study of 185 women with pregnancy-induced hypertension who delivered vaginally found no harmful effects of epidural blockade. The incidence of maternal hypotension (6% vs 7%), abnormal

fetal heart rate tracings, low Apgar scores, and neonatal intensive care unit admissions did not differ whether women received local or epidural anesthesia.[87] These authors concluded that epidural anesthesia was safe and effective in this patient population. Epidural blockade provokes little hemodynamic change in women with severe preeclampsia. Neither PCWP, CVP, nor cardiac index change in women hydrated to a PCWP of 8 to 12 mm Hg. Before blockade, SVR falls slightly, whereas mean arterial pressure falls significantly (from 121.4 mm Hg to 97.7 mm Hg).[88] Prudent use of fluids guided by clinical judgment and invasive monitoring when indicated will minimize any risk of precipitous hypotension when using regional anesthesia in the preeclamptic patient. Obstetric or medical complications, not fluids given before epidural placement, most often predispose to pulmonary edema.[46] In experienced hands, epidural anesthesia is a safe and beneficial technique for the preeclamptic patient that allows maximal flexibility for the obstetrician and anesthesiologist.

Magnesium and Epidural Anesthesia

In North America, essentially all patients with preeclampsia will receive magnesium sulfate. Because magnesium has vasodilating properties, there could be an increase in the incidence or severity of hypotension after epidural anesthesia when parturients are receiving magnesium therapy. Vincent et al[89] recorded slightly lower blood pressure during epidural anesthesia in ewes receiving magnesium compared to controls (18% below baseline vs 5% below baseline). Maternal cardiac output, uterine blood flow, and fetal oxygenation did not change in either group. Additional animal work has compared ephedrine and phenylephrine as vasopressors to correct hypotension after epidural anesthesia in the presence of a therapeutic magnesium level. Ephedrine restored both maternal blood pressure and uterine blood flow to baseline, whereas phenylephrine corrected maternal blood pressure but failed to improve uterine blood flow.[90]

Some Technical Issues

EPINEPHRINE Controversy surrounds the use of epinephrine in local anesthetic solutions in obstetric anesthesia, in general, and in women with preeclampsia, in particular. Normal pregnant patients have attenuated responses to endogenous and exogenous catecholamines. Isolated uterine arteries from pregnant animals are less sensitive to vasoconstrictive drugs than are vessels from nonpregnant animals.[91] Arteries exposed to norepinephrine, epinephrine, and phenylephrine generate a less effective and weaker vasoconstrictive response during pregnancy. Norepinephrine infusion increases blood pressure in normal parturients not by vasoconstriction but by increasing cardiac output. In nonpregnant patients, norepinephrine infusion increases SVR while lowering cardiac output.[92] Parturients also become resistant to the chronotropic effects of isoproterenol. Pregnancy reduces the response to this synthetic catecholamine fivefold (Fig. 27-6).[93] Women who develop preeclampsia do not make these adaptations. Preeclamptic patients have an exaggerated hypertensive response to norepinephrine infusion. As in nonpregnant women, SVR increases but cardiac output does not change. Preeclamptic patients also respond to isoproterenol as though they were not pregnant (see Fig. 27-6).[94] Accidental intravascular injection or excessive systemic absorption of epinephrine might cause an exaggerated heart rate or blood pressure response in a woman with preeclampsia.

Epidural epinephrine also may impair uteroplacental blood flow. Early studies reported no change in intervillous blood flow following epidural injection of 2-chloroprocaine with 50 μg of epinephrine. Because blood pressure fell significantly, these authors postulated that the placental bed undergoes vasodilation when perfusion pressure decreases. They concluded that epinephrine had no deleterious effect on placental perfusion.[95] Epinephrine-containing local anesthetics caused no apparent complications in four preeclamptic mothers during vaginal or cesarean delivery.[96] These authors concluded that the use of epinephrine did not exacerbate pre-existing hypertension.

More recent work contradicts these conclusions. Using dynamic placental scintigraphy, one group of investigators found a 34% decrease in placental blood flow when patients underwent cesarean section with epidural anesthesia using 0.5% bupivacaine with 2.5 μg/mL of epinephrine (1:400,000).[97] Placental blood flow fell despite a median fall in blood pressure of only 3 mm Hg. These authors noted a negative correlation between changes in maternal blood pressure and changes in placental flow. They speculated that maternal blood pressure was maintained at the expense of placental blood flow. Unfortunately, this study had no control group, and the women received a relatively small bolus of fluid (10 mL/kg) during induction. All infants had normal Apgar scores and umbilical artery pH values.

Doppler ultrasound can measure uterine artery resistance. When healthy primigravidae receive plain lidocaine for labor epidural analgesia, they respond

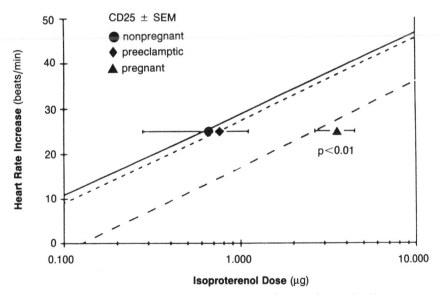

Figure 27–6. The chronotropic response to isoproterenol in preeclamptic, healthy pregnant, and nonpregnant women. The heart rate response is significantly attenuated in healthy pregnant patients, but not in preeclamptic women. (Leighton BL, Norris MC, De Simone CA, Darby MJ, Menduke H. Pre-eclamptic and healthy term pregnant patients have different chronotropic responses to isoproterenol. Anesthesiology 1990;72:392)

with a fall in umbilical artery resistance. In contrast, patients receiving lidocaine with epinephrine (40 µg) fall into two groups. Those who exhibited an initially normal umbilical arterial resistance also responded with a decline in uterine artery resistance. In contrast, those with an initially high resistance reacted to the local anesthetic solution with a further rise in resistance; one third developed fetal heart rate decelerations.[98] Thus, in a subgroup of normal parturients, the addition of epinephrine may have adverse consequences. The risks of epinephrine might be even greater in preeclamptic patients with generalized arteriolar vasospasm.

Although lower concentrations of epinephrine can be used in the local anesthetic solution, we have no way of knowing what amount of epinephrine is "safe" for a particular fetus. Because of the increased responsiveness to vasopressors, maternal and fetal sequelae could be disastrous should unintentional intravenous injection or excessive systemic absorption of epinephrine occur. To date, however, no one has reported any harm to mother or infant from epinephrine-containing local anesthetics. If you decide to include epinephrine in your local anesthetic solution, use small incremental doses and meticulous technique to avoid intravascular injection.

PATIENT PREPARATION. Several points must be addressed before placing an epidural catheter in a patient with preeclampsia. First, check a recent coagulation profile. We require at least a platelet count and fibrinogen level. These two values can be obtained within 30 minutes. We prefer to see sequential values to evaluate whether or not a downward trend exists. We do not recommend routinely measuring bleeding time. If the platelet count is less than 100,000/mm³ or the fibrinogen concentration is less than 200 mg/dL, we avoid regional anesthesia. If ultrasound examination suggests abruption, also check the prothrombin and partial thromboplastin times. Next, evaluate volume status. A hematocrit above 36% or a urine output below 0.5 mL/kg/h suggests significant volume contraction. Patients who are not severely volume-contracted need only 500 mL of crystalloid before induction of epidural block. In seriously ill patients, raise the CVP to a positive value or PCWP to 5 to 10 mm Hg. Some would elevate COP to at least 17 mm Hg using albumin or other colloid;[47] however, colloid infusion correlates with elevated filling pressures after delivery. These women then require diuretics to prevent pulmonary edema. Whatever the preload, give the local anesthetic slowly. This precaution allows adequate time to respond if hypotension develops as the level of blockade rises.

Suggested Technique

A parturient with preeclampsia may receive epidural analgesia whenever the obstetrician has committed her to delivery and she feels discomfort. While continuously monitoring the fetus, give the mother oxygen by face mask and have her assume the lateral or sitting position for insertion of the epidural catheter. Then, position the patient comfortably while ensuring good uterine displacement and provide pain relief with incremental doses (3–5 mL) of 0.25% bupivacaine, with or without 0.0002% fentanyl (2 µg/mL). The issue of an appropriate test dose for obstetric patients is controversial. I prefer to use small incremental doses of local anesthetic to avoid toxic reactions due to intravascular or subarachnoid placement. Monitor blood pressure by arterial catheter or at least every 2 minutes by automated cuff for 20 minutes after the initial dose and then less frequently. A continuous infusion of 0.125% plain bupivacaine or 0.0625% bupivacaine with fentanyl at a rate of 10 mL/h helps maintain a steady level of pain relief. I avoid lidocaine for prolonged infusions because preeclampsia significantly prolongs its clearance.[99] If mean arterial pressure falls more than 30% from baseline or if fetal distress occurs at any time, use further left uterine displacement, a fluid bolus, and 2.5 to 5.0 mg of intravenous ephedrine to correct the hypotension rapidly. In severely ill patients, evaluate filling pressures and SVR repeatedly as the level of sympathetic blockade rises. Following trends in these measurements will help guide fluid and vasopressor therapy.

Intrathecal Opioids

Intrathecal opioids for pain relief during labor are becoming increasingly popular in obstetrics (see Chap. 20). They may offer some advantages to these patients. Opioids can be given by single injection or via a subarachnoid catheter. Intrathecal injection of morphine (0.25 mg), fentanyl (10 to 25 µg), sufentanil (5 to 10 µg), or meperidine (10 to 20 mg) can provide analgesia for the first stage of labor.[100,101] This technique avoids sympathectomy and the need for volume loading (with the possible exception of meperidine). Supplemental analgesia is usually required for the second stage of labor and certainly for instrumental delivery. Either pudendal block or a low "saddle" block with local anesthetic are effective. As with epidural anesthesia, consider coagulation status before placing a spinal catheter. If the patient requires cesarean delivery, the rapid onset of sympathectomy initiated by use of subarachnoid local anesthetic may make hypotension difficult to avoid.

Other Choices

Other anesthetic options must be considered for the parturient who cannot have, or does not want, a regional anesthetic. Although traditionally obstetricians or labor and delivery personnel have administered narcotics and tranquilizers for labor analgesia, anesthesiologists have much to offer in their knowledge of the pharmacokinetics, efficacy, and side effects of the available drugs.[102] Intravenous fentanyl, 1 μg/kg, can provide rapid onset of intense analgesia with minimal neonatal effects. However, its short duration and accumulation with repeated doses make it appropriate only for short, painful procedures late in labor or at delivery.

Two of the agonist–antagonist drugs, butorphanol and nalbuphine, have been shown to provide more effective analgesia than meperidine with fewer side effects. Because their metabolites are inactive, neonatal depression is uncommon. Psychomimetic effects are rare, although marked maternal drowsiness can occur. Their "ceiling effect" on respiratory depression is unfortunately also associated with a ceiling effect on analgesia. Both nalbuphine and meperidine have been used during labor by patient-controlled analgesia with greater maternal satisfaction than intermittent bolus doses by nursing personnel. Total drug required and side effects were less using patient-controlled analgesia, and neonatal outcomes were similar between the two groups. This technique will likely continue to gain in popularity (see Chap. 16).

ANESTHESIA FOR CESAREAN DELIVERY

The incidence of cesarean delivery in the parturient with preeclampsia is increased for both maternal and fetal reasons. The anesthesiologist should be prepared to provide an anesthetic for operative delivery whether initially planned or not. Subarachnoid block is rarely chosen in these patients because of the risk of severe, profound hypotension. A spinal catheter allows slower titration of dose, but the onset of sympathetic block will still be more rapid than with epidural blockade.

Epidural Anesthesia

Advantages

STRESS RESPONSE. Epidural anesthesia provides a number of advantages over general anesthesia. Epidural blockade markedly blunts the hormonal and hemodynamic responses to surgery. Extensive epidural blockade prevents adrenocortical and hyperglycemic responses to stress in women undergoing hysterectomy.[103] In women undergoing elective cesarean section, epidural anesthesia correlates with lower maternal plasma cortisol, glucose, insulin, and ACTH concentrations. These women also have lower mean blood pressures and heart rates, and their infants have higher Apgar scores when compared to parturients having general anesthesia.[104,105] Epinephrine and norepinephrine levels markedly increase in patients given a general anesthetic, whereas the amounts of these compounds decrease in patients given an epidural anesthetic. Severely preeclamptic patients undergoing cesarean section have similar responses. Although the concentrations of epinephrine, norepinephrine, ACTH, and beta-endorphin increase with general anesthesia, they remain unchanged in parturients having an epidural anesthetic.[106]

HEMODYNAMIC CHANGES. Because hormonal concentrations are so well controlled in patients receiving epidural anesthesia, it is not surprising that their hemodynamic course also is smoother. Hodgkinson et al[107] followed the MAP, PA pressure (PAP), PCWP, and CVP in patients with severe preeclampsia undergoing cesarean delivery (Fig. 27-7). Those who had a general anesthetic experienced significant increases in MAP, PAP, and PCWP at intubation and extubation. The hemodynamic measurements in the group receiving epidural anesthesia remained unchanged.[107]

UTEROPLACENTAL BLOOD FLOW. The data on placental blood flow during epidural anesthesia for cesarean section are less clear. Two studies found an inconsistent effect among patients with both pronounced increases and decreases in placental blood flow. The overall effect in both studies was a small but insignificant fall in flow.[108,109] Apgar scores and umbilical cord blood gases were normal in all infants regardless of changes in uteroplacental perfusion. On the other hand, induction of general anesthesia with 4 mg/kg of thiopental and succinylcholine consistently decreases intervillous blood flow by 35% (Fig. 27-8).[110]

Mean and SE of MAP, PAP, and PwP of Pre-Eclamptic Patients Undergoing Caesarean Section Under Thiopental and Nitrous Oxide (40%) Anesthesia with 0.5% Halothane

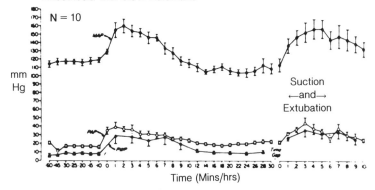

Mean and SE of MAP, PAP, and PwP of Pre-Eclamptic Patients Undergoing Caesarean Section Under Epidural Anesthesia

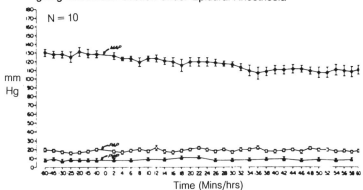

Figure 27–7. A comparison of systemic and pulmonary pressures during cesarean delivery under general or epidural anesthesia in preeclamptic parturients. General anesthesia consisted of thiopental, 3 mg/kg; succinylcholine, 100 mg; nitrous oxide, 40%; halothane, 0.5%; and a succinylcholine 0.2% infusion. Epidural block was established using 0.75% bupivacaine injected at time 0. (MAP = mean arterial pressure, PAP = pulmonary arterial pressure, PWP = pulmonary wedge pressure.) (Hodgkinson R, Husain FJ, Hayashi RH. Systemic and pulmonary blood pressure during caesarean section in parturients with gestational hypertension. Can Anaesth Soc J 1980;27: 389)

MISCELLANEOUS ADVANTAGES. In addition to blunting maternal stress responses during surgery and avoiding excessive hypertension during intubation and extubation, epidural anesthesia also maintains maternal consciousness and decreases the risk of aspiration. When the patient is awake, neurologic status can be monitored if there is concern about recovery after an eclamptic seizure or changing level of consciousness. Epidural blockade avoids the increases in ICP associated with a rapid-sequence induction of general anesthesia. This anesthetic also exposes the often premature neonate to less drug than does general anesthesia.

Some Technical Issues

The issues of coagulopathy and the safety of added epinephrine remain. Fluid management becomes more difficult. These women may require larger volumes of crystalloid to maintain hemodynamic stability. There will be rapid volume shifts of 1000 mL or more at the time of delivery. For these reasons, careful monitoring of volume status can help avoid sudden and potentially dangerous changes in blood pressure. You will need large-bore intravenous access for the following reasons:

- Fluids can be given rapidly during induction of epidural anesthesia.
- Magnesium therapy may cause some degree of tocolysis and can contribute to uterine atony and blood loss.
- Patients with HELLP syndrome or liver injury may require rapid infusion of blood products.

The optimal choice of local anesthetic for cesarean delivery is not clear. 2-Chloroprocaine has the most rapid onset, making timely intervention to correct hypotension more difficult. Slow titration to raise the anesthetic level is difficult with chloroprocaine. Dosing at intervals of more than a few minutes will often fail to raise the anesthetic level. Finally, redosing will have to be done about every 30 minutes, so you may be faced

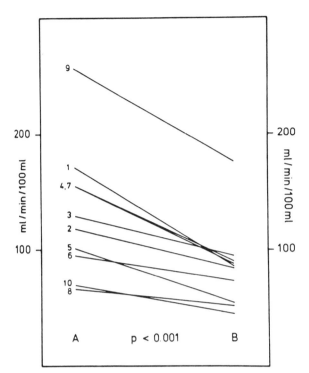

Figure 27–8. The individual intervillous flow changes. (*A*), Before anesthesia (mean intervillous blood flow = 131 ± 57 mL/min/100 mL). (*B*), During induction of general anesthesia (mean intervillous blood flow = 84 ± 37 mL/min/100 mL). (Jouppila P, Kuikka J, Jouppila R, Hollmen A. Effect of induction of general anesthesia for cesarean section on intervillous blood flow. Acta Obstet Gynecol Scand 1979;58:249)

extending the block for cesarean section will significantly improve the quality of blockade. In animals, magnesium appears to have no effect on the plasma concentration of bupivacaine at which seizures or cardiovascular collapse occurred. Magnesium did prevent cardiac dysrhythmias.[111]

Suggested Technique
(Table 27-3)

Give oral sodium citrate just before going to the operating room. Use your invasive monitoring to guide fluid and vasopressor therapy. Treat hypotension with additional fluids and small doses of a vasopressor (ephedrine before delivery or phenylephrine after delivery). Maintain adequate uterine displacement at all times. I initiate the block in a labor room with 10 mL of 0.5% bupivacaine containing 100 µg of fentanyl in incremental doses. This dose of bupivacaine usually provides a sensory level of T-8–T-10. After each dose, reassess hemodynamic values to determine the need for additional preload or a small dose of vasopressor. Slow titration of local anesthetic and continuous assessment of hemodynamics should avoid or allow rapid correction of hypotension. Once the sympathectomy has sta-

with giving a bolus of drug just after delivery, when the incidence of hypotension is already high. Lidocaine is metabolized less efficiently in the preeclamptic patient,[99] but this should not be of concern with the single bolus dose used for cesarean section. A more difficult problem is the maximum allowable dose of lidocaine that can be used without adding epinephrine. If the toxic dose of plain lidocaine is assumed to be 5 mg/kg and the average-sized woman is 60 kg, her toxic dose of 2% lidocaine is only 15 mL. This volume may prove inadequate to produce sensory block to T-4. Finally, although 0.5% bupivacaine probably best allows slow titration of anesthetic level, it is not as potent as 3% 2-chloroprocaine or 2% lidocaine. Because bupivacaine provides less dense motor and sensory blockade, the mother may require supplemental analgesia. Adding 100 µg of fentanyl to the local anesthetic solution will improve the quality of analgesia. Injecting the epidural catheter several times during labor before

Table 27-3

A Suggested Technique for Elective Cesarean Section in a Preeclamptic Parturient Under Epidural Anesthesia

1. Assess coagulation status.
2. Assess volume status and determine need for invasive hemodynamic monitoring.
3. Administer aspiration prophylaxis.
4. Insert additional 16-gauge IV catheter, separate from medication infusions. Hydrate with 20 mL/kg or until CVP is positive or PCWP is 5–10 mm Hg.
5. After identifying the epidural space, administer 0.5% bupivacaine, 10 mL, with fentanyl, 100 µg, in incremental doses.
6. Assess hemodynamic changes before each additional increment of drug, and give additional intravenous fluids or vasopressor as needed.
7. When hemodynamics are stable, proceed to the operating room and administer an additional 10 mL of 2% plain lidocaine in increments as needed to raise sensory level to T-4.
8. Treat hypotension at delivery as dictated by hemodynamic changes (*i.e.*, volume vs pressor vs inotropic support).
9. Administer 4–5 mg of preservative-free morphine through the epidural catheter after the umbilical cord is clamped.

bilized (in about 20 min), move the patient to the operating room and raise the level of sensory block to T-4 with an additional 10 mL of plain 2% lidocaine in incremental doses. This approach provides denser sensory blockade than using bupivacaine alone. Within a few minutes of delivery, a short period of moderate to severe hypotension often occurs. Air or amniotic fluid embolus or the sudden loss of a significant amount of blood in a relatively vasoconstricted patient may all contribute to this fall in blood pressure. Treat with fluid replacement and vasopressors if the mother is symptomatic. In the presence of maternal tachycardia, phenylephrine will improve vascular tone while lowering heart rate. Chose an appropriate vasopressor based on the patient's hemodynamic profile.

A functioning epidural catheter also often proves effective for urgent cesarean delivery. Use lidocaine or 2-chloroprocaine to provide a more rapid onset of sensory blockade. Infuse additional fluids simultaneously as needed to maintain a stable blood pressure. If there are earlier indications during labor that cesarean delivery may be needed (*i.e.,* slow progress), I give 0.5% bupivacaine to achieve a more dense block and sacral analgesia (but a level no higher than T-10). Then I change the continuous infusion solution to 0.25% bupivacaine. Again, good communication with the obstetric service should provide adequate warning of an impending operative procedure.

General Anesthesia

The anesthesiologist may have to resort to general anesthesia in some instances. Patients may refuse regional block or they may have a significant coagulopathy. General anesthesia may be the only choice for an emergent cesarean delivery in a woman without an epidural catheter. Several important issues must be considered when preparing a woman with preeclampsia for general anesthesia.

Airway

The generalized edema seen in preeclampsia may produce glottic edema, which makes endotracheal intubation extremely difficult.[112] Be aware of a potential airway problem if you note marked facial edema or the patient complains of hoarseness, difficulty swallowing, or respiratory distress. Glottic edema cannot be adequately assessed on routine airway exam. If you anticipate difficulty, consider gentle awake laryngoscopy under topical anesthesia to visualize the glottis. Respi-

ratory distress or other symptoms strongly suggest the need for awake intubation.[113]

AWAKE INTUBATION. The vascularity of the pregnant airway and our reluctance to premedicate parturients heavily just before delivery can make awake nasal or oral intubation traumatic for all involved. A simple, comfortable method of anesthetizing the airway involves nebulizing 4 mL of 4% lidocaine and 1 mL of 1% phenylephrine by mask.[114] If desired, this can be preceded by phenylephrine nasal drops to facilitate nasal breathing and a small amount of intravenous fentanyl to prevent coughing. A lubricated nasal airway is then placed and removed gently to dilate the nares, and an appropriately sized endotracheal tube is introduced over the fiberoptic bronchoscope. This technique can obtund protective airway reflexes; aspiration prophylaxis should be given beforehand, if possible. The technique is rapid, painless for the patient, and provides reliable anesthesia for nasotracheal intubation. Whatever technique is used for induction, a variety of smaller endotracheal tubes should be immediately available in the delivery room.

Blood Pressure

Dramatic and dangerous hypertension can complicate intubation and cause pulmonary edema or cerebral hemorrhage.[115] Numerous approaches can obtund this hypertensive response. Hood *et al*[116] used nitroglycerin to lower blood pressure by 20% before induction. This treatment limited the hypertensive response to intubation. These patients had no central hemodynamic monitoring. The authors did not mention what fluid therapy the women received. At our institution, we attempted to use nitroglycerin in a similar fashion after volume loading to a PCWP of 10 to 15 mm Hg.[117] At intubation, despite very high infusion rates of nitroglycerin, heart rate, MAP (from 134–164 mm Hg), and SVR all increased significantly. Because nitroglycerin primarily affects venous capacitance and ventricular preload, it will be less effective in the volume-expanded patient. Labetalol in doses up to 1 mg/kg may prove effective.[118] In some patients, this dose of labetalol will not induce a 20% reduction in MAP. Even in these women, however, some fall in blood pressure occurs without reflex tachycardia.

Opioids also can blunt the response to intubation. They are generally avoided in parturients because of the risk of neonatal depression. In healthy parturients, alfentanil (10 μg/kg) given just before induction effectively controls the pressor response to intubation without adversely affecting Apgar scores in the neonate.[119] Alfentanil readily crosses the placenta with a transfer ratio of 0.35. A comparison of lidocaine (1.5 mg/kg), magnesium sulfate (40 mg/kg), and alfentanil (10 μg/kg) given intravenously just before induction favored alfentanil and magnesium for controlling the cardiovascular responses to intubation, but alfentanil caused significant neonatal respiratory depression.[120] These patients had moderate to severe preeclampsia, and mean birth weight was 1726 g, so it may be that these premature neonates were more sensitive to the depressant effects of alfentanil; however, there was no indication of neonatal depression in the group who received magnesium, and no correlation between neonatal magnesium concentration and Apgar scores or ventilatory status. Recent work varying the time interval between intravenous lidocaine administration and tracheal intubation found that 1.5 mg/kg of lidocaine helped control the hemodynamic response to intubation only if administered more than 2 minutes beforehand.[121]

Maintenance

The choice of an inhalation agent for maintenance of the parturient with severe preeclampsia is not critical. Neither renal toxicity with enflurane nor liver dysfunction with halothane occur in preeclamptic parturients.[122] Isoflurane may be the agent of choice, however. In addition to being an excellent vasodilator, it avoids the issue of hepatic dysfunction (common in preeclampsia) and halothane. Enflurane may lower the seizure threshold, not a desirable feature in this patient population.

Remember, P_{50} shifts to the left in preeclampsia. Mechanical hyperventilation will shift the oxyhemoglobin dissociation curve even further to the left. Mechanical hyperventilation also decreases venous return and cardiac output. Both events decrease oxygen delivery to an already compromised fetus.

Magnesium and Muscle Relaxants

Therapeutic serum magnesium concentrations significantly potentiate nondepolarizing muscle relaxants. Neuromuscular transmission studies of preeclamptic women receiving magnesium therapy have documented a defect in neuromuscular transmission that increases in severity with increasing magnesium exposure.[123] Magnesium depresses neuromuscular transmission at multiple sites. It decreases presynaptic release of acetylcholine, lowers the sensitivity of the postjunctional muscle end-plate, and depresses the excitability of the muscle fiber membrane. Both animal and human studies have documented increased density of neuromuscular blockade and prolongation of nondepolarizing muscle relaxants by magnesium (Fig. 27-9).[124–126]

The interaction of magnesium with depolarizing muscle relaxants is more complicated. The neuromuscular effects of magnesium should antagonize the effects of succinylcholine. (Succinylcholine mimics acetylcholine at the nerve terminal. Magnesium inhibits the action of acetylcholine.) However, patients treated with magnesium require less succinylcholine by infusion than normal parturients (4.73 mg/kg/h vs 7.39 mg/kg/h) during uncomplicated cesarean section.[127] Likewise, in an isolated nerve preparation, magnesium doubles the potency of succinylcholine.[128] Preparation of the isolated nerve model, however, involved multiple washings to remove plasma cholinesterase. Therefore, these results probably represent the direct neuromuscular effect of succinylcholine or phase II block. The prolongation of succinylcholine after repeated

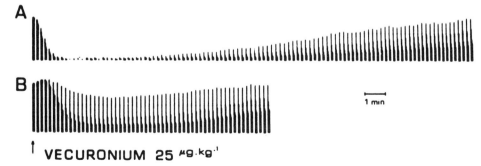

Figure 27–9. Electromyographic tracing comparing the neuromuscular blockade achieved by vecuronium, 25 μg/kg, in an eclamptic patient receiving intravenous magnesium sulfate at 2 g/h. (**A**) to that achieved in a control parturient (**B**). (Baraka A, Yazigi A. Neuromuscular interaction of magnesium with succinylcholine vecuronium sequence in the eclamptic parturient. Anesthesiology 1987;67:806)

doses or continuous infusion also may represent development of phase II block potentiated by magnesium. Human studies have failed to document any prolongation of onset or duration of succinylcholine after a single intubating dose in patients receiving magnesium (Fig. 27-10).[126,129] In clinical use, parturients receiving magnesium therapy will respond normally to a bolus injection of succinylcholine. Recovery after repeated doses or continuous infusion may be prolonged. Carefully monitor neuromuscular function with a nerve stimulator when giving any muscle relaxant to a woman with preeclampsia who has received magnesium.

Suggested Technique

The following is a suggested technique for general anesthesia for cesarean section in a woman with preeclampsia (Table 27-4). Before beginning, give appropriate aspiration prophylaxis. Carefully assess the patient's airway. Place any needed invasive monitors. During preoxygenation in the left tilt position, carefully control maternal blood pressure. Aim for a blood pressure of 140/90 mm Hg, but do not allow it to fall by more than 20%. Stop if a nonreassuring fetal heart rate pattern develops. I recommend either trimethaphan, in doses of 1 to 2 mg or as an infusion, nitroprusside by infusion, or labetalol in increments of 5 to 10 mg. Once you have lowered maternal blood pres-

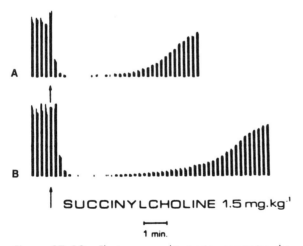

Figure 27-10. Electromyographic tracing comparing the neuromuscular blockade achieved by succinylcholine, 1.5 mg/kg, in an eclamptic patient (receiving intravenous magnesium sulphate at 2 g/h) (**A**) to that achieved in a control parturient (**B**). (Baraka A, Yazigi A. Neuromuscular interaction of magnesium with succinylcholine vecuronium sequence in the eclamptic parturient. Anesthesiology 1987;67:806)

Table 27-4

A Suggested Technique for Cesarean Section in a Preeclamptic Parturient under General Anesthesia

1. Administer aspiration prophylaxis.
2. Determine need for invasive hemodynamic monitoring.
3. Insert additional 16-gauge IV catheter, separate from medication infusions.
4. Evaluate the airway. Have spare, smaller endotracheal tubes (5.5, 6.0 mm) available in the operating room.
5. In the operating room, place the patient in the left-tilt position and begin preoxygenation with 100% oxygen.
6. Lower blood pressure to a mean of approximately 105–110 mm Hg or as the fetus tolerates using labetalol or vasodilators depending on the patient's hemodynamic status.
7. Induction sequence:
    Lidocaine, 1.5 mg/kg
    Alfentanil, 10 µg/kg
    Thiopental, 4 mg/kg
    Succinylcholine, 1 mg/kg
8. Maintain anesthesia before delivery with 50% nitrous oxide in oxygen and 0.75% isoflurane. Maintain normocarbia. If there is fetal distress, consider using 100% oxygen and 1.0%–1.5% isoflurane.
9. After delivery, increase nitrous oxide to 60%–70% as tolerated and titrate morphine, 0.2–0.3 mg/kg intravenously. Discontinue isoflurane. Treat hypotension at delivery based on hemodynamic changes (*i.e.*, volume vs pressor vs inotropic support).
10. Using a neuromuscular blockade monitor, titrate a succinylcholine infusion if the procedure is expected to last less than 1 h. For longer procedures, titrate atracurium in 10-mg increments to maintain 80%–90% blockade.
11. At emergence, reverse neuromuscular blockade if a nondepolarizing relaxant was used. Discontinue nitrous oxide. Treat emergence hypertension with agents used at induction. Extubate when patient is awake and can maintain 5s head lift.

sure adequately, begin a rapid sequence induction of general anesthesia. I use 1.5 mg/kg of lidocaine, 4 mg/kg of thiopental, and 1.0 mg/kg of succinylcholine. In severely hypertensive mothers or if I am concerned about rapid increases in ICP, I add alfentanil, 10 µg/kg, to the induction sequence. I then advise the pediatricians that the neonate may be narcotized. If fetal distress is the indication for delivery, maintain anesthesia with 100% oxygen and 1.0% to 1.5% isoflurane to assure maternal amnesia. If the fetus appears healthy, a lower oxygen concentration and 50% nitrous oxide can be used with 0.75% isoflurane. After delivery, increase the concentration of nitrous oxide, give incremental doses of morphine (total dose:

0.2–0.3 mg/kg), and a muscle relaxant as needed. I find the vasodilating properties of morphine helpful in controlling blood pressure after stopping the halogenated agent. Morphine also provides longer postoperative analgesia than fentanyl. If the surgery lasts less than 1 hour, a succinylcholine infusion can be used. I prefer to avoid nondepolarizing muscle relaxants, which are more difficult to titrate and reverse completely in the presence of high levels of magnesium sulfate. [Editors Note: I find succinylcholine infusions difficult to use even under normal circumstances. In this setting, I carefully titrate atracurium in increments of 5 or 10 mg. I strongly agree on the need to monitor neuromuscular function.] If the procedure is expected to require more than 1 hour, however, atracurium may be preferable to vecuronium because it is not dependent on hepatic metabolism. The laudanosine metabolite of atracurium does produce an arousal pattern on electroencephalogram but does not cause seizure activity in usual clinical doses. Oxytocin infusion must begin immediately at delivery to counteract the tocolytic effects of magnesium. Be prepared for hypotension shortly after delivery. Treat significant hypotension with vasopressors and additional fluids as guided by your invasive hemodynamic monitors. Vasodilators will probably be needed during emergence to control hypertension until the patient is fully awake and ready to be extubated.

POSTPARTUM CONSIDERATIONS

Care of the preeclamptic patient does not end immediately postoperatively. Monitoring should continue for at least 24 hours postpartum, or until diuresis begins. Mobilization of fluid should begin by 24 hours, and if a spontaneous diuresis does not occur, filling pressures will rise. If the patient had an epidural anesthetic, resolution of the sympathectomy with return of vascular tone may cause central pressures to rise as well. Elevated filling pressures put the patient at risk for pulmonary edema. If invasive monitoring is in place, follow CVP and PCWP carefully, and if they begin to rise without diuresis occurring, small doses of diuretics or low-dose dopamine may help.

In HELLP syndrome, thrombocytopenia may not reach its nadir until 2 or 3 days postpartum. An upward trend in platelet count should be apparent by the third postpartum day. Resolution to a count above 100,000/mm^3 may require 5 to 6 days. Fourteen percent to 27% of eclamptic seizures occur after delivery. Women with HELLP syndrome are at especially high risk of postpartum eclampsia.[40,130]

Patients will need to be changed from acute (parenteral) to long-term (oral) blood pressure medications. Most patients will need treatment of their hypertension for up to 6 weeks postpartum. Oral medications may include nifedipine, alpha-methyldopa, labetalol, or clonidine. Their efficacy and the patient's compliance should be documented before she is discharged from the hospital.

CONCLUSION

The preeclamptic patient requires the same meticulous attention from the anesthesiologist as a seriously ill patient in the general operating room—perhaps more, because only in the obstetric patient can mortality be 200%! This attention includes detailed preoperative preparation, selection of appropriate monitors, development of an anesthetic plan for all possible modes of delivery, and close postoperative follow-up. A good working relationship with our obstetric colleagues and the development of open lines of communication for consultation and planning will best serve the parturient in our care.

REFERENCES

1. Kambam JR, Entman S, Mouton S, Smith BE. Effect of preeclampsia on carboxyhemoglobin levels: A mechanism for a decrease in p50. Anesthesiology 1988; 68:433.
2. Trofatter KF, Howell ML, Greenberg CS, Hage ML. Use of the fibrin D-dimer in screening for coagulation abnormalities in preeclampsia. Obstet Gynecol 1989;73:435.
3. Pritchard JA, Cunningham FG, Mason RA. Coagulation changes in eclampsia: Their frequency and pathogenesis. Am J Obstet Gynecol 1976;124:855.
4. Kelton JG, Hunter DJS, Neame PB. A platelet function defect in preeclampsia. Obstet Gynecol 1985;65:107.
5. Ramanathan J, Sibai BM, Vu T, Chauhan D. Correlation between bleeding times and platelet counts in women with preeclampsia undergoing cesarean section. Anesthesiology 1989;71:188.
6. Schindler M, Gatt S, Isert P, Morgans D, Cheung A. Thrombocytopenia and platelet functional defects in pre-eclampsia: Implications for regional anaesthesia. Anaesth Intensive Care 1990;18:169.
7. Rolbin SH, Abbott D, Musclow E, Papsin F, Lie LM, Freedman J. Epidural anesthesia in pregnant patients with low platelet counts. Obstet Gynecol 1988;71:918.
8. Rasmus KT, Rottman RL, Kotelko DM, Wright WC, Stone JJ, Rosenblatt RM. Unrecognized thrombocytopenia and regional anesthesia in parturients: a retrospective review. Obstet Gynecol 1989;73:943.

9. Hew-Wing P, Rolbin SH, Hew E, Amato D. Epidural anaesthesia and thrombocytopenia. Anaesthesia 1989; 44:775.

10. Burrows RF, Kelton JG. Incidentally detected thrombocytopenia in healthy mothers and their infants. N Engl J Med 1988;319:142.

11. Kopacz DJ, Gibbs CP. Training anesthesia residents to perform bleeding times. Reg Anesth 1991;161:16.

12. Rodgers RPC, Levin J. A critical reappraisal of the bleeding time. Semin Thromb Hemost 1990;16:1.

13. Benigni A, Gregorini G, Frusca T, et al. Effect of low-dose aspirin on fetal and maternal generation of thromboxane by platelets in women at risk for pregnancy-induced hypertension. N Engl J Med 1989; 321:357.

14. Voulgaropoulos DS, Palmer CM. Coagulation studies in the parturient: How do we practice? [Abstract] Presented at the Society for Obstetric Anesthesia and Perinatology, May, 1991.

15. Barker P, Callander CC. Coagulation screening before epidural analgesia in pre-eclampsia. Anaesthesia 1991; 46:64.

16. Maltin JN, Blake PG, Lowry SL, Perry KG, Files JC, Morrison JC. Pregnancy complicated by preeclampsia-eclampsia with the syndrome of hemolysis, elevated liver enzymes, and low platelet count: How rapid is postpartum recovery? Obstet Gynecol 1990;76:737.

17. Smith LG, Moise KJ, Dildy GA, Carpenter RJ. Spontaneous rupture of liver during pregnancy: Current therapy. Obstet Gynecol 1991;77:171.

18. Cotton DB, Lee W, Huhta JC, Dorman KF. Hemodynamic profile of severe pregnancy-induced hypertension. Am J Obstet Gynecol 1988;158:523.

19. Clark SL, Divon MY, Phelan JP. Preeclampsia/eclampsia: Hemodynamic and neurologic correlations. Obstet Gynecol 1985;66:337.

20. Milliez J, Dahoun A, Boudraa M. Computed tomography of the brain in eclampsia. Obstet Gynecol 1990;75:975.

21. Montan S, Ingemarsson I. Intrapartum fetal heart rate patterns in pregnancies complicated by hypertension. Am J Obstet Gynecol 1989;160:283.

22. Naidoo DP, Bhorat I, Moodley J, Naidoo JK, Mitha AS. Continuous electrocardiographic monitoring in hypertensive crises in pregnancy. Am J Obstet Gynecol 1991;164:530.

23. Clark SL, Cotton DB. Clinical indications for pulmonary artery catheterization in the patient with severe preeclampsia. Am J Obstet Gynecol 1988;158:453.

24. Clark SL, Horenstein JM, Phelan JP, Montag TW, Paul RH. Experience with the pulmonary artery catheter in obstetrics and gynecology. Am J Obstet Gynecol 1985;152:374.

25. Woodward DG, Romanoff ME. Is central venous pressure monitoring "contraindicated" in patients with severe preeclampsia? Am J Obstet Gynecol 1989;161:837.

26. Clark SL, Divon MY, Phelan JP. Preeclampsia/eclampsia: Hemodynamic and neurologic correlations. Obstet Gynecol 1985;66:337.

27. Benedetti TJ, Cotton DB, Read JC, Miller FC. Hemodynamic observations in severe preeclampsia with a flow-directed pulmonary artery catheter. Am J Obstet Gynecol 1980;136:465.

28. Cotton DB, Gonik B, Dorman K, Harrist R. Cardiovascular alterations in severe pregnancy-induced hypertension: relationship of central venous pressure to pulmonary capillary wedge pressure. Am J Obstet Gynecol 1985;151:762.

29. Easterling TR, Benedetti TJ, Carlson KL, Watts DH. Measurement of cardiac output in pregnancy by thermodilution and impedance techniques. Br J Obstet Gynaecol 1989;96:67.

30. Easterling TR, Watts DH, Schmucker BC, Benedetti TJ. Measurement of cardiac output during pregnancy: Validation of Doppler technique and clinical observations in preeclampsia. Obstet Gynecol 1987;69:845.

31. Benedetti TJ, Carlson RW. Studies of colloid osmotic pressure in pregnancy-induced hypertension. Am J Obstet Gynecol 1979;135:308.

32. Cotton DB, Lee W, Huhta JC, Dorman KF. Hemodynamic profile of severe pregnancy-induced hypertension. Am J Obstet Gynecol 1988;158:523.

33. Benedetti TJ, Cotton DB, Read JC, Miller FC. Hemodynamic observations in severe preeclampsia with a flow-directed pulmonary artery catheter. Am J Obstet Gynecol 1980;136:465.

34. Rafferty TD, Berkowitz RL. Hemodynamics in patients with severe toxemia during labor and delivery. Am J Obstet Gynecol 1980;138:263.

35. Phelan JP, Yurth DA. Severe preeclampsia: Peripartum hemodynamic observations. Am J Obstet Gynecol 1982;144:17.

36. Groenendijk R, Trimbos JBMJ, Wallenburg HCS. Hemodynamic measurements in preeclampsia: Preliminary observations. Am J Obstet Gynecol 1984; 150:232.

37. Clark SL, Greenspoon JS, Aldahl D, Phelan JP. Severe preeclampsia with persistent oliguria: Management of hemodynamic subsets. Am J Obstet Gynecol 1986; 154:490.

38. Easterling TR, Benedetti TJ, Schmucker BC, Millard SP. Maternal hemodynamics in normal and preeclamptic pregnancies: A longitudinal study. Obstet Gynecol 1990;76:1061.

39. Easterling TR, Benedetti TJ. Preeclampsia: A hyperdynamic disease model. Am J Obstet Gynecol 1989; 160:1447.

40. Sibai BM, McCubbin JH, Anderson GD, Lipshitz J, Dilts PV. Eclampsia. I. Observations from 67 recent cases. Obstet Gynecol 1981;58:609.

41. Pritchard JA, Cunningham FG, Pritchard SA. The Parkland Memorial Hospital protocol for treatment of eclampsia: Evaluation of 245 cases. Am J Obstet Gynecol 1984;148:951.

42. Sibai BM. Magnesium sulfate is the ideal anticonvulsant in preeclampsia–eclampsia. Am J Obstet Gynecol 1990;162:1141.

43. Watson KV, Moldow CF, Ogburn PL, Jacob HS. Magnesium sulfate: Rationale for its use in preeclampsia. Proc Natl Acad Sci USA 1986;83:1075.

44. Friedman SA, Lim KH, Baker CA, Repke JT. A comparison of phenytoin infusion versus magnesium sulfate infusion in preeclampsia [Abstract]. Soc Perinat Obstet 1990;10:12.

45. Kirshon B, Lee W, Mauer MB, Cotton DB. Effects of low-dose dopamine therapy in the oliguric patient with preeclampsia. Am J Obstet Gynecol 1988;159:604.

46. Sibai BM, Mabie BC, Harvey CJ, Gonzalez AR. Pulmonary edema in severe preeclampsia–eclampsia: Analysis of thirty-seven consecutive cases. Am J Obstet Gynecol 1987;156:1174.

47. Kirshon B, Moise KJ, Cotton DB, et al. Role of volume expansion in severe preeclampsia. Surg Gynecol Obstet 1988;167:367.

48. Cotton DB, Jones MM, Longmire S, Dorman KF, Tessem J, Joyce TH. Role of intravenous nitroglycerin in the treatment of severe pregnancy-induced hypertension complicated by pulmonary edema. Am J Obstet Gynecol 1986;154:91.

49. Cotton DB, Gonik B, Dorman KF. Cardiovascular alterations in severe pregnancy-induced hypertension: Acute effects of intravenous magnesium sulfate. Am J Obstet Gynecol 1984;148:162.

50. Ring G, Krames E, Shnider SM, Wallis KL, Levinson G. Comparison of nitroprusside and hydralazine in hypertensive ewes. Obstet Gynecol 1977;50:598.

51. Cotton DB, Gonik B, Dorman KF. Cardiovascular alterations in severe pregnancy-induced hypertension seen with an intravenously given hydralazine bolus. Surg Gynecol Obstet 1985;161:240.

52. Wheeler AS, James FM, Meis PJ, et al. Effects of nitroglycerin and nitroprusside on the uterine vasculature of gravid ewes. Anesthesiology 1980;52:390.

53. Naulty J, Cefalo RC, Lewis PE. Fetal toxicity of nitroprusside in the pregnant ewe. Am J Obstet Gynecol 1981;139:708.

54. Stempel JE, O'Grady JP, Morton MJ, Johnson KA. Use of sodium nitroprusside in complications of gestational hypertension. Obstet Gynecol 1982;60:533.

55. Craft JB, Co EG, Yonekura ML, Gilman RM. Nitroglycerin therapy for phenylephrine induced hypertension in pregnant ewes. Anesth Analg 1980;59:494.

56. Cotton DB, Longmire S, Jones MM, Dorman KF, Tessem J, Joyce TH. Cardiovascular alterations in severe pregnancy-induced hypertension: Effects of intravenous nitroglycerin coupled with blood volume expansion. Am J Obstet Gynecol 1986;154:1053.

57. Ishikawa T, Funatsu N, Okamoto K, Takeshita H, McDowall DG. Cerebral and systemic effects of hypotension induced by trimethaphan or nitroprusside in dogs. Acta Anaesth Scand 1982;26:643.

58. Karlin A, Hartung J, Cottrell JE. Rate of induction of hypotension with trimetaphan modifies the intracranial pressure response in cats. Br J Anaesth 1988;60:161.

59. Sklar GS, Lanks KW. Effects of trimethaphan and sodium nitroprusside on hydrolysis of succinylcholine in vitro. Anesthesiology 1977;47:31.

60. Poulton TJ, James FM, Lockridge O. Prolonged apnea following trimethaphan and succinylcholine. Anesthesiology 1979;50:54.

61. MacCarthy EP, Bloomfield SS. Labetalol: A review of its pharmacology, pharmacokinetics, clinical uses and adverse effects. Pharmacotherapy 1983;3:193.

62. Nylund L, Lunell N-O, Lewander R, Sarby B, Thornstrom S. Labetalol for the treatment of hypertension in pregnancy. Acta Obstet Gynecol Scand Suppl 1984;118:71.

63. Jouppila P, Kirkinen P, Koivula A, Ylikorkala O. Labetalol does not alter the placental and fetal blood flow or maternal prostanoids in pre-eclampsia. Br J Obstet Gynaecol 1986;93:543.

64. Eisenach JC, Mandell G, Dewan DM. Maternal and fetal effects of labetalol in pregnant ewes. Anesthesiology 1991;74:292.

65. MacPherson M, Pipkin FB, Ruker N. The effect of maternal labetalol on the newborn infant. Br J Obstet Gynaecol 1986;93:539.

66. Mabie WC, Gonzalez AR, Sibai BM, Amon E. A comparative trial of labetalol and hydralazine in the acute management of severe hypertension complicating pregnancy. Obstet Gynecol 1987;70:328.

67. Östman PL, Chestnut DH, Robillard JE, Weiner CP, Hdez MJ. Transplacental passage and hemodynamic effects of esmolol in the gravid ewe. Anesthesiology 1988;69:738.

68. Eisenach JC, Castro MI. Maternally administered esmolol produces fetal beta-adrenergic blockade and hypoxemia in sheep. Anesthesiology 1989;71:718.

69. Kjellmer I, Dagbjartsson A, Hrbek A, Karlsson K, Rosen KG. Maternal beta-adrenoceptor blockade reduces fetal tolerance to asphyxia. Acta Obstet Gynecol Scand Suppl 1984;118:75.

70. Losasso TJ, Muzzi DA, Cucciara RF. Response of fetal heart rate to maternal administration of esmolol. Anesthesiology 1991;74:782.

71. Larson CP Jr, Shuer LM, Cohen SE. Maternally administered esmolol decreases fetal as well as maternal heart rate. J Clin Anesth 1990;427:2.

72. Horvath JS, Phippard A, Korda A, Henderson-Smart DJ, Child A, Tiller DJ. Clonidine hydrochloride—a safe and effective antihypertensive agent in pregnancy. Obstet Gynecol 1985;66:634.

73. Eisenach JC, Castro MI, Dewan DM, Rose JC, Grice SC. Intravenous clonidine hydrochloride toxicity in pregnant ewes. Am J Obstet Gynecol 1988;160:471.

74. Norris MC, Rose JC, Dewan DM. Nifedipine or verapamil counteracts hypertension in gravid ewes. Anesthesiology 1986;65:254.

75. Belfort M, Anthony J, Buccimazza A, Davey DA. Hemodynamic changes associated with intravenous infusion of the calcium antagonist verapamil in the treatment of severe gestational proteinuric hypertension. Obstet Gynecol 1990;75:970.

76. Belfort M, Kirshon B, Akovic K, Anthony J, Mari G, Cotton DB. Umbilical and uterine artery impedance following volume expansion and verapamil therapy in severe preeclampsia [Abstract]. Soc Perinat Obstet 1990;10:407.

77. Ducsay CA, Thompson JS, Wu AT, Novy MJ. Effects of calcium entry blocker (nicardipine) tocolysis in rhesus macaques: Fetal plasma concentrations and cardiorespiratory changes. Am J Obstet Gynecol 1987;157:1482.

78. Walters BNJ, Redman CWG. Treatment of severe pregnancy-associated hypertension with the calcium antagonist nifedipine. Br J Obstet Gynaecol 1984;91:330.

79. Barton JR, Hiett AK, Conover WB. The use of nifedipine during the postpartum period in patients with severe preeclampsia. Am J Obstet Gynecol 1990;162:788.

80. Thorp JM, Spielman FJ, Valea FA, Payne FG, Mueller RA, Cefalo RC. Nifedipine enhances the cardiac toxicity of magnesium sulfate in the isolated perfused Sprague-Dawley rat heart. Am J Obstet Gynecol 1990;163:655.

81. Snyder SW, Cardwell MS. Neuromuscular blockade with magnesium sulfate and nifedipine. Am J Obstet Gynecol 1989;161:35.

82. Mehta N, Modi N. ACE inhibitors in pregnancy. Lancet 1989;2:96.

83. Gutsche B. Is epidural block for labor and delivery and for cesarean section a safe form of analgesia in severe preeclampsia or eclampsia? Surv Anesthesiol 1986;30:304.

84. Abboud T, Artal R, Sarkis F, Henriksen EH, Kammula RK. Sympathoadrenal activity, maternal, fetal, and neonatal responses after epidural anesthesia in the preeclamptic patient. Am J Obstet Gynecol 1982;144:915.

85. Jouppila R, Jouppila P, Hollmen A, Koivula A. Epidural analgesia and placental blood flow during labour in pregnancies complicated by hypertension. Br J Obstet Gynaecol 1979;86:969.

86. Jouppila P, Jouppila R, Hollmen A, Koivula A. Lumbar epidural analgesia to improve intervillous blood flow during labor in severe preeclampsia. Obstet Gynecol 1982;59:158.

87. Moore TR, Key TC, Reisner LS, Resnik R. Evaluation of the use of continuous lumbar epidural anesthesia for hypertensive pregnant women in labor. Am J Obstet Gynecol 1985;152:404.

88. Newsome LR, Bramwell RS, Curling PE. Severe preeclampsia: Hemodynamic effects of lumbar epidural anesthesia. Anesth Analg 1986;65:31.

89. Vincent RD, Chestnut DH, Sipes SL, Weiner CP, DeBruyn CS, Bleuer SA. Magnesium sulfate decreases maternal blood pressure but not uterine blood flow during epidural anesthesia in gravid ewes. Anesthesiology 1991;74:77.

90. Chestnut DH, Vincent RD, Sipes SL, DeBruyn CS, Bleuer SA, Chatterjee P. Which vasopressor should one give to treat hypotension during magnesium sulfate infusion and epidural anesthesia [Abstract]? Presented at the Society for Obstetric Anesthesia and Perinatology, May, 1991.

91. Weiner CP, Martinez E, Chestnut DH, Ghodsi A. Effect of pregnancy on uterine and carotid artery response to norepinephrine, epinephrine, and phenylephrine in vessels with documented functional endothelium. Am J Obstet Gynecol 1989;161:1605.

92. Nisell H, Hjemdahl P, Linde B. Cardiovascular responses to circulating catecholamines in normal pregnancy and in pregnancy-induced hypertension. Clin Physiol 1985;5:479.

93. DeSimone CA, Leighton BL, Norris MC, Chayen B, Menduke H. The chronotropic effect of isoproterenol is reduced in term pregnant women. Anesthesiology 1988;69:626.

94. Leighton BL, Norris MC, DeSimone CA, Darby MJ, Menduke H. Pre-eclamptic and healthy term pregnant patients have different chronotropic responses to isoproterenol. Anesthesiology 1990;72:392.

95. Albright GA, Jouppila R, Hollmen AI, Jouppila P, Vierola H, Koivula A. Epinephrine does not alter human intervillous blood flow during epidural anesthesia. Anesthesiology 1981;54:131.

96. Heller PJ, Goodman C. Use of local anesthetics with epinephrine for epidural anesthesia in preeclampsia. Anesthesiology 1986;65:224.

97. Skjoldebrand A, Eklund J, Lunell N-O, Nylund L, Sarby B, Thronstrom S. The effects on uteroplacental blood flow of epidural anaesthesia containing adrenaline for caesarean section. Acta Anaesthesiol Scand 1990;34:85.

98. Marx GF, Elstein ID, Schuss M, Anyaegbunam A, Fleischer A. Effects of epidural block with lignocaine and lignocaine-adrenaline on umbilical artery velocity wave ratios. Br J Obstet Gynaecol 1990;97:517.

99. Ramanathan J, Bottorff M, Jeter JN, Khalil M, Sibai BM. The pharmacokinetics and maternal and neonatal effects of epidural lidocaine in preeclampsia. Anesth Analg 1986;65:120.

100. Leighton BL, DeSimone CA, Norris MC, Ben-David B. Intrathecal narcotics for labor revisited: The combination of fentanyl and morphine intrathecally provides rapid onset of profound, prolonged analgesia. Anesth Analg 1989;69:122.

101. Honet JE, Arkoosh VA, Huffnagle HJ, Norris MC, Leighton BL. Comparison of fentanyl, meperidine, and sufentanil for intrathecal labor analgesia [Abstract]. Presented at the Society for Obstetric Anesthesia and Perinatology, May, 1991.

102. Heyman HJ. Systemic analgesia in labor: Still a viable option? Anesthesiol Clin North Am 1990;8:43.

103. Engquist A, Brandt MR, Fernandes A, Kehlet H. The blocking effect of epidural analgesia on the adrenocortical and hyperglycemic responses to surgery. Acta Anaesth Scand 1977;21:330.

104. Lindahl S, Norden N, Nybell-Lindahl G, Westgren M. Endocrine stress response during general and epidural anaesthesia for elective caesarean sections. Acta Anaesthesiol Scand 1983;27:50.

105. Loughran PG, Moore J, Dundee JW. Maternal stress response associated with caesarean delivery under general and epidural anaesthesia. Br J Obstet Gynaecol 1986;93:943.

106. Ramanathan J, Sibai B. Maternal stress response during cesarean delivery in severe preeclampsia [Abstract]. Soc Obstet Anesth Perinatol 1988;20:G28.

107. Hodgkinson R, Husain FJ, Hayashi RH. Systemic and pulmonary blood pressure during caesarean section in parturients with gestational hypertension. Can Anaesth Soc J 1980;27:389.

108. Jouppila R, Jouppila P, Kuikka J, Hollmen A. Placental blood flow during caesarean section under lumbar extradural analgesia. Br J Anaesth 1978;50:275.

109. Skjolderbrand A, Eklund J, Johansson H, Lunell N-O, Nylund L, Sarby B, Thornstrom S. Uteroplacental blood flow measured by placental scintigraphy during epidural anaesthesia for caesarean section. Acta Anaesthesiol Scand 1990;34:79.

110. Jouppila P, Kuikka J, Jouppila R, Hollmen A. Effect of induction of general anesthesia for cesarean section on intervillous blood flow. Acta Obstet Gynaecol Scand 1979;58:249.

111. Solomon D, Bunegin L, Albin M. The effect of magnesium sulfate administration on cerebral and cardiac toxicity of bupivacaine in dogs. Anesthesiology 1990;72:341.

112. Jouppila R, Jouppila P, Hollmen A. Laryngeal oedema as an obstetric anaesthesia complication. Acta Anaesth Scand 1980;24:97.

113. Heller PJ, Scheider EP, Marx GF. Pharyngolaryngeal edema as a presenting symptom in preeclampsia. Obstet Gynecol 1983;62:523.

114. Bourke DL, Katz J, Tonneson A. Nebulized anesthesia for awake endotracheal intubation. Anesthesiology 1985;63:690.

115. Fox EJ, Sklar GS, Hill CH, Villanueva R, King BD. Complications related to the pressor response to endotracheal intubation. Anesthesiology 1977;47:524.

116. Hood DD, Dewan DM, James FM, Floyd HM, Bogard TD. The use of nitroglycerin in preventing the hypertensive response to tracheal intubation in severe preeclampsia. Anesthesiology 1985;63:329.

117. Longmire S, Leduc L, Jones MM, Hawkins JL, Joyce TH, Cotton DB. The hemodynamic effects of intubation during nitroglycerin infusion in severe preeclampsia. Am J Obstet Gynecol 1991;164:551.

118. Ramanathan J, Sibai BM, Mabie WC, Chauham D, Ruiz AG. The use of labetalol for attenuation of the hypertensive response to endotracheal intubation in preeclampsia. Am J Obstet Gynecol 1988;159:650.

119. Cartwright DP, Dann WL, Hutchinson A. Placental transfer of alfentanil at caesarean section. Eur J Anaesthesiol 1989;6:103.

120. Allen RW, James MFM, Uys PC. Attenuation of the pressor response to tracheal intubation in hypertensive proteinuric pregnant patients by lignocaine, alfentanil and magnesium sulphate. Br J Anaesth 1991;66:216.

121. Wilson IG, Meiklejohn BH, Smith G. Intravenous lignocaine and sympathoadrenal responses to laryngoscopy and intubation. Anaesthesia 1991;46:177.

122. Crowhurst JA, Rosen M. General anaesthesia for caesarean section in severe preeclampsia. Br J Anaesth 1984;587:56.

123. Ramanathan J, Sibai BM, Pillai R, Angel Jl. Neuromuscular transmission studies in preeclamptic women receiving magnesium sulfate. Am J Obstet Gynecol 1988;158:40.

124. Giesecke AH, Morris RE, Dalton MD, Stephen CR. Of magnesium, muscle relaxants, toxemic parturients, and cats. Anesth Analg 1968;47:689.

125. Sinatra RS, Philip BK, Naulty JS, Ostheimer GW. Prolonged neuromuscular blockade with vecuronium in a patient treated with magnesium sulfate. Anesth Analg 1985;64:1220.

126. Baraka A, Yazigi A. Neuromuscular interaction of magnesium with succinylcholine vecuronium sequence in the eclamptic parturient. Anesthesiology 1987;67:806.

127. Morris R, Giesecke AH. Potentiation of muscle relaxants by magnesium sulfate therapy in toxemia of pregnancy. South Med J 1968;61:25.

128. Ghoneim MM, Long JP. The interaction between magnesium and other neuromuscular blocking agents. Anesthesiology 1970;32:23.

129. James MFM, Cork RC, Dennett JE. Succinylcholine pretreatment with magnesium sulfate. Anesth Analg 1986;65:373.

130. Miles JF, Martin JN, Blake PG, Perry KG, Martin RW, Meeks GR. Postpartum eclampsia: a recurring perinatal dilemma. Obstet Gynecol 1990;76:328.

CHAPTER 28

Vaginal Birth After Cesarean Section

Divina Juson Santos

Between 1970 and 1986, the cesarean rate in the United States more than quadrupled from 5.5% to 24%.[1] The rate increased approximately 1% a year for almost two decades and now approaches 25%. At nearly 1 million operations a year, cesarean section is the most frequently performed major surgical procedure in this country. More cesarean sections are done than tonsillectomies, appendectomies, and mastectomies combined. The practice of automatic repeat cesarean section has contributed significantly to this trend. By 1980, close to 40% of cesarean sections were repeat procedures. Reducing the rate of repeat cesarean section could have a dramatic impact on the total cesarean section rate.[2] Leveno *et al*[3] estimate that for every 100 women with prior cesarean delivery who deliver vaginally, the cesarean section rate at the Parkland Hospital will fall by 1% (Fig. 28-1). Unless the current trend changes, the cesarean section rate may reach 40% by the year 2000 (Fig. 28-2).[1]

HISTORICAL BACKGROUND

Before the late 19th century, when antiseptic surgical technique and suturing of the uterine wound became common, too few mothers survived the cesarean delivery to even worry about subsequent pregnancies. Then the fundal vertical or classical incision in the thick upper uterine segment was the most common way to deliver the baby (Fig. 28-3A). As early as 1882, Kehrer advocated making the incision in the thinner lower uterine segment (Fig. 28-3B). This idea was revived 40 years later by Kerr.[4]

As maternal mortality from cesarean section decreased and patients became pregnant again, the question arose how to deliver subsequent pregnancies. As early as 1903, Williams recognized the danger of rupture of the previous uterine scar in subsequent pregnancies. At that time, uterine rupture carried with it a maternal mortality of 50% to 75% and a fetal mortality of nearly 100%. Cragin's 1916 recommendation of "once a cesarean, always a cesarean" was well received. The cesarean section rate then was 1% to 2%, all using the classical uterine incision. Cragin's other plea for conservatism in the use of primary cesarean section was largely forgotten. However, even as early as 1917, Williams thought that the fear of uterine rupture following cesarean section was greatly exaggerated. He recognized that this complication occurred only if the uterus was not properly sutured and its healing was complicated by infection.[4]

Because the classical incision ruptured 4% of the time with catastrophic results, Kerr in 1921 revived the use of the transverse incision in the lower uterine seg-

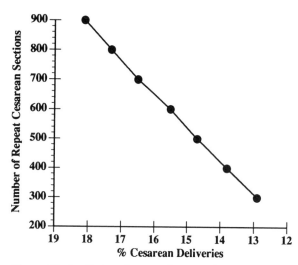

Figure 28–1. Projected impact of increased vaginal births in patients with prior cesarean section on the overall cesarean section rate at Parkland Hospital in Houston. Projections are based on 1983 data. (After Leveno KJ, Cunningham FG, Pritchard JA. Cesarean section: An answer to the House of Horne. Am J Obstet Gynecol 185;153:838)

ment (see Fig. 28-3B). The use of this incision rapidly gained in popularity. By 1976, 90% of uterine incisions were of this type.[4]

In subsequent pregnancies, a low transverse incision behaves differently than a classical one (Table 28-1).[5] The classical scar is more than four times as likely to rupture as is the low-segment transverse scar. It is also more likely to rupture before labor, accompanied by sudden severe symptoms. Rupture of the classical incision carries a higher fetal and maternal mortality. After analyzing the data from the British literature, Dewhurst concluded that vaginal birth after a previous cesarean section could be undertaken with considerable safety.[5] Indeed, "trial of scar" was common in Europe but rarely practiced in the United States and Canada.

To allow time for the lower uterine segment to develop, Riva and Teich intentionally delayed repeat cesarean section after the onset of labor.[6] In some patients, labor progressed rapidly to vaginal delivery before the repeat operation could be done. Because they found few uterine defects after delivery, by serendipity, the practice of deliberate trial of labor after previous cesarean section for selected patients began to evolve. From 1953 to 1960, 158 out of 214 patients with a prior uterine scar attempted vaginal delivery and 74% succeeded. These women awaited labor in the hospital for the last 2 weeks of their pregnancy. Neither uterine rupture nor maternal death occurred in the women who delivered vaginally.

In 1968, Sloan polled a group of obstetricians and asked if they would consider permitting labor in patients with previous low transverse cesarean scar if provided with overwhelming evidence of the safety of such practice. Eighty percent said "No!"[7] Despite reports of the relative safety of vaginal birth after cesarean section, by 1978, 99% of patients had an automatic repeat cesarean section.[4]

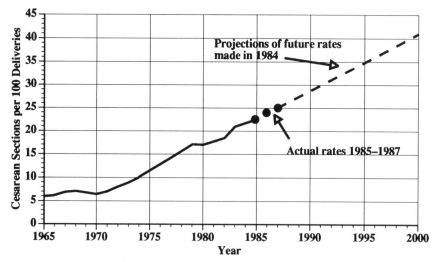

Figure 28–2. Projected growth of cesarean delivery rate nationally up to the year 2000 if the current rate of rise is not limited. (After Cesarean section in America: Dramatic trends, 1970 to 1987. Stat Bull 1989;70:2)

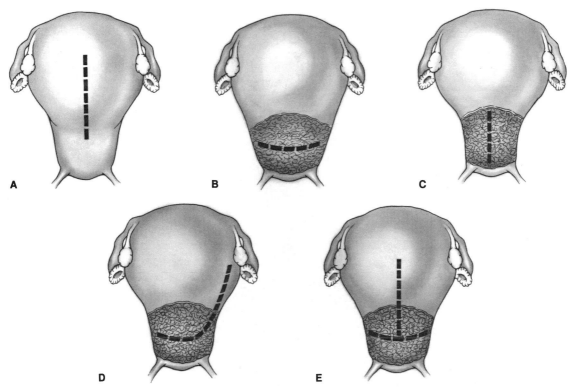

Figure 28–3. Types of cesarean section scars. (**A**) Classical incision. (**B**) Transverse incision in the lower uterine segment. (**C**) Vertical incision in the lower uterine segment. (**D**) "J" incision, extension of a low transverse incision curvilinearly into the upper uterine segment. (**E**) "T" incision, a combined low transverse with a low vertical incision. (Santos DJ, Ahlering CL, Hickey JL. Vaginal birth after cesarean section at St. John's. Res Medica [in press])

Concerned about the rising cesarean delivery rate, the National Institute of Health (NIH) Consensus Development Conference on Cesarean Section met in 1980. They recommended revoking the practice of automatic repeat cesarean section.[8] The American College of Obstetrics and Gynecology (ACOG) published and revised Guidelines for Vaginal Birth After Cesarean (VBAC) in 1982 and in 1985. Despite these recommendations and reports of the low risk and successful outcomes of trials of labor, US and North American obstetricians responded very slowly. Trial of labor increased fourfold, from 2.1% to 8%, between 1979 and 1984. Only a fraction of eligible gravidae were offered a choice other than automatic repeat cesarean section.[9]

In October, 1988, the ACOG Committee on Obstetrics: Maternal and Fetal Medicine published "Guidelines for Vaginal Delivery After a Previous Cesarean Birth." They suggest that repeat cesarean section should no longer be automatic; instead, VBAC should be the norm. Because any hospital with an obstetric

service should be able to do an emergency cesarean section within 30 minutes of making the decision, such hospital should be able to offer VBAC. The report emphasized the data collected in the past 10 years that extolled the virtues and safety of trial of labor. A plethora of media coverage followed this announcement. Today, the option of VBAC slowly continues to gain popularity.

WHY VBAC?

Collected series from 1950 to 1985 show that approximately 80% of patients with an earlier cesarean section may deliver vaginally.[9,10] The success rate for patients with two or more previous cesarean sections is 69%.[10] Attempted VBAC will most likely succeed regardless of the indication for the original operation (Table 28-2).[10] It appears that given a chance, almost four out of five patients can deliver vaginally and

Table 28–1

Differences in Behavior of Classical and Low Transverse Scars

	CLASSICAL SCAR	LOW TRANSVERSE SCAR
Incidence of rupture	2.2%	0.5%
Maternal mortality	5%	0%
Fetal mortality	73%	12.5%
Time of scar rupture		
Before labor	57%	24%
During labor	43%	76%
Clinical rupture before labor		
Symptomatic rupture	84%	18%
Incidental finding	16%	82%
Severity of symptoms		
No symptoms	13%	47%
Symptoms, but no collapse	21%	43%
Collapse	66%	8%

Clinical Features

	Sudden severe pain	Pain may be absent
	Contractions may cease	Contractions may continue
	Abnormal uterine shape	Bulging lower uterine segment
	Readily palpable fetus	Recession of fetal presenting part
	Absent fetal heart tones	Fetal distress
	Explosive, sudden collapse	Slower progression of symptoms
	Diffuse tenderness	Suprapubic tenderness

(Data from Dewhurst CJ. The ruptured caesarean section scar. J Obstet Gynaecol 1957;64:113)

avoid repeat cesarean birth. By adopting a liberal VBAC program, a group of university obstetricians successfully reduced their repeat cesarean section rate by 54%.[9] At the University of Chicago, routine VBAC has stabilized the cesarean delivery rate at 16% to 17% between 1985 and 1988, despite a continuing increase in primary cesarean sections. In 1982, women with a previous cesarean delivery were 10 times as likely to deliver abdominally than were patients without a uterine scar. By 1988, the relative risk of cesarean section had fallen to five times that of nonoperated women.[11]

Table 28–2

Success of Vaginal Delivery Following Cesarean Section and the Original Indications for Cesarean Section

INDICATION FOR PRIOR CESAREAN SECTION	TRIAL OF LABOR	VAGINAL DELIVERY
Cephalopelvic disproportion/failure to progress	774	509 (66%)
Fetal distress	317	238 (75%)
Breech	467	391 (84%)
Others	584	426 (73%)

(After Davies JA, Spencer JAD. Trial of scar. Br J Hosp Med 1988;40:379)

BENEFITS OF VBAC

Maternal

The practice of allowing patients to attempt VBAC offers many distinct advantages over automatic repeat cesarean section (Table 28-3). It is safer for the mother. Women are 5 to 10 times more likely to die after cesarean than vaginal birth.[12,13] Patients delivering abdominally are more likely to die of sepsis, pulmonary embolism, hemorrhage, and complications from anesthesia. On the other hand, there has been no maternal death from uterine rupture from VBAC in more than 11,000 patients over the past 30 years.[2]

Women who fail VBAC have a good chance of developing infection, but their risk approaches that of women undergoing primary cesarean section in labor. Because about 70% of VBAC patients succeed in delivering vaginally, the total febrile morbidity of VBAC patients is lower than patients delivering by elective repeat cesarean section.[14,15] Endometritis and urinary tract infection are the usual causes of fever in the puerperium. Vaginal birth after cesarean avoids operative complications such as injury to vital organs, blood transfusions, anesthetic complications, postoperative adhesions, and wound infections.[13] Patients delivering vaginally experience less discomfort and require less analgesia and nursing care.[16] They also recover more quickly, and care for their infants and return to work sooner.[17] The hospital stay is shorter by 2 to 3 days.[14] The psychological benefits of a shared labor and delivery experience for the patient and her spouse are immeasurable. Fetal–maternal bonding is more readily established.[15,18]

Shunning elective repeat cesarean section saves from $2,000 to $3,000 per delivery.[19,20] Assuming a cost differential of $3,000, avoiding 200,000 elective repeat cesarean deliveries would save approximately $600,000,000![22] Approximately 1.2 million hospital days could be saved if half the 1 million repeat cesarean sections could have delivered vaginally.[22] In developing countries where a large family size is desired, successful VBAC allows the patient to have more pregnancies.[23] Even a failed VBAC ending in repeat abdominal delivery offers the advantage of shorter operating time when compared to elective repeat cesarean section.[24]

Fetal

Vaginal delivery avoids certain fetal risks associated with cesarean section (Table 28-4).[25] Elective cesarean section increases the risk of iatrogenic prematurity and neonatal respiratory morbidity.[26] In the term newborn, the absence of labor before abdominal delivery can result in the syndrome of transient tachypnea or "neonatal wet lung." The completion of fetal lung adaptation to extrauterine respiration may require a few hours of labor.[25,26] Transient tachypnea may require admission to the intensive care nursery.[27] Occasionally, this

Table 28-3

Maternal Benefits of VBAC

MATERNAL BENEFITS	VAGINAL DELIVERY	CESAREAN SECTION
Maternal mortality	1.7/10,000 0–2.7/100,000	10.8/10,000[12] 0–10/100,000[13]
Febrile morbidity[12,14,15]	0.6%–3.6%	27%–35% (1° C/S) 13%–18% (repeat C/S)
Overall morbidity*[12]	3.2%	48% (1° C/S) 27% (repeat C/S)
Discomfort[16]	Less	More
Recovery[17]	Quicker	Slower
Hospital stay[14,19]	1–3 d	5–6 d
Cost[20,21]	Less	$2,000–$3,000 more
Number of pregnancies[23]	No limit	More limited

*Overall morbidity includes endometritis, mastitis, thrombophlebitis, infected wound, peritonitis, septicemia, pyelonephritis, urinary retention, oliguria/anuria, thrombosis/emboli, psychosis, respiratory diseases, abdominal wound dehiscence, postspinal symptoms, neurologic events.
Abbreviations: C/S = cesarean section.
1° C/S = primary cesarean section

Table 28-4

Fetal Risks from Cesarean Delivery

Fetal asphyxia due to anesthesia or maternal supine hypotension

Increased neonatal respiratory morbidity due to
   Iatrogenic prematurity
     Transient tachypnea of the newborn or "wet lung"
     Persistent pulmonary hypertension

Accidental fetal scalpel lacerations

Uterine rupture and abnormalities of placentation with subsequent pregnancies

---

syndrome leads to pulmonary hypertension and its severe infant morbidity and mortality. Heritage and Cunningham[28] described this syndrome in 12 babies delivered by elective cesarean section at term. Only two of the patients had any labor before operation. Unexplained respiratory distress occurred in four infants by 1 hour of age, and the rest of the infants by 8 hours of age. By 12 hours of age, all infants required mechanical ventilation. Three of the 12 infants died, 2 at 3 and 4 days of age, and the third at 6 months. The absence of labor may prevent fluid resorption, lung maturation, and surfactant release. These changes appear to be essential to decrease the pulmonary vascular resistance.[28]

Accidental scalpel lacerations can occur when the lower uterine segment thins and the surgeon is relatively inexperienced.[25,29] Subsequent pregnancies in patients with previous cesarean section present high risk to the fetus owing to the increased likelihood of abnormal placentation or possible catastrophic uterine rupture.[25]

RISKS OF VBAC

Uterine Rupture

Of greatest concern when considering VBAC is the danger of rupture of the previous uterine scar. There are two types of uterine rupture (see Table 28-1).

Complete or true rupture involves the entire thickness of the uterine wall, usually with extrusion of uterine contents. Symptoms occur suddenly and explosively. There is usually pain, hemorrhage, shock, and significant fetal and maternal morbidity and mortality. A classical uterine scar usually splits this way. The unscarred uterus also may suffer true rupture following trauma. It is rarely seen in low transverse uterine scars.[21]

Incomplete uterine rupture does not involve the entire thickness of the uterine wall. Because there is frequently no associated bleeding or extrusion of uterine contents, symptoms may be absent, and fetal or maternal morbidity or mortality rarely occur. This is the type usually seen in the low transverse uterine scar. Synonyms include *occult, silent, window,* or *dehiscence.*[21]

The risk of uterine rupture depends largely on the location of the uterine scar. A classical incision is a vertical cut in the thicker, more contractile upper uterine segment. It is rarely performed today. Specific indications include anterior placenta previa, transverse lie with the fetal back down, or dense scarring in the lower uterine segment.[29]

Most uterine incisions (90%) are transverse in the passive, less contractile lower uterine segment (see Fig. 28-3B). This portion of the uterus is thinner, less vascular, and only becomes fully formed during labor. Uterine contractions originate from a "pacemaker" region near the uterotubal junctions. The muscle fibers of the myometrium are uniquely arranged in a spiral fashion from the outer layer inward and from the fundus toward the lower uterine segment. Such an arrangement pulls on the circumferentially arranged muscles of the lower uterine segment. The contracting upper portion of the uterus thickens after each contraction because the muscle fibers do not relax to their original length. To maintain normal tension, the lower uterine segment thins out and expands as it is pulled upward. Meanwhile, it becomes distended as the presenting part is pushed toward the birth canal. The formation of the lower uterine segment has been compared to pulling a tight turtleneck sweater over one's head. As the sweater is pulled down, the head naturally flexes to present the smallest diameter to the neckline. Gradually, the turtleneck opens up by stretching over the head on each side. Finally, the head delivers through the turtleneck.[30] The gradual stretching that occurs in the formation of the lower uterine segment may explain why it is more prone to dehiscence instead of complete rupture. In addition, peritoneal signs may be absent because the loose bladder peritoneum covering the lower uterine segment may prevent peritoneal soiling during uterine rupture.[31]

If the lower uterine segment is not well developed, the obstetrician may choose to do a vertical incision in the lower uterine segment (Fig. 28-3C). Because the incision may not remain confined in the lower uterine segment, a low vertical scar may rupture more often than a transverse scar.

The "J" (Fig. 28-3D) incision also may be more prone to rupture than the uncomplicated low transverse scar because the incision extends into the thicker upper segment.[29] The "T" (Fig. 28-3E) could be a dangerous incision because of the combined use of a low transverse and low vertical incisions, and a weak junction where the two incisions meet.

Uterine rupture can occur in the intact or unscarred uterus. It can occur before or during labor. Most ruptures of the intact uterus result from accidents, traumatic obstetric maneuvers (*i.e.,* version and extraction, forceps delivery), obstructed labor, or oxytocin use in the grand multipara. Following rupture of the intact uterus, maternal mortality is 14% and fetal mortality is 76%. In contrast, fetal mortality falls to 35% and maternal death rarely occurs with rupture of previous cesarean scars.[32]

The most common cause of uterine rupture is reportedly the separation of a prior cesarean section scar;[33] however, a review of recent reports of uterine ruptures during pregnancy shows that 70% of uterine ruptures occurred in the unscarred uterus (Table 28-5).[33–35] With increasing numbers of women with previous cesarean scar undergoing trial of labor, and with fewer traumatic obstetric maneuvers, these numbers may change in the future.

Shy et al[36] estimated 73 uterine ruptures during labor per 10,000 planned VBACs. Many reports of VBAC emphasize the high success rate of vaginal delivery even in patients whose first cesarean section was for failure to progress or cephalopelvic disproportion (CPD).[37,38] Although uterine rupture and dehiscence do occur during trial of labor, this complication does not present a higher risk of maternal or fetal mortality than elective repeat cesarean section.[17,36]

However, three recent articles dealing with rupture of the previous cesarean section scar emphasize that VBAC is not completely risk-free. Chazotte and Cohen[39] presented 17 cases of catastrophic complications in patients with one or more cesarean section scars delivering between January, 1986 to June, 1989. The authors called the following complications catastrophic:

- Fetal or maternal death
- Hemorrhage requiring transfusion of five or more units of blood
- Hysterectomy or major artery ligation
- Uterine rupture requiring emergent surgery, associated with fetal extrusion or neonatal depression

Ten of 17 cases involved a low-segment transverse scar (4 after primary cesarean section done preterm). Six cases involved an unknown type of scar, and one involved a vertical scar. Eight patients had more than one scar. Twelve infants were born preterm; eight required admission to the neonatal intensive care unit.

Two mothers died. One suffered intractable hemorrhage from placenta previa/percreta. The other had a pulmonary embolus 4 weeks after cesarean hysterectomy. Rupture of her vertical scar was diagnosed during elective cesarean section at 34 weeks. She was a grand multipara with a history of prior uterine rupture at 20 weeks.

Table 28-5

Incidence of Rupture of the Pregnant Uterus

| YEAR | TOTAL RUPTURES | SCARRED UTERUS | | | INTACT UTERUS |
		Vertical	Low Transverse	Other	
1976	335	10	50	15	260
1978	47	15	9	1	22
1979	15	2	5	0	8
1980	93	6	23	3	61
1983	23	8	4	2	9
1986	24	3	2	0	19
1987	15	1	6	9	8
Total	552	45 (8%)	99 (18%)	21 (4%)	387 (70%)

(Data from Plauche WC, Von Almen W, Muller R. Catastrophic uterine ruptures. Obstet Gynecol 1984;64:792; Eden RD, Parker RT, Gall SA. Rupture of the pregnant uterus: A 53-year review. Obstet Gynecol 1986;68:671; and Fedorkow DM, Nimrod CA, Taylor PJ. Ruptured uterus in pregnancy: A Canadian hospital's experience. Can Med Assoc J 1987;137:27.)

There were three fetal deaths. Two died after uterine rupture with fetal extrusion. One infant, at 22 weeks of gestation, died of exsanguinating maternal hemorrhage from a placenta previa. This latter case required internal iliac ligation, hysterectomy, and a 13-unit transfusion. These maternal and fetal deaths were *not* related to trial of labor.

Serious hemorrhage occurred in 11 patients, resulting in eight hysterectomies. Of seven elective repeat cesarean sections, five had placenta previa with varying degrees of accreta. In three patients, uterine rupture caused the hemorrhage. The other eight women had placenta previa associated with some degree of placenta accreta. Only two of the hemorrhages occurred during VBAC.

Nine of 17 patients had serious uterine rupture. Five of the ruptures were associated with VBAC (1.4% of patients allowed a trial of labor). Three of the five patients who had a rupture during labor received oxytocin. In one rupture, the fetus, and in another, the umbilical cord, extruded through the rupture, resulting in Apgar scores of 3 and 5, and 3 and 4, at 1 and 5 minutes, respectively. One fetus was severely depressed after rupture of an unknown scar in a patient with severe preeclampsia, late decelerations, and clinical diagnosis of abruptio placentae, who also received oxytocin and epidural anesthesia. All three patients who received epidural anesthesia complained of pain. All five low transverse scar ruptures were repaired.

The overall risk of catastrophic complication in patients with previous cesarean section was 1 in 42 (2.4%), whereas the risk of maternal or fetal death was 0.7%, or 1 in 143 pregnancies. Patients with prior cesarean section scar were twice as likely to have placenta previa with accreta. Uterine rupture and placenta previa/accreta were the major causes of mortality and serious morbidity.

Rupture of the low transverse scar is not always benign. Scott[40] reports a total of 14 serious uterine ruptures during trial of labor: 3 from the University of Utah, and 9 from four community hospitals in Salt Lake City. These ruptures were symptomatic and endangered the life of the fetus or mother. All the hospitals where the ruptures occurred had obstetricians who were readily available to evaluate labor, and they had the capability to perform a cesarean section within 30 minutes of the decision to do so.

Continuous fetal monitoring was started upon admission. Ten patients had spontaneous labor, whereas two patients were induced at 38 and 42 weeks. Oxytocin was used in four patients and epidural anesthesia in three. Fetal distress was seen in nine (64%) cases.

Four patients had surgery less than 1 hour after admission to the hospital. Six patients (43%) experienced abdominal pain. Three patients (21%) had vaginal bleeding. Three patients had recession of the presenting part. At laparotomy, there was partial to complete extrusion through the uterine rupture in nine patients. The estimated blood loss was 1000 to 4000 mL, with four patients requiring blood transfusion. There was one hysterectomy and one internal iliac ligation. Thirteen cases were amenable to repair of the uterine rupture.

Six infants were severely depressed at birth. There were three perinatal deaths, all of which occurred when the fetal monitor tracing was not under direct observation of the physician. One infant was severely damaged owing to delay in diagnosis of uterine rupture and fetal distress. Two fetuses died after uterine rupture with fetal extrusion. One infant died within a year after suffering severe perinatal asphyxia and severe neurologic damage. Another infant continues to show neurologic damage.

Scott[40] could only guess at the incidence of uterine rupture of 1.5% (reported incidence in other studies was 0 to 2.3%). The author concludes that although VBAC is generally successful, it is not always uncomplicated. He advocates a more cautious approach to VBAC, with careful patient selection, discussion of risks and possible sequelae of uterine rupture, and a specific management plan.

Jones *et al*[41] also reported eight cases of rupture of the low-segment scar during trial of labor. These cases occurred in five hospitals in the Denver metropolitan area over a 13-month period. All patients had electronic fetal monitoring, and seven patients had an intrauterine pressure catheter. Table 28-6 shows the details of the cases presented. All but one patient (Case 2) received oxytocin: four for induction (three had earlier cervical ripening with prostaglandin E_2) and three for augmentation. There were two instances of uterine hyperstimulation. Of four patients who received both epidural anesthesia and oxytocin, two experienced pain during rupture. The diagnosis of uterine rupture was not always immediately apparent. Four patients had severe variable decelerations before the fetal head receded. The most frequent finding was sudden deterioration of the fetal heart rate. Recession of the fetal head (50%) and suprapubic bulging were associated with the most accurate and rapid diagnosis. Five women complained of pain or tenderness in the suprapubic area. All eight parturients underwent emergency exploratory laparotomy. Rupture of the uterus was an incidental finding at surgery in two patients. Uterine repair was possible in seven. Three cases of bladder

Table 28–6

Details of Eight Uterine Ruptures During Trial of Labor

CASE NO.	WEEK	OBSTETRIC MANAGEMENT	FETAL FINDINGS (EXTRUSION)	APGAR SCORES	UA pH	OUTCOME
1	37	PGE$_2$ oxy, epid	Head	8/9	—	Normal
2	37	expectant (three previous C/S)	Complete	7/9	7.24	Normal
3	41	oxy, epidural	Head	8/8	—	Normal
4	41	oxy induction	Head	1/2	6.76	Asphyxia, normal
5	40	PGE$_2$, oxy ind	Complete	1/3	6.90	Asphyxia, normal
6	40	oxy aug, epid	Complete	0/0	—	Neonatal death
7	40	oxy aug, epid	Umbilical cord	2/7	7.15	Normal
8	41	PGE$_2$, oxy ind	Head and shoulder	8/9	7.14	Normal

(Data from Jones RO, Nagashima AW, Hartnett-Goodman MM, Goodlin RC. Rupture of low transverse cesarean scars during trial of labor. Obstet Gynecol 1991;77:815.)
Abbreviations: aug = augmentation, C/S = cesarean section, epid = epidural anesthesia, ind = induction, oxy = oxytocin, UA = umbilical artery.

perforation were repaired. Estimated blood loss ranged from minimal to 1900 mL. There was one neonatal death due to fetal extrusion and abruptio placentae. Two infants with perinatal asphyxia were normal at discharge. Although the use of oxytocin during VBAC is safe, this study serves as a reminder that it may not be used with impunity. Oxytocin use must be carefully titrated, and any evidence of fetal distress must be viewed with a high index of suspicion that uterine rupture may be occurring.

Diagnosis of Uterine Rupture

Because of its rarity and protean manifestations, early diagnosis of uterine rupture is not easy. The clinician must maintain a high index of suspicion in any patient with a uterine scar. The few premonitory signs may be indistinguishable from the normal aches, pains, and "bloody show" of labor. The classic symptoms of uterine rupture arise in only 17% of cases (Table 28-7).[34] Even when suprapubic pain is present, uterine rupture was confirmed at operation in only 1 of 20 cases.[42]

Abdominal pain is an inconsistent finding that is neither sensitive nor specific.[34,43-45] If present, the pain usually is described as a severe sensation of shearing or tearing in the suprapubic area.[46] Some fear that epidural anesthesia may mask the pain of uterine rupture. However, a growing consensus believes that this apprehension is not valid.[47] A properly administered epidural anesthetic at analgesic concentrations will fre-

quently allow the patient to perceive the so-called "breakthrough pain" associated with abruptio placenta or complete uterine rupture.[48]

Fetal distress signals uterine rupture in 20% to 60% of monitored patients.[40,41,45] There may be fetal bradycardia or severe variable decelerations. Uterine pressure monitoring may show a progressive rise in intrauterine baseline pressure of up to 35 mm Hg associated with severe variable decelerations (Fig. 28-4)[49] or a sudden loss of uterine tone (Fig. 28-5).[50] When pain, vaginal bleeding, and fetal distress are present, abruptio placentae is a more common preoperative diagnosis than uterine rupture. Placental abruption may result from

Table 28–7

Signs and Symptoms of Uterine Rupture of the Gravid Uterus (Scarred or Unscarred)

SIGNS AND SYMPTOMS OF UTERINE RUPTURE	INCIDENCE
Pain	0% to 50%–80%
Fetal distress	50%–75%
Vaginal bleeding	17%–67%
Recession of presenting part	25%–50%
Shock	0%–50%
Readily palpable fetal parts	17%
Peritoneal signs	17%

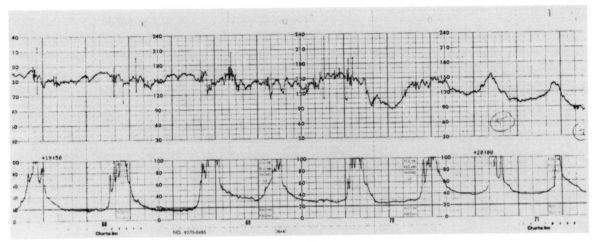

Figure 28–4. The monitor tracing shows fetal heart rate decelerations associated with an increase in intrauterine pressure of up to 35 to 40 mm Hg in a patient with uterine rupture during trial of labor. (Rodriguez MH, Masaki DI, Phelan JP, Diaz FG. Uterine rupture: Are intrauterine pressure catheters useful in the diagnosis? Am J Obstet Gynecol 1989;161:666)

sudden uterine decompression as the uterus ruptures and its contents are extruded. Recession of the fetal presenting part, readily palpable fetal parts, peritoneal signs, and shock are late signs.[40]

Treatment of Uterine Rupture

Early diagnosis is the key to minimizing maternal and fetal morbidity and mortality. Resuscitation of the mother must start simultaneously with preparations for immediate surgical intervention. Procrastination may be devastating: 13 of 20 patients with uterine rupture associated with severe hemorrhage died when treated medically. Shock does not contraindicate surgery when intraperitoneal hemorrhage is suspected.[46] Fetal outcome depends largely on the timeliness of the operation. Repair of the uterine rent should be the operative goal, especially if the woman desires future pregnancy, or if she is hemodynamically unstable. However, if hemostasis cannot be achieved by internal iliac ligation, hysterectomy should be done. Total hysterectomy is preferred if the patient can tolerate the procedure; otherwise, subtotal hysterectomy should suffice.[51]

Failed VBAC

Patients who fail a trial of labor have a higher likelihood of febrile morbidity following repeat cesarean section when compared to patients who have an elective operation. This risk, however, is no greater than that seen in patients undergoing primary cesarean section during labor.[14] Indications for repeat cesarean section in these patients include arrest disorders or failure to progress (72%), fetal distress (15%), and other indications (13%).[14] Despite the failure and accompanying disappointment, most patients do not seem to regret having tried to deliver vaginally.[52,53]

Increased Perineal Lacerations

The risk of significant perineal lacerations in VBAC patients who delivered spontaneously was higher than in a control group of nulliparas (31% vs 18%).[54] The incidence of lacerations increased when the babies weighed more than 3600 g.

Fetal Risks

Although the low transverse scar is more likely to dehisce than rupture, delay in diagnosis of complete rupture is associated with poor perinatal outcome. In Jones's report from Denver, there was one neonatal death and two cases of severe perinatal asphyxia in eight cases of uterine rupture of the low-segment transverse incision.[41] Scott[40] presented two stillbirths, two neonatal deaths, and three severely depressed infants (two have persistent neurologic deficits) in 14 VBAC patients.

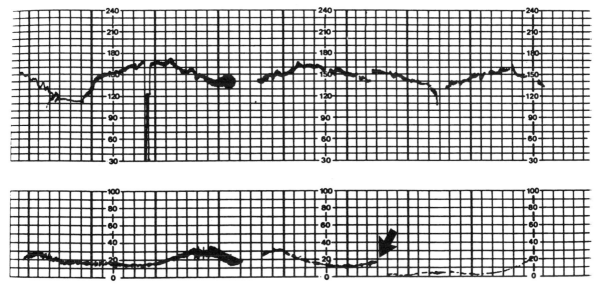

Figure 28–5. The monitor tracing of a patient with uterine rupture of a low transverse scar during trial of labor. Late decelerations of the fetal heart associated with an abrupt decrease in intrauterine pressure are indicated by the *arrow*. (Stovall TG, Shaver DC, Solomon SK, Anderson GD. Trial of labor in previous cesarean section patients, excluding classical cesarean sections. Obstet Gynecol 1987;70:713)

Medicolegal Risks

Patients are increasingly aware of the option of VBAC from a variety of sources, including the media. Some patients choose a particular physician or hospital because of the availability of this alternative to automatic repeat cesarean section. Review of the operative note and counseling must begin early in the pregnancy. Analysis, perception, and acceptance of risk must be faced by patients and obstetricians alike.[55] For patients awaiting labor, Gibbs[15] and Phelan *et al*[14] have noted a few cases of unexplained stillbirths after 38 weeks of gestation that might have been averted by an elective repeat cesarean section. Whether the VBAC patient is at greater risk for late fetal demise than her unscarred counterpart is unknown. Nevertheless, Phelan[14] recommends routine antepartum fetal surveillance beginning at or around 38 weeks of gestation for these patients.

During discussions of risks, it will be useful to know if there are defects in the uterine scar. Michaels *et al*[56] prospectively studied 70 patients with prior low-segment scar by ultrasonography and compared them with 12 nulliparous controls. They found a 21% incidence of scar defects that were confirmed at repeat cesarean section. It appears that the optimum time to study the lower uterine segment is between 26 and 36 weeks. At this time, the lower uterine segment has

begun to develop, the presenting part is not too deep in the pelvis, and the amniotic fluid volume is still copious. Lonky *et al*[57] saw 28% of 47 scars. All scars visualized were low transverse; no vertical scars could be identified. The value of these observations needs further evaluation.

Medicolegal problems can arise if there is an adverse result from trial of labor. Scott[40] mentions that litigation has been initiated in four cases with poor perinatal outcome. All cases appeared to have followed the ACOG guidelines. The media coverage regarding VBAC may be partly responsible for the cavalier attitude of a few patients. One patient at 43 weeks of gestation tried to deliver at home with a lay midwife; this resulted in fetal death from uterine rupture. The patient claimed that she had read that VBAC was safe.[40] It is important to involve the patient actively in the decision process. She must be made aware that there are risks associated with both VBAC and repeat cesarean section. The mere presence of a prior scar puts her at risk for subsequent uterine rupture not present in a patient with an unscarred uterus. The patient must be made aware of the risks and behavior of the different types of uterine scars. As patients seek greater control of their health care, they also must begin to assume some of the responsibilities involved. For instance, she should know the details of her prior operation, keep a copy of the operative report, obtain early and regular prenatal care, be familiar with the signs of labor, and promptly report anything unusual.

PATIENT SELECTION

In October, 1988, the Committee on Obstetrics: Maternal and Fetal Medicine of the ACOG issued "Guidelines for Vaginal Delivery After a Previous Cesarean Birth." Each hospital was encouraged to develop its own protocol for management of patients who are planning VBAC (Figs. 28-6 and 28-7). The protocol should include the following:

- The practice of routine repeat cesarean birth should be replaced by a specific indication for a subsequent abdominal delivery. In the absence of a contraindication, a woman with one previous low-segment transverse cesarean delivery should be counseled and encouraged to attempt labor in her current pregnancy.
- A woman who has had two or more previous cesarean deliveries with low transverse incisions who now wishes to attempt vaginal birth should not be discouraged from doing so in the absence of contraindications.
- In circumstances in which specific data on risks are lacking, the question of whether to allow trial of labor must be assessed on an individual basis.

- A previous classical incision is a contraindication to labor.
- Professional and institutional resources must have the capacity to respond to acute intrapartum emergencies, such as performing cesarean delivery within 30 minutes from the time the decision is made until the surgical incision is begun (the standard for any obstetric patient in labor).
- Normal activity should be encouraged during the latent phase of labor. There is no need for restriction to a labor bed before actual labor has begun.
- A physician who can evaluate labor and do a cesarean delivery should be readily available.

No specific guidelines were given regarding the use of oxytocin. Recent reports on the use of oxytocin for augmentation of labor indicate that oxytocin appears to pose no greater risk in patients with prior low transverse incision than in the general population. There was no noted evidence that epidural anesthesia is contraindicated for these patients.

Specific Contraindications to a Trial of Labor

Absolute contraindications for VBAC include the following:

- Classical scar, extensive uterine surgery, "T" or "J" extensions of low transverse incisions

---

St. Joseph's Hospital, Milwaukee, Wisconsin
Nursing Policy and Procedure
Vaginal Birth After Cesarean Section

1.00   *PURPOSE*
This statement lists requirements necessary for patients wishing to have vaginal birth after cesarean section

2.00   *REQUIREMENTS*
These are requirements for patients wishing to have a vaginal birth after having had a previous cesarean section.

     2.01   The previous c-section must have been a low transverse incision.
     2.02   The patient shall be admitted in early labor.
     2.03   The patient shall have blood drawn for a CBC and type and screen/cross-match.
     2.04   The patient shall have a peripheral IV line established.
     2.05   A fetal monitor shall be applied.
     2.06   Anesthesia personnel shall be available and notified of patient's admission.
     2.07   An obstetrical resident shall be in-house.
     2.08   There must be no contraindications to vaginal delivery.

Figure 28-6. Protocol for vaginal birth after cesarean section at St. Joseph's Hospital in Milwaukee, Wisconsin.

St. John's Mercy Medical Center, St. Louis, Missouri
Vaginal Delivery After Previous Cesarean Section

I.   **PURPOSE:**   To provide guidelines for physicians wishing to offer patients the option to attempt vaginal delivery after a previous cesarean birth.

II. **POLICY:**   **A.**   The patient will have previously discussed the option of a trial labor with her physician and will be aware of the benefits and potential risks.

   B.   The patient will have an IV infusing during labor and delivery.

   C.   The patient will have continuous electronic monitoring of fetal heart rate and uterine activity.

   D.   The patient will be allowed to deliver in the LDR room.

   E.   Anesthesia will be decided upon by the physician and the anesthesiologist on duty.

   F.   The use of oxytocin will be at the discretion of the physician and according to the established protocol of the department.

   G.   The obstetrician will not be required to remain in the labor/delivery area during the entire labor. A resident physician capable of evaluating labor and performing emergency cesarean delivery will be immediately available.

   H.   All patients requiring a repeat cesarean section must have their chart stamped with the C-section stamp and filled out by an OB resident or attending physician.

Figure 28–7.   Protocol for vaginal delivery after previous cesarean section at St. John's Mercy Medical Center in St. Louis, Missouri.

- Absolute cephalopelvic disproportion
- Obstetric contraindication to vaginal delivery
- Patient refusal
- Lack of personnel or facilities

There must not be any obstetric contraindication to vaginal delivery. The patient must consent to VBAC, and it should only be allowed if facilities and personnel are available. The obstetrician should reserve the right and responsibility to exercise individual judgment based on a case-by-case basis, especially when experience with specific obstetrical conditions is limited.[9] It is only appropriate that the patient and her spouse be actively involved in the decision process. The couple then can share in the responsibility for the chosen plan of management.

OBSTETRIC CONSIDERATIONS FOR VBAC

Use of Oxytocin for Induction or Augmentation of Labor

Some investigators fear that use of oxytocin increases the risk of uterine rupture during trial of labor. There seems to be no reason to believe that a given uterine pressure achieved by oxytocin administration is any more dangerous to the uterine scar than the same pressure produced during natural labor. A uterus strong enough to withstand spontaneous labor should be able to withstand a properly induced labor as well.[21] In properly selected cases, with careful surveillance and precisely controlled administration, the use of oxytocin for induction or augmentation of labor in patients with a prior low-segment cesarean section is safe.

Oxytocin use in this group of patients does not seem to increase the risk of uterine dehiscence or rupture, transfusion, birth trauma, or adverse maternal and neonatal outcome.[58,59] If oxytocin is required to augment labor, the incidence of repeat operative delivery increases,[50,60] as is true in any patient with dysfunctional labor. In studies in which oxytocin was withheld because of fear of uterine rupture, the success rate for vaginal delivery was lower than in those studies in which oxytocin was used to treat uterine inertia (Table 28-8).[21,37,50,60,61,63–65] More recent studies find no difference in success rates in patients with or without oxytocin.[37,62] This trend may suggest increased confidence in the safety of the use of oxytocin in these patients. There does appear to be a difference in successful outcome when using oxytocin for induction (58%)

Table 28-8

Reports of Oxytocin Use During Trial of Labor

		OXYTOCIN			NO OXYTOCIN		
		VBAC	Vaginal Delivery		VBAC	Vaginal Delivery	
SERIES	YEAR	(n)	(n)	(%)	(n)	(n)	(%)
McGarry et al	1969	83	51	62	191	145	76
Saldana et al[66]	1979	3	3	100	142	51	38
Carlsson et al[48]	1980	76	64	84	43	41	95
Benedetti et al	1982	16	12	75	73	59	81
Demianczuk et al[92]	1982	23	10	43	69	40	58
Meier and Porreco[53]	1982	42	34	81	165	141	85
Martin et al[72]	1983	25	17	68	137	84	61
Horenstein et al[58]	1984	58	31	56	234	168	84
Flamm et al[94]	1984	94	61	65	136	120	88
Horenstein et al[59]	1985	289	200	69	443	395	89
Flamm et al[60]	1987	485	309	64	1291	1005	78
Silver and Gibbs[103]	1987	98	58	59			
Lao and Leung[63]	1987	102	86	84	564	485	86
Stovall et al[50]	1987	133	98	74	139	116	85
Molloy et al[61]	1987	719	600	83	1363	1244	91
Targett et al[104]	1988	127	88	69	1450	1109	76
Ollendorf et al[76]	1988	46	27	59	51	34	67
Flamm et al[37]	1990	1686	1140	68	4047	3151	78
Total		4105	2889	70	10,538	8388	80

(After Flamm BL, Goings JR, Fuelberth N, Fischermann E, Jones C. Hersh E. Oxytocin during labor after previous cesarean section: Results of a multicenter study. Obstet Gynecol 1987;70:709)

compared to using it for augmentation of labor (88%).[66]

Oxytocin had been used safely in more than 10,000 cases in the literature. Its use is not without risk, however. Patients must be selected carefully. Oxytocin must be titrated carefully under the guidance of an internal uterine pressure catheter whenever possible. Although the internal uterine pressure catheter does not appear to increase the chances of diagnosing uterine rupture,[49] it remains useful for assessing the adequacy of uterine contractions and detecting hyperstimulation during oxytocin use.

Multiple Prior Cesarean Section Scars

The success rate of VBAC in women after multiple previous cesarean deliveries varies between 45% and 81%. The largest available study included 501 patients and reported a 69% success rate.[67] Of patients requiring oxytocin, 53% delivered vaginally. In contrast, the success rate was 83% in patients not requiring oxytocin. Thirty percent of patients received epidural anesthesia without problems. The number of previous scars did not affect the dehiscence rate. The VBAC group had a 1.8% dehiscence rate versus 4.6% in patients undergoing elective repeat cesarean section.[65] Even patients with more than one previous cesarean section can safely and often successfully attempt VBAC (Table 28-9).[6,68-72]

Previous Low-segment Vertical Incision

The incidence of rupture of the low vertical scar is 1.3%, compared to 2.2% for the classical and 0.7% for the low transverse scar.[73] Most studies exclude patients that have this scar.[37] However, three papers suggest that VBAC in patients with one or more low vertical scars is safe.[14,50,74]

Table 28-9

Success Rate of Trial of Labor in Patients with Two or More Low-Segment Transverse Scars

AUTHORS	YEAR	VAGINAL DELIVERY		REPEAT CESAREAN SECTION		TOTAL
		(n)	(%)	(n)	(%)	
Riva and Teich[6]	1961	50	66	26	34	76
Saldana et al[66]	1979	22	58	16	42	38
Porreco and Meier[67]	1983	17	81	4	19	21
Farmakides[68]	1987	44	77	13	33	57
Pruett et al[69]	1988	25	45	30	55	55
Phelan et al[65]	1989	346	69	155	31	501
Novas et al[70]	1989	29	80	7	20	36
Total		533	68	251	36	784

Unknown Type of Uterine Scar

Vaginal birth after cesarean section in patients with unknown uterine scar is a highly controversial issue. At the Women's Hospital in Los Angeles County, Beall *et al*[75] found that they could only document the type of uterine scar in 48% of their patients. Ninety-two percent had a low transverse scar, and 8% had vertical scars. There was no difference in the success of VBAC in patients with unknown and low transverse scars (86% vs 72%). Pruett *et al*[76] found more unknown uterine incisions (76%) in their patients at Jefferson Davis Hospital in Houston, Texas. Vaginal birth after cesarean succeeded in 62% of patients with unknown scars and 52% of patients with low transverse scars. The uterine dehiscence rate was 3.4% for the low transverse, and 2.6% for the unknown scar.[76] Oxytocin was used in about 35% of patients in both series. A total of 397 patients with unknown uterine scars from both studies attempted VBAC. The authors concluded that patients with an unknown uterine scar can attempt labor without undue risk to them or the fetus provided that intensive maternal and fetal monitoring are carried out and facilities are available to perform emergency operation when indicated.

Previous Cesarean Section for Failure to Progress

Patients with a previous history of cesarean section for failure to progress or cephalopelvic disproportion should not be automatically excluded from considering a trial of labor. Sixty-eight percent of these women will deliver vaginally.[77] There is no difference in the rate of success if the primary cesarean section was done for arrest of labor in the latent, active, or second stages of labor. Also, the maximum cervical dilatation obtained in the earlier labor does not correlate with the likelihood of success in achieving vaginal delivery in the subsequent pregnancy.[64]

Macrosomic Fetus

Fetal macrosomia is present when the fetus weighs more than 4000 g. Some investigators recommend cesarean delivery for these infants to avoid traumatic birth injuries, including shoulder dystocia.[78] There is greater concern in delivering these babies in the presence of a uterine scar. Phelan *et al*[79] allowed VBAC in 140 patients with prior uterine scar whose babies were estimated to weigh more than 4000 g. Sixty-seven percent (94 out of 140) delivered vaginally. Eighty-three percent of women whose babies weighed less than 4000 g had a successful VBAC. Patients who had an intervening vaginal delivery after the first cesarean section whose primary cesarean section was not for cephalopelvic disproportion were more likely to succeed. Eighty-nine percent of babies were delivered spontaneously. The most serious complication was shoulder dystocia, which occurred in three patients (3.2%) who also received oxytocin augmentation. This incidence is higher than the generally quoted risk of 0.37% of vertex deliveries. The incidence is 1.7% for babies weighing more than 4000 g and 10% for babies weighing more than 4500 g (in patients without prior uterine scar).[30] Ollendorf *et al*[64] achieved an 81% successful VBAC rate when the infant weighed less than 4000 g but only 40% if it weighed more than 4000 g. Flamm and Goings[80] studied a total of 301 macrosomic babies. Fifty-eight percent and 43% of babies weighing between 4000 and 4499 g and greater than 4500 g, respectively, were delivered vaginally.[80] Vaginal birth cannot be recommended routinely in the presence of fetal macrosomia, with or without a previous cesarean section. It is reasonable to allow labor in selected patients provided that labor is progressing normally and the pelvis seems adequate.

Post-term Pregnancy

A pregnancy is considered post term when it exceeds 42 weeks. This entity occurs in 7% to 12% of pregnancies.[81] The fetal dangers associated with prolonged pregnancy include oligohydramnios and possible cord accidents; macrosomia and birth trauma; meconium passage and aspiration; and placental insufficiency, perinatal hypoxia, and death.[82] Elective repeat cesarean section, usually scheduled shortly after completion of 38 weeks, should theoretically avoid these problems. MacKenzie[83] induced labor in 143 post-term patients who wanted to attempt VBAC with vaginal prostaglandins and achieved a 76% success rate. This series included 77 patients with unfavorable cervix, 68% of whom delivered vaginally. Meehan[84] had to induce 38% of his post-term VBAC patients with good success. Yeh *et al*[85] followed 78 post-term patients who attempted VBAC and reported a 73% success rate with no increase in morbidity. Post-term pregnancy does not appear to be a contraindication to VBAC.

Multiple Gestation

Gravidas with twin gestation and previous cesarean section generally are excluded from attempting VBAC because of concern that the uterine scar may not withstand the stress of overdistention. However, Strong *et al*[86] reported a 72% success rate in 25 patients who tried to deliver vaginally. The dehiscence rate of 4% was twice that seen in singleton pregnancies. The authors concluded that trial of labor appears reasonable in properly motivated and monitored patients.

Breech Presentation

Breech presentation, which occurs in 4% of term pregnancies, is nearly universally delivered by cesarean section in an attempt to avoid fetal trauma and asphyxia. The incidence of cesarean delivery for breech presentation has increased fourfold, from 22% (from 1963–1973) to 94% (in 1978), with no improvement in fetal outcome and an increased incidence of maternal morbidity.[87] Ophir *et al*[88] studied 47 patients with a prior uterine scar and breech presentation in the current pregnancy who chose to attempt VBAC. Seventy-nine percent delivered vaginally. Neonatal morbidity did not increase. A smaller study of 13 patients reported a 48% success rate with no increase in fetal or maternal morbidity.[89] Vaginal birth seems reasonable in carefully selected cases of breech presentation after a previous cesarean section.

ANESTHETIC CONSIDERATIONS

The anesthesiologist must be involved in the formulation of the hospital protocol for patients planning a trial of labor after previous cesarean section. When planning an anesthetic for these women, the anesthesiologist must consider a variety of issues.

What Is the Incidence of Emergent Cesarean Section in Patients Attempting VBAC?

Finley and Gibbs[90] studied this question by reviewing their experience over a 5-year period involving 1156 VBAC patients. They found 18 patients who required emergent operation (1.56%). This rate did not differ from patients laboring without a uterine scar (Table 28-10).

In another group of 751 women attempting VBAC, 7 (0.9%) needed emergent cesarean section. In contrast, 2 of 458 (0.4%) patients who planned elective repeat cesarean section required emergent abdominal delivery for fetal distress.[91]

What Is the Risk of Epidural Anesthesia for Labor Analgesia in VBAC Patients?

A concern about the use of epidural anesthesia in women attempting VBAC is that it may mask pain and delay the diagnosis of uterine rupture. Maternal hypo-

Table 28-10

Emergent Cesarean Section During Trial of Labor

PREOPERATIVE DIAGNOSIS	n	% OF VBAC PATIENTS (n=1156)	GENERAL INCIDENCE (%)
Uterine scar complication	3	0.26	
Abruptio placenta	3	0.26	0.49–1.3
Cord prolapse	4	0.35	0.2–0.5
Fetal distress	8	0.69	0.32–1.9
Total	18	1.56	

(Data from Finley BE, Gibbs CE. Emergent cesarean delivery in patients undergoing trial of labor with a transverse lower segment scar. Am J Obstet Gynecol 1986;155:936)

tension and compensatory tachycardia caused by hemorrhage from uterine rupture may be mistaken for the fall in blood pressure frequently observed from the sympathetic blockade of epidural anesthesia. Another possible hazard is the reduction in the capability of the patient to vasoconstrict in the presence of hypovolemia that may accompany uterine rupture. In addition, the cessation of uterine contractions after fetal extrusion may be misinterpreted as the temporary decrease in uterine activity seen after induction of epidural anesthesia. These concerns were raised and answered by Uppington in 1983.[92] Because pain and suprapubic tenderness are not reliable signs, and hemorrhage and shock are rarely observed, epidural analgesia did not delay the diagnosis of uterine rupture. Instead, fetal distress seemed the more reliable and consistent sign. The presence of a previous cesarean section is not a relative contraindication to the use of epidural anesthesia.

Table 28-11[45,93,94] compiles the results of 16 studies in which epidural analgesia was used for trial of labor. A total of 1915 patients received epidural anesthesia among 12,212 patients attempting VBAC. The incidence of uterine rupture for the entire group is 0.38%.[93-98]

Table 28-12 compares the clinical presentation of uterine rupture in 14 patients with epidural anesthesia and 29 without it.[93] Abdominal pain alone (19%) was not a prominent symptom. Fetal distress alone (51%) was the most common symptom. The incidence of uterine rupture was higher in the group receiving epidural anesthesia (0.76% vs 0.28%), but the presenting symptoms did not differ between the two groups. Of the patients who had uterine rupture, 38% had epidural anesthesia and 62% did not. Nineteen percent received a combination of epidural anesthesia and a

uterine stimulant (18 oxytocin, 1 prostaglandin), 28% had oxytocin alone, and 34% received neither epidural analgesia nor oxytocin. Half the patients with uterine rupture (47%) received some form of uterine stimulant, whereas the other half (53%) did not (Table 28-13).

The diagnosis of uterine rupture may be simplified in the presence of epidural analgesia. Any pain that "breaks through" a functioning epidural must be viewed with suspicion. At low anesthetic concentrations used to relieve labor pain, it is possible that axons are blocked just slightly above the minimal blocking concentration of the drug. A more intense stimulus, such as uterine rupture, abruptio placentae, or acute bladder distention, can provoke an impulse that may be conducted through the "blocked" segment of the axon. Crawford[99] called this phenomenon "epidural sieve." Similarly, peritoneal irritation from blood or amniotic fluid underneath the diaphragm can cause referred pain in the shoulder. A recent case report described a patient who complained of shoulder pain after epidural injection of 2% lidocaine for cesarean section. Complete uterine rupture was found at operation.[100]

When providing epidural analgesia during a trial of labor, limit the concentration and dose of local anesthesia to maintain analgesic levels not much above T-10. A small amount of narcotic administered with the local anesthetic may allow a further decrease in the dose of local anesthetic.[95] Establish good bilateral blockade. Monitor the anesthetic level frequently. Continuous epidural infusions allow the maintenance of steady levels of analgesia. The level of sensory blockade can usually be rapidly extended if immediate operative intervention is required. Three percent 2-chloropro-

(text continues on page 548)

Table 28–11

Trial of Labor and Epidural Analgesia

STUDY	YEAR	TOTAL	EPIDURAL (n)	NO EPIDURAL (n)	RUPTURED UTERUS (n)	RUPTURED UTERUS (%)
Carlsson et al[48]	1980	119	77	42	2	1.7
Demianczuk et al[92]	1982	92	41	51	2	2.2
Meier et al[53]	1982	207	19	188	0	0
Martin et al[72]	1983	717	98	619	3	0.42
Uppington et al[91]	1983	222	71	151	4	1.8
Rudick et al[93]	1984	115	115	0	1	0.87
Flamm et al[94]	1984	230	73	157	0	0
Horenstein et al[59]	1985	732	0	732	2	0.27
Stovall et al[50]	1987	272	153	119	1	0.37
Molloy et al[61]	1987	1781	85	1696	8	0.45
Phelan et al[14]	1987	1796	178	1618	5	0.28
Flamm et al[2]	1988	1776	181	1595	3	0.17
Meehan et al[95]	1989	1498	187	1311	4	0.27
Meehan et al[44]	1989	1350	345	1005	6	0.44
Nielsen et al[45]	1989	1008	205	803	6	0.6
Sakala et al[97]	1991	237	87	150	0	0
Totals		12,212	1,915	10,297	47	0.38%

(After Johnson C, Oriol N. The role of epidural anesthesia in trial of labor. Reg Anesth 1990; 15:304)

Table 28–12

Presenting Signs and Symptoms of Uterine Rupture During Trial of Labor in Women With and Without Epidural Blockade

PRESENTING SIGNS AND SYMPTOMS OF RUPTURE	NO. OF RUPTURES	EPIDURAL (n=1828)	NO EPIDURAL (n=10,147)
Abdominal pain	8 (19%)	3 (21%)	5 (17%)
Fetal distress	22 (51%)	7 (50%)	15 (52%)
Incidental finding at C/S	3 (7%)	1 (2%)	2 (5%)
Fetal distress and abdominal pain	6 (14%)	2 (14%)	4 (14%)
Postpartum bleeding	4 (9%)	1 (7%)	3 (10%)
Total rupture incidence	43	14 (0.76%)	29 (0.28%)

(After Johnson C, Oriol N. The role of epidural anesthesia in trial of labor. Reg Anesth 1990;15:304)
Abbreviation: C/S = cesarean section.

Table 28-13

Uterine Rupture During Trial of Labor Related to Use of Epidural Analgesia and Uterine Stimulation

PRESENTATION	EPIDURAL	EPIDURAL + OXYTOCIN	EPIDURAL + PROSTAGLANDIN	OXYTOCIN	PROSTAGLANDIN	NOTHING	TOTAL
Abdominal pain alone	0	3	1	0	1	4	9(19%)
Abdominal pain + fetal distress	1	1	0	2	0	2	6(13%)
Fetal distress alone	7	3	0	5	0	6	21(45%)
Incidental finding at C/S	1	0	0	2	0	0	3(6%)
Postpartum bleeding	0	1	0	0	0	3	4(8%)
Presentation not given	0	0	0	3	0	1	4(8%)

(After Johnson C, Oriol N. The role of epidural anesthesia in trial of labor. Reg Anesth 1990;15:304)

Abbreviation: C/S = cesarean section

caine or 2% lidocaine are equally useful for this purpose. Some obstetricians routinely palpate the scar during labor[100] or after vaginal delivery.[102] Others have questioned this practice.[103]

Does the Use of Epidural Anesthesia Decrease the Likelihood of Successful VBAC?

Another concern regarding the use of epidural anesthesia for VBAC is its possible effect on success rate. For instance, Stovall *et al*[50] noted a 25.5% cesarean section rate in patients receiving epidural analgesia, compared to 14.3% in patients not given epidural anesthesia. Of the 39 patients who received an epidural and subsequently required a repeat cesarean section, 28 (72%) had a history of labor dystocia in their primary cesarean section. Twenty three of these same 28 patients (82%) were given oxytocin during the trial of labor. Epidural administration correlated with the use of oxytocin. Seventy-seven percent of patients receiving oxytocin (103 of 133) also used epidural anesthesia. In contrast, only 36% (50 of 139) of patients not receiving oxytocin had an epidural. The estimated risk of cesarean section in patients receiving both an epidural and oxytocin was 31%, compared to 14% in patients who only received an epidural.[50] Sakala *et al*[94] reported similar findings when they compared the outcome in 87 patients who received epidural block for labor analgesia with 150 patients who did not. The operative vaginal delivery was higher in the epidural group compared to the nonepidural group (37% vs 23%). More patients in the epidural group who failed the trial of labor used oxytocin. The cervical dilatation was less, and the presenting part was at a higher station at the time of epidural placement. Patients in the epidural group had a greater weight gain and larger infants. When the oxytocin subjects were excluded from the data analysis, both epidural and nonepidural groups had the same high rates of successful outcome (94% and 92%) and spontaneous vaginal delivery (70% and 76%).[97]

Does the Sitting Position for Epidural Anesthesia Increase the Risk of Uterine Rupture?

Golan *et al*[51] reported five cases of uterine rupture (four intact, one scarred) occurring during epidural placement in the sitting position. Plauche *et al*[32] also reported two cases of uterine rupture of the low transverse scar under similar circumstances. Both in-

vestigators suggest that the uterus may have ruptured because of the marked increase in intra-abdominal pressure caused by acute anteflexion of the torso. It is difficult to imagine that the sitting position could cause a greater rise in intra-abdominal pressure than the same degree of flexion obtained with the patient in lateral decubitus position.

CASE REPORTS

Uterine rupture in a patient with a previous cesarean section can present in many different ways. The following are illustrative cases.

Case 1

A pregnant patient with no prenatal care presented to labor and delivery complaining of abdominal pain. On examination, she was noted to be about 32 weeks pregnant, with a midline suprapubic scar, abdominal tenderness, and absent fetal heart tones. She admitted a previous cesarean section for placenta previa but did not know the type of scar. She had a history of intravenous drug abuse but denied recent drug use. On admission, blood pressure was 105/70 and pulse was 96/minute. An intravenous line was started. While evaluation progressed, her vital signs deteriorated. An exploratory laparotomy was performed under general anesthesia. A stillborn fetus and placenta inside intact membranes floating free in the abdomen (Fig. 28-8) and a completely ruptured classical scar (Fig. 28-9) were found. Although this patient was not undergoing a trial of labor, this case underscores the danger presented by a patient with a cesarean section scar. Patients often do not know what type of uterine scar they have. The classical scar usually ruptures catastrophically before the onset of labor. The lower uterine scar can rupture similarly, albeit less frequently (Santos D, Lachica R: unpublished data).

Case 2

A gravida 2, para 1 patient with one previous low transverse cesarean section was attempting VBAC. At 4 cm of cervical dilation, she received an epidural for labor analgesia. A bilateral T-9 sensory level developed within 30 minutes of injection of 3 mL of 2% lidocaine and 10 mL of 0.25% bupivacaine. Analgesia was maintained with a continuous infusion of 0.125% bupivacaine at 10 mL/h. When the patient was comfortable, oxytocin augmentation was begun for hypotonic uter-

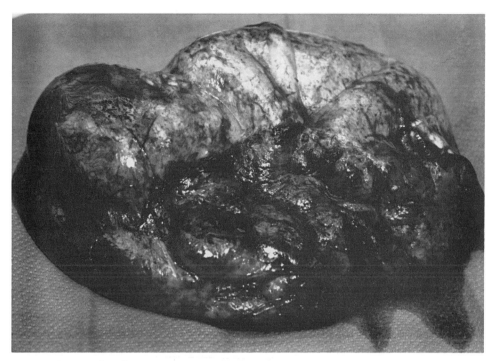

Figure 28–8. A free-floating dead 32-week-old fetus, complete with placenta, inside an intact sac. It was seen during exploratory laparotomy of a patient with an unknown uterine scar who developed deterioration of vital signs.

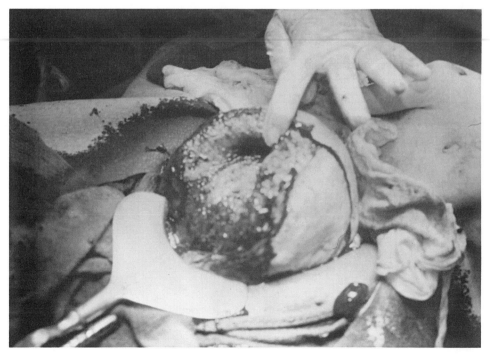

Figure 28–9. Ruptured classical uterine scar

ine contractions. After excellent labor analgesia for 4 hours, the patient suddenly complained of severe suprapubic pain. Anesthetic level to pin prick was T-10 bilaterally, and both feet were warm and vasodilated. Severe variable decelerations in fetal heart rate were noted. Because the cervix had not changed despite good labor, a decision was made to proceed with a repeat section for failure to progress. The suprapubic pain lessened after administration of 18 mL of 2% lidocaine with 1:200,000 epinephrine. At cesarean section, a meconium-stained fetal elbow was seen protruding through the ruptured low-segment scar. The bladder peritoneum was still intact. The Apgar scores were 8 and 9 at 1 and 5 minutes. The uterus was repaired in the usual fashion. Both mother and baby did well. This case shows that epidural anesthesia at analgesic concentration does not mask the pain of uterine rupture. However, surgical analgesia did abolish the pain (Lachica R, Koh C: personal communication, 1991).

Case 3

A 31-year-old gravida 2, para 1, patient with a history of low transverse cesarean section presented to labor and delivery at 40+ weeks of gestation in early labor. Several hours after admission, membranes were ruptured artificially and internal fetal and uterine pressure monitors were placed. Dilute oxytocin was administered to improve the labor pattern. Intermittent variable decelerations occurred. Epidural anesthesia was initiated when the patient was 4 cm dilated using 3 mL of 1% lidocaine, followed by 3 mL of 0.5% bupivacaine with 1:200,000 epinephrine and 12.5 µg of sufentanil in an 8-mL total volume. The patient had excellent labor analgesia with a T-8 sensory level bilaterally. A continuous infusion of 0.075% bupivacaine at 14 mL/h provided ongoing pain relief. Throughout labor, the patient had occasional mild variable decelerations. The cervix was completely dilated 6 hours after epidural placement. When she started to push, severe repetitive variable decelerations in fetal heart rate began (Fig. 28-10). She was given oxygen to breathe, and the vacuum extractor was used to deliver a 7 lb, 12 oz baby who had Apgar scores of 7 and 8 at 1 and 5 minutes, respectively. The anterior placenta was removed manually with no difficulty, and the lower uterine segment was noted to be intact. Postpartum, the patient did well until 1.5 hours later, when her blood pressure fell to 90/60 mm Hg. The uterus was firm, and vaginal bleeding was minimal. Her blood pressure did not re-

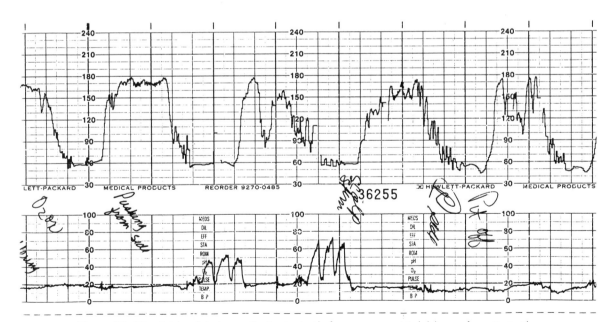

Figure 28–10. Fetal and uterine monitor tracing just before vacuum-assisted delivery of a patient with a previous cesarean section undergoing trial of labor. The fetal heart rate shows repetitive deep variable decelerations with quick return to the baseline and good beat-to-beat variability. There is no notable change in uterine tone. The infant's Apgar scores were 7 and 8 at 1 and 5 minutes, respectively.

spond to fluid infusion. She had postural hypotension. Her abdomen was diffusely tender with rebound. Her hemoglobin and hematocrit dropped to 8.2 g% and 25.3 volumes%, from 11.9 g% and 36.3 volumes%, respectively. An exploratory laparotomy was performed under general anesthesia. Upon entering the peritoneal cavity, about 500 mL of blood was seen coming from the completely ruptured lower segment transverse scar. The defect was repaired, and hemostasis was secured. The patient did well postoperatively except for mild ileus and a hemoglobin of 6.5 g% and a hematocrit of 19.2 volumes%. The uterine rupture probably occurred during the second stage of labor, when repetitive severe variable decelerations were occurring with each contraction. After the variable deceleration, there was a quick return to the baseline and no change in uterine tone. This case emphasizes the need to continue to be vigilant in the immediate postpartum period (Santos D, Ahlering C: unpublished data).

CONCLUSION

The studies of VBAC in the literature must be taken in proper perspective. The information based on reports of VBAC experiences both here and abroad have primarily addressed the question of success of trial of labor. These studies are not randomized. Many are retrospective and compiled from multiple centers. Most hospitals with a VBAC program have ideal settings, teaching institutions with housestaff coverage, and in-house anesthesia coverage. The frequently quoted incidence of uterine rupture of 0.7% to 2.2% is many times higher than the overall rate of rupture of both scarred and unscarred uteri. It is a mistake to think that VBAC patients are so low risk that they can be managed as if they did not have a uterine scar. The mere presence of a uterine scar places a woman at greater risk for uterine rupture than her unscarred counterpart. Although low-segment ruptures are more rare, more benign, and more forgiving than the rupture of the classical scar, the clinician should not be lulled into complacency in managing these patients during labor. Low-segment scar incisions are safer than the classical type because the slower progress of the tear allows the clinician more time to make the diagnosis and act before catastrophe occurs; however, the signs and symptoms are less definite. Recent reports should serve as reminders that rupture of the low-segment scar may occur with serious consequences for the fetus and mother if the diagnosis is not made early and managed promptly.[39–41]

REFERENCES

1. Cesarean section in America: Dramatic trends, 1970 to 1987. Stat Bull 1989;70:2.
2. Flamm BL, Lim OW, Jones C, Fallon D, Newman LA, Mantis JK. Vaginal birth after cesarean section: Results of a muticenter study. Am J Obstet Gynecol 1988; 158:1079.
3. Leveno KJ, Cunningham FG, Pritchard JA. Cesarean section: An answer to the House of Horne. Am J Obstet Gynecol 1985;153:838.
4. Enkin M. Labour and delivery following previous caesarean section. In: Chalmers I, Enkin M, Keirse MJNC, eds. Effective care in pregnancy and childbirth. Oxford: Oxford University Press, 1989:1196.
5. Dewhurst CJ. The ruptured caesarean section scar. J Obstet Gynaecol 1957;64:113.
6. Riva HL, Teich JC. Vaginal delivery after cesarean section. Am J Obstet Gynecol 1961;81:501.
7. Sloan D. Inconclusive conclusion. Am J Obstet Gynecol 1968;101:133.
8. The Cesarean Birth Task Force. NIH Consensus Development Statement on Cesarean Childbirth. Obstet Gynecol 1981;57:537.
9. Martin JN, Morrison JC, Wiser WL. Vaginal birth after cesarean section: The demise of routine repeat abdominal delivery. Obstet Gynecol Clin North Am 1988;15:719.
10. Davies JA, Spencer JAD. Trial of scar. Br J Hosp Med 1988;40:379.
11. Pridjian G, Hibbard JU, Moawad AH. Cesarean: Changing trends. Obstet Gynecol 1991;77:195.
12. Minkoff HL, Schwarz RH. The rising cesarean section rate: Can it be safely reversed? Am J Obstet Gynecol 1980;56:135.
13. Canady C, Goldstein PJ. Elective repeat cesarean section: Old controversy, new concepts. M Med J 1988;37:133.
14. Phelan JP, Clark SL, Diaz D, Paul RH. Vaginal birth after cesarean. Am J Obstet Gynecol 1987;157:1510.
15. Gibbs CE. Planned vaginal delivery following cesarean section. Clin Obstet Gynecol 1980;23:507.
16. Graham AR. Trial labor following previous cesarean section. Am J Obstet Gynecol 1984;149:35.
17. Rosen MG, Dickinson JC, Westhoff CL. Vaginal birth after cesarean: a meta-analysis of morbidity and mortality. Obstet Gynecol 1991;77:465.
18. Petitti DB. Maternal mortality and morbidity in cesarean section. Clin Obstet Gynecol 1985;28:763.
19. Costs of normal births: Regional variations, 1986. Stat Bull 1988;69:25.
20. Births by cesarean: Cost changes, 1982-83 to 1986. Stat Bull 1988;69:18.
21. Flamm BL. Vaginal birth after cesarean section: Controversies old and new. Clin Obstet Gynecol 1985; 28:735.
22. Placek PJ, Taffel SM. Vaginal birth after cesarean

(VBAC) in the 1980s. Am J Public Health 1988; 78:512.

23. De Jong P. Trial of labor following cesarean section—a study of 212 patients. Int J Gynaecol Obstet 1987; 25:405.

24. Boucher M, Tahilramaney MP, Eglinton GS, Phelan JP. Maternal morbidity as related to trial of labor after previous cesarean delivery: A quantitative analysis. J Reprod Med 1984;29:12.

25. Minton SD. Resuscitation of the newborn infant. In: Phelan JP, Clark SL, eds. Cesarean delivery. New York: Elsevier, 1988:320.

26. Bowes WA Jr. Clinical aspects of normal and abnormal labor. In: Creasy RK, Resnik R, eds. Maternal-fetal medicine: Principles and practice. 2nd ed. Philadelphia: WB Saunders, 1989:530.

27. Faranoff AA, Martin RJ, Miller MJ. Other pulmonary problems. In: Fanaroff AA, Martin RJ, eds. Neonatal-perinatal medicine: Diseases of the fetus and infant. 4th ed. St. Louis: CV Mosby, 1987:608.

28. Heritage CK, Cunningham MD. Association of elective repeat cesarean delivery and persistent pulmonary hypertension of the newborn. Am J Obstet Gynecol 1985;152:627.

29. Hibbard LT. Cesarean section and other surgical procedures. In: Gabbe SGI, Neibyl JR, Simpson JL, eds. Obstetrics: Normal and problem pregnancies. New York: Churchill Livingstone, 1986:517.

30. Sokol RJ, Brindley BA. Practical diagnosis and management of abnormal labor. In: Scott JR, DiSaia PJ, Hammond CB, Spellacy WN, eds. Danforth's obstetrics and gynecology. 6th ed. Philadelphia: JB Lippincott, 1990:602.

31. Pedowitz P, Schwartz RM. The true incidence of silent rupture of cesarean section scars: A prospective analysis of 403 cases. Am J Obstet Gynecol 1957;74:1071.

32. Plauche WC, Von Almen W, Muller R. Catastrophic uterine ruptures. Obstet Gynecol 1984;64:792.

33. Injuries to the birth canal. In: Cunningham FG, MacDonald PC, Gant NF, eds. Williams Obstetrics. 18th ed. Norwalk: Appleton and Lange, 1989:406.

34. Eden RD, Parker RT, Gall SA. Rupture of the pregnant uterus: A 53-year review. Obstet Gynecol 1986;68:671.

35. Fedorkov DM, Nimrod CA, Taylor PJ. Ruptured uterus in pregnancy: A Canadian hospital's experience. Can Med Assoc J 1987;137:27.

36. Shy KK, LoGerfo JP, Karp LE. Evaluation of elective repeat cesarean section as a standard of care: An application of decision analysis. Am J Obstet Gynecol 1981;139:123.

37. Flamm BL, Newman LA, Thomas SJ, Fallon D, Yoshida MJ. Vaginal birth after cesarean delivery: Results of a 5-year multicenter collaborative study. Obstet Gynecol 1990;76:750.

38. Lavin JP, Stevens RJ, Miodovnik M, Barden TP. Vaginal delivery in patients with a prior cesarean section. Am J Obstet Gynecol 1982;59:135.

39. Chazotte C, Cohen WR. Catastrophic complications of previous cesarean section. Am J Obstet Gynecol 1990;163:738.

40. Scott JR. Mandatory trial of labor after cesarean delivery: An alternative viewpoint. Obstet Gynecol 1991;77:811.

41. Jones RO, Nagashima AW, Hartnett-Goodman MM, Goodlin RC. Rupture of low transverse cesarean scars during trial of labor. Obstet Gynecol 1991;77:815.

42. Case BD, Corcoran R, Jeffcoate N, Randle GH. Caesarean section and its place in modern obstetric practice. J Obstet Gynaecol Br Commonwealth 1971;78:203.

43. Horenstein J, Clark SL. Epidural anesthesia in patients undergoing trial of labor after a previous cesarean birth. In: Phelan JP, Clark SL, eds. Cesarean delivery. New York: Elsevier, 1988:497.

44. Meehan FP, Magani IM. True rupture of the caesarean section scar (a 15-year review, 1972-1987). Eur J Obstet Gynecol Reprod Biol 1989;30:129.

45. Nielsen TF, Ljungblad UI, Hagberg H. Rupture and dehiscence of cesarean section scar during pregnancy and delivery. Am J Obstet Gynecol 1989;160:569.

46. Schrinsky DC, Benson RC. Rupture of the pregnant uterus: A review. Obstet Gynecol Surv 1978;33:217.

47. Chestnut DH. Anesthetic considerations for vaginal birth after previous cesarean section [lecture]. Obstetric Anesthesia 1991. San Francisco: March 15, 1991.

48. Carlsson C, Nybell-Lindahl, Ingemarsson I. Extradural block in patients who have previously undergone caesarean section. Br J Anaesth 1980;52:827.

49. Rodriguez MH, Masaki DI, Phelan JP, Diaz FG. Uterine rupture: Are intrauterine pressure catheters useful in the diagnosis? Am J Obstet Gynecol 1989;161:666.

50. Stovall TG, Shaver DC, Solomon SK, Anderson GD. Trial of labor in previous cesarean section patients, excluding classical cesarean sections. Obstet Gynecol 1987;70:713.

51. Golan A, Sandbank O, Rubin A. Rupture of the pregnant uterus. Obstet Gynecol 1980;56:549.

52. Roumen FJME, Janssen AAJM, Vrouenraets FPJM. The course of delivery after previous cesarean section. Eur J Obstet Gynecol Reprod Med 1990;34:15.

53. Meier PR, Porreco RP. Trial of labor following cesarean section: A two-year experience. Am J Obstet Gynecol 1982;144:671.

54. Yetman TJ, Nolan TE. Vaginal birth after cesarean section: A reappraisal of risk. Am J Obstet Gynecol 1989;161:1119.

55. Mariona FG. Discussion of Martin et al paper on vaginal birth following previous cesarean birth. Am J Obstet Gynecol 1983;146:261.

56. Michaels WH, Thompson HO, Boutt A, Schreiber FR, Michaels SL, Karo J. Ultrasound diagnosis of defects in the scarred lower uterine segment during pregnancy. Obstet Gynecol 1988;71:112.

57. Lonky NM, Worthern N, Ross MG. Prediction of cesarean section scars with ultrasound imaging during pregnancy. J Ultrasound Med 1989:8:15.

58. Horenstein JM, Eglinton GS, Tahilramaney MP, Boucher M, Phelan JP. Oxytocin use during a trial of labor in patients with previous cesarean section. J Reprod Med 1984;29:26.

59. Horenstein JM, Phelan JP. Previous cesarean section: The risks and benefits of oxytocin usage in a trial of labor. Am J Obstet Gynecol 1985;151:564.

60. Flamm BL, Goings JR, Fuelberth N, Fischermann E, Jones C, Hersh E. Oxytocin during labor after previous cesarean section: Results of a multicenter study. Obstet Gynecol 1987;70:709.

61. Molloy BG, Sheil O, Duignan NM. Delivery after caesarean section: A review of 2176 consecutive cases. Br Med J 1987;294:1645.

62. Meehan FP, Burke G, Kehoe JT. Update of delivery following prior cesarean section: a 15-year review 1972–1987. Int J Gynecol Obstet 1989;30:205.

63. Lao TT, Leung BFH. Labor induction for planned vaginal delivery in patients with previous cesarean section. Acta Obstet Gynecol Scand 1987;66:413.

64. Ollendorf DA, Goldberg JM, Minogue JP, Socol ML. Vaginal birth after cesarean section for arrest of labor: Is the success determined by maximum cervical dilatation during prior labor? Am J Obstet Gynecol 1988;159:636.

65. Targett C. Caesarean section and trial of scar. Aust NZ Obstet Gynaecol 1988;28:249.

66. Sakala EP, Kaye S, Murray RD, Munson LJ. Oxytocin use after previous cesarean: Why a higher rate of failed labor trial? Obstet Gynecol 1990;75:356.

67. Phelan JP, Ahn MC, Diaz F, Brar H, Rodriguez MH. Twice a cesarean, always a cesarean? Obstet Gynecol 1989;73:161.

68. Saldana LR, Schulman H, Reuss L. Management of pregnancy after cesarean section. Am J Obstet Gynecol 1979;135:555.

69. Porreco RP, Meier PR. Trial of labor in patients with multiple previous cesarean sections. J Reprod Med 1983;28:770.

70. Farmakides G, Duvivier R, Schulman H. Vaginal birth after two or more cesarean sections. Am J Obstet Gynecol 1987;156:565.

71. Pruett KM, Kirshon B, Cotton DB, Poindexter AN. Is vaginal birth after two or more cesarean safe? Obstet Gynecol 1988;72:163.

72. Novas J, Myers SA, Gleicher N. Obstetric outcome of patients with more than one previous cesarean section. Am J Obstet Gynecol 1989;160:364.

73. Palerme GR, Friedman EA. Rupture of the gravid uterus in the third trimester. Am J Obstet Gynecol 1966;94:571.

74. Martin JN, Harris BA, Huddleston JF, et al. Vaginal delivery following previous cesarean birth. Am J Obstet Gynecol 1983;146:255.

75. Beall M, Eglinton GS, Clark SL, Phelan JP. Vaginal delivery after cesarean section in women with unknown types of uterine scar. J Reprod Med 1984;29:31.

76. Pruett KM, Kirshon B, Cotton DB. Unknown uterine scar and trial of labor. Am J Obstet Gynecol 1988;159:807.

77. Duff P, Southmayd K, Read JA. Outcome of trial of labor in patients with a single previous low transverse cesarean section for dystocia. Obstet Gynecol 1988;71:380.

78. Hollingsworth D, Moore TR. Diabetes and pregnancy. In: Creasy RK, Resnik R, eds. Maternal–fetal medicine: Principles and practice. 2nd ed. Philadelphia: WB Saunders, 1989:970.

79. Phelan JP, Eglinton GS, Horenstein JM, Clark SL, Yeh S. Previous cesarean birth: Trial of of labor in women with macrosomic infants. J Reprod Med 1984;29:36.

80. Flamm BL, Goings JR. Vaginal birth after cesarean section: Is suspected fetal macrosomia a contraindication? Obstet Gynecol 1989;74:694.

81. Resnik R. Post-term pregnancy. In: Creasy RK, Resnik R. Maternal–fetal medicine: Principles and practice. 2nd ed. Philadelphia: WB Saunders, 1989:505.

82. Spellacy WN. The postdate pregnancy. In: Scott JR, DiSaia PJ, Spellacy WN. Danforth's Obstetrics and gynecology. 6th ed. Philadelphia: JB Lippincott, 1990:375.

83. MacKenzie IZ. Vaginal prostaglandins and labour induction for patients previously delivered by caesarean section. Br J Obstet Gynaecol 1984;91:7.

84. Meehan FP. Trial of scar with induction/oxytocin in delivery following prior section. Clin Exp Obstet Gynecol 1988;15:117.

85. Yeh S, Huang X, Phelan JP. Postterm pregnancy after previous cesarean section. J Reprod Med 1984;29:41.

86. Strong TH, Phelan JP, Ahn MO, Sarno AP Jr. Vaginal birth after cesarean delivery in the twin gestation. Am J Obstet Gynecol 1989;161:29.

87. Cruikshank DP. Malpresentations and umbilical cord complications. In: Scott JR, DiSaia PJ, Spellacy WN. Danforth's Obstetrics and gynecology. 6th ed. Philadelphia: JB Lippincott, 1990:570.

88. Ophir E, Oettinger M, Yagoda et al. Breech presentation after cesarean section: Always a section? Am J Obstet Gynecol 1989;161:25.

89. Sarno MP Jr, Phelan JP, Ahn MO, Strong TH Jr. Vaginal birth after cesarean delivery: Trial of labor in women with breech presentation. J Reprod Med 1989;34:831.

90. Finley BE, Gibbs CE. Emergent cesarean delivery in patients undergoing trial of labor with a transverse lower segment scar. Am J Obstet Gynecol 1986;155:936.

91. Paul RP, Phelan JP, Yeh S. Trial of labor in the patient with a prior cesarean birth. Am J Obstet Gynecol 1985;151:297.

92. Uppington J. Epidural analgesia and previous caesarean section. Anaesthesia 1983;38:336.

93. Johnson C, Oriol N. The role of epidural anesthesia in trial of labor. Reg Anesth 1990;15:304.

94. Sakala EP, Kaye S, Murray RD, Munson LJ. Epidural analgesia: Effect on the likelihood of successful trial of labor after cesarean section. J Reprod Med 1990;35:886.

95. Demianczuk NN, Hunter DJS, Taylor DW. Trial of labor after previous cesarean section: Prognostic indicators of outcome. Am J Obstet Gynecol 1982;142:640.

96. Rudick V, Niv D, Hetman-Peri M, Geller E, Avni A, Golan A. Epidural analgesia for planned vaginal delivery following previous cesarean section. Obstet Gynecol 1984;64:621.

97. Flamm BL, Dunnett C, Fischermann E, Quilligan EJ. Vaginal delivery following cesarean section: Use of oxytocin augmentation and epidural anesthesia with internal tocodynamic and internal fetal monitoring. Am J Obstet Gynecol 1984;148:759.

98. Meehan FP, Burke G, Casey C, Sheil JG. Delivery following cesarean section and perinatal mortality. Am J Perinatol 1989;6:90.

99. Crawford JS. The epidural sieve and MBC (minimum blocking concentration): An hypothesis. Anaesthesia 1976;31:1277.

100. Shin YK. Shoulder pain in a trial of labor after cesarean delivery. South Med J 1989;82:1320.

101. Meehan FP, Moolgaoker AS, Stallworthy J. Vaginal delivery under caudal analgesia after caesarean section and other major uterine surgery. Br Med J 1972;2:740.

102. Phelan JP, Clark SL. Reply to Jakobi et al. Am J Obstet Gynecol 1989;160:1539.

103. Jakobi P, Zimmer EZ, Weissman A. Oxytocin administration and uterine exploration in the management of vaginal birth after cesarean—not a routine procedure. Am J Obstet Gynecol 1989;160:1538.

104. Silver RK, Gibbs RS. Predictors of vaginal delivery in patients with previous cesarean section who require oxytocin. Am J Obstet Gynecol 1987;156:57.

CHAPTER 29

Intra-amniotic Infection

Divina Juson Santos

Intra-amniotic infection (IAI) is also called chorioamnionitis, amnionitis, intrapartum infection, or amniotic fluid infection.[1] This common infectious process can involve the chorionic and amniotic membranes, placenta, uterus, umbilical cord, and fetus. It may have serious consequences for both mother and fetus.[2] Rupture of membranes (ROM) frequently, but not always, accompanies IAI. Clinically evident IAI complicates 0.5% to 2.0% of pregnancies.[3] In women with ROM longer than 24 hours, the incidence reaches 3% to 25%.[4]

OBSTETRIC CONSIDERATIONS

Diagnosis

To diagnose IAI early in its course, the clinician must maintain a high index of suspicion. The clinical criteria for diagnosis (Table 29-1) are neither specific nor sensitive.[1,5] Nonspecific signs include fever and maternal or fetal tachycardia. Maternal fever greater than 100.2° F or 37.8° C is the most frequent sign. Rupture of membranes is almost universally present.[6] More specific criteria such as uterine tenderness or foul-smelling amniotic fluid or fetus occur in only a minority of cases.[7] In the work-up of the parturient with fever and tachycardia, it is important to exclude other causes, such as infection outside the uterus, dehydration, hypotension, anxiety, pain, or drug effects. Similarly,

prematurity, hypoxia, arrhythmia, and drug effect must be ruled out in evaluating fetal tachycardia.[1,8]

Laboratory tests can provide some help in making the diagnosis of IAI (Table 29-2).[9–11] The blood leukocyte count varies from 5,000 to 12,000/mm³ during pregnancy. During labor, white cell count may rise to 25,000/mm³ or more (average 14,000–16,000/mm³).[12] Because peripheral leukocytosis is frequent during normal labor, only markedly elevated white cell counts or toxic changes reliably suggest infection.[13] A single value of greater than 20,000 white blood cells/mm³ with a leftward shift or an increase of more than 5000 white blood cells/mm³ might indicate of IAI, especially if the patient is not in labor.[14]

C-reactive protein (CRP), an acute-phase reactant protein, rises a thousand-fold in the early stages of infection, inflammation, or tissue necrosis. Normal CRP concentration in the nonpregnant patient ranges from 0.6 to 0.8 mg/dL.[15] During pregnancy and labor, the upper limit of normal for CRP ranges from 1.25 to 1.9 mg/dL.[16] A rising CRP concentration may antedate other parameters of infection. Intrauterine infection is rarely present if the CRP is normal, but an isolated elevation of CRP greater than 2 mg/dL or a 30% rise may suggest impending IAI.[15]

Cultures are useful for confirmation of infection and as a guide for antibiotic management.[8] In patients with fever, two sets of blood cultures at least an hour apart should be drawn, even though bacteremia occurs

Table 29-1

Clinical Criteria for Diagnosis of Intra-amniotic Infection

	INCIDENCE	SENSITIVITY	SPECIFICITY
Maternal			
Fever (> 100.2° F or 37.8° C)	85%–100%	62%	91%
Rupture of membranes	98%–100%		
Tachycardia (> 120/min)	33%–84%		
Uterine tenderness	13%–25%		
Foul or purulent amniotic fluid	7%–22%		
Fetal			
Tachycardia (> 160/min)	37%–70%	62%	81%
Foul smell	9%		

(After Gibbs RS, Castillo MS, Rodgers PJ. Management of acute chorioamnionitis. Am J Obstet Gynecol 1980;136:709)

in only 10% of patients.[3] Bacteremia by itself is nonspecific because it does not identify the source of infection. Direct examination of the amniotic fluid gives the greatest specificity of diagnosis.[8] The fluid sample can be obtained either by transabdominal amniocentesis or by aspiration from an intrauterine pressure catheter. The specimen can be analyzed for the presence of bacteria using the Gram's stain, and neutrophils can be analyzed using the Wright's stain.[13,14]

Mere presence of bacteria in amniotic fluid or inflammation of fetal membranes does not predict development of maternal and neonatal sepsis. In a study of 28 high-risk patients, Bobbitt and Ledger[17] found that clinical IAI developed in only 56% of patients with bacterial colony counts greater than 10^3/mL. On the other hand, no patient with a negative Gram's stain or culture of fluid obtained by transabdominal amniocentesis developed IAI.[18]

Gas–liquid chromatography is a direct assay of bacterial metabolism that does not depend on maternal or fetal response to infection. Leukocyte esterase indicates the presence of significant amounts of leukocytes in amniotic fluid.[5] These tests have not been adopted for routine clinical use at the present time.

Compounds that inhibit bacterial infection (*e.g.*, neutrophils, lysosomes, beta-lysine, transferrin, immunoglobulins) reside in amniotic fluid.[1,8] This antibacterial activity is absent or insignificant until 30 weeks of gestation; it then increases until term. It is diminished in patients who are poor and malnourished.[18] The lack of these factors in early gestation may

explain the high risk of chorioamnionitis in preterm patients, especially in the presence of ruptured membranes.[3] A low molecular weight peptide–zinc complex seems to inhibit bacterial growth of aerobic gram negative rods.[19] Beta-lysine appears to act against the cytoplasmic membrane of gram-positive bacteria and, like the lysosomes, is effective against gram-positive organisms.[3]

After delivery, the placenta and fetal membranes can be examined histologically to confirm the presence or absence of infection. Even here, a discrepancy exists because 11% to 16% of patients have histologic IAI, yet only 0.5% to 1% develop clinical amnionitis.[8] Vintzileos *et al*[20] found, in patients with premature rupture of membranes (PROM), that the fetal biophysical profile predicted the development of IAI. When the biophysical score was greater than 8, 3% developed IAI, whereas if the score was less than 7, 96% got infected.[20] The biophysical profile is difficult to obtain when the quantity of amniotic fluid is significantly diminished.

To make matters more confusing, overt infection may be absent in the mother or fetus even in the presence of bacteria or inflammation in the amniotic fluid, fetal membranes, or placenta.[17,21,22] When Garite *et al*[23] found bacteria in amniotic fluid obtained by transabdominal amniocentesis in a group of patients with PROM, only 55% of mothers and 25% of infants developed clinical infection. It has been estimated that only 1 in 10 patients with histologic chorioamnionitis develop clinical infection in the mother or neonate.[8,23]

Table 29–2

Laboratory Diagnosis of Intra-amniotic Infection*

MOTHER/FETUS			
	Abnormal Test Value	Sensitivity	Specificity
Maternal Blood			
White blood cells (cells/mm³)	> 12,500	80%	62%
White blood cell bands (%)	> 9%	52%	75%
Erythrocyte sedimentation rate (mm/first hour)	> 60	65%	100%
C-reactive protein (mg/dL)	> 1.25	88%	96%
Blood cultures	Positive		
Amniotic Fluid			
Gram stain	Positive for bacteria	62%	81%
Wright's stain	Positive for white blood cells		
Culture	> 10² colony forming units	86%	91%
Gas–liquid chromatography pattern	abnormal	94%	95%
Leukocyte esterase	Positive	91%	95%
Biophysical Profile	< 7		
HISTOPATHOLOGY OF PLACENTA AND FETAL MEMBRANES			

Neonate	Abnormal Test Value
White blood cells (cells/mm³)	
Leukopenia	< 3500
Leukocytosis	> 25,000
Latex particle agglutination (group B streptococcus)	Positive
Blood culture	Positive
Cerebrospinal fluid culture	Positive
Urine culture	Positive
Chest radiograph	Positive
(Data from references 5, 9, 10, 11, and 20)	

Microbiologic Concept of Infection

Infection is a general term that describes any interaction between a host and a parasite. The only requirement is that the parasite be present in or on the host. Figure 29-1 shows the interaction that occurs between host and parasite (bacteria, virus, or fungus). Clinical manifestations of injury to the host (fever, malaise, etc.) signal overt infection. If the parasite proliferates in the host without inciting any reaction, there is colonization. Between overt infection and colonization lies covert or subclinical infection. The parasite has not

yet sufficiently injured the host to produce a clinically obvious response. A given parasite does not always provoke an identical disease in all infected individuals. The parasite's ability to produce disease depends on the size of the inoculum, port of entry, virulence, pathogenicity, and invasiveness. Whether or not an infection becomes established and produces disease depends largely on host-resistance factors.[24]

These microbiologic concepts can help explain the confusing picture seen with intra-amniotic infections. The amniotic cavity is colonized if the amniotic fluid culture is positive for bacteria in the absence of clinical

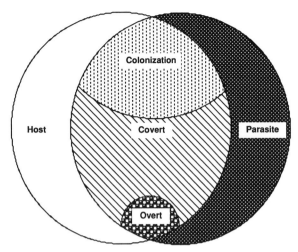

Figure 29–1. Any interaction between host and bacteria may result in infection. Such interactions may consist of colonization (bacterial proliferation without host reaction) and infectious disease. This disease may be either covert (subclinical) or overt (symptomatic). (After Hoeprich PD. Host–parasite relationships and the pathogenesis of infectious diseases. In: Hoeprich PD, Jordan MC, eds. Infectious diseases. 4th ed. Philadelphia: JB Lippincott, 1989:48)

or histologic evidence of infection in the mother or neonate. Subclinical or covert infection exists when there is histologic evidence of infection in the fetal membranes and placenta in the absence of clinical infection in the mother or fetus. Clinical IAI represents overt infection.

Pathophysiology

The amniotic cavity and its contents are usually sterile before labor and ROM. The intact fetal membranes and closed cervix with its mucus plug usually prevent entry of bacteria from the vagina.[25] Although thin, the amnion is very strong and able to withstand rupture in spite of a variety of stresses (*i.e.,* multiple pregnancy, hydramnios).[26] However, fetal membranes rupture readily when exposed in vitro to collagenase and collagenase-producing bacteria.[27] Asymptomatic cervical dilation during pregnancy exposes the fetal membranes to the vaginal flora. Microorganisms that contact fetal membranes can cause it to rupture and subsequently initiate labor (Fig. 29-2).[28,29]

The most common pathway of IAI is by the *ascending* route. When membranes are ruptured, infection commonly starts at the fetal membranes closest to the cervical os (Fig. 29-3A). Bacteria then colonize the amniotic fluid and inactivate the antibacterial systems commonly present there. Through aspiration of infected amniotic fluid, the fetus may develop pneumonia, enteritis, meningitis, or generalized sepsis. The 1% to 19% incidence of IAI associated with cervical cerclage probably is effected by this route.[1] Microorganisms also can invade the amniotic cavity through intact membranes.

In the presence of intact membranes, bacteria proliferate in the chorion and decidua basalis. Colonization spreads to involve an extensive area of the amniotic sac until it reaches the placenta producing a placentitis. From here, bacteria spread *hematogenously* through the intervillous space to infect the fetus (Fig. 29-3B), or they produce disseminated infection in the mother (*e.g.,* disseminated gonorrhea).[30] Bacteria that produce IAI by hematogenous spread include *Listeria monocytogenes,* Group A streptococcus, and *Neisseria gonorrhoeae.*[30,31]

Intra-abdominal infections producing peritonitis (*e.g.,* appendicitis, cholecystitis, pyelonephritis) can infect the uterine cavity through *retrograde seeding* of the fallopian tubes (Fig. 29-3C).[29]

Lastly, bacteria may be accidentally introduced during obstetric procedures (Fig. 29-3D). Intra-amniotic infection rarely (< 1%) follows amniocentesis, but it may complicate 5% to 10% of intrauterine transfusions.[3]

Rupture of Membranes

Rupture of membranes before the onset of labor complicates about 10% of pregnancies. Most (80%) of

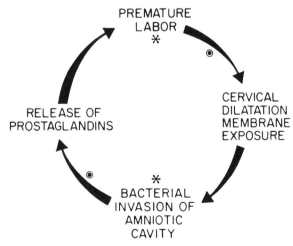

Figure 29–2. Premature labor and infection. (*=point of initiation of labor.) (Minkoff H. Prematurity: infection as an etiologic factor. Obstet Gynecol 1983;62:137)

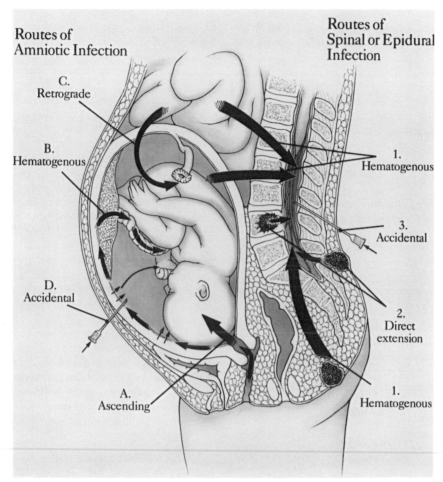

Figure 29–3. Routes of intra-amniotic and neuraxial infection. The left side illustrates the following routes of intra-amniotic infection: (**A**) ascending pathway, (**B**) hematogenous, (**C**) retrograde, and (**D**) accidental. The right side illustrates the following routes of epidural or spinal infection: (*1*) hematogenous, (*2*) direct extension, and (*3*) accidental. (Santos DJ. Chorioamnionitis and the anesthesiologist. Res Medica [in press])

these ruptures happen at term, and labor will begin within 24 hours in 90% of patients. When ROM occurs between 28 to 34 weeks, only 50% are in labor within 24 hours, and 80% to 90% by 1 week. Before 24 to 26 gestation, only half will be in labor after a week. The three main complications associated with PROM are as follows:

- Maternal and fetal infection
- Premature labor and delivery
- Hypoxia and asphyxia due to umbilical cord compression

The longer the time interval from ROM to onset of labor, the greater the risk of IAI from ascending infec-

tion. Premature ROM complicates up to 34% of preterm deliveries. The risk of umbilical cord prolapse is 1.5% when ROM occurs before labor. With preterm labor and PROM, the incidence of fetal distress due to cord compression is 8.5% compared to 1.5% in patients in premature labor with intact membranes. Umbilical cord compression may account for the higher incidence of stillbirths in patients with preterm PROM (1%–6%) who were being managed expectantly.[25]

The risk of developing overt IAI is higher in patients with PROM and oligohydramnios. With no pocket of amniotic fluid larger than 1 × 1 cm on ultrasound, IAI manifested in 47% of patients; it manifested in 14% of patients who had such a pocket.[32] Differences in the degree of membrane disruption may account for these findings. High amniotic membrane leaks distant from the cervical os may reseal and allow normal amniotic fluid volume to reaccumulate. In contrast, patients with frank rupture at the cervical os may continue to leak, preventing amniotic fluid reaccumulation. Because of oligohydramnios and diminished inhibitory factors in the amniotic fluid, these latter patients may be more likely to develop an ascending infection.[32]

Role of Bacteria in Initiation of Labor

Large amounts of arachidonic acid accumulate in fetal membranes. They are not usually mobilized until term. Bacteria and neutrophils that contain phospholipase induce the release of arachidonic acid. Different organisms contain varying amounts of phospholipase (Fig. 29-4). High-virulence organisms, such as *Bacillus fragilis* and *Peptostreptococcus,* contain the highest con-

centrations of phospholipase. These pathogens are likely to have a role in initiating and maintaining labor.[33,34] Arachidonic acid rapidly converts to prostaglandin E_2 and prostaglandin $F_{2\alpha}$. Prostaglandin E_2 causes cervical dilatation, and prostaglandin $F_{2\alpha}$ initiates uterine contractions. Unlike oxytocin, which is most effective in producing contractions at or near term, prostaglandins can cause uterine contractions at any gestational age.[29,31]

A close association exists between intrauterine infection and preterm labor. In the presence of infection, prostaglandin E, prostaglandin $F_{2\alpha}$, and leukotriene B_4 production by fetal membranes and placenta is significantly increased. Moreover, other chemical mediators, such as histamine, bradykinins, serotonin, platelet-activating factor, and bacterial endotoxins may also provoke myometrial contractions and preterm labor.[34] Intra-amniotic infection accounts for nearly 70% of spontaneous preterm deliveries between 24 and 26 weeks, and 30% between 34 and 36 weeks of gestation.[31] Tocolysis to arrest premature labor is usually futile once infection arises.[35]

Gibbs *et al*[36] collected and cultured amniotic fluid aspirated from intrauterine pressure catheters during labor in women with clinical IAI. They found polymicrobial cultures (2.2 isolates per culture) and isolated many high-virulence organisms (Table 29-3). The rate of isolation of these high-virulence organisms was lower in matched uninfected controls.[36]

Consequences of Intra-amniotic Infection

Maternal Effects

As many as 75% of patients with IAI develop dysfunctional labor and require higher doses of oxytocin than uninfected patients (Table 29-4).[37] The apparent paradox of increased uterine irritability leading to premature labor and the 35% to 45% cesarean section rate for failure to progress may be due to dissociation of uterine activity and cervical dilatation. Bacteria may interfere with labor progress by affecting the number or sensitivity of oxytocin receptors. Sustained prostaglandin synthesis is essential to maintain adequate uterine contractions during active labor. Intra-amniotic infection may deplete the available pool of arachidonic acid substrate and thereby impede prostaglandin production and then labor.[37,38] Uterine atony and postpartum hemorrhage are more likely to develop after cesarean section, but not after vaginal delivery.[39]

Maternal infections from IAI include endometritis, parametritis, pelvic thrombophlebitis, wound infec-

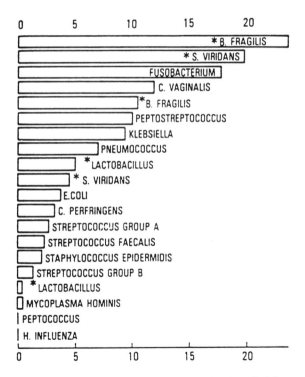

Figure 29–4. Phospholipase A activity of bacteria isolated from the female genital tract. Anaerobes are among the bacteria showing the highest levels of phospholipase activity. (*=different strains of *Bacteroides fragilis*.) (Bejar R, Curbello V, Davis C, Gluck L. Premature labor. II. Bacterial sources of phospholipase. Obstet Gynecol 1981;57:479)

Table 29-3

Bacteriology of Different Infections Processes

Intra-amniotic Infection		Spinal/Epidural Procedure–Related Meningitis*	
Bacteroides species	25%	Pseudomonas (11)	46%
Group B streptococcus	12%	Group D streptococcus (1)	4%
Other aerobic streptococci	13%	Staphylococcus aureus (1)	4%
Escherichia coli	10%	Streptococcus mitis (1)	4%
Other gram-negative rods	10%	Streptococcus sanguis (1)	4%
Clostridium species	9%	Escherichia coli (1)	4%
Peptococcus species	7%	Pneumococcus (1)	4%
Fusobacterium	6%	Unknown (7)	29%
Meningitis		**Spinal/Epidural Procedure–Related Epidural Abscess***	
Hemophilus influenzae	48%	Staphylococcus aureus (13)	68%
Neisseria meningititis	20%	Staphylococcus epidermis and	
Streptococcus pneumoniae	13%	Bacteroides (1)	5%
Group B streptococcus	3%	Pseudomonas (1)	5%
Listeria monocytogenes	2%	Proteus (1)	5%
Other	8%	Escherichia coli (1)	5%
Unknown	6%	Mixed flora (1)	5%
Spontaneous Epidural Abscess		Unknown (1)	5%
Staphylococcus aureus	62%	**Urinary Tract Infection During Pregnancy**	
Aerobic gram-positive rods	18%	Escherichia coli	75%
Staphylococcus epidermis	2%	Staphylococcus epidermis	7%
Anaerobes	2%	Klebsiella-Enterobacter	7%
Other	1%	Enterococcus	6%
Unknown	6%	Proteus mirabilis	2%
		Group B streptococcus	2%
		Other	1%

(Data from references 36, 63, 84, 93)

*Collated from 41 cases of epidural abscess or meningitis developing in patients having lumbar puncture or epidural or spinal anesthesia (see Table 29–6). The infectious agents causing epidural abscess are different from those causing IAI meningitis, or urinary tract infection.

tion, septicemia, and septic shock. In women with IAI, postoperative endomyometritis occurs 10 to 30 times more frequently after abdominal delivery than vaginal delivery.[3] Twenty percent to 85% of patients with IAI develop endometritis after cesarean section. Incision through infected tissue and spillage of infected amniotic fluid into the abdominal cavity may account for this increased risk.[40]

A short course of prophylactic antibiotics started at the time of cesarean section may reduce the incidence of endometritis.[41] This practice has little microbiologic rationale. Short-term antibiotic use does not significantly alter the uterine or cervicovaginal flora. Possibly, prophylactically administered antibiotics prevent clinical infection by inhibiting the multiplication of potential pathogens. These bacteria then cannot overwhelm host defenses. Administration of prophylactic antibiotics after umbilical cord clamping, even up to 1 hour postpartum, seems as effective as predelivery administration and has the advantage of not interfering with neonatal cultures. The efficacy of single-dose regimen versus multiple-dose administration remains unresolved. Also unclear is whether intraoperative pelvic and wound irrigation with antibiotic solution inhibits bacterial multiplication by direct local action or by systemic absorption. Anaphylaxis, antibiotic-induced coli-

Table 29–4

Maternal and Fetal Consequences of Intra-amniotic Infection

	NO IAI	WITH IAI	REFERENCE
Maternal			
Dysfunctional labor	20%	75%	37
Increased use and dose requirement for oxytocin	5 ± 5 mU/min	10 ± 8 mU/min	38
Cesarean section rate	25%	58%	38
Postpartum hemorrhage	—	Increased	39
Endometritis, parametritis	—	20%–85%	40
Wound infection	2%	5%–20%	3,42
Pelvic thrombophlebitis	—	Increased	3
Septicemia and septic shock	—	Increased	3
Fetal			
Preterm labor and delivery	—	Increased	50
Fetal distress and hypoxia	—	Increased	52
Respiratory distress syndrome	—	Increased	50,52
Neonatal pneumonia and sepsis	—	Increased	52
Fetal death	—	Increased	52

tis, and selection of antibiotic-resistant organisms are potentially serious risks of antibiotic prophylaxis.[42]

Wound infection complicates 2% to 20% of abdominal deliveries. Elective "clean" cases usually have a 2% wound infection rate. Contaminated cases (those with clinically recognized amnionitis and urgent cases with shortened abdominal prep time) have a 20% rate of infection. "Clean-contaminated" cases (cesarean section during labor with ruptured membranes) have an intermediate incidence. Approximately 10^5 bacteria/mL or gram of tissue are required to establish an infection. However, in the presence of tissue damage, sutures, drains, and so forth, the required inoculum may fall to 10^2 bacterial colonies. Aerobic gram-positive organisms (*i.e., Staphylococcus,* Group A or Group B *Streptococcus*) are the most common causes of wound infection. Anaerobic organisms are also problematic because they outnumber aerobes 10:1 in skin and 100:1 in vagina. Early wound infections are usually due to *Streptococcus*. If the patient has IAI, the infectious organisms are more likely to be mixed aerobic–anaerobic bacteria. Late wound infections, occurring on the sixth to eighth postoperative day, are usually due to *Staphylococcus* or mixed aerobe–anaerobes. Prophylactic antibiotics do not seem to reduce the incidence of wound infection. The role of wound irrigation in preventing wound infections is controversial.[3,42]

Most investigators agree that intrapartum antibiotic treatment limits maternal sepsis.[43–46] Intrapartum anti-biotics may also prevent neonatal sepsis. They interfere with epithelial attachment and surface colonization of bacteria, and might prevent vertical transmission by eradicating pathogenic vaginal and perineal organisms.[43] However, predelivery antibiotic administration may invalidate neonatal cultures. As a result, some healthy infants born of high-risk mothers may receive unneeded therapy. Inadequate neonatal cultures also may delay treatment of infected infants or expose them to a costly septic work-up.[43,47] Furthermore, there is some doubt about whether the fetus can be adequately treated by antimicrobials given to the mother.[43] In a randomized study, Gibbs *et al*[45] found fewer infections and a shorter hospital stay for both mother and fetus in the group treated antepartum when compared to those treated postpartum. Moreover, Gilstrap *et al*[48] measured significant levels of ampicillin, gentamicin, cefoxitin, mezlocillin, and clindamycin in cord blood and placenta after maternal administration. Ampicillin and gentamicin had the highest cord blood–to–maternal blood ratios. Some experts merely stop antibiotic treatment of the neonates at 72 hours if they are clinically well and the cultures are negative.[49]

Fetal Effects

Rupture of membranes and IAI increases the risk of preterm delivery. When neither ROM nor IAI is present, 5% of infants deliver before term. Intra-amniotic infection without ROM raises the frequency of preterm delivery to 12%. Fifty-seven percent of pregnancies complicated by both IAI and ROM end prematurely.[50] Only 8% of histopathologically diagnosed cases of IAI had maternal antepartum fever, and only 3% had neonatal sepsis. The rarity of clinical infection in the mother and fetus suggests that subclinical infection may be an important cause of preterm labor.[51] A number of investigators who obtained amniotic fluid for culture by amniocentesis as part of their evaluation of preterm labor have found occult amnionitis (positive cultures) in 3% to 26% of patients.[2]

Infants born prematurely as a result of IAI frequently are depressed as a result of antenatal hypoxia and immaturity. Respiratory distress syndrome is more severe owing to the combined effects of immaturity, antenatal hypoxic damage to the lungs, and bacterial destruction of surfactant.[50] Villous edema interferes with gas and nutrient exchange across the placenta by compressing the blood vessels in the placental villi. Mean Apgar scores are significantly lower when villous edema is severe.[31]

The premature infant is more likely than the term infant to develop neonatal sepsis.[31] The host defense mechanism in the newborn is inadequate because of defective opsonic activity, insufficient granulocyte function, and deficient cell-mediated immunity.[43] Hence, the preterm neonate is considered a "compromised host." These infants cannot limit infection, which readily spreads to meninges and other organs.[51]

Morales[52] showed that infants delivered of women with IAI had a fourfold increase in neonatal mortality and a threefold greater incidence of respiratory distress syndrome, neonatal sepsis, and intraventricular hemorrhage. Antibiotic therapy before delivery appears to reduce these complications and may prolong the critical time interval from ROM to delivery.[29]

Group B *Streptococcus* infection in the neonate carries a high risk of mortality.[3] Vaginal cultures are positive for Group B *Streptococcus* in 10% to 35% of parturients. Nearly 50% of male partners are also colonized. The more heavily colonized mother is more likely to transmit the disease to her infant. Premature and low-birth-weight infants are more susceptible to this infection, although the term infant is not immune.[3,53]

Obstetric Management

In the absence of well-controlled comparative studies in the literature, the management of patients with IAI is arbitrary and conflicting. Despite agreement among investigators about the need for antibiotics and ex-

peditious delivery for both preterm and term pregnancies, the specifics are unclear. The optimal diagnosis-to-delivery interval is unknown. Most obstetricians strive to achieve delivery within 1 to 12 hours after diagnosis.[1,3] The cesarean section rate may be as high as 35% to 45%, although the preferred route of delivery is vaginal.[37] Failure to progress or fetal distress is the most frequent indication for cesarean section.[3]

ANESTHETIC CONSIDERATIONS

The Febrile Parturient

Fever, being an almost universal response to infection, cannot be ignored in any patient.[54] Its presence in the parturient presents specific concerns for the anesthesiologist.[55]

The normal body temperature at rest varies within a narrow range of 36.7°C to 37.0°C or 98.0°F to 98.6°F (orally) and 0.6°C higher when measured rectally.[55] The body temperature is lowest in the morning and rises toward evening, following a normal circadian rhythm that is more pronounced in women than men. Temperature also normally increases during physical activity or exercise.[56] Normally, a delicate balance between heat production and heat loss maintains body temperature. The hypothalamus contains a thermoregulatory center that operates like a thermostat with a "set point" of about 98.6°F. The thermoregulatory center responds to superficial and deep thermoreceptors located in the skin and the hypothalamus.[54,55]

The term *fever* refers to a more sustained temperature elevation in response to disease.[56] Leukocytes, macrophages, and Kupffer cells phagocytize bacteria or their breakdown products and release endogenous pyrogen or interleukin-1. This substance produces fever directly, at the preoptic area of the hypothalamus, or indirectly, by inducing prostaglandin synthesis (Fig. 29-5).[57] During fever, the body attempts to dissipate heat by vasodilatation of the skin, evaporation through increased sweating, and decreased heat production.[54,56]

Changes in body temperature from whatever cause profoundly alter biologic systems within the body. High temperature reduces the body's ability to withstand stress. It elevates heart rate, cardiac output, and basal metabolic rate. Fever during pregnancy and labor can overwhelm the maternal resources, resulting in increased maternal and fetal morbidity and mortality. The body's response to fever exaggerates the normal physiologic changes during pregnancy (Table 29-5).[58]

Renal bicarbonate excretion usually compensates for the chronic hyperventilation of pregnancy to main-

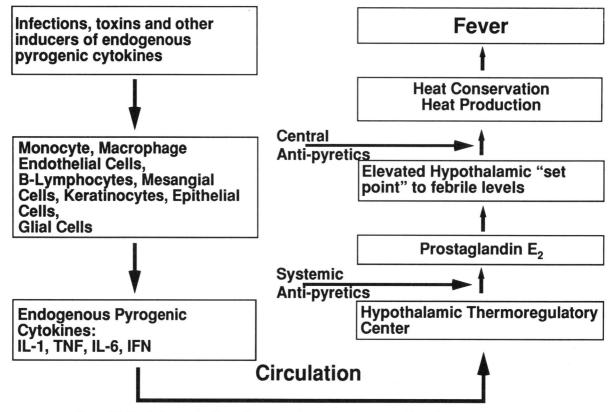

Figure 29–5. Pathogenesis of fever. Bacteria and toxins are phagocytized by inflammatory cells (monocytes, macrophages, etc.) resulting in the release of endogenous pyrogens, including interleukin-1. These pyrogens stimulate the hypothalamus to produce fever through prostaglandin E_2, which elevates the "set point" to produce a febrile response. (After Dinarello CA, Wolff SM. Pathogenesis of fever. In: Mandell GL, Douglas RG Jr, Bennett JE, eds. Principles and practice of infectious diseases, 3rd ed. New York: Churchill Livingstone, 1990:462)

tain a normal pH. Fever stimulates greater hyperventilation in an attempt to increase heat loss.[56] This increased hyperventilation can aggravate the leftward shift of the oxyhemoglobin dissociation curve and hinder placental oxygen transport.[58] Owing to decreased maternal buffering capacity, lactic acidemia occurs more readily in both mother and fetus. In addition, maternal fever causes uterine irritability, which can lead to premature labor and delivery.[58] The elevated uterine tone can impair uterine blood flow by more than 50% when maternal temperature is elevated 1°C to 2.5°C above normal.[59]

Fetal tachycardia frequently accompanies maternal fever and may even precede it.[60] Umbilical cord compression is more likely in patients with PROM and especially those who also have IAI.[61] Depending on the fetal cardiovascular reserve and etiology and duration of the maternal fever, the fetal scalp pH may become

progressively acidotic, indicating progressive fetal distress. The neonate frequently needs resuscitation and evaluation by the pediatrician at delivery.[58]

Regional Anesthesia in the Presence of Fever

Inducing regional anesthesia in a febrile parturient who may have a systemic infection raises the possibility of fomenting meningitis or epidural abscess. How significant is this risk is the key question.

Lumbar puncture–induced meningitis or epidural abscess are both extremely rare disease entities. Although the reported overall incidence of epidural abscess appears to be rising (from 0.2–1.2/10,000[62] to 2.8/10,000[63] hospital admissions), this increase has not been attributed to the use of epidural anesthesia.

Table 29–5

Changes Due to Fever in Nonpregnant and Pregnant Patients

PARAMETER	NONPREGNANT	PREGNANT
Heart rate	Increased 10 bpm/°F	Increased 15 bpm > nonpregnant
Cardiac output	Increased 50%–75% at 39.2°C	Increased 15%–30% > nonpregnant
Oxygen consumption	Increased 60% at 41°C	Increased 21% > nonpregnant
Basal metabolic rate	Increased 13%/°C	Increased 14% > nonpregnant
Alveolar ventilation	—	Increased 70% > nonpregnant
Uterine blood flow	—	Decreased 50% when temperature increased 1–2.6°C
Norepinephrine	Increased	Increased
Prostaglandins	Increased	Increased
Uterine irritability	—	Increased
Resistance to infection	—	? Decreased

After Storniolo FR, Cheek TG, Shelley WC, Gutsche BB. The febrile parturient. In: James FM III, Wheeler AS, Dewan DM, eds. Obstetric anesthesia: The complicated patient. 2nd ed. Philadelphia: FA Davis, 1988:439. Additional data from references 28, 29, 42, 56, 57, and 59.)

On the other hand, there are no data indicating that the 1:22,000 to 1:30,000 incidence of meningitis resulting from spinal anesthesia is changing.[64]

The following sources of bacteria can lead to epidural abscess formation or meningitis (Fig. 29-3):

- The primary source is a distant infection that spreads *hematogenously* (Fig. 29-3[1]) in an immunocompromised host. This route accounts for 26% to 72% of reported cases of epidural abscess.[62,65] Infection reaches the epidural veins when blood shunts to the intervertebral venous plexus during episodes of inferior venocaval obstruction. Trauma to the spine during regional anesthesia may produce a hematoma that can act as a culture medium for bacterial growth.
- Another route is by *direct extension* from a nearby infection (18%),[61] such as vertebral osteomyelitis (Fig. 29-3[2]).
- Rarely, bacteria may be *iatrogenically introduced* through a break in sterile technique, such as the use of contaminated solution or equipment (Fig. 29-3[3]).

Trauma and subsequent bleeding into the epidural space may create a nidus for infection that can lead to the development of an abscess. Most epidural abscesses reported occur spontaneously and are not related to instrumentation of the spine, although some cases were associated with mild trauma, such as a fall.[62] With increasing numbers of surgery performed on the spine,

procedure-related infections now account for 13% to 24% of recent cases.[66,67]

Table 29-6 reviews 41 cases (reported from 1971–1991) of epidural abscess or meningitis that occurred after regional anesthesia. Of the 19 epidural abscesses, 9 arose after epidural catheter placement.[67–76] Five occurred in conjunction with lumbar puncture.[64,70,77-80,82,83] Paravertebral blocks preceded three abscesses.[70,81] Lastly, one abscess followed local anesthetic infiltration in the coccygeal area.[73] Of the cases involving epidural catheter placement, four were inserted to treat acute pain,[68,74,75] four were inserted for noncancer chronic pain,[69,70,72] and one involved a chronically implanted epidural catheter for cancer pain.[71] Twenty-seven reported cases of dural puncture correlated with 22 cases of meningitis and 5 epidural abscesses.[64,70,76,77,82,83]

Of five verified contaminations, three were due to *Pseudomonas* traced to a common saline solution used to flush the spinal needles,[64] and two were due to *Staphylococcus aureus*. This pathogen was cultured from a common vial of local anesthetic solution used for repeated injections and from the nares of the anesthetist.[75]

Four cases of meningitis involved parturients. Three followed spinal anesthesia for delivery in one hospital in Rhode Island.[64] One involved an afebrile patient with a 12-hour history of ROM. In this patient, the first epidural placement resulted in a "wet tap." The second attempt was successful and provided good labor anal-

Table 29–6

Case Reports of Epidural Abscess and/or Meningitis Compiled from the Literature

AUTHORS	YEAR	DETAILS
Corbett and Rosenstein	1971	*Pseudomonas* meningitis due to contaminated saline flush solution (3 cases)
Saady	1976	*Staphylococcus aureus* EA from catheter for postoperative analgesia (40 h)
Berman and Eiselle	1978	Group D streptococcal meningitis after spinal anesthesia
Loarie and Fairley	1978	*Staphylococcus epidermis* and bacteroides EA detected during second spinal anesthetic for below-knee amputation (diabetic)
North and Brophy	1979	*Staphylococcus aureus* EA from infected local anesthetic solution during 72-h epidural for priapism. *S. aureus* EA from 4-d epidural for trauma (possible source, anesthetist nares)
Rustin et al	1983	*Staphylococcus aureus* EA from local anesthetic injection in coccygeal area
Kilpatrick and Girgis	1983	Seventeen cases of meningitis associated with recent spinal anesthesia (8 *Pseudomonas*, 1 *S. aureus*, 1 *Streptococcus* mitis)
Bergman et al	1983	*Staphylococcus aureus* EA from multiple, traumatic lumbar punctures in a premature infant for posthemorrhagic hydrocephalus
McDonogh and Cranney	1984	*Staphylococcus aureus* EA from 80-h epidural for trauma analgesia
Beaudoin and Klein	1984	*Pseudomonas* EA following five spinal anesthetics in 10 d for infected toe (diabetic)
Schmutzhard et al	1986	Two cases of *S. aureus* EA from paravertebral blocks for pain
Fine et al	1988	EA from 72-h thoracic epidural for chronic pain
Berga and Trierweiler	1989	*Streptococcus sanguis* meningitis following a "wet tap" and successful epidural labor analgesia, 12-h SROM, afebrile
Abdel-Magid and Kotb	1990	*Proteus* EA 15 d after spinal anesthesia for hemorrhoidectomy
Ericsson et al	1990	One *Escherichia coli* EA, 1 *Pneumococcus* meningitis, and EA from repeated spinal taps; 1 mixed-flora EA from epidural for pain; 1 *S. aureus* EA after paravertebral local anesthetic injection
Reynolds and Hahn	1991	*Staphylococcus aureus* coagulase-negative EA 4 wk after epidural catheter implantation for cancer analgesia
Strong	1991	Two *S. aureus* EA from two epidural catheter placements, each for pain control, lasting 3–5 d each

Abbreviations: EA = epidural abscess, SROM = spontaneous rupture of membranes.

gesia for 6 hours. On the first postpartum day, an epidural blood patch was done for postdural puncture headache with good relief. Six hours after the blood patch, the woman developed a fever of 38.5°C that resolved without treatment. On the third postpartum day, the patient received another epidural blood patch for recurrence of head and neck pain, this time without any relief. When fever of 39.5°C to 40.2°C developed, she was evaluated and found to have meningitis due to *Streptococcus sanguis* (an oral pathogen), which responded well to antibiotics.[76]

Sixty-eight percent of the epidural abscesses reported were due to *Staphylococcus aureus* (see Table 29-3). The cases of spinal meningitis were mostly due to *Pseudomonas* (11 cases). This bacteria was established as a definite contaminant in three cases[64] and suspected of being a contaminant in the other cases.[82] The pathogens isolated from the cases of meningitis associated with regional anesthesia were quite different from the usual microorganisms causing meningitis[84] or epidural abscess[63] (see Table 29-3). As many as 73% of spinal infections were likely iatrogenic owing to a break in aseptic technique.[64,75] Epidural abscesses arising during the use of an epidural catheter for pain control involved intermittent dosing, which could increase the risk of contamination.[68,69,71,72,74,75] Hematogenous spread from a distant focus may account for the other 27% of cases reported.

The anesthesiologist must consider several factors when considering options for a parturient with fever. Does fever correlate with bacteremia? Because trauma may be associated with subsequent epidural abscess formation, what is the likelihood of vein puncture during spinal or epidural anesthesia? What do the "experts" recommend in this situation? The following sections of this chapter consider these questions.

Incidence of Bacteremia

The incidence of bacteremia in the febrile parturient is 10%.[85] Ninety percent of febrile parturients had no bacteremia when blood cultures were obtained.[86] Bacteremia was found in only 8% of patients with clinically overt IAI (estimated to occur in 0.5%–2% of pregnancies).[85] Half of the patients with positive blood cultures had temperatures below 38.8°C. In the usual clinical setting, blood cultures are obtained only during a fever spike. However, there appears to be no consistent relationship between the occurrence of bacteremia and the severity of fever. Bacteremia has been known to occur in the absence of fever.[87–89] The presence of fever does not imply bacteremia; conversely, absence of fever does not exclude bacteremia.

Bacteremia occurs commonly in a wide variety of clinical settings (Table 29-7).[87,90] Less than 1% of healthy individuals not undergoing instrumentation experience bacteremia.[87] Even in the presence of sterile urine, bladder catheterization or instrumentation can induce bacteremia in 57% of patients.[91] In the healthy individuals undergoing dental procedures, 18% to 88% have a transient bacteremia for 1 to 15 minutes.[87] The incidence of bacteremia after vaginal delivery may be as high as 8%.[89] After cesarean section, the incidence ranges from 8% to 20%.[3]

The relationship between bacteremia and metastatic infection after epidural or spinal anesthesia is unknown. Many factors, including the size of the inoculum, route of introduction, virulence of the bacteria, and host defenses, determine if infection becomes established.[24] For instance, septic abscesses occur more frequently in the immunosuppressed host, and defective cardiac leaflets are more susceptible to endocarditis during episodes of bacteremia than normal valves.[90]

Bacteremia probably occurs frequently in otherwise healthy laboring parturients. Instrumentation of the lower genital tract is associated with a significant bacteremia, especially if the urine is infected.[92] Bladder catheterization alone can produce bacteremia in 8% of patients, even if the urine is sterile. During urologic procedures, the risk of bacteremia increases in the presence of infected urine. Because 5% to 10% of pregnant women have asymptomatic bacteriuria, the likelihood of bacteremia during routine bladder catheterization during labor should be higher. Given the frequent use of epidural analgesia and the frequent need to catheterize these women, if bacteremia and epidural infections were causally related, many more cases of epidural abscess should have occurred in this population.[55,86] In reality, the probability of this event occurring is remote.

Table 29-7

Incidence of Bacteremia in Health and Various Clinical Conditions and Procedures

PROCEDURE	INCIDENCE
Healthy individuals, no instrumentation	< 1%
Obstetric/Gynecologic conditions/ procedures	
Parturition	1%–8%
Cesarean section	8%–20%
Intra-amniotic infection	8%–12%
Endometrial biopsy	10%
Urologic procedures/conditions	
Urethral catheterization (sterile urine)	8%
Pyelonephritis	15%–20%
Urethral dilatation	19%–33%
Transurethral resection	11%–58%
Retropubic prostatectomy	13%–82%
Dental	
Gingival disease before instrumentation	10%
Dental extraction	18%–85%
Periodontal surgery	32%–88%
Tooth brushing	0%–26%
Flossing	20%
Upper airway	
Oral intubation	0%
Nasal intubation or suctioning	16%
Rigid bronchoscopy	15%
Fiberoptic bronchoscopy	0%
Gastrointestinal	
Upper gastrointestinal endoscopy	8%–12%
Appendectomy	21%
Primary peritonitis	75%
Secondary peritonitis	20%–30%

(After Scheld WM, Sande MA. Endocarditis and intravenous infections. In: Mandell GL, Douglas RG, Jr., Bennett JE, eds. Principles and practice of infectious diseases. 3rd ed. New York: Churchill Livingstone, 1989:673; and Everett ED, Hirschmann JY. Transient bacteremia and endocarditis prophylaxis. Medicine 1977;56:61. Additional data from references 3, 87, 88, and 89.)

It is important to note that the microorganisms causing urinary tract infection during pregnancy[93] are quite different from those seen in meningitis or epidural abscess (Table 29-3). Moreover, 73% of the spinal infections associated with lumbar puncture or epidural catheter reviewed were likely due to a break in aseptic technique rather than bacteremia (Table 29-6).

Vein Disruption During Epidural and Spinal Anesthesia

The incidence of epidural vein puncture by a needle or catheter varies (Table 29-8).[94] As many as 12% of

Table 29–8

Reported Incidence of Epidural Vein Puncture

EVENT	FREQUENCY	REFERENCE
Trauma with needle or catheter	1%–10%	Verniquet (1980)
Blood vessel trauma with catheter	12%	Rolbin and Farine (1991)
Intravascular placement of catheter	4.8%	Kenepp and Gutsche (1981)
Vessel puncture with 16-gauge Tuohy needle	1.7%	Dawkins (1969)
Vessel puncture with Harris needle	0.3%	Dawkins (1969)
Air emboli during identification of epidural space	43%	Naulty et al (1982)

catheters may perforate an epidural vein.[55] Needle size may relate to the likelihood of vessel trauma. Dawkins[95] recorded a 1.7% incidence of trauma when using a 16-gauge Tuohy needle, but he reported only a 0.3% incidence with the thinner Harris needle.[95] Naulty *et al*[96] detected Doppler sounds that suggested air entry into the right atrium in 43% of women when using air for loss of resistance during epidural insertion. Whether this result truly represents the incidence of epidural vein puncture is debatable.

A successfully placed epidural catheter also can change location during labor. In one study, 54% of catheters moved after insertion. Eighteen percent migrated inward, and 36% moved outward.[97] After the catheter has been in place for some time, 0.3% may enter a blood vessel.[98] Because of this possibility, some anesthesiologists advocate removal of the epidural catheter when a parturient develops fever;[99] however, it seems unreasonable to terminate the benefits of epidural anesthesia on the remote possibility of developing an epidural or spinal infection. These patients require more pitocin, have a higher likelihood of abdominal delivery, and therefore reap significant benefits from epidural block.[100] In one case, the epidural catheter was removed when fever developed during labor. Subsequently, the anesthetist had difficulty during intubation for cesarean section. If the epidural catheter had not been removed, it could have been used for surgery, and the problem may have been averted.[99]

"Traumatic tap," which occurs in up to 20% of lumbar punctures, may help seed the meninges during bacteremia.[101] Scattered reports since the early 1900s have suggested the possibility that lumbar puncture may induce meningitis.[102,103] Two retrospective studies failed to establish that lumbar puncture induces meningitis in bacteremic patients. Patients with bacteremia due to *Streptococcus pneumoniae, Hemophilus influenzae, Neisseria meningitidis,* or Group A or B *Streptococcus* had a 14% incidence of spontaneous meningitis due to the predilection of these organisms for the meninges. On the other hand, bacteremia due to organisms that rarely cause meningitis (*Staphylococcus aureus, Klebsiella,* etc.) resulted in a 0.8% incidence of spontaneous meningitis, which was not significantly different from the 2.1% risk of meningitis after diagnostic lumbar puncture.[103,104] The development of bacterial meningitis in patients with bacteremia strongly correlates with the species of bacteria causing the infection, not lumbar puncture.[104]

What Is the Risk of Epidural or Spinal Anesthesia in the Patient with Intra-amniotic Infection?

Vaddadi *et al*[105] reviewed the clinical course of 139 patients with IAI, 113 of whom received epidural anesthesia, 63 for cesarean section and 50 for vaginal delivery. In 74 patients, IAI developed after epidural placement. Thirty-nine patients with signs of systemic infection were given epidural anesthesia, only 23 of whom had antibiotics before epidural placement. Amniotic fluid cultures were positive in 20 patients, 11 of whom had epidural anesthesia. No epidural abscesses developed in any of the patients.[105]

At St. John's Mercy Hospital in St. Louis, Missouri, where more than 5000 epidurals per year are done for labor and delivery, no case of epidural abscess has been reported in the past 13 years. Our usual practice is to avoid epidural anesthesia in clearly septic women. Once an epidural catheter is in place, however, we do not remove it if the parturient develops fever during labor.

Clinical Recommendations

Carefully assess the risks and benefits of regional anesthesia in the febrile parturient who may have IAI. In the absence of acute sepsis, regional anesthesia may be justifiable in patients who will clearly benefit from it (*e.g.,* patients in preterm labor or those suffering from severe labor pain unrelieved by narcotics). The parturient and her spouse must be involved in the decision-making. The alternatives, risks, and benefits must be presented based on available data. Based on analysis of data in the literature, Thistlewood[86] concludes that withholding epidural anesthesia only because of a fever of 38.5°C is too conservative a stance.

In the presence of systemic symptoms suggesting bacteremia or septicemia (*i.e.,* fever, chills, myalgia), most anesthesiologists avoid regional anesthesia. The use of antibiotics to decrease the bacterial load may fail in up to 22% of patients because of subinhibitory plasma concentrations.[58] The risk of regional anesthesia in the presence of obvious bacteremia or septicemia involves not only the possibility of inducing spinal or epidural infection but also the task of maintaining cardiovascular stability in the face of sympathetic blockade. Fortunately, patients with IAI are rarely clinically unstable or grossly septic.

Despite the 8% to 12% incidence of bacteremia seen in IAI and the increasing use of epidural anesthesia, there have been no reported cases of epidural abscess associated with this infection.[55,58] Only one reported case even remotely suggests a correlation between IAI, epidural analgesia, and neuraxial infection (meningitis) (Table 29-6).[76] In this case, the pathogen (*Streptococcus sanguis*) is also an oral pathogen. It could have spread from the operator. Concern that the use of epidural anesthesia in patients with IAI increases the likelihood of developing epidural abscess may be misplaced.

There appears to be no reason to terminate epidural analgesia in a patient who subsequently develops signs and symptoms of IAI. These patients are prone to dysfunctional labor and frequently require oxytocin, and they are at increased risk of cesarean section for failure to progress or fetal distress.[37] Develop a management plan with the obstetrician that may include antibiotic therapy and delivery within a finite time frame.

Single subarachnoid or epidural injections appear less likely to introduce exogenous infection than do continuous techniques requiring several injections that provide multiple chances of contamination. The use of continuous-infusion pumps during labor may reduce the likelihood of contamination. The role of micropore filters in decreasing bacterial contamination of solutions used for prolonged administration is unknown.

To exclude common bacterial contaminants and particulate matter, the filter size must be less than or equal to 0.22 μm.[106]

If general anesthesia is chosen for the febrile parturient, the risks of aspiration and hypoxemia must be recognized and precautions taken to minimize them. In addition, make allowance for the increased basal metabolic rate, oxygen consumption, and cardiac output (see Table 29-5). Thorough preoxygenation coupled with use of high inspired oxygen concentration may help lower the risk of maternal and fetal hypoxemia. Similar precautions must be taken during emergence and early postoperative course.

EPIDURAL ABSCESS

Diagnosis

A high index of suspicion is essential for the early diagnosis of epidural abscess. In most series reported, epidural infection was suspected at initial presentation in only 25% of cases.[62,63] Diagnosis of epidural abscess in a patient who has no history of recent spinal instrumentation can be difficult because of subtle symptoms and variable presentation early in the course of the disease (Table 29-9). Back pain is usually severe, intensified by coughing, sneezing, and ventral flexion of the spine. Neck rigidity is frequently present. Although described as a "painful, febrile spinal syndrome,"[107] fever and other signs of sepsis initially may be absent in up to 43% of patients.[63] Neurologic deficit usually is a late sign.[67]

If diagnosis is delayed, the abscess produces a space-occupying lesion and exerts pressure on the spinal cord and nerve roots. The vascular supply to the spinal cord may be compromised, leading to ischemia, infarction, and subsequent neurologic damage.[66,108] Weakness, sensory loss, urinary and bowel retention, paralysis, and even death may result. The neurologic deterioration may take as little as 0.5 to 2 hours.[66]

Early diagnosis is the key to complete neurologic recovery. In one series, when epidural abscess was the primary diagnosis, confirmation and treatment were accomplished within 1.3 ± 1.0 days, with 86% complete recovery. In contrast, when the initial impression was other than epidural abscess, 12.7 ± 2.9 days were required for diagnosis and treatment. Only 46% of these patients recovered completely.[63] Appearance of neurologic abnormality worsens the prognosis. Delay in surgery may be disastrous. Total recovery may still be possible if surgery is done before the onset of paralysis, or if paralysis is less than 36 hours in duration. Paralysis

Table 29–9

Clinical and Radiologic Diagnosis of Epidural Abscess

	INCIDENCE
Signs and Symptoms of Epidural Abscess	
Severe back pain	89%–100%
Localized overlying tenderness	95%
Fever	57%–95%
Leukocytosis (> 10,000/mm³)	76%
Neurologic deficit	69%
Diagnostic Tests for Epidural Abscess	
Myelogram	
Computed Tomography	
Magnetic resonance imaging	
(Data from references 62, 63, 66, and 67.)	

for more than 48 hours risks incomplete recovery and even death. In Baker's series (1975), all five patients who were not operated on died.[62]

Diagnostic tests include myelography, computed tomography (CT), or magnetic resonance imaging (MRI). By injecting contrast intrathecally, myelography can demonstrate the level of spinal block or compression due to the abscess (Fig. 29-6).[109] Computed tomography using intravenous contrast material can demonstrate the presence of the epidural abscess (Fig. 29-7) as well as its location, extent, and volume. If desired, guided needle aspiration can follow.[110–112]

More recently, MRI has emerged as the examination of choice in patients suspected of epidural abscess.[111,113] This test has the advantage of being noninvasive, painless, and safe because it uses no ionizing radiation. It is superior to myelography and CT because it allows visualization of the degree of cord compression and extent of the lesion in all directions. Transverse, coronal, and sagittal slices can be obtained without moving the patient. Magnetic resonance imaging penetrates bone and visualizes contents of the spinal canal with no need for contrast.[113–115]

Treatment

Antibiotics and laminectomy to drain pus are the mainstay of therapy. The initial antibiotic should include coverage for coagulase-positive *Staphylococcus aureus,* the most commonly cultured pathogen. Before 1945 and the use of antibiotics, laminectomy alone was associated with a 55% mortality rate. Adding antibiotics lowered the death rate to 25%. The most recent report shows a 6.9% mortality rate, attributed to early diagnosis and treatment with operative decompression and antibiotics. Abscesses located in the lumbar area, which produce cauda equina syndrome rather than cord compression, have a better prognosis.[67]

Nonoperative treatment of epidural abscess has been successful in patients who do not have any neurologic deficits at the time of diagnosis.[110,111,114,115] Early diagnosis and follow-up with MRI and CT allow this approach. In some patients, percutaneous needle aspiration of pus in the epidural space has avoided laminectomy. This approach may require longer treatment with parenteral and oral antibiotics.[110,114,115] If neurologic deterioration occurs, laminectomy and drainage are necessary.[110] Repeat MRI or CT documents regression of the abscess.[111]

CASE REPORTS

What follows are two cases of epidural abscess involving healthy parturients who received uncomplicated epidural anesthesia for repeat cesarean section. Both were in very early labor with intact membranes. These are unpublished observations obtained by the author from two different hospitals. I present them here to emphasize the variable presentation of this potentially devastating complication.

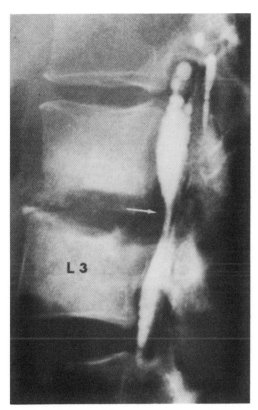

L 3

Figure 29–6. Myelography shows a partial, elongated anterior defect of the dye column at L-2–3 (*arrow*) due to the presence of an anterior epidural abscess. (Shapiro R. Inflammatory lesions. In: Shapiro R, ed. Myelography, 4th ed. Chicago: Yearbook Medical Publishers, 1962:301)

Case 1

A 25-year-old gravida 2, para 1 patient delivered a healthy infant by repeat cesarean section under epidural anesthesia during early labor. Mild paralytic ileus responded to conservative measures postoperatively. She had mild back pain at the time of discharge on the fifth postoperative day. She was readmitted on the 11th postoperative day for worsening back and leg pain and fever of 103°F. The epidural site was well healed and nontender. Severe back spasms occurred with any movement. Her complete blood count included 13,000 white blood cells/mm³, with 76% neutrophils. Initial therapy consisted of cefazolin, 1 g IV every 6 hours, morphine by patient-controlled analgesia, diazepam 2 mg three times a day, and Tylox as needed at bedtime. Her temperature ranged from 101°F to 103°F. The CT scan showed a mass at L-2–3. A translumbar myelogram showed poor filling at lL-2–3.

On the 13th day after cesarean section, a left L-2 laminectomy was performed under general anesthesia; about 4 mL of thick pus was drained. The epidural space was copiously irrigated and drained. Gram's stain showed many white blood cells and a moderate amount of gram-positive cocci, while the culture grew coagulase-positive *Staphylococcus aureus*. The antibiotic was switched to nafcillin. Postoperatively, she defervesced within 24 hours. Urinary retention responded to intermittent bladder catheterization. She was discharged 10 days after the laminectomy on oral doxycycline for another 2 weeks. The patient continues to do well.

Case 2

A 26-year-old gravida 2, para 1 patient, weighing 98 kg and measuring 168 cm, delivered a healthy baby by uncomplicated repeat cesarean section under epidural anesthesia. On the third postoperative day, the patient complained of diffuse pain around the epidural site. She also had a low-grade fever. These symptoms did not deter discharge on the fourth postoperative day. At home, the patient developed a fever of 102°F and increasing back pain. She was readmitted on the sixth postoperative day. She was treated with ampicillin, gentamicin, and clindamycin for presumed endometritis. The white blood cell count was 22,000/mm³, with 87% neutrophils. The anesthesiologist who evaluated the patient because of increasing back pain on the seventh postoperative pain sought immediate neurosurgical consultation.

The neurosurgeon found the sensory and motor tests to be grossly normal, although range of movement of the lower extremities was severely limited by pain. The MRI (Fig. 29-8A) showed findings consistent with an epidural abscess with circumferential narrowing of the thecal sac at the level of L-2–3. There was probable cellulitis involving the overlying paraspinous tissues. There was no evidence of discitis or osteomyelitis. After careful discussion of the findings and treatment options with the patient and her husband, the neurosurgeon aspirated the epidural abscess percutaneously under radiologic and CT guidance. About 10 mL of pus was obtained. The overlying soft-tissue abscess and cellulitis were incised and drained. Gram stain showed many white blood cells and gram-positive cocci. The culture showed moderate growth of beta-hemolytic Group A *Streptococcus,* which is sensitive to penicillin and many other antibiotics. The patient was treated with intravenous penicillin for 10 days and then received 4 weeks of oral therapy.

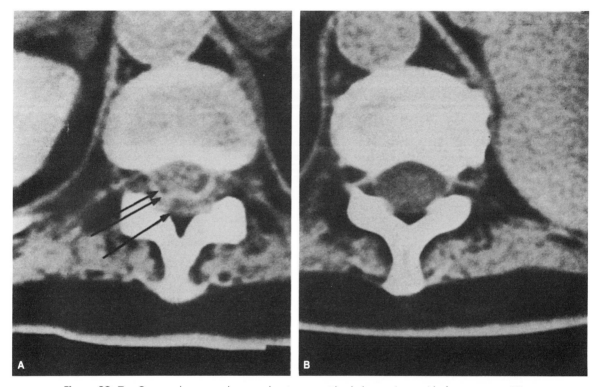

Figure 29–7. Computed tomography scan showing an epidural abscess (*arrows*) before treatment (**A**), and its disappearance after percutaneous aspiration and antibiotics (**B**). (Leys D, Lesoin F, Viaud C, et al. Decreased morbidity from acute bacterial spinal epidural abscesses using computed tomography and nonsurgical treatment in selected patients. Ann Neurol 1985;17:350)

Two days after drainage, the white blood cell count was 12,000/mm³, with 82% neutrophils and 12% bands. A follow-up MRI, performed 3 days after drainage of the abscess, showed marked decrease in the size of the epidural abscess with disappearance of the thecal sac narrowing (Fig. 29-8B). She was discharged in good condition 2 weeks after drainage of the abscess. At discharge, the white blood cell count was 6300/mm³, with 61% neutrophils.

Discussion

These two cases of epidural abscess occurred in the absence of fever or obvious antecedent illness after routine epidural anesthesia for repeat cesarean section. Because both patients were at term in very early labor with intact membranes, it is highly unlikely that IAI was present. *Staphylococcus aureus* and Group A *Streptococcus* are both carried in the nasopharynx and both can

produce skin infections.[116,117] *Staphylococcus aureus* is a frequent pathogen in folliculitis, acne, furuncles, and carbuncles,[116] whereas Group A *Streptococcus* causes impetigo, cellulitis, and pharyngitis.[117] The patient in the second case had acne-type lesions on the back, with some clearing in the lower lumbar area where the epidural catheter was placed. Bacteremia as a possible source of epidural infection is difficult to imagine in these afebrile patients, although spontaneous *Staphylococcus aureus* bacteremia in young adults has been reported.[115] The more likely source of infection is a break in sterile technique, such as introduction of bacteria from the patient's skin (Case 2) or from the nasopharynx of the anesthetist (Case 1 or 2).

CONCLUSION

A team approach must be adopted when dealing with the febrile parturient. Early consultation and planning

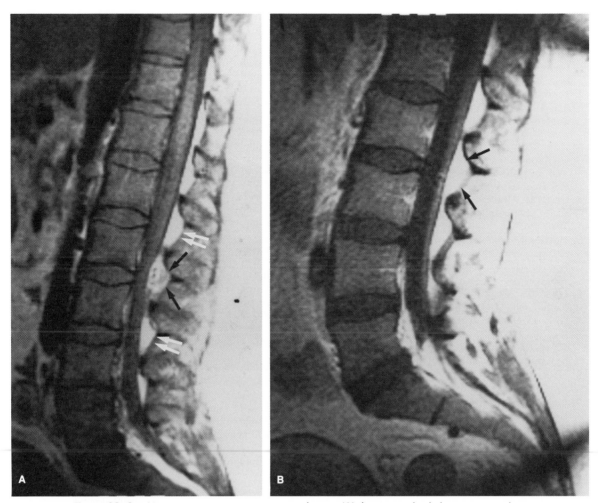

Figure 29–8. Magnetic resonance imaging sagittal image (**A**) showing epidural abscess as a nonhomogeneous area within the epidural fat (*black arrows*) in contrast to the normal bright signal intensity fat at adjacent levels (*white arrows*). Follow-up sagittal image (**B**) showing normalization of the epidural fat (*black arrows*) 3 days after percutaneous needle aspiration of the epidural abscess. (Courtesy of Radiological Associates, St. Louis, Missouri)

between the obstetrician, anesthesiologist, and pediatrician are important. In considering options for labor analgesia or operative anesthesia in the febrile parturient who may have IAI, carefully present the risks and benefits of each choice to the patient and her family so that they may actively participate in the decision process.

A well-conducted epidural anesthetic for labor and delivery provides benefits for many obstetric patients. Lumbar puncture in febrile patients does not increase the incidence of meningitis or epidural abscess.[103,104]

The theoretical risk of inducing epidural abscess or spinal meningitis in parturients with IAI, although not to be ignored, should not override the benefits of regional anesthesia for labor analgesia and cesarean section. Review of the literature has not uncovered a single case of epidural abscess or meningitis resulting from epidural or spinal anesthesia in patients with IAI.[55,58] The difference in bacteriology of IAI, meningitis, epidural abscess, and urinary tract infection makes it highly unlikely that these infections are causally related (Table 29-3).

REFERENCES

1. Sweet RL, Gibbs RS. Intraamnionitic infections (intrauterine infection in late pregnancy). In: Sweet RL, Gibbs RS, eds. Infectious diseases of the female genital tract. Baltimore: Williams & Wilkins, 1985:263.
2. Landers DV, Sweet RL. Perinatal infections. In: Scott RG, DiSaia PJ, Hammond CB, Spellacy WN, eds. Danforth's Obstetrics and gynecology. 6th ed. Philadelphia: JB Lippincott, 1989:535.
3. Gibbs RS, Sweet RL. Maternal and fetal infections: Clinical disorders. In: Creasy RK, Resnik R, eds. Maternal-fetal medicine: Principles and practice. Philadelphia: WB Saunders, 1989:656.
4. Gibbs RS, Castillo MS, Rodgers PJ. Management of acute chorioamnionitis. Am J Obstet Gynecol 1980;136:709.
5. Hoskins IA, Johnson TRB, Winkel CA. Leucocyte esterase activity in human amniotic fluid for rapid detection of chorioamnionitis. Am J Obstet Gynecol 1987;157:730.
6. Looff JD, Hager WD. Management of chorioamnionitis. Surg Gynecol Obstet 1984;158:161.
7. Gibbs RS. Obstetric factors associated with infections of the fetus and newborn infant. In: Remington JS, Klein JO, eds. Infectious diseases of the fetus and newborn infant. 3rd ed. Philadelphia: WB Saunders, 1990:981.
8. Hollander D. Diagnosis of chorioamnionitis. Clin Obstet Gynecol 1986;29:816.
9. Hawrylyshyn P, Bernstein P, Milligan JE, Soldin S, Pollard A, Papsin FR. Premature rupture of membranes: The role of C-reactive protein in the prediction of chorioamnionitis. Am J Obstet Gynecol 1983;147:240.
10. Gravett MG, Eschenbach DA, Speigel-Brown CA, Holmes KK. Rapid diagnosis of amniotic-fluid infection by gas-liquid chromatography. N Engl J Med 1982;306:725.
11. Feigin RD, Abramson SL, Edwards MS. Infections in the fetus and neonate. In: Fanaroff AA, Martin RJ, eds. Neonatal-perinatal medicine. Diseases of the fetus and infant. 4th ed. St. Louis: CV Mosby, 1987:763.
12. Maternal adaptations to pregnancy. In: Cunningham FG, MacDonald PC, Gant NF, eds. William's obstetrics. 18th ed. Norwalk, CT: Appleton & Lange, 1989:143.
13. Gibbs RS. Diagnosis of intra-amniotic infection. Semin Perinatol 1977;1:71.
14. Arias F, Peskin EG. Premature rupture of the membranes. In: Arias F, ed. High-risk pregnancy and delivery. St. Louis: CV Mosby, 1984:63.
15. Bek KM, Nielsen FR, Qvist I, Rasmussen PE, Tobiassen M. C-reactive protein (CRP) and pregnancy. An early indicator of chorioamnionitis. A review. Eur J Obstet Gynecol Reprod Biol 1990;35:29.
16. Watts DH, Krohn MA, Wener MH, Eshenbach DA. C-reactive protein in normal pregnancy. Obstet Gynecol 1991;77:176.
17. Bobitt JR, Ledger WJ. Amniotic fluid analysis: Its role in maternal and neonatal infection. Obstet Gynecol 1978;51:56.
18. Broekhuizen FF, Gilman M, Hamilton PR. Amniocentesis for Gram stain and culture in preterm premature rupture of the membranes. Obstet Gynecol 1985; 66:316.
19. Schlievert P, Johnson W, Galask RP. Amniotic fluid antibacterial mechanisms: Newer concepts. Semin Perinatol 1977;1:59.
20. Vintzileos AM, Campbell WA, Nochimson DJ, Connolly ME, Fuenfer MM, Hoehn GJ. The fetal biophysical profile in patients with premature rupture of the membranes—an early predictor of fetal infection. Am J Obstet Gynecol 1985;152:510.
21. Zhang J, Kraus FT, Aquino TI. Chorioamnionitis: A comparative histologic, bacteriologic and clinical study. Int J Gynecol Pathol 1985;4:1.
22. Dong Y, St. Clair PJ, Ramzy I, Kagan-Hallet KS, Gibbs RS. A microbiologic and clinical study of placental inflammation at term. Obstet Gynecol 1987;70:175.
23. Garite TJ, Freeman RK. Chorioamnionitis in preterm gestation. Am J Obstet Gynecol 1982;59:539.
24. Hoeprich PD. Host–parasite relationships and the pathogenesis of infectious diseases. In: Hoerpich PD, Jordan MC, eds. Infectious diseases. 4th ed. Philadelphia: JB Lippincott, 1989:41.
25. Garite TJ. Premature rupture of membranes. In: Scott JR, DiSaia PJ, Hammond CB, Spellacy WN, eds. Danforth's Obstetrics and gynecology, 6th ed. Philadelphia: JB Lippincott, 1990:353.
26. Manabe Y, Himeno N, Fukumoto M. Tensile strength and collagen content of amniotic membrane do not change after second trimester or during delivery. Obstet Gynecol 1991;78:24.
27. McGregor JA, French JI, Lawellin D, Franco-Buff A, Smith C, Todd JK. Bacterial protease-induced reduction of chorioamniotic membrane strength and elasticity. Obstet Gynecol 1987;69:167.
28. Minkoff H. Prematurity: Infection as an etiologic factor. Obstet Gynecol 1983;62:137.
29. Romero R, Mazor M, Wu YK, et al. Infection in the pathogenesis of preterm labor. Semin Perinatol 1988;12:262.
30. Smith LG, Summers PR, Miles RW, Biswas MK, Pernoll ML. Gonococcal chorioamnionitis associated with sepsis: A case report. Am J Obstet Gynecol 1989;160:573.
31. Naeye RL. Acute bacterial chorioamnionitis. In: Scarpelli DG, Migaki G, eds. Transplacental effects on fetal health: Proceedings of a symposium held in Bethesda, Maryland, November 5-6, 1987:73.
32. Gonik B, Bottoms SF, Cotton DB. Amniotic fluid volume as a risk factor in preterm premature rupture of membranes. Obstet Gynecol 1985;65:456.
33. Bejar R, Curbello V, Davis C, Gluck L. Premature labor. II. Bacterial sources of phospholipase. Obstet Gynecol 1981;57:479.

34. van der Elst CW, Bernal AL, Sinclair-Smith CC. The role of chorioamnionitis and prostaglandins in premature labor. Obstet Gynecol 1991;77:672.

35. Harger JH, Meyer MP, Amortegui A, MacPherson TA, Kaplan L, Mueller–Heubach E. Low incidence of positive amniotic fluid cultures in preterm labor at 27-32 weeks in the absence of clinical evidence of chorioamnionitis. Obstet Gynecol 1991;77:228.

36. Gibbs RS, Blanco JD, St. Clair PJ, Castaneda YS. Quantitative bacteriology of amniotic fluid from women with clinical intraamniotic infection at term. J Infect Dis 1982;145:1.

37. Duff P, Sanders R, Gibbs RS. The course of labor in term patients with chorioamnionitis. Am J Obstet Gynecol 1983;147:391.

38. Silver RR, Gibbs RS, Castillo M. Effect of amniotic fluid bacteria on the course of labor in nulliparous women at term. Obstet Gynecol 1986;68:587.

39. Combs CA, Murphy EL, Laros RK Jr. Factors associated with hemorrhage in cesarean deliveries. Obstet Gynecol 1991;77:77.

40. Azzizz R, Cumming J, Naeye R. Acute myometritis and chorioamnionitis during cesarean section of asymptomatic women. Am J Obstet Gynecol 1988;159:1137.

41. Stovall TG, Ambrose SE, Ling FW, Anderson GD. Short-course antibiotic therapy for the treatment of chorioamnionitis and postpartum endomyometritis. Am J Obstet Gynecol 1988;159:404.

42. Isada NB, Grossman JH III. Perinatal infections. In: Gabbe SG, Niebyl JR, Simpson JL, eds. Obstetrics: Normal and problem pregnancies. New York: Churchill Livingstone, 1986:979.

43. Sperling RS, Ramamurthy RS, Gibbs RS. A comparison of intrapartum versus immediate postpartum treatment of intraamniotic infection. Obstet Gynecol 1987;70:861.

44. Gilstrap LC, Leveno EJ, Cox SM, Burris JS, Mashburn M, Rosenfeld CR. Intrapartum treatment of acute chorioamniotis: Impact on neonatal sepsis. Am J Obstet Gynecol 1988;159:579.

45. Gibbs RS, Dinsmoor MJ, Newton ER, Ramamurthy RS. A randomized trial of intrapartum versus immediate postpartum treatment of women with intra-amniotic infection. Obstet Gynecol 1988;72:823.

46. Johnston MM, Sanchez-Ramos L, Vaughn AJ, Todd MW, Renrubi GI. Antibiotic therapy in preterm premature rupture of membranes: A randomized, prospective, double-blind trial. Am J Obstet Gynecol 1990;163:743.

47. Cunningham FG, Leveno KJ, DePalma RT, Roark M, Rosenfeld CR. Perioperative antimicrobials for cesarean delivery: Before or after cord clamping. Obstet Gynecol 1983;62:151.

48. Gilstrap LC III, Bawdon RE, Burris J. Antibiotic concentration in maternal blood, cord blood and placental membranes in chorioamnionitis. Obstet Gynecol 1988;72:124.

49. Hauth JC, Gilstrap LC III, Hankins GDV, Connor KD.

50. Guzick DS, Winn K. The association of chorioamnionitis with preterm delivery. Obstet Gynecol 1985;65:11.

51. Mustafa MM, McCracken GH Jr. Neonatal septicemia and meningitis. In: Rudolf AM, ed. Pediatrics. 19th ed. Norwalk, CT: Appleton & Lange, 1991:551.

52. Morales WJ. The effect of chorioamnionitis on the developmental outcome of preterm infants at one year. Obstet Gynecol 1987;70:183.

53. Pass MA, Gray BM, Dillon HC Jr. Puerperal and perinatal infections with group B steptococci. Am J Obstet Gynecol 1982;143:147.

54. Weinstein B, Swartz MN. Host responses to infection. In: Sodeman WA Jr, Sodeman TM, eds. Sodeman's Pathologic physiology mechanisms of disease, 7th ed. Philadelphia: WB Saunders, 1985:540.

55. Rolbin S, Farine D. The febrile parturient. In: Datta S, ed. Anesthetic and obstetric management of high-risk pregnancy. St. Louis: Mosby–Year Book, 1991:596.

56. Body temperature, temperature regulation and fever. In: Guyton AC, ed. Textbook of medical physiology. 8th ed. Philadelphia: WB Saunders, 1991:797.

57. Dinarello CA, Wolff SM. Pathogenesis of fever. In: Mandell GL, Douglas RG Jr, Bennett JE, eds. Principles and practice of infectious diseases, 3rd ed. New York: Churchill Livingstone, 1990:462.

58. Storniolo FR, Cheek TG, Shelley WC, Gutsche BB. The febrile parturient. In: James FM III, Wheeler AS, Dewan DM, eds. Obstetric anesthesia: The complicated patient, 2nd ed. Philadelphia: FA Davis, 1988:439.

59. Cefalo RC, Hellegers AE. The effects of maternal hyperthermia on maternal and fetal cardiovascular and respiratory function. Am Obstet Gynecol 1978;131:687.

60. Hager WD, Pauly TH. Fetal tachycardia as an indicator of maternal and neonatal morbidity. Obstet Gynecol 1985;66:191.

61. Moberg LJ, Garite TJ, Freeman RK. Fetal heart rate patterns and fetal distress in patients with preterm premature rupture of membranes. Obstet Gynecol 1984; 64:60.

62. Baker AS, Ojemann RG, Swartz MN, Richardson EP. Spinal epidural abscess. N Engl J Med 1975;293:463.

63. Danner RL, Hartman BJ. Update of spinal epidural abscess: 35 cases and review of the literature. Rev Infect Dis 1987;9:265.

64. Corbett JJ, Rosenstein BJ. *Pseudomonas* meningitis related to spinal meningitis: Report of three cases with a common source of infection. Neurology 1971;21:946.

65. Grant FC. Epidural spinal abscess. JAMA 1945; 128:509.

66. Hlavin ML, Kaminski HJ, Ross JSI Ganz E. Spinal epidural abscess: A ten year perspective. Neurosurgery 1990;27:177.

67. Del Curling O, Gower DJ, McWhorter JM. Changing

Term maternal and neonatal complications of acute chorioamnionitis. Obstet Gynecol 1985;66:59.

concepts in spinal epidural abscess: A report of 29 cases. Neurosurgery 1990;27:185.

68. McDonogh AJ, Cranney BS. Delayed presentation of an epidural abscess. Anaesth Intensive Care 1984;12:364.

69. Fine PG, Hare BD, Zahniser JC. Epidural abscess following epidural catheterization in a chronic pain patient: A diagnostic dilemma. Anesthesiology 1988; 69:422.

70. Ericsson M, Algers G, Schliamser SE. Spinal epidural abscesses in adults: Review and report of iatrogenic cases. Scand J Infect Dis 1990;22:249.

71. Reynolds PC, Hahn MB. Early diagnosis of a spinal epidural abscess. Reg Anesth 1991;16:57.

72. Strong WE. Epidural abscess associated with epidural catheterization: A rare event? Report of two cases with markedly delayed presentation. Anesthesiology 1991; 74:943.

73. Rustin MHA, Flynn MD, Coomes EN. Acute sacral epidural abscess following local anaesthetic injection. Postgrad Med J 1983;59:399.

74. Saady A. Epidural abscess complicating thoracic epidural analgesia. Anesthesiology 1976;44:244.

75. North JB, Brophy BP. Epidural abscess: A hazard of spinal epidural anaesthesia. Aust NZ J Surg 1979;49:484.

76. Berga S, Trierweiler MW. Bacterial meningitis following epidural anesthesia for vaginal delivery: A case report. Obstet Gynecol 1989;74:437.

77. Berman RS, Eisele JH. Bacteremia, spinal anesthesia and development of meningitis. Anesthesiology 1978; 48:376.

78. Loarie DJ, Fairley HB. Epidural abscess following spinal anesthesia. Anesth Analg 1978;57:351.

79. Beaudoin MG, Klein L. Epidural abscess following multiple spinal anaesthetics. Anaesth Intensive Care 1984;12:163.

80. Abdel-Magid RA, Kotb HIM. Epidural abscess after spinal anesthesia: A favorable outcome. Neurosurgery 1990;27:310.

81. Schmutzhard E, Aichner F, Dierckx RA, Gerstenbrand F, Willeit J. New perspectives in acute epidural spinal abscess illustrated by two case reports. Acta Neurochir 1986;80:105.

82. Kilpatrick ME, Girgis NI. Meningitis—a complication of spinal anesthesia. Anesth Analg 1983;62:513.

83. Bergman I, Meyer JD, Painter MJ. Epidural abscess and vertebral osteomyelitis following serial lumbar puncture. Pediatrics 1983;72:476.

84. Miller JR, Jubelt B. Infections of the nervous system. In: Rowland LR, ed. Merritt's Textbook of neurology. 8th ed. Philadelphia: Lea & Febiger, 1989:63.

85. Blanco JD, Gibbs RS, Castaneda YS. Bacteremia in obstetrics: Clinical course. Obstet Gynecol 1981;58:621.

86. Thistlewood JM. The febrile parturient. Can J Anaesth 1988;35:270.

87. Everett ED, Hirschmann JY. Transient bacteremia and endocarditis prophylaxis. Medicine 1977;56:61.

88. Livengood CH, Land MR, Addison WA. Endometrial biopsy, bacteremia, and endocarditis risk. Obstet Gynecol 1985;65:678.

89. McCormack WM, Rosner B, Lee Y, Rankin JS, Lin J. Isolation of genital mycoplasmas from blood obtained shortly after vaginal delivery. Lancet 1975;1:596.

90. Scheld WM, Sande MA. Endocarditis and intravenous infections. In: Mandell GL, Douglas RG Jr, Bennett JE, eds. Principles and practice of infectious diseases. 3rd ed. New York: Churchill Livingstone, 1989:673.

91. Drach GW, Cox CE II. Bladder bacteria: Common but unique response for sepsis. Postoperative endotoxin responses. J Urol 1971;106:67.

92. Sullivan NM, Sutter VL, Mims MM, Marsh VH, Finegold SM. Clinical aspects of bacteremia after manipulation of the genitourinary tract. J Infect Dis 1973;127:49.

93. Simpson ML, Gaziano EP, Lupo VR, Peterson PK. Bacterial infections during pregnancy. In: Burrow GN, Ferris TF, eds. Medical complications during pregnancy. 3rd ed. Philadelphia: WB Saunders, 1988:345.

94. Verniquet AJW. Vessel puncture with epidural catheters. Anaesthesia 1980;35:660.

95. Dawkins CJM. An analysis of the complications of extradural and caudal block. Anaesthesia 1969;24:554.

96. Naulty JS, Ostheimer GW, Datta S, Knapp R, Weiss JB. Incidence of venous air embolism during epidural catheter insertion. Anesthesiology 1982;57:410.

97. Phillips DC, Macdonald R. Epidural catheter migration during labour. Anaesthesia 1987;42:661.

98. Kenepp NB, Gutsche BB. Inadvertent intravascular injections during lumbar epidural anesthesia. Anesthesiology 1981;54:172.

99. Thomas DG. Epidural analgesia in the presence of fever. Anaesthesia 1986;41:553.

100. Behl S. Epidural analgesia in the presence of fever. Anaesthesia 1985;40:1241.

101. Marton KI, Gean AD. The spinal tap: A new look at an old test. N Engl J Med 1981;305:1079.

102. Teele DW, Dashefsky B, Rakusan T, Klein JO. Meningitis after lumbar puncture in children with bacteremia. N Engl J Med 1981;305:1079.

103. Eng RH, Seligman SJ. Lumbar puncture-induced meningitis. JAMA 1981;245:1456.

104. Shapiro ED, Aaron NH, Wald ER, Chiponis D. Risk factors for development of bacterial meningitis among children with occult bacteremia. J Pediatr 1986;109:15.

105. Vaddadi A, Ramanathan J, Angel JJ, Sibai B. Epidural anesthesia in women with chorioamnionitis (a retrospective study). Anesthesiology 1989;71:A863.

106. Abouleish E, Amortegui AJ, Taylor FH. Are bacterial filters needed in continuous epidural analgesia for obstetrics? Anesthesiology 1977;46:351.

107. Hancock DO. A study of 49 patients with acute spinal extradural abscess. Paraplegia 1973;10:285.

108. Heusner AP. Nontuberculous spinal epidural infections. N Engl J Med 1948;239:845.

109. Shapiro R. Inflammatory lesions. In: Shapiro R, ed. Myelography. 4th ed. Chicago: Year Book Medical Publishers, 1962:301.

110. Leys D, Lesoin F, Viaud C, et al. Decreased morbidity

from acute bacterial spinal epidural abscesses using computed tomography and nonsurgical treatment in selected patients. Ann Neurol 1985;17:350.

111. Mampalam TJ, Rosegay H, Andrews BT, Rosembaum ML, Pitts LH. Nonoperative treatment of spinal epidural infections. J Neurosurg 1989;71:208.

112. Post MJD, Quencer RM, Montalvo BM, Katz BH, Eismont FJ, Green BA. Spinal infection: Evaluation with MR imaging and intraoperative US. Radiology 1988;169:765.

113. Erntell M, Holtas S, Norlin K, Dahlquist E, Nilsson-Ehle I. Magnetic resonance imaging in the diagnosis of spinal epidural abscess. Scand J Infect Dis 1988;20:323.

114. Larsson EM, Holtas S, Cronquist S. Emergency mag-netic resonance examination of patients with spinal cord symptoms. Acta Radiol 1988;29:69.

115. Andrew ER. Perspectives in NMR imaging. In: Partain CL, James AE Jr, Rollo FD, Price RR. Nuclear magnetic resonance imaging. Philadelphia: WB Saunders, 1983:1.

116. The *Staphylococcus*. In: Brooks GF, Butel JS, Ornston LN, Jawetz E, Melnick JL, Adelberg EA, eds. Medical microbiology, 19th ed. Norwalk, CT: Appleton & Lange, 1991:194.

117. The streptococci. In: Brooks GF, Butel JS, Ornston LN, Jawetz E, Melnick JL, Adelber EA, eds. Medical microbiology. 19th ed. Norwalk, CT: Appleton & Lange, 1991:200.

CHAPTER 30

Obstetric Hemorrhage

Steven Goldberg
Mark C. Norris

Although rare, maternal death during childbirth still occurs. Maternal morbidity and mortality complicate approximately 5% of obstetric deliveries. Obstetric hemorrhage is responsible for about 75% of maternal complications during gestation. Life-threatening blood loss, (that requiring surgical intervention) arises in 0.05% to 0.1% of obstetric hemorrhages.[1]

One could organize a discussion of obstetric hemorrhage in any of the following ways:

- By the causes of hemorrhage
- By the setting of the event, either antepartum, intrapartum, or postpartum
- By management options

These divisions are artificial and potentially confusing. Hemorrhage from a particular cause can occur at many times throughout gestation. Also, blood loss from multiple sources can arise simultaneously. Management decisions by both the obstetrician and anesthesiologist are often subject to frequent and rapid reassessment of the clinical situation.

The obstetric management of active obstetric hemorrhage is straightforward and requires the following:

1. Maternal resuscitation
2. Delivery of the fetus
3. Removal of the placenta
4. Contraction of the uterus

5. Surgical repair of tissue laceration and restoration of anatomy

Continued in utero management of obstetric hemorrhage is primarily reserved for the mother who is clinical stable without active bleeding who has a preterm fetus with a reassuring fetal monitoring assessment.

The anesthetic management of obstetric bleeding focuses on maternal resuscitation, replacement of blood and blood products, and, when needed, provision of analgesia or anesthesia for delivery of the fetus or repair of tissue laceration. Key considerations include the following:

- Timing and circumstances surrounding the initial consultation. Specifically, does the clinical situation allow for an interview, intravenous access, initial laboratory studies, or placement of regional anesthesia?
- Time until and route of delivery
- Hemodynamic status of the mother

The goal of this chapter is to review obstetric hemorrhage and its management. By presenting the concerns of both the obstetrician and the anesthesiologist, we hope to simplify communication and joint management during these emergencies. Efficient, coherent care of these women should limit the potential maternal and fetal morbidity and mortality.

CLINICAL DEFINITION OF OBSTETRIC HEMORRHAGE

An obstetric hemorrhage has traditionally been defined as a blood loss of 500 mL after completion of the third stage of labor (ending with placenta delivery and uterine contraction).[2] However, the average blood loss with vaginal delivery is 500 mL (800–1000 mL at cesarean section) (Fig. 30-1). In addition, estimates of obstetric blood loss are notoriously inaccurate. Thus, the preceding definition of obstetric hemorrhage has limited clinical utility.

The gravida at term has an average increase in blood volume of 30% to 60% (1–2 L), so she tolerates considerable blood loss at delivery without a significant fall in hematocrit. After cesarean delivery in a sample population (average blood loss of 1000 mL), hematocrit changes little from predelivery values in spite of a fall in blood volume and total erythrocyte volume of nearly 25% (Fig. 30-2).[2] Despite this "reserve capacity," significant blood loss can arise rapidly. Approximately 600 mL/min of blood flows through the placenta and into the intervillous spaces.[3] Placental separation or removal abruptly severs the many arteries and veins carrying blood to and from this organ. Without rapid hemostasis and contraction of the uterus around these exposed vessels, continued profound blood loss occurs.

Baker[4,5] has described a method of assessing blood loss that was later adapted to the parturient (Table 30-1). This approach is based on the correlation between clinical findings and volume of blood lost. It offers a clinically useful method for estimating blood loss.

INITIAL EVALUATION

All patients admitted to Labor and Delivery at Thomas Jefferson University Hospital undergo an anesthesia interview. This discussion provides an opportunity to screen for risk factors for obstetric hemorrhage. A problem list or a prenatal history sheet often identifies medical, surgical, or obstetric conditions that predispose to hemorrhage (Table 30-2). Immediate problems of interest include antepartum bleeding, ultrasound evidence of a placenta previa, and placental location in patients with a previous cesarean section.

After completing the examination, consider making a (mental) risk assessment for obstetric hemorrhage. Although the assessment is artificial and not needed in entirety with each interview, Table 30-3 provides a model for evaluating all patients at risk for obstetric hemorrhage. After consultation with the obstetrician, the anesthesiologist can then formulate an appropriate plan for analgesia or anesthesia.

ANTEPARTUM HEMORRHAGE

Although most obstetric hemorrhages occur postpartum, bleeding can occur at any time during pregnancy. Placenta previa and abruptio placenta are the most likely causes of bleeding before term and account for two thirds of hemorrhages in the antepartum period.[6]

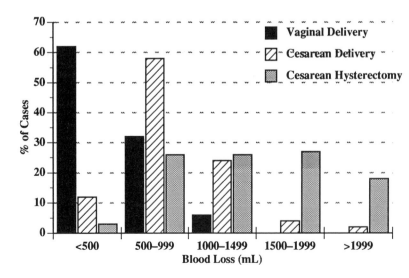

Figure 30–1. Blood loss associated with vaginal delivery, repeat cesarean section, and repeat cesarean section plus total hysterectomy. (After Prichard JA, Baldwin RM, Dickey JC, Wiggins KM, Reed GP, Bruce DM. Blood volume changes in pregnancy and the puerperium. Am J Obstet Gynecol 1962;84:1271)

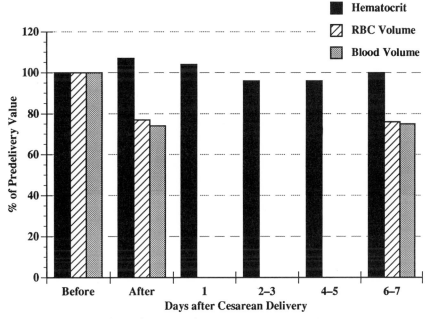

Figure 30–2. In a group of women undergoing cesarean section, the hematocrit postpartum changed insignificantly from the predelivery value in spite of an average blood loss of 1000 mL. At the same time, blood volume and total erythrocyte volume dropped nearly 25%. (Data from Prichard JA, Baldwin RM, Dickey JC, Wiggins KM, Reed GP, Bruce DM. Blood volume changes in pregnancy and the puerperium. Am J Obstet Gynecol 1962;84:1271)

Placenta Previa

The placenta usually implants well away from the lower uterine segment and high in the body or fundus of the uterus. Placenta previa is positioning of the placenta over or very near the cervical os. This condition is responsible for one third of antepartum hemorrhages.[7] The proximity of the placenta to the cervical os risks its disruption during cervical dilation, or a placenta previa could block the passage of the fetus through the birth canal. Placenta previa can be total (20%–43% of cases), partial (31%), or marginal (Fig. 30-3).[5,8] Placental separation often contributes to bleeding seen with a partial placenta previa. Placenta previa is often identified early in gestation by ultrasound. More than 90% of these will resolve by term.[9] This phenomenon, often called *placental migration,* does not represent separation and reattachment of the placenta at a more cephalad site. Instead, proportionally greater development of the fundus and body of the uterus during the second and third trimester pulls the placenta away from the cervical os. If a placenta previa is complete or persists after 37 weeks of gestation, it is not likely to resolve (Table 30-4). The incidence of placenta previa at delivery is 1/58 to 1/345.[10,11] Risk factors for placenta previa include the following:

- Previous cesarean delivery
- Multiparity
- Advanced maternal age
- Large placenta
- Previous placenta previa
- Other uterine surgery

The classic sign and symptom of placenta previa, painless vaginal bleeding appearing after the end of the second trimester, occurs in 90% of patients.[10] Thinning of the lower uterine segment and dilation of the internal os tears the placental attachments. Bleeding from exposed uterine vessels follows. The lower uterine segment cannot contract and compress the torn vessels, exacerbating the bleeding. The lower uterine segment (the site of implantation) contains significantly less contractile tissue (muscle) in comparison to the uterine fundus. It is less effective at compressing the extensive uterine vessels supplying the placenta. Placenta previa, then, increases the risk of both antepartum and postpartum hemorrhage.

Table 30–1

Classification of Hemorrhage in the 60-kg Gravida at 30 weeks' Gestation

CLASS	VOLUME LOST	CLINICAL FINDINGS
Modest bleeding	≤ 15% of blood volume (≤ 900 mL)	Mild tachycardia Variable pallor Normal blood pressure Normal respirations Negative capillary blanching test Negative tilt test Normal urine output
Moderate bleeding	20% to 25% of blood volume (1200–1500 mL)	Tachycardia (heart rate 110–130) Diastolic hypertension, decreased pulse pressure Moderate tachypnea Positive capillary blanching test Positive tilt test Urine output 25–40 mL/h
Severe bleeding	30%–35% of blood volume (1800–2100 mL)	Marked tachycardia (heart rate 120–160) Cold, clammy, pallid skin Hypotension Tachypnea (respirations 30–50/min) Oliguria
Massive bleeding	≥ 40% of blood volume (≥ 2400 mL)	Profound shock No peripheral blood pressure discernible (systolic blood pressure < 80 mm Hg) Peripheral pulses absent Marked tachycardia Circulatory collapse Oliguria or anuria

(After Baker RN. Evaluation and management of critically ill patients. In: Wynn RM, ed. Obstetrics and gynecology Annual: 1977. Vol 6. New York: Appleton-Century-Crofts, 1977:295, and Beneditti TJ. Obstetric hemorrhage. In: Gabbe SG, Niebyl JR, Simpson JL, eds. Obstetrics: Normal and problem pregnancies. 2nd ed. New York: Churchill Livingstone, 1991:573)

The accuracy of placental location by prenatal ultrasound approaches 98%.[2] Vaginal examination to confirm the diagnosis is rarely required. It is done, after a commitment to delivery is made, to distinguish a nonobstructing, low-lying placenta from a partial abruption. The examination is done in the operating room after preparations for cesarean section are made (double set-up). The double set-up was traditionally used, before the wide availability of ultrasound, to confirm the diagnosis of placenta previa. Although finding of a nonobstructing placenta usually allows for a trial of labor, the presence of a placenta previa requires a cesarean section.

Although the first bleeding episode of a placenta previa is usually small and stops spontaneously, 25% of patients present with symptomatic hypovolemia.[10] Before term, patients with placenta previa who are hemodynamically stable, are not actively bleeding, and are not in labor can be candidates for conservative (expectant) management. Ultimately, cesarean section is the accepted method of delivery in most cases of placenta previa. Blood loss varies and increases with the number of previous cesarean sections (Fig. 30-4). If the mother is bleeding, cesarean delivery is appropriate even in the presence of a dead fetus.

The prognosis with placenta previa is good, with rare maternal mortality. Fetal mortality is 4% to 8%.[12] Hemorrhage is most likely fatal when blood components are not immediately available. Coagulation defects characteristic of consumptive coagulopathy are rare, because factors likely to incite coagulopathy (*e.g.,* placental thromboplastin) pass per

Table 30-2

Conditions that Predispose to Obstetric Hemorrhage

Abnormal Placentation

Placenta previa
Abruptio placenta
Placenta accreta
Hydatidiform mole

Trauma During Labor and Delivery

Complicated vaginal delivery
Cesarean section or hysterectomy
Uterine rupture

Uterine Atony

Overdistended uterus
Multiple fetuses
Hydramnios
Distention with clots
Halogenated anesthetics
Previous uterine atony

Coagulation Defects (Intensifies Other Causes)

Placental abruption
Prolonged retention of dead fetus
Amniotic fluid embolism
Sepsis
Severe intravascular hemolysis
Massive transfusion
Severe preeclampsia and eclampsia
Congenital or acquired coagulopathies

(After Obstetric hemorrhage. In: Cunningham FG, MacDonald PC, Gant NF, eds. Williams Obstetrics, 18th ed. Norwalk, CT: Appleton & Lange, 1989:697)

vagina instead of entering the maternal system, as occurs with abruption.

Placenta Accreta, Increta, and Percreta

Placenta accreta, increta, and percreta are other types of abnormal placentation and are associated with catastrophic blood loss. Whereas *placenta previa* describes the abnormal location of the placenta, these terms describe placental implantation directly into the myometrium, without intervening endometrium. Lacking the natural endometrial cleavage plane, the placenta adheres to the uterine wall and cannot be removed without disruption of the myometrium. The degree of invasion into the myometrium gives rise to the dif-

ferent terms. Placenta accreta is implantation of the placenta on the myometrial surface. Placenta increta is implantation into the myometrium. Placenta percreta is invasion through the full thickness of the myometrium (Fig. 30-5).

These complications are rare, occurring in 1 in 2500 deliveries.[13] Abnormal implantation is more common in the presence of a placenta previa (1/26 cases). The incidence of accreta rises even higher if the placenta implants over a uterine scar.[14] Twenty-five percent to 31% of women with placenta previa and a previous cesarean section have a placenta accreta. The risk increases with the number of previous cesarean sections (Fig. 30-6).[15]

Obstetric management is individualized, with immediate hysterectomy traditionally associated with the least mortality. Operative blood loss and fluid requirements can be significant (see Fig. 30-4).[14] Indications for conservative (nonhysterectomy) management include partial accreta and blood loss less than 1750 mL. There is a higher risk for uterine rupture. The overall maternal mortality is 5%.[15]

Placental Abruption

Placental abruption (abruptio placentae) is the separation of a normally implanted placenta from the uterus before delivery of the infant. Separation allows bleeding into the layer (decidua basalis) between the placenta and myometrium. The decidual hematoma that develops isolates, compresses, and impairs the function of adjacent placental tissue. Continued bleeding from the decidual spiral arteries enlarges the hematoma. Maternal hemorrhage is varyingly concealed within the uterine cavity or passed per vagina (Fig. 30-7).

The past decade has seen an increasing association of placental abruption with maternal cocaine use.[16] Maternal risk factors include the following:

- Pregnancy-induced or chronic hypertension
- Trauma
- Short umbilical cord
- Sudden uterine decompression
- Multiparity
- Uterine abnormalities or tumors
- Cocaine
- Previous abruption

The most common risk factor is hypertension. One study of placental abruption associated with fetal death found a 50% correlation with hypertension.[17] Placental abruption complicates 1 in 37 to 1 in 500 deliveries.[2] It

Table 30–3

Assessment of Obstetric Hemorrhage

Hemodynamic Status of Mother

Vital signs

Response to position change ("tilt test")

Appearance (skin turgor, color of conjunctiva, etc.)

Evidence of, or Potential for, Ongoing Hemorrhage

Medical (idiopathic thrombocytopenic purpura, von Willebrand's disease, heparin therapy, etc.)

Surgical (trauma)

Obstetric (placenta previa, hydramnios, multiple gestation, etc.)

Need for Transfusion

Vital signs

Hemoglobin/hematocrit

Fetal condition

Coagulation Status

Prothrombin time, partial thromboplastin time, fibrinogen

Platelet count, bleeding time

Clinical signs of bleeding

Need for Invasive Monitoring

Maternal condition

Risk of ongoing blood loss

Need for Vasopressor Agents

Vital signs

Maternal symptoms (nausea, light-headedness, etc.)

Fetal condition

New Problem Development

(*e.g.*, acute tubular necrosis, acute respiratory distress syndrome)

Fetal Status

Fetal heart rate pattern

Acid–base balance

occurs most often in the third trimester; half the episodes arise after 36 weeks of gestation.

The diagnosis of abruption is based primarily on clinical signs and symptoms. The presentation varies, but it is classically described as painful vaginal bleeding. Ultrasound may identify a retroplacental clot in the uterine cavity, yet the absence of clot does not exclude a severe abruption. The amount of blood loss, percentage of functioning placenta, and development of coagulopathy affect the severity of clinical presentation. Blood loss is usually underestimated. The amount of blood passed vaginally may often mislead. The uterus can hide significant blood loss without maternal evidence of hypotension or anemia. The more concealed the bleeding, the greater the risk of coagulopathy. Mild or moderate abruption comprises 85% to

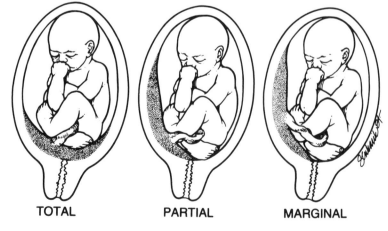

TOTAL   PARTIAL   MARGINAL

Figure 30–3. Three variations of placenta previa. (Gabbe SG, Niebyl JR, Simpson JL, eds. Obstetrics: Normal and problem pregnancies. 2nd ed. New York: Churchill Livingstone, 1991:585)

Table 30–4

Sonographic Identification of Placenta Previa and Subsequent Clinical Disease

GESTATIONAL AGE AT TIME OF SONOGRAPHY (WKS)	PLACENTA PREVIA OR HEMORRHAGE AT DELIVERY (%)
< 20	2.3
20–25	3.2
25–30	5.2
30–35	23.9
> 37	90

(Data from Comeau J, Shaw L, Marcell CC, Lavery JP. Early placenta previa and delivery outcome. Obstet Gynecol 1983;61:577, and Rizos N, Doran T, Mikskin M, et al. Natural history of placenta previa ascertained by diagnostic ultrasound. Am J Obstet Gynecol 1979;133:287)

90% of cases and correlates with good neonatal outcome.[18] Maternal hypotension and coagulopathy are characteristics of severe abruption and are poor prognostic indicators. Continued blood loss with extravasation of blood, placental tissue, and amniotic fluid into the systemic circulation may cause systemic clotting abnormalities and consumptive coagulopathy. These problems complicate up to 50% of abruptions.[18]

The definitive management of placental abruption is to empty the uterus. If the mother is hemodynamically stable without evidence of active bleeding or coagulopathy, and the fetal condition is reassuring, a conservative approach may be chosen and is favored for a viable preterm fetus. Continued surveillance of the mother and fetus is critical. Sholl[19] conservatively managed women with gestations of 26 to 37 weeks. Half the patients delivered within 3 days of admission because of progression to serious hemorrhage or fetal distress. These patients, interestingly, did not require an increased frequency of cesarean section than did those managed for longer intervals. Controversy surrounds tocolysis for uterine hypertonus or preterm contractions with the diagnosis of abruption. Vaginal delivery is preferred for fetal death.

Immediate cesarean section is indicated either for a viable distressed fetus remote from delivery or maternal evidence of continued bleeding, hypovolemia, or disseminated intravascular coagulation (DIC). Placental abruption can occur just before birth. Management decisions are most difficult when delivery is imminent in the presence of maternal bleeding or fetal distress. Under these circumstances, options for delivery include operative vaginal delivery (forceps, vacuum) or emergent cesarean section. Extravasation of blood into the uterus (Couvelaire uterus) can predispose to uterine atony. Resuscitation of the mother occurs with preparation for delivery.

Prognosis varies with the severity of abruption. Maternal mortality is between 1% and 5%. Fetal mortality with vaginal delivery is 19% to 67%; with cesarean section, it is 8% to 22%.[20,21] Some have identified neurologic sequelae in infants surviving placental abruption.[22] The incidence of maternal coagulopathy is as high as 50%. The recurrence risk is 1 in 6 to 1 in 25.[2]

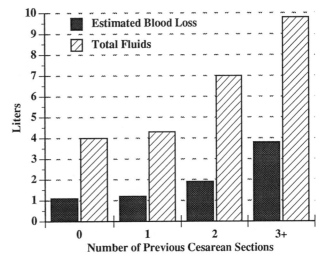

Figure 30–4. Intraoperative blood loss and fluid requirements in parturients with placenta previa undergoing cesarean section. Patients with previous cesarean deliveries were more likely to require hysterectomy for placenta accreta. (After Arcario T, Greene M, Ostheimer GW, Datta S, Naulty JS. Risks of placenta previa/accreta in patients with previous cesarean deliveries. Anesthesiology 1988;69: A659)

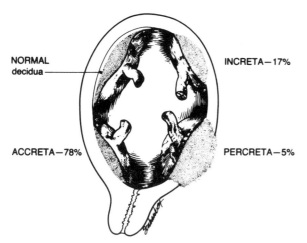

NORMAL
decidua

INCRETA—17%

ACCRETA—78%

PERCRETA—5%

Figure 30–5. Uteroplacental relationships found in abnormal placentation. (Gabbe SG, Niebyl JR Simpson JL, eds. Obstetrics: Normal and problem pregnancies. 2nd ed. New York: Churchill Livingstone, 1991:588)

Uterine Rupture

Uterine rupture involves any disruption of the uterine cavity. There are, however, two clinical entities with significantly different prognoses. One involves the dehiscence ("incomplete rupture") of a uterine scar, most commonly in a patient with a previous cesarean section. The other, much more catastrophic, is the complete rupture of an unscarred uterus, from obstetric or other causes.[23,24]

The lower uterine segment at term consists predominantly of connective tissue and is not near vascular uterine beds or placenta. Therefore, dehiscence of a low transverse uterine scar often incites very little bleeding. In contrast, with the intense blood supply to the body of uterus and surrounding tissues, complete rupture is potentially catastrophic and accounts for one third of hemorrhage-related maternal morbidity.[25] True uterine rupture is rare (1 in 1500 deliveries). Risk factors are those that predispose to a "weakened" uterine wall and encompass the following:

- Grand multiparity
- Uterine distention with macrosomia or hydramnios
- Dysfunctional or precipitous labor
- Previous uterine scars from cesarean section, curettage, or myomectomy
- Infection
- Adenomyosis or trophoblastic invasion (placenta accreta)
- Forceps application
- Excessive fundal pressure

Complete rupture most likely occurs during labor. Only 4.3% of cases happened before labor in one large series.[24] Thirty-five percent of cases are recognized before delivery, 20% at emergency cesarean section, and 45% after vaginal delivery.[26] Signs and symptoms of uterine rupture include the following:

- Severe constant abdominal pain
- Hypotension
- Bradycardia

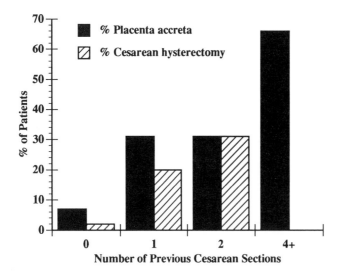

Figure 30–6. The incidence of placenta accreta in parturients with placenta previa. Only 7% of women who have a previa with no uterine scar have placenta accreta. In contrast, a pre-existing uterine scar markedly increases the risk of accreta should the placenta implant over the scar. (Data from Arcario T, Greene M, Ostheimer GW, Datta S, Naulty JS. Risks of placenta previa/accreta in patients with previous cesarean deliveries. Anesthesiology 1988; 69:A659 and Clark SL, Koonings PP, Phelan JP. Placenta previa/accreta and prior cesarian section. Obstet Gynecol 1985;66:89)

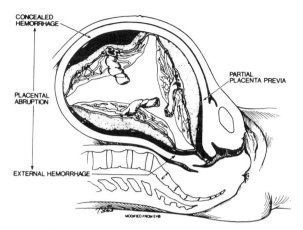

Figure 30–7. Hemorrhage from premature placental separation. (*Upper left*) Extensive placental abruption with the periphery of the placenta and the membranes still adherent to the endometrium. Hemorrhage is completely concealed. (*Lower left*) Placental abruption with the placenta detached peripherally and with the membranes between the placenta and cervical canal stripped from the underlying decidua. External hemorrhage follows. (*Right*) Partial placenta previa with placental separation and external hemorrhage. (Cunningham FG, MacDonald PC, Gant NF, eds. Williams' Obstetrics. 18th ed. Norwalk, CT: Appleton & Lange, 1989:702)

- Cessation of uterine contractions
- Fetal distress or arrest

Maternal mortality after scar dehiscence is very rare. In contrast, rupture of an intact uterus has proved lethal in 4% of cases.[24] Outcome worsens with delayed therapy. Fetal mortality is 50% to 75% with uterine rupture.[27] Fetal compromise is much less frequent with scar dehiscence, with mortality estimated at 1 in 1000.[28] With uterine rupture, fetal death is often rapid.

The treatment is emergent laparotomy with uterine repair and, often, postpartum hysterectomy. The abdomen may hold 2 to 3.5 L of blood after catastrophic uterine rupture.[25] Resuscitation centers on volume and blood replacement.

FETAL HEMORRHAGE

Fetal hemorrhage is a rare event and poses no threat to the mother. However, because its occurrence can alter obstetric management, a brief discussion is included.

The fetus at term has a blood volume of 78 mL/kg, or approximately 300 mL.[29] A loss of 30 to 40 mL may produce evidence of fetal stress. A loss of 100 mL is life-threatening. Fetal blood loss most often occurs into the maternal circulation. Although microscopic bleeding is common with delivery, more extensive loss is rare. Loss of up to 10 mL happens in 1 in 200 to 1 in 714 births.[30] Life-threatening hemorrhage (greater than 150 mL) complicates 1 in 800 births.[31] Possible causes of fetal hemorrhage are as follows:

- Scalp sampling
- Forceps delivery
- Umbilical cord trauma
- Medical conditions (von Willebrand's disease, ideopathic thrombocytopenic purpura)
- Velamentous insertion of the umbilical cord
- Vasa previa

Umbilical cord trauma and vasa previa can lead to rapid exsanguination.

Umbilical cord trauma can occur with a "velamentous insertion" of the umbilical cord. In this situation, umbilical vessels travel to the fetus from the placenta within the thin membrane of the amniotic sac instead of the cushioning, protective Wharton's jelly of the umbilical cord. The vessels are much more susceptible to trauma with labor and delivery. This abnormality is variable in its degree. It is more common in multiple gestations.

Vasa previa, "vessels going ahead," describes velamentous insertion of the umbilical cord in front of the presenting part of the fetus. The diagnosis is made upon palpation of pulsatile vessels in an unruptured sac during vaginal exam. The condition is most often diagnosed accidentally with elective rupture of the membranes. Tragically, perinatal mortality with rupture is 75% to 100%.[32] Signs include fetal bradycardia and hemorrhage. Treatment involves immediate delivery, usually by emergent cesarean section. When the diagnosis is entertained in the setting of a less vigorous bleed, testing of vaginal blood will detect fetal hemoglobin.[33] Fetal salvage requires a high index of suspicion, with plans for infant volume resuscitation at delivery.

ANESTHETIC MANAGEMENT OF THE BLEEDING PARTURIENT

Normal Cesarean Section

Although variable, the incidence of cesarean section in North America is 15% to 20%.[34] Most cesarean deliveries occur via a transverse incision in the lower cervical segment of the uterus (low transverse cervical segment or Monroe–Kerr incision). If the pregnancy is at term or the patient has labored, this segment is usually thin. Also, it has less muscle than the uterine corpus. These factors limit surgical blood loss.

The average blood loss for an elective low transverse cervical segment cesarean section is 800 to 1200 mL, approximately 10% to 15% of circulating blood volume of the normal parturient at term. The pregnant woman can lose more than 1 L of blood without a drop in hematocrit (Fig. 30-1).[2] In one large series of high-risk patients, significant hemorrhage, defined either as a 10% fall in hematocrit or the need for blood transfusion, complicated 6.4% of cesarean deliveries.[35] Risk factors for significant hemorrhage include the following:

- General anesthesia
- Amnionitis
- Preeclampsia
- Protracted active phase of labor
- Second-stage arrest of labor
- Hispanic ethnicity.[34]

Incisions into an unlabored lower segment or into the corpus of the uterus; lacerations of the uterus, cervix, or broad ligament; and uterine atony increase blood loss.

Anesthesia for the Parturient at Risk for Hemorrhage

Assessment

When planning an anesthetic for a gravida at risk for significant blood loss, consider the urgency of the clinical situation as well as the patient's current volume status. The clinical presentation of placenta previa and placental abruption varies. A woman may present at term for elective cesarean section, or, at the other extreme, a parturient may arrive with acute, severe bleeding and be carrying a gravely compromised fetus. Close communication with the obstetrician aids in initial assessment.

Careful assessment of blood loss and current volume status are important steps in formulating an anesthetic plan. Patients who are significantly hypovolemic or who are still bleeding are poor candidates for regional anesthesia. On the other hand, if the woman is stable, well hydrated, and has little or no active bleeding, regional block may be an appropriate technique. Women with placental abruption also may have coagulation abnormalities.

Preparation

Check the availability of blood and blood products. When anesthetizing women with placenta previa or suspected placenta accreta, have 2 to 4 units of packed red blood cells immediately available. Even stable parturients presenting for elective cesarean delivery because of placenta previa can have significant, rapid hemorrhage. Insert two large-bore intravenous catheters to allow rapid fluid resuscitation. Warming blood and intravenous fluids will help maintain temperature stability. Having extra personnel available to help may prove life-saving.

Management

Either regional or general anesthesia is appropriate for elective or urgent cesarean delivery in a hemodynamically stable mother. Appreciate that sympathectomy induced by regional block does impair the mother's ability to cope with sudden hypovolemia. However, many experts consider regional anesthesia an appropriate choice for parturients with placenta previa or at high risk for placenta accreta.[36] For short periods of hypovolemia, intermittent boluses of ephedrine or phenylephrine should be adequate treatment. If blood loss and hypotension persist, a continuous infusion of epinephrine or norepinephrine can be titrated to maintain maternal blood pressure. Use maternal symptoms (*i.e.*, nausea, lightheadedness) to guide therapy. In addition, if cesarean hysterectomy becomes necessary, the operation may outlast a single-injection spinal anesthetic. Plan ahead. If needed, induce general anesthesia in a calm, controlled manner. Do not wait until the block has significantly regressed and the patient is suffering severe pain. Continuous spinal or continuous epidural block is an appropriate alternative if you suspect a prolonged procedure at the outset.

In some clinical situations, general anesthesia is the only safe choice. Actively bleeding, hypovolemic parturients can develop profound hypotension with regional anesthesia. Women with chronic abruption and significant coagulopathy should not receive regional block. If the maternal or fetal condition mandates immediate delivery (within 10 minutes), general anesthesia also may be the best choice.

The choice of induction agent depends on volume status. A reduced dose of thiopental ($\leq$ 3 mg/kg) or ketamine (0.8–10 mg/kg) is a safe choice in moderately hypovolemic women.[25] In the severely compromised parturient, muscle relaxant alone may be the only safe choice. Ketamine causes central nervous system–mediated catecholamine release. In most hypo-volemic patients, this effect supports heart rate and blood pressure; however, peripheral vasoconstriction may have reached its maximum in a severely volume-depleted patient. In this situation, ketamine cannot induce further vasoconstriction, and its cardiac depressant effects can result in hypotension and potentially cardiac arrest.[37] The remainder of a rapid sequence induction, including application of cricoid pressure, succinylcholine (1–2 mg/kg IV), and endotracheal intubation, proceeds as usual.

Ongoing Hemorrhage

Operative management (Fig. 30-8) begins with identifying the source of bleeding. Uterine atony, uterine lacerations, and injury to vessel supply of the uterus, broad ligament, or other structures can all produce rapid hemorrhage. If a laceration of the uterus or otherwise is identified, it is repaired. In the absence of lacerations, uterine atony responds to massage and contractile agents (Table 30-5). Continued bleeding from the myometrial surface, despite removal of all membrane and adequate massage, is due to atony or surface disruption (*i.e.,* placenta accreta). Initial surgical options aim at decreasing uterine artery perfusion pressure to facilitate hemostasis. Choices include uterine artery ligation[38] and hypogastric (internal iliac) artery ligation.[39,40] "Packing" the uterus is effective only in cases of confined, continued lower-segment bleeding.[41] In the face of severe ongoing or life-threatening hemorrhage, the obstetrician must consider hysterectomy (Table 30-6).[42] If hysterectomy fails to control bleeding, the few options that remain include arterial embolization[43] and pelvic packing of the vaginal cuff.[44] Keep the obstetrician advised about the patient's hemodynamic status. This information is helpful when deciding among surgical alternatives.

POSTPARTUM HEMORRHAGE

Blood loss greater than 500 mL constitutes postpartum hemorrhage. Other authorities consider a 10% decrease in hematocrit or blood loss requiring a transfusion as hemorrhage.[45] Using these criteria, hemorrhage complicates 3.9% of vaginal deliveries.[45] In descending order of frequency, the following factors raise the risk of significant blood loss after vaginal delivery:[45]

1. Prolonged third stage of labor
2. Preeclampsia
3. Mediolateral episiotomy
4. Previous postpartum hemorrhage
5. Twin pregnancy
6. Arrest of descent
7. Soft tissue lacerations
8. Augmented labor
9. Forceps or vacuum delivery
10. Asian or Hispanic descent
11. Midline episiotomy
12. Multiparity

Multiple factors can simultaneously cause bleeding after delivery in a given patient. Diagnosis and treatment of hemorrhage after vaginal delivery requires a cooperative, comfortable patient. The obstetric anesthesiologist may be called upon to monitor such a patient or provide varying degrees of analgesia and, occasionally, anesthesia.

Once consulted, approach the patient in an orderly fashion. Confirm or establish adequate intravenous access. Initiate fluid replacement with crystalloids. Place the appropriate monitoring devices. Determine the availability of blood products. Assess the amount of blood loss and maternal volume status (especially important if considerable time has passed since delivery). Discuss the situation with the obstetrician; focus on the cause of the blood loss, the prognosis for its continuing, and treatment plans. The need for anesthesia and analgesia will depend on the answers to these questions.

Anesthesia for Vaginal Exam and Repair

Perineal and Distal Vaginal Anesthesia

Submucosal lesions involving the distal vagina, vestibule, or perineum usually can be repaired with local infiltration. For more extensive perineal lacerations (of the external and sphincter or rectal mucosa), bilateral pudendal blocks using 20 mL of local anesthetic may be chosen.[46] If already in place, an epidural or spinal catheter also can provide analgesia for hemorrhage evaluation and repair; however, they produce sympathectomy and loss of vasomotor tone in the affected areas and may impair the normal vasoconstrictor response to hemorrhage. Thus, major regional anesthesia is relatively contraindicated in the actively bleeding patient and absolutely contraindicated in the presence of uncorrected hypovolemia. Inhaled nitrous oxide in oxygen or intravenous opioid also can provide analgesia for exam (but not repair).

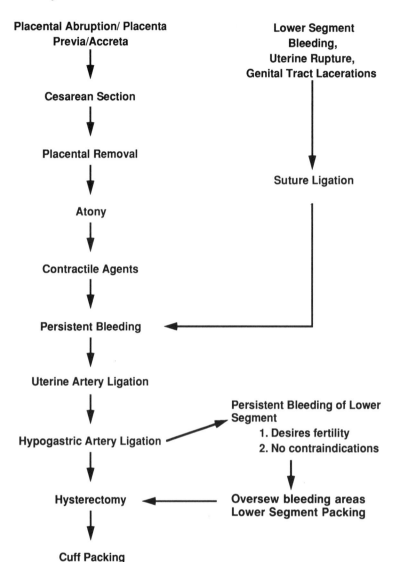

Figure 30–8. Flow chart for the obstetric management of persistent bleeding at delivery. (After Druzin ML. Packing of the lower uterine segment for control of post cesarean bleeding in instances of placenta previa. Surg Gynecol Obstet 1989;169:543, by permission of Surgery, Gynecology & Obstetrics)

Proximal Vagina, Cervix, and Uterine Anesthesia

Examination of the proximal vagina, cervix, and uterus is potentially difficult and painful. Additional assistants are needed for retraction to visualize the superior parts of the vagina. Stretching and distention of the cervix or uterus with manipulation produces pain. Patients with spinal, lumbar, epidural, or caudal block to at least T-10 often need no further anesthesia. Despite an intact block, additional analgesia or anesthesia may be required depending on the skill of the examiner, adequacy of the block, and sensitivity of the patient. Options include inhaled nitrous oxide, 40% to 50%, in oxygen, intravenous opioid, or ketamine. More extensive examination might require general endotracheal anesthesia.

Uterine Atony, Lacerations, Retained Placenta, and Uterine Inversion

Uterine Atony

Normally, the uterus contracts as the placenta delivers. The myometrium compresses the spiral arteries and rapidly stops the flow of blood. Failure of the uterus to contract (atony) can allow rapid maternal hemorrhage.

Table 30-5

Uterine Contractile Agents

DRUG	DOSE	CONTRAINDICATIONS	SIDE EFFECTS	FREQUENCY	TOTAL DOSE
Oxytocin	10 μ/min IV, 10 μ IM or intramyometrially	Hypotension	Hypotension, antidiresis		
Ergonovine maleate	0.2 mg IM or intramyometrially	Hypersensitivity, hypertension, sepsis	Nausea, vomiting, hypertension, headache	q 2–4 h	1 mg
15-methyl prostaglandin F$_{2\alpha}$	250 μg IV, IM, or intramyometrially	Asthma	Nausea, vomiting, diarrhea, fever, hypotension	q 1.5–3.5 h	12 mg

Blood loss can exceed 2000 mL in less than 5 minutes.[47] Uterine atony is the most common cause of obstetric hemorrhage, complicating 4% to 5% of deliveries.[48] Risk factors for uterine atony are those contributing to ineffective myometrial contraction (Table 30-7). General causes include overdistention of the uterus, use of tocolytic or contractile agents, and disruption of myometrial fibers.

The diagnosis is made by palpating an atonic uterus and observing "excess" vaginal bleeding. Management begins with external massage of the uterus. Internal (bimanual) massage allows for uterine exploration and clot removal. In the absence of lacerations or retained placenta, additional management options include administration of contractile agents. When mechanical and pharmacologic intervention fail, the obstetrician proceeds to laparotomy (see Fig. 30-8).

Lacerations

Lacerations after a vaginal delivery are most often caused by shear forces against the mucosa and soft tissue of the birth canal with passage of the fetus. They rarely produce major hemorrhage. Other causes of obstetric lacerations include the following:

- Valsalva against closed cervix
- Macrosomia
- Excess manipulation
- Precipitous cervix dilation or delivery
- Forceps or vacuum-extractor injury
- Dehiscence of cesarean section scar

With the increased vascularity of the perineum, cervix, and uterus, significant blood loss can transpire over a short period. Exploration of the vagina, cervix,

Table 30-6

Indications for Emergency Obstetric Hysterectomy

DIAGNOSIS	PERCENT OF CASES
Ruptured uterus	53.8
Intractable postpartum hemorrhage	20.5
Placenta accreta	7.7
Placenta previa	7.7
Hemorrhage at cesarean section	4.5
Couvelaire uterus	< 1
Abdominal pregnancy	< 1

(Data from Al-Sibai MH, Rahman J, Rahman MS, Butalack F. Emergency hysterectomy in obstetrics—a review of 117 cases. Aust NZ J Obstet Gynaecol 1987;27:180)

Table 30-7

Risk Factors for Uterine Atony

Dysfunctional labor
Multiple gestations
Macrosomia
Hydramnios
Precipitous delivery
Previous atony
Placental abruption (Couvelaire uterus)
Tocolytic or contractile agents
Retained placenta
Operative intervention (internal version and extraction for malpresentation)
Infection (chorioamnionitis)

and, when indicated, lower uterine segment is difficult to do in the unanesthetized patient. Actively bleeding lesions require surgical repair. The obstetrician needs assistance with retraction, good lighting, and a comfortable, cooperative patient.

Retained Placenta

Retention of the placenta in situ beyond 30 minutes after delivery is abnormal and occurs in 1 in 300 vaginal births.[48] If all or part of the placenta remains within the uterus, it prevents contraction, inciting atony and ongoing blood loss. The initial procedure of choice for removal of the intact in situ placenta is its manual extraction. Before attempting extraction, some suggest the use of intra-umbilical vein oxytocin to contract the placenta off the uterine wall.[49] Good maternal analgesia, either with systemic medications or regional block, eases manual removal of the placenta.

If the uterus or cervix is firmly contracted, inhibiting removal of the placenta, uterine relaxation is required. This task can be done under general endotracheal anesthesia. Do a rapid sequence induction and intubate the trachea. Then, administer a potent inhalation agent in oxygen to provide uterine relaxation. All potent agents produce significant uterine relaxation in concentrations above 0.5 MAC. Higher concentrations (2 MAC) also block the response to oxytocin infusion.[50] Inhaled anesthetics produce rapid relaxation that abates rapidly when withdrawn. Turn off the agent once the uterus relaxes enough to allow exam and placental removal. Begin oxytocin infusion immediately after removal of the placenta. Nitroglycerin offers an alternative to general anesthesia for many of these patients. In one series, nitroglycerin (50 to 100 µg IV) provided rapid, short-lived uterine relaxation in 22 parturients.[51]

If, after removal is attempted, placental fragments remain or active bleeding persists, the risk of significant morbidity increases. The most common cause of this scenario is a form of placenta accreta. Obstetric management at this point proceeds with repeat attempts at manual removal and possible curettage. If hemostasis is achieved after maximal debulking, modest accretas are best managed expectantly. More severe myometrial invasion with continued hemorrhage requires exploratory laparotomy (see Fig. 30-8).

Uterine Inversion

Uterine inversion involves the collapse of the fundus into the body of the uterus. The (endometrial) placental surface becomes the most caudal part of the uterus (and is potentially visible per vagina). The incidence is 1 in 1700 deliveries.[52] Although it can occur spontaneously, uterine inversion most commonly follows manual traction on the umbilical cord.[53] If uncorrected, exsanguination follows as bleeding continues. Management requires prompt reversion. Firm pressure against the fundus by a hand in the vagina usually succeeds.

Previously established regional block can ease this process. Other anesthetic options include nitrous oxide and intravenous sedation, or general endotracheal anesthesia. The uterus usually can be reduced without active relaxation.

If the uterus has contracted in an inverted position, uterine relaxation is required and is classically achieved with halothane anesthesia.[25] Again, any potent agent will work. [Editor's Note: My one attempt to use intravenous nitroglycerin in this situation did not succeed.] Failed vaginal correction requires prompt laparotomy for replacement of the uterus to an intraperitoneal position.

Distant or Secondary Postpartum Hemorrhage

Distant postpartum hemorrhage is not a strictly defined entity. Excessive bleeding more than 6 to 12 hours after delivery through to the 6-week postpartum examination usually qualifies. King *et al*[54] identified 83 cases of secondary postpartum hemorrhage with bleeding occurring most frequently between the 8th and 14th day after delivery. Seventy-three percent of the patients had been discharged and required readmission. Suction evacuation was performed in 72 of the patients and stopped the bleeding in all patients. Interestingly, histology confirmed retained gestational products in only 42%. No predictive factors for either distant postpartum hemorrhage or for retained products were identified.[54]

COAGULOPATHY AND DISSEMINATED INTRAVASCULAR COAGULATION

This section focuses on mechanisms, diagnosis, and management of coagulopathy as they occur in relation to obstetric hemorrhage. Disturbance of clotting with hemorrhage most commonly occurs in association with inadequate surgical hemostasis. Normally, the following four components interact to allow localized clot formation at the local site of vascular injury:

- Vessel factors
- Platelet function
- The coagulation system
- Clot lysis

In obstetrics, disseminated intravascular circulation (DIC) may involve any of the four mechanisms involved in the coagulation process. Activation of the coagulation cascade through the extrinsic system by introduction of large amounts of tissue phospholipids (thromboplastin) into the maternal vascular system is a common stimulus for DIC in obstetrics. Conditions that can incite DIC include the following:

- Retained dead fetus
- Amniotic fluid embolism
- Most commonly, placental abruption. (Conservatively, 10%–30% of patients with this diagnosis have some degree of coagulation disturbance.)[48]

Placental abruption may induce maternal coagulopathy by enhancing entry of decidual placental thromboplastin into the maternal circulation. Thromboplastin then activates the extrinsic clotting pathway generating thrombin.[25] Thrombin acts on fibrinogen to generate fibrin. Fibrin diffusely deposits in the microcirculation, resulting in DIC. This process breeds hypofibrinogenemia, and the consumption of platelets and clotting factors V and VIII. Subsequently, plasmin degrades the fibrin clots, yielding fibrin split products. These compounds have their own physiologic activity, which inhibits fibrin cross-linking and induces platelet dysfunction. The net result of factor consumption, fibrin disruption, and platelet disfunction occurring diffusely in the vasculature is maternal bleeding.[5,55]

Other causes of coagulopathy in obstetrics include infections that lead to bacteremia and septic shock. Septic abortion, antepartum pyelonephritis, and puerperal sepsis are most common. Bacterial endotoxins initiate intrinsic clotting through activation of factor XII or extrinsic clotting through release of thromboplastic activity from leukocytes.[56]

Evidence of delayed hemostasis or bleeding from unexpected sites, such as the gums or intravenous entry, in the appropriate clinical setting suggests the diagnosis of DIC.[55] A delayed or nonclotting sample of blood, placed in a clear glass tube, make a preliminary diagnosis. Laboratory evidence of abnormal coagulation, such as low platelets, low fibrinogen, and elevated fibrin split products, partial thromboplastin time, and prothrombin time in the clinical setting are sufficient for diagnosis.[55] Treatment begins with removing the initiating agent. Coagulation disturbances most often develop rapidly after the acute inciting episode and resolve after correction of the initial stimulus. In some settings (*i.e.,* sepsis, amniotic fluid embolus), DIC may persist.

Treat by replacing coagulation factors. Use the results of coagulation studies to guide therapy. Heparin therapy, although occasionally suggested, is of no proven benefit. In the immediate postdelivery period, heparin may worsen blood loss from the uterus or surgical sites.

Although the overall prognosis is good, hypovolemic shock associated with DIC may initiate other problems. Acute tubular necrosis and Sheehan's syndrome (hypoperfusion and posthemorrhagic necrosis of the anterior pituitary) have been reported.[57]

BLOOD AND BLOOD PRODUCTS

Autologous Blood Donation

Autologous blood donation conserves blood-product resources and may avoid the significant morbidity risk associated with a volunteer donor pool. Only with sufficient use is this option cost-effective for patients. In obstetrics, even the identification of risk factors for obstetric hemorrhage has proved a poor predictor of the need for transfusion with delivery. A large study in a high-risk population found a transfusion rate of 0.57%. Sixty-three percent of these women lacked risk factors for obstetric hemorrhage.[58] Therefore, programs for autologous blood donation from parturients at risk for obstetric hemorrhage may not prove cost-effective. Selective use in patients with placenta previa may be the one exception to this conclusion.[58]

Transfusion of Blood Products

Guidelines regarding the indications and amounts of products for transfusion vary between institutions. No specific guidelines are available for managing hemorrhage in the obstetric patient. In Tables 30-8 and 30-9, we offer guidelines for transfusion compiled from review of several sources, including the Technical Bulletin on Blood Component Therapy from the American College of Obstetrics and Gynecology,[59] Thomas

(text continues on page 596)

Table 30-8

Guidelines for Transfusion of Blood and Blood Products*

PRODUCT	CONTENTS	VOLUME	INDICATIONS	DOSAGE	COST
Whole blood	Red and white blood cells, co-agulation fac-tors (50% factor V, 50% factor VIII after 7 d), plasma proteins	500 mL	Hypovolemia due to blood loss with hypotension and tachycardia, or a 20% blood loss; symptomatic defi-cit in oxygen-carrying capaci-ty combined with hypovolemia and shock; im-mediate transfusion in an un-known blood type warrants type (O, Rh-negative blood	To achieve suffi-cient oxygen-carrying capaci-ty (hemoglobin of 7–9 mg/dL)	$54.00/unit
Red blood cells	Red blood cells, usual hematocrit of 65%–80%; white blood cells, less than whole blood	240–300 mL	1. Hypovolemia due to blood loss in patients with a symp-tomatic deficit of oxygen-carrying capacity 2. Hemoglobin < 10% or hematocrit < 30% with symptoms of anemia or be-fore surgery 3. With evidence of hemor-rhage in conjunction with crystalloid solution to main-tain hematocrit about 7–9 mg/dL and urine output be-tween 30 and 60 mL/h	One unit increases hemoglobin 1 g/dL and hematocrit 2–3% for a 70-kg adult.	$106.00/unit
Fresh frozen plasma	The fluid portion of 1 unit of human blood, centri-fuged, separat-ed, and frozen solid within 6 h of collection	250 mL	1. Congenital coagulation fac-tor deficiency in factors V, VII, IX, XI, and XIII 2. Acquired coagulation factor deficiencies with bleeding and failure to respond to vitamin K (PT > 16 s, PT ratio > 1.5, or APTT > 60 s) 3. Preoperative patients with or without bleeding and post-operative patients with PT ratio > 1.3 4. Blood loss > than 1 blood volume in an adult within 24 h	At least 2 units. After transfusion of 4–5 units of PRBC, if PT/PTT abnormal, give 1 unit FFP/4 units PRBC. One unit increases fi-brinogen 10 mg/dL	$55.00/unit
Cryopre-cipitate	Fibrinogen (usually 150 mg), factor VIII (> 80 units), and von Willebrand's factor; poor source of fac-tors II, V, IX, X, XI, and XII	15–40 mL	1. Patients with factor VIII defi-ciency due to hemophilia A or von Willebrand's disease 2. Active bleeding in patients with primary hypofibrinogenemia 3. Blood loss of greater than 1 blood volume in an adult within 24 h	Average dose at TJUH: 10 units. More specific dosage calcula-tions in the American Red Cross Circular of Information, February 15, 1991.	$35.00/unit

(continued)

Table 30–8

(Continued)

PRODUCT	CONTENTS	VOLUME	INDICATIONS	DOSAGE	COST
Platelets	55×10^6 platelets/unit	50 mL	1. Less than 30,000 platelets/mm³, 30,000–80,000 platelets/mm³ with bleeding, before surgery or with platelet dysfunction 2. Evidence of hemodilution coagulopathy caused by a blood loss > 1 blood volume in an adult within 24 h	Usually given in 6-unit doses. Each unit raises the platelet count by 7,000–10,000 platelets/uL.	$55.00/unit

Abbreviations: APTT = activated partial thromboplastin time, FFP = fresh frozen plasma, PRBC = packed red blood cells, PT = prothrombin time, PTT = partial thromboplastin time, TJUH = Thomas Jefferson University Hospital.
*Platelet notes: Following replacement of 1 blood volume, 35% to 40% of the platelets usually remain. Accelerated platelet destruction, which sometimes occurs in bleeding patients, accentuated thrombocytopenia. Monitor platelet count frequently to guide therapy.

Table 30–9

Fresh Frozen Plasma Versus Cryoprecipitate

	FRESH FROZEN PLASMA	CRYOPRECIPITATE
Advantages	Greater concentration of factor VIII Larger volume Only source of factors V, XI, and XII	Allows rapid infusion of fibrinogen Smaller volume
Monitoring	If persistent bleeding after transfusion of 4–5 units of PRBC, check coagulation studies. If PT, PTT abnormal, give 1 unit of FFP for every 4 units transfused PRBC.	Periodic PT, PTT, and fibrinogen
Use	Massive hemorrhage/replacement Those on warfarin, bleeding before surgery Disseminated intravascular coagulation	Rarely used in obstetric hemorrhage. Consider in massive hemorrhage requiring rapid infusion of fibrinogen and clotting factors, or when patient is refractory to FFP infusion. Disseminated intravascular coagulation (controversial)
Disadvantages		Multiple donors/unit; significantly higher risk of disease transmission
Notes	Nonsurgical bleeding in the patient receiving massive transfusion is caused more frequently by thrombocytopenia than by depletion of coagulation factors.	Controversial for DIC due to absence of several clotting factors, and the (theoretical) concern that its content of activated factors will promote DIC

Abbreviations: FFP = fresh frozen plasma, PRBC = packed red blood cells, PT = prothrombin time, PTT = partial thromboplastin time.

Table 30-10

Risks of Blood Transfusion from Volunteer Donors

COMPLICATION	RISK/UNIT TRANSFUSED	INCIDENCE OF DEATH/UNIT TRANSFUSED
Human immunodeficiency virus	1/40,000–1/1,000,000	1/500,000
Hepatitis B	1/100,000	1/2,000,000
Non-A, non-B hepatitis	1/50–1/100	Unknown
Hemolytic transfusion reaction	Unknown	1/100,000–1/600,000
Nonhemolytic transfusion reaction	1/100	1/10,000,000

(After Benedetti TJ. Obstetric hemorrhage. In: Gabbe SG, Niebyl JR, Simpson JL, eds. Obstetrics: normal and problem pregnancies. 2nd ed. New York: Churchill Livingstone, 1991:570)

Jefferson University Hospital blood bank transfusion protocols, Circular of Transfusion Information from the American Red Cross (1991), and consensus conferences on blood-product replacement supported by the National Institutes of Health.[60–62] More extensive information regarding indications, contraindications, and hazards of transfusion are discussed in "Blood Transfusion Therapy" from the American Association of Blood Banks.[63] An assessment of the risks of transfusion-related illness is shown in Table 30-10.

RELATED TOPICS TO OBSTETRIC HEMORRHAGE

Fetal Death and Delayed Delivery

Most women enter spontaneous labor within 2 weeks of fetal death. Gross disruption of maternal coagulation mechanism rarely develops in less than 1 month after fetal death. Then, 25% of women will have coagulation changes.[2] Management of fetal death has evolved from awaiting spontaneous labor to more active intervention. Appreciation of the emotional stress of carrying a dead fetus and of the dangers of coagulation defects, as well as more effective methods of induction of labor have lead to this change.

Amniotic Fluid Embolism

Entry of amniotic fluid into the maternal circulation can prove fatal. The major risk factors include prolonged labor, oxytocin augmentation, and the presence of meconium (toxic amniotic fluid). Signs and symptoms range from mild peripheral desaturation to respiratory distress, circulatory collapse, cardiac arrest, serious hemorrhage, and severe coagulation defect. Treatment relates to the severity of the disease. In general, treatment requires rapid recognition, ventilatory and hemodynamic support, and treatment of DIC (see Chap. 31).[2]

REFERENCES

1. Chattopadhyay SK, Roy BD, Edrees YB. Surgical control of obstetric hemorrhage: Hypogastric artery ligation or hysterectomy? Int J Gynecol Obstet 1990;32:345.
2. Obstetric hemorrhage. In: Cunningham FG, MacDonald PC, Gant NF, eds. Williams' Obstetrics, 18th ed. Norwalk, CT: Appleton & Lange, 1989:695.
3. The morphological and functional development of the fetus. In: Cunningham FG, MacDonald FC, Gant NF, eds. Williams' Obstetrics, 18th ed. Norwalk, CT: Appleton & Lange, 1989:94.
4. Baker RN. Evaluation and management of critically ill patients. In: Wynn RM, ed. Obstetrics and gynecology annual: 1977. Vol 6. New York: Appleton-Century-Crofts, 1977:295.
5. Benedetti TJ. Obstetric hemorrhage. In: Gabbe SG, Niebyl JR, Simpson JL, eds. Obstetrics: Normal and problem pregnancies. 2nd ed. New York: Churchill-Livingstone, 1991:573.
6. Biehl DR. Antepatum and postpartum hemorrhage. In: Shnider SM, Levinson C, eds. Anesthesia for obstetrics. 2nd ed. Baltimore: Williams & Wilkins, 1987:281.
7. Abdul-Karim RW, Chevli RN. Antepartum hemorrhage and shock. Clin Obstet Gynecol 1976;19:533.
8. Greenhill JP, Friedman EA. Biological principles and

modern practice of obstetrics. Philadelphia: WB Saunders, 1974:418.

9. Rizos N, Doran T, Mikskin M, et al. Natural history of placenta previa ascertained by diagnostic ultrasound. Am J Obstet Gynecol 1979;133:287.

10. Hibbard LT. Placenta previa: Am J Obstet Gynecol 1969;104:173.

11. Crenshaw C, Jones DE, Parker RT. Placenta previa: A survey of twenty years' experience with improved perinatal survival by expectant therapy and cesarean delivery. Obstet Gynecol Surv 1973;28:461.

12. McShane PN, Heyl PS, Epstein MF. Maternal and perinatal morbidity resulting from placenta previa. Obstet Gynecol 1984;150:15.

13. Singh PN, Rodrigues C, Gupta AN. Placenta previa and previous cesarean section. Acta Obstet Gynecol Scand 1981;60:367.

14. Arcario T, Greene M, Ostheimer GW, Datta S, Naulty JS. Risks of placenta previa/accreta in patients with previous cesarean deliveries. Anesthesiology 1988;69:A659.

15. Read JA, Cotton DB, Miller FM. Placenta accreta: Changing clinical aspects and outcome. Obstet Gynecol 1980;56:31.

16. Chasnoff IJ, Burns WJ, Schnoll SH, Burns KA. Cocaine use in pregnancy. N Engl J Med 1985;313:666.

17. Pritchard JA, Mason R, Corley M, Pritchard S. Genesis of severe placental abruption. Am J Obstet Gynecol 1970;108:22.

18. Baker RN. Hemorrhage in obstetrics. Obstet Gynecol Annu 1977;6:295.

19. Sholl JS. Abruptio placentae: Clinical management in nonacute cases. Am J Obstet Gynecol 1987;156:40.

20. Clark SL, Yen SY, Phelan JP, et al. Emergency hysterectomy for obstetrical hemorrhage. Obstet Gynecol 1984;64:376.

21. Green-Thompson RW. Antepartum hemorrhage. Clin Obstet Gynaecol 1982;9:479.

22. Abdella TN, Sibai BM, Hays JM Jr, Anderson GD. Perinatal outcome in abruptio placentae. Obstet Gynecol 1984;63:365.

23. Schrinsky DC, Benson RC. Rupture of the pregnant uterus: A review. Obstet Gynecol Surv 1978;33:217.

24. Eden RD, Parker RT, Gall SA. Rupture of the pregnant uterus: A 53-year review. Obstet Gynecol 1986;68:671.

25. Plumer MH. Bleeding problems. In: James FM, Wheeler AS, Dewan DM, eds. Obstetric anesthesia: The complicated patient. 2nd ed. Philadelphia: FA Davis, 1988:327.

26. Lachman E, Moodley J, Pitsoe SB, Philpott RH. Rupture of the gravid uterus. S Afr Med J 1985;67:333.

27. Injuries to the birth canal. In: Cunningham FG, MacDonald PC, Gant NF, eds. Williams' Obstetrics, 18th ed. Norwalk, CT: Appleton & Lange, 1989:411.

28. Lavin JP. Vaginal delivery after cesarean birth: Frequently asked questions. Clin Perinatol 1983;10:439.

29. Usher R, Shephard M, Lind J. The blood volume of the newborn infant and placental transfusion. Acta Paediatr 1963;52:497.

30. Fay RA. Fetal maternal haemorrhage as a cause of fetal morbidity and mortality. Br J Obstet Gynaecol 1983;90:443.

31. Hoag RW. Fetomaternal hemorrhage associated with umbilical vein thrombosis: Case report. Am J Obstet Gynecol 1986;154:1271.

32. Antoine C, Young BK, Silverman F, Greco MA, Alvarez SP. Sinusoidal fetal heart rate pattern with vasa previa in twin pregnancy. J Reprod Med 1982;27:295.

33. Diseases and abnormalities of the placenta and fetal membranes. In: Cunningham FG, MacDonald PC, Gant NF, eds. Williams' Obstetrics, 18th ed. Norwalk, CT: Appleton & Lange, 1989:538.

34. Lavin JP, Stephens RJ, Miodovaik M, et al. Vaginal delivery in patients with prior cesarean section. Obstet Gynecol 1982;59:135.

35. Combs CA, Murphy EL, Laros RK Jr. Factors associated with hemorrhage in cesarean deliveries. Obstet Gynecol 1991;77:77.

36. Chestnut DH, Dewan DM, Redick LF, Caton D, Spielman FJ. Anesthetic management for obstetric hysterectomy: A multi-institutional study. Anesthesiology 1989;71:607.

37. Bieh DR. The anesthetic management of obstetrical hemorrhage. Int Anesth Clin 1990;28:53.

38. O'Leary JL, O'Leary JA. Uterine artery ligation for control of post cesarean section hemorrhage. Obstet Gynecol 1984;43:849.

39. Burchell CR. Physiology of internal iliac artery ligation. J Obstet Gynaec Br Commonwealth 1968;75:642.

40. Evans S, McShane P. The efficacy of internal iliac artery ligation in obstetric hemorrhage. Surg Gynecol Obstet 1985;160:250.

41. Druzin ML. Packing of lower uterine segment for control of postcesarean bleeding in instances of placenta previa. Surg Gynecol Obstet 1989;169:543.

42. Al-Sibai MH, Rahman J, Rahman MS, Butalack F. Emergency hysterectomy in obstetrics—a review of 117 cases. Aust NZ J Obstet Gynaecol 1987;27:180.

43. Pais SO, Glickman M, Schwartz P, Pingoud E, Berkowitz R. Embolization of pelvis arteries for control of postpartum hemorrhage. Obstet Gynecol 1980;55:754.

44. Robie GF, Morgan MA, Payne GG Jr, Wasemiller-Smith L. Logothetopulos pack for the management of uncontrollable postpartum hemorrhage. Am J Perinatol 1990;7:327.

45. Combs CA, Murphy EL, Laros RK Jr. Factors associated with postpartum hemorrhage with vaginal birth. Obstet Gynecol 1991;77:69.

46. Analgesia and anesthesia. In: Cunningham FG, MacDonald PC, Gant NF, eds. Williams' obstetrics. 18th ed. Norwalk, CT: Appleton & Lange, 1989:332.

47. Newton M. Postpartum hemorrhage. Am J Obstet Gynecol 1967;54:51.

48. Herbert WP, Afalo RC. Management of postpartum hemorrhage. Clin Obstet Gynecol 1984;27:139.

49. Wilken-Jensen C, Strom V, Neilson MD, Rosenkilde-

Gram B. Removing a retained placenta by oxytocin—a controlled study. Am J Obstet Gynecol 1989;1671:155.

50. Naftolin NJ, McKay DM, Phear WC, Goldberg AH. The effects of halothane on pregnant and non-pregnant human myometrium. Anesthesiology 1977;46:15.

51. De Simone CA, Norris MC, Leighton BL. Intravenous nitroglycerin aids manual extraction of a retained placenta. Anesthesiology 1990;73:787.

52. Watson P, Besch N, Bowes WA Jr. Management of acute and subacute puerperal inversion of the uterus. Obstet Gynecol 1980;55:12.

53. Harris BA Jr. Acute puerperal inversion of the uterus. Clin Obstet Gynecol 1984;27:134.

54. King PA, Buthie SJ, Dong ZG, Ma H. Secondary postpartum haemorrhage. Aust NZ J Obstet Gynaecol 1984;29:394.

55. Nanmann RO, Weinstein L. Disseminated intravascular coagulation: The clinician's dilemma. Obstet Gynecol Surv 1985;40:487.

56. Lerner RG, Rappaport SI, Siemsen KJ, Spitzer JM. Disappearance of fibrinogen ^{131}I after endotoxin: Effects of a first and second injection. Am J Physiol 1968;214:532.

57. Abnormalities of the third stage of labor. In: Cunningham FG, MacDonald PC, Gant NF, eds. Williams' obstetrics. 18th ed. Norwalk, CT: Appleton & Lange, 1989:417.

58. Andras RL, Piacquadio KM, Resnik R. A reappraisal of the need for autologous blood donation in the obstetric patients. Am J Obstet Gynecol 1990;163:1551.

59. Blood component therapy. Washington, DC: American College of Obstetricians and Gynecologists, July, 1984 (Rev. January, 1988) Technical Bulletin No. 78.

60. Fresh-frozen plasma: Indications and risks. JAMA 1985;253:551.

61. Platelet transfusion therapy. JAMA 1987;275:1777.

62. Perioperative red blood cell transfusion. JAMA 1988;260:2700.

63. Blood components. In: Pisciotto PT, ed. Blood transfusion therapy. 3rd ed. Arlington, VA: American Association of Blood Banks, 1989:1:7.

CHAPTER 31

Amniotic Fluid Embolism

Christopher M. Viscomi
John E. Heusner

Amniotic fluid embolism (AFE) is an incompletely understood syndrome with the potential for catastrophic effects on mother and fetus. Classically, the syndrome presents with a triad of symptoms consisting of hypoxia, hypotension, and coagulopathy. The speed of onset and lethality of the physiologic derangements induced by AFE are remarkable. As many as 86% of cases prove fatal; death occurs within half an hour of symptom onset in more than 50% of cases.[1,2] Although it is a rare event, AFE still ranks among the leading causes of maternal death in the peripartum period.

HISTORICAL DESCRIPTION

The first clinical report of AFE is generally credited to Meyer[4] in 1926; however, the syndrome may have been described more than 100 years earlier.[5] In 1941, Steiner and Lushbaugh[5] described eight cases of cardiovascular collapse in the peripartum period that they attributed to AFE. Autopsy findings of fetal squamous cells and mucin in the pulmonary circulation in all eight cases and the absence of this material in the lungs of parturients who died of other causes supported their diagnosis. A later series of 14 fatal AFE cases showed the presence of fetal debris in the pulmonary circulation.[7] Amniotic fluid components were also identified in maternal brain, kidney, liver, spleen, and pancreas,

although the route of access into the maternal arterial circulation remains speculative.

For many years, antemortem diagnosis of AFE was based only on clinical signs. Definitive diagnosis awaited autopsy findings of amniotic fluid debris such as fetal squamous cells, lanugo hair, meconium, mucin, or vernix caseosa in the maternal pulmonary circulation. Use of central venous and pulmonary artery catheters in AFE patients introduced a new method for antemortem diagnosis (Fig. 31-1). Resnik *et al*[8] first applied this technique. They confirmed a suspected case of AFE by showing mucin and fetal squamous cells in blood obtained from central venous catheter. Subsequently, amniotic fluid components have been found in mixed venous blood obtained from the pulmonary arteries of AFE patients.[8,9]

EPIDEMIOLOGY OF AMNIOTIC FLUID EMBOLISM

Based on their series of eight cases, Steiner and Lushbaugh[5] calculated an incidence rate for AFE of 1 in 8000 deliveries. When they observed no additional cases in the next 26,000 deliveries, it appeared that this rate was an overestimate. Larger series have found frequencies as low as 1 in 92,000.[2] Most studies fall somewhere between these two extremes. In a review of AFE

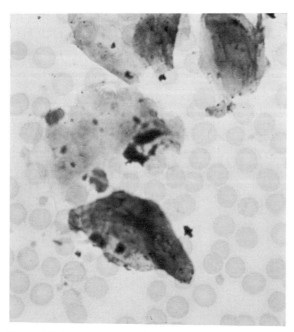

Figure 31–1. Squamous cells present in aspirate of maternal central venous blood. Several studies have proposed this finding as diagnostic of amniotic fluid embolism. (Photomicrograph provided by Steven L. Clark, MD)

cases in the United States, Resnik *et al*[7] noted an incidence of approximately 1 in 55,000 during the years 1968 to 1973.

Amniotic fluid embolism carries a high risk of fatal outcome. In a review of 272 cases, Morgan[1] describes a mortality rate of 86%. This rate may be artifactually high. All but four reports in this review predate the use of central venous blood aspiration as an aid in antemortem diagnosis. Because the definitive diagnostic measure in this series was autopsy, it is difficult to know how many nonfatal cases of AFE went undiagnosed and unreported. Recent literature clearly supports a higher survival rate.[10] This trend may reflect either increased sensitivity of diagnosis or an improvement in treatment modalities.

Several series have found that AFE causes between 4.5% and 9% of maternal deaths in the peripartum period.[1,2,11] In the US population, AFE ranks behind preeclampsia/eclampsia, obstetric hemorrhage, pulmonary thromboembolism, and obstetric infection as a cause of death (Table 31-1). Amniotic fluid embolism causes nearly twice as many obstetric deaths as does anesthesia.[11] The number of deaths due to hemorrhage, infection, and hypertensive disorders has declined with improved obstetric and anesthetic care. In contrast, the number of deaths of embolic origin has not decreased proportionately. This trend reflects the difficulty inherent in prevention, diagnosis, and treatment of embolic disease in the parturient.

Our understanding of the predisposing factors for AFE comes largely from anecdotal evidence. Increased maternal age, multiparity, large fetal size, rapid progression of labor, and the use of oxytocin augmentation may increase the risk of AFE. Most cases occur in somewhat older parturients, with a mean age of 32 years. A third of cases in an Australian series occurred in patients over 34 years of age.[2] The incidence of AFE increases in multiparous patients; covariation in maternal age with increased parity may at least partly explain this association. Little evidence exists for macrosomia as a risk factor; the mean birth weight in a large series was 3.3 kg. Tumultuous labor was present in less than a third of cases. Uterine stimulants were used in only 22%. To quote Morgan: "In view of the very wide use of accelerated labor and the rarity of amniotic fluid embolism, it must be concluded that there is no direct association between the two."[1] Placental abruption occurs in up to 50% of AFE cases; fetal death precedes clinical presentation of AFE in 40% of cases.[12]

By far, the most common situation in which AFE presents is labor (90% of cases in an extensive review).[1] Amniotic fluid embolism also occurs during cesarean delivery, first- and second-trimester abortion, amniocentesis, and abdominal trauma.[13–16] Some cases even present in the postpartum period.[17] In an unusual presentation, AFE syndrome occurred spontaneously in the second trimester of a previously uncomplicated pregnancy.[18]

Table 31-1

Principal Causes of Peripartum Maternal Death

SOURCE	INCIDENCE
Preeclampsia/eclampsia	19.2%
Obstetric hemorrhage	16.0%
Pulmonary thromboembolism	13.1%
Obstetric infection	9.6%
Amniotic fluid embolism	9.1%
Cerebrovascular accident	5.2%
Anesthetic complications	4.7%

(Data modified from Kaunitz AM, Hughes JM, Grimes DA, Smith JC, Rochat RW, Kafrissen ME. Causes of maternal mortality in the United States. Obstet Gynecol 1985;65:605)

CLINICAL PRESENTATION

Presenting Symptoms

The clinical presentation of AFE syndrome is often dramatic. Shnider and Moya[19] offered the following description, which remains vivid 30 years later: "Suddenly and without warning, the signs of amniotic fluid infusion appear: hyperpnea or tachypnea, cyanosis and shock progressing into profound coma. In addition, there is often rigor, clonic–tonic convulsions and acute pulmonary edema. If the patient survives this initial phase, incoagulability of the blood develops with excessive bleeding from raw surfaces in the uterus, vagina, and perineum." Sometimes, nonspecific prodromal symptoms (nausea, vomiting, agitation, chills, apprehension, and restlessness) may precede overt evidence of AFE. The prevalence of these symptoms in the obstetric population renders them of limited use in predicting onset of AFE. Most cases continue to present as completely unheralded cardiorespiratory collapse.

Rapid onset of severe cardiopulmonary compromise characterizes the initial phase of AFE syndrome. In most cases, respiratory distress is the presenting symptom (Table 31-2), usually followed by severe hypotension and frequently within minutes by cardiac arrest. Alternate initial presentations include cardiovascular collapse, uncontrolled hemorrhage, and seizures.[1,2] More atypical presentations of AFE have included abdominal pain, chest pain, and ventricular tachycardia. Mortality is very high during the initial phase. In one review, over half the women died within 30 minutes of initial onset of symptoms. A later hemorrhagic phase

Table 31-2

Presenting Symptoms in Amniotic Fluid Embolism

SYMPTOM	INCIDENCE*
Respiratory distress	57%
Hypotension	37%
Coagulopathy	13%
Seizures	10%

(Data from Morgan M. Amniotic fluid embolism. Anaesthesia 1979;34:20, and Ratten GJ. Amniotic fluid embolism—2 cases and a review of maternal deaths from this cause in Australia. Aust NZ J Obstet Gynaecol 1988;28:33)
*Because of frequent overlap of presenting symptoms, percentages sum to greater than 100%.

develops in 40% to 50% of patients with AFE. Considering the very high immediate mortality, it is likely that this percentage underestimates the true incidence of coagulopathy.[12]

Cardiopulmonary Effects

The chief cardiovascular manifestation of AFE is severe hypotension, which is usually out of proportion to any blood loss. Significant tachycardia typically accompanies the rapid drop in blood pressure. Clinical and invasive monitoring data frequently suggest left ventricular dysfunction. Electrocardiogram findings are nondiagnostic. The electrocardiogram may be normal or reflect sinus tachycardia or other arrhythmias, with or without accompanying ST-segment changes.

Usually, clinical evidence of pulmonary edema, such as rales, frothy pink sputum, and jugular venous distention, develops rapidly. In up to 70% of patients, chest radiograph reveals some degree of pulmonary edema. Although left ventricular filling pressures may increase, the degree of pulmonary edema is often out of proportion to this rise, suggesting involvement of both cardiogenic and noncardiogenic mechanisms. Adult respiratory distress syndrome will frequently develop as a delayed complication in those that survive the acute event. Arterial blood gas tensions in AFE typically reveal severe hypoxemia and metabolic acidosis with incomplete respiratory compensation. Continuous pulse oximetry provided the initial evidence of AFE in one report. A patient's room air oxyhemoglobin saturation during cesarean section dropped abruptly without any other signs or symptoms. Within hours, she suffered a cardiac arrest and died. The autopsy findings suggested AFE.[20]

Invasive Monitoring Data

At present, only a few published cases report data from early invasive central hemodynamic monitoring. In contrast to the pulmonary hypertension and elevated pulmonary vascular resistance of several animal models,[5,21–24] left ventricular failure is the only consistent finding in humans.[10,12] Several patients had elevations of pulmonary artery pressures that appeared to reflect elevated pulmonary capillary wedge pressures and left ventricular failure rather than intrinsic pulmonary artery vasospasm. These case reports consistently describe significant left ventricular dysfunction based on clinical criteria, nuclear scanning, or calculation of left ventricular stroke work index (Fig. 31-2). Echocardiography has similarly shown severe left ventricular dysfunction in AFE.[25] Diminished coronary artery blood flow, as noted in an animal model of AFE,[26] provides a possible basis for these observations. In addition to left ventricular failure, Clark noted that several patients had low calculated systemic vascular resistance.

Shortcomings of Clark's work include the absence of hemodynamic data early in AFE. The earliest data from any of these patients was obtained 70 minutes after the onset of clinical symptoms. Much of the information reflects events occurring after vasoactive agents had been administered in efforts to stabilize the patient. In Ratten's[2] review of 54 cases, mortality in excess of 65% occurs within 30 minutes of initial symptoms. Thus, invasive monitoring data from longer-term survivors may not be representative of all victims of AFE, especially those with more sudden and catastrophic presentations.

An additional report exists of a presumed AFE in a woman with a pulmonary artery catheter already in place.[13] A 41-year-old patient with severe chronic hypertension and classic angina had invasive monitoring established for elective cesarean section. During delivery, under epidural anesthesia, left-sided chest pain developed, coincident with a rise in pulmonary artery pressures from 35/9 to 38/16. Neither cardiac output nor pulmonary capillary wedge pressure was measured then. The chest pain did not respond to nitroglycerin infusion. The patient had several transient episodes of ventricular tachycardia. Examination of pulmonary artery catheter aspirate revealed squamous cells and fetal debris. No other signs of AFE (hypoxia, pulmonary edema, hypotension, or coagulopathy) developed. Unfortunately, the incomplete nature of the hemodynamic monitoring plus the patient's coexisting diseases and absence of classic signs of AFE render this case of little value in evaluating the hemodynamic course of AFE.

Coagulopathy

Some degree of coagulopathy will develop in 40% of patients who survive the immediate hemodynamic and pulmonary effects of AFE. Anything from subclinical coagulopathy with transient abnormalities in laboratory studies to fully developed disseminated intravascular coagulation with life-threatening hemorrhage may arise. Laboratory values will reflect consumption of clotting factors with decreased fibrinogen and platelet count, elevated fibrin split products, and prolonged prothrombin and partial thromboplastin times. Clinically, the patient will exhibit persistent vaginal or incisional bleeding and oozing from venipuncture sites. The simultaneous development of uterine atony, possibly secondary to direct inhibition of myometrial contractility by amniotic fluid, often complicates the coagulopathy.[12] The underlying mechanism of AFE-associated disseminated intravascular coagulation is unclear. Amniotic fluid contains an activator of factor X, but in an amount that appears inadequate to initiate disseminated intravascular coagulation.[27] Clark[12] has proposed that systemic release of trophoblastic material may play a significant role. Clinical signs of coagulopathy may precede other evidence of AFE. Rarely, coagulopathy has been the sole manifestation of presumptive AFE,[2] although diagnosis in this setting might reflect a tendency to overdiagnose AFE in unexpected cases of peripartum death.[11]

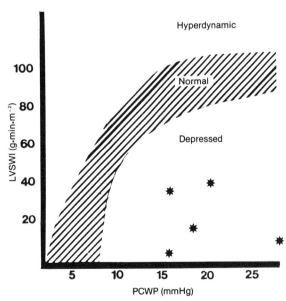

Figure 31–2. Left ventricular performance in five victims of amniotic embolism. (LVSWI = left ventricular stroke work index, PCWP = pulmonary capillary wedge pressure) (SL Clark, Phelan JP, Cotton DB. Amniotic fluid embolism. In: Critical care obstetrics, 2nd ed. Cambridge: Blackwell Scientific Publications, 1991)

Neurologic and Other Manifestations

Seizures, likely secondary to cerebral hypoxia, may occur in 10% to 20% of AFE cases. They may complicate management by increasing oxygen demand. Hypoxic brain injury, a potentially devastating complication of AFE, has caused severe disability in survivors of the acute event.[28] Acute renal failure due to prolonged hypoperfusion also may follow. Amniotic fluid embolism appears to have no permanent cardiac or pulmonary sequelae; survivors generally return to baseline cardiopulmonary function.

Fetal distress is inevitable following onset of AFE symptoms. Maternal hypoxemia and hypotension drastically reduce transplacental oxygen delivery. The fetus rarely survives unless delivered immediately. A report by Barrows illustrates that fetal distress also may precede the development of maternal symptoms, reflecting the extreme sensitivity of the fetus to even asymptomatic maternal hypoxemia.[29]

Differential Diagnosis

It is difficult to differentiate the clinical presentation of AFE from that of other potential peripartum complications (Table 31-3). Pulmonary thromboembolism, venous air embolism, systemic sepsis, myocardial infarction, decompensation of significant valvular disease, and peripartum cardiomyopathy can cause acute cardiovascular collapse in the parturient. Venous air embolism, detectable by Doppler ultrasound in up to 65% of cesarean deliveries, often produces dyspnea and oxyhemoglobin desaturation.[30] Both severe preeclampsia and placental abruption cause a coagulopathy that is clinically indistinguishable from that of AFE. Other complications to be considered in the differential diagnosis of AFE include eclampsia, cerebral hemorrhage, aspiration of gastric contents, severe supine hypotensive syndrome, uterine rupture, and systemic toxicity of local anesthetic agents.

AMNIOTIC FLUID IN THE MATERNAL CIRCULATION

Amniotic Fluid Composition

Amniotic fluid volume increases rapidly during pregnancy from approximately 50 mL at 12 weeks of gestation to a maximum of 1 L at term. In the first half of pregnancy, amniotic fluid has essentially the same electrolyte composition as maternal plasma. Particulate matter is nearly absent. As the pregnancy progresses, fetal urine output makes the fluid hypotonic and increases its concentration of urea and creatinine. Varying amounts of particulate matter of fetal origin ac-

Table 31-3

Differential Diagnosis of Amniotic Fluid Embolism

CONDITION	SYMPTOM			
	Respiratory Distress	Hypotension	Coagulopathy	Seizures
Pulmonary thromboembolism	✔	✔		
Venous air embolism	✔	✔		
Septic or hypovolemic shock		✔	✔	
Myocardial infarction		✔		
Peripartum cardiomyopathy	✔	✔		
Decompensation of cardiac valvular disease	✔	✔		
Uterine rupture		✔		
Supine hypotensive syndrome		✔		
Preeclampsia/eclampsia			✔	✔
Local anesthetic toxicity				✔
Placental abruption		✔	✔	
Cerebrovascular accident	✔			✔
Aspiration of gastric contents	✔			

cumulate. This debris consists of desquamated fetal skin cells, lanugo and scalp hairs, vernix caseosa, mucin, and, occasionally, meconium. Amniotic fluid also contains prostaglandins and other arachidonic acid metabolites that may play an important role in the pathophysiology of AFE.[31]

Entry into Maternal Circulation

Entry of amniotic fluid into the maternal circulation requires communication between the amniotic sac and the maternal venous system. This communication can occur through either the uteroplacental junction or uterine or cervical veins disrupted by incision or trauma. Endocervical veins are commonly lacerated during labor as the upper portion of the uterus becomes part of the lower uterine segment.[32] Following membrane rupture, uterine contractions may force amniotic fluid into these vessels. Cervical veins frequently tear during normal labor with no apparent ill effects on the parturient. This mechanism, therefore, most likely does not have a primary role in the onset of AFE syndrome. Placental abruption commonly occurs in cases of AFE. Possibly, premature separation of the placenta allows amniotic fluid entry through the placental implantation site. Disruption of the fetal membranes appears necessary for the development of AFE. The amniotic sac breaks before the onset of symptoms in most cases. When not apparent, concealed rupture has occurred, with intact membranes continuing to cover the cervical os.

Evidence exists for and against the routine entry of amniotic fluid into the maternal circulation. Sparr and Pritchard[33] examined this question in 1958 by injecting Cr[51]-labeled red blood cells into the amniotic fluid of parturients shortly before vaginal or cesarean delivery. They found only trace amounts of radioactivity in the maternal circulation after delivery and calculated the volume of amniotic fluid entry at less than 2 mL.[33] A contrasting study by Talbert *et al*[34] found significant transfer of radiolabeled albumin from the amniotic fluid into the maternal circulation during abortion induced with hypertonic saline.[34] Intra-amniotic injection of hypertonic saline may raise intrauterine pressure to levels well above those achieved during normal labor. Taken together, these two studies lend some support to the long-standing clinical impression that AFE occurs more frequently in cases of uterine tetany or a "hard" course of labor.

Autopsy studies have consistently found no evidence of amniotic fluid debris in maternal lung sections without clinical signs of AFE. Roche and Norris[35] compared lung biopsies obtained from 20 fatal cases of AFE with control samples from 20 parturients who died of complications of preeclampsia/eclampsia. Nineteen of 20 AFE patients had evidence of amniotic fluid debris on examination of a single tissue sample. The remaining case was positive in a second sample. None of the control samples contained evidence of amniotic fluid debris.[35] In contrast to amniotic fluid, trophoblastic embolism is somewhat common during pregnancy. In a postmortem study, Attwood and Park[36] found evidence of trophoblastic tissue in maternal lung in 96 out of 220 cases studied. Between 30% and 80% of parturients have trophoblastic cells in their peripheral circulation.[37]

Significance of Fetal Debris

Pulmonary artery catheterization may allow the rapid diagnosis of AFE and enable differentiation of AFE from other causes of peripartum cardiovascular compromise.[9] Detection of fetal squamous cells in the maternal pulmonary circulation has been proposed as pathognomonic for AFE; however, reliable differentiation of fetal from adult squamous cells may not be possible. Recent evidence suggests that examination of mixed venous blood from patients with indwelling pulmonary artery catheters may commonly reveal squamous cells. Clark *et al*,[38] in a series of 16 pregnant and 17 nonpregnant patients who underwent pulmonary artery catheterization for a variety of indications, recovered squamous cells from the central circulation in all 33 cases. The cell count, slightly higher in the pregnant patients and tending to increase postpartum, suggested that perhaps some cells were of fetal origin. Most were presumed to be contaminants introduced into the circulation secondary to intravenous cannulation. Of interest, the series included one patient who eventually died of apparent AFE; her cell count was no higher than in nonpregnant controls. In a similar study, Kuhlman *et al*[39] examined pulmonary artery blood samples from a series of parturients without clinical signs of AFE. They compared these women to a nonpregnant control patient and a patient with clinical symptoms of AFE syndrome. Only the nonpregnant control patient tested completely negative for amniotic fluid components. Although the patient with suspected AFE had the most fetal debris, all the other parturients also had squamous cells, lanugo hair, or mucin in their pulmonary artery blood. There is evidence, therefore, that the presence of squamous cells or other fetal debris in the parturient's central circulation is not pathognomonic for AFE. "In a critically ill obstetric patient, such a finding should not deter the clinician from a thorough search for other causes of hemodynamic instability."[38]

Animal Models of Amniotic Fluid Embolism

Although the clinical presentation of AFE has been well described in many reviews, the underlying mechanism of the maternal response to AFE remains elusive. Because AFE occurs so rarely and the early mortality is so high, controlled clinical trials of alternative therapeutic regimens are nearly impossible. Thus, we must rely heavily on animal models and in vitro experiments to explain the pathogenesis and promising treatment modalities for this vexing syndrome.

Unfortunately, no consensus exists for the proper animal model of AFE (Table 31-4). Rabbit, dog, sheep, monkey, cat, and calf models have all been developed. Further complicating analysis of these studies is whether the investigators used heterologous (from another species) or autologous (same animal) amniotic fluid in their attempts to create experimental AFE. In addition, the amniotic fluid administered in these various models has varied from a particulate-free filtrate to highly meconium-enriched solutions.

Heterologous Models

Steiner and Luschbaugh[5] first studied AFE in animals. Rabbits and dogs received intravenous injection of either unaltered or meconium-enriched human amniotic fluid. Particulate-free human amniotic fluid was innocuous in rabbits. Thick, meconium-enriched, human amniotic fluid usually proved fatal in both rabbits and dogs.

At least 12 later heterologous AFE studies exist, with widely varying findings (Table 31-4). Certain species, such as the rabbit, seem particularly sensitive to intravenous heterologous amniotic fluid.[5] In contrast, calves,[21] dogs,[22] and sheep[23] suffer only transient alterations in pulmonary or systemic hemodynamics or temporary coagulopathy. The obstetric literature often quotes a study by Attwood and Downing that employed a canine model of AFE.[25] The authors evaluated both left- and right-sided cardiac function. Intravenous injection of human amniotic fluid or suspended human meconium transiently decreases blood pressure, cardiac output, and systemic vascular resistance while significantly elevating pulmonary vascular resistance. None of the animals developed hypofibrinoge-

nemia or pulmonary edema. Some clinicians accept these data as a valid basis upon which to base therapeutic recommendations. On the other hand, others claim that heterologous models of AFE only prove "that it is possible to kill animals by the systemic injection of large boluses of foreign material from another species."[12]

Autologous Models

Several groups of investigators have attempted to address some criticisms of heterologous AFE models by using autologous amniotic fluid. They have used both primate and lower animal models. In a highly invasive study of near-term ewes, Reis *et al*[40] harvested amniotic fluid at the time of cesarean section (done under local anesthesia). Then, they induced general anesthesia, did a median sternotomy, and placed flow probes and pressure sensors. Amniotic fluid was injected into the inferior vena cava or the left atrium. Transient decreases in blood pressure and systemic vascular resistance that were accompanied by substantial increases in pulmonary artery pressures and pulmonary vascular resistance followed. Cardiac output did not change consistently. The absence of a difference in response between inferior vena caval and left atrial injections, or between filtered and particulate-rich amniotic fluid, suggests a humoral mechanism of AFE, rather than a mechanical–obstructive process.[40] It is particularly interesting that, at necropsy, the lungs were normal, in strong contrast to the typical findings of amniotic fluid debris in the lungs of humans who succumb to this syndrome.

Reports of two primate models of autologous AFE are available.[41,42] Nonpregnant, pregnant, and postpartum monkeys were injected with autologous amniotic fluid. These injections proved totally innocuous. The authors concluded that AFE syndrome is not caused by the introduction of "normal" amniotic fluid into the maternal vasculature.

The various animal models produce inconsistent maternal responses to amniotic fluid injection. Studies of heterologous amniotic fluid in nonprimates usually find significant pathology; however, these models are probably the least relevant to human AFE. Autologous amniotic fluid injection in nonprimates produces transient hemodynamic effects. Most frequently, it causes pulmonary vasospasm and diminished systemic vascular resistance. Primate models, however, reveal few sequelae after amniotic fluid injection. These findings have led some to question the belief that "normal" amniotic fluid can account for the clinical picture of human AFE.

Table 31–4

Animal Models of Amniotic Fluid Embolism

Investigator	Year	Animal	Anesthetized	Pregnant	Filtered AF	Pathology with Whole/Concentrated AF
Steiner and Luschbaugh	1941	Rabbit/dog	No	No	No	Yes
Gron	1952	Rabbit	No	No	NE	Yes
Schneider	1953	Dog	No	No	NE	Yes
Jaques	1960	Dog	Yes	No	NE	Yes
Halmagyi	1962	Sheep	Yes	No	No	Yes
Attwood	1965	Dog	Yes	No	Yes (mild)	Yes
Stolte	1967	Monkey	Yes	Yes	No	No
Macmillan	1968	Rabbit	No	No	No	Yes
Reis	1969	Sheep	Yes	Yes	Yes	Yes
Dutta	1970	Rabbit	Yes	No	NE	Yes
Adamsons	1971	Monkey	Yes	Yes	NE	No
Kitzmiller	1972	Cat	Yes	No	No	Yes
Spence	1974	Rabbit	No	Yes	No	No
Reeves	1974	Calf	No	No	NE	Yes
Azegami	1986	Rabbit	No	No	No	Yes
Richards	1988	Rat*	Yes	No	Yes	NE

(After Clark SL, Phelan JP, Cotton DB: Amniotic fluid embolism. In: Critical care obstetrics, 2nd ed. Cambridge, MA: Blackwell Scientific Publications, 1991:318)
*Isolated heart preparation.
Abbreviations: AF = amniotic fluid, BP = blood pressure, CO = cardiac output, CVP = central venous pressure, LAP = left atrial pressure, NE = not examined, NI = normal, P = pulse, PAP = pulmonary arter pressure, PCWP = pulmonary capillary wedge pressure, PVR = pulmonary vascular resistance, RR = respiratory rate, SVR = systemic vascular resistance.

Several workers have attempted to reconcile animal and human data by postulating a "biphasic" pattern of pulmonary and cardiovascular response to AFE.[10,43] They suggest an initial phase involving pulmonary hypertension and elevated pulmonary vascular resistance, as seen in several animal experiments. In this model, those surviving the initial insult experience a secondary phase of left-heart failure with normalization of pulmonary artery pressures. This hypothesis remains purely speculative; no evidence of the proposed initial phase exists in humans.

MODELS OF AMNIOTIC FLUID EMBOLISM: ROLE OF PROSTAGLANDINS AND LEUKOTRIENES

Amniotic fluid contains significant amounts of prostaglandins, leukotrienes, and other arachidonic acid metabolites.[44] Figure 31-3 reviews the activation of arachidonic acids and the subsequent formation of prostaglandins and leukotrienes. Many arachidonic acid metabolites possess hemodynamic and coagula-

AF Species	Injection Arterial	Injection Venous	Hemodynamic Changes	Coagulopathy	Autopsy
Human	NE	Yes	NE (death)	No	Debris in pulmonary artery
Human	No	Yes	NE (death)	No	Debris in pulmonary artery
Human	NE	Yes	NE (death)	5 of 8	Debris in pulmonary artery
Human/dog	NE	Yes	↑ PAP, Nl BP	Fibrionogen 12 of 13	Debris in pulmonary artery
Human	NE	Yes	↑ PAP, Nl SVR, nl CO,	No	NE
Human	Yes	Yes ↑ LPA, BP	↑ PAP, ↑PVR, ↓ SVR, Nl to	4 of 12	NE
Human/monkey	No	No	Nl BP, Nl P	1 of 12	NE
Human	Yes	Yes	NE (death)	2 of 12	Minimal debris, hemorrhage
Sheep	Yes	Yes Nl LAP, Nl PCWP	↑ PAP, ↑ PVR, ↓ SVR, ↓ BP,	No	Normal
Human	NE	Yes	NE (death)	No	Minimal debris, massive infarction
Monkey	NE	No	Nl BP, Nl P, Nl RR	No	NE
Human	NE	Yes	↓ BP, ↑ P, ↑ CVP	No	NE
Rabbit	NE	No	Nl BP, Nl P, Nl RR	No	NE
Calf	NE	Yes	↓ BP, ↑ PAP, Nl CO Nl PCWP		
Human	NE	Yes	NE (death)	No	Pulmonary edema, debris in pulmonary vessels
Human	NE	Yes	Coronary flow		

tion cascade effects that mimic clinical AFE. Considerable effort has been applied to characterizing both the changing production of these substances during human gestation and their effects on maternal physiology. The amount and type of these compounds in the amniotic fluid change throughout pregnancy. Early in gestation, only prostaglandins of the E series are found. With the onset of labor, prostaglandin $F_2\alpha$ becomes detectable and prostaglandin F_1 levels increase. Simultaneously, the concentration of prostaglandin E falls.[45,46]

Kitzmiller[47] first noted the increased toxicity of amniotic fluid obtained from laboring versus nonlaboring women.[47] The changing prostaglandin content of amniotic fluid during labor may account for its increased toxicity. Other investigators have shown that a lipid extract of amniotic fluid causes the observed pulmonary hypertension in the bovine model of AFE.[21] Furthermore, aspirin (a potent inhibitor of prostaglandin synthesis) totally prevents the occurrence of pulmonary hypertension. Azegami and Mori[45] have recently demonstrated that leukotrienes also may play a role in the

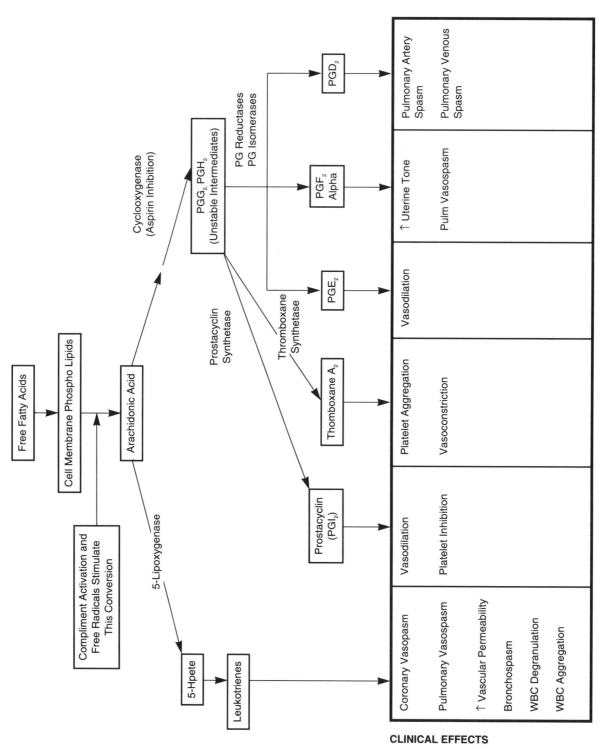

Figure 31-3. Arachidonic acid synthesis, metabolites, and clinical effects.

pathology of rabbit AFE. Prior administration of 5-lip-oxygenase inhibitors, which block the formation of leukotrienes, prevents acute death in these animals.[45]

Preliminary data from humans also indirectly implicate arachidonic acid metabolites in the genesis of AFE syndrome. Hankins et al[48] reported a series of women who developed severe hypoxemia after intramuscular or intramyometrial injection of 15 methyl prostaglandin $F_{2\alpha}$. Intrapulmonary shunts of up to 28% developed. The authors suggest that this compound can induce severe bronchoconstriction and pulmonary vasospasm leading to V/Q mismatch. Douglas[49] reported fulminant pulmonary edema and cardiovascular collapse in a parturient receiving high-dose intramyometrial prostaglandin $F_{2\alpha}$. These reports imply that amniotic fluid from laboring parturients, which contains large amounts of this prostaglandin, could initiate similar pathology if it entered the maternal circulation in any significant amount.

A study by Hammerschmidt et al[50] provides further evidence for a possible role of prostaglandins in AFE syndrome. Their work was stimulated by the finding of extensive leukostasis in pulmonary sections of human AFE victims. Leukostasis of this degree usually involves extensive complement and granulocyte activation and has been described in acute respiratory distress syndrome and extracorporeal circulation induced pulmonary dysfunction. Their experiments proved the ability of human amniotic fluid to activate complement, principally via the alternative pathway. Complement activation was more likely to occur in plasma samples from gravid women than in samples from nongravid women. Furthermore, the amniotic fluid of "stressed" pregnancies (stressors include toxemia, diabetes, amnionitis, and hydrops fetalis) was a more potent activator of complement than fluid from uncomplicated pregnancies. In response to complement activation, leukocytes produce toxic-free radicals that stimulate the arachidonic acid pathway.[51] High levels of arachidonic acid, present in maternal serum and amniotic fluid during labor,[52,53] provide an expanded substrate pool for the production of thromboxanes and leukotrienes. These compounds have well-known vasoactive, leukocyte-aggregating, and platelet-stimulating properties. Hammerschmidt et al[50] proposed that a gravid woman is "primed" for an exaggerated cellular and vascular response in the event of complement activation (as in AFE). They proposed that clinical AFE occurs when a significant volume of amniotic fluid, rich in complement-activating property, enters the circulation of women unfortunate enough to have plasma that can be activated. This line of research appears most promising in explaining the underlying mechanisms of clinical AFE.

TREATMENT

Historically, therapeutic recommendations have been based upon animal models of AFE. Efforts focused on relieving presumed pulmonary vasospasm with atropine, papaverine, aminophylline, steroids, and vasodilators.[1,12,54–56] In light of more recent human invasive monitoring data, a more rational approach involves initial stabilization, consideration of the differential diagnosis, and the use of appropriate vasoactive drugs guided by invasive monitoring (Fig. 31-4).

Cardiopulmonary Resuscitation

With a potential first-hour mortality of 65%, considerable attention should be focused on the ABCs of cardiopulmonary resuscitation. Hypoxemia is a nearly universal finding in early AFE. Many patients have survived the initial insult, yet ultimately die of complications of cerebral hypoxia.[12,57] Thus, early oxygen supplementation, preferably via an endotracheal tube, is imperative. The AFE patients will frequently require blood-pressure support to provide acceptable perfusion pressures for maternal vital organs and the fetus. Ephedrine has long been the acute vasopressor of choice in obstetrics, as it usually preserves uterine blood flow.[58] Left uterine displacement should accompany other resuscitative efforts.

Should full cardiac arrest occur, controversy surrounds the effectiveness of closed-chest cardiopulmonary resuscitation in parturients.[59–61] Diminished venous return in the supine position impairs cardiopulmonary resuscitation in the antepartum patient. Lateral tilt introduces technical difficulty and mechanical disadvantage. Even optimal cardiopulmonary resuscitation produces only 30% of normal cardiac output.[62] Thus, it is unlikely that adequate placental and fetal oxygen delivery can be sustained during cardiopulmonary resuscitation. In several reports of maternal cardiac arrest, expeditious delivery correlated with improve maternal and neonatal outcome.[63,64] To end, immediate and rapid preparation for cesarean delivery must commence should maternal cardiac arrest occur.

Once initial stabilization has been accomplished, and appropriate noninvasive monitoring (electrocardiogram, pulse oximetry, blood pressure monitor) is ongoing, attention should focus on the differential diagnosis. Clinical AFE syndrome is rare. Conditions that could easily mimic AFE include complications of toxemia (severe cerebral hemorrhage, hepatic rupture, eclamptic seizure with aspiration), overwhelming sepsis, concealed abruptio placenta, and intravenous or

AFE TREATMENT ALGORITHM

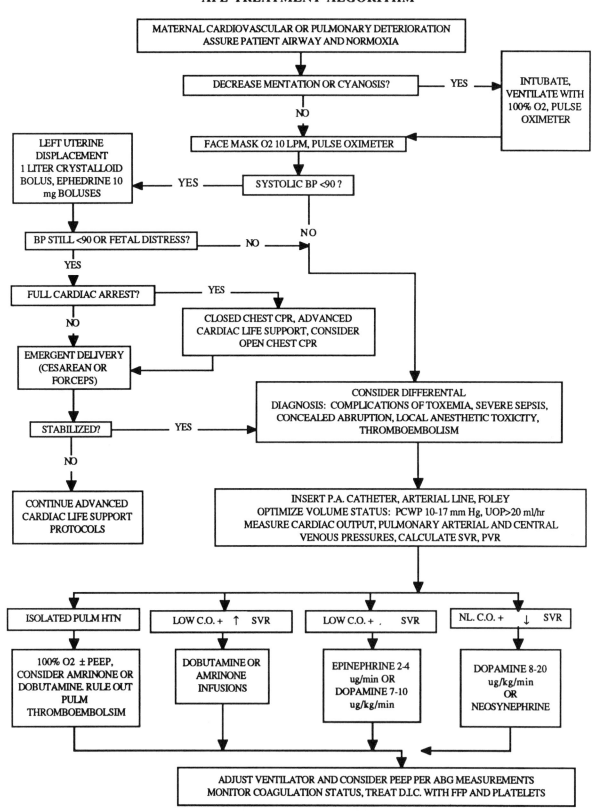

MATERNAL CARDIOVASCULAR OR PULMONARY DETERIORATION
ASSURE PATIENT AIRWAY AND NORMOXIA

DECREASE MENTATION OR CYANOSIS? — YES → INTUBATE, VENTILATE WITH 100% O2, PULSE OXIMETER

NO

FACE MASK O2 10 LPM, PULSE OXIMETER

LEFT UTERINE DISPLACEMENT 1 LITER CRYSTALLOID BOLUS, EPHEDRINE 10 mg BOLUSES ← YES — SYSTOLIC BP <90 ?

NO

BP STILL <90 OR FETAL DISTRESS? — NO →

YES

FULL CARDIAC ARREST? — YES → CLOSED CHEST CPR, ADVANCED CARDIAC LIFE SUPPORT, CONSIDER OPEN CHEST CPR

NO

EMERGENT DELIVERY (CESAREAN OR FORCEPS)

STABILIZED? — YES → CONSIDER DIFFERENTAL DIAGNOSIS: COMPLICATIONS OF TOXEMIA, SEVERE SEPSIS, CONCEALED ABRUPTION, LOCAL ANESTHETIC TOXICITY, THROMBOEMBOLISM

NO

CONTINUE ADVANCED CARDIAC LIFE SUPPORT PROTOCOLS

INSERT P.A. CATHETER, ARTERIAL LINE, FOLEY
OPTIMIZE VOLUME STATUS: PCWP 10-17 mm Hg, UOP>20 ml/hr
MEASURE CARDIAC OUTPUT, PULMONARY ARTERIAL AND CENTRAL VENOUS PRESSURES, CALCULATE SVR, PVR

ISOLATED PULM HTN | LOW C.O. + ↑ SVR | LOW C.O. + , SVR | NL. C.O. + ↓ SVR

100% O2 ±PEEP, CONSIDER AMRINONE OR DOBUTAMINE. RULE OUT PULM THROMBOEMBOLSIM | DOBUTAMINE OR AMRINONE INFUSIONS | EPINEPHRINE 2-4 ug/min OR DOPAMINE 7-10 ug/kg/min | DOPAMINE 8-20 ug/kg/min OR NEOSYNEPHRINE

ADJUST VENTILATOR AND CONSIDER PEEP PER ABG MEASUREMENTS
MONITOR COAGULATION STATUS, TREAT D.I.C. WITH FFP AND PLATELETS

cerebrospinal fluid–mediated local anesthetic toxicity (Table 31-3).

Invasive Monitoring

Placement of arterial and pulmonary artery catheters is the next priority. Periodic arterial blood gas measurement will guide ventilator therapy. Intelligent use of a pulmonary artery catheter can be invaluable in choosing and titrating vasoactive drugs, as well as optimizing volume status (see Fig. 31-4).

Blood Product Therapy

Delayed coagulopathy (disseminated intravascular coagulation) develops in 40% of patients who survive the initial insult of AFE. Concomitant uterine atony also may occur. Frequent laboratory evaluation of coagulation profiles (fibrinogen, fibrin split products, prothrombin time, partial thromboplastin time, and platelet counts) provides a basis for therapy. Treat this usually self-limited coagulopathy with factor (fresh frozen plasma) and platelet replacement. Treatment of uterine atony includes uterine massage, oxytocin, methergonovine, and avoidance of volatile anesthetic agents. Use prostaglandin $F_{2\alpha}$ only with extreme caution, as it may further complicate matters by inciting severe hypoxemia and hypotension.[48,49]

CONCLUSIONS

Amniotic fluid embolism syndrome remains a significant cause of maternal morbidity and mortality. Although the symptom complex involving maternal hypotension, hypoxemia, and coagulopathy clearly exists, the link to amniotic fluid remains unproved. Amniotic fluid commonly enters the maternal circulation, yet clinical AFE syndrome is very rare. Amniotic fluid has a highly variable ability to activate complement and the arachidonic acid pathways. Women vary tremendously in their susceptibility to complement activation and prostaglandin synthesis. Current knowledge suggests that clinical AFE syndrome results when a significant volume of amniotic fluid high in complement-ac-

tivating ability enters the circulation of a woman predisposed to excessive complement and arachidonic acid metabolite response.

The diagnosis rests upon excluding potential imitators of AFE, whereas therapy remains essentially supportive. Early invasive monitoring appears essential to optimize intravascular volume and to choose appropriate vasoactive drugs. The finding of squamous cells and fetal debris in a pulmonary artery catheter aspirate is necessary but not sufficient for the diagnosis.

More than 40 years ago, Eastman[65] advised against making AFE syndrome "a wastebasket for all cases of unexplained death in labor." An equally sage observation is that "the diagnosis of amniotic fluid embolism has been the escape hatch through which makers of errors in judgement can gain freedom."[66] Our challenge remains to identify correctly this vexing syndrome, so that we can treat it optimally and understand it better.

REFERENCES

1. Morgan M. Amniotic fluid embolism. Anaesthesia 1979;34:20.
2. Ratten GJ. Amniotic fluid emboism—2 cases and a review of maternal deaths from this cause in Australia. Aust NZ J Obstet Gynaecol 1988;28:33.
3. Meyer JR. Embolis pulmonar-caseosa. Brazil-Med 1926;2:301.
4. Attwood HD. Matthew Baillie—a possible early description of amniotic fluid embolism. Aust NZ Obstet Gynaecol 1979;19:176.
5. Steiner PE, Lushbaugh CC. Maternal pulmonary embolism by amniotic fluid as a cause of obstetric shock and unexplained death in obstetrics. J Am Med Assoc 1941;117:1245.
6. Liban E, Raz S. A clinicopathologic study of fourteen cases of amniotic fluid embolism. Am J Clin Pathol 1969;51:477.
7. Resnik R, Swartz WH, Plumer MH, Benirschke K, Stratthaus ME. Amniotic fluid embolism with survival. Obstet Gynecol 1976;47:295.
8. Dolyniuk M, Orfei E, Vania H, Karlman R, Tomich P. Rapid diagnosis of amniotic fluid embolism. Obstet Gynecol 1983;61:28S.
9. Agia G, Wyatt L, Re E. Pulmonary microvascular cytology: A new diagnostic application of the pulmonary artery catheter. Chest 1986;90:627.

◄

Figure 31–4. A therapeutic algorithm for amniotic fluid embolism syndrome. (ABG = arterial blood gas, BP = blood pressure, CO = cardiac output, CPR = cardiopulmonary resuscitation, FFP = fresh frozen plasma, HTN = hypertension, PA = pulmonary artery, PCWP = pulmonary capillary wedge pressure, PEEP = positive end-expiratory pressure, PVR = pulmonary vascular resistance, SVR = systemic vascular resistance, UOP = urine output)

10. Clark SL, Cotton DB, Gonick B, Greenspoon J, Phelan JP. Central hemodynamic alterations in amniotic fluid embolism. Am J Obstet Gynecol 1988;158:1124.

11. Kaunitz AM, Hughes JM, Grimes DA, Smith JC, Rochat RW, Kafrissen ME. Causes of maternal mortality in the United States. Obstet Gynecol 1985;65:605.

12. Clark SL. New concepts of amniotic fluid embolism: A review. Obstet Gynecol Surv 1990;45:360.

13. Shah K, Karlman R, Heller J. Ventricular tachycardia and hypotension with amniotic fluid embolism during cesarean section. Anesth Analg 1986;65:533.

14. Guidotti RJ, Grimes DA, Cates W. Fatal amniotic fluid embolism during legally induced abortion in the United States, 1972–1978. Am J Obstet Gynecol 1981;141:257.

15. Dodgson J, Martin J, Boswell J, Goodal HB, Smith R. Probable amniotic fluid embolism precipitated by amniocentesis and treated by exchange transfusion. Br Med J 1987;294:1322.

16. Olcott CO, Robinson AJ, Maxwell TM, et al. Amniotic fluid embolism and disseminated intravascular coagulation after blunt maternal trauma. J Trauma 1973:13:737.

17. Masson RG, Ruggieri J, Siddiqui MM. Amniotic fluid embolism: Definitive diagnosis in a survivor. Am Rev Respir Dis 1979;120:187.

18. Meier PR, Bowes WA. Amniotic fluid embolus-like syndrome presenting in the second trimester of pregnancy. Obstet Gynecol 1983;61:31S.

19. Shnider SM, Moya F. Amniotic fluid embolism. Anesthesiology 1961;22:108.

20. Quance D. Amniotic fluid embolism: Detection by pulse oximetry. Anesthesiology 1988;68:951.

21. Reeves JT, Daoud FS, Estridge M, Stone WH, McGary D. Pulmonary pressor effects of small amounts of bovine amniotic fluid. Respir Physiol 1974;20:231.

22. Jacques WE, Hampton JW, Bird RM, et al. Pulmonary hypertension and plasma thromboplastin antecedent deficiency in dogs. Arch Pathol 1960;69:248.

23. Halmajyi D, Starzecki B, Shearman RP. Experimental amniotic fluid embolism: Mechanism and treatment. Am J Obstet Gynecol 1962;84:251.

24. Attwood HD, Downing SE. Experimental amniotic fluid embolism. Surg Gynecol Obstet 1965;120:255.

25. Girard P, Mal H, Laine J-F, et al. Left heart failure in amniotic fluid embolism. Anesthesiology 1986;64:262.

26. Richards DS, Carter LS, Corke B, Spielman F, Cefalo RC. The effect of human amniotic fluid on the isolated perfused rat heart. Am J Obstet Gynecol 1988;158:210.

27. Phillips LL, Davidson EC. Procoagulant properties of amniotic fluid. Am J Obstet Gynecol 1972;113:911.

28. Mainprize TC, Maltby JR. Amniotic fluid embolism: A report of four probable cases. Can Anaesth Soc J 1986;33:382.

29. Barrows JJ. A documented case of amniotic fluid embolism presenting as fetal distress. Am J Obstet Gynecol 1982;143:599.

30. Vartikar JV, Johnson MD, Datta S. Precordial Doppler monitoring and pulse oximetry during cesarean delivery:

31. Detection of venous air embolism. Reg Anesth 1989;14:145.

31. Clark SL. Arachidonic acid metabolites and the pathophysiology of amniotic fluid embolism. Semin Reprod Endocrinol 1985;3:253.

32. Price TM, Baker VV, Cefalo RC. Amniotic fluid embolism. Three case reports with a review of the literature. Obstet Gynecol Surv 1985;40:462.

33. Sparr RA, Pritchard JA. Studies to detect the escape of amniotic fluid into the maternal circulation during parturition. Surg Gynecol Obstet 1958;107:560.

34. Talbert LM, Adcock DF, Weiss AE, et al. Studies on the pathogenesis of clotting defects during salt-induced abortions. Am J Obstet Gynecol 1973;115:656.

35. Roche WD, Norris HJ. Detection and significance of maternal pulmonary amniotic fluid embolism. Obstet Gynecol 1974;43:729.

36. Attwood HD, Park WW. Embolism to the lungs by trophoblast. J Obstet Gynaecol Br Commonwealth 1961;68:611.

37. Covone AE, Johnson PM, Mutton D, et al. Trophoblastic cells in peripheral blood from pregnant women. Lancet 1984;1:841.

38. Clark SL, Pavlova Z, Greenspoon J, Horenstein J, Phelan JP. Squamous cells in the maternal pulmonary circulation. Am J Obstet Gynecol 1986;154:104.

39. Kuhlman K, Hidvegi D, Tamura RK, Depp R. Is amniotic fluid in the central circulation of peripartum patients pathologic? Am J Perinatol 1985;2:295.

40. Reis RL, Pierce WS, Behrendt DM. Hemodynamic effects of amniotic fluid embolism. Surg Gynecol Obstet 1965;129:45.

41. Adamson K, Mueller-Heubach E, Myers R. The innocuousness of amniotic fluid infusion in the pregnant rhesus monkey. Am J Obstet Gynecol 1971;109:977.

42. Stolte L, Kessel HV, Seelen J, Eskes T, Wagatsuma T. Failure to produce the syndrome of amniotic fluid embolism by infusion of amniotic fluid and meconium into monkeys. Am J Obstet Gynecol 1967;98:694.

43. Clark SL, Motz FJ, Phelan JP. Hemodynamic alterations associated with amniotic fluid embolism: A reappraisal. Am J Obstet Gynecol 1985;151:617.

44. Ostergard DR. The physiology and clinical importance of amniotic fluid. Obstet Gynecol Surv 1970;25:297.

45. Azegami M, Mori N. Amniotic fluid embolism and leukotrienes. Am J Obstet Gynecol 1986;155:1119.

46. Karim SM, Delvin J. Prostaglandin content of amniotic fluid during pregnancy and labour. J Obstet Gynaecol Br Commonwealth 1967;74:230.

47. Kitzmiller JL, Lucas WE. Studies on a model of amniotic fluid embolism. Obstet Gynecol 1972;39:626.

48. Hankins GD, Berryman GK, Scott RT, Hood D. Maternal arterial desaturation with 15-methyl prostaglandin F$_2$ alpha for uterine atony. Obstet Gynecol 1988;72:367.

49. Douglas MJ, Farquharson DF, Ross PLE, Renwick JE. Cardiovascular collapse following an overdose of pros-

taglandin F$_2$ alpha: A case report. Can J Anaesth 1989;36:466.

50. Hammerschmidt DE, Ogburn PL, Williams JE. Amniotic fluid activates complement: A role in amniotic fluid embolism syndrome? J Lab Clin Med 1984; 104:901.

51. Horrow JC. Heparin reversal of protamine toxicity: Have we come full circle? J Cardiothorac Anesth 1990;4:539.

52. Ogburn PL, Johnson S, Williams PP, Holman RT. Levels of free fatty acids and arachidonic acid in pregnancy and labor. J Lab Clin Med 1980;95:943.

53. Keirse MJ, Hicks BR, Mitchell MD, Turnbull AC. Increase in the prostaglandin precursor, arachidonic acid, in amniotic fluid during spontaneous labor. Br J Obstet Gynaecol 1977;84:937.

54. Courtney LD. Amniotic fluid embolism. Obstet Gynecol Surv 1974;29:169.

55. Dutta D, Bhargava KC, Chakravarti RN, et al. Therapeutic studies in experimental amniotic fluid embolism in rabbits. Am J Obstet Gynecol 1970;106:1201.

56. Peterson EP, Taylor HB. Amniotic fluid embolism: An analysis of 40 cases. Obstet Gynecol 1970;35:787.

57. Steingrub JS, Lopez T, Teres D, Steingart R. Amniotic fluid embolism associated with castor oil ingestion. Crit Care Med 1988;16:642.

58. James FM. An evaluation of vasopressor therapy for maternal hypotension during spinal anesthesia. Anesthesiology 1970;33:35.

59. Forester D. Amniotic fluid embolism and emergency cardiac care. Ann Emerg Med 1984;13:1172.

60. Sterner S, Campbell B, Davies S. Amniotic fluid embolism. Ann Emerg Med 1984;343.

61. Oates S, Williams G, Rees GAD. Cardiopulmonary resuscitation in late pregnancy. Br Med J 1988;297:404.

62. DelGuercio LR, Feins NR, Cohn JD, et al. Comparison of blood flow during external and internal cardiac massage in man. Circulation 1982;31:1171.

63. Albright GA. Clinical aspects of bupivacaine toxicity: Report to the Anesthetic and Life-Support Drugs Advisory Committee. Rockville, MD: U.S. Department of Health and Human Services, 1983.

64. Rees GAD, Willis BA. Resuscitation in late pregnancy. Anaesthesia 1986;43:347.

65. Eastman NJ. Editorial. Obstet Gynecol Surv 1948;3:35.

66. Cron RS, Kilkenny GS, Wirthwein C, et al. Amniotic fluid embolism. Am J Obstet Gynecol 1952:64:1360.

CHAPTER 32

Anesthetic Complications: Intraoperative

Barbara L. Leighton

Obstetric anesthesia is remarkably safe, but many minor and major complications can and do occur. Some complications, such as hypotension, occur frequently despite our best attempts to prevent them. The incidence and consequences of complications can be minimized by understanding the relevant pathophysiology and treatment options. Other complications, such as failed intubation, occur only rarely but can be catastrophic. In this setting, careful patient evaluation and planning are necessary preventive measures.

This chapter attempts to describe some common and uncommon obstetric anesthesia complications that are diagnosed and treated intraoperatively. Chapter 38 discusses complications presenting or treated postoperatively.

I hope the reader will finish this chapter with the answers to the following questions:

- Why is a given event harmful to mother or fetus?
- Why is the parturient at greater risk of a given complication than her nonpregnant counterpart?
- Can the complication be prevented?
- Can the effects of the complication be minimized or eliminated even if the complication occurs?
- How can one best manage the consequences of a complication?

HYPOTENSION

Hypotension is the most common complication of obstetric regional anesthesia. Using available techniques to prevent hypotension repays tremendous dividends. The incidence of hypotension during spinal anesthesia for cesarean section decreases from 79% to 100% to 0% to 15% by using left uterine displacement, intravenous fluid preload, and intravenous venoconstrictor drugs (Table 32-1).[1-3]

Why Are Obstetric Anesthesiologists So Worried About Hypotension?

Severe hypotension can prove fatal for both mother and fetus; "spinal shock" was once a common cause of maternal mortality.[4] Infants delivered after severe hypotension lasting more than 4 minutes may be acidotic and have poor Apgar scores.[5,6] Mild hypotension produces few maternal symptoms but is poorly tolerated by the fetus. Uterine blood flow falls in proportion to the decrease in maternal blood pressure.[7] Infants of hypotensive mothers (mean arterial pressure < 70 mm Hg during epidural anesthesia for cesarean section) had normal Apgar scores but weak rooting and sucking reflexes for 2 days.[8]

Table 32-1

Incidence of Hypotension During Spinal Anesthesia for Cesarean Section

	CLARK		MARX
	Labor	No Labor	No Labor
No prophylaxis, supine patient	50%	92%	—
No fluid, LUD	—	—	100%
Fluid (1 L D$_5$RL), supine patient	46%	57%	—
Ephedrine (25 mg IM), LUD	—	—	56%
Fluid (1 L D$_5$RL), LUD	15%	53%	0%
Ephedrine (25 mg IM), fluid (1L D$_5$RL), LUD	—	—	10%*

(Data from Clark RB, Thompson DS, Thompson CH. Prevention of spinal hypotension associated with cesarean section. Anesthesiology 1976;45:670, and Marx GF, Cosmi EV, Wollman SB. Biochemical status and clinical condition of mother and infant at cesarean section. Anesth Analg 1969;48:986)
*The authors felt that the degree of left uterine tilt employed was insufficient to relieve aortocaval compression in one obese parturient.
Abbreviations: LUD = left uterine displacement, RL = Ringer's lactate.

What Constitutes Treatment-requiring Hypotension in a Parturient?

Maternal blood pressure does not affect maternal or fetal condition if the systolic pressure remains above 100 mm Hg or the maternal systolic blood pressure falls less than 30% (whichever is greater).[2,5,9] The fetal effects of mild-to-moderate maternal hypotension depend on the duration of hypotension and maternal hydration. A healthy fetus tolerates hypotension that persists for less than 4 minutes.[5,6] Generous maternal intravenous fluid administration blunts the fetal acidosis following maternal hypotension during spinal anesthesia for cesarean section. Fetal umbilical acidemia occurred less frequently if mothers received 1000 to 1500 mL of crystalloid intravenously before induction than if they received only 500 to 999 mL.[10] When mothers received 1500 to 2000 mL of balanced salt solution intravenously, the incidence of fetal umbilical acidemia did not differ between the offspring of mildly to moderately hypotensive mothers (systolic blood pressure 70–100 mm Hg for 0–15 min) and normotensive mothers.[11]

Why Are Parturients So Susceptible to Hypotension?

Aortocaval Compression

Compression of the inferior vena cava and the aorta by the abdominal contents occurs rarely in nonpreg-

nant patients but almost universally among parturients. The inferior vena cava is an easily collapsed blood vessel that frequently gets caught between a rock (the gravid uterus) and a hard place (the maternal vertebral bodies).[12]

The following factors increase the incidence and severity of aortocaval compression.

SUPINE POSITION. Obstruction of the inferior vena cava produces supine hypotension (a decrease in systolic blood pressure of $\geq$ 30 mm Hg or a systolic blood pressure $\leq$ 80 mm Hg) in 6% to 11% of term parturients (Fig. 32-1).[13,14] Aortic compression can occur in 37% of supine term parturients.[15]

HYPOVOLEMIA. The uterus compresses the vena cava in supine parturients. This compression worsens as the pressure within the vena cava falls.

SPINAL OR EPIDURAL ANESTHESIA. Spinal and epidural blockade induce a form of distributive hypovolemia. Hypotension during spinal or epidural anesthesia occurs when the cardiac preload (not the afterload) decreases.[16,17] Using impedance cardiography during epidural anesthesia for cesarean section, Ramanathan and Grant[17] found that stroke volume and end-diastolic volume diminished significantly during hypotension, whereas systemic vascular resistance barely changed (Fig. 32-2). Ephedrine or phenylephrine treatment restored the blood pressure, stroke volume, and end-diastolic volume to baseline values, whereas the systemic vascular resistance decreased further.[17] Central venous pressure (CVP) falls in both

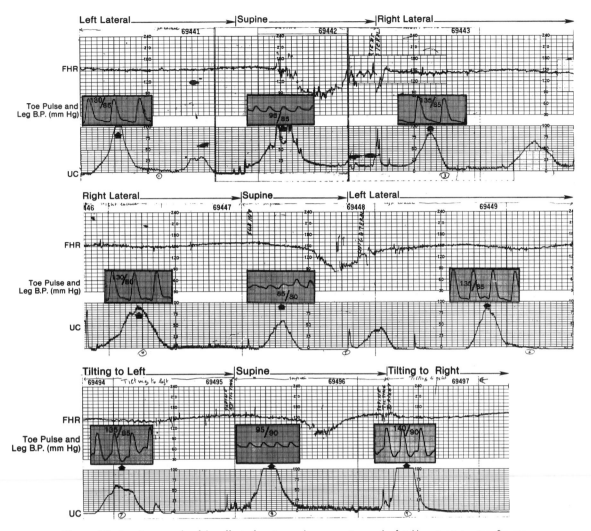

Figure 32–1. An example of the effect of aortocaval compression on the fetal heart rate tracing. Severe late decelerations and lower limb hypotension are seen only in the supine position. (BP = blood pressure, FHR = fetal heart rate, UC = uterine contraction) (Arbitol MM. Supine position in labor and associated fetal heart rate changes. Obstet Gynecol 1985;65:481)

Figure 32–2. Stroke volume (SV), end-diastolic volume (EDV), and systemic vascular resistance (SVR) at three time points: (1) before anesthesia, (2) during hypotension, and (3) after treatment with ephedrine or phenylephrine. (* = significantly different from time points 1 and 3. Measurements in the control group were obtained before anesthesia and at T-6 sensory level.) (Ramanathan S, Grant GJ. Vasopressor therapy for hypotension due to epidural anesthesia for cesarean section. Acta Anaesthesiol Scand 1988;32:559)

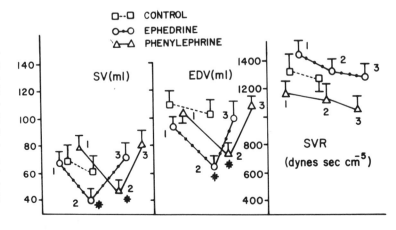

normotensive and hypotensive parturients during spinal anesthesia, attaining lower values in the hypotensive patients.[16]

UTERINE CONTRACTIONS. The uterus compresses the more posteriorly placed vena cava only *between* contractions (Fig. 32-3).[13] Maternal hypotension occurs more frequently during caval obstruction (between contractions). Aortic occlusion occurs almost exclusively *during* uterine contractions (Fig. 32-4).[12,15,18] Despite maternal body position, the uterus squeezes the aorta during contractions in up to 86% of laboring women.[12]

OTHER OBSTETRIC FACTORS. Laboring patients have a lower incidence of hypotension than do nonlaboring parturients during epidural or spinal anesthesia for cesarean section.[3,19] Aortic compression is more frequent if the cervix is dilated less than 5 cm or if the fetal head is not engaged in the pelvis.[12,15,20] Occiput–posterior fetal head position also increases the risk of aortic compression.[12]

Rapid Development of Sympathetic Nerve Block

Sympathetic nerve block develops more quickly in pregnant than in nonpregnant women during regional anesthesia. Intrinsic homeostatic mechanisms then cannot compensate for this sympatholysis as it develops.[21]

What Is the Best Way to Prevent or Treat Hypotension?

The anesthesiologist has the following three weapons in the fight against hypotension:

- Manipulation of maternal body position to prevent aortocaval compression
- Infusion of balanced salt or colloid solution intravenously
- Administration of a drug to constrict maternal capacitance vessels

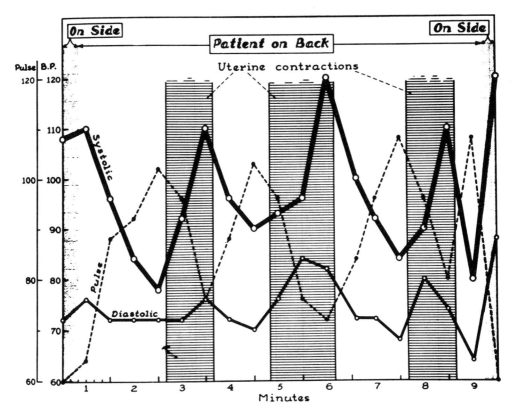

Figure 32–3. An example of the effect of inferior venocaval compression on maternal pulse and blood pressure (BP). Note that the pulse and blood pressure normalize during uterine contractions. (Howard BK, Goodson JH, Mengert WF. Supine hypotensive syndrome in late pregnancy. Obstet Gynecol 1953;1:373)

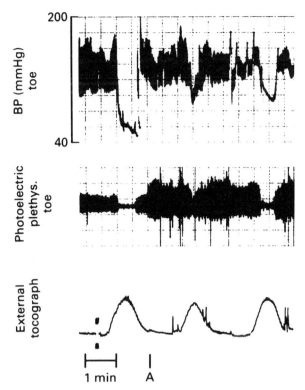

Figure 32–4. An example of intermittent aortic compression during uterine contractions. (BP = blood pressure, Plethys = plethysmograph) (Kinsella SM, Whitwam JG, Spencer JAD. Aortic compression by the uterus: identification with the Finapres digital arterial pressure instrument. Br J Obstet Gynaecol 1990;97:700)

None of these ways is sufficient by itself; a combination approach must be used.

Left Uterine Displacement

Hypotension following the initiation of modified saddle block anesthesia was completely relieved by left uterine displacement in 93% of the laboring parturients.[22] Left uterine displacement decreased the incidence of hypotension from 46% to 15% at cesarean section in hydrated, laboring patients.[3]

The full left or right lateral position completely relieves aortocaval compression (Fig. 32-1).[12] Elevating the mother's right hip 10 to 15 cm improves femoral arterial blood pressure in all women and completely relieves aortocaval compression in 58% of term parturients.[20] In some patients, tilting the uterus to the right is more effective than leftward tilt.[20] Inserting a wedge under the right hip instead of using a mechanical uterine displacement device better preserves femoral (and presumably uterine) arterial pressure.[20,23,24]

Intravenous Hydration

Despite a 40% increase in blood volume, parturients appear hypovolemic when facing the twin assaults of a total sympathectomy and compressed abdominal blood vessels. The CVP of healthy parturients increased from 8 to 10 cm H_2O after rapid intravenous infusion of 1 L of D_5 Ringer's lactate with no evidence of heart failure.[16] The CVP of both hydrated and nonhydrated patients fell 4 cm H_2O after induction of high spinal anesthesia. Only the nonhydrated women became hypotensive. After delivery, both groups of women had similar CVP and blood pressure.[16] One liter of the hypertonic fluid (D_5 Ringer's lactate) prevents hypotension efficiently, but rapid infusion of this amount of dextrose can lead to neonatal hypoglycemia.[3,16,25,26] One liter of balanced salt solution without dextrose before high spinal or epidural anesthesia fails to prevent hypotension reliably.[19] Colloid solutions offer no advantages over larger volumes of crystalloid solution in healthy parturients.[27] Infusion of 2 L of dextrose-free balanced salt solution immediately before high spinal or epidural anesthesia in healthy parturients produces excellent conditions in the mother (7% hypotension incidence, all CVPs <12 cm H_2O) and the infant (low incidence of acidosis).[11,28]

Pressors

Pressors are double-edged swords. Administration of a small amount of a venoconstrictor to a hydrated, laterally tilted parturient can restore cardiac preload without affecting uterine blood flow.[5,17] On the other hand, large doses of potent arterial constrictors decrease uterine blood flow (especially in poorly hydrated women) and further the fetal insult.[5,29] The drug dose, drug venous/arterial selectivity, and patient hydration status determine whether the pressor will improve or worsen the intrauterine environment.

EPHEDRINE. Ephedrine remains the pressor of choice in most obstetric situations. No other agent surpasses its performance in clinical or animal studies. In hydrated parturients during cesarean section, prompt treatment of hypotension with intravenous ephedrine rapidly restores maternal blood pressure and cardiac output. Timely therapy also ensures excellent neonatal outcome.[1,3,17] Ephedrine also elevates maternal heart rate and cardiac inotropy.[30] Ephedrine returned uterine blood flow to 90% of baseline during spinal anesthesia–induced hypotension in gravid ewes.[7] Ephedrine did not decrease uterine blood flow in unanesthetized ewes despite producing a 50% increase in maternal blood pressure.[29] Ephedrine crosses the placenta, increases fetal heart rate and beat-to-beat variability, and transiently affects the neonatal electroencephalogram.[31-33]

Ephedrine, 5 to 10 mg intravenously, when the maternal blood pressure starts to drop, or prophylactic intravenous ephedrine infusion following spinal injection, prevents maternal hypotension, nausea, and vomiting, and neonatal acidosis.[1,8] Although prophylactic intramuscular ephedrine worked well in one case series, other authors have reported a high incidence of hypotension as well as excessive hypertension with this regimen.[2,34,35]

Occasionally I find that ephedrine fails. Despite more than 2 L of prehydration and left lateral tilt, 50 mg or more of ephedrine increases maternal heart rate but not maternal blood pressure. Ephedrine, a mixed alpha- and beta-adrenergic agonist, occasionally shows predominately beta-adrenergic effects. Switching to phenylephrine, an alpha-1 agonist, usually corrects the hypotension quickly.

PHENYLEPHRINE. In well-hydrated, laterally tilted parturients, phenylephrine, 20 to 100 µg, and ephedrine, 5 to 10 mg, are equally effective. Both restore maternal blood pressure and cardiac preload (see Fig. 32-2) while ensuring good neonatal acid–base status, Apgar scores, and neurobehavioral scores.[17,36,37]

MEPHENTERMINE. In gravid ewes made hypotensive with spinal anesthesia, mephentermine increases uterine blood flow to 90% of baseline (as does ephedrine).[5] However, in unanesthetized hypertensive gravid ewes, mephentermine decreases uterine blood flow 20%.[29]

METARAMINOL AND METHOXAMINE. These agents decrease uterine blood flow in unanesthetized and spinally anesthetized gravid ewes.[5,29]

Leg Wrapping

Wrapping both legs with elastic Esmarch bandages after spinal placement prevented hypotension in hydrated, tilted parturients at cesarean section.[38] Inflatable boots and splints have not been effective in preventing hypotension.[39,40]

All effective hypotension prevention and treatment regimens have the same goal: maintenance of an adequate maternal cardiac preload. Position all parturients receiving regional anesthesia properly to avoid aortocaval compression. Infuse an adequate intravenous fluid preload of balanced salt solution. Give pro-

phylactic venopressors if desired. Always be prepared to treat decreases in blood pressure with an appropriate intravenous pressor.

UNINTENDED DURAL PUNCTURE DURING EPIDURAL CATHETER PLACEMENT

Diagnosis

The gold standard for clinical diagnosis of subarachnoid needle or catheter position is the development of spinal anesthesia after the injection of an appropriate amount of local anesthetic. In parturients, this event is usually defined as the onset of sensory anesthesia 2 to 3 minutes after injection and motor nerve block 3 to 5 minutes after injection of one of the following local anesthetics: lidocaine, 30 to 45 mg; bupivacaine, 12.5 mg; or 2-chloroprocaine, 100 mg.[41-43] Test all epidural catheters (or needles, if local anesthetic is to be injected through the epidural needle) in this manner before giving larger doses of local anesthetic.

Recognizing a dural puncture is simple if clear fluid flows in a continuous stream from the epidural needle or catheter. Occasionally, one can aspirate a small (0.2–2 mL) amount of clear fluid after injecting saline or local anesthetic. On which side of the dura did the fluid originate?

A urine dipstrip is a convenient, but not infallible, testing method.[44,45] The most reliable assay is the pH (local anesthetic is pH 5, cerebrospinal fluid [CSF] is pH 7; see Table 32-2). Cerebrospinal fluid itself is only weakly positive for glucose. Local anesthetic tests false positive for protein; however, 0.2 to 0.6 mL amounts of fluid aspirated from epidural catheters before reinjection may have a physiologic pH and test positive for glucose despite the absence of a dural puncture.[46]

Table 32–2

Urine Test Strip Properties of Fluids that Might be Aspirated from the Epidural Space

FLUID	pH	GLUCOSE	PROTEIN
Cerebrospinal fluid	7	0–1+	Trace–1+
Saline	5	0	0
Local anesthetic	5	0	2+–4+
Epidural aspirate, no dural puncture	7	0–2+	Trace

Initial Management

Puncture of the dura with either the epidural needle or catheter occurs in 1% to 2.5% of attempted obstetric lumbar epidural anesthetics.[47,48] Mostly, the dura is punctured with the needle and the problem is immediately obvious, for CSF is visible in the needle hub.[47,48] Four courses of action are then possible:

- *Pull the needle out and insert an epidural catheter at another interspace.* This choice introduces the risk of puncturing the dura a second time[49] but permits administration of a prophylactic epidural blood patch if desired.[50] One must test the catheter for subarachnoid position (as described above) and inject drug slowly, for the incidence of unintended subdural and subarachnoid cannulation is higher than if the previous dural puncture had not occurred.[51]
- *Convert to a single-shot spinal anesthetic.* Insert a longer spinal needle through the epidural needle, see freely flowing CSF, and inject drug. I do not recommend injecting drug through the epidural needle itself. The tip of the epidural needle may be partially subarachnoid and partially epidural. Even if CSF is flowing freely, injection of bupivacaine, 15 mg, may lead to a two-dermatome epidural.
- *Thread a catheter and manage as a continuous catheter spinal anesthetic.* Remember, aspirating CSF is no guarantee that the catheter is in the subarachnoid space; the catheter may be subdural or epidural and should be handled with care.[52,53] A spinal catheter (of whatever gauge) can be an excellent technique for analgesia for labor or cesarean section (see Chap. 20). Unfortunately, the prolonged presence of a spinal catheter does not decrease the incidence of postdural puncture headache in parturients.[49]
- *Pull the needle back until CSF no longer drips and thread a catheter into the "epidural space."* Kalas and Hehre[47] attempted this maneuver in a series of 11 patients. Eight patients had successful epidural blocks, two patients had spinal anesthetics, and in one patient, no block developed. This is a tempting course of action, but I have rarely seen it successfully done and cannot recommend it.

Occasionally, the dura appears to have been punctured by the catheter; no fluid is seen in the epidural needle, but CSF is freely aspirated through the catheter. In this situation, leave the catheter in situ and initiate a continuous spinal catheter anesthetic or remove the catheter entirely and replace it at another interspace. Withdrawing the catheter until CSF can no longer be aspirated and injecting local anesthetic is a riskier course of action that Kalas and Hehre[47] attempted four times. Two of the catheters remained subarachnoid, whereas two were correctly withdrawn into the epidural space.

Management of Epidural Catheters Placed After Dural Puncture

The presence of a fresh dural puncture raises several management issues.

Should One Decrease the Epidural Dose of Local Anesthetic?

If the catheter is truly in the epidural space (as opposed to being subarachnoid, subdural, or out in left field), I usually find that little reduction in the local anesthetic dose is needed or desired.

Can One Safely Administer 2-Chloroprocaine?

Neurotoxicity following subarachnoid injection of massive amounts of the old, metabisulfite formulation of 2-chloroprocaine was so well known and feared that many anesthesiologists refused to administer epidural 2-chloroprocaine to patients with a fresh dural puncture. 2-Chloroprocaine has been reformulated with EDTA instead of metabisulfite to minimize the risk of nerve damage. Although no neurotoxicity cases have been reported, the new formulation still has a short track record.

Should One Administer a Prophylactic Epidural Blood Patch Through the Catheter at the End of the Anesthetic?

Early attempts at prophylactic epidural blood patch were unsuccessful, and the technique fell into disrepute. Loeser *et al*[54] reported a 71% failure rate among epidural blood patches with 10 mL of autologous blood performed within 24 hours of the dural puncture. The recent push to discharge all parturients from the hospital quickly has led several investigators to reexamine this practice using larger volumes of blood. Following unintended dural puncture with an 18-gauge epidural needle, 16 patients in two case series received 15 to 20 mL of freshly drawn autologous blood through an epidural catheter placed at an adjacent interspace.[55,56] Only one patient developed any headache, and that did not require further treatment. The one randomized trial performed to date reports a definite but more realistic clinical effect. Thirty-nine patients with unintended 18-gauge dural punctures were randomized to receive an epidural injection of 15 mL of autologous blood or no injection following delivery.[50] Prophylactic epidural blood patch decreased the headache incidence from 80% to 35% ($P<0.005$). The decrease in the need for therapeutic blood patch (7 vs 3 patients) did not reach statistical significance.

If one decides to do a prophylactic epidural blood patch, one should wait until the local anesthetic blockade has receded before injecting the blood. In one case, injection of 15 mL of blood through an epidural catheter when the sensory level was T-4 produced a block that was either a total subdural or a total spinal but was certainly a total clinical problem.[57]

Many anesthesiologists are concerned about the possibility of causing meningitis or an epidural abscess by injecting blood through an epidural catheter that has been used intermittently for many hours. No such cases have been reported yet, but the technique of prophylactic blood patch has only recently become popular.

Does a Dural Puncture Decrease the Incidence of Successful Epidural Block in a Subsequent Pregnancy?

In one large review, dural puncture in a previous pregnancy lowered the incidence of successful epidural analgesia from 89% to 92% to 59% to 65%.[58] Previous epidural blood patch did not affect the success rate.

HIGH OR TOTAL SPINAL ANESTHESIA

Excessively extensive spinal anesthesia is most frequently seen in the following clinical circumstances:

- *Unrecognized dural puncture by the epidural needle or catheter.* Dawkins[48] reports that this event complicates 0.2% of epidural anesthetics. Be vigilant with every epidural dose. There are many reports of catheters that eroded into the subarachnoid space after one or more apparently normal epidural doses.[59–61] Although no one catheter type is implicated in the available case reports, there are theoretical reasons to suspect that this problem occurs more frequently with multiholed epidural catheters. Multiorifice catheters have been placed with the holes in different bodily compartments.[62] Flow through the more distal holes increases with increasing injection pressure.[63] A multiholed catheter with only its tip in the subarachnoid space may behave as an epidural during initial, slow injection. Later, if injected rapidly, high spinal block may result.

- *Spinal anesthesia for cesarean section initiated immediately following institution of a patchy epidural anesthetic.* There is at least one such case in the literature,[64] and I am aware of several unreported cases from my institution. In this circumstance, I decrease the amount of subarachnoid bupivacaine from 15 mg to 8 to 10 mg.

- *Unexpectedly high block during a primary spinal anesthetic for cesarean section.*[65]

- *High spinal block following administration of the initial local anesthetic "test dose."* Spinal anesthesia requiring intubation and ventilation has occurred after injection of a mere 2.5 mL of 2% 2-chloroprocaine[66] and 3.0 mL of 0.5% bupivacaine.[67]

In the first case, the diagnosis and needed management are rarely in doubt. Within 2 minutes of injection, the patient develops extensive sensory and motor block, profound hypotension, apnea, and loss of consciousness. The following actions need to be taken quickly:

- Turn the patient supine with left uterine displacement.

- Ventilate with 100% oxygen via mask with cricoid pressure until intubation can be safely accomplished. Do not attempt to intubate unless appropriate supplies and a competent assistant are in the room and the patient is well oxygenated (if possible). Inject succinylcholine, 1 mg/kg intravenously, to optimize visualization, preceded by a small dose of thiopental if the blood pressure permits. I advocate ventilation before intubation because the long-term consequences of hypoxia to the mother and the fetus are usually worse than the morbidity from aspiration. Once an airway is established, continue ventilation until the patient regains consciousness and can maintain a good 5-second head lift or hand grip.

- Administer fluids and pressors vigorously to maintain an adequate blood pressure. The hypotension seen in this situation can be profound and difficult to treat.

Proper management of the remaining situations just listed may not be so obvious. At what point is a spinal too high? Most of the patients who complain vigorously of shortness of breath, appear anxious, and have a weaker-than-normal hand grip are, in fact, fine and need only reassurance. I recommend induction of general anesthesia and endotracheal intubation in the following situations:

- When the patient is unable to maintain oxygen saturation greater than 95% despite breathing 100% oxygen via face mask
- When the patient can whisper but can no longer phonate. I am concerned here about the patient's ability to prevent aspiration.

I recommend applying cricoid pressure, administering 1 to 3 mg/kg of thiopental (based on blood pressure) and 1.5 mg/kg of succinylcholine, ventilating with 100% oxygen until the patient is well oxygenated (if necessary), intubating, and finishing the case as a general anesthetic.

SUBDURAL ANESTHESIA

Unintended subdural, epiarachnoid anesthesia, a complication first reported by de Saram[68] and reviewed by Massey Dawkins,[48] Lubenow,[69] and Reynolds and Speedy,[70] is clinically recognized during 0.1% to 0.8% of attempted epidural anesthetics. The true incidence may be much higher. Mehta[71] radiographically showed partial subdural Tuohy needle position in 7 of 100 attempted epidural anesthetics. Subdural injection occurs more frequently during attempted subarachnoid needle placement; it complicates 10% to 13% of attempted myelograms.[72] Subdural injection may be a more important cause of failed spinal anesthesia than is generally realized, for general anesthesia may be induced before the signs of subdural anesthesia appear.

The clinical picture can be confusing, for the characteristics of a subdural anesthetic are *not* halfway between those of spinal and epidural anesthetics. The chief clinical features of subdural anesthesia following injection of 2 to 10 mL of local anesthetic are as follows:[68]

- *Extremely delayed anesthetic onset.* Most authors report a delay of 5 to 45 minutes between local anesthetic injection and the first signs of sensory block.
- *Extensive sensory block, frequently extending to cervical levels.* Although the sensory block is extensive, it is frequently patchy or asymmetric and may be entirely one-sided.[73,74]
- *Loss of consciousness accompanying high sensory blocks.* Unlike the epidural space, the subdural space does extend intracranially.[75]
- *Hypotension.* Maternal blood pressure requires treatment, but the severity of hypotension is less than that accompanying total spinal anesthesia.
- *Variable motor block.*
- *Respiratory depression.* Respiration is usually compromised, although total apnea is uncommon.

- *Prolonged time to complete clinical recovery.* Most patients recover fully in 2 to 6 hours, although an 11-hour recovery has been reported.[76]

Subdural anesthesia is rarely reported following injection of larger volumes of local anesthetic. Perhaps the fluid pressure from larger volume injections ruptures the arachnoid membrane and produces a total spinal anesthetic.

Risk Factors

Factors that increase the risk of subdural anesthesia include previous back surgery,[69] dural puncture at the same or adjacent interspace,[77–79] and rotation of the Tuohy needle 180 degrees (with gentle needle advancement) following identification of the epidural space.[80]

A word here in defense of the practice of rotating the epidural 90 degrees with gentle needle retraction: This technique permits one to identify the epidural space with the bevel of the epidural needle oriented parallel to the longitudinal dural fibers. In the event of a dural puncture, parallel needle bevel orientation decreases the headache incidence from 80% to 52% and the epidural blood patch rate from 50% to 19%.[81] Following rotation, the catheter can then be threaded in the midline. Our department has used this technique in the performance of approximately 4000 obstetric epidurals and has observed no increase in the dural puncture or subdural catheterization rates.[81]

Management

The initial subdural injection usually provides a more extensive block than is clinically desired. Provide hemodynamic and respiratory support as needed. Although few authors report a second, deliberate subdural injection, the nature of a subdural block (extensive sensory analgesia with little motor or sympathetic nerve block) makes it appropriate for labor. I consider trying to continue to use the catheter. The arachnoid membrane can be punctured easily, so, before any injection, attempt slow, careful aspiration of the catheter with a 1- or 3-mL syringe. Then, inject a small volume of dilute local anesthetic (such as 1–3 mL of 0.5% lidocaine) and carefully monitor the patient for at least 45 minutes. Of course, most anesthesiologists, once burned, opt to replace the subdural with an epidural catheter at a different (usually more rostral) interspace.

UNINTENDED INTRAVENOUS PLACEMENT OF EPIDURAL NEEDLE OR CATHETER

Placing a needle or catheter into an epidural vein instead of the epidural space is all too easy to do in term-pregnant patients. During attempts to identify the epidural space, veins are cannulated in 5% to 15% of parturients versus 2.8% of nonpregnant patients.[48,82–84] To make matters worse, systemic local anesthetic toxicity occurs at lower drug doses in pregnant than in nonpregnant patients.

Can One Lower the Incidence of Epidural Venous Cannulation?

Injecting 10 mL of saline before threading an epidural catheter halved the incidence of venous cannulation in one study.[84] Injection of 3 mL of fluid did not affect the incidence of blood-vessel puncture.[85] Blood can be aspirated more frequently through three-holed than through single-holed catheters. It is unclear if three-holed catheters puncture veins more frequently or if intravenous placement is less readily diagnosed with single-holed catheters.[86]

How Can One Detect Catheters Located in Epidural Veins?

Doppler Method

Precordial Doppler monitoring during injection of 1 to 2 mL of air through the epidural catheter detects most intravenously located epidural catheters.[83,87] Because this method is independent of changes in maternal heart rate or chronotropic responsiveness, it is more appropriate than epinephrine for use in laboring women. In 313 consecutive laboring patients, aspiration for blood or the Doppler test identified all 21 of the intravenously placed epidural catheters.[83] Occasionally, the Doppler is too sensitive; epidural anesthesia developed normally in six (2%) of the patients who had a positive Doppler test. Because tinnitus also occurred in two of these six patients after lidocaine injection, some communication between a vein and the epidural space probably existed.[83]

The Doppler test is simple to perform. Insert an epidural catheter and administer a small dose of local anesthetic to test for unintended intrathecal catheter placement. Place the Doppler probe (an external fetal heart rate monitor works well for this purpose) slightly to the right of the lower maternal sternum and maneuver it

until clear maternal heart sounds are heard (Fig. 32-5). Inject 1 to 2 mL of air through the epidural catheter and listen for 15 seconds for changes in maternal heart sound changes. If the epidural catheter is in a vein, valvular maternal heart sounds ("lub-dub") become indistinct, and you will hear a loud, irregular, swishing sound.

The safety of the Doppler test in routine clinical practice has yet to be determined. Still, intravenous entrainment of air occurs so frequently and with such rare sequelae that safety problems with the Doppler test seem unlikely. Epidural injection of 10 mL of air during the air loss-of-resistance technique for identifying the epidural space (which has been used in millions of parturients) produces Doppler-detectable intracardiac air 43% of the time.[88] Unlike the air emboli that occur in 10% to 65% of cesarean section patients, the Doppler test involves a small, known amount of air.[89–91] By capitalizing on the diagnostic potential of a common clinical occurrence, the Doppler test avoids exposing the mother and fetus to the risks of intravenous local anesthetic or epinephrine.

Epinephrine

Epinephrine, 15 µg, detects unintended epidural venous cannulation in most nonpregnant patients.[92] It does not work as well in parturients, especially those in labor.[93] The problems are fourfold.

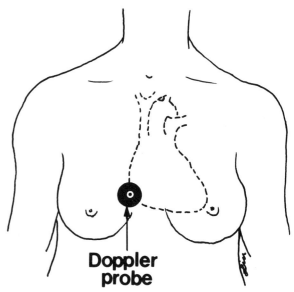

Figure 32–5. Correct probe position on the maternal chest during performance of the Doppler test to detect unintended intravascular epidural catheter location.

- Healthy pregnant women are comparatively insensitive to chronotropic agents. Increasing the heart rate by 25 beats/minute requires five times as much isoproterenol in healthy pregnant women as in nonpregnant women or mildly pre-eclamptic patients.[94,95]

- Epinephrine, a mixed alpha- and beta-adrenergic agonist, does not consistently produce maternal tachycardia. The mean maternal heart rate effect of epinephrine, 15 µg intravenously, is tachycardia for 80 seconds followed by mild bradycardia lasting at least 3 minutes.[93] However, some laboring women never become tachycardic (Fig. 32-6).

- Cyclic maternal heart rate changes occur in unanesthetized laboring women. In 12% to 45% of actively laboring women, maternal heart rate increases more than 30 beats/minute with each painful uterine contraction (Fig. 32-7).[93,96] Maternal heart rate is more stable in nonlaboring parturients. Epinephrine seems a more reliable indicator before elective cesarean section.[96]

- The fetal effects of unintended intravenous epinephrine injection remain unclear. Epinephrine doses comparable to 15 µg in a 70-kg patient decrease uterine blood flow for 2 to 5 minutes in gravid ewes and guinea pigs.[97,98] Ominous fetal heart rate patterns lasting 10 to 12 minutes occurred in 2 of 10 previously healthy fetuses after maternal intravenous injection of epinephrine, 15 µg.[93] On the other hand, sheep fetuses stressed by partial umbilical cord occlusion were equally acidotic after maternal intravenous injection of bupivacaine, 12.5 mg, and fentanyl, 50 µg, with or without epinephrine, 16.5 µg.[99]

If one uses an epinephrine test dose, one must monitor the maternal pulse with a device that provides an accurate digital display of the instantaneous maternal heart rate. A finger on an artery does not suffice.[94] Commercial electrocardiograms or internal fetal heart rate monitors can be used.[93,96] Pulse oximeters frequently display a time-averaged heart rate; many mod-

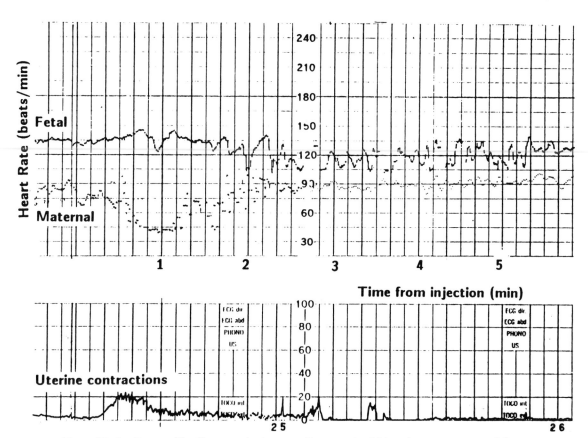

Figure 32–6. Tracing of fetal heart rate (*top*), maternal heart rate (*middle*), and uterine contractions following maternal injection of epinephrine, 15 µg IV, at time 0. Note the maternal bradycardia at 1 minute; maternal mean arterial pressure at the time was 152 mm Hg.

els cannot display rapid changes in maternal heart rate. In nonlaboring patients with a stable baseline maternal heart rate, one should monitor the maternal heart rate for at least 1 minute before and after injecting the epinephrine. A 25 beats/minute increase in maternal heart rate lasting at least 15 seconds suggests that the catheter is located in a vein. In actively laboring women, one must monitor the maternal heart rate through at least one contraction (generally 2–3 min) to establish a baseline. An increase of 10 beats/minute in the peak maternal heart rate during a contraction indicates intravenous catheter location (see Fig. 32-7). A maternal heart rate increase of 25 beats/minute lasting at least 15 seconds that does not occur during a uterine contraction also shows intravenous location.

When Should One Test Epidural Catheters for Intravenous Location?

One tests epidural catheters for intravenous location to avoid delaying the onset of epidural anesthesia and to avoid systemic local anesthetic toxicity. Test all catheters immediately after insertion. If one is using an existing catheter for cesarean section or tubal ligation, test it again just before local anesthetic injection. I do not routinely test catheters before reinjecting labor epidurals because the local anesthetic dose used and the risk of catheter migration are so low.

What Should One Do with the Catheter After Determining that It Is in a Vein?

Usually, remove the catheter and replace it at another interspace. If you have placed a labor epidural only after great difficulty, you may attempt to rescue it by withdrawing the catheter slightly. Use it only if a repeat Doppler test is negative. Inject 5 to 8 mL of lidocaine 1% (not bupivacaine). Watch carefully for symptoms of intravenous local anesthetic injection. The amount of local anesthetic needed for cesarean section is so large that I would abandon an intravenously located catheter and proceed to a spinal or repeat epidural anesthetic.

BUPIVACAINE: A POTENT CARDIOELECTROPHYSIOLOGIC POISON

Bupivacaine is the most popular and the most arrhythmogenic local anesthetic currently used in parturients. Epidural injection of dilute bupivacaine pro-

vides sensory analgesia with minimal motor block, a valuable attribute during labor. Epidural bupivacaine is also widely used for cesarean section anesthesia. Initial animal studies did not suggest that bupivacaine was particularly arrhythmogenic.[100,101] However, a rash of maternal deaths following unintended intravenous bupivacaine injection in cesarean section patients led the Food and Drug Administration to ban the obstetric epidural use of 0.75% bupivacaine in the United States.[102–104]

Pathophysiology

Bupivacaine causes arrhythmias because it dissociates from myocardial sodium channels much more slowly than it binds to them, particularly at physiologic maternal heart rates.[105,106] The lidocaine:bupivacaine dose ratio for clinical effect, seizure induction, and myocardial depression is 4:1; however, bupivacaine is 16 times as potent as lidocaine in inducing cardiac arrhythmias.[107] Bupivacaine blocks fast sodium channels,[104] slow calcium channels,[108] and potassium channels.[109] Although both lidocaine and bupivacaine enter myocardial sodium channels quickly during the action potential, lidocaine is much less toxic because it dissociates 10 times more quickly during diastole (time constants: 154 vs 1557 ms).[104] Bupivacaine accumulates in myocardial sodium channels at heart rates of 60 to 150 beats/minute (Fig. 32-8).[104] Bupivacaine impairs impulse conduction at all levels of the myocardial conduction system but does not affect sinus node automaticity.[110] In addition to the direct effect of bupivacaine on cardiac conduction tissue, intracerebral bupivacaine produces ventricular arrhythmias and hypertension by increasing autonomic nervous system outflow from the brain stem.[111,112]

Arrhythmias

There is no one pathognomonic cardiac rhythm disturbance after unintended intravenous bupivacaine injection. The following electrocardiographic changes are frequently reported:

- Wide QRS complex
- Atrioventricular nodal block of varying degree
- Polymorphic ventricular tachycardia, which can progress to torsades de pointes (Fig. 32-9)
- Bradycardia with electromechanical dissociation, leading to:
- Asystole.

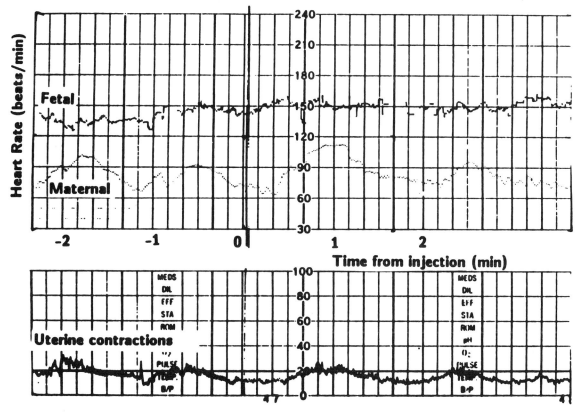

Figure 32–7. Tracing of fetal heart rate (*top*), maternal heart rate (*middle*), and uterine contractions following maternal injection of epinephrine, 15 μg IV, at time 0. Note the marked contraction-induced variation in maternal heart rate. Maternal heart rate increases 20 to 30 beats/minute with most uterine contractions and increases 40 beats/minute after the epinephrine injection. (Leighton BL. New advances in obstetric anesthesia. In: Barash PG, ed. Refresher courses in anesthesiology. Vol 19. Philadelphia: JB Lippincott, 1991:59)

Confounding Factors

Factors that increase bupivacaine electrophysiologic toxicity include the following:

- *Pregnancy.* Pregnant ewes develop arrhythmias and circulatory collapse at lower bupivacaine doses and blood concentrations than nonpregnant ewes (Fig. 32-10).[113] Pregnancy reduces bupivacaine binding by serum proteins, so more free drug is available to block sodium channels.[114]
- *Bupivacaine administration by rapid intravenous bolus injection.* Bupivacaine is very lipid soluble and highly protein bound. At steady state, plasma-free drug concentration is low. During rapid intravenous injection, toxic amounts of free drug can reach the heart and the brain before lipid uptake, and protein binding can occur. In addition, the percent of bound drug decreases with increasing serum concentrations of bupivacaine.[114]
- *Hypoxia and acidosis.*[115,116] Profound hypoxia and acidosis can develop within 90 seconds of the start of bupivacaine-induced convulsions in both humans and anesthetized dogs.[117,118]
- *Co-administration of small doses of epinephrine or phenylephrine.* Bupivacaine mixed with either epinephrine or phenylephrine is more toxic than plain bupivacaine.[119] This finding is surprising, because administration of massive doses of intravenous epinephrine is an integral feature of most successful animal resuscitation protocols.
- *Hyperkalemia or hyponatremia.*[120]
- *Presence of other drugs that decrease electrical conduction in the heart.* This is a long list, including class I antiarrhythmics (quinidine, procainamide, lidocaine, disopyramide, etc.), calcium entry blockers,[121] and beta-blockers.[122,123]

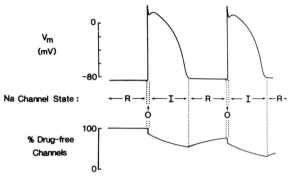

Figure 32–8. Schematic diagram showing local anesthetic block of cardiac sodium (Na) channels. The drug binds to sodium channels in open (O) and inactivated (I) states (*i.e.*, during the action potential [V$_m$]) but has a very low affinity for channels in the rested (R) state. Drug dissociation during diastole is time-dependent and incomplete, resulting in an accumulation of drug-associated (blocked) channels with successive beats. (Clarkson CW, Hondeghem LM. Mechanism for bupivacaine depression of cardiac conduction: Fast block of sodium channels during the action potential with slow recovery from block during diastole. Anesthesiology 1985;62:396)

Available Antiarrhythmics

Bupivacaine-induced arrhythmias have been treated successfully in animals with the following agents: bretylium, isoproterenol, magnesium, and diazepam or midazolam.

Bretylium

In anesthetized dogs with constant serum bupivacaine concentrations of 7 μg/mL, bretylium, 20 mg/kg, proved beneficial. Bretylium corrected bupivacaine-induced alterations in cardiac output, stroke volume,

heart rate, and systemic vascular resistance.[123] In this model, bupivacaine infusion produced no spontaneous ventricular arrhythmias, but bupivacaine infusion did lower the threshold for inducing sustained ventricular tachycardia. Bretylium administration returned this threshold to the normal range.[123]

Isoproterenol

In isolated rabbit hearts, isoproterenol, 1 to 2 μg/mL, corrects bupivacaine-induced prolongation of electrical conduction.[124] This treatment is counterintuitive, for isoproterenol induces tachycardia, which should increase sodium channel accumulation of bupivacaine; however, isoproterenol raises intracellular cyclic AMP concentration, thereby opening more calcium channels and compensating for the impaired sodium flux.[108] Isoproterenol is an effective antiarrhythmic in other torsades de pointes conditions.

Magnesium

Pretreatment of dogs with magnesium sulfate prevented widening of the QRS complex and QT interval but did not affect prolongation of the PR interval or the seizure dose of bupivacaine.[125] Magnesium has not been used to treat bupivacaine-induced arrhythmias, although magnesium successfully treats torsades de pointes arrhythmias due to other causes.

Diazepam or Midazolam

Benzodiazepines terminate arrhythmias caused by minute bupivacaine doses applied to the brain stem and, thus, may treat confounding GABA-mediated cerebral autonomic components of the arrhythmia.[111,112] Benzodiazepines also can treat or prevent further seizure activity.

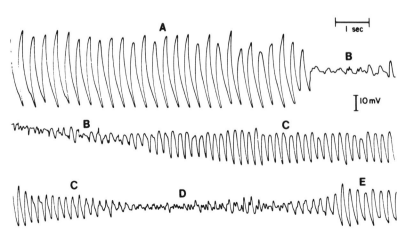

Figure 32–9. Bupivacaine-induced "torsades de pointes" ventricular tachycardia in the dog. Note that periods of "typical" ventricular tachycardia (*A* and *C*) are followed by what appears to be ventricular fibrillation (*B* and *D*), only to have "typical" ventricular tachycardia occur again (*E*). Visual inspection revealed regular organized contractions consistent with ventricular tachycardia throughout this time. (Kasten GW, Martin ST. Bupivacaine cardiovascular toxicity: Comparison of treatment with bretylium and lidocaine. Anesth Analg 1985; 64:911)

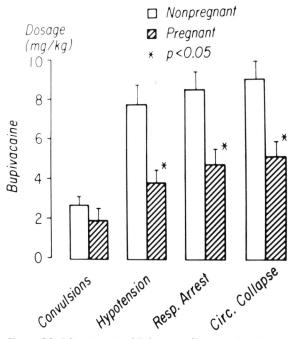

Figure 32–10.   Mean (± SE) dosages of bupivacaine administered to nonpregnant and pregnant ewes up to the onset of each toxic manifestation. (* = significantly different from nonpregnant ewes, Circ = circulatory, Resp = respiratory) (Morishima HO, Pedersen H, Finster M, et al. Bupivacaine toxicity in pregnant and nonpregnant ewes. Anesthesiology 1985;63:134)

Treatment

Treatment frequently involves a prolonged and difficult cardiac resuscitation. Because cardiac arrest caused by bupivacaine occurs so rarely and volunteer studies obviously have not been done, the following treatment recommendations are based on animal studies, case reports, and treatments that work in related conditions.

1. *Ventilate and oxygenate immediately.* This is not a trivial matter in the setting of an unexpected cardiac arrest. Profound hypoxia, hypercapnia, and acidosis occur more quickly in bupivacaine cardiotoxicity than in almost any other condition (*i.e.,* profound hypoxia develops within 90 s in previously well-ventilated dogs!).[118] Resuscitation is more difficult in response to hypoxia and acidosis. Intubate the trachea as quickly as possible, but do not delay ventilation pending tracheal intubation.
2. *Institute closed chest cardiac massage as needed.*
3. *Prevent any aortocaval compression.* In anesthetized dogs, partial inferior vena cava compression lengthened the time to successful resuscitation (22 vs 2 min) and significantly increased the amounts of epinephrine (7 vs 1 mg) and bicarbonate (46 vs 22 mEq) required (Table 32-3).[126] Because preventing aortocaval compression while maintaining effective closed chest cardiac massage may prove nearly impossible, one should strongly consider an emergency cesarean section.
4. *Emergency cesarean section.* In one case report, a mother could not be resuscitated until after the fetus was removed.[127] Both the mother and the baby survived.
5. *Antiarrhythmics.* The following drug therapy scheme has worked successfully in dogs weighing 20 to 25 kg and in sheep weighing 40 to 50 kg.[118,128]
   a. *Ventricular tachycardia.* Administer bretylium, 5 mg/kg intravenously, every 30 seconds to a maximum dose of 30 mg/kg.
   b. *Ventricular fibrillation.* Administer bretylium as above, plus epinephrine, 1 mg intravenously, followed by DC cardioversion.

Table 32-3

Time and Drug Doses Required to Resuscitate Dogs from Bupivacaine-induced Cardiovascular Toxicity During Partial Inferior Vena Cava Occlusion*

	CONTROL	PARTIAL IVC OCCLUSION
Resuscitation time (min)	2.1 ± 0.5	22.2 ± 6.9[†]
Epinephrine dose (mg)	1.3 ± 0.4	7.1 ± 2.5[†]
NaHCO₃ dose (mEq)	22.4 ± 4.5	45.9 ± 10.1[†]
Survivors	6/6	5/6

(Data from Kasten GW, Martin ST. Resuscitation from bupivacaine-induced cardiovascular toxicity during partial inferior vena cava occlusion. Anesth Analg 1986;65:341)
*Data are mean ± SD.
†Significantly different from control.
Abbreviation: IVC = inferior vena cava.

c. *Bradycardia with electromechanical dissociation or asystole.* Administer epinephrine, 0.75 mg, and atropine, 0.8 mg intravenously, followed by epinephrine, 0.5 mg, and atropine, 0.4 mg intravenously, every 45 seconds until the pulse and blood pressure are stable.

Obviously, prevention is better than cure. One of the epidural needle and catheter testing schemes first described should be used (and used correctly!) whenever the total incremental bupivacaine dose exceeds 35 mg.[103] Electrophysiologic toxicity also can occur with any other local anesthetic; however, the safety margins are larger.

MISCELLANEOUS

Broken Needles and Catheters

Needles

Open-ended needles are most prone to breakage at the junction of the hub and the shaft of the needle.[129,130] Do not bury needles to the hub, for surgical exploration then may be necessary for needle retrieval if the hub and shaft separate.[131] Needles with recessed holes (such as the Sprotte needle) may bend (and, very rarely, break) at the thinnest point of the metal after a high-velocity impact with bone. Broken needles should be removed because they can migrate and cause further tissue damage.

Epidural Catheters

The tip of an epidural catheter may shear off if it is withdrawn through the epidural needle.[132,133] Catheter shearing occurs more frequently with Teflon-coated polyvinyl chloride than with nylon or polyamide catheters.[134,134a] Such catheter tips may be left in situ if the patient is asymptomatic.[48] Catheters may knot on themselves if excessive amounts of catheter are threaded into the epidural space. Most such catheters have been removed intact with gentle steady traction on the catheter.[135,136]

Spinal Catheters

The new 28- to 32-gauge spinal catheters break frequently if they are not removed extremely carefully.[137,138] The catheters usually stretch during attempted removal and snap off just below the skin. Although expectant management is usually chosen, one catheter was easily removed surgically after positioning the patient prone on a Wilson frame.[139] Because these catheter fragments frequently connect the subarachnoid and subcutaneous spaces, surgical removal may be considered.

It is far easier to prevent than treat sheared catheters. If you encounter any resistance during attempted removal or if the catheter starts to stretch, tape the catheter in place and leave it in situ for 12 to 24 hours. The catheter works its way out of the entrapping ligaments with time and is usually easily removed the next day. My group has removed several recalcitrant catheters in this fashion.

Headache of Immediate Onset

Immediate, severe headache can follow subarachnoid or subdural injection of air during attempted identification of the epidural space.[75,140,141] Unlike headaches caused by low CSF pressure, subarachnoid or subdural air injection can instantly produce a headache that is not relieved, and may be exacerbated, by lying down. Patients usually recover spontaneously over 1 to 5 days.

Ulnar or Radial Nerve Injury

Automatic blood pressure cuffs positioned over the elbow of thin parturients who are actively moving their arms may cause acute radial or ulnar nerve injury.[142,143] Injury may occur after less than 1 hour of use of the automated cuff.[142] Unlike nerve injuries under general anesthesia, which are primarily caused by ischemia of the vasa nervorum, these injuries are probably caused by mechanical intussusception of the myelin sheath.[142,144]

Hypertension Secondary to Ergot Compounds and Pressors

Ergot compounds, especially when administered intravenously, can cause hypertension or coronary artery spasm in healthy parturients.[35,145] Following large doses of long-acting vasopressors such as ephedrine or methoxamine, ergonovine can increase the maternal blood pressure by up to 160 mm Hg.[35] Hypertension severe enough to rupture a subarachnoid aneurysm has been reported.[145]

Prevention is clearly better than cure. Use oxytocin for initial uterotonic therapy in patients who have received large doses of long-acting vasopressors. If an ergot compound is administered after pressors, give a small dose intramuscularly, not intravenously. Check the blood pressure frequently for at least 3 hours. Ergot-induced hypertension can be treated with small doses of labetalol, trimethaphan, nitroglycerin, or nitroprusside. Chlorpromazine, 12.5 mg intravenously, has also been used successfully.[145]

Air Emboli

Air can enter the venous sinuses of the gravid uterus, especially during sexual intercourse, manual placental extraction, cesarean section with massive blood loss, and in patients with placenta previa.[146-148] Precordial Doppler monitoring detects venous air embolism in 10% to 65% of cesarean section patients.[89-91] Placing the operating table in a 5-degree reverse Trendelenburg position decreases the incidence of air emboli, although flexing the head of the operating table up 5 to 10 degrees does not.[149,150] Two-dimensional echocardiography verifies that the emboli detected are indeed air.[151] Awake patients experiencing air emboli may complain of chest pain or dyspnea. Cyanosis, low oxygen saturation, or end-tidal carbon dioxide tension, hypotension, and cardiac arrhythmias, may occur when larger amounts of air embolize.[90] Treatment of a clinically significant air embolism consists of flooding the operative field, stopping nitrous oxide administration, placing the patient in steep head-down and left-tilted position, and providing cardiac resuscitation as needed.[152]

Although cardiac arrest and death due to massive air embolism have been reported, morbid events occur in only a minute fraction of cesarean patients with air emboli.[152,153] One should maintain a high index of suspicion for air emboli in all cesarean patients, but the use of routine precordial Doppler monitoring does not seem warranted.

Electrocardiographic Changes During Cesarean Section

Electrocardiographic changes consistent with ischemia occurred in 37% to 39% of cesarean section patients.[154,155] Although the cause of this phenomenon is not known, the leading hypotheses are myocardial ischemia secondary to air emboli or hypervolemia and sympathectomy. Palmer *et al*[154] did not employ precordial Doppler monitoring, so the incidence of air emboli in his series is unknown.[154] Vartikar *et al*[91] monitored both Doppler and serial electrocardiograms. The incidence of electrocardiographic changes in this series was low (4%), but all electrocardiographic changes oc-

curred during Doppler-detected air emboli. On the other hand, sudden hypervolemia in the presence of high epidural anesthesia can overdistend the cardiac ventricles and markedly increase myocardial oxygen demand and myocardial work.[156] Rapid infusion of 1500 mL of intravenous fluid during sympathetic nerve block increases stroke volume (53%–55%) and left ventricular stroke work (108%) in healthy nonpregnant and term-pregnant patients.[157,158]

GENERAL ANESTHESIA

Failed Intubation

Failed intubation occurs roughly 10 times as often during general anesthesia in obstetric patients as in other surgical patients.[159,160] Samsoon and Young[161] reported that 1:280 obstetric versus 1:2230 other surgical patients could not be intubated. The failed intubation incidence during general anesthetic cesarean sections ranges from 1 in 140 to 1 in 300 cases.[162,163]

Intubation difficulties, with or without pulmonary aspiration, contribute heavily to maternal deaths associated with cesarean section. Thirty-three percent of such deaths occurred in Georgia from 1975 to 1976, and 26% of such deaths occurred in England and Wales from 1982 to 1984 (Table 32-4).[164-166] Pulmonary aspiration frequently complicates the intubation difficulties, which accompany up to 5% of obstetric general anesthetics.[167] Half the cases of pulmonary aspiration in the obstetric closed-claim study occurred in association with difficult tracheal intubation, esophageal intubation, or inadequate ventilation.[168]

Why is tracheal intubation of obstetric patients so difficult? Anatomic changes due to the pregnancy undoubtedly contribute to the difficulty: Edema of the larynx, nasopharynx, and tongue, which is present to some degree in all parturients, contributes to difficult intubation in some preeclamptic patients[169] and healthy patients following strenuous bearing-down efforts.[170] Capillary engorgement makes the mucosa of the airway friable and prone to bleed more easily. Finally, mammary hyperplasia and increased anteroposterior chest diameter decrease the distance from the chin to the chest and make it more difficult to insert the laryngoscope blade in the mouth.

Another factor is pregnancy-induced anatomic changes that turn a difficult airway into an impossible airway. Fahy[163] used x-ray laryngoscopy under local anesthesia to evaluate nonpregnant women with a history of failed intubation during pregnancy. The laryngoscopist could not view the glottis in five of the

Table 32–4

Incidence of Maternal Aspiration and Maternal Deaths from Aspiration or Failed Intubation

STUDY	ASPIRATION	DEATHS
	Cases/100,000 Live Births	
Mendelson, 1932–1945	149.92	4.54
Merrill, 1945–1949	39.06	2.36
Georgia 1975–1976		1.88
Michigan, 1979–1984		0.82
United States, 1979–1986		0.30
New York City, 1980–1984		0.70
England and Wales, 1982–1984		0.63*

(Data from references 164, 165, 186, 213, 217, and 219)
*Rate per 100,000 total births (live and stillbirths).

eight patients. Even when not pregnant, these women would be considered at risk for airway difficulty.

Lastly, the urgent or emergent clinical situation, in which many obstetric general anesthetics take place, leads many to proceed without sufficient airway assessment or consideration of other options.

Prevention

Decreasing the incidence of intubation failures requires careful preparation of personnel and equipment, much of which needs to occur long before the case is anticipated. Use the following guidelines:

- Carefully assess the airway in all obstetric patients before inducing general anesthesia (Fig. 32-11). This assessment need not take much time. Honesty, not egotism, is essential in this endeavor.
- Be prepared to suggest or insist on an anesthetic plan <u>not</u> involving rapid-sequence general anesthesia. This can be difficult when facing an agitated obstetrician concerned about fetal well-being, but an excessively fetocentric view of the anesthetic does not help either mother or baby.
- Anticipate difficult situations and plan ahead for regional anesthesia. Spinal anesthesia for emergent cesarean section can be induced more quickly and is accepted more readily if the anesthesiologist also uses this technique during nonemergent cesarean sections. If you anticipate airway difficulty or are seeing a preeclamptic woman with an adequate but falling platelet count, insert an epidural catheter and test its location with a small dose of local anesthetic (*e.g.*, 5 mL of 1% lidocaine) early in the obstetric

course. The epidural anesthetic does not have to be maintained if the patient is in latent labor or is feeling no pain.

- Optimize the position of the bed and the patient's head before inducing general anesthesia. In my experience, elevating the back of the operating table 5 to 15 degrees while keeping the head and the legs parallel to the floor (Fig. 32-12) improves laryngeal visualization in most obstetric patients. This maneuver is extremely important in obese parturients (see Chap. 26). This body position permits gravity to keep the breasts and chest out of the way of the laryngoscope handle and minimizes the amount of lift necessary to expose the larynx. Although this bed position is easily accomplished on most standard operating room tables, many delivery rooms (including the one at the author's institution) have operative delivery tables in the cesarean room that do not have a separate head section. One must then use a wedge or a stack of towels and sheets to achieve this position, which cannot then be flattened for improved surgical access.
- Never induce general anesthesia with inadequate or unchecked equipment or inadequate assistance. I feel that general anesthetic inductions proceed most smoothly with three people: one person whose only job is to hold cricoid pressure and hand the laryngoscopist the endotracheal tube, an experienced assistant who injects the drugs and assists the laryngoscopist, and the laryngoscopist. An inexperienced but reliable and well-instructed assistant can hold cricoid pressure. This assistant should adequately demonstrate cricoid-holding technique on the awake patient or the anesthetist before the induction begins.

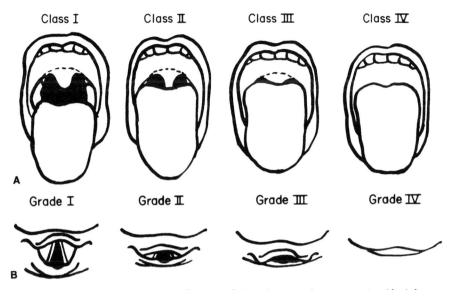

Figure 32–11. (**A**) Pictorial classification of the pharyngeal structures (modified from Mallampati). Note that in class III, the soft palate is visible and in class IV, the soft palate is not visible. (**B**) Grades of laryngoscopic views (modified from Cormack and Lehane). (Samsoon GLT, Young JRB. Difficult tracheal intubation: A retrospective study. Anaesthesia 1987;42:487)

- Learn and habitually use a technique for laryngoscope blade insertion that is effective in patients with increased chest anteroposterior diameter. Many anesthetists insert the laryngoscope blade in the mouth in the midsagittal plane and pivot in that plane to expose the larynx. Parturients often do not have enough space between the sternum and the mouth to permit this maneuver with a standard laryngoscope handle. An alternate technique (Fig. 32-13A and B) is to insert the laryngoscope straight into the mouth in a plane angled 45 degrees to the right (or left) of the midsagittal plane, with the tip of the blade following the midline of the tongue, until the tip of the blade is near the uvula. Gently rotate the laryngoscope into the midsagittal plane and

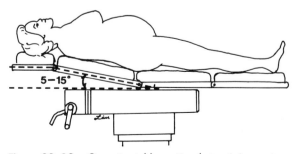

Figure 32–12. Operating table position that optimizes maternal airway visualization in obese parturients.

advance as usual. Be careful to keep the tip of the blade in the midsagittal plane to avoid getting caught in the tonsillar pillar. Learn this technique on healthy patients; don't try it for the first time during rapid-sequence induction for cesarean section. The advantage of this technique is that the laryngoscope handle is never near the chest wall. Few experiences are more frustrating than an inability to get the laryngoscope in the mouth during a rapid-sequence induction.

- Use smaller endotracheal tubes than one would use in nonpregnant women. I routinely use a cuffed 6.0- or 6.5-mm tube and always keep a cuffed 5.5-mm tube available.

- Develop a failed intubation protocol and review and practice it periodically. The protocol used at my institution is described in Figure 32-14.[171]

- If the failed intubation protocol includes the use of unusual equipment, one must develop familiarity with the equipment during routine general anesthetics in nonpregnant patients at low risk of aspiration. Examples of such equipment include special laryngoscope blades, the light wand, the fiberoptic bronchoscope, the Bullard intubating laryngoscope, and the laryngeal mask airway.[172]

- All personnel administering general anesthesia to obstetric patients must know where the relevant emergency airway/ventilation equipment is stored. Although this seems like an elementary point, it is often overlooked.

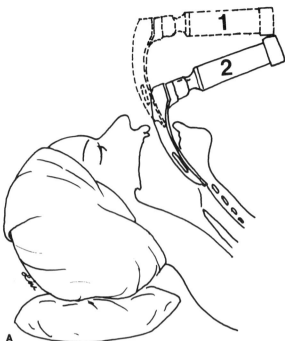

A

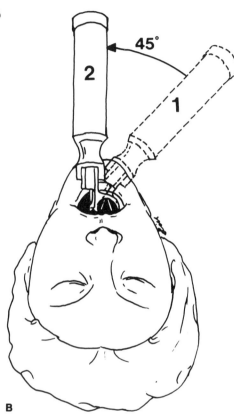

B

Figure 32–13. Recommended technique for insertion of laryngoscopic blade in obstetric patients. Insert the laryngoscopic blade into the mouth parallel to the floor (**A-1**) and at a 45-degree angle to the midsagittal plane (**B-1**). Advance the blade tip along the midline of the tongue until the blade tip is at the level of the uvula. Then rotate the laryngoscopic blade into the midsagittal plane (**B-2**) and advance into the vellecula (**A-2**).

Difficult or failed intubation remains distressingly common in obstetric anesthesia. We must all work to improve our track record in this area.

Aspiration

Pulmonary aspiration has long been recognized as a clinical problem; Hippocrates described the syndrome and warned of its dangers.[173] Sir James Simpson[173] reported the first anesthetic (chloroform)-associated aspiration death. The problem remains with us to this day. In the closed-claim study (cases from 1975–1985), 35% of the obstetric versus 2% of the nonobstetric suits involved the pulmonary aspiration of gastric contents.[168]

Compared to nonpregnant women, parturients maintain a large gastric volume and frequently reflux gastric contents into the esophagus. Intragastric pressure is twice as high in pregnant as in nonpregnant women.[174,175] A parturient may suffer severe reflux in the absence of heartburn or a hiatal hernia.[176] Pregnant women have low concentrations of plasma motilin[177] (and, thus, low gastric motility) and high concentrations of plasma gastrin[178] (and, thus, high gastric acid production[179]). Gastric emptying, which is slowed slightly by the pain of labor and is unaffected by epidural analgesia, is profoundly delayed by parenteral narcotics.[180,181] Labor is scarcely a planned experience; patients may eat before labor begins or during a prolonged latent phase of labor. Consequently, emergency cesarean section patients have much larger volumes of gastric residue than elective cesarean patients.[182]

Pathophysiology

Tracheal instillation of 1 to 4 mL/kg of any liquid produces hypoxia, hypotension, and wheezing. The further clinical course depends on the nature of the liquid aspirated.[173,183–189]

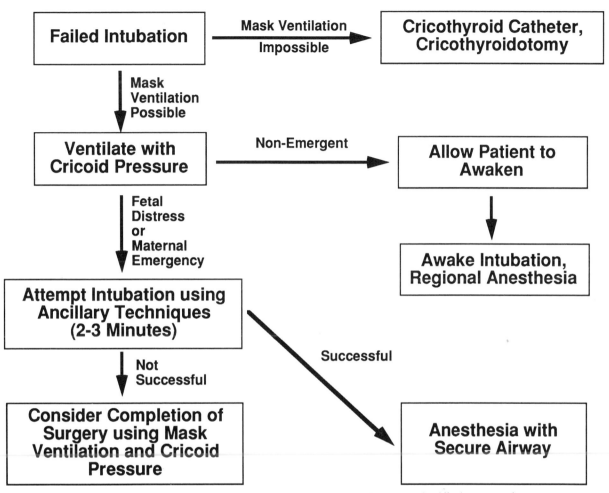

Figure 32–14. Sample protocol for failed intubation. (Malan TP, Johnson MD. The difficult airway in obstetric anesthesia: techniques for airway management and the role of regional anesthesia. J Clin Anesth 1988;1:104)

SALINE. Hypoxia and hypotension are mild and completely resolve in 30 minutes with no sequelae.

ACID. Acid produces an immediate chemical pneumonitis, the severity of which depends on the liquid's pH and volume. Instillation of liquid with a pH below a critical value (in man, somewhere between 1.75 and 2.5) produces severe lung injury. Severe injury occurs with instillation of 0.4 mL/kg of 0.1N of hydrochloric acid in one lung in the monkey; however, at least 0.8 mL/kg of the same acid is required to produce the same injury in both lungs.

Acid instillation produces moderate to severe hypoxemia and hypotension. Transudation of plasma occurs rapidly, producing intravascular hypovolemia and pulmonary edema. Adult respiratory distress syndrome then develops, with alveolar hyaline membrane formation. If the patient survives the initial event, the lungs may heal without scarring. Patients with acid aspiration uncomplicated by bacterial pneumonia recover in 4 to 5 days.

FOOD. Large chunks can obstruct airways. Liquid food produces less hypoxemia, hypotension, and fluid transudation than acid but more hypercapnia and acidosis. Food aspiration heals with granuloma formation.

BILE-CONTAMINATED GASTRIC JUICE. This is usually fatal in both patients and animal models.

Diagnosis

Frequently, the aspiration is observed. However, one should suspect aspiration in a patient who presents with some or all the following signs: hypoxia, pulmonary edema, bronchospasm, isolated laryngospasm,[190] cough, or apnea followed by tachypnea, tachycardia, or hypotension.[173,184]

Symptoms usually present within 2 hours.[184] Roentgenograms show localized or diffuse patchy alveolar infiltrates or, in severe cases, opacification of large lung fields. Aspiration occurs most often in the right lower lobe (the straightest path from the trachea) or the most dependent lung area (frequently the right upper lobe in supine patients). The chemical pneumonitis itself can cause an initial temperature elevation; fever from bacterial overgrowth usually occurs several days later.[173,184] The clinical course usually follows one of three paths: rapid deterioration and death (12%); rapid, sustained clinical improvement (62%); or rapid improvement followed by decline due to bacterial pneumonia (26%).[184] Superimposed bacterial pneumonia is fatal in more than 60% of the cases.[184]

Therapy

Recommended therapy for symptomatic aspiration includes the following procedures:

- Intubation and positive-pressure ventilation with positive end-expiratory pressure (PEEP). Use just enough oxygen to maintain oxygen saturation above 90%.[173,191] Dogs receiving mechanical ventilation (tidal volume 15 mL/kg, 10 cm H_2O PEEP) for 5 hours following tracheal instillation of 2 mL/kg of hydrochloric acid had significantly higher oxygen saturation and improved lung histology compared to dogs not ventilated after the acid instillation.[191] Because ventilation may need to be continued for several days, avoid excessively high oxygen concentrations in order to prevent additional lung damage from oxygen toxicity.
- Careful intravascular fluid replacement. Plasma volume can decrease 35% within 2 hours of a massive acid aspiration.[183] Institution of mechanical ventilation with PEEP can further depress cardiac output and arterial pressure.[191] Central venous or pulmonary artery pressure monitoring may be needed to guide therapy. These patients frequently have obvious pulmonary edema yet are oliguric secondary to hypovolemia.[173,183] Reflex treatment of pulmonary edema with phlebotomy and diuretics may have unnecessarily elevated mortality in early case series. One author found that patients resuscitated with colloid had less pulmonary shunt than patients resuscitated with crystalloid fluids only.[185]

- Bronchoscopy *only* if needed to clear food chunks from the airway. Although patients can die of pure mechanical airway obstruction (a fate that should be prevented),[186] bronchoscopy does not improve the course of patients who aspirate liquid gastric contents only.[183]
- Rigid maintenance of asepsis during tracheal tube care. More than 60% of the patients who develop a superimposed bacterial pneumonia die.[184]

Therapies that are not recommended include the following:

- *Lavage.* Bronchial transudation neutralizes bronchial fluid pH within 30 minutes of massive acid aspiration.[183] Lavage spreads the noxious aspirate to previously uninvolved lung areas and adds the negative effects (slight but appreciable) of a saline aspiration.[183] In dogs, 40% of lavage fluid was unrecoverable, and the dogs receiving lavage were more hypoxic than the dogs that did not.[183]
- *Steroids.* Steroids, once enthusiastically prescribed after aspiration,[187] are ineffective clinically[173] and impede recovery in animal models.[192-194]
- *Prophylactic antibiotics.* Prophylactic antibiotics, also clinically ineffective, may increase late mortality by promoting the growth of resistant bacteria.[173,184,187] Obtain bronchial fluid cultures regularly, and use antibiotics to treat documented bacterial infections.

Prophylaxis

Pharmacologic agents are frequently used to decrease the risk that a parturient possesses a dangerous amount or acidity of gastric fluid. These agents, which are discussed in greater detail in Chapter 22, include the following:

- *Antacids.*[195] Bicitra, 0.3 molar sodium citrate,[196] is currently recommended. Magnesium- and aluminum-containing antacids are *not* recommended. Initial animal studies suggested that aspiration of gastric fluid was a benign clinical event as long as the pH was neutral.[187,197] The first antacids widely used in laboring parturients contained magnesium or aluminum particles.[198] Several parturients developed classic aspiration symptoms despite aspiration of particulate–antacid containing gastric fluid of neutral pH.[199-201] Gibbs *et al*[202] then showed, in the dog, that aspiration of aluminum/magnesium hydroxide produces acute pulmonary pathology (as severe as that produced by acid instillation) that evolves into chronic granulomatous bronchopneumonitis and heals with extensive scar formation.
- *Agents to raise the gastric pH.* Ranitidine is now the most widely used agent from this class.[203] Cimetidine or omeprazole also can be used.[204]

- *Metoclopramide.*[205] Metoclopramide increases gastric motility[206] (an effect that is blocked by narcotics[180,207] or atropine[208]) and increases lower esophageal sphincter pressure.[209]
- *Anticholinergics.* I do not recommend these agents for this purpose. Atropine increases gastric volume.[210] Atropine and glycopyrrolate either increase[211] or do not affect[212] gastric pH. Atropine decreases lower esophageal sphincter pressure.[208]

Prevention

Avoiding mask general anesthesia in obstetric patients is the primary way to prevent maternal pulmonary aspiration. Most anesthesiologists preferentially do regional anesthesia for cesarean as well as vaginal deliveries. When general anesthesia is necessary, use a rapid sequence anesthetic induction and insert a cuffed tracheal tube. Routine intubation of obstetric patients during general anesthesia has lowered the incidence of maternal aspiration from 39 to 150 cases per 100,000 live births in the 1940s to 9 cases per 100,000 live births in the late 1960s.[186,213,214]

Although the incidence of maternal aspiration has decreased greatly in the past 50 years, the incidence of anesthesia-associated pulmonary deaths in obstetric patients has declined much more slowly (see Table 32-4).[165,215–217] Why has the prevention of maternal aspiration had so little affect on maternal mortality? Several reasons follow:

- Now that obstetric patients receiving general anesthesia are routinely intubated, deaths from failed intubation are replacing deaths from aspiration.[168,218,219]
- Many patients with anesthesia-related aspiration pneumonia aspirated while awake following a planned extubation.[173,220]
- Most deaths due to aspiration or failed intubation occur during cesarean section, and the cesarean section rate has increased greatly in the past 50 years. In Georgia, from 1975 to 1976, the incidence of maternal deaths due to aspiration or failed intubation was 1 in 53,078 live births but 1 in 5063 cesarean sections.[164]
- Several agents used before 1980 for aspiration prophylaxis or treatment are ineffective or harmful. Particulate-containing antacids, steroids, and prophylactic antibiotics fall into this category.
- Aspiration pneumonia is a rare disease. Information on its incidence can only be gleaned from large epidemiologic studies, which usually lag 6 to 10 years behind the period studied.

No completely effective measures exist to prevent aspiration or failed intubation in parturients. A major factor is that awake intubation in parturients, as currently performed, is usually so uncomfortable and time-consuming that the technique is rarely seriously considered. Can new awake intubation techniques improve this situation?

SUMMARY AND CONCLUSIONS

Intraoperative complications that require prompt and effective treatment can and do occur in obstetric anesthesia. This chapter reviewed the diagnosis, pathophysiology and intraoperative management of hypotension, unintended dural puncture, high/total spinal anesthesia, subdural anesthesia, unintended intravascular catheter placement, systemic bupivacaine toxicity, failed intubation, and pulmonary aspiration.

Maternal hypotension during regional anesthesia can decrease uterine perfusion, which can depress neonatal Apgar and neurobehavioral scores, even if the mother is asymptomatic. The gravid uterus is heavy enough to compress the inferior vena cava and the aorta, further hindering maternal blood pressure and uterine perfusion. Generous maternal prehydration, avoidance of aortocaval compression, and judicious intravenous pressor administration can minimize the incidence and impact of maternal hypotension.

All anesthesiologists occasionally puncture the dura during epidural anesthetics. It is important to administer a "spinal size" local anesthetic dose and wait long enough for spinal anesthesia to develop before injecting larger volumes of local anesthetic through epidural needles or catheters. If one is in the subarachnoid space, one must then decide whether to continue with a single shot or continuous spinal anesthetic or reidentify the epidural space.

High or total spinal anesthesia during cesarean section occurs most frequently when spinal anesthesia with an undiminished local anesthetic dose is initiated to compensate for a patchy epidural block. Extremely high spinal blocks also occur during intended spinal anesthetics and during epidural anesthesia if dural puncture is not recognized. Prompt ventilatory and hemodynamic support is critical.

Subdural anesthesia probably occurs more frequently than is clinically recognized. The classic presentation is an extremely delayed anesthetic onset, extensive sensory blockade with less motor and sympathetic nerve block, and delayed anesthetic regression.

Unintended intravenous placement of epidural needles and catheters occurs much more often in pregnant than in nonpregnant patients. Aspiration for blood and fractionation of the local anesthetic dose fail to detect many intravenously placed needles and catheters. Although 15 μg of epinephrine can be used before elective cesarean section in healthy patients, the Doppler test is more appropriate for laboring or preeclamptic women.

Although bupivacaine has many desirable clinical attributes, it is extremely toxic to the conduction system of the heart. Bupivacaine binds avidly to sodium channels (and, to a lesser extent, to calcium and potassium channels) but dissociates slowly at physiologic heart rates. Hypoxia, acidosis, hyperkalemia, and the presence of other class I antiarrhythmics increase bupivacaine toxicity. Ventilation, oxygenation, external cardiac massage, if needed, and elimination of aortocaval compression (which may require cesarean section) must be started rapidly. Large doses of epinephrine and atropine can reverse ventricular fibrillation or bradycardia. In animal models, bretylium, isoproterenol, and magnesium successfully combat the torsades de pointes ventricular tachycardia that can occur.

Failed intubation occurs 10 times as often in obstetric as in surgical patients. Meticulous preparation of personnel and equipment and honest airway assessment, leading to the use of alternate anesthetic plans when needed, are crucial in avoiding failed intubation.

Pulmonary aspiration of gastric contents still occurs, albeit less frequently. The avoidance of general anesthesia when possible, rapid-sequence induction of general anesthesia, and minimization of maternal gastric volume and acidity before anesthetic induction may limit the incidence and severity of aspiration.

Careful technique and knowledge of the pathophysiology and management of obstetric anesthetic complications are crucial for all practitioners who conduct general or regional anesthesia in pregnant women.

REFERENCES

1. Kang YG, Abouleish E, Caritis S. Prophylactic intravenous ephedrine infusion during spinal anesthesia for cesarean section. Anesth Analg 1982;61:839.
2. Marx GF, Cosmi EV, Wollman SB. Biochemical status and clinical condition of mother and infant at cesarean section. Anesth Analg 1969;48:986.
3. Clark RB, Thompson DS, Thompson CH. Prevention of spinal hypotension associated with cesarean section. Anesthesiology 1976;45:670.
4. Klein MD, Clahr J. Factors in the decline of maternal mortality. JAMA 1958;168:237.
5. Ebner H, Barcohana J, Bartoshuk AK. Influence of postspinal hypotension on the fetal electrocardiogram. Am J Obstet Gynecol 1960;80:569.
6. Hon EH, Reid BL, Hehre FW. The electronic evaluation of fetal heart rate. II. Changes with maternal hypotension. Am J Obstet Gynecol 1960;79:209.
7. James FM, Greiss FC, Kemp RA. An evaluation of vasopressor therapy for maternal hypotension during spinal anesthesia. Anesthesiology 1970;33:25.
8. Hollmen AI, Joupilla R, Koivisto M, et al. Neurologic activity of infants following anesthesia for cesarean section. Anesthesiology 1978;48:350.
9. Datta S, Alper MH, Ostheimer GW, Weiss JB. Method of ephedrine administration and nausea and hypotension during spinal anesthesia for cesarean section. Anesthesiology 1982;56:68.
10. Caritis SN, Abouleish E, Edelstone DI, Mueller-Heubach E. Fetal acid–base state following spinal or epidural anesthesia for cesarean section. Obstet Gynecol 1980;56:610.
11. Norris MC. Hypotension during spinal anesthesia for cesarean section: Does it affect neonatal outcome? Reg Anesth 1987;12:191.
12. Kinsella SM, Whitwam JG, Spencer JAD. Aortic compression by the uterus: Identification with the Finapres digital arterial pressure instrument. Br J Obstet Gynaecol 1990;97:700.
13. Howard BK, Goodson JH, Mengert WF. Supine hypotensive syndrome in late pregnancy. Obstet Gynecol 1953;1:371.
14. Wright L. Postural hypotension in late pregnancy. Br Med J 1962;1:760.
15. Goodlin RC. Importance of the lateral position during labor. Obstet Gynecol 1971;37:698.
16. Wollman SB, Marx GF. Acute hydration for prevention of hypotension of spinal anesthesia in parturients. Anesthesiology 1968;29:374.
17. Ramanathan S, Grant GJ. Vasopressor therapy for hypotension due to epidural anesthesia for cesarean section. Acta Anaesthesiol Scand 1988;32:559.
18. Bieniarz J, Maqueda E, Caldeyro-Barcia R. Compression of aorta by the uterus in late human pregnancy. Am J Obstet Gynecol 1966;95:795.
19. Brizgys RV, Dailey PA, Shnider SM, Kotelko DM, Levinson G. The incidence and neonatal effects of maternal hypotension during epidural anesthesia for cesarean section. Anesthesiology 1987;67:782.
20. Eckstein KL, Marx GF. Aortocaval compression and uterine displacement. Anesthesiology 1974;40:92.
21. Butterworth JF, Walker FO, Lysak SZ. Pregnancy increases median nerve susceptibility to lidocaine. Anesthesiology 1990;72:962.
22. Kennedy RL, Friedman DL, Katchka DM, Selmantis S, Smith RN. Hypotension during obstetrical anesthesia. Anesthesiology 1959;20:153.
23. Colon-Morasel MA. A self-supporting device for continuous left uterine displacement during cesarean section. Anesth Analg 1970;49:223.
24. Kennedy RL. An instrument to relieve inferior vena cava occlusion. Am J Obstet Gynecol 1970;107:331.

25. Mendiola J, Grylack LJ, Scanlon JW. Effects of intrapartum maternal glucose infusion on the normal fetus and newborn. Anesth Analg 1982;61:32.

26. Kenepp NB. Effects on newborn of hydration with glucose in patients undergoing cesarean section with regional anesthesia. Lancet 1980;1:1150.

27. Ramanathan S, Masih A, Rock I, Chalon J, Turndorf H. Maternal and fetal effects of prophylactic hydration with crystalloids or colloids before epidural anesthesia. Anesth Analg 1983;62:673.

28. Lewis M, Thomas P, Wilkes RG. Hypotension during epidural analgesia for Cæsarean section. Anaesthesia 1983;38:250.

29. Ralston DH, Shnider SM, deLorimier AA. Effects of equipotent ephedrine, metaraminol, mephentermine, and methoxamine on uterine blood flow in the pregnant ewe. Anesthesiology 1974;40:354.

30. Zaimis E. Vasopressor drugs and catecholamines. Anesthesiology 1968;29:732.

31. Hughes SC, Wark MG, Levinson G, et al. Placental transfer of ephedrine does not affect neonatal outcome. Anesthesiology 1985;63:217.

32. Wright RG, Shnider SM, Levinson G, Rolbin SH, Parer JT. The effect of maternal administration of ephedrine on fetal heart rate and variability. Am J Obstet Gynecol 1981;57:734.

33. Kangas-Saarela T, Hollmen AI, Tolonen U, et al. Does ephedrine influence newborn neurobehavioural responses and spectral EEG when used to prevnet maternal hypotension during cæsarean section? Acta Anaesthesiol Scand 1990;34:8.

34. Gutsche BB. Prophylactic ephedrine preceding spinal analgesia for cesarean section. Anesthesiology 1976;45:462.

35. Moya F, Smith B. Spinal anesthesia for cesarean section. JAMA 1962;179:609.

36. Moran DH, Perillo M, Bader AM, Datta S. Phenylephrine in treating maternal hypotension secondary to spinal anesthesia. Anesthesiology 1989;71:A857.

37. Ramanathan S, Friedman S, Moss P, Arismendy J, Turndorf H. Phenylephrine for the treatment of maternal hypotension due to epidural anesthesia. Anesth Analg 1984;63:262.

38. Bhagwanjee S, Rocke DA, Rout CC, Koovarjee RV, Brijball R. Prevention of hypotension following spinal anæsthesia for elective cæsarean section by wrapping of the legs. Br J Anaesth 1990;65:819.

39. James FM, Greiss FC. The use of inflatable boots to prevent hypotension during spinal anesthesia for cesarean section. Anesth Analg 1973;52:246.

40. Goudie TA, Winter AW, Ferguson DJM. Lower limb compression using inflatable splints to prevent hypotension during spinal anaesthesia for Caesarean section. Acta Anaesthesiol Scand 1988;32:541.

41. Abraham RA, Harris AP, Maxwell LG, Kaplow S. The efficacy of 1.5% lidocaine with 7.5% dextrose and epinephrine as an epidural test dose for obstetrics. Anesthesiology 1986;64:116.

42. van Zundert AA, de Wolf AM, Vaes L, Soetens M. High-volume spinal anesthesia with bupivacaine 0.125% for cesarean section. Anesthesiology 1988;69:998.

43. Foldes FF, McNall PG. 2-Chloroprocaine: A new local anesthetic agent. Anesthesiology 1952;13:287.

44. Reisner LS. Epidural test solution or spinal fluid? [correspondence] Anesthesiology 1976;44:451.

45. Rosenberg H. pH in differentiating CSF from local anesthetics in epidural anesthesia [correspondence]. Anesthesiology 1976;45:579.

46. Waters J, Chuba JV, Ramanathan S, Turndorf H. Epidural catheter aspirate [Abstract]. Anesthesiology 1990;73:A959.

47. Kalas DB, Hehre FW. Continuous lumbar peridural anesthesia in obstetrics. VIII. Further observations on inadvertent lumbar puncture. Anesth Analg 1972;51:192.

48. Massey Dawkins CJ. An analysis of the complications of extradural and caudal block. Anaesthesia 1969;24:554.

49. Norris MC, Leighton BL. Continuous spinal anesthesia after unintentional dural puncture in parturients. Reg Anesth 1990;15:285.

50. Colonna-Romano P, Shapiro BE. Unintentional dural puncture and prophylactic epidural blood patch in obstetrics. Anesth Analg 1989;69:522.

51. Hodgkinson R. Total spinal block after epidural injection into an interspace adjacent to an inadvertent dural puncture. Anesthesiology 1981;55:593.

52. Schultz EH, Brogdan BG. The problem of subdural placement in myelography. Radiology 1962;79:91.

53. Blomberg RG. The lumbar subdural extraarachnoid space of humans: An anatomical study using spinaloscopy in autopsy cases. Anesth Analg 1987;66:177.

54. Loeser EA, Hill GE, Bennett GM, Sederberg JH. Time vs. success rate for epidural blood patch. Anesthesiology 1978;49:147.

55. Check TG, Banner R, Sauter J, Gutsche BB. Prophylactic extradural blood patch is effective: a preliminary communication. Br J Anaesth 1988;61:340.

56. Ackerman WE, Colclough GW. Prophylactic epidural blood patch: the controversy continues. Anesth Analg 1987;66:913.

57. Leivers D. Total spinal anesthesia following early prophylactic epidural blood patch. Anesthesiology 1990;73:1287.

58. Ong BY, Graham CR, Ringaert KRA, Cohen MM, Palahniuk RJ. Impaired epidural analgesia after dural puncture with and without subsequent blood patch. Anesth Analg 1990;70:76.

59. Fobson JA, Brodsky JB. Latent dural puncture after lumbar epidural block. Anesth Analg 1977;56:725.

60. Philip JH, Brown WU. Total spinal anesthesia late in

the course of obstetric bupivacaine epidural block. Anesthesiology 1976;44:340.

61. Park R. A migrating epidural cannula. Anaesthesia 1984;39:289.

62. Beck H, Brassow F, Doehn M, et al. Epidural catheters of the multi-orifice type: Dangers and complications. Acta Anaesthesiol Scand 1986;30:549.

63. Power I, Thorburn J. Differential flow from multihole epidural catheters. Anaesthesia 1988;43:876.

64. Stone PA, Thorburn J, Lamb KSR. Complications of spinal anæsthesia following extradural block for cæsarean section. Br J Anaesth 1989;62:335.

65. Russell IF. Inadvertent total spinal for Cæsarean section. Anaesthesia 1985;40:199.

66. Kim YI, Mazza NM, Marx GF. Massive spinal block with hemicranial palsy after a "test dose" for extradural analgesia. Anesthesiology 1975;43:370.

67. Stonham J, Moss P. The optimal test dose for epidural anesthesia. Anesthesiology 1983;58:389.

68. de Saram M. Accidental total spinal analgesia: A report of three cases. Anaesthesia 1956;11:77.

69. Lubenow T, Keh-Wong E, Kristof K, Ivankovich O, Ivankovich AD. Inadvertent subdural injection: A complication of an epidural block. Anesth Analg 1988;67:175.

70. Reynolds F, Speedy HM. The subdural space: The third place to go astray. Anaesthesia 1990;45:120.

71. Mehta M. Extradural block. Confirmation of the injection site by X-ray monitoring. Anaesthesia 1985; 40:1009.

72. Jones MD, Newton TH. Inadvertent extra-arachnoid injections in myelography. Radiology 1963;80:18.

73. Manchanda VN, Murad SHN, Shilyansky G, Mehringer M. Unusual clinical course of accidental subdural local anesthetic injection. Anesth Analg 1983;62:1124.

74. Brindle Smith G, Barton FL, Watt JH. Extensive spread of local anæsthetic solution following subdural insertion of an epidural catheter during labour. Anaesthesia 1984;39:355.

75. Katz JA, Lukin R, Bridenbaugh PO, Gunzenhauser L. Subdural intracranial air: An unusual cause of headache after epidural steroid injection. Anesthesiology 1991;74:615.

76. Maycock E. An epidural anæsthetic with unusual complications. Anaesth Intensive Care 1978;6:263.

77. Stevens RA, D'Arcy Stanton-Hicks M. Subdural injection of local anesthetic: A complication of epidural anesthesia. Anesthesiology 1985;63:323.

78. Cohen CA, Kallow T. Failure of spinal anesthesia due to subdural catheter placement. Anesthesiology 1972; 37:352.

79. Collier C. Total spinal or massive subdural block? Anaesth Intensive Care 1982;10:92.

80. Mehta M, Maher R. Injection into the extra-arachnoid subdural space; experience in the treatment of intractable cervical pain and in the conduct of extradural (epidural) analgesia. Anaesthesia 1977;32:760.

81. Norris MC, Leighton BL, DeSimone CA. Needle bevel direction and headache after inadvertent dural puncture. Anesthesiology 1989;70:729.

82. Kenepp NB, Gutsche BB. Inadvertent intravascular injections during lumbar epidural anesthesia. Anesthesiology 1981;54:172.

83. Leighton BL, Norris MC, DeSimone CA, Rosco T, Gross JB. The air test is a clinically useful indicator of intravenously placed epidural catheters. Anesthesiology 1990;73:610.

84. Ahn NN, Ung DA, DeFay S, Cannelli G, Rudy TE, McKenzie R. Blood vessel puncture with epidural catheters. Anesthesiology 1989;71:A916.

85. Rolbin SH, Halpern SH, Braude BM, Kapala D, Unger R, Radhakrisnan S. Fluid through the epidural needle does not reduce complications of epidural catheter insertion. Can J Anaesth 1990;37:337.

86. Morrison LMM, Buchan AS. Comparison of complications associated with single-holed and multi-holed extradural catheters. Br J Anaesth 1990;64:183.

87. Leighton BL, Gross JB. Air: An effective marker of intravenously located catheters. Anesthesiology 1989; 71:848.

88. Naulty JS, Ostheimer GW, Datta S, Knapp R, Weiss JB. Incidence of venous air embolism during epidural catheter insertion. Anesthesiology 1982;57:410.

89. Handler JS, Bromage PR. Venous air embolism during cesarean delivery. Reg Anesth 1990;15:170.

90. Malinow AM, Naulty JS, Hunt CO, Datta S, Ostheimer GW. Precordial ultrasonic monitoring during cesarean delivery. Anesthesiology 1987;66:816.

91. Vartikar JV, Johnson MD, Datta S. Precordial Doppler monitoring and pulse oximetry during cesarean delivery: Detection of venous air embolism. Reg Anesth 1989;14:145.

92. Moore DC, Batra MS. The components of an effective test dose prior to epidural block. Anesthesiology 1981;55:693.

93. Leighton BL, Norris MC, Sosis M, Epstein R, Chayen B, Larijani GE. Limitations of epinephrine as a marker of intravascular injection in laboring women. Anesthesiology 1987;66:688.

94. Leighton BL, DeSimone CA, Norris MC, Chayen B. Isoproterenol is an effective marker of intravenous injection in laboring women. Anesthesiology 1989;71:206.

95. Leighton BL, Norris MC, DeSimone CA, Darby MJ, Menduke H. Pre-eclamptic and healthy term pregnant patients have different chronotropic responses to isoproterenol. Anesthesiology 1990;72:392.

96. Chestnut DH, Owen CL, Brown CK, Vandewalker GE, Weiner CP. Does labor affect the variability of maternal heart rate during induction of epidural anesthesia? Anesthesiology 1988;68:622.

97. Hood DD, Dewan DM, James FM. Maternal and fetal effects of epinephrine in gravid ewes. Anesthesiology 1986;64:610.

98. Chestnut DH, Weiner CP, Herrig JE, Wang J. Effect of

intravenous epinephrine upon uterine blood flow velocity in the pregnant guinea pig. Anesthesiology 1986;65:633.

99. Youngstrom P, Hoyt M, Veille JC, Cohen I, Amini S, Herman M. Effects of intravenous test dose epinephrine on fetal sheep during acute fetal stress and acidosis. Reg Anesth 1990;15:237.

100. Munson ES, Tucker WK, Ausinsch B, Malagodi MH. Etidocaine, bupivacaine, and lidocaine seizure thresholds in monkeys. Anesthesiology 1975;42:471.

101. Liu P, Feldman HS, Covino BM, et al. Acute cardiovascular toxicity of intravenous amide local anesthetics in anesthetized ventilated dogs. Anesth Analg 1982; 61:317.

102. Albright GA. Cardiac arrest following regional anesthesia with etidocaine or bupivacaine. Anesthesiology 1979;51:285.

103. Albright GA. Epinephrine should be used with the theraputic dose of bupivacaine in obstetrics. Anesthesiology 1984;61:217.

104. Clarkson CW, Hondeghem LM. Mechanism for bupivacaine depression of cardiac conduction: fast block of sodium channels during the action potential with slow recovery from block during diastole. Anesthesiology 1985;62:396.

105. de Jong RH, Ronfeld RA, DeRosa RA. Cardiovascular effects of convulsant and supraconvulsant doses of amide local anesthetics. Anesth Analg 1982;61:3.

106. de Jong RH, Bonin JD. Deaths from local anesthetic-induced convulsions in mice. Anesth Analg 1980; 59:401.

107. Nath S, Haggmark S, Johansson G, Reiz S. Differential depressant and electrophysiologic cardiotoxicity of local anesthetics: An experimental study with special reference to lidocaine and bupivacaine. Anesth Analg 1986;65:1263.

108. Coyle DE, Sperelakis N. Bupivacaine and lidocaine blockage of calcium-mediated slow action potentials in guinea pig ventricular muscle. J Pharmacol Exp Ther 1986;242:1001.

109. Courtney KR, Kendig JJ. Bupivacaine is an effective potassium channel blocker in heart. Biochim Biophys 1988;939:163.

110. Lacombe P, Blaise G, Loulmet D, Hollmann C. Electrophysiologic effects of bupivacaine in the isolated rabbit heart. Anesth Analg 1991;72:62.

111. Bernards CM, Carpenter RL, Rupp SM, et al. Effect of midazolam and diazepam premedication on central nervous system and cardiovascular toxicity of bupivacaine in pigs. Anesthesiology 1989;70:318.

112. Bernards CM, Artu AA. Hexamethonium and midazolam terminate dysrhythmias and hypertention caused by intracerebroventricular bupivacaine in rabbits. Anesthesiology 1991;74:89.

113. Morishima HO, Pedersen H, Finster M, et al. Bupivacaine toxicity in pregnant and nonpregnant ewes. Anesthesiology 1985;63:134.

114. Santos AC, Pedersen H, Harmon TW, et al. Does pregnancy alter the systemic toxicity of local anesthetics? Anesthesiology 1989;70:991.

115. Rosen MA, Thigpen JW, Shnider SM, Foutz SE, Levinson G, Koike M. Bupivacaine-induced cardiotoxicity in hypoxic and acidotic sheep. Anesth Analg 1985;64:1089.

116. Sage DJ, Feldman HS, Arthur R, et al. Influence of lidocaine and bupivacaine on isolated guinea pig atria in the presence of acidosis and hypoxia. Anesth Analg 1984;63:1.

117. Moore DC, Crawford RD, Scurlock JE. Severe hypoxia and acidosis following local anesthetic-induced convulsions. Anesthesiology 1980;53:259.

118. Kasten GW, Martin ST. Successful cardiovascular resuscitation after massive intravenous bupivacaine overdosage in anesthetized dogs. Anesth Analg 1985;64:491.

119. Kambam JR, Kinney WW, Matsuda F, Wright W, Holaday DA. Epinephrine and phenylephrine increase cardiorespiratory toxicity of intravenously administered bupivacaine in rats. Anesth Analg 1990;70:543.

120. Timour Q, Freysz M, Mazze R, Couzon P, Bertrix L, Faucon G. Enhancement by hyponatremia and hyperkalemia of ventricular conduction and rhythm disorders caused by bupivacaine. Anesthesiology 1990;72:1051.

121. Edouard AR, Berdeaux A, Ahmad R, Samii K. Cardiovascular interactions of local anesthetics and calcium entry blockers in dogs. Reg Anesth 1991;16:95.

122. Timour Q, Freysz M, Couzon P, et al. Possible role of drug interactions in bupivacaine-induced problems related to intraventricular conduction disorders. Reg Anesth 1990;15:180.

123. Kasten GW, Martin ST. Bupivacaine cardiovascular toxicity: Comparison of treatment with bretylium and lidocaine. Anesth Analg 1985;64:911.

124. Lacombe P, Blaise G, Hollmann C, Tanguay M, Loulmet D. Isoproterenol corrects the effects of bupivacaine on the electrophysiologic properties of the isolated rabbit heart. Anesth Analg 1991;72:70.

125. Solomon D, Bunegin L, Albin M. The effect of magnesium sulfate administration on cerebral and cardiac toxicity of bupivacaine in dogs. Anesthesiology 1990;72:341.

126. Kasten GW, Martin ST. Resuscitation from bupivacaine-induced cardiovascular toxicity during partial inferior vena cava occlusion. Anesth Analg 1986;65:341.

127. DePace NC, Betesh JS, Koller MN. 'Postmortem' cæsarean section with recovery of both mother and fetus. JAMA 1982;248:971.

128. Kasten GW, Martin ST. Comparison of resuscitation of sheep and dogs after bupivacaine-induced cardiovascular collapse. Anesth Analg 1986;65:1029.

129. Eng M, Zorotovich RA. Broken-needle complication with a disposable spinal introducer. Anesthesiology 1977;46:147.

130. Schlake PT, Peleman RR, Winnie AP. Separation of the

hub from the shaft of a disposable epidural needle. Anesthesiology 1988;68:611.

131. Snow JC, Kripke BJ, Sakellarides H, et al. Broken disposable needle during an axillary approach to block the brachial plexus. Anesth Analg 1974;53:89.

132. Bonica JJ. Peridural block: Analysis of 3,637 cases and a review. Anesthesiology 1957;18:723.

133. Chun L, Karp M. Unusual complications from placement of catheters in caudal canal in obstetrical anesthesia. Anesthesiology 1966;27:96.

134. Hurley RJ, Lambert DH. Microcatheters for continuous spinal anesthesia. Anesth Analg 1990;71:201.

134a. Belatti RG, Fromme GA, Danielson DR. Relative resistance to shearing of commercially available epidural catheters versus available epidural needles. Anesthesiology 1985;63:A189.

135. Hehre FW, Muechler HC. Complications associated with use of extradural catheter in obstetric anesthesia. Anesth Analg 1965;45:245.

136. Nash TG, Openshaw DJ. Unusual complication of epidural anaesthesia. Br Med J 1968;2:700.

137. Hurley RJ, Lambert DH. Continuous spinal anesthesia with a microcatheter technique: preliminary experience. Anesth Analg 1990;70:97.

138. Baxter AD. Microcatheters for continuous spinal anesthesia [correspondence]. Anesth Analg 1990;71:200.

139. DeVera HV, Ries M. Complications of continuous spinal microcatheters: Should we seek their removal if sheared? [correspondence] Anesthesiology 1991; 74:794.

140. Wolfson B, Siker E, Gray G. Post-pneumoencephalography headache. Anaesthesia 1970;25:328.

141. Heaney GAH. An interesting dural tap. Anaesthesia 1984;39:386.

142. Bickler PE, Schapera A, Bainton CR. Acute radial nerve injury from use of an automatic blood pressure monitor. Anesthesiology 1990;73:186.

143. Sy WP. Ulnar nerve palsy possibly related to use of automatically cycled blood pressure cuff. Anesth Analg 1981;60:687.

144. Ochoa J, Noordenbos W. Pathology and disordered sensation in local nerve lesions. In: Bonica JJ, Liebeskind JC, Albe-Fessard DG, eds. Advances in pain research and therapy. New York: Raven Press, 1979:68.

145. Casady GN, Moore DC, Bridenbaugh LD. Postpartum hypertension after use of vasoconstrictor and oxytocic drugs. JAMA 1960;172:1011.

146. Durant TM, Long J, Oppenheimer MJ. Pulmonary venous air embolism. Am Heart J 1947;33:269.

147. Lifschultz BD, Donoghue ER. Air embolism during intercourse in pregnancy. J Forensic Sci 1983;28:1021.

148. Aronson ME, Nelson PK. Fatal air embolism in pregnancy resulting from an unusual sexual act. Obstet Gynecol 1967;30:127.

149. Fong J, Galadalla F, Druzin M. Venous emboli occurring during Cæsarean section: The effect of patient position. Can J Anaesth 1991;38:191.

150. Karuparthy VR, Downing JW, Husain FJ, et al. Incidence of venous air embolism during cesarean section is unchanged by the use of a 5 to 10 degree head-up tilt. Anesth Analg 1989;69:620.

151. Fong J, Gadalla F, Pierri K, Druzin M. Are Doppler-detected venous emboli during cesarean section air emboli? Anesth Analg 1990;71:254.

152. Younker D, Rodriguez V, Kavanagh J. Massive air embolism during cesarean section. Anesthesiology 1986;65:77.

153. Waldrop GS. Fatal air embolism during term labor and the pueriperium. Obstet Gynecol 1953;1:454.

154. Palmer CM, Norris MC, Giudici MC, Leighton BL, DeSimone CA. Incidence of electrocardiographic changes during cesarean delivery under regional anesthesia. Anesth Analg 1990;70:36.

155. Mathew JP, Fleisher LA, Sevarino FB, Rosenbaum SH. Silent myocardial ischemia in healthy parturients during cesarean delivery. Anesthesiology 1990;73:A992.

156. Nishimura N, Kajimoto Y, Kabe T, Sakamoto A. The effects of volume loading during epidural analgesia. Resuscitation 1985;13:31.

157. Frye RL, Braunwald E. Studies on Starling's law of the heart. I. The circulatory response to acute hypervolemia and its modification by ganglionic blockade. J Clin Invest 1960;39:1043.

158. Elstein ID, Marx GF. Electrocardiographic changes during cesarean section under regional anesthesia. Anesth Analg 1990;71:100.

159. King TA, Adams AP. Failed tracheal intubation. Br J Anæsth 1990;65:400.

160. Cohen SE. Aspiration syndromes in pregnancy. Anesthesiology 1979;51:375.

161. Samsoon GLT, Young JRB. Difficult tracheal intubation: A retrospective study. Anaesthesia 1987;42:487.

162. Lyons G. Failed intubation. Six years' experience in a teaching maternity unit. Anaesthesia 1985;40:759.

163. Fahy L, Horton WA, Charters P. Factor analysis in patients with a history of failed tracheal intubation during pregnancy. Br J Anaesth 1990;65:813.

164. Rubin GL, Peterson HB, Rochat RW, McCarthy BJ, Terry JS. Maternal death after cesarean section in Georgia. Am J Obstet Gynecol 1981;139:681.

165. Department of Health. Report on confidential enquiries into maternal deaths in England and Wales, 1982–84. London: Her Majesty's Stationery Office, 1989.

166. Gibb D. Confidential enquiry into maternal death. Br J Obstet Gynaecol 1990;97:97.

167. Gibbs CP. Gastric aspiration: Prevention and treatment. Clin Anesthesiol 1986;4:47.

168. Chadwick HS, Posner K, Caplan RA, Ward RJ, Cheney FW. A comparison of obstetric and nonobstetric anesthesia malpractice claims. Anesthesiology 1991;74:242.

169. Joupilla R, Joupilla P, Hollmen A. Laryngeal edema as an obstetric anæsthetic complication. Acta Anaesthesiol Scand 1980;24:97.

170. Mackenzie AI. Laryngeal oedema complicating obstetric anæsthesia. Anaesthesia 1978;33:271.

171. Malan TP, Johnson MD. The difficult airway in ob-

stetric anesthesia: Techniques for airway management and the role of regional anesthesia. J Clin Anesth 1988;1:104.

172. McClune S, Regan M, Moore J. Laryngeal mask airway for cæsarean section. Anaesthesia 1990;45:227.

173. LeFrock JL, Clark TS, Davies B, Klainer AS. Aspiration pneumonia: A ten-year review. Am Surgeon 1979; 45:305.

174. Spence AA, Moir DD, Finlay WEI. Observations on intragastric pressure. Anaesthesia 1967;22:249.

175. Lind JF, Smith AM, McIver DK, Coopland AT, Crispin JS. Heartburn in pregnancy—a manometric study. Can Med Assoc J 1968;98:571.

176. Hey VMF, Cowley DJ, Ganguli PC, Skinner LD, Ostick DG, Sharp DS. Gastro-oesophageal reflux in late pregnancy. Anaesthesia 1977;32:372.

177. Christofides ND, Ghatei MA, Bloom SR, Borberg C, Gillmer MDG. Decreased plasma motilin concentrations in pregnancy. Br Med J 1982;285:1453.

178. Attia RR, Ebeid AM, Fischer JE, Goudsouzian NG. Maternal fetal and placental gastrin concentrations. Anaesthesia 1982;37:18.

179. Murray FA, Erskine JP, Fielding J. Gastric secretion in pregnancy. J Obstet Gynaecol 1957;64:373.

180. Wilson J. Gastric emptying in labour: Some recent findings and their clinical significance. J Int Med Res 1978;6(Suppl 1):54.

181. LaSilvia LA, Steffen EA. Delayed gastric emptying time in labor. Am J Obstet Gynecol 1950;59:1075.

182. Holdsworth JD. Relationship between stomach contents and analgesia in labour. Br J Anaesth 1978; 50:1145.

183. Awe WC, Fletcher WS, Jacob SW. The pathophysiology of aspiration pneumonitis. Surgery 1966;60:232.

184. Bynum LJ, Pierce AK. Pulmonary aspiration of gastric contents. Am Rev Respir Dis 1976;114:1129.

185. Lewis RT, Burgess JH, Hampson LG. Cardiorespiratory studies in critical illness: Changes in aspiration pneumonitis. Arch Surg 1971;103:335.

186. Mendelson CL. The aspiration of stomach contents into the lungs during obstetric anesthesia. Am J Obstet Gynecol 1946;52:191.

187. Hamelberg W, Bosomworth PP. Aspiration pneumonitis: Experimental studies and clinical observations. Anesth Analg 1964;43:669.

188. Teabeaut JR. Aspiration of gastric contents: An experimental study. Am J Pathol 1952;28:51.

189. Schwartz DJ, Wynne JW, Gibbs CP, Hood CI, Kuck EJ. The pulmonary consequences of aspiration of gastric contents at pH values greater than 2.5. Am Rev Respir Dis 1980;121:119.

190. Sarwar H, Sprague DH. Laryngospasm as an early indicator of aspiration. Anesth Analg 1978;57:119.

191. Chapman RL, Modell JH, Ruiz BC, Calderwood HW, Hood CI, Graves SA. Effect of continuous positive-pressure ventilation and steroids on aspiration of hydrochloric acid (pH 1.8) in dogs. Anesth Analg 1974;53:556.

192. Wynne JW, Reynolds JC, Hood CI, Auerbach D, Ondrasick J. Steroid therapy for pneumonitis induced in rabbits by aspiration of foodstuff. Anesthesiology 1979;51:11.

193. Wynne JW, DeMarco FJ, Hood CI. Physiological effects of corticosteroids in foodstuff aspiration. Arch Surg 1981;116:46.

194. Chapman RL, Downs JB, Modell JH, Hood CI. The ineffectiveness of steroid therapy in treating aspiration of hydrochloric acid. Arch Surg 1974;108:858.

195. James CF, Modell JH, Gibbs CP, Kuck EJ, Ruiz BC. Pulmonary aspiration—effects of volume and pH in the rat. Anesth Analg 1984;63:665.

196. Gibbs CP, Spohr L, Schmidt D. The effectiveness of sodium citrate as an antacid. Anesthesiology 1982; 57:44.

197. Hamelberg W, Bosomworth PP. Aspiration pneumonitis: Experimental studies and clinical observations. Anesth Analg 1964;43:669.

198. Roberts RB, Shirley MA. Reducing the risk of acid aspiration during cesarean section. Anesth Analg 1974;53:859.

199. Taylor G. Acid pulmonary aspiration syndrome after antacids: A case report. Br J Anaesth 1975;47:615.

200. Whittington RM, Robinson JS, Thompson JM. Fatal aspiration (Mendelson's) syndrome despite antacids and cricoid pressure. Lancet 1979;ii:228.

201. Bond VK, Stoelting RK, Gupta CD. Pulmonary aspiration syndrome after inhalation of gastric fluid containing antacids. Anesthesiology 1979;51:452.

202. Gibbs CP, Schwartz DJ, Wynne JW, Hood CI, Kuck EJ. Antacid pulmonary aspiration in the dog. Anesthesiology 1979;51:380.

203. Tordoff SG. Acid-aspiration prophylaxis in 288 obstetric anæsthesia departments in the United Kingdom. Anaesthesia 1990;45:776.

204. Ewart MC, Yau G, Gin T, Kotur CF, Oh TE. A comparison of the effects of omeprazole and ranitidine on gastric secretion in women undergoing elective Cæsarean section. Anaesthesia 1990;45:527.

205. Bylsma-Howell M, Riggs KW, McMorland GH, et al. Placental transport of metoclopramide: assessment of maternal and neonatal effects. Can Anaesth Soc J 1983;30:487.

206. Howard FA, Sharp DS. Effect of metoclopramide on gastric emptying during labor. Br Med J 1973;1:446.

207. Nimmo WS, Wilson J, Prescott LF. Narcotic analgesics and delayed gastric emptying during labor. Lancet 1975;i:890.

208. Brock-Utne JG, Rubin J, Downing JW, Dimopoulos GE, Moshal MG, Naiker M. The administration of metoclopramide with atropine. Anaesthesia 1976; 31:1186.

209. Brock-Utne JG, Rubin J, Welman S, Dimpoulos GE, Moshal MG, Downing JW. The action of commonly used antiemetics on the lower oesophageal sphincter. Br J Anaesth 1978;50:295.

210. Howells TH, Khaam T, Kreel L, Seymour C, Oliver B,

Davies JAH. Pharmacological emptying of the stomach with metoclopramide. Br Med J 1971;2:558.

211. Baraka A, Saab M, Salem M, et al. Control of gastric acidity by glycopyrrolate premedication in the parturient. Anesth Analg 1977;56:642.

212. Stoelting RK. Responses to atropine, glycopyrrolate and Riopan of gastric fluid pH and volume in adult patients. Anesthesiology 1978;48:367.

213. Merrill RB, Hingson RA. Study of incidence of maternal mortality from aspiration of vomitus during anesthesia occurring in major obstetric hospitals in United States. Anesth Analg 1951;30:121.

214. Hutchinson BR. Acid aspiration syndrome [correspondence]. Br J Anaesth 1979;51:75.

215. Scott DB. Mendelson's syndrome. Br J Anaesth 1978; 50:81.

216. Cohen SE. Aspiration syndromes in pregnancy. Anesthesiology 1979;51:375.

217. Syverson CJ, Chavkin W, Atrash HK, Rochat RW, Sharp ES, King GE. Pregnancy-related mortality in New York City, 1980 to 1984: Causes of death and associated risk factors. Am J Obstet Gynecol 1991;164:603.

218. Bassell GM, Marx GF. Anesthesia-related maternal mortality. In: Shnider SM, Levinson G, eds. Anesthesia in obstetrics. 2nd ed. Baltimore: Williams & Wilkins, 1987:326.

219. Endler GC, Mariona G, Sokol RJ, Stevenson LB. Anesthesia-related maternal mortality in Michigan, 1972 to 1984. Am J Obstet Gynecol 1988;159:187.

220. Gibbs CP, Rolbin SH, Norman P. Cause and prevention of maternal aspiration. Anesthesiology 1984;61:111.

CHAPTER 33

Anesthesia for the Stressed Fetus

Kathleen A. Leavitt

The obstetric anesthesiologist strives to provide safe, effective analgesia to the parturient while simultaneously avoiding detrimental effects to the fetus. The presence of chronic or acute fetal compromise can complicate the realization of this goal. In recent years, obstetric management of the complicated pregnancy has focused on prompt intervention in an attempt to limit the risk of adverse neurologic outcome. In obstetric anesthesia, investigators have tried to determine if specific anesthetic agents or techniques harm or help the stressed fetus. This chapter first reviews the risk factors associated with, and the criteria used to diagnose, fetal distress. Then, it discusses anesthetic options for both elective and emergent delivery.

ETIOLOGY

Chronic Fetal Stress

Chronic fetal stress is an ongoing physiologic imbalance between fetal nutritional supply and metabolic demand. Long-standing deprivation of oxygen or nutrients leads to intrauterine growth retardation (IUGR), the hallmark of a chronically stressed fetus (Table 33-1). Intrauterine growth retardation can follow one of two patterns: symmetric or asymmet-

ric.[1] These patterns differ in terms of etiology and prognosis for ultimate neonatal development.

Viral infections, chromosomal anomalies, and exposure to teratogens all can cause symmetric IUGR. Infants suffer an equal reduction in all growth parameters, including birth weight, length, and head circumference. Symmetric IUGR is due to an insult that occurs early in gestation. It has little to do with deprivation of fetal nutritional supply. The prognosis for neonatal outcome is poor.

In contrast, asymmetric IUGR arises later in gestation and produces an infant with low birth weight and body length, but with normal head circumference. Chronic deprivation of fetal nutritional supply by an assortment of maternal or uteroplacental factors causes this pattern of IUGR. This type of chronic fetal stress induces a redistribution of blood flow, sparing brain growth at the expense of body growth. With an improved nutritional supply, these infants have a favorable prognosis for normal growth and development. However, because it is difficult to correct the underlying cause of chronic uteroplacental insufficiency, the fetus is extremely susceptible to perinatal asphyxia because of its limited physiologic reserve. Thus, both patterns of IUGR place the small-for-gestational-age fetus at greatly increased risk for perinatal morbidity and mortality.[2]

Table 33–1

Causes of Intrauterine Growth Retardation and Chronic Fetal Stress

Maternal

Extremes of maternal age

Lack of prenatal care

Low socioeconomic status

Malnutrition

Drug exposure: tobacco, ETOH, cocaine

Vascular disease: diabetes, chronic hypertension, preeclampsia, systemic lupus erythematosus

Cyanotic heart disease

Anemia, hemoglobinopathies

Previous history of IUGR

Uteroplacental

Placentation errors
  Accreta
  Previa

Placental insufficiency
  Infarction
  Fibrosis
  Calcification

Fetal

Chromosomal abnormalities

Intrauterine infections
  Cytomyolovirus
  Rubella

Cardiovascular anomalies

Multiple gestation

Acute Fetal Distress

A sudden interruption in fetal nutritional supply or an increase in metabolic demand causes acute fetal distress. Most often, acute fetal distress results from decreased blood flow to the fetus (asphyxia). Asphyxia leads to fetal hypoxia, anaerobic metabolism, and acidosis from production and accumulation of metabolic wastes. Fetal hypoxia also can result from delivery to the fetus of blood with a decreased oxygen content.

The fetal response to asphyxia has been studied in a variety of animal models.[3–5] Asphyxia causes a redistribution of blood flow to the brain, heart, and adrenal glands at the expense of flow to the gut and periphery. The sympathetic and parasympathetic nervous systems, baroreceptors, chemoreceptors, and a variety of hormones such as vasopressin and prostacyclin mediate this cardiovascular response.[6,7] Hypoxemia causes sym-

pathetically mediated systemic vasoconstriction, hypertension, and reflex bradycardia. In addition, fetal oxygen consumption decreases and anaerobic metabolism begins in certain vascular beds.

Maternal, uteroplacental, and fetal problems can all induce acute fetal distress (Table 33-2). Placental perfusion depends on uterine blood flow. The uterine vessels are dilated maximally at term, and, unlike other vascular beds that undergo autoregulation, these vessels cannot dilate further in response to decreased aortic blood flow or increased fetal metabolic demand. Therefore, uteroplacental blood flow varies directly with maternal arterial perfusion pressure. Hypotension, from decreased maternal cardiac output due to aortocaval compression, sympathetic blockade, or hypovolemia, directly lowers placental perfusion. Uterine blood vessels constrict markedly in response to alpha-adrenergic stimulation from endogenous or exogenous catecholamines. Uterine contractions also increase uterine vascular resistance and result in a transient fall in

Table 33–2

Causes of Acute Fetal Distress

Maternal

Hypotension

Aortocaval compression

Sympathetic blockade

Hypovolemia
  Dehydration
  Hemorrhage
  Placental abruption, previa

Decreased oxygen delivery

Anemia

Hypoxemia

Uteroplacental

Uterine artery vasoconstriction due to catecholamines, alpha-adrenergic agonists

Uterine tetany
  Overstimulation with oxytocin
  Placental abruption

Umbilical cord compression
  Oligohydramnios
  Maternal position

Umbilical cord prolapse

Umbilical vein/artery vasoconstriction

Fetal

Anemia

Arrhythmia

intervillous blood flow. Sustained or tetanic uterine contractions from overstimulation with oxytocin or placental abruption induce a much more significant interruption in placental perfusion.

Acute umbilical cord occlusion dramatically reduces blood flow to the fetus. The risk of umbilical cord compression is enhanced by oligohydramnios and may depend on maternal position. Umbilical blood vessels may have sympathetic innervation and vasoconstrict in response to endogenous and exogenous catecholamines.[8] Finally, conditions that interfere with oxygen delivery within the fetal circulation, such as anemia or arrhythmias, may result in acute fetal distress.

Not all fetuses will develop hypoxia and acidosis in response to these insults. The consequences of asphyxia depend upon the magnitude and duration of the insult and the pre-existing status of the uteroplacental circulation. The chronically stressed fetus, because of its limited physiologic reserve, is much more susceptible to acute decompensation when confronted with even transient reductions in oxygen supply. Therefore, the clinician must try to identify the fetus at risk of developing acute fetal distress and take steps to minimize the likelihood of this occurrence.

DIAGNOSIS

Table 33-3 lists the antepartum, intrapartum, and postpartum diagnostic modalities used to detect both acute and chronic fetal compromise. A few of these techniques are discussed briefly.

Antepartum

Several antepartum surveillance techniques can identify the fetus at risk of distress during labor. Nonstress testing and contraction stress testing are two long-standing modalities that use fetal heart rate analysis to detect fetal stress (see Chap. 7). The value of these tests lies in the prognostic significance of a negative test; that is, a normal or "reactive" fetal heart rate response during either a nonstress test or a contraction stress test correlates with 99% fetal survival for at least 1 week. Because of the high false-positive rate, however, both a nonreactive nonstress test and an abnormal fetal heart rate response during a contraction stress test require further evaluation.[9]

Ultrasound imaging is another essential modality of fetal surveillance. This technique allows the clinician to follow the growth of the fetus throughout gestation.

Table 33-3

Diagnostic Modalities Used to Detect Acute and Chronic Fetal Compromise

Antepartum

Nonstress test

Contraction stress test

Ultrasound
  Fetal size, weight
  Biophysical profile
    Fetal breathing movements
    Gross body movements
    Fetal tone
    Amniotic fluid volume
    Fetal heart rate
Doppler ultrasound
  Umbilical blood flow velocity

Intrapartum

Continuous electronic fetal heart rate monitoring

Intermittent auscultation of fetal heart rate

Fetal scalp capillary blood pH

Meconium-stained amniotic fluid

Postpartum

Apgar scores

Umbilical cord blood gas analysis

Neurobehavioral testing

The diagnosis of low fetal weight for gestational age identifies a fetus at high risk of perinatal morbidity and mortality. Unfortunately, estimates of fetal weight late in gestation may be inaccurate by as much as 20%.[10,11] A more comprehensive test, using ultrasound, is the biophysical profile. The biophysical profile has been likened to an in utero Apgar score in that it evaluates five discrete biophysical variables: fetal breathing movements, gross body movement, fetal tone, amniotic fluid volume, and fetal heart rate. A low score predicts a high risk of perinatal mortality, and there are few false-negative results. Thus, the biophysical profile is a very sensitive and specific test for identifying fetal compromise.[12-14]

Doppler ultrasound measurement of umbilical arterial blood flow velocity offers a newer, more sophisticated means of antepartum detection of fetal compromise. Because the use of this technique is becoming more widespread, it is important to understand its basic principles. Doppler ultrasound measures blood flow velocity by transmitting an ultrasound beam that is scattered and reflected as it encounters a moving column of red blood cells. The frequency of the reflected ultrasound beam is directly proportional to the blood flow velocity.[15] Pulsatile blood flow has a characteristic velocity waveform depending on the vascular site recorded. The waveform represents a summation of the forward velocity of blood ejected by the heart and of reflected waves as the blood encounters arterial branching and termination points. These reflected waves serve to cancel or diminish the forward velocity of blood flow. Their affect is greatest during the later or diastolic portion of the waveform. If blood encounters a distal vascular bed of high impedance, the incident waveform will be highly reflected. This results in reduced velocity or even reversal of blood flow during diastole (Fig. 33-1). If the distal vascular bed is of low impedance, the incident waveform will not be highly reflected, resulting in maintained forward blood flow during diastole (Fig. 33-2).

The ratio of the peak systolic to the least diastolic blood flow velocity (S/D ratio) in the umbilical artery correlates with placental vascular resistance.[16] The placenta is normally a vascular bed of extremely low resistance. In fact, placental vascular resistance should decrease with increasing gestational age with growth of more vascular channels and increased cross-sectional area. Therefore, the incident waveform from blood traveling through the umbilical artery toward the fetal side of the placenta should be reflected less and less throughout gestation. Thus, blood flow velocity during diastole increases and S/D ratio decreases as gestation progresses. If, however, placental vascular resistance is abnormally high, diastolic flow falls or even

reverses owing to greater reflection of the incident waveform. A decline in diastolic flow produces a rise in S/D ratio; therefore, the S/D ratio serves as a measure of placental blood flow resistance and, thus, of potential fetal compromise (Fig. 33-3).

As yet, Doppler ultrasound measurement of umbilical blood flow velocity is not used as criteria for emergent delivery of the fetus. In the research setting, it has predicted fetal growth retardation as well as perinatal hypoxia, acidosis, and fetal distress.[17] Clinically, velocimetry can help monitor the fetus with suspected placental insufficiency and assess the effects of therapeutic maneuvers designed to improve placental blood flow.[18,19] For example, Giles *et al*[20] showed that, in well-hydrated, nonlaboring parturients, lumbar epidural blockade improved diastolic blood flow.[20] Future studies should use this modality to evaluate the effects of major conduction blockade on maternal and fetal blood flow in the presence of placental insufficiency.

Intrapartum

The diagnosis of intrapartum fetal distress has traditionally relied upon two modalities: electronic fetal heart rate monitoring (EFM) and fetal scalp capillary blood gas analysis. Electronic fetal heart rate monitoring largely replaced intermittent auscultation of fetal heart rate in the early 1970s as a more sensitive means of detecting potential fetal compromise. Observation of the baseline heart rate, variability, and periodic

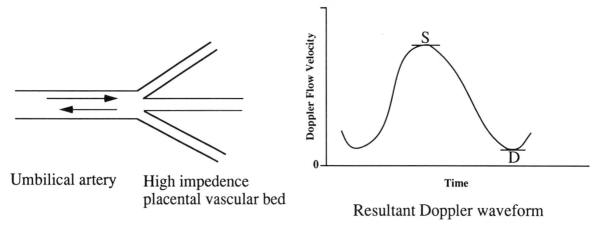

Figure 33–1. Schematic diagram of pulsatile blood flow through the umbilical artery during systole (S) and diastole (D) as it travels toward a placental vascular bed of high resistance. The resultant Doppler waveform shows diminished blood flow during diastole because reflection of incident waves serves to cancel forward blood flow velocity.

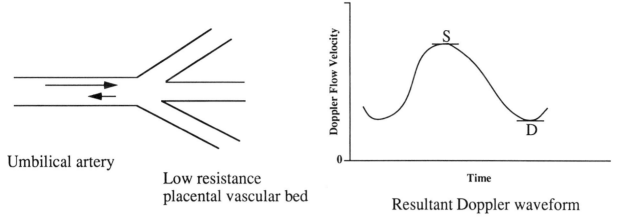

Figure 33–2. Schematic diagram of pulsatile blood flow through the umbilical artery during systole (S) and diastole (D) as it travels toward a placental vascular bed of low resistance. The resultant Doppler waveform shows preserved forward blood flow during diastole because of less reflection of incident waves.

changes in heart rate associated with uterine contractions provides an indirect assessment of fetal status. Because these parameters are under the direct control of the central nervous system (CNS), a normal fetal heart rate pattern is thought to represent an intact axis between the CNS and cardiovascular system. Asphyxia interferes with this axis and produces characteristic changes in the fetal heart rate tracing. Common alterations include baseline tachycardia or bradycardia, variable and late decelerations, and loss of beat-to-beat variability. Variable decelerations probably represent umbilical cord compression. They are most often treated by altering maternal position into right lateral, left lateral, or knee-chest position. Umbilical cord compression often occurs in the setting of decreased amniotic fluid volume. Transvaginal infusion of saline into the amniotic cavity lessens the frequency of variable decelerations.[21] Prophylactic intrapartum amnioinfusion reduced the incidence of severe variable decelerations, end-stage bradycardia, and operative delivery for fetal distress.[22] Because the infusion of an adequate volume of saline may take up to 30 minutes, amnioinfusion may be ineffective for acute fetal distress, which requires more rapid intervention.

Late decelerations are the most serious periodic changes in fetal heart rate. Recurrent late decelerations are frequently associated with significant fetal acidemia from uteroplacental insufficiency. They can signify both chronic and acute fetal compromise and require prompt evaluation and intervention.

When all abnormalities in the fetal heart rate tracing are considered, the baseline variability is the single most important characteristic in predicting fetal status.

Baseline variability represents the constant push–pull effect of the sympathetic and parasympathetic nervous systems on the fetal heart rate. Its presence shows an intact CNS. Fetal heart rate variability is affected by maternally administered drugs such as narcotics and by fetal sleep–wake cycles. Nevertheless, loss of variability may signify fetal asphyxia and always warrants further investigation.

Intrapartum analysis of fetal scalp capillary blood pH can help further evaluate a nonreassuring fetal heart rate pattern. Sampling can be done only when the cervix has dilated to at least 2 to 3 cm and membranes are ruptured. A fetal scalp pH of 7.25, or greater, is normal. A pH between 7.20 and 7.25 is borderline and should be followed every 15 to 30 minutes with repeat sampling. A value below 7.20 suggests significant fetal acidemia and requires prompt intervention (Table 33-4).

Despite their widespread use, neither fetal acid–base analysis nor electronic fetal heart rate monitoring can predict newborn complications attributable to asphyxia. Part of the inaccuracy is inherent in the tests themselves. Maternal pH, fetal scalp blood flow, and the presence of air bubbles in the sample will all affect fetal scalp pH.[23] Also, some have suggested that the pH value that truly shows significant acidemia is much below the accepted criteria of 7.20.[24]

Interpretation of fetal heart rate tracings is very subjective. In a recent analysis, experts in the field differed widely in their interpretations of sample fetal heart rate tracings.[25] Electronic fetal heart rate monitoring is a very sensitive, yet nonspecific, test. The incidence of a false-positive diagnosis of fetal distress will be high

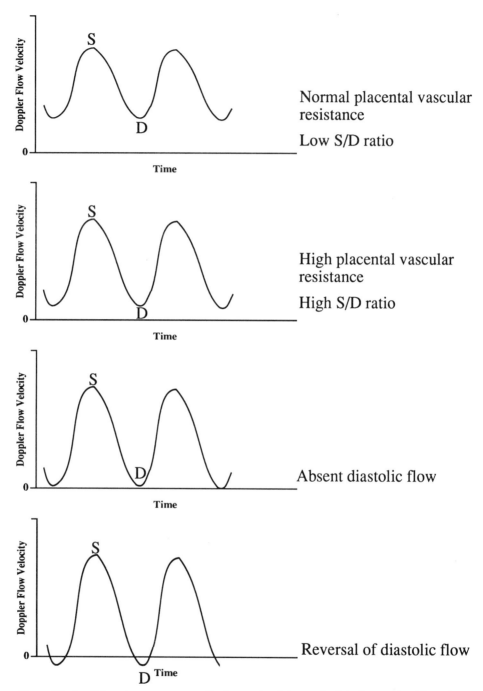

Figure 33–3. Schematic representation of both normal and abnormal umbilical artery blood flow velocity waveforms. The ratio of blood flow velocity during systole compared to diastole (S/D ratio) is used to quantify placental vascular resistance.

Table 33-4

Interpretation and Clinical Management of Fetal Scalp pH Results

pH	INTERPRETATION	CLINICAL ACTION
> 7.25	Normal	—
7.20–7.25	Borderline	Follow, repeat in 20–30 min
< 7.20	Significant acidemia	Prompt delivery

when using EFM in a population in which the incidence of fetal asphyxia is low.[26]

Many anticipated a dramatic reduction in the incidence of poor neurologic outcome with the introduction of continuous fetal heart rate analysis during labor. Unfortunately, this expectation has not been realized. Instead, a dramatic increase in the incidence of instrumental and cesarean deliveries has occurred. The cause of adverse neurologic outcome is poorly understood. Only severe and prolonged asphyxia increases the risk of permanent neurologic dysfunction.[27,28] However, the vast majority of infants diagnosed with severe intrapartum asphyxia develop without any detectable neurologic deficit. As a corollary, most children with neurologic disabilities displayed no evidence of perinatal asphyxia. This is a contradiction to the commonly held belief that adverse neurologic sequelae, particularly cerebral palsy, can be prevented by early diagnosis and treatment of intrapartum asphyxia. Cerebral palsy occurs in approximately 2 in 1000 live births. At most, 10% of these cases are associated with perinatal asphyxia, suggesting a prenatal rather than perinatal etiology of the disease.[29,30] Therefore, intrapartum events may be responsible for the development of two cases of cerebral palsy in 10,000 deliveries. Given these statistics, is the routine use of continuous electronic fetal monitoring warranted in all pregnancies?

The obstetric community is currently debating the use of intermittent auscultation versus continuous EFM to detect fetal compromise during labor. Advocates of intermittent auscultation point to the increased cesarean delivery rate and lack of significant improvement in neonatal outcome associated with the use of EFM. Eight randomized prospective studies have recently appeared in the literature comparing perinatal outcome with the use of intermittent auscultation versus continuous EFM.[31–38] None of the studies shows any reduction in perinatal mortality with the use of continuous EFM. Two of them report improved umbilical cord blood gas values and decreased incidence of neonatal seizures in the group monitored continuously but no difference in the incidence of long-term neurologic deficits.[31,34] The remaining six studies found no difference in neonatal morbidity in terms of Apgar scores, umbilical cord blood gases, or need for resuscitation.

Because no clear benefit can be attributed to the use of EFM, the American College of Obstetricians and Gynecologists states that intermittent auscultation is equivalent to continuous EFM in detecting fetal compromise.[39] If intermittent auscultation is used, it should be done during a contraction and for 30 seconds following its resolution, according to the schedule outlined in Table 33-5. It remains to be seen whether or not these recommendations will be ac-

Table 33-5

Recommended Guidelines for Use of Intermittent Auscultation to Monitor Fetal Heart Rate During Labor

PREGNANCY CATEGORY	FREQUENCY OF AUSCULTATION	
	First Stage	Second Stage
Low risk	Every 30 min	Every 15 min
High risk	Every 15 min	Every 5 min

cepted by the medical community and intermittent auscultation again becomes the standard of care for intrapartum fetal monitoring.

A discussion of intrapartum fetal monitoring would not be complete without mentioning meconium. Meconium-stained amniotic fluid has traditionally been regarded as a sign of intrapartum fetal stress. However, the significance of meconium passage is poorly understood, and some suggest that it is merely a sign of a normally functioning fetal gastrointestinal tract.[40] Meconium-stained amniotic fluid occurs in up to 44% of pregnancies and has never been consistently associated with abnormal fetal heart rate tracings, acidosis, or low Apgar scores.[41] Therefore, passage of meconium does not by itself signify fetal distress. However, it should prompt the obstetrician to look for other signs of fetal compromise and to take special precautions at the time of delivery to prevent the potentially devastating consequences of meconium aspiration syndrome. Intrapartum amnioinfusion of saline can reportedly wash out the meconium from the amniotic cavity and decrease the incidence and severity of meconium aspiration.[42]

Postpartum

Apgar scores, umbilical cord blood gas analysis, and neurobehavioral testing are all used in the routine evaluation of the neonate. Persistently low Apgar scores (less than 5) at 10, 15, and 20 minutes identify an infant at high risk of death or of severe neurologic impairment.[43,44] However, do not *retrospectively* attribute low Apgar scores to intrapartum asphyxial events. Many factors are known to affect Apgar scores, including the following:

- Maternally administered sedatives
- Prematurity
- Birth weight
- Congenital malformations
- Genetic defects[45]

Acidosis identified by umbilical cord blood gas analysis also correlates poorly with neonatal status and subsequent neurologic development.[46] Most neonates with an umbilical cord blood pH less than 7.20 are vigorous at birth and show no adverse short- or long-term sequelae.[47,48] The value of routinely obtaining an umbilical cord blood gas sample is in documenting a normal pH value, refuting the presence of intrapartum asphyxia.[49]

Neurobehavioral tests are an additional means of detecting more subtle or delayed effects of perinatal events but are predominantly used in the research setting (see Chap. 6).[50-52] Therefore, their prognostic significance in identifying neonates at risk of abnormal neurologic development is not known.

TREATMENT

Once diagnosed, it is important first to determine and correct the underlying etiology of antepartum or intrapartum fetal distress before proceeding to emergent operative delivery. Because of the nonspecific nature of the diagnostic modalities, determining the exact etiology of fetal distress is often difficult. Once fetal distress is suspected, however, several maneuvers may improve blood flow and oxygen delivery to the fetus (Table 33-6).

Alter Maternal Position

The first step is to place the parturient in left or right lateral, knee–chest, or Trendelenburg position. Altering maternal position improves fetal blood flow by relieving aortocaval compression or umbilical cord compression. Aortocaval compression impairs uterine perfusion by two mechanisms. First, the gravid uterus directly compresses the aorta proximal to the origin of the uterine blood vessels. Second, it compresses the inferior vena cava, decreasing venous return, right ventricular preload, and maternal cardiac output. Some refer to the effects of aortocaval compression as the *supine hypotensive syndrome,* but remember that uterine artery perfusion pressure is not accurately reflected in maternal brachial artery pressure. Maternal blood pressure measured in the brachial artery may be entirely normal owing to compensatory vasoconstriction.[53] A

Table 33–6

Treatment of Fetal Distress

Alter maternal position
   Aortocaval compression
   Umbilical cord compression
Correct maternal hypotension
   Fluids
   Vasopressors
Decrease uterine tone
   Stop oxytocin
   Give tocolytics
Administer maternal oxygen

towel or blanket place under the parturient's right hip will usually relieve aortocaval compression. In some patients, the right or left lateral decubitus positions more effectively displace the gravid uterus. If fetal distress persists, Trendelenburg or knee–chest positions may relieve umbilical cord compression by the presenting fetal part. Vaginal examination may detect umbilical cord prolapse. Finally, intra-amniotic infusion of saline also may be effective in relieving umbilical cord compression when oligohydramnios is present.

Correct Hypotension

Because uteroplacental blood flow varies directly with maternal arterial perfusion pressure, it is extremely important to avoid and to treat maternal hypotension rapidly. Adequate fluid prehydration, left uterine displacement, use of dilute local anesthetic/narcotic infusions for labor analgesia, and slow, incremental titration of more concentrated local anesthetics for cesarean delivery can limit or prevent hypotension caused by sympathetic blockade from regional anesthesia.[54–57] Fluid prehydration should entail the use of 1 to 2 L of non–glucose-containing isotonic crystalloid. Several studies illustrate the importance of using non–glucose-containing fluids.[58–62] Philipson *et al*[58] evaluated the fetal and maternal metabolic effects of hydration with either 5% dextrose, Ringer's lactate, or isotonic saline in healthy parturients undergoing elective cesarean delivery. Infusion of 1 L of 5% dextrose yields maternal and fetal hyperglycemia, and significantly decreases umbilical venous and arterial pH and fetal oxygen saturation. Chronic glucose infusion increases fetal metabolic rate and oxygen consumption, leading to acidemia and hypoxemia.[60–62] Other adverse effects of fetal hyperglycemia include neonatal hypoglycemia and the potential for worsened neurologic outcome after global cerebral ischemia.

Besides adequate fluid prehydration, administer a vasopressor at the first sign of falling maternal blood pressure.[63] The vasopressor of choice is ephedrine. Its beta-adrenergic effects increase maternal heart rate, contractility, cardiac output, and uterine blood flow.[64,65] Pure alpha-adrenergic agonists, such as phenylephrine, have not been widely used in obstetrics because they can constrict the uterine vasculature.[66,67] Clinically, phenylephrine lacks adverse effects on neonatal status when used to treat maternal hypotension during cesarean delivery.[68,69] However, these data come from healthy, nonlaboring parturients without evidence of fetal compromise. These healthy fetuses may have sustained significant reduction in uterine

blood flow, yet suffered no measurable effects because of sufficient placental reserve. Therefore, the use of alpha-adrenergic agonists to treat maternal hypotension cannot be recommended without further evaluation of their effects on the compromised fetus.

Decreased Uterine Tone

Uterine contractions can have a profoundly ischemic effect on the placental circulation. The tension developed within the myometrium increases uterine vascular resistance in proportion to the intensity, frequency, and duration of contractions. Because of limited placental reserve, the stressed fetus cannot tolerate significant reductions in uterine blood flow. Thus, frequent or sustained uterine contractions often result in acute decompensation. When a nonreassuring fetal heart rate tracing or acidosis exists during labor, immediately stop exogenous oxytocin administration. In addition, beta$_2$-sympathomimetics have been used to decrease uterine tone, abolish uterine contractions, and improve umbilical blood flow in acute intrapartum fetal distress. Either intravenous or subcutaneous administration of terbutaline, 0.25 mg, significantly improves fetal acid–base status, fetal heart rate tracing, and neonatal outcome.[70–74] One randomized study found significant improvement in acid–base status and Apgar scores in parturients who received subcutaneous terbutaline compared to those who did not (Table 33-7).[70] Umbilical vascular resistance declines after subcutaneous administration of terbutaline.[71] In contrast, magnesium did not alter umbilical vascular resistance. A single dose of terbutaline to treat acute intrapartum fetal distress produces a mild maternal tachycardia but no other side effects.[72]

Administer Maternal Oxygen

Maternal hyperoxia can increase oxygen delivery to the fetus if blood flow is not drastically impeded by uterine hypoperfusion, umbilical cord compression, or uterine hypertonus. Supplemental oxygen delivered by high-flow face mask increased maternal and fetal transcutaneous P_{O_2} in both normal and "high-risk" parturients in labor.[75] During elective cesarean delivery under epidural anesthesia, supplemental oxygen by face mask progressively increases fetal P_{O_2} as FiO_2 rises to 1.0 (Table 33-8).[76] Although the rise in fetal P_{O_2} seems small, fetal hemoglobin lies on the steep portion of its oxyhemoglobin dissociation curve, and a small increment in P_{O_2} greatly increases oxygen saturation and

Table 33–7

Intrauterine Fetal Resuscitation with Terbutaline

	TERBUTALINE (n = 11)	CONTROL (n = 9)
Initial pH (fetal scalp)	7.15	7.18
Final pH (umbilical artery)	7.25	7.17
1 min Apgar > 7 (n)	10/11	4/9

(Data from Shekarloo A, Mendez-Bauer C, Cook V, Freese U. Terbutaline (intravenous bolus) for the treatment of acute intrapartum fetal distress. Am J Obstet Gynecol 1989;160:615)

content. The increase in umbilical venous oxygen saturation from 65% to 87% can provide substantial oxygen reserve.

Earlier studies, however, reported a plateau or decline in fetal oxygen tension when maternal Po_2 exceeded 300 mm Hg.[77–79] These authors studied patients undergoing elective cesarean delivery under general anesthesia with nitrous oxide and volatile agent. In one study, increasing maternal inspired oxygen concentration from 50% to 100% did not improve fetal oxygenation.[77] Marx and Mateo[78] also reported this "ceiling" effect of maternal oxygen administration at an FiO_2 between 50% and 65%. Another investigation even reported a decline in fetal oxygen tension with inspired oxygen concentrations above 50%.[79] These authors suggested a vasoconstricting effect of maternal hyperoxia. However, these studies have been criticized for the lack of control over several variables, including the following:

- Anesthetic depth
- Maintenance of left uterine displacement
- Uterine incision to delivery interval
- Maternal $Paco_2$

Increasing the maternal FiO_2 without also increasing the delivered concentration of volatile agent may result in an inadequate depth of anesthesia, maternal catecholamines, and placental vasoconstriction. A more recent study controlled the anesthetic depth during general anesthesia for both elective and emergent cesarean delivery.[80] The investigators gave isoflurane in either 100% oxygen or 50% nitrous oxide in oxygen. All women received 1.5 MAC of anesthesia for the first 5 minutes after induction and then 1.0 MAC. Administration of 100% oxygen and isoflurane resulted in a small but significant increase in umbilical venous Po_2. This effect was most notable in patients undergoing emergency cesarean delivery. Fewer newborns needed resuscitation with supplemental oxygen in this group. Administration of 100% oxygen to patients undergoing nonemergent cesarean delivery did not seem to offer these same advantages. No adverse maternal ef-

Table 33–8

Effect of Maternal Oxygen Administration on Maternal and Fetal Oxygenation

FiO_2	0.21	0.47	0.74	1.00
Maternal PaO_2 (mm Hg)	96	232	312	423
UV Po_2 (mm Hg)	28	36	41	47
UVo_2Sat (%)	65			87
UA Po_2 (mm Hg)	15	19	21	25
UA O_2Sat (%)	26			59

(Data obtained from 40 healthy term parturients undergoing elective cesarean delivery with epidural anesthesia. Ramanathan S, Gandhi S, Arismendy J, Chalon J, Turndorf H. Oxygen transfer from mother to fetus during cesarean section under epidural anesthesia. Anesth Analg 1982;61:576)
Abbreviations: UA = umbilical artery, UV = umbilical vein.

fects (*i.e.*, decreased uterine contractility or increased blood loss) correlated with the use of higher concentrations of volatile agent.[80–82]

Therefore, maternal oxygen administration during either general or regional anesthesia will increase umbilical venous and arterial oxygen tensions. The seemingly small rise in fetal P_{O_2} substantially increases hemoglobin saturation and oxygen content. This effect may significantly improve the physiologic reserve of the stressed fetus. However, maternal oxygen administration will do little to improve fetal status if fetal blood supply is interupted.

ANESTHETIC MANAGEMENT

Vaginal Delivery

The route of anticipated delivery is probably the most important determining factor in the choice of anesthetic technique. Given the diagnosis of chronic fetal stress, obstetricians will attempt to effect either spontaneous or instrumental vaginal delivery, because this is associated with less maternal morbidity and mortality than cesarean delivery.[83] The anesthetic options available to the parturient include Lamaze techniques, parenteral narcotics, regional blocks such as paracervical, pudendal, and perineal infiltration, subarachnoid block, and, finally, continuous lumbar epidural analgesia. Although any of these options is appropriate in a parturient with an uncompromised fetus, the woman with a stressed fetus should be strongly encouraged to undergo placement of a continuous lumbar epidural catheter for several reasons.

The diagnosis of fetal stress places these parturients at higher risk of requiring urgent or emergent operative delivery. When a fetus with already marginal reserve is subjected to the additional stress of labor, acute fetal distress often follows. Continuous lumbar epidural analgesia begun early in labor can then be extended to provide surgical anesthesia should the need to perform emergent cesarean delivery arise. This option can improve maternal safety. A prospective observational study by Morgan *et al*[84] examined the benefits of both preoperative assessment and early institution of epidural analgesia in 360 patients requiring emergency cesarean delivery. Routine preoperative evaluation identified a group of women who seemed likely to require abdominal delivery (Table 33-9). Preoperative evaluation alone allowed them to predict the need for emergency cesarean delivery for fetal distress in 87% of cases. Only 13% developed fetal distress with no prior warning. This study illustrates that the need for cesarean delivery can be anticipated simply by a knowledge

Table 33-9

Characteristics of Parturients Who Seem Likely to Require Abdominal Delivery

Failure to progress in labor
Cephalopelvic disproportion
Nonengaged fetal head
Persistent occiput posterior head
Breech presentation
Abnormal fetal heart rate tracing
Need for fetal scalp pH analysis
Multiple gestation
Suspected IUGR
Vaginal birth after cesarean delivery
Preeclampsia

of risk factors and by preoperative assessment of all patients who present to the labor suite. In addition, institution of epidural analgesia early in labor allowed 70% of patients to undergo operative delivery by extension of the epidural blockade. Twenty-two percent did not receive epidural analgesia despite preoperative assessment and thus required general anesthesia for cesarean delivery. Finally, an additional 7% required general anesthesia in spite of receiving an epidural block in labor. Neonatal condition did not differ between the epidural and general anesthesia groups, but no mention was made of the specific anesthetic agents used. The authors note that complications of general anesthesia are less common but more serious and include difficult intubation, bronchospasm, and awareness. Epidural anesthesia is associated with more frequent but less serious complications. These included discomfort during surgery requiring opiate administration (9%), hypotension treated with fluids and ephedrine (18%), nausea (20%), and vomiting (5%). Morgan *et al*[84] draw the following conclusions:

- Preoperative assessment should be done on all patients admitted to the labor suite. Risk factors that predispose to cesarean delivery can be identified.
- Induction of epidural analgesia early in labor may avoid the need for a rushed general anesthetic if fetal distress arises.
- Epidural block nearly eliminates the risk of maternal aspiration of gastric contents and of failed intubation—the two most common causes of maternal morbidity and mortality.

Lumbar epidural analgesia also can have a beneficial effect on uteroplacental perfusion. Probably, sympathetic blockade and maternal pain relief serve to lower maternal catecholamine concentrations. This effect then relieves any catecholamine-induced uterine artery vasoconstriction that may have been limiting placental oxygen delivery. In 12 laboring women, Doppler measurement of umbilical artery flow velocity waveforms showed decreased placental vascular resistance after epidural analgesia with 1.5% lidocaine.[8] An earlier study reported the same effect in 13 out of 16 laboring patients who received epidural analgesia with 3% 2-chloroprocaine.[85] Umbilical artery vascular resistance did not change in three patients, probably because they were studied during a less active phase of labor. Both studies were done in normal, healthy laboring patients with no evidence of fetal stress. Jouppila *et al*[86] measured intervillous blood flow during labor in nine patients with severe preeclampsia. They noted dramatic improvement in intervillous blood flow measured by xenon[133] clearance after epidural analgesia with 0.25% bupivacaine. This evidence supports the beneficial effect of continuous lumbar epidural analgesia on uteroplacental perfusion, especially in the presence of a vasoconstricted placental bed.

Several controversies still surround the use of continuous lumbar epidural analgesia for vaginal delivery in the presence of chronic fetal stress. These include the choice of local anesthetic, the use of epidural narcotics, and the use of epinephrine-containing solutions.

Choice of Local Anesthetic

The most commonly used local anesthetics to provide lumbar epidural analgesia are 2-chloroprocaine, lidocaine, and bupivacaine. Theoretically, 2-chloroprocaine should be the local anesthetic of choice in the presence of fetal stress. It is rapidly hydrolyzed by maternal plasma cholinesterase to an inactive metabolite resulting in limited placental transfer.[87] The maternal and neonatal in vitro half-lives of 2-chloroprocaine are 21 and 43 seconds, respectively.[88] Also, Philipson *et al*[89] showed that fetal acid–base status did not affect fetal plasma concentrations of 2-chloroprocaine and its major metabolite.

However, this drug has several major disadvantages. Its short duration of action makes it impractical to use as the sole local anesthetic for continuous epidural analgesia for labor. There also are several recent reports of significant back pain in ambulatory surgical patients who received epidural anesthesia with 2-chloroprocaine.[90,91] Hypocalcemic tetany of the paraspinal muscles induced by the preservative and calcium-chelating agent disodium EDTA remains the most probable mechanism. As yet, no reports of this phenomenon in the obstetric population have appeared.

One final unfavorable characteristic of 2-chloroprocaine is its antagonistic effect on both epidural narcotics and amide local anesthetics. Epidural fentanyl provides significantly less analgesia after cesarean delivery when 2-chloroprocaine is used compared to either bupivacaine or lidocaine.[92,93] Epidural fentanyl provided postoperative analgesia for less than 90 minutes when used with 2-chloroprocaine compared to 4 hours with bupivacaine or lidocaine. Altering the pH of 2-chloroprocaine does not reverse this antagonism.[94] Subsequent investigators have attempted to find a narcotic that does provide analgesia after 2-chloroprocaine. There is some evidence that butorphanol, a kappa-agonist, might be such a narcotic.[95]

Several studies have illustrated the antagonistic effect of 2-chloroprocaine on amide local anesthetics. Mixtures of 2-chloroprocaine with longer-acting local anesthetics are used to speed the onset of analgesia and as safe "test doses" to detect intravascular epidural catheter placement. Cohen *et al*[96] and DeCampo *et al*[97] first reported that the duration of analgesia produced by a mixture of 2-chloroprocaine and bupivacaine was shorter than that produced by bupivacaine alone. 2-Chloroprocaine–bupivacaine mixtures have both a slow onset and provide poor analgesia.[98] Raising the pH of 2-chloroprocaine slightly hastens the onset of the block, but the duration of analgesia obtained with bupivacaine remains shortened.[99] Finally, Grice *et al*[100] reported that 2-chloroprocaine used to confirm location of the epidural catheter tip significantly shortened the duration of analgesia obtained with a mixture of bupivacaine, fentanyl, and epinephrine.

Therefore, despite its rapid metabolism and minimal fetal transfer, 2-chloroprocaine presents too many disadvantages to be advocated as the local anesthetic of choice for epidural analgesia for labor in the presence of fetal stress. Reserve this drug for those situations in which acute fetal distress requires expedient delivery and rapid onset of anesthesia.

The amide local anesthetics bupivacaine and lidocaine are alternatives that present a unique set of problems. Both undergo a phenomenon known as "ion trapping" when given in the presence of fetal acidosis (see Chap. 6). As a result, local anesthetic accumulates in fetal plasma and tissues, predisposing to cardiac and CNS toxicity.[101,102] In addition, asphyxia enhances the toxic effects of local anesthetics.[101] An asphyxiated fetus will develop seizures and cardiac arrest at much lower plasma concentrations of local anesthetics than a nonasphyxiated fetus.

Epidural analgesia using 0.5% bupivacaine also may increase the incidence of fetal heart rate decelerations during labor.[103–105] Furthermore, amide local anesthetics have been associated with decreased fetal heart rate variability.[106,107] A recent study, however, showed no evidence of fetal heart rate decelerations or diminution in variability in parturients undergoing elective cesarean delivery using epidural anesthesia with either lidocaine or bupivacaine.[108] Labor itself may be responsible for the fetal heart rate changes sometimes observed. There is a 6% incidence of fetal heart rate decelerations during labor in the absence of epidural analgesia.[109]

Finally, Scanlon *et al*[110] in the early 1970s, reported an increased incidence of "floppy but alert" newborns when lumbar epidural analgesia with lidocaine was used for vaginal delivery. Although this study has several major methodologic flaws, it prompted many subsequent investigations of the neurobehavioral effects of local anesthetics.[104,111–116] Although these studies never confirmed Scanlon's findings of neonatal hypotonia, they did detect subtle neurobehavioral effects of all local anesthetics, including 2-chloroprocaine. These effects are short-lived and correlate better with the route of delivery than the particular local anesthetic used. Infants delivered by cesarean delivery perform better than those born vaginally, despite exposure to higher concentrations of local anesthetics.[115] A very important report by Kuhnert *et al*[81] showed that even 2-chloroprocaine, the local anesthetic associated with minimal placental transfer, can affect neurobehavioral performance. It must be emphasized, however, that the neuro-

behavioral effects of local anesthetics have not been studied in the presence of fetal acidosis, and the potential for different findings exists.

When choosing a local anesthetic to provide continuous lumbar epidural analgesia in the presence of fetal stress, the amide agents offer potential important advantages (Table 33-10). When used in dilute concentrations and administered in fractionated doses, bupivacaine causes minimal maternal hemodynamic effects because of its slower onset of action. It also offers the advantages of longer duration, minimal motor blockade, and potentiation with narcotics. Despite the limited placental transfer of 2-chloroprocaine, this agent has too many adverse effects to warrant its use in the setting of chronic fetal stress. Reserve it for situations in which serious concerns about fetal well-being require expedient delivery and speed of onset of anesthesia is paramount.

Epidural Opioids

Opioids are widely used as adjuvants to local anesthetics during continuous lumbar epidural analgesia. Epidural opioids hasten the onset of lumbar epidural analgesia. In addition, they potentiate the analgesia supplied by epidural local anesthetics and allow the use of more dilute solutions of these drugs. This property, in turn, limits local anesthetic–induced motor blockade, hypotension, and toxicity. Are epidural opioids safe in the presence of fetal stress? To answer this ques-

Table 33–10

Choice of Local Anesthetics

ESTERS (2-CHLOROPROCAINE)	AMIDES (LIDOCAINE, BUPIVACAINE)
Advantages	
Limited placental transfer	Longer duration of analgesia potentiated by narcotics
Low risk of maternal CNS and cardiac toxicity	Preferential sensory block with bupivacaine
Disadvantages	
Short duration of action	Ion trapping
Reports of paraspinal muscle spasm	Maternal cardiac toxicity with bupivacaine
Antagonism of amide local anesthetics and narcotics	Fetal heart rate decelerations*
	Decreased fetal heart rate variability*
	Neurobehavioral effects*

*controversial

tion, two issues must be addressed. First, how do epidural opioids change the fetal heart rate tracing? Second, do epidural opioids adversely affect neonatal status?

FETAL HEART RATE VARIABILITY. The fetal heart rate tracing is an essential monitor of intrapartum fetal status. Loss of beat-to-beat variability and late or variable decelerations raise serious concerns about fetal well-being. It is important that the anesthetic management not interfere with fetal heart rate analysis by either obscuring or mimicking the signs of fetal distress.

Parenteral administration of opioids such as fentanyl, morphine, and meperidine reduce fetal heart rate variability.[117,118] Systemic absorption of epidurally administered opioids occurs, but resulting maternal plasma concentrations vary widely. After epidural fentanyl, 1 µg/kg, some studies report undetectable maternal plasma concentrations, whereas others show peak concentrations of 0.5 to 1.0 ng/mL within 5 to 20 minutes.[119–121] Factors that determine maternal uptake of drug include total dose, lipid solubility, pKa, protein binding, and metabolism.

Viscomi *et al*[122] evaluated the fetal heart rate effects of epidural administration of either saline or fentanyl, 75 µg, during stable lidocaine analgesia. Both fentanyl and saline produced similar reductions in fetal heart rate variability and number of accelerations in fetal heart rate. Decreased fetal heart rate variability occurred with equal frequency with bolus administration of either plain bupivacaine or bupivacaine with 100 µg of fentanyl.[123] Therefore, reductions in fetal heart rate variability may follow administration of lumbar epidural analgesia, but the addition of fentanyl to the local anesthetic does not increase the frequency or severity of these changes.

NEONATAL EFFECTS. Evaluation of the effects of epidurally administered opioids on the newborn consists mainly of Apgar scores, incidence of respiratory depression, and neurobehavioral status. Fentanyl is extremely safe when given in the absence of fetal compromise. Neonatal depression occurs only after large, repeated doses are given immediately before delivery. Trapping of fentanyl in the acidotic fetal circulation has been postulated but thus far never documented. Thus, there is no absolute contraindication to the administration of epidural opioids in the presence of fetal stress. However, several recommendations should be made.

Like all other medications given to the parturient, use the smallest effective dose to minimize fetal ex-

posure. The optimal dose of epidural fentanyl is 50 µg diluted in 10 mL of saline.[124] Consider using sufentanil, another lipid-soluble opioid with a high affinity for the mu-opioid receptor. Continuous epidural infusion of bupivacaine with sufentanil yields undetectable maternal venous and umbilical vein sufentanil concentrations.[125] Neonatal depression, as assessed by Apgar score and respiratory rate, did not occur. Sufentanil, 10 to 30 µg, with bupivacaine did not depress Apgar or neurobehavioral scores.[126] Much smaller doses of sufentanil (5 µg) may be equally effective and have even lower risk of adverse neonatal effects.[127] More studies are needed comparing the potency of sufentanil to fentanyl in the epidural space and of the effects of these opioids on the stressed fetus.

Epinephrine

The use of epinephrine-containing local anesthetics in the presence of fetal stress raises the following two controversial questions:

- Is it safe to use an epinephrine test dose to detect intravascular placement of an epidural catheter?
- Do epinephrine-containing local anesthetics have detrimental effects on uterine blood flow that can further compromise the stressed fetus?

THE EPINEPHRINE TEST DOSE. Epinephrine-containing local anesthetics are widely used at many institutions as a means to detect intravascular placement of an epidural catheter. However, many question the reliability and safety of this practice in the laboring parturient, especially in the presence of fetal compromise. Epinephrine injected intravenously causes dose-related uterine artery vasoconstriction and can precipitate acute fetal distress (Fig. 33-4).[128–131] In nonlaboring gravid ewes, intravenous injection of as little as 10 µg of epinephrine lowers uterine blood flow by 50% to 65%.[132] The magnitude of this decrease in blood flow is similar to that observed during a normal uterine contraction; however, the decrease in uterine blood flow persisted for more than 3 minutes following the injection, much like a tetanic uterine contraction. This transient decline in uterine perfusion may have an insignificant impact on the uncompromised fetus. When the effects of epinephrine are superimposed upon uterine contractions or uteroplacental insufficiency, however, uterine perfusion and fetal condition may deteriorate. Another study of gravid ewes looked at fetal effects of intravascular administration of 16.5 µg of epinephrine in the presence of fetal asphyxia and acidosis.[133] Epinephrine lacked adverse effects on fetal status, as measured by fetal heart rate, mean arte-

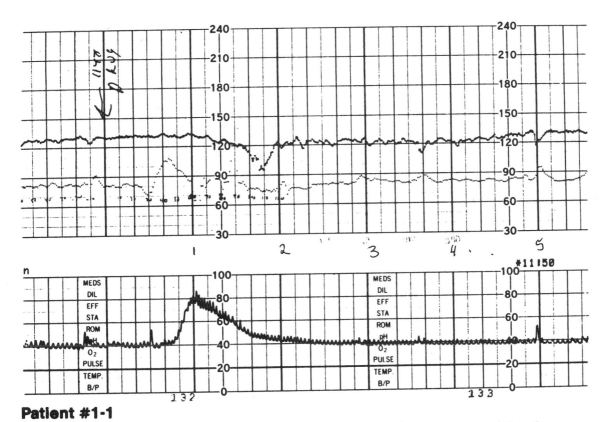

Patient #1-1

Figure 33–4. Late deceleration in a previously normal fetus after maternal intravenous injection of 15 µg of epinephrine. (Courtesy of Barbara L. Leighton, MD, Philadelphia, PA)

rial pressure, aortic blood flow, or pH; however, these investigators did not measure uterine artery or umbilical blood flow. They observed the ewe for only 15 minutes following injection of epinephrine. This may have been insufficient time to detect worsening acidosis or fetal heart rate abnormalities. In addition, the epinephrine test dose contained bupivacaine and 50 µg of fentanyl, obscuring what the effects of epinephrine alone might be. Clearly, more studies looking at the effects of epinephrine administered as an intravascular test dose in the presence of fetal asphyxia must be performed.

Given that most of the data show detrimental effects on uterine blood flow of even small doses of intravenous epinephrine, I do not recommend the use of an epinephrine-containing test dose in the presence of fetal distress. As an alternative test dose, consider 100 mg of 2-chloroprocaine without epinephrine. In male volunteers, this dose of drug reliably produces symptoms of intravascular injection.[134] Doses of 2-chloroprocaine of this magnitude have been shown to have no

effect on uterine blood flow. However, 2-chloroprocaine antagonizes the analgesic effect of subsequently injected amide local anesthetics and opioids.[100] Alternatively, the following measures can detect or limit the consequences of intravascular placement of epidural catheters:

- Carefully aspirate through the needle or catheter, preferably with a small syringe before each injection.
- Fractionate doses of local anesthetics into 3- to 5-mL aliquots.
- Frequently assess the patient for signs and symptoms of local anesthetic toxicity.
- Monitor for onset of appropriate analgesia.
- Use the Doppler test (see Chap. 32).

EPINEPHRINE-CONTAINING LOCAL ANESTHETICS AND UTERINE BLOOD FLOW. Does the addition of epinephrine to epidural local anesthetics have any adverse effects on fetal well-being? There are several studies that measure uterine artery blood flow after lumbar epidural anesthesia using local anesthetics with and without epinephrine. Lumbar epidural anesthesia with 2-chloroprocaine plus epinephrine 1:200,000 produce a transient but significant fall in uterine blood flow in gravid ewes.[135] Plain 2-chloroprocaine did not impair uterine blood flow. Two mechanisms may incite the observed effects. First, systemically absorbed epinephrine may directly constrict the uterine artery (alpha-effect). Alternatively, epinephrine-containing local anesthetics cause an exaggerated hemodynamic response to epidural anesthesia.[136] Epinephrine absorbed from the epidural space exerts beta$_2$-effects, producing vasodilation in the skeletal muscle vascular bed. This action potentiates the drop in mean arterial pressure caused by sympathetic blockade. Adequate fluid prehydration and vasopressors should preserve uterine artery perfusion pressure.

Epinephrine-containing local anesthetics may have differing effects on uteroplacental blood flow, depending on the initial placental vascular resistance. Veille *et al*[137] measured umbilical artery flow velocity waveforms in patients with normal placental vascular resistance undergoing elective cesarean delivery with epidural anesthesia using 2-chloroprocaine plus epinephrine 1:300,000. They reported no adverse effects on the S/D ratio of the umbilical artery, provided hypotension is avoided with adequate fluid preload. Marx *et al*[8] used this technique in laboring patients to compare the effects of lumbar epidural anesthesia with either plain lidocaine or lidocaine plus epinephrine 1:200,000. They found differential effects depending

upon the initial S/D ratio. In patients with initially normal placental vascular resistance, both plain lidocaine or lidocaine with epinephrine decreased the S/D ratio, indicating decreased placental vascular resistance. However, a subgroup of seven patients had initially high placental vascular resistance (Table 33-11). Four or these women received epinephrine-containing local anesthetic. All showed a rise in S/D ratios, suggesting a further increase in placental vascular resistance. One fetus in this group developed late decelerations for 8 minutes. In the three patients with initially high placental vascular resistance who received plain lidocaine, the placental vascular resistance remained unchanged or even declined. The effects of epinephrine on the S/D ratio are transient. The S/D ratio returned to baseline with the second measurement, 30 minutes after the initial bolus injection. However, the effects of continued administration or the use of more than 40 µg (8 mL of 1:200,000 solution) of epinephrine were not evaluated.

The aforementioned study suggests that epinephrine-containing local anesthetics, when administered to parturients with evidence of uteroplacental insufficiency, may further compromise placental perfusion. When providing lumbar epidural anesthesia for either labor or cesarean delivery in the presence of fetal stress, the benefits of using epinephrine must be weighed against the detrimental effects on placental vascular resistance. Table 33-12 summarizes my anesthetic recommendations for spontaneous vaginal delivery in the presence of fetal stress.

Table 33-11

Umbilical Artery S/D Ratios Before and After Epidural Injection of 8 mL of Local Anesthetic in Seven Women with Initial Ratios Above 3.0

NO.	ANESTHETIC	DIAGNOSIS	INITIAL S/D	S/D AT 10 MIN	S/D AT 30 MIN
1	Lido + Epi	PIH	3.10	5.00*	3.46
2	Lido + Epi	Asthma	3.08	4.23*	3.30
3	Lido	PIH, SGA	3.01	2.71	2.70
4	Lido + Epi	Diabetes	3.10	4.20*	3.30
5	Lido	Diabetes	3.08	2.76	2.70
6	Lido	PIH	3.11	3.10	3.10
7	Lido + Epi	PIH, SGA	3.57	4.25*	3.60

(After Marx GF, Elstein ID, Schuss M, Anyaegbunam A, Fleischer A. Effects of epidural block with lignocaine and lignocaine–adrenaline on umbilical artery velocity wave ratios. Br J Obstet Gynaecol 1990;97:517)
*$P < 0.001$
Abbreviations: PIH = pregnancy-induced hypertension, SGA = small for gestational age, Lido = 1.5% lidocaine plain, Lido + Epi = 1.5% lidocaine with epinephrine 1:200,000.

Table 33-12

Anesthetic Recommendations for Vaginal Delivery in the Presence of Fetal Stress/Distress

---

1. Assess all parturients upon admission to labor and delivery and begin epidural anesthesia early in labor if risk factors for fetal distress are present.
2. Provide labor analgesia with a continuous lumbar epidural infusion of a dilute bupivacaine/opioid solution.
3. Monitor patient hourly for signs of increasing or decreasing anesthetic level to detect intrathecal or intravascular epidural catheter migration.
4. Use minimum effective dose of epidural opioids.
5. Avoid use of epinephrine-containing local anesthetics in the test dose, bolus dose, or by continuous infusion.

Obstetric Forceps Delivery

Often obstetrical forceps or a vacuum extractor can speed vaginal delivery. Indications for these instruments include the following:

- Prolonged second stage of labor
- Maternal exhaustion
- Malrotation of the fetal head
- Fetal distress during advanced second stage

Anesthetic options are the same as for spontaneous vaginal delivery. Regional anesthesia (epidural or spinal) offers the distinct advantages of selectively providing dense perineal anesthesia and relaxed pelvic musculature. The specific technique and agents chosen are based on fetal station and degree of fetal distress. Low or outlet forceps have a high success rate and require a T-10 through sacral level of dense sensory anesthesia. Mid-forceps application, however, has a much lower success rate and yields a higher incidence of maternal and fetal trauma. In this situation, a flexible anesthetic technique like continuous epidural or spinal block offers distinct advantages. Table 33-13 summarizes the anesthetic recommendations for obstetrical forceps delivery.

Nonemergent Forceps Delivery

When a lumber epidural catheter is in place, 10 mL of 2% lidocaine without epinephrine will provide dense sensory anesthesia. A T-10 sensory level usually develops within 10 minutes. The block is sufficiently dense without the addition of epinephrine, avoiding the adverse effects of catecholamines on uteroplacental perfu-

sion. With a functioning epidural catheter in place, the block can be extended to the T-4 dermatome should the need to perform cesarean delivery arise. Because cesarean delivery requires more dense sensory block than plain lidocaine provides, I use 0.5% bupivacaine (15–20 mL) in nonemergent situations.

When the parturient does not have an epidural catheter in place, single-shot or continuous spinal anesthesia can be used. Hyperbaric lidocaine, 50 mg, will produce anesthesia to T-10 for low or outlet forceps. For mid-forceps application, aim for a T-4 level with hyperbaric bupivacaine, 12 to 15 mg, to prepare for possible cesarean delivery.

Emergent Forceps Delivery

An obstetrician may elect low or outlet forceps delivery late in the second stage of labor when delivery is imminent. Epidural injection of 10 mL of 3% 2-chloroprocaine will rapidly provide the necessary dense perineal anesthesia. Alternatively, a pudendal block done by the obstetrician may suffice. Finally, subarachnoid block with 50 mg of hyperbaric lidocaine can be performed if one is facile with the technique. Inhalational anesthesia by mask risks maternal aspiration of gastric contents. If inhalational anesthetics are required, first secure the airway with a rapid sequence induction and endotracheal intubation.

Cesarean Delivery

Cesarean delivery may be done in the presence of fetal stress for several reasons, which follow:

- Failure to progress in labor due to cephalopelvic disproportion
- Malpresentation

Table 33-13

Anesthetic Recommendations for Instrumental Vaginal Delivery: Forceps and Vacuum Extractor

---

Epidural anesthesia	
Nonemergent	(2% lidocaine without epinephrine, 10 mL)
Emergent	(3% 2-chloroprocaine, 10 mL)
Spinal anesthesia	
Low/outlet forceps	(hyperbaric lidocaine, 50 mg)
Midforceps	(hyperbaric bupivacaine, 12–15 mg, ± epinephrine, 0.2 mg)
Pudendal block	
General endotracheal anesthesia	

- Deteriorating fetal status
- Nonreassuring fetal heart rate (fetal distress)
- Maternal decompensation, hemorrhage, worsening preeclampsia/eclampsia

The urgency of the situation and indication for delivery will mostly decide the choice of anesthetic technique. Also consider maternal factors, such as hemodynamic status, coagulopathy, airway anomalies, and general medical condition. Table 33-14 outlines the anesthetic options available for cesarean delivery and particular advantages and disadvantages.

Regional Versus General Anesthesia

For elective or nonemergent cesarean delivery, most anesthesiologists choose regional anesthesia because of the lower risk of maternal morbidity and mortality from aspiration and failed intubation. Regional anesthesia also minimizes fetal exposure to depressants, resulting in better Apgar and neurobehavioral scores in the immediate postdelivery period.[138] However, major conduction blockade can have profound hemodynamic effects. A compromised fetus may not tolerate even small reductions in uteroplacental perfusion. Studies on fetal blood flow after either epidural or spinal anesthesia show that both techniques are safe provided prolonged maternal hypotension is avoided.[139-142] However, most of these studies did not include large numbers of fetuses with evidence of distress. Many clinicians prefer general anesthesia because of its reliability and its rapid onset. Currently, investigators are evaluating fetal cerebral protection with the use of general anesthetic agents. These benefits must be weighed against the potential for difficult intubation, neonatal depression, and increased blood loss associated with the use of general anesthesia for cesarean delivery.

Table 33–14

Anesthetic Options for Cesarean Delivery

ADVANTAGES	DISADVANTAGES
Regional Anesthesia	
Spinal anesthesia	
Increased maternal safety	Hypotension
Rapid onset	Headache
Definitive endpoint	
Decreased fetal exposure to LA	
Decreased maternal exposure to LA	
Continuous spinal anesthesia	
All of the above plus better control of	"Microcatheter"
anesthetic level	Technical difficulties
	Catheter breakage
	Cauda equina syndrome
	Headache
Epidural Anesthesia	
Rapid extension of block possible if	Hypotension
catheter already in place	
LA toxicity	
General Anesthesia	
Reliable, fast onset	Increased maternal morbidity and mortality
? Fetal cerebral protection	Aspiration
	Hemorrhage
	Awareness
	Failed intubation
Local Anesthetic Infiltration	
Rapid onset	Unsatisfactory analgesia
Abbreviation: LA = local anesthetic	

There are few well-conducted studies that compare neonatal outcome of distressed fetuses delivered by cesarean delivery under regional versus general anesthesia. Marx et al[143] evaluated neonatal condition in 126 parturients requiring emergency cesarean delivery for fetal distress. The mothers chose the anesthetic technique. Seventy-one parturients chose general anesthesia, 33 chose spinal, and 22 chose extension of their epidural blockade. A fluid bolus of at least 800 mL was infused before induction of the regional anesthetic. The incidence of hypotension did not differ between the groups. Vasopressors were not required, even in the patients receiving spinal anesthesia. Infants delivered under regional anesthesia had significantly better 1-minute Apgar scores. At 5 minutes, Apgar scores did not differ among the groups. Fetal blood gas and pH data did not differ between regional and general anesthesia. These authors concluded that regional anesthesia is a suitable, and perhaps a better, alternative to general anesthesia in the setting of fetal distress. In experienced hands, spinal anesthesia can be induced rapidly, is not associated with hemodynamic instability or worsening fetal acid–base status, and results in slightly improved neonatal condition.

A similar study evaluated neonatal outcome in 101 parturients following emergency cesarean delivery for fetal distress.[144] General anesthesia was administered to 67 patients, whereas 34 underwent extension of their epidural blockade with 3% 2-chloroprocaine. Apgar scores and fetal acid–base status did not differ between the two groups.

Finally, Ong et al[145] retrospectively evaluated fetal outcome in 319 cesarean deliveries performed for fetal distress under either epidural or general anesthesia. Infants whose mother received regional anesthesia had better Apgar scores and less need for active respiratory resuscitation.

Anesthetic Recommendations

NONEMERGENT CESAREAN DELIVERY.
When a cesarean delivery is done nonemergently in the presence of fetal stress, I prefer regional anesthesia for the reasons discussed above. Pay close attention, however, to maternal hemodynamics, and promptly correct hypotension using left uterine displacement, intravenous fluids, and vasopressors. Women presenting for cesarean delivery who are already in labor seem to have a lower risk of hypotension (see Chap. 32).[142]

If an epidural catheter is already in place, extend the block to the T-4 dermatome with either 0.5% bupivacaine or 2% lidocaine with epinephrine 1:200,000. When rapid onset of anesthesia is not required, I prefer

0.5% bupivacaine because it offers many advantages in the setting of fetal stress. It provides excellent sensory anesthesia without the use of epinephrine. The slow onset of 0.5% bupivacaine minimizes hypotension and allows for early detection and prompt intervention. Lidocaine provides a faster onset of anesthesia than bupivacaine, but epinephrine must be added to produce sufficient density of the block to perform cesarean delivery. Fentanyl, 50 µg, diluted in 10 mL of preservative-free normal saline can be given with either local anesthetic to potentiate the block.

When an epidural catheter is not in place and a nonemergent cesarean delivery must be done, subarachnoid block is an appropriate technique. It offers the advantages of fast onset, dense sensory and motor block, and use of extremely small doses of local anesthetics and opioids. Again, any decrease in maternal blood pressure must be detected and promptly treated to maintain uteroplacental perfusion. A single injection of hyperbaric bupivacaine, 12 mg, with fentanyl, 10 µg, provides satisfactory anesthesia for 60 to 90 minutes. Epinephrine, 0.2 mg, also can be added to the spinal anesthetic to augment the block without causing adverse maternal hemodynamic or fetal effects.[146,147] This approach may prove especially useful in the obese parturient or with repeat cesarean delivery when the procedure often takes longer and involves more vigorous tissue manipulation.

The use of continuous spinal anesthesia also must be considered in the setting of a nonemergent cesarean delivery. Intrathecal catheters permit the slow titration of incremental doses of local anesthetic, providing better control over the height of the anesthetic level. This property is desirable in the morbidly obese parturient with a difficult airway. The major obstacle with the use of conventional catheters is the high incidence of postdural puncture headache in the obstetric population. The so-called microcatheters produce a much lower incidence of this complication but are technically more difficult to insert and therefore are not as reliable. In addition, there are reports of catheter breakage upon removal and of cauda equina syndrome when high concentrations of glucose-containing local anesthetics are used.[148–150] When one is familiar with their use, however, microcatheters offer all the advantages of a "single-shot" spinal, plus the added benefit of a more controlled segmental level of anesthesia.

Emergent Cesarean Delivery

When a properly functioning epidural catheter is in place, the block should be extended rapidly using pH-adjusted 3% 2-chloroprocaine. 2-Chloroprocaine is the only local anesthetic that is appropriate in this situation because of its rapid onset and rapid elimination. I inject a total dose of 20 to 25 mL over 1 to 2 minutes with careful aspiration after each 5 mL. Continuously monitor the patient for signs and symptoms of local anesthetic toxicity. A negative aspirate does not rule out the possibility of intravascular or intrathecal injection. This circumstance emphasizes the need to assess the laboring parturient who is on a continuous epidural infusion frequently in order to detect catheter misplacement or migration. Always be prepared to treat maternal hypotension, local anesthetic–induced seizures, and total spinal anesthesia. To prevent or treat maternal hypotension, rapidly infuse intravenous fluids once the obstetrician chooses cesarean delivery. Rigorously maintain left uterine displacement. Give vasopressors at the first sign of decreasing blood pressure.

Local anesthetic–induced seizures from intravascular injection of 2-chloroprocaine are short-lived owing to its rapid plasma hydrolysis. (A common scenario is for the patient to seize after the total dose of local anesthetic has been injected and she is being transported to the operating room.) First, give oxygen and support the airway with either assisted or controlled ventilation by mask. The seizure is usually self-limited and most often stops before barbiturates or benzodiazepines can be given. If not, upon arrival in the operating room, rapidly induce general anesthesia and intubate the trachea. Cesarean section may begin after confirmation of correct endotracheal tube placement.

Unintentional intrathecal injection of 2-chloroprocaine resulting in total spinal anesthesia is managed in a similar way. Profound and prolonged hypotension may require aggressive fluid and vasopressor therapy. Assess maternal ventilation. If inadequate, intubate.

If an epidural catheter is not in place, an attempt at spinal anesthesia is warranted if one is facile with the technique. The goal in acute fetal distress is to administer the block as quickly as possible so that preparations for operation can proceed without excessive delay. Spinal anesthesia can be done with the patient in either the lateral decubitus or sitting position, the latter being preferable in the obese parturient. Sterile technique should be strictly maintained. In the interest of time, omit the addition of adjuvants to the local anesthetic such as epinephrine or opioids. Hyperbaric bupivacaine, 12 to 15 mg, will provide satisfactory anesthesia for cesarean delivery. Parenteral narcotics can be used if necessary to supplement the block after delivery of the fetus. If the placement of the spinal proves technically difficult and is unsuccessful after several attempts, abort the procedure and induce general anesthesia. Continuously monitoring fetal heart rate while at-

tempting to induce spinal anesthesia can help decide how long one can safely persist. If, for some reason, there is a major contraindication to general anesthesia (*i.e.,* difficult airway), more time and effort can be expended toward placement of the spinal anesthetic because maternal welfare should always be placed above fetal status. Ideally, these patients should be identified and have an epidural or continuous spinal catheter in place. Also, placement of continuous catheters early in labor avoids the danger of having to administer a rushed general anesthetic should fetal distress arise. Unfortunately, patients occasionally present to the hospital needing urgent cesarean delivery. In this setting, anesthetic options are limited to rapid institution of either spinal or general anesthesia.

Table 33-15 summarizes the anesthetic recommendations for both emergent and nonemergent cesarean delivery.

General Anesthesia

Not uncommonly, general anesthesia must be done for emergent cesarean delivery. The technique of general anesthesia for cesarean delivery is described in detail elsewhere (see Chap. 22). There are several points to consider when giving a general anesthetic in the presence of fetal stress.

EQUIPMENT. In the setting of acute fetal distress, cesarean delivery must proceed at a much more rapid pace than in the nonemergent setting. Therefore, equipment and supplies necessary to deliver general anesthesia must always be readily available and working. These items include, but are not limited to, the following:

- A properly functioning anesthesia machine with breathing circuit
- Equipment for endotracheal intubation
- Suction apparatus
- Medications for induction and maintenance of general anesthesia

EVALUATION OF THE PARTURIENT. Although emergent operative delivery must be done expeditiously, careful evaluation of the parturient cannot be neglected. In particular, ask about a history of medical problems (asthma, hypertension, diabetes) and medication allergies. On physical examination, pay particular attention to the airway and hemodynamic status. Check intravenous access and infuse non–glucose-containing isotonic crystalloid solution. Give 30 mL of a nonparticulate antacid just before induction of anesthesia. Metoclopramide, 10 mg, also can be injected before induction of general anesthesia, mainly

Table 33–15

Regional Anesthesia for Cesarean Delivery of the Stressed Fetus

INTRAOPERATIVE	POSTOPERATIVE
Epidural Anesthesia	
Nonemergent	
0.5% bupivacaine (20–25 mL)	Morphine, 3–5 mg, in 10 mL of PFNS
	Fentanyl, 50 μg, in 10 mL of PFNS
Emergent	
3% 2-chloroprocaine (20–25 mL)	Patient-controlled analgesia
pH-adjusted (1 mEq NaHCO$_3$/10 mL)	
Inject over 1–2 min	
Aspirate after each 5 mL	
Be prepared to treat complications	
Hypotension	
Total spinal	
Local anesthetic–induced seizures	
Spinal Anesthesia	
Nonemergent	
Hyperbaric bupivacaine, 12–15 mg	Morphine, 150–500 μg
Fentanyl, 10 μg, ± epinephrine, 0.2 mg	
Emergent	
Hyperbaric bupivacaine, 12–15 mg	Patient-controlled analgesia
Abbreviation: PFNS = preservative-free normal saline.	

to increase lower esophageal sphincter tone. The gastrokinetic effects of this drug begin in 30 to 60 minutes and therefore play a more important role during emergence.

PREOXYGENATION. When induction of general anesthesia must proceed rapidly, four maximal inspirations of 100% oxygen provide adequate preoxygenation.[151]

DEFASCICULATION. I do not routinely give a defasciculating dose of a nondepolarizing muscle relaxant before induction of general anesthesia for several reasons. First, the time required to draw up and administer the drug is better spent applying monitors and preoxygenating the patient. Second, pregnant women do not have intense muscle fasciculations or a high incidence of postoperative myalgias. Finally, administration of nondepolarizing muscle relaxants increases the intubating dose of succinylcholine and may interfere with optimal relaxation.

INDUCTION AGENTS. If you think you can intubate the patient, do a rapid sequence induction of general anesthesia with cricoid pressure. The ideal induction agent in the presence of fetal distress is unknown. Studies to date comparing induction agents have been performed mostly on patients undergoing elective cesarean delivery.

Thiopental is the standard to which other induction agents are compared. Peak fetal exposure after a dose of 4 mg/kg occurs within 1.5 to 3 minutes.[152] Although it crosses the placenta rapidly, thiopental is rarely associated with neonatal depression due to at least three factors:

- Rapid redistribution in the maternal circulation
- Dilution in the fetal inferior vena cava
- Uptake by the fetal liver[153,154]

Therefore, delaying delivery after induction with thiopental, 4 mg/kg, offers no benefit. Large doses of thiopental (30 mg/kg) after delivery have been proposed for providing fetal cerebral protection in the presence of asphyxia.[155] However, significant hemodynamic instability results, with no improvement in neurologic outcome. Methohexital, despite its shorter half-life, does not offer any advantage over thiopental.[156]

Ketamine is a less popular induction agent mainly because of the high incidence of unpleasant dreams and dysphoria upon emergence. This unwanted side effect can be reduced by limiting the induction dose to 1 mg/kg and by administering a benzodiazepine before emergence.[157] Like thiopental, ketamine is transferred rapidly across the placenta, resulting in peak fetal blood concentrations in 1 to 2 minutes.[158] Because of its sympathomimetic effects, ketamine better preserves maternal mean arterial pressure and uterine blood flow.[159] Therefore, it is an ideal drug in the presence of maternal hypotension. In high doses (5 mg/kg), however, ketamine may increase both resting uterine tone and the frequency and intensity of uterine contractions, and thus can adversely affect uterine blood flow.[160,161]

Several investigators have studied the effects of ketamine on the asphyxiated fetus. In acidotic fetal lambs, ketamine abolishes the usual hypertensive response to umbilical cord occlusion. Nevertheless, cerebral, myocardial, and renal blood flow remain unchanged and acid–base status does not deteriorate.[162] Ketamine (2 mg/kg) preserves fetal blood pressure and cerebral blood flow better than thiopental (6 mg/kg).[163] Several studies have compared neonatal outcome in humans after induction with ketamine (1 mg/kg) versus thiopental (3–4 mg/kg).[164,165] Apgar scores and umbilical cord blood gas values are similar with both drugs. One study, however, does point to improved neurobehavioral status of infants born after induction with ketamine compared to thiopental for vaginal delivery.[166] Therefore, ketamine is well suited as an induction agent in the presence of fetal distress. It is especially useful when maternal hypotension or asthma is also present.

Etomidate, 0.3 mg/kg, is sometimes used as an induction agent for cesarean delivery. Studies comparing it to thiopental (4 mg/kg) show that it produces fewer hemodynamic changes and perhaps slightly better neonatal status as measured by time to sustained respiration.[167,168] Propofol has been evaluated as an induction agent for elective cesarean delivery and has been shown to have no adverse effects on umbilical blood gas values or neurobehavioral scores.[169] Unfortunately, these induction agents have not been studied in the asphyxiated fetus.

MAINTENANCE OF ANESTHESIA. The anesthetist's primary goal during cesarean delivery for fetal distress is to maximize fetal blood flow and oxygen delivery. Maintain left uterine displacement. Give intravenous fluids and vasopressors as needed. Use a high inspired oxygen concentration. Nitrous oxide and a low dose of potent agent in 50% oxygen is appropriate for routine cesarean delivery. For the stressed fetus, however the small increase in Po_2 provided by giving the mother 100% oxygen may prove beneficial.[75,76,80,81] Giving 100% oxygen with 1.5 MAC

isoflurane for emergency cesarean delivery increases umbilical Po_2 and improves neonatal status.[80,81] Use enough volatile agent to provide sufficient depth of anesthesia to limit maternal catecholamine release. (Catecholamines can impair placental perfusion by constricting the uterine artery.[170]) Because of the limited duration of exposure, the high concentration of volatile agent has little depressant effect on either the neonate or uterine contractility.[80–82]

Is there any evidence to suggest that one inhalational agent is superior to another in the setting of fetal distress? Several studies have looked at the effects of inhalational agents on the fetal compensatory response to asphyxia.[171–175] Asphyxia induced by uterine artery occlusion in the ewe incites fetal hypertension and bradycardia with redistribution of blood flow to the brain, heart, and adrenals. Most studies show that 1.0% to 1.5% halothane blunts this response yet preserves both the compensatory increase in cerebral blood flow and decrease in cerebral oxygen consumption,[171–173] thus maintaining a favorable ratio of cerebral oxygen supply to demand. Some feel that isoflurane could improve this ratio, because this agent produces the greatest reduction in cerebral oxygen consumption. However, 1.0% isoflurane blunts the compensatory increase in cerebral blood flow observed with asphyxia alone.[175] Halothane may offer greater cerebral protection to the asphyxiated fetus than isoflurane.

Maintain normocarbia. Low maternal $Paco_2$ shifts the oxyhemoglobin dissociation curve to the left, impairing oxygen delivery to the fetus.[176] Aggressive positive-pressure ventilation decreases venous return, impairing maternal cardiac output and uterine perfusion.[177] Marked maternal respiratory alkalosis ($Paco_2 <$ 17 mm Hg) may directly cause uterine artery vasoconstriction.[178] Maternal respiratory acidosis is also deleterious because it leads to fetal carbon dioxide retention and worsening acid–base status.

LOCAL ANESTHETIC INFILTRATION

This anesthetic option is used under rare circumstances for emergent cesarean delivery of the distressed fetus. Indications include the following:

- Failed or contraindicated regional anesthesia with an inaccessible airway
- Failed intubation
- Supplementation of inadequate regional block
- Unavailability of trained personnel to administer other types of of anesthesia

The obstetrician infiltrates sequential layers in the midline of the lower abdominal wall with a large volume of dilute local anesthetic (0.5% lidocaine with epinephrine).[179] The technique requires little technical skill, has a rapid onset, preserves maternal airway reflexes, and produces minimal fetal effects. However, the disadvantages of incomplete and often unsatisfactory anesthesia combined with the potential for local anesthetic toxicity make the use of local anesthetic infiltration uncommon.

SUMMARY AND CONCLUSIONS

Fetal distress may arise at any time, even in uncomplicated pregnancies. In certain parturients, fetal condition is more likely to decompensate acutely. The anesthesiologist, by screening all women presenting to the labor and delivery suite, can identify most of these high-risk pregnancies. Encourage those with risk factors predisposing to fetal distress to have an epidural or continuous spinal catheter placed early in labor. This precaution can greatly diminish the need to administer a rushed general anesthetic if the need for emergent operative delivery arises. Regardless of the anesthetic technique chosen, efforts to maintain fetal blood flow and oxygen delivery remain the cornerstone of management of the distressed fetus.

REFERENCES

1. Fanaroff AA, Martin RJ, Miller MJ. Identification and management of high-risk problems in the neonate. In: Creasy RK, Resnik R, eds. Maternal fetal medicine: principles and practice, 2nd ed. Philadelphia: WB Saunders, 1989:1162.
2. Koops BL, Morgan LJ, Battaglia FC. Neonatal mortality risk in relation to birth weight and gestational age: Update. J Pediatr 1982;101:969.
3. Sheldon RE, Peeters LLH, Jones MD Jr, Makowski EL, Meschia G. Redistribution of cardiac output and oxygen delivery in the hypoxemic fetal lamb. Am J Obstet Gynecol 1979;135:1071.
4. Block BS, Llanos AJ, Creasy RK. Responses of the growth-retarded fetus to acute hypoxemia. Am J Obstet Gynecol 1984;148:878.
5. Cohn HE, Sacks E, Heymann MA, Rudolph AM. Cardiovascular responses to hypoxemia and acidemia in fetal lambs. Am J Obstet Gynecol 1974;120:817.
6. Parer J. The influence of beta-adrenergic activity on fetal heart rate and the umbilical circulation during hypoxia in fetal sheep. Am J Obstet Gynecol 1983;147:592.
7. Cohn HE, Piasecki GJ, Jackson BT. The effect of beta-

adrenergic stimulation on fetal cardiovascular function during hypoxemia. Am J Obstet Gynecol 1982; 144:810.
8. Marx GF, Elstein ID, Schuss M, Anyaegbunam A, Fleischer A. Effects of epidural block with lignocaine and lignocaine-adrenaline on umbilical artery velocity wave ratios. Br J Obstet Gynaecol 1990;97:517.
9. Thacker SB, Berkelman RL. Assessing the diagnostic accuracy and efficacy of selected antepartum fetal surveillance techniques. Obstet Gynecol 1986; 41:121.
10. Shepard MJ, Richards VA, Berkowitz RL, et al. An evaluation of two equations for predicting fetal weight by ultrasound. Am J Obstet Gynecol 1982;152:47.
11. Romero R, Jeanty P. The detection of fetal growth disorders. Semin Ultrasound CT MR 1984;5:130.
12. Manning FA, Morrison I, Lange IR, et al. Fetal assessment based on fetal biophysical profile scoring: Experience in 12,620 referred high-risk pregnancies. I. Perinatal mortality by frequency and etiology. Am J Obstet Gynecol 1985;151:343.
13. Manning FA, Morrison I, Harman CR, et al. Fetal assessment by fetal BPS: Experience in 19,221 referred high-risk pregnancies. II. The false-negative rate by frequency and etiology. Am J Obstet Gynecol 1987;157:880.
14. Vintzileos AM, Fleming AD, Scorza WE, et al. Relationship between fetal biophysical activities and umbilical cord blood gas values. Am J Obstet Gynecol 1991;165:707.
15. Gill RW. Pulsed doppler with B-mode imaging for quantitative blood flow measurement. Ultrasound Med Biol 1979;5:223.
16. Trudinger BJ, Giles WB, et al. Fetal umbilical artery flow velocity waveforms and placental resistance: clinical significance. Br J Obstet Gynaecol 1985;92:23.
17. Low JA. The current status of maternal and fetal blood flow velocimetry. Am J Obstet Gynecol 1991; 164:1049.
18. Brar HS, Platt LD. Antepartum improvement of abnormal umbilical artery velocimetry: does it occur? Am J Obstet Gynecol 1989;160:36.
19. Lombardi SJ, Rosemond R, Ball R, Entman SS, Boehon FH. Umbilical artery velocimetry as a predictor of adverse outcome in pregnancies complicated by oligohydramnios. Obstet Gynecol 1989;74:338.
20. Giles WB, Lah FX, Trudinger BJ. The effect of epidural anaesthesia for cesarean section on maternal uterine and fetal umbilcia artery blood flow velocity waveforms. Br J Obstet Gynaecol 1987;94:55.
21. Nageotte MP, Freeman RK, Garite TJ, Dorchester W. Prophylactic intra-amnioinfusion in patients with preterm premature rupture of membranes. Am J Obstet Gynecol 1985;153:557.
22. Strong TH, Hetzler G, Sarno AP, Paul RH. Prophylactic intrapartum amnioinfusion: a randomized clinical trial. Am J Obstet Gynecol 1990;162:1370.
23. Quilligan EJ. Monitoring the fetus using fetal acid–base status. Clin Obstet Gynecol 1979;6:309.

24. Parer JT, Livingston EG. What is fetal distress? Am J Obstet Gynecol 1990;162:1421.

25. Cohen AB, Klapholz H, Thompson MS. Electronic fetal monitoring and clinical practice: A survey of obstetric opinion. Med Decis Making 1982;2:79.

26. Frigoletto FD, Nadel AS: Electronic fetal heart rate monitoring: Why the dilemma? Clin Obstet Gynecol 1988;31:1:179.

27. Ergander U, Eriksson M, Zetterstrom R. Severe neonatal asphyxia, incidence and prediction of outcome in the Stockholm area. Acta Paediatr Scand 1983;72:321.

28. Nelson KB, Ellenberg JH. Apgar scores as predictors of chronic neurologic disability. Pediatrics 1981;68:36.

29. Nelson KB, Ellenberg JH. Antecedents of cerebral palsy. N Engl J Med 1986;315:81.

30. Shields JR, Schifrin BS. Perinatal antecedents of cerebral palsy. Obstet Gynecol 1988;71:899.

31. Haverkamp AD, Orleans M, Langendoerfer S, et al. A controlled trial of the differential effects of intrapartum fetal monitoring. Am J Obstet Gynecol 1979;134:399.

32. Haverkamp AD, Thompson HE, McFee JG, et al. The evaluation of continuous fetal heart rate monitoring in high-risk pregnancy. Am J Obstet Gynecol 1976;125:310.

33. Kelso IM, Parson RJ, Lawrence GF, et al. An assessment of continuous fetal heart rate monitoring in labor. Am J Obstet Gynecol 1978;131:526.

34. Renou P, Chang A, Anderson I, et al. Controlled trial of fetal intensive care. Am J Obstet Gynecol 1976;126:470.

35. Wood C, Renou P, Oats J, et al. Controlled trial of fetal heart rate monitoring in a low-risk obstetric population. Am J Obstet Gynecol 1981;141:527.

36. Leveno KJ, Cunningham FG, Nelson S, et al. A prospective comparison of selective and universal electronic fetal monitoring in 34,995 pregnancies. N Engl J Med 1986;315:615.

37. MacDonald D, Grant A, Sheridan-Pereira M, et al. The Dublin randomized controlled trial of intrapartum fetal heart rate monitoring. Am J Obstet Gynecol 1985;152:523.

38. Luthy DA, Shy KK, van Belle G, et al. A randomized trial of electronic fetal monitoring in preterm labor. Obstet Gynecol 1987;69:687.

39. American College of Obstetricians and Gynecologists. Intrapartum fetal heart rate monitoring. Am Coll Obstet Gynecol Tech Bull 1989;132.

40. Woods JR, Dolkart LA. Significance of amniotic fluid meconium. In: Creasy RK, Resnik R, eds. Maternal-fetal medicine: Principles and practice. 2nd ed. Philadelphia: WB Saunders, 1989:404.

41. Meis PJ, Hobel CJ, Ureda JR. Late meconium passage in labor—a sign of fetal distress? Obstet Gynecol 1982;59:332.

42. Wenstrom KD, Parsons MT. The prevention of meconium aspiration in labor using amnioinfusion. Obstet Gynecol 1989;73:647.

43. Levene M, Grindulis H, Sands C, Moore J. Comparison of two methods of predicting outcome in perinatal asphyxia. Lancet 1986;1:67.

44. Schmidt B, Kirpalani H, Rosenbaum, et al. Strengths and limitations of the Apgar score: A critical appraisal. J Clin Epidemiol 1988;41:843.

45. American College of Obstetricians and Gynecologists: Use and misuse of the Apgar score [Committee Opinion]. 1986;49.

46. Fee SC, Malee K, Deddish R, et al. Severe acidosis and subsequent neurologic status. Am J Obstet Gynecol 1990;162:802.

47. Tucker JM, Hauth JC. Intrapartum assessment of fetal well-being. Clin Obstet and Gynecol 1990;33:3:515.

48. Josten BE, Hohnson RE, Nelson JP. Umbilical cord blood pH and Apgar scores as an index of neonatal health. Am J Obstet Gynecol 1987;157:843.

49. Thorp JA, Sampson JE, Parisi VM, Creasy RK. Routine unbilical cord blood gas determinations? Am J Obstet Gynecol 1989;161:600.

50. Brazelton TB. Neonatal behavioral assessment scale. Philadelphia: JB Lippincott, 1973.

51. Scanlon JW, Brown WU, Weiss JB, Alper MH. Neurobehavioral response of newborn infants after maternal epidural anesthesia. Anesthesiology 1974;40:121.

52. Amiel-Tison C, Barrier G, Shnider SM, Levinson G, Hughes SC, Stephani SJ. A new neurologic and adaptive capacity scoring system for evaluating obstetric medications in full-term newborns. Anesthesiology 1982;56:340.

53. Eckstein KL, Marx GF. Aortocaval compression and uterine displacement. Anesthesiology 1974;40:92.

54. Hallworth D, Jellicoe JA, Wilkes RG. Hypotension during epidural anesthesia for caesarean section: A comparison of intravenous loading with crystalloid and colloid solutions. Anaesthesia 1982;37:53.

55. Lewis M, Thomas PK, Wilkes RG. Hypotension during epidural analgesia for caesarean section: Arterial and central venous pressure changes after acute intravenous loading with two litres of Hartmann's solution. Anaesthesia 1983;38:250.

56. Clark RB, Thompson DS, Thompson CH. Prevention of spinal hypotension associated with cesarean section. Anesthesiology 1976;45:670.

57. Wollman SB, Marx GF. Acute hydration for prevention of hypotension of spinal anesthesia in parturients. Anesthesiology 1968;29:374.

58. Philipson EH, Kalhan SC, Riha MM, Pimentel R. Effects of maternal glucose infusion on fetal acid–base status in human pregnancy. Am J Obstet Gynecol 1987;157:866.

59. Kenepp NB, Shelley WC, Gabbe SG, et al. Fetal and neonatal hazards of maternal hydration with 5% dextrose before cesarean section. Lancet 1982;1:1150.

60. Robillard JE, Sessions C, Kennedy RL, Smith FG. Metabolic effects of constant hypertonic glucose infusion in well-oxygenated fetuses. Am J Obstet Gynecol 1978;130:199.

61. Philipps AF, Dubin JW, Matty PJ, Raye JR. Arterial hy-

poxemia and hyperinsulinemia in the chronically hyperglycemic fetal lamb. Pediatr Res 1982;16:653.

62. Philipps AF, Porte PJ, Stabinsky S, Rosenkrantz TS, Raye JR. Effects of chronic fetal hyperglycemia upon oxygen consumption in the ovine uterus and conceptus. J Clin Invest 1984;74:279.

63. Datta S, Alper MH, Ostheimer GW, Weiss JB. Method of ephedrine administration and nausea and hypotension during spinal anesthesia for cesarean section. Anesthesiology 1982;56:68.

64. James FM III, Greiss FC Jr, Kemp RA. An evaluation of vasopressor therapy for maternal hypotension during spinal anesthesia. Anesthesiology 1970; 33:25.

65. Hollmen AJ, Jouppila R, Albright GA, Jouppila P, Vierola H, Koivula A. Intervillous blood flow during caesarean section with prophylactic ephedrine and epidural anaesthesia. Acta Anaesthesiol Scand 1984; 28:396.

66. Ralston DH, Shnider SM, DeLorimier AA. Effects of equipotent ephedrine, mephentermine and methoxamine on uterine blood flow in the pregnant ewe. Anesthesiology 1974;40:354.

67. Magness T, Rosenfeld C. Systemic and uterine responses to alpha-adrenergic stimulation in pregnant and nonpregnant ewes. Am J Obstet Gynecol 1986; 155:897.

68. Moran DH, Perillo M, LaPorta RF, Bader AM, Datta S. Phenylephrine in the prevention of hypotension following spinal anesthesia for cesarean delivery. J Clin Anesth 1991;3:301.

69. Ramanathan S, Grant GJ. Vasopressor therapy for hypotension due to epidural anesthesia for cesarean section. Acta Anaesthesiol Scand 1988;32:559.

70. Patriarco MS, Viechnicki BM, Hutchinson TA, Klasko SK, Yeh SY. A study on intrauterine fetal resuscitation with terbutaline. Am J Obstet Gynecol 1987;157:384.

71. Wright JW, Patterson RM, Ridgway LE III, Berkus MD. Effect of tocolytic agents on fetal umbilical velocimetry. Am J Obstet Gynecol 1990;163:748.

72. Shekarloo A, Mendez-Bauer C, Cook V, Freese U. Terbutaline (intravenous bolus) for the treatment of acute intrapartum fetal distress. Am J Obstet Gynecol 1989;160:615.

73. Mendez-Bauer C, Shekarloo A, Cook V, Freese U. Treatment of acute intrapartum fetal distress by beta$_2$-sympathomimetics. Am J Obstet Gynecol 1987;156:638.

74. Burke MS, Porreco RP, Day D, et al. Intrauterine resuscitation with tocolysis; an alternate-month clinical trial. J Perinatol 1989;9:296.

75. Willcourt RJ, King JC, Queenan JT. Maternal oxygenation administration and fetal transcutaneous Po$_2$. Am J Obstet Gynecol 1983;146:714.

76. Ramanathan S, Gandhi S, Arismendy J, Chalon J, Turndorf H. Oxygen transfer from mother to fetus during cesarean section under epidural anesthesia. Anesth Analg 1982;61:576.

77. Baraka A. Correlation between maternal and foetal Po$_2$ and Pco$_2$ during caesarean section. Br J Anaesth 1970;42:434.

78. Marx GF, Mateo C. Effects of different oxygen concentrations during general anaesthesia for elective caesarean section. Can Anaesth Soc J 1971;18:587.

79. Rorke MJ, Davey DA, DuToit HJ. Foetal oxygenation during caesarean section. Anaesthesia 1968;23:585.

80. Piggott SE, Bogod DG, Rosen M, Rees GAD, Harmer M. Isoflurane with either 100% oxygen or 50% nitrous oxide in oxygen for caesarean section. Br J Anaesth 1990;65:325.

81. Bogod DG, Rosen M, Rees GAD. Maximum FiO$_2$ during caesarean section. Br J Anaesth 1988;61:255.

82. Tunstall ME, Sheikh A. Comparison of 1.5% enflurane with 1.25% isoflurane in oxygen for caesarean section. Br J Anaesth 1989;62:138.

83. Frigoletto FD Jr, Ryan KJ, Phillippe M. Maternal mortality rate associated with cesarean section: An appraisal. Am J Obstet Gynecol 1986; 136:969.

84. Morgan BM, Magni V, Goroszenuik T. Anaesthesia for emergency caesarean section. Br J Obstet Gynaecol 1990;97:420.

85. Marx GF, Patel S, Berman JA, Farmakides G, Schulman H. Umbilical blood flow velocity waveforms in different maternal positions and with epidural analgesia. Obstet Gynecol 1986;68:61.

86. Jouppila P, Jouppila R, Hollmen A, Koivula A. Lumbar epidural analgesia to improve intervillous blood flow during labor in severe preeclampsia. Obstet Gynecol 1982;59:158.

87. Kuhnert BR, Kuhnert PM, Prochaska AL, Gross TL. Plasma levels of 2-chloroprocaine in obstetric patients and their neonates after epidural anesthesia. Anesthesiology 1980;53:21.

88. O'Brien JE, Abbey V, Hinsvark O, et al. Metabolism and measurement of chloroprocaine, an ester-type local anesthetic. J Pharm Sci 1979;68:75.

89. Philipson EH, Kuhnert BR, Syracuse CD. Fetal acidosis, 2-chloroprocaine, and epidural anesthesia for cesarean section. Am J Obstet Gynecol 1985; 151:322.

90. Fibuch EE, Opper SE. Back pain following epidurally administered nesacaine–MPF. Anesth Analg 1989; 69:113.

91. Hynson JM, Sessler DI, Glosten B. Back pain in volunteers after epidural anesthesia with chloroprocaine. Anesth Analg 1991;72:253.

92. Naulty JS, Hertwig L, Hunt CO, et al. Duration of analgesia of epidural fentanyl following cesarean delivery—effects of local anesthetic drug selection [Abstract]. Anesthesiology 1986;65:A180.

93. Malinow AM, Mokriski BLK, Wakefield ML, et al. Anesthetic choice effects postcesarean epidural fentanyl analgesia [Abstract]. Anesth Analg 1988;67:S138.

94. Malinow AM, Mokriski BL, Wakefield ML et al. Does pH adjustment reverse nesacaine antagonism of postcesarean epidural fentanyl analgesia? [Abstract] Anesth Anal 1988;67:S137

95. Camann WR, Hartigan PM, Gilbertson LI, et al.

Chloroprocaine antagonism of epidural opioid analgesia: a receptor-specific phenomenon. Anesthesiology 1990;73:860.

96. Cohen SE, Thurlow A. Comparison of a chloroprocaine–bupivacaine mixture with chloroprocaine and bupivacaine used individually for obstetric epidural analgesia. Anesthesiology 1979;51:288.

97. DeCampo T, Macias-Loza M, Cohen H, Galindo A. Lumbar epidural anaesthesia and sensory profiles in term pregnant patients. Can Anaesth Soc J 1980; 27:274.

98. Hodgkinson R, Husain FJ, Bluhm C. Reduced effectiveness of bupivacaine 0.5 to relieve labor pain after prior injection of chloroprocaine 2% [Abstract]. Anesthesiology 1982;57:A201.

99. Chestnut DH, Geiger M, Bates JN, Choi WW. The influence of *p*H-adjusted 2-CP on the quality and duration of subsequent epidural bupivacaine analgesia during labor: A randomized, double-blind study. Anesthesiology 1989;73:437.

100. Grice SC, Eisenach JC, Dewan DM. Labor analgesia with epidural bupivacaine plus fentanyl: Enhancement with epinephrine and inhibition with 2-chloroprocaine. Anesthesiology 1990;72:623.

101. Morishima HO, Covino BG. Toxicity and distribution of lidocaine in nonasphyxiated and asphyxiated baboon fetuses. Anesthesiology 1981;54:182.

102. Pickering B, Biehl D, Meatherall R. The effect of foetal acidosis on bupivacaine levels in utero. Can Anaesth Soc J 1981;28:544.

103. Lavin JP, Samuels SV, Miodovnik M, Holroyde J, Loon M, Joyce T. The effects of bupivacaine and chloroprocaine as local anesthetics for epidural anesthesia on fetal heart rate monitoring parameters. Am J Obstet Gynecol 1981;141:717.

104. Abboud TK, Khoo SS, Miller F, Doan T, Henriksen EH. Maternal, fetal and neonatal responses after epidural anesthesia with bupivacaine, 2-chloroprocaine or lidocaine. Anesth Analg 1982;61:638.

105. Abboud TK, Afrasiabi A, Sarkis F, et al. Continuous infusion epidural analgesia in parturients receiving bupivacaine, chloroprocaine or lidocaine: Maternal, fetal and neonatal effects. Anesth Analg 1984;63:421.

106. Boehm FH, Woodruff LF, Growdon JH. The effect of lumbar epidural anesthesia on fetal heart rate variability. Anesth Analg 1975;54:779.

107. Hehre FW, Hook R, Hon EH. Continuous lumbar peridural anesthesia in obstetrics. VI. The fetal effects of transplacental passage of local anesthetic agents. Anesth Analg 1969;48:909.

108. Loftus JR, Holbrook RH, Cohen SE. Fetal heart rate after epidural lidocaine and bupivacaine for elective cesarean section. Anesthesiology 1991;75:406.

109. Krebs HB, Petres RE, Dunn LJ, Segretti A. Intrapartum fetal heart rate monitoring. IV. Observations on elective and nonelective fetal heart rate monitoring. Am J Obstet Gynecol 1980;138:213.

110. Scanlon JW, Brown WU, Weiss JB, Alper MH. Neurobehavioral responses of newborn infants after maternal epidural anesthesia. Anesthesiology 1974; 40:121.

111. Scanlon JW, Ostheimer GW, Lurie AO, Brown WU, Weiss JB, Alper MH. Neurobehavioral responses and drug concentrations in newborns after maternal epidural anesthesia with bupivacaine. Anesthesiology 1976;45:400.

112. Abboud TK, Sarkis F, Blikian A, Varakian L, Earl S, Henriksen E. Lack of adverse neonatal neurobehavioral effects of lidocaine. Anesth Analg 1983; 62:473.

113. Abboud TK, Kim KC, Noueihed R, et al. Epidural bupivacaine, chloroprocaine, or lidocaine for cesarean section—maternal and neonatal effects. Anesth Analg 1983;62:914.

114. Kileff ME, James FM, Dewan DM, Floyd HM. Neonatal neurobehavioral responses after epidural anesthesia for cesarean section using lidocaine and bupivacaine. Anesth Analg 1984;63:413.

115. Kuhnert BR, Harrison MJ, Linn PL, Kuhnert PM. Effects of maternal epidural anesthesia on neonatal behavior. Anesth Analg 1984;63:301.

116. Kuhnert BR, Kennard MJ, Linn PL. Neonatal neurobehavior after epidural anesthesia for cesarean section: a comparison of bupivacaine and chloroprocaine. Anesth Analg 1988;67:64.

117. Petrie RH, Yeh S, Murata Y. The effect of drugs on fetal heart rate variability. Am J Obstet Gynecol 1978;130:294.

118. Zimmer EZ, Divon MY, Vadasz A. Influence of meperidine on fetal movements and heart rate beat-to-beat variability in the active phase of labor. Am J Perinatol 1988;5:197.

119. Lampl E, Garen D, Levron P, Pathier D, Cousin MT. Pharmacokinetics of fentanyl given by the epidural route in women in labour. J Gynecol Obstet Biol Reprod 1986;15:603.

120. Gaffud MP, Bansal P, Lawton C. Surgical analgesia for cesarean delivery with epidural bupivacaine and fentanyl. Anesthesiology 1986;65:331.

121. Gourlay GK, Murphy TM, Plummer JL, Kowalski SR, Cherry DA, Cousins MJ. Pharmacokinetics of fentanyl in lumbar and cervical CSF following lumbar epidural and intravenous administration. Pain 1989;38:253.

122. Viscomi CM, Hood DD, Melone PJ, Eisenach JC. Fetal heart rate variability after epidural fentanyl during labor. Anesth Analg 1990;71:679.

123. Cohen SE, Tan S, Albright GA, Halpern J. Epidural fentanyl/bupivacaine mixtures for obstetric analgesia. Anesthesiology 1987;67:403.

124. Hunt CO, Naulty JS, Bader AM, et al. Perioperative analgesia with subarachnoid fentanyl–bupivacaine. Anesthesiology 1987;67:A621.

125. Phillips G. Continuous infusion epidural analgesia in labor: the effect of adding sufentanil to 0.125% bupivacaine. Anesth Analg 1988;67:462.

126. Vertommen JD, Vandermeulen E, Van Aken H, et al.

The effects of the addition of sufentanil to 0.125% bupivacaine on the quality of analgesia during labor and on the incidence of instrumental deliveries. Anesthesiology 1991;74:809.

127. Naulty JS, Ross R, Bergen W. Epidural sufentanil–bupivacaine for analgesia during labor and delivery. Anesthesiology 1989;71:A842.

128. Chestnut DH, Weiner CP, Martin JG, Herrig JE, Wang J. Effect of intravenous epinephrine upon uterine artery blood flow velocity in the pregnant guinea pig. Anesthesiology 1986;65:633.

129. Greiss FC. The uterine vascular bed: Effect of adrenergic stimulation. Obstet Gynecol 1963;21:295.

130. Rosenfeld CR, Barton MD, Meschia G. Effects of epinephrine on distribution of blood flow in the pregnant ewe. Am J Obstet Gynecol 1976;124:156.

131. Leighton BL, Norris MC, Sosis M, Epstein R, Chayen B, Larijani GE. Limitations of epinephrine as a marker of intravascular injection in laboring women. Anesthesiology 1987;66:688.

132. Hood DD, Dewan DM, James FM. Maternal and fetal effects of epinephrine in gravid ewes. Anesthesiology 1986;64:610.

133. Youngstrom P, Cohen I, Hoyt M, Amini S, Veille JC, Herman M. Effects of intravenous test dose epinephrine on fetal sheep during acute fetal stress and acidosis. Reg Anesth 1990;15:237.

134. Grice SC, Eisenach JC, Dewan DM, Mandell G. Evaluation of 2-chloroprocaine as an effective intravenous test dose for epidural analgesia [Abstract]. Anesthesiology 1987;67:A627.

135. Wallis KL, Shnider SM, Hicks JS, et al. Epidural anesthesia in the normotensive pregnant ewe: Effects on uterine blood flow and fetal acid–base status. Anesthesiology 1976;44:481.

136. Grant GJ, Ramanathan S, Turndorf H. The maternal hemodynamic effects of bupivacaine-epinephrine mixture used for obstetrical anesthesia. Acta Anaesthesiol Scand 1990;34:543.

137. Veille JC, Youngstrom P, Kanaan C, Wilson B. Human umbilical artery flow velocity waveforms before and after regional anesthesia for cesarean section. Obstet Gynecol 1988;72:890.

138. Abboud T, Nagappala S, Murakawa K, et al. Comparison of the effects of general and regional anesthesia for cesarean section in Neonatal Neurologic and Adaptive Capacity scores. Anesth Analg 1985;64:996.

139. Lindblad A, Marsal K, Vernersson E, Renck H. Fetal circulation during epidural analgesia for caesarean section. Br Med J 1984;288:1329.

140. Lindblad A, Bernow J, Marsal K, Vernersson E. Effects of epidural anaesthesia on human fetal blood flow in utero: A comparison of three local anaesthetic solutions. Br J Anaesth 1987;59:1265.

141. Lindblad A, Bernow J, Marsal K. Fetal blood flow during intrathecal anaesthesia for elective caesarean section. Br J Anaesth 1988;61:376.

142. Brizgys RV, Dailey PA, Shnider SM, Kotelko DM, Levinson G. The incidence and neonatal effects of maternal hypotension during epidural anesthesia for cesarean section. Anesthesiology 1987;67:782.

143. Marx GF, Luykx WM, Cohen S. Fetal–neonatal status following caesarean section for fetal distress. Br J Anaesth 1984;56:1009.

144. Ramanathan J, Ricca DM, Sibai BM, Angel JJ. Epidural vs general anesthesia in fetal distress with various abnormal fetal heart rate patterns [Abstract]. Anesth Analg 1988;67:S180.

145. Ong BY, Cohen MM, Palahniuk RJ. Anesthesia for cesarean section—effects on neonates. Anesth Analg 1989;68:270.

146. Abouleish EI. Epinephrine improves the quality of spinal hyperbaric bupivacaine for cesarean section. Anesth Analg 1987;66:395.

147. Moore DC. Spinal anesthesia: bupivacaine compared with tetracaine. Anesth Analg 1980;59:743.

148. Hurley RJ, Lambert DH. Continuous spinal anesthesia with a microcatheter technique: Preliminary experience. Anesth Analg 1990;70:97.

149. Rigler ML, Drasner K, Krejcie TC, et al. Cauda equina syndrome after continuous spinal anesthesia. Anesth Analg 1991;72:275.

150. Lambert DH, Hurley FJ. Cauda equina syndrome and continuous spinal anesthesia. Anesth Analg 1991;72:817.

151. Norris MC, Dewan DM. Preoxygenation for cesarean section: A comparison of two techniques. Anesthesiology 1985;62:827.

152. Kosaka Y, Takahashi T, Mark LC. Intravenous thiobarbiturate anesthesia for cesarean section. Anesthesiology 1969;31:489.

153. Finster M, Morishima HO, Mark LC, et al. Tissue thiopental concentration in the fetus and newborn. Anesthesiology 1972;36:155.

154. Woods WA, Stanski DR, Curtis J, et al. The role of the fetal liver in the distribution of thiopental from mother to fetus. Anesthesiology 1982; 57:A390.

155. Goldberg R, Moscoso P, Bauer C, et al. Use of barbiturate therapy in severe perinatal asphyxia: A randomized controlled trial. J Pediatr 1986; 109:851.

156. Sliom CM, Frankel L, Holbrook RA. A comparison between methohexitone and thiopentone as induction agents for caesarean section anesthesia. Br J Anaesth 1962;34:316.

157. Peltz B, Sinclair DM. Induction agents for cesarean section—a comparison of thiopentone and ketamine. Anaesthesia 1973;28:37.

158. Ellingson A, Haram K, Sagen N, et al. Transplacental passage of ketamine after intravenous administration. Acta Anaesth Scand 1977;21:41.

159. Levinson G, Shnider SM, Gildea JE, DeLorimer AA. Maternal and foetal cardiovascular and acid–base changes during ketamine anaesthesia in pregnant ewes. Br J Anaesth 1973;45:1111.

160. Craft JB, Coaldrake LA, Yonekura JL, et al. Ketamine, catecholamines, and uterine tone in pregnant ewes. Am J Obstet Gynecol 1983;146:429.

161. Marx G, Hwang H, Chandra P. Postpartum uterine pressures with different doses of ketamine. Anesthesiology 1979;50:163.

162. Swartz J, Cumming M, Biehl D. The effect of ketamine anaesthesia on the acidotic fetal lamb. Can J Anaesth 1987;34:233.

163. Pickering BG, Palahniuk RJ, Cote J, et al. Cerebral vascular responses to ketamine and thiopentone during foetal acidosis. Can Anaesth Soc J 1982;29:463.

164. Peltz B, Sinclair DM. Induction agents for caesarean section—a comparison of thiopentone and ketamine. Anaesthesia 1973;28:37.

165. Bernstein K, Gisselsson L, Jacobsson L, et al. Influence of two different anaesthetic agents on the newborn and the correlation between foetal oxygenation and induction–delivery time in elective caesarean section. Acta Anesthesiol Scand 1985;29:157.

166. Hodgkinson R, Marx GF, Kim SS, et al. Neonatal neurobehavioral test following vaginal delivery under ketamine, thiopental, and extradural anesthesia. Anesth Analg 1977;56:548.

167. Downing JW, Buley RJF, Brock-Utne JG, et al. Etomidate for induction of anaesthesia at caesarean section: Comparison with thiopentone. Br J Anaesth 1979;51:135.

168. Ionescu T, Besse TC, Smalhout B. Etomidate during caesarean section, general anaesthesia in obstetrics. Seventh World Congress of Anaesthesiologists, Hamburg, West Germany. International Congress Series, No. 533, 17:318, Amsterdam: Excerpta Medica, 1980.

169. Dailland P, Cockshott ID, Lirzin JD, et al. Intravenous propofol during cesarean section: placental transfer, concentrations in breast milk, and neonatal effects. A preliminary study. Anesthesiology 1989;71:827.

170. Shnider SM, Wright RG, Levinson G, et al. Plasma norepinephrine and uterine blood flow changes during endotracheal intubation and general anesthesia in the pregnant ewe. [Abstract]. Annual Meeting of the American Society of Anesthesiologists, Chicago, 1978:115.

171. Swartz J, Cummings M. The effects of general anaesthesia on the asphyxiated foetal lamb in utero. Can Anaesth Soc J 1985;32:577.

172. Yarnell R, Biehl D, Tweed W, et al. The effect of halothane anaesthesia on the asphyxiated foetal lamb in utero. Can Anaesth Soc J 1983;30:474.

173. Cheek DB, Hughes SC, Dailey PA, et al. Effect of halothane on regional cerebral blood flow and cerebral metabolic oxygen consumption in the fetal lamb in utero. Anesthesiology 1987;67:361.

174. Palahniuk R, Doig G, Johnson G, et al. Maternal halothane anesthesia reduces cerebral blood flow in the acidotic sheep fetus. Anesth Analg 1980;59:35.

175. Baker BW, Hughes SC, Shnider SM, Field DR, Rosen MA. Maternal anesthesia and the stressed fetus: Effects of isoflurane on the asphyxiated fetal lamb. Anesthesiology 1990;72:65.

176. Ralston DH, Shnider SM, deLorimier AA. Uterine blood flow and fetal acid–base changes after bicarbonate administration to the pregnant ewe. Anesthesiology 1974;40:348.

177. Levinson G, Shnider SM, deLorimier AA, Steffenson JL. Effects of maternal hyperventilation on uterine blood flow and fetal oxygenation and acid–base status. Anesthesiology 1974;40:340.

178. Morishima HO, Daniel SS, Adamsons K Jr, James LS. Effects of positive pressure ventilation of the mother upon the acid-base state of the fetus. Am J Obstet Gynecol 1965;93:269.

179. Ranney B, Stanage WF. Advantages of local anesthesia for cesarean section. Obstet Gynecol 1975;45:163.

CHAPTER 34

The Premature Fetus

Holly A. Muir
Brett B. Gutsche
Theodore G. Cheek

Today, preterm birth is defined as delivery before 37 weeks' completed gestation, or 259 days after the first day of the last menstrual period. Low birth weight is a birth weight of less than 2500 g regardless of gestational age. A very-low-birth-weight infant weighs less than 1500 g at birth. Five percent to 10% of births in developed nations are preterm. In 1980 preterm delivery accounted for 8.9% of births in the United States.[1] Prematurity is by far the leading cause of perinatal morbidity and mortality. In 1976, it accounted for 75% of perinatal deaths in the United States[2] and 85% of nonanomalous-related neonatal mortality in England.[3]

Presently, nearly 100% of nonanomalous neonates survive after preterm birth at 32 weeks or greater. When birth takes place in a tertiary care center, 90% of 29- to 30-week gestations and nearly 50% of 26-week gestations survive.[4] Fewer than 15% of neonates born before 26 weeks of gestation or with a birth weight of less than 800 g who survive have neurologic handicaps.[4] These data show that efforts to salvage these infants are worthwhile and often are rewarded with a normal child.

The causes of morbidity in the preterm birth neonate are many and formidable (Table 34-1). The leading cause of mortality and morbidity in the preterm birth neonate is no longer respiratory distress but periventricular and intraventricular hemorrhage. These complications occur in more than 50% of preterm birth neonates with birth weights of less than 1200 g.[5] Evidence suggests that avoiding asphyxia, birth trauma, and hypothermia in the peripartum period will minimize the incidence and severity of respiratory distress syndrome, bronchopulmonary dysplasia, necrotizing enterocolitis, and retrolental fibroplasia in the preterm infant. An appropriate, skillfully administered anesthetic can help avoid perinatal asphyxia and provide for the atraumatic delivery of the premature newborn.[6]

To provide the most effective care during preterm birth, the anesthesiologist must understand the evaluations, procedures, and medications employed by the obstetrician. Many therapeutic modalities used have significant anesthetic implications. Table 34-2 outlines the more important obstetric considerations of preterm birth.

In utero fetal evaluation is important for the rational therapy of premature labor. Estimation of gestational age by the last menstrual period is often in error, even with the most reliable patients. Diagnostic ultrasound can accurately date the pregnancy within a week if done in early gestation. Fetal maturity, particularly fetal lung maturity, is usually determined from amniotic fluid analyzed for components of lung surfactant. Initially, the lecithin/sphingomyelin (L/S) ratio was deter-

Table 34-1

Causes of Morbidity and Mortality in the Premature Neonate

Respiratory

Respiratory distress syndrome or hyaline membrane disease
Bronchopulmonary dysplasia
Sudden Infant death syndrome from apneic episodes
Interstitial emphysema, pneumothorax

Neurologic

Periventricular and intraventricular hemorrhage
Neurologic damage causing cerebral palsy, hydrocephalus, and seizure disorders
Retinopathy of prematurity (benign and reversible) progressing to irreversible retrolental fibroplasia

Circulatory

Persistent fetal circulation with patent ductus arteriosus and resultant pulmonary hypertension

Gastrointestinal

Necrotizing enterocolitis
Hyperbilirubinemia

Obstetric

Increased breech presentation (premature > 25%, term < 3%)
Birth asphyxia
Birth trauma
Infection from prolonged rupture of membranes and chorioamnionitis

Miscellaneous

Increased incidence of congenital anomalies
Decreased thermoregulation
Decreased maternal interaction and bonding

---

mined. Between 33 and 35 weeks, the L/S ratio rapidly increases, reaching a value of 2 or greater at 35 weeks of gestation. In the nondiabetic parturient, a ratio of 2 or greater correlates with minimal risk of respiratory distress syndrome. A value below 1.5 suggests a greater likelihood that the neonate will develop significant respiratory distress syndrome. Other amniotic fluid determinations of lung maturity include both phosphatidylinositol and phosphatidylglycerol. The presence of phosphatidylglycerol in amniotic fluid almost assures the absence of respiratory distress syndrome. A newer measure of fetal lung maturity is the TDx assay.[7] This automated assay measures the relative concentrations of surfactant and albumin in the amniotic fluid. Its greatest advantage over the other assays is time. The

TDx assay is complete within 30 minutes. This short time itself has anesthetic implications. A decision can be made to allow delivery much quicker than previously possible. The anesthetist has much less time to prepare.

TOCOLYTIC DRUGS

Table 34-3 shows various methods of tocolysis used in the past and today. Beta-agonists and magnesium sulfate are the primary tocolytics now used in the United States. These agents act by a variety of mechanisms and have many side effects, some of which can be life-threatening to the patient, especially in combination with anesthesia.

Beta-agonists

Many initially thought that beta-agonist tocolytic drugs would effectively lower the incidence of the preterm birth. Unfortunately, tocolytic therapy in

Table 34-2

Obstetric Considerations with Preterm Labor

Determine if preterm labor does indeed exist
   Contractions
   Cervical dilation and effacement
Treat underlying causes of preterm labor, if possible
   Infection
   Incompetent cervix (use of cerclage in early second trimester)
   Medical conditions
   Surgical correction of uterine abnormalities in nonpregnant state
Fetal evaluation
   Gestational age
   Weight
   Lung maturity
   Presence of fetal anomalies
   Fetal well-being (biophysical profile)
Evaluation of state of pregnancy
   Membranes (intact or ruptured)
   Placental abnormalities (previa or abruptio)
   Presentation and station of fetus
Tocolysis, when indicated
Enhancement of fetal lung maturity (glucocorticoids when not contraindicated)
Delivery plan
   Induction or trial of labor
   Cesarean section
   Attempt external version

Table 34–3

Methods of Tocolysis

Methods of the Past and Rarely Used Methods

Progesterone injections

Ethanol (often required inebriation, associated with pulmonary acid aspiration)

Phosphodiesterase inhibitors (aminophylline)

Diazoxide

Methods Used Today

First step
  Bed rest
  Intravenous fluids
Second step
  Beta$_2$-agonists (ritodrine, terbutaline)
  Magnesium sulfate
Special use or occasional
  Prostaglandin synthesis inhibitors (indomethacin)
  Calcium channel blockers

Methods of the Future

Oxytocin analogue (1-deamino-2-D-Try-[OEt]-4-Thr-8-Orn-Oxytocin)

Western Europe and in North America has not significantly reduced the rate of preterm birth.[4,8] By way of explanation, less than 30% of patients presenting with premature labor are candidates for tocolysis. A recent study by King *et al*[9] reviewed 16 different randomized controlled trials of the beta-agonist tocolytics (ritodrine, terbutaline, or isoxsuprine). Conducted between 1966 and 1986, these reports included 484 women versus 406 controls.[9] The authors concluded that the data showed ". . . an unequivocal effect of beta-mimetic tocolytic administration in delaying delivery and this is reflected in a reduction in the frequency of preterm birth and low birth weight. However, no beneficial effect of this treatment on perinatal mortality or severe neonatal respiratory disorders could be detected." Despite these rather pessimistic findings, tocolysis is still widely used today. Contraindications to tocolysis are summarized in Table 34-4.

Physiologic Effects

The physiologic actions of the beta-adrenergic agonists are multisystemic (Table 34-5). These drugs can produce major side effects (Table 34-6),[10] many of which have important anesthetic implications. Those

Table 34–4

Contraindications to Tocolysis in Premature Labor

ABSOLUTE	RELATIVE
Fetal	
Mature fetus	Rupture of membranes without chorioamnionitis
Fetal anomalies incompatible with life	
Severe intrauterine fetal growth retardation	Fetal anomaly,
Chorioamnionitis	Mild intrauterine fetal growth retardation
Fetal death	Fetal distress
Maternal	
Severe preeclampsia or eclampsia	Controlled metabolic diseases (*e.g.*, diabetes, hyperthyroidism)
Decompensated cardiac disease	
Chorioamnionitis	Cervix > 4–5 cm dilated
Severe bleeding	
Maternal refusal or noncompliance	
Placental	
Significant bleeding of any cause	Stable abruption or previa
Coagulopathy	
Severe abruption	

Table 34–5

The Physiologic Effects of Beta-agonists

BETA$_1$	BETA$_2$
Cardiac	**Smooth Muscle**
Increased stroke volume	Decreased uterine activity
Increased heart rate	Vasodilation
	Bronchiolar relaxation
Renal	**Renal**
Increased renal blood flow	Increased renin and aldosterone production
Decreased urinary output	
Metabolic	**Metabolic**
Lipolysis with increase in ketones	Increased insulin release
Increased potassium with decrease in serum potassium	Increased glycogenolysis with increase in blood sugar
Metabolic lactic acidosis	

involving the cardiovascular system are especially troublesome. Tachycardia with rates usually above 100 beats/minute occurs commonly, often with associated tremor, palpitations, and chest pain. This tachycardia can exceed 120 beats/minute. If, simultaneously, the mother receives drugs such as epinephrine, ephedrine, anticholinergics, or intravenous bolus oxytocin, her pulse rate may surpass 140 beats/minute. Consider deleting epinephrine from the local anesthetic solution and using a pure alpha-agonist as a vasopressor in a patient with beta-agonist–induced tachycardia. Arrhythmias, including premature ventricular contractions, premature nodal contractions, and atrial fibrillation have been reported with beta-agonist therapy.[10] Although some of these arrhythmias may be benign changes in normal pregnancy, they are often reasons for stopping beta-agonist therapy. The ventricular arrhythmias associated with beta-agonist therapy may become more apparent and troublesome with concomitant exposure to anesthetic agents such as halothane.

Cardiac output, elevated 40% in the third trimester of normal pregnancy, may rise to 80% above the nonpregnant level with use of beta-agonists. Despite some beta-receptor selectivity, both inotropic and chronotropic effects contribute to the elevated cardiac output.[11]

Side Effects

ANGINA PECTORIS. Angina pectoris has been reported as a complication of beta-agonist therapy in preterm labor.[12–14] The angina is usually diagnosed symptomatically and may correlate with changes on the electrocardiogram (ECG). It predictably resolves on stopping the beta-agonist and is usually not associated with enzyme changes. Hendricks *et al*[15] found ECG changes suggesting myocardial ischemia (including ST depression and T-wave inversion) in over 70% of asymptomatic patients studied.[15] They found no statistical correlation between patient symptoms, rate or dose of beta-agonist administration, serum potassium concentration, cardiac enzyme changes, and ECG changes. These findings lead one to question the validity of ECG changes in the diagnosis of myocardial ischemia in patients receiving beta-agonist therapy.

PULMONARY EDEMA. The most serious complication associated with the use of beta-agonists is pulmonary edema, with a reported incidence as high as 5%.[16] Oral, subcutaneous, and continuous intravenous infusions have all been associated with pulmonary edema. This complication does not correlate with either total dose administered or infusion rate. Pulmonary edema may arise during or after therapy.[17]

The etiology of the pulmonary edema is unclear. Various mechanisms have been proposed, including both cardiogenic and noncardiogenic. Cardiogenic causes may include the following:

- Fluid overload
- Catecholamine-related myocardial necrosis
- Cardiac failure secondary to the tachycardia

Table 34-6

Maternal Side Effects of the Beta-agonist Tocolytics

Cardiac

Tachycardia and palpitations

Dysrhythmias and myocardial sensitization

Vasodilation and postural hypotension

Cardiomyopathy

Electrocardiographic changes of hypokalemia and ischemia

Pulmonary edema

Fluid retention

Metabolic

Hypokalemia

Hyperglycemia

Lactic acidosis

Central Nervous System

Apprehension

Insomnia

Tremor

Headache and exacerbation of migraine

Other

Nausea and vomiting

Uterine atony and postpartum hemorrhage

■ Down regulation of the beta-receptors on the heart after chronic exposure to high concentrations of beta-agonist.[16,18]

Evaluation of cardiac function by pulmonary artery catheterization or echocardiography, however, has failed to show left ventricular failure.[10,19] Increased pulmonary vascular permeability and decreased colloid oncotic pressure may contribute to noncardiogenic pulmonary edema. Increases in pulmonary hydrostatic pressure and vascular permeability can lead to displacement of fluid into the extravascular space of the lung. The usual rapid resolution of the pulmonary edema with treatment makes this idea less plausible. It is difficult to envision a membrane defect that would resolve so quickly.

The mechanism of the pulmonary edema is likely multifactorial. One hypothesis proposes that the pulmonary edema results from a beta$_1$ effect of the drug. In dogs, a beta$_1$-selective antagonist (metoprolol) seems to protect against the development of pulmonary edema.[20] Although these animal data must be interpreted with caution, they may shed some light on the etiology of the pulmonary edema.

Several predisposing factors have correlated with the pulmonary edema seen with beta-agonist tocolysis (Table 34-7).[20] Simultaneous administration of the beta-agonists and glucocorticoids does not increase the incidence of pulmonary edema as previously thought.[10] The association between pulmonary edema and combined beta-agonist and glucocorticoid therapy now seems incidental.[18] Pulmonary edema arising during general anesthesia may represent the effect of a myocardial depressant on an already stressed cardiovascular system.

Pulmonary edema usually occurs between 24 and 72 hours after initial intravenous administration of the beta-agonist tocolytics, as the dose is being rapidly elevated, or when tocolysis is unsuccessful and the mother receives general anesthesia for delivery. It is unrelated to dosage and occurs with equal frequency for all the beta-agonists. It is only occasionally seen once the mother is on oral maintenance. It has a significant mortality and hence requires rapid recognition and effective treatment, which follows:

1. Stop the beta-agonist and avoid other tocolytic drugs.
2. Restrict fluids.
3. Place the patient in the sitting position.
4. Give a high inspired Fio$_2$.
5. Induce diuresis with furosemide.
6. Occasionally, invasive central venous or pulmonary artery monitoring may be helpful as a guide to fluid and cardiac therapy in severe cases
7. Rarely, intubation, positive-pressure ventilation, and the addition of positive end-expiratory pressure may be required.

Table 34-7

Factors Predisposing to Development of Pulmonary Edema with Beta-agonist Tocolytic Use

---

Changes specific to pregnancy

    Capillary wall alterations

    Hypervolemia

    Hypoproteinemia

    Decreased colloid oncotic pressure

Fluid overload

Diseases of the heart, lungs, kidneys, and metabolism

Chorioamnionitis

Co-administration of prostaglandin antagonist

General anesthesia

Multiple gestation

Because the etiology is almost never cardiac failure, digitalis therapy is rarely indicated. Cardiac glycosides may predispose to serious arrhythmias owing to the coexisting hypokalemia.[18]

METABOLIC EFFECTS. Metabolic changes accompanying beta-agonist tocolytic therapy include hypokalemia, hyperglycemia, and lactic acidosis.[21,22] Potassium concentrations may fall to less than 3.0 mEq/L owing to an intracellular influx of potassium. The body does not lose potassium, so replacement is seldom necessary. Hyperinsulinemia and direct $beta_1$-adrenoreceptor stimulation induce this intracellular flux of potassium.[23] Serum potassium concentration declines during the first few hours of therapy. After 24 hours of continuous therapy or within a few hours of abrupt cessation of the tocolytic, potassium concentration returns toward normal (Fig. 34-1).[23,24] Maternal hyperventilation may exaggerate hypokalemia. Some changes associated with hypokalemia have significant anesthetic implications (Table 34-8).

Beta$_2$-receptor stimulation causes glycogenolysis and hyperglycemia. Metabolic lactic acidosis and a rise in maternal serum insulin follows. Blood glucose concentrations in nondiabetic parturients commonly reach 140 to 160 mg/dL. Hyperglycemia may incite a reactive neonatal hypoglycemia. Use glucose-free intravenous solutions antenatally to limit this problem. Using beta-agonist tocolytics in the diabetic requires careful glucose monitoring and a concomitant infusion of insulin.

Maternal fluid retention is common and may result in a lowered hemoglobin concentration and plasma oncotic pressure. Other side effects of the beta-agonist tocolytics include nausea, vomiting, insomnia, tremors, and headache, with an exacerbation of migraine-type headaches. When these tocolytics are given near delivery, especially with a cesarean birth, postpartum recalcitrant uterine atony and excessive maternal blood loss may occur. Uterine atony is usually treated with one or a combination of the following: oxytocin, ergotamine, or prostaglandin. Use ergotamine with caution, as it may predispose these women to pulmonary edema.[25]

The side effects of beta-agonists may contraindicate their use in a variety of situations (see Table 34-4). These include cardiac lesions that contraindicate tachycardia (stenotic valvular lesions or idiopathic hypertrophic subaortic stenosis) or are associated with myocardial ischemia. In addition, these drugs should be used with extreme caution in parturients with severe preeclampsia or eclampsia, diabetes, hyperthyroidism, chorioamnionitis, chronic hypertension, hypovolemia, and a history of cerebrovascular disorder.

Anesthetic Implications

Because beta-agonists produce vasodilatation and increased cardiac output, they may attenuate the maternal hypotension associated with epidural or subarachnoid block. Chestnut *et al*[26] asked the question "Does ritodrine worsen maternal hypotension during epidural anesthesia in gravid ewes?" They concluded that prior administration of ritodrine did not worsen maternal hypotension but, rather, helped maintain maternal cardiac output and uterine blood flow during epidural anesthesia. Aggressive preblock intravenous hydration may predispose to fluid overload and decreased serum colloid oncotic pressure, increasing the risk of pulmonary edema.[17,18] Incorrectly interpreting a tachycardia

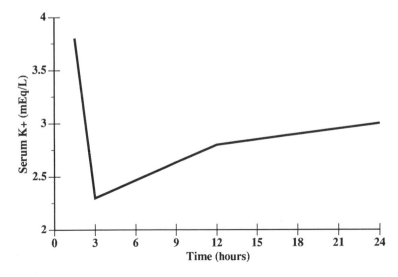

Figure 34–1. Changes in serum potassium during ritodrine tocolysis. (Data from Young D, Leveno KJ. Potassium and glucose concentrations without treatment during ritodrine tocolysis. Am J Obstet Gynecol 1983;145: 105, and Cano A, Tovar I, Parilla JJ. Metabolic disturbances during intravenous use of ritodrine: Increased insulin levels and hypokalemia. Obstet Gynecol 1985;65:359)

Table 34–8

Anesthetic Considerations in the Presence of Hypokalemia

Autonomic neuropathy
   Orthostatic hypotension
   Decreased sympathetic reserve
Impaired myocardial contractility
   Aggravated by anesthetic agent with myocardial
     depressant properties
Electrical conduction abnormalities
   Electrocardiographic changes
     Widened QRS
     S-T segment abnormalities
     Decreased T-wave amplitude
     Increased U-wave amplitude
   Arrhythmias
     Sinus tachycardia
     Atrial and ventricular dysrhythmia
     Ventricular fibrillation
Potentiation of hypokalemic state with alkalosis
Increased myocardial sensitivity to digoxin, calcium, and
   potassium infusion
Muscle weakness
Hypoperistalsis (delayed gastric emptying)
Peripheral nephropathy

---

as a sign of hypovolemia may result in further unnecessary intravenous fluids. The vasodilated state induced by beta-agonists suggests that the use of rapid-acting local anesthetics such as 2-chloroprocaine or lidocaine is safe in these patients.

Beta-agonists also may interfere with pulmonary hypoxic vasoconstriction.[27] This effect will increase the risk of maternal hypoxemia, particularly under general anesthesia. Using a higher F_{IO_2} will help minimize this risk.[28]

Earlier estimates suggested that the serum half-life of ritodrine was 50 ± 20 minutes.[29] Recent work by Caritis *et al*[30] now suggests a mean half-life of 156 minutes. The traditional teaching that general anesthesia should be delayed 30 minutes, when possible, after stopping intravenous administration of a beta-agonist should be revised because of these data. A delay of 2 hours or longer may be more prudent if time allows.

Fetal Effects

The beta-agonist tocolytics have few adverse effects on the fetus. High intravenous infusion rates may cause a mild fetal tachycardia. If the neonate is born within 24 hours of cessation of the drugs, neonatal hypoglycemia, hypocalcemia, and hypotension may occur.

No neonatal effects are evident if delivery is more than 24 hours after stopping therapy.

Magnesium Sulphate

Intravenous magnesium sulphate is an effective tocolytic in doses similar to or slightly higher than those used for the treatment of preeclampsia and eclampsia.[31] Like the beta-agonists, magnesium sulphate therapy induces many maternal side effects. These sequelae include vasodilation, flushing, headache, and postural hypotension. Magnesium acts at the myoneural junction to cause generalized skeletal muscle weakness and loss of deep tendon reflexes; in overdose, it can cause respiratory depression and arrest. Gross overdose can cause cardiac arrest. Other side effects may include drowsiness without analgesia, blurred vision, nausea, constipation, and chest pain.[32,33] In a series of 355 patients receiving magnesium for tocolysis, 1.1% developed pulmonary edema.[34] Because magnesium is excreted primarily through the kidneys, it must be used with caution in patients with compromised renal function. Deep tendon reflexes are monitored during magnesium therapy. Loss of the patellar reflex occurs with a serum magnesium concentration of about 10 mg/dL. This sign is an early indicator of magnesium toxicity. Respiratory depression occurs at concentrations of 12 to 15 mg/dL (Table 34-9).

Magnesium tocolysis is preferable to beta-agonists in some groups of patients. Its use is not associated with hyperglycemia and metabolic lactic acidosis, rendering it more suitable for the diabetic parturient. In therapeutic doses, it does not have inotropic and chronotropic effects, making it safer for use in women with various cardiac disorders. It does not increase metabolic rate and is not contraindicated in hypermetabolic disorders such as hyperthyroidism. It is inexpensive and effective. Currently, its use requires hospitalization for intravenous tocolysis. Oral use is impractical. A new oral preparation of the gluconate salt of magnesium is now being developed that could have great therapeutic benefits.

Some advocate magnesium sulphate as the drug of choice in the patient at risk of hemorrhage and in need of tocolysis. They argue that beta-agonist–induced vasodilation may worsen the magnitude of the hemorrhage and blunt the normal hemodynamic response to hemorrhage.[10] However, a study by Chestnut *et al*[35] found the opposite effect. In the gravid ewe, magnesium sulphate, but not ritodrine, worsened the maternal hypotensive response to hemorrhage. A further

Table 34–9

Effects of Increasing Plasma Magnesium Concentration

OBSERVED CONDITION	MAGNESIUM CONCENTRATION (MEQ/L)
Normal plasma	1.5–2.0
Therapeutic range (may see diplopia and mild skeletal muscle weakness)	4.0–6.0
Electrocardiographic changes (widened QRS and prolonged P-Q interval)	5.0–10.0
Loss of deep tendon reflexes	10.0
Sinoatrial and atrioventricular block	15.0
Respiratory paralysis	15.0
Cardiac arrest	25.0

study showed no improvement in the maternal response to hemorrhage in the presence of magnesium sulphate with the administration of calcium chloride.[36]

Anesthetic Implications

Magnesium tocolysis also interacts with anesthetic drugs and techniques. In its own right, magnesium causes muscle weakness. Combined with muscle relaxants, it increases the degree and duration of action of depolarizing and especially nondepolarizing relaxants,[37] including the newer relaxant vecuronium.[38] Reversal of a nondepolarizing muscle relaxant with an anticholinesterase may be incomplete. Magnesium decreases the sensitivity of the motor end-plate to applied acetylcholine, reducing the efficacy of the reversal process.[39]

Magnesium attenuates succinylcholine fasciculations.[40] Its effect on the action of succinylcholine is variable. It does not affect the response to or duration of a single dose of succinylcholine. Full intubating doses are required.[41] Magnesium does, however, increase the duration of paralysis after repeated doses or continuous infusion of succinylcholine. Use a peripheral nerve stimulator to judge the response to and recovery from muscle relaxants in a patient receiving magnesium.

Like the beta-agonists, magnesium produces vasodilation, but without increasing cardiac output; therefore, postural hypotension is more likely with magnesium than with beta-agonist drugs. Sympathetic block during regional anesthesia should be unlikely to produce hypotension. Marked preblock hydration is usually not necessary and may predispose to pulmonary edema. Magnesium also can interfere with uterine contractions following delivery, which increases the likeli-

hood of postpartum uterine atony and excessive blood loss.

Fetal Effects

Fetal blood concentration parallels maternal blood concentration of magnesium. Fetal heart rate variability may decrease. Clinical experience suggests that magnesium induces decreased muscle tone, ileus, and poor feeding. A prospective study from 1988, however, reported that magnesium was more likely to affect color than muscle tone.[41] Significantly decreased muscle tone and respiratory or cardiac depression is not likely in the absence of maternal toxicity. If neonatal toxicity is seen in the absence of maternal magnesium toxicity, it is important to look for other causes. If neonatal renal function is normal, the effects of magnesium dissipate within 48 hours.[42–44]

Prostaglandin Synthesis Inhibitors

Indomethacin, a prostaglandin synthetase inhibitor, is an effective tocolytic agent.[45] Maternal side effects (nausea, vomiting, gastritis, peptic ulcer formation, and masking of fever) are essentially those of aspirin. Like aspirin, it can be associated with thrombocytopenia, and it interferes with platelet function. Unlike aspirin, its effects on platelets are reversible and usually dissipate within a few days of its discontinuation.[46] Controversy surrounds this issue of bleeding times before regional anesthesia in patients receiving ASA or nonsteroidal anti-inflammatory agents.[47,48] The usefulness of the bleeding time is now being questioned, even by hematologists.[49] A bleeding time may be useful in patients with a history or clinical signs of a bleeding problem with an otherwise normal coagulogram. Otherwise, it is not needed in these patients. We rarely use bleeding time in our practice.

In animals, indomethacin, like aspirin, can induce premature closure of the ductus arteriosus, pulmonary vascular constriction, and pulmonary hypertension. These effects appear to be related to gestational age. The ductus arteriosus becomes more sensitive to prostaglandin inhibitors close to term. In clinical use, indomethacin is usually reserved for refractory premature labor before 34 weeks of gestation.[45,50] Indomethacin also may be associated with reversible oligohydramnios.[51] However, because of its lack of maternal cardiovascular and other side effects and its ease of administration, it is finding increased use for initial tocolysis in early pregnancy. Indomethacin also may prove a useful adjunct for the temporary control of premature labor in the mother being transported to a tertiary care center for delivery.

Calcium Channel Blockers

Calcium channel blockers, particularly nifedipine, are potent relaxants of uterine muscle.[52] Several of these drugs are undergoing investigation for their efficacy as tocolytics. They are potent vasodilators and often incite flushing and hypotension. Other bothersome side effects include nausea and headache, but, compared to the beta-agonist ritodrine, nifedipine yields fewer maternal side effects. The cardiovascular alterations, although significant, are less than those associated with ritodrine. Maternal heart rate increases, whereas diastolic pressure and mean arterial pressure decrease (Fig. 34-2). Changes in glucose homeostasis accompany both nifedipine and ritodrine. The magnitude of these changes is much less with nifedipine. Nifedipine does not significantly alter serum electrolyte values.[52,53]

Initial animal studies with rhesus monkeys and ewes suggested an increased incidence of intrauterine fetal death with the use of calcium channel blockers. In these models, nifedipine lowered uterine blood flow and induced fetal acidosis and hypoxia.[54] To date, these findings have not been substantiated in humans. Current data show no difference in fetal outcome after tocolytic use of nifedipine or ritodrine.[52,55]

Anesthetic Effects

Calcium channel blockers interact with various anesthetic agents. Both inhalation and local anesthetics exhibit some calcium channel blocking properties. Researchers have used animal models to look at the

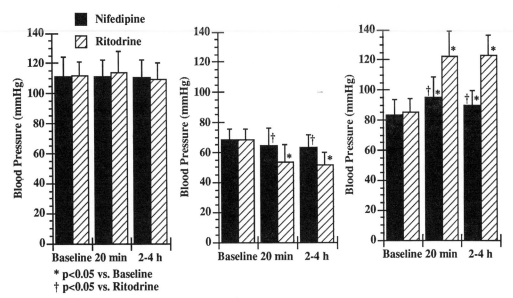

Figure 34–2. Comparison of cardiovascular parameters at 20 minutes and 2 to 4 hours after the last sublingual dose of nifedipine or at the intravenous infusion rate of ritodrine necessary to achieve tocolysis. Data are mean ± SD. (Data from Ferguson JE, Dyson DC, Holbrook RH, Schutz T, Stevenson DK. Cardiovascular and metabolic effects associated with nifedipine and ritodrine tocolysis. Am J Obstet Gynecol 1989; 161:788)

hemodynamic effects of calcium channel blockers and inhalational anesthetics. These agents both have similar impact on the cardiovascular system, namely vasodilation and myocardial depression. In the dog, during light halothane anesthesia (1%), nifedipine induced transient hypotension with a compensatory increase in cardiac output and heart rate. More significant hypotension arose under deep halothane anesthesia (2%), presumably because of an attenuation of the compensatory increase in heart rate.[56] Combinations of isoflurane or enflurane and the other calcium channel blocking agents yield similar results.[57] Although deep volatile anesthesia is rarely used in the obstetric population, there are circumstances when uterine relaxation may be needed, and this drug interaction could have significant consequences.

The interactions of lidocaine and bupivacaine with verapamil and diltiazem have been examined in conscious dogs in an attempt to reproduce the clinical situation of epidural anesthesia.[58] Either bupivacaine or lidocaine was infused to achieve serum concentrations seen with epidural anesthesia. When calcium channel blockers were then given, mean arterial pressure and myocardial contractile force decreased significantly. Both lidocaine and bupivacaine lengthened the P-R interval when used in combination with a calcium channel blocker. High-degree atrioventricular nodal block was seen more frequently with bupivacaine. This drug's enhanced cardiodepressant effects, when used in combination with calcium channel blockers, warrant further investigation.

Other Tocolytic Drugs

An oxytocin analogue, 1-deamino-2-D-Try-(OEt)-4-Thr-8-Orn-oxytocin, is effective for initial tocolysis.[59] No cardiovascular or other side effects were seen in either the mother or fetus. This preliminary study suggests great promise for the drug as an effective, rapid-acting, safe tocolytic. Its clinical application, however, remains on the distant horizon.

Tocolytic Interactions

Both the mechanism of action of the various tocolytic drugs and the complex mechanisms responsible for regulating uterine contractions rely on multiple cellular functions. Preterm labor is a syndrome of disorders resulting from a variety of causes associated with different cellular mechanisms. It is therefore not unreasonable to use different tocolytic agents concur-

rently in the hope that their synergistic action may halt more resistant cases of preterm labor. However, the simultaneous use of various tocolytics increases the risk of adverse drug interaction and potentiates some side effects. The simultaneous use of magnesium sulphate reportedly augments the hypotensive effects of nifedipine.[60] In the isolated, perfused Sprague–Dawley rat heart, the combination of nifedipine and magnesium produced a greater decrease in left ventricular systolic pressure and left ventricular contractility than either drug alone.[61] Also, nifedipine potentiates the effects of magnesium on neuromuscular function.[62] This interaction may result in a further exaggeration of the response of patients on magnesium sulphate to nondepolarizing muscle relaxants.

ANESTHETIC MANAGEMENT OF THE PRETERM DELIVERY

The obstetric anesthesiologist has several goals when planning for the delivery of a preterm infant. Try to ensure the least traumatic delivery possible. Also, take all possible measures to prevent asphyxia and hypothermia. A sudden, uncontrolled delivery will markedly increase the likelihood of intercerebral hemorrhage, which is now the leading cause of morbidity and mortality in preterm birth. For vaginal delivery, the ideal is a controlled, atraumatic delivery over a wide episiotomy. Likewise, the premature infant tolerates asphyxia poorly. The asphyxiated preterm infant has an increased incidence of respiratory distress syndrome, intraventricular hemorrhage, and necrotizing enterocolitis. Before vaginal or cesarean delivery, position the mother carefully to prevent aortocaval compression. Give supplemental oxygen. Avoid or aggressively treat maternal hypotension. Continuous electronic fetal monitoring may detect early signs of fetal asphyxia.

Maternal hemorrhage from placenta previa, abruption, or uterine atony from attempted tocolysis can complicate preterm birth. The incidence of breech in the preterm birth is 25%, compared to a 3% incidence at term. Fetal distress, prolapsed cord, and maternal hemorrhage are more common in premature labor. Expeditious cesarean section is indicated if the fetus shows any evidence of compromise.

Delivery in a tertiary care center, instead of transfer after birth, lowers neonatal mortality.[63,64] The preterm fetus and newborn, with its less developed lungs, liver, and kidneys, may have difficulty metabolizing and excreting depressant analgesic and anesthetic drugs. Despite this possibility, Myers and Myers[65] recommend the use of analgesics in appropriate doses when needed.

Lastly, the anesthetist involved in a preterm birth must be acquainted with the side effects of the various tocolytic agents and their interaction with anesthetic techniques and drugs.

Vaginal Delivery

When the mother delivering a preterm infant is to have a trial of labor, lumbar epidural analgesia, initiated early and maintained throughout labor and delivery, is the most desirable option (Table 34-10). Begin epidural block early in labor. Use an adequate volume and concentration of local anesthetic (*i.e.,* 10–12 mL 0.375% bupivacaine or 1.5% lidocaine). The goal is complete perineal analgesia and a sensory level to at least T-8. With such a level, should an emergency cesarean section become necessary, adequate analgesia will be present to allow immediate incision. Simultaneously, the sensory level can be raised with 1.5% to 2.0% lidocaine or 3% 2-chloroprocaine. The pre-existing T-8 sensory block limits the risk of precipitous hypotension during elevation of the sensory level with these rapid-acting agents. Add epinephrine 1:300,000 to the local anesthetic just before injection. This adjuvant drug increases the duration and quality of the block and shortens the onset time without hindering uterine or intervillous blood flow.

The choice of local anesthetic agent has generated controversy over the years. In the mid-1970s, Scanlon et al[66] described the alert but floppy baby after delivery with epidural block using both lidocaine and mepivacaine. Biehl et al[67] in 1978 showed that fetal acidosis increased the fetal uptake of lidocaine. These findings led to a marked decrease in the use of lidocaine for epidural anesthesia. This trend was especially marked when neonatal performance was critical and the risk of fetal asphyxia was high, as with the preterm fetus. 2-Chloroprocaine became favored. It seemed to have no adverse neonatal effects. It has a very short half-life (43 s in cord blood).

Many experts disputed that lidocaine anesthesia produced alert but floppy babies. Subsequent studies could show no clinically significant differences attributable to the use of epidural lidocaine.[68–73] Further studies also couldn't prove the superiority of 2-chloroprocaine. Indeed, a 1988 study by Kuhnert et al[74] suggested that infants delivered after bupivacaine anesthesia did better on neurobehavioral tests than those after 2-chloroprocaine anesthesia.[74] A recent study by Morishima et al[75] reported some adverse effects of lidocaine in the asphyxiated preterm lamb. The pH of lambs who were acutely asphyxiated while receiving lidocaine was significantly lower than that of control lambs receiving saline. These findings may be significant enough to alter the choice of local anesthetic during preterm birth, especially in the presence of acute asphyxia. [Editor's Note: Until confirming data from humans become available, I urge caution in interpreting the clinical implications of animal studies.]

We are not concerned by lack of reflex urge to bear down and the early relaxation of the perineum induced by our anesthetic technique. To provide a completely controlled delivery, we intentionally seek these conditions. Our technique includes repeat doses of 10 to 12 mL of 0.25% to 0.375% bupivacaine with epinephrine, depending on the level of the block, every 2 hours by the clock. This approach maintains analgesia and assures the lack of maternal reflex bearing down. A continuous infusion technique also may be used. Bupivacaine, 0.187% (3/16) to 0.25%, with epinephrine, 1:400,000, works well. When using a continuous infusion, closely monitor the level and density of sensory blockade to ensure adequate perineal analgesia and obtund the urge to push. If, during the second stage of labor, the obstetrician wants the mother to bear down, she can do so on command, unaccompanied by any reflex urge. Out of concern for their possible neonatal effects, we normally do not continuously infuse narcotics with epidural local anesthetics for labor with a preterm fetus. Give supplemental oxygen throughout labor.

If labor is progressing rapidly, a modified saddle block to T-10 can provide analgesia and relaxation for an atraumatic delivery. Any hyperbaric solution with added epinephrine (5% lidocaine in 7.5% dextrose [1.0

Table 34-10

Advantages of Epidural Analgesia for Vaginal Delivery of the Preterm Infant

> Alert, cooperative, pain-free mother
> Ideal conditions for a vaginal delivery
>   Mother can control pushing on command
>   Allows operative delivery (forceps or vacuum extraction)
>   Allows wide episiotomy and repair
>   Decreases likelihood of precipitous delivery
> Minimizes the risk of pulmonary edema associated with beta-agonists, magnesium, and general anesthesia
> Not associated with newborn drug depression
> Stable maternal cardiovascular system protects mother and fetus from the stress of painful labor with associated metabolic acidosis and increased maternal catecholamines
> Can be rapidly extended for an emergency cesarean section

mL, 60–75 min], 0.75% bupivacaine in 8.25% dextrose [0.8–1.0 mL, 90–120 min], or 0.5% tetracaine in 5% dextrose [1.0–1.2 mL, 150–180 min]) will prove adequate. In the event that delivery has not occurred before regression of the subarachnoid block, epidural analgesia can then be initiated. If the fetal head is low in the vagina, or if labor is progressing rapidly, do the epidural or subarachnoid block with the mother on her side to prevent fetal head compression. Induce regional anesthesia in the lateral position in other similar situations (*i.e.*, a small infant whose head is not yet engaged, breech presentation, or ruptured membranes). Placing these women upright risks trauma to the fetal head; uncontrolled, precipitous delivery; and umbilical cord prolapse.

Should epidural or subarachnoid block be contraindicated, inhalation of 40% nitrous oxide in oxygen can provide analgesia for delivery. Careful titration of up to 0.5% enflurane also can help. Check maternal consciousness frequently, because the airway is not protected by an endotracheal tube. Intravenous ketamine, 0.25 mg/kg (15–25 mg), at delivery is an alternative to the use of a potent inhalation agent. Ketamine provides rapid, intense analgesia lasting 3 to 5 minutes. Should the situation require additional analgesia, further 0.125 to 0.25 mg/kg doses may be used. Monitor maternal consciousness and limit the total dose of ketamine to 1.0 mg/kg before delivery. With inhalational or intravenous analgesia, pudendal block or at least local infiltration of the perineum, is required. Systemic medications alone cannot assure adequate analgesia for episiotomy, or application of forceps or vacuum. Although the aforementioned technique is useful, it is not nearly as ideal as epidural or subarachnoid block. It does not abolish the reflex urge to bear down. The mother is less likely to be cooperative and quiet on the delivery table, hindering a controlled, atraumatic delivery.

General anesthesia is rarely required for vaginal delivery. Should it be, take all the usual precautions to prevent pulmonary aspiration. Do a rapid sequence induction with cricoid pressure. Avoid induction of anesthesia in the lithotomy position.

Cesarean Delivery

Obstetricians often chose to deliver viable preterm neonates abdominally. If not contraindicated by other factors, we choose either lumbar epidural or subarachnoid block for anesthesia for cesarean delivery. Several points need to be reemphasized. In a breech or non-vertex presentation, doing the block in the sitting position may predispose to prolapse of the umbilical cord. A mother who has just received a beta-agonist tocolytic should have cautious and minimal intravenous prehydration. An FiO_2 of 0.5 from the time of block until delivery may significantly improve fetal and neonatal oxygenation at birth.

The following conditions may demand general anesthesia:

- Severe fetal distress in a mother without a functioning continuous lumbar epidural
- Maternal refusal of an epidural or subarachnoid block
- Conditions contraindicating a major conduction block such as severe coagulopathy, septicemia, hypovolemia, gross neurologic abnormalities, etc.

Do not avoid general anesthesia out of fear of exposing the neonate to depressant drugs. With proper technique, such exposure is minimal and not associated with perinatal asphyxia. As with all general anesthetics given to the parturient, take appropriate maneuvers to prevent aspiration. Maintain left uterine displacement until delivery. Give an FiO_2 of at least 0.5 until delivery. Add 0.50 to 0.67 MAC of a potent anesthetic plus nitrous oxide. Avoid maternal hyperventilation to a $Paco_2$ below 25 mm Hg. Remember the potential for interactions between the tocolytics (particularly the beta-agonists, magnesium, and the calcium channel blockers) and the anesthetic agents and muscle relaxants.

CARE OF THE PRETERM NEWBORN

Before the birth, qualified pediatricians or neonatologists should be aware of the pending birth and be prepared for care of the newborn. Initial care focuses primarily on two aspects—prevention or treatment of asphyxia and maintenance of body temperature. Despite the risks of hyperoxia (retrolintal fibroplasia and pulmonary oxygen toxicity), do not hesitate to give a high FiO_2 (> 0.9) to treat signs of hypoxemia.[76] A pale or markedly cyanotic premature infant requires oxygen to avoid the devastating consequences of hypoxemia. If intubation is required, either continuous positive airway pressure or positive end-expiratory pressure will be necessary to maintain alveolar expansion. The premature infant has a large surface area for a small mass and rapidly loses heat, for which he or she cannot compensate. Hypothermia can lead to acidosis and increased oxygen consumption. Prevent a drop in temperature by immediately drying the neonate at birth, and placing him or her under radiant heat in an area protected from drafts.

Premature infants are prone to develop hypoglycemia and hypocalcemia, particularly those whose mothers recently received beta-agonists for tocolysis. Finally, because these neonates, especially those weighing less than 2000 g, require much monitoring and intensive care, mother and fetus, as a unit, should be transported to a tertiary center where this care is available at delivery.

SUMMARY

Premature birth still accounts for about 75% of perinatal mortality. Although great strides in the care of the premature infant over the past 2 decades have markedly decreased mortality, the incidence of premature birth unfortunately has not greatly changed. The use of tocolysis, particularly beta-agonists and magnesium sulfate, may delay birth and allow maturation. However, these drugs have many side effects that, if not recognized, can cause serious maternal morbidity and even mortality. These drugs, and other less widely used tocolytics, have important implications for the anesthetist. To assure optimal outcomes, preterm infants should be delivered in a tertiary center that is equipped and ready to attend to their needs.

Major conduction analgesia, particularly continuous lumbar epidural blockade is an ideal form of analgesia for the delivery of most premature neonates. Properly administered, this technique can accomplish the following:

- Maintains maternal physiology
- Does not produce newborn drug depression
- Provides for a controlled atraumatic vaginal delivery
- Has little interaction with tocolytics and may protect against some of their potential side effects

Epidural block is ideal for a trial of labor and, if initiated early, will allow for emergency cesarean delivery. Continuous lumbar epidural or subarachnoid block is superb for the elective or urgent cesarean section. When their use is contraindicated, however, inhalation analgesia for vaginal delivery or general anesthesia for cesarean section can be safely administered without compromise of either mother or child. Expertly administered anesthesia is not a luxury but an indispensable requirement for an optimal outcome in a premature delivery.

REFERENCES

1. US Department of Health and Human Services, Public Health Service, National Center for Health Statistics: Vital Statistics of the United States 1980. Hyattsville, MD: US Department of Health and Human Services, 1984:1.
2. Fuchs F. Prevention of prematurity. Am J Obstet Gynecol 1976;126:809.
3. Rush RW, Keirse MJNC, Howat P, Baum JD, Anderson ABM, Turnbull AC. Contribution of preterm delivery to perinatal mortality. Br Med J 1976;2:965.
4. Main DM, Main EK. Management of preterm labor and delivery. In Gabbe SG, Neibyl JR, Simpson JL, eds. Obstetrics: Normal and problem pregnancies. New York: Churchill Livingstone, 1986:689.
5. Horbar JD, Pasnick M, McAuliffe TL, Lucey JF. Obstetric events and risks of periventricular hemorrhage in premature infants. Am J Dis Child 1983;137:678.
6. Mayhew JF, Bourke DL, Guinee WS. Evaluation of the premature infant at risk for postoperative complications. Can J Anaesth 1987;34:627.
7. Russell JC, Cooper CM, Ketchum CH, et al. Multicenter evaluation of TDx test for assessing fetal lung maturity. Clin Chem 1989;35:1005.
8. Eggleston MK. Management of preterm labor and delivery. Clin Obstet Gynecol 1986;29:230.
9. King JF, Grant A, Keirse MJNC, Chalmers I. Beta-mimetics in preterm labor: an overview of the randomized controlled trials. Br J Obstet Gynaecol 1988;95:211.
10. Benedetti T. Maternal complications of parenteral beta-sympathomimetic therapy for premature labor. Am J Obstet Gynecol 1983;154:1.
11. Hosenpud JD, Morton MJ, O'Grady JP. Cardiac stimulation during ritodrine hydrochloride tocolytic therapy. Obstet Gynecol 1983;62:52.
12. Ying YK, Tejani NA. Angina pectoris as a complication of ritodrine hydrochloride therapy in premature labor. Obstet Gynecol 1982;60:385.
13. Tye KH, Desset KB, Benchimol A. Angina pectoris associated with terbutaline treatment for preterm labor. JAMA; 1980;244:692.
14. Michalak D, Klein V, Marquette G. Myocardial ischemia: A complication of ritodrine tocolysis. Am J Obstet Gynecol 1983;146:861.
15. Hendricks SK, Keroes J, Katz M. Electrocardiographic changes associated with ritodrine-induced maternal tachycardia and hypokalemia. Am J Obstet Gynecol 1986;154:921.
16. Hawker F. Pulmonary edema associated with β_2-sympathomimetic treatment of premature labor. Anesth Intensive Care 1984;12:143.
17. Jacobs MM, Knight AB, Arias F. Maternal pulmonary edema resulting from beta-mimetic and glucocorticoid therapy. Obstet Gynecol 1980;56:56.
18. Pisani J, Rosenow EC. Pulmonary edema associated with tocolytic therapy. Ann Intern Med 1989;110:714.

19. Philipsen T, Eriksen PS, Lynggard F. Pulmonary edema following ritodrine–saline infusion in premature labor. Obstet Gynecol 1981;58:304.

20. Strigl R, Pfeiffer U, Aschenbrenner G. Influence of the beta-1 selective blocker, metoprolol on the development of pulmonary edema in tocolytic therapy. Obstet Gynecol 1986;67:537.

21. Gross TL, Sokol RJ. Maternal metabolic complications following ritodrine or terbutaline therapy. Birth Defects 1982;18:191.

22. Cotton DB, Strassner HT, Lipson LG, Goldstein DA. The effect of terbutaline on acid base, serum electrolytes and glucose homeostasis during the management of preterm labor. Am J Obstet Gynecol 1981;141:617.

23. Cano A, Tovar I, Parilla JJ. Metabolic disturbances during intravenous use of ritodrine: Increased insulin levels and hypokalemia. Obstet Gynecol 1985;65:359.

24. Young DC, Toofanian A, Leveno KJ. Potassium and glucose concentration without treatment during ritodrine tocolysis. Am J Obstet Gynecol 1983;145:105.

25. Adverse reactions from treating premature labor with beta-agonist. FDA Drug Bull 1981;11:13.

26. Chestnut DH, Pollack KL, Thompson CS. Does ritodrine worsen maternal hypotension during epidural anesthesia in gravid ewes? Anesthesiology 1990;72:315.

27. Conover WB, Benumof JL, Key TL. Ritodrine inhibition of hypoxic pulmonary vasoconstriction. Am J Obstet Gynecol 1983;146:652.

28. Marx GF, Mateo CV. Effects of different oxygen concentrations during general anesthesia for elective cesarean section. Can Anesth Soc J 1971;18:587.

29. Holleboom CAG, Merkus JMWM, van Elferen LWN. Loading dose infusion scheme for intravenous tocolysis with ritodrine: a pilot study. Eur J Obstet Gynaecol Reprod Biol 1987;26:119.

30. Caritis SN, Venkataramanan R, Darby MJ, et al. Pharmacokinetics of ritodrine administered intravenously: recommendations for changes in the current regime. Am J Obstet Gynecol 1990;162:429.

31. Hollander DI, Nagey DA, Pupkin MJ. Magnesium sulfate and ritodrine hydrochloride: A randomized comparison. Am J Obstet Gynecol 1987;156:631.

32. Skaredoff MN, Roaf ER, Datta S. Hypermagnesemia and anesthetic management. Can J Anesth 1982;29:35.

33. Gambling DR, Birmingham CL, Jenkins C. Magnesium and the anesthetist. Can J Anesth 1988;35:644.

34. Elliott J. Magnesium sulfate as a tocolytic agent. Am J Obstet Gynecol 1983;147:277.

35. Chestnut DH, Thompson CS, McLaughlin GL. Does the infusion of ritodrine or magnesium sulphate alter the hemodynamic response to hemorrhage in gravid ewes? Am J Obstet Gynecol 1988;159:1467.

36. Vincent RD, Chestnut DH, Sipes SL, et al. Calcium chloride administration during hemorrhage hypotension does not increase maternal pressure or uterine blood flow in hypermagnesiemic gravid ewes [Abstract]. Boston: SOAP Meeting, 1991.

37. Giesecke AG, Morris RE, Dalton MD, Stephen CR. On magnesium, muscle relaxants, toxemic patients and cats. Anesth Analg 1980;47:689.

38. Sinatra RS, Phillip BK, Naulty JS, Ostheimer GW. Prolonged neuromuscular blockade with vecuronium in a patient treated with magnesium sulfate. Anesth Analg 1985;64:1220.

39. James MFM, Cork RC, Dennett JE. Succinylcholine pretreatment with magnesium sulphate. Anesth Analg 1986;65:373.

40. DeVore JS, Astrani R. Magnesium sulfate prevents succinylcholine-induced fasciculations in toxemic parturients. Anesthesiology 1980;52:76.

41. Pruett KM, Kirshon B, Cotton D, Adam K, Doody K. The effects of magnesium sulphate on Apgar scores. Am J Obstet Gynecol 1988;159:1047.

42. Lipsitz PJ. The clinical and biochemical effects of excess magnesium in the newborn. Pediatrics 1971;47:3.

43. Peaceman AM, Meyer BA, Thorp JA. The effect of magnesium sulphate tocolysis on the fetal biophysical profile. Am J Obstet Gynecol 1989;161:771.

44. Green KW, Key TC, Coen R. The effects of maternally administered magnesium sulphate on the neonate. Am J Obstet Gynecol 1983;146:29.

45. Dudley DKL, Hardie MJ. Fetal and neonatal effects of indomethacin used as a tocolytic agent. Am J Obstet Gynecol 1985;151:181.

46. Kocsis JJ, Hernandovich J, Silver JJ, et al. Duration of inhibition of platelet prostaglandin formation and aggregation by ingested aspirin or indomethacin. Prostaglandins 1973;3:141.

47. MacDonald R. Aspirin and extradural blocks. Br J Anaesth 1991;66:1.

48. Hindman BJ, Koka BV. Usefulness of post-aspirin bleeding time. Anesthesiology 1986;64:368.

49. Channing Rodgers RP, Levin J. A critical reappraisal of the bleeding time. Semin Thromb Hemos 1990;16:1.

50. Moise KJ, Huhta JC, Sharif DS. Indomethacin in the treatment of premature labor: Effects on the fetal ductus arteriosus. N Eng J Med 1988;319:327.

51. Hickok DE, Hollenbach KA, Reilly SF. The association between deceased amniotic fluid volume and treatment with nonsteroidal anti-inflammatory for preterm labor. Am J Obstet Gynecol 1989;160:1525.

52. Read MD, Wellby DE. The use of a calcium antagonist (nifedipine) to suppress preterm labor. Br J Obstet Gynaecol 1986;93:933.

53. Ferguson JE, Dyson DC, Holbrook RH, Schutz T, Stevenson DK. Cardiovascular and metabolic effects associated with nifedipine and ritodrine tocolysis. Am J Obstet Gynecol 1989;161:788.

54. Harake B, Gilbert RD, Ashwal S, Power GG. Nifedipine: Effects on fetal and maternal hemodynamics in pregnant sheep. Am J Obstet Gynecol 1987;157:1003.

55. Ferguson JE, Dyson DC, Schutz T, Stevenson DK. A comparison of tocolysis with nifedipine or ritodrine: analysis of efficacy and maternal, fetal and neonatal outcome. Am J Obstet Gynecol 1990;163:105.

56. Tosone S, Reves J, Kissin I, Smith L, Fournier S. Hemodynamic responses to nifedipine in dogs anesthetized with halothane. Anesth Analg 1983;62:903.

57. Merin R. Calcium channel blocking drugs and anesthetics: Is the drug interaction beneficial or detrimental? Anesthesiology 1987;66:111.

58. Eduard A, Berdeaux A, Ahmand R, Samii, K. Cardiovascular interactions of local anesthetics and calcium entry blockers in conscious dogs. Reg Anesth 1991;16:95.

59. Akerlund M, Stromberg P, Hauksson A, et al. Inhibition of uterine contractions of premature labor with an oxytocin analog. Results from a pilot study. Br J Obstet Gynaecol 1984;94:1040.

60. Waisman GD, Mayorga LM, Camera Ml. Magnesium plus nifedipine: Potentiation of the hypotensive effect in preeclampsia? Am J Obstet Gynecol 1988;159:308.

61. Thorp JM, Spielman FJ, Valea FA, et al. Nifedipine enhances the cardiac toxicity of magnesium sulphate in the isolated perfused Sprague–Dawley rat heart. Am J Obstet Gynecol 1990;163:655.

62. Snyder S, Cardwell MS. Neuromuscular blockade with magnesium sulphate and nifedipine. Am J Obstet Gynecol 1989;161:35.

63. Crenshaw C, Payne P, Blackmon L, et al. Prematurity and the obstetrician. Am J Obstet Gynecol 1983;147:125.

64. Kitchen W, Ford G, Orgill A, et al. Outcome in infants with a birth weight 500 to 999 gm: A regional study of 1979 and 1980 births. J Pediatr 1984;104:921.

65. Myers RE, Myers SE. Use of sedative, analgesic, and anesthetic drugs during labor and delivery: Bane or boon? Am J Obstet Gynecol 1979;133:83.

66. Scanlon JW, Brown WU, Weiss JB, et al. Neurobehavioral responses of newborn infants after maternal epidural anesthesia. Anesthesiology 1974;40:121.

67. Biehl D. Placental transfer of lidocaine: Effects of fetal acidosis. Anesthesiology 1978;48:409.

68. Abboud TK, Williams V, Miller F, et al. Comparative fetal, maternal, and neonatal responses following epidural analgesia with bupivacaine, chloroprocaine and lidocaine. Anesthesiology 1981;55:A315.

69. Abboud TK, Khoo SS, Miller F, et al. Maternal, fetal, and neonatal responses after epidural anesthesia with bupivacaine, 2-chloroprocaine or lidocaine. Anesth Analg 1982;61:638.

70. Datta S, Corke BC, Alper MH, et al. Epidural anesthesia for cesarean section: A comparison of bupivacaine, chloroprocaine and etidocaine. Anesthesiology 1980;52:48.

71. Kileff M, James FM, Dewan D, et al. Neonatal neurobehavioral responses after epidural anesthesia for cesarean section with lidocaine and bupivacaine. Anesthesiology 1982;57:A403.

72. Merkow AJ, McGuinness GA, Erenberg A, et al. The neonatal neurobehavioral effects of bupivacaine, mepivacaine, and 2-chloroprocaine used for pudendal block. Anesthesiology 1980;52:309.

73. Kuhnert BR, Harrison MJ, Linn PL, Kuhnert PM. Effects of maternal epidural anesthesia on neonatal behavior. Anesth Analg 1984;63:301.

74. Kuhnert BR, Kennard MJ, Linn PL. Neonatal neurobehavior after epidural anesthesia for cesarean section. Anesth Analg 1988;67:64.

75. Morishima HO, Pedersen H, Santos AC, et al. Adverse effects of maternally administered lidocaine on the asphyxiated preterm fetal lamb. Anesthesiology 1989;71:110.

76. Merritt JC, Kraybill EN. Retrolental fibroplasia: A five-year experience in a tertiary perinatal center. Ann Ophthalmol 1988;65:67.

CHAPTER 35

Fetal Malpresentation and Multiple Birth

Barbara L. Hartwell

BREECH PRESENTATION

Definitions and Incidence

Breech presentation is the entrance of the fetal lower extremities or pelvis into the maternal pelvic inlet. There are three types of breech presentation (Fig. 35-1), which follow:

- Frank breech, with the hips flexed and knees extended
- Complete breech, with hips flexed and knees flexed
- Incomplete or footling breech, with one or both hips not flexed and one or both feet below the buttocks

Breech presentation complicates 3% of deliveries. Before 28 weeks' gestation, 25% of fetuses are breech. To fit to the shape of the uterine cavity, most fetuses convert to cephalic presentation as gestational age and fetal size increase. Of singleton breech infants weighing less than 2500 g, 38% are frank breech, 12% are complete breech, and 50% are footling breech. The distribution is different in breech infants over 2500 g: 51% to 73% are frank breech, 4.6% to 11.5% are complete breech, and 20% to 24% are footling breech (Fig. 35-2).[1]

Fetal Risks

The most common cause of breech presentation is prematurity. Approximately 30% of breech infants weigh less than 2500 g at birth.[2,3] Often, the infant has not yet turned to the cephalic position. This event usually occurs by 34 weeks' gestation. Other causes of breech presentation include uterine anomalies, fetal anomalies, hydramnios, multiple gestation, placenta previa, contracted maternal pelvis, and tumors obstructing the birth canal (Table 35-1).[1]

Historically, the increased risks to the breech infant are well-documented. In 1956, Hall and Kohl[2] reviewed 1011 term breech deliveries and reported a perinatal mortality five times greater than that of term cephalic presentations.[2] Morgan and Kane,[3] in 1964, reviewed 16,327 breech births and found a perinatal death rate 5.5 times that of the total rate for the 463,847 deliveries studied. Of infants weighing over 2500 g, the perinatal mortality rate was still 3.5 times that of the entire group.[3] Prematurity is not the sole reason for this risk.

Other factors that increase morbidity and mortality of breech presentation are congenital anomalies, birth asphyxia, and birth trauma. Six percent of breech infants have congenital anomalies, an incidence that is

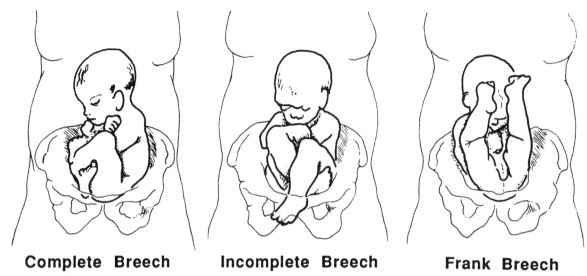

Complete Breech   **Incomplete Breech**   **Frank Breech**

Figure 35–1. Three types of breech presentation. (After Gabbe SG, Niebyl JR, Simpson JL, eds. Obstetrics: Normal and problem pregnancies. 2nd ed. New York: Churchill Livingstone 1991)

two to three times that occurring in cephalic presentation.[4] These anomalies include chromosomal, skeletal, and neuromuscular diseases. These problems may cause breech presentation by physically preventing the fetus from attaining the normal cephalic presentation.[5]

Birth asphyxia can occur secondary to umbilical cord prolapse, arrest of the after-coming head, or umbilical cord compression.[1] Umbilical cord prolapse occurs in approximately 0.5% of cephalic presentations and in 4% to 7% of breech presentations.[2,4,6] With a frank breech, the risk of cord prolapse approaches that of the cephalic presentation. The presenting part fills

the maternal pelvic inlet and does not readily allow cord prolapse. By contrast, umbilical cord prolapse complicates 4% to 5% of complete breech and 10% of footling breech presentations.[6]

Arrest of the after-coming head may occur when the body of a premature breech infant passes through the cervix before full dilation. Other causes of arrest of the after-coming head include small maternal pelvis and hyperextension of the fetal head.[1] Prolonged umbilical cord compression occurs when the fetal head or shoulders exert pressure on the umbilical cord during delivery.

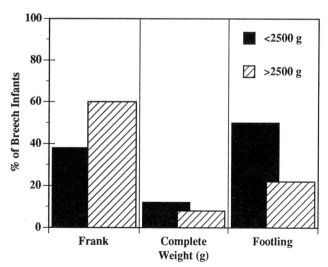

Figure 35–2. The position of singleton breech fetuses changes as their weight increases. The incidence of footling breech presentation falls, whereas that of frank breech presentation rises.

Table 35-1

Known Factors Associated with Breech Presentation and Potential Reasons for Failure to Assume the Vertex Presentation

FACTORS	POTENTIAL REASONS
Uterine and Placental	
Bicornuate to double uterus	Aberrant shape of pregnant uterine cavity
Placenta previa or placenta in cornua of uterus	Aberrant shape of pregnant uterine cavity
Fetal	
Twins	Aberrant crowding
Prematurity	Less uterine constraint to fetal positioning
Low birth weight	Less uterine constraint to fetal positioning
Polyhydramnios	Less uterine constraint to fetal positioning
Oligohydramnios	Undue uterine constraint to fetal movement
Abnormalities in form or function of the fetus	Limitation in the capacity of the fetus to assume the vertex position

Birth trauma can occur during breech extraction, most commonly in emergency situations when the fetus is also at risk of birth anoxia. The types of trauma include tentorial tears, intracranial hemorrhages, cephalhematoma, damage to the spinal cord, nerve trauma, bony fractures, and injury to intraabdominal organs.[1]

Maternal Risks

The breech presentation also places the mother at increased risk. Postpartum infection may occur after cervical or birth canal trauma from manipulation or operative intervention. Because of the need for uterine relaxation for manipulative procedures, the risk of uterine atony and postpartum hemorrhage is also higher.[7]

The high rate of cesarean delivery for breech presentation subjects the parturient to the inherent risks associated with operative delivery. In 1980, a prospective study of breech deliveries by Collea *et al*[8] found a 49.3% incidence of maternal morbidity in women delivered by cesarean section, compared to 6.7% morbidity in women delivered vaginally. Infection and hemorrhage were the most common complications.

Obstetric Management

Because of the complexity of perinatal and maternal risks associated with breech presentation, the percentage of breech infants delivered by cesarean section over the past 35 years has increased dramatically. Hall and Kohl[2] reported a 10.7% cesarean section rate for breech presentation in 1956. By contrast, Parkland Memorial Hospital reports a 75% cesarean section rate in recent years.[9] At the Brigham and Women's Hospital, with more than 10,000 deliveries between 1989 and 1990, only 32 singleton breech infants delivered vaginally. These infants were all very premature, nonviable, or unrecognized as breech.

There are three methods of breech delivery: spontaneous, assisted or partial breech extraction, and total breech extraction.[10] In a spontaneous breech delivery, the entire infant delivers without any traction or manipulation. In a partial breech extraction, the infant delivers spontaneously to the umbilicus and the obstetrician extracts the remainder of the body. The entire body of the infant is extracted in a total breech extraction. Forceps may deliver the head in both partial and total breech extractions. Because of the risks of birth anoxia and trauma, few breech infants are delivered vaginally. Term frank breech infants weighing between 2500 and 3800 g, with the fetal head in the flexed position, may deliver vaginally with little increased risk.[1,8] The remainder of breech fetuses (and, in many institutions, almost all viable breech fetuses) are delivered by cesarean section.

Anesthetic Management

The goals of providing anesthesia for vaginal breech delivery are as follows:

- Adequate pain relief
- Prevention of a premature bearing-down reflex
- Maternal cooperation in a slow, controlled delivery over a relaxed perineum
- The ability to relax the uterus rapidly if needed

Ideally, these goals can be accomplished without risk to the fetus and with optimal neonatal outcome.

When a parturient with a breech fetus is admitted to labor and delivery, the obstetrician must discuss the obstetric plan with the anesthesiologist. The anesthesiologist should then interview the patient and discuss the options and goals of providing anesthesia for delivery. Because of the potential emergencies that may follow, the anesthesiologist must remain immediately available. The patient should have adequate venous access and restricted oral intake.

Labor Analgesia and Vaginal Delivery

Anesthetic technique for vaginal breech delivery has been controversial over the last 20 years (Table 35-2). For many years, both obstetricians and anesthesiologists believed that epidural analgesia was inappropriate for breech delivery. In 1971 Crawford[11] discouraged the use of epidural analgesia for breech deliveries because of a direct correlation with increased perinatal morality. He attributed this problem to the need for breech extraction because of diminished maternal expulsive efforts. Crawford then hinted that low concentrations of local anesthetics might serve to provide analgesia without abolishing maternal expulsive efforts. In fact, 3 years later, in 1974, Crawford presented a review of 247 singleton breech deliveries, of which 162 had vaginal deliveries, 56 with epidural analgesia.[12] After analysis of Apgar scores and postnatal course, he concluded that the incidence of neonatal depression was less with epidural analgesia. Despite a prolonged second stage of labor (44 vs 34 min), there were no more extractions in the epidural group.

Bowen-Simpkins and Fergusson[13] conducted a similar retrospective study in 1974. They evaluated 133 breech deliveries, including 72 with epidural analgesia. They reported an increased duration of the second stage of labor but no adverse effects on the fetus as assessed by Apgar scores, and no increased incidence of manipulative delivery. Donnai and Nichols,[14] in another retrospective study, added umbilical vein pH analysis to neonatal assessment. These authors deemed epidural analgesia "beneficial." By allowing maternal cooperation, it lowered the incidence of breech extraction. It also allowed rapid and safe extraction when necessary.

In 1976, Darby *et al*[15] reviewed 226 singleton breech deliveries. One hundred and one of the 180 patients undergoing vaginal delivery had epidural analgesia; 79 received parenteral analgesia. Although both first and second stages were longer in the epidural group, the incidence of breech extraction or emergency cesarean section did not increase. Also, the 5-minute Apgar scores were higher in the epidural group.

In 1978, Breeson *et al*[16] published one of the few prospective studies of epidural analgesia for vaginal breech delivery. Fifty-one parturients received epidural analgesia early in the first stage of labor. They compared these women to a "control group" from a previous study. Based on fetal blood sampling during the second stage of labor and Apgar scores, the fetal condition was better in the epidural group. Compared to their previous study, the duration of labor remained unchanged and the frequency of breech extraction declined. Despite its limitations, this study clearly showed a lack of adverse maternal or fetal effects of epidural analgesia.

Confino *et al*,[17] in 1985, reviewed 4 years of vaginal breech deliveries with and without epidural analgesia. In this somewhat large series (94 patients with epidural blockade, 277 without), the duration of the first stage of labor did not increase. Epidural analgesia did correlate with a longer second stage of labor if the baby weighed more than 2500 g. The 1-minute Apgar scores were lower in the epidural group, but the 5-minute scores were similar in both groups. There was no difference in perinatal morbidity. The authors suggested that lower concentrations of local anesthetic in the second stage might increase maternal cooperation and shorten the second stage, possibly improving the 1-minute Apgar scores. Van Zundert *et al*[18] recently reviewed 10 years of vaginal breech deliveries under epidural analgesia using 0.125% bupivacaine plus epinephrine, 1:800,000, by intermittent injection. They gave additional doses of drug if needed to abolish the bearing-down reflex. Their study included examination of duration of second stage of labor, "expulsion time" (the time from the first expulsion effort to delivery), Apgar scores, and resuscitation efforts. The average times of the second stage of labor and expulsion were 31 and 8.7 minutes, respectively. Instrumental assistance was employed in 6% of the vaginal breech deliveries, 80% of which were done by one obstetrician. Seventy-six percent of the infants had 1-minute Apgar scores of 7 or greater, and 96% had 5-minute Apgar scores of 7 or greater. The authors concluded that "epidural analgesia with good perineal analgesia is particularly indicated in vaginal breech deliveries."

Table 35–2

Epidural Analgesia for Vaginal Breech Deliveries

AUTHORS	STUDY DESIGN	EFFECTS ON LABOR AND DELIVERY	EFFECTS ON NEONATAL OUTCOME	METHOD(S) OF NEONATAL EVALUATION
Crawford[12] (1974)	Retrospective: epidural vs no epidural	Prolonged second stage; no increase in breech extractions	Decreased neonatal depression	Apgar scores, "postnatal course"
Bowen-Simpkins and Fergusson[13] (1974)	Retrospective: epidural vs "other forms of analgesia"	Prolonged second stage; no increase in manipulative delivery	No adverse effects	Apgar scores
Donnai and Nichols[14] (1975)	Retrospective: no control	Low incidence of breech extraction	87% 1-min Apgar scores ≥ 6	Umbilical vein pH, Apgar scores
Darby et al[15] (1976)	Retrospective: epidural vs parenteral	Prolonged first and second stage; no increase in breech extractions or emergency cesarean section	Higher 5-min Apgar scores	Apgar scores
Breeson et al[16] (1978)	Prospective: epidural vs historical control group	No increase in duration of labor; decrease in breech extraction	Improved fetal condition	Fetal blood sampling, Apgar scores
Confino et al[17] (1985)	Retrospective: epidural vs no epidural	Prolonged second stage if birth weight > 2500 g	Lower 1-min Apgar scores but similar 5-min Apgar scores; no change in perinatal morbidity	Apgar scores
Van Zundert et al[18] (1991)	Retrospective: vaginal breech vs vaginal vertex and cesarean breech, all with epidural	Mean duration second stage: 31 min; mean "expulsion time": 9 min; 6% instrumental deliveries	Lower 1-min Apgar scores vs vertex or cesarean section; similar 5-min Apgar scores	Apgar scores

Over the last 20 years, epidural analgesia has become the anesthetic of choice for vaginal breech delivery (see Table 35-2). Advantages include the following:

- The ability to conduct comfortable, accurate vaginal examinations
- Abolition of pain and of the bearing-down reflex
- Maternal cooperation

- The ability to do breech extraction if necessary
- The avoidance of general anesthesia
- Safe delivery of the fetus without increased perinatal morbidity, and perhaps even improved neonatal outcome

A low concentration of local anesthetic such as 0.25% bupivacaine dosed intermittently or 0.125% bupivacaine as a continuous infusion will provide analgesia and obtund the bearing-down reflex. Sometimes, perineal analgesia is desired early to prevent premature pushing. If perineal analgesia is inadequate, a dose of 0.25% bupivacaine will improve perineal analgesia without significant motor block. If breech extraction becomes necessary, 2% lidocaine or 3% 2-chloroprocaine through the epidural catheter will provide anesthesia rapidly. All parturients should receive supplemental oxygen by mask during vaginal breech delivery.

Spinal anesthesia may find occasional use for breech delivery if rapid anesthesia is desired. Possible settings include the precipitous delivery or a breech extraction in a patient who does not have an epidural catheter in place. In this situation, 1.5% lidocaine in 7.5% dextrose provides anesthesia with less motor block than 5% lidocaine or 0.75% bupivacaine.[19]

If the obstetrician suddenly needs uterine relaxation to deliver the after-coming head, general anesthesia is often employed. After preoxygenation, induce anesthesia with thiopental, 4 mg/kg, and succinylcholine, 1.5 mg/kg, followed by endotracheal intubation with cricoid pressure. Maintain anesthesia with 50% nitrous oxide in oxygen with anesthetic concentrations of halothane, enflurane, or isoflurane. All three volatile agents will relax the uterus in equipotent doses.[20,21] Stop the inhalation agent after delivery to avoid uterine atony and hemorrhage.

Amyl nitrate, crushed in the reservoir bag, also can provide uterine relaxation,[22] but it is unpleasant to breathe and not readily available in many delivery units. Intravenous nitroglycerin, in 50- to 100-µg doses, relaxes the uterus for extraction of retained placenta without serious adverse effects.[23,24] Nitroglycerin also effectively provides uterine relaxation during breech extraction.[25]

Anesthesia for Cesarean Delivery

Cesarean delivery may be done under epidural, spinal, or general anesthesia. Emergency delivery for cord prolapse or fetal distress requires general anesthesia unless an epidural catheter is already in place. Epidural injection of 3% 2-chloroprocaine will rapidly provide good operating conditions.[26] In emergency cesarean deliveries, Darby *et al*[15] noted that 1-minute Apgar scores were lower with epidural compared to general anesthesia. The two groups of infants had similar 5-minute Apgar scores. If the patient does not have an epidural catheter, administer general anesthesia as for any emergency cesarean section.[27]

If time permits, spinal anesthesia may be used for the "urgent" cesarean delivery. Hyperbaric 0.75% bupivacaine or 5% lidocaine provides excellent surgical anesthesia. Rapid intravenous hydration with Ringer's lactate (1500–2000 mL) and prompt treatment of hypotension ephedrine in 10-mg doses will prevent the untoward effects of hypotension in mother and fetus.

For elective cesarean delivery, regional anesthesia is the technique of choice. Crawford and Davies,[28] in 1982, studied neonates delivered by elective cesarean section. They compared vertex versus breech presentation and epidural versus general anesthesia. By evaluating umbilical vein and artery blood gases and Apgar scores, they concluded that a prolonged uterine incision–delivery (U–D) interval under general anesthesia related to poor neonatal condition at delivery. Yet, a prolonged U–D interval with epidural anesthesia did not correlate with poor neonatal condition. Crawford and Davies concluded that, particularly for breech infants, the clinical condition of the infant was better under epidural than general anesthesia. Thus, there appears to be a clear advantage to both mother and fetus in avoiding general anesthesia.

The premature breech fetus warrants special consideration. Even during cesarean delivery, the after-coming head may become trapped, causing fetal asphyxia. The asphyxiated premature fetus is particularly sensitive to maternal depressants, making regional anesthesia even more desirable.[29] Head entrapment during cesarean delivery under regional technique requires the same maneuvers described under vaginal delivery to relax the uterus emergently. Remember that the patient in preterm labor may have received tocolytic therapy that may predispose her to pulmonary edema with aggressive hydration. She also may develop severe hypotension secondary to the tachycardia caused by beta-mimetic tocolytic agents.[30] For any breech delivery, a qualified team (anesthesiologist or pediatrician and support personnel) and equipment must be present for neonatal evaluation and resuscitation.

FETAL MALPRESENTATION

Fetal malpresentation other than breech includes abnormal cephalic presentations such as face and brow. Other malpresentations include shoulder presentation and compound presentation.

Face Presentation

Face presentation occurs when the fetal head hyperextends and the mentum presents. Approximately 1 in 600 to 1 in 1200 singleton infants present in this manner.[9] Face presentation is associated with multiparity, anencephaly, pelvic contraction, and very large fetuses.[31] Successful vaginal delivery usually follows unless the pelvis is contracted or the fetus is very large; in these instances, delivery is by cesarean section. Epidural anesthesia is appropriate for vaginal delivery with low concentrations of local anesthetic to maximize maternal expulsive efforts.

Brow Presentation

Brow presentation is very rare, occurring in 1 in 1000 to 1 in 4470 deliveries.[9,31] The area between the orbital ridge and the anterior fontanel presents. Pelvic contraction and large infants correlate with brow presentation. About 65% to 70% of these fetuses convert to face or vertex presentations; the remainder persist as brow presentations, and cesarean delivery is recommended.[31] There are no specific anesthetic considerations, and regional or general anesthesia may be employed as appropriate.

Shoulder Presentation

The shoulder presents in approximately 1 in 322 to 1 in 420 singleton deliveries.[9,31] Etiologic factors include multiparity, prematurity, cephalopelvic disproportion, and placenta previa.[31] Cesarean delivery is necessary to avoid uterine rupture. Shoulder presentation slightly increases maternal mortality. Placenta previa, increased incidence of cord prolapse, surgical intervention, and potential sepsis after rupture of the membranes if the fetal arm appears through the vagina all increase maternal risk.[9] Anesthetic considerations include those associated with prematurity, placenta previa, and the possible need for emergency anesthesia for a cord accident. For a neglected shoulder presentation, treat sepsis, hemorrhage, and uterine rupture with supportive and resuscitative measures.

Compound Presentation

Compound presentation refers to the presentation of an extremity with the presenting part and occurs in 1 in 1192 to 1 in 2235 deliveries.[9,20] The most common of these is the vertex/arm presentation. Other types include vertex/arm and foot, vertex/foot, and breech/hand presentations. Prematurity is the most common etiologic factor, but often the cause is unknown. Cord prolapse can occur in up to 12.5% of compound presentations.[31] Prematurity and cord prolapse increased perinatal morbidity. Without cord prolapse, the patient may labor, and often the extremity will rise out of the way.[32] Anesthetic considerations are those associated with prematurity and with cord prolapse.

MULTIPLE GESTATION

Incidence and Presentation

Twin gestation occurs in approximately 1 in 90 pregnancies. However, the use of ultrasound early in pregnancy has identified a much higher incidence of twin conceptions, many of which eventually end in singleton births owing to early (previously unrecognized) fetal loss. The incidence of triplets is about 1 in 9800; the incidence of quadruplets is 1 in 70,000. Perinatal morbidity increases markedly when three or more fetuses are present. Current practice, after in vitro fertilization produces a multiple gestation, includes pregnancy reduction, usually to twins.[33,34]

Twins most often present as vertex/vertex (40%). Other presentations include vertex/breech (26%), breech/vertex (10%), breech/breech (10%), and vertex/transverse (8%). The presentation of the fetuses is an important consideration in the obstetric and anesthetic management of the parturient.

Fetal Risks

Both maternal and fetal risks increase with multiple gestation (Table 35–3). Risks to the fetus are often due to the associated prematurity or growth retardation. Forty percent of twin gestations deliver before 37 weeks,[35] and length of gestation progressively shortens with increasing numbers of fetuses. Besides the shorter length of gestation, the rate of growth is also slower in multiple gestations. After about 28 weeks of gestation, growth rate steadily declines. This depression is greater as the number of fetuses increases.[36]

The high incidence of malpresentation, with its associated risks of birth trauma and asphyxia, warrant the same considerations discussed in the first part of this chapter. Congenital abnormalities are approximately twice as common in twins as in singleton pregnancies.[37] The risk of prolapsed umbilical cord is increased, especially for the second twin.

Monozygotic twins result from the division of one fertilized ovum, whereas dizygotic twins result from two fertilized ova (Fig. 35-3). The number of days after fertilization that division occurs determines the number of chorions and amnions that will develop (Table

Table 35-3

Perinatal Problems Associated with Multiple Gestation

Maternal

Physiologic Considerations
   Anemia
   Increased cardiac stress
   Aspiration
   Supine hypotension
   Respiratory difficulty
   Increased lumbar lordosis, back edema
Obstetric Risks
   Preeclampsia
   Gestational hypertension
   Uterine atony, hemorrhage
   Abruption
   Placenta previa
   Preterm labor
   Premature rupture of membranes
   Polyhydramnios

Fetal

Prematurity

Intrauterine growth retardation

Malpresentation

Birth trauma

Asphyxia

Congenital malformation

Prolapsed umbilical cord

Twin transfusion syndrome

35-4). Cord abnormalities and placental vascular anastomoses are more likely to occur with monozygotic twins. Monoamniotic twins have a high mortality rate owing to intertwining umbilical cords.[38]

The second twin warrants special consideration. The second twin may face twice the mortality risk faced by the first twin.[37,39,40] The birth weight of the second twin may be an important factor affecting survival. Increased mortality occurs only when the second twin weighs less than 2000 g.[27] Modern obstetric practices and better intrapartum monitoring have led to improved survival of the second twin, but there are specific problems that do result in increased morbidity. The second twin suffers increased likelihood of abnormal presentation, with its inherent risks. After delivery of the first twin, partial separation of the placenta, contraction of the placental site, or reduced placental circulation may cause hypoxia in the second twin.[41]

As the number of fetuses in a pregnancy increases, the risks to the fetus increase. Although twin neonatal mortality rate is 6 times the singleton rate, the rate for triplets is 20 times that of singletons.[42] As previously mentioned, duration of gestation decreases with increasing number of fetuses, and intrauterine growth retardation becomes more severe. At delivery, each successive fetus has a less efficient placental circulation.

Maternal Risks

When carrying multiple fetuses, the mother faces both physiologic and obstetric risks (see Table 35-3). Many physiologic alterations that occur during single gestation are more dramatic in multiple gestation. Plasma volume increases to 67% above normal in twin pregnancies compared to a 48% rise in singleton pregnancies; with triplets, the values are even higher.[43] Anemia results from greater increases in plasma volume than in red blood cell volume and with increased blood loss at delivery.

Robson *et al*[44] studied hemodynamic parameters in twin pregnancies using Doppler and M-mode echocardiography every 4 weeks from 20 to 36 weeks' gestation. They found that in twin pregnancy, heart rate and, consequently, cardiac output were significantly higher than in singleton pregnancy. Cardiac output was 60% higher than that of nonpregnant women and 15% higher than that of single-gestation subjects. Other studies have found increased stroke volume in twin pregnancy.[45] Clearly, multiple gestation presents greater cardiac stress than single gestation.

Mechanical effects of the greatly enlarged uterus make the parturient with multiple gestation especially susceptible to supine hypotension syndrome. Gastric emptying slows, the cardioesophageal angle changes, and the risk of aspiration of gastric contents increases. Respiratory changes include elevation of the diaphragm, decreased functional residual capacity, and increased closing volume.[46] With multiple gestation, the lumbar lordosis can be exaggerated, and back edema due to bed rest can make regional anesthesia more difficult.

Multiple gestation also increases the incidence of obstetric complications (see Table 35-3). Pregnancy-induced hypertension may complicate up to 20% of twin or greater gestations.[35] Uterine atony from overdistention and subsequent hemorrhage can occur, and the average blood loss at delivery is twice that of singleton deliveries. Other causes of hemorrhage include a possible increased incidence of placenta previa and abruption.[47] Preterm labor is common, and the use of beta-adrenergic therapy for tocolysis places the mother at risk for relative fluid overload and pulmonary edema. Polyhydramnios arises in 6% to 12 % of multiple gestations and can cause placental abruption, uterine dysfunction, and postpartum hemorrhage.[48]

Obstetric Management

Obstetric management of multifetal pregnancies focuses on the following:

- Prevention of preterm labor, which may include bed rest and tocolysis

- Aggressive antepartum monitoring with nonstress tests
- Ultrasound determinations of the presentation of the fetuses

Twins presenting as vertex/vertex are usually delivered vaginally. If the first twin is breech, cesarean delivery is usually chosen. Management varies when the presenting twin is vertex and the second twin is nonvertex; external version of the second twin may be

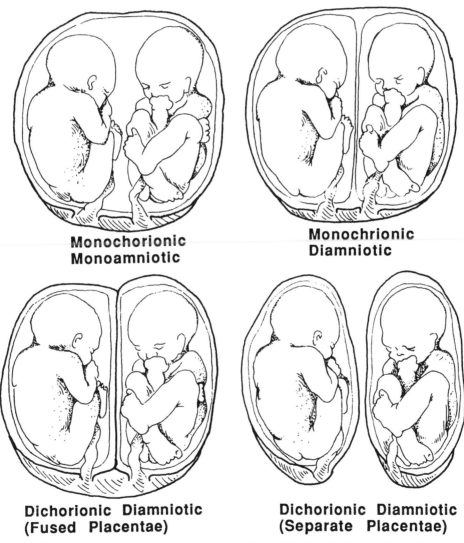

Monochorionic Monoamniotic

Monochrionic Diamniotic

Dichorionic Diamniotic (Fused Placentae)

Dichorionic Diamniotic (Separate Placentae)

Figure 35–3. Placentation in twin pregnancies. (After Gabbe SG, Niebyl JR, Simpson JL, eds. Obstetrics: Normal and problem pregnancies. 2nd ed. New York: Churchill Livingstone, 1991)

Table 35-4

Monozygotic Twinning

TIME OF DIVISION	COMMENTS
Diamnionic, dichorionic 1–3 d	Two distinct placentas or single fused placenta
Diamnionic, monochorionic 4–8 d	Cord anomalies, placental vascular anastomoses
Monoamnionic, monochorionic 9–12 d	High mortality due to cord intertwining
Conjoined twins >13 d	

attempted. If internal version is necessary, it must be carried out swiftly by a skilled obstetrician while the uterus is flaccid after delivery of the first infant. Otherwise, once contractions have resumed, general anesthesia will be necessary to relax the uterus. Often in this setting cesarean delivery is a safer choice than internal podalic version. Triplets and higher pluralities are delivered by cesarean section unless the fetuses are extremely immature or there are extraordinary maternal complications that make cesarean delivery very hazardous to the mother.[38] Table 35-5 summarizes the factors favoring cesarean delivery with multiple gestation.

Anesthetic Management

The anesthetic management of multiple gestation requires close communication with the obstetrician regarding the obstetric plan. The anesthesiologist must consider the causes of increased maternal and fetal risk and plan accordingly. Whatever the anticipated mode of delivery, the usual preparations are important. Consult with the patient soon after her admission to the labor suite. Insert a large-bore intravenous catheter and prohibit further food intake.

Labor Analgesia and Vaginal Delivery

Many investigators have looked at the safety and advantages of epidural analgesia for labor and delivery of twins. As early as 1954, Aaron *et al*[49] reported a lower fetal mortality rate with conduction anesthesia (Fig.

35-4). Early studies by Crawford[50] showed an increased interval between full cervical dilatation and delivery of the first twin but a shorter interval between delivery of the first and second twin under epidural analgesia. Apgar scores were lower in the second twin at 1 minute, but no other differences arose. Gullestad and Sagen[51] compared epidural versus "conventional analgesics" in a randomized study of twin mothers. They found an increase in the duration of labor by 2 hours and an increased incidence of operative deliveries in the epidural group, but there were no differences between groups in Apgar scores or acid–base values. Eleven of the 24 mothers in the control group required general anesthesia for operative delivery. There were also no differences in the clinical condition of the first and second twin in the epidural group. James *et al*[52] compared the outcome of 14 twin deliveries with epidural analgesia to singleton deliveries with epidural analgesia to singleton deliveries with epidural analgesia. The first twin fared as well as singleton newborns as determined by Apgar scores and umbilical blood gas tensions and acid–base values. Second twins showed a small degree of compromise that was worse when the presentation of the fetus was nonvertex. A study by Weekes *et al*[53] compared 52 twin pregnancies with epidural blockade for labor to 92 twin pregnancies with parenteral analgesia for labor. They found similar duration of labor, mode of delivery, and Apgar scores. A recent prospective study by Crawford[54] of 200 twin deliveries suggested that the second twin's condition as determined by acid–base status was better under epidural analgesia. One can conclude from these studies that epidural analgesia for labor does not harm and may even benefit the neonate in twin gestation.

Epidural analgesia for twin deliveries offers many advantages. Some include the following:

Table 35-5

Factors Favoring Cesarean Delivery with Multiple Gestation

Malpresentation of twin A
Discordancy, with twin B larger than twin A
Intrauterine death of one fetus
Twin–twin transfusion
Congenital deformities
Decreased uteroplacental reserve (positive oxytocin challenge test or nonreactive nonstress test)
Fetal cardiac decelerations of either twin
Prematurity
Three or more fetuses

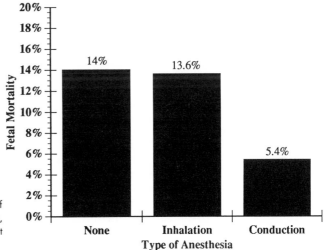

Figure 35–4. Conduction anesthesia lowers the risk of fetal mortality in twin deliveries. (Data from Aaron JB, Halperin J. Fetal survival in 376 twin deliveries. Am J Obstet Gynecol 1955;69:794)

- Elimination of the need for parenteral narcotics and sedatives (especially desirable in premature infants)
- Pain relief, which may allow the mother to avoid unnecessary muscle activity and may diminish the work of the cardiovascular system[52]
- Prevention of the bearing-down reflex, therefore allowing a controlled delivery
- The ability to do an operative delivery if needed
- The ability to operate emergently to deliver the second twin without inducing general anesthesia

Specifically, I suggest using a local anesthetic that will provide analgesia with little motor block. Bupivacaine, 0.25%, administered intermittently or continuous infusion of bupivacaine, 0.125%, with 2 μg/mL of fentanyl are satisfactory choices. The parturient should labor on her side to avoid aortocaval compression. Monitor blood pressure very closely. Treat hypotension immediately with oxygen, fluids, and intravenous ephedrine in 10-mg doses.

Because of the uncertainties and potential problems that can arise, twin deliveries should take place in an operative delivery room. Give the mother oxygen by face mask. Have blood pressure, electrocardiogram, and pulse oximeter monitors in place. Careful titration of a more concentrated local anesthetic at the time of delivery will provide perineal anesthesia without abolishing effective pushing. Give larger doses to raise the level of anesthesia if emergency cesarean section becomes necessary for the second twin. There may be an interval of time after delivery of the first twin in which the uterus is flaccid enough to allow intrauterine manipulation of the second twin. Once contractions resume, if uterine relaxation is needed, general anesthesia, or perhaps intravenous nitroglycerine, becomes necessary.

"Single-shot" spinal anesthesia is rarely used for vaginal twin delivery and should be reserved for urgent situations in which epidural anesthesia is not practical.[7] Use a long-acting local anesthetic because of the possible delay between delivery of the twins. A dose of drug adequate for cesarean section will abolish maternal expulsive efforts. Sensory blockade to T-10 will impair expulsive efforts to a lesser degree but will not provide complete comfort for intrauterine fetal manipulation nor for cesarean section. The use of a catheter for continuous spinal anesthesia will allow for repeated doses as needed and for titration to the appropriate level of block. General anesthesia is the least desirable anesthetic. Its depressant effects may be especially marked in the second twin.

Anesthesia for the Elective Cesarean Delivery of Twins

There are no prospective studies comparing anesthetic techniques for cesarean twin delivery. Regardless of the technique employed, insert a large-bore intravenous catheter and give a nonparticulate antacid. Be careful to minimize aortocaval compression. Aggressively treat hypotension with ephedrine in 10-mg doses and fluids. Most anesthesiologists prefer regional anesthesia for cesarean twin delivery. This approach minimizes the risk of anesthetic depression of the preterm or second twin. The exaggerated physiologic changes of pregnancy place the mother at increased risk for aspiration and hypoxemia during induction of general anesthesia.

Infuse 20 to 30 mL/kg of crystalloid solution before inducing epidural or spinal anesthesia. Identifying the epidural or subarachnoid space may prove especially difficult in these women. They have an increased lumbar lordosis. They cannot assume a good position because of the obstruction presented by their greatly enlarged uterus. Edema caused by bed rest prescribed for preterm labor may further complicate identification of anatomic landmarks.

Lumbar epidural anesthesia offers a slower onset of action, which may allow better hemodynamic stability and control of the upper level of sensory blockade. Careful titration of 2% lidocaine with epinephrine 1:200,000 or 0.5% bupivacaine will accomplish these goals. Smaller-than-usual doses of local anesthetic may be needed owing to exaggerated spread in these women.[42] Give oxygen by face mask during placement of the epidural catheter and at least until delivery of the infants.

Spinal anesthesia may be used for cesarean twin delivery. Some avoid this technique because of the unpredictability of the cephalad spread anesthesia and the high incidence of hypotension. Still, at our institution, we frequently administer spinal anesthesia for cesarean twin delivery. With adequate hydration, good left uterine displacement, and aggressive use of ephedrine, hypotension is minimized.

General endotracheal anesthesia is carried out in the standard fashion. Pay particular attention to adequate preoxygenation and rapid sequence induction with cricoid pressure. Turn off the volatile anesthetic immediately following the last delivery because of the increased risk of uterine atony in these patients.

Whatever the type of anesthesia, infuse intravenous oxytocin, 20 units/L of crystalloid, following delivery. Pay close attention to the condition of the uterus. Uterine atony may require the use of additional oxytocin, methylergonovine, and occasionally 15-methyl prostaglandin $F_{2\alpha}$. Increased fluid administration or blood transfusion may be necessary. Two pediatric teams should be present at the delivery, one to take care of each infant.

Special Anesthetic Considerations for Cesarean Delivery of Triplets and Higher Plurality

In the presence of three or more fetuses, do a thorough preoperative assessment of the parturient. Give particular attention to the gestational age of the fetuses and the use of tocolytics. Look for preeclampsia, back edema, exaggerated lumbar lordosis, supine hypoten-

sion, and a significant degree of dyspnea. Insert large-bore intravenous catheters. Have fluid warmers and blood immediately available. Separate neonatal teams are needed for each infant.

If possible, avoid general and spinal anesthesia. With multiple fetuses, each successive fetus receives more general anesthetic.[55,56] Because of the tremendously enlarged uterus, spinal anesthesia can prove dangerously unpredictable. Therefore, I recommend using a carefully titrated epidural anesthetic. Pay careful attention to avoiding aortocaval compression. Treat hypotension promptly. Bear in mind the high likelihood of uterine atony and hemorrhage. Start oxytocin infusion immediately after delivery of the last infant.

The mother of multiple infants is likely to be especially apprehensive and possibly depressed as well. The prospect of caring for so many infants who are often premature, the time spent at bed rest, and the discomfort of the pregnancy all contribute to these feelings. The anesthesiologist should be aware of these emotions and can play an important role in trying to encourage the parturient and allaying her anxieties.

REFERENCES

1. Collea JV. Current management of breech presentation. Clin Obstet Gynecol 1980;23:525.
2. Hall JE, Kohl S. Breech presentation. A study of 1,456 cases. Am J Obstet Gynecol 1956;72:977.
3. Morgan HS, Kane SH. An analysis of 16,327 breech births. JAMA 1964;187:262.
4. Brenner WE, Bruce RD, Hendricks CH. The characteristics and perils of breech presentation. Am J Obstet Gynecol 1974;118:700.
5. Braun FHT, Jones KL, Smith DW. Breech presentation as an indicator of fetal abnormality. J Pediatr 1975;86:419.
6. Morley GW. Breech presentation—a 15-year review. Obstet Gynecol 1967;30:745.
7. Murray NP. Anesthesia for breech presentation and multiple gestation. Probl Anesth 1989;3:45.
8. Collea JV, Chein C, Quilligan EJ. The randomized management of term frank breech presentation: A study of 208 cases. Am J Obstet Gynecol 1980;137:235.
9. Cunningham FG, MacDonald PC, Gant NF. Williams' Obstetrics. 18th ed. Norwalk, CT: Appleton and Lange, 1989:349.
10. Cunningham FG, MacDonald PC, Gant NF. Williams' Obstetrics. 18th ed. Norwalk, CT: Appleton and Lange, 1985:393.
11. Crawford JS. Anæsthesia for obstetric emergencies. Br J Anaesth 1971;43:864.
12. Crawford JS. An appraisal of lumbar epidural blockade in patients with a singleton fetus presenting by the breech. J Obstet Gynaecol Br Commonwealth 1974;81:867.

13. Bowen-Simpkins P, Fergusson ILC. Lumbar epidural block and the breech presentation. Br J Anaesth 1974;46:420.

14. Donnai P. Epidural analgesia, fetal monitoring and the condition of the baby at birth with breech presentation. Br J Obstet Gynaecol 1975;82:360.

15. Darby S, Thornton CA, Hunter DJ. Extradural analgesia in labour when the breech presents. Br J Obstet Gynaecol 1976;83:35.

16. Breeson AJ, Kovacs GT, Pickles BG, Hill JG. Extradural analgesia—the preferred method of analgesia for vaginal breech delivery. Br J Anaesth 1978;50:1227.

17. Confino E, Ismajovich B, Rudick V, David MP. Extradural analgesia in the management of singleton breech delivery. Br J Anaesth 1985;57:892.

18. Van Zundert A, Vaes L, Soetens M, et al. Are breech deliveries an indication for lumbar epidural analgesia? Anesth Analg 1991;72:399.

19. James FM. Anesthetic considerations for breech or twin delivery. Clin Perinatol 1982;9:77.

20. Marx GF, Kim YI, Lin C, Halevy S, Schulman H. Postpartum uterine pressures under halothane or enflurane anesthesia. Obstet Gynecol 1978;51:695.

21. Munson ES, Embro WJ. Enflurane, isoflurane and halothane and isolated human uterine muscle. Anesthesiology 1977;46:11.

22. Donchin Y, Evron S. Relaxation of uterus with amyl nitrite in cases of multiple deliveries and breech presentation [Abstract]. San Diego: The 13th Annual Meeting of the Society for Obstetric Anesthesia and Perinatology, 1981:29.

23. Peng ATC, Gorman RS, Shulman SM, DeMarchis E, Nyunt K, Blancato LS. Intravenous nitroglycerin for uterine relaxation in the postpartum patient with retained placenta. Anesthesiology 1989;71:172.

24. DeSimone CA, Norris MC, Leighton BL. Intravenous nitroglycerin aids manual extraction of a retained placenta. Anesthesiology 1990;73:787.

25. Effer SB, McMorland GH. Breech presentation, malpresentation, multiple gestation. In: Datta S, ed. Anesthetic and obstetric management for high-risk pregnancy. 1st ed. Chicago: Mosby–Year Book, 1991:74.

26. Marx GF, Luykx WM, Cohen S. Fetal-neonatal status following cesarean section for fetal distress. Br J Anaesth 1984;56:1009.

27. Hartwell BL, Ostheimer GW. Emergency cesarean section. In: Rogers MC, ed. Current practice in anesthesiology. 1st ed. Toronto: BC Decker, 1988:176.

28. Crawford JS, Davies P. Status of neonates delivered by elective caesarean section. Br J Anaesth 1982;54:1015.

29. Barrier G, Sureau C. Effects of anaesthetic and analgesic drugs on labour, fetus and neonate. Clin Obstet Gynaecol 1982;9:351.

30. Helton B. Preterm labor: Anesthesiologist's view. In: Datta S, Ostheimer GW, eds. Common problems in obstetric anesthesia. 1st ed. Chicago: Year Book Medical Publishers, 1987:271.

31. Cruikshank DP, White CA. Obstetric malpresentations: twenty years' experience. Am J Obstet Gynecol 1973;116:1097.

32. Goplerud J, Eastman NJ. Compound presentation: Survey of 65 cases. Obstet Gynecol 1953;1:59.

33. Lynch L, Berkowitz RL, Chitakara U, Alvarez M. First-trimester transabdominal multifetal pregnancy reduction: A report of 85 cases. Obstet Gynecol 1990;75:735.

34. Tabsh KA. Transabdominal multifetal pregnancy reduction: Report of 40 cases. Obstet Gyencol 1990;75:739

35. Dewan DM. Anesthesia for preterm delivery, breech presentation, and multiple gestation. Clin Obstet Gynecol 1987;30:566.

36. McKeown T, Record RG. Observations on foetal growth in multiple pregnancy in man. J Endocrinol 1952;8:386.

37. Guttmacher AF, Kohl SG. The fetus of multiple gestations. Obstet Gynecol 1958;12:528.

38. Cunningham FG, MacDonald PC, Gant NF. Williams' Obstetrics. 18th ed. Norwalk, CT: Appleton and Lange, 1989:629.

39. Corston JM. Twin survival. A comparison of mortality rates of the first and second twin. Obstet Gynecol 1957;10:181.

40. Graves LR, Adams JQ, Schreier PC. The fate of the second twin. Obstet Gynecol 1962;19:246.

41. MacDonald RR. Management of the second twin. Br Med J 1962;1:518.

42. Writer WDR. Breech presentation and multiple pregnancy: Obstetrical aspects and anaesthetic management. Clin Anaesthesiol 1986;4:305.

43. Rovinsky JJ, Jaffin H. Cardiovascular hemodynamics in pregnancy. I. Blood and plasma volumes in multiple pregnancy. Am J Obstet Gynecol 1965;93:1.

44. Robson SC, Hunter S, Boys RJ, Dunlop W. Hemodynamic changes during twin pregnancy. A doppler and M-mode echocardiography study. Am J Obstet Gynecol 1989;161:1273.

45. Veille JC, Morteon MJ, Burry KJ. Maternal cardiovascular adaptations to twin pregnancy. Am J Obstet Gynecol 1985;153:261.

46. Malinow AM, Ostheimer GW. Anesthesia for the high-risk parturient. Obstet Gynecol 1987;69:951.

47. Cetrulo CL, Ingardia CJ, Sbarra AJ. Management of multiple gestation. Clin Obstet Gynecol 1980;23:533.

48. Cunningham FG, MacDonald PC, Gant NF. Williams' Obstetrics. 18th ed. Norwalk, CT: Appleton and Lange, 1989:533.

49. Aaron JB, Halperin J. Fetal survival in 376 twin deliveries. Am J Obstet Gynecol 1955;69:794.

50. Crawford JS. An appraisal of lumbar epidural blockade in labour in patients with multiple pregnancy. Br J Obstet Gynaecol 1975;82:929.

51. Gullestad S, Sagen N. Epidural block in twin labour and delivery. Acta Anaesth Scand 1977;2:730.

52. James FM III, Crawford JS, Davies P, Naiem H. Lumbar epidural analgesia for labor and delivery of twins. Am J Obstet Gynecol 1977;127:176.

53. Weekes ARL, Cheridjian VE, Mwanje DK. Lumbar epidural analgesia in labour in twin pregnancy. Br Med J 1977;2:730.

54. Crawford JS. A prospective study of 200 consecutive twin deliveries. Anaesthesia 1987;42:33.

55. Abouleish E. Caudal analgesia for quadruplet delivery. Anesth Analg 1976;55:61.

56. Craft JB, Levinson G, Shnider SM. Anæsthetic considerations in caesarean section for quadruplets. Can Anaesth Soc J 1978;25:236.

CHAPTER 36

Anesthesia for Postpartum Tubal Ligation

Richard Elgart

The postpartum period starts immediately after delivery of the neonate. In a matter of minutes, the term parturient begins a rapid reversal of her pregnant state. Although extraordinary changes occur in the immediate postpartum period, the transition to a normal anatomic and physiologic state remains incomplete. This intermediate state poses a special challenge to the anesthesiologist. Frequently, these patients present for surgical tubal sterilization in the immediate postpartum period. This unique patient population requires special considerations for a safe and successful anesthetic.

Nearly half of all tubal sterilizations in the United States are performed in the immediate postpartum period.[1] Postpartum tubal ligation (PPTL) offers a variety of advantages. As a matter of convenience and cost savings, only one hospitalization is required. For many women, hospitalization for delivery may be their sole involvement with the health care system. Elective tubal ligation at this time may provide their best option. Also, women are highly motivated after childbirth to select tubal ligation as a contraceptive option.

Multiple factors decide the timing of PPTL. The procedure is usually done immediately after delivery or early the following day. Performing the procedure expediently allows surgical and postpartum recovery to be combined. This practice avoids unnecessary delays in patient discharge. If maternal health or neonatal status is uncertain, future interval tubal sterilization is a better alternative. Debate surrounds the appropriate delivery-to-surgery interval for safe administration of anesthesia during the postpartum period. Some question whether a previously laboring patient, who may have received narcotic analgesics, is a candidate to receive anesthesia for immediate surgery.

Nonetheless, PPTL is a safe procedure. Combined surgical and anesthetic mortality from all tubal sterilization procedures is approximately 8 per 100,000 women.[2] Although anesthetic risk is low, the postpartum patient requires special attention to prevent a potentially catastrophic complication.

GENERAL ANESTHESIA FOR PPTL

Because of incomplete postpartum transition of pregnancy-induced anatomic and physiologic changes, general anesthesia for PPTL requires special consideration. The risk of aspiration of gastric contents remains a significant concern. Also, incomplete postpartum changes significantly alter certain drug requirements during general anesthesia.

Regurgitation and Aspiration of Gastric Contents

The prepartum patient is at risk for regurgitation and aspiration of gastric contents during general anesthesia. Many mechanical and hormonal changes associated with gestation persist into the postpartum period. During pregnancy, intra-abdominal pressure and intra-gastric volume increase, lower esophageal sphincter pressure declines, and gastric emptying slows. In the immediate postpartum period, these factors partially reverse. The gravid uterus markedly decreases in size, which lowers intra-abdominal pressure and decompresses the duodenum. Progesterone concentrations fall dramatically, possibly raising lower esophageal sphincter pressure. The effects of labor pain and narcotics, which prolong gastric emptying, diminish in the postpartum period. Even though mechanical and hormonal changes occur rapidly in the immediate postpartum period, it is unclear when these changes are complete. It is unknown when the increased risk of gastric regurgitation resolves after delivery. Clinical studies have not yet defined the safe delivery-to-surgery interval.

Studies of postpartum patients have attempted to show when it is safe to give a general anesthetic without increased risk of pneumonitis from aspiration of gastric contents. Blouw *et al*,[3] in a study of gastric volume and pH in postpartum patients, suggested that postpartum patients undergoing PPTL more than 8 hours after delivery were at no more risk for aspiration than elective nonpregnant patients. However, 33% of postpartum patients and 64% of control patients had large gastric volumes with pH less than 2.5. Uram *et al*[4] also could not define a safe delivery-to-surgery interval for postpartum patients. They concluded that delaying PPTL more than 2 hours after delivery did not lower the risk of aspiration. In a study of early (1–8 h) and late (9–45 h) postpartum patients undergoing PPTL, James *et al*[5] could not show any differences in gastric pH and volume between postpartum and nonpregnant control subjects (Figs. 36-1 and 36-2). However, 60% of the subjects met criteria for risk of aspiration (Table 36-1).

Both postpartum and nonpregnant patients have high gastric volumes (> 25 mL) with low pH (< 2.5). Both seem at equal risk for chemical pneumonitis should aspiration occur. Passive regurgitation of gastric contents, however, may be more likely to occur during general anesthesia in the postpartum patient. Delivery may only partially alleviate the pregnancy-induced risk of gastric regurgitation. Delayed gastric emptying, a significant risk factor for regurgitation in prepartum patients, has been studied in postpartum patients. Using epigastric impedance to measure gastric empty-

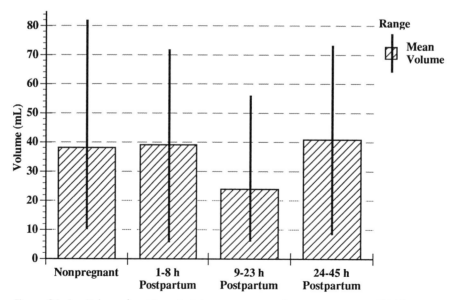

Figure 36–1. Volume of gastric contents in nonpregnant and postpartum women. *Thick line* represents the range of volumes. Mean volume at 9 to 23 h postpartum is significantly lower than mean volumes at 1 to 8 h and 24 to 45 h postpartum. (Data from James CF, Gibbs CP, Banner T. Postpartum perioperative risk of aspiration pneumonia. Anesthesiology 1984;61:756)

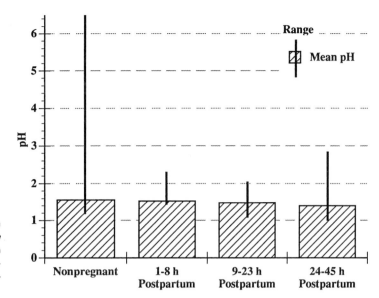

Figure 36–2. pH of gastric contents in nonpregnant and postpartum women. *Thick line* represents the range of pH values. (Data from James CF, Gibbs CP, Banner T. Postpartum perioperative risk of aspiration pneumonia. Anesthesiology 1984;61:756)

ing, O'Sullivan *et al*[6] found slowed gastric emptying in the immediate postpartum period (Table 36-2). They noted, however, that the use of meperidine and promethazine during labor was the principal factor in the delay in gastric emptying in the postpartum period (Table 36-3). Whitehead *et al*[7] measured paracetamol absorption in the postpartum period. They found no differences in gastric emptying between early and late postpartum patients and nonpregnant controls. In sum, no clinical study has definitively shown that postpartum patients are at greater risk of gastric regurgitation than nonpregnant control subjects. Even so, most experts recommend precautionary measures to protect against regurgitation and aspiration during induction of a general anesthetic.

Altered Anesthetic Requirements

Inhalation Agents

Pregnancy decreases the MAC of potent inhalation agents. Increased progesterone concentration during pregnancy may be responsible for this phenomenon. Although the mechanism is not clear, progesterone-induced changes may increase neuronal susceptibility to local and general anesthetics. Available evidence strongly suggests that progesterone increases central and peripheral neuronal sensitivity to local anesthetic conduction blockade. A similar phenomenon also may explain the greater sensitivity to potent inhalation agents. Palahniuk *et al*[8] reported significantly lower

Table 36–1

Gastric Volume and pH in Nonpregnant and Postpartum Women

GROUP	Volume > 25 mL (%)	pH < 2.5 (%)	Volume > 25 mL (%) and pH < 2.5 (%)
Nonpregnant	67	80	60
1–8 h postpartum	73	100	73
9–23 h postpartum	40	100	40
24–45 h postpartum	73	80	67

(Data from James CF, Gibbs CP, Banner T. Postpartum perioperative risk of aspiration pneumonia. Anesthesiology 1984;61:756)

Table 36-2

Values for Gastric Emptying Times of 500 mL of Water in Women as Measured by Gastric Impedance*

TIME	NONPREGNANT	THIRD TRIMESTER	POSTPARTUM
$T_{0.7}$ (min)	5.2 ± 0.6	4.4 ± 0.5	8.8 ± 1.6[†]
$T_{0.5}$ (min)	8.3 ± 0.9	7.2 ± 0.6	13.0 ± 1.9[†]
$T_{0.3}$ (min)	11.1 ± 1.3	9.8 ± 0.8	15.8 ± 2.3[‡]

(Data from O'Sullivan GM, Sutton AJ, Thompson SA, Carrie LE, Bullingham RE. Non-invasive measurement of gastric emptying in obstetric patients. Anesth Analg 1987;66:505)
*Data are mean ± SEM. $T_{0.7}$, $T_{0.5}$, and $T_{0.3}$ represent the time at which gastric impedance had decreased to 70%, 50%, and 30% of the maximum deflection.
[†]$P < 0.05$ versus other two groups.
[‡]$P < 0.05$ versus third trimester.

MAC in pregnant compared to nonpregnant ewes. Pregnancy reduced halothane MAC by 25% and isoflurane MAC by 40%. Datta *et al*[9] showed that administration of exogenous progesterone to oophorectomized rabbits significantly decreased halothane requirements. High plasma progesterone concentrations correlated with a lower halothane MAC.

Postpartum animal studies, however, have not supported this conclusion. Halothane MAC falls in pregnant rats and returns to control levels by postpartum day 5.[10] Interestingly, plasma progesterone concentration did not correlate with changes in MAC. Although postpartum rats have elevated progesterone levels during lactation, halothane MAC requirements return to nonpregnant levels. These investigators concluded that progesterone is not responsible for decreased

MAC requirements of potent inhalation agents during pregnancy.

In humans, the interval for normalization of MAC is unknown. Most likely, MAC rises gradually after delivery. Consider MAC decreased in the postpartum patient undergoing immediate PPTL. If one is using potent inhalation agents to maintain general anesthesia for PPTL, carefully titrate these agents to avoid potential overdosage and delayed emergence.

Neuromuscular Blocking Drugs

Studies of succinylcholine and vecuronium in the postpartum period have found significantly prolonged duration of neuromuscular blockade. This effect may have clinical implications when choosing appropriate

Table 36-3

Gastric Emptying in Postpartum Women Who Had and Had Not Received Opioid Analgesia for Labor and Delivery*

TIME	NO ANALGESIA OR EPIDURAL ANALGESIA	MEPERIDINE AND PROMETHAZINE
$T_{0.7}$ (min)	6.6 ± 1.4	13.1 ± 3.0[†]
$T_{0.5}$ (min)	10.3 ± 1.4	18.2 ± 4.0[†]
$T_{0.3}$ (min)	12.9 ± 1.5	21.8 ± 5.6[†]

(Data from O'Sullivan GM, Sutton AJ, Thompson SA, Carrie LE, Bullingham RE. Non-invasive measurement of gastric emptying in obstetric patients. Anesth Analg 1987;66:505)
*Data are mean ± SEM. $T_{0.7}$, $T_{0.5}$, and $T_{0.3}$ represent the time at which gastric impedance had decreased to 70%, 50%, and 30% of the maximum deflection.
[†]$P < 0.05$ versus no analgesia or epidural analgesia.

drug and dosage for neuromuscular blockade during PPTL.

Prepartum patients normally have reduced serum cholinesterase activity. Plasma cholinesterase activity falls further immediately after delivery. Shnider[11] noted reductions in serum cholinesterase activity of 27.7% in late pregnancy and 32.3% at 2 days postpartum (Fig. 36-3).[11] This decrease reflects a quantitative, rather than qualitative, change in the plasma cholinesterase enzyme. Postpartum patients have normal dibucaine numbers. The lower plasma cholinesterase activity in postpartum patients increases sensitivity to succinylcholine and prolongs recovery time. In a comparison of the response to succinylcholine in postpartum and nonpregnant patients, Ganga *et al*[12] observed that postpartum women needed significantly less succinylcholine to produce 80% depression of control twitch height. They noted that maximal recovery times after a bolus injection (20 mg) were significantly prolonged in the postpartum group. Leighton *et al*[13] used a larger dose of succinylcholine (1 mg/kg). The duration of succinylcholine was approximately 3 minutes longer in postpartum compared to nonpregnant and term pregnant patients. Diminished plasma cholinesterase activity probably accounts for the longer duration of action of succinylcholine in postpartum women. Although prepartum patients also have low plasma cholinesterase activity, they do not show increased sensitivity to succinylcholine or longer recovery times. Pregnancy-induced increases in the volume of distribution raise the minimum effective dose of succinylcholine and compensate for decreased enzyme concentrations.[13]

Although the duration of action of succinylcholine is prolonged during the early postpartum period, this fact is more interesting than clinically relevant. A typical intubating dose of succinylcholine (1 mg/kg) lasts a clinically insignificant 180 seconds longer in a postpartum patient. The intubating dose of succinylcholine must not be reduced to compensate for the increased duration of action. The appropriate dose of succinylcholine is required to secure the postpartum airway safely. Underdosing could cause less than adequate paralysis for intubation, and increase the risk of postpartum aspiration of gastric contents. If a patient does show evidence of prolonged neuromuscular blockade after succinylcholine, suspect atypical plasma cholinesterase.

The duration of vecuronium-induced neuromuscular blockade is also prolonged in the postpartum period (Fig. 36-4). Camp *et al*[14] observed a nearly 50% increase in duration of vecuronium, 0.1 mg/kg, in postpartum subjects compared to nonpregnant subjects. An intubating dose of vecuronium lasted over 60 minutes in the postpartum patient. Subsequent studies have also shown a prolonged duration of action of vecuronium in early postpartum patients.[15] The exact reason for the prolonged duration of action is not clear at this time. Khuenl-Brady *et al*[16] compared vecuronium and atracurium in postpartum patients. The duration of action of atracurium was not prolonged (see Fig. 36-4). Because of its preserved intermediate duration of action, atracurium is the muscle relaxant of choice for PPTL. If vecuronium must be used, reduce the dose and monitor the effect carefully with a peripheral nerve stimulator.

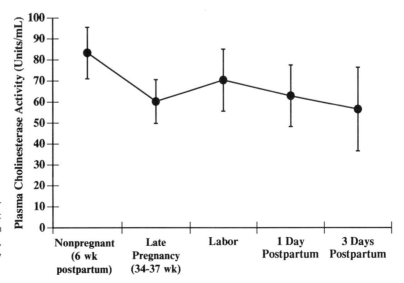

Figure 36–3. Changes in plasma cholinesterase activity (mean ± SD) in obstetric patients. (Data from Shnider SM. Serum cholinesterase activity during pregnancy, labor and the puerperium. Anesthesiology 1965;26:335)

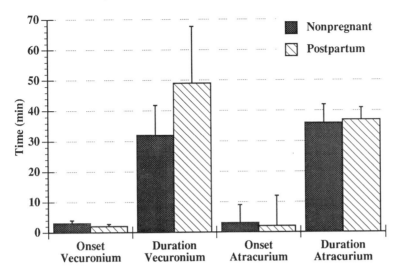

Figure 36–4. Onset (95%–100% twitch depression) and duration (time to appearance of fourth twitch in a train-of-four sequence) of vecuronium, 0.1 mg/kg, and atracurium, 0.5 mg/kg, in nonpregnant and postpartum women. The duration of vecuronium blockade is significantly longer in the postpartum women. Data are mean ± SD. (Data from Khuenl-Brady KS, Koller J, Mair P, Puhringer F, Mitterschiffthaler G. Comparison of vecuronium and atracurium-induced neuromuscular blockade in postpartum and nonpregnant patients. Anesth Analg 1991;72:110)

Clinical Suggestions

In conclusion, the postpartum patient requires special considerations before administration of a general anesthetic. Although little clinical evidence proves that postpartum patients are at increased risk of regurgitation or aspiration, prophylactic measures have become standard. These women should be fasted for at least 8 hours before surgery. Limit the use of narcotics after delivery because they may delay gastric emptying. Preoperatively, give an oral nonparticulate antacid (*i.e.,* 0.3 M sodium citrate, 30 mL) shortly before induction. H$_2$-Antagonists and gastrokinetic agents also are options, although drug interactions and side effects may limit their role to high-risk patients only. James *et al*[5] recommend rapid sequence induction with cricoid pressure and endotracheal intubation to secure the airway. Succinylcholine is the muscle relaxant of choice for rapid sequence induction, unless contraindicated. If the condition of the airway is suspect or if the risk of gastric regurgitation is high, consider awake, oral endotracheal intubation. Remember, PPTL is an elective procedure. Interval tubal sterilization, well after delivery, may lower the risks of general anesthesia in certain women. When giving potent inhalation agents or vecuronium during the maintenance phase of anesthesia, titrate reduced dosages carefully to avoid potential overdose.

REGIONAL ANESTHESIA FOR PPTL

Spinal and epidural blockade offer reasonable and safe alternatives to general anesthesia for PPTL. Both techniques minimize the risk of aspiration of gastric con-

tents. The rapid anatomic and physiologic changes of the postpartum period influence the administration of a regional anesthetic. The postpartum patient is less sensitive to local anesthetics when compared to prepartum patients. The hemodynamic response to sympathetic blockade diminishes after delivery.

Spread of Sensory Blockade

Sensory blockade spreads to more dermatomes after neuraxial injection of local anesthetic in prepartum compared to postpartum and nonpregnant patients. Bromage[17] noted that parturients required one-third less local anesthetic than nonpregnant patients. After delivery, spread of neuraxial local anesthetics decreases. Early studies by Assali and Prystowsky[18] showed that postpartum patients required three or four times the amount of local anesthetic (procaine) to achieve the same level of anesthetic blockade as prepartum patients. More recent clinical studies confirm this observation. Abouleish[19] reported decreased dermatomal spread of subarachnoid local anesthetic in postpartum woman. His postpartum patients developed lower levels of sensory block than term parturients, despite injection of 25% more local anesthetic (0.75% bupivacaine). De Simone *et al*[20] showed that the same dose of bupivacaine blocked fewer dermatomes in postpartum compared to prepartum women. Subarachnoid 0.75% bupivacaine, 12 mg, produced sensory blockade to the T-1–T-2 dermatome in parturients, but blockade extended only to T-4 in postpartum women.

It is unclear when the postpartum patient develops a normal, nonpregnant response to local anesthetics. Marx[21] noted a progressive decline in the height and duration of spinal blockade over the first 3 days following delivery. Brooks and Mandel,[22] in a study of early postpartum dermatomal spread of epidural local anesthetic, found that epidural dose requirements for postpartum patients were no different than those for nonpregnant patients after 36 postpartum hours. However, De Simone et al[20] found no correlation between the hours postpartum (2–51.5) and the level of sensory blockade.

The etiology of these changes in local anesthetic sensitivity is also uncertain. Both mechanical and hormonal factors probably play a role.

Mechanical Factors

Mechanical changes induced by pregnancy may partly explain the increased spread of local anesthetics in prepartum patients. Early studies attempted to show that inferior vena cava compression by the gravid uterus increased the cephalad spread of local anesthetic. Barclay et al[23] augmented the dermatomal spread of a spinal anesthetic in nonpregnant subjects by fitting them with an abdominal binder. They felt the binder simulated inferior vena cava compression by the gravid uterus. This study suggested that inferior vena cava compression alone could account for the increased spread of neuraxial local anesthetics during pregnancy. Other mechanical factors also may be involved. Increased intra-abdominal pressure, epidural vein distention, increased intravascular blood volume, or exaggerated lumbar lordosis also could contribute to the observed changes. After delivery, anatomic changes occur rapidly. Regression of the gravid uterus minimizes aortocaval compression and decreases intra-abdominal pressure. These changes may partially explain the decreased spread of neuraxial local anesthetics in the postpartum patient.

Hormonal Factors

Fagraeus et al[24] reported increased epidural local anesthetic spread in first-trimester parturients, despite minimal inferior vena cava compression by the pregnant uterus. In addition, parturients continue to be sensitive to local anesthetics despite left uterine displacement. Therefore, mechanical factors alone cannot explain the increased spread of local anesthetics during pregnancy. Most current evidence suggests that hormone-induced neuronal changes also increase the parturient's sensitivity to local anesthetics.

Hormones, primarily progesterone, increase neuronal susceptibility to conduction blockade by local anesthetics. Isolated, intact vagal nerve fibers from pregnant rabbits develop conduction blockade more rapidly than nerves from nonpregnant rabbits when exposed to local anesthetics.[25] Greater sensitivity to local

anesthetic or enhanced diffusion with higher intraneuronal concentrations of drug could explain this observation. To further support this theory, the administration of exogenous progesterone to oophorectomized rabbits increased their susceptibility to conduction blockade.[26] A recent human study showed that the median nerve is more susceptible to conduction blockade by local anesthetic in third-trimester parturients than nonpregnant patients.[27] Most experts now think that progesterone induces intrinsic neuronal changes that increase neural sensitivity to local anesthetics. In the immediate postpartum period, cerebrospinal fluid progesterone concentration falls rapidly, decreasing threefold from prepartum values within 12 to 18 hours postpartum (Fig. 36-5).[28] Progesterone-induced neuronal changes may then slowly regress. This effect may, in part, contribute to the postpartum decrease in susceptibility to conduction blockade.

Summary

The decreased spread of local anesthetics in the postpartum period is the result of the rapid mechanical and hormonal changes that follow delivery. It is unclear to what degree each contributes to this effect. Possibly, postpartum reductions in uterine size and intra-abdominal pressure cause the initial decline in dermatomal spread of local anesthetics. Although blood and cerebrospinal fluid progesterone concentrations fall rapidly in the postpartum period, hormone-induced neuronal changes may persist for some time. Progesterone effects may persist well into the postpartum period, and explain why sensory blockade does not return to nonpregnant levels immediately.

Hemodynamic Response to Sympathetic Blockade

The postpartum patient is more hemodynamically stable during regional anesthesia than prepartum patients. Maternal hypotension during regional anesthesia is very common in the prepartum period, but the incidence of hypotension decreases significantly after delivery. Assali and Prystowsky[18] studied the hemodynamic response to incremental spinal anesthesia in pregnant and postpartum women. During high spinal anesthesia, parturients experienced marked hypotension with bradycardia and shock. In contrast, postpartum women showed only small changes in blood pressure during high spinal block (Fig. 36-6).[18] Abouleish[19] gave ephedrine to correct maternal hypotension in 83% of parturients receiving spinal anesthesia for cesarean

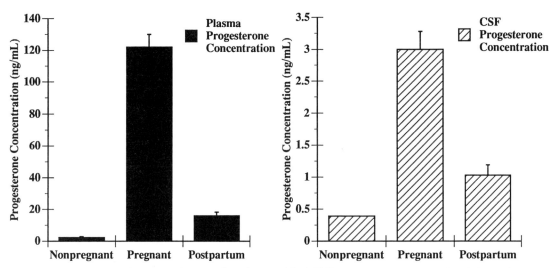

Figure 36-5. Changes in plasma and cerebrospinal fluid (CSF) progesterone concentration during and after pregnancy. Samples for plasma and cerebrospinal fluid progesterone concentration determination were obtained from 12 nonpregnant patients, 21 parturients at cesarean section, and 8 postpartum women at postpartum tubal ligation. Data are mean ± SEM. (Data from Datta S, Hurley, RJ, Naulty SJ, et al. Plasma and cerebrospinal fluid progesterone concentrations in pregnant and nonpregnant women. Anesth Analg 1986;65:950)

delivery compared to only 7% of women during PPTL under spinal block.

There are several possible explanations for this improved hemodynamic stability. Decreased dermatomal spread of local anesthetics in the postpartum period, however, is an unlikely reason. The level of sensory blockade achieved in postpartum women is usually only two or three dermatomes below that obtained in parturients.[20] It seems unlikely that small differences in sympathetic block could account for such a marked change in the incidence of hypotension. In addition, the study by Assali and Prystowsky[18] showed that postpartum women were significantly more hemodynamically stable despite having the same degree of sympathetic blockade as parturients. Perhaps postpartum increases in intravascular volume caused by fluid mobilization may have a role. Also, complete relief of aortocaval compression with delivery may allow unimpeded venous return during regional anesthesia in the postpartum woman. Finally, yet undescribed hormonal factors may promote the exaggerated hemodynamic responses to sympathetic block in parturients. Reversal of the effects of these hormones with delivery may allow the return of normal hemodynamic adaptation to sympathectomy.

Regional Technique Selection

The choice of spinal or epidural anesthesia for PPTL is made, in part, by previous placement of an epidural catheter for labor analgesia. If a well-functioning epidural catheter is already in situ, it can be used for immediate PPTL in the fasted patient, or remain in place for 24 to 48 hours for a later surgical time. Only a patient with a well-functioning epidural catheter is a candidate for immediate PPTL. At Thomas Jefferson Hospital, if an epidural catheter is not in place or does not function properly, we delay PPTL for at least 8 hours after delivery. We choose a spinal anesthetic to avoid the technical delays associated with placement and incremental dosing of a new epidural catheter.

Epidural Anesthesia

A well-functioning epidural catheter can provide excellent operating conditions for PPTL. With epidural anesthesia, the same anesthetic technique can be used for labor, delivery, and subsequent postpartum surgery. Use of an epidural catheter for surgery 24 to 48 hours after placement is unique to the postpartum patient. Although proper use of this technique is convenient and time-saving, approach these catheters with caution. Epidural catheters can migrate into the sub-arachnoid, subdural, or intravascular space. Cata-strophic intrathecal overdose or systemic toxicity may follow drug injection into a wayward catheter. Exclude the possibility of catheter migration by aspirating and injecting an appropriate test dose before giving addi-tional incremental doses of local anesthetic (see Chap. 32). Even if a catheter has functioned well during labor and delivery, it may fail to provide adequate surgical blockade. When using this technique for PPTL, I main-tain a high degree of skepticism, and abandon the epi-dural for a spinal anesthetic if it does not behave in the usual expected manner.

Spinal Anesthesia

Spinal anesthesia provides excellent regional block-ade for PPTL. This technique offers the following advantages:

- Ease of application
- Certainty of needle location
- Rapid onset of sensory and motor blockade
- Low local anesthetic toxicity potential
- Dense sensory blockade

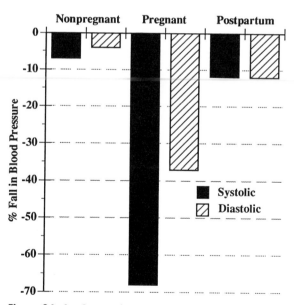

Figure 36–6. Percent decrease in systolic and diastolic blood pressure in nonpregnant, term pregnant, and postpartum women during continuous procaine spinal anesthesia. The level of sensory blockade reached at least T-2 in all patients. (Data from Assali NS, Prystowsky H. Studies on autonomic blockade. I. Comparison be-tween the effects of tetraethylammonium chloride [TEAC] and high selective spinal anesthesia on blood pressure of normal and toxe-mic pregnancy. J Clin Invest 1950;29:1354)

Spinal anesthesia, still, may be complicated by sys-temic hypotension, excessive sensory blockade, or post-lumbar puncture headache. Hypotension is only rarely a problem during spinal anesthesia for PPTL (see Fig. 36-6). These women require little additional hydration before induction of spinal block. Because of post-partum decreases in dermatomal spread of local anes-thetics, the postpartum patient may be less likely to ex-perience high levels of spinal blockade than prepartum patients. Postlumbar puncture headache is always a consideration when administering a spinal anesthetic. Young age and pregnancy increase the risk of postdural puncture headache. The exact incidence of headache in postpartum women has not been reported. Small-gauge needles, parallel needle bevel direction, and atraumatic conical-tipped needles may all limit the risk of this complication.

Clinical Suggestions

A T-4 dermatomal level provides optimal surgical conditions for PPTL. Although the operation may pro-ceed with a T-8 level, peritoneal traction may prove intolerable to the patient. Because PPTL is a short sur-gical procedure, local anesthetics with short and inter-mediate durations are most useful. Subarachnoid injec-tion of hyperbaric 5% lidocaine, 75 mg, provides 30 to 45 minutes of surgical anesthesia. For slower surgeons or longer procedures (*i.e.,* the woman with previous pelvic surgery), 12 mg of hyperbaric 0.75% bupivac-aine provides up to 90 minutes of operating time. For epidural anesthesia, 15 to 20 mL of 3% 2-chloropro-caine or 2% lidocaine with 1:400,000 epinephrine usu-ally will prove adequate. Dose the epidural catheter in 5-mL increments. Maintain optimal operating condi-tions by giving additional incremental doses of local anesthetic. Provide maternal sedation, if needed, with small doses of intravenous midazolam.

SUMMARY AND CONCLUSIONS

Tubal sterilization after delivery offers many advan-tages but is not without risks. Physiologically, post-partum women are in a state of flux. Their true anes-thetic risk remains undefined. Studies of the post-partum risk of aspiration have not yielded a safe delivery-to-surgery interval. Delaying surgery does not necessarily reduce the risk of aspiration.

Currently, only a fasted patient with a well-func-tioning epidural catheter is a candidate for immediate PPTL. If the previously placed epidural catheter does not work properly, a new regional or general anesthetic cannot be initiated for immediate surgery. Still, the patient must remain fasted for at least 8 hours before receiving a new anesthetic.

Little clinical evidence suggests that postpartum patients are at increased risk of regurgitation or aspiration of gastric contents; however, empirically applied prophylactic therapies and procedures to prevent aspiration have become standard. All postpartum patients for PPTL receive aspiration prophylaxis, despite the anesthetic technique administered.

General anesthesia for PPTL presents unique considerations. Most experts recommend rapid sequence induction with cricoid pressure and endotracheal intubation to secure the airway and protect against aspiration of gastric contents. Unless specifically contraindicated, succinylcholine is the muscle relaxant of choice for rapid sequence induction. When giving potent inhalation agents or vecuronium during the maintenance phase of anesthesia, carefully monitor the clinical response to avoid potential overdosage.

A previously placed epidural can provide excellent operative conditions for PPTL. Spinal anesthesia is an effective alternative should the patient lack a functioning epidural catheter. Postpartum patients require little prehydration before a regional anesthetic. With either technique, aim for a T-4 level of sensory blockade. If using epidural anesthesia, test and dose the catheter carefully. When spinal anesthesia is selected, use the smallest possible needle size to minimize the risk of postlumbar puncture headache.

REFERENCES

1. Moses VI, Hughes JM. Surgical surveillance: Tubal sterilization in women aged 15–44 years: 1979–1980. Atlanta: United States Centers for Disease Control (CDC), Division of Reproductive Health, 1983:1.

2. Peterson HB, DeStefano F, Greenspan JR, Ory HW. Mortality risk associated with tubal sterilization in United States hospitals. Am J Obstet Gynecol 1982;143:125.

3. Blouw R, Scatliff J, Craig DB, Palahniuk RJ. Gastric volume and pH in postpartum patients. Anesthesiology 1976;45:456.

4. Uram M, Abouleish E, McKenzie R, Phitykorn P, Tantisira B, Uy N. The risk of aspiration pneumonitis with postpartum tubal ligation [Abstract]. Jackson Hole, WY: Society for Obstetric Anesthesia and Perinatology, 1982:2.

5. James CF, Gibbs CP, Banner T. Postpartum perioperative risk of aspiration pneumonia. Anesthesiology 1984; 61:756.

6. O'Sullivan GM, Sutton AJ, Thompson SA, Carrie LE, Bullingham RE. Non-invasive measurement of gastric emptying in obstetric patients. Anesth Analg 1987; 66:505.

7. Whitehead EM, Smith M, O'Sullivan G. An evaluation of gastric emptying times in pregnancy and the puerperium [Abstract]. Madison, WI: Society for Obstetric Anesthesia and Perinatology, 1990:F1.

8. Palahniuk RJ, Shnider SM, Eger EI II. Pregnancy decreases the requirement for inhaled anesthetic agents. Anesthesiology 1974;41:82.

9. Datta S, Migliozzi RP, Flanagan HL, Krieger NR. Chronically administered progesterone decreases halothane requirements in rabbits. Anesth Analg 1989;68:46.

10. Strout CD, Nahrwold ML. Halothane requirement during pregnancy and lactation in rats. Anesthesiology 1981;55:322.

11. Shnider SM. Serum cholinesterase activity during pregnancy, labor and the puerperium. Anesthesiology 1965;26:335.

12. Ganga CC, Heyduk JV, Marx GF, Sklar GS. A comparison of the response to suxamethonium in postpartum and gynaecological patients. Anaesthesia 1982;37:903.

13. Leighton BL, Cheeck TG, Gross JB, et al. Succinylcholine pharmacodynamics in peripartum patients. Anesthesiology 1986;64:202.

14. Camp CE, Tessem J, Adenwala J, Joyce TH III. Vecuronium and prolonged neuromuscular blockade in postpartum patients. Anesthesiology 1987;67:1006.

15. Hawkins JL, Adenwala J, Camp C, Joyce TH III. The effect of H-2 receptor antagonist premedication on the duration of vecuronium-induced neuromuscular blockade in postpartum patients. Anesthesiology 1989;71:175.

16. Khuenl-Brady KS, Koller J, Mair P, Puhringer F, Mitterschiffthaler G. Comparison of vecuronium- and atracurium-induced neuromuscular blockade in postpartum and nonpregnant patients. Anesth Analg 1991;72:110.

17. Bromage PR. Continuous lumbar epidural analgesia for obstetrics. Can Med Assoc J 1961;85:1136.

18. Assali NS, Prystowsky H. Studies on autonomic blockade. I. Comparison between the effects of tetraethylammonium chloride (TEAC) and high selective spinal anesthesia on blood pressure of normal and toxemic pregnancy. J Clin Invest 1950;29:1354.

19. Abouleish E. Postpartum tubal ligation requires more bupivicaine for spinal anesthesia than does cesarean section. Anesth Analg 1986;65:897.

20. DeSimone CA, Norris MC, Leighton BL, Epstein RH, Palmer C. Spinal anesthesia for cesarean section and postpartum tubal ligation [Abstract]. Anesthesiology 1989;71:A837.

21. Marx GF. Regional analgesia in obstetrics. Der Anaesth 1972;21:84.

22. Brooks GZ, Mandel ALZ. The early postpartum dermatomal spread of epidural 2-chloroprocaine [Abstract]. San Antonio, TX: Society for Obstetric Anesthesia and Perinatology, 1984:25.

23. Barclay DL, Renegar OJ, Nelson EW Jr. The influence of

inferior vena cava compression on the level of spinal anesthesia. Am J Obstet Gynecol 1968;101:792.

24. Fagraeus L, Urban BJ, Bromage PR. Spread of epidural analgesia in early pregnancy. Anesthesiology 1983; 58:184.

25. Datta S, Lambert DH, Gregus J, Gissen AJ, Covino BG. Differential sensitivities of mammalian nerve fibers during pregnancy. Anesth Analg 1983;62:1070.

26. Flanagan HL, Datta S, Muller RA, Covino BG. Effect of exogenously administered progesterone on susceptibility of rabbit vagus nerves to bupivicaine [Abstract]. Anesthesiology 1988;69:A676.

27. Butterworth JF IV, Walker FO, Lysak SZ. Pregnancy increases median nerve susceptibility to lidocaine. Anesthesiology 1990;72:962.

28. Datta S, Hurley RJ, Naulty JS, et al. Plasma and cerebrospinal fluid progesterone concentrations in pregnant and nonpregnant women. Anesth Analg 1986;65:950.

Postoperative Care

CHAPTER 37

Postoperative Analgesia

Craig M. Palmer
Thomas H. Kramer

Cesarean delivery is one of the most frequently performed operations in the United States. Such a large number of procedures in a relatively homogeneous population of patients provides a ready opportunity to evaluate and compare many analgesic options. Although differences in study design often complicate comparison between investigations, in few other areas of medicine have such a variety of techniques and drugs been investigated. The first section of this chapter examines our current understanding of postoperative pain. It examines pain pathways, neuropharmacology, and the mechanisms of analgesia. The following section discusses specific clinical experience with postoperative analgesia in the obstetric population. Systemic narcotics have long been the mainstay of pain therapy after cesarean section. However, clinicians have also tried other drugs and approaches. Some of these alternatives are presently gaining popularity.

PSYCHOSOCIAL AND CULTURAL ASPECTS OF THE POSTOPERATIVE PAIN EXPERIENCE

Definition of Pain

Pain is a purely subjective phenomenon. Only the individual can fully interpret a painful experience. Noxious sensation alone is not pain; the latter term has a far broader interpretation with extensive emotional associations. Pain, as defined by the International Association for the Study of Pain, is "an unpleasant sensory and emotional experience associated with actual or potential tissue damage, or described in terms of such damage."[1]

Pain cannot be objectively quantified. However, various subjective assessments of pain intensity and relief attempt this task. Most of these methods use the report of the patient or subject experiencing the pain as the principal basis of the measurement. In the simplest sense, therefore, pain is whatever the patient says it is. Interpretation of the patient's report of pain (or lack thereof) is probably the most challenging aspect of pain management.

Non-noxious Components of Pain Behavior

Reiterating the message of the previous paragraph, we are unable to observe or measure pain per se; instead we observe pain behavior. Pain cannot be equated in some way to the number of nerve impulses reaching the brain via the spinothalamic tract. Instead, pain behavior is the net result of such impulses after they have been integrated with the patient's emotional state, understanding and expectations of her current physical condition and environment, and cultural and social conditioning with respect to her pregnancy, delivery, and newborn infant.

The emotional condition of a patient can significantly influence her response to a noxious stimulus. Anxiety, either transient or as an established personality trait, can aggravate the experience of pain.[2,3] A woman experiencing even routine childbirth, let alone the invasiveness of a cesarean section, is likely to be anxious. This anxiety may be compounded or alleviated by the presence of family members, depending on their experience with and preparation for the events surrounding parturition and surgery. Also, the attitude and behavior of the medical staff can have salutary or adverse effects on the woman's emotional state. Although it is not always necessary to alleviate anxiety completely, particularly when drastic measures would be required (*e.g.*, sedation, isolation from particular family members), it is important to recognize the contribution of emotional state to pain behavior.

Certain cognitive factors also can strongly influence the experience and expression of postoperative and obstetric pain. The context of pain experience is critical.[3] The parturient often regards the anticipated birth of a healthy child after the pain of labor or the postoperative pain from cesarean section as a positive experience.[4] This circumstance likely causes a significant reduction in pain expression compared to that observed with a similar degree of noxious stimulation resulting from a pathologic condition. Conversely, when the outcome of the birthing process is complicated or not entirely welcome, as when labor fails to progress and cesarean delivery is required, expression of pain may be increased.

Besides context, understanding and expectations about the experience are highly important in determining the patient's response to pain. Accurate, reasonable expectations can modify the response to pain. Patients who are actively informed before surgery about the expected intensity and duration of postoperative pain have shorter recovery times, less analgesic use, and an abridged hospital stay.[5] Effective teaching before cesarean section, therefore, may improve the patient's postoperative pain experience. Absence of teaching, or patient ignorance regarding the effects of childbirth and surgery, may result in considerable anxiety and increased expression of pain.

Lastly, the effect of cultural factors on the patient's response to and expression of pain must be remembered. People of particular cultures or ethnic origins are often characterized (accurately or not) as particularly stoic or, in contrast, "expressive."[4] Not only will cultural training influence a patient's expression of pain, expectations based on the patient's ethnic origin may color the staff's interpretation of pain complaints. Similar considerations apply to the attitude of patients, family, and staff about the use of analgesics, particularly opiates. Owing to cultural influences, many individuals associate the use of opiates for analgesia with weakness and even addictive behavior. These associations may manifest themselves in particularly complex fashion; for example, a patient may desire analgesics, but her family will not wish her to receive potentially addictive drugs. The staff may further complicate such a picture by initially encouraging the use of analgesics, then reversing their position and discouraging analgesic use if, in their perception, the patient is manipulative or complains excessively.

The primary purpose in discussing these emotional, cognitive, and cultural aspects of pain behavior is to remind the reader that the most appropriate and simplest way of interpreting pain complaints is to take them at face value.

MEASUREMENT OF PAIN AND PAIN RELIEF

The preceding discussion should not imply that we cannot evaluate a report of pain by a patient because of the presence of a variety of modifying factors. It is meant, instead, to reinforce the idea that a patient's complaint should be viewed as legitimate. The practitioner should not upgrade or downgrade a pain report based on his or her perceptions or opinions. The patient's expression of distress is a highly useful tool in assessing the response to analgesic therapy.[6]

Depending on the requirements of the situation, patient reports may be quantitated in varying degrees of detail. Certain objective criteria, distinct from pain complaints per se, are often useful adjuncts in assessing the severity of pain and response to analgesics. The following is a brief overview of some more common methods and instruments that are used to evaluate pain intensity.

Interview Techniques

The simplest ways to measure pain intensity are also the ones most likely to find use in routine clinical practice. Straightforward questions and answers provide the maximum amount of information with the least effort by both patient and practitioner. Questions may be purely quantal, such as "Do you have pain?" "Yes" (or "No"). Graded scales ("Describe your pain using one of these five words: none, mild, moderate, severe, excruciating") are a more complex approach. Also in this category is the verbally administered digitized analog scale. The patient is instructed to rate her pain on a scale from 0 to 9 (or a similar range), with 0 representing no pain and 9 representing the worst pain imaginable. This scale is particularly useful for repeated evaluation of pain intensity over time.

These standardized techniques offer advantages over a simple, unstructured interview. The responses are easily evaluated by other practitioners who may question the patient about pain. Inclusion of these quantitative responses in the patient's progress notes can then help guide pain management.

Direct patient interview also can provide information about physical function. Such data may be of supporting value in assessing pain intensity. The patient's mobility often directly reflects pain intensity. Responses to questions about the subject's willingness to get out of bed, success at negotiating a trip to the toilet, tolerance of ambulation, and the like can be highly illuminating. Sleep disturbance is a sensitive and useful indicator of pain intensity (however, see the following discussion on distinctions between acute and chronic pain and, with acute pain, the relative roles of constant and incident factors). Appetite also may be of modest use in assessing the overall effect of the patient's pain.

A final effective interview tool is to ask the patient to distinguish the severity of various sources of discomfort that she may have. If the presence of a nasogastric tube or stiffness from prolonged bed rest is more significant than pain of the operative site or incision, pain intensity is likely low.

Physiologic Effects

Acute pain is a syndrome with aspects that distinguish it from other pain states. Of particular significance is the stimulatory effect of acute pain on physiologic parameters such as heart and respiratory rate and blood pressure. When used carefully, these physical signs may support the assessment of pain intensity.[7] Truly marked and obvious increases in heart rate or blood pressure usually suggest very severe pain. Moderate (but still undesirable) degrees of pain may not reliably produce such elevations in all subjects. Also, these parameters adapt in the face of persistent pain. They become essentially useless for evaluation of pain intensity in chronic, established pain states.[8] Therefore, one should *never* discount or downgrade a patient's complaint of pain based on the absence of elevations of cardiorespiratory parameters or signs of stress.

Constant Versus Incident Pain

Acute pain states, especially postoperative pain, also may be characterized as having one or both of two grades of pain: constant and incident. Usually, the constant component is lesser in intensity but persistent. Incident pain, resulting from movement, coughing, deep breathing, and other activities, is more severe but transient. Mild to moderate constant pain may be primarily responsible for the sleep disturbance, stress, and irritability noted with inadequately relieved acute pain. The incident component most likely produces the adverse effects on mobility and ventilation. These limitations may lead to atelectasis and pneumonitis and are the medically significant effects of acute pain.[9] The distinction between constant and incident pain is important for two reasons. First, the differing intensities of pain require different strategies for relief. Constant low-grade pain will usually respond to a modest amount of continuously present analgesic medication. In contrast, relief of incident pain may require high doses of analgesic. This amount of drug is potentially unsafe for continuous administration but is acceptable for intermittent brief periods. For this reason, patient-controlled analgesia (PCA) modalities, which allow both rapid titration and continuous administration of opiates, have met with great success. Second, interview techniques for assessing acute pain must address both the constant and incident components. The unwary practitioner may mistakenly believe that a patient is comfortable based on assessment of only one component of the pain. Thus, in interviewing the patient about pain and pain relief, a multifaceted approach works best. Relying on a single question or pain scale to decide pain intensity runs the risk of ignoring significant discomfort (*i.e.,* a patient at rest who reports no pain, but is not questioned regarding her comfort when coughing or getting out of bed).

Analgesic Consumption

A particularly useful tool for assessing changes in pain intensity for an individual patient is the rate of analgesic self-administration. Physicians often attempt to gauge the severity of a patient's pain by quantifying her analgesic use. Unfortunately, this method has significant drawbacks when the patient does not have direct control over the rate and amount of analgesic available. In the presence of an as-needed analgesic order, with some latitude given to nursing staff on dose and interval (*i.e.,* 3–5 mg of morphine sulfate IM every 3 to 6 h, as needed), the total amount of analgesic administered per day may bear little or no relationship to the patient's pain severity. Evidence exists to show that this traditional strategy for pain relief often results in considerable undermedication and inadequate analgesia.[9] With the use of patient-controlled ("demand") analgesia, tracking of analgesic use becomes more useful as a pain-assessment tool. Many PCA devices available today keep extensive electronic histories of a patient's demands and dosages. Such information is highly useful in evaluating the patient's progress toward decreased pain and recovery.

Written Instruments

Finally, more extensive evaluation of pain is possible with written pain-evaluation instruments. The two best known and most commonly used instruments are the visual analog scale[10,11] and the McGill Pain Questionnaire.[12] These methods have been used and validated extensively in research on clinical pain. Many excellent articles dealing with these instruments, individually or in comparison, are available to the interested reader.[13,14]

NEUROANATOMIC BASIS OF POSTOPERATIVE OBSTETRIC PAIN

Underlying a successful approach to preventing and treating postoperative pain is an adequate appreciation of the structures and processes that function to produce it. The experience of postoperative pain is the result of a chain of events beginning with the actual disruption of somatic tissue by the surgical procedure. Activation of afferent nerves, specifically designated to convey information about tissue damage to the central nervous system, occurs because of this injury. The specificity of these afferent fibers for noxious stimuli is fortunate because these fibers respond selectively to particular classes of pharmacologic agents. The connection of afferent nerves to the central nervous system is organized in a highly specific fashion. The afferent nerves innervating the site of surgical manipulation come from a specific place in the spinal cord. This high degree of correlation also is propitious; it allows administration of drugs in an anatomically selective fashion. Either or both neuroanatomic factors may be exploited in the treatment of postsurgical pain.

Simple cesarean section disrupts both somatic and visceral tissue. The somatic site is normally a small incision in the lower abdomen, innervated via the T-11 and

T-12 dermatomes. The visceral (uterine) site, whether a low transverse incision or a classic upper fundus approach, is not innervated by the same region of the spinal cord as the somatic site. Although the ovaries, fallopian tubes, and upper vagina are innervated via the lower thoracic segments, the uterus receives its afferent fibers from the upper sacral area of the spinal cord.[15] Thus, after cesarean section, sensation of pain will be transmitted to the central nervous system via two discrete spinal regions. More extensive surgical procedures (*e.g.*, cesarean hysterectomy) broaden the number of spinal segments involved.

There are several important distinctions in the number and type of nerve fibers that innervate somatic and visceral tissue. In somatic tissue, there are three general types of afferent fibers, designated A-delta (A_δ), A-beta (A_β), and C. A_δ-fibers are small in diameter and myelinated, with rapid conduction velocities. A_β-fibers are larger in diameter and are myelinated. They have very fast conduction velocities. The C-fiber type, in contrast, is small in diameter and unmyelinated. It conducts impulses slowly.[16]

The anatomic locations of these neurons are similar. The cell bodies of all three types lie in the dorsal root ganglia of the spinal cord. The individual nerve fibers reside in the somatic nerves and terminate peripherally in a variety of sensory receptors in cutaneous and muscular tissue.

The function of each receptor is highly specific. Receptors responding selectively to cold, heat, and mechanical stimuli that are damaging, or potentially damaging, are located on C-fibers.[17] Another population of C-fibers possesss polymodal receptors that may respond to a variety of noxious stimuli, including chemical types.[17] In contrast, A_δ-fibers respond almost exclusively to high-intensity mechanical stimulation and are therefore called high-threshold mechanical nociceptors.[17] Another class of mechanoreceptors respond to low-intensity, non-noxious stimuli; these are located on A_β-fibers that extensively innervate muscle and cutaneous structures.[17]

Perhaps the most important consideration in the translation of somatic stimuli into painful or nonpainful perceptions by the brain is in the spinal termination of the individual types of nerve fibers. All afferent fibers terminate on the dorsum of the spinal cord. The dorsal horns of the spinal cord may be anatomically divided into a series of layers or laminae, numbered in increasing fashion beginning with the most superficial (dorsal) layer.[18] Laminae I and II are often called the substantia gelatinosa, because of its high content of unmyelinated nerve fibers and resulting gelatinous appearance. The substantia gelatinosa is of great importance to the perception of pain, as most of the small, unmyelinated afferent neurons (C-fibers) terminate in this region alone.[16] The large-diameter myelinated fibers (A_β) penetrate to much deeper levels (laminae III–VI) before synapsing with central neurons.[16] A_δ-fibers are somewhat more complex, in that they provide collateral innervation to both superficial and deep laminae. The majority of their synaptic connections are located in the substantia gelatinosa. So, fiber types that sense and relay information only about damaging or potentially damaging stimuli, namely the C and A_δ types, synapse very selectively with a discrete region of the spinal cord. In contrast, the synapses of fibers that respond to nonnoxious stimuli are located elsewhere (see Fig. 37-1, for example).

Another significant factor in the afferent innervation of somatic tissue is the degree to which the spinal terminations of afferent neurons spread in the rostrocaudal direction. Overlap of the cutaneous fields served by each spinal segment is minimal. Afferent fibers entering via a particular spinal nerve terminate on the spinal cord at that level. They do not synapse extensively with the cord in regions above or below the point of entry.[15] This organization results in the well-defined pattern of dermatomes that can be observed in the pres-

ence of discrete neuropathies or epidural anesthesia, for example. Combined with the distinct functions of the individual types of sensory receptors and neurons, and the discrete nature of their connection with the spinal cord, this anatomic factor provides for the precise degree of localization and qualitative description that is characteristic of somatic and cutaneous sensation.

The afferent innervation of visceral tissue, by contrast, is considerably less well defined. As with somatic tissue, the cell bodies of visceral afferents are located in the dorsal root ganglia of the spinal cord; however, the nerve fibers are located in autonomic nerves. Within the sympathetic division, the afferents access the thoracic and lumbar spinal roots after passing through either the hypogastric or preaortic plexuses and the sympathetic chain. Those afferents contained in the parasympathetic division travel in the pudendal nerves and enter the spinal cord at the sacral level.[15] The sensory receptors in visceral tissue are less specific than those found in somatic tissue. Most nociceptors in the viscera are of the polymodal C-fiber type, responding to multiple noxious stimuli rather than a single type.[15] Some high-threshold mechanoreceptors (A_δ) are present too. The termination of visceral afferents in the spinal cord follows the same pattern as the somatic afferents in the sense of fiber type and depth of synapse in

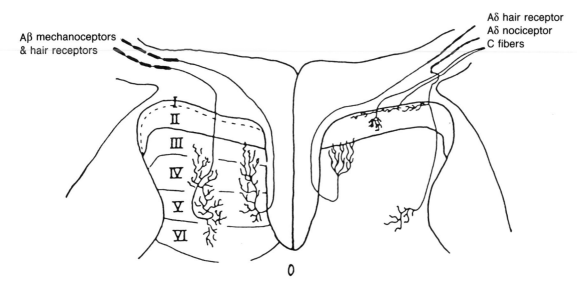

Figure 37–1. Schematic diagram of the different types of cutaneous afferent terminations in the dorsal horn of the spinal cord. On the left side, Rexed's lamination of the dorsal horn is shown along with terminal arbors of large myelinated afferent fibers. The termination of the medial afferent is a typical flame-shaped arbor. On the right are the terminal arbors of small myelinated and unmyelinated afferents. Although not shown here, lamina II is often divided into inner (IIi) and outer (IIo) zones. (Fitzgerald M. The course and termination of primary afferent fibers. In: Wall PD, Melzack R, eds. Textbook of pain. New York: Churchill Livingstone, 1984:34)

the dorsal horn. However, the rostrocaudal spread of the spinal terminations is somewhat more diffuse for visceral afferents.[15] This wider spread, combined with the nonspecific nature of the visceral nociceptors, results in visceral stimuli being perceived with considerably less localization and quality compared to somatic stimuli. Rostrocaudal spread also may be the basis of referred pain, in which stimuli originating in the viscera are perceived as localized in a particular somatic area. For cesarean section, referred pain might present as dull or aching pain in the lower back or sacrum. Figure 37-2 shows a diagrammatic representation of the presumed human viscerotomes.

The neuropharmacology of the afferent nervous system is a subject in rapid evolution. Because many strategies for pain relief are directed at specific pharmacologic interruption of afferent transmission, a brief review of the afferent neurotransmitters and their receptors is appropriate. These afferent neurotransmitters were largely unknown until the recent past; developments in analytical technology and molecular biology are revealing novel neurotransmitters at a

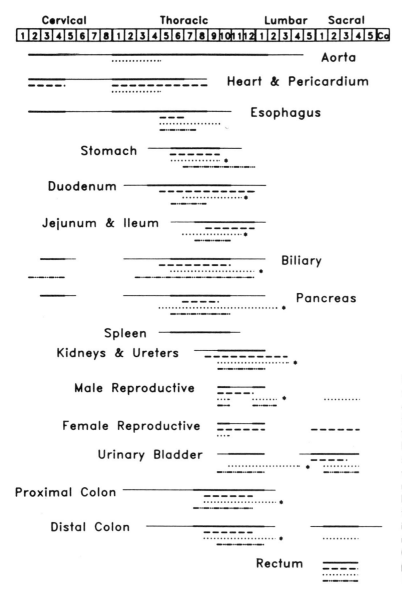

Figure 37–2. Diagrammatic representation of presumed viscerotomes in humans as determined by the following: sites of 'referred' pathologic pain (⎯⎯⎯ indicates typical dermatomes of referral; thickness of line relates to the frequency of occurrence); sites of cutaneous hyperalgesia associated with visceral disease (– – – –); neurosurgical destruction of dorsal roots or local anesthetic blocks that lead to relief from pathologic visceral pain (· · · · · ·, * indicates splanchnectomy effective in pain relief); sites of referred experimental pain (– · – · ·). (Ness TJ, Gebhart GF. Visceral pain: A review of experimental studies. Pain 1990;41:167)

phenomenal rate. The common characteristic of most afferent neurotransmitters is that they are peptides, in contrast to the well-described monoamines present in the autonomic nervous system.

Perhaps the best characterized class of peptide neurotransmitters is the tachykinins. Two distinct genes produce these peptides, the neurokinin-A gene (NKA) and the neurokinin-B gene (NKB).[19] The NKA gene generates the best-known tachykinin, substance P. The NKA gene also produces at least four related peptides, including neuropeptide K and neuropeptide gamma.[20–22] The NKB gene, thus far, is known to produce only one peptide, neurokinin B.[23,24] These peptides have shown affinity for the various tachykinin receptors, which currently number three, the NK-1, NK-2, and NK-3 receptors.[19]

The NK-1 (substance P) receptor exists in particularly high density in the superficial dorsal horn of the spinal cord. Its location corresponds to the sites of termination of small-diameter primary afferent fibers that transmit nociceptive impulses.[25,26] Substance P is synthesized in the cell bodies of these afferent fibers, is found in high concentrations in the nerve terminals, and is released by stimulation of these neurons.[27–31] The NK-3 receptor also is found in the dorsal horn, but in a distribution different from that of the NK-1 receptor.[32] The peptide NKB, which has greater affinity for the NK-3 receptor than the NK-1, has a similar, corresponding distribution (Fig. 37-3).[33]

These findings suggest an additional level of complexity in afferent transmission. Both the type and anatomic location of the peripheral afferent neuron, and the precise sequence of the peptide that it expresses and releases, govern the type of signal transmitted.

Other peptides that are currently the subject of intense scrutiny for their role in afferent neurotransmission include calcitonin gene-related peptide (CGRP), somatostatin, vasoactive intestinal polypeptide, cholecystokinin, and others.[17,34] The CGRP appears to play a role highly analogous to that of substance P and other tachykinins. It is contained in the terminals of small-diameter A_δ and C primary afferent fibers that synapse in the superficial lamina of the dorsal horn and is released in response to noxious stimulation.

Some authors suggest that release of various afferent neurotransmitters is stimulus-specific. For example, exposure of the tail of a rat to noxious heat releases somatostatin, but not substance P. Inversely, noxious cold emits substance P but not somatostatin.[35]

Besides neurotransmitters, several chemical modulators of afferent neurotransmission are important in the process of nociception. These structurally diverse agents exert a variety of actions depending on the organ system in question. They are generically called the *autocoids*. This class of substances includes the following:

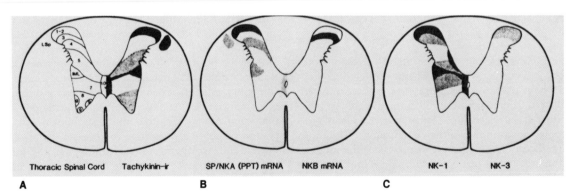

Figure 37–3. Schematic illustrations of (**A**) laminar divisions of the thoracic spinal cord in the rat (left side) and the distribution and relative density of tachykinin-ir in the rat thoracic spinal cord. The tachykinin-ir was assessed with a monoclonal antibody to substance P (SP), which cross-reacts extensively with neurokinin A (NKA) (and presumably other NKA-related peptides) and neurokinin B (NKB). (**B**) The distribution and relative density of cell bodies containing PPT mRNA (left side) or NKB precursor mRNA. (**C**) The distribution and relative density of NK-1 binding sites (left side) as labeled with [125I] BH-SP and of NK-3 binding sites as labeled with [125I] BH-eledoisin. (IML = intermediolateral cell column, ir = immunoreactivity, LSp = lateral spinal nucleus, PPT = preprotachykinin) (Helke CJ, Krause JE, Mantyh, PW, Couture R, Bannon MJ. Diversity in mammalian tachykinin peptidergic neurons: Multiple peptides, receptors, and regulatory mechanisms. FASEB J 1990;4:1606)

- The aromatic monoamines, 5, 17 hydroxytryptamine (serotonin, 5-HT) and histamine
- The plasma kinins bradykinin and kallikrein, both peptides
- The various products of the arachidonic acid cascade, such as the prostaglandins, thromboxanes, and leukotrienes

In their roles as modulators of pain sensation, the autocoids are synthesized and released in areas of injury or inflammation. For this reason, they also are called "local hormones."[36] These agents share in common the ability to sensitize or stimulate the peripheral terminals of afferent neurons. They are released and act locally, not regionally or systemically. They serve to amplify the sensitivity of the afferent nervous system, especially the nociceptive components, in discrete areas of damaged tissue.

Although the neurotransmitters and modulators discussed thus far are primarily stimulatory in nature, other transmitters exist that play an inhibitory role in the sensation of pain. The endogenous opioids are the most widely recognized inhibitory transmitters. They are distributed extensively throughout the afferent nervous system and many other organs. The endogenous opioids are all peptides and come from the following distinct precursor peptides: proopiomelanocortin, proenkephalin (or proenkephalin A), and prodynorphin (or proenkephalin B).

Proopiomelanocortin is the precursor for the melanocyte-stimulating hormones and adrenocorticotrophic hormone (ACTH) and the opioid peptide beta-endorphin.[37] Beta-endorphin is found in the highest concentrations in the pituitary gland.[38] Although beta-endorphin is released into the blood in response to stress, it is currently unclear whether circulating beta-endorphin plays a role in stress- or exercise-induced analgesia. Its presence in the blood may simply be a byproduct of the release of ACTH (also derived from proopiomelanocortin) under these conditions. A large and contradictory body of literature exists on this subject. It does not appear that beta-endorphin is important in peripheral afferent or spinal sensory pathways.[39]

In contrast, the significance of peptides derived from the remaining two opioid precursors, proenkephalin and prodynorphin, in afferent nerves and spinal cord is much more clear. A variety of peptides may come from these two precursors. The most significant agents identified thus far are leucine enkephalin (primarily from prodynorphin), methionine enkephalin (from proenkephalin), and dynorphin (from prodynorphin).[38]

Most experts agree that enkephalins are the endogenous agonists for the delta-opioid receptor, and dynorphin is the corresponding agonist for the kappa-receptor. Considerable controversy exists regarding the most likely endogenous agonist(s) for the mu-opioid receptor type. Each of these receptors will be treated in more detail in the section on the pharmacologic management of pain. The superficial dorsal horn (the substantia gelatinosa) of many mammalian species contains high densities of mu- and delta-opioid receptors. These receptors are concentrated on the synaptic terminals of small-diameter primary afferent fibers of the C and A_δ type.[40] Neurons in this region contain high concentrations of the enkephalins and their precursor molecules.[41,42] Kappa receptors exist in spinal cord in lower concentrations.[43] Dynorphin-containing neurons also are found there.[34,44]

Extensive evidence obtained using a variety of experimental techniques shows that the endogenous opioids play a critically important role in processing nociceptive impulses that reach the spinal cord via the primary afferent neurons. This anatomic region (the substantia gelatinosa), and, in particular, the receptors for the endogenous opioids located within it, is a principal site of action for the analgesic action of exogenous opiate drugs.[45]

GOALS OF POSTOPERATIVE PAIN MANAGEMENT IN OBSTETRICS

Pain therapy aims to prevent or reduce the medically and psychologically deleterious effects of pain. Especially for acute pain, these goals must be balanced against the positive, physiologically appropriate functions of pain sensation. Clearly, acute pain is a warning to the individual that something is wrong, and in this sense it also serves the physician as a diagnostic aid. The inhibition of mobility that often accompanies acute pain is probably a protective mechanism, helping to prevent further aggravation of injury.[9] In the postoperative period, however, unrelieved pain can have strongly negative consequences for a patient's health and well-being. This section outlines the most significant of these consequences and states the goals of postoperative pain management in terms of avoiding them.

Spinal and supraspinal reflexes produce several characteristic responses to pain.[9] Increased muscle tension, particularly in the thorax, breeds decreased chest wall compliance with resultant falls in inspiratory capacity, vital capacity, and functional residual capacity. Increased sympathetic tone mediated by these reflexes impairs gastrointestinal motility and bladder function and elevates peripheral vascular resistance, blood pressure, cardiac output, and myocardial oxygen demand. A typical stress response, with release of ACTH and cortisol with secondary catabolic changes, arises.[46,47] Stress and anxiety also may influence hematologic parameters, increasing blood viscosity and coagulability.[48,49] With respect to postoperative pain, the most significant consequences of these physiologic responses to pain and stress are thrombus formation and pulmonary complications, such as atelectasis, that may lead to pneumonitis. Thrombus formation likely results from prolonged periods of immobility, coupled with the potential changes in hematologic parameters discussed previously.[48,49] Pulmonary effects may stem from a combination of factors. Chest wall rigidity, abdominal distention (from decreased gastrointestinal motility) generating diminished diaphragmatic excursion, and fear of pain from deep breathing and coughing all contribute.[9,45,50]

In most common postoperative settings, therefore, pain management therapy is directed at maintaining or optimizing pulmonary toilet, improving mobility and allowing ambulation at the earliest reasonable time, and minimizing psychological stress and anxiety. This last consideration is of particular relevance in the obstetric setting, when interaction between the newborn, mother, and family are of great importance.

THE PHARMACOLOGIC TREATMENT OF PAIN

Classes of Agents

The prevention and treatment of postoperative pain is largely pharmacologic. It rests on the interruption of sensory neuronal transmission of noxious impulses to the central nervous system. The selectivity with which this task is achieved (*i.e.,* the extent to which noxious input is eliminated and other, non-noxious sensation is preserved) must be balanced against the intensity of the effect required.

Three general regions of opportunity exist for such interruptions. The first is in the periphery, where tissue injury activates sensory receptors. Drugs that counter the effects of the various autocoids or "local hormones" produced in response to injury and inflammation can reduce the genesis of nociceptive impulses in the small-diameter sensory afferent neurons. The principal drugs acting in this fashion are the prostaglandin synthetase inhibitors, or nonsteroidal anti-inflammatory drugs

(NSAIDs). Next, progressing toward the central nervous system, are the axons of nerve fibers that carry the nociceptive input. Drugs that block conduction in electrically excitable tissue, namely, local anesthetics, can prevent impulse transmission. A final opportunity lies at the point of synapse with the central nervous system. Agents that selectively impair synaptic communication by a specific drug–receptor interaction inhibit transmission from peripheral afferent nociceptive fibers to central neurons. Opioids are the principal example in this class.

Opioids

Receptors

Opioid analgesics cause their effects via interaction with specific opioid receptors. Not one, but a minimum of three, distinct opioid receptor types and potentially several subtypes exist in mammalian systems. This discussion focuses on the currently accepted receptor types, their biochemical mechanisms, anatomic distribution, and the effects produced by them in response to the binding of opioid agonists.

The earliest indications of the existence of multiple opioid-receptor types came from two discrete lines of evidence, one functional in nature and derived from experiments in dogs, and the other based on in vitro studies of smooth muscle and brain homogenates. Martin *et al*[51] postulated the existence of three receptors, mu, kappa, and sigma. They based this conclusion on the diverse physiologic responses of chronically spinalized dogs to various opioid agonists (morphine, cyclazocine, oxilorphan, nalorphine, and ketocyclazocine). Almost simultaneously, Lord *et al*[52] showed that leucine enkephalin and a variety of enkephalin derivatives interacted with more than one receptor site in brain homogenates and smooth muscle preparations. They defined the new receptor as delta. Subsequently, investigators using a variety of experimental techniques have examined evidence for the existence and function of mu-, delta-, kappa-, sigma-, and epsilon-receptors. Leslie[53] has written an excellent and extensive review of this subject that provides additional detail regarding methodology and controversies in the field.

Briefly, the mu-, delta-, and kappa-receptors are considered the true opioid receptors, based on both receptor binding and functional pharmacologic studies. Sigma-receptors are probably nonopioid in nature. Some exogenous opioid compounds have moderate affinity for this receptor; none of the endogenous opioid peptides possess significant affinity for this site. Drugs such as phencyclidine, SKF 10,047, and haloperidol bind sigma-receptors with good affinity.[54] The epsilon-receptor is not universally recognized as legitimate entity and lacks any known physiologic function.[55–59]

Various lines of evidence suggest the existence of subtypes of mu-, delta-, and kappa-receptors. In particular, the putative subtypes of the mu-receptor have received considerable attention.[60] However, agonist drugs selective for these subtypes do not exist. Current evidence has not clearly shown functional correlates supporting the existence of distinct subtypes.[61] These arguments also apply to putative subtypes of delta- and kappa-receptors.

In discussing drugs that interact with the opioid receptors, one must distinguish between the prototypic ligands used in scientific research and the agents employed clinically. With very few exceptions, these two groups of drugs are entirely separate. The two opioids most commonly used as clinical analgesics are also the two oldest opioids of their kind—morphine, the alkaloidal natural product derived from the opium poppy *Papaver somniferum,* and meperidine (pethidine in the British idiom), the first successful synthetic opioid analgesic. Extensive research has resulted in the development of both agonist and antagonist drugs with extraordinary potency and specificity for the mu-,[62,63] delta-,[64–66] and kappa-.[67,68] Only the potent opioid sufentanil, a highly selective mu-agonist, is both a clinically useful opioid drug and an appropriate research tool. (Many studies of opioid pharmacology still include morphine, mainly because of its widespread use and historical significance.)

Biochemical Mechanisms

Regardless of the opioid-receptor type (mu, delta, or kappa) or its anatomic location, the immediate result of receptor activation is an inhibitory effect. Investigations into the biochemical mechanism of action of the opioids have shown that the known opioid receptors belong to the larger family of guanine nucleotide binding protein (G-protein) coupled receptors.[69] The effect of an opioid agonist binding to a receptor is transduced to a second messenger system via an associated protein that binds guanosine triphosphate. [In this sense, the opioid receptors are related to other types of receptors such as the adrenergics and muscarinics. They are distinctly different from receptors such as the GABA/benzodiazepine/chloride ionophore complex or the nicotinic acetylcholine receptors of the neuromuscular junction, in which the effector system (an ion channel) is actually part of the receptor itself.]

Two separate second-messenger systems activated by opioid receptors have been characterized at this time. In discrete brain regions such as the nigrostriatum, and in certain neuronal tumor cell lines, activation of opioid receptors inhibits adenylate cyclase and thereby reduces the formation of intracellular cyclic AMP.[70] In other neuronal tissue, such as primary afferent neurons[71] and the myenteric plexus of the enteric nervous system,[72] opioid receptors are coupled to a potassium channel. Activation of the receptor leads to hyperpolarization of the cell (or, more probably, the local region of the synaptic terminal). This change lowers the calcium current through voltage-dependent calcium channels in response to depolarization,[73,74] which in turn inhibits the calcium-dependent release of a neurotransmitter (such as substance P). This mechanism underlies the analgesic effect of opioids in the spinal cord.[71] The final common pathway in producing analgesia is a decrease in intracellular calcium (and voltage-dependent calcium flux).[69] Calcium channel antagonists, calcium, and calcium chelators significantly potentiate opioid actions.[75,76] The effect of drugs active on calcium channels on the action of opioid analgesics is a current topic of intense interest.[77–79]

Physiologic Effects

Opioid receptors are anatomically widespread and, in addition to producing analgesic effects, influence a huge array of physiologic functions. The succeeding paragraphs outline the distribution of the three types of opioid receptors according to their influence on the following physiologic functions or organ systems:

- Pain sensation
- The gastrointestinal tract
- Ventilation (respiration)
- The urinary bladder
- Behavior (addiction/reinforcement)
- The endocrine/immune systems

PAIN SENSATION. Opioid receptors exist at several levels of the nervous system, and therefore can influence nociception at multiple points. The best-described distribution of opioid receptors is in the superficial dorsal horn of the spinal cord. High densities of mu- and delta-receptors lie on the presynaptic terminals of primary afferent neurons terminating in laminae I and II (the substantia gelatinosa). In most mammalian systems studied thus far, kappa-receptors have not been found in significant quantities at this site. However, evidence is accumulating that supports the existence of kappa-receptors on the cell bodies of spinal neurons (*i.e.*, postsynaptic to the primary afferent neurons).[34] Besides the widely accepted role of the mu-receptor in producing analgesia at this site, extensive evidence obtained from animal studies proves that delta-receptors also produce significant antinociceptive effects in this area.[80–82] It is less clear at this time to what extent the kappa-receptor mediates analgesia at the spinal level. Some nociceptive endpoints (in animal studies) are sensitive to drugs selective for the kappa-receptor, but others are not.[83,84]

Opioid receptors are also present at supraspinal levels and clearly produce analgesia at these sites as well. Again, the mu-receptor is most strongly implicated. It exists in high densities in the periaqueductal gray matter and thalamus.[85,86] So, mu-receptors are strategically located to interrupt transmission of nociceptive information through the spinothalamic tract. Considerable controversy has existed for some time over the role of supraspinal delta-receptors in producing analgesia.[87] Currently, most evidence (again, derived exclusively from studies in animal models) supports such a role.

Agonists for the kappa-receptor produce supraspinally mediated analgesia in selected pain models, but, as with spinally mediated analgesia, not in all tests.[88] Studies of a kappa-selective drug, spiradoline, have been done in human subjects. At this time, kappa-agonist analgesics remain mired in early clinical development. Significant adverse effects related to sedation and dysphoria are a problem.[88]

THE GASTROINTESTINAL TRACT. It may be argued that opioid receptors and endogenous opioids are more important in the regulation of gastrointestinal function than in the regulation of any other organ system of the body. The use of opium for its antidiarrheal properties is at least as old as its use as an analgesic and sedative.[89] With respect to the gastrointestinal tract and the neural systems that control it, opioid receptors are ubiquitous. Biochemical and functional studies have shown the presence and importance of opioid receptors at every level of the gastrointestinal system, including the following:

- Submucosa[90–92]
- Smooth muscle of stomach[93]
- Gall bladder[94]
- Small and large intestine[95]
- Myenteric plexus[93,96]
- Areas of the brain and spinal cord[58,96–99] that exert direct control over gastrointestinal motility and secretion

The types of opioid receptors involved in gastrointestinal regulation vary with the anatomic site and sometimes with the species.[93,96] A reasonable generalization is that the effect of kappa-receptor activation on gastrointestinal transit is minimal. Delta-receptor activation causes some degree of inhibition, particularly at the spinal level. Mu-receptor activation (as occurs with most clinically useful opioids) results in constipation despite site (*i.e.*, brain, spinal cord, or gastrointestinal tract).[96] The inhibitory effects of opioid analgesics on gastrointestinal function represent a significant problem that complicates their use for the relief of pain, particularly in the chronic setting.

Despite the extensive body of basic knowledge that has grown from research on opioids and the gastrointestinal tract, sound clinical data that would guide the selection of less-constipating opioid analgesics, or better define the effects of opioids in aggravating or prolonging postoperative ileus, are generally lacking. Although traditional clinical teachings often hold that particular opioids (*e.g.*, meperidine) are less constipating than morphine, data to prove this effect are absent.

Several generalizations about the clinical effects of opioid analgesics on gastrointestinal function are offered here, mainly to prevent the undertreatment of pain based on misconceptions about the constipating effects of opioids. First, the inhibitory potency of opioids on gastrointestinal transit generally parallels their analgetic potency. Equipotent amounts of two different opioids will produce approximately similar degrees of constipation. The observation that particular analgesics, such as meperidine, are less constipating than morphine likely arises from the unfortunate customary clinical practice of using small or infrequent and, therefore, less effective doses of these medications. Constipation cannot be avoided by using epidural or intrathecal opioids, as the spinal cord is a prominent site for opioid inhibition of gastrointestinal function.[96] However, some data exist suggesting that intrathecal or epidural analgesia inhibits gastric emptying less[100] and allows earlier recovery of bowel function[101] than equieffective doses of parenteral opioids. The prominent local effects of opioids on the bowel may be absent or much diminished after spinal administration. In animals, the most constipating routes of administration for morphine are oral and intraperitoneal, which likely result in the highest concentrations of drug in the region of the bowel.[102–104] Based on this fact, the conversion of a patient's analgesic regimen from parenteral to oral medications to decrease constipation is counterproductive, unless, of course, a less-effective analgesic dose is given orally.

VENTILATION. The negative effects of opioids on respiration are greatly feared as the most severe and potentially life-threatening consequences of the use of these drugs for pain. In contrast to the opioid receptors that regulate other physiologic functions, those influencing ventilation are located in a very discrete distribution within the ventral medulla.[105-107] At this site, they act very specifically on medullary neurons to reduce the ventilatory response to hypercapnia. Opioids produce characteristic changes of the minute ventilation/end-tidal carbon dioxide curve generated by rebreathing of expired air in a spirometer.[108] Opioid analgesics cause retention of carbon dioxide, with resultant respiratory acidosis and, in cases of extreme toxicity, respiratory arrest.

The respiratory depressant effects of opioids are primarily due to mu-receptor activation. The role of the delta- and kappa-receptor in this response is still unclear.[109,110] Thus, respiratory depression continues to be of some degree of concern with all clinically useful opioid analgesics. All exert most of their effects via the mu-receptor. However, the presumed risk of ventilatory compromise is rarely sufficient reason to justify withholding analgesics.[9]

THE URINARY BLADDER. Opioid receptors are present on the smooth muscle of the ureters, urinary bladder, and urethra,[89] as well as on neurons of the central nervous system that govern function of the urinary bladder.[111] Administration of opioids often causes urinary retention by interruption of the micturition reflex and by inciting contraction of the vesical sphincter.[89] Opioids also enhance tone of the detrusor muscle, sometimes generating urinary urgency.

BEHAVIOR AND ENDOCRINE AND IMMUNOLOGIC EFFECTS. Considerable interest in the endocrine and immunologic effects of the opioids is evident in the recent literature. Opioids influence the release of a variety of hormones from the pituitary and hypothalamus.[112] Disruption of the cyclic nature of prolactin secretion may induce the effects of opioid addiction on the menstrual cycle. It is unclear what effect the short-term administration of opioids for analgesia may have on menstruation and other prolactin-dependent processes.

Another well-described endocrine effect of opioid administration is stimulation or suppression of the release of antidiuretic hormone (vasopressin or ADH). Whereas morphine usually stimulates vasopressin release and causes antidiuresis, kappa-selective opioids suppress vasopressin release, yielding diuresis.[113,114]

Opioid receptors exist on the surfaces of the many circulating cellular components of the immune system. Morphine and beta-endorphin appear to inhibit stimulated mitogenesis in lymphocytes.[112,115] The meaning of these findings in terms of the use of opioids as analgesics is unclear, and awaits considerable further study before major changes in clinical practice should occur.

Available Agents and Properties

FULL-AGONIST OPIOIDS. This class of drugs encompasses all agents that can produce very intense analgesia and relieve the most severe forms of pain. Morphine is the prototypic drug of this class. Several other types of opioid drugs, with highly diverse chemical structures, produce nearly identical pharmacologic effects. Three principal groups are of interest to the clinician. The first is the 4, 5 epoxymorphinans, also called the *opiates*. They are directly obtained from opium (*i.e.,* codeine, morphine), or they are chemically derived from codeine or morphine, as in the cases of diacetylmorphine (heroin), hydromorphone (Dilaudid), hydrocodone (Dicodid), oxymorphone (Numorphan), and oxycodone (contained in Percodan). Another highly significant group is the piperidine-based drugs. These can be subdivided into the phenylpiperidines and the anilinopiperidines. The phenylpiperidines are represented in clinical use almost exclusively by meperidine (Demerol). The anilinopiperidines include the fentanyl series of opioid analgesics, fentanyl (Sublimaze), sufentanil (Sufenta), and alfentanil (Alfenta) being the agents available for use in man. A final group is the diphenylpropylamines, which for practical purposes include only methadone and propoxyphene (Darvon), the latter being a low-efficacy analgesic.

The pharmacologic effects of these drugs are highly similar. The principle opioid receptor activated by these drugs is the mu-receptor. The available full-agonist opioids have variable but low activity at delta- and kappa-receptors. To date, no clinically important effect at these latter receptors has been identified. Thus, administration of any of these drugs would be expected to produce, in addition to analgesic effects, some degree of sedation, possibly euphoria or dysphoria, depression of ventilatory drive, and decreases in intestinal propulsion. The potential for cardiovascular depression and certain endocrine effects (*e.g.,* prolactin release) also must be considered.

Pharmacokinetic properties account for many apparent differences between the drugs. It is useful to generalize the pharmacokinetic behavior of the drugs based on their chemical class. The opiate drugs (represented by morphine) tend to be the least lipophilic of the three general chemical classes of full agonists. Morphine itself is the least lipophilic of this group. The other derivatives (codeine, heroin, hydromorphone) are somewhat more lipid-soluble; however, these drugs are all considerably less lipid-soluble than the piperidines and methadone.[116] This lipophobia contributes to smaller apparent volumes of distribution and somewhat slower onset of action compared to the piperidines (such as meperidine and fentanyl).

Another significant characteristic of this group is the role of hepatic conjugative metabolism, particularly glucuronidation, in their elimination. Glucuronidation of the 3- and 6-position hydroxyl groups accounts for most of morphine's metabolism. These glucuronide conjugates are subsequently excreted in urine.[117] 6-Glucuronidation of morphine does not inactivate the molecule. Instead, it produces a highly potent mu-opioid agonist.[118-123] Extensive research is currently attempting to delineate the part the 6-glucuronide of morphine plays in the production of clinical analgesia after morphine administration.[124-128]

The other opiate compounds have been less well characterized with respect to their metabolism. All undergo some degree of conjugation. Many sustain various hepatic oxidative reactions first, resulting in N-demethylation, O-demethylation, or O-deacetylation. Hepatic extraction of opiate molecules is modest, particularly in comparison to the piperidines. Because of this effect, oral administration provides good systemic amounts of drug. This class of drugs has the greatest number of useful oral opioid analgesics.

In contrast, the piperidines experience primarily hepatic oxidative dealkylation and hydroxylation reactions. These changes produce inactive, water-soluble compounds that are easily excreted in the urine.[129-131] The important exception to this generalization is the phenylpiperidine meperidine. This compound is dealkylated by the hepatic microsomal enzymes to normeperidine, which retains weak opioid agonist activity and is neurotoxic.[132,133] Reviewing the literature reveals many case reports of neurologic manifestations (seizures) of normeperidine accumulation.[134-136] Because this metabolite is excreted primarily in the urine, these occurrences are usually associated with renal impairment, high dosages of meperidine for extended periods, or both.[131,133] Although oral absorption of meperidine is good, hepatic extraction is high, resulting in low bioavailability (approximately 25%) and extensive production of a toxic metabolite. Because of these considerations, use of meperidine by the oral route is discouraged, particularly considering the many good alternatives available in the opiate class. Hepatic extraction of the anilinopiperidines (the fentanyl series) is nearly complete, making oral administration of these compounds useless.[129]

The most important differences between the anilinopiperidines (fentanyls) and the opiates lie in lipophilicity and distributive characteristics. Rapid distribution away from the site of action, not metabolic clearance, mostly determines the duration of action of anilinopiperidines. The extremely low concentrations of these drugs that appear in blood under clinical circumstances have proved extremely difficult to measure. As a result, older reports may have significantly underestimated important pharmacokinetic parameters such as volume of distribution and clearance.[129,137] Recent studies using more sensitive assays and larger dosages have yielded much larger volumes of distribution and longer elimination half-lives for fentanyl and sufentanil than previously described.[138-140]

Methadone does not find extensive use in the management of acute pain, owing mainly to its unique pharmacokinetic properties. The plasma protein binding of methadone is very high, resulting in a slow rate of distribution into a high apparent volume. Thus, despite its high lipophilicity, methadone has a somewhat slow onset of action. Methadone has an extremely long elimination half-life, resulting in a prolonged approach to steady-state conditions. Its slow onset and protracted elimination make rapid titration of methadone to effect very difficult.[141-143] The related drug propoxyphene is a poor analgesic and is not available for parenteral administration. Many more effective opioids are available for oral administration. Table 37-1 summarizes the pharmacokinetic properties of the full opioid agonists.

Partial Agonists and Mixed Agonist/Antagonist Opioids

This group of compounds encompasses a variety of chemical structures and pharmacokinetic characteristics. In developing these agents, pharmacologists hope to produce analgesics with reduced dependence liability and decreased respiratory-depressant properties. They attempt to achieve this goal by making drugs that are lower in efficacy than standard compounds (*e.g.,* morphine) or act on different opioid receptors (kappa or delta, rather than mu), or both. Efficacy in this context refers to the maximal degree of pharmacologic effect a drug can produce in a given system or organism. Agonists of low efficacy, besides producing less robust pharmacologic effects than full agonists, also can function as antagonists of their full-agonist counterparts.

The first drug of this type introduced into clinical practice, nalorphine (Nalline), was initially used as an opioid antagonist. It is no longer in routine use.

Table 37-1

Pharmacokinetic Properties of Full-agonist Opioids

OPIOID	VOLUME OF DISTRIBUTION (L/kg)	CLEARANCE (L/kg/h)	ELIMINATION HALF-LIFE (h)
Morphine	3.2–5.2	0.7–2.0	1.7–3.5
Meperidine	2.8–4.8	0.7–1.1	3.1–4.1
Fentanyl	2.9–8.1	0.42–0.72	4.6–11.6
Sufentanil	4.0–19.0	0.61–1.2	5.0–20.0
Alfentanil	0.3–0.4	0.1–0.3	1.5
Methadone	1.7–5.3	0.05–0.12	13.0–51.0

Today, commonly used mixed agonist/antagonist opioids include nalbuphine (Nubain), pentazocine (Talwin), and butorphanol (Stadol). All have activity at kappa-opioid receptors besides being partial mu-opioid agonists. Other drugs include buprenorphine (Buprenex) and the newly introduced analgesic dezocine (Dalgan). Drugs with kappa-opioid receptor activity have marked sedative and dysphoria-inducing properties.[54,88] None of these agents are listed on Schedule II of the Controlled Substances Act, owing to their demonstrably lower abuse potential compared to morphine. Similarly, these drugs appear to produce respiratory depression in a limited way. They have an apparent "ceiling" effect. No additional increases in respiratory depression occur with repeated or escalated dosages.[144] Although these drugs yield effective analgesia under controlled conditions, clearly their reduced efficacy also is associated with reduced analgesic effectiveness. They find no routine employment in the treatment of severe pain, particularly cancer pain. They are not used in anesthesia to the same extent as the full-agonist opioids, such as morphine and fentanyl. Pentazocine is the only member of this group currently available for oral administration; the tablet formulation is a combination with the opioid-antagonist naloxone, to nullify its potential misuse by intravenous injection.[145] Nalbuphine is not uncommonly employed as an opioid antagonist in the postoperative setting. Butorphanol is widely used to treat the pain of labor. Pharmacokinetic properties of these drugs are summarized in Table 37-2.

Local Anesthetics

The local anesthetics are the least specific of the various pharmacologic agents available for use as analgesics. Unlike the opioids and antiprostaglandin drugs, their effects are not limited to neuronal systems subserving nociception but apply to all forms of conducting tissue.

Table 37-2

Pharmacokinetic Properties of Partial/Mixed-agonist Opioids

OPIOID	VOLUME OF DISTRIBUTION (L/kg)	CLEARANCE (L/kg/h)	ELIMINATION HALF-LIFE (h)
Pentazocine	3.5–7.7	0.8–1.5	2.0–5.1
Nalbuphine	3.4–7.4	1.4–2.0	1.3–2.7
Butorphanol*	5	2.3	2.7
Buprenorphine*	2.8	1.13	3.0
Dezocine	6.8–15.2	1.7–4.1	1.8–5.2

*Mean data. Ranges are unavailable.

Their principal pharmacologic action is to block the fast sodium conductance responsible for generating action potentials.[146] Their significant toxicities are a direct extension of their pharmacologic action, applied to whatever particular organ system is relevant. In practical terms, when used for postoperative analgesia, the local anesthetics are applied almost exclusively epidurally. In addition to analgesia, the effects that might be observed include anesthesia (due to blockade of non-nociceptive afferent neurons), paralysis or weakness (due to blockade of efferent motor neurons), hypotension (due to blockade of efferent sympathetic fibers), myocardial depression, and central nervous system effects (after systemic uptake of the anesthetic due to normal absorption or inadvertent intravascular administration).

Nonsteroidal Anti-inflammatory Drugs

The nonsteroidal anti-inflammatory drugs have long been appreciated for their analgesic properties as well as their anti-inflammatory effects. Salicylate, derived from the bark of the willow tree (*Salix alba vulgaris*, has been used alone as a therapeutic agent and modified to produce methyl salicylate, diflunisal, and acetylsalicylic acid or aspirin. This last compound has been employed as an analgesic, an anti-inflammatory, and an antipyretic since the turn of the century.[147] Many other NSAIDs have subsequently been introduced. Some of these agents are particularly useful in the management of acute pain; thus, their relevant pharmacology will be reviewed briefly here.

The nonsteroidal anti-inflammatory drugs, including the salicylates, inhibit the cyclooxygenase enzyme (formerly known as prostaglandin synthetase). This enzyme is crucial in production of the various prostanoids from the arachidonic acid precursor molecule. *All* the prostanoids (thromboxane, prostacyclin, and the various prostaglandins) require the cyclooxygenase enzyme for their synthesis. The production of leukotrienes, the other major category of arachidonic acid metabolites, proceeds via the lipoxygenase pathway, is not associated with cyclooxygenase, and thus is unaffected by the NSAIDs.[147] The prostaglandins and their synthetic enzymes are ubiquitous and produce effects on a variety of organ systems. The analgesic actions of the NSAIDs can be ascribed to their effect on prostaglandin sensitization and activation of afferent nociceptors (see the discussion of autocoids) and their impact on afferent nerves. The adverse consequences of the NSAIDs also directly relate to inhibition of prostaglandin synthesis in various tissues. An understanding of the actions of the prostaglandins in relevant organ systems leads directly to an appreciation of the effects of the NSAIDs.

Thromboxane A_2 and prostacyclin have diametrically opposing actions on the cardiovascular system and on blood platelets. Thromboxane A_2 is a potent vasoconstrictor and platelet-aggregating agent. In contrast, prostacyclin is a potent vasodilator and inhibitor of platelet aggregation. The predominant effect of NSAID administration (and thus cyclooxygenase inhibition) on hemostasis is an increase in bleeding time due to platelet inhibition. Platelet count, prothrombin time, or partial thromboplastin time do not change.[147] Changes in platelet function caused by acetylsalicylic acid (aspirin) are permanent. New platelets must be generated to restore bleeding time to normal. This process requires 4 to 7 days.[147] In contrast, the increased bleeding time associated with the newer NSAIDs is reversible, essentially resolving when the drug is eliminated.

The prostaglandins have effects on most forms of smooth muscle. In the gastrointestinal tract, the impact depends on the muscle type and the particular prostaglandin. Both prostaglandin E and prostaglandin F contract longitudinal muscle. On the other hand, circular muscle contracts in response to prostaglandin F and is relaxed by prostaglandin E.[148] Bronchial and tracheal smooth muscle respond similarly to gastrointestinal circular muscle. Prostaglandins are probably involved in the aspirin hypersensitivity that can result in the severe bronchoconstriction observed in some individuals.[149] Perhaps of most significance in the obstetric field, uterine smooth muscle requires the production of prostaglandins for contraction. This dependence underlies both the utility of NSAIDs in the treatment of painful uterine cramping associated with menstruation and the ability of NSAID administration to prolong gestation.[150]

Prostaglandins (in particular, prostaglandin E and prostacyclin) perform the following roles in the regulation of the function of gastrointestinal mucosa:

- Promote secretion of electrolyte and water in the small intestine
- Regulate blood flow in mucosa
- Stimulate production of cytoprotective mucus in stomach
- Inhibit gastric acid secretion[151,152]

In these regions, inhibition of prostaglandin synthesis yields the following:

- Loss of regulation of local blood flow
- Decreased mucus production
- Back-diffusion of luminal acid into mucosal cells

These effects predispose to ulceration, the most common serious adverse effect associated with NSAID administration.[152] Gastrointestinal discomfort, not necessarily associated with ulceration, is a frequent complaint and is the most common limitation of NSAID use. Note that these effects are not produced only by orally administered NSAIDs.[147] Injectable forms, such as the newly introduced analgesic ketorolac (Toradol), share these detractions.

The anti-inflammatory and antipyretic activities of the NSAIDs have some minor negative consequences that bear mentioning. Although few of the NSAIDs are promoted specifically for their antifebrile activities, all act as antipyretics. Little evidence is available to suggest that NSAID administration may mask signs of infection, but in the acute postoperative setting, this point is worth considering. Also, the prostanoids play a positive role in the inflammatory response to injury. They are involved in wound healing and, in particular, bone reformation and fusion.[153] Debate and research continue on the significance of NSAID effects on wound healing, especially after orthopedic procedures.[154–157]

Prostaglandins stimulate renal blood flow and inhibit chloride reuptake in the kidney. The NSAIDs antagonize these as well as the effects of diuretics.[158] In otherwise healthy individuals, the NSAIDs have little effect on blood pressure or fluid and electrolyte balance. In individuals with congestive heart failure or chronic renal disease, however, sodium retention may occur, the action of diuretics may be lessened, and, rarely, acute renal failure may be precipitated. Although these issues will be of little importance in the healthy parturient, they should be considered before one uses NSAIDs in patients with pregnancy-associated hypertension, for example.

A variety of nonsteroidal anti-inflammatory drugs are now available that encompass several chemical classes and possess differing pharmacokinetic profiles. Many, if not most, of these drugs are more appropriate for the symptomatic treatment of rheumatic disease than for use as postoperative analgesics. A selected few with desirable characteristics are described here; all but one are available only for oral administration. Dosages and durations of action are summarized in Table 37-3.

Aspirin is the oldest and best-studied NSAID. It is also the most toxic. It has a smaller therapeutic index than most NSAIDs and causes long-lasting inhibitory effects on platelet aggregation.[147] The usual dose is 650 to 1000 mg, given every 4 hours, preferably with food to reduce gastrointestinal irritation. Aspirin is commonly incorporated in combination analgesics, such as Percodan. Although it is inexpensive and widely available, aspirin is being supplanted by ibuprofen. Also available over the counter, ibuprofen is less toxic, better tolerated, and arguably both more effective and as economical as aspirin.

Acetaminophen (Tylenol) lacks potent antiprostaglandin activity, does not affect platelet function, and is not effective as an anti-inflammatory. It does produce analgesia and antipyresis via an apparently central mechanism involving prostaglandins.[147] It is a weak analgesic when used alone, but it finds common use in the postoperative setting in combination with opiates such as codeine (Tylenol #3 and #4) and oxycodone (Percocet, Tylox). Excessive dosages of acetaminophen cause hepatic toxicity. Limit the total daily dose of acetaminophen to 4000 mg.

Ibuprofen (Motrin)[159] and naproxen (Naprosyn)[160] are the best choices of strong, orally administered NSAIDs for postoperative pain. Naproxen may be ad-

Table 37–3

Suggested Dosages of Nonsteroidal Anti-inflammatory Drugs

DRUG	DOSE RANGE (mg)	INTERVAL RANGE (h)
Ibuprofen	200–600	4–6
Naproxen	250–500	6–12
Indomethacin	25–50	4–8
Aspirin	650–1000	4–6
Ketorolac*	30	6
Acetaminophen†	650–1000	4–6

*Intramuscular use only; begin with a 60-mg loading dose.
†Do not exceed 4000 mg/24 h.

ministered as infrequently as twice per day to good effect. The sodium salt of naproxen (Anaprox) has a more rapid onset of action than the free acid and finds frequent use in the treatment of painful cramping associated with menstruation. Due to prior familiarity, it may be easily accepted as an analgesic by both patients and surgeons. Suggested doses and schedules are presented in Table 37-3. As with all analgesics, the NSAIDs are most effective if used on a schedule, not on an as-needed basis. Because the acute adverse effects of the NSAIDs are dramatically less serious than those of the opioids, there is no reason to limit administration of these drugs to on request.

The potent nonsteroidal anti-inflammatory drug ketorolac, as its tromethamine salt (Toradol), was recently introduced for use as a postoperative analgesic.[161] This agent represents a significant advance. Unlike previous NSAIDs, it is potent enough that an effective dose is soluble in a sufficiently small volume to allow parenteral administration, particularly via intramuscular injection. Do not confuse the issue of potency with efficacy. No evidence exists to suggest that ketorolac is a more effective analgesic than appropriate doses of other strong NSAIDs. In all respects, this drug mimics the other NSAIDs, including effects on bleeding and gastrointestinal mucosa. Nevertheless, this agent is an effective analgesic and can be used in the immediate postoperative period when oral intake is unreliable or contraindicated. It lacks the sedative, constipating, and respiratory-depressant effects of the opioids, and has little or no potential for diversion or abuse.[161] When ketorolac is used for moderate to severe postoperative pain, the manufacturer recommends, that an opioid analgesic also be available (package insert, Toradol/ketorolac tromethamine, Syntex, Inc., Palo Alto, CA 94304, 1989).

Transition to Oral Therapy

Oral analgesics are an integral part of the management of acute and chronic pain. Remember that with appropriate drug and dose selection, orally administered opiates can be just as effective for the relief of pain, even severe pain, as parenterally administered opiates. In addition to being markedly less expensive than parenteral administration, the oral route is particularly convenient and safe. Oral administration is clearly the method of choice for the patient who will be discharged home with a significant degree of pain. An important aspect of postoperative pain management is the promotion and maintenance of mobility of the patient. Oral analgesics are frequently used after a period of paren-

teral therapy to facilitate patient mobility. Giving insufficiently strong oral analgesics after discontinuation of powerful modalities such as the epidural or PCA returns the patient to a state of marked discomfort and defeats this purpose. Knowledge of the relative potencies of orally administered analgesics is therefore critical to their successful employment.

Oral analgesics are indicated for patients with appropriate pain complaints that require analgesia, who would be expected to respond to the drug selected (based on type of pain), and who can tolerate oral intake (clear liquids at a minimum). Contraindications to oral therapy include a nothing-by-mouth status or presence of ileus; persistent nausea and vomiting that prevent reliable oral intake; and very severe acute pain that demands immediate titration (with parenteral opiates). A high parenteral dosage requirement should not be considered a contraindication. Successful transition to oral therapy can easily be achieved if appropriate conversion factors for oral to parenteral potency are observed.

A short summary of typically useful opioid analgesics for oral administration is given in Table 37-4. Pay particular attention to the potency equivalence of a given analgesic to the parenteral morphine standard. Using these equivalencies, patients can be converted from known dosages (or, for PCA, rates of self-administration) of parenteral opioids to equivalent dosages of oral analgesics, providing for a smooth transition unmarked by a sudden loss of analgesia or onset of excessive sedation.

CLINICAL EXPERIENCE

Intramuscular and intravenous narcotics have long been the mainstay of analgesic therapy following cesarean delivery. In many hospitals, they still represent the most widely practiced analgesic technique. Information on dosage and administration is available elsewhere and will not be repeated here.

The last two decades have seen a major shift in the methods used to provide postoperative analgesia to obstetric patients. This change stems from two main factors. Obstetric anesthesiologists have increasingly preferred regional anesthetic techniques and avoided general anesthesia. The discovery, in the 1970s, of widely distributed opiate receptors in the central nervous system, combined with the predominate use of regional anesthesia, produced a radically different approach to postoperative pain control.

Table 37-4

Analgesic Equivalencies of Orally Administered Opioids

DRUG	DOSE (mg)	DURATION (h)	IM/IV MORPHINE EQUIVALENT (mg)
Morphine	30	4	10
Morphine sustained release	30	8–12	10
Meperidine	300	3–4	10
Codeine	60	3–4	3
Oxycodone	10	3–4	5
Hydromorphone	4	2–3	5
Methadone	20	4–6/12–24	10

EPIDURAL ANALGESIA

Morphine

In 1979, Behar *et al*[162] reported that epidurally injected morphine effectively relieved pain in nonobstetric patients. Subsequently, multiple studies appeared in the literature analyzing the analgesic efficacy of epidural morphine.

Youngstrom *et al*,[163] in 1982, reported the results of a prospective, double-blind study of 35 patients who randomly received either morphine, 4 mg epidurally, or morphine, 4 mg intramuscularly, after epidural anesthesia for cesarean. A single dose of epidural morphine provided more profound and prolonged analgesia than the same dose of intramuscular morphine (Table 37-5).

Forty patients who had received lumbar epidural anesthesia for cesarean delivery participated in an early dose-response study of epidural morphine. They were prospectively randomized to one of four groups for postoperative analgesia: morphine, 7.5 mg intramuscularly, or morphine, 2.0, 5.0, or 7.5 mg epidurally. Women in the intramuscular morphine group had pain relief for 1 to 3 hours after injection. Most patients receiving morphine, 2 mg epidurally, did not gain any significant pain relief. All patients who got either 5 or 7.5 mg of morphine epidurally had significant analgesia for an extended period—over 12 hours (Fig. 37-4).[164]

Writer *et al*[165] studied a larger series (207) of both obstetric and nonobstetric patients. Subjects randomly received either morphine, 5 mg epidurally, or an epi-

Table 37-5

Median of Hourly and Total 6-hour Visual Analog Pain Scores After Epidural or Intramuscular Morphine

GROUP*	NO.	MS DOSE (mg)	HOUR 1	2	3	4	5	6	TOTAL
A	5	4 IM	4	3	3	4	4	3	19
BC	19	4 epidural	2	1	1†	1†	1†	1†	7‡

(After Youngstrom PC, Cowan RI, Sutheimer C, et al. Pain relief and plasma concentrations from epidural and intramuscular morphine in post-cesarean patients. Anesthesiology 1982;57:404)
*Group A received morphine, 4 mg IM, and epidural placebo. Groups B and C received epidural morphine, 4 mg, in 10 mL of normal saline and intramuscular placebo. In group C, 1:200,000 epinephrine was added to the epidural morphine solution.
†$P<0.05$.
‡$P<0.01$, Wilcoxon rank sum test.

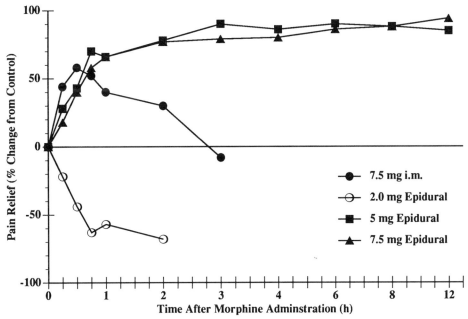

Figure 37–4. Percent changes in pain relief (from control) in parturients after cesarean section with either epidural or intramuscular morphine. Data represent average values with 10 women in each group. (After Rosen MA, Hughes SC, Shnider SM, et al. Epidural morphine for the relief of postoperative pain after cesarean delivery. Anesth Analg 1983;62:666)

dural placebo. Both the obstetric and nonobstetric patient groups who received epidural morphine obtained longer postoperative analgesia with lower supplemental narcotic requirements than the placebo patients. Parturients had longer pain relief after the same dose of morphine than nonobstetric patients (18.3 ± 1.3 h vs 9.2 ± 1.2 h, respectively).[165] In a similar study of only parturients, 83% of women receiving 5 mg of epidural morphine reported good to excellent postoperative analgesia. Fifty-two percent of parturients who got this dose needed no other analgesics for over 24 hours (Figs. 37-5 and 37-6).[166]

Today, morphine remains the most widely used epidural narcotic for analgesia after cesarean section. Work by other investigators has confirmed the efficacy of epidural morphine and further clarified the dose–response relationship.[167–170] Morphine, 5 mg epidurally, is the most commonly administered dose. Patients usually have good analgesia with lower doses. Four mg provides comparable analgesia for most patients with fewer of the troublesome side effects.[168] Some clinicians prefer 3.5 mg, but a higher failure rate becomes apparent if the dose is reduced to 3 mg.

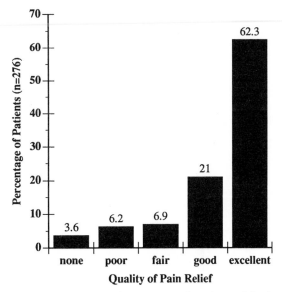

Figure 37–5. Maternal assessment of analgesia following epidural morphine, 5 mg, after cesarean delivery. (After Kotelko DM, Dailey PA, Shnider SM, et al. Epidural morphine analgesia after cesarean delivery. Obstet Gynecol 1984;63:409)

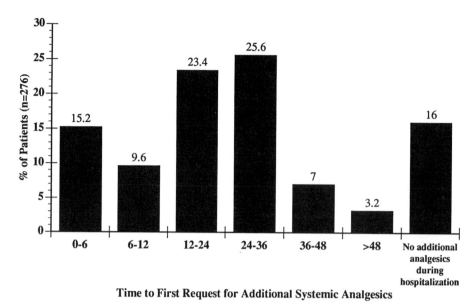

Figure 37–6. Time to first request for additional analgesia following epidural morphine, 5 mg, after cesarean delivery. (After Kotelko DM, Dailey PA, Shnider SM, et al. Epidural morphine analgesia after cesarean delivery. Obstet Gynecol 1984;63:409)

Side Effects of Epidural Morphine

The frequent occurrence of troublesome side effects has dampened the initial enthusiasm for epidural morphine as a postoperative analgesic. This problem has also prompted investigators to study the epidural use of other narcotics in hopes of finding a suitable alternative to morphine. The following section characterizes the side effects of epidural morphine in more detail before reviewing the use of other narcotics for epidural analgesia.

PRURITUS. Nearly all investigators studying epidural morphine have reported itching as a side effect. They only report some variation in its frequency and severity (Table 37-6).[166,170–172] The pruritus associated with epidural morphine is characteristically mild. It occurs most commonly on the face or trunk, although it also may be generalized.

The exact mechanism by which epidural morphine causes pruritus is unknown. Zakowski *et al*[173] measured plasma histamine in patients receiving either epidural or intrathecal morphine after cesarean section. Plasma histamine concentration increased significantly after administration of intrathecal morphine, whereas concurrent plasma morphine concentrations remained very low (Fig. 37-7). These authors speculated that intrathecal morphine may induce histamine release via a central histaminergic system.

Table 37-6

Pruritus After Epidural Morphine

STUDY	DOSE EPIDURAL MORPHINE (mg)	PRURITUS	SEVERE (OR REQUIRING TREATMENT)
Ackerman et al[171]	5	60%	
Gieraerts et al [172]	5	80%	
Kotelko et al[166]	5	68%	28%
Leicht et al[170]	5	27%	4%

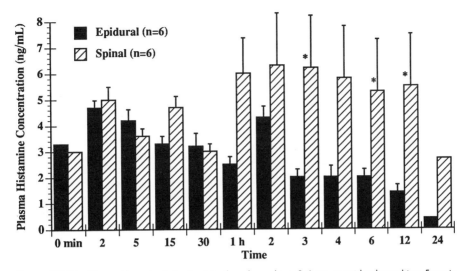

Figure 37–7. Plasma histamine following intrathecal morphine, 0.6 mg, or epidural morphine, 5 mg, in 12 parturients after cesarean delivery. (After Zakowski M, Ramanathan S, Khoo P, Turndorf H. Plasma histamine with intraspinal morphine in cesarean section. Anesth Analg 1990;70:S448)

NAUSEA AND VOMITING. Nausea or vomiting occur less frequently than pruritus after administration of epidural morphine. Without differentiating the nausea from vomiting, Leicht et al[170] reported an incidence of 20% in a survey of 1000 parturients. Kotelko et al[166] reported nausea in 18% and vomiting in 11% of parturients who received 5 mg of morphine. Fuller et al[174] reported a 30% incidence of nausea and vomiting after unspecified doses of epidural morphine in their retrospective review of 4880 parturients. Not all nausea and vomiting after cesarean delivery is due to the epidural narcotic. Writer et al,[165] in a report that included both obstetric and nonobstetric patients, found a 34% incidence of nausea and vomiting after intra-abdominal surgery and epidural morphine and a 13% incidence after similar surgery and epidural placebo.

Epidural morphine causes nausea and vomiting by stimulating the chemoreceptor trigger zone in the base of the fourth ventricle of the brain. Morphine, a highly hydrophilic compound, remains free in the cerebrospinal (CSF) fluid for a long time. Morphine concentration in the cervical CSF rises slowly. It is undetectable for the first hour after lumbar epidural injection. The concentration of morphine in the cervical CSF peaks 3 to 4 hours after injection (Fig. 37-8).[175] Radiographic studies of other water-soluble compounds confirm that cephalad migration of such compounds in the CSF does occur.[176]

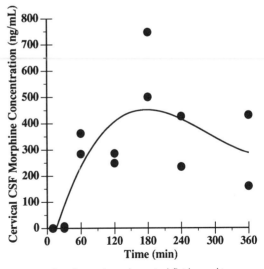

Figure 37–8. Cervical cerebrospinal fluid morphine concentrations at various times following lumbar epidural administration of 10 mg of morphine. The patients were randomly allocated to have the cerebrospinal fluid collected done at the recorded times. Each point represents data from a single patient. Each patient had only one cerebrospinal fluid sample collected from the C-7–T-1 interspace. (Data from Gourlay GK, Cherry DA, Cousins MJ. Cephalad migration of morphine in CSF following lumbar epidural administration in patients with cancer pain. Pain 1985;23:317)

RESPIRATORY DEPRESSION. Respiratory depression was recognized as a serious complication of the use of epidural morphine shortly after its introduction to clinical use.[177,178] The true incidence of this potentially disastrous complication, and whether it is lower in the obstetric population, has been the subject of some debate. The incidence is low enough that only a large series of patients can characterize it. A retrospective review of 4880 parturients receiving an unspecified dose of epidural morphine after cesarean delivery found a respiratory rate below 10 in only 12 patients, or 0.25%.[174] A prospective study of 1000 parturients who received morphine, 5 mg epidurally, reported 4 patients with a respiratory rate below 10.[170] Two of these women were observed and received no treatment. One with a respiratory rate of nine breaths per minute and a normal arterial blood gas received naloxone. The last had a rate of four to six breaths per minute and a $Paco_2$ of 76 mm Hg, and recovered without sequelae after receiving intravenous naloxone. These reports suggest that the incidence of clinically significant respiratory depression after neuraxial opioids in the obstetric population is 0.2% to 0.3%.

Respiratory depression following the administration of epidural morphine is usually described as "late," with an onset between 6 and 12 hours after administration. It usually manifests as a gradual decline in respiratory rate that, if untreated, will lead to progressive respiratory acidosis. The cause, as with nausea and vomiting, is the cephalad migration of morphine within the CSF, which incites direct central depression of respiration. The risk of respiratory depression rises with increasing dose.

Early respiratory depression after epidural administration of morphine also is possible. This event probably arises from rapid systemic uptake or intravascular injection of the narcotic.

In the absence of cephalad migration causing central depression of respiration, epidural morphine does not appear to have any characteristic effect on respiratory patterns. Slow respiratory rates and brief apneic periods occur both in patients who receive epidural morphine and those who receive intramuscular morphine. Recordings of pulse oximetry and respiratory impedance plethysmography for 24 hours after cesarean delivery find no difference with analgesic technique.[179] Brose and Cohen[180] monitored oxygen saturation in parturients receiving either epidural, intramuscular, or intravenous opioids after cesarean delivery. Patients in all three groups experienced periods of arterial desaturation ($Sao_2 < 95\%$). Patients receiving epidural morphine or intramuscular meperidine were at greatest risk of transient periods of severe desaturation ($Sao_2 < 85\%$).[180]

HERPES SIMPLEX LABIALIS. In 1987, Gieraerts et al[172] reported the results of a prospective, nonrandomized study of 44 parturients after cesarean delivery. Twenty-six of these patients received epidural morphine, 5 mg intraoperatively, and 3 to 5 mg up to twice daily thereafter. Another 18 women received intramuscular morphine 10 mg, every 6 hours as needed for pain. Recurrent herpes simplex labialis (HSL) lesions appeared in 9 of the 26 patients in the epidural group, but none of the patients in the intramuscular group. The authors speculated that scratching to relieve epidural morphine-induced pruritus lead to reactivation of the virus.[172] Crone et al[181] corroborated this report a year later. They published a retrospective study of 291 patients who received epidural anesthesia for either cesarean or vaginal delivery. The HSL lesions recurred in 9.7% of patients who received epidural morphine but in only 0.6% of those who did not. This group then reported a prospective follow-up study.[182] Again, they found an association between epidural morphine and HSL. Patients who received intramuscular morphine were not at increased risk. The groups did not differ in their history of previous oral lesions. Other investigators have been unable to verify this association. Cancer patients who had received either epidural morphine or epidural lidocaine for pain control did not differ in the incidence of oral HSL.[183] Weiss et al[184] prospectively followed 203 parturients after cesarean delivery: 24 patients received morphine, 3 to 5 mg epidurally; 81 patients received morphine, 0.15 mg intrathecally; and 98 patients received systemic narcotics. They found that HSL developed in 6 of 105 patients receiving central narcotics, and in 4 of the 98 patients receiving systemic narcotics. Further, they noted no difference between general and regional anesthesia, or spinal and epidural anesthesia (Fig. 37-9). Clarification of any association between epidural morphine and the recurrence of oral herpes awaits further studies and a better understanding of the possible mechanism.

TEMPERATURE EFFECTS. Bernstein et al[185] investigated the effects of both epidural and subarachnoid morphine on body temperature at cesarean delivery. In a prospective, randomized study, they found a clinically and statistically significant decrease in body temperature in patients receiving subarachnoid morphine compared to those not receiving subarachnoid morphine. Epidural morphine did not have any effect on body temperature after epidural anesthesia for cesarean section.[185] (The large decrease in body temperature

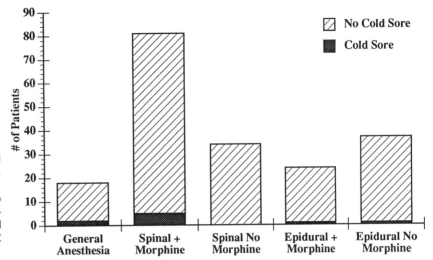

Figure 37–9. Incidence of cold sore versus type of anesthesia, ± neuraxial morphine (n = 203). Neither type of anesthetic nor the use of neuraxial morphine correlated with the development of oral lesions. (Graph courtesy of MC Norris, Philadelphia, PA.)

with epidural anesthesia alone may have prevented detection of any drop due solely to the morphine.) The mechanism of a morphine-induced decrease in body temperature is unclear. Similar effects occur in animals. Suggested mechanisms include interference with temperature modulation via the ventrolateral spinothalamic tract or a direct effect on the thermoregulatory center of the hypothalamus.[186,187]

Treatment of Side Effects

Most mild cases of pruritus do not require treatment. Diphenhydramine, 25 to 50 mg intramuscularly, usually provides adequate symptomatic relief in mild cases requiring treatment. The sedation associated with diphenhydramine may be as instrumental in providing relief as its antihistamine effects. Naloxone, 0.04 to 0.2 mg intravenously, also can relieve the itching. One must titrate naloxone carefully to eliminate the pruritus without reversing analgesia. Because of its short duration of action, a continuous infusion of naloxone may be needed to prevent recurrence of the pruritus. An effective rate is probably 0.4 to 0.6 mg/h. Again, titration is necessary. In a case report, intravenous nalbuphine successfully stopped both pruritus and nausea.[188] A randomized, double-blind comparison between intravenous naloxone, 0.2 to 0.6 mg, and nalbuphine, 5 to 15 mg, found nalbuphine better at relieving the side effects of epidural morphine.[189] This author (CMP) has had good success treating morphine-induced pruritus with nalbuphine, 10 to 20 mg intravenously. This treatment also can augment analgesia from the epidural narcotic.[188] Nalbuphine lasts longer than naloxone, making a con-

tinuous infusion unnecessary. Further, nalbuphine reportedly reverses epidural narcotic-induced respiratory depression.[190,191] However, prophylactic nalbuphine does not prevent the occurrence of side effects after administration of epidural morphine.[192]

Treatment options for nausea and vomiting include narcotic antagonists and antiemetics. Intravenous nalbuphine, 5 to 10 mg, can relieve narcotic-induced nausea and vomiting.[188] Likewise, intravenous naloxone, 0.1 to 0.2 mg, also should work if the nausea is due to a morphine effect in the fourth ventricle. Droperidol, 2 mg intramuscularly, suffices.[166] In this author's experience, intravenous droperidol, 0.625 mg, is a faster, more effective treatment. Rosen reported that 10 to 20 mg of prochlorperazine administered intramuscularly was a useful treatment.[164] All the preceding reports are anecdotal. Blinded comparisons between agents are not available.

Early or late, the treatment of choice for respiratory depression is intravenous naloxone. Institute artificial or mechanical support of ventilation immediately if the patient is obtunded while waiting for naloxone to have effect.

Prevention of Side Effects

Several investigators have studied ways to prevent side effects following epidural morphine. Naloxone will reverse pruritus, nausea, and respiratory depression due to epidural morphine but also can reverse analgesia. Naloxone infusion can prevent side effects as well. Because naloxone must be carefully titrated and it can only be given intravenously, it has not found wide use as prophylactic therapy. Nalbuphine, although an effective treatment, does not prevent side effects after epidural morphine.[192]

Naltrexone is a long-acting, orally administered narcotic antagonist. Cullen *et al*[193] administered naltrexone, 5 mg orally, to parturients 1 hour after they received epidural morphine, 5 mg, after cesarean delivery. Parturients receiving the naltrexone had a lower incidence of pruritus and nausea and vomiting than a control group who received a placebo. Neither pain scores nor the need for supplemental narcotics differed between the two groups. Abboud *et al*[194] studied the effects of two different doses of naltrexone on analgesia and side effects. These women received 4 mg of epidural morphine for pain after cesarean section. The women receiving naltrexone experienced significantly less pruritus compared to a control group receiving placebo. The incidence of inadequate analgesia increased as the dose of naltrexone rose from 6 to 9 mg. The duration of analgesia (as determined by time to first remedication) decreased as the dose of naltrexone increased. Other studies involving the use of oral naltrexone following intrathecal morphine found that naltrexone decreased the incidence of side effects after intrathecal morphine but also tended to reverse the analgesia.[195,196]

Finally, prophylactic transdermal scopolamine decreases the incidence of nausea and vomiting during the first 24 hours after cesarean delivery.[197] The scopolamine patch must be applied several hours in advance. Some patients then complain of dry mouth (Fig. 37-10).

Other Epidural Opioids

Fentanyl

Morphine, although a good epidural analgesic, has limitations. A high incidence of side effects and a prolonged latency and duration complicate its use. These restraints have led investigators to try other compounds in a quest for the "perfect" epidural analgesic. An early alternative explored was fentanyl, a phenylpiperidine derivative. Unlike morphine, fentanyl is highly lipid-soluble. This characteristic accounts for much of the difference between the two compounds. Fentanyl is much more rapid-acting, has a shorter duration, and a greater potency.

In a dose–response study, 30 patients undergoing cesarean delivery with epidural bupivacaine randomly received one of six doses of epidural fentanyl. The investigators injected epidural fentanyl, 0 to 100 μg intraoperatively, after delivery (no intravenous fentanyl control group was included). Visual analog scales were used to measure postoperative pain. The onset of analgesia was rapid and dependent on the dosage. At doses of 50 μg or more, all patients reported pain scores of 0 (Fig. 37-11). Twenty-five micrograms provided partial analgesia. Duration of pain relief increased as dose escalated up to 50 μg. The duration of complete analgesia at this dose was about 4.5 hours from the time of drug injection (Fig. 37-12). Epidural fentanyl, 50 to 100 μg, significantly reduced 24-hour morphine consumption. Giving more than 50 μg of epidural fentanyl offered no clear advantage.[198]

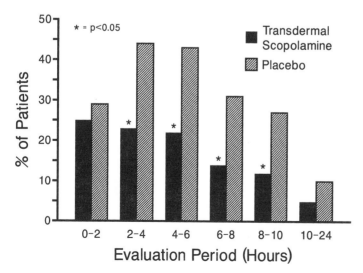

Figure 37–10. Nausea and transdermal scopolamine. All women received 4 mg of epidural morphine for analgesia after cesarean section. Patients receiving transdermal scopolamine experienced significantly less nausea during the first 12 hours after surgery. (Kotelko DM, Rottman FL, Wright WC, Stone JJ, Yamashiro AY, Rosenblatt RM. Transdermal scopolamine decreases nausea and vomiting following cesarean section in patients receiving epidural morphine. Anesthesiology 1989;71:675)

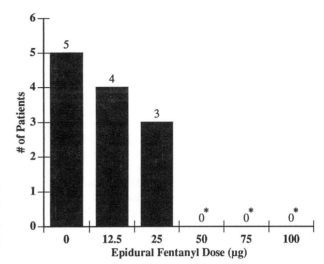

Figure 37–11. Number of patients feeling pain during cesarean section after varying doses of epidural fentanyl. There were six patients in each group. All patients received 0.75% bupivacaine for epidural blockade for cesarean delivery. (* = $P < 0.1$ vs 0 μg) (After Naulty JS, Datta S, Ostheimer GW, et al. Epidural fentanyl for postcesarean delivery pain management. Anesthesiology 1985;63:694)

The analgesic properties of fentanyl differ significantly from those of morphine. Epidural fentanyl, 75 μg, provided faster pain relief than epidural morphine, 2 mg. The morphine had a markedly longer duration of analgesia.[199]

Adding epidural fentanyl to epidural morphine may offer some advantages. Retrospectively, Kotelko *et al*[200] reviewed 219 patients who received either no epidural narcotics or epidural morphine, 3.5 mg, with either 100, 50, or 0 μg fentanyl. Only 4% of the patients who had received epidural fentanyl required further intraoperative narcotics, compared to 37% who had received epidural morphine alone, and 71% of those who had received no epidural narcotics. The time to first request for narcotics tended to be longer with the highest

dose of fentanyl (100 μg) compared to the other groups.[200]

Because of its short duration of action, continuous infusions have been used to provide prolonged epidural fentanyl analgesia. Continuous infusion of 75 μg/h provides a longer duration of effective analgesia than does a fentanyl bolus.[201]

A recent study has questioned whether epidural fentanyl offers any advantages over systemic fentanyl. In blinded, randomized study of 28 parturients, Ellis *et al*[202] compared the analgesia, side effects, and plasma concentrations attained with epidural and intravenous infusions of fentanyl following cesarean delivery. The women received a bolus of 1.5 μg/kg of fentanyl either epidurally or intravenously. Infusion rates were then

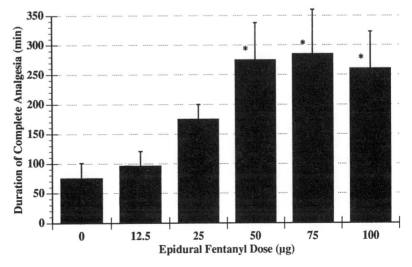

Figure 37–12. Duration of complete analgesia (pain score = 0) after varying doses of epidural fentanyl. Values represent the mean ± SEM of six patients in each group. All patients received 0.75% bupivacaine for epidural blockade for cesarean delivery. (* = $P < 0.1$ vs 0 μg) (After Naulty JS, Datta S, Ostheimer GW, et al. Epidural fentanyl for postcesarean delivery pain management. Anesthesiology 1985;63:694)

adjusted until the patient was comfortable. Plasma concentrations of fentanyl were lower in the epidural group at 12 hours after beginning the infusion, but there was no difference by 24 hours. Neither infusion rate, pain scores, nor the incidence of side effects differed between the groups. Three of the patients in the intravenous group were dropped from the study because of failure to obtain adequate analgesia. The authors concluded that epidural infusion of fentanyl for postoperative analgesia offered no clinical advantage over intravenous fentanyl infusion.[202]

With regard to side effects, epidural fentanyl shares many limitations with epidural morphine. Forty percent of patients who receive 25 μg or more of epidural fentanyl complain of itching.[198] James *et al*[201] reported pruritus in 75% of their patients with the bolus technique and 100% of the patients receiving a continuous epidural infusion. Itching required treatment in only 12.5% to 20% of their patients.[201] Nausea and vomiting occurred less frequently, between 4% with a bolus technique,[198] and 30% in patients on an epidural infusion.[201] Some patients also will complain of drowsiness.[198] Respiratory depression has been reported in one woman who received epidural fentanyl, 100 μg, at cesarean delivery. The depression responded rapidly to intravenous naloxone.[203]

Gourlay *et al*[204] studied the pharmacokinetics of lumbar epidural fentanyl, 1 μg/kg, in chronic pain patients. The fentanyl rapidly crossed the dura, and underwent cephalad migration. Cervical CSF fentanyl concentrations were approximately 10% of lumbar CSF concentrations. Peak cervical CSF concentration varied considerably between patients. The mean time to peak concentration was 22 minutes (Fig. 37-13).[204]

In summary, epidural fentanyl, 50 to 100 μg, provides rapid onset of profound analgesia; further increasing the dose does not improve or prolong analgesia. Analgesia lasts up to 4 hours after 50 to 100 μg. Like epidural morphine, epidural fentanyl can cause both bothersome and life-threatening side effects.

Sufentanil

Sufentanil, like fentanyl, is a phenylpiperidine derivative. Intravenously, sufentanil is approximately 10 times as potent as fentanyl, with about half the duration of action. Sufentanil is even more lipid-soluble than fentanyl and possesses a high affinity for the mu-receptor. In 1987, Madej *et al*[205] compared the analgesia provided by a single 100-μg bolus of epidural fentanyl to four different doses of epidural sufentanil in a randomized, blinded study of 50 parturients.[205] The duration of pain relief was dose-related, but sim-

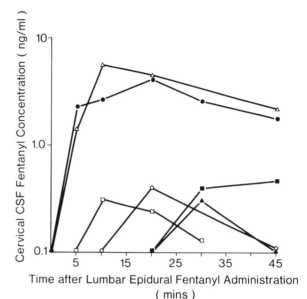

Figure 37–13. Cerebrospinal fluid (CSF) fentanyl concentrations as a function of time following lumber epidural administration of 1 μg/kg body weight of fentanyl to chronic pain patients. Each line represents values from a single patient. (Gourlay GK, Murphy TM, Plummer JL, Kowalksi SR, Cherry DA, Cousins MJ. Pharmacokinetics of fentanyl in lumbar and cervical CSF following lumbar epidural and intravenous administration. Pain 1989;38:253)

ilar, after either drug (Fig. 37-14). Drowsiness and sedation appeared to increase with larger doses of sufentanil. Parturients given 30 μg or more of sufentanil had significantly more nausea and vomiting than those given 20 μg or less, or fentanyl. Pruritus was common in all groups. Others have compared intravenous to epidural sufentanil[206] and epidural morphine to epidural sufentanil.[207] Epidural administration of sufentanil, 50 μg, produced more prolonged pain relief than intravenous administration of sufentanil, 30 μg. Epidural sufentanil, 30 to 60 μg, delivered prompt, short-lasting analgesia. In contrast, epidural morphine, 5 mg, had a long latency and a long duration of action (Fig. 37-15). Side effects were common in both studies. Itching occurred regardless of sufentanil dose or route of administration. Both epidural morphine and sufentanil, 60 μg, incited nausea and vomiting in 20% of patients. Both studies concluded that 30 μg of epidural sufentanil was an effective dose for postoperative analgesia.

The major advantage of epidural sufentanil over epidural morphine is its more rapid onset. The incidence of side effects is comparable to epidural morphine at

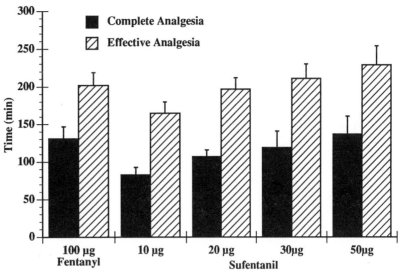

Figure 37-14. Duration of complete analgesia (pain score = 0) and effective analgesia (time to first request for additional analgesia) after 100 μg of epidural fentanyl or varying doses of epidural sufentanil. All patients received 2% lidocaine with 1:200,000 epinephrine for epidural anesthesia for cesarean delivery. Values represent the mean ± SEM. The duration of pain relief was dose-related but similar after either drug. (Data from Madej TH, Strunin L. Comparison of epidural fentanyl with sufentanil. Anaesthesia 1987;42:1156)

equianalgesic doses. Larger doses slightly prolong epidural sufentanil analgesia. Nonetheless, morphine provides a much longer duration of pain relief. None of the currently available studies are large enough to evaluate the risk of respiratory depression. When given intravenously at these doses, sufentanil can produce profound respiratory depression.

Meperidine

Meperidine, another phenylpiperidine derivative, is also known as pethidine in Great Britain and Australia. Most reports of its epidural use are from these countries. In a study that combined both cesarean section and lower abdominal surgery patients, Brownridge *et al*[208] compared epidural meperidine, 50 mg, to epi-

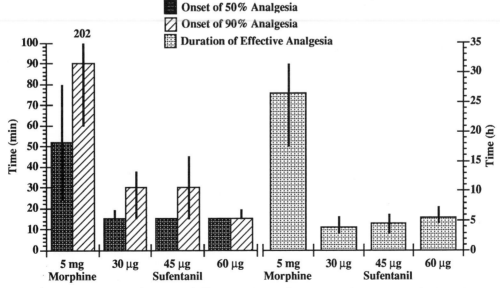

Figure 37-15. Onset and duration of effective analgesia after cesarean delivery with epidural morphine or various doses of epidural sufentanil. Values represent the mean ± SEM. All patients received 2% lidocaine with 1:200,000 epinephrine for epidural anesthesia. Sufentanil, at all doses had a significantly shorter latency and duration than morphine. (Data from Rosen MA, Daily PA, Hughes SC, et al. Epidural sufentanil for postoperative analgesia after cesarean section. Anesthesiology 1988;68:448)

dural bupivacaine, 25 mg, or intramuscular meperidine, 100 mg. Epidural meperidine produced a greater decrease in pain scores than intramuscular meperidine, and a slightly greater decrease than epidural bupivacaine. The duration of all three treatments ranged between 150 and 200 minutes. Patients preferred epidural meperidine to the other two analgesics. No information regarding side effects was reported. Perriss et al[209] compared epidural meperidine, 50 mg, to intramuscular meperidine, 100 mg, in post–cesarean section patients. They assessed pain with visual analog scales. The onset of epidural meperidine was faster than intramuscular meperidine, but the duration of analgesia did not differ. Epidural meperidine provided significantly better analgesia in all patients. The incidence of sedation and nausea and vomiting was low in both groups, and pruritus was not reported.[209] Although epidural meperidine would appear to be an effective postoperative analgesic, its clinical utility is limited by its short duration of action.

Hydromorphone

Hydromorphone, commonly known as Dilaudid, is a semisynthetic derivative of morphine that is readily available in a preservative-free solution. Its analgesic potency when administered systemically is roughly twice that of morphine. Epidural hydromorphone, 1.0 to 1.25 mg, provided 6.2 hours of pain relief. Slightly fewer side effects were noted than in a comparison group receiving epidural morphine.[210] Henderson et al[211] compared epidural hydromorphone, 1.0 mg, to intramuscular hydromorphone, 2 mg, in 30 parturients following cesarean delivery. The mean time to first request for additional analgesia was 19.3 hours in the epidural group versus 5.0 hours in the intramuscular group. Visual analog pain scores were significantly lower in the epidural group between 4 and 12 hours after injection.[211] In a randomized, blinded study of 40 parturients, epidural injection of both hydromorphone, 1.0 mg, and morphine, 5.0 mg, provided good pain relief, but morphine provided significantly longer analgesia (21.1 h vs 12.0 h for hydromorphone).[212]

Side effects following epidural administration of hydromorphone are comparable to those following epidural administration of morphine. Chestnut et al[213] reported a 42% incidence of nausea and vomiting and a 58% incidence of pruritus after epidural administration of 1.0 mg of hydromorphone. Other studies have reported no significant difference in the incidence of side effects between epidural morphine and hydromorphone.[210] None of these series reported respiratory depression, although the numbers of patients were too small to gauge the risk of this complication accurately.

These studies show no advantage to the use of epidural hydromorphone over epidural morphine as a postoperative analgesic.

Other Opioids

Epidural methadone provides more rapid onset of analgesia than epidural morphine. In one study the mean duration of analgesia after epidural methadone 4 mg was 4.8 hour.[214]

Even diamorphine (heroin) has been used as an epidural analgesic. McCrae et al[215] reported it to be an effective analgesic, with a mean duration of 8.39 hours, and side effects comparable to epidural morphine. It appears to have no advantage over morphine. It is not readily available in the United States.

Butorphanol

Butorphanol is a mixed opioid agonist/antagonist. It has both agonist and antagonist actions at the mu-receptor. It is a pure agonist at the delta- and kappa-receptors. Several investigators studied the epidural use of butorphanol in the obstetric population hoping to avoid the side effects of epidural morphine, specifically nausea, pruritus, and respiratory depression.

Naulty et al,[216] in a blinded, randomized study, found that 2 mg or more of epidural butorphanol prolonged postoperative analgesia following cesarean delivery under epidural anesthesia.[216] Increasing the dose of butorphanol increased the duration of analgesia and led to a dose-related decrease in supplemental narcotic usage. No patient complained of nausea or pruritus. The only side effect reported was somnolence, occurring in 13 of 14 patients who received 2 mg or more of epidural butorphanol. The somnolence lasted approximately 6 hours, although patients were reportedly "easily arousable." Epidural butorphanol has a faster onset but a shorter duration of action than epidural morphine (Fig. 37-16).[217] Epidural injection of both morphine and butorphanol slightly decreases central sensitivity to carbon dioxide.[217]

The low incidence of pruritus after epidural butorphanol is its major advantage. The short duration of action and the high incidence of somnolence represent significant shortcomings of this drug. It may not be appropriate to give a new mother a drug that is almost certain to make her drowsy during an important time in her and her new baby's life.

A promising technique involves the combined administration of epidural morphine and butorphanol.[218] Parturients who received 4 mg of morphine and 3 mg of butorphanol had a mean duration of analgesia of over 24 hours, without any reported pruritus or nau-

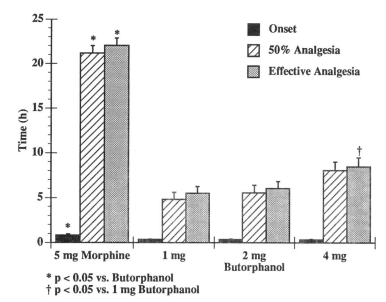

Figure 37–16. Onset and duration of 50% analgesia (pain relief ≥ 50% by visual analog scale) and effective analgesia with epidural morphine or various doses of epidural butorphanol. Values represent the mean ± SEM. All patients received 2% lidocaine with 1:200,000 epinephrine for epidural anesthesia for cesarean delivery. (Data from Abboud TK, Moore M, Zhu J, et al. Epidural butorphanol or morphine for the relief of section pain: Ventilatory responses to carbon dioxide. Anesth Analg 1987;66:887)

sea. Adding butorphanol to epidural morphine did not appear to cause significant sedation. Unfortunately, another group of investigators did not find any advantage to giving epidural butorphanol to parturients receiving epidural morphine.[219]

Nalbuphine

Nalbuphine is another mixed opioid agonist/antagonist. It has antagonist effects at the mu-receptor, agonist effects at the sigma-receptor, and partial agonist effects at the kappa-receptor. The antagonist properties of the compound may limit the potential for respiratory depression and other side effects following epidural administration, but also may limit its analgesic potency.

Varying doses of epidural nalbuphine (5, 10, 15, and 20 mg) produced "fair, and somewhat inconsistent" pain relief when compared to epidural morphine, 5 mg, in parturients after cesarean section.[220] Still, nalbuphine produced neither side effects nor detectable depression of respiration in response to a carbon dioxide challenge. Similarly, after thoracotomy, nalbuphine analgesia was "distinctly inferior" to epidural morphine.[221]

Clonidine

Clonidine is an alpha-adrenergic type 2 receptor agonist. After oral administration, it has significant antihypertensive actions. After epidural or spinal injection, it produces significant analgesia. Only a few of the

data on the analgesic effects of neuraxial clonidine come from parturients.

In 1989, a report appeared describing the use of epidural clonidine in six women after cesarean delivery.[222] These women received epidural clonidine, 800 to 900 μg, upon the first complaint of pain. They self-administered morphine via patient-controlled analgesia for additional pain relief. No patient required further analgesics for over 4 hours after clonidine injection. Twenty-four hour morphine use (23 mg) was less than a historical control group (62 mg). Sedation was the only side effect reported, and was described as "prominent" in the first hour after injection.

This group of investigators then studied the analgesic effects of continuous infusions of epidural clonidine.[223] One group received clonidine, 400 μg epidurally, followed by an infusion at 10 μg/h; a second group received clonidine, 800 μg epidurally and a 20 μg/h infusion; and a control group received a saline bolus and a saline infusion. Further analgesia was provided by intravenous morphine through a PCA pump. Both clonidine groups reported complete analgesia for 4 to 6 hours after injection. Only the higher infusion rate decreased 24-hour narcotic usage (Fig. 37-17). Decreased heart rates and lower blood pressures occurred in both clonidine groups. Transient sedation and prolonged motor and sensory block followed the injection of clonidine. The decreased narcotic usage may have reflected the prolonged sensory blockade produced by epidural clonidine.

In nonpregnant patients, Bonnet *et al*[224] found epidural clonidine to be equivalent to intramuscular clo-

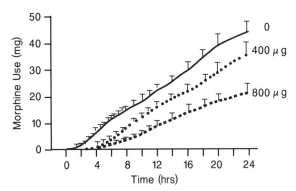

Figure 37–17. Cumulative mean patient-controlled analgesia morphine use by patients receiving either 800 μg, 400 μg, or no epidural clonidine as a bolus following cesarean delivery under epidural anesthesia. (Mendez RM, Eisenach JC, Kashtan K. Epidural clonidine infusion following cesarean section. Anesthesiology 1990;73:A919)

nidine for postoperative analgesia. Boico *et al*[225] found epidural clonidine to produce analgesia of rapid onset but short duration. Epidural clonidine has been tried in combination with epidural nalbuphine,[226] morphine,[227] and sufentanil.[228] Clonidine appears to speed onset and provide some early potentiation of analgesia with these opioids, without offering any other major advantage.

These studies have revealed several consistent side effects associated with epidural clonidine. Sedation is common, as is decreased blood pressure. In sheep, epidural clonidine consistently lowers heart rate, cardiac output, and central venous pressure.[229] Sympathectomy and decreased cardiac filling pressures probably cause this effect. An infusion of crystalloid restores all variables to baseline. Epidural clonidine appears to have no negative inotropic effects.

Although further study of epidural clonidine is necessary, this early work suggests that the usefulness of the drug will be limited. Epidural clonidine is largely without the usual side effects associated with epidural opioids (pruritus, nausea, vomiting, respiratory depression), but appears to have its own set of side effects (sedation, decreased blood pressure) that could prove to be equally bothersome. Finally, the short duration of action of epidural clonidine means an infusion is necessary for any effect beyond the immediate postoperative period. Using the drug as an adjunct to other analgesics may be the limit of its clinical utility.

Epinephrine

Epinephrine, a naturally occurring catecholamine with both alpha- and beta-adrenergic agonist effects, has been used with a variety of epidural analgesics. The primary aim of this combination is to prolong analgesia, and the secondary goal is to decrease the incidence of side effects. A point often overlooked when discussing the effects of epinephrine is the alpha-2-adrenergic agonism it possesses. Alpha-2 agonism is presumed to be the basis for clonidine-mediated analgesia, and this mechanism may give epinephrine some intrinsic analgesic properties.[230,231]

Most investigators have focused on using epinephrine to enhance the duration of the shorter-acting epidural opioids. One randomized, blinded study compared analgesia after cesarean delivery with epidural fentanyl alone to epidural fentanyl with epinephrine 1:400,000.[232] Each patient received two injections of her assigned study solution. No difference was found between groups in speed of onset or duration of analgesia following the first injection. Interestingly, duration of analgesia following the *second* injection was longer in the epinephrine group. More women (44%) in the epinephrine group complained of itching than in the control group (17%).

Epinephrine, 300 μg, significantly prolonged the duration of analgesia provided by epidural sufentanil, 50 μg (348 vs 266 min).[233] Side effects occurred with equal frequency in both groups, but with greater severity in the epinephrine group.

Dougherty *et al*[234] added epinephrine 1:200,000 to hydromorphone, 1.5 mg, epidurally for analgesia after cesarean delivery. Compared to patients who received the same amount of epidural hydromorphone alone, the epinephrine group had a slightly faster onset and slightly better analgesia over the initial 12 hours after injection. The duration of effective analgesia was somewhat longer in the epinephrine group—24.3 hours versus 18.2 hours. The epinephrine patients requested fewer additional narcotics. Pruritus was common in both groups (over 70%). All patients received "prophylactic" intravenous nalbuphine and droperidol, however, making comparison to other series difficult.

In a small study involving nonpregnant patients, Parker *et al*[235] added epinephrine to epidural fentanyl, sufentanil, and hydromorphone and could not find any increase in duration of analgesia compared to the plain solutions. Finally, in a slightly different twist, Dobson *et al*[236] found that adding epinephrine to epidural bupivacaine for cesarean delivery did not prolong the analgesia of subsequently administered epidural morphine.

In parturients, epinephrine may prolong the analgesia resulting from some shorter-acting opioids. This prolongation often comes at the expense of an increased incidence or severity of side effects. Except for hydromorphone, the duration of analgesia still falls well short of that obtained with epidural morphine alone. If used as a component of a continuous epidural infusion, epinephrine may reduce the infusion rate and total amount of opioid necessary for adequate postoperative analgesia.

Controversies

Youngstrom[163] reported a marked and prolonged lowering of pain scores in parturients who had received epidural morphine after 2-chloroprocaine epidural anesthesia. Later, Kotelko *et al*[237] reported that the use of 2-chloroprocaine for epidural anesthesia adversely affected the efficacy of epidural morphine in their patients after cesarean section.[237] They speculated that the low pH of the chloroprocaine solution interfered with the action of epidural morphine, possibly by causing the morphine to remain highly ionized in the epidural space.[238] 2-Chloroprocaine was and continues to be a popular local anesthetic agent in obstetrics, and this observation ignited a controversy that lingers still.

Several other authors have looked at this issue. In a retrospective review, women who received 2-chloroprocaine had more pain (assessed via VAS) than those who received bupivacaine or lidocaine. The duration of epidural morphine analgesia was similar in all patients.[239] A randomized, prospective comparison of epidural morphine pain relief after either 2-chloroprocaine or lidocaine for cesarean section also found poorer analgesia in the 2-chloroprocaine group.[240] Using even small (2–5 mL) doses of 2-chloroprocaine to "test" epidural catheters significantly impairs subsequent epidural morphine analgesia.[241] Other investigators have reported no differences in the duration of epidural morphine analgesia following different local anesthetics.[242]

These reports have led other investigators to study the effect of 2-chloroprocaine on pain relief after other epidural narcotics. Epidural fentanyl, 50 μg, provides significantly shorter analgesia after lidocaine or 2-chloroprocaine than after bupivacaine or lidocaine with epinephrine.[243] The shorter duration of pain relief from epidural narcotics after 2-chloroprocaine may simply reflect the more rapid regression of chloroprocaine sensory block and not a specific antagonistic effect.[244]

Adding a small dose of 2-chloroprocaine to epidural bupivacaine during cesarean section significantly shortens the duration of subsequent epidural fentanyl analgesia.[245] 2-Chloroprocaine also inhibits the effect of epidural fentanyl labor analgesia. Epidural catheters placed in laboring parturients were tested with either lidocaine or 2-chloroprocaine, followed by an epidural bolus injection of a bupivacaine–fentanyl–epinephrine mixture. A decreased duration of action was noted in the group that received 2-chloroprocaine.[246]

An explanation or mechanism for this interaction has proved elusive. A metabolite of 2-chloroprocaine, 4-amino-2-chlorobenzoic acid, may be responsible for a partial inhibition of bupivacaine or opiate action.[247] 2-Chloroprocaine may alter the pH of the epidural space; however, raising the pH of 2-chloroprocaine does not alter the duration of action of subsequently injected morphine.[238] Recently, Camann *et al*[248] compared fentanyl and butorphanol as epidural analgesics after cesarean delivery with either lidocaine or 2-chloroprocaine. Women who received fentanyl, but not butorphanol, after 2-chloroprocaine obtain a shorter duration of analgesia. Because butorphanol's primary action after epidural administration is as a kappa-receptor agonist, with little or no mu-receptor activity, the possibility arises that the inhibition is somehow mu-receptor mediated. Clarification of this issue awaits further study.

Although not all clinicians accept the reality of 2-chloroprocaine antagonism of epidural opioids, there clearly exists enough clinical data to suggest its actuality. Epidural administration of opioids has become so widespread in obstetrics; when using 2-chloroprocaine, be aware that analgesia obtained from epidural opioids may not be ideal, and be prepared to offer an alternative form of analgesia.

Summary

There are a variety of ways to provide epidural opioid analgesia following cesarean delivery. The following recommendations reflect the current practice at the University of Arizona. Most commonly, we rely on fentanyl and morphine for postoperative analgesia after a bupivacaine or lidocaine epidural anesthetic. We avoid using 2-chloroprocaine except in the most urgent situations owing to its negative interaction with epidural opioids. Fentanyl, 50 to 100 μg, mixed with the local anesthetic, enhances intraoperative comfort and provides early postoperative analgesia.[37] Morphine is still the longest-lasting epidural opioid available, and is the mainstay of postoperative analgesia in our practice. Immediately after delivery, we give morphine, 4 mg, in a volume of 8 mL.

Because of the risk of respiratory depression and the frequency of side effects, we find standard postoperative orders very useful (Table 37-7). Nurses check and record respiratory rates hourly for 24 hours after epidural morphine. If respiratory rate falls below eight breaths per minute, the nurse immediately injects naloxone and notifies the anesthesiologist. In the ab-

Table 37–7

Postoperative Neuraxial Opioid Orders

1. Epidural/intrathecal _____, _____mg, administered at _____ hours on _____(date).
2. No sedatives or narcotics administered except by order of anesthesiologist.
3. One ampule naloxone at bedside at all times.
4. Maintain intravenous access or heparin lock at all times.
5. Measure and record respiratory rate q 1 h; for respiratory rate < 8/min, give naloxone 0.2 mg IV, slowly over 2 min; notify anesthesiologist.
6. Supplemental analgesics: nalbuphine, 10–20 mg IV q 4 h as needed for pain.
7. For pruritus: nalbuphine, 10–20 mg IV q 4 h as needed for itching.
8. For nausea/vomiting: nalbuphine, 10–20 mg IV q 4 h as needed for nausea and vomiting.
9. For pain, pruritus, or nausea/vomiting unresponsive to above, page anesthesiologist on call.
10. This protocol covers 24 h after each dose of spinal narcotic.

sence of other sedatives or narcotics, respiratory depression of this degree should be rare. We have had good success treating pruritus, pain, and, to lesser extent, nausea and vomiting with intravenous nalbuphine. Not all patients will respond predictably, however, so the anesthesiologist must be available to manage patients if the standing orders are inadequate.

SUBARACHNOID OPIOIDS

The past decade has seen the resurgence of spinal anesthesia as a technique of regional anesthesia for cesarean delivery. As the use of spinal anesthesia has increased, so has the use of intrathecally administered opioids for postoperative analgesia.

Morphine

In 1979, Wang *et al*[249] reported that small doses of intrathecal morphine could provide prolonged, effective analgesia in patients with chronic pain. In parturients, subarachnoid morphine also produces excellent pain relief after cesarean section. The duration of analgesia ranges from 18.6 hours after 0.1 mg to 27.7 hours after 0.25 mg.[250] Women not getting subarachnoid morphine typically request analgesics 3.4 hours after delivery (Fig. 37-18). In a retrospective review, 0.3 to 0.5 mg of intrathecal morphine provided pain relief for over 20 hours in 78% of women.[251] A tendency to

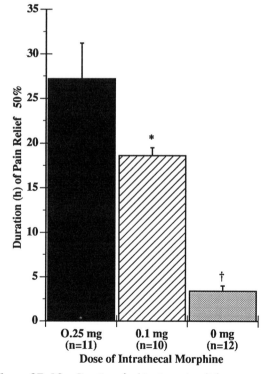

Figure 37–18. Duration of subjective pain relief as assessed by visual analogue scale in parturients receiving intrathecal morphine after cesarean delivery. (* = $P < 0.05$ vs 0.1 mg morphine, † = $P < 0.05$ vs 0.1 and 0.25 mg morphine) (Data from Abboud TK, Dror A, Mosaad P, et al. Mini-dose intrathecal morphine for the relief of post-cesarean section pain: safety, efficacy, and ventilatory responses to carbon dioxide. Anesth Analg 1988;67:13)

longer analgesia was noted with higher doses. Zakowski *et al*[252] prospectively compared the duration of analgesia after 0.2, 0.4, or 0.6 mg of intrathecal morphine administered with 12 mg of bupivacaine for spinal anesthesia. After 0.6 mg, analgesia lasted 44 hours.

Side effects reported in these studies are comparable to those seen after administration of epidural morphine. Pruritus occurs in 40% to 80% of patients and appears dose-dependent.[250,251] Vomiting occurs rarely after low doses (0.1 mg) of morphine but in up to one third of patients receiving larger doses (0.25 mg).[250,251] Clinically significant respiratory depression is rare.[251] Abboud *et al*[250] could detect no depression of respiratory response to carbon dioxide in patients receiving subarachnoid morphine (Fig. 37-19). Subarachnoid morphine, 0.2 mg, rarely produced clinically significant respiratory depression in a series of over 1600 parturients.[253] Eight markedly obese patients had episodes of respiratory depression ($Sao_2 \leq 85\%$ or respiratory rate $< 10/\min$). Although respiratory depression was not seen in these series, it has been reported elsewhere following subarachnoid morphine.[254–257] The optimal dose of subarachnoid morphine is around 0.2 to 0.3 mg; this dose should provide over 20 hours of good analgesia while avoiding an excessive incidence of side effects.

Following a report by Johnson *et al*,[258] both Abboud *et al*[259] and Carney *et al*[260] studied the effect of subarachnoid morphine on the incidence of postspinal headache. Neither of these prospective series could find any effect of subarachnoid morphine on incidence or severity of postoperative headache.

Finally, McDonald *et al*[261] investigated the interaction of subarachnoid morphine and local anesthetics, specifically bupivacaine, in rats. They found that bupivacaine reduced the time to onset of maximal morphine effect but did not prolong morphine antinociception.

Fentanyl

Fentanyl has also been used with local anesthetics for spinal anesthesia at cesarean delivery. Hunt *et al*[262] published a prospective, randomized dose–response study of subarachnoid fentanyl in combination with bupivacaine in parturients. The amount of fentanyl administered varied between 0 and 50 µg, whereas the bupivacaine dose was dependent on patient height. Addition of fentanyl caused no difference in speed of onset of the anesthetic, but it did transiently slow regression of blockade at the higher dose ranges. The duration of complete analgesia increased with the dose of fentanyl and plateaued at 6.25 µg. Likewise, the duration of effective analgesia increased from 71.8 minutes without fentanyl to 192 minutes with 6.25 µg of fentanyl (Fig. 37-20). Twenty-four hour narcotic usage did not vary among any of the groups. Pruritus occurred frequently in all the fentanyl groups, and nausea occurred less often. The short duration of effective analgesia even at the higher dose ranges limits the value of subarachnoid fentanyl as a true postoperative analgesic. No respiratory depression was noted in this study, but a recent report implicates fentanyl as a cause of respiratory depres-

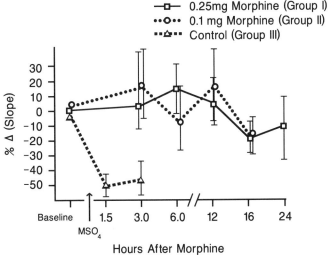

Figure 37–19. Percent change in slope of carbon dioxide–response curve following administration of either 0.1 mg or 0.25 mg of intrathecal morphine at cesarean delivery in healthy parturients. Control patients received no morphine. (After Abboud TK, Dror A, Mosaad P, et al. Mini-dose intrathecal morphine for the relief of post-cesarean section pain: Safety, efficacy, and ventilatory responses to carbon dioxide. Anesth Analg 1988;67:137)

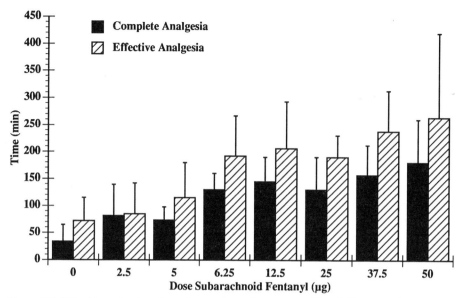

Figure 37–20. Mean duration of complete analgesia (pain score = 0) and effective analgesia (time to first request for additional analgesia) after varying doses of intrathecal fentanyl and hyperbaric bupivacaine for cesarean section. (* = $P < 0.05$ vs 0 μg fentanyl) (Data from Hunt CO, Naulty JS, Bader AM, et al. Perioperative analgesia with subarachnoid fentanyl–bupivacaine for cesarean delivery. Anesthesiology 1989;71:535)

sion in this population at a similar dose range.[263] Subarachnoid fentanyl should not be perceived as innocuous in this regard until wider experience is reported.

A single report by Johnson *et al*[258] suggests that the combination of fentanyl and a local anesthetic decreases the incidence of postdural puncture headache. This retrospective report remains unconfirmed. Many other factors may have contributed to the decrease in headache rate noted.

Finally, epinephrine added to a lidocaine–fentanyl mixture, but not to a lidocaine anesthetic alone, prolonged analgesia in patients who had undergone postpartum tubal ligation.[264] Epinephrine may have acted to delay absorption of fentanyl, or acted synergistically to prolong analgesia. Either way, it may be useful in prolonging the short duration of analgesia of subarachnoid fentanyl.

Other Opioids

Subarachnoid sufentanil, 10 μg, provided 5.4 hours of analgesia after cesarean delivery.[265] Patients who did not receive sufentanil needed pain medications 2.8 hours after induction. The sufentanil patients used fewer narcotics in the first 4 postoperative hours, but by 8 hours both groups required similar amounts of additional pain medications. Pruritus, usually of short duration, occurred in over half the sufentanil patients. Like fentanyl, a short duration of action limits the usefulness of sufentanil as a postoperative analgesic.

Subarachnoid buprenorphine, 0.045 mg, in combination with bupivacaine for spinal anesthesia at cesarean delivery, prolonged the pain-free interval from 109 minutes in controls to 420 minutes.[266] Nausea and vomiting developed slightly more often in the buprenorphine group. The incidence of pruritus after buprenorphine was 13.3%.

Subarachnoid narcotics that have been used in nonpregnant populations include methadone and oxymorphone. Methadone produces analgesia of shorter duration and less consistent quality than morphine, even at doses as high as 20 mg.[267,268] Oxymorphone provides approximately 16 hours of analgesia when administered intrathecally, with side effects of pruritus and nausea and vomiting.[269] Optimal dose ranges and advantages and disadvantages await further study.

Marando *et al*[270] injected subarachnoid nalbuphine in pregnant rats and did not find any suppression of writhing in response to visceral pain. They speculated that the mu-receptor antagonism of nalbuphine may have reduced the endogenous suppression of visceral nociception due to the pregnant state, offsetting the weak kappa analgesic effects of nalbuphine.

Nonopioids: Clonidine

Clonidine has been studied as a subarachnoid analgesic, although only in the nonpregnant population. Nakagawa et al[271] found that clonidine depressed the activity of wide-dynamic-range neurons in the dorsal horn of the spinal cord in response to noxious stimuli in cats. They also found a synergistic interaction between morphine and clonidine, the combination producing greater depression of activity at lower doses than either drug alone. Coombs et al[272] evaluated the analgesic potential of clonidine in 30 patients after lumbar laminectomy. Study groups received either 100 μg of subarachnoid clonidine or 100 μg of clonidine with 100 μg of morphine. The authors found that the combination of clonidine and morphine decreased postoperative PCA use for at least 8 hours, but they also found a confusing trend toward higher pain scores after 12 hours in the patients who had received clonidine alone or in combination with morphine.

Summary

Based on the aforementioned evidence, morphine remains the best choice for postoperative subarachnoid analgesia. Our current practice is to combine 0.25 mg of morphine and 10 to 15 μg of fentanyl with either hyperbaric lidocaine or bupivacaine in a single syringe to induce spinal anesthesia for cesarean delivery. The morphine provides up to 24 hours of good to excellent postoperative analgesia. Many parturients advance directly to oral pain medications on the first postoperative day, eliminating completely the need for parenteral analgesics. Fentanyl may enhance intraoperative comfort and provide some early postoperative analgesia. Because of the very small volumes of opioids used with this technique, we draw the narcotics up separately in tuberculin syringes to minimize the risk of accidental overdose. Although the addition of the opioids to the hyperbaric local anesthetic solution will predictably lower the baricity of the resulting solution, we have not found the dermatomal level of anesthesia to be appreciably different from a plain local anesthetic solution. As with epidural opioid analgesia, close postoperative monitoring of patients is essential. Postoperative orders are identical to those used following epidural opioids (see Table 37-3).

PATIENT-CONTROLLED ANALGESIA

In recent years, PCA has become a popular and effective method of providing postoperative analgesia following a wide range of surgical procedures. Several studies have focused on the use of PCA in the obstetric population. A prospective, randomized study compared intramuscular narcotics on an as-needed schedule; morphine, 5 mg epidurally; and PCA morphine for analgesia in 60 patients after cesarean delivery.[273] Following a loading dose of morphine in the recovery room, patients in the PCA group received a morphine bolus with a 15-minute lockout interval. The intramuscular group received either meperidine or morphine intramuscularly as ordered by their obstetrician. Patients rated their pain on a five-point scale every 2 hours while awake for 24 hours. Twenty-four hour narcotic usage was lowest in the epidural group. Analgesia, as determined by patient ratings, did not differ significantly between the intramuscular and PCA groups. Analgesia was significantly better in the epidural group than the intramuscular group. Patient satisfaction was higher in both the PCA and epidural groups when compared to the intramuscular group, with patient satisfaction being highest in the PCA group (Table 37-8).

Harrison et al[274] confirmed these results in a very similar study. Patients receiving epidural morphine had significantly lower pain scores in the first 16 hours postoperatively than did women receiving either intramuscular or PCA narcotics. Again, no difference in analgesia was found between intramuscular and PCA groups. The incidence of pruritus was highest in the epidural morphine group. Patient satisfaction with PCA was comparable to that with epidural morphine, despite poorer pain control in the PCA group.

Sinatra et al[275] compared postcesarean analgesia using PCA between morphine, meperidine, and oxymorphone. Equipotent solutions of each opioid were used (1 mL contained either 1.5 mg of morphine, 15 mg of meperidine, or 0.25 mg of oxymorphone). Upon first complaint of pain, patients received 1-mL increments of one of the opioids until comfortable, then could self-administer 1.2-mL boluses with a lockout interval of 8 minutes. Patient satisfaction scores were very high with all three opioids, and no differences in analgesia at rest were found. A few very slight differences were reported: The meperidine group reported severe pain with movement more frequently; nausea was highest in the oxymorphone group; and sedation was highest in the morphine group.

The effect of using a basal infusion plus intermittent bolus PCA also was studied by Sinatra's group.[276]

Table 37–8

Patient Responses to Questions About Analgesia and Satisfaction with Three Alternate Methods of Postoperative Analgesia

PARAMETER	INTRAMUSCULAR THERAPY (%)	PATIENT-CONTROLLED ANALGESIA (%)	EPIDURAL MORPHINE (%)
Analgesia (overall quality)			
Comfortable	25	40	65*
Mildly uncomfortable	55	60	30*
Very uncomfortable	10	0	0
In pain	10	0	5
Satisfaction (vs previous cesarean section)			
Much prefer current therapy	25	90†	65*
Prefer current therapy	30	10	30
Don't care	30	0*	0*
Prefer as-needed intramuscular therapy	15	0	5

(Data from Eisenach JC, Grice SC, Dewan DM. Patient-controlled analgesia following cesarean section: A comparison with epidural and intramuscular narcotics. Anesthesiology 1988;68:444)
*P<0.05 versus intramuscular group.
†P<0.001 versus intramuscular group.

Thirty-two patients received either morphine or oxymorphone PCA, with or without a basal infusion of the same opioid, following cesarean delivery. Basal infusion did not change 24-hour opioid usage, but it did significantly decrease pain scores with movement. The incidence of nausea was higher in the groups receiving the basal infusion.

Epidural PCA allows the use local anesthetics and opioids. In two separate series, Parker *et al*[277] compared epidural opioid PCA to intravenous PCA in patients after cesarean delivery. In a prospective, randomized series, they studied epidural hydromorphone PCA versus intravenous hydromorphone PCA.[277] Both groups reported comparable pain relief. The epidural PCA group used 60% to 80% less opioid. The incidence of side effects (nausea, vomiting, pruritus) was much higher in the epidural group. A second series studied the effect of the use of a basal infusion via the epidural route on analgesia, side effects, and opioid requirements on epidural hydromorphone PCA.[278] No difference in pain or sedation scores, or side effects, was found between groups, although the basal infusion group received significantly more opioid.

In another study, epidural PCA using a buprenorphine–bupivacaine combination provided similar pain relief as a fentanyl–bupivacaine combination.[279] The concentration of bupivacaine in both groups was 0.03%. A basal infusion of the study solution was used in both groups. Pain relief was comparable in both groups, but patient satisfaction was higher in the fentanyl group, due apparently to a lower incidence of nausea and vomiting. Lower extremity sensory loss was a side effect even with this low concentration of bupivacaine and was noted to be "of concern"; whether or not patients were ambulatory was not reported.

Intravenous PCA also can be used in combination with neuraxial opioids. Intraoperative injection of either epidural (3.0 mg) or subarachnoid (0.25 mg) meperidine significantly decreases postoperative PCA morphine usage.[280] This combination may prove an effective way to titrate postoperative analgesia.

Intravenous PCA offers an alternative to epidural or intrathecal morphine for postcesarean analgesia. Although intravenous PCA may not provide the same degree of analgesia as neuraxial opioids do, the control they allow the patient over her analgesia provides a significant level of satisfaction. In terms of maternal satisfaction, no one opioid appears to have distinct advantages over the others. Morphine, however, may have fewer neonatal effects. Breast-feeding neonates of mothers using morphine PCA scored consistently higher in "alertness" and "human orientation" measures on the Brazelton Neonatal Assessment Scale than did neonates whose mothers used meperidine PCA.[281] The incidence and severity of maternal side effects with PCA is usually lower than with neuraxial opioids. Further study of epidural PCA for postoperative analgesia will decide if this technique provides distinct advantages. The combination of intravenous PCA and neuraxial opioids may be the optimal solution for providing the best analgesia to the greatest number of patients.

ALTERNATE APPROACHES

Ilioinguinal Nerve Block

Bunting and McConachie,[282] in 1988, reported the use of ilioinguinal nerve block to provide postoperative analgesia following cesarean delivery (via Pfannenstiel incision). In a prospective study, patients receiving general anesthesia for cesarean delivery randomly received either bilateral ilioinguinal nerve blocks or conventional intramuscular papaveretum injections for postoperative analgesia. Ilioinguinal nerve block was performed using bupivacaine 0.5%, 10 mL bilaterally (Fig. 37-21). Patients in both groups had equal access to intramuscular analgesics. Patients in the nerve block group had significantly lower visual analog pain scores at four of the five intervals recorded between 0 and 24 hours postoperatively. The mean 24-hour dose of papaveretum administered was significantly lower in the block group.

Witkowski *et al*[283] studied ilioinguinal nerve block as an alternative or supplement to intrathecal morphine in patients receiving spinal anesthesia for cesarean delivery, again via Pfannenstiel incision. Patients received either morphine, 0.15 mg intrathecally, bilateral ilioinguinal nerve block with bupivacaine 0.5%, 10 mL, or both. Postoperative narcotic orders were standardized. The three groups did not differ in pain scores or supplemental narcotic usage. The women getting intrathecal morphine had a higher incidence of pruritus. These authors concluded that bilateral ilioinguinal nerve block could be used as a substitute for, or supplement to, intrathecal morphine

Transnasal

Transnasal administration of medications has recently proved effective in pediatric patients undergoing anesthetic procedures. Abboud *et al*[284] reported the efficacy of transnasal butorphanol for postoperative analgesia in parturients. In a prospective, randomized series, they compared intravenous butorphanol to several doses of transnasal butorphanol. All patients had effective pain relief. Intravenous butorphanol worked faster. Butorphanol, 2 mg transnasally, either as a single dose or in two equal portions, provided longer analgesia than did butorphanol, 2 mg intravenously (4.5 vs 3.0 h). Somnolence was a frequent side effect (over 70%) in both groups.

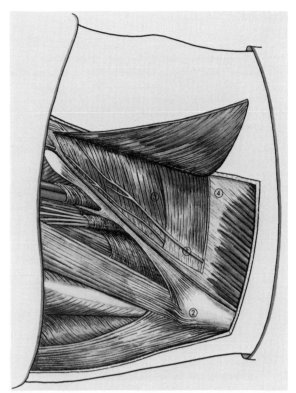

Figure 37–21. Course of the ilioinguinal nerve (1) as it proceeds between the internal oblique muscle (3) and the external oblique muscle (4), just medial to the anterior superior iliac spine (2). Block the nerve at a point 2.5 cm medial to the anterior superior iliac spine on a line between this landmark and the umbilicus. (Nolte W. Ilioinguinal nerve block. In: Hoerster W, Kreuscher H, Niesel HC, Zenz M, eds. Regional anesthesia. 2nd ed. St. Louis: Mosby–Year Book, 1990:278)

CONCLUSION

Over the past 2 decades, we have seen remarkable advances in our understanding of pain pathways and central opioid receptors. We also have the technology to make use of this knowledge. These developments have provided anesthesiologists with myriad options to provide postoperative analgesia to women after cesarean delivery. Neuraxial opioids and PCA are no longer interesting topics for research, but are therapies that can and should be incorporated into every clinical practice. The days of as-needed intramuscular analgesics after cesarean deliveries may soon be of merely historic interest.

REFERENCES

1. IASP Subcommittee on Taxonomy. Pain terms: A list with definitions and notes on usage. Pain 1979;6:247.

2. Barber J. Managing acute pain. In: Barber J, Adrian C, eds. Psychological approaches to the management of pain. New York: Brunner/Mazel, 1982:168.

3. Elton D, Stanley G, Burrows G. Psychological control of pain. New York: Grune & Stratton, 1983:25.

4. Fagerhaugh SY, Strauss A. Politics of pain management—staff-patient interaction. Menlo Park, CA: Addison-Wesley, 1977.

5. Egbert LD, Battit GE, Welch CD, Bartlett MK. Reduction of postoperative pain by encouragement and instruction of patients. N Engl J Med 1965;270:825.

6. Houde R, Wallenstein S, Rogers A. Clinical pharmacology of analgesics. Clin Pharmacol Ther 1960;1:163.

7. Houde R, Wallenstein S, Beaver W. Clinical measurement of pain. In: de Stevens G, ed. Analgesics. New York: Academic Press, 1964:75.

8. Houde R. Methods for measuring clinical pain in humans. Acta Anaesthesiol Scand 1982;74:25.

9. Bonica JJ. Importance of effective pain control. Acta Anaesthesiol Scand 1987;31:1.

10. Huskisson EC. Measurement of pain. Lancet 1974; 2:1127.

11. Scott J, Huskisson EC. Graphic representation of pain. Pain 1976;2:175.

12. Melzack R. The McGill Pain Questionnaire: Major properties and scoring methods. Pain 1975;1:277.

13. Wallenstein S, Heidrich G, Kaiko R, Houde R. Clinical evaluation of mild analgesics: The measurement of clinical pain. Br J Clin Pharmacol 1980;10:319S.

14. Seymer AS, Simpson JM, Charlton JED, Philips ME. An evaluation of length and end-phase of visual analogue scales in dental pain. Pain 1985;21:177.

15. Ness TJ, Gebhart GF. Visceral pain: A review of experimental studies. Pain 1990;41:167.

16. Fitzgerald M. The course and termination of primary afferent fibers. In: Wall PD, Melzack R, eds. Textbook of pain. New York: Churchill Livingstone, 1984:34.

17. Lynn B. The detection of injury. In: Wall PD, Melzack R, eds. Textbook of pain. New York: Churchill Livingstone, 1984:19.

18. Wall PD. The dorsal horn. In: Wall PD, Melzack R, eds. Textbook of pain. New York: Churchill Livingstone, 1984:80.

19. Helke, CJ, Krause JE, Mantyh, PW, Couture R, Bannon MJ. Diversity in mammalian tachykinin peptidergic neurons: Multiple peptides, receptors, and regulatory mechanisms. FASEB J 1990;4:1606.

20. Nawa H, Kotani H, Nakanishi S. Tissue-specific generation of two preprotachykinin mRNAs from one gene by alternative RNA splicing. Nature 1984;312:729.

21. Nawa H, Hirose T, Takashima H, Inayama S, Nakanishi S. Nucleotide sequences of cloned cDNA's for two types of bovine brain substance P precursor. Nature 1983; 306:32.

22. Krause JE, Chirgwin JM, Carter MS, Xu ZS, Hershey AD. Three rat preprotachykinin mRNAs encode the neuropeptides substance P and neurokinin A. Proc Natl Acad Sci USA 1987;84:881.

23. Kotani H, Hoshimaru M, Nawa H, Nakanishi S. Structure and gene organization of bovine neuromedin K precurser. Proc Natl Acad Sci USA 1986;83:7174.

24. Bonner TI, Affolter HU, Young AC, Young WS. A cDNA encoding the precursor of the rat neuropeptide, neurokinin B. Mol Brain Res 1987;2:243.

25. Charlton CG, Helke CJ. Autoradiographic localization and characterization of spinal cord substance P binding sites: High densities in sensory, autonomic, phrenic, and Onuf's motor nuclei. J Neurosci 1985;5:1653.

26. Helke CJ, Charlton CG, Wiley RG. Studies on the cellular localization of spinal cord substance P receptors. Neuroscience 1986;19:523.

27. Lembeck F. Zur frage zentralen ubertagung afferenter impulse. III. Das vorkommen und die bedeutung der substanz P in den dorsalen wurzeln des ruckenmarks. Naunyn Schmiedebergs Arch Pharmacol 1953;219: 197.

28. OtsukaM, Konishi S. Electrophysiological and neurochemical evidence for substance P as a transmitter of primary sensory neurons. In: Von Euler US, Pernow B, eds. Substance P (Nobel Symposium 37). New York: Raven Press, 1977:207.

29. Ljungdahl A, Hokfelt T, Nilsson G. Distribution of substance P like immunoreactivity in the central nervous system of the rat. I. Cell bodies and nerve terminals. Neuroscience 1978;3:861.

30. Nicoll RA, Schenker C, Leeman SE. Substance P as a transmitter candidate. Annu Rev Neurosci 1980;3:227.

31. Pernow B. Substance P. Pharmacol Rev 1983;35:85

32. Mantyh PW, Gates TS, Mantyh CI, Maggio JE. Autoradiographic localization and characterization of tachykinin receptor binding sites in the rat brain and peripheral tissues. J Neurosci 1989;9:258.

33. Warden MK, Young WS III. Distribution of cells containing mRNAs encoding substance P and neurokinin B in the rat central nervous system. J Comp Neurol 1988;272:90.

34. Carlton S, Hayes E. Dynorphin A(1-8) immunoreactive cell bodies, dendrites and terminals are postsynaptic to calcitonin gene-related peptide primary afferent terminals in the monkey dorsal horn. Brain Res 1989; 504:124

35. Tiseo P, Adler M, Liu-Chen L. Differential release of substance P and somatostatin in the rat spinal cord in response to noxious cold and heat; effect of dynorphin A(117). J Pharmacol Exp Ther 1990;252:539.

36. Douglas WW. Autocoids. In: Gilman AG, Goodman LS, Rall TW, Murad F, eds. Goodman and Gilman's The pharmacological basis of therapeutics. 7th ed. New York: Macmillan Publishing, 1985:604.

37. Eipper BA, Mains RE. Structure and biosynthesis of proadrenocorticotropin/endorphin and related peptides. Endocr Rev 1980;1:1.

38. Akil H, Watson SJ, Young E, et al. Endogenous opioids: Biology and function. Annu Rev Neurosci 1984; 7:223.

39. Quirion R. Pain, nociception and spinal opioid receptors. Prog Neuropsychopharmacol Biol Psychiatry 1984;8:571.

40. Fields HL, Emson PC, Leigh BK, Gilbert RFT, Iversen LL. Multiple opiate receptors in primary afferent fibres. Nature 1980;214:351.

41. Hokfelt T, Ljungdahl A, Elde R, Nilsson G, Terenius L. Immunohistochemical analysis of peptide pathways possible related to pain and analgesia: Enkephalin and substance P. Proc Natl Acad Sci USA 1977;74:3081.

42. Basbaum AI, Fields HL. Endogenous pain control systems: Brainstem spinal pathways and endorphin circuitry. Annu Rev Neurosci 1984;7:309.

43. Mack KJ, Killian A, Weyhenmeyer JA. Comparison of mu, delta and kappa opiate binding sites in rat brain and spinal cord. Life Sci 1984;34:281.

44. Zamir N, Palkovits M, Weber E, Mezey E, Brownstein MJ. A dynorphinergic pathway of leu-enkephalin production rat substantia nigra. Nature 1984;307:643

45. Yaksh TL, Jessell TM, Gause R, Mudge AW, Leeman SE. Intrathecal morphine inhibits substance P release from mammalian spinal cord in vivo. Nature 1980; 286:155.

46. Bonica JJ. Current status of postoperative pain therapy. In: Yokota T, Dubner R, eds. Current topics in pain research and therapy. Tokyo: Excerpta Medica, 1983:169.

47. Wilmore DW, Long JM, Mason AD, Pruitt BA. Stress in surgical patients as a neurophysiologic reflex response. Surg Gynecol Obstet 1976;142:257.

48. Dreyfuss F. Coagulation time of the blood, level of blood eosinophyles and thrombocytes under emotional stress. J Psychosom Res 1956;1:252.

49. Cash JD, Allan AGE. The effect of mental stress on the fibrinolytic reactivity. Br Med J 1967;2:545.

50. Benedetti C, Bonica JJ, Bellucci G. Pathophysiology and therapy of postoperative pain. In: Benedetti C, Chapman CR, Moricaa G, eds. Advances in pain research and therapy. Vol 2. New York: Raven Press, 1984:373

51. Martin WR, Eades CG, Thompson JA, Huppler RE, Gilbert PE. The effects of morphine-and nalorphine-like drugs in the nondependent and morphine-dependent chronic spinal dog. J Pharmacol Exp Ther 1976; 197:517.

52. Lord JAJ, Waterfield AA, Hughes J, Kosterlitz HW. Endogenous opioid peptides: Multiple agonists and receptors. Nature 1977;267:495.

53. Leslie FM. Methods used for the study of opioid receptors. Pharmacol Rev 1987;39:197.

54. Martin WR. Pharmacology of opioids. Pharmacol Rev 1983;35:283.

55. Garzon J, Schulz R, Herz A. Evidence for the epsilon-type of opioid receptor in the rat vas deferens. Mol Pharmacol 1985;28:1.

56. Lemaire S, Magnan J, Regoli D. Rat vas deferens: A specific bioassay for endogenous opioid peptides. Br J Pharmacol 1978;64:327.

57. Liao CS, Day AR, Freer RJ. Evidence for a single opioid receptor type on the field-stimulated rat vas deferens. Life Sci 1981;29:2617.

58. Schulz R, Faase E, Wuster M, Herz A. Selective receptors for B-endorphin on the rat vas deferens. Life Sci 1979;24:843.

59. Smith CFC, Rance MJ. Opiate receptors in the rat vas deferens. Life Sci 1983;33:327

60. Pasternak GW, Wood PJ. Multiple mu opiate receptors. Life Sci 1986;38:1889.

61. Goldstein A, Naidu A. Multiple opioid receptors: Ligand selectivity profiles and binding site signature. Mol Pharmacol 1989;36:265.

62. Chang KJ, Wei ET, Killian A, Chang JK. Potent morphiceptin analogs: Structure activity relationships and morphine-like activities. J Pharmacol Exp Ther 1983;227:403.

63. Kramer TH, Shook JE, Kazmierski W, et al. Novel peptidic mu opioid antagonists: Pharmacologic characterization in vitro and in vivo. J Pharmacol Exp Ther 1989;249:544.

64. Mosberg HI, Hurst R, Hruby VJ, et al. BIS-penicillamine enkephalins possess highly improved specificity towards delta opioid receptors. Proc Natl Acad Sci USA 1983;80:5871.

65. Cotton R, Giles MG, Miller L, Shaw JS, Timms D. A highly selective antagonist for the opioid delta-receptor. Eur J Pharmacol 1984;97:331.

66. Portoghese PS, Sultana M, Takemori AE. Naltrindole, a highly selective and potent non-peptide delta opioid receptor antagonist. Eur J Pharmacol 1988;146:185.

67. Lahti RA, Mickelson MM, McCall JM, Von Voigtlander P. A highly selective ligand for the opioid κ-receptor. Eur J Pharmacol 1985;109:281.

68. Portoghese PS, Lipkowski AW, Takemori AE. Binaltorphimine and norbinaltorphimine, potent and selective κ-opioid receptor antagonists. Life Sci 1987; 40:1287.

69. McFadzean I. The ionic mechanisms underlying opioid actions. Neuropeptides 1988;11:173.

70. Simonds WF. The molecular basis of opioid receptor function. Endocr Rev 1988;9:200.

71. Werz MA, MacDonald RL. Opioid peptides selective for mu and delta-opiate receptors reduce calcium-dependent action potential duration by increasing potassium conductance. Neurosci Lett 1983;42:173.

72. North RA, Williams JT, Suprenant A, Christie MJ. Mu and delta receptors belong to a family of receptors that are coupled to potassium channels. Proc Natl Acad Sci USA 1987;84:5487.

73. Munoz FG, Cerreta KV, Guerrero ML, Way EL. Effect of morphine on synaptosomal Ca^{++} uptake. J Pharmacol Exp Ther 1979;209:132.

74. End DW, Carchman RA, Dewey WL. Interactions of narcotics with synaptosomal calcium transport. Biochem Pharmacol 1981;30:674.

75. Contreras E, Tamayo L, Amigo M. Calcium channel antagonists increase morphine-induced analgesia and antagonize morphine tolerance. Eur J Pharmacol 1988;148:463.

76. Chapman DB, Way EL. Metal ion interactions with opiates. Annu Rev Pharmacol Toxicol 1980;20:552.

77. Del Pozo E, Caro G, Baeyens JM. Analgesic effects of several calcium channel blockers in mice. Eur J Pharmacol 1987;137:155.

78. Munoz FG, Fearon Z. Opioids/opiates analgesic response modified by calcium. Life Sci 1982;31:1237.

79. Welch SP, Cooper CW, Dewey WL. An investigation of the antinociceptive activity of calcitonin gene-related peptide alone and in combinate with morphine: Correlation to 45 Ca^{++} uptake by synaptosomes. J Pharmacol Exp Ther 1988;244:28

80. Porreca F, Mosberg H, Hurst R, Hruby V, Burks T. Roles of mu, delta and kappa opioid receptors in spinal and supraspinal mediation of gastrointestinal transit effects and hot-plate analgesia in the mouse. J Pharmacol Exp Ther 1984;230:341.

81. Dickenson AJ, Sullivan AF, Roques BP. Evidence that endogenous enkephalins and a delta opioid receptor agonist have a common site of action in spinal antinociception. Eur J Pharmacol 1988;148:437.

82. Sullivan AF, Dickenson AH, Roques BP. Delta-opioid mediated inhibitions of acute and prolonged noxious-evoked responses in rat dorsal horn neurones. Br J Pharmacol 1989;98:1039.

83. Parsons CG, Headley PM. Spinal antinociceptive actions of mu and kappa opioids: The importance of stimulus intensity in determining "selectivity" between reflexes to different modalities of noxious stimulus. Br J Pharmacol 1989;98:523.

84. Parsons CG, West DC, Headley PM. Spinal antinociceptive actions and naloxone reversibility in intravenous mu and kappa opioids in spinalized rats: Potency mismatch with values reported for spinal administration. Br J Pharmacol 1989;98:533.

85. Mansour A, Khachaturian H, Lewis ME, Akil H, Watson SJ. Anatomy of CNS opioid receptors. Trends Neurol Sci 1988;11:308.

86. Fedynyshyn JP, Kwiat G, Lee NM. Characterization of high-affinity opioid binding sites in rat periaqueductal gray P2 membrane. Eur J Pharmacol 1989;159:83.

87. Heyman JS, Vaught JL, Raffa RB, Porreca F. Can supraspinal delta opioid receptors mediate antinociception? Trends Pharmacol Sci 1988;9:134.

88. Millan MJ. Kappa opioid receptors and analgesia. Trends Pharmacol Sci 1990;11:70

89. Jaffe JH, Martin WR. Opioid analgesics and antagonists. In: Gilman AG, Goodman LS, Rall TW, Murad F, eds. Goodman and Gilman's The pharmacological basis of therapeutics. 7th ed. New York: Macmillan Publishing, 1985:491.

90. Primi M, Fargeas M, Bueno L. Central mu, sigma, and kappa opioid influences on intestinal water and electrolyte transport in dogs. Regul Pept 1988;21:107.

91. Coupar I. Opioid action on the intestine: The importance of the intestinal mucosa. Life Sci 1987; 41:917.

92. Sheldon B, Malarchik M, Fox D, Burks T, Porreca F. Pharmacological characterization of neural mechanisms regulating mucosal ion transport in mouse jejunum. J Pharmacol Exp Ther 1989;249:572.

93. Bitar K, Makhlouf G. Specific opiate receptors on isolated mammalian gastric smooth muscle cells. Nature 1982;297:72.

94. Severi C, Grider J, Makhlouf G. Characterization of opioid receptors on isolated canine gallbladder smooth muscle cells. Life Sci 1988;42:2373.

95. Kromer W. Endogenous and exogenous opioids in the control of gastrointestinal motility and secretion. Pharmacol Rev 1988;40:121.

96. Burks TF, Fox DA, Hirning LD, Shook JE, Porreca F. Regulation of gastrointestinal function by multiple opioid receptors. Life Sci 1988;43:2177.

97. Manara L, Bianchetti A. The central and peripheral influences of opioids on gastrointestinal propulsion. Annu Rev Pharmacol Toxicol 1985;25:249.

98. Galligan J, Burks T. Opioid peptides inhibit intestinal transit in the rat by a central mechanism. Eur J Pharmacol 1982;85:61.

99. Galligan J, Burks T. Centrally mediated inhibition of small intestinal transit and motility by morphine in the rat. J Pharmacol Exp Ther 1983;226:356

100. England D, Davis I, Timmins A, Downing R, Widsor W. Gastric emptying: A study to compare the effects of intrathecal morphine and IM papaveretum analgesia. Br J Anaesth 1987;59:1403.

101. Scheinin B, Asantila R, Orka R. The effect of bupivacaine and morphine on pain and bowel function after colonic surgery. Acta Anaesthesiol Scand 1987;31:161.

102. Tavani A, Bianchi G, Manara L. Morphine no longer blocks gastrointestinal transit but retains antinociceptive action in diallylnormorphine-pretreated rats. Eur J Pharmacol 1979;59:151.

103. Tavani A, Bianchi G, Ferretti P, Manara L. Morphine is most effective on gastrointestinal propulsion in rats by intraperitoneal route: Evidence for local action. Life Sci 1980;27:2211.

104. Stewart J, Curd C. Antipropulsive effects of central and peripheral morphine in the rat gastrointestinal tract. J Pharm Pharmacol 1984;36:476

105. Florez Z, Hurle MA, Mediavilla A. Respiratory responses to opiates applied to the medullary ventral surface. Life Sci 1982;31:2189.

106. Hurle MA, Mediavilla A, Florez J. Morphine, pentobarbital and naloxone in the ventral medullary chemosensitive areas: Differential respiratory and cardiovascular effects. J Pharmacol Exp Ther 1982;220:642.

107. Traviera da Silva AM, Dias Souza JA, Quest JA, et al. Central nervous system site of action for the respiratory depressant effects of diacetylmorphine (heroin) in the cat. J Clin Invest 1983;72:1209.

108. Bromage PR, Camporesi E, Leslie J. Epidural narcotics

in volunteers: sensitivity to pain and to carbon dioxide. Pain 1980;9:145.

109. Kiritsy-Roy JA, Marson L, Van Loon GR. Sympatho-adrenal, cardiovascular and blood gas responses to highly selective mu and delta opioid peptides. J Pharmacol Exp Ther 1989;251:1096.

110. May CN, Dashwood MR, Whitehead CJ, Mathias CJ. Differential cardiovascular and respiratory responses to central administration of selective opioid agonists in conscious rabbits: Correlation with receptor distribution. Br J Pharmacol 1989;98:903.

111. Dray A, Metsch R. Opioids and central inhibition of urinary bladder motility. Eur J Pharmacol 1984;98:155

112. Holaday JW. Endogenous opioids and their receptors. Current concepts. Kalamazoo, MI: The Upjohn Company, 1985:28.

113. Firemark HM, Weitzaman RE. Effects of beta-endorphin, morphine and naloxone on arginine vasopressin secretion and the electroencephalogram. Neuroscience 1979;4:1895.

114. Leander JD, Zerbe RL, Hart JC. Diuresis and suppression of vasopressin by kappa opioids: Comparison with mu and delta opioids and clonidine. J Pharmacol Exp Ther 1985;234:463.

115. Yahya MD, Watson RR. Immunomodulation by morphine and marijuana. Life Sci 1987;41:2503

116. Hansch C, Bjorkroth JP, Leo A. Hydrophobicity and central nervous system agents: On the principle of minimal hydrophobicity in drug design. J Pharm Sci 1987;76:663.

117. Glare PA, Walsh TD. Review: Clinical pharmacokinetics of morphine. Ther Drug Monit 1991;13:1.

118. Abbott FV, Palmour RM. Morphine-6-glucuronide: Analgesic effects and receptor binding profile in rats. Life Sci 1988;43:1685.

119. Oguri K, Yamada-Mori I, Shigezane J, Hirano T, Yoshimuro H. Enhanced binding of morphine and nalorphine to opioid delta receptor by glucuronate and sulfate conjugations at the 6 position. Life Sci 1987;41:1457.

120. Christensen B, Jorgensen LN. Morphine-6-glucuronide had affinity for the opioid receptor. Pharmacol Toxicol 1987;60:75.

121. Pasternak GW, Bodnar RJ, Clark JA, Inturrisi CE. Morphine 6-glucuronide, a potent mu agonist. Life Sci 1987;41:2845.

122. Paul D, Standifer KM, Inutrrisi CE, Pasternak GW. Pharmacological characterization of morphine-6B-glucoronide, a very potent morphine metabolite. J Pharmacol Exp Ther 1989;25:477

123. Yoshimura H, Ida S, Oguri K, Tsukamoto H. Biochemical basis for analgesic activity of morphine-6-glucuronide. Biochem Pharmacol 1973;22:1423.

124. Hanna MH, Peat SJ, Knibb AA, Fung C. Disposition of morphine-6-glucuronide and morphine in healthy volunteers. Br J Anaesth 1991;66:103.

125. Hanks GW, Aherne GW, Hoskin PJ, Turner P, Poulain P. Explanation for potency of repeated oral doses of morphine? Lancet 1987;2:723.

126. Osborne R, Joel S, Trew D, Slevin M. Analgesic activity of morphine-6-glucuronide. Lancet 1988;1:828.

127. Osborne R, Joel S, Trew D, Slivin M. Morphine and metabolite behavior after different routes of morphine administration: Demonstration of the importance of the active metabolite morphine-6-glucuronide. Clin Pharmacol Ther 1990;47:12.

128. Hasselstrom J, Berg U, Lofgren A, Sawe J. Long-lasting respiratory depression induced by morphine-6-glucuronide? Br J Pharmacol 1989;27:515

129. Mather LE. Clinical pharmacokinetics of fentanyl and its newer derivatives. Clin Pharmacokinet 1983;8:422.

130. Mather LE, Meffin PJ. Clinical pharmacokinetics pethidine. Clin Pharmacokinet 1978;3:352.

131. Edwards DJ, Svensson CK, Visco JP, Lalka D. Clinical pharmacokinetics of pethidine: 1982. Clin Pharmacokinet 1982;7:421.

132. Kaiko RF, Foley KM, Grabinski PY, et al. Central nervous system excitatory effects of meperidine in cancer patients. Ann Neurol 1983;13:180.

133. Szeto HH, Inturrisi CE, Houde R, Saal S, Cheigh J, Reidenberg MM. Accumulation of normeperidine, an active metabolite of meperidine, in patients with renal failure or cancer. Ann Intern Med 1977;86:738.

134. Tang R, Shimomura SK, Rotblatt M. Meperidine-induced seizures in sickle cell patients. Hosp Formulary 1980;15:764.

135. Goetting MG, Thirman MJ. Neurotoxicity of meperidine. Ann Emerg Med 1985;14:1007.

136. Mauro VF, Bonfiglio MF, Spunt AL. Meperidine-induced seizure in a patient without renal dysfunction or sickle cell anemia. Clin Pharm 1986;837.

137. Bovill JG, Sebel PS, Blackburn CL, Oei-Lim V, Heykants JJ. The pharmacokinetics of sufentanil in surgical patients. Anesthesiology 1984:61:502.

138. Chauvin M, Ferrier C, Haberer JP, et al. Sufentanil pharmacokinetics in patients with cirrhosis. Anesth Analg 1989;68:1.

139. Hudson RJ, Thomson IR, Cannon JE, Friesen RM, Metherall RC. Pharmacokinetics of fentanyl in patients undergoing abdominal aortic surgery. Anesthesiology 1986;64:334.

140. Hudson RJ, Bergstrom R, Thomson IR, Sabourin MA, Rosenbloom M, Strunin L. Pharmacokinetics of sufentanil in patients undergoing abdominal aortic surgery. Anesthesiology 1989;70:426.

141. Verebely K, Volavka J, Mule S, Resnick R. Methadone in man: Pharmacokinetic and excretion studies in acute and chronic treatment. Clin Pharmacol Ther 1975; 18:180.

142. Inturrisi CE, Verebely K. Disposition of methadone in man after a single oral dose. Clin Pharmacol Ther 1972;13:923.

143. Nilsson MI, Meresaar U, Anggard E. Clinical pharmacokinetics of methadone. Acta Anaesthesiol Scand 1982;74:66.

144. Zola EM, McLeod DC. Comparative effects and analgesic efficacy of the agonist–antagonist opioids. Drug Intell Clin Pharm 1983;17:411.

145. Ehrnebo M, Boreus LO, Lonroth U. Single-dose kinetics and bioavailability of pentazocine. Acta Anaesthesiol Scand 1982;74:70.

146. Ritchie JM, Greene NM. Local anesthestics. In: Gilman AG, Goodman LS, Rall TW, Murad F, eds. Goodman and Gilman's The pharmacological basis of therapeutics. 7th ed. New York: Macmillan Publishing, 1985:302.

147. Moncada S, Flower RJ, Vane JR. Prostaglandins, prostacyclin, thromboxane-A2, and leukotrienes. In: Gilman AG, Goodman LS, Rall TW, Murad F, eds. Goodman and Gilman's The pharmacological basis of therapeutics. 7th ed. New York: Macmillan Publishing, 1985:660.

148. Bennett A. The role of prostaglandins in gastrointestinal tone and motility. In: Berti F, Samuelsson B, Velo GP, eds. Prostaglandins and thromboxanes. New York: Plenum Press, 1977:275.

149. Cuthbert MF. Prostaglandins and respiratory smooth muscle. In: Cuthbert MF, ed. The prostaglandins: Pharmacological and therapeutic advances. Philadelphia: JB Lippincott, 1973:253.

150. Goldberg VJ, Ramwell PW. Role of prostaglandins in reproduction. Physiol Rev 1975;55:325.

151. Cohen MM. Gastric mucosal protection with prostaglandins. In: Pfeiffer CJ, ed. Drugs and pepetic ulcer. Vol 1. Boca Raton: CRC Press, 1982;133.

152. Price A, Fletcher M. Mechanisms of NSAID-induced gastroenteropathy. Drugs 1990;40:1.

153. Waterbury L, Kunysz EA, Beuerman R. Effects of steroidal and non-steroidal anti-inflammatory agents on corneal wound healing. J Ocular Pharmacol 1987;3:43.

154. Elves MW, Bayley I, Roylance PJ. The effect of indomethacin upon experimental fractures in the rat. Acta Orthop Scand 1982;53:35.

155. Sudman E, Dregelid E, Bessesen A, Morland J. Inhibition of fracture healing by indomethacin in rats. Eur J Clin Invest 1979;9:333.

156. Allen HL, Wase A, Bear WT. Indomethacin and aspirin: Effect of nonsteroidal anti-inflammatory agents on the rate of fracture repair in the rat. Acta Orthop Scand 1980;51:595.

157. Ro J, Sudmann E, Marton PF. Effect of indomethacin on fracture healing in rats. Acta Orthop Scand 1976;47:588.

158. Nakano J, Koss MC. Pathophysiologic roles of prostaglandins and the action of aspirin-like drugs. South Med J 1973;66:709.

159. Kantor TG. Ibuprofen. Ann Intern Med 1979;91:877.

160. Todd P, Clissold S. Naproxen: A reappraisal of its pharmacology and therapeutic use in rheumatic diseases and pain states. Drugs 1990;40:91.

161. Buckley MMT, Brogden RN. Ketorolac: A review of its pharmacodynamic and pharmacokinetic properties, and therapeutic potential. Drugs 1990;39:86.

162. Behar M, Magora F, Olshwang D, et al. Epidural morphine in treatment of pain. Lancet 1979;1:527.

163. Youngstrom PC, Cowan RI, Sutheimer C, et al. Pain relief and plasma concentrations from epidural and intramuscular morphine in post-cesarean patients. Anesthesiology 1982;57:404.

164. Rosen MA, Hughes SC, Shnider SM, et al. Epidural morphine for the relief of postoperative pain after cesarean delivery. Anesth Analg 1983;62:666.

165. Writer WDR, Hurtig JB, Edelist G, et al. Epidural morphine prophylaxis of postoperative pain: Report of a double-blind multicentre study. Can Anæsth Soc J 1985;32:330.

166. Kotelko DM, Dailey PA, Shnider SM, et al. Epidural morphine analgesia after cesarean delivery. Obstet Gynecol 1984;63:409.

167. Chambers WA, Mowbray A, Wilson J. Extradural morphine for the relief of pain following caesarean section. Anaesthesia 1983;55:1201.

168. Kanto J, Erkkola R, Aaltonen L, et al. Epidural morphine as postoperative analgesic following cesarean section under epidural analgesia. Int J Clin Pharm Ther Toxicol 1985;23:43.

169. Webster NR, Lyons G, Macdonald R. Forum: Sleep and comfort after caesarean section. Anaesthesia 1986; 41:1143.

170. Leicht CH, Hughes SC, Dailey PA, et al. Epidural morphine sulfate for analgesia after cesarean section: a prospective report of 1000 patients. Anesthesiology 1986;65:A366.

171. Ackerman WE, Juneja MM, Kaczoramski DM, Colclough GW. A comparison of the incidence of pruritus following epidural opioid administration in the parturient. Can J Anæsth 1989;36:388.

172. Gieraerts R, Navalgund A, Vaes L, et al. Increased incidence of itching and herpes simplex in patients given epidural morphine after cesarean section. Anesth Analg 1987;66:1321.

173. Zakowski M, Ramanathan S, Khoo P, Turndorf H. Plasma histamine with intraspinal morphine in cesarean section. Anesth Analg 1990;70:S448.

174. Fuller JG, McMorland GH, Douglas J, et al. Epidural morphine for postoperative pain after caesarean section: A report of 4880 patients. Can J Anaesth 1990; 37:636.

175. Gourlay GK, Cherry DA, Cousins MJ. Cephalad migration of morphine in CSF following lumbar epidural administration in patients with cancer pain. Pain 1985;23:317.

176. Drayer BP, Rosenbaum AE. Studies of the third circulation, amipaque CT cisternography and ventriculography. J Neurosurg 1978;48:946.

177. Christensen V. Respiratory depression after extradural morphine. Br J Anaesth 1980;52:841.

178. Glynn CJ, Mather LE, Cousins MJ, Wilson PR, Graham JR. Spinal narcotics and respiratory depression. Lancet 1979;2:356.

179. Turner K, Sandler AN, Vosu H, et al. Respiratory pat-

tern in post-cesarean section patients after epidural or intramuscular morphine. Anesth Analg 1989;68:S296.

180. Brose WG, Cohen SE. Oxyhemoglobin saturation following cesarean section in patients receiving epidural morphine, PCA, or IM meperidine analgesia. Anesthesiology 1989;70:948.

181. Crone LA, Conly JM, Clark KM, et al. Recurrent herpes simplex virus labialis and the use of epidural morphine in obstetric patients. Anesth Analg 1988;67:318.

182. Crone LA, Conly JM, Storgard C, et al. Herpes labialis in parturients receiving epidural morphine following cesarean section. Anesthesiology 1990;73:208.

183. Jain S, Kestenbaum A, Khan Y, et al. Does epidural morphine predispose to herpes simplex in cancer patients? A comparison with epidural lidocaine. Anesth Analg 1990;70:S174.

184. Weiss JH, Carney M, Norris MC, et al. Incidence of recurrent herpes simplex virus labialis after cesarean section. Anesthesiology 1990;73:A951.

185. Bernstein J, Ramanathan S, Ramabadran K, et al. Body temperature changes with epidural and intrathecal morphine. Anesthesiology 1988;69:A688.

186. Van Ree JM, Spaapen-Kok WB, De Weid D. Differential localization of pituitary–adrenal activation and temperature changes following intrahypothalamic microinjection of morphine in rats. Neuroendocrinology 1976;22:318.

187. Rudy TA, Yaksh TL. Hyperthermic effects of morphine: Set-point manipulation by a direct spinal action. Br J Pharm 1977;61:91.

188. Henderson SK, Cohen H. Nalbuphine augmentation of analgesia and side effects following epidural hydromorphone. Anesthesiology 1986;65:216.

189. Cohen SE, Archer JH, Ratner EF, Kreitzman TR, Mignano LR. Nalbuphine is better than naloxone for treatment of side effects after epidural morphine. Anesthesiology 1991;75:A845.

190. Latasch L, Probst S, Dudziak R. Reversal by nalbuphine of respiratory depression caused by fentanyl. Anesth Analg 1984;63:814.

191. Penning JP, Samson B, Baxter A. Nalbuphine reverses epidural morphine induced respiratory depression. Anesth Analg 1986;65:S119.

192. Morgan PJ, Mehta S. Prophylactic nalbuphine in caesarean section patients treated with epidural morphine. Anesth Analg 1989;68:S203.

193. Cullen M, Altstatt AH, Kwon NJ, Benzuly S, Naulty JS. Naltrexone reversal of the side effects of epidural morphine. Anesthesiology 1988;69:A336.

194. Abboud TK, Afrasiabi A, Davidson J, et al. Prophylactic oral naltrexone with epidural morphine: Effect on adverse reactions and ventilatory responses to carbon dioxide. Anesthesiology 1990;72:233.

195. Norris MC, Leighton BL, DeSimone CA. Naltrexone and subarachnoid morphine following cesarean section. Anesthesiology 1989;71:A873.

196. Abboud TK, Lee K, Zhu J, et al. Prophylactic oral naltrexone with intrathecal morphine for cesarean sec-

tion: Effects on adverse reactions and analgesia. Anesth Analg 1990;71:367.

197. Kotelko DM, Rottman RL, Wright WC, Stone JJ, Yamashiro AY, Rosenblatt RM. Transdermal scopolamine decreases nausea and vomiting following cesarean section in patients receiving epidural morphine. Anesthesiology 1989;71:675.

198. Naulty JS, Datta S, Ostheimer GW, et al. Epidural fentanyl for postcesarean delivery pain management. Anesthesiology 1985;63:694.

199. Blanco J, Blanco E, Carceller JM, et al. Epidural analgesia for post-caesarean pain relief: A comparison between morphine and fentanyl. Eur J Anaesth 1987;4:395.

200. Kotelko DM, Rottman RL, Wright WC, et al. Improved surgical and post-cesarean analgesia with epidural fentanyl/morphine combination. Anesthesiology 1987;67:A622.

201. James CF, Banner CE, Hanna PG, et al. Comparison of epidural fentanyl via bolus with or without continuous infusion after cesarean section. Anesthesiology 1988;69:A682.

202. Ellis DJ, Millar WL, Reisner LS. A randomized double-blind comparison of epidural versus intravenous fentanyl infusion for analgesia after cesarean section. Anesthesiology 1990;72:981.

203. Brockway MS, Noble DW, Sharwood-Smith GH, McClure JH. Profound respiratory depression after extradural fentanyl. Br J Anaesth 1990;14:243.

204. Gourlay GK, Murphy TM, Plummer JL, Kowalksi SR, Cherry DA, Cousins MJ. Pharmacokinetics of fentanyl in lumbar and cervical CSF following lumbar epidural and intravenous administration. Pain 1989;38:253.

205. Madej TH, Strunin L. Comparison of epidural fentanyl with sufentanil. Anaesthesia 1987;42:1156.

206. Cohen SE, Tan S, White PF. Sufentanil analgesia following cesarean section: Epidural versus intravenous administration. Anesthesiology 1988;68:129.

207. Rosen MA, Daily PA, Hughes SC, et al. Epidural sufentanil for postoperative analgesia after cesarean section. Anesthesiology 1988;68:448.

208. Brownridge P, Frewin DB. A comparative study of techniques of postoperative analgesia following caesarean section and lower abdominal surgery. Anaesth Intensive Care 1985;13:123.

209. Perriss BW, Latham BV, Wilson IH. Analgesia following extradural and i.m. pethidine in post-caesarean section patients. Br J Anaesth 1990;64:355.

210. Albright G. Epidural morphine, hydromorphone, and meperidine for post c-section pain relief utilizing a respiratory apnea monitor. Anesthesiology 1983;59:A416.

211. Henderson SK, Matthew EB, Cohen H, Avram MJ. Epidural hydromorphone: A double-blind comparison with intramuscular hydromorphone for postcesarean section analgesia. Anesthesiology 1987;66:825.

212. Matthew EB, Henderson SK, Avram MJ, et al. Epidural hydromorphone versus epidural morphine for postcesarean section analgesia. Anesth Analg 1987;66:S112.

213. Chestnut DH, Choi WW, Isbell TJ. Epidural hydromorphone for postcesarean analgesia. Obstet Gynecol 1986;68:65.

214. Beeby D, MacIntosh KC, Bailey M, Welch DB. Postoperative analgesia for caesarean section using epidural methadone. Anaesthesia 1984;39:61.

215. Macrae DJ, Munishankrappa S, Burrow LM, et al. Double-blind comparison of the efficacy of extradural diamorphine, extradural phenoperidine and i.m. diamorphine following caesarean section. Br J Anaesth 1987;59:354.

216. Naulty JS, Weintraub S, McMahon, et al. Epidural butorphanol for post-cesarean delivery pain management. Anesthesiology 1984;61:A415.

217. Abboud TK, Moore M, Zhu J, et al. Epidural butorphanol or morphine for the relief of section pain: Ventilatory responses to carbon dioxide. Anesth Analg 1987;66:887.

218. Lawhorn CD, McNitt J, Fibuch EE, Leadle RJ. Epidural morphine with butorphanol for postoperative analgesia following cesarean delivery. Anesth Analg 1991;72:53.

219. Gambling DR, Huber C, Howell P, Kozak S. Epidural butorphanol does not reduce side effects from epidural morphine post-caesarean section [Poster presentation]. Boston: Annual Meeting of the Society for Obstetric Anesthesia and Perinatology, 1991:17.

220. McMorland GH, Douglas MJ, Fuller J, et al. Epidural nalbuphine for postcaesarean section analgesia [Poster presentation]. Seattle: Annual Meeting of the Society for Obstetric Anesthesia and Perinatology, 1989:D2.

221. Baxter AD, Samson B, Laganiere S, et al. Is nalbuphine an effective epidural analgesia? Anesthesiology 1989;71:A701.

222. Viscomi CM, Eisenach JC. Epidural clonidine for post cesarean section analgesia [Poster presentation]. Seattle: Annual Meeting of the Society for Obstetric Anesthesia and Perinatology, 1989:D24.

223. Mendez RM, Eisenach JC, Kashtan K. Epidural clonidine infusion following cesarean section. Anesthesiology 1990;73:A919.

224. Bonnet F, Boico O, Rostaing S, et al. Clonidine for postoperative analgesia: epidural versus IM study. Anesthesiology 1988;69:A395.

225. Boico O, Bonnet F, Rostaing S, et al. Epidural clonidine produces postoperative analgesia. Anesthesiology 1988;69:A388.

226. Mok MS, Wang JJ, Chan JH, et al. Analgesic effect of epidural clonidine and nalbuphine in combined use. Anesthesiology 1988;69:A398.

227. Petit J, Oksenhendler G, Colas G, et al. Comparison of the effects of morphine, clonidine and a combination of morphine and clonidine administered epidurally for postoperative analgesia. 1989;71:A647.

228. Vercauteren M, Meese G, Lauwers E, et al. Addition of clonidine potentiates postoperative analgesia of epidural sufentanil. Anesth Analg 1990;70:S416.

229. Weiler RL, Wardell GC. Hemodynamic study of epidural clonidine in awake sheep. Anesth Analg 1988;67:S252.

230. Collins JG, Kitahata LM, Matsumoto M, Homma E, Suzukawa M. Spinally administered epinephrine suppresses noxiously evoked activity of WDR neurons in the dorsal horn of the spinal cord. Anesthesiology 1984;6:269.

231. Reddy SVR, Maderdrut JL, Yaksh TL. Spinal cord pharmacology of adrenergic agonist-mediated antinociception. J Pharmacol Exp Ther 1980;213:525.

232. Robertson K, Douglas MJ, McMorland GH. Epidural fentanyl, with and without epinephrine for post-caesarean section analgesia. Can Anaesth Soc J 1985;32:502.

233. Leicht CH, Kelleher AJ, Robinson DE, Dickerson SE. Prolongation of postoperative epidural sufentanil analgesia with epinephrine. Anesth Analg 1990;70:323.

234. Dougherty TB, Baysinger CL, Henenberger JC, Gooding DJ. Epidural hydromorphone with and without epinephrine for postoperative analgesia after cesarean delivery. Anesth Analg 1989;68:318.

235. Parker EO, Brookshire GL, Bartel SJ, et al. Effects of epinephrine on epidural fentanyl, sufentanil and hydromorphone for postoperative analgesia. Anesthesiology 1985;63:A235.

236. Dobson CE, Eisenach JC, Lysak SZ. Adding epinephrine to bupivacaine does not prolong epidural morphine analgesia following cesarean section [Poster presentation]. San Francisco: Annual Meeting of the Society for Obstetric Anesthesia and Perinatology, 1988:122.

237. Kotelko DM, Thigpen JW, Shnider SM, et al. Postoperative epidural morphine analgesia after various local anesthetics. Anesthesiology 1983;59:A413.

238. Hughes SC, Wright RG, Murphy D, et al. The effect of pH adjusting 3% 2-chloroprocaine on the quality of postcesarean section analgesia with epidural morphine. Anesthesiology 1988;69:A689.

239. Cuplin SR, Chadwick HS. Effect of local anesthetic agent on postcesarean epidural morphine analgesia. [Scientific exhibits]. San Francisco: Annual Meeting of the Society for Obstetric Anesthesia and Perinatology, 1988:120.

240. Phan CQ, Azar I, Osborn IP, et al. The quality of epidural morphine analgesia following epidural anesthesia with lidocaine or chloroprocaine for cesarean delivery. Anesth Analg 1988;67:S172.

241. Schlairet TJ, Eisenach JC, Dobson CE. Effect of catheter testing with 2-chloroprocaine on the duration of epidural morphine analgesia following cesarean section. Anesthesiology 1989;71:A916.

242. Durkan WJ, Baker LT, Leicht CH. Postoperative epidural morphine analgesia after 3% 2-chloroprocaine (Nesacaine-MPF) or lidocaine epidural anesthesia. Anesthesiology 1989;71:A834.

243. Naulty JS, Hertwig L, Hunt CO, et al. Duration of analgesia of epidural fentanyl following cesarean delivery—effects of local anesthetic drug selection. Anesthesiology 1986;65:A180.

244. Malinow AM, Mokriski BLK, Wakefield ML, et al. An-

esthetic choice affects postcesarean epidural fentanyl analgesia. Anesth Analg 1988;67:S138.

245. Ackerman WE, Colclough GW, Juneja MM. The addition of 2-chloroprocaine to 0.5% bupivacaine decreases the duration of analgesia of epidural fentanyl. San Francisco: Eighth Scientific Session of the Annual Meeting of the Society for Obstetric Anesthesia and Perinatology, 1988:97.

246. Grice SC, Eisenach JC, Dewan DM. Effect of 2-chloroprocaine test dosing on the subsequent duration of labor analgesia with epidural bupivacaine–fentanyl–epinephrine. Anesthesiology 1988;69:A668.

247. Corke BC, Carlson CG, Dettbarn WD. The influence of 2-chloroprocaine on the subsequent analgesic potency of bupivacaine. Anesthesiology 1984;60:25.

248. Camann WR, Hartigan PM, Gilbertson LI, et al. Chloroprocaine antagonism of epidural narcotic analgesia: A receptor-specific phenomenon? Anesthesiology 1990;73:A934.

249. Wang JK, Nauss LA, Thomas JE. Pain relief by intrathecally applied morphine in man. Anesthesiology 1979;50:149.

250. Abboud TK, Dror A, Mosaad P, et al. Mini-dose intrathecal morphine for the relief of post-cesarean section pain: Safety, efficacy, and ventilatory responses to carbon dioxide. Anesth Analg 1988;67:137.

251. Chadwick HS, Ready LB. Intrathecal and epidural morphine sulfate for postcesarean analgesia—a clinical comparison. Anesthesiology 1988;68:925.

252. Zakowski M, Ramanathan 5, Turndorf H. Intrathecal morphine for postcesarean section analgesia. Anesthesiology 1989;71:A870.

253. Abouleish E, Rawal N, Rashad MN. The addition of 0.2 mg subarachnoid morphine to hyperbaric bupivacaine for cesarean delivery: A prospective study of 856 cases. Reg Anesth 1991;16:137.

254. Cousins MJ, Mather LE. Intrathecal and epidural administration of opioids. Anesthesiology 1984; 61:271.

255. Yaksh TL. Spinal opiate analgesia: Characteristics and principles of action. Pain 1981;11:293.

256. Gloss PSA. Respiratory depression following only 0.4 mg of intrathecal morphine [letter]. Anesthesiology 1984;60:256.

257. Odoom JA, Sih IL. Respiratory depression after intrathecal morphine [letter]. Anesth Analg 1982;61:70.

258. Johnson MD, Hertwig L, Datta S. Fentanyl may reduce the incidence of spinal headache. Anesthesiology 1989;71:A911.

259. Abboud TK, Reyes A, Zhu J, et al. Effect of intrathecal morphine on the incidence of spinal headache. Anesthesiology 73:A937, 1990 96.

260. Carney MD, Weiss JH, Norris MC, Leighton BL. Intrathecal morphine and postdural puncture headache. Anesthesiology 1990;73:A949.

261. McDonald JS, Rattan AK, Tejwani GA. Effect of intrathecal bupivacaine on morphine analgesia. Anesthesiology 1989;71:A679.

262. Hunt, CO, Naulty JS, Bader AM, et al. Perioperative analgesia with subarachnoid fentanyl–bupivacaine for cesarean delivery. Anesthesiology 1989;71:535.

263. Palmer CM. Case report: Early respiratory depression following intrathecal fentanyl-morphine combination. Anesthesiology 1991;74:1153.

264. Malinow AM, Mokriski BLK, Nomura MK, et al. Effect of epinephrine on intrathecal fentanyl analgesia. Anesthesiology 1990;73:381.

265. de Sousa H, de la Vega S. Spinal sufentanil. Reg Anesth 1988;13:23.

266. Celleno D, Capogna G. Spinal buprenorphine for postoperative analgesia after caesarean section. Acta Anaesthesiol Scand 1989;33:236.

267. Jacobson L, Chabal C, Brody MC, et al. Intrathecal methadone and morphine for postoperative analgesia: A comparison of the efficacy, duration and side effects. Anesthesiology 1988;69:A352.

268. Jacobson L, Chabal C, Brody MC, et al. Intrathecal methadone: A dose–response study and comparison with intrathecal morphine. Anesthesiology 1989; 71:A695.

269. de Sousa H, Klein E. Intrathecal and epidural oxymorphone. Anesthesiology 1989;71:A699.

270. Marando R, Sinatra RS, Collins JG. Failure of intrathecally administered nalbuphine to suppress visceral pain in pregnant rats. Anesthesiology 1987;67:A447.

271. Nakagawa I, Kitahata LM, Murata K. Spinal mechanism of clonidine analgesia and its synergism with morphine. Anesth Analg 1988;67:S157.

272. Coombs DW, Lawrence BJ, Murphy C. Microdose intrathecal clonidine and morphine for postoperative analgesia. Anesthesiology 1987;67:A238.

273. Eisenach JC, Grice SC, Dewan DM. Patient-controlled analgesia following cesarean section: A comparison with epidural and intramuscular narcotics. Anesthesiology 1988;68:444.

274. Harrison DM, Sinatra R, Morgese L, Chung JH. Epidural narcotic and patient-controlled analgesia for post-cesarean section pain relief. Anesthesiology 1988;68:454.

275. Sinatra RS, Lodge K, Sibert K, et al. A comparison of morphine, meperidine, and oxymorphone as utilized in patient-controlled analgesia following cesarean delivery. Anesthesiology 1989;70:585.

276. Sinatra R, Chung KS, Silverman DG, et al. An evaluation of morphine and oxymorphone administered via patient-controlled analgesia (PCA) or PCA plus basal infusion in postcesareandelivery patient. Anesthesiology 1989;71:502.

277. Parker RK, Berberich N, Helfer DL, White PF. Use of epidural-PCA versus IV-PCA after obstetrical anesthesia. Anesthesiology 1989;71:A872.

278. Parker RK, Baron M, Helfer DL, Berberich N, White PF. Epidural PCA: Effect of a continuous (basal) infusion on the postoperative opioid requirement. Anesth Analg 1990;70:S296.

279. Cohen S, Amar D, Pantuck CB, Pantuck EJ, Weisman A, Lustig C. Continuous epidural-PCA post-cesarean section: Buprenorphine—-bupivacaine 0.03% vs

fentanyl-bupivacaine 0.03%. Anesthesiology 1990;73:A975.

280. Kempen PM, Treiber H. Neuraxial morphine plus intravenous patient controlled analgesia—new method in postcesarean analgesia. Anesth Analg 1990;70:S198.

281. Wittels B, Scott DT, Sinatra RS. Exogenous opioids in human breast milk and acute neonatal behavior: A preliminary study. Anesthesiology 1990;73:864.

282. Bunting P, McConachie I. Ilioinguinal nerve blockade for analgesia after cesarean section. Br J Anaesth 1988;61:773.

283. Witkowski TA, Leighton BL, Norris MC. Ilioinguinal nerve blocks: An alternative or supplement to intrathecal morphine. Anesthesiology 1990;73:A962.

284. Abboud TK, Zhu J, Gangolly J, et al. Transnasal butorphanol: A new method for pain relief in postcesarean section pain. Acta Anaesthesiol Scand 1991;35:14.

CHAPTER 38

Complications Associated with Regional Anesthesia in the Obstetric Patient

Pontus L. Östman

This chapter describes some maternal complications associated with epidural or spinal anesthesia. It concentrates only on problems that become apparent after sensory and motor block should have regressed. Most of the chapter focuses on the diagnosis and treatment of postdural puncture headache (PDPH). Other topics, including back pain, neck ache, infectious complications, foreign-material contamination, paresthesia, motor nerve dysfunction, and the potential neurotoxicity of the commonly used local anesthetics, also are discussed. Every anesthesiologist caring for obstetric patients should be familiar in the diagnosis, treatment, and prognosis of potential complications associated with regional anesthesia. Because, regarding complications, the major difference between spinal and epidural anesthesia is the size of the needle, these techniques are considered together.

Maternal morbidity from conduction anesthesia is a challenging area to study. Most of the available studies are retrospective and reveal only a fraction of the actual complication rate. In one review of 505,000 epidural blocks for 2,580,000 deliveries between 1982 and 1986, there were 108 serious complications associated with epidural anesthesia (Table 38-1).[1] The incidence of paresthesia (abnormal sensation, not necessarily unpleasant, vs dysesthesia, an unpleasant sensation[2]) or motor dysfunction after epidural anesthesia ranges between 0 and 40 in 10,000 according to several studies (Tables 38-2 and 38-3). A prolonged and difficult instrumental delivery requiring regional or general anesthesia in the primipara coincides with a greater frequency of paresthesia and motor dysfunction than an uncomplicated delivery in the multipara (Table 38-4).[3]

This chapter does not intend to review the possible late complications caused by maternal labor analgesia to the fetus. It suffices to say that infants delivered with normal Apgar and acid–base values may still be affected in subtle ways by medications received by the mother during labor. These effects can be measured by the Brazelton Neonatal Behavioral Assessment Scale, the Scanlon Early Neonatal Neurobehavioral Scale, or the Neurologic and Adaptive Capacity Scoring System. These neonatal scoring systems evaluate reflex, autonomic, motor, arousal, behavioral, and other physiologic parameters. Little agreement exists about which tests should be used and how to interpret their long-term implications (see Chap. 6).

Table 38-1

Serious Complications Associated with Epidural Block in an Obstetric Population

1982–1986	
Deliveries	2,580,000
Epidurals	505,000
Serious complications	76
Permanent	4
Fatal	0

(Data from Scott DB, Hibbard BM. Serious non-fatal complications associated with extradural block in obstetric population. Br J Anaesth 1990;64:537)

POSTDURAL PUNCTURE HEADACHE

Headache is a common neurologic symptom during and after gestation. Pregnancy complicates the clinical symptoms of headache. Presence of headache after delivery raises special concerns about diagnosis and treatment. Thirty percent to 40% of parturients who do not receive anesthesia complain of a headache during the first week after delivery. Headache after spinal anesthesia, or after accidental puncture of the dura with an epidural needle, is unpleasant, especially for the obstetric patient who wishes to participate in the care of her newborn. The severe nature and postural character of the headache may render the parturient incapable of participating in normal daily activities.

Postdural puncture headache is the most common complication associated with epidural or spinal anesthesia. No method exists to predict whether a given dural puncture will cause a headache. The symptoms of PDPH may occur simultaneously with a nonpostural headache. Patients with a history of headaches have a higher incidence of postural and nonpostural headache after dural puncture than those who do not have such history.[4,5] Also, obstetric patients have a much higher incidence of PDPH than the general nonpregnant population. The symptoms of PDPH vary tremendously in character and severity. The diagnosis is sometimes difficult to make, especially if the headache develops after an uncomplicated epidural anesthetic. The prognosis of PDPH is usually good, but rarely the outcome is devastating if the cerebrospinal fluid (CSF) flow and pressure physiology is not restored. The incidence of PDPH is highest in younger patients, especially if a large-diameter needle punctured the dura. The technique used while doing spinal anesthesia can affect the incidence of PDPH. The treatment of PDPH can be challenging. Over the years, more than 50 treatment modalities have been described, but only a few have withstood the test of time.

Symptoms of Postdural Puncture Headache

The common symptoms and postural nature of PDPH were described nearly 100 years ago.[6] Postdural puncture headache may arise immediately or up to several months after the dural puncture (Fig. 38-1). The pain is usually occipital, bifrontal, or both. Typically, the headache starts 1 to 2 days after delivery as the patient begins to ambulate. Occasionally, pain extends to the neck and shoulders. Standing, coughing, and moving make the headache worse. Laying down usually relieves some of the pain. Bed rest sometimes postpones the headache; it does not prevent it.[7] Postdural postural headache can be associated with nausea, vomiting, neck ache, back pain, and visual disturbances. Diminished

Table 38-2

The Incidence of Paresthesia After Epidural Anesthesia

AUTHOR	NO.	NUMBER OF PARESTHESIA/ 10,000 EPIDURALS
Bonica (1957)[132]	3,637	24.7
Eisen (1960)[188]	9,532	16.8
Lund (1962)[187]	10,000	7.0
Crawford (1972)[174]	2,035	14.7
Ong (1987)[3]	9,403	36.2

Table 38-3

The Incidence of Motor Dysfunction After Epidural Anesthesia

AUTHOR	NO.	NUMBER OF MOTOR DEFICITS/ 10,000 EPIDURALS
Bonica (1957)[132]	3,637	2.7
Lund (1962)[187]	10,000	1.0
Hellman (1965)[196]	26,127	0
Dawkins (1969)[180]	32,718	1.7
Crawford (1972)[174]	2,035	0
Bleyaert (1979)[185]	9,404	0.8

hearing, unilateral deafness, tinnitus, and hyperacusis are common complaints besides the headache (Table 38-5).

Differential Diagnosis of Postdural Puncture Headache

When a patient who received conduction anesthesia develops postpartum headache, the anesthesiologist is confronted with the problem of differential diagnosis. Postpartum headaches often result from causes other than the anesthetic technique. These alternate sources include neurologic, vascular, musculoskeletal, and metabolic causes. Underlying illness such as migraine, preeclampsia, pseudotumor cerebri, intracranial hemorrhage, rapid expansion of a brain tumor, cortical vein thrombosis, or postpartum exhaustion and hypoglycemia can all produce headaches. Myofascial pain, also common after vaginal delivery, resembles PDPH but is not positional in nature.

Obstetric patients are prone to peripartum thrombotic complications. Besides hypercoagulable blood, these patients may have traumatic vascular endothelial damage and stasis of intracerebral blood flow. Cortical vein thrombosis, caused by thrombosis of the superior

Table 38-4

The Incidence of Postpartum Paresthesia and Motor Dysfunction According to Anesthetic and Patient Characteristics

	PARESTHESIA OR MOTOR DEFICIT/10,000 DELIVERIES	P
Anesthetic Technique		
No anesthesia	2.4	
Inhalation anesthesia	6.3	Not significant
Epidural anesthesia	36.2	< 0.001
General anesthesia	34.7	< 0.001
Patient characteristics		
Multipara	11.7	
Primipara	27.9	0.02
Spontaneous delivery	11.0	
Instrumental delivery	28.5	0.03

(After Ong BY, Cohen MM, Esmail A, Cumming M, Kozody R, Palahniuk RJ. Paresthesias and motor dysfunction after labor and delivery. Reprinted with permission from the International Anesthesia Research Society (Anesthesia and Analgesia 1987;66:18)

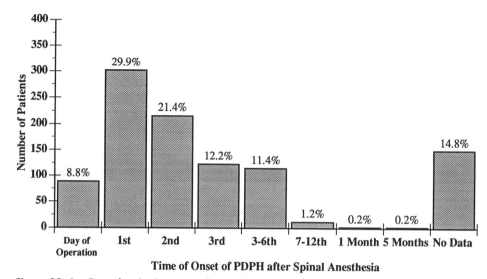

Figure 38–1. Time after dural puncture of onset of symptoms of PDPH in 1011 untreated patients. Patients ranged in age from 10 to 89 years. Spinal anesthesia was performed with 24- to 16-gauge needles. (Data from Vandam LD, Dripps RD. Long-term follow-up of patients who received 10,098 spinal anesthetics. JAMA 1956;161:586)

longitudinal sinus, may increase CSF pressure and cause a headache. The incidence of cortical venous thrombosis is estimated at approximately 1 in 6000 deliveries.[8] Symptoms of puerperal cortical vein thrombosis may mimic PDPH and are often initially treated as such. Within 1 to 3 days, the symptoms usually progress to focal or generalized seizures.[8,9] Contrast computed tomography or magnetic resonance imaging confirms the diagnosis.

Although hypomagnesemia occurs in up to 10% of hospitalized patients, it is a rare cause of neurologic symptoms in the parturient. The symptoms of hypomagnesemia include tremors, restlessness and convulsions. Two postpartum patients have been reported

Table 38–5

Patients' Descriptions of Postdural Postural Headache

Pain
Constricting band
Sharp
Shooting

Heaviness
Vacuum-like
Dead weight
Lead weight
Worse on moving
Echo-like

Location
Occipital
Nuchal
Stiff neck
Bifrontal

Ocular signs
Double vision
Blurred vision
Photophobia
Inability to read

Auditory
Decreased hearing
Obstruction
Plugging
Popping
Tinnitus
Buzzing
Roaring
Dizziness

whose neurologic symptoms were attributed to hypo-magnesemia. One of these women received an epidural blood patch in an unsuccessful attempt to treat her headache.[10]

Pathophysiology of Postdural Puncture Headache

Leakage of spinal fluid through the dural hole into the epidural space probably incites PDPH.[11] In the adult, the CSF volume is close to 150 mL. The CSF is produced at a rate of 200 to 500 mL/day. The volume of CSF escaping through the dural hole in a patient suffering from PDPH may be as high as 200 mL in a 24-hour period.[12] Leakage from the needle opening has been seen at laminectomy and at postmortem examination up to 14 days after dural puncture. When the patient resumes an upright position, a relative spinal fluid deficit occurs in the cranium. The upright position creates high intraspinal lumbar pressure, whereas the lumbar epidural pressure changes little. This pressure gradient forces more spinal fluid out through the hole in the dura. In the horizontal position, the CSF pressure at lumbar level is about 10 cm of H_2O. Pressure rises to 50 cm of H_2O in the upright position. Loss of CSF can cause a shift in the brain in relation to the dura and create traction on pain-sensitive tentorial and meningeal structures, and pain-sensitive cerebral vessels (Fig. 38-2).[13] Concomitant compensatory cerebrovasodilatation also may cause a vascular type of headache in patients with PDPH (Fig. 38-3). Draining as little as 20 mL of CSF with a subject in the erect position produces the symptoms of PDPH. Increasing CSF pressure with saline infusion relieves the headache.[13,14]

When the headache is severe and progresses into a nonpostural type, or when there are ocular symptoms, other factors may contribute to the pathophysiology. The sudden shift of brain matter may cause tears in the intracranial subdural bridging veins, resulting in subdural hematoma. The downward sagging of the brain may cause herniation of the cerebral uncus against the tentorium cerebelli.[15-25] Small subdural hematomas often clear spontaneously; thus, their incidence during PDPH remains unknown.

Prognosis of Postdural Puncture Headache

Physically, dural puncture in humans shows no signs of healing during the first few days.[12] Macroscopically, the opening in the dura persists for at least 14 days. At 40 days, newly formed tissue partially fills the puncture site.

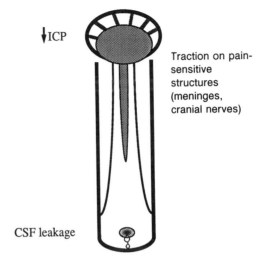

Figure 38–2. Mechanical pathophysiology of PDPH. Cerebrospinal fluid (CSF) loss lowers lumbar and intracranial CSF pressure. When the patient assumes the upright position, this loss of CSF causes a shift in the brain relative to the dura and creates traction on pain-sensitive tentorial and meningeal structures and pain-sensitive cerebral vessels. Headache follows. (Drawing courtesy M. Norris, MD)

Clinically, the symptoms of PDPH can be mild and regress within 2 to 3 days without therapy, or they may be debilitating and persist from weeks to months (Fig. 38-4). Usually, PDPH will spontaneously resolve within 7 days (70%), 6 weeks (95%), or 6 months (96%), but some may last as long as 19 months.[26–28]

When PDPH is severe, perhaps because of a large CSF leak, symptomatology can include cranial nerve palsy and intracranial hemorrhage. The incidence of abducens nerve paresis following PDPH is 1 in 5000 to 8000 patients with PDPH. The likelihood that a patient with PDPH will develop cranial nerve paresis correlates positively with the gauge of the needle used and the severity of the headache. The mechanism of the nerve injury is probably stretching of the nerve when low CSF pressure causes descent of the neural structures in the cranial cavity.

Cranial subdural hematoma is an unlikely, yet nonetheless a possible and dreadful, complication of severe CSF leakage into the epidural space.[15–22,29] The CSF volume lost from the ventricles allows the brain to descend. This drop may cause stretching and tearing of the bridging veins in the subdural space.

Cerebral herniation can follow lumbar puncture in patients with increased CSF pressure. This complication is also possible in patients with normal CSF volume. Eerola *et al*[30] reported a case of fatal uncus herniation against the tentorium cerebelli following spinal anesthesia. Here, the patient suffered severe headache,

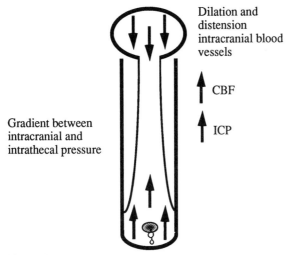

Figure 38–3. Vascular mechanism of PDPH. Acute loss of cerebrospinal fluid produces a gradient between lumbar and intracranial CSF pressure. A reflex increase in cerebral blood flow (CBF) follows. This augmented CBF increases intracranial pressure (ICP) and produces dilation and distension of intracranial blood vessels. Both of these effects can incite headache. (Drawing courtesy M. Norris, MD)

nausea, and vomiting for several days before becoming unresponsive. Before unresponsiveness, the neurologic examination had been normal, and conservative treatment was chosen.

Incidence of Postdural Puncture Headache

Dural puncture complicates 1% to 3% of epidural anesthetics done in residency training programs.[31] The likelihood of a patient developing PDPH in this situation can be as high as 85%.[32] In the nonobstetric population, the most significant predictors of PDPH after spinal anesthesia are age, direction of the bevel of the needle, and a history of previous PDPH.[33,34] The incidence of PDPH was 36% among patients with a history of previous PDPH and 7% for those patients who did not suffer PDPH after previous spinal anesthesia. The incidence was 17% for those patients who had spinal anesthesia for the first time.[34]

Postdural postural headache bothers both the patient and the physician. We do not know why some patients will develop PDPH, whereas others, in the same clinical situation, will not. When headache does not arise after dural puncture, spontaneous closure of the hole might occur, perhaps by an arachnoid or dural flap occluding the opening. Several patient and technical variables might modify the risk of PDPH.

Age and Gender

The incidence of PDPH clearly decreases after the fifth decade of life (Table 38-6).[26,33,35,36] Traditionally, PDPH has been considered almost twice as common in women as in men.[26,34] However, when considering patient age, in addition to gender, sex does not influence the incidence of PDPH (Table 38-7).[33] In the parturient, PDPH is almost twice as common as in the nonpregnant patient.[26] Some reasons for this higher incidence of PDPH may reflect the physiologic changes that occur after delivery. Postpartum diuresis and bed rest may contribute to relative hypovolemia and decreased CSF production. Reduction in the intra-abdominal pressure and subsequent decrease in the epidural venous pressure may increase the gradient between lumbar and cranial CSF pressure.

Psychological Factors

Some anesthesiologists believe that a detailed description of PDPH as part of the informed consent may predispose patients to headache postoperatively. This headache is often then diagnosed as PDPH. Vandam and Dripps[26] examined this dilemma by giving spinal anesthesia to 100 patients who were already under general anesthesia and were not aware that they had received a spinal anesthetic. These patients had a similar incidence of PDPH as those patients who knew they were having a spinal anesthetic.

Distance from Surface of Skin to Epidural Space

Approximation of the distance from the skin surface to the lumbar epidural space may help avoid some unintentional dural punctures. In pregnant patients, this distance relates directly to body weight.[37] The mean distance is approximately 5 cm. The range is from 2 to 10 cm (Fig. 38-5).[38]

Equipment and Technique

The use of intrathecal anesthesia in obstetrics has been limited because of the high incidence of PDPH in this population. However, recent improvements in technique and equipment may considerably reduce this risk and make this technique more appealing to the patient and the anesthesiologists.

NEEDLE SIZE. The larger the hole in the dura (from the needle), the higher the incidence of PDPH (Table 38-8). The risk of PDPH after unintentional dural puncture with an epidural needle can be as low as

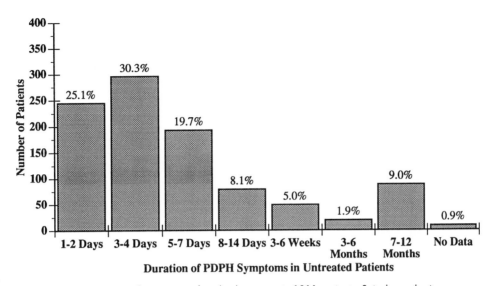

Figure 38–4. Duration of symptoms after dural puncture in 1011 patients. Spinal anesthesia was performed with 24- to 16-gauge needles in patients ranging between 10 and 89 years of age. (Data from Vandam LD, Dripps RD. Long-term follow-up of patients who received 10,098 spinal anesthetics. JAMA 1956;161:586)

9.3% in general surgical patients or as high as 85% in obstetric patients.[32,39] In vitro studies with human thoracolumbar dura have clearly shown that fluid leakage through the dura is a function of the needle size (Table 38-9).[40,41] Besides the higher incidence, PDPH is more severe and prolonged when the dura is punctured with larger-diameter needle.

As needle size decreases (to 30 gauge), the incidence of PDPH after spinal anesthesia approaches zero. The technical difficulties and the failure rate in performing spinal anesthesia increase.[42] Free flow of spinal fluid through the needle becomes delayed with decreasing needle diameter. Normal CSF pressure is 12 cm H_2O. With 29-gauge spinal needles, CSF does not appear at

Table 38–6

The Patient's Age Versus Incidence of PDPH After Spinal Anesthesia

AGE (Y)	PERCENT
10–19	10
20–29	16
30–39	14
40–49	11
50–59	8
60–69	4
70–79	2
80–89	3

(Data from Vandam LD, Dripps RD. Long-term follow-up of patients who received 10,098 spinal anesthetics. III. Syndrome of decreased intracranial pressure [headache, ocular, and auditory difficulties]. JAMA 1956;161:586)

Table 38–7

Multivariate Relationship Between PDPH and Other Factors After Spinal Anesthesia in General Surgical Patient Population

FACTOR	P
Age	0.0001
Previous PDPH	0.0018
Direction of needle bevel	0.022
Gender	0.118
Needle size	0.105
Multiple attempts	0.091
Duration of postoperative recumbency (> or < 4 h)	0.65

(After Lybecker H, Moller JT, May O, Nielsen HK. Incidence and prediction of postdural puncture headache: a prospective study of 1201 spinal anesthesias. Reprinted with permission from the International Anesthesia Research Society [Anesthesia and Analgesia 1990;70:389])

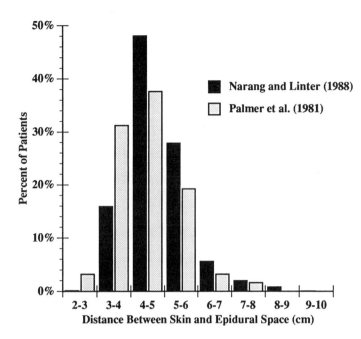

Figure 38–5. Distribution of the distance between the skin surface and the epidural space in parturients. (Data from Palmer SK, Abram SE, Maitra AM, Von Colditz JH. Distance from the skin to the lumbar epidural space in an obstetric population. Anesth Analg 1981;62:944, and Narang VPS, Linter SPK. Failure of extradural blockade in obstetrics. Br J Anaesth 1988;60:402)

the hub for up to 42 seconds. With 26-gauge needles, this time is about 9 seconds.[40]

NEEDLE TYPE. In addition to the size of the needle, its shape is an important factor in determining the patient's chance of developing PDPH.[43] Studies of dural puncture using human cadaveric dura found a significantly slower rate of leakage when using a noncutting, pencil-point needle instead of a cutting type of needle (see Table 38-9).[40,41,44]

Clinically, the type of needle (cutting vs pencil point) does significantly influence the incidence of PDPH. Pencil-point needles produce fewer headaches than do needles with a cutting bevel.[43] The incidence of PDPH after spinal anesthesia for cesarean section using a 24-gauge noncutting, pencil-point Sprotte needle can be as low as 0%.[45] In another study, the incidence of PDPH using a 22-gauge, noncutting, Whitacre needle was 4%, compared to 25% with a 26-gauge cutting bevel Quincke needle.[46] Pencil-point needles may spread dural fibers without cutting them (Fig. 38-6A). The fibers retain their elasticity and snap back into place when the needle is withdrawn.

MULTIPLE DURAL PUNCTURES. A higher incidence of PDPH is generally thought to be associated with multiple punctures. In a study of 1021 spinal anesthetics, however, multiple attempts did not increase the risk of headache (see Table 38-7).[33]

PARAMEDIAN VERSUS MIDLINE APPROACH. Some clinicians prefer the paramedian approach when performing epidural or spinal anesthesia.[47–49] When identifying the epidural space, the paramedian approach may offer some benefits. Studies in cadavers suggest that the paramedian approach holds the following advantages:

- There is less risk of dural puncture and intravascular cannulation.
- The catheter avoids the dorsomedian band and does not tent the dura.
- The catheter is more likely to advance straight ahead.[50]

Catheters placed using the midline approach incline to deviate from the midline. This tendency may increase the possibility of nerve-root contact with accompanying paresthesia.

In urologic patients, the paramedian approach offers less difficulty in identifying the epidural space, a lower incidence of paresthesia during catheter placement, and less resistance to advancement of the catheter than the midline approach.[49] In obstetric patients, some studies have shown fewer side effects (paresthesia, intravascular catheter placement), and some have shown no differences when comparing the midline and paramedian approaches to epidural catheter insertion.[51,52] If one encounters significant paresthesia or resistance while attempting to advance the catheter through the midline, it may be appropriate to withdraw the needle with the catheter and approach the epidural space through the paramedian route in another attempt.

Dural puncture with the paramedian approach also may create separate holes in the dura and arachnoid. Theoretically, this event provides two flap-valve mechanisms to prevent CSF leak. In vitro, even at 55 cm H_2O, only minor leaks through the dura occurred after tangential (paramedian) puncture with 20-, 22-, or 25-gauge needles. With the perpendicular approach, however, significant leakage began at pressures of 10 cm H_2O.[53]

The low incidence of spinal headache when using small-diameter spinal needles may partially arise from fact that these thin, pliable needles seldom keep their initial direction upon insertion. Tangential puncture of the dura may be common.[53,54] In cadavers, a 20-gauge needle, introduced perpendicularly in the midline, stayed in the midline and entered the subarachnoid space in the midline. When 22- or 25-gauge needles were used in the same manner, they tended to deviate from the midline course and enter the dura on a tangent. Bending occurred even when using an intro-

ducer. There may be less bending of the fine needles in younger patients and in the obstetric population, in whom the ligaments tend to be more compliant than in the older population. This tendency would partially explain the high incidence of PDPH in the parturient even when using small-diameter spinal needles.

BEVEL DIRECTION. When using a cutting type needle for spinal anesthesia, needle bevel direction significantly influences the risk of PDPH. Entering the dura with the needle bevel parallel to the longitudinal axis of the thecal sack splits rather than cuts the dural fibers. This approach minimizes the number of transected dural fibers and lowers the incidence of PDPH (see Fig. 38-6B, C).[12,43,55]

Laboratory studies offer conflicting information when attempting to explain this clinical observation. Electron microscopy of human dura shows that collagen fibers do not lie in a strongly marked longitudinal direction.[56] In one in vitro study of puncture of cadaveric dura with a 22-gauge spinal needle, the most important factor in determining the size of the dural tear was the size of the needle. Direction of the needle bevel had only a minor role in the size of the dural hole; it did not influence the rate of fluid leakage.[44] How-

Table 38-8

Needle Gauge Versus Incidence of PDPH After Spinal Anesthesia*

NEEDLE GAUGE	SPINALS (NO.)	PDPH (%)	AUTHOR
16	839	8.0	Vandam (1956)[26]
19	54	10.0	Vandam (1956)[26]
20	2698	14.0	Vandam (1956)[26]
20	98	28.0[†]	Rasmussen (1989)[36]
20	93	11.0[‡]	Rasmussen (1989)[36]
22	952	9.0	Vandam (1956)[26]
24	634	6.0	Vandam (1956)[26]
25	95	13.0[‡]	Rasmussen (1989)[36]
25	88	19.0[§]	Flaatten (1987)[4]
25	64	33.0[‖]	Flaatten (1987)[4]
25	90	8.0[†]	Rasmussen (1989)[36]
26	99	10.1	Flaatten (1987)[4]
29	50	0.0	Flaatten (1987)[4]

*Vandam (1956)[26] recorded PDPH after 10,098 spinal anesthetics in a mixed population.
† and ‡Rasmussen (1989)[36] recorded the incidence of headache in young (mean age 29 y[†]) and old (mean age 69 y[‡]) men.
§and ‖Flaatten[4] followed men § and women ‖ (mean age both groups 33 y), after dural puncture with 25-gauge needle and a mixed population after dural puncture with 26- and 29-gauge needles.

Table 38-9

Loss of Cerebrospinal Fluid* Through Dural Holes

NEEDLE	ALIGNMENT	MEDIAN VOLUME (mL/MIN)
22-gauge Quinke	Parallel	5.9
22-gauge Whitacre (pencil-point needle)		4.6
26-gauge Quinke	Parallel	0.94
29-gauge Quinke	Parallel	0.03
		RATE (mL/MIN)
22-gauge Quinke	Parallel	11.9
22-gauge Quinke	Perpendicular	15.5
22-gauge Whitacre (pencil-point needle)		7.7
25-gauge Quinke	90 degrees parallel	3.3
25-gauge Quinke	60 degrees parallel	2.5
25-gauge Quinke	30 degrees parallel	0.3

(Data from Cruickshank RH, Hopkinson JM. Fluid flow through dural puncture sites: an in vitro comparison of needle-point types. Anaesthesia 1989;44:415, and Ready LB, Cuplin S. Haschke RH, Nessly M. Spinal needle determinants of rate of transdural fluid leak. Anesth Analg 1989;69:457)

ever, other studies have shown that the dural leak may vary significantly depending on the bevel direction and the type of needle (see Table 38-9).[41]

In clinical practice, it is evident that the direction of the bevel and the type of needle play a major role in the subsequent development of PDPH.[33,54] In one study of general surgical patients, PDPH developed in 16% of the subjects when the bevel of the needle (22 or 25 gauge) was at a right angle to the longitudinal axis of the spine. In contrast, when the needle bevel was parallel to the longitudinal axis of the spine, the frequency of PDPH was only 0.24%.[54]

Because of the lower risk of PDPH when the bevel of the spinal needle is oriented parallel to the longitudinal axis of the spine, some authors suggest inserting an epidural needle in the same manner. When in the epidural space, the needle bevel can then be rotated for catheter insertion. In 1558 patients about to receive epidural analgesia for labor pain, 2.6% suffered a dural puncture.[31] In 20 women, the dura was entered with the needle perpendicular to the spine, and in 21 the needle bevel was parallel to the spine. Seventy-three percent of the perpendicular and 31% of the parallel group developed PDPH (Fig. 38-7). In this study, rotating the needle within the epidural space did not increase the risk of dural puncture.

However, rotating the epidural needle significantly decreases the force required to puncture the dura.[57]

The mean weight required for dural puncture was 180 g without rotation and 148 g with rotation. Modern disposable epidural needles have sharp tips, which can drill a hole in the dura if held against it while rotating the needle. Until more clinical data are available about the safety of needle rotation, I do not recommend this practice for routine use. [Editor's Note: I do recommend it. See Chap. 32]

PATIENT POSITION DURING PLACEMENT. Anesthesiologists differ in opinion concerning the optimum patient position during the placement of an epidural catheter in the parturient. Obese parturients usually prefer a sitting position, whereas other women prefer the lateral one.[58] The lateral position may offer some advantages because the decrease in subarachnoid pressure may decrease dural tension, and subsequently decrease the possibility of perforating the dura. In addition, the venous pressure in the epidural veins is lower when the patient is in the lateral position. This can diminish the diameter of the vessels and decrease the chance of vascular perforation. The actively laboring parturient also may have difficulty remaining in the sitting position.

Choice of Local Anesthetic

One study suggested that the local anesthetic for spinal anesthesia for cesarean section influenced the incidence of PDPH. In this prospective study, 2511 patients had a cesarean delivery with spinal anesthesia. All the patients received approximately the same amount of hydration. All spinals were done with disposable 26-gauge needles with the bevel of the needle parallel to the longitudinal axis of the spine. The patients received tetracaine/procaine (n = 804), bupivacaine/glucose (n = 942), or lidocaine/glucose (n = 765). Significantly more women in the lidocaine group (9.54%) and the bupivacaine group (7.64%) had a postural

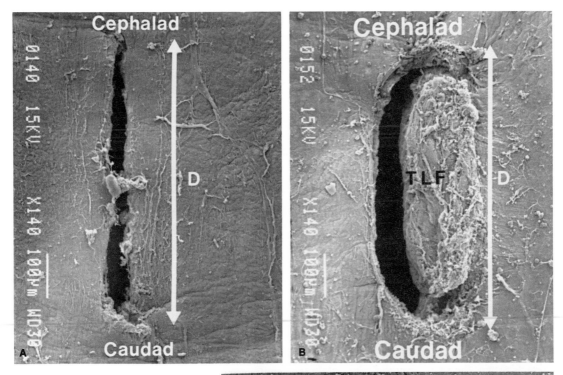

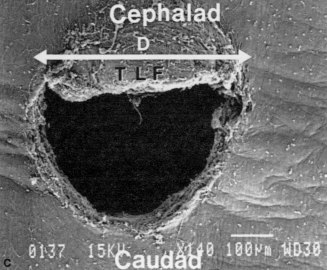

Figure 38–6. Micrographs of dural defects produced by 22-gauge needles: (**A**) Whitacre type (pen point); (**B**) Quinke, with the bevel oriented parallel to the longitudinal dural axis; (**C**) Quinke, with the bevel oriented perpendicular to the longitudinal dural axis. Magnification × 140. (D = diameter of the defect, TLF = "tin-lid" flap) (Photograph courtesy of K. Sami, MD., Naperville, IL)

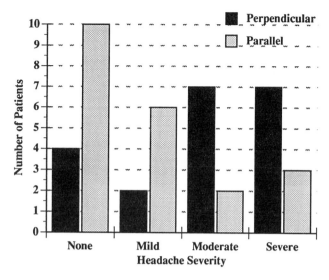

Figure 38–7. Incidence and severity of headache in parturients after accidental dural puncture with 17- or 18-gauge needles. Orienting the needle bevel parallel to the longitudinal axis of the back significantly ($P < 0.05$) reduces the incidence and severity of headache. Parallel needle bevel orientation also lowers the need for therapeutic epidural blood patch (data not shown). (After Norris MC, Leighton BL, DeSimone CA. Needle bevel direction and headache after inadvertent dural puncture. Anesthesiology 1989;70:729)

PDPH than in the tetracaine/procaine group (5.85%) (Fig. 38-8).[59]

The choice of local anesthetic did not influence the number of epidural blood patches required. The authors speculated that at least two different mechanisms may be involved in the development of PDPH. The initial headache, appearing soon after the anesthetic had worn off, seemed influenced by the local anesthetic used. This headache may be caused by the effects of the local anesthetic or the glucose injected on cerebrovascular smooth muscle. Differences between local anesthetics in lipid solubility, protein binding, or metabolism may produce variable vasodilatation. Increased CSF concentrations of glucose also may dilate cerebral blood vessels. Then, the more severe, chronic PDPH

develops. This headache is independent of the local anesthetic.

Similarly, one retrospective review noted a reduced rate of PDPH in patients who received intrathecal fentanyl.[60] Subsequent studies using intrathecal morphine in obstetric patients could not confirm this finding.[61]

Continuous Spinal After Dural Puncture

Continuous spinal anesthesia is an alternative if the epidural needle accidentally enters the subarachnoid space. If the initial passage was troublesome, subsequent attempts also may be difficult. This difficulty could produce several dural punctures. In addition,

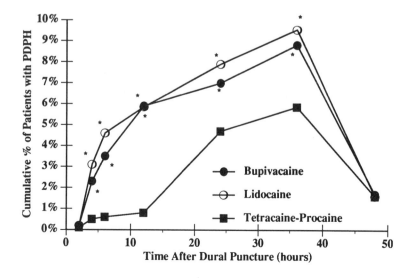

Figure 38–8. The cumulative percentage of patients reporting symptoms of PDPH for 48 h after spinal anesthesia for cesarean delivery. Significantly more patients receiving bupivacaine–glucose and lidocaine–glucose had headaches during the first 36 h. (* = $P < 0.05$). (After Naulty JS, Hertwig L, Hunt CO, Datta S, Ostheimer GW, Weiss JB. Influence of local anesthetic solution on postdural puncture headache. Anesthesiology 1990;72:450)

some reports claim that continuous spinal anesthesia, even with large-diameter epidural catheters, carries a much lower incidence of PDPH than the dural puncture alone.

In the elderly surgical patient population, continuous spinal anesthesia produces PDPH in fewer than 1 in 100 patients.[62-64] This incidence is considerably less than the frequency of PDPH (37%) after dural puncture with an 18-gauge needle.[13] However, a recent prospective study comparing "single-shot" spinal anesthesia to continuous spinal anesthesia found no differences in the incidence of PDPH.[65] The mechanism of the possible lower incidence of PDPH with a continuous spinal catheter is unknown. An inflammatory reaction may occur that seals the dural hole after removing the catheter.

At this time, it is not clear if parturients benefit from continuous spinal anesthesia after accidental dural puncture. A 16% incidence of PDPH was reported in obstetric patients who received continuous spinal anesthesia for cesarean section.[66] In a retrospective review of obstetric patients who had dural puncture with a 17-gauge epidural needle, however, the incidence of PDPH was 60% when the epidural was converted to continuous spinal anesthesia. The patients who received continuous epidural following dural puncture had a 43% incidence of PDPH.[67] This difference was not statistically significant (Fig. 38-9).

An emerging method in obstetric anesthesia is the use of continuous spinal analgesia via a 32-gauge microcatheter. The catheter is introduced into the spinal space through a 25- or 26-gauge needle. Three of 26 patients (11%) in one trial had an orthostatic headache following the delivery.[68]

Prevention and Treatment of Postdural Puncture Headache

The treatment of PDPH has significantly improved since 1918, when the only effective treatment was a week's stay in bed with the head low.[11] Considering the natural course of PDPH, the treatment of PDPH is generally very successful. One goal of therapy for PDPH is to return CSF volume to normal. Because of the usually short duration of the headache, it is not surprising that many treatments have been claimed to be successful. Over the years, multiple treatment modalities, including radiation of the head, intravenous infusion of pituitary gland extract, and the placement of pieces of catgut in the epidural space, have been recommended. Only epidural blood patch, epidural saline, and conservative therapy with caffeine and analgesics while the patient waits for spontaneous recovery have stood the test of time (Fig. 38-10). Because of the rare possibility of subdural hematoma, cerebral herniation, and cranial nerve palsy, PDPH should be treated to increase the CSF pressure. Definitive therapy is especially important when the headache is severe and prolonged.

The main role of conservative treatment is to offer the patient some comfort while she waits for spontaneous recovery. If the PDPH is severe and interferes with all normal activity, conservative treatment is only an adjunct to epidural blood patch.

Hydration

Although it does not increase CSF production, hydration has traditionally been recommended as a way

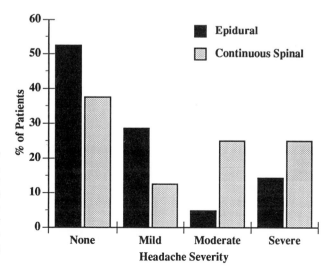

Figure 38-9. Headache severity in parturients after dural puncture with a 17- or 18-gauge Hustead needle. Women in the epidural group received conventional lumbar epidural analgesia for labor and delivery. Women in the continuous spinal group had a 20-gauge polyamide catheter inserted into their subarachnoid space for relief of labor pain. (After Norris MC, Leighton BL. Continuous spinal anesthesia after unintentional dural puncture in parturients. Reg Anesth 1990;15:285)

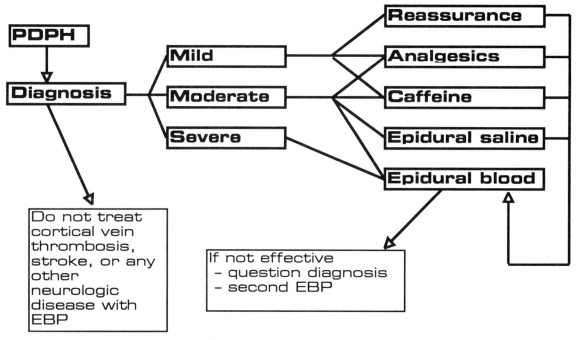

Figure 38–10. Algorithm for the treatment of PDPH. (EBP = epidural blood patch)

to decrease the risk of spinal headache.[69] The greatest consequence of excessive hydration is the increased need for urination. Walking to the bathroom unmasks the postural headache and makes the patient feel miserable. Hydration, as a means to prevent or treat PDPH, is not effective.

Supine Position

Some clinicians recommend remaining supine for variable times to prevent PDPH. Laying flat after dural puncture lessens the CSF pressure gradient across the dural tear. This position might promote spontaneous closure of the tear. Certainly, while the patient is supine, postural headache is eliminated. On the contrary, others recommend early ambulation because controlled studies have shown no benefit to the supine position.[7,33,34,70,71] In one prospective, controlled study of parturients, the incidence of PDPH was 36% in the group that remained supine for at least 24 hours. The group of patients who mobilized 6 hours after delivery had a 23% incidence of PDPH.[71] This difference is not statistically significant. The bed-rested patients did, however, have more severe headaches. These studies show that enforced bed rest offers no benefit in the prevention of PDPH in the postpartum period. On the contrary, prolonged bed rest can significantly inconvenience both the mother caring for her infant and the nursing staff.

Abdominal Binder

Use of an abdominal binder may reduce the incidence of PDPH.[72] The abdominal binder reproduces venocaval obstruction and causes shunting of blood through the vertebral veins. This altered blood flow increases intracerebral venous pressure. No recent studies exist on the efficacy of the abdominal binder in the treatment of PDPH.

Method of Delivery

In addition, bearing down during the second stage of labor might increase the risk of spinal headache. By increasing CSF pressure, pushing might force CSF out through the dural tear. In a controlled study, however, neither bearing down nor the method of delivery altered the incidence of PDPH.[73]

Caffeine

Cerebrospinal fluid hypotension associated with PDPH may cause compensatory dilatation of cerebral vessels. The resultant increase in cerebral blood flow can induce headache (see Fig. 38-3). Caffeine, a methylated xanthine, is a cerebral vasoconstrictor. Clinicians first used caffeine to treat spinal headache almost 50 years ago.[74] Intravenous caffeine sodium benzoate (500 mg) initially relieves PDPH in 75% to 89% of patients;[75,76] however, symptoms often recur. Caffeine does not stop the CSF leak, nor does it treat the CSF hypotension caused by the CSF leak. Caffeine's main action is on cerebrovascular dynamics, where it causes an increase in cerebral arteriolar resistance and a decrease in cerebral blood volume and blood flow. If a vascular type of headache is the main component of the patient's PDPH, then caffeine does offer some relief while waiting for spontaneous closure of the dural hole. Reported side effects from intravenous caffeine include transient dizziness and flushing.[77,78]

Oral caffeine via tablets or caffeinated beverages also has been advocated for the treatment of PDPH. In a controlled study of obstetric patients who had PDPH, 300 mg of oral caffeine relieved the headache for about 4 hours in 90% of the patients. In the control group, 60% of the patients had relief from their headache during the first 4 hours. At 24 hours, there were no differences in the frequency of headache when the caffeine group was compared to the placebo group. In addition, similar numbers of women in each group received a therapeutic epidural blood patch (Fig. 38-11).[78]

Nonsteroidal Anti-inflammatory Drugs

Indomethacin (100 mg) given orally 6 hours after spinal anesthesia decreased the incidence of PDPH from 17.8% to 10.3% in one open study. The authors speculated that indomethacin diminished the inflammatory reaction produced by traction of the cranial nerves created by low CSF volumes.[35] In another study, the incidence of PDPH was 16.8% in the prophylactic indomethacin group and 24.5% in the placebo group.[79] This difference was not statistically significant.

Epidural Saline

The administration of large volumes of saline as a bolus injection (20–100 mL) or an infusion (1000–2000 mL over 24 hours) into the epidural space increases epidural and, thus, subarachnoid pressure.[32,80,81] This increased pressure correlates with relief of the headache. The rise in the epidural pressure is short-lived and lasts only for the duration of the infusion. Often the headache returns. Twenty milliliters of epidural saline increase the subarachnoid pressure immediately to as high as 85 cm of H_2O. After injection of saline, pressure remains elevated for 3 to 10 minutes.[82] Rapid injections produce higher pressures than slow injections. Side effects, such as dizziness, nausea, and spasm of the lumbar muscles, occur more commonly after rapid injection. Occasional patients report immediate and permanent relief of postural headache from epidural saline injection. The rapid rise in epidural pressure may push the dural flap back through the opening and seal the dural hole.

Several researchers have studied the efficacy of epidural saline infusion for PDPH. The results of these studies remain contradictory. Generally, the results were good when the patients were followed for a limited time, and discouraging if longer follow-up was utilized.[80,81,83–85]

After accidental dural puncture in parturients, prophylactic injections of 60 mL of saline immediately following delivery and the following morning decreased the incidence of PDPH from 76.5% to 12.5%.[81] Prophylactic infusion of 1 to 1.5 L of Hartman's solution in obstetric patients after accidental dural puncture resulted in a 39% incidence of PDPH.[86] These

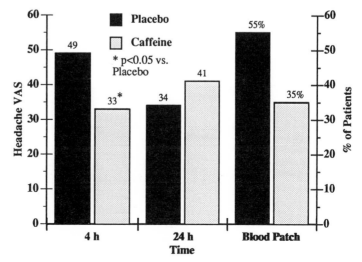

Figure 38-11. Oral caffeine provides transient relief of PDPH. Forty parturients who complained of PDPH received either placebo or a single 300-mg dose of oral caffeine. Women in the caffeine group had less pain 4 hours later. Both groups had the same degree of pain by 24 hours. The need for therapeutic epidural blood patch did not differ between the groups. (Data from Camman WR, Murray RS, Muschlin PS, Lambert DH. Effects of oral caffeine for postdural puncture headache. A double-blind placebo controlled study. Anesth Analg 1990;70:181)

same authors had previously reported a 77.5% headache rate with no prophylactic measures. In other studies, epidural saline provided minimal benefits. One study with obstetric PDPH patients reported a 0% success rate with epidural saline injection.[85]

A recent study followed patients for 4 days after epidural saline treatment. The parturients treated with prophylactic crystalloid infusion did not have headache initially. By the fourth day, they were just as likely to have a headache as the control patients (Fig. 38-12).[84]

The main component of dura is collagen. Collagen is a potent stimulus to platelet aggregation and adherence.[87] When the needle enters the epidural space, especially in the parturient, one should expect some bleeding. Infusing saline into the epidural space dilutes the released coagulation factors and thus may not be the most logical action when hoping for a hemostatic plug. In addition, a continuous epidural saline infusion adds to the potential of accidental epidural infusion of other medications. Infused saline must be preservative-free lest neurotoxic effects follow.[88]

Symptoms associated with epidural saline infusion include back pain, orbital pain, and even retinal hemorrhage.[89] If large volumes of saline are used, sharp back and neck pain may last for several days.[86]

Prophylactic Epidural Blood Patch

For accidental dural puncture and subsequent epidural anesthesia, prophylactic epidural blood patch given immediately before withdrawing the needle or catheter is tempting. If successful, this approach would eliminate most instances of PDPH. Patient suffering, and the related increased hospital costs, would be avoided. Several authors have successfully reduced the incidence of PDPH with prophylactic epidural blood patch.

In parturients, epidural blood patch (15 mL) given a few hours after delivery reduced the incidence of PDPH from 80% to 21% during the following 4 days.[90] In a similar study, prophylactic epidural blood patch lowered the incidence of PDPH from 57.1% to 14.3%.[91] One investigator injected blood epidurally immediately after local anesthetic injection in seven patients. None of these subjects developed PDPH.[92] In another study, obstetric patients who had dural punctures with 18-gauge Tuohy needles were allocated to three treatment groups. In the oral fluid/narcotic group, 21 of 24 patients (87.5%) developed PDPH. The patients who received prophylactic epidural saline (40–60 mL) had a 66.7% incidence of PDPH (20 of 30 patients). The third group of 20 patients received epidural injection of 15 mL of autologous blood shortly after delivery. One patient in this group developed a headache. Her headache persisted after subsequent therapeutic epidural blood patch.[83] In a blinded study, patients undergoing extracorporeal lithotripsy received spinal anesthesia via a 25-gauge needle. Half the patients received 10 mL of epidural saline and the other half received 10 mL of epidural blood at the same interspace immediately after the spinal injection. In the blood group, 8.3% of patients experienced a headache, whereas 45% in the saline group suffered PDPH. Both groups had a similar incidence of back pain.[93] The incidence of PDPH in the epidural saline group equalled that found with no prophylactic treatment.

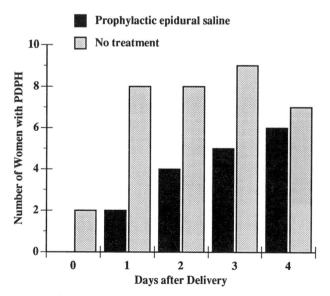

Figure 38–12. The efficacy of prophylactic epidural saline infusion after accidental dural puncture in obstetric patients. (Data from Okell RW, Sprigge JS. Unintentional dural puncture. A survey of recognition and management. Anaesthesia 1987;42:1110)

Other studies have reported a failure rate of blood patch given soon after the dural puncture as high as 54% to 71%. When delaying the blood patch until 24 hours after dural puncture, the failure rate fell to 4% (Table 38-10).[94,95]

Reported complications from early prophylactic blood patch include total spinal anesthesia.[96] In the reported case, the author postulated that the injection of blood into the epidural space forced CSF upward, producing extensive spinal blockade.

The success rate of prophylactic epidural blood patch seems low (<80%–90%) if the blood is injected soon after the dural puncture. In addition, 20% to 40% of the patients do not develop PDPH after dural puncture with an epidural needle and thus do not require epidural blood patch. An alternate method is to leave the catheter in place for 24 hours and inject the blood through the catheter if postural headache should develop. This treatment plan lessens the frequency of unnecessary epidural blood patches while it maintains early treatment of postural headache without delaying the discharge of the patient and increasing hospital costs.

Therapeutic Epidural Blood Patch

Epidural blood patch, thought to be a benign procedure, is often used to treat PDPH; however, complications are not uncommon. Up to 35% of patients may experience paresthesia, radiculitis, cranial nerve dysfunction, neck ache, or back pain.[97,98] Back pain and neck ache are the most common residual symptoms after epidural blood patch. These may persist up to 3 months.[97] The enzymatic coagulation cascade produces bradykinin and nociceptive mediators. These compounds may play a role in the observed side effects.[99]

Nelson (1930) first suggested that a bloody tap may help seal the dural hole and prevent PDPH.[100] Blood injected into the epidural space has been successfully used in the treatment of PDPH since the 1960s.[101,102]

The injection of autologous blood into the epidural space increases the pressure in that space, increases CSF pressure, and forms a sealing clot over the dural tear. The immediate rise in the CSF pressure gives initial relief for the headache. Later, new CSF production and the sealed dural hole maintain normal intracerebral pressure/volume homeostasis.

An in vitro study of dura, suspended between two chambers and punctured with a spinal needle, examined the ability of epidural blood to seal a dural tear. The CSF filled one side of the chamber and blood the other. After 30 minutes, the dura was inspected. Small sheets of coagulated blood appeared on the epidural side of the dura. In some specimens, the blood also emerged on the subdural side. The specimens with the blood patch showed only minor leakage when stressed with pressures of up to 40 mm Hg. The clots remained adherent to the dura throughout the testing. The control specimens all leaked profusely at 1.5 mm Hg of pressure.[103]

Sheep injected epidurally with autologous blood after a spinal tap initially showed widespread fibroblastic activity in the epidural space. Seven days later, collagen formation prevailed. Focal areas of fat necrosis, but no significant inflammation, also were present. Both the spinal cord and the nerve roots remained intact without evidence of demyelinization. Dura from control animals that had only dural puncture first developed a layer of fibroblasts. This fibroblastic activity continued, particularly in the area of dural puncture. After 3 weeks to 6 months, the reaction in some control animals was indistinguishable from the animals that received epidural blood.[104]

Table 38-10

The Incidence of PDPH (%) with or Without Prophylactic Epidural Blood Patch

PDPH (%)		PEBP VOLUME (mL)	AUTHOR
+ PEBP (NO.)	− PEBP (NO.)		
21 (19)	80 (20)	15	Calonna–Romano (1989)[90]
14.3 (7)	57.1 (7)	18–20	Ackerman (1989)[91]
0 (7)		15–17	Quaynor (1985)[92]
5 (20)	88 (24)	15	Trivedi (1989)[83]
54 (75)	59 (11)	5–10	Palahniuk (1979)[95]
Abbreviation: PEBP = prophylactic epidural blood patch.			

INDICATIONS AND CONTRAINDICATIONS FOR EPIDURAL BLOOD PATCH.

The indication for epidural blood patch is PDPH when other etiologies are ruled out. The headache is usually severe enough to prevent normal daily child-care activities, and conservative therapy fails. Contraindications to epidural blood patch are similar to those of epidural anesthesia. These include local or systemic infection, patient refusal, and coagulation disorders.

EFFICACY OF EPIDURAL BLOOD PATCH.

The success rate for the first epidural blood patch is more than 90% (Table 38-11).[104,105] After the second blood patch, 97.5% of headaches are cured.[97] Faulty diagnosis or misplaced blood may result in the failure of epidural blood patch to cure PDPH.

VOLUME OF BLOOD FOR EPIDURAL BLOOD PATCH.

There is no consensus about the volume of autologous blood that should be administered epidurally for the treatment of PDPH. In his original description of the technique, Gormley[101] recommended using 2 to 3 mL of blood. Twenty years later, Crawford[105] advocated injecting as much as 20 mL (or until the patient feels discomfort). In parturients, 7 to 10 mL of blood injected into the epidural space is 97.5% successful (although some patients will require two procedures).[97]

Szeinfeld *et al*[106] studied the spread of technetium[99]-labeled autologous blood injected into the epidural space. The spread of blood in the epidural space ranged between 7 and 14 spinal segments and varied with the volume of the injectate (Fig. 38-13). The average volume of the blood introduced was 14.8 mL (1.6 mL/ spinal segment). The injected blood tended to flow in the cephalad direction and passed through the intervertebral foramina into the paravertebral space. In all but one patient, blood spread caudally to S_1 or S_2. In that one patient, blood did not extend below the injection site. Based on this study, it seems logical to inject the blood in an interspace at or below the dural puncture to ensure that the blood will cover the dural puncture site. A 10-mL volume will cover approximately six segments, which should be adequate to seal the dural hole. A volume of 20 mL, recommended by some anesthesiologists, may be excessive and will bring more discomfort and side effects to some patients. [Editor's Note: I think a larger volume of blood (15–20 mL) is more likely to produce an immediate cure and, if injected carefully, will not produce significant side effects.]

TECHNIQUE FOR EPIDURAL BLOOD PATCH.

Place the patient in the lateral position. This posture avoids excessive epidural CSF leakage during the needle placement and may make the woman more comfortable. Using strict aseptic technique, identify the epidural space in the usual manner. Once the needle is in the epidural space, an assistant draws 10 mL of the patient's blood, usually from the antecubital vein, into a syringe in a sterile fashion. Then, inject the blood into the epidural space over 30 to 60 seconds. Keep the patient supine for 10 to 30 minutes, then test the effectiveness of the blood patch.

If working alone, you can do a PDPH by placing an epidural catheter, and then injecting blood through it.[107] However, in vitro, passing blood through an epidural catheter delays its coagulation.[108]

Table 38-11

Efficacy of Epidural Blood Patch

AUTHOR	NO. OF PATIENTS	RELIEF AFTER FIRST EBP (%)	NO RELIEF (%)
Gormley (1960)	7	100	0
DiGiovanni (1970)	45	91.1	8.9
DiGiovanni (1972)	63	92.8	3.2
Glass (1972)	50	94.0	6.0
DuPont (1972)	42	95.2	2.4
Vondrell (1973)	60	96.7	3.3
Ostheimer (1974)	185	98.4	1.6
Abouleish (1975)	118	89.0	2.5
Abbreviation: EBP = epidural blood patch.			

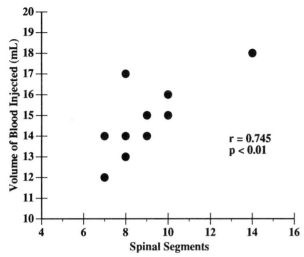

Figure 38–13. Correlation between the amount of radiolabeled blood injected into the epidural space and the spread of gamma radiation. (After Szeinfeld M, Ihmeidan IH, Moser MM, Machado R, Klose KJ, Serafini AN. Epidural blood patch: Evaluation of the volume and spread of blood injected into the epidural space. Anesthesiology 1986;64:820)

What should you do if you find CSF dripping from the epidural needle when attempting an epidural blood patch? The spinal fluid leaking through the dural tear into the epidural space may accumulate faster than it can be reabsorbed. If one waits a few minutes with the epidural needle in place, the CSF leak usually stops. One can then proceed with the autologous blood injection.[109] Other options include placing the needle in another interspace or abandoning the procedure. If a significant volume of CSF leaks or if you can easily aspirate CSF, the needle is in the subarachnoid space. At this point, abandon the procedure at this interspace. Withdrawing the needle until the CSF leak stops does not guarantee that the blood would not be injected into the subarachnoid space. Injection of a small amount of short-acting spinal anesthetic can distinguish spinal and epidural placement of the tip of the needle.[109]

SIDE EFFECTS OF EPIDURAL BLOOD PATCH. Transient side effects of epidural blood patch include back pain, neck ache, paresthesia in the legs and toes, dizziness, radicular pain, cramping in the abdomen, cranial nerve palsy, and epidural hematoma.[97,98,105,110–112] Possible complications, such as adhesive arachnoiditis, abscess formation, or obliteration of the epidural space, have not been reported. Meningitis is a rare complication.[113] More than 95% of obstetric patients accept this technique.[97]

Pain and discomfort from excessive volume of the blood can last for several days unless the injection stops immediately when the symptoms occur. In the sitting position, the transdural pressure can be between 21 and 48 cm H_2O.[114] If large volumes of epidural blood are injected, this pressure gradient may be reversed, and blood may enter the spinal space.[103] Blood in the spinal fluid also may clot if the entry rate is rapid. In dogs, the subarachnoid injection of 2 mL of autologous blood caused spasms in the lower extremities. However, no permanent neurologic deficits occurred.[115]

WHEN THE EPIDURAL BLOOD PATCH DOES NOT WORK. When the blood patch does not work, reevaluate the patient's diagnosis. A single epidural blood patch is more than 90% effective. A true PDPH may require a second, and very rarely a third, blood patch before resolving. Baysinger *et al*[116] reported two patients whose headaches persisted after three and four blood patches. Normal saline epidural infusion at 15 to 30 mL/h (rate-limited by the patient) for 24 hours relieved both of the patients' symptoms. No reasonable explanations exist why these patients responded to epidural saline but not to autologous blood.

Epidural Dextran

Because of the potential for bacterial contamination and other complications associated with epidural blood patch, alternate agents have been advocated for the treatment of PDPH. One group of researchers reported positive results with epidural injection of dextran 40 (20–30 mL) in 52 patients.[117] Treatment with dextran was initiated when other approaches had failed. Apart from dysesthesias (7.1%) and burning sensation (3.5%), no long-term adverse effects were noted.

Limited neurotoxicology data are available concerning dextran. No systematic neurotoxicity studies have been performed, and the safety of spinal or epidural dextran is unknown. In the only two toxicity studies available, dextran injected epidurally caused no significant changes in the histopathology of epidural, subdural, or subarachnoid structures, nor did it cause tissue irritation when injected into the intercostal space.[99,118]

Dextran 40 may successfully treat PDPH because it is slowly absorbed from the epidural space. Thus, dextran produces a more prolonged pressure effect on the dura than saline. This extra time may allow the dural hole to heal. Because dextran effectively cures PDPH, coagulation per se may not be an essential part of the successful treatment of PDPH.[99]

Dural Puncture and Subsequent Epidural Anesthesia

Previous dural puncture or epidural blood patch usually do not pose a clinical problem for the success of a later epidural anesthetic.[119-121] However, case reports and retrospective reviews exist that conclude that previous dural puncture significantly impairs the quality of a subsequent epidural anesthetic.[122,123]

Ong *et al*[123] retrospectively reviewed their experience with epidural block after an earlier accidental dural puncture. Ninety percent of women with an earlier uncomplicated epidural anesthetic had a successful later block. Only 59% of parturients with a history of dural puncture and epidural blood patch had a successful epidural in a subsequent pregnancy. Those women with a history of dural puncture alone had a 65% success rate (Table 38-12).[123] These women did not have a high incidence of failed blocks with their initial anesthetic. Only one woman who suffered a dural puncture had poor analgesia with her first epidural. In the 29 women with a history of dural puncture and epidural blood patch, five patients had missed segments, and three required a large volume (35–37 mL) of local anesthetic. In four patients, epidural anesthesia was abandoned for general anesthesia. Of the 17 women who had previous dural puncture only, without epidural blood patch, 6 had missed segments, and 4 of these women required general anesthesia to complete the cesarean section. The authors postulated a role for one or more of the following factors: previous dural puncture, previous epidural anesthetic, technical failure of the anesthesia staff, and anatomic abnormality of the epidural space that initially caused the dural puncture.[123]

BACK PAIN

Back pain occurs commonly after labor and delivery. Epidural analgesia does not appear to alter the incidence of this complication.[124] Low back pain may occur in up to 50% of parturients.[125] Magnetic resonance imaging studies detect abnormal lumbar disc bulge or herniation of an intervertebral disc in up to 53% of pregnant patients, symptomatic or not.[126] In the nonobstetric population, the incidence of postoperative localized back pain after spinal or epidural anesthesia varies from 2% to 32%.[127-132]

One retrospective study found an 18.9% incidence of back pain after vaginal delivery in patients who had epidural analgesia. The incidence was 10.5% in those parturients who did not receive epidural anesthesia.[133] In another study in which no one received an epidural or spinal anesthetic, parturients had a 40% incidence of back pain after spontaneous delivery and a 25% incidence after forceps/vacuum delivery.[134] Similar numbers of women complained of back pain after cesarean delivery with either regional or general anesthesia. In a recent study using 25- or 29-gauge spinal needles in young patients, 11.3% complained of back pain.[135] The incidence of back pain did not correlate with needle size or the number of attempts to identify the subarachnoid space. In a prospective study, 32% of 1036 parturients suffered back pain after delivery. The three main risk factors associated with subsequent postpartum back pain were a history of previous back pain, multiparity, and epidural anesthesia (Fig. 38-14).

Epidural anesthesia coincided with the development of back pain only in multiparas.[136] A history of previous back pain was the strongest risk factor for the development of postpartum back pain. In another pro-

Table 38-12

Epidural Anesthesia After Previous Dural Puncture in Parturients

PATIENT CHARACTERISTICS	NO. OF PATIENTS	SUCCESSFUL EPIDURALS (%)
Previous dural puncture and EBP	29	59*
Previous dural puncture	17	65*
Previous epidural	928	90
First epidural (primigravida)	5691	92
First epidural (multigravida)	1973	89

(After Ong BY, Graham CR, Ringaert KRA, Cohen MM, Palahniuk RJ. Impaired epidural analgesia after dural puncture with and without subsequent blood patch. Reprinted with permission from the International Anesthesia Research Society [Anesthesia and Analgesia 1990;70:76])
*$P < 0.05$ versus previous epidural and first epidural groups.
Abbreviation: EBP = epidural blood patch.

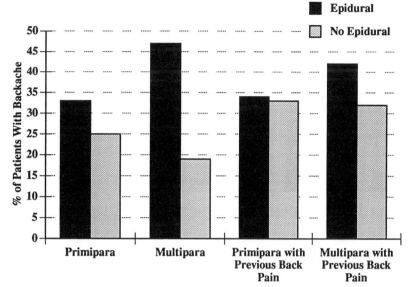

Figure 38–14. Risk factors associated with back pain in 1036 obstetric patients. Multiparity, epidural anesthesia, and a previous history of back pain significantly ($P < 0.01$) increased the risk of postpartum back pain. Epidural anesthesia significantly ($P < 0.001$) increases the risk of back pain in multiparous women with no previous history of back pain. (Data from Lecoq G. Hamza J, Narchi P, Jullien P, Attane D. Risk factors associated with postpartum backache in obstetric patients. Anesthesiology 1990;73:A966)

spective study of 466 parturients, the only factors related to the epidural procedure that correlated with back pain were local pain associated with the placement of the epidural needle and unilateral block (Fig. 38-15). Other factors, such as patient position, local skin infiltration, the interspace used, volume of the local anesthetic, and technical problems while placing the epidural catheter, were not associated with postpartum back pain.[137]

A cause for back pain following spinal and epidural anesthesia could be the flattening of the normal lumbar lordosis, with resultant minor sprains due to anesthetic-induced muscular relaxation. This effect can stretch joints and muscles of the back beyond the nor-

mal range and subsequently cause back pain.[138] Needle trauma to supraspinous and interspinous ligaments also may lead to localized aseptic periostitis, tendonitis, and inflammation of the ligaments. Other causes for back pain are epidural hematoma, epidural abscess, and, rarely, symphyseal rupture.

Severe lumbar paraspinal muscle pain and spasm have recently been associated with the epidural use of 2% or 3% 2-chloroprocaine (MPF).[139] The older chloroprocaine formulation, which contains a higher bisulfite concentration, did not appear to produce this type of back pain. Disodium ethylenediaminetetra-acetic acid (EDTA) in the MPF formulation of 2-chloroprocaine could cause hypocalcemic tetany in the par-

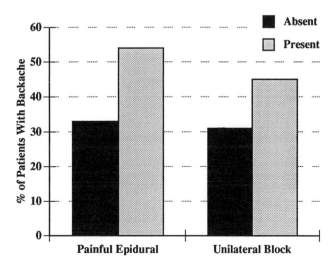

Figure 38–15. Incidence of postpartum backache in 466 parturients receiving epidural labor analgesia. Painful epidural insertion and unilateral analgesia significantly ($P < 0.05$) increased the risk of backache. (After Benlabed M, Hamza J, Jullien P, Troche G, Lecoq G. Risk factors for postpartum backache associated with epidural anesthesia. Anesthesiology 1990;73:A996)

aspinous muscles. Recently, Dirkes[140] successfully treated this back pain with intravenous calcium chloride. Epidurally injected EDTA causes tetanic muscle contractions in the rat.[141] Others have attributed this pain to infiltration of the skin and subcutaneous tissues with acidic chloroprocaine solution before epidural needle placement.[142] Hynson *et al*[143] reported a volunteer study using larger volumes of epidural chloroprocaine (30–50 mL). Before block, the paraspinal muscles were infiltrated with 1% lidocaine or 0.75% bupivacaine. One of 10 volunteers who received 1% epidural lidocaine developed back pain. Four of five subjects in the chloroprocaine (MPF) group suffered back pain.[143] These results eliminated local infiltration with acidic chloroprocaine as the cause of back pain.

Field block to anesthetize the segmental recurrent spinal nerves before conduction anesthesia may significantly reduce the incidence of the back pain and may eliminate prolonged back pain (Fig. 38-16).[131] Treat back pain after spinal or epidural anesthesia with conservative physical therapy and reassurance. Encourage patients to ambulate early. Because about 3% of patients may suffer from back pain for prolonged periods, appropriate follow up is necessary.[131]

NECK PAIN

The epidural space is commonly identified by detecting the loss of resistance to the injection of air. Injecting too much air can produce emphysema of the neck with neck pain.[144–146] Excessive amounts of epidural air also may cause venous air embolism. Large volumes of air are not needed when identifying the epidural space

with loss-of-resistance technique. A volume of 0.1 to 0.2 mL is sufficient to define the loss of resistance. This amount of air should cause no clinical problems no matter where it is injected.

PROLONGED BLOCK

The cause of prolonged blockade after epidural anesthesia is not known. Perhaps large amounts of local anesthetic accumulate in the epidural fat with repeated injections. Slow release of drug from this depot may persistently block nerve conduction. Prolonged blockade is totally reversible and does not involve any neural injury.[147,148]

INFECTION

Infection of the spinal or epidural space is an uncommon, but potentially devastating, condition. Any regional anesthetic risks bacterial or viral infection. Equipment, catheters, or drugs may all transmit microorganisms. The infecting agent also can come from the anesthesiologist or the patient. The most common sites of infection are the skin and subcutaneous tissues. The more serious central neural infections are extremely rare.

Theoretically, bacteremic blood that escapes into the spinal or epidural space during needle insertion can cause localized infection. Many anesthesiologists agree that an elevated body temperature contraindicates spinal and epidural anesthesia. Thirty percent of bacteremic rats subjected to percutaneous cisternal punc-

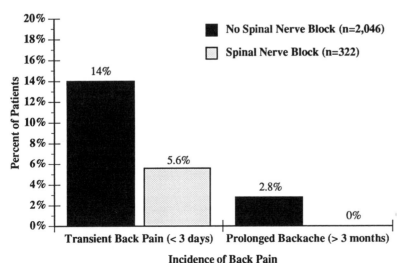

Figure 38–16. Recurrent spinal nerve block and the incidence of backache following epidural anesthesia. (Data from Peng ATC, Behar S, Blancato LS. Reduction of post lumbar puncture backache by the use of field block anesthesia prior to lumbar puncture. Anesthesiology 1985;63:277)

ture showed evidence of meningitis 24 hours later.[149] On the other hand, lumbar puncture for CSF collection is a standard procedure in the evaluation of fever of unknown etiology. This procedure does not appear to increase the risk of central nervous system or epidural infection.

Chorioamnionitis is a common systemic infection in the parturient (see Chap. 29). Conduction anesthesia is sometimes denied to these women out of fear of spreading bacteria into the epidural and spinal space. It is not known if chorioamnionitis predisposes the patient who receives spinal or epidural anesthesia to meningitis. The literature contains no reports of epidural abscess or meningitis in association with conduction anesthesia in these patients. In a retrospective study, 113 parturients with chorioamnionitis received epidural anesthesia without any infectious complications.[150] However, a zero incidence in a study with few patients does not equal to zero risk. For example, if the true risk for developing epidural abscess was 1 in 1000, then the probability of not developing epidural infection would be 0.999. In this setting, the chance that none of the 113 patients in the preceding study would develop epidural infection is 0.999[113] or 89%.

Systemic Infection

The method of anesthesia for cesarean section may affect the maternal immune reaction toward certain viruses (*i.e.,* herpes simplex). Natural killer cell activity falls significantly after cesarean section in patients who received general anesthesia, but not in those who had epidural anesthesia.[151] Newborns show no such changes. Clinically, the technique of anesthesia for cesarean section lacks influence on postcesarean infectious morbidity.[152]

Aseptic Meningitis

Aseptic meningitis mimics infectious meningitis. Aseptic meningitis is a rare complication after epidural or spinal anesthesia. Two cases of aseptic meningitis occurred in a series of 780,000 conduction anesthetics.[130] With modern conduction anesthesia equipment, technique, and drugs, aseptic meningitis is practically nonexistent unless a breech in technique occurs.[153] Aseptic meningitis is a clinical syndrome of unknown etiology, although chemical irritation of the subarachnoid space is often blamed. Aseptic meningitis was more common when nondisposable spinal trays were used.[154,155] The few reported cases often occurred in a single hospital as

an epidemic, suggesting a breech in technique. Incomplete rinsing of a detergent solution (Alconox) was implicated as the cause in one series of cases.[156] Unsatisfactory sterile preparation of instruments also may lead to aseptic meningitis.

As recently as 1985, a report of aseptic meningitis after dibucaine spinal anesthesia appeared.[153] In this case, the spinal tray was prepared in the hospital. The tray included a disposable spinal needle but a reusable glass syringe for injection of the local anesthetic. In further study of the incident, the authors detected detergent residue in some syringes.

Symptoms of aseptic meningitis include headache, fever, and nuchal rigidity. These symptoms typically begin 6 to 24 hours after spinal anesthesia. The headache is severe, generalized, and not postural. A CSF culture with no growth of bacteria in spite of the high white cell count confirms the diagnosis. Treatment is supportive and conservative. The prognosis is invariably good. Aseptic meningitis must be differentiated from purulent meningitis, in which the consequences are severe if not treated promptly. Diagnostic lumbar puncture in symptomatic patients is of utmost importance.

Septic Meningitis

Bacterial meningitis associated with conduction anesthesia is a rare but serious event. Case reports of septic meningitis in healthy obstetric patients have been published.[113,157] Causative organisms are usually nosocomial.[158] Absolute and meticulous sterile technique is mandatory. In the author's institution, all personnel in the labor/delivery room don a cap and mask during the placement of an epidural catheter.

Epidural Abscess

Spinal epidural abscess is a rare complication in the obstetric patient. Only one case of epidural abscess would be expected per year in a tertiary care hospital in this country (all causes combined).[159] Crawford[160] reported one case of epidural infection in 26,490 epidurals given to obstetric patients. This patient was bacteremic, and developed an epidural abscess 16 days after delivery.[160] In another survey of 516,000 lumbar epidural blocks in obstetric patients, one diabetic patient developed epidural abscess 11 months after her delivery.[1]

Despite improvements in therapy and diagnostic tests, mortality in the general patient population from spinal epidural abscess approaches 25%.[161] The initial symptoms associated with epidural abscess are often fever, malaise, back pain, headache, and bladder and bowel dysfunction. Nuchal rigidity is also common. Lower extremity pain, weakness, and paralysis are late symptoms.

The diagnosis is suspected from symptoms and confirmed with myelography, computed tomography, or magnetic resonance imaging. The treatment is acute surgical intervention and appropriate antibiotic therapy. Once present, the neurologic signs are usually irreversible if decompressive surgery is delayed for more than 6 hours.

Adhesive Arachnoiditis

Arachnoiditis is a delayed inflammatory reaction of the arachnoid mater of multifactorial etiology. It may coincide with epidural anesthesia in some circumstances.[162,163] It produces thickened membranes around the spinal cord and the cauda equina. Sometimes, newly formed connective tissue totally obliterates the subarachnoid space. Adhesions develop between the pia and dura mater. This pathology may obstruct CSF flow and blood supply to the spinal cord and nerve roots. Causative factors include chemical damage from disinfectants, detergents, preservatives, and local anesthetics. The symptoms usually start weeks to months after the inciting event. Gradual progressive weakness and sensory loss of the lower extremities over the months may lead to paraplegia. Myelography confirms the diagnosis. No effective treatment is available.

RETAINED CATHETER AND FOREIGN-MATERIAL CONTAMINATION

Withdrawal of the catheter through the epidural needle is not recommended in any situation because it may shear off. In one case, an anesthesiologist sheared approximately 2 cm of an epidural catheter. Computed tomography localized the catheter to the interspinous muscles. The patient was informed, and the catheter was left in place.[164]

Several cases of knotted epidural catheters have been described in the literature.[165-167] Because the catheter often curls after a short passage in the epidural space, one can *maximize* the chance of the catheter knotting by passing it as far as possible into the epidural space and then withdrawing it to the appropriate distance.[168]

If an epidural catheter cannot be removed easily, wait until the block has completely regressed. A lodged catheter, besides knotting, may encircle a nerve root. Under epidural anesthesia, the patient may not feel pain when such a catheter damages a nerve. Before pulling out a tightly lodged catheter, consider taking a radiograph to try to locate the path of the catheter.

Epidural and spinal needles also may carry various materials into the epidural and spinal space.[169] Needles can carry glass, rubber, and other foreign material such as skin, muscle, and disinfecting solution. Seventy-five percent of 22-gauge spinal needle tips with the stylet in place introduced 1-inch deep in the lumbar interspace contain pieces of skin and epidermis covered with betadine.[170] A 17-gauge Tuohy needle with the stylet in place produces a skin core 87% of the time.[171] The consequences or the magnitude of this type of contamination are unknown. Could, for example, spinal introduction of dermoid cells cause an epidermoid tumor?

Puncturing of rubber stoppers in medication vials with hollow needles cores out a rubber plug 60% to 70% of the time. When injected intramuscularly, these particles cause an acute inflammatory reaction.[172] Later, a fibrous sheath forms around these particles. Macrophages can transport some rubber particles. Drug manufacturers should develop appropriate vials to avoid this unnecessary contamination. Similarly, breaking a glass ampule often results in the introduction of glass particles into the local anesthetic solution and creates the possibility of injection of these particles into the epidural or spinal space.[173]

To minimize foreign-body contamination of the epidural or spinal space, always use a filtered needle when filling a syringe. Always inject through the filter provided in the epidural kits.[173] Remove the filter temporarily to allow aspiration of the catheter before drug injection.

BLADDER DYSFUNCTION

The incidence of bladder dysfunction in parturients not receiving a spinal or epidural anesthetic is 14.2% after spontaneous vaginal delivery and 37.5% after forceps/vacuum delivery.[134] Women receiving epidural analgesia are at similar risk.[174] Some causes for the inability to urinate are decreased bladder tone, perineal tears, edema, episiotomy scar, and sutures.

NEUROLOGIC COMPLICATIONS

A woman who develops a neurologic deficit after delivery is a major concern for the obstetric anesthesiologist. Differential diagnosis presents a sizable problem. Is conduction anesthesia causative, or is it only temporally associated with the patient's symptoms?[175] Could the labor and delivery have caused the damage? Motor weakness, sensory deficit, or bladder or bowel dysfunction may accompany paresthesia (abnormal sensation). Most of the literature relating to postpartum neurologic complications consists of case reports. Only a few extensive reviews are available. Many neurologic disorders are liable to occur during pregnancy, labor, and delivery.[176] Conduction anesthesia causes only a small number of temporally associated complications. After ensuring appropriate treatment for the patient, the anesthesiologist should direct his or her attention to the proper diagnosis of these complications.[177]

Trauma, compression, or ischemia may incite neurologic complications coincident with, but not caused by, conduction anesthesia (Table 38-13). Sites of injury may include the brain, spinal cord, nerve roots, nerve trunks, and peripheral nerves. Trauma by the descending fetal head may cause nerve injuries and muscular sprains. Hematoma, tumor, hemangioma, or abscess may generate symptoms of nerve compression. Vascular causes, such as anterior spinal artery syndrome, may be associated with hypotension. Other causes may include multiple sclerosis, polyneuritis, herniated intervertebral disc, or uncommon myopathic disorders. In addition, a simple strain can yield muscle weakness.[178] Pregnancy can precipitate several neurologic conditions, including carpal tunnel syndrome, sciatica, and Bell's palsy. Most (98.2%, excluding PDPH) of the postoperative neurologic symptoms temporally connected to spinal anesthesia have no causal relationship with the anesthetic technique.[179]

However, since the early part of this century, derangements of nerve function ranging from minor sensory dysfunction to severe paraplegia have been recognized as sequelae of major conduction anesthesia. With the introduction of strict sterile technique, disposable and improved instruments, and preservative-free medications, the complications caused by major conduction anesthesia are becoming increasingly rare.

Postpartum neurologic complications require immediate attention. These patients need prompt, detailed, and ongoing evaluation while the complaint persists. A thorough history and physical examination, in addition to a detailed neurologic examination, is important to delineate the extent, site, and etiology of the patient's symptoms. Diagnostic tests may include plain and contrast radiographs, magnetic resonance imaging studies, coagulation profile, diagnostic lumbar puncture, and nerve conduction studies.

Sensory and Motor Dysfunction

Nerve injuries following delivery usually happen to the lumbosacral trunk. Sensory and motor dysfunction are commonly limited to one nerve or nerve root and have a duration of a few days to a few months. Difficult labor, instrumental delivery, or maternal–fetal disproportion can all cause nerve damage. Anesthetic factors include direct needle trauma, intraneural or intraspinal injection, local anesthetic toxicity, or contamination of the equipment and medications used.

Nerve palsies occur also after uncomplicated delivery. The frequency of paresthesia and motor dysfunction is higher in primiparas, in women who had forceps or vacuum deliveries, and in patients who received epidural anesthesia.[3] At a Canadian hospital, between 1975 and 1983, paresthesia and motor dysfunction complicated 18.9 in 10,000 deliveries.[3] Patients who had epidural anesthesia suffered paresthesia and motor dysfunction in 36.2 in 10,000 deliveries. Those who received general anesthesia had an incidence of 34.7 in 10,000 deliveries (see Table 38-3). In the primigravida, prolonged and difficult instrumental delivery requiring regional anesthesia correlates with an increased frequency of paresthesia and motor dysfunction.

Paraplegia is a rare complication after conduction anesthesia.[180,181] Temporal relationship to conduction anesthesia does not necessary imply a causal relationship. Pre-existing pathology may be causative.[182-184]

Surveys report the frequency of minor neurologic complications following epidural anesthesia as between 0 and 40 in 10,000.[3,26,39,128,130,132,177,180,185-192] Most of the surveys presented are retrospective and may lack sensitivity. In contrast to these surveys, the literature contains many case reports of adverse outcome after conduction anesthesia.[88,155,163,181,193-199] Retrospective

Table 38–13

Causes of Postpartum Paresthesia and Motor Dysfunction

Nerve entrapment
Adhesive arachnoiditis
Cauda equina syndrome
Tumor
Hematoma
Vascular malformation
Muscle strain
Prolapsed intervertebral disc
Anterior spinal artery syndrome
Meralgia paresthetica
Conduction anesthesia

studies may grossly under-report the frequency of neurologic complications. Anesthesiologists, obstetricians, and nursing staff recorded only 22% of the complications reported in a prospective Canadian study.[3] Only the study nurse, who made all postoperative visits, recorded the majority (78%) of these neurologic events. Most of the deficits found were transient paresthesia, numbness, and tingling in the thighs and feet. The incidence of motor dysfunction was 0.8 in 10,000. The incidence of these symptoms was similar after general anesthesia and epidural anesthesia. The duration of these symptoms ranged from hours to months.

Cranial Nerve Involvement

Cranial nerve paresis is an infrequent but well-recognized complication of dural puncture. It is often preceded by spinal headache and associated symptoms. The frequency is reported at 1 in 250 to 400 spinal anesthetics.[200] Paralysis of the abducens nerve has been reported more often than paralysis of the other cranial nerves.[110,200] Often, cranial nerve palsy is positional and responds to epidural blood patch. Recovery is commonly complete within 3 months. Usually these patients have had their dura pierced with a large-bore needle with an ensuing severe headache. Nerve palsies can occur up to a week after anesthesia and persist for several weeks.[1,201] Displacement and traction of the brain can compress and stretch the individual nerves with resultant paresis.

Vestibulocochlear nerve dysfunction is not uncommon after spinal anesthesia.[202-205] Hearing loss may occur.[26] In addition to decreased hearing, other auditory sensations, such as plugging, popping, tinnitus, and buzzing, occur in up to 0.4% of spinal anesthetics.[26] The deficits in hearing are transient, but some may take several months to normalize. Significant hearing loss may be associated with PDPH. One controlled study evaluated the incidence of hypoacusis after spinal anesthesia using 22- or 26-gauge needles.[202] A statistically significant reduction in hearing was found after dural puncture with 22-gauge needles. Dural leak of CSF lowers intracranial pressure and endolymphatic pressure. Audiometry may be a sensitive indicator of low CSF pressure if this hypothesis is accurate. Hearing loss can be postural and sometimes resolves after epidural blood patch.[206] Uncomplicated epidural anesthesia does not cause hearing loss.[203]

Patients with spinal headache occasionally develop visual disturbances. Abducens nerve palsy occurs infrequently in association with severe PDPH.[128,207] The sixth nerve nuclei lie in the floor of the fourth ventricle and directly contact CSF. The nerve has a long and tortuous course over the temporal bone before entering the cavernous sinus to innervate the lateral rectus muscle. Diplopia following the sixth nerve palsy associated with conduction anesthesia may last from weeks to months. Other than epidural blood patch, there is no specific treatment for sixth nerve palsy. Symptomatic treatment includes alternate eye occlusion or prism, which provides single vision.[207] Causes of bilateral sixth nerve paresis include diabetes, myasthenia gravis, herpes zoster, pseudotumor cerebri, cavernous sinus thrombosis, and thyroid disease. Permanent pericentral ring scotomata also has been described following spinal anesthesia for cesarean section.[208,209]

Interruption of the sympathetic nerve supply to the ipsilateral arm and head cause Horner's syndrome. Lumbar epidural blockade may induce a transient Horner's syndrome if high unilateral spread local anesthetic occurs.[210] Horner's syndrome arises in 1.3% to 4% of patients receiving epidural anesthesia.[211]

Nerve Entrapments

The incidence of maternal paresis can be as high as 1 in 2600 deliveries.[212,213] The descending fetal head alone, or in combination with forceps delivery, can cause lumbosacral plexus injury with resulting muscle weakness, sensory loss, or pain. A herniated intervertebral disc may produce similar symptoms and must be part of the differential diagnosis. The lateral popliteal nerve may be injured by forceps compressing the lumbosacral trunk. Fetal head compression can cause obturator nerve damage. The common peroneal nerve, the lateral popliteal nerve, or the femoral/sciatic nerve may be damaged in the lithotomy position by the stirrups.

Cauda Equina Syndrome

The use of continuous spinal anesthesia has been recently recommended for the treatment of labor pain. The neurotoxic effects and the pharmacokinetics of repeated intraspinal drug injections are not known. Multiple injections of local anesthetics through a spinal catheter may produce persistent high spinal fluid drug concentrations. Several recent case reports have suggested that this technique may incite the cauda equina syndrome.

The cauda equina syndrome encompasses bowel and bladder disturbances, perineal sensory loss ("saddle area"), and lower extremity weakness.[214] The bladder symptoms (urinary retention) usually start immediately after the block has worn off; fecal incontinence and other neurologic symptoms follow later. Once present, the symptoms may be permanent or last from weeks to months. The nerve filaments in the cauda may be more sensitive to the toxic actions of agents injected into the CSF because they are not covered with protective sheaths as they pass through the dural sac.

The cauda equina syndrome rarely occurs after modern conduction anesthesia. Ferguson (1937) reported 14 cases of cauda equina syndrome after spinal anesthesia with "heavy" durocaine.[214] This anesthetic was formulated in 15% alcohol, which, in addition to 10% procaine, may have been the causative factor.

Recently, cases of cauda equina syndrome, similar to those reported by Ferguson, were reported after continuous spinal anesthesia with a small-gauge spinal catheter.[215] These patients needed a somewhat high dose of local anesthetic to produce a sufficient level of sensory block. The authors postulated that the use of a small-gauge spinal catheter for continuous spinal anes-thesia caused a maldistribution of the local anesthetic (local and prolonged displacement of the CSF). Both misdirection of the catheter and the very low flow rate of injection might encourage nonuniform distribution of local anesthetic; therefore, the cauda equina was exposed to high (toxic) local anesthetic concentrations for a prolonged period. These authors recommended abandoning the continuous spinal technique when the block does not spread normally after initial dosing. A study using a simplified spinal canal model and a small-gauge spinal catheter showed that the infused anesthetic tended to have a very limited spread that localized according to gravitational forces (Figs. 38-17 and 38-18).[216]

Needle Trauma

One common anesthesia-related variable for postoperative paresthesia is difficult location of the spinal or the epidural space (numerous puncture sites and par-

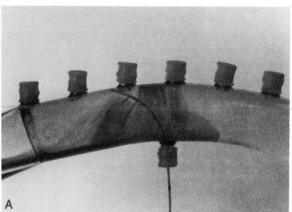

Figure 38–17. Injection of 1 mL of lidocaine/dye mixture (4.76% lidocaine hydrochloride) over 10 s via laterally placed catheters. (**A**) A 20-gauge multiple sideport. (**B**) A 20-gauge endport. (**C**) A 28-gauge endport. The 20-gauge multiple sideport catheter dispersed local anesthetic in a cephalad direction. With the other two catheters, dye concentrates in the dependent (sacral) area. (Rigler ML, Drasner K. Distribution of catheter-injected local anesthetic in a model of the subarachnoid space. Anesthesiology 1991;75:684)

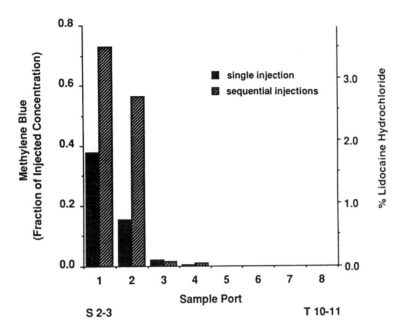

Figure 38–18. Effect of three sequential injections on distribution of the lidocaine/dye mixture. Two experiments are compared. In the first, 1 mL of lidocaine/dye mixture (4.76% lidocaine hydrochloride) was injected over 60 s; in the second, three sequential 1-mL injections (5 min apart) were made with the catheter fixed in the same position. (Rigler ML, Drasner K. Distribution of catheter-injected local anesthetic in a model of the subarachnoid space. Anesthesiology 1991;75: 684)

esthesia during the attempted needle placement).[3] Advancing the needle close to the nerve root or spinal cord causes severe and immediate pain. In this situation, withdraw the needle immediately and advance it in a new direction to avoid nerve injury. Paresthesia may follow even if the needle was withdrawn to avoid further nerve contact.

Rotating the spinal needle (four quadrants), as advocated by some anesthesiologists to ensure intraspinal needle tip placement, may result in removal of some nerves or meningeal tissue when the needle is withdrawn (spaghetti fork technique).[217] Needle rotation has not been shown to produce a higher success rate of spinal anesthesia and is not recommended because of the possibilities for adverse outcome. Although a prevalent "common sense" technique is widely used, it should not mandate implementation by the anesthesiologist when supporting data of the technique do not exist.

Hematoma

Hematoma has occurred as a complication of conduction anesthesia in every spinal compartment. In addition, excessive bleeding from the skin has been reported.[218] Epidural hematoma usually presents hours to days after the anesthetic. Severe back pain with or without a radicular component signals hematoma formation. Neurologic deficit, such as paresthesia, bowel and bladder dysfunction, or paraplegia, follows.

Spinal subarachnoid or epidural hematoma after conduction anesthesia in obstetrics is extremely rare. No spinal hematomas were reported in several large studies on spinal anesthesia.[128,177,189,192] Reports of hematomas are mainly single cases with a variety of causative factors. Epidural hematoma can occur spontaneously in patients who are anticoagulated.[219] Bleeding and hematoma formation in the subcutaneous tissue, periosteum, and epidural space are common during insertion of spinal or epidural needles. Controversy surrounds the use of spinal or epidural anesthesia in patients with coagulopathy. Several cases of epidural hematoma following epidural anesthesia in anticoagulated patients have been reported.[194,220–222] A review of the literature found 33 cases of spinal hematoma.[223] In 26 of these patients, impaired hemostasis accompanied the hematoma. Only 15 of the patients had partial or good recovery of neurologic function.

Cortical vein thrombosis may mimic PDPH but usually progresses to focal or generalized seizures within 1 to 3 days. Associated factors include a hypercoagulable state during pregnancy, decreased fibrinolysis, and dehydration.

Anterior Spinal Artery Syndrome

Insufficient perfusion through the anterior spinal artery during prolonged hypotension can produce ischemia of the spinal cord and cause paraplegia after epidural anesthesia.[181,193,195] The syndrome is most common after abdominal vascular surgery but has also occurred after cesarean section.[224] The supine hypotensive syndrome combined with the hypercoagulable state of pregnancy also may promote anterior spinal artery syndrome in a laboring patient.

Chemical Injury

The spinal cord is remarkably resistant to a variety of agents, as proven by the positive outcome after accidental epidural injection of many drugs. Potassium chloride and diazepam injected epidurally caused profound sensory and motor block to T-10. Five hours later, motor and sensory function returned to normal.[225] Magnesium sulfate was infused epidurally in a preeclamptic patient.[226] The patient complained of a burning sensation for 3 hours after the erroneous infusion was discontinued. No residual paresthesia or motor weaknesses developed. Thiopental injected epidurally and followed by epidural bupivacaine and lidocaine caused no long-term neurologic symptoms.[227] Accidental epidural methohexital, followed by methylprednisolone and hyaluronidase to dilute the methohexital, caused no neurologic sequelae.[228] Four milligrams of the muscle relaxant pancuronium was injected through a spinal needle in a patient about to have cesarean section. She later received a second spinal injection containing 2 mL of 1% hyperbaric bupivacaine. The patient, besides a good anesthetic level, developed generalized weakness. The paralysis responded promptly to neostigmine and atropine. No long-term neurologic sequelae developed.[229]

TOXICITY OF EPIDURAL AND SPINAL AGENTS

Neurologic complications following conduction or regional anesthesia are unusual. Often, faulty technique is blamed; however, local anesthetics, preservatives, or contaminants can produce injury. In addition to direct neuronal injury, local anesthetics can produce vascular damage, impaired perfusion, or injuries to the meninges and other supporting structures of the spinal cord. The greatest concern regarding neurotoxicity involves spinal use of anesthetic and analgesic agents. Nerve damage from the commonly used local anesthetics is not a major clinical problem. However, case reports claiming neurotoxicity from local anesthetics appear occasionally in the literature. Most of these toxic reactions clear spontaneously. The frequency of these complications may be far greater than reported.

Local Anesthetics

Studies on the neurotoxic effects of local anesthetics have a long tradition. The rabbit has been a popular model for spinal neurotoxicity studies. The relative absence of spinal fluid in this animal limits the dilution of injected drugs. Over the years, several clinically used local anesthetics such as stovaine, tropocaine, alypin, nupercaine, gravocaine, scurocaine, spinocaine, and monocaine have been discarded because of neurotoxicity.[230,231] The clinical risk of local anesthetic neurotoxicity is minimal. However, few studies have examined the subtle neurotoxic effects of modern local anesthetics. Preservatives or the nonphysiologic pH of these drugs also may produce toxic effects.

The therapeutic safety of local anesthetics varies. Local anesthetic agents, like most anesthetic medications, have a narrow therapeutic margin. Etidocaine, 0.5% to 2%, and tetracaine, 0.25% to 1%, produce no permanent neurologic deficits when injected intraspinally in the rabbit. However, 4% etidocaine and 2% tetracaine hydrochloride caused neuropathologic abnormalities in some rabbits studied.[232] Also in the rabbit, intrathecal 4% tetracaine, 8% lidocaine, and 0.4% sodium bisulfite consistently yielded prolonged neurologic deficits.[233] Several animals exhibited damage to the cauda equina (axonal degeneration, central necrosis of the cord, and subpial degeneration). Many animals showed similar histologic changes despite apparently normal neurologic function after subarachnoid injection of clinically used anesthetic concentrations. 2-Chloroprocaine and bupivacaine in amounts up to the solubility limit caused no derangements in neurologic function.

2-Chloroprocaine

2-Chloroprocaine hydrochloride was first introduced as a local anesthetic in clinical practice in 1952.[234] Initially, it was marketed in crystal powder form. Later, additives and preservatives increased the shelf-life of the agent. Two formulations were marketed—one with preservatives for local infiltration and the other formulated with sodium bisulfite (antioxidant) for conduction anesthesia. Because of low systemic toxicity and fast onset of action, chloroprocaine became a popular epidural analgesic, especially in obstetric anesthesia.

In 1980, several anesthesiologists reported cases of prolonged neurologic deficits after unintentional injection of large volumes of 2-chloroprocaine (Nesacaine-CE) into the subarachnoid space.[235–237] The pathology varied from prolonged motor and sensory deficits to cauda equina syndrome and adhesive arachnoiditis.

The etiology of these adverse effects is not known. The formulation of Nesacaine-CE had not changed since 1964. Usually, intraspinal injection of more than 200 mg of Nesacaine-CE was required to produce neurotoxic symptoms.[237] 2-Chloroprocaine or its preservative, sodium bisulfite (0.2%), alone or in combination with a large volume injected accidentally in the CSF, appeared to produce the pathology. The large volume may have caused a pressure effect, temporarily impairing spinal cord blood flow. After these reports, the formulation of 2-chloroprocaine changed. The new formulation of Nesacaine-MPF does not contain bisulfite.

These case reports prompted several experimental studies aimed at discovering the mechanisms of the neurotoxic actions of Nesacaine-CE. In some experiments, either 2-chloroprocaine or bisulfite had neurotoxic effects. Some studies found no differences in neurotoxicity of any of the modern local anesthetic agents.

Rabbits subjected to repeated injections of either 2% 2-chloroprocaine or 0.2% sodium bisulfite developed spastic paralysis when the bisulfite bolus dose was more than 1.2 to 2.4 mg.[238] Repetitive injections of small doses of bisulfite did not result in neurologic deficits. Dogs subjected to single spinal injection of 3% 2-chloroprocaine developed persistent neurologic deficits in 35% of the experiments. No such deficits arose in the control dogs who received either normal saline or bupivacaine.[239] Sheep subjected to a single spinal injection of either 2% lidocaine, 0.75% bupivacaine, 3% 2-chloroprocaine, or the dilutent in 3% 2-chloroprocaine developed prolonged neurologic abnormalities. This study concluded that no local anesthetic was more neurotoxic than another in this laboratory model.[240]

Kalichman *et al*[241] using an in vivo peripheral nerve (sciatic) preparation, found neurotoxic effect with several clinically used local anesthetics. In the rabbit carotid sheath/vagus nerve preparation, only 3% 2-chloroprocaine (but not 0.75% bupivacaine or 2% lidocaine) caused abnormal nerve conduction of electrical impulses, perineural fibrosis, edema, axonal degeneration, and pinpoint hemorrhages.[242] The addition of epinephrine made the histopathologic changes worse.

The aforementioned studies have shown that any of the clinically used local anesthetics have the potential to cause neurologic deficits in certain situations. When the commonly used dosages are exceeded, high local concentrations of the drug are unintentionally delivered (intraspinal microcatheters) or accepted clinical practice is violated, and the risk of toxicity increases. The latest formulation of 2-chloroprocaine (Nesacaine-

MPF) has not been associated with any neurologic deficits.

Preservatives and Detergents

Additives also may cause nerve damage (*e.g.*, benzyl alcohol, a common preservative, can cause neurologic damage).[88] After delivery, 40 mL of 0.9% normal saline with 1.5% benzyl alcohol was injected epidurally as a prophylactic measure against PDPH in a parturient. The patient gradually developed severe left-sided flaccid paraparesis. Nine weeks after the delivery, she could walk with crutches. Sixteen months after delivery, her motor function approached baseline, although she still suffered from severe leg cramps.

Similarly, detergents used to clean nondisposable instruments can be neurotoxic. In a series of 11 patients with varying degrees of neurologic damage following spinal anesthesia, it was suggested that a detergent solution, inadequately rinsed from needles and syringes, caused the injury.[199] Although the role of the detergent was only speculative, other experimental studies have confirmed the toxicity of detergents.[243,244]

Spinal Cord Blood Flow

Little information is available on the effects of spinally administered drugs on spinal cord blood flow. This deficit may reflect the difficulty in performing these studies in a chronically instrumented animal model. The control of spinal cord blood flow is similar to that of the cerebral circulation. The knowledge of the effects of spinally administered drugs on spinal blood flow is important because permanent spinal cord injury can result from critical decreases in spinal cord blood flow. Spinally or epidurally administered drugs may alter spinal cord blood flow through several of the following mechanisms:

- An action on the smooth muscle of the vessels in the spinal cord directly changing blood flow
- An indirect action via changes in systemic circulation
- Autonomic nervous system effects
- A change the local metabolic rate

Changes in spinal cord blood flow induced by preeclampsia, arteriosclerosis, collagen vascular disease, or tumor compression may coincide with the injection of local anesthetics, confounding the diagnostic picture.[224] Because of the anatomy of the vascular supply to the spinal cord, anterior cord ischemia is more common than posterior cord ischemia. Symptoms and signs of spinal cord ischemia include localized back pain, paraplegia, burning pain in the feet, loss of temperature sensation, and urinary and bowel incontinence.

The results of experimental studies on the effects of local anesthetic agents on spinal cord blood flow are confusing and contradictory. Tetracaine (dog,[245] cat[246]), lidocaine (dog,[247] cat[246]), morphine (dog,[248]), and mepivacaine (cat[246]) did not change spinal cord blood flow. On the other hand, bupivacaine and tetracaine have been reported to produce a decrease in spinal cord blood flow (rat[249]). Epidurally administered lidocaine, but not saline, decreased spinal cord blood flow in dogs.[250] Another study observed spinal cord hyperemia after spinally administered lidocaine in dogs.[251] Epinephrine and phenylephrine generally decrease spinal cord blood flow.[247]

EPIDURAL/SPINAL NARCOTIC ANALGESIA

Other than itching, urinary retention, and respiratory depression, no late (more than 24 h) untoward effects of epidural narcotics have been reported. Reports on neurotoxicity during labor analgesia do not exist. Some researchers have associated reactivation of the herpes simplex virus with epidural narcotics. Of the less frequently mentioned side effects of anesthesia, alopecia areata has been associated with use of epidural morphine.[252]

SUMMARY

Despite the tremendous number of possible complications that can arise after a regional anesthetic in the obstetric patient, these techniques have proved themselves to be remarkably safe. Headache, the most common late complication of regional anesthesia, is usually self-limiting and easily treated; however, do not allow the relative safety of regional anesthesia in obstetrics to lull you into a false sense of security. Rarely, devastating complications do arise. Only meticulous technique, careful follow-up, astute diagnosis, and prompt treatment can prevent disaster.

Acknowledgments

The contributions of Helen Petty, Chief, and Lisbeth Maas, Library Technician of the Veterans Administration Medical Center Library Service in Iowa City were invaluable in the preparation of this manuscript.

REFERENCES

1. Scott DB, Hibbard BM. Serious non-fatal complications associated with extradural block in obstetric population. Br J Anaesth 1990;64:537.
2. Bonica JJ. The management of pain. Philadelphia: Lea & Febiger, 1990:21.
3. Ong BY, Cohen MM, Esmail A, Cumming M, Kozody R, Palahniuk RJ. Paresthesias and motor dysfunction after labor and delivery. Anesth Analg 1987;66:18.
4. Flaatten H, Rodt S, Rosland J, Vamnes J. Postoperative headache in young patients after spinal anæsthesia. Anaesthesia 1987;42:202.
5. Stein GS. Headaches in the first postpartum week and their relationship to migraine. Headache 1981;21:201.
6. Bier AKG, von Esmarch JFA. Versuche über Cocainiseirung des Rückenmarkes. Deutsch Z Chir 1899;51:361.
7. Carbaat P, Van Crevel H. Lumbar puncture headache: Controlled study on the preventive effect of 24 hours' bed rest. Lancet 1981;2:1133.
8. Younker D, Jones M, Adenwala J, Citrin A, Joyce TH III. Maternal cortical vein thrombosis and the obstetric anesthesiologist. Anesth Analg 1986;65:1007.
9. Gewirtz EC, Costin M, Marx G. Cortical vein thrombosis may mimic postdural puncture headache. Reg Anesth 1987;12:188.
10. Ravindran RS, Carrelli A. Neurologic dysfunction in postpartum patients caused by hypomagnesemia. Anesthesiology 1987;66:391.
11. MacRobert RG. The cause of lumbar puncture headache. JAMA 1918;70:1350.
12. Franksson C, Gorth T. Headache after spinal anesthesia and a technique for lessening its frequency. Acta Chir Scand 1946;94:443.
13. Kunkle EC, Ray BS, Wolf HG. Experimental studies on headache. Arch Neurol Psych 1943;49:323.
14. Wolff HG. Headache. New York: Oxford University Press, 1948:103.
15. Reynolds AF, Slavin L. Postpartum acute subdural hematoma; a probable complication of saddle block analgesia. Neurosurgery 1980;7:398.
16. Jack TM. Postpartum intracranial subdural hæmatoma: A possible complication of epidural analgesia. Anaesthesia 1979;34:176.
17. Pavlin DJ, McDonald JS, Child B, Rusch V. Acute subdural hematoma—an unusual sequelae to lumbar puncture. Anesthesiology 1979;51:338.
18. Schube PG, Raskin N. Cerebral hemorrhages following lumbar puncture. J Nerv Ment Dis 1936;84:636.
19. Edelman JD, Wingard DW. Subdural hematomas after lumbar dural puncture. Anesthesiology 1980;52:166.
20. Welch K. Subdural hematoma following spinal anesthesia. AMA Arch Surg 1959;79:49.
21. Wedel DJ, Mulroy MF. Hemiparesis following dural puncture. Anesthesiology 1983;59:474.
22. Marshall S, Hinman F. Subdural hematoma following

administration of urea for hypertension. JAMA 1962;182:813.

23. Blake DW, Donnan G, Jensen D. Intracranial subdural hematoma after spinal anæsthesia. 1987;15:341.

24. Mantia AM. Clinical report of the occurence of an intracerebral hemorrhage following post-lumbar puncture headache. Anesthesiology 1981;55:684.

25. Newrick P, Read D. Subdural haematoma as a complication of spinal anæsthesia. Br Med J 1982;285:341.

26. Vandam LD, Dripps RD. Long-term follow-up of patients who received 10,098 spinal anesthetics. III. Syndrome of decreased intracranial pressure (headache, ocular, and auditory difficulties). JAMA 1956;161:586.

27. Casement BA, Danielson DR. The epidural blood patch: Are more than two ever necessary? Anesth Analg 1984;63:1033.

28. Wilton NCT, Globerson JH, de Rosayro AM. Epidural blood patch for postdural puncture headache: It's never too late. Anesth Analg 1986;65:895.

29. Jonsson LO, Einarsson P, Olsson GL. Subdural hematoma and spinal anæsthesia. A case report and an incidence study. Anaesthesia 1983;38:144.

30. Eerola M, Kaukinen L, Kaukinen S. Fatal brain lesion following spinal anæsthesia. Report of a case. Acta Anæsth Scand 1981;25:116.

31. Norris MC, Leighton BL, DeSimone CA. Needle bevel direction and headache after inadvertent dural puncture. Anesthesiology 1989;70:729.

32. Brownridge P. The management of headache following accidental dural puncture in obstetric patients. Anaesthesia and Intensive Care 1983;11:4.

33. Lybecker H, Moller JT, May O, Nielsen HK. Incidence and prediction of postdural puncture headache. A prospective study of 1201 spinal anesthesias. Anesth Analg 1990;70:389.

34. Poukkula E. The problem of postspinal headache. Ann Chir Gynæcol 1984;73:139.

35. Kaukinen S, Kaukinen L, Kannisto K, Kataja M. The prevention of headache following spinal anesthesia. Ann Chir Gynaecol 1981;70:107.

36. Rasmussen BS, Blom L, Hansen P, Mikkelsen SS. Postspinal headache in young and elderly patients. Two randomized, double-blind studies that compare 20- and 25-gauge needles. Anaesthesia 1989;44:571

37. Palmer SK, Abram SE, Maitra AM, Von Colditz JH. Distance from the skin to the lumbar epidural space in an obstetric population. Anesth Analg 1981;62:944.

38. Narang VPS, Linter SPK. Failure of extradural blockade in obstetrics. Br J Anaesth 1988;60:402.

39. Moore DC, Bridenbaugh LD, Bagdi BA, Bridenbaugh PO, Stander H. The present status of spinal (subarachnoid) and epidural (peridural) block: A comparison of the two techniques. Anesth Analg 1968;47:40.

40. Cruickshank RH, Hopkinson JM. Fluid flow through dural puncture sites. An in vitro comparison of needle-point types. Anaesthesia 1989;44:415.

41. Ready LB, Cuplin S, Haschke RH, Nessly M. Spinal needle determinants of rate of transdural fluid leak. Anesth Analg 1989;69:457.

42. Herman NL, Knape KG, Husain FJ, Karuparthy VR, Downing JW. Incidence of postdural puncture headache after subarachnoid block for postpartum tubal ligation: comparison of 26- vs 30-gauge needles. Anesthesiology 1990;73:A972.

43. Hart JR, Whitacre RJ. Pencil-point needle in prevention of postspinal headache. JAMA 1951;147:657.

44. Cuplin SR, Ready LB, Haschke RH. Influence of spinal needle tip design and bevel orientation on fluid leak across human dura [Abstract]. Society of Obstetric Anesthesia and Perinatology, San Francisco, May 1988.

45. Sears DH, Leeman MI, O'Donnell RH, Kelleher JF, Santos GC. Incidence of postdural puncture headache in cesarean section patients using the 24G Sprotte needle. Anesthesiology 1990;73:A1003.

46. Snyder GE, Person DL, Flor CE, Wilden RT. Headache in obstetrical patients: comparison of Whitacre versus Quincke needle. Anesthesiology 1990;71:A860.

47. Armitage EN. The paramedian approach to lumbar epidural analgesia. Anaesthesia 1976;31:1287.

48. Baretto C, Hook R, Seah CH. Use of the Tuohy needle in paramedian approach for peridural block. Anesth Analg 1977;56:582.

49. Blomberg RG, Jaanivald A, Walther S. Advantages of the paramedian approach for lumbar epidural analgesia with catheter technique. A clinical comparison between midline and paramedian approaches. Anaesthesia 1989;44:742.

50. Blomberg RG. Technical advantages of the paramedian approach for lumbar epidural puncture and catheter introduction. A study using epiduroscopy in autopsy subjects. Anaesthesia 1988;43:837

51. Griffin RM, Scott RPF. A comparison between the midline and paramedian approaches to the extradural space. Anaesthesia 1984;39:584.

52. Jaucot J. Paramedian approach of the peridural space in obstetrics. Acta Anaesth Belg 1986;37:187.

53. Hatfulvi BI. The dynamics of post-spinal headache. Headache 1977;17:64.

54. Mihic DN. Postspinal headache and relationship of needle bevel to longitudinal dural fibers. Reg Anesth 1985;10:76

55. Greene HM. Lumbar puncture and the prevention of postpuncture headache. JAMA 1926;86:391.

56. Fink BR, Walker S. Orientation of fibers in human dorsal lumbar dura mater in relationship to lumbar puncture. Anesth Analg 1989;69:768.

57. Meiklejohn BH. The effect of rotation of an epidural needle. Anaesthesia 1987;42:1180

58. Vincent RD, Chestnut DH, Russell PK, Walker BJ, Östman PLG. What position is more comfortable for the parturient during induction of epidural anesthesia. Anesthesiology 1990;73:A978.

59. Naulty JS, Hertwig L, Hunt CO, Datta S, Ostheimer GW, Weiss JB. Influence of local anesthetic solution on postdural puncture headache. Anesthesiology 1990;72:450.

60. Johnson MD, Hertwig L, Vehring PH, Datta S.

Intrathecal fentanyl may reduce the incidence of spinal headache. Anesthesiology 1989;71:A911.

61. Abboud TK, Reyes A, Zhu J, et al. Effect of intrathecal morphine on the incidence of spinal headache. Anesthesiology 1990;73:A936.

62. Denny N, Masters R, Pearson D, Read J, Sihota M, Selander D. Postdural puncture headache after continuous spinal anesthesia. Anesth Analg 1987;66:791.

63. Peterson DO, Borup JL, Chestnut JS. Continuous spinal anesthesia: Case review and discussion. Reg Anesth 1983;8:109.

64. Kallos T, Smith TC. Continuous spinal anesthesia with hypobaric tetracaine for hip surgery in lateral decubitus. Anesth Analg 1972;51:766.

65. Moote CA, Varkey GP, Komar WE. Similar incidence of post-dural puncture headache after conventional vs. continuous spinal anesthesia. Anesth Analg 1991; 72:S190.

66. Giuffrida JD, Bizarri DV, Masi R, Bondoc R. Continuous spinal anesthesia for cesarean section. Anesth Analg 1972;51:117.

67. Harris A, Whitehead D. Continuous spinal anesthesia does not prevent headaches following unintentional dural puncture in pregnant patients [Abstract]. Society of Obsteric Anesthesia and Perinatology, Seattle, WA, May 1989.

68. Benedetti C, Chadwick HS, Mancuso JJ, Ross BK, Tiengo M. Incidence of postspinal headache after continuous subarachnoid analgesia for labor using a 32-gauge microcatheter. Anesthesiology 1990;73:A922.

69. Jacobs MW. Prevention of the postpartum, postspinal headache. Am J Obstet Gynecol 1962:83:320.

70. Jones RL. The role of recumbency in the prevention and treatment of postspinal headache. Anesth Analg 1974; 53:788.

71. Thornberry EA, Thomas TA. Posture and post-spinal headache. A controlled trial in 80 obstetric patients. Br J Anaesth 1988;60:195.

72. Beck WW. Prevention of the postpartum spinal headache. Am J Obstet Gynecol 1973;115:354.

73. Ravindran RS, Viegas OJ, Tasch MD, Cline PJ, Deaton RL, Brown TR. Bearing down at the time of delivery and the incidence of spinal headache in parturients. Anesth Analg 1981;60:524.

74. Holder HG. Reactions after spinal anesthesia. JAMA 1944;124:56.

75. Sechzer PH, Abel L. Post-spinal anesthesia headache treatment with caffeine. Evaluation with demand method. Part I. Curr Ther Res 1978;24:307.

76. Jarvis AP, Greenwalt JW, Fagraeus L. Intravenous caffeine for postdural puncture headache. Anesth Analg 1986;65:316.

77. Sechzer PH. Post-spinal headache treated with caffeine. Part II. Intracranial vascular distension, a key factor. Curr Ther Res 1979;26:440.

78. Camman WR, Murray RS, Muschlin PS, Lambert DH. Effects of oral caffeine for postdural puncture headache. A double-blind placebo controlled study. Anesth Analg 1990;70:181

79. Flaaten H, Rodt SA, Vamnes J, Rosland J, Wisborg T, Koller ME. Postdural puncture headache. A comparison between 26- and 29-gauge needles in young patients. Anaesthesia 1989;44:147

80. Rice GC, Dabbs HC. The use of peridural and subarachnoid injections of saline solution in the treatment of severe postspinal headache. Anesthesiology 1950; 11:17.

81. Craft JB, Epstein BS, Coakley CS. Prophylaxis of dural puncture headache with epidural saline. Anesth Analg 1973;52:228.

82. Usubiaga JE, Usubiaga LE, Brea LM, Goyena R. Effect of saline injections on epidural and subarachnoid space pressures and relation to postspinal anesthesia headache. Anesth Analg 1967;46:293.

83. Trivedi N, Eddi D, Shevde K. Prevention of headache following inadvertent dural puncture [Abstract]. Society of Obstetric Anesthesia and Perinatology, Seattle, WA, May 1989:C-3.

84. Okell RW, Sprigge JS. Unintentional dural punctue. A survey of recognition and management. Anaesthesia 1987;42:1110.

85. Bart AJ, Wheeler AS. Comparison of epidural saline placement and epidural blood patch in the treatment of postlumbar puncture headache. Anesthesiology 1978; 48:221.

86. Crawford JS. The prevention of headache consequent upon dural puncture. Br J Anaesth 1972;44:598.

87. Deykin D. Emerging concepts of platelet function. N Engl J Med 1974;290:144.

88. Craig DB, Habib GG. Flaccid paraparesis following obsterical epidural anesthesia: Possible role of benzyl alcohol. Anesth Analg 1977;53:228.

89. Clark CJ, Whitwell J. Intraocular hemorrhage after epidural injection. Br Med J 1961;1612.

90. Colonna-Ramano P, Shapiro BE. Unintentional dural puncture and prophylactic epidural blood patch in obstetrics. Anesth Analg 1989;69:522.

91. Ackerman WE, Juneja MM, Kaczorowski DM. The attenuation of postdural puncture headache with a prophylactic blood patch in labor patients. Anesth Analg 1989;68:S1.

92. Quaynor H, Corbey M. Extradural blood patch—why delay? Br J Anaesth 1985;57:538.

93. Sengupta P, Bagley G, Lim M. Prevention of postdural puncture headache after spinal anesthesia for extracorporeal shockwave lithotripsy. An assessment of prophylactic epidural blood patching. Anaesthesia 1989; 44:54.

94. Loeser EA, Hill GE, Bennett GM, Sederberg JH. Time vs. success rate for epidural blood patch. Anesthesiology 1978;49:147.

95. Palahniuk RJ, Cumming M. Prophylactic blood patch does not prevent post lumbar puncture headache. Can Anaesth Soc J 1979;26:132.

96. Leivers D. Total spinal anesthesia following early prophylactic epidural blood patch. Anesthesiology 1990;73:1287.

97. Abouleish E, Vega S, Blendinger I, Tio T. Long-term

follow-up of epidural blood patch. Anesth Analg 1975;54:459.

98. Shanta TR, McWhirter WR, Dunbar RW. Complications following epidural "blood patch" for postlumbar-puncture headache. Anesth Analg 1973;52:67.

99. Lander CJ, Korbon GA. Histopathologic consequences of epidural blood patch and epidurally administered dextran 40. Anesthesiology 1988;69:A410.

100. Nelson MO. Postpuncture headaches: A clinical and experimental study of the cause and prevention. Arch Derm Syphilol 1930;21:615.

101. Gormley JB. Treatment of postspinal headache. Anesthesiology 1960;21:565.

102. DiGiovanni AJ, Dunbar BS. Epidural injection of autologous blood for postlumbar-puncture headache. Anesth Analg 1970;49:268.

103. Rosenberg PH, Heavner JE. In vitro study of the effect of epidural blood patch on leakage through a dural puncture. Anesth Analg 1985;64:501.

104. DiGiovanni AJ, Galbert MW, Wahle WM. Epidural injection of autologous blood for postlumbar-puncture headache. II. Additional clinical experiences and laboratory investigation. Anesth Analg 1972;51:226.

105. Crawford JS. Experiences with epidural blood patch. Anaesthesia 1980;35:513.

106. Szeinfeld M, Ihmeidan IH, Moser MM, Machado R, Klose KJ, Serafini AN. Epidural blood patch: Evaluation of the volume and spread of blood injected into the epidural space. Anesthesiology 1986;64:820.

107. Shah JL, Veness AM. Epidural blood patch using a catheter. Diagnosis of an unrecognised dural tap. Anaesthesia 1985;40:1120.

108. Humphreys HK, Jones BR. Blood coagulation is delayed after passage through an epidural catheter. Anesth Analg 1991;72:S117.

109. Cucciara RF, Wedel DJ. Finding cerebrospinal fluid during epidural blood patch: How to proceed. Anesth Analg 1984;63:1121.

110. Heyman HJ, Salem MR, Klimow I. Persistent sixth cranial nerve paresis following blood patch for postdural puncture headache. Anesth Analg 1982;61:948.

111. Cornwall RD, Dolan WM. Radicular pain following lumbar epidural blood patch. Anesthesiology 1975;54:459.

112. Lowe DM, McCullough AM. 7th nerve palsy after extradural blood patch. Br J Anaesth 1990;65:721.

113. Berga S, Trierweiler MW. Bacterial meningitis following epidural anesthesia for vaginal delivery: a case report. Obstet Gynecol 1989;74:437.

114. Kalso E, Tuominen M, Rosenberg PH. Effect of posture and some CSF characteristics on spinal anesthesia with isobaric 0.5% bupivacaine. Br J Anaesth 1982;54:1179.

115. Ravindran RS, Tasch MD, Baldwin SJ, Hendrie M. Subarachnoid injection of autologous blood in dogs is unassociated with neurologic deficits. Anesth Analg 1981;60:603.

116. Baysinger CL, Menk EJ, Harte E, Middaugh R. The succesful treatment of dural puncture headache after failed epidural blood patch. Anesth Analg 1986;65:1242.

117. Barrios-Alarcon J, Aldrete JA, Paragas-Tapia D. Relief of post-lumbar puncture headache with epidural Dextran 40: A preliminary report. Reg Anesth 1989;14:78.

118. Kaplan JA, Miller ED, Gallager EG. Postoperative analgesia for thoracotomy patients. Anesth Analg 1975;54:773.

119. Abouleish E, Wadhwa RK, de la Vega S, Tan RN, Lim Uy NT. Regional anesthesia following epidural blood patch. Anesth Analg 1975;54:634.

120. Naulty JS, Herold R. Successful epidural anesthesia following epidural blood patch. Anesth Analg 1978;57:272.

121. Bray MC, Carrie LES. Unblocked segments in obsteric epidural blocks. Anaesthesia 1978;33:232.

122. Rainbird A, Pfitzner J. Restricted spread of analgesia following epidural blood patch. Anaesthesia 1983;38:481.

123. Ong BY, Graham CR, Ringaert KRA, Cohen MM, Palahniuk RJ. Impaired epidural analgesia after dural puncture with and without subsquent blood patch. Anesth Analg 1990;70:76-79.

124. Crawford JS. Lumbar epidural block in labour: A clinical analysis. Br J Anaesth 1972;44:66.

125. Berg G, Hammar M, Moller-Nielsen J, Linden V, Thornblad J. Low back pain during pregnancy. Obstet Gynecol 1988;71:71.

126. Weinreb JC, Wolbarst LB, Cohen JM, Brown CEL, Maravilla KR. Prevalence of lumbosacral intervertebral disk abnormalities on MR images in pregnant and asymptomatic nonpregnant women. Radiology 1989;170:125.

127. Cotev S, Robin GC, Davidson JT. Back pain after epidural analgesia. Anesth Analg 1969;46:259.

128. Phillips OC, Ebner H, Nelson AT, Black MH. Neurologic complications following spinal anesthesia with lidocaine: A prospective review of 10440 cases. Anesthesiology 1969;30:284.

129. Bromage PR. Epidural anesthesia. Philadelphia: WB Saunders, 1978:661.

130. Usubiaga JE. Neurological complications following epidural anesthesia. Int Anaesth Clin 1975;13:1.

131. Peng ATC, Behar S, Blancato LS. Reduction of post-lumbar puncture backache by the use of field block anesthesia prior to lumbar puncture. Anesthesiology 1985;63:277.

132. Bonica JJ, Backup PH, Anderson CE, Hadfield D, Crepps WF. Peridural block: analysis of 3,637 cases and a review. Anesthesiology 1957;18:723.

133. MacArthur C, Lewis M, Knox EG, Crawford JS. Epidural anæsthesia and long-term backache after childbirth. Br Med J 1990;301:9.

134. Grove LH. Backache, headache, and bladder dysfunction after delivery. Br J Anaesth 1973;45:1147.

135. Geurts JW, Haanschotten RM, van Wijk RM, Kraak H, Besse TC. Postdural puncture headache in young patients. A comparative study bewtween the use of 0.52-mm (25-gauge) and 0.33-mm (29-gauge) spinal needles. Acta Anaesthesiol Scand 1990;34:350.

136. Lecoq G, Hamza J, Narchi P, Jullien P, Attane D. Risk

factors associated with postpartum backache in obstetric patients. Anesthesiology 1990;73:A966.

137. Benlabed M, Hamza J, Jullien P, Troche G, Lecoq G. Risk factors for postpartum backache associated with epidural anesthesia. Anesthesiology 1990;73:A996.

138. Middleton MJ, Bell CR. Postoperative backache: Attempts to reduce the incidence. Anesth Analg 1965; 44:446.

139. Fibuch EE, Opper SE. Back pain following epidurally administered Nesacaine-MPF. Anesth Analg 1989; 69:113.

140. Dirkes WE. Treatment of Nescaine-MPF-induced back pain with calcium cloride. Anesth Analg 1990;70:461.

141. Wang BC, Li D, Hiller JM, Simon EJ, Budzilovich G, Turndorf H. Epidural EDTA induces tetanic contractions in the rat. Anesth Analg 1991;72:S312.

142. Ackerman WE. Back pain after epidural Nesacaine-MPF. Anesth Analg 1990;70:222.

143. Hynson JM, Sessler DI, Glosten B. Back pain in volunteers after epidural anesthesia with chloroprocaine. Anesth Analg 1991;72:253.

144. Carter MI. Cervical surgical emphysema following extradural analgesia. Anaesthesia, 1984;39:1115.

145. Kilpatrick SM. Emphysema of the neck after epidural anesthesia. Anaesthesia 1984;39:499.

146. Munro HM. Pain in the neck. Anæsthesia 1990;45:173.

147. Pathy GV, Rosen M. Prolonged block with recovery after extradural analgesia for labor. Br J Anaesth 1975; 47:520.

148. Cuerden C, Buley R, Downing JW. Delayed recovery after epidural block in labor. Anaesthesia 1977;32:773.

149. Carp H, Bailey S. Meningitis after dural puncture in bacteremic rats. Anesthesiology 1990;71:A862.

150. Vaddadi A, Ramanthan J, Angel JJ, Sibai B. Epidural anesthesia in women with chorioamnionitis. Anesthesiology 1990;70:A863.

151. Ryhanen P, Jouppila R, Lanning M, Jouppila P, Hollmen A, Kouvalainen K. Natural killer cell activity after elective cesarean section under general and epidural anesthesia in healthy parturients and their newborns. Gynecol Obstet Invest 1985;19:139.

152. Chestnut DH, Noe AL. Effect of anesthesia for primary cesarean section on postoperative infectious morbidity. Obstet Gynecol 1986;68:667.

153. Bert AA, Laasberg LH. Aseptic meningitis following spinal anesthesia—a complication of the past? Anesthesiology 1985;62:674.

154. Denson JS, Joseph SI, Koons RA, Murry WE, Bissonette HW. Effects of detergents intrathecally. Anesthesiology 1957;18:143.

155. Goldman WM, Sanford JP. An "epidemic" of chemical meningitis. Am J Med 1960;29:94.

156. Gibbons RB. Chemical meningitis following spinal anesthesia. JAMA 1969;5:900.

157. Roberts SP, Petts HV. Meningitis after obstetric spinal anesthesia. Anaesthesia 1990;45:376.

158. Kilpatrick ME, Girgis NI. Meningitis—a complication of spinal anesthesia. Anesth Analg 1983;62:513.

159. Danner RL, Hartman BJ. Update of spinal epidural abscess: 35 cases and review of the literature. Rev Infect Dis 1987;9:265.

160. Crawford JS. Some maternal complications of epidural anæsthesia for labour. Anaesthesia 1985;40:1219.

161. Hlavin ML, Kaminski HJ, Ross JS, Ganz E. Spinal epidural abscess: A ten-year perspective. Neurosurgery 1990;27:177.

162. Sghirlanzoni A, Marazzi R, Pareyson D, Olivieri A, Bracchi M. Epidural anæsthesia and spinal arachnoiditis. Anaesthesia 1989;44:317.

163. Braham J, Saia A. Neurological complications of epidural anæsthesia. Br Med J 1958;2:657.

164. Moore DC, Artu AA, Kelly WA, Jenkins D. Use of computed tomography to locate a sheared epidural catheter. Anesth Analg 1987;66:795.

165. Saberski LR, Schwartz JI, Greenhouse BB, Kennedy TM, Ullman DA. Unique complication of a lumbar epidural catheter. Anesthesiology 1988;69:634.

166. Fibuch EE, McNitt JD, Cussen T. Knotting of the Theracath after an uneventful epidural insertion for cesarean delivery. Anesthesiology 1990;73:1293.

167. Browne RA, Politi VL. Knotting of an epidural catheter: A case report. Can Anaesth Soc J 1979;26:142.

168. Muneyuki M, Shirai K, Inamoto A. Roentgenographic analysis of the positions of catheters in the epidural space. Anesthesiology 1970;33:19.

169. Crawford JS, Williams ME, Veales S. Particulate matter in the epidural space. Br J Anaesth 1975;47:807.

170. Brandus V. The spinal needle as a carrier of foreign material. Can Anaesth Soc J 1968;15:197.

171. Charlebois PA. Coring: The unseen menace. Can Anaesth Soc J 1966;13:585.

172. Magath TB, McClellan JT. Reaction to accidentally injected rubber plugs. Am J Clin Path 1950;20:829-833.

173. Sabon RL, Cheng EY, Stommeil KA, Hennen CR. Glass particle contamination: Influence of aspiration methods and ampule types. Anesthesiology 1989;70:859-862

174. Crawford JS. The second thousand epidural blocks in an obstetric hospital practise. Br J Anaesth 1972;44:1277.

175. Chaudhari LS, Kop BR, Dhruva AJ. Paraplegia and epidural analgesia. Anaesthesia 1978;33:722.

176. Aminoff MJ. Neurological disorders and pregnancy. Am J Obstet Gynecol 1978;132:325.

177. Sadove MS, Levin MJ, Rant-Sejdinaj I. Neurological complications of spinal anesthesia. Can Anaesth Soc J 1961;8:405.

178. Shin YK, Lee VC, Kim YD. Unusual cause of weakness of the lower extremity following vaginal delivery under epidural analgesia: Iliopsoas muscle strain. Anesthesiology 1985;63:531.

179. Kane RE. Neurologic deficits following epidural or spinal anesthesia. Anesth Analg 1981;60:150.

180. Dawkins CJM. An analysis of the complications of extradural and caudal block. Anæsthesia 1969;24:554.

181. Urquhart-Hay D. Paraplegia following epidural anesthesia. Anaesthesia 1969;24:461.

182. Hirsch NP, Child CS, Wijetilleka SA. Paraplegia caused

by spinal angioma—possible association with epidural analgesia. Anesth Analg 1985;64:937.

183. Hirlekar G. Paraplegia after epidural analgesia associated with an extradural spinal tumour. Anaesthesia 1980;35:363.

184. Sghirlanzoni A, Gemma M, Pareyson D, Cimino C, Boiardi A. Spinal arteriovenous fistula. A possible cause of paraparesis after epidural anæsthesia. Anaesthesia 1989;44:831.

185. Bleyaert A, Soetens M, Vaes L, Van Steeberg AL, Vanderdonck A. Bubivacaine, 0.125%, in obstetric epidural anesthesia. Anesthesiology 1979;51:435.

186. Holdcroft A, Morgan M. Maternal complications of obstetric epidural analgesia. Anaesth Intensive Care 1976; 4:108.

187. Lund PC. Peridural anesthesia. A review of 10,000 administrations. Acta Anaesth Scand 1962;6:143.

188. Eisen SM, Rosen N, Winesanker H, et al. The routine use of lumbar epidural anaesthesia in obstetrics: A clinical review of 9,532 cases. Can Anaesth Soc J 1960;7:280.

189. Moore DC, Bridenbaugh LD. Spinal (subarachnoid) block: A review of 11574 cases. JAMA 1966;195:907.

190. Dripps RD, Vandam LD. Long-term follow-up of patients who received 10,098 spinal anesthetics: Failure to discover major neurologic sequelae. JAMA 1954; 156:1486.

191. Vandam LD, Dripps RD. A long-term follow-up of 10,098 spinal anesthetics. II. Incidence and analysis of minor sensory neurological defects. Surgery 1955; 38:463.

192. Vandam LD, Dripps RD. Long-term folow-up of patients who received 10,098 spinal anesthetics. IV. Neurological disease incident to traumatic lumbar puncture during spinal anesthesia. JAMA 1960;172:1483.

193. Davies A, Solomon B, Levene A. Paraplegia following epidural anæsthesia. Br Med J 1958;2:654.

194. Gingrich TF. Spinal epidural hematoma following continuous epidural anesthesia. Anesthesiology 1968; 29:162.

195. Harrison PD. Paraplegia following epidural analgesia. Anaesthesia 1974;30:778.

196. Hellman K. Epidural anæsthesia in obsterics: A second look at 26,127 cases. Can Anaesth Soc J 1965;12:398.

197. Kennedy F, Effron AS, Perry G. The grave spinal cord paralysis caused by spinal anesthesia. Surg Gynecol Obstet 1950;91:385.

198. Paddison RM, Alpers PJ. Role of intrathecal detergents in pathogenesis of adhesive arachnoiditis. Arch Neurol Psychiatry 1954;71:87.

199. Winkelman NW. Neurologic symptoms following accidental intraspinal detergent injection. Neurology 1952;2:284.

200. Lee JJ, Roberts RB. Paresis of the fifth cranial nerve following spinal anesthesia. Anesthesiology 1978;49:217.

201. Bryce-Smith RM, Macintosh HH. Sixth-nerve palsy after lumbar puncture and spinal analgesia. Br Med J 1971;1:275.

202. Fog J, Wang LP, Sundberg A, Mucciano C. Hearing loss after spinal anesthesia is related to needle size. Anesth Analg 1990;70:517.

203. Wang LP, Fog J, Bove M. Transient hearing loss following spinal anæsthesia. Anaesthesia 1987;42:1258.

204. Wang LP. Sudden bilateral hearing loss after spinal anæsthesia. A case report. Acta Anaesthesiol Scand 1986;30:412.

205. Panning B, Mehler D, Lehnhardt E. Transient low-frequency hypoacusia after spinal anæsthesia. Lancet 1983;ii:582.

206. Lee CM, Peachman FA. Unilateral hearing loss after spinal anesthesia treated with epidural blood patch. Anesth Analg 1986;65:312.

207. Richer S, Ritacca D. Sixth nerve palsy after lumbar anesthesia. Optometry Vision Sci 1989;66:320.

208. Stilma JS, De Lange JJ, Crezee FC. Bilateral central scotoma with preservation of central vision in two patients following cæsarean section under spinal anæsthesia. Doc Ophthalmol 1987;67:59.

209. DeLange JJ, Stilma JS, Crezee F. Visual disturbances after spinal anæsthesia. Anaesthesia 1988;43:570.

210. Evans JM, Gauci CA, Watkins G. Horner's syndrome as a complication of lumbar epidural block. Anaesthesia 1975;30:774.

211. Clayton KC. The incidence of Horner's syndrome during lumbar extradural for elective cæsarean section and provision of analgesia during labour. Anaesthesia 1983;38:583.

212. Hill EC. Maternal obstetric paralysis. Am J Obstet Gynecol 1962;83:1452.

213. Murray RR. Maternal obstetric paralysis. Am J Obstet Gynecol 1964;88:399.

214. Ferguson FR, Watkins KH. Paralysis of the bladder and associated neurological sequelae of spinal anæsthesia (cauda equina syndrome). Br J Surg 1937;25:735.

215. Rigler ML, Drasner K, Krejcie TC, et al. Cauda equina syndrome after continuous spinal anesthesia. Anesth Analg 1991;72;275.

216. Lambert DH, Hurley RJ. Cauda equina syndrome and continuous spinal anesthesia. Anesth Analg 1991; 72:817.

217. Scheller MS, Sarnat AJ, Astarita RW. Unintentional removal of meningeal tissue with a 25-gauge spinal needle during spinal anesthesia: A case report. Anesthesiology 1984;61:593.

218. Haley S. Prolonged bleeding from epidural insertion site. Can J Anaesth 1988;35:322.

219. Harik SI, Raichle ME, Reis DJ. Spontaneously remitting spinal epidural hematoma in a patient on anticoagulants. N Engl J Med 1971;284:1355.

220. Butler AB, Green CD. Haematoma following epidural anesthesia. Can Anaesth Soc J 1970;17:635.

221. Frumin MJ, Schwartz H. Continuous segmental peridural anesthesia. Anesthesiology 1952;13:488.

222. DeAngelis J. Hazards of subdural and epidural anesthesia during anticoagulant therapy: A case report and review. Anesth Analg 1972;51:676.

223. Owens EL, Kasten GW, Hessel EA. Spinal subarachnoid hematoma after lumbar puncture and heparinization: A case report, review of the literature, and discussion of anesthetic implications. Anesth Analg 1986;65:1201.

224. Ackerman WE, Juneja MM, Knapp RK. Maternal paraparesis after epidural anesthesia and cesarean section. South Med J 1990;83:695.

225. Lin D, Becker K, Shapiro HM. Neurologic changes following epidural injection of potassium chloride and diazepam: A case report with laboratory correlations. Anesthesiology 1986;65:210.

226. Dror A, Henricksen E. Accidental epidural magnesium sulfate injection. Anesth Analg 1987;66:1020.

227. Forester JE, Raj PP. Inadvertent epidural injection of thiopental: A case report. Anesth Analg 1975;54:406.

228. Wells D, Davies G, Wagner D. Accidental injection of epidural methohexital. Anesthesiology 1987;67:846.

229. Peduto VA, Gungui P, Martino MR, Napoleone M. Accidental subarachnoid injection of pancuronium. Anesth Analg 1989;69:516.

230. Davis L, Haven H, Givins JH, Emmett J. Effects of spinal anesthetics on the spinal cord and its membranes. JAMA 1931;97:1781.

231. Tui C, Preiss AL, Barcham I, Nevin MI. Local nervous tissue changes following spinal anesthesia in experimental animals. J Pharmacol Exp Ther 1944;81:209.

232. Adams HJ, Mastri AR, Eicholzer AW, Kilpatrick G. Morphologic effects of intrathecal etidocaine and tetracaine on the rabbit spinal cord. Anesth Analg 1974;53:904.

233. Ready LB, Plumer MH, Haschke RH, Austin E, Sumi SM. Neurotoxicity of intrathecal local anesthetics in rabbits. Anesthesiology 1985;63:364.

234. Foldes FF, McNall PG. 2-chlorprocaine, a new local anesthetic agent. Anesthesiology 1952;13:287.

235. Ravindran RS, Bond JK, Tasch MD, Gupta CD, Luersen TG. Prolonged neural blockade following regional analgesia with 2-chloroprocaine. Anesth Analg 1980;59:447.

236. Reisner LS, Hochman BN, Plumer MH. Persistent neurologic deficit and adhesive arachnoiditis following intrathecal 2-chloroprocaine injection. Anesth Analg 1980;59:452.

237. Moore DC, Spierdijk J, vanKleef JD, Coleman RL, Love GF. Chloroprocaine neurotoxicity: Four additional cases. Anesth Analg 1982;61:155.

238. Wang BC, Hillman DE, Spielholz NI, Turndorf H. Chronic neurological deficits and Nesacaine-CE: An effect of the anesthetic, 2-chloroprocaine, or the antioxidant, sodium bisulfite. Anesth Analg 1984;63:445.

239. Ravindran RS, Turner MS, Muller J. Neurologic effects of subarachnoid administration of 2-chloroprocaine-CE, bupivacaine, and low pH normal saline in dogs. Anesth Analg 1982;61:279.

240. Rosen MA, Baysinger CL, Shnider SM, et al. Evaluation of neurotoxicity after subarachnoid injection of large volumes of local anesthetic solutions. Anesth Analg 1983;62:802.

241. Kalichman MW, Powell HC, Myers RR. Pathology of local anesthetic-induced nerve injury. Acta Neuropathol 1988;75:583.

242. Barsa J, Batra M, Fink BR, Sumi SM. A comparative in vivo study of local neurotoxicity of lidocaine, bupivacaine, 2-chlorprocaine and a mixture of 2-chlorprocaine and bupivacaine. Anesth Analg 1982;61:961.

243. Joseph SI, Denson JS. Spinal anesthesia, arachnoiditis and paraplegia. JAMA 1958;168:1330.

244. Smith RA, Conner EH. Experimental study of intrathecal detergents. Anesthesiology 1962;23:5.

245. Dohi S, Takeshima R, Naito H. Spinal cord blood fow during spinal anesthesia in dogs: The effects of tetracaine, epinephrine, acute blood loss, and hypercapnia. Anesth Analg 1987;66:599.

246. Porter SS, Albin MS, Watson WA, Bnegin J, Pantoja G. Spinal cord and cerebral blood flow responses to intrathecal local anesthetics with and without epinephrine. Acta Anaesthesiol Scand 1985;20:330.

247. Dohi S, Matsumiya N, Takeshima R, Naito H. The effects of subarachnoid lidocaine and phenylephrine on spinal cord and cerebral blood flow in dogs. Anesthesiology 1984;61:238.

248. Matsumiya N, Dohi S. Effects of intravenous or subarachnoid morphine on cerebral and spinal cord hemodynamics and antagonism with naloxone in dogs. Anesthesiology 1983;59:175.

249. Crosby G. Local spinal cord blood flow and glucose utilization during spinal anesthesia with bupivacaine in consciuous rats. Anesthesiology 1985;63:55-60.

250. Mitchell P, Goad R, Erwin CW, et al. Effect of epidural lidocaine on spinal cord blood flow. Anesth Analg 1989;68:312.

251. Kozody R, Swartz J, Palahniuk RJ, Biehl DR, Wade JG. Spinal blood flow following subarachnoid lidocaine. Can Anaesth Soc J 1985;32:472.

252. Andersen PT. Alopecia areata after epidural morphine. Anesth Analg 1984;63:1142.

FOUR

Managing an Obstetric Anesthesia Service

CHAPTER 39

Standards of Care: Managing an Obstetric Anesthesia Service

John W. Downing
Walter U. Brown

"Ideally, hospitals in which obstetric care is provided should have anesthesia services available on a 24-hour basis. These units require the availability of sophisticated monitoring equipment and specially trained professional nursing personnel." (ACOG Tech Bull January, 1988: 112)

The combined life expectancy of a woman and her child is 110 to 130 years. The delivery of a healthy baby to a happy mother represents a significant investment in the future. Obstetric health care providers, including obstetric anesthesiologists and anesthetists, thus bear a singular responsibility toward their community.

Obstetrics and obstetric anesthesia are high-risk medical and medicolegal environments. Obstetric anesthesiologists and anesthetists are unique in that they care for more than one patient at a time. Furthermore, the legal statutory limit for the fetus is 21 years. Injuries that occur during administration of an obstetric anesthetic can alter the lives of two people and haunt the anesthesiologist for years to come. The largest punitive award following an obstetric anesthetic misadventure of which the authors are aware is 13 million dollars.[1] Against this amount, funding required to establish an obstetric anesthesia service pales into insignificance.

The goals of this chapter are as follows:

- To justify the creation of a dedicated obstetric anesthesia service
- To present guidelines for how this task may best be accomplished
- To define the short- and long-term implications, social and financial, of this type of community service

HISTORICAL PERSPECTIVE

In 1942, Bert Hershenson was appointed Chief of Anesthesiology at the Boston Hospital for Women, making him the first Director of Obstetric Anesthesia in the United States.[2] Meanwhile in New York, Gertie Marx pioneered the idea that obstetric anesthesia should meet the special needs of the parturient, and championed the cause of obstetric anesthesia resident education. Before that time, "anesthesiology residents received meager instruction in obstetric anesthesia, which was still thought to be a superfluous subspecialty."[3] In October of 1952, Daniel Moore and colleagues at the Virginia Mason Clinic in Seattle, inaugurated a full-time obstetric anesthesia service and were the first to share their experiences in print.[4-6]

The early 1970s saw recognition of the need to consolidate obstetric services and to provide dedicated 24-hour obstetric anesthesia care.[7,8] "Even though it has been estimated that 60% to 90% of obstetric patients deliver their babies without complications, obstetrics must be considered an emergency service. Various support equipment, material, and personnel must be available quickly to support life in situations of hemorrhage, cardiorespiratory collapse, and metabolic disturbances. It is logical to assume that anesthesiology support is an integral part of modern obstetrics, not only to provide pain relief with conduction and inhalation anesthesia but also to maintain vital functions during both normal and surgical deliveries."[8]

In the last decade, American hospitals competing for business in an increasingly cutthroat market have realized the need to cater specifically to women and their babies. A hospital's future prosperity may depend upon its ability to satisfy the parturient. She may then choose to bear her next child at that hospital and refer family or friends for medical attention there too.

Obstetric services delivering 2000 to 2500 babies annually have the best morbidity and mortality statistics.[8] To be cost-effective, an obstetric service should do no less than 2000 and no more than 5000 deliveries a year. The safety and success of an obstetric program depend largely on the ready availability of a good obstetric anesthesia service. A delivery rate of less than 2000 per annum may provide too little work to justify a dedicated obstetric anesthesia service. In contrast, a workload that exceeds 5000 deliveries in a year can easily overburden anesthesia staff and hospital facilities. We consider a delivery rate of 3000 ($\pm$ 500) a year as "ideal."

"STANDARDS" OF ANESTHESIA CARE FOR OBSTETRIC PATIENTS

In 1958, Sappenfield, as president of the American Society of Anesthesiologists (ASA), established a Committee on Maternal Welfare to address the special problems related to the administration of obstetric anesthesia. A link was forged between the ASA Committee on Maternal Welfare and the American College of Obstetricians and Gynecologists (ACOG) Committee on Maternal Welfare in 1963. These committees formulated standards for obstetric analgesia–anesthesia and published them in the ACOG Manual of Standards 1 year later. In 1966, John Bonica, then president of the

ASA, changed the committee's name to Committee on Obstetrical Anesthesia, to emphasize that obstetric anesthesiologists were equally concerned with fetal/neonatal, as well as maternal, welfare.[3,9]

Both the ASA and ACOG have since periodically updated their published guidelines for the safe practice of obstetric anesthesia. These proclamations focus on several main issues. Personnel on the labor and delivery floor should be trained in resuscitation and life-support techniques. Qualified anesthetic care for the parturient should be available within 30 minutes. The quality and availability of equipment, facilities, and support personnel in labor and delivery suites should at least equal, or perhaps exceed, that provided in the surgical operating suite. Anesthesia care providers working in obstetrics should study and follow these ASA/ACOG guidelines in the interest of safe obstetric anesthesia.

There has been some confusion concerning the 1988 joint ACOG/ASA statement on the optimal goals for obstetric anesthesia care (App. A). These issues are again being addressed by the bodies concerned. In addition, the ASA Committee on Obstetrical Anesthesia and the ASA Committee on Standards of Care will shortly issue a revised set of "guidelines" rather than "standards" (App. B). A court of law might construe "standards" as inviolate. "Experts in setting practice guidelines have defined standards as hard and fast rules that should always be followed. . . . Guidelines are intended to be more flexible. They should be followed under most circumstances, but depending on the patient, the circumstances, and other factors, they can and should be tailored to fit individual needs."[10]

As recently as 1991, the Joint Commission published its anesthesia and obstetric indicators for quality assurance of obstetric and anesthesia care of the parturient (App. C).[11] These indicators were developed and rigorously tested over a period of 2.5 years. In January, 1990, the Board of Commissioners recommended that hospitals use these quality-assurance indicators to evaluate their obstetric anesthesia programs.

THE PERINATAL TEAM

Adoption of the perinatal team concept (Fig. 39-1) is essential for proper care of the mother and her infant(s). Anesthesiologists and anesthetists can make a major contribution to the perinatal team. To create and preserve a spirit of camaraderie and cooperation, team members need to meet regularly for patient rounds and medical seminars. Informal communication in a communal recreational setting over coffee and doughnuts is equally important to team morale. We highly recom-

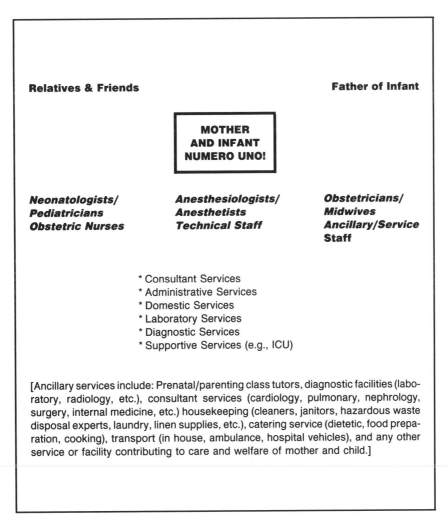

Figure 39-1. The perinatal team approach.

mend acceptance of the "Cardinal Cs" (Table 39-1) by the perinatal team as guiding principles for interpersonal relationships. Kindness and humanity to patients and coworkers alike are the keys to the success of the perinatal team.

MANAGING AN OBSTETRIC ANESTHESIA SERVICE

"Obstetric anesthesia is immediate, not emergent."
(Attributed to the late Robert Hodgkinson, M.D.)

Obstetric anesthesia services fall broadly into two categories—teaching and nonteaching. A teaching division in a "public" institution, university hospital, or university-affiliated medical center, whether private or state funded, caters to resident and certified registered nurse anesthetist (CRNA) education and practical training. A "private" institution or smaller state-controlled hospital does not.

Management of an Obstetric Anesthesia Teaching Program

Staffing Requirements

An academic obstetric anesthesia program begins with a structured staff cohort, headed by a director of obstetric anesthesia and affiliated with the faculty of a recognized anesthetic teaching department.[7,12] The di-

Table 39–1

The "Cardinal C's"

Compassion
Cooperation
Concern
Courtesy
Communication
Consideration
Coordination
Confidence

(After Bonica JJ, Principles and practice of obstetric analgesia and anesthesia. Philadelphia: FA Davis, 1967;1:6)

rector should provide a balanced academic program based upon the "academic tripod" of excellent patient care: resident, nurse anesthetist, and medical student teaching (practical and didactic); and clinical and laboratory research (Fig. 39-2). Each leg of the tripod is equally important and deserves the same amount of attention and dedication.

An additional priority for the director is personnel management. A happy workforce produces the best team effort. The director should offer constructive criticism and, when necessary, issue reprimands. He or she also should give praise and place trust where they are due. Recognition of a job well done boosts self-worth, reinforces morale, and inspires loyalty. Delegation of duties and responsibilities provides a singular challenge. The director, by appropriate delegation, can in turn make time to do other important matters. Staying current with the anesthesia literature, writing, and doing research are prime examples of the latter.

(As an aside, most chairpersons, directors, and chiefs of clinical academic departments and divisions are appointed based on their clinical skills and academic prowess. Few boast a background in modern personnel and departmental management methods. This glaring deficiency in medical leadership should be addressed.)

An adequate number of clinically capable but academically oriented obstetric anesthesia faculty is essential. An obstetric anesthesia faculty cohort large enough to enjoy a 50:50 clinical to nonclinical time ratio is the goal. Between six and eight staff anesthesiologists are needed to reach this goal. Owing to the "fire drill" nature of obstetric anesthesia, this ideal is unlikely to be fulfilled. Cost and insufficient faculty recruitment (obstetric anesthesiologists can be difficult to come by) interfere with achieving this goal.

General anesthesia faculty, without specific obstetric anesthesia training but with an interest in the field can participate. They may be recruited to help

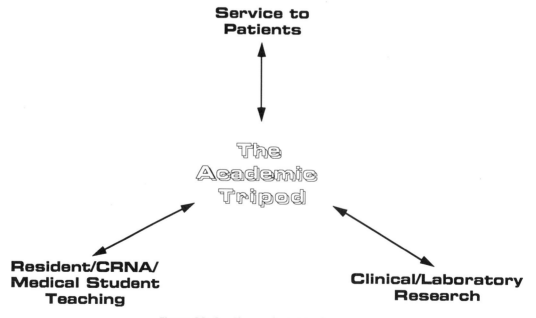

Figure 39–2. The academic tripod.

teach residents and provide staff coverage for nights, weekends, and holidays. Resident supervision during working hours can then be furnished by three to four designated obstetric anesthesiologists. The entire anesthesia department staff can provide coverage for both the surgical operating rooms and the obstetric suite at night and over weekends and holidays. Obstetric anesthesia faculty should contribute to the surgical/obstetric attending call roster. In addition, an obstetric anesthesiologist must constantly be available for consultation or assistance. To help communication, he or she should carry a cellular telephone in addition to a beeper.

Obstetric anesthesia faculty should attend the day-to-day general surgical anesthesia service too. The following skills, which are seldom used but vital to obstetric anesthetic practice thus can be retained:

- Placement of arterial and central lines
- Interpretation of data derived from them
- Elective management of "the difficult airway," including fiberoptic laryngoscopy
- Appropriate management of the hemodynamically compromised patient

Severe pregnancy-induced hypertension serves as an example of the latter. This diverse syndrome demands the latest and best in monitoring technology as well as an intimate knowledge of its pathophysiology.

The Trainees

PREPARATION. Residents and nurse anesthetist trainees should administer analgesia for vaginal delivery as well as regional and general anesthesia for cesarean section. Obstetric patients present special difficulties in placing epidural catheters and face greater danger from general anesthesia. Therefore, trainees should have successfully performed a reasonable number of epidural and subarachnoid blocks and be able to do a rapid sequence induction of general anesthesia and cardiopulmonary resuscitation before entering the obstetric anesthesia teaching program.

Recommendations on "a reasonable number" range from 20 to 100, depending on the authority consulted. We suggest 50 epidural and an equal number of subarachnoid blocks as a compromise. [Editor's Note: In some anesthesia residency programs, residents learn how to do epidural and subarachnoid blocks *during* their obstetric anesthesia rotation. These residents first need an adequate background in general anesthesia (4–6 mo) to ensure their ability to manage complica-

tions. This arrangement requires close supervision of new residents but allows the opportunity to teach technique as well as management. (The authors of this chapter disagree with the editor on this point.)]

Aspiring anesthesiologists and nurse anesthetists entering the program should have at least 6 months' experience in a busy anesthetic teaching program, affording each resident at least 1000 procedures a year. For less active departments, we recommend a 1-year background of practical anesthesia. A higher incidence of anesthetic complications such as accidental dural puncture (due to maternal lumbar lordosis, softening of the ligaments of the back during pregnancy), and failed intubation (but we hope not failed ventilation) can be expected in a teaching environment. Attending supervision and assistance for obstetric anesthesia trainees is essential. Protocols dealing with immediate obstetric anesthesia complications should be taught conscientiously and displayed prominently by poster.*

THE ROTATION. Obstetric anesthesia guidelines must be issued to residents at the start of their rotation. These notes should not be so detailed that they distract resident attention from the published obstetric anesthesia literature. Relevant books and journals should be on hand in a separate obstetric anesthesia library close by where residents can study when the service is quiet.

An obstetric anesthesia resident rotation should last for 2 to 3 months. Senior residents with a special interest in the field can take an optional 3- to 6-month "clinical fellowship." Those planning an academic career dedicated to obstetric anesthesia should undertake a more rigorous 1- to 2-year academic fellowship that allows time for involvement in clinical and laboratory research.

With the population of anesthesia trainees changing every 2 to 3 months, familiarity with the unit layout, anesthesia equipment, and functional aspects of the service can be deficient. Staggering rotations so that trainees overlap month by month can offset this difficulty. The constant presence of competent anesthesia faculty also helps provide continuity. If inadequate staffing makes these approaches impractical, a 24-hour CRNA commitment to obstetric anesthesia offers a sensible alternative.

"Failed Intubation/Ventilation Regime or Drill" poster obtainable from John W. Downing, MD, Division of Obstetric Anesthesia, Vanderbilt University School of Medicine, 526 Medical Arts Building, Nashville, TN 37232-1127.

A Recommended System

Considering our suggested "ideal" obstetric service, which performs 3000 deliveries a year,† with a 70% "epidural rate" (Fig. 39-3) and a cesarean section rate of 20%, we recommend the following staffing structure:

- Academic director of obstetric anesthesia—1
- Obstetric anesthesia faculty anesthesiologists—3
- CRNAs providing 24-hour coverage—5
- Residents/nurse anesthetists in training—4
- Anesthetic technicians, working hours only—2‡

The preceding suggestions would provide each resident/trainee with a chance to do an average of 88 epidural blocks for labor and delivery in a 2-month rotation (Fig. 39-4). A 3-month rotation would yield approximately 132 epidural procedures. Each resident/trainee will anesthetize on the average of 25 patients for cesarean section in a 2-month rotation and 36 in a 3-month rotation (Fig. 39-5). However, 70% of these patients will likely receive regional anesthesia and only 30% will receive general anesthesia. Therefore, resident experience in the performance of rapid sequence induction of general anesthesia will be limited. This deficiency should be corrected by exposure of residents to the emergency surgical and trauma anesthesia service before their obstetric anesthesia rotation.

CRNAs

In the authors' view, CRNAs assigned to obstetrics should do conduction anesthesia when necessary (*e.g.,* when one case commands the attention of the resident and attending anesthesiologist and a parturient urgently needs pain relief). Qualified CRNAs doing epidural blocks under these conditions should not seriously dilute trainee experience. A CRNA presence on

---

†*Others consider an annual delivery rate of 2000 to 2500 optimal. We believe this number too low, tertiary care obstetric and neonatal referral units excepted.*
‡*As an alternative to CRNAs, 24-hour technical coverage with five technicians may be entertained. The latter decrees dedicated full-time attending coverage.*

the obstetric floor is a source of educated assistance and resident back-up as well. The preceding view is controversial in the light of the ASA Statement on Regional Anesthesia (App. K). This promulgation recommends that only physicians do regional blocks.

Qualified anesthesiologists interested in obstetric analgesia/anesthesia are at a premium.[13–22] At least 60% to 70% of primigravid women experience "severe to excruciating pain" during labor and delivery.[23] Epidural block can control the pain of childbirth in 85% of these women and at least reduce suffering in a further 12% to 13%. Also, once an American mother has experienced a successful epidural block for childbirth, she is likely to choose to do so again. Institutions in which skilled obstetric anesthesia personnel practice therefore can expect an epidural rate between 60% and 80%. Only 22% of patients delivering in hospitals with more that 1500 deliveries per year received epidural blockade, however. An anesthesiologist or CRNA did only 70% of these procedures.[20] These statistics suggest a shortage of qualified physician and nonphysician anesthetists willing to provide obstetric labor analgesia. Limiting regional blocks to physicians would only worsen this situation.

Early in 1991, we canvassed 802 members of the Society for Obstetric Anesthesia and Perinatology (SOAP). They were quizzed about the role of CRNAs in their obstetric anesthetic practice and their opinions concerning the 1983 ASA Statement on Regional Anesthesia. Of the 802 questionnaires mailed, 60 were returned undelivered. Of the remaining 742 questionnaires, 216 replies were received, a response rate of 29.3%. After review, we considered 210 out of 216 eligible for inclusion.

Of these 210 respondents, 102 (48.6%) did not work with CRNAs and 108 (51.4%) did. Of the latter, 46 of 108 (42.6%) reported that CRNAs administered conduction anesthesia for obstetrics versus 62 of 108 (57.4%) who did not. Thus, 46 of 210 (21.9%) respondents worked with CRNAs who administered obstetric conduction anesthesia; of the remaining 62 who admitted functioning with CRNA help, 25.8% (16/62) did not permit CRNAs to do conduction anesthesia because of the 1983 ASA Statement on Regional Anesthesia; 29.0% (18/62) gave other reasons; and 45.2% (28/62) chose not to answer the question.

We conclude from this survey that CRNAs currently administer many obstetric conduction anesthetics in

$$\frac{\#\ \textbf{Epidurals Performed} \times \textbf{100}}{\textbf{Total}\ \#\ \textbf{Deliveries} - \#\ \textbf{Cesarean Deliveries}} = \%\ \textbf{Epidural Anesthetics}$$

Figure 39–3. Calculation of epidural rate.

$$\frac{3{,}000 \text{ Deliveries/Year} \times 70\% \text{ Epidural Rate}}{4 \text{ Trainees/Month} \times 12 \text{ Months/Year} \times 100} = 43.75 \text{ Epidurals/Trainee/Month}$$

Figure 39–4. Average number of epidural anesthetics per month per trainee.

the United States. Only 14.8% (16/108) of SOAP members canvassed who worked with CRNAs knowingly adhere to the 1983 ASA Statement on Regional Anesthesia.

We concur with Frederick Hehre, who in 1975 stated that "I firmly believe that an elite group of nurse anesthetists should be developed into obstetrical anesthesia specialists, and, after training and certification, be allowed to administer conduction anesthesia. Pragmatically, the nurse anesthetist presently makes certain medical decisions and administers drugs and treatment; for example, treatment of hypotension with vasopressors, administration of blood, choice of anesthetic agent, etc." (An important analogy seems to exist here between the obstetric nurse anesthetist and the intensive care nurse.) "It is more sensible to allow qualified individuals to make the decision to administer conduction anesthesia to an obstetrical patient with a known full stomach than to risk aspiration of vomitus with inhalation anesthesia, which is the leading anesthetic cause of maternal death."[24]

Two more recent statements, one issued jointly by ACOG/ASA and the other by the ASA alone, appear to recognize that American CRNAs do, in practice, administer conduction anesthesia for obstetrics:

Qualifications for administering anesthesia.
A qualified anesthesiologist responsible for all anesthetics administered should be appointed. In many obstetric units, obstetricians or obstetrician-supervised nurse anesthetists administer the anesthetics. The administration of general or regional anesthesia requires numerous medical judgments and technical skills. Nurse anesthetists are not trained as physicians and cannot be expected to make medical decisions. Obstetricians seldom have sufficient training or experience in administering anesthesia to allow them to properly supervise nurse anesthetists." (ACOG and ASA recommended obstetric anesthesia goals. ACOG Newsletter: 32: #9 [September] 1988:9-10).

"Major conduction blocks in obstetrics shall be initiated and maintained by or under the direction of a physician with appropriate privileges.
Physicians must be approved through the institutional credentialing process to administer or supervise the administration of obstetric anesthesia and must be qualified to manage procedurally related complications." (Guidelines for Conduction Anesthesia in Obstetrics: Approved by the House of Delegates on October 12, 1988 and last amended on October 23, 1990.)

These guidelines stress direct CRNA supervision by a qualified anesthesiologist instead of the obstetrician. The latter's training cannot guarantee that he or she possesses the prerequisite anesthetic skills and knowledge needed for adequate CRNA surveillance. We concur with this more pragmatic approach. It provides sensible latitude for those institutions that, whether of necessity or by choice, approve the administration of obstetric regional anesthesia by appropriately supervised CRNAs.

Regrettably, the authors are reliably informed that the latter ASA Guideline II has again been modified to recommend that CRNAs be excluded entirely from administering regional analgesia in the labor suite. In rural areas, small towns, and some large cities, however, anesthesiologists interested in the practice of obstetric anesthesia are scarce. Here CRNAs do most obstetric anesthesia care, including epidural analgesia. The actual number of obstetric regional blocks done by CRNAs annually in North America is presently unknown, but it is undoubtedly significant.

The dearth of obstetric anesthesiologists can be met by employing CRNAs trained in obstetric conduction anesthesia and methods of dealing with its complications. This fact needs to be acknowledged and addressed by both the ASA and the American Association of Nurse Anesthetists. These two organizations should resolve their differences on this issue for the benefit of our patients.

$$\frac{3{,}000 \text{ Deliveries/Year} \times 20\% \text{ Cesarean Sections}}{4 \text{ Trainees/Month} \times 12 \text{ Months/Year} \times 100} = \frac{12.5 \text{ Cesarean}}{\text{Sections/Trainee/Month}}$$

Figure 39–5. Average number of anesthetics given by each trainee for cesarean section per month.

Obstetric Anesthesia Teaching and Research

A balanced academic program ensures good resident education.[7,25] A series of didactic presentations on obstetric anesthesia must be included in the departmental lecture program. Time must be set aside during the working day for faculty and residents to meet informally. Another anesthesiologist or a qualified CRNA can cover clinical duties during these sessions to avoid interruptions. Tutorials and literature discussions may be scheduled two to three times a week. The goal should be to inculcate in residents the lifelong habit of reading current literature as a means of keeping up-to-date.

Productive obstetric anesthesia clinical and laboratory research depends upon the motivation of the director and faculty. Funding is essential, particularly for laboratory research. Faculty need reasonable (50%) nonclinical time to draft protocols, write grant proposals, and do research studies. (A substantial portion of this nonclinical time also must be allotted to reading current literature, preparing and delivering lectures and tutorials, and writing abstracts, papers, and book chapters.) Sharing laboratory space, facilities, and staff within the Department of Anesthesiology cuts costs.

Obstetric anesthesia research fellowships of 1 to 2 years in duration should be created to attract young, free-thinking people. Fellows should aim to complete one or two worthwhile projects each that are likely to benefit patients. After completing their research projects, Fellows may be invited to remain on the faculty or move elsewhere to further the cause of obstetric anesthesia there. Either way, the reputation of the obstetric anesthesia fellowship and resident programs will be enhanced.

Management of a Nonteaching Obstetric Anesthesia Service

The basic management tenets outlined previously also stand in the organization of a nonteaching obstetric anesthesia service. However, important differences exist regarding staffing. Two distinct staffing patterns prevail in larger (>1500 deliveries per annum) nonteaching obstetric anesthesia units. Structural differences are mainly dictated by local anesthesiologists' attitudes to nurse anesthetists in obstetrics.

Many nonteaching institutions, including some with large obstetric services (4000–5000 deliveries per year) provide obstetric analgesia/anesthesia through a cohort of CRNAs. A suitably qualified physician directs obstetric anesthesia. Helped by other members of the anesthesiology practice, he or she is responsible for the supervision of the obstetric anesthesia CRNAs day and night. The anesthesiologist is usually free to help if immediate problems or complications arise.

The contrasting situation can be found where CRNAs are barred from administering conduction analgesia/anesthesia. In this situation, the obstetric anesthesia service is physician-based. Although this arrangement is exemplary in theory, the situation may not be so ideal in practice. A single anesthesiologist services the obstetric floor on a 24-hour basis. This arrangement works well if patient turnover is modest; however, if the hospital concerned is busy and boasts a 70% epidural rate, matters may get out of hand. The scenario then changes to one of a harassed, weary anesthesiologist racing from room to room placing epidural catheters and documenting the case briefly. He or she then leaves the care of the patient to the obstetric nurse. Not all obstetric nurses are ACLS certified or familiar with complications of epidural blockade. The anesthesiologist may be called to an immediate cesarean section. Should an anesthetic complication needing urgent treatment then arise in a labor room, can the obstetric nurse respond appropriately?

Staffing with a cohort of CRNAs offers a better way to cope with this situation. A CRNA inserts the epidural catheter under the direct or indirect supervision of the duty anesthesiologist. He or she then monitors the patient's vital signs at the bedside for the next 30 minutes or until the patient is comfortable and hemodynamically stable. The CRNA is trained to respond appropriately to maternal hypotension, seizures, high subarachnoid or insidious subdural block, and so forth. Other CRNAs are available to help should an obstetric emergency arise that demands immediate assisted vaginal or abdominal delivery. The need for an epidural "top-up," infusion syringe refills, or treatment of an anesthetic complication draws a quick and appropriate reaction. Such dedicated patient cover by physicians is expensive, and, in areas where anesthesiologists are hard to find, impossible.

OTHER MATTERS

Patient Evaluation and Anesthetic Documentation

A thorough preanesthetic assessment is vital to patient safety. Complete medical, surgical, anesthetic, drug, allergic, and family histories are prerequisite. They alert the anesthesiologist to the presence of any medical "time bombs" the patient may be secreting. The ASA Basic Standards for Preanesthesia Care (App. E) and the more current Guideline III in the ASA Guidelines for Conduction Anesthesia in Obstetrics (see App. B) provide direction here.

A further ASA statement, which appears in Documentation of Anesthesia Care (App. H), emphasizes the importance of documenting the preanesthetic patient evaluation and maintaining a detailed perianesthesia time-based record of events. Part of it reads as follows: "Documentation is a factor in the provision of quality care, and is the responsibility of an anesthesiologist." For this task, we recommend a preprinted, boxed preanesthetic form that is considered part of the patient's hospital record; thus, important questions that the patient should answer will not be overlooked.

An obstetric anesthesia record differs from that used in the main operating rooms, but the two should originate from the same root and bear a close resemblance (Apps. M and N). The task of keeping good anesthetic records will be simplified by familiarity for those working in both the main operating rooms and the obstetric suite. The recovery period the patient spends in the Post-Anesthesia Care Unit also must be charted.

All anesthesia documentation should be of the highest caliber. Medicolegally, a meticulous anesthesia record is considered evidence of good anesthetic care, an important consideration in the highly charged legal climate of obstetrics. Computer technology will soon offer the option of automated anesthesia records.[26] Automated anesthesia records offer accurate documentation and better patient care. Computerized anesthesia data management systems bear consideration by all directors of obstetric anesthesia services.

Analgesia and Anesthesia Techniques

Indications for obstetric epidural blockade vary from one institution to the next depending on obstetric opinion. "Ultraconservative" obstetricians believe that epidural block causes maternal hypotension, compromises the fetus, prolongs labor, increases the incidence of assisted vaginal delivery, and may even predispose toward dystocia-related cesarean section. They therefore advocate a single indication for epidural analgesia, namely severe pain. Then, their recommended period for epidural catheter placement is limited to 6 to 8 cm of cervical dilatation.

More "radical" obstetricians believe that their patients should experience no pain and little discomfort, that the epidural catheter should be inserted early in labor (1–2 cm of cervical dilatation), and that labor can

be stimulated with intravenous oxytocin if delay results from premature epidural blockade.

Differences exist, too, even within the same obstetric practice, on the anesthetic management of the complicated parturient (*e.g.*, Should patients with pregnancy-induced hypertension, breech presentation, multiple gestation, preterm labor, or diabetes receive epidural blockade?). Controversy over these and other issues can make life difficult for the informed obstetric anesthesiologist. It is therefore advisable that anesthesiologists meet regularly with their obstetric colleagues for discussion so that they can formulate mutually acceptable indications for epidural block. Frequent communication and mutual agreement help preserve cordial relations and a healthy, stress-free working environment for all.

Fortunately, modern infusion techniques of labor epidural analgesia that combine a local anesthetic with a synthetic opioid, or other analgesic agents acting upon the spinal cord (*e.g.*, alpha-adrenergic agonists), offer increased flexibility. Continuous spinal analgesia for labor and delivery is another technique that was recently revived following the introduction of new microcatheter technology. (The recent FDA ruling that these microcatheters be withdrawn from the market by their manufacturers will, however, hinder this endeavor.) These new methods widen the options for coping with diverse obstetric opinion. Good pain relief compatible with the best physiologic outcome can be obtained with these diverse methods.

Acute Pain Service

The role of the Acute Pain Service in obstetrics deserves attention. Patient mobility postoperatively is a key factor in avoiding deep vein thrombosis and pulmonary venous embolism. Satisfactory patient analgesia after perineal repair or cesarean section enables the mother to walk and exercise her venous pump. She is free to interact with and care for her baby. The patient can cough and breathe deeply, too, making postoperative bronchopneumonia less likely. Good recovery from surgery and patient satisfaction with anesthesia depend on effective postoperative pain relief.

The juxtapositioning of obstetric anesthesia and the Acute Pain Service makes good sense. Both are concerned with acute pain management. In some institutions, anesthesiologists share duties in these two mutually compatible areas. Involvement in the Acute Pain Service benefits patients, expands the interests of obstetric anesthesiologists, and adds stature to the specialty.

Management of the "High-Risk" Obstetric Patient

Clinical management regimens for "high-risk" obstetric patients who are hypertensive, bleeding, or suffering from a critical medical or surgical condition are detailed elsewhere. However, we would be remiss if we didn't address the issues of facilities and staffing for the care of these women.[27,28] Intensive care facilities should include sophisticated electronic monitors for the direct measurement and display of arterial, central venous, pulmonary artery, and pulmonary artery wedge pressures. Evaluation of cardiac output and peripheral and mixed venous oxygen saturation should be possible. Monitors must be situated permanently in the obstetric suite and placed in an area designated for the care of the critically ill. A versatile lung ventilator that can compensate for decreased lung compliance and increased airway resistance should be at hand. A nearby automated biochemical laboratory performing arterial and mixed venous blood–gas/acid–base analyses provides data for calculation of tissue oxygen consumption, oxygen delivery, and Vo_2/Do_2 ratios. Other biochemical parameters essential to patient management can be measured as well.

A major component in the successful treatment of the critically ill parturient is the constant presence of an ICU-trained obstetric nurse. Vanderbilt University Medical Center in Nashville maintains an elite cadre of ICU-trained nurses, one of whom is always on duty. The obstetric anesthesia service has the technical expertise for the insertion of arterial and central lines. The obstetric anesthesiologists help with interpretation of monitored data and, in consultation with their obstetric and nursing colleagues, advise on patient management.

Obstetricians, anesthesiologists, and obstetric nurses commissioned to develop an obstetric intensive care program should meet in advance to review and agree upon management strategies and define treatment protocols. This goal particularly applies to severe preeclampsia, in which singular controversy exists. Obstetric anesthesiologists largely agree about anesthetic management and intravenous fluid therapy for this complex syndrome. Consensus among obstetricians working together is far less frequent. More conservative obstetric ideas may even hamper anesthesia care of the severe preeclamptic. As an example, patients are kept "dry" without the benefit of central venous or pulmonary artery pressure monitoring to "avoid iatrogenic pulmonary edema." This strategy may be considered safer obstetrically in a poorly equipped and understaffed peripheral hospital, but profound volume depletion makes induction of anesthesia, regional or general, perilous. Nowadays, swift transport by air or road argues for transfer of critically ill parturients to tertiary obstetric care centers with intensive care facilities.

Established management guidelines should be reviewed and amended when necessary on a monthly or quarterly basis. A "chain of command" must be fashioned in which a single physician (the duty obstetric chief/senior resident) is designated to prescribe *all* patient therapy in writing. This precaution ensures that orders given to the ICU obstetric nurses do not conflict.

Seriously ill parturients may need to be delivered hurriedly, frequently by cesarean section. Sophisticated anesthesia equipment, ventilators, and electronic monitors should be ready in the obstetric operating rooms. A modular system of monitors reduces the need for costly duplication. Expensive cardiac output and mixed venous oxygen saturation modules can be moved between the operating room and intensive care area as required.

In short, we agree with the statement made by Palmer and Gibbs: "No matter what obstetric anesthesia protocols are adopted, one overriding rule applies—that obstetric patients receive the same standard of care, including quality of anesthetic equipment and monitors, that patients in the general operating room receive. In fact, because the risk of a malpractice suite is much higher in obstetrics, the standard of care and record keeping should exceed that of surgical patients."[29]

Management of the Patient Requiring Abortion

Controversy exists over whether patients undergoing mid-trimester abortion need conduction analgesia. Staff opposed to abortion on religious or conscientious grounds may refuse to be involved. Some anesthesiologists consider the risks of epidural blockade for abortion too high. Because the baby's welfare is not at issue, they argue for the liberal intravenous use of potent analgesic, anxiolytic, and amnestic agents to control the patient's anxiety and pain.

An induced abortion can be painful. Conduction analgesia is then indicated. Whether or not abortion is indicated for medical or social reasons, the mental and physical suffering experienced by the patient is always real. No patient in this situation should be denied regional analgesia on other than medical grounds. The feelings of the patient's husband, significant other, or immediate family concerning relief of her anxiety and pain should not be overlooked, but their opinions should not supersede the patient's wishes and needs. Divisional guidelines should therefore be established to avoid any embarrassment or unpleasantness for all concerned.

Medicolegal Issues: Informed Consent

Others have succinctly confronted the medicolegal implications of obstetric anesthesia.[30] Excellent guidelines are also available for obstetric anesthetic risk management.[29] The idea of informed consent, highly relevant to the matter at hand, has recently been addressed.[31] We think that the most important caveat in avoiding litigation is straightforward: Always adopt an open and honest approach to the patient, her spouse or significant other, and close relatives. Take the time to explain the proposed anesthetic procedure, with its risks and complications, frankly, in plain language, and without being patronizing. Most patients, even the less educated, usually have enough common sense to understand their circumstances.

The patient should appreciate that, in a training institution, some complications are more common. A fair estimate of the degree of extra risk involved based on current literature should be provided. For example, accidental dural puncture will occur in 2% to 3% of patients managed by residents. The incidence in more experienced hands should be less than 0.5%. The risks of more serious complications, such as intraspinal abscess or blood clot, permanent nerve damage, or local anesthetic–induced seizures or cardiac arrest, should be no greater in a well-supervised resident program. The patient can be reassured that these latter major complications seldom arise.

Providing the patient with information so that she can give informed consent demands a delicate and individual approach.[32] Too detailed a description of anesthesia-related complications in pursuit of the doctrine of informed consent can frighten even the most balanced individual. But emphasis placed on the fact that effective methods exist to deal with anesthetic complications helps allay patient anxiety and fear. After discussion of severe postpartum spinal headache as a consequence of dural puncture, stress the efficacy of autologous blood patch in its treatment. Admit the possibility of an imperfect or failed intraspinal block, but highlight the likely remedies, including general anesthesia. Underscore the success of early surgical intervention in avoiding paralysis due to epidural abscess or hematoma.

Should a serious complication occur, we strongly recommend an honest and forthright approach to all concerned. Accurately appraise all the patient's support persons of the situation quickly and keep them abreast of developments, good or bad. Convey to the patient that the perinatal team has her best interests at heart. Sometimes a patient or member of her family is unable, in the heat of the moment, to comprehend or remember what they have been told concerning complicated medical events. Once the crisis is over, again take time to explain matters to ensure reasonable understanding. A further visit or telephone call about a month after the patient leaves hospital will impress upon her that she has been and continues to be well cared for. As her anesthesiologist, you in turn will be reassured that no misconceptions exist about the recent critical events. Misinformation and misunderstanding cause confusion, which can lead to anger and frustration on behalf of the patient, a surefire recipe for litigation.

Financial Implications of an Obstetric Anesthesia Service

American medicine is based upon free-market principles. Rivalry for patients between community hospitals is, and will continue to become, increasingly competitive. Hospital administrators and marketing divisions view the parturient as a potential source of patient referral. Therefore, to attract women to give birth at their hospital or attend to female ailments, many hospitals have adopted the idea of a "Women's Pavilion." This approach offers convenient, specialized obstetric and gynecologic patient care all under one roof.

A significant factor contributing toward patient satisfaction is the presence of an efficient, round-the-clock obstetric analgesia/anesthesia service. Many private institutions have established such services, and 60% to 90% of their clients are now delivered under epidural blockade. An obstetric anesthesia service can be profitable despite the major commitment to workers and equipment involved, even when anesthesiologists, not CRNAs, provide the service. If the hospital fails to make a direct profit out of obstetric anesthesia, it can still benefit from an increase in patient referrals.

The emphasis for state and university-based hospitals is somewhat different. An academic division of obstetric anesthesia must not only provide superb clinical care but also coordinate theoretical teaching with practical training. Equally important, but sometimes neglected, is clinical and laboratory research. According to our recent SOAP survey, many teaching departments avoid using CRNAs for obstetrics to ensure adequate practical resident experience. The provision of 24-hour resident/attending physician cover, coupled with equal dedication to patient care, resident education, and research, demands people and funding. We believe that the institution must share in the running expenses of an obstetric anesthesia division. Augmented patient referrals offset financial losses thus incurred by the hospital. Furthermore, a good obstetric anesthesia division enhances a hospital's reputation and prestige within the community it serves. These facts are worth emphasizing when negotiating with hospital administrators.

Marketing and Communication

There are few anesthetic subspecialties in which marketing and communication are more important. It is the responsibility of the Obstetric Anesthesia Director to ensure that both verbal and printed information about anesthesia is available to prospective parents. Institutional parenting classes must incorporate spoken information about methods of pain relief in childbirth and anesthesia for cesarean section. A lively presentation given in lay terms by an entertaining speaker provides a firm foundation for establishing good patient/physician rapport later in pregnancy. If this is not feasible, a brief but professionally produced and narrated videotaped presentation on the subject is useful. An information pamphlet about obstetric anesthesia, easily understandable and without medical jargon, allows the patient and her partner to read about conduction analgesia and general anesthesia at their leisure. The patient and her support person can then devise an informed "game plan" for pain control well before labor.

Due respect must be paid to "natural childbirth" methods featuring regulated breathing patterns and muscle relaxation.[23,33] Patients who practice these techniques frequently cannot control their pain adequately throughout labor and delivery and often request epidural blockade. Our preference is to indicate strongly to the mother and her partner that she may well deliver successfully "naturally" without "artificial" analgesia/anesthesia, but they should both appreciate that relaxation and breathing methods are not always effective. To quote Melzack: "Those whose expectations of labor are violated by the actual labor experience report more severe pain."[23] Therefore, the patient should enter hospital with a comprehensive "game plan" that includes conduction blockade as an option.

CONCLUSION

A pregnant woman and her anesthesiologist can usually expect a smooth course and joyous outcome to childbirth, but obstetric anesthesia can provide some of the greatest immediate challenges to an anesthesiologist's technical skills. A case in point is the parturient with an unsuspected difficult airway. The knowledge and expertise of the obstetric anesthesiologist are also called upon in less acute, but equally menacing, situations. An example of the latter is the management of severe preeclampsia, a syndrome so diverse in its presentation that it sometimes confuses even the most erudite clinician.

A well-staffed and efficiently organized obstetric anesthesia division equipped with "state-of-the-art" anesthesia and monitoring equipment promotes patient well-being and safety. It also provides a happy and challenging work environment. Communication is essential. There are few relationships in anesthesia, or in medicine as a whole, in which open communication is more important than that between the parturient and her anesthesiologist or anesthetist. An open and honest approach to the patient and her supporters will help in making all anesthetic-related decisions. Complications associated with conduction analgesia and general anesthesia should be discussed frankly beforehand. Untoward events, should they occur, must be dealt with efficiently and candidly. This approach should largely offset any concurrent medicolegal threat.

Despite the risks and frustrations they confront, obstetric anesthesiologists and anesthetists generally lead a demanding but exciting and satisfying existence.[7] American communities are surprisingly aware of the standard of obstetric anesthesia care provided by the hospitals that serve them, and often choose where to deliver their babies accordingly. Therefore, from the departmental or practice viewpoint, as well as in the interests of the institution and the citizens of the community to which it caters, obstetric anesthesia deserves both moral and financial backing. The authors look forward to the day when all American women bearing children can count on the support of a strong obstetric anesthesia service.

REFERENCES

1. Medical Malpractice: Verdicts, settlements, and experts. 1988;4:1.
2. Marx GF. Foreward. In: Datta S, ed. Anesthetic and ob-

stetric management of high-risk pregnancy. St Louis: Mosby–Year Book, 1991:XI.

3. Marx G. Personal reflections on 50 years of obstetric anesthesia. Reg Anesth 1990;15:232.

4. Moore DC, Bridenbaugh LD. Is it practical for medical anesthetists to supply a twenty-four hour obstetrical service? Surg Obstet Gynecol 1955:382.

5. Moore DC. Twenty-four hour coverage of obstetrical deliveries by physician anesthetists. Acta Anaesthesiol Scand Suppl 1966;25:350.

6. Moore DC, Bridenbaugh LD, Bridenbaugh PO. Twenty-four hour coverage of obstetric deliveries by anesthesiologists. Anesth Analg Curr Res 1969;48:401.

7. Kalas DB, Hehre FW. Departmental evolution of obstetric anesthesia: a 12-year survey. Obstet Gynecol 1970;36:156.

8. Sheldon RS. Consolidation of hospital obstetric services. Med Clin North Am 1974;58:885.

9. Marx GF. Obstetric anesthesia organizations in the United States. Anesthesiology 1974;41:308.

10. Cohen SE. Obstetrical anesthesia: An overview of growth and change. ASA Newsletter 1991;55:17.

11. Accreditation manual for hospitals, 1991. Appendix C, Joint Commission on Anesthesia and Obstetric Indicators. Joint Commission for Accreditation of Healthcare Organizations (JCAHO).

12. Marx GF. Obstetric anesthesia in New York City. Am J Obstet Gynecol 1976;124:440.

13. Phillips OC, Frazier TM. Obstetric anesthetic care in the United States. Obstet Gynecol 1962;19:796.

14. Shnider SM. Obstetric anesthesia coverage: Problems and solutions. Obstet Gynecol 1969;34:615.

15. Taylor G. Obstetric anaesthesia services in the United Kingdom. Br Med J 1971;1:101.

16. Rasmussen J, George T, Reisman A, Cull WA, Gravenstein JS. Obstetric anesthesiology practices and attitudes in hospitals in Cuyahoga County, Ohio: A survey. Ohio State Med J 1977;73:139.

17. Palahniuk RJ. Editorial: Survey of obstetric anaesthesia practice in British Columbia. Can Anaesth Soc J 1986;33:123.

18. McMorland GH, Jenkins LC, Douglas MJ. A survey of obstetric anaesthesia practice in British Columbia. Can Anaesth Soc J 1986;33:185.

19. Levinson G, Shnider SM. Editorial: Obstetric anesthesia coverage—a continuing problem. Anesthesiology 1986;65:245.

20. Gibbs CP, Krischer J, Peckham BM, Sharp H, Kirschbaum TH. Obstetric anesthesia: A national survey. Anesthesiology 1986;65:298.

21. Reynolds F. Obstetric anaesthetic services [Editorial]. Br Med J 1986;293:403.

22. MacDonald R, Webster DCS. Obstetric anaesthetic services in the Yorkshire region. Br Med J 1986;293:431.

23. Melzack R. The myth of painless childbirth [The John J.Bonica Lecture]. Pain 1984;19:321.

24. Hehre FW. Observations, philosophic and opionated, on obstetric anesthesia coverage. In: Safer P, ed. Clinical anesthesia: Public health aspects of critical care medicine and anesthesiology. Philadelphia: FA Davis, 1976; 10:324.

25. Shnider SM. Training in obstetric anesthesia in the United States. Am J Obstet Gynecol 1965;93:243.

26. Merritt TW. Can anesthesiologists adopt and benefit from use of automated record-keeping devices? In: Anesthesiology News. New York: The McMahon Group, July, 1991.

27. Graham SG, Luxton MC. The requirement for intensive care support for the pregnant population. Anaesthesia 1989;44:581.

28. Mabie WC, Sibai BM. Treatment in an obstetric intensive care unit. Am J Obstet Gynecol 1990;162:1.

29. Palmer SK, Gibbs CP. Risk management in obstetric anesthesia. Int Anesthesiol Clin 1989;27:188.

30. Karp D, Craddick M. Obstetric anesthesia and lawsuits. In: Shnider SM Levinson G, eds. Obstetric anesthesia. 2nd ed. Baltimore: Williams & Wilkins, 1987:334.

31. Gild WM. Informed consent: A review. Anesth Analg 1989;68:649.

32. Stenchever MA. Too much informed consent? [Editorial] Am J Obstet Gynecol 1991;77:631.

33. Hetherington SE. A controlled study of the effect of prepared childbirth classes on obstetric outcomes. Birth 1990;17:86.

APPENDIX A

ACOG and ASA Recommend Obstetric Anesthesia Goals: Joint Statement on the Optimal Goals for Anesthesia Care in Obstetrics

This joint statement was adopted by the ASA and ACOG and was designed to address issues of concern to both specialties. Good obstetric care requires the availability of qualified personnel and equipment to administer general or regional anesthesia on either an elective or emergent basis.

OPTIMAL GOALS

The extent and degree to which anesthesia services are available varies widely among hospitals. However, for any hospital providing obstetric care, certain optimal anesthesia goals should be sought.

Availability of Personnel

A person qualified to administer an appropriate anesthetic should be available whenever necessary. For many women, regional anesthesia (spinal or epidural) will be the most appropriate anesthetic.

A person qualified to maintain support of vital functions in any obstetric emergency should be available.

Anesthesia and surgical personnel able to start emergency cesarean deliveries within 30 minutes of recognition of need should be available.

Qualifications for Administering Anesthesia

A qualified anesthesiologist responsible for all anesthetics administered should be appointed. In many obstetric units, obstetricians or obstetrician-supervised nurse anesthetists administer the anesthetics. The administration of general or regional anesthesia requires numerous medical judgments and technical skills. Nurse anesthetists are not trained as physicians and cannot be expected to make medical decisions. Obstetricians seldom have sufficient training or experience in administering anesthesia to allow them to properly supervise nurse anesthetists.

Persons administering or supervising obstetric anesthesia should be qualified to manage the infrequent but occasionally life-threatening complications of major regional anesthesia such as respiratory and cardiovascular failure, toxic local anesthetic convulsions, or vomiting and aspiration. Mastering and retaining the skills and knowledge necessary to manage these complications require adequate training and frequent application.

To ensure the safest and most effective anesthesia for obstetric patients, the director of anesthesia services, with the approval of the medical staff, must develop and enforce written policies regarding provision of obstetric anesthesia. It is the responsibility of the director of anesthesia services and the medical staff to review each individual's qualifications and competence and to determine which agents and techniques may be used.

The Obstetrician

A qualified obstetrician should be available during administration of anesthesia. Neither major conduction anesthesia (epidural, caudal, or spinal) nor general anesthesia should be administered until the patient has been examined and the fetal status and progress of labor have been evaluated by a qualified physician who is readily available to supervise the labor and to deal with any obstetric complications that may arise.

Equipment, Facilities, and Support Personnel

Equipment, facilities, and support personnel equal to those provided in the surgical suite should be available. This should include the availability of a properly equipped and staffed recovery room capable of receiving and caring for all patients recovering from major regional or general anesthesia. Birthing facilities, when used for anesthesia, must be appropriately equipped to provide safe anesthetic care during labor and delivery and postanesthesia recovery care.

Resuscitation of the Depressed Newborn

Personnel other than the surgical team should be immediately available to assume responsibility for resuscitation of the depressed newborn. The surgeon and anesthesiologist are responsible for the mother and may not be able to leave her to care for the newborn even when a regional anesthetic is functioning adequately. An individual qualified to perform neonatal resuscitation should demonstrate the following:

- Skills in rapid and accurate evaluation of the newborn condition, including Apgar scoring
- Knowledge of the pathogenesis and causes of a low Apgar score (asphyxia, drugs, hypovolemia, trauma, anomalies, and infection), as well as specific indications for resuscitation
- Skills in airway management, laryngoscopy, endotracheal intubation, suctioning of airways, artificial ventilation, cardiac massage, and maintenance of thermal stability.

In larger maternity units and those functioning as high-risk centers, 24-hour in-house anesthesia and obstetric and neonatal specialists are usually necessary. Preferably, the obstetric anesthesia services should be directed by an anesthesiologist with special training or experience in obstetric anesthesia. These units will also frequently require the availability of more sophisticated monitoring equipment and specially trained nursing personnel.

RECOMMENDATIONS

A recent survey jointly sponsored by ASA and ACOG found that many hospitals in the United States have not yet achieved the aforementioned goals. Deficiencies were most evident in smaller delivery units. Some small delivery units are necessary because of geographic considerations. Currently, 54% of hospitals providing obstetric care perform fewer than 500 deliveries per year. Providing comprehensive care for obstetric patients in these small units is extremely inefficient, not cost-effective, and frequently impossible. Thus, the following recommendations would seem appropriate:

1. Whenever possible, small units should consolidate.*
2. When geographic factors require the existence of smaller units, these units should be part of a well-established perinatal regionalizations system.

The availability of the appropriate personnel to assist in the management of a variety of obstetric problems is a necessary feature of good obstetric care. The presence of a pediatrician at a high-risk cesarean section or that of an anesthesiologist at a breech delivery are examples. Frequently, these professionals spend a considerable amount of time waiting but eventually may not be required to perform the tasks for which they are present. Reasonable compensation for these standby services is justifiable and necessary.

A variety of other mechanisms have been suggested to increase the availability and quantity of anesthesia services in obstetrics. Improved hospital design to place labor and delivery suites closer to the operating room would allow for more efficient supervision of nurse anesthetists. Anesthesia equipment in the labor and delivery area must be comparable to that in the operating room.

Finally, interpersonal relations between obstetricians and anesthesiologists could be improved. Joint meetings between the two departments should be encouraged. Anesthesiologists should recognize the special needs and concerns of the obstetrician, and obstetricians should recognize the anesthesiologist as a consultant in the management of pain and life-support measures. Both should recognize the need to provide high-quality care for all patients.

ACOG, ANESTHESIOLOGISTS CLARIFY STANDARDS ISSUES FOR OBSTETRIC ANESTHESIA†

The joint statement adopted by ACOG and the ASA on optimal goals for obstetric anesthesia and the subsequent standards for conductive (sic) anesthesia

---

*The National Foundation–March of Dimes, Committee on Perinatal Health: Toward improving the outcome of pregnancy—recommendations for the regional development of maternal and perinatal health services. New York: The National Foundation–March of Dimes, 1977.

†ACOG Newsletter, September, 1988:9

published by ASA in December, 1988, have been subject to misinterpretation. This has caused problems at the local institutional level.

Concern is primarily directed towards the portion of the document delineating responsibilities of the obstetrician, which states that anesthesia should not be administered until the patient has been examined, and the fetal status and progress of labor evaluated by a qualified physician who is readily available to supervise the labor. The passage in question also appeared in ASA's Standards for Conduction Anesthesia as Standard III, which is reprinted as follows:

Major conduction anesthesia should not be administered until the patient has been examined and the fetal status and progress of labor evaluated by a qualified physician who is readily available to supervise the labor and to deal with any obstetric complications that may arise.

Both ACOG and the ASA have responded to concerns over this standard with a clarification of intent. The intent of this standard is that the examination of the patient may be performed by the physician responsible for obstetric management or may be delegated to a qualified individual, who may be a nurse or midwife. Standard III has been referred back to ASA's Committee on Obstetrical Anesthesia and Standards for further study, with clarification and rewording to be done in conjunction with ACOG. In the interim, this explanation is meant to clear up some of the confusion caused by its misinterpretation.

ANESTHESIOLOGISTS SEND STATEMENT BACK FOR REWORDING[‡]

About 2 years ago, ACOG consulted with the ASA about issues pertaining to the availability and quality of obstetric anesthesia. Their findings were summarized in the joint statement, "Optimal Goals for Anesthesia in Obstetrics," published in the September, 1988 ACOG Newsletter and in the December, 1988 ASA Newsletter under the title "Standards for Conduction Anesthesia in Obstetrics."

In the intervening time, concerns have been raised about a passage stating that major conduction anesthesia should not be administered "until the patient has been examined and the fetal status and progress of labor have been evaluated by a qualified physician who is readily available to supervise the labor and to deal with any obstetric complications that may arise." In the ASA version, the same passage is incorporated under the first part of Standard III.

The intent of the standard, ASA notes, "is that the examination of the patient may be performed by the physician responsible for obstetric management or may be delegated to a qualified individual who may be a nurse or midwife."[§] The statement has been referred to the ASA Committees on Obstetrical Anesthesia and Standard of Care[**] for clarification and rewording.

[‡]*ACOG Newsletter, December, 1989:7*

[§]*American Society of Anesthesiologists. Clarification of standards for conduction anesthesia in obstetrics. ASA Newsletter 1989; 53(12):19.*

[**]*ACOG Newsletter, February, 1990:9*

APPENDIX B

Guidelines for Regional Anesthesia in Obstetrics

(Approved by the House of Delegates on October 12, 1988 and last amended on October 30, 1991)

These guidelines apply to the use of regional anesthesia or analgesia in which local anesthetics are administered to the parturient during labor and delivery. They are intended to encourage quality patient care but cannot guarantee any specific patient outcome. Because the availability of anesthesia resources may vary, members are responsible for interpreting and establishing the guidelines for their own institutions and practices. These guidelines are subject to revision from time to time as warranted by the evolution of technology and practice.

GUIDELINE I

Regional anesthesia should be initiated and maintained only in locations in which appropriate resuscitation equipment and drugs are immediately available to manage procedurally related problems.

> Resuscitation equipment should include, but is not limited to, sources of oxygen and suction, equipment to maintain an airway and perform endotrachael intubation, a means to provide positive-pressure ventilation, and drugs and equipment for cardiopulmonary resuscitation.

GUIDELINE II

Regional anesthesia should be initiated by a physician with appropriate privileges and maintained by or under the medical direction[1] of such an individual.

Physicians should be approved through the institutional credentialing process to initiate and direct the maintenance of obstetric anesthesia and to manage procedurally related complications.

GUIDELINE III

Regional anesthesia should not be administered until (1) the patient has been examined by a qualified individual,[2] and (2) the maternal and fetal status and progress of labor have been evaluated by a physician with privileges in obstetrics who is readily available to supervise the labor and manage any obstetric complications that may arise.

> Under circumstances defined by department protocol, qualified personnel may perform the initial pelvic examination. The physician responsible for the patient's obstetrical care should be informed of her status so that a decision can be made regarding present risk and further management.[2]

GUIDELINE IV

An intravenous infusion should be established before the initiation of regional anesthesia and maintained throughout the duration of the regional anesthetic.

GUIDELINE V

Regional anesthesia for labor and/or vaginal delivery requires that the parturient's vital signs and the fetal heart rate be monitored and documented by a qualified individual. Additional monitoring appropriate to the clinical condition of the parturient and the fetus should be employed when indicated. When extensive regional blockade is administered for complicated vaginal delivery, the standards for basic intraoperative monitoring[3] should be applied.

GUIDELINE VI

Regional anesthesia for cesarean delivery requires that the standards for basic intraoperative monitoring[3] be applied and that a physician with privileges in obstetrics be immediately available.

GUIDELINE VII

Qualified personel, other than the anesthesiologist attending the mother, should be immediately available to assume responsibility for resuscitaion of the newborn.[2]

> The primary responsibility of the anesthesiologist is to provide care to the mother. If the anesthesiologist is also requested to provide brief assistance in the care of the newborn, the benefit to the child must be compared to the risk to the mother.

GUIDELINE VIII

A physician with appropriate privileges should remain readily available during the regional anesthetic to manage anesthetic complications until the patient's postanesthesia condition is satisfactory and stable.

GUIDELINE IX

All patients recovering from regional anesthesia should receive appropriate postanesthesia care. Following cesarean delivery and/or extensive regional blockade, the standards for postanesthesia care[4] should be applied.

- A Postanesthesia Care Unit (PACU) should be available to receive patients. The design, equipment, and staffing should meet requirements of the facility's accrediting and licensing bodies.
- When a site other than the PACU is used, equivalent postanesthesia care should be provided.

GUIDELINE X

There should be a policy to assure the availability in the facility of a physician to manage complications and to provide cardiopulmonary resuscitation for patients receiving postanesthesia care.

REFERENCES

1. Anesthesia care team (approved by ASA House of Delegates 10/14/87).
2. Guidelines for perinatal care. American Academy of Pediatrics and American College of Obstetricians and Gynecologists, 1988.
3. Standards for basic intra-operative monitoring (approved by ASA House of Delegates 10/21/86; last amended 10/23/90).
4. Standards for postanesthesia care (approved by ASA House of Delegates 10/12/88; last amended 10/23/90).

(ASA Member Directory, American Society of Anesthesiologists, 1992:693)

APPENDIX C

Joint Commission Anesthesia and Obstetrics Indicators

OBSTETRIC INDICATORS

1. Patients with primary cesarean section for failure to progress
2. Patients with attempted vaginal birth after cesarean section (VBAC), subcategorized by success or failure
3. Patients with excessive maternal blood loss defined by either postdelivery red blood cell transfusion or a low postdelivery hematocrit or hemoglobin (Hct < 22%, Hgb < 7 gms) or a significant pre- to post-delivery decrease in hematocrit ($\geq$ 11%) or hemoglobin ($\geq$ 3.5 gms) excluding patients with abruptio placenta or placenta previa.
4. Patients with the diagnosis of eclampsia
5. The delivery of infants weighing less than 2500 grams following either induction of labor or repeat cesarean section without medical indications
6. Term infants admitted to an NICU within 24 hours of delivery and with NICU stay greater than 24 hours, excluding admission for congenital anomalies
7. Neonates with an Apgar score of 3 or less at 5 minutes and a birth weight greater than 1500 g
8. Neonates with a discharge diagnosis of massive aspiration syndrome requiring either oxygen therapy or NICU admission for greater than 24 hours
9. Neonates with a discharge diagnosis of significant birth trauma*

10. Term infants with a diagnosis of hypoxic encephalopathy or clinically apparent seizure prior to discharge from the hospital of birth
11. Deaths of infants or fetuses weighing 500 grams or more subcategorized by intrahospital neonatal deaths, prepartum stillborns, and intrapartum stillborns
12. Intrahospital neonatal deaths of infants with a birth weight of 750 to 999 g born in a hospital with an NICU
13. Maternal readmissions within 14 days of delivery
14. Intrahospital maternal deaths occurring within 42 days postpartum
15. Infants weighing less than 1800 grams delivered in a hospital without an NICU
16. Neonates transferred from a non-NICU hospital to a NICU hospital.

ANESTHESIA INDICATORS

1. Patients diagnosed with a central nervous system (CNS) complication occurring during procedures involving anesthesia administration or within 2 postprocedure days of its conclusion, subcategorized by American Society of Anesthesiologists-Physical Status (ASA-PS) class, patient age, and CNS versus non–CNS-related procedures
2. Patients developing a peripheral neurologic deficit during procedures involving anesthesia administration or within 2 postprocedure days of its conclusion
3. Patients with an acute myocardial infarction during procedures involving anesthesia administration or within 2 postprocedure days of its conclusion, subcategorized by ASA-PS class, patient age, and cardiac versus noncardiac procedures

---

*The lists of significant birth traumas and medical indications for induction and repeat cesarean section are specified in the JCAHO Clinical Indicator Abstract Forms for these indicators.
Note: The final wording of each indicator may be subject to revision based on the results of further testing

4. Patients with a cardiac arrest during procedures involving anesthesia administration or within 24 postprocedure hours of its conclusion, excluding patients with required intraoperative cardiac arrest, subcategorized by ASA-PS class, patient age, and cardiac versus noncardiac procedures

5. Patients with unplanned respiratory arrest during procedures involving anesthesia administration or within 24 postprocedure hours of its conclusion

6. Death of patients during procedures involving anesthesia administration or within 48 postprocedure hours of its conclusion, subcategorized by ASA-PS class and patient age

7. Unplanned admission of patients to the hospital within 1 postprocedure day following outpatient procedures involving anesthesia administration

8. Unplanned admission of patients to an intensive care unit within 1 postprocedure day of procedures involving anesthesia administration

9. Patients with a discharge diagnosis of fulminant pulmonary edema developed during procedures involving anesthesia administration or within 1 postprocedure day of its conclusion

10. Patients diagnosed with an aspiration pneumonitis occurring during procedures involving anesthesia administration or within 2 postprocedure days of its conclusion

11. Patients developing a postural headache within 4 postprocedure days following procedures involving spinal or epidural anesthesia administration

12. Patients experiencing dental injury during procedures involving anesthesia care

13. Patients experiencing an ocular injury during procedures involving anesthesia care

(Accreditation Manual for Hospitals, Appendix C. Joint Commission for Accreditation of Healthcare Organizations 1991: 301)

APPENDIX D

Guidelines for Patient Care in Anesthesiology

(Approved by House of Delegates on October 3, 1967 and last amended on October 16, 1985)

I. Definition of Anesthesiology
Anesthesiology is a discipline within the practice of medicine specializing in:
   A. The medical management of patients who are rendered unconscious and/or insensible to pain and emotional stress during surgical, obstetrical and certain other medical procedures (involves preoperative, intraoperative and postoperative evaluation and treatment of these patients)
   B. The protection of life functions and vital organs (*e.g.,* brain, heart, lungs, kidneys, liver) under the stress of anesthetic, surgical, and other medical procedures
   C. The management of problems in pain relief
   D. The management of cardiopulmonary resuscitation
   E. The management of problems in pulmonary care
   F. The management of critically ill patients in special care units

II. Anesthesiologist's Responsibilities
Anesthesiologists are physicians who, after college, have graduated from an accredited medical school and have successfully completed an approved residency in anesthesiology. Anesthesiologists' responsibilities to patients should include:
   A. Preanesthetic evaluation and treatment
   B. Medical management of patients and their anesthetic procedures
   C. Postanesthetic evaluation and treatment
   D. On-site medical direction of any nonphysician who assists in the technical aspects of anesthesia care to the patient

III. Guidelines for Anesthesia Care
   A. The same quality of anesthetic care should be available for all patients
      1. Twenty-four hours a day, 7 days a week
      2. Emergency as well as elective patients
      3. Obstetric, medical, and surgical patients
   B. Preanesthetic evaluation and preparation means that the responsible anesthesiologist:
      1. Reviews the chart
      2. Interviews the patient to
         a. Discuss medical history, including anesthetic experiences and drug therapy.
         b. Perform any examinations that would provide information that might assist in decisions regarding risk and management.
      3. Orders necessary tests and medications essential to the conduct of anesthesia
      4. Obtains consultations as necessary
      5. Records impressions on the patient's chart

C. Perianesthetic care means:
   1. Re-evaluation of patient immediately prior to induction
   2. Preparation and check of equipment, drugs, fluids, and gas supplies
   3. Appropriate monitoring of the patient
   4. Selection and administration of anesthetic agents to render the patient insensible to pain during the procedure
   5. Support of life functions under the stress of anesthetic, surgical, and obstetric manipulations
   6. Recording the events of the procedure
D. Postanesthetic Care means:
   1. The individual responsible for administering anesthesia remains with the patient as long as necessary.
   2. Availability of adequate nursing personnel and equipment necessary for safe postanesthetic care
   3. Informing personnel caring for patients in the immediate postanesthetic period of any specific problems presented by each patient
   4. Assurance that the patient is discharged in accordance with policies established by the Department of Anesthesiology

5. The period of postanesthetic surveillance is determined by the status of the patient and the judgment of the anesthesiologist. (Ordinarily, when a patient remains in the hospital postoperatively for 48 hours or longer, one or more notes should appear in addition to the discharge note from the postanesthesia care unit).

IV. Additional Areas of Expertise:
   A. Resuscitation procedures
   B. Pulmonary care
   C. Critical (intensive) care
   D. Diagnosis and management of pain
   E. Trauma and emergency care

V. Quality Assurance
   The anesthesiologist should participate in a planned program for evaluation of quality and appropriateness of patient care and resolving identified problems.

(ASA Member Directory. American Society of Anesthesiologists, 1992:698)

APPENDIX E

Basic Standards for Preanesthesia Care

(Approved by House of Delegates on
October 14, 1987)

These standards apply to all patients who receive anesthesia or monitored anesthesia care. Under unusual circumstances (*e.g.,* extreme emergencies), these standards may be modified. When this is the case, the circumstances shall be documented in the patient's record.

STANDARD I

An anesthesiologist shall be responsible for determining the medical status of the patient, developing a plan of anesthesia care, and acquainting the patient or the responsible adult with the proposed plan.

The development of an appropriate plan of anesthesia care is based upon:

1. Reviewing the medical record
2. Interviewing and examining the patient to

a. Discuss the medical history, previous anesthetic experiences, and drug therapy.
b. Assess those aspects of the physical condition that might affect decisions regarding perioperative risk and management.

3. Obtaining and/or reviewing tests and consultations necessary to the conduct of anesthesia
4. Determining the appropriate prescription of preoperative medications as necessary to the conduct of anesthesia.

The responsible anesthesiologist shall verify that the above has been properly performed and documented in the patient's record.

(ASA Member Directory. American Society of Anesthesiologists, 1992:702)

APPENDIX F

Standards for Basic Intra-Operative Monitoring

(Approved by House of Delegates on October 21, 1986 and last amended on October 23, 1990, to become effective by January 1, 1991)

These standards apply to all anesthesia care, although, in emergency circumstances, appropriate life-support measures take precedence. These standards may be exceeded at any time based on the judgment of the responsible anesthesiologist. They are intended to encourage high-quality patient care, but observing them cannot guarantee any specific patient outcome. They are subject to revision from time to time, as warranted by the evolution of technology and practice. This set of standards addresses only the issue of basic intraoperative monitoring, which is one component of anesthesia care. In certain rare or unusual circumstances, some of these methods of monitoring may be clinically impractical, and appropriate use of the described monitoring methods may fail to detect untoward clinical developments. Brief interruptions of continual† monitoring may be unavoidable. Under extenuating circumstances, the responsible anesthesiologist may waive the requirements marked with an asterisk (*). It is recommended that when this is done, it should be so stated (including the reasons) in a note in the patient's medical record. These standards are not intended for application to the care of the obstetric patient in labor or in the conduct of pain management.

STANDARD I

Qualified anesthesia personnel shall be present in the room throughout the conduct of all general anesthetics, regional anesthetics, and monitored anesthesia care.

Objective

Because of the rapid changes in patient status during anesthesia, qualified anesthesia personnel shall be continuously present to monitor the patient and provide anesthesia care. In the event there is a direct known hazard (*e.g.,* radiation) to the anesthesia personnel which might require intermittent remote observation of the patient, some provision for monitoring the patient must be made. In the event that an emergency requires the temporary absence of the person primarily responsible for the anesthetic, the best judgment of the anesthesiologist will be exercised in comparing the emergency with the anesthetized patient's condition and in the selection of the person left responsible for the anesthetic during the temporary absence.

---

†*Note that* continual *is defined as "repeated regularly and frequently in steady rapid succession," whereas* continuous *means "prolonged without any interruption at any time."*

STANDARD II

During all anesthetics, the patient's oxygenation, ventilation, circulation, and temperature shall be continually evaluated.

Oxygenation

Objective

To ensure adequate oxygen concentration in the inspired gas and the blood during all anesthetics

Methods

1. Inspired gas: During every administration of general anesthesia using an anesthesia machine, the concentration of oxygen in the patient breathing system shall be measured by an oxygen analyzer with a low oxygen concentration limit alarm in use.*
2. Blood oxygenation: During all anesthetics, a quantitative method of assessing oxygenation such as pulse oximetry shall be employed.* Adequate illumination and exposure of the patient is necessary to assess color.*

Ventilation

Objective

To ensure adequate ventilation of the patient during all anesthetics

Methods

1. Every patient receiving general anesthesia shall have the adequacy of ventilation continually evaluated. While qualitative clinical signs such as chest excursion, observation of the reservoir breathing bag, and auscultation of breath sounds may be adequate, quantitative monitoring of the CO_2 content and/or volume of expired gas is encouraged.
2. When an endotracheal tube is inserted, its correct positioning in the trachea must be verified by clinical assessment and by identification of carbon dioxide in the expired gas.* End-tidal CO_2 analysis, in use from the time of endotracheal tube placement, is encouraged.
3. When ventilation is controlled by a mechanical ventilator, there shall be in continuous use a device that is capable of detecting disconnection of components of the breathing system. The device must give an audible signal when its alarm threshold is exceeded.
4. During regional anesthesia and monitored anesthesia care, the adequacy of ventilation shall be evaluated, at least, by continual observation of qualitative clinical signs.

Circulation

Objective

To ensure the adequacy of the patient's circulatory function during all anesthetics

Methods

1. Every patient receiving anesthesia shall have the electrocardiogram continuously displayed from the beginning of anesthesia until preparing to leave the anesthetizing location.*
2. Every patient receiving anesthesia shall have arterial blood pressure and heart rate determined and evaluated at least every 5 minutes.*
3. Every patient receiving general anesthesia shall have, in addition to the above, circulatory function continually evaluated by at least one of the following: palpation of a pulse, auscultation of heart sounds, monitoring of a tracing of intra-arterial pressure, ultrasound peripheral pulse monitoring, or pulse plethysmography or oximetry.

Body Temperature

Objective

To aid in the maintenance of appropriate body temperature during all anesthetics

Methods

There shall be readily available a means to continuously measure the patient's temperature. When changes in body temperature are intended, anticipated, or suspected, the temperature shall be measured.

(ASA Member Directory. American Society of Anesthesiologists, 1992:675)

APPENDIX G

Standards for Postanesthesia Care

(Approved by House of Delegates on October 12, 1988 and last amended on October 23, 1990)

These Standards apply to postanesthesia care in all locations. These Standards may be exceeded based on the judgment of the responsible anesthesiologist. They are intended to encourage high-quality patient care but cannot guarantee any specific patient outcome. They are subject to revision from time to time as warranted by the evolution of technology and practice. Under extenuating circumstances, the responsible anesthesiologist may waive the requirements marked with an asterisk (*). It is recommended that when this is done, it should be so stated (including the reasons) in a note in the patient's medical record.

STANDARD I

All patients who have received general anesthesia, regional anesthesia, or monitored anesthesia care shall receive appropriate postanesthesia management.

1. A Postanesthesia Care Unit (PACU) or an area which provides equivalent postanesthesia care shall be available to receive patients after surgery and anesthesia. All patients who receive anesthesia shall be admitted to the PACU except by specific order of the anesthesiologist responsible for the patient's care.
2. The medical aspects of care in the PACU shall be governed by policies and procedures which have been reviewed and approved by the Department of Anesthesiology.

3. The design, equipment, and staffing of the PACU shall meet requirements of the facility's accrediting and licensing bodies.
4. The nursing standards of practice shall be consistent with those approved in 1986 by the American Society of Post Anesthesia Nurses (ASPAN).

STANDARD II

A patient transported to the PACU shall be accompanied by a member of the Anesthesia Care Team who is knowledgeable about the patient's condition. The patient shall be continually evaluated and treated during transport with monitoring and support appropriate to the patient's condition.

STANDARD III

Upon arrival in the PACU, the patient shall be reevaluated and a verbal report provided to the responsible PACU nurse by the member of the Anesthesia Care Team who accompanies the patient.

1. The patient's status on arrival in the PACU shall be documented.
2. Information concerning the preoperative condition and the surgical/anesthetic course shall be transmitted to the PACU nurse.
3. The member of the Anesthesia Care Team shall remain in the PACU until the PACU nurse accepts responsibility for the nursing care of the patient.

STANDARD IV

The patient's condition shall be evaluated continually in the PACU.

1. The patient shall be observed and monitored by methods appropriate to the patient's medical condition. Particular attention should be given to monitoring oxygenation, ventilation, and circulation. During recovery from all anesthetics, a quantitative method of assessing oxygenation such as pulse oximetry shall be employed in the initial phase of recovery.[†] This is not intended for application during the recovery of the obstetrical patient in whom regional anesthesia was used for labor and vaginal delivery.

2. An accurate written report of the PACU period shall be maintained. Use of an appropriate PACU scoring system is encouraged for each patient on admission, at appropriate intervals prior to discharge, and at the time of discharge.

3. General medical supervision and coordination of patient care in the PACU should be the responsibility of an anesthesiologist.

4. There shall be a policy to assure the availability in the facility of a physician capable of managing complications and providing cardiopulmonary resuscitation for patients in the PACU.

STANDARD V

A physician is responsible for the discharge of the patient from the postanesthesia care unit.

1. When discharge criteria are used, they must be approved by the Department of Anesthesiology and the medical staff. They may vary depending upon whether the patient is discharged to a hospital room, to the ICU, to a short stay unit, or home.

2. In the absence of the physician responsible for the discharge, the PACU nurse shall determine that the patient meets the discharge criteria. The name of the physician accepting responsibility for discharge shall be noted on the record.

[†]*To become effective as soon as feasible, but no later than January 1, 1992.*

(ASA Member Directory. American Society of Anesthesiologists 1991:672)

APPENDIX H

Documentation of Anesthesia Care

(Approved by the House of Delegates on
October 12, 1988)

Documentation is a factor in the provision of quality care, and is the responsibility of an anesthesiologist. While anesthesia care is a continuum, it is usually viewed as consisting of preanesthesia, perianesthesia, and postanesthesia components. Anesthesia care should be documented to reflect these components and to facilitate review.

The record should include documentation of:

I. Preanesthesia evaluation*
   A. Patient interview to review
      1. Medical history
      2. Anesthesia history
      3. Medication history
   B. Appropriate physical examination
   C. Review of objective diagnostic data (*e.g.,* laboratory, ECG, X-ray).
   D. Assignment of ASA physical status
   E. Formulation and discussion of anesthesia plan with the patient and/or responsible adult

II. Perianesthesia (time-based record of events)
   A. Immediate review prior to initiation of anesthetic procedures:
      1. Patient re-evaluation
      2. Check of equipment, drugs, and gas supply

B. Monitoring of the patient[†] (*e.g.,* recording of vital signs)
C. Amounts of all drugs and agents used, and times given
D. The type and amounts of all intravenous fluids used, including blood and blood products, and times given
E. The technique(s) used
F. Unusual events during the anesthesia period
G. The status of the patient at the conclusion of anesthesia

III. Postanesthesia
   A. Patient evaluation on admission and discharge from the postanesthesia care unit
   B. A time-based record of vital signs and level of consciousness
   C. All drugs administered and their dosages
   D. Type and amounts of intravenous fluids administered, including blood and blood products
   E. Any unusual events including postanesthesia or postprocedural complications
   F. Postanesthesia visits

[†]*See Appendix F: Standards for Basic Intra-Operative Monitoring*

(*ASA Member Directory. American Society of Anesthesiologists 1992:682.*)

See Appendix E: Basic Standards for Preanesthesia Care.

APPENDIX I

The Anesthesia Care Team

(Approved by House of Delegates on
October 26, 1982 and last amended on
October 14, 1987)

Anesthesiology is a recognized specialty of medicine. Anesthesia care personally performed or medically directed by an anesthesiologist, a physician who has completed an approved residency in anesthesiology, constitutes the practice of medicine. Certain aspects of anesthesia may be delegated to other properly trained individuals. This group of people, medically directed by the anesthesiologist, comprises the Anesthesia Care Team.

Such delegation and direction should be specifically defined by the anesthesiologist director of the Anesthesia Care Team and approved by the hospital medical staff. Although selected functions of overall anesthesia care may be delegated to appropriate members of the Anesthesia Care Team, responsibility and direction of the Anesthesia Care Team rest with the anesthesiologist.

The Society does not intend that its recognition of the Anesthesia Care Team concept shall limit the availability of anesthesia care personally delivered by an anesthesiologist. The Society strongly encourages practice arrangements that provide patient access to the direct care of an anesthesiologist.

Members of the medically directed Anesthesia Care Team may include physicians and nonphysician personnel.

I. Those who assist in providing direct patient care during the perioperative period, for example:

A. Anesthesiology resident—a physician who is presently in an approved anesthesiology residency program
B. Nurse anesthetist—a registered nurse who has satisfactorily completed an approved nurse anesthesia training program
C. Anesthesiologist assistant—a graduate physician's assistant who has satisfactorily completed an approved anesthesiologist's assistant training program.

II. Others who have patient care functions during the perioperative period include
A. Postanesthesia nurse—a nurse who cares for patients recovering from anesthesia
B. Critical care nurse—a nurse who cares for patients in a special care area such as the Intensive Care Unit
C. Respiratory therapist—an allied health professional who provides respiratory care to patients

III. Support personnel whose efforts deal with technical expertise, supply, and maintenance, for example: anesthesia technicians, anesthesia aides, blood gas technicians, respiratory technicians, and monitoring technicians.

In order to apply the Anesthesia Care Team concept in a manner consistent with the highest standards of patient care, the following essentials should be observed:

I. Medical direction: Anesthesia direction, management, or instruction provided by an anesthesiologist whose responsibilities include
   A. Preanesthetic evaluation of the patient
   B. Prescription of the anesthesia plan
   C. Personal participation in the most demanding procedures in this plan, especially those of induction and emergence
   D. Following the course of anesthesia administration at frequent intervals
   E. Remaining physically available for the immediate diagnosis and treatment of emergencies
   F. Providing indicated postanesthesia care.

An anesthesiologist engaged in medical direction should not personally be administering another anesthetic, and should use sound judgment in initiating other concurrent anesthetic and emergency procedures.

II. Delegation of any part of anesthesia care by an anesthesiologist to a member of the Anesthesia Care Team under his or her medical direction should be fully disclosed to all concerned.

III. Exploitation of patients, institutions, Anesthesia Care Team members, colleagues, or payors is unethical.

(ASA Member Directory. American Society of Anesthesiologists, 1992:672)

APPENDIX J

Guidelines for Delegation of Technical Anesthesia Functions to Nonphysician Personnel

(Approved by House of Delegates on October 17, 1984)

I. Anesthesiology is the practice of medicine. Anesthesia, in all its forms, should be administered by a physician who is trained in the administration of anesthesia, preferably an anesthesiologist, a physician who has completed an approved residency in Anesthesiology. Accordingly, an anesthesiologist should be personally responsible to each patient for all aspects of anesthesia care.

II. While optimal anesthesia care involves a one-to-one relationship between anesthesiologist and patient, manpower shortages may necessitate the utilization of nonphysician personnel to perform technical functions relating the administration of anesthesia under the personal direction of an anesthesiologist or other qualified physician.

III. Delegation of functions to nonphysician personnel should be based on specific criteria (*i.e.,* the individual's education, training, and demonstrated skills) approved by the medical staff on the recommendation of the physician responsible for anesthesia care. Such criteria should include competence to follow the anesthesia plan prescribed by the anesthesiologist and the technical ability to

A. Induce anesthesia under the direction of an anesthesiologist
B. Maintain anesthesia at prescribed levels
C. Monitor and support life functions during the perioperative period
D. Recognize and report to the anesthesiologist any abnormal patient responses during anesthesia

(ASA Member Directory. American Society of Anesthesiologists, 1992:692)

APPENDIX K

Statement on Regional Anesthesia
(Approved by House of Delegates on October 12, 1983)

There has been an increased interest in the question of whether nurse anesthetists and other nonphysicians should be trained and permitted to perform spinal and other regional anesthesia procedures. While the permissible scope of practice by nurses and other nonphysicians is a matter to be determined by appropriate licensing and credentialing authorities, the Committee on Anesthesia Care Team believes that it is appropriate for the Society, as an organization of physicians dedicated to enhancing the safety and quality of anesthesia care, to state its views concerning the responsibilities of anesthesiologists for patient care in anesthesia and the role of nonphysicians in participating in such care. The Committee believes that these views are well and adequately set forth in guidelines and policy statements adopted by the House of Delegates.

These guidelines and policy statements emphasize that anesthesiology is the practice of medicine and that anesthesia, in all its forms, should be administered by, or under the medical direction of, a physician who is trained in the administration of anesthesia, preferably an anesthesiologist. Accordingly, anesthesiologists should assume responsibility for all aspects of anesthesia care, including obstetric anesthesia, outpatient anesthesia, and anesthesia for emergency surgery. Spinal and other regional anesthesia procedures involve diagnostic assessment, indications, contraindications, the prescription of drugs, and the institution of corrective measures and treatment in response to complications, and are not merely technical parts of patient care. In common with other medical practices, these procedures require a sound basic science background and experienced medical judgment.

Regional anesthesia should be performed only by an anesthesiologist or other physician trained in the administration of anesthesia.

(ASA Member Directory. American Society of Anesthesiologists, 1992:707)

APPENDIX L

Statement on Invasive Monitoring in Anesthesiology

(Approved by House of Delegates on
October 17, 1984)

A major contribution to the current practice of medicine is made by the galaxy of monitoring equipment and techniques developed in the past two decades. They have played a vital role in improving our ability to prevent, and to recognize and treat many conditions that previously contributed to morbidity and mortality.

These techniques, particularly those involving insertion of central venous pressure monitoring lines, intra-arterial catheters, and Swan-Ganz catheters (PA lines), carry with their application some varying degree of risk to the patient.

This statement attempts to minimize such risk by outlining our position on the provision of such procedures in the delivery of anesthesia care by Anesthesia Care Team personnel:

- The decision to use invasive monitoring is a medical judgment and should, therefore, be made only by a qualified physician.
- Invasive monitoring techniques should be prescribed by a physician. Depending upon its risk, each should be applied only by a competent and trained physician, or under the personal and immediate medical direction of such a competent and responsible physician.
- Training and credentialing of nonphysician members of the Anesthesia Care Team who may perform invasive monitoring techniques should be approved at the local medical staff level by the anesthesia department and the active medical staff.
- Some of the invasive monitoring tasks, namely the insertion of CVP lines placed via the upper extremity and of arterial lines (A-lines), may be delegated to properly trained and credentialed members of an Anesthesia Care Team. Performance, however, should be under the immediate and personal medical direction of the leader of the Team, preferably an anesthesiologist.
- Insertion of pulmonary artery catheters is a relatively hazardous procedure and should only be done by a properly trained physician.

(ASA Member Directory. American Society of Anesthesiologists, 1992:689)

APPENDIX M

Policy Statement on Standards of Care
(Approved by House of Delegates on
October 18, 1989)

The Committee on Standards of Care recommends Standards for the safe conduct of anesthesia care to the ASA Board of Directors and House of Delegates. Members are responsible for interpreting the application of the Standards to their own institutions and practices. The Committee is not empowered and declines to define interpretations for specific institutions, organizations or practices.

The Standards adopted by the ASA are not necessarily the only evidence of appropriate measures of due care, and an individual physician has the opportunity to show that the care rendered, even if departing from the Standards in some respects, nevertheless satisfies the physician's duty to the patient under all the facts and circumstances.

(ASA Member Directory. American Society of Anesthesiologists, 1992:706)

APPENDIX N

Vanderbilt University Medical Center Anesthesia Record

PREANESTHETIC EVALUATION

Date _____ Time _____ Age _____ Sex _____ Race _____

Procedure _____

_____

Diagnosis _____

_____

Last P.O. _____ ☐ Solids   ☐ Liquids

Allergies ☐ YES ☐ NO _____

Print Clearly

Name: _____

Number: _____

Age: _____

Sex: _____

Review of Systems

	YES	NO	Cardiovascular Disease
	☐	☐	MI
	☐	☐	Hypertension
	☐	☐	Dysrhythmia
	☐	☐	Angina
	☐	☐	CHF
	☐	☐	Valvular Disease
	☐	☐	Peripheral Vasc. Disease
	☐	☐	Past Cardiac Surgery
	☐	☐	Other

Renal Disease

☐ ☐ Renal Failure
☐ ☐ Other

Pulmonary Disease YES NO
☐ ☐ Smoking History
☐ ☐ COPD/Emphysema
☐ ☐ Asthma
☐ ☐ Other

Hepatic Disease
☐ ☐ Hepatitis
☐ ☐ Other

Endocrine Disease
☐ ☐ Diabetes
☐ ☐ Other

Infectious Disease
☐ ☐ Sepsis
☐ ☐ Other

Neurologic Disease YES NO
☐ ☐ Seizures
☐ ☐ Elevated ICP
☐ ☐ Cerebrovasc. Disease
☐ ☐ Neuromuscular Disorder
☐ ☐ Other

Gastrointestinal Disease
☐ ☐ G.E. Reflux/Hiatal Hernia
☐ ☐ Other

Hematologic Disease
☐ ☐ Sickle Cell
☐ ☐ Coagulopathy
☐ ☐ Other

Pediatrics YES NO
☐ ☐ Prematurity
☐ ☐ Congenital Abnormalities
☐ ☐ Apnea
☐ ☐ Other

Anesthetic Difficulties
☐ ☐ Difficult Intubation
☐ ☐ Family History
☐ ☐ History suggests MH
☐ ☐ Other

Drug Abuse
☐ ☐ ETOH
☐ ☐ Other

☐ HISTORY UNKNOWN EXCEPT AS NOTED ABOVE

Explanation of Positive Patient Data

_____
_____
_____
_____
_____
_____
_____
_____
_____
_____
_____

Physical Exam

BP (Range) _____ Pulse _____ Resp. _____ Temp. _____ Weight _____ Kg.

_____
_____
_____
_____
_____
_____
_____
_____

Medications: _____

Impression: ASA Status   1 2 3 4 5 6 E _____

_____
_____
_____

Plan: _____

_____
_____
_____

_____ **Completed By:** _____

Figure 39–Appendix N–1.

© Copyright Dept. of Anesthesiology, VUMC, 1991

Vanderbilt Anesthesia Record

Machine Checklist

_____ Anesthesia Machine

☐ Primary ✴ ☐ Secondary

Yes		No
✴ ☐ Unused Controls Off	☐
✴ ☐ Cylinder Pressures OK	☐
☐ O₂ Failure Alarm OK	☐
☐ Pipeline Gas Press. OK	☐
☐ Gas Flow Controls Off	☐
✴ ☐ Vaporizers Full and Off	☐
☐ Machine Leak Test OK	☐
☐ O₂ Monitor/SARA OK	☐
✴ ☐ Absorber OK ☐ N/A	☐
✴ ☐ Circuit OK	☐
✴ ☐ Vent. and Alarms OK	☐
☐ Scavenging System On	☐
✴ ☐ Suction Ready	☐

Special Techniques

☐ Induced Hypothermia
☐ Induced Hypotension
☐ Field Avoidance

Preanesthetic Meds

Monitoring

Oxygenation:
☐ # _____ Pulse Oximeter
☐ # _____ O₂ Analyzer

Ventilation:
☐ # _____ Ventilator
☐ Mass Spectrometer
☐ # _____ Capnometer
☐ # _____ Volume Monitor
☐ # _____ Pressure Monitor
☐ Precordial Stethoscope
☐ Esophageal Stethoscope

Circulation:
☐ # _____ ECG
☐ # _____ NIBP
☐ # _____ PC Doppler
☐ Arterial Line
☐ Central Line
☐ Swan-Ganz
☐ Cardiac Output

Other:
☐ Temperature
☐ Nerve Stimulator
☐ Evoked Potentials
☐ ICP
☐ _____

Airway Information

Intubation:
☐ Awake
☐ Oral
☐ Nasal
☐ Trach.
☐ Cuff
☐ Blind
☐ Fiberoptic
☐ Mask Only

Airway:
☐ Oral
☐ Nasal
☐ None

Circuit Type:
☐ Circle
☐ MJR
☐ Humid.
☐ Other

ET Tube Type:
☐ Standard   ☐ Anode
☐ Preformed ☐ Dbl. Lumen
☐ Laser _____ Size

Anesthesia Type

☐ General - induction:
  ☐ IV   ☐ Inhalation
☐ Regional
  ☐ Spinal   ☐ Epidural
Other: _____
  ☐ Single Bolus
  ☐ Multiple Bolus
  ☐ Continuous
☐ MAC

Special Equipment

☐ # _____ Fluid Warmer
☐ Rapid Infusion Device

Date

Anes Start	
Pt in Room	
Anes Induc	
Surg Start	
Surg Finish	
Pt Out Of Rm	
Anes Finish	

| Weight | Hct. | Allergies |
| kg | | |

Diagnosis

Operation

Attending Anesthesiologist   CS   Surgeon

Resident/CRNA

1.   2.

Print Clearly

Name _____
Number _____
Age _____
Sex _____

ASA Physical Status
1 2 3 4 5 6 E

OR # _____
☐ VUH ☐ TVC ☐ CSC

| Time | | | | | | | | | | | | Comments: |

| Oxygen | | | | | | |

End Tidal: O₂ / N₂O/N₂ / Agent / CO₂

BP ∨ ∧	40	100	220
MAP X	38	90	200
Pulse ●	36	80	180
	34	70	160
Temp △	32	60	140
SaO₂ ○	30	50	120
Start Anes X	°C	40	100
	SaO₂		80
Start Op ⊙			60
End Anes ⊗			40
			20

TV / RR / PIP
Temp. Es / Nas
UOP Int / Tot
EBL Int / Tot
Fluid In Int / Tot
Blood In Int / Tot

Position:

Post Anesthesia

HR _____ BP _____ / _____ RR _____
SaO₂ _____ % Intubated: ☐ Yes ☐ No

Drugs		Ordered		Fluid Summary - Input		Laboratory				
Drug	Total	Drug	Total	Type	Total	Time	pH	pCO₂	pO₂	BE	Other
A.		H.								
B.		I.								
C.		J.								
D.		K.								
E.		L.								
F.		M.								
G.		N.								

© Copyright Dept. of Anesthesiology, VUMC, 1991

CHART COPY

Figure 39–Appendix N–2.

APPENDIX O

Vanderbilt University Medical Center
Obstetric Anesthesia/Analgesia Record

OBSTETRIC PREANESTHETIC EVALUATION

Date _____ Time _____ Age _____ Sex _____ Race _____

GEST:_____ wks. Cx Dil. _____ cms. PARITY: G ____ P ____

PROCEDURE: ○ LEP ○ C/S ○ IVF ○ Cerc. ○ BTL ○ D&C _____
            ○ Ret. Plac. ○ Abort. ○ Other

DIAGNOSIS: ○ IUP. ○ Labor ○ PIH/PAH ○ Plac. Prev. _____
           ○ Abrupt ○ Diabetes ○ IUFD ○ Abnorm. Fetus ○ Other

Print Clearly

Name: _____

Number: _____

Age: _____

Sex: _____

Last P.O. _____ ○ Solids   ○ Liquids

Allergies ○ YES ○ NO _____

Review of Systems

Cardiovascular Disease
- ○ MI
- ○ Hypertension
- ○ Dysrhythmia
- ○ Angina
- ○ CHF
- ○ Valvular Disease
- ○ Peripheral Vasc. Disease
- ○ Past Cardiac Surgery
- ○ Other ○ NONE

Renal Disease
- ○ Renal Failure
- ○ Other ○ NONE

Pulmonary Disease
- ○ Smoking History
- ○ COPD/Emphysema
- ○ Asthma
- ○ Other ○ NONE

Hepatic Disease
- ○ Hepatitis
- ○ Other ○ NONE

Endocrine Disease
- ○ Diabetes
- ○ Other ○ NONE

Infectious Disease
- ○ Sepsis
- ○ Other ○ NONE

Neurologic Disease
- ○ Seizures
- ○ Elevated ICP
- ○ Cerebrovasc. Disease
- ○ Neuromuscular Disorder
- ○ Other ○ NONE

Gastrointestinal Disease
- ○ G.E. Reflux/Hiatal Hernia
- ○ Other ○ NONE

Hematologic Disease
- ○ Sickle Cell
- ○ Coagulopathy
- ○ Other ○ NONE

Family History
- ○ Hypertension
- ○ Cardiac Disease
- ○ Diabetes
- ○ Other ○ NONE

Anesthetic Difficulties
- ○ Difficult Intubation
- ○ Family History
- ○ History suggests MH
- ○ Other ○ NONE

Drug Abuse
- ○ ETOH
- ○ Other ○ NONE

○ HISTORY UNKNOWN EXCEPT AS NOTED ABOVE

Explanation of Positive Patient Data

Surg:_____ C-section _____ Other_____

Med: _____

Surg: _____

Physical Exam Wt: _____ kg Ht: _____ cms

BP (Range) _____ Pulse _____ Resp. _____ Temp. _____

Morphology:
○ ENDO ○ ECTO ○ MESO

AIRWAY DIFFICULT? ○ No ○ Yes Class: ○ I ○ II ○ III ○ IV _____

LAB. RESULTS:	**PCV**	Plts		Bleed. Time	Min.	TEG: R	K	MA	DC
	LDH	SGOT	SGPT	Na+	K+	Cl-			
	Gluc.	pH	p_aCO_2	p_aO_2	BE	HCO_3			

Medications: _____

Impression: ASA Status 1 2 3 4 5 6 E _____

Plan: ANESTHESIA: ○ LEP ○ SAB ○ GETA ○ MAC. ○ Other _____

Signature: _____

CONSENT: ○ Informed ○ Signed   Completed By: _____

© Copyright Dept. of Anesthesiology, VUMC, 1991

Figure 39–Appendix O–1.

Vanderbilt Obstetric Anesthesia Record

Print Clearly

Machine Checklist

\#_____ Anesthesia Machine

○ Primary *○ Secondary

	Yes		No
*○ Unused Controls Off		○	
*○ Cylinder Pressures OK		○	
○ O₂ Failure Alarm OK		○	
○ Pipeline Gas Press. OK		○	
○ Gas Flow Controls Off		○	
*○ Vaporizers Full and Off		○	
○ Machine Leak Test OK		○	
○ O₂ Monitor/SARA OK		○	
*○ Absorber OK ○ N/A		○	
*○ Circuit OK		○	
*○ Vent. and Alarms OK		○	
○ Scavenging System On		○	
*○ Suction Ready		○	

Preop Medications

○ Alkaseltzer
○ Metoclopramide
○ Ranitidine

○ _____
○ _____

Monitoring

Oxygenation:
○ \#_____ Pulse Oximeter
○ \#_____ O₂ Analyzer

Ventilation:
○ \#_____ Ventilator
○ Mass Spectrometer
○ \#_____ Capnometer
○ \#_____ Volume Monitor
○ \#_____ Pressure Monitor
○ Precordial Stethoscope
○ Esophageal Stethoscope

Circulation:
○ \#_____ ECG
○ \#_____ NIBP
○ \#_____ PC Doppler
○ Arterial Line
○ Central Line
○ Swan-Ganz
○ Cardiac Output

Other:
○ Temperature
○ Nerve Stimulator
○ _____
○ _____
○ _____

Airway Information

Intubation:
○ Awake
○ Oral
○ Nasal
○ Trach.
○ Cuff
○ Blind
○ Fiberoptic
○ Mask Only

Airway:
○ Oral
○ Nasal
○ None

Circuit Type:
○ Circle
○ MJR
○ Humid.
○ Other

ET Tube Type:
○ Standard ○ Anode
○ Preformed ○ Dbl. Lumen
○ Laser _____ Size

Anesthesia Type

○ General - induction:
  ○ IV   ○ Inhalation
○ Regional
  ○ Spinal   ○ Epidural
Other: _____
○ Single Bolus
○ Multiple Bolus
○ Continuous
○ MAC

Special Equipment

○ \#_____ Fluid Warmer
○ Rapid Infusion Device

Date

Anes Start	
Pt in Room	
Anes Induc	
Surg Start	
Surg Finish	
Pt Out Of Rm	
Anes Finish	

Name: _____

Number: _____

Age: _____

Sex: _____

Weight	Height.		Gest	Hct.	ASA Physical Status
kg	cms		wks		1 2 3 4 5 6 E

Allergies:

Diagnosis:

\# Fetus: ○ Single ○ Breech
○ Multiple ○ Abnormal lie

Operation:

Room \#

Attending Anesthesiologist   CS Obstetrician:

Resident/CRNA
1.   2.

Techniques / Comments: Page \# _____

Time chart

Time	
Oxygen	

Bup/Fent Infusion (ml/hr)

End tidal	O₂ / SAT
	N₂O/N₂
	Agent
	CO₂

BP ∨ ∧
MAP X
Pulse ●
Temp △
SaO₂ ○

	°C			SaO₂
BP	40	100	220	
	38	90	200	
MAP	36	80	180	
Pulse	34	70	160	
Temp	32	60	140	
SaO₂	30	50	120	
Start Anes X	40	100		
		80		
Start Op ○		60		
End Anes ⊗		40		
		20		

TV / RR / PIP
Temp. Es / Nas
UOP Int / Tot
EBL Int / Tot
Fluid In Int / Tot
Blood In Int / Tot

Position:

Post Anesthesia

HR _____ BP _____ / _____ RR _____
SaO₂ _____ % Intubated: ○ Yes ○ No

Drugs

	Drug	Total
A.		
B.		
C.		
D.		
E.		
F.		
G. Infusion Vol	Bup 0.125 % Fent 0.0002 %	

Ordered

	Drug	Total
H.		
I.		
J.		
K.		
L.		
M.		
N. Oxytocin		

Fluid Summary

Type	Total
LR	
EBL	
UOP	

Infant Data

INFANT DATA	INFANT #1	INFANT #2
Sex		
Alive or Stillborn		
Time of Delivery		
Mode of Delivery		
Apgar Score	1 5	1 5
Time Placenta Expressed:		○ Man. ○ Spont.
Infant Resuscitation and Condition		

© Copyright Dept. of Anesthesiology, VUMC, 1991

Figure 39—Appendix O-2.

Vanderbilt University Medical Center
OBSTETRIC ANESTHESIA/ANALGESIA

RECORD and NOTES

N.B. Enter TOTAL DRUG DOSAGE in Last Column.*

Time													
Lidocaine													
Bup / Ropivacaine													
Chloroprocaine													
Fent / Suf / Alfent													
Thiop / Etom / Ketamine													
Suxameth													
Atracur / Vecur													
Droperidol / Scopol													
Diazed / Midazol													
Atrop / Glycop.													
Ephedrine													
Ketorolac													

			O₂ / SAT			

E T
n i
d d
  a
  l
			N₂O / N₂			

			Agent			
			CO₂			

BP v ^	40	100	240			
MAP x	38	90	220			
	36	80	200			
Pulse •	34	70	180			
Temp Δ	32	60	160			
Sao↑ o	30	50	140			
Start Anes x	C 40	120				
	SaO	100				
Start Op O		80				
End Anes ⊗		60				
		40				

TV / RR / PIP						
Temp. Es / Nas						
UOP Int / Tot						
EBL Int / Tot						
Fluid In Int / Tot						
Blood In Int / Tot						
Position:						

GAS / ANES: ☐ N₂O ☐ O₂ ☐ Hal ☐ Isofl ☐ Enfl ☐ Desfl ☐ Sevfl ☐ Other _____

VASODIL: ☐ SNP ☐ NTG ☐ TMP ☐ Hydral ☐ Labet ☐ Ca⁺⁺CB ☐ Other _____

COMPLICATIONS: ☐ BP↓ ☐ BP↑ ☐ "Wet Tap" ☐ Heme ☐ CSF ☐ Para ☐ Obese ☐ PPSH ☐ APH ☐ PPH

MEDICAL:

*	INFANT DATA	INFANT #1	INFANT #2
	Sex		
	Alive or Stillborn		
	Time of Delivery		
	Mode of Delivery		
	TSR (Secs)		
AT ONE MINUTE	Heart Rate		
	Reflexes		
	Muscle Tone		
	Color		
	Apgar Score		
	Infant Resuscitation		
	Infant(s) Condition When Leaving Delivery Room		
	Time Placenta Expressed:		

☐ Spont.   ☐ Man.

OXYTOCICS	TIME	DOSE	ROUT
Oxytocin			
Methergine			
Prostacyclin			

TECHNIQUE:

POST ANESTHESIA
HR _____   BP ____/____   RR _____
O₂ / SAT% _____   Intubated: ☐ Yes ☐ No

Figure 39–Appendix O–3.

MC 4101 (9/91)

Vanderbilt University Medical Center

OBSTETRIC ANESTHESIA DISMISSAL NOTE:

DATE: _____ / _____ / _____   TIME: _____

CONSCIOUSNESS: ○ awake   ○ drowsy   ○ semi-conscious   ○ comatosed
     B.P.   /   mm hg   H.R.   /min.   R.R.   /min. O_2 Sat   %
     CVP   cms H_2O PAP   /   mm hg   Hct   %

SENSORY BLOCK: ○ none   ○ residual   levels [-   ]

MOTOR BLOCK: ○ none   PARTIAL: ○ minimal   ○ marked   ○ complete
CATHETER: REMOVED   ○ YES   ○ NO   ○ EPIDURAL   ○ SUBARACH
POSTOP. ANALG: ○ EPI Opioid   ○ SAB Opioid   PCA: ○ IV   ○ EPI
DISMISSED TO: ○ post-part   ○ labor suite   ○ OBICU
Other (specify): _____
_____
_____

COMMENTS/COMPLICATIONS: _____   SIGNATURE/NAME (Print):
_____   _____
_____   _____

POST-ANESTHESIA NOTE:

DATE: _____ / _____ / _____   TIME: _____

ANESTHESIA: ○ GETA   ○ Spinal   ○ Epidural   ○ Caudal   ○ MAC
Other (specify): _____
_____

RESIDUAL BLOCK: ○ None   ○ Sensory   ○ Motor
Detail: _____
Complications: _____

CATHETERS: ○ None   ○ epidural   ○ subarach   ○ removed   ○ intact
HEADACHE   ○ None   ○ mild   ○ moderate   ○ severe   ○ incapacitating
BACKACHE   ○ None   ○ mild   ○ moderate   ○ severe   ○ incapacitating
TENDERNESS   ○ None   ○ back   ○ sacrum   ○ IV   ○ ART   ○ Other

Detail: _____
_____

○ Sore Throat   ○ Nausea   ○ Vomiting   ○ Pyrexia   Cough: ○ Dry ○ Productive ○ Pruritis ○ Urine Retention

Detail: _____
_____
_____

SATISFACTION WITH: PAIN RELIEF   SATISFACTION WITH: ANESTHESIA
(0 = Very Dissatisfied; 10 = Extremely Satisfied)   (0 = Very Dissatisfied; 10 = Extremely Satisfied)

0 _____ 10   0 _____ 10

COMMENTS/COMPLICATIONS: _____   SIGNATURE/NAME (Print):
_____   _____
_____   _____

Figure 39–Appendix O–4.

CHAPTER 40

Legal and Ethical Issues in Obstetric Anesthesia

Jeannine C. Salvesen
Fred J. Spielman

LEGAL ISSUES

Few topics strike more fear into the heart of physicians than malpractice. All patients are potentially litigious.[1] Despite our best intentions, and the most careful, vigilant care, complications will occur. Whether the complications lead a patient or a patient's family to take legal action depends on several factors. Many claims are unfounded or frivolous. Some are legitimate. The remainder fall into a grey area between these two extremes. In this grey area, a physician's behavior may well prove a deciding factor. Usually, if the patient and family feel well informed about a procedure or anesthetic and its risks, and if the physician has established a good relationship with them, they will not sue. Yet, if the physician seemed callous, impersonal, or uninformative, and the patient or the family feels dissatisfied with the medical care, legal action may follow. The outcome of a malpractice suit depends on both the validity of the claim and the current legal climate in the state of jurisdiction.

The incidence and cost of malpractice suits have changed greatly over the past 20 years. A sharp rise in the number of malpractice claims occurred between 1970 and 1975. The number of claims then fell, but 3 years later, another waxing occurred. In 1985, a second decline began. We are currently experiencing this second downturn. Unlike the events of the late 1970s and early 1980s, experts do not expect another jump in the number or cost of claims.

This chapter discusses recent malpractice history and its relationship to anesthesiology. It explains issues specific to obstetric anesthesia as well as malpractice prevention techniques. Finally, we cover steps to take if you are sued.

Malpractice Demographics

Following World War II, a rise in malpractice activity occurred. In 1971, a Presidential commission examined the impact of liability insurance and medical malpractice on the rising cost of health care.[2] The commission suggested the following reasons for the increase in malpractice activity:

- More people were receiving health care.
- Health care had become more complex.
- The diagnostic and therapeutic interventions that saved lives also led to increased numbers of adverse effects.

Eighty percent of the malpractice claims filed between 1935 and 1975 were filed during the last 5 years of that period.[2] By 1975, the medical and insurance industries experienced a "crisis of availability."[3] Insurance became unavailable at any price. Insurance companies changed their policies from occurrence policies to claims-made policies. Occurrence policies cover physicians against all claims relating to events that happened during a given year of coverage. Claims-made policies, in contrast, cover only claims actually filed while the policy is in force. Claims-made coverage requires physicians to purchase costly "tails" that cover possible future claims following termination of their insurance policies.

The number of claims declined briefly between 1975 and 1978 with the institution of tort reform legislation in many states. Tort reform sought several ends, such as the following:

- A shorter statute of limitations
- Ceilings on awards
- Limits on the plaintiff lawyer's contingency fees
- The establishment of screening and arbitration panels to decide whether a claim merits further action

Despite these improvements, the cost of settling a claim increased by 44%. Insurance company actuaries feared total losses would continue to escalate. Nationwide, insurance company payments increased from $817 million in 1975 to $2 billion in 1983. The cost of medical liability coverage increased by 80%.[2]

Between 1981 and 1985, the number of professional liability claims per 100 physicians almost doubled, mimicking the events of a decade earlier. By 1988, however, a report issued by the AMA Center for Health Policy Research cited a subsequent change. The number of malpractice claims fell from 10.2 per 100 physicians in 1985, to 6.7 per 100 physicians in 1987—an annual decline of 19%[3] (Table 40-1). Physicians view this recent improvement in medical liability with cautious optimism. Several authors believe that the institution of risk-management and quality-assurance programs may have helped improve loss experience.

Anesthesia Malpractice

The incidence of anesthesia malpractice suits relates directly to anesthesia-associated morbidity and mortality. In 1984, approximately 1 in 10,000 patients in the United States died of anesthesia-related causes,[4] with 1 in 200,000 deaths due solely to anesthesia.[5] A 1987 study from the University of Manitoba suggested that at least 17.5% of patients experienced some type of anesthetic complication, whereas 0.45% suffered significant morbidity from the anesthetic exposure.[6]

It is difficult to estimate the current incidence of anesthesia-associated morbidity and mortality in the United States. The current medicolegal climate inhibits prospective confidential inquiry.[8] Most available data come from either multicenter retrospective reviews or prospective findings from individual institutions. Definitions of anesthesia-associated deaths vary. Some investigators include only deaths occurring within 24 hours of an anesthetic,[9] whereas others include deaths occurring within 6 days.[10] Finally, much of these data come from the years before 1985. Since then, the use of

Table 40-1

Annual Claims per 100 Physicians by Specialty

	YEAR			AVERAGE ANNUAL RATE OF CHANGE (%)
	1985	1986	1987	
All Physicians	10.2	9.2	6.7	−19.0
Specialty				
General practice	5.7	7.6	5.7	0.0
Internal medicine	6.2	5.5	4.5	−14.8
Surgery	16.8	15.8	12.7	−13.1
Obstetrics/gynecology	25.8	13.0	8.0	−44.3
Anesthesiology	7.5	8.7	4.6	−21.7

(After Holzer JF. Liability insurance: Issues in anesthesiology. Int Anaesthesiol Clin 1989;27:206)

oximetry and capnography has become routine. Therefore, older numbers may overestimate current statistics.

The most recent inquiry into anesthetic-associated morbidity and mortality comes from the ASA Closed Claims Study. These investigators undertook an exhaustive review of anesthesia malpractice claims (excluding dental) closed between 1974 and 1988. They reviewed files from 17 insurance companies. They described the following items:

- The type and severity of anesthetic mishap
- The possible effect of additional monitoring
- Risk associated with some anesthesia subspecialties
- Whether "standard of care" was met

Additionally, they correlated meeting of the standard of care with the likelihood of financial recovery.[10]

Adverse outcome associated with respiratory events constitutes the single largest class of injury in the ASA Closed Claims Study (522 of 1541 cases, or 34%).[11] Seventy-three percent of these claims resulted from inadequate ventilation, esophageal intubation, or difficult intubation. Death or brain damage occurred in 85% of the cases studied, and better monitoring (*e.g.,* oximetry and capnography) may have prevented 72% of these deaths. Nerve damage (15%) was the second most frequent claim. Cheney *et al*[10] found that even when reviewers judged anesthesia to be appropriate, payment was made in 40% of cases! Conversely, when they judged care to be substandard, payment was made in 82% of cases (Fig. 40-1). Table 40-2 lists the specific allegations leading to lawsuits. Table 40-3 compares the outcome, payment, and payment frequency of respiratory versus nonrespiratory events.

Analysis of malpractice claims closed between 1975 and 1978 shows that anesthesia injuries accounted for 3% of claims paid, but a disproportionate 11% of dollars paid.[3] In 1984, anesthesia allegations increased to 5.3% of claims paid, but indemnity payments fell to a proportionate 5.6%.[3] Figures released for 1986 to 1987 reflect further improvement. Anesthesia allegations accounted for 3.5% of claims paid and 3.6% of losses incurred.[3] According to the 1984 United States General Accounting Office (GAO) report, 43% of claims made against physicians succeeded. The average indemnity payment was $80,741. Anesthesia allegations had a similar average indemnity, $84,451, but 62.5% of claims made succeeded That victory rate is the highest for all specialties (Table 40-4). Despite this troubling information, many risk managers believe that liability issues in the speciality of anesthesiology will only improve.[3]

Malpractice Insurance Cost

Since the early 1980s, many institutions, at the urging of their insurance carriers, developed stringent risk-management programs and instituted minimal standards for anesthetic care. Harvard Hospitals mandated use of oximetry and capnography in 1985. The ASA established basic intraoperative monitoring standards in October, 1986. These standards "encouraged" the use of capnography and oximetry.[5] The following year, the Massachusetts Board of Registration in Medicine mandated that all licensees "shall adhere to the ASA monitoring standards." An organization that insures many Massachusetts anesthesiologists, the Medical

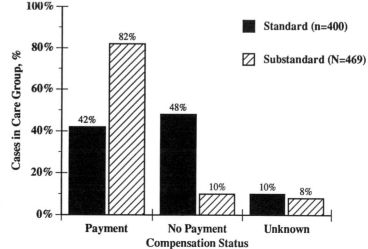

Figure 40–1. Incidence of compensation among patients (n = 869) who did or did not receive appropriate care (for whom appropriateness of care could be judged). There is a significant association between incidence of compensation and standard of care. (*P* < 0.01). (Cheney FW, Posner KL, Caplan RA, Ward RJ. Standard of care and anesthesia liability. JAMA 1989;261:1599)

Table 40-2

Type and Severity of Common Anesthesia-related Complications*

COMPLICATION	NO. OF LAWSUITS (%)	NO. OF DEATHS (%)[†]
Death	372 (37)	NA
Nerve damage	157 (15)	1 (1)
Permanent brain damage	119 (12)	NA
Cardiovascular collapse	70 (7)	45 (64)
Prolonged vent support	33 (3)	16 (48)
Eye injury	32 (3)	0 (0)
Hepatic dysfunction	28 (3)	12 (43)
Burn	27 (3)	0
Pneumothorax	19 (2)	2 (11)
Aspiration	17 (20)	10 (59)
Pulmonary edema	17 (20)	10 (59)
Stroke	17 (20)	10 (59)

(After Cheney FW, Posner KL, Caplan RA, Ward RJ. Standard of care and anaesthesia liability. JAMA 1989;261:1599)
*Only complications with an occurrence rate of 2% or greater are included. Some lawsuits involved multiple complications.
[†]Percentages of deaths in lawsuits associated with this complication (percentage of column 1).
Abbreviation: NA = not available.

Malpractice Joint Underwriting Association (JUA), offered a 20% discount on liability insurance premiums to those who agreed to use oximetry and capnography.[5] Evaluation of 1 million anesthetics delivered at Harvard Hospitals between 1976 and mid-1988 revealed 11 events of major morbidity or mortality solely attributable to anesthesia. Of these, eight were preventable by using monitors (disconnect and low oxygen flow alarms, pulse oximetry, and capnography). Since mandating use of these monitors in 1985, only one such event has occurred.[5]

Insurance companies calculate premium relativities to define the differences in risk between various subspecialties based on their susceptibility to claims and the degree of risk of financial loss. Factors involved in determining the premium relativity class include the following:

- Claim losses for a specified period
- The number of years covered
- The dollar loss per covered year

Note that the frequency of claims is not directly factored into the risk. Typically, physicians who do no surgical, obstetric, or invasive procedures have a relativity of 1.0. A class 5.0 anesthesiologist would pay approximately 5 times that of a class 1 internist.

The insurance industry believes risk management and adherence to standards will result in fewer lawsuits and lower total losses. They have lowered the premium relativity class assigned to some anesthesiologists. In 1988, the St. Paul Fire and Marine Insurance Company decreased the relativity for anesthesiologists from 4.5 to 4.0. The Harvard and the JUA-insured anesthesiologists had their relativities lowered to 2.5 and 3.0, respectively.[3]

Obstetric Anesthesia

The lay public commonly believes that anesthetic risk should be zero. Anesthesia itself is not therapeutic. The public presumes that anesthetic agents are not lethal unless misused.[7] This certainty joins with the expectation that a healthy pregnant woman who enters the hospital should leave with a healthy baby. Therefore, when complications involving the mother or infant arise, lawsuits invariably follow.[12] The angry and grieving patient and family often resort to the "shotgun" approach and sue all providers involved in their care.[13] In addition, the statute of limitations (2 years for patient injury) increases to 18 years for injury to newborns. These factors significantly increase the

Table 40–3

Outcome, Payment, and Payment Frequency Following Adverse Respiratory Events*

	ALL RESPIRATORY EVENTS (N = 522)	INADEQUATE VENTILATION (N = 196)	ESOPHAGEAL INTUBATION (N = 94)	DIFFICULT TRACHEAL INTUBATION (N = 87)	ALL NON RESPIRATORY EVENTS (N = 1019)
Outcome (percent of cases)					
Death	66[†]	71[†]	81[†]	6[†]	22
Permanent brain damage	19[†]	23[†]	17[†]	10	8
Other permanent injury	5[†]	1[†]	1[†]	18	25
Temporary injury	9[†]	4[†]	1[†]	25[†]	39
No injury	1[†]	1[†]	0[†]	1[†]	6
Payment (in $1,000)					
Range	1–6,000	1.5–6,000	30–3,400	1–4,700	<1–5,400
Median	200[†]	240[†]	217[†]	76[†]	35
Payment Frequency (percent of claims paid)	72[†]	73[†]	82[†]	67[†]	51

(After Caplan RA, Posner KL, Ward RJ, Cheney FW. Adverse respiratory events in anesthesia: A closed claims analysis. Anesthesiology 1990;72:828)
*Percentages do not always sum to 100 because of rounding error.
[†]$P<0.05$ versus nonrespiratory events.

risk of malpractice action in obstetrics. As of 1987, 57% of obstetricians had been sued at least once in their career.[3] The same ingredients that put an obstetrician at high risk for malpractice litigation also place the obstetric anesthesiologist at risk.

The medical profession has also contributed directly to liability in the obstetric area. Anesthesiology depart-ments often neglect obstetrics and may stock the obstetric suite with older anesthesia equipment.[12] Hospital designs may place the suite at a distance from the operating rooms. An anesthesiologist called for epidural placement may feel inconvenienced by the additional patient responsibility. When called for an emergency cesarean section, he or she may have to

Table 40–4

United States General Accounting Office: Characteristics of Claims Closed in 1984

	PAID CLAIMS		INDEMNITY PAYMENTS			
Type of Error	Number	Percent of Total*	Median	Average	Lowest	Highest
All claims	31,786	43.3	$18,000	$80,741	$1	$2,472,020
Surgery	7235	38.7	$25,000	$76,255	$108	$1,616,185
Diagnosis	7647	44.0	$30,000	$95,747	$28	$1,315,996
Obstetrics	3186	57.8	$65,000	$216,464	$100	$2,000,000
Anesthesia	1699	62.5	$1,500	$84,451	$20	$2,472,020

(After Holzer JF. Liability insurance: Issues in anesthesiology. Int Anaesthesiol Clin 1989;27:207)
*Shows paid claims as a percentage of total claims. For example, an estimated 2720 claims involved anesthesia errors; of these, 1699 (or 62.5%) were closed with payment.

anesthetize quickly an unfamiliar patient with a stressed fetus. The anesthesiologist may not have enough time for a complete preoperative evaluation and certainly not enough time to develop good patient rapport. A small hospital may not have an anesthesiologist "in house." Indeed, 26% of general anesthetics for cesarean section are done by a certified registered nurse anesthetist (CRNA) without supervision by an anesthesiologist.[14]

The cost of a malpractice claim in the obstetric population is extremely high. Multiple parties often contribute to the indemnity, or total of monies awarded to the plaintiff. In 1984, the median jury verdict for injuries to newborns was $1.45 million.[14] The median anesthesiology payment was $500,000.[15] The financial impact on physicians notwithstanding, haphazard care of the obstetric patient is illogical. Barnes[12] clearly emphasized this point in the following statement: It is anachronistic that in some of the finest hospitals in the country, a 70-year-old patient undergoing craniotomy for brain tumor will be attended by a team of six or seven people, including an anesthesiologist and one assistant, while a woman delivering a baby is attended by one physician, one nurse, and haphazard or inadequate anesthesia coverage. The life expectancy of the tumor patient is at best 18 months, while that of the mother and baby exceeds 100 years.

Complications in Obstetric Anesthesia

Current information about the complications in obstetric anesthesia come primarily from the following two sources: (1) the Confidential Enquiry into Maternal Mortality in England and Wales, which gives mortality data, and (2) the ASA Closed Claims Study.[15]

The Confidential Enquiry into Maternal Mortality in England and Wales suggested that between 1979 and 1982, anesthetic mortality was 1 in 8821. The two leading antecedents to maternal death were inhalation of stomach contents and difficult tracheal intubation.[16] The ASA Closed Claims Study analyzed obstetric anesthesia suits. The authors compared claims emanating from regional versus general anesthesia, and vaginal versus cesarean delivery. They also compared the type and severity of injury, award figures, and standard of care for obstetric claims versus nonobstetric claims. Although their data cannot estimate anesthesia-associated morbidity and mortality, they provide valuable information regarding anesthetic mishaps and claims in the obstetric population.

Both the Confidential Enquiry and the ASA Closed Claims Study noted similar causes of maternal injury. For obstetric patients receiving general anesthesia, 53% of the complications involved the respiratory system, and 33% involved problems with intubation or aspiration. The most common adverse outcomes were maternal death, newborn brain damage, and headache. Table 40-5 outlines the most common anesthetic injuries and contrasts them with nonobstetric claims. Convulsions represented the single most common damaging event. Ninety-five percent of the convulsions occurred in patients having epidural anesthesia, and 83% of the convulsions resulted in neurologic injury to the mother, newborn, or both. Almost 25% of claims paid were for seemingly minor complications, such as headache, emotional distress, and backache. There were 38 cases alleging newborn brain injury, with 17 (45%) attributable solely to anesthetic care.[15] Table 40-6 lists the events that led to adverse outcome. There were proportionally more deaths in the nonobstetric group. Practitioners met the expected standard of care in 46% of obstetric cases, similar to that found in nonobstetric cases. In the obstetric group, payments, especially those for brain injury, were typically higher. Payments were made in 59% of nonobstetric claims, with a median payment of $85,000. Fifty-three percent of obstetric claims were paid, but the median payment was $203,000 (Table 40-7).

Malpractice Prevention

Quality Assurance and Risk Management

The goals of risk management are to prevent patient injury and prevent or limit subsequent financial loss to the hospital and physicians. Quality assurance is the discipline that focuses on clinical care in an attempt to identify human and system errors. The success of the risk-management and quality-assurance programs depends on the degree to which all hospital departments and staff understand and participate in the process. Thus, the first step in setting up a risk-management and quality-assurance program involves conducting an educational campaign to inform the hospital community.

Published data suggest that human error causes between 50% and 80% of critical incidents.[17–19] A critical incident is a "human error or equipment failure which, if not detected and corrected in time, could have caused morbidity or mortality."[20] Repeatedly, case histories published in *Anesthesia Malpractice Protector*

Table 40-5

Most Common Injuries in the Obstetric Anesthesia Claims*

	NONOBSTETRIC CLAIMS (N = 1351)	OBSTETRIC CLAIMS (N = 190)	OBSTETRIC REGIONAL (N = 124)	OBSTETRIC GENERAL (N = 62)
Patient/maternal death	39% (525)[†]	22% (41)	12% (15)[†]	42% (26)
Newborn brain damage	NA	20% (38)	19% (23)	24% (15)
Headache	1% (10)[†]	12% (23)	19% (23)[†]	0% (0)
Newborn death	< 0.5% (1)[†]	9% (17)	7% (8)	10% (6)
Pain during anesthesia	< 0.5% (5)[†]	8% (16)	13% (16)[†]	0% (0)
Patient/maternal nerve damage	16% (209)[†]	8% (16)	10% (12)	7% (4)
Patient/maternal brain damage	13% (174)[†]	7% (14)	7% (9)	8% (5)
Emotional distress	2% (30)	6% (12)	7% (9)	5% (3)
Back pain	1% (8)	5% (9)	7% (9)	0% (0)

(After Chadwick HS, Posner KL, Caplan RA, Ward RJ, Cheney FW. A comparison of obstetric and non-obstetric anesthesia malpractice claims. Anesthesiology 1991;74:242)
*Table shows, in order of decreasing frequency, the most common injuries for which claims were made in the obstetric group. Percentages are based on the total claims in each group. Some claims had more than one injury and are represented more than once. Brain damage only includes patients who were alive when the claim was closed. Statistical comparisons are made between obstetric and nonobstetric claims and between obstetric regional and obstetric general anesthetics. [†]$P \leq 0.01$
abbreviation: NA = not applicable.

describe damaging events potentially preventable by the following:

- Increased vigilance
- More careful supervision of a CRNA or resident
- A more thorough preoperative evaluation

The quality-assurance committee must review adverse patient outcomes related to inadequate monitoring, machine malfunction, or human error. The committee should establish and monitor specific outcome criteria, such as the following:

- ASA I patients should not suffer death or organ damage.
- Post Anesthesia Care Unit stays should be less than 2 hours.
- No more than two patients per month should be admitted from day surgery for anesthesia causes.

These items are "clinical indicators." They have an expected frequency of occurrence determined by an individual department's practice characteristics and training center status. Examples of some obstetric anesthesia clinical indicators include the following:

- Failed epidural or spinal blockade
- Regional anesthesia converted to general anesthesia

- Hypotension requiring ephedrine
- Inadvertent dural puncture

Collection of these data usually involves a simple check list with space for further explanation. The quality-assurance forms should be part of a department's internal audit rather than the patient's chart. Indicators that occur more frequently than the established threshold require further investigation. Repeated positive indicators for individual practitioners (*e.g.,* four esophageal intubations per week for Dr. X) also must be analyzed. Departments should discuss these issues at quality-assurance and morbidity and mortality conferences. Record objective follow-up in the patient's chart. Describe the event, the patient's condition, and the information that has been transmitted to the family. When damaging events (*i.e.,* complications) occur, report them to the hospital risk management or legal department. The legal department will give further advice regarding potential liability.

Informed Consent

Before administering an anesthetic or treatment, one must first obtain consent. Anglo–American common law recognizes an individual's right to autonomy.[21] A 1914

Table 40–6

Most Common Damaging Events in the Obstetric Anesthesia Claims*

	NONOBSTETRIC CLAIMS (N = 1351)	OBSTETRIC CLAIMS (N = 190)	OBSTETRIC REGIONAL (N = 124)	OBSTETRIC GENERAL (N = 62)
Respiratory System	35% (476)[†]	24% (46)	11% (13)[†]	53% (33)
Inadequate ventilation	14% (186)[†]	5% (10)	4% (5)	7% (5)
Difficult intubation	6% (77)	5% (10)	1% (1)[†]	15% (9)
Aspiration	1% (18)[†]	4% (8)	2% (2)	10% (6)
Esophageal intubation	6% (87)	4% (7)	2% (2)	8% (5)
Bronchospasm	2% (27)	3% (5)	1% (1)	7% (4)
Inadequate Fio_2	1% (7)	2% (4)	1% (1)	5% (3)
Airway obstruction	3% (39)	1% (1)	1% (1)	0% (0)
Premature extubation	1% (20)	1% (1)	0% (0)	2% (1)
Convulsions	1% (19)[†]	10% (19)	15% (18)[†]	2% (1)
Equipment problems	4% (56)	6% (11)	6% (7)	6% (4)
Wrong drug/dose	3% (47)	4% (8)	2% (2)	10% (6)
Cardiovascular system	7% (94)[†]	3% (6)	3% (4)	2% (1)
Inappropriate fluid therapy	2% (29)	2% (4)	3% (4)	0% (0)
Excessive blood loss	2% (28)	1% (1)	0% (0)	2% (1)
Wrong blood administered	1% (10)	1% (1)	0% (0)	0% (0)

(After Chadwick HS, Posner KL, Caplan RA, Ward RJ, Cheney FW. A comparison of obstetric and non-obstetric anesthesia malpractice claims. Anesthesiology 1991;74:242)
*Table illustrates the most common damaging events in the obstetric claims. Percentages are based on the total claims in each group. Specific damaging events were not identified in all cases. Some claims had more than one damaging event. However, for events related to the respiratory system, only the most significant is listed. Statistical comparisons are made between obstetrics and nonobstetric claims and between obstetric regional and obstetric general anesthetics.
[†]$P \leq 0.01$.
[‡]$P \leq 0.05$.

ruling (Schloendorff v Society of NY Hosp 211NY 125, 105NY 92, 93[1914]) stated that individuals have the "right to be free from any unconsented harmful or offensive touching." Informed consent law varies from state to state, but the basic principles remain the same.

Older consent law (pre-1970s) stated that adequate disclosure consisted of what a reasonable physician would reveal in a similar case. In contrast, recent consent law focuses on the patient. It requires the physician to disclose those facts that a "reasonably prudent person" would likely deem significant.[21] The actual legal requirements for informed consent come from individual state laws. Anesthesiologists should be aware of the current legal requirements in the state in which they practice. Valid informed consent must include discussion of the following:

- Nature of the proposed anesthetic or procedure
- Possible complications of the proposed anesthetic
- Alternatives available
- Possible complications of the alternative

Many liability attorneys recommend that anesthesiologists obtain written informed consent. They also suggest that the anesthesia consent form be separate from any other consent forms the patient may sign. Just which risks should be discussed is only sometimes clear. Most anesthesiologists agree that patients need to know that postdural puncture headache may develop after spinal anesthesia. Should total spinal or convulsions be discussed as a complication of epidural placement? Should the physician discuss how he or she plans to avoid this complication? These questions come under the heading of therapeutic privilege; the physician and patient must decide their answers. Factors that should guide the anesthesiologist in his or her discussion with the patient are as follows:

- Severity and likelihood of the complication occurring
- Nature of the proposed surgery
- Patient's age
- Concurrent illness

The law does not require full disclosure when such knowledge would impose undue psychological trauma to the patient. In an emergency, when there is no time to obtain consent from the patient or next of kin, the adequate disclosure doctrine is also relaxed. In such a case, consent is implied because the patient has presented for treatment. Both instances still require documentation of lack of disclosure or consent and the reasons for their absence. Only a competent adult, emancipated minor, or legal guardian of a child or incompetent adult may give informed consent.

Many anesthesiologists feel that the stress and pain of labor invalidate consent given at that time. Grice *et al*[22] have found, however, that for laboring women, a verbal discussion plus a written consent form resulted in significantly higher recall scores than a verbal discussion alone. In addition, they concluded that most laboring women are at least as mentally and physically competent to give consent as are cardiac patients. A review of the Lexis legal database by Knapp[24] has revealed that the courts have not expressed concern about the inability to obtain an informed consent in laboring patients. In each case reviewed, the court ruled for the anesthesiologist. In none of these cases did the court conclude that the stresses of labor prevented the patient from giving informed consent. The courts found that factors that supported informed consent include patient cooperation with the procedure and notation in the record of the consent discussion. Although thorough documentation of informed consent is not a defense against malpractice, it does provide tangible evidence that a discussion of risks occurred.

Malpractice Litigation

When complications with negative outcome occur, a patient may resort to legal action to seek compensation. Malpractice litigation is a matter of civil not criminal law.[12] This distinction means that the plaintiff is seeking damages (money) instead of punishment (jail sentence). The alleged malpractice is a tort (wrong) and may be intentional or negligent. Examples of intentional torts include assault, battery, fraud, deceit, breach of contract, and invasion of privacy. Performing a procedure over the patient's objections is battery. If the patient experiences fear and terror, one is liable for assault and battery. The responsible individual (physician) is the tort–feasor, and in this situation committed malpractice. Depending on patient outcome, the court may find guilt with negligence or guilt without negligence. Many malpractice insurance policies do not cover intentional torts.[13]

When a patient enters a physician's care, a fiduciary relationship arises. This term means that each person trusts the other to live up to his or her responsibility. An anesthesiologist's obligations are to provide care as agreed, to respect confidence, to maintain standards, and not to cease care unilaterally. A patient's duties are to disclose pertinent information, follow advice, and pay as agreed.[13] For a malpractice suit to succeed, the plaintiff (patient) must prove the following four elements:[12]

- Duty—A fiduciary relationship existed and the physician owed the patient a certain standard of care.

Table 40–7

Payment Data*

	NONOBSTETRIC CLAIMS (N = 1351)	OBSTETRIC CLAIMS (N = 190)	OBSTETRIC REGIONAL (N = 124)	OBSTETRIC GENERAL (N = 62)
No payment	2% (431)	38% (72)	43% (53)	27% (17)
Payment made	59% (745)	53% (100)	48% (59)	63% (39)
Median payment	$85,000	$203,000†	$91,000	$225,000†
Range	$15–6 million	$675–5.4 million	$675–2.5 million	$750–5.4 million

(After Chadwick HS, Posner KL, Caplan RA, Ward RJ, Cheney FW. A comparison of obstetric and non-obstetric anesthesia malpractice claims. Anesthesiology 1991;74:242)
*Frequency and amount of payments are illustrated. Percentages are based on the total claims in each group and do not sum to 100% because of missing data. Statistical comparisons are made between payment distributions for obstetric and non-obstetric claims. Claims with no payments were excluded from calculations of median payment and range.
†$P \leq 0.05$

- Breach of duty—The physician violated the standard of care.
- Causation—There was a causal connection between the physician's acts and the injury.
- Damages—Physical, financial, or emotional injury occurred to the patient or relatives.

Duty is owed when the doctor–patient relationship is established. A patient may invalidate this obligation if she purposefully withholds information from a physician. Breach of duty is established by "expert witnesses." They are engaged by both sides to establish "standard of care" and answer the question, "Did the physician act as any 'reasonable and prudent practitioner' in the United States would have acted?" The plaintiff must present evidence that the physician's actions were the most likely cause of the injury. One exception is when *res ispsa loquitur*, or "the thing speaks for itself," is invoked.[12] For instance, if an anesthetized patient falls from the operating room table and suffers an injury while under the anesthesiologist's care, the anesthesiologist is responsible. Three types of damages may be sought:

- General damages—pain and suffering and loss of consortium
- Special damages—actual costs for past and present medical care, loss of income, or funeral expenses
- Punitive or exemplary damages—awarded to the plaintiff to punish or make an example of the physician

What to Do If You Are Sued

Developing a good doctor–patient relationship is vital in all areas of medicine. In the field of anesthesia, it is the most important measure a practitioner can take to prevent a lawsuit. Patients often initiate malpractice suits if they feel poorly informed about procedures and risks.[24] A thorough and appropriately detailed discussion of anesthetic plans may well reduce the risk of litigation when complications occur.

When untoward events do occur, a report should be filed with your quality-assurance department, and possibly with the hospital risk-management or legal department. If you feel the event is likely to cause a claim or suit, notify your insurance carrier immediately. They probably will instruct you to obtain all pertinent medical records, begin your file on the case and start damage control measures. Damage-control measures include the following:[25]

- Thorough documentation of the event, outcome, and treatment

- Frequent honest discussions with the patient and family members
- Obtaining consultations from other physicians to help diagnosis or treatment of the complications
- Not accepting or assigning blame for the complication

If you are notified of an impending lawsuit, try to remain calm. Only one of 20 malpractice cases reach a jury trial.[13]

You should take the following steps in preparation for your defense:[1,13,25–27]

1. Notify your department chief, hospital legal department, and insurance carrier, if you have not already done so.
2. *Do not* alter the patient's chart. The patient's lawyer probably has a copy of the chart and will try to make alterations look like a "smoking gun." Amend, clarify, or correct the medical record as separate, dated entries.
3. Have no further communication with the patient or the patient's attorney. This will prevent you from making comments that they may use against you later. Let your attorney handle all correspondences.
4. *Do not* discuss the case with friends or colleagues. Any comment you make about the patient can be viewed as breach of confidentiality. Defense lawyers have, on occasion, planted individuals in hopes of overhearing such discussions.
5. Review the case with your hospital and insurance attorneys. Use these meetings to educate them. The attorneys will need as much medical information as possible to select expert witnesses and to decide crucial points for further investigation.
6. When suggesting expert witnesses for your case, suggest experts, not your friends or individuals who owe you favors. The plaintiff's attorney will look to discredit them. Witnesses with the best credentials are usually those who have a university affiliation. They are usually the best teachers, and you want someone who will educate the jury.
7. Check your claim status regularly. Request that your defense attorney and malpractice adjuster send you copies of reports and communications about your case. Ask questions about things you do not understand.
8. Be familiar with the financial aspects of your case. You should know about the reserves the insurance company has set. This is the sum of money the insurance company puts aside to cover the expected cost of the claim. Ask how they arrived at the figure, because it will impact on your policy renewal costs.
9. Consider engaging your personal attorney if you have no confidence in the insurance attorney, if your

hospital privileges are at risk, or if the expected cost of settlement is more than your policy limits. You may be personally liable for the difference.

The case will go through the following phases before it is settled:[1,27]

1. Answering the compliant: This is a statement prepared with your attorney that addresses specific points the plaintiff has made.
2. Discovery: Both sides will gather facts and clarify issues before a trial.
3. Interrogatory: This is a written list of questions filed by the plaintiff's attorney. Frequently, it contains hundreds of questions, some of which may not be relevant. If you doubt the relevance of the questions, consult your attorney.
4. Deposition: This is a sworn statement given by the defendant anesthesiologist and other anesthesiologists appearing as expert witnesses. The setting is usually informal, but one must be on guard because anything said in the deposition can be introduced as evidence in court. Dress and act professionally. Don't appear condescending.
5. Negotiations and settlements: The attorneys jockey for position based on their perceptions of the strengths of each side of the case. Most cases settle before a trial. The defendant should agree to settle when so advised by the defense attorney unless it will have an effect on privileges or licensure. The cost of defending a malpractice suit is very high, and there is always a chance the jury will decide an award higher than the settlement.

After a Lawsuit

Before June, 1990, there were few repercussions following a malpractice settlement. A physician usually continued his or her practice. Although one's malpractice insurance costs might have risen, it was unlikely that hospital privileges or licensure would be affected. In 1986, Congress passed the Health Care Quality Improvement Act authorizing the formation of the National Practitioner Data Bank. The Data Bank opened in September, 1990. Its purpose is to collect and release certain information relating to the professional competence and conduct of physicians, dentists, and other health care practitioners.[28] Hospitals, insurance companies, licensing boards, and professional review committees must report any malpractice awards paid for a practitioner, disciplinary action, or refusal of licensure or privileges to the bank within 30 days of the action. They must also query the bank before issuing a health care provider a license or privileges. Failure to do either could result in a $10,000 penalty.

The purpose of the National Practitioner Data Bank is to centralize information collection and retrieval. The required report form contains demographic information and space for a short narrative of the action against the practitioner. The practitioner has access to this information, but does not have to agree with it. They may query the Data Bank and petition for changes in wording or content of reports, but until they complete the petition process, the information on file is released at the request of authorized entities.

The system has already had difficulties managing the volume of information and queries received.[29] Some individuals question confidentiality protection. Others fear that false reports may be filed. It is too early to decide if the National Practitioner Data Bank will succeed as a "one-stop clearing house" for information about health care providers and if the overall impact is positive or negative.

Although all obstetric anesthesiologists make mistakes, some who injure their patients never see a summons, and many who have done no harm are sued. Usually, a patient decides to sue or to forgive based on her relationship with the physician before and immediately after the incident. Remember this often-repeated comment: Always try to treat your patients the way you would want to be treated if you were sick. This advice is not new, but neither is it outdated.

ETHICAL ISSUES

Many ethical issues exist in the field of obstetrics. Some of these issues, such as court-ordered intervention, in vitro fertilization, and fetal abuse prosecution, have been the topics of legal debate. Other potential dilemmas surround procedures such as fetal surgery and fetal tissue transplantation, which are still experimental. Public policy and ethical guidelines for these issues are still evolving. This section presents the history and status of some of these questions.

Fetal well-being is usually best achieved by promoting the health of the pregnant woman. A parturient usually acts in a reasonable way to enhance the health of her fetus.[30] Advances in medicine that enable the physician to treat the fetus directly have created the perception of the fetus as a separate patient.[30] Still, therapy for this patient requires the participation and cooperation of his or her mother. A woman may refuse a procedure or treatment her physician believes would benefit the fetus. Parturients also can behave in ways that may harm the fetus. Such situations of "maternal versus fetal rights" can produce conflicts between the pregnant woman and her obstetrician. These events address the question: Who is the primary patient—mother or fetus? The courts have ordered several women to submit to operative procedures. Courts have also detained women against their will to promote the health of the fetus. Judges ruling for interventions frequently cite Roe versus Wade, the abortion rights decision, as their justification. They argue that when a woman forgoes her right to end a pregnancy, she becomes morally and legally obligated to ensure the well-being of the fetus by all means at her disposal. Still, there are indications that the opinion of the courts is changing. Both the American Medical Association and the American College of Obstetricians and Gynecologists have issued policy statements supporting a woman's right to autonomy. Ethicist George Annas agrees. He asserts that while a pregnant woman has a moral obligation to act in a way to ensure the well-being of her fetus, she lacks a legal obligation to do so. Legally forcing her violates her right to autonomy.[32] Court-ordered interventions force women to assume medical risks and forfeit autonomy in a manner not required of nonpregnant individuals.[33]

Maternal versus Fetal Rights

Court-ordered Cesarean Sections

The first reported court-ordered cesarean section occurred in Colorado on March 6, 1979.[33] A morbidly obese 33-year-old woman with a term fetus was in early labor. Shortly after her admission to the labor unit, meconium-stained amniotic fluid appeared and the fetal heart rate tracing showed signs of fetal stress with loss of variability and late decelerations. The physicians recommended cesarean section. The patient, who was "angry and uncooperative,"[33] refused the procedure, citing fear for her health. Neither her physician nor family could sway her decision. A psychiatrist's evaluation found that the patient was "neither delusional nor incompetent."[33] The obstetricians and hospital attorneys petitioned the juvenile court for legal intervention. The court appointed separate attorneys for the mother and the fetus. A judge presided over a hearing convened in the patient's room. The judge ruled that the fetus was a dependent and neglected child within the meaning of the Colorado Code. He ordered a cesarean section to "safeguard the life of the unborn child."[33] The cesarean section took place, under general anesthesia, 4 hours after the initial notification of the juvenile court. Both mother and infant did well.

Courts have ordered at least 19 cesarean sections since then.[34] The first decision published in the legal literature, Jefferson versus Griffin Spalding County Hospital, is the precedent most often cited in subsequent cases. In this case, Mrs. Jefferson's physicians diagnosed complete placenta previa by ultrasound examination on one of her routine prenatal visits. Her physicians recommended a cesarean section to save the life of her fetus, and probably her life, as well. Mrs. Jefferson refused on religious grounds, stating that "surgery was wrongful."[35] Her physicians requested and obtained a court order, but before they could do the cesarean section, Mrs. Jefferson had an uneventful vaginal delivery.

The most publicized case of court-ordered cesarean section, "In Re AC" (1987), came to a tragic end. In 1987, a 27-year-old woman with a 25-week pregnancy was admitted to George Washington Hospital with shortness of breath and back pain. She had been diagnosed with Ewing's sarcoma at age 14 and had numerous rounds of chemotherapy and surgery. She had been in remission for 3 years at the time of her pregnancy. A large recurrent tumor in her lung was causing her current symptoms. Her oncologist from the National Cancer Institute recommended chemotherapy and radiation therapy. He hoped to temporarily improve AC's condition so she could reach the 28th week of pregnancy, thereby improving the chance of fetal survival. The George Washington physicians did not order these therapies. After 5 days, AC's condition worsened. She was intubated, sedated, and considered "terminally ill." The medical staff and family supported passive treatment only, but the hospital general counsel sought a court order to perform a cesarean section and protect the legal rights of the 25-week fetus. The superior court ruled in favor of the cesarean section. AC's lawyer filed an appeal stating that a "court-ordered cesarean would in effect be terminating her life." This appeal was denied. The surgery was performed despite the patient's, family's, and physician's objections. The female infant died 2 hours after birth and AC died 2 days later.[34]

LEGAL OPINION. After the death of AC and her baby, the Superior Court vacated its original order and reheard the case. AC's attorney, American Civil Liberties Union, National Organization of Women Legal Defense and Education Fund, American Medical Association, and American Public Health Association all filed briefs. On April 26, 1990, the court upheld "the pregnant woman's right to decide the course of medical treatment for herself and for her fetus."[34] AC's family subsequently sought $3 million in damages in a suit charging George Washington Hospital with malpractice and civil rights violations.[36] They charged that the cesarean section was performed without the patient's consent. Because of this case, George Washington Hospital has developed a policy for dealing with maternal–fetal conflicts. It states that the hospital will heed a competent pregnant patient's treatment wishes whenever possible, even if it risks the life of the mother or her fetus.[21]

A National Survey conducted in 1987 by Kolder *et al*[32] found that 15 court orders for cesarean section were sought in 11 states, and 13 court orders were granted. Most opinions granting court-ordered intervention cited Roe versus Wade 410 US 113, 93 S. ct.705(1973), which dictates that "a state assert important interests in safeguarding health, in maintaining medical standards, and protection of potential life once the fetus has become viable." The judge at the bedside will likely grant the petition if the surgery involves some risk but is a common and generally safe obstetric procedure. In addition, attempted vaginal delivery must place mother or fetus at risk of death or substantial impairment.[37]

The overriding question that faces obstetricians and the petitioned justices is this: Who is the primary patient—fetus or mother?[33] Is the mother's right to autonomy and self-determination overridden by the rights of a "potential person?"[21,34,37] Should a mother's moral responsibility to help fetal well-being be legally enforced?[38] Courts, in attempting to answer this question, have compared the maternal–fetal relationship to the parent–child relationship. Legal sanctions under "Samaritan Law" enforce the parent's duty to a child.[30] Samaritan Law states that people who have special relationships to another person, such as parent to a child, have a legal obligation to the come to the aid of that person; however, one does not have to endanger himself or herself to render aid. For example, a parent must provide medical care for his or her children, but the parent cannot be forced to donate a kidney or bone marrow to the child. Conclusions reached by the AMA Board of Trustees[30] are as follows:

- The legal enforcement of a pregnant woman's moral responsibility to her fetus should not exceed the legal enforcement of a parent's moral duty to his or her child.
- A pregnant woman's refusal of treatment should not be overridden for the benefit of the fetus.

Although the need for informed consent may be overridden when a patient is incompetent, the next of kin is the guardian and must give consent according to most states' consent law. It is interesting that in none

of the cases reviewed by Kolder *et al*[32] was a pregnant woman deemed incompetent nor was guardianship granted to the next of kin.

PROBLEMS WITH COURT-ORDERED INTERVENTIONS. Physicians who seek court-ordered interventions destroy their physician–patient relationship. Doctor and patient become adversaries. As with the George Washington physicians in the case of AC, petitioning doctors may incur liability for malpractice as well.[36]

The timing of these interventions also presents problems. The hospital attorney petitions the court for guardianship of the mother or fetus or both. The court appoints both a lawyer to represent the mother and, usually, one ad litem (in law) to represent fetal interests.[37] Usually, a hearing is hurriedly convened in the patient's room. In others, guardianship may be obtained on the telephone.[32] According to Kolder's survey, the court issued orders within 6 hours of notification in 88% of the cases. In 19%, the court decided in less than 1 hour. This haste often leads to unchallenged due-process violations, including "absence of timely prior notice, adequate representation, explicit standards of proof, and right of appeal."[34] The judge hearing the case has little time to deliberate; review legal precedents; or seek additional legal, medical, or ethical information.[32]

Socioeconomic bias also may play a role in petitions for court-ordered intervention. The women in Kolder's survey showed the following traits:[32,37]

- All were poor.
- Eighty-one percent were black, Hispanic, or Asian.
- Twenty-five percent did not speak English as their primary language.

Religious or cultural beliefs led to maternal refusal in several instances.[35] Two women cited "risk of life."[33,34] At least one woman stated that the death of the fetus would solve her already complicated life situation.[40] Although this last position seems immoral, is it ethical to treat her "as a fetal container, a nonperson without rights to bodily integrity"[41] when a physician disagrees with her decision?

ANESTHESIA IMPLICATIONS. Although the women involved in the aforementioned cases refused surgery, the use of force to administer anesthesia has not been noted. Conversely, there is no mention in the literature of the court ordering an anesthesiologist to anesthetize a patient, nor, fortunately, of any untoward events because of anesthesia. Administration of anesthesia without patient consent could make anesthesiologists liable for a civil suit.[21] Should severe maternal injury or death result from the anesthetic or surgery, all parties involved could be held personally liable for malpractice and possibly homicide.[39]

Court-ordered Transfusion

A major advance in antenatal diagnosis occurred in 1952 with the measurement of amniotic fluid bilirubin through amniocentesis.[42] Intrauterine blood transfusion, practiced since 1963 with great success,[41] has become a routine, accepted fetal therapy for of Rh hemolytic disease.[43] The procedure is done under ultrasound guidance. A needle is passed into the amniotic sac through the mother's abdomen, and a small dose of muscle relaxant may be injected into a uterine artery.[42] Once the fetus becomes still, the blood transfusion begins. This treatment can prolong fetal intrauterine life in cases of severe hemolytic disease.

Kolder *et al*[32] cited three instances in which court orders for intrauterine transfusion were sought. All patients cited religious reasons for refusal. The court granted two orders, and the transfusions took place without significant maternal morbidity.[32]

Maternal Detention

There are many instances in which a fetus may benefit from an alteration in maternal behavior. These changes include bed rest, hospitalization, tight diabetic control, administration of cardiac medications for fetal arrhythmias, or medications for fetal hyper- or hypothyroidism. What if a woman refuses to comply? Should the courts intervene and force the prescribed therapy?

Between 1981 and 1987, physicians sought three court-ordered hospital detentions and obtained two. Both cases involved noncompliant diabetic women with 31- to 33-week pregnancies.[32] Unwilling detention is incarceration and raises serious legal and ethical questions. Previous attempts to declare a noncompliant pregnant woman mentally ill have failed.[43] In one instance, the court ordered a fetus, and therefore its mother, to be detained while deliberating the guardianship of the fetus.[43] The California Court of Appeals overturned this decision, stating that fetuses were not "persons" within the meaning of the statute (and therefore could not be detained). They argued that when a statute intended to include fetuses, it would so state. Ironically, this decision occurred after the birth of the child and a 2-month maternal detention.

Fetal Abuse Prosecution

The debate of fetal versus maternal rights has gained national attention over the past several years. The future of abortion rights is uncertain, and several women have incurred criminal prosecution for "fetal abuse," defined as behaviors deleterious or harmful to the unborn child.[44] Some authors feel that the mother's interest in freedom and bodily integrity must be balanced against the offspring's interest in being born healthy. They also believe that, depending on this balance, some maternal prenatal conduct standards should be obligatory.[45] Education and ensuring access to treatment are the most desirable avenues available to effect maternal behavioral changes.[45] What measures should be available to physicians and the state to ensure maternal compliance when an informed woman chooses to engage in behaviors harmful to her fetus? Excessive alcohol intake produces cardiac and craniofacial defects and developmentally retarded infants.[46] Mothers with phenylketonuria have microcephalic mentally retarded infants if they do not resume their low phenylalanine diet.[46] Narcotic-addicted mothers have addicted infants. Smokers have low-birth-weight infants. Should measures such as prebirth seizures (*i.e.,* incarceration) be employed? Should a mother be held civilly and criminally liable if she does not produce a "normal" infant?[46]

Obstetricians are sued by mothers for damages to their infants. They may be sued until the child is age 18. Children have sued their mothers for damages occurring in the prenatal period.[10] Maternal prosecution for fetal abuse may seem a logical next step in assigning responsibility for damaged or harmed infants.[45]

This issue gained wide publicity in 1987. Pamela Rae Stewart, a 27-year-old mother of two, had a high-risk pregnancy with a placenta previa. She was told to seek medical attention at the "first sign of bleeding."[35] When bleeding occurred, she waited 12 hours before seeking medical attention. During this time, she allegedly had sex with her husband, smoked marijuana, and took amphetamines. She gave birth to a severely impaired infant who died 6 weeks later.[47] Ms. Stewart was criminally charged with violating a statute that requires parents to "furnish necessary clothing, food, shelter or medical attention or other remedial care for his or her child."[35] The charges against Ms. Stewart were eventually dropped.

On July 3, 1989, a Florida woman became the first person convicted of giving birth to a drug-exposed infant.[47] Felony charges of child abuse and possession and delivery of a controlled substance to a minor were brought when a urine drug screen on her newborn infant was positive.[48] Several states (Illinois, Indiana, Nevada, Oklahoma, Florida) modified their juvenile codes to include infants born with controlled substances in their system as "neglected minors." Other states mandate that health officials report drug use by pregnant women to social service departments. Failure to report this behavior may be charged as a misdemeanor.[47] Who is to be tested? Women who are poor or nonwhite may be the group labeled "high risk."[47]

Bias also occurs in the reporting of "fetal abuse." A study done in Pinellas County, Florida in 1989 found that African–American women were almost 10 times as likely to be reported as their white counterparts.[47] The authors tested 715 women, 335 of whom were in private care. A total of 14.8% of the women tested positive for alcohol, cocaine, or opiates. White women were equally likely to have used alcohol or drugs before their first physician visit, yet African–American women were 9.6 times as likely to be reported to the state for this "fetal abuse."

Will these mandates do more harm than good? Will women avoid prenatal care and withhold information from their physicians to avoid being reported?[47]

In Vitro Fertilization

Chang[49] first achieved success with in vitro fertilization (IVF) using rabbits in 1959. Veterinarians have used the procedure ever since. In 1976, Edwards and Steptoe[50] devised the technique for human IVF. The first live birth occurred, amid great public uproar, in England in 1978. Since then IVF has become a widely practiced and accepted solution for infertile couples. Several thousand infants have been born via IVF to date. Over 50 centers in the United States practice this technique.[51]

Because several embryos are transferred, multiple gestation occurs 10 times more often following IVF than in natural conception.[52] If the maximum number of embryos transferred is four, multiple pregnancy should complicate no more than 25% of successful attempts.[53] Multiple gestation is a high-risk situation associated with marked increases in maternal and perinatal mortality and morbidity.[54] These risks are proportional to the number of fetuses. Average length of gestation is approximately 35 weeks for twins, 33 weeks for triplets, and 29 weeks for quadruplets.[55] Infants from multifetal pregnancies usually have low birth weight and may suffer complications associated with prematurity. Lengthy intensive care unit stays are extremely expensive and emotionally costly. To decrease the risk of multiple gestations, some practitioners do selective terminations.[56,56] Done between

the 9th and 11th weeks of pregnancy, the procedure involves placement of a needle into a fetal thorax under ultrasound guidance through the maternal abdomen.[55] Once the needle is in place, the obstetrician injects 0.5 mL of potassium chloride into the fetus, which causes its death. The goal is to reduce the pregnancy to two fetuses. The main risk associated with this procedure is pregnancy loss. In a report by Evans *et al*,[55] the pregnancy loss rate was 22.7%. One patient lost the pregnancy 1 week after the procedure; the other losses occurred later in the pregnancy. Ethical justification of the procedure is the same as that of elective abortion. Performance of the procedure during the first trimester allows the idea of selective termination to remain within the realm of ethical standards acceptable to the general populous.[57]

The most controversial IVF issue of recent years revolves around the fate of frozen pre-embryos. Because the fertilized eggs are frozen before the embryonic stage of development, they are pre-embryos.[57] Two recent court cases have brought this issue into the public consciousness. The Davis case began in 1988, when Mr. and Mrs. Davis had nine pre-embryos frozen. Two were transferred, but did not result in a pregnancy. The remaining seven were kept for later use. Unfortunately, the Davis' filed for divorce and disagreed about the disposition of their frozen pre-embryos.[58] Mrs. Davis wanted to become a mother; Mr. Davis preferred to remain childless. The court, faced with an unusual custody issue, decided that human life begins at conception.[57] Mrs. Davis was granted custody so she could try to become a mother.[58] Mr. Davis planned an appeal. The second case involved a couple involved with an IVF program in Virginia. The couple moved to California and wanted their frozen pre-embryos transferred to a new IVF center. The Virginia clinic refused the request, stating that the uterine transfer should only be done at their clinic. Before this case came to trial, the Virginia clinic agreed to release the pre-embryos to the couple.[56]

In May, 1990, the Board of Trustees of the American Medical Association issued a report addressing these issues.[57] Their findings are as follows:

- The gamete providers have a fundamental interest in their potential for procreation. The government does not grant decision-making authority to third parties, but it does restrict potential course of action.
- An advance agreement should be reached by gamete providers concerning disposition of unused pre-embryos in the event of divorce, death, or withdrawal from the IVF program.

- Gamete providers may donate their pre-embryos for use by other couples or for research use.
- The gamete providers have the authority to decide when the pre-embryos should be thawed for transfer, and they can change physicians and move their pre-embryos to another facility for transfer.

Conclusions

Except for court-ordered operative interventions, the ethical issues in obstetrics rarely involve anesthesiologists directly. There are no right or wrong answers to the ethical dilemmas posed. There are only personal beliefs and individual rights. Finding the balance is often a difficult process that requires input from the legal system, medical ethics boards, and the individuals involved. It is also a dynamic process, in need of constant reassessment and rethinking.

REFERENCES

1. Kroll DA. What to do when you are sued: Medical-legal issues in anesthesiology. ASA Annual Refresher Course Lectures 1989:115.
2. Cheney FW. Anesthesia and the law: The North American experience. Br J Anaesth 1987;59:891.
3. Holzer JF. Liability insurance: Issues in anesthesiology. Int Anaesthesiol Clin 1989;27:3.
4. Cooper JB. Preventable mishaps in anesthesia practice. ASA Annual Refresher Course Lectures 1984:217.
5. Eichorn JH. Prevention of intraoperative anesthesia accidents and related severe injury through safety monitoring. Anesthesiology 1989;70:572.
6. Duncan PG, Cohen MM. Postoperative complications: Factors of significance to anesthetic practice. Can J Anaesth 1987;34.
7. Gaba DM, Maxwell M, DeAnda, A. Anesthetic mishaps: Breaking the chain of evolution. Anesthesiology 1987;66:670.
8. Holland R. Anaesthetic mortality in New South Wales. Br J Anaesth 1987;59:834.
9. Lunn JN, Muskin WW. Mortality associated with anæsthesia. Nuffield Provincial Hospitals Trust, 1982.
10. Cheney FW, Posner KL, Caplan RA, Ward RJ. Standard of care and anesthesia liability. JAMA 1989;261:1599.
11. Caplan RA, Posner KL, Ward RJ, Cheney FW. Adverse respiratory events in anesthesia: A closed claims analysis. Anesthesiology 1990;72:828.
12. Dewan DM. Medical/legal aspects of obstetric anesthesia. Clin Anesthesiol 1985;19:2.
13. Ablouleish E. Litigation in obstetric anesthesia. Curr Rev Clin Anesth 1987;7:174.
14. Palmer SK, Gibbs CP. Risk management in obstetric anesthesia. Int Anesthesiol Clin 1989;27:188.
15. Chadwick HS, Posner KL, Caplan RA, Ward RJ, Cheney FW. A comparison of obstetric and non-obstetric anesthesia malpractice claims. Anesthesiology 1991;74:242.
16. Norman J. Education in anaesthetic safety. Br J Anaesth 1987;59:922
17. Herr GP. Anesthesia mishaps: Occurrence and prevention. Semin Anesthesiol 1983;2:213.
18. Kumar V, Barcellos WA, Mehta MP, Carter JG. An analysis of critical incidents in a teaching department for quality assurance. Anaesthesia 1988;43:879.
19. Pierce EC. Reducing preventable anesthetic mishaps: A need for greater risk management inititatives. Risk Management Foundation Forum 1985;6:2.
20. Gaba DM. Human error in anesthetic mishaps. Int Anaesthesiol Clin 1989;27:137.
21. Sullivan DR. Informed consent. Anesth Rev 1989;16:31.
22. Grice SC, Eisenach JC, Dewan DM, Robinson ML. Evaluation of informed consent for anesthesia for labor and delivery. Anesthesiology 1988;69:A664.
23. Knapp RM. Legal view of informed consent during labor. Anesthesiology 1990;72:211.
24. Gibbs RF. Ten commandments of anesthesia risk management. Legal Perspec Anesth 1983;1.
25. Quinley KM. Twelve tips for defending yourself in a malpractice suit. Am J Nurs January, 1990:37.
26. Langson SH. Exploration of a medical malpractice claim from the plaintiff's attorney's perspective. NC Bar Foundation Continuing Education, Professional Liability Meeting. NC Bar Foundation, 1990.
27. Lawing SA. Preparation of the defense of a medical malpractice claim. NC Bar Foundation Continuing Education, Professional Liability Meeting. NC Bar Foundation, 1990.
28. The National Practitioner Data Bank. American Hospital Association, May, 1990.
29. Holoweiko M. The malpractice data bank is turning into a Frankenstein. Med Econ May 6, 1991.
30. AMA Board of Trustees Report. Legal interventions during pregnancy. JAMA 1990;246:266
31. Annas G, Elias S. Legal and ethical issues in perinatology. In: Gabbe ES, Niebyl J, Simpson JL, eds. Obstetrics: Normal and problem pregnancies. New York: Churchill Livingstone, 1986:1079.
32. Kolder VEB, Gallagher J, Parsons MT. Court-ordered obstetrical interventions. N Engl J Med 1987;316:1192.
33. Bowes WA Jr, Selgestad B. Fetal versus maternal rights: Medical and legal perspectives. Obstet Gynecol 1981;58:209.
34. Lew JB. Terminally ill and pregnant: State denial of a woman's right to refuse cesarean section. Buffalo Law Rev 1990;38:619.
35. Field MA. Controlling the woman to protect the fetus. Law Med Health Care 1989;17:114.
36. Gianelli DM. Am Med News, December 14, 1990;14.
37. Curran WJ. Court-ordered cesarean sections receive judicial defeat. N Engl J Med 1990;323:7:489.
38. Johnson D. A new threat to pregnant women's autonomy. Hastings Center Rep, August, 1987;33.

39. Jurow R, Paul RH. Cesarean delivery for fetal distress without maternal consent. Obstet Gynecol 1984;63:596.

40. Annas GJ. Protecting the liberty of pregnant patients. N Engl J Med 1987;316:1213.

41. Rosner F, Bennett AJ, Cassell EJ, et al. Fetal therapy and surgery. NY State J Med 1989;89:2:80.

42. Bowman J. Hemolytic disease. In: Creasy RK, Resnik R, eds. Maternal–Fetal medicine—principles and practice. 2nd ed. Philadelphia: WB Saunders, 1989:613.

43. Nelson LJ, Buggy BP, Weil CJ. Forced medical treatment of pregnant women: "Compelling each to live as seems good to the rest." Hastings Law J 1986;37:703.

44. Blank RH. Emerging notions of women's rights and responsibilities during gestation. J Legal Med 1986;7:441.

45. Robertson JA, Schulman JD. Pregnancy and prenatal harm to offspring: The case of mothers with PKU. Hastings Center Rep, August, 1987;23.

46. Fleisher LD. Wrongful births. When is there liability for prenatal injury? Am J Dis Child 1987;141:1260.

47. Moss K. Substance abuse during pregnancy. Harvard Women's Law J 1990;13:278.

48. Ahmann S. Mother to be tried for exposing fetus to cocaine. OB Gynecol News March, 1989;1:26.

49. Chang MC. Fertilization of rabbit ova in vitro. Nature 1959;84:877.

50. Steptoe PC, Edwards RG. Reimplantation of a human embryo with subsequent tubal pregnancy. Lancet 1976;1:880.

51. Gonik B. Pregnancy management following in vitro fertilization and embryo transfer. In: Wolf DP, Quigley MM, eds. Human in vitro fertilization and embryo transfer. New York: Plenum Press, 1984:365.

52. Lancaster PAL. Obstetric outcome. Clin Obstet Gynecol 1985;12:847.

53. Laufer N, Navot D. Human in vitro fertilization. In: DeCherndy AH, ed. Reproduction failure. Edinburgh: Churchill Livingstone, 1986:219.

54. Mueller-Heubach E. Complications of multiple gestation. Clin Obstet Gynecol 1984;27:1003.

55. Evans MI, May M, Drugan A, Fletcher JC, Johnson MP, Sokol RJ. Selective termination: Clinical experience and residual risks. Am J Obstet Gynecol 1990;162:1568.

56. Berkowitz RL, Lynch L. Selective reduction: An unfortunate misnomer. Obstet Gynecol 1990;75:873.

57. AMA Board of Trustees Report. Frozen pre-embryos. JAMA 1990;263:2484.

58. New York Times. September 22, 1989:A13.

Index

Page numbers followed by f indicate figures; those followed by t indicate tabular material.

ISBN 0-397-51115-9